Date Due

White House

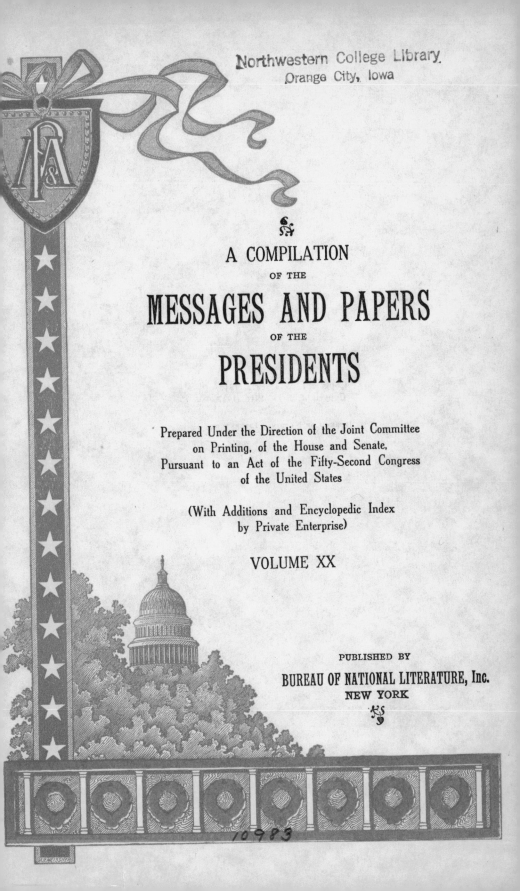

A COMPILATION

OF THE

MESSAGES AND PAPERS

OF THE

PRESIDENTS

Prepared Under the Direction of the Joint Committee
on Printing, of the House and Senate,
Pursuant to an Act of the Fifty-Second Congress
of the United States

(With Additions and Encyclopedic Index
by Private Enterprise)

VOLUME XX

PUBLISHED BY

BUREAU OF NATIONAL LITERATURE, Inc.
NEW YORK

Mabina, case of his oath of allegiance to United States, 6735.

McCall, E. & Co., agents to receive installments from Peru, 2587.

McCulloch vs. Maryland.—A case brought before the Supreme Court of the United States in 1819, in which the right of a State to interfere with the execution of Federal laws was denied. McCulloch was cashier of the Baltimore branch of the Bank of the United States, which had been incorporated by an act of Congress in 1816 and had headquarters in Philadelphia. The action brought by the State of Maryland against McCulloch was one of debt, he, it was averred, having refused to comply with an act of the Maryland general assembly of 1818 which imposed a tax upon all banks or branches of banks doing business in Maryland and not chartered by the State legislature. The court of appeals of Maryland decided against the plaintiff. The Supreme Court reversed this decision, declaring that the act under which the bank was chartered was constitutional, and that therefore the act of the Maryland legislature of 1818 was contrary to the Constitution of the United States, and therefore void, because States have no power, by taxation or otherwise, to impede or control the operations of constitutional laws enacted by Congress to carry into execution any of the powers of the Federal Government.

McKinley, William.—March 4, 1897-Sept. 14, 1901.

Twenty-eighth Administration—Republican.
(FIRST TERM, 1897-1901.)
Vice-President—Garret A. Hobart.
Secretary of State—
John Sherman.
William R. Day.
John Hay.
Secretary of the Treasury—
Lyman J. Gage.
Secretary of War—
Russel A. Alger.
Elihu Root.
Attorney-General—
Joseph McKenna.
John W. Griggs.
Postmaster-General—
James A. Gary.
Charles E. Smith.
Secretary of the Navy—
John D. Long.
Secretary of the Interior—
Cornelius N. Bliss.
Ethan A. Hitchcock.
Secretary of Agriculture—
James Wilson.

McKinley was elected by the Republican party at the elections of 1896 and 1900. At the Republican National Convention at St. Louis, June 16, 1896, he was nominated on the first ballot, overwhelmingly defeating Reed and Quay, his closest rivals.

Platform.—The platform on this occasion caused much discussion over the money plank, and Senator Teller's resolution seeking to commit the party to an endorsement of gold and silver, with free coinage on a basis of 16 to 1, was defeated. The platform as adopted severely arraigned the Democratic administration; blamed it for the period of financial depression through which the country had just passed; confirmed the party's allegiance to the doctrine of protection; advocated a continuance and revival of reciprocity; favored the restoration of discriminating duties; stood unreservedly for sound money; opposed the debasing of currency by free coinage; pledged ample provisions for veterans; urged the control of Hawaii by the United States, the building of the trans-Isthmian canal, and the purchase of the Danish West Indies; condemned the Armenian massacres; reasserted the Monroe Doctrine; urged the restoration of peace to, and the securing of independence for Cuba, by the United States; insisted upon rigid enforcement of immigration laws; supported civil service reform; condemned lynching; recommended a Board of Arbitration to adjudicate between labor and capital; urged free-homestead laws upon Congress; favored the extension of statehood to the remaining territories, and proper recognition of Alaska; sympathized with temperance; and recognized the rights of women.

Opposition.—The Democratic National Convention at Chicago, July 7, 1896, nominated William J. Bryan on the fifth ballot, over Bland and Pattison. The People's party, or Populists, in convention at St. Louis on July 22, 1896, agreed to support Bryan, and nominated Watson as Vice-President. The National Silver party, at the same place and time, agreed to support Bryan for President and nominated Sewall for Vice-President. The sound-money Democrats in convention at Indianapolis, on Sept. 2, 1896, nominated General John W. Palmer and General Simon B. Buckner as their candidates. The National Prohibition party was split over the money question into "Narrow Gaugers," who wanted the platform confined to Prohibition, and the "Broad Gaugers," who wanted free coinage and other national issues incorporated. The Narrow Gaugers nominated Joshua Levering and Hale Johnson as candidates. The Broad Gaugers nominated Rev. Charles E. Bentley and James A. Southgate. The Socialist Labor Party, at New York, on July 4, 1896, nominated Charles H. Matchett and Matthew Maguire as their candidates.

Vote.—The popular vote gave McKinley 7,111,607; Bryan, 6,509,052; Palmer, 222,-583; Levering, 134,645; Bentley, 13,968, and Matchett, 36,373. The electoral vote gave McKinley 271, Bryan 176.

(SECOND TERM—MARCH 4, 1901-SEPT. 14, 1901.)

Twenty-ninth Administration—Republican.
Vice-President—Theodore Roosevelt.
Secretary of State—
John Hay (continued).
Secretary of the Treasury—
Lyman J. Gage (continued).
Leslie M. Shaw.
Secretary of War—
Elihu Root (continued).
William H. Taft.
Attorney-General—
Philander C. Knox.
William H. Moody.
Postmaster-General—
Charles E. Smith (continued).
Henry C. Payne.
Robert J. Wynne.
Secretary of the Navy—
John D. Long (continued).
William H. Moody.
Paul Morton.
Secretary of the Interior—
E. A. Hitchcock (continued).
Secretary of Agriculture—
James Wilson (continued).
Secretary of Commerce and Labor.—
George B. Cortelyou.
Victor H. Metcalf.

The Republican National Convention held at Philadelphia in June, 1900, nominated President McKinley for a second term.

SECOND TERM—Opposition.—The Democratic National Convention, at Kansas City, Mo., nominated William J. Bryan. The

People's party, or Fusionists, at Sioux Falls, S. D., endorsed Bryan's candidacy; while the "Middle-of-the-Road" Anti-Fusionist faction of the People's party, at Cincinnati, nominated Wharton Barker. The Prohibitionists, at Chicago, nominated John G. Woolley. The Socialist Labor party, in New York City, nominated Joseph F. Maloney. The Social Democratic party, at Indianapolis, nominated Eugene Debs. The United Christian party, at Rock Island, Ill., nominated Silas C. Swallow. The Silver Republican Convention, at Kansas City, endorsed Bryan. The National party, in New York City, nominated Donelson Caffrey of Louisiana, but he declined the nomination.

Vote.—The popular vote ran: McKinley, 7,207,923; Bryan, 6,358,133; Woolley, 208,-914; Barker, 50,373; Debs, 87,814; Maloney, 39,379. The electoral vote stood: McKinley, 292; Bryan, 155.

Party Affiliation.—From his youth William McKinley was an ardent Republican. After his return from the war, he was admitted to the bar, and settled in Canton, Unio, then an opposition county, where his political ability had abundant scope and where he quickly attained considerable political prominence. In 1867, he favored negro suffrage, a most unpopular topic in his neighborhood; in 1875, at the height of the greenback craze, he spoke for sound money and the resumption of specie payment. In Congress, in 1878, he opposed the Wood Tariff Bill; in 1879 and 1880, he opposed the repeal of the Federal election laws; in 1882, he advocated the protective policy in Congress and the tariff commission; in 1884, he opposed the Morrison Tariff Bill; in 1884, he supported Blaine for the Presidency; in 1886, he favored arbitration between labor and capital; in 1887, he conducted a brilliant campaign against the Mills Bill, which was supposed to embody Cleveland's policy and ideas on the tariff; his final address in Congress on this bill has been characterized as "the most effective and eloquent tariff speech ever heard in Congress." This speech served as a textbook of the campaign. On April 16, 1890, Major McKinley introduced the tariff bill since known by his name, which became a law on Oct.-6, 1890. Defeated for Congress in 1890, he was elected Governor of Ohio. His inauguration as Governor took place shortly before the commencement of the Presidential campaign.

Public Debt.—The public debt of the United States for the years to which President McKinley was elected to serve stood as follows: July 1, 1897, $986,656,086.14; 1898, $1,627,085,492.14; 1899, $1,155,320,-235.19; 1900, $1,107,711,257.89; 1901, $1,044,739,119.97; 1902, $969,457,241.04; 1903, $925,011,637.31; 1904, $967,231,-773.75.

Tariff.—In his Inaugural Address (page 6238) President McKinley took up the tariff question. He said: "Nothing was ever made plainer at a general election than that the controlling principle in the raising of revenues from duties on imports is zealous care for American interests and American labor. The people have declared that such legislation should be had as will give ample protection and encouragement to the industries and development of our country. . . . To this policy we are all, of whatever party, firmly bound by the voice of the people—a power vastly more potential than the expression of any political platform." Further, he says: "In the revision of the tariff especial attention should be given to the re-enactment and extension of the reciprocity principle of the law of 1890, under which so great a stimulus was given to our foreign trade in new and advantageous mar-

kets for the surplus of our agricultural and manufactured products." In his message at the special session (page 6246) he said: "The necessity of the passage of a tariff law which shall provide ample revenue, need not be further urged. The imperative demand of the hour is the prompt enactment of such a measure." In his Third Annual Message (page 6439) the President said: "I recommend that the Congress at its present session reduce the internal revenue taxes imposed to meet the expenses of the war with Spain in the sum of thirty millions of dollars. This reduction should be secured by the remission of these taxes which experience has shown to be the most burdensome to the industries of the people." In his Second Inaugural Address (page 6465) the President said: "Now I have the satisfaction to announce that the Congress just closed has reduced taxation in the sum of $41,000,000."

Foreign Policy.—In his First Inaugural Address (page 6241) President McKinley summed up the foreign policy of his administration in these words: "We want no wars of conquest; we must avoid the temptation of territorial aggression. War should never be entered upon until every agency of peace has failed; peace is preferable to war in almost every contingency. Arbitration is the true method of settlement of international as well as local or individual differences." In a special message to Congress (page 6277) the President announces the destruction of the battleship *Maine* in Havana waters and the conclusion of the court of inquiry. His special message (page 6281) deals with the revolution in Cuba and its effects upon the United States. In it he says: "The issue is now with Congress. It is a solemn responsibility. I have exhausted every effort to relieve the intolerable condition of affairs which is at our doors. Prepared to execute every obligation imposed upon me by the Constitution and the law, I await your action." By act of Congress, April 25, 1898, a state of war was declared to exist between the United States of America and the Kingdom of Spain. President McKinley's proclamation of war (page 6474) followed on April 26, 1898. The President discussed the future relations which should exist between the United States and Cuba in his Second Inaugural Address (page 6467). As to the war in the Philippines, the President said: "Our countrymen should not be deceived. We are not waging war against the Philippine Islands. A portion of them are making war against the United States. . . . We will not leave the destiny of the loyal millions in the islands to the disloyal thousands who are in rebellion against the United States."

Civil Service.—In his Inaugural Address (page 6241) the President said: "Reforms in the civil service must go on; but the changes should be real and genuine, not perfunctory, or prompted by a zeal in behalf of any party simply because it happens to be in power." Among the reforms instituted, the President lays especial stress upon dismissals, and says: ". . . a distinct advance has been made in giving a hearing before dismissals upon all cases where incompetency is charged or demand made for the removal of officials in any of the Departments." In his Fourth Annual Message (page 6455) the President recommends the extension of such parts of the Civil Service regulations as may be practicable to the Philippines.

McKinley, William:

Advancement and progress of the United States discussed by, 6618.

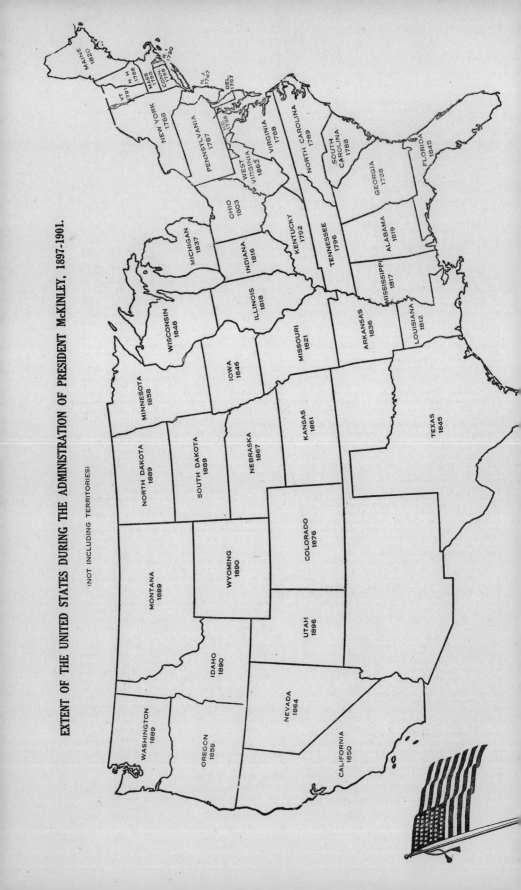

EXTENT OF THE UNITED STATES DURING THE ADMINISTRATION OF PRESIDENT McKINLEY, 1897-1901.

(NOT INCLUDING TERRITORIES)

Peace Commission, Spanish-American, discussed by, 6321, 6322.
At The Hague, discussed by, 6383, 6432.
Pennsylvania, riots at Latimer, 6324, 6363.
Pensions, discussed by, 6345, 6388, 6452.
Peru, affairs in, discussed by, 6335, 6432.
Philippine Islands, affairs in, 6441.
Government for, discussed, 6391, 6395, 6441.
Thanks tendered to commanders and men by, 6319, 6579.
Victory of squadron over Spanish fleet in bay of Manila, discussed by, 6297, 6315.
Force, etc., for suggestions from commanders regarding, requested by, 6392, 6580.
Portrait of, 6233.
Postal Service, discussed by, 6344, 6386, 6451.
Proclamations of—
Blockade of Cuban ports, 6472, 6481.
Cessation of Tariff, Puerto Rico, 6564.
Copyright—
Costa Rica, 6515.
Netherlands, 6522.
Existence of War—Spain, 6474.
Extraordinary session of—
Congress, 6470.
Senate, 6544.
Harrison, Benjamin, death of, 6545.
Hawaiian Cable Concession, 6493,
Lands, Public—
Set apart as public reservation, 6475, 6477, 6482, 6487, 6492, 6495, 6497, 6499, 6500, 6504, 6505, 6516, 6519, 6523, 6536, 6541, 6546, 6549, 6551, 6561, 6566.
Opened to settlement, 6486, 6506, 6525, 6547, 6553.
Louisiana Purchase Exposition, 6567.
Germany, 6538.
Italy, 6539.
Revocation of suspension of port dues—
Tobago, 6502.
Trinidad, 6503.
Sherman, John, death of, 6543.
Southern Ute Indians, Colorado, 6506.
Suspension of hostilities, Spain, 6487.
Suspension of tonnage dues—
Mexico, 6471, 6496.
Denmark, 6485.
Thanksgiving, 6470, 6491, 6518, 6544.

Treatment to be accorded foreign vessels, 6474.
Volunteers called for, 6473, 6477.
Puerto Rico, Legislation for, suggested by, 6402, 6447.
Relief for, discussed by, 6403.
Reconcentrados, 6256, 6283, 6284, 6285, 6308.
Red Cross, American National, aid furnished Cubans by, discussed by, 6284, 6308.
Samoan Islands, Affairs of, and policy of the United States, concerning, discussed by, 6336, 6375, 6428, 6435.
Spanish-American War, discussed by, 6295, 6297, 6298, 6302, 6305, 6307.
Trusts, discussed by, 6240, 6360.
Veto messages of—
Navajo, 6411.
Water Boundary Commission, discussed by, 6334, 6374, 6432.
McKinley Tariff Act, discussed, 5556, 5626.

McLane, The. (See Cedar Keys, Fla.)
McLeod Case.—In 1840 Alexander Mc Leod, a Canadian sojourning in New York, boasted of having taken part in the seizure of the steamer *Caroline* during a rebellion in Canada a few years previously. He was arrested and indicted for murder in Lockport, N. Y. The British minister demanded his release on the ground that McLeod had acted under orders and that the New York State courts had no jurisdiction in a case that lay only between the two Governments of Great Britain and the United States. The Federal Government admitted the justice of the British contention, but held that McLeod could only be released by operation of the law. The Attorney-General instituted *habeas corpus* proceedings, but the court held that there was no ground for releasing him. McLeod finally proved an alibi in October, 1841, and was acquitted.
"Macedonian."—A British gun boat, captured by the gun boat *The United States* in the War of 1812.
Macedonian, The, 1822, 3015, 3064.
Award of arbiter referred, 3381.
Capture of, 506.
Claims for, adjusted, 2116.
Second claim discussed, 2193.
Payment of, 3445.
Machine Tools, should be defined before being put on free list, 8131.
Mackinaw, Mich.:
Extension of civil authority over recommended, 190.
Lands ceded for post of, discussed, 421, 426.
Proclamation granting privileges of other ports to, 2859.
Reduction of, discussed, 534.
Macon Bill No. 2.—A bill introduced in Congress by Nathaniel Macon and passed in May, 1810, to relieve American commerce from the depredations of English and French cruisers and privateers. It provided

that commerce should be free and carried on under sanction of the Berlin and Milan decrees of France and the orders in council of England, but that if either of these nations should withdraw from these conventions commerce should be prohibited with the nation which retained them.

Madagascar:

Affairs of, report on, referred to, 5399, 5400.

Imprisonment of American citizen in, by French authorities, 6060, 6098.

Treaty with, 3780, 4653.

Referred to, 4757.

Madeira River, Brazil, exploration of, referred to, 4449. (See also Brazil, Physical Features.)

Madison, James.—1809-1817.

(FIRST TERM, 1809-1813.)

Sixth Administration—Democratic-Republican.

Vice-President—George Clinton.

Secretary of State—
Robert Smith.
James Monroe.

Secretary of the Treasury—
Albert Gallatin (continued).

Secretary of War—
William Eustis.
John Armstrong.

Secretary of the Navy—
Paul Hamilton.
William Jones.

Attorney-General—
Cæsar A. Rodney (continued).
William Pinkney.

Postmaster-General—
Gideon Granger (continued).

Nomination.—Madison was elected by the Democratic-Republicans in 1808 and 1812. Virginia, in separate caucuses, nominated James Madison and James Monroe as Presidential candidates to succeed Jefferson. But the Congressional Republican caucus, by an almost unanimous vote, chose Madison for President and George Clinton for Vice-President. Monroe had many supporters, but reconciled them to the choice of Madison by the suggestion that Monroe should succeed Madison. The Federalists held no caucus and made no formal nomination; but they accepted C. C. Pinckney and Rufus King. The election was held Nov. 8, 1808, and seventeen States took part in it.

Vote.—The electoral vote, counted Feb. 8, 1809, gave Madison 122 votes and Clinton 113 votes, against 47 each for Pinckney and King. The New England Federalists by a determined effort, redeemed some of their lost States. The votes of New York, North Carolina, and Maryland were divided.

(SECOND TERM, 1813-1817).

Seventh Administration—Democratic-Republican.

Vice-President—Elbridge Gerry.

Secretary of State—
James Monroe (continued).

Secretary of the Treasury—
Albert Gallatin (continued).
G. W. Campbell.
Alex. J. Dallas.

Secretary of War—
John Armstrong (continued).
James Monroe (acting).
Wm. H. Crawford.

Secretary of the Navy—
William Jones (continued).
B. W. Crowninshield.

Attorney-General—
William Pinkney (continued).
Richard Rush.

Postmaster-General—
Gideon Granger (continued).
Return J. Meigs.

SECOND TERM—Nomination.—In the election of 1812, Madison was nominated by the Republican Congressional caucus, at which New York State was represented by only one member. The other New York members formed a faction which nominated DeWitt Clinton. The Federalists, at a caucus held in New York City, agreed to support DeWitt Clinton for President and Jared Ingersoll for Vice-President.

Vote.—The federal election was held Nov. 3, 1812, and the electoral vote, which was counted Feb. 13, 1813, gave Madison 128, against 89 for Clinton; and Gerry 131, against 86 for Ingersoll. Eighteen States took part, for Louisiana was admitted in 1812. Maryland's was the only divided vote, and it was cast 6 to 5.

Party Affiliation.—In the early construction of the Government, Madison was a pronounced Federalist. He played a most important part in carrying the Constitution through the Virginia Assembly, despite the well-organized opposition of such leaders as Patrick Henry and Lee. His work in the First National Congress included tariff resolutions, creation of executive departments, and the proposal of amendments to the Constitution. He did not support Hamilton's financial measures and it was not long before he became one of the leaders of the new Republican party. Especially did he oppose the assumption of state debts and the institution of a national bank. While he sympathized with the French Revolutionists he did not go so far in this direction as did Jefferson. He led the debates in opposition to Jay's treaty with Great Britain. In 1798 he drew up the resolutions passed by the Virginia Assembly denouncing the Alien and Sedition Acts.

Political Complexion of Congress.—The Eleventh Congress (1809-1811) was made up of a Senate of 34 members, of whom 10 were Federalists and 24 Democrats; and the House, of 141 members, of whom 46 were Federalists and 95 Democrats. In the Twelfth Congress (1811-1813) the Senate, of 36 members, was made up of 6 Federalists and 30 Democrats; the House, of 141 members, was made up of 36 Federalists and 105 Democrats. In the Thirteenth Congress (1813-1815) the Senate, of 36 members, was made up of 9 Federalists and 27 Democrats, and the House, of 182 members, was made up of 67 Federalists and 115 Democrats. In the Fourteenth Congress (1815-1817) the Senate, of 38 members, was made up of 12 Federalists and 26 Democrats; and the House, of 183 members, was made up of 61 Federalists and 122 Democrats.

Foreign Policy.—In his First Inaugural Address, Madison outlines his foreign policy (page 451): "To cherish peace and friendly intercourse with all nations having corresponding dispositions; to maintain strict neutrality toward belligerent nations; to prefer in all cases amicable discussion and reasonable accommodation of differences to a decision of them by an appeal to arms; to exclude foreign intrigues and foreign partialities, so degrading to all countries and so baneful to free ones; to foster a spirit of independence too just to invade the rights of others, too proud to surrender our own, too liberal to indulge unworthy prejudices ourselves, and too elevated not to look down upon them in others; to hold the union of the states

EXTENT OF THE UNITED STATES DURING THE ADMINISTRATION OF PRESIDENT MADISON, 1809-1817.

(NOT INCLUDING TERRITORIES)

N. H. 1788
VT. 1791
MASSACHUSETTS 1788
CONN. 1788
R. I. 1790
N. J. 1787
DEL. 1787
NEW YORK 1788
PENNSYLVANIA 1787
MD. 1788
VIRGINIA 1788
NORTH CAROLINA 1789
SOUTH CAROLINA 1788
GEORGIA 1788
OHIO 1803
INDIANA 1816
KENTUCKY 1792
TENNESSEE 1796
LOUISIANA 1812

FLAG OF 1817

as the basis of their peace and happiness. . . ." The embargo act of 1807 was repealed and the non-intercourse act substituted in 1809. This proved ineffectual and was repealed in 1810, but was revived against Great Britain in 1811. Great Britain conceded the rights of neutrals, but refused to accommodate the impressment of sailors, to the satisfaction of the United States.

War with England.—During 1811, hostilities began on land and sea. By proclamation of June 19, 1812, Madison (page 497) declared war against Great Britain, and this followed closely upon his special message of June 1, 1812 (page 484), in which he reviewed the acts of hostility and offense of which Great Britain had been guilty. Throughout the several messages the progress of the war is discussed. It is generally conceded that the conduct of the war was feeble on the part of the United States. So far as Madison's connection with it is concerned, it may be remembered that he was essentially a man of peace and that the war, so important in the annals of the country and in the life history of those who bore themselves valiantly in defense of their country, becomes a mere incident in Madison's life. Eventful as his administration was, the part which he contributed was slight in comparison with his preeminently brilliant record before he reached the highest office.

Public Debt.—The public debt of the United States during the Madison administration stood as follows: Jan. 1, 1810, $53,173,217.50; 1811, $48,005,587.76; 1812, $45,209,737.90; 1813, $55,962,827.57; 1814, $81,487,846.24; 1815, $90,833,660.15; 1816, $127,334,933.74; 1817, $123,491,965.16.

Tariff.—July 1, 1812, there was passed a tariff act for imposing "additional duties upon all goods, wares, and merchandise, imported from any foreign port or place, and for other purposes." By this act, the duties were increased 100 per cent., and an additional tax of 10 per cent. was levied on all goods imported in foreign vessels. Feb. 25, 1813, a duty was imposed on the importation of iron wire; and July 29 of the same year the duty was imposed on imported salt, a bounty was granted on pickled fish exported, and certain vessels employed in the fisheries were entitled to allowances. In his Seventh Annual Message (page 552) Madison brings up the question of tariff for protection: "In adjusting the duties on imports to the object of revenue, the influence of the tariff on manufactures will necessarily present itself for consideration. However wise the theory may be which leaves to the sagacity and interest of individuals the application of their industry and resources, there are in this as in other cases exceptions to the general rule. Besides the condition which the theory itself implies of a reciprocal adoption by other nations, experience teaches that so many circumstances must concur in introducing and maturing manufacturing establishments, especially of the more complicated kinds, that a country will remain long without them, although sufficiently advanced and in some respects even peculiarly fitted for carrying them on with success."

Slavery.—In his Second Annual Message (page 470) President Madison says: "Among the commercial abuses still committed under the American flag, and leaving in force my former reference to that subject, it appears that American citizens are instrumental in carrying on a traffic in enslaved Africans, equally in violation of the laws of humanity and in defiance of those of their own country. The same just and benevolent motives which pro-

duced the interdiction in force against this criminal conduct will doubtless be felt by Congress in devising further means of suppressing the evil."

Commerce.—The commercial status of the United States in the year 1810 was as follows: Area, 1,999,775 square miles; population, 7,239,881; population per square mile, 3.62; gold coined, $501,435; silver coined, $638,774; money in circulation, $26,500,000; imports, $85,400,000; exports, $66,757,970; vessels built, 127,575 tons; vessels in foreign trade, 984,269 tons; vessels in coastwise trade, 440,175 tons; post-offices, 2,300.

Madison, James:

Mafia.—A Sicilian secret order which aims to substitute its own authority for that legally constituted by the state. It first became prominent in 1860. It depends upon community of sentiment rather than thorough organization for its strength, and its members are bound neither to seek redress at law nor give evidence in court. The boycott and blackmail are the usual means of offense, but violence is often resorted to. Members of the society emigrating to the United States have established branches in New York, New Orleans and elsewhere. On the night of Oct. 15, 1890, David C. Hennessy, chief of police of New Orleans, was assassinated before his own house by members of the Mafia to whose band he had traced a number of crimes. The officer received six wounds. Eleven Italians were arrested charged with the murder. By the 15th of the following March several of the prisoners had been acquitted, and, despairing of convicting any of them, on account of their disregard of oaths, a mob of enraged citizens, headed by a lawyer named Parkerson, broke into the jail and put to death the eleven prisoners, including those who had been acquitted. In consequence of the delay in bringing to justice the perpetrators of this deed the Italian Government made a protest against this violation of the rights of Italian citizens, and the United States arranged the matter amicably by paying an indemnity to the families of the murdered Italians.

Magazine.—In military parlance, a place for storing powder, shells and other war munitions.

Magazines. (See Arsenals and Magazines.)

Magicienne, The, appropriation to pay claims of owners of, recommended, 3580.

Maha Indians. (See Indian Tribes.)

Mail Matter.—Mail matter is divided into four classes, as follows: First Class—Postal cards and private mailing cards, one cent each; letters and other sealed matter, two cents each ounce or fraction of ounce. "Drop" letters not involving delivery may be mailed for one cent each. Letters may be mailed also to Great Britain for two cents each, and at the same rate to Germany, provided that they take the direct ocean route to the latter country. Second Class—Newspapers and periodicals. When mailed by the publisher in bulk, one cent per pound. Singly, one cent each for four ounces or fraction thereof. Delivery in the county in which second-class matter is published is free. Third Class—Comprises all other printed matter, and may be mailed at the rate of one cent for each two ounces or fraction thereof. Fourth Class—All other mailable matter, including parcel post (q. v.). Mail carried for the Government is free, as is mail sent under the frank of a member of Congress. (See Post-Office Department.)

Mail Matter. (See Postal Service.)

Mail Service. (See Postal Service; Railway Mail Service.)

Mail Steamers. (See Postal Service.)

Mails, Foreign, transmission of, through United States, referred to, 2175. (See also Postal Service.)

Maine.—One of the New England states; nickname, "The Pine Tree State"; motto, "Dirigo" ("I direct"). The most northeasterly state of the Union. It extends from lat. 43° 4′ to 47° 28′ north and from long. 66° 57′ to 71° 7′ west. It is bounded on the north by the Province of Quebec, on the east by New Brunswick, on the southeast and south by the Atlantic, and on the west by New Hampshire and Quebec. The area of the State is 33,040 square miles.

Settlements were made by the French under Du Monts in 1604 and by the English in 1607. The first permanent settlement dates from 1623. Maine was a part of the province of Massachusetts Bay in 1691 and became a separate state in 1820. The Webster-Ashburton treaty of 1842 settled the long-standing dispute regarding its northeastern boundary.

The products of Maine are chiefly those derived from forestry, fishing, farming and quarrying. The most fertile portion, the Aroostook Valley, is well adapted for the growing of fruits and vegetables.

Statistics of agriculture collected for the last Federal census place the number of farms in the State at 60,016, comprising 6,296,859 acres, valued, with stock and improvements, at $199,271,998. The average value of farm land advanced from about $8 an acre in 1900 to $14 an acre in 1910. The value of domestic animals, poultry, etc., was $25,161,889, including 256,523 cattle, valued at $7,784,384; 107,574 horses, $14,364,756; 358 mules, $72,446; 87,156 swine, $948,094; 206,430 sheep, $813,976. The yield and value of field crops for 1911 is given as follows: Corn, 18,000 acres, 792,000 bushels, $713,000; wheat, 3,000 acres, 63,000 bushels, $69,000; oats, 135,-000 acres, 5,198,000 bushels, $2,807,000; potatoes, 118,000 acres, 21,240,000 bushels, $16,355,000; hay, 1,400,000 acres, 1,540,000 tons, $23,176,000.

In the value of feldspar, Maine has ranked first in the United States during the last three years, and in 1913 according to the United States Geological Survey its output showed an increase of more than 100 per cent, both in quantity and value, over that of the preceding year. The principal mineral product of the state, however, is granite, in which Maine ranks third, being exceeded only by Vermont and Massachusetts. More than half the granite quarried is used in buildings and monuments, but considerable quantities are made into paving blocks and curbing, and a small quantity—chiefly waste—is crushed and screened for road making, concrete, and railroad ballast. The total value of the stone production in 1913 was $1,792,079, against $1,810,590 in 1912. The quantity of lime produced in 1913 was valued at $906,604. Maine is also one of the leading states in the production of slate, the output of which in 1913 was valued at $323,998. The production of feldspar in 1913 was 38,248 short tons, valued at $347,-499. Other commercial minerals produced in Maine in 1913 were mineral waters, sand and gravel, and a small quantity of gem material.

The valuation of property in 1910 was $428,252,465, and the assessed tax was $2,143,156, at the rate of five mills. The State treasurer reported receipts for the fiscal year as $4,030,356, and expenditures of $3,970,457, net cash balance, $135,722.

There are 2,144 miles of steam railway and 383 miles of electric line in the State. The population was 742,371 in 1910.

The number of manufacturing establishments in Maine having an annual output valued at $500 or more at the beginning of 1915 was 3,378. The amount of capital invested was $233,744,000, giving employment to 90,758 persons, using material valued at $117,655,000, and turning out finished goods worth $200,371,000. Salaries and wages paid amounted to $50,525,000.

Maine:

Claims of, presented, 1496, 1687.

Controversy with New Brunswick referred to, 1805.

Depredations in, committed by lawless men from British provinces, 1733.

    Correspondence regarding, 1738, 1784, 1785, 1791.

Northeastern boundary correspondence regarding. (See Northeastern Boundary.)

Usurpation of jurisdiction within, by New Brunswick, 990.

Maine, The.—One of the second-class battleships of the United States Navy. This vessel was sent to Havana, Cuba, in January, 1898, on a peaceful mission. She was received by the Spanish forts and naval vessels in the harbor with the courtesies usually extended to visiting war ships of a friendly power. Her anchorage was selected by the Spanish authorities. On the night of Feb. 15, 1898, the *Maine* was destroyed by a submarine mine (6277). It was believed that the Spaniards, who at the time were very much incensed at the interest Americans were taking in the Cuban insurrection, had maliciously destroyed the vessel and crew. Two officers and 258 sailors and marines lost their lives by the explosion (6296). An investigation failed to place the responsibility for the catastrophe, and Spain hastened to send a message of regret at what she called an "incident." The blowing up of the *Maine* was among the causes of the war with Spain, begun soon afterwards. A new battleship has since been added to the navy bearing the name Maine. (See illustrations opposite 5645, 5709, 5775.)

Maine, The, destruction of, in Havana Harbor, Cuba, 6277, 6290, 6308.

Findings of court of inquiry, discussed, 6277, 6290.

Number of lives lost in, report on, 6296.

Proposition of Spain to investigate causes of, referred to, 6290.

Removal of wreck of, appropriation for, recommended, 7630.

Makah Indians. (See Indian Tribes.)

Malay Archipelago.—The largest and most important island group or congeries of groups in the world, stretching from lat. 25° north to 12° south and from long. 93° to 105° east. It is bounded on the north by the China Sea, on the east by the Pacific Ocean, and on the south and west by Australia and the Indian Ocean. The principal groups are the Sunda Islands, including Sumatra, Java, Bali, Sumbawa, Flores,

Sandalwood, Timor, and several smaller ones; the Philippines in the north; Celebes and the Salayer Islands, north of Flores; the Moluccas and others east of Celebes. The chief islands for trade are Java, Sumatra, Borneo, and the Moluccas. The Dutch division of Papua is considered a part of the Malay Archipelago. The Philippines were taken by the United States from Spain in 1898. Great Britain is in possession of Singapore, Penang, Malacca, and Labuan. Native rajas rule most of the islands. The Dutch East Indies, including Sumatra, Borneo, Java, and the Celebes, comprise the greater and richer portion of the archipelago, having rights of suzerainty over the active princes.

Malefactors of Great Wealth.—A phrase used by President Roosevelt, (7138), and afterwards popular in political discussions as denoting men of riches who defied the law.

Malefactors of Wealth and Position, attitude of Roosevelt administration toward, 7137.

Proceeded against by the Department of Justice, 7085.

Malfeasance.—Official conduct of a fraudulent or wilfully illegal character.

Malvern Hill (Va.), Battle of.—The last of the Seven Days' Battles before Richmond. On the morning of July 1, 1862, the Second, Third, and Sixth corps of McClellan's army, under command of Keyes, Franklin, Sumner, Heintzelman, and Porter, were united on Malvern Hill, a plateau near the James River. The approaches to the position were commanded by about 70 guns, several of them heavy siege cannon. The Confederate attack, under D. H. Hill and Magruder, was made about 3 P. M., and it continued until 9 P. M. The assailants were repulsed. During the night McClellan continued his retreat to Harrison's Landing. (See illustration opposite 3469.)

Manassas (Va.), or Bull Run, Second Battle of.—On the morning of Aug. 30, 1862, the day after the battle of Groveton, the conflict between the forces under Pope and those under Jackson was renewed. The latter, having been reenforced, massed his forces on the left of the Federal army with the intention of turning Pope's flank and securing a position on the road to Centerville, in Pope's rear. The fiercest fighting of the day took place about 5 o'clock in the afternoon on the ground where the battle of Bull Run had been fought July 21, 1861. By night the left wing of the Union army had been driven back about half a mile, the right not so far. Pope, being defeated, retreated to Centerville. Federal loss, about 15,000; Confederate, 8,400. (See also Groveton (Va.), Battle of.)

Manassas, Va.:

Army manœuvers at, 6927.
Encampment at, 6774.

Manassas (Va.), Battle of. (See Bull Run (Va.), Battle of.)

Mandan Indians. (See Indian Tribes.)

Maneuvering.—In war parlance, the orderly movement of military or naval forces for the acquisition of tactical advantage over the enemy. (See Tactics.)

Manila Harbor (Philippine Islands), Battle of.—Prior to the beginning of the war with Spain the Asiatic Squadron of the United States had been lying for several weeks at Hongkong, under the command of Commodore (now Admiral) George

Dewey. Upon the issuance of the colonial proclamation of neutrality, the usual 24 hours' notice having been given, Dewey repaired to Mirs Bay, near Hongkong. From there he proceeded, under telegraphic orders, to capture or destroy the Spanish fleet then assembled at Manila, capital of the Philippine Islands, a Spanish possession off the southeast coast of Asia. At daybreak May 1, 1898, the American fleet entered Manila Bay and before noon effected the total destruction of the Spanish fleet, consisting of 10 warships and a transport, besides capturing the naval station and forts at Cavite. Thus at one blow, in a few hours, was annihilated Spain's naval power in the Pacific. Nor was this all. The victory secured to the American commander complete control of the bay of Manila, with the ability to take the city at will. Not a life was lost on the American ships. The wounded numbered only seven. The Spanish loss was 412 officers and men killed and wounded. Aug. 15, after a brief assault upon the works of Manila by the land forces under Gen. Merritt, in which the squadron assisted, the last scene of the war was enacted at its starting place, resulting in the unconditional surrender of the city.

Manila, Philippine Islands (see also Philippine Islands):

Cable communications with, recommended, 6348, 6373, 6449.

Expeditions to, under command of Gen. Merritt, 6315.

Gen. Otis directed to avoid conflict with insurgents, 6584.

Victory of—

American squadron over Spanish fleet in bay of, discussed, 6297, 6315.

Commander of American squadron—

Appointed acting rear-admiral, 6297, 6568.

Sword to be presented to, and medals to men under, 6302.

Thanks of Congress to, and men under, 6298.

Recommended, 6297.

Reply of, 6302.

Thanks of President tendered, 6568.

Referred to, 6297.

Commander of the *Hugh McCulloch* in, recognition of services of, recommended, 6305.

American squadron and land forces at, discussed, 6319.

Thanks of President tendered commanders and men, 6579.

Mann Law. (See White Slavery.)

Manor.—In English law a freehold estate held by the lord of the manor, who is entitled to maintain a tenure between himself and conyhold tenants, whereby a sort of feudal relation is kept up between them. Manors closely resemble the feudal estates held in Scotland by all proprietors of land. Manors of the English type were granted in the United States in several of the Colonies on such terms that property right carried right of jurisdiction. In 1636 the proprietor of Maryland ordered that every grant of 2,000 acres should be made a manor.

Manual of Parliamentary Practice.—The manual prepared by Thomas Jefferson after he was elected Vice President in 1796 was the first such in this country, and it still holds the premier position as a guide for deliberative bodies, and is usually referred to as the Jefferson Manual.

Manufactory Bank. (See Bank, Manufactory.)

Manufacturers, Association of.—In order to combat the encroachments of organized labor and offset the growing tendency of public opinion and state legislatures to acquiesce in the demands of labor men, no matter how ruinous to employers, the National Association of Manufacturers was formed. A platform of ten principles for the guidance of members in dealing with the labor question was formulated, as follows:

1. Fair dealing is the fundamental and basic principle on which relations between employees and employers should rest.

2. The National Association of Manufacturers is not opposed to organizations of labor as such, but it is unalterably opposed to boycotts, blacklists and other illegal acts of interference with the personal liberty of employer or employee.

3. No person should be refused employment or in any way discriminated against on account of membership or non-membership in any labor organization, and there should be no discriminating against or interference with any employee who is not a member of a labor organization by members of such organizations.

4. With due regard to contracts, it is the right of the employee to leave his employment whenever he sees fit, and it is the right of the employer to discharge any employee when he sees fit.

5. Employers must be free to employ their work people at wages mutually satisfactory, without interference or dictation on the part of individuals or organizations not directly parties to such contracts.

6. Employers must be unmolested and unhampered in the management of their business in determining the amount and quality of their product, and in the use of any methods or systems of pay which are just and equitable.

7. In the interest of employees and employers of the country, no limitation should be placed upon the opportunities of any person to learn any trade to which he or she may be adapted.

8. The National Association of Manufacturers disapproves absolutely of strikes and lockouts, and favors an equitable adjustment of all differences between employers and employees by any amicable method that will preserve the rights of both parties.

9. Employees have the right to contract for their services in a collective capacity, but any contract that contains a stipulation that employment should be denied to men not parties to the contract is an invasion of the constitutional rights of the American workman, is against public policy, and is in violation of the conspiracy laws. This association declares its unalterable antagonism to the closed shop and insists that the doors of no industry be closed against American workmen because of their membership or non-membership in any labor organization.

10. The National Association of Manufacturers pledges itself to oppose any and all legislation not in accord with the foregoing declaration.

Manufactures.—The following table is taken from a summary issued by the Director of the Census in 1914.

Number of establishments	275,793
Persons engaged in manufactures	8,265,426
Proprietors and firm members	264,872
Salaried employees	964,217
Wage earners (average number employed during the year)	7,036,337
Wage earners, by months:	
January	7,075,682
February	7,141,594
March	7,242,752
April	7,217,320
May	7,148,650
June	7,100,368
July	7,018,867
August	7,020,682
September	7,086,804
October	7,006,342
November	6,736,699
December	6,640,284
Primary horsepower	22,537,129
Capital	$22,790,880,000
Services	5,367,249,000
Salaries	1,287,917,000
Wages	4,079,332,000
Materials	14,368,089,000
Value of products	24,246,323,000
Value added by manufacture (value of products less cost of materials)	9,878,234,000

In the following table the several industries are arranged in the order of the value of their output.

MANUFACTURING INDUSTRIES.

	Average Number of Wage-Earners.	Value of Products.
Slaughtering and packing	89,728	$1,370,568,000
Foundries and machine shops	531,011	1,228,475,000
Lumber and timber	695,019	1,156,129,000
Iron and steel, steel works	240,076	985,723,000
Flour and grist mills	39,453	883,584,000
Printing and publishing	258,434	737,876,000
Cotton goods	378,880	628,392,000
Clothing, men's	239,696	568,077,000
Boots and shoes	198,297	512,798,000
Woollen, worsted and felt goods	168,722	435,979,000
Tobacco	166,810	416,695,000
Car shops	282,174	405,601,000
Bread and bakeries	100,216	396,865,000
Iron and steel, blast furnaces	38,429	391,429,000
Clothing, women's	153,743	384,752,000
Copper, smelting and refining	15,628	378,806,000
Liquors, malt	54,579	374,730,000
Leather	62,202	327,874,000
Sugar and molasses, not including beet	13,526	279,249,000
Butter, cheese and milk	18,431	274,558,000
Paper and wood pulp	89,492	267,657,000
Automobiles	75,721	249,202,000
Furniture	128,452	239,887,000
Petroleum refining	13,929	236,998,000
Electrical machinery	87,256	221,309,000
Liquors, distilled	6,430	204,699,000
Hosiery and knit goods	129,275	200,144,000
Copper, tin and sheet iron	73,615	199,824,000
Silk and silk goods	99,037	196,912,000
Lead, smelting and refining	7,424	167,406,000
Gas, illuminating and heating	37,215	166,814,000
Carriages and wagons	69,928	159,893,000
Canning and preserving	59,968	157,101,000
Brass and bronze	40,618	149,989,000
Oil, cottonseed	17,071	147,868,000
Agricultural implements	50,551	146,329,000
Patent medicines	22,895	141,942,000
Confectionery	44,638	134,796,000
Paint and varnish	14,240	124,889,000
Cars, steam railroad	43,086	123,730,000
Chemicals	23,714	117,689,000
Marble and stone work	65,603	113,093,000
Leather goods	34,907	104,719,000
All other industries	1,634,927	4,561,002,000
All industries, total	6,615,046	$20,672,052,000

One of the important duties of the federal census is to take account of the number and extent of the manufacturing establishments of the country and report on the number of persons engaged in the various industries, the value of finished products and the value added to raw material in the process of manufacture, as in the preceding tables.

Manufactures:

Capital—

Invested in, discussed, 5741.

Should be applied to internal, 443.

Depression in, mentioned, 559.

Encouragement of, recommended, 58, 60, 193, 197, 318, 454, 469, 480, 538, 630, 979.

Increase of, 676, 760, 979, 1108, 3991.

Prosperous condition of, 2404.

Referred to, 95, 175, 361, 456, 667, 979.

Statistics of, referred to, 3066, 3067.

"Man Without a Country, The."—The title of a story written in 1863 by Edward Everett Hale, which has been widely read and has made a strong patriotic appeal.

Maps of United States, joint resolution providing for printing of, vetoed, 5292.

Marauder.—One who plunders; in the plural especially applied to a group of soldiers organized for illicit foraging or stealing.

Marblehead, The, mentioned, 6317, 6766, 6768, 6769.

Marbury vs. Madison.— The first important case wherein the Supreme Court set aside an act of Congress because of conflict with the Constitution. William Marbury and others had been appointed justices of the peace in the District of Columbia by President John Adams, with the consent of the Senate. Before their commissions were issued Adams was succeeded by Thomas Jefferson and James Madison was appointed Secretary of State. Failing to receive his commission, Marbury moved the Supreme Court to issue a mandamus to Madison commanding him to issue it. The court decided that Marbury was legally entitled to his commission, but that the court had no constitutional authority to issue a mandamus in such a case, thus declaring unconstitutional a portion of the judiciary act of 1789, which purported to grant such authority.

Marietta, The, voyage and arrival of, from San Francisco discussed, 6316.

Marine Conference, International, at Washington discussed and recommendations regarding, 5180, 5370, 5468, 5493, 5498, 5543.

Marine Corps.—The United States Marine Corps is an independent branch of the military service of the United States, serving generally under the direction of the Secretary of the Navy. The corps may be detached by order of the President for service with the army, and on various occasions parts of the corps have so served.

Marines served on shore and on board vessels of the navy throughout the Revolutionary war, two battalions having been authorized by the Continental Congress Nov. 10, 1775, but the present organization dates from July 11, 1798, when an act of Congress was approved for establishing and organizing a marine corps to consist of one major, four captains, sixteen first lieutenants, twelve second lieutenants, forty-eight sergeants, forty-eight corporals, thirty-two drums and fifes and 720 privates.

The following duties are assigned to the marine corps: To garrison the different navy yards and naval stations, both within and beyond the continental limits of the United States. To furnish the first line of the mobile defence of naval bases and naval stations beyond the continental limits of the United States. To man such naval defences, and to aid in manning, if necessary, such other defences as may be erected for the defence of naval bases and naval stations beyond the continental limits of the United States. To garrison the Isthmian Canal Zone, Panama. To furnish such garrisons and expeditionary forces for duties beyond the seas as may be necessary in time of peace. To serve on board all battleships and armored cruisers of the navy, and such other vessels as may be directed, in detachments of not less than 8 per cent of the strength of the enlisted men of the navy on said vessels. In case of disturbances in foreign countries marines are landed to protect American interests.

The marine corps garrisons the following places:

Naval Proving Ground, Indian Head, Md.
American Legation, Peking, China.
American Legation, Managua, Nicaragua.
Marine Barracks, Washington, D. C., and San Diego, Cal.
Rifle Range, Winthrop, Mass.

Navy Yards.—Boston, Mass.; Charleston, S. C.; Mare Island, Cal.; New York, N. Y.; Norfolk, Va.; Philadelphia, Pa.; Puget Sound, Wash.; Portsmouth, N. H.; Washington, D. C.

Recruit Depots.—Mare Island, Cal., and Port Royal, S. C.

Naval Stations.—Cavite, Philippine Islands; Guam, Mariana Islands; Guantanamo, Cuba; Pearl Harbor, Hawaii; Key West, Fla.; Olongapo, Philippine Islands.

Naval Academy.—Annapolis, Md.

Naval Hospitals.—Boston, Mass.; Las Animas, Colo.; New York, N. Y.; Norfolk, Va.; Washington, D. C.

Naval Home.—Philadelphia, Pa.

Staff Offices.—New York, N. Y., San Francisco, Cal., and Philadelphia, Pa.

Naval Magazines.—Dover, N. J.; Fort Mifflin, Pa.; Illingham, Mass.; Iona Island, N. Y.; St. Julien's Creek, Va.

Naval Prisons.—Cavite, Philippine Islands; Mare Island, Cal.; Portsmouth, N. H. Also 38 vessels of the U S. Navy.

Commissioned officers are appointed from graduates of the Naval Academy, from worthy non-commissioned officers, and from civil life. Applicants must be twenty-one years of age and not over twenty-seven, and must pass such mental, moral and physical examinations as are prescribed by the president.

The term of enlistment in the marine corps is four years. Applicants must be nineteen years of age and not over thirty-five, able-bodied and of good character. Minors must have consent of parents or guardian. Apprentices to learn the drum and trumpet are enlisted between the ages of fifteen and seventeen, with consent of parents or guardian, to serve during minority. All recruits, after acceptance, are sent for three months to a recruit depot for

Instruction. Permanent marine corps recruiting stations as follows:

Atlanta, Ga., 29½ Marietta Street.
Baltimore, Md., 311 U. S. Custom House Building.
Boston, Mass., 22 Tremont Row.
Buffalo, N. Y., 215 Federal Building.
Chicago, Ill., 628 South State Street.
Cincinnati, Ohio, 23 Pickering Building.
Cleveland, Ohio, Federal Building.
Denver, Colo., 1605 Larimer Street.
Detroit, Mich., 22 Munroe Avenue.
Houston, Tex., 915 Prairie Avenue.
Kansas City, Mo., 1324 Main Street.
Louisville, Ky., 414 West Jefferson Street.
Memphis, Tenn., 206 South Main Street.
New Orleans, La., 638½ Gravier Street.
New York, N. Y., 24 E. Twenty-third Street.
Philadelphia, Pa., 130 South 15th Street.
Pittsburgh, Pa., Smithfield and Water Streets.
Portland, Ore., Third and Alder Streets.
Richmond, Va., Postoffice Building.
Salt Lake City, Utah., 216½ Main Street.
San Francisco, Cal., 36 Annie Street.
Seattle, Wash., 101 First Ave., So.
St. Louis, Mo., 122 Seventh Street.
St. Paul, Minn., 47 Baltimore Building.
The authorized strength of the corps (September 1, 1916) was 346 officers and 9,-921 enlisted men, as follows: One major-general commandant, eleven colonels, twelve lieutenant-colonels, twenty-eight majors, 107 captains, ninety-seven first lieutenants, ninety second lieutenants, twelve sergeant majors, seventy-nine quartermaster sergeants, one drum major, 114 first sergeants, eighty-six gunnery sergeants, 480 sergeants, 897 corporals, 124 drummers, 124 trumpeters, one leader of the band, one second leader of the band, thirty first-class musicians, thirty second-class musicians and 7,-942 privates. The Commandant is Major-General George Barnett.

Marine Corps:

Appointment in, referred to, 1965.

Compensation to officers of, referred to, 906, 1097.

Expenditures of, 2670.

Appropriation for, recommended, 1045.

Nominations for, referred to, 2586, 3236.

Plan for peace establishment of, 764.

Rank and position in, discussed, 3235.

Recommendation for, 2502.

Should be merged into artillery or infantry, 1023.

Marine Corps Reserve. (See Naval Reserve.)

Marine Hospitals. (See also Health Service.)

Construction of, referred to, 2747.

Patients treated by, during 1885, 4931.

Plan for, referred to, 1613.

Provision for, recommended, 324.

Service discussed, 4931, 5877.

Sites for, referred to, 1796, 1835.

Appropriation for, recommended, 1953.

Marine Insurance.—Eighteen marine insurance companies reporting to the New York State Insurance Department had on January 1, 1912, assets of $34,043,259, net surplus of $14,274,876 and premiums

received $13,745,122, losses paid $5,450,268, risks written $10,305,373,098.

Marine, Secretary of.—Up to 1781 the Board of Admiralty had supervision of all naval affairs. Feb. 7 of that year the Continental Congress created the office of Secretary of Marine, whose duties corresponded with those of the present Secretary of the Navy. Before the end of that year, however, the duties of the office were transferred to the Treasury Department.

Marine Signals, international conference at Washington for adoption of system of, etc., 5468.

Marines:

Arrest of, in Mexico, 7934.

Funeral of, in Brooklyn Navy Yard, 7939.

Mariposa Big Tree Grove, presented to Nation by California, 7013.

Maritime Canal Company, referred to, 5623, 6185, 6326.

Maritime Law, declaration concerning referred to, 2917, 2945.

Maritime Policy, adoption of, by United States recommended 6340.

Maritime Rights, correspondence with foreign powers, regarding, referred to, 7854.

Maritime War, rights of neutrals and belligerents in, discussed, 821.

Uniform action of the powers regarding, 866.

Markets and Rural Organization Service, Agriculture Department.—A branch office of the Department of Agriculture devoted to the study of the many problems of rural organization, including studies of marketing and distributing farm products and bettering country life. It is not generally appreciated, said Secretary Houston, in his report for 1915, to what extent marketing troubles have their origin in irregularity of production or lack of a stable and balanced agriculture. In years when a destructive disease prevails, the yield from an acreage normally sufficient to supply consuming requirements is insufficient to meet the demand, and high prices follow. High prices also may result from reduced acreage caused by low prices at planting time. High prices one year stimulate heavy planting the next. The solution of evils of this sort is the problem which confronts the Markets and Rural Organization Service. It is also an object of the service to supply shippers and distributors of perishable products with accurate information concerning the quantities arriving in the large markets.

Marmion Case.—The South Carolina legislature in 1822 passed a law providing that any free negroes entering the ports of that State on ships could be imprisoned until the departure of the vessels. This was done in the case of negroes on board the *Marmion*. The district court of the United States in 1823 decided that this law was contrary to the Constitution and incompatible with the international obligations of the United States. The Attorney-General rendered a similar opinion in 1824.

Marriages of American citizens abroad, recommendations regarding, 4246, 4301, 4360.

Marriage, Divorce and Polygamy, discussed, 7428.

Collection of statistics of States by Director of Census, recommended, 6942.

Marseillaise.—The French National Hymn. Composed in Strassburg in 1792 by a young officer, Claude Joseph Rouget de Lisle, it was sung by volunteers coming from the city of Marseilles when they entered Paris during the French Revolution, and later was shouted aloud with glee at the attack upon the King's Palace. First called the Hymn of the Marseillians, the title soon was shortened to the Marseillaise. The hymn is decidedly stirring in both words and music, and is distinctively republican in its import, as is shown by the fact that it was prohibited during the later French empire and monarchy, and also by the fact that it has received recognition as the official hymn of the Socialist and of other revolutionary movements.

Marshal.—(a) A military officer. (b) A civil officer in the jurisdiction of each United States Circuit and District Court. The marshal is under the direct control of the Circuit or District Court, or of the Supreme Court, according to the jurisdiction of the case.

Marshals, United States:

Acts making appropriations to pay fees of, vetoed, 4493, 4497, 4543, 4544.

Appropriations for maintenance of service of, recommended, 4474, 4525.

Necessity for, referred to, 4535.

Compensation to, discussed, 2666, 2714, 4770, 4836, 4939, 5103.

Referred to, 91.

Martha's Vineyard, Mass., lands designated by proclamation for lighthouses on, 1221.

Martial.—Characteristic of wars; war-like. (See Martial-Law.)

Martial Law.—A system of government under the direction of military authority. It is an arbitrary kind of law, proceeding directly from the military power and having no immediate constitutional or legislative sanction. It is only justified by necessity and supersedes all civil government. Sir Matthew Hale said: "Martial law is built on no settled principle, but is arbitrary, and, in truth, no law, but sometimes indulged, rather than allowed, as law." Suspension of the writ of *habeas corpus* is essentially a declaration of martial law. "In this case," says Blackstone, "the nation parts with a portion of liberty to secure its permanent welfare, and suspected persons may then be arrested without cause assigned."

Martin vs. Hunter's Lessee.—In 1791 Martin brought suit of ejectment against the defendant in the district court of Virginia for the recovery of certain lands. The court decided for the defendant. The court of appeals of Virginia reversed this decision, and their judgment was reversed by the United States Supreme Court in 1816. The court of appeals of Virginia refused to execute this judgment, declaring that the "appellate power of the Supreme Court of the United States does not extend to this court under a sound

construction of the Constitution of the United States," and that the "act of Congress to that effect is not in pursuance of said Constitution." The Supreme Court overruled this decision and thus established its jurisdiction upon such points.

Martinique, Island of, Lesser Antilles; French; 381 square miles; population, 203, 781.

Volcanic eruption on, detroying St. Pierre, formerly populated by 26,000, 6679.

Tonnage on American vessels at, referred to, 1123.

Mary Lowell, The, seizure of, by Spanish authorities, referred to, 3986.

Mary, The, capture and sequestration of, by Netherlands, 1612.

Claims arising out of, 1693.

Maryland.—One of the thirteen original states of the Union; nickname, "Old Line State;" motto, "Fatti maschii; parole femine" ("Deeds are men; words are women"). It was founded by Lord Baltimore in 1634 and named in honor of Henrietta Maria, wife of Charles I. Maryland extends from lat. 37° 53' to 39° 43' north and from long. 75° 4' to 79° 33' west. It is bounded on the north by Pennsylvania, on the east by Delaware and the Atlantic Ocean, on the south by the Chesapeake Bay, on the southwest by Virginia and West Virginia (separated by the Potomac), and on the west by West Virginia. It is divided into two parts by the Chesapeake Bay, and has an area of 12,327 square miles.

Maryland was first settled at St. Marys in 1634 as a proprietary colony of the Calvert family, but was governed as a royal province from 1691 to 1716. The Mason and Dixon line was established as the boundary between Maryland and Pennsylvania about 1766.

The fisheries of the State are important, the oysters of Chesapeake Bay being widely famous. Other fishery products are shad, bass, perch, and shell fish. Agriculture is an important industry, about 82 per cent of the area being in farms, and these mostly worked by their owners.

Statistics of agriculture collected for the last Federal census place the number of farms in the State at 49,923; comprising 5,057,140 acres, valued, with stock and improvements, at $286,167,028. Native white farmers operated 40,669 farms, about one-eighth of the farmers being negroes. The value of domestic animals, poultry, etc., was $32,570,134, including 287,751 cattle, valued at $7,869,526; 155,438 horses, $16,787,467; 22,667 mules, $3,043,581; 301,583 swine, $1,765,857; 237,137 sheep, $1,142,965. The yield and value of field crops for 1911 is given as follows: corn, 670,000 acres, 24,455,000 bushels, $15,407,000; wheat, 605,000 acres, 9,378,000 bushels, $8,534,000; oats, 46,000 acres, 1,242,000 bushels, $609,000; rye, 28,000 acres, 406,000 bushels, $349,000; potatoes, 30,000 acres, 1,755,000 bushels, $1,597,000; hay, 276,000 acres, 199,000 tons, $4,458,000; tobacco, 26,000 acres, 19,110,000 pounds.

The mineral products of the State for 1910 were valued at $15,440,207, of which $5,835,058 was coal, and $5,230,824 pig iron. The coal business of the State benefited indirectly from the six months' strike of mine workers in the middle western states, and as a result 1,193,884 tons more were mined than during the previous year, giving employment to 5,889 men, who worked an average of 270 days.

The receipts of the State treasurer for the fiscal year ended Sept. 30, 1911, were $5,875,598, and disbursements $6,328,557; balance, $875,111. The State debt was $7,529,926, an increase of $811,000 during the year.

There are 1,469 miles of steam railway and 538 miles of electric line. The population in 1910 was 1,295,346.

The number of manufacturing establishments in Maryland having an annual output valued at $500 or more at the beginning of 1915 was 4,799. The amount of capital invested was $295,934,000, giving employment to 131,333 persons, using material valued at $238,982,000, and turning out finished goods worth $377,764,000. Salaries and wages paid aggregate $71,829,000. This report showed a decrease in the number of establishments since the last report, which was in 1909, but an increase in the amount of capital invested. The number of employees also increased.

Maryland (see also Baltimore):

Act of general assembly of, relating to Chesapeake and Delaware Canal Co., 870.

Census of, referred to, 321.

Cession of Government interest in Chesapeake and Ohio Canal to, considered, 1776.

Claims of, against United States for expenditures during War of 1812, 894.

Combinations, unlawful in, discussed and proclamations against, 4400, 4424.

Constitutional amendments received from governor, 63.

District of Columbia, portion of, ceded to Congress by, 92.

Referred to, 86.

Legislature of, arrest and dispersion of members of, would not be justifiable, 3218.

Loan of, to Washington City, payment of, guaranteed by United States, 321.

Ratification of amendment to Federal Constitution by, referred to, 63, 249.

Unlawful combinations in, discussed, and proclamations against, 4400, 4424.

Maryland in Liberia.—A negro colony to the eastward of Cape Palmas, in what is now the Republic of Liberia, Africa, founded by the Maryland State Colonization Society in 1834. Expeditions sent to Monrovia in 1831 and 1832 proved unsuccessful. John Russworm, a citizen of Monrovia, was chosen the first governor in 1836. In 1857 it became part of Liberia.

Mason and Slidell, Confederate envoys to Great Britain and France, removal of, from British steamer *Trent,* 3262, 3263, 3264, 3267, 3268.

Mason and Dixon's Line.—The boundary line between Pennsylvania and Maryland. It is coincident with the parallel of 39° 43', beginning at the Delaware River and running 244 miles to the westward, and was laid out by two eminent English mathematicians and astronomers, Charles Mason and Jeremiah Dixon, about 1766. Lord Baltimore and William Penn having disputed the boundary between their adjoining grants, the case was taken to London for adjudication and the parties to the suit were ordered to have the line run. The surveyors marked the line with boundary posts, having on one side the arms of Penn and on the other those of Lord Baltimore. The line became famous in later days as marking in part the boundary between free and slave states. During the discussion in Congress on the Missouri compromise John Randolph of Roanoke made free use of this phrase, which contributed to its more popular use as such dividing line.

Masonic, The, confiscation of, attempted by Spain, discussed, 4626, 4759.

Indemnity for, awarded, 4919.

Massachusetts.—One of the thirteen original states of the Union; nickname, "The Old Bay State"; motto, "Ense petit placidam sub libertate quietem" ("With the sword she seeks quiet peace under liberty"). It was named from the Massachusetts Indians, who occupied the eastern part of the territory. The name means "At the Great Hills." Massachusetts extends from lat. 41° 14' to 42° 53' north and from long. 69° 53' to 73° 32' west. It is bounded on the north by Vermont and New Hampshire, on the east by the Atlantic Ocean, on the south by the Atlantic Ocean, Rhode Island and Connecticut, and on the west by New York, and has an area of 8,266 square miles.

Massachusetts chartered the first college in America. It has produced more eminent literary men than any other state in the Union. It is the leading state in the manufacture of boots and shoes and cotton and woolen goods. It was visited by Gosnold in 1602 and settled at Plymouth in 1620. This was the third in the order of settlement of the British Colonies in America. Later settlements were made at Salem and Boston in 1628 and 1630. A Confederate union of the Massachusetts, Plymouth, New Haven, and the Connecticut Colonies existed from 1643 to 1684 for defensive purposes. Massachusetts took an important part in the Revolutionary War and the organization of the Government. It was the scene of Shay's Rebellion in 1786-1787.

Statistics of agriculture collected for the last Federal census place the number of farms in the State at 36,917, comprising 2,875,941 acres, valued, with stock and improvements, at $226,474,025. The average value of land per acre was $36.69, as compared with $27.62 in 1900. The value of domestic animals, poultry, etc., was $20,-741,366, including 252,416 cattle, valued at $9,348,076; 64,283 horses, $8,671,997; 268 mules, $43,385; 103,108 swine, $978,989; 32,708 sheep, $156,498. The yield and value of field crops for 1911 is given as follows: corn, 47,000 acres, 2,068,000 bushels, $1,716,000; oats, 8,000 acres, 280,000 bushels, $162,000; rye, 3,000 acres, 48,000 bushels, $46,000; potatoes, 25,000 acres, 2,325,000 bushels, $2,232,000; hay, 584,-000 acres, 631,000 tons, $14,513,000; tobacco, 5,600 acres, 9,240,000 pounds, $1,-848,000. The mineral products of the State in 1910 were $6,077,370. Of this, stone, of which Massachusetts is one of the largest producers, was valued at $3,539,794. The total bonded debt of the State at the end of the fiscal year ending Nov. 30, 1910, was $81,077,452. The net receipts during the year amounted to $11,992,395, and the expenditures were $13,481,137; cash balance, $2,186,431.

The salt water fisheries of the State for 1905 produced $8,986,186.

The first mercantile census ever taken in the United States was taken in Massachusetts in 1905. It showed that the value of goods sold by the establishments of the State was $1,384,241,383, of which $967,-009,354 was credited to Boston. In 1907 there were 181 national banks in the State, of which 20 were in Boston; 189 savings banks, 135 co-operative banks and 45 trust companies. The population in 1910 was 3,366,416.

The number of manufacturing establishments in Massachusetts having an annual output valued at $500 or more at the beginning of 1915 was 12,013. The amount of capital invested was $1,548,961,000, giving employment to 676,640 persons, using material valued at $931,384,000, and turning out finished goods worth $1,641,373,000. Salaries and wages paid amounted to $425,024,000.

Massachusetts (see also Boston; Lynn):

Claims of, for services rendered by militia in War of 1812, discussed, 795, 854.

Constitution of United States, ratification of certain articles of, evidences of, 166.

Governor of—

Referred to, 65.

Refusal of, to furnish militia for defense of frontier, 501.

Prisoners in, provision for, recommended, 183.

Massachusetts Bay Company.—A colonizing company chartered in England, March 19, 1628, by John Humphrey, John Endicott, and others. The company grew out of the preexisting Dorchester Company, and was the result of imperiled political and religious rights in England under Charles I. The patentees received a grant of land extending from the Atlantic to the "Western Ocean," in width from a line running three miles north of the Merrimac to one running three miles south of the Charles. Endicott headed a colony which settled at Salem in September, 1628. March 4, 1629, a new charter was granted to the governor and company of Massachusetts Bay, and the old officers of the company were succeeded by John Winthrop as governor, with a deputy and eighteen assistants. In 1630 Winthrop, at the head of a large body of settlers, transferred the company 'headquarters to America and founded Boston. Under this charter Massachusetts carried on her government for fifty-five years.

Massachusetts, The, appropriation to owners for detention of the *Perthshire* by, recommended, 3247.

Massachusetts, The (battleship), mentioned, 6396.

Massacre of Christians. (See Armenians.)

Matanzas, Cuba, harbor and forts shelled by American squadron, 6315.

Mayflower Compact.—Before the landing of the Pilgrim Fathers the company gathered in the cabin of the *Mayflower*, in Provincetown Harbor, Nov. 11, 1620, and there bound themselves into a body politic and pledged themselves to abide individually and collectively by the laws they should make.

Mayflower Descendants.—Organized in the City of New York, Dec. 22, 1894, by lineal descendants of the *Mayflower* pilgrims, "to preserve their memory, their records, their history, and all facts relating to them, their ancestors, and their posterity." Every lineal descendant over eighteen years of age, male or female, or any passenger of the voyage of the *Mayflower* which terminated at Plymouth, Mass., December, 1620, including all signers of "The Compact," are eligible to membership. The initiation fee is $10 and the annual dues are $5. The Triennial Congress is held in September at Plymouth, Mass. Societies have been organized in New York, Connecticut, Massachusetts, Pennsylvania, Illinois, District of Columbia, Ohio, New Jersey, Wisconsin, Rhode Island, Michigan, Minnesota, Maine, Colorado, and California.

Maysville, Washington, Paris and Lexington Turnpike Road Co., act authorizing subscription of stock in, vetoed, 1046.

Mazzei Letter.—A private letter written by Thomas Jefferson to an Italian named Mazzei in 1796. The letter was translated and published in an English paper. It aroused much animosity against Jefferson by its supposed allusion to Washington and others as those "Samsons in the field and Solomons in the council" who had formed an Anglican monarchical aristocratic party in America whose avowed object was "to draw over us the substance, as they had already done the forms, of the British Government."

Meat Packing and Slaughtering.—The art of refrigeration has been so perfected in recent years that fresh meat may be shipped thousands of miles and its quality so preserved that it is even more desirable and palatable at its destination than at the point where slaughtered. The present methods of curing and preserving by salting, smoking, etc., differ from the ancient methods only in the extent and system adopted. Preservation in hermetically sealed cans or jars is a comparatively recent process, introduced into the United States in 1873. The utilization of the by-products of slaughtering, such as hides, hoofs, horns, bones, hair, fats, intestines, blood, etc., has broadened the scope of the business and added from $1 to $2 per head to the value of animals.

The present day meat packing establishment, with a constant demand, arranges for a constant supply of live animals by maintaining stock yards which are regularly fed by accession from the farmer and herder. Machinery, too, has employed an important part in bringing the modern meat packing establishment to completion. In the up-to-date plant operations are continuous, lighted at night by electricity and surrounded always by the latest sanitary precautions and appliances.

The rise of slaughtering and meat packing as a distinct industry in the United States dates back to 1818, when a packer is recorded as conducting business in Cincinnati. Similar operations were begun in Chicago in 1823, but the packing statistics of the latter city were of small account until 1850, though it is said 9,600 hogs were packed there in 1834. It was not until 1861-62 that Chicago attained pre-eminence as a packing centre.

During the winter of 1832-33 there were several packing establishments in Cincinnati, and it is claimed that 85,000 hogs were slaughtered there that season. The development of the agricultural resources of the Ohio Valley cheapened the cost of raising stock, and the demands of the Eastern and Southern markets caused increased production, particularly of hogs. Cincinnati's pre-eminence in the meat packing industry was maintained up to the beginning of the Civil War, when Chicago took the lead it has since maintained.

Cincinnati's advantage was due to its situation in the centre of the stock-raising region and to its superior banking facilities, for the packing industry demanded that large sums be expended in ready cash. It was also necessary often to employ large gangs of laborers and coopers at short notice and these could be had at Cincinnati. An ample supply of salt was always readily obtainable there. In 1844 there were twenty-six packing houses in Cincinnati, and in 1856, forty-two. During the season of 1848-49 475,000 hogs were slaughtered there.

About 20,000 hogs were killed in Chicago in 1850-51, and since that time the business has steadily increased. The Union Stock Yards were laid out on 320 acres of land in 1865. This area has been doubled since, and the plant is now worth $10,000,000, and employs 50,000 men. The amount of capital invested was given in 1900 as $67,000,000. Within the yards are twenty miles of water troughs, seventy-five miles of drainage pipes and 150 miles of railroad track.

Efforts to shorten the overland journey of live cattle, sheep and hogs from the western farms and ranges where raised to the place of slaughter caused the establishment of yards and packing houses further west. With the development of the country west of the Mississippi St. Louis took its rise as a packing and slaughtering centre. The importance of Kansas City as a meat packing centre dates from 1870. The stock yards there cover about 200 acres. There were only three packing houses in the city in 1873. Other meat packing centres are St. Joseph, Mo., and Omaha, Neb.

According to the census of 1910 there were 1,641 establishments engaged in meat packing and slaughtering. These were capitalized at $383,249,170, employed 108,716 persons and paid out $71,698,677 in salaries and wages. They turned out finished goods to the value of $1,370,568,101, of which $1,202,827,784 represented the cost of material. The business is divided into three classes—slaughtering and meat packing, slaughtering not including meat packing, and the manufacture of sausage. Those engaged primarily in slaughtering and meat packing formed 40 per cent of the whole number, and employed more than 90 per cent. of the wage-earners. Establishments engaged chiefly in slaughtering formed one-third of the whole number, but they employed only 7.2 per cent. of the wage-earners. The 420 establishments engaged in the manufacture of sausage reported 2.1 per cent of the wage-earners and contributed 1.1 per cent of the value of the finished goods.

The number of establishments as a whole increased 20 per cent. during the twenty years preceding the last census. The number of wage-earners more than doubled during this period, and the value of products increased 142.7 per cent. The business is well distributed throughout the country, being reported on from 43 states and the District of Columbia. Illinois is by far the most important state in the industry. The value of the business in that state increased 35 per cent. in ten years.

There were slaughtered for food in wholesale establishments in 1914, 7,149,042 beeves, 2,019,004 calves, 15,951,860 sheep and lambs and goats and kids, and 34,441,913 hogs.

Reports made to the Department of Commerce in 1914 show the following values of products for the preceding year:

PRODUCTS	POUNDS	VALUE
Fresh Meat:		
Beef	3,658,333,660	$421,296,794
Veal	104,698,880	26,299,446
Mutton and lamb and goat and kid	629,232,690	74,675,627
Pork	1,877,099,071	226,535,734
Edible offal and all other fresh meat	296,666,701	20,576,245
Cured Meat:		
Beef, pickled and other cured	91,571,753	14,395,316
Pork, pickled and other cured	2,929,309,741	393,605,600
Canned goods	160,798,955	26,417,624
Sausage:		
Canned	74,004,380	9,845,669
All other	435,146,931	58,349,853
Lard, oils and fats:		
Lard	1,119,188,675	120,414,007
Lard compounds and substitutes	396,397,950	33,037,467

	GALLONS	VALUE
Oleo oil	16,501,585	$ 11,925,832
Other oils	6,715,497	4,009,602
Tallow and oleo stock	209,614,135	$ 13,731.756
Stearin	30,091,991	2,752,421
Oleomargarine	60,387,881	8,818,557
All other products, value*		185,076,874
Total value		$1,651,765,424

*Includes value of baked beans, confectionery, fertilizers' fertilizer materials, glue, head cheese, hides and skins, hog hair, ice, meat puddings, peanut butter, preserves, sausage casings, scrapple, wool, etc., and amount received for slaughtering and refrigeration for others.

Location of Establishments.—With the exception of North Dakota, every state in the Union reported one or more abattoirs for 1914. Of the 1,279 establishments which made up the total for that year, 184 were located in New York, 152 in Ohio, 146 in Pennsylvania, 81 in California, 70 in Illinois, 65 in Indiana, 56 in New Jersey, 46 each in Maryland and Massachusetts, 31 in Missouri, 28 each in Iowa and Kentucky, 26 in Kansas, 22 in Wisconsin, 21 each in Maine and Virginia, 19 each in Delaware and Minnesota, 18 each in Tennessee and Texas, 17 in Michigan, 16 in Colorado, 14 each in Oregon and Utah, 11 each in Florida and Washington, 10 each in Nebraska and Rhode Island, 9 in Idaho, 8 in Montana, 7 each in Alabama and West Virginia, 5 each in Connecticut, District of Columbia, and New Hampshire, 4 each in Georgia, Louisiana, Nevada, Oklahoma, and South Dakota, 3 each in Arkansas and Vermont, 2 in South Carolina, and 1 each in Arizona, Mississippi, New Mexico, North Carolina, and Wyoming.

Meat Products. (See Animals and Animal Products.)

Mechanicsville (Va.), Battle of.—One of the Seven Days' Battles before Richmond. On June 26, 1862, Lee massed his troops on his left, A. P. Hill crossing to the north side of the Chickahominy and being supported by Longstreet and D. H. Hill. Jackson joined the Confederate forces later. The Confederate attack on Fitz-John Porter at dawn was repulsed, but the Federal army subsequently retired. According to Federal accounts, the Confederate loss was 1,500, the Union 361. This battle is also called the battle of Beaver Dam Creek.

Mecklenburg Declaration.—A series of resolutions purporting to have been adopted by the citizens of Mecklenburg County, N. C., May 20, 1775, declaring their independence of Great Britain, followed by a second series of resolutions, adopted on the 31st of May, providing for a local government. The independence resolutions were first published in 1819 and created much discussion as to their genuineness. They contained several phrases almost or quite identical with portions of the document adopted at Philadelphia, July 4, 1776. Thomas Jefferson immediately declared them fraudulent. It was admitted that the original Mecklenburg resolutions were burned in 1800 and that those published in 1819 were reproduced from memory by a son of one of the secretaries of the meeting. The North Carolina legislature investigated the matter and secured enough evidence to warrant them in making May 20 a state holiday. The historians are divided in opinion. Hildreth, one of the most critical, admits the validity of the Declaration, but, curiously enough, says it was made May 31. Bancroft contends that only a provisional government was formed, and that on the date of the 31st. There is no dispute as to the fact that a government was organized. In North Carolina, among the Scotch-Irish people, there exists little doubt that the Mecklenburgers declared their independence on May 20, 1775. William A. Graham, Secretary of the Navy from 1850 to 1852 and candidate of the Whigs for vice-president in 1852, was the son of Joseph Graham, who was present at the meeting in Charlotte which declared independence, and testified to the fact.

Mecklenburg-Schwerin:
Treaty with, 2417, 2479.
Vessels of, discriminating duties on, suspended by proclamation, 1365.

Medal of Honor Legion.—Composed of officers and enlisted men of the United States army and navy who have been awarded medals of honor for most distinguished gallantry in action during any war in which the United States has been engaged. At the present time it has 440 such members.

Medals.—Congress has from time to time awarded gold and silver medals for distinguished services in the army and navy. Since the civil war most of the medals have been awarded for heroic rescues from dangers at sea. Under resolutions of 1874, 1878 and 1882 several hundred medals of honor have been awarded by the Secretary of the Treasury for life saving. Among the recipients of the latter have been eight women.

The following is a list of persons who have been awarded medals by Congress for distinguished services in the army and navy:

Gen. George Washington, (gold medal) for the Capture of Boston.
Brig.-Gen. Horatio Gates, (gold) Defeat of Burgoyne.
Maj.-Gen. Anthony Wayne, (gold) Storming of Stony Point.
Lieut.-Col. De Fleury, (silver) Storming of Stony Point.
Maj. John Stewart, (silver) Storming of Stony Point.
Maj. Henry Lee, (gold) Surprise of Paulus Hook.
John Paulding, (silver) Capture of Andre.
David Williams, (silver) Capture of Andre.

Isaac Van Wart, (silver) Capture of Andre.
Brig.-Gen. Daniel Morgan, (gold) Victory of Cowpens.
Lieut.-Col. William A. Washington, (silver) Victory of Cowpens.
Lieut. John E. Howard, (silver) Victory of Cowpens.
Maj.-Gen. Nathaniel Greene, (gold) Victory at Eutaw Springs.
Capt. John Paul Jones, (gold) Capture of the *Serapis* 1779.
Capt. Thomas Truxtun, (gold) Action with the *Vengeance* (fr).
Com. Edward Preble, (gold) Tripoli.
Capt. Isaac Hull, (gold) Capture of the *Guerriere.*
Capt. Jacob Jones, (gold) Capture of the *Frolic.*
Capt. Stephen Decatur, (gold) Capture of the *Macedonian.*
Capt. William Bainbridge, (gold) Capture of the *Java.*
Lieut. Edward R. McCall, (gold) Capture of the *Boxer.*
Com. Oliver H. Perry, (gold) Victory on Lake Erie.
Capt. Jesse D. Elliott, (gold) Victory on Lake Erie.
Capt. James Lawrence, (gold) Capture of the *Peacock.*
Com. Thomas Macdonough, (gold) Victory on Lake Champlain.
Capt. Robert Henley, (gold) Victory on Lake Champlain.
Lieut. Stephen Cassin, (gold) Victory on Lake Champlain.
Capt. Lewis Warrington, (gold) Capture of the *Empervier.*
Capt. Johnston Blakely (to the widow), (gold) Capture of the *Reindeer.*
Maj.-Gen. Jacob Brown, (gold) Victory of Chippewa, etc.
Maj.-Gen. Peter B. Porter, (gold) Victory of Chippewa, etc.
Brig.-Gen. E. W. Ripley, (gold) Victory of Chippewa, etc.
Brig.-Gen. James Miller, (gold) Victory of Chippewa, etc.
Maj.-Gen. Winfield Scott, (gold) Victory of Chippewa, etc.
Maj.-Gen. Edmund P. Gaines, (gold) Victory of Erie.
Maj.-Gen. Alexander Macomb, (gold) Victory of Plattsburg.
Maj.-Gen. Andrew Jackson, (gold) Victory of New Orleans.
Capt. Charles Stewart, (gold) Capture of *Cyane* and *Levant.*
Capt. James Biddle, (gold) Capture of *Penguin.*
Maj.-Gen. William H. Harrison, (gold) Victory of the Thames.
Gov. Isaac Shelby, (gold) Victory of the Thames.
Col. Geo. Croghan (22 yrs. after), (gold) Defence of Fort Stephenson, 1813.
Maj.-Gen. Zachary Taylor, (gold) Victory on Rio Grande.
Maj.-Gen. Zachary Taylor, (gold) Capture of Monterey.
British, French and Spanish officers and crews, (gold and silver) Rescuing Crew of the U. S. Brig-of-war *Somers* before Vera Cruz, Dec. 7, 1846.
Maj.-Gen. Winfield Scott, (gold) Mexican Campaign.
Maj.-Gen. Zachary Taylor, (gold) Victory of Buena Vista.
Capt. Duncan N. Ingraham, (gold) Release of Martin Koszta.
Dr. Frederick H. Rose of the British Navy, (gold) Humanity—care of yellow fever patients from Jamaica to N. Y. on the U. S. S. *Susquehanna.*
Maj.-Gen. Ulysses S. Grant, (gold) Vic-

tories of Fort Donelson, Vicksburg, Chattanooga.

Cornelius Vanderbilt, (gold) Gift of ship *Vanderbilt.*

Capts. Creighton, Low and Stouffler, (gold) Rescuing 500 passengers from the S. S. *San Francisco,* July 26, 1853.

Cyrus W. Field, (gold) Laying the Atlantic Cable.

George Peabody, (gold) Promotion of Education.

Capt. Crandall and others, Long Island lighthouse keeper and crew, (gold) Saving passengers from the *Metis* of the N. Y. and Providence Line, Aug. 31, 1872.

George F. Robinson, (gold) Saving William H. Seward from assassination Apr. 14, 1865. Besides the medal $5,000.

Under resolutions of July 12, 1862, and March 3, 1863, 2,000 army medals of bronze were provided for non-commissioned officers and privates for gallantry in action. All the members of the twenty-seventh Maine volunteers received these medals for remaining in service for the battle of Gettysburg after their terms had expired.

Naval medals were authorized in 1861 and 1862 to be bestowed on petty officers, seamen and marines for gallantry in action. Two hundred were issued.

Medals, Life-Saving, government grant of, 7026.

Mediation and Conciliation, Board of.— (Created by act of Congress approved July 15, 1913.) The purpose for which the Board of Mediation and Conciliation was established is to settle by mediation, conciliation and arbitration controversies concerning wages, hours of labor or conditions of employment that may arise between common carriers engaged in interstate transportation and their employees engaged in train operation or train service.

In any case where an interruption of traffic is imminent and fraught with serious detriment to the public interest, the Board of Mediation and Conciliation may, if in its judgment such action seem desirable, proffer its services to the respective parties to the controversy.

Whenever a controversy concerning wages, hours of labor, or conditions of employment arises between such railroads and such employees, interrupting or threatening to interrupt the operation of trains to the serious detriment of the public interest, upon the request of either party the Board of Mediation is required to use its best efforts, by mediation and conciliation, to bring about an agreement. If such efforts to bring about an amicable adjustment through mediation and conciliation are unsuccessful, the board endeavors to induce the parties to submit their controversy to arbitration and, if successful, makes the necessary arrangements for such arbitration. The board is an independent office, not connected with any department.

Medical Museum, Army, building for, recommended, 4572, 4780, 4833.

Medicine and Surgery, Bureau of, Navy Department. (See Bureau of Medicine and Surgery.)

Medicines, Patent.—For purposes of valuation and enumeration the federal census bureau classifies under this heading many patent compounds and druggists' preparations. The patent office has a list of synthetical chemicals, the formulas of which are protected by letters patent, but most of the special remedies are protected only in the use of their distinctive names. The value of patent medicines manufactured in the United States as ascertained in 1910 amounted to $141,942,000. This figure represents the wholesale price, indicating that the public spends about $200,000,000 in retail purchases. The census of 1900 gave the value of the annual product at $59,611,355. Comparison of these figures shows the rapid growth of the business in recent years.

The cost of material entering into the manufacture of patent medicines is smaller in proportion to the retail price than that of perhaps any other business. The profits to the manufacturers, however, are largely reduced by the discounts allowed dealers and the cost of advertising, upon which the success of the business largely depends. Patent medicine manufacturers are among the largest general advertisers in the country. It is estimated that $40,000,000 is spent annually for periodical advertising. The number of establishments reported by the last census was 3,642, employing an average of 22,895 wageworkers.

"Druggists' preparations" include all materials for use by druggists in compounding medicines to be dispensed upon physicians' prescriptions or orders. These comprise tinctures, fluid extracts, medicinal sirups, and other liquid preparations; pills, tablets, powders, etc.; alkaloids and derivatives (cocaine, codein, morphine, quinine, and strychnine); synthetic medicinal preparations, such as acetanilid, acetphenetidin, phenolphthalein, saccharin, methylsalicylate, etc.; medicinal metals and their salts (bromides, acetates, citrates, bismuth, etc.); and biological products, such as serums, vaccines, toxins, etc.

"Patent and proprietary medicines" are those sold under the protection of a patent, copyright, or trademark, or prepared according to a secret formula; and "patent and proprietary compounds" include all such compounds not intended for medicinal use, such as fire-extinguisher compounds, household ammonia, insecticides, etc.

"Perfumery and cosmetics" comprise cologne, toilet waters, face powders, cold cream, etc., and perfumes.

Reports for 1914 were received from 4,082 establishments, with products valued at $172,008,946.

Of the 4,082 establishments reported for all three branches of the industry, 850 were located in New York, 391 in Illinois, 353 in Pennsylvania, 267 in Ohio, 234 in Missouri, 179 in Massachusetts, 161 in Indiana, 155 in Michigan, 142 in California, 134 in New Jersey, and 107 in Minnesota, and the remaining 1,109 establishments were distributed among 34 states, ranging from 99 in Iowa to 1 in Arizona. The states for which no establishments were reported are Idaho, Nevada, New Mexico, and Wyoming.

Druggists' Preparations.—The manufacture of druggists' preparations in 1914 was reported by 438 establishments, with products valued at $48,624,966. At the census of 1909 there were reported 375 establishments, with products valued at $43,958,479. The increase in number of establishments thus amounted to 16.8 per cent, and in value of products to 10.6 per cent.

The production of liquid preparations, such as tinctures, fluid extracts, and medicinal sirups, reported for 1914 was valued at $13,900,402; and of pills, tablets, powders, etc., at $10,903,056. These figures, however, are to be considered as representing only an approximate distribution of these classes of goods because of the inability of the manufacturers in many cases to make separate reports for certain products.

The manufacture of alkaloids and their derivatives in 1914 was reported by 142 establishments, with products valued at $11,493,168. Of these establishments, 27 were located in New York, 17 in Pennsylvania, 13 in Illinois, 8 in Ohio, and 7 in New Jersey, and the remaining 70 were distributed among 27 states.

The production of synthetic medicinal preparations to the value of $1,384,996 was reported by 72 establishments, of which 17 were located in New York and 10 in Pennsylvania, the remaining 45 being distributed among 20 states.

The manufacture of medicinal metals and their salts, valued at $732,307, was reported by 47 establishments, of which 16 were located in New York and 11 in Pennsylvania, the remaining 20 being distributed among 11 states.

The manufacture of serums, vaccines, toxins, and other biological products, to the value of $6,223,475, was reported by 93 establishments, of which 19 were located in Kansas, 10 each in Illinois, Missouri, and Nebraska, 7 in Pennsylvania, 6 each in Indiana, Iowa, and New York, 5 in Montana, 3 each in Michigan and Wisconsin, 2 each in Minnesota and South Dakota, and 1 each in California, District of Columbia, Kentucky, and Tennessee.

Patent and Proprietary Medicines and Compounds.—The manufacture of patent and proprietary medicines and compounds in 1914 was reported by 3,085 establishments, with products valued at $105,665,611.

Patent and proprietary medicines to the value of $83,455,264 were manufactured by 2,271 establishments in 1914 (including some which were engaged primarily in the manufacture of druggists' preparations and perfumery and cosmetics), the leading five states in this branch of the industry being New York, with 406 establishments; Illinois, 203; Pennsylvania, 192; Ohio, 156; and Missouri, 126; and patent and proprietary compounds to the value of $16,514,352 were manufactured by 1,006 establishments, the leading five states being New York, with 211 establishments; Illinois, 97; Pennsylvania, 83; Missouri, 73; and Massachusetts, 60. Some of these establishments manufactured both medicines and compounds.

Perfumery and Cosmetics.—The manufacture of perfumery and cosmetics in 1914 was reported by 559 establishments, with products valued at $17,718,369. These figures, however, do not include the products of establishments classified, according to their principal products, in the other two branches of this industry.

The value of the production of perfumery and cosmetics and other toilet preparations in 1914, by all establishments including those engaged primarily in the manufacture of druggists' preparations and of patent and proprietary medicines and compounds, was $19,160,427.

The leading five states reporting the 559 establishments classified in this branch of the industry were New York, with 175; Illinois, 67; Pennsylvania, 45; Ohio, 34; and Michigan, 28.

Mediterranean Sea:
Naval force in, should be increased, 333, 356, 826.
Piracies in, 929.
Trade with, 75, 77, 78.
Vessels sent to, for protection of commerce, 314, 347, 358, 631, 826, 874, 928, 1008.

Mediterranean Squadron, referred to, 1905, 1953.

Medium of Exchange. (See also Currency):
Augmentation of, discussed, 643.
Discussed by President—
Buchanan, 2968.
Grant, 3983, 4198, 4239.
Johnson, 3769, 3877.
Madison, 550, 563.
Monroe, 643.
Tyler, 1897, 1935, 2119.
Gold and silver—
Hope expressed that use of, for, will become general, 1383.
To take place of bills below $20 recommended, 1385.
Paper used as, discussed, 1897, 1935.
Restoration of uniform system of, recommended, 563.

Mee-sée-qua-guilch Indians. (See Indian Tribes.)

Melbourne, Australia:
International exhibition at, to celebrate centenary of founding of New South Wales, 5176.
International Exhibition of Arts and Industries at, discussed, 4519, 4559, 4625.

Melton, Miss, assailants of, in Turkey, conviction of, discussed, 5962.

Members of Congress. (See Congress.)

Memorial and Remonstrance. (See Religious Freedom.)

Memphis (Tenn.), Capture of.—After the evacuation of Corinth, Miss., by Beauregard, Fort Pillow, forty miles above Memphis, was useless, as the Union army could take it from the rear. The Confederates therefore spiked the guns, burned the barracks, and what supplies they could not take away, and in their gunboats dropped down the river to Memphis. The Confederate fleet consisted of 8 vessels, mounted 28 guns, commanded by Commodore Montgomery. On June 6, 1862, Commodore Davis, with 5 Union gunboats and 2 rams, appeared before the city, and Montgomery went forth to give him battle. After one hour and twenty minutes of fierce fighting the Confederate fleet was defeated. Col. Ellet, who built the rams, was the only person injured on the Federal side. The number of killed and wounded on the Confederate side is not known, but was probably between 80 and 100.

Memphis, Tenn., navy-yard to be established at, 2202.
Proposition of city authorities of, relative to, 2829.

Mercantile Marines of France, Germany, Great Britain, and Italy, referred to, 4978.

Merchant Marine.—The British navigation acts, beginning in 1645, prohibited importations into the Colonies except in English or colonial built ships. Though seriously restricting commerce, these acts served to stimulate the shipbuilding interest.

Between 1789 and 1797 the registered tonnage of United States commercial ships increased 384 per cent. From 1837 to 1857 the tonnage increased from 810,000 to

2,268,000, and in 1861 the aggregate tonnage of American registered vessels reached the highest point—5,539,813. This nearly equaled the combined tonnage of all other nations excepting Great Britain, which alone was slightly in excess of it. For various reasons American shipping fell off after the Civil War, until it became quite insignificant. During recent years, however, a revival has taken place, more especially in the coastwise trade, the number of vessels (1915) engaged in it being 26,701, with a tonnage of 8,389,429.

For many years no country of importance other than the United States has required that ships flying the national flag shall be of domestic construction, although practically every country has made this requirement in the case of steamships receiving postal subventions. England has granted registers to foreign-built ships, in other words has pursued the free-ship policy, since about 1850. At that time, it is interesting to note, wooden sailing vessels were predominant and these could be secured more cheaply in the United States, which had larger supplies of timber and naval stores and a more efficient ship-building industry. As a result of this free-ship policy the merchant marine of England received large accessions during the Civil War, when more than 750,000 tons of American shipping secured English registers to avoid capture or destruction.

The policy of granting loans to shipowners at low interest or without interest was begun, it is believed, by Austria. The only instance of such a loan by the British Government was that made to the Cunard Steamship Line under the mail and admiralty subvention contract of 1903. Under this contract the British Government loaned the steamship company $12,652,900, for building two steamers that would be suitable for use by the admiralty and be the fastest afloat. This loan brought into being the Lusitania and Mauretania. The loan was made at the rate of 2¾ per cent, which was about 2 per cent lower than the rate at which the company could have borrowed a similar amount in the open market.

Exemption from taxation is a form of indirect assistance granted by only Austria-Hungary and by a few of our own States. A notable law in New York State exempts from all taxation for State and local purposes all American-owned ships registered at any port in the State if engaged in the foreign trade of the United States. Corporations owning such ships are exempt until December 31, 1922, from all taxation upon their stock, franchises, and earnings. Alabama exempts all ships engaged in foreign commerce from taxation, while the State of Washington exempts all ships built or in process of construction in the coastwise as well as in the foreign trade of the United States.

The granting of postal subventions to steamship lines antedates the bounty or subsidy system and is in more general use throughout the world. Great Britain was probably the first to pay subventions of this kind, the first contract of the sort being made in 1838. The United States and France soon followed suit—the United States in 1847 and France in 1851. Germany did not adopt the policy until 1886, when a contract with the North German Lloyd was concluded. The purpose of mail subvention contracts is primarily to encourage the maintenance of fast mail services on regular routes and schedules. In many instances a motive of almost equal weight is that of maintaining the fastest possible communication between the mother country and her colonies. Incidentally a

third object is commonly achieved, namely, that of providing vessels suitable for auxiliary cruisers and transports in time of war, and, in many cases a fourth object, namely, that of fostering the domestic shipbuilding industry by requiring that the subventions shall be paid only to domestic-built ships. With only two important exceptions, all financial aid extended by the British Government has been in the form of postal and admiralty subventions. The United States and Germany, whose merchant navies rank next to that of Great Britain, have extended financial aid to shipping only in the form of mail subventions.

The system of paying direct general bounties or subsidies to shipping lines may be said to have been instituted by France, which entered upon this policy in 1881, and has made a more extensive use of bounties than any other country, although as a whole the results have **not** been satisfactory. Italy, Austria-Hungary, Japan, and Spain have followed the French plan, with indifferent success except in the case of Japan. Unquestionably the merchant marine of Japan has developed more rapidly during the last 35 years than that of any other nation, although this development is in part due to the phenomenal development of Japanese industries in recent years.

Some specific opportunities that now exist for American shipping are as follows: The west coast of South America imports large quantities of coal from Australia and Wales. Since the construction of the efficient coal-carrying railroads, such as the Norfolk and Western, the Chesapeake and Ohio, the Virginian, and the Carolina, Clinchfield and Ohio, Virginia steam coal of excellent quality can be delivered at low cost at the Atlantic seaboard ports of Norfolk, Newport News, and Charleston, where it can be delivered to vessel quickly, efficiently, and at low cost. It is believed that increasingly large quantities of this coal can be sold in Chile and Peru at lower cost than Australian or Welsh coal. If this proves to be the case, the vessels carrying coal from the United States can return with nitrates from Chile, copper from American-owned mines and smelters in Chile and Peru, tin ore from American-owned mines in Bolivia, and iron ore from American-owned mines in Chile. The development of coal exports would cause reductions in return freights (a factor which goes far toward accounting for the maritime supremacy of Great Britain) and an extension of American shipping.

Merchant Marine:

Development of, hindered, 8016.

Need for, discussed by Taft, 7674.

Merchant Vessels:

Claims resulting from destruction of United States vessels by Confederate vessels, referred to, 3964.

Condition of American, 6653, 6654, 7005.

Discussed, 6239, 6241, 6338, 6359, 6381, 6436, 6460, 6653.

Naval force for protection of, in Mexican ports, etc., recommended, 3100.

Meridian Conference, International:

At Washington, discussed, 4718, 4800, 4827, 4841, 5180.

Invitation of Italian Government to attend, 5546.

Merrimac, The (Confederate ram), engagement of, with—
Cumberland, 3345.
Monitor, 3313.
See Hampton Roads (Va.), Battle of, and illustration opposite 3309, 3910.

Merrimac, The.—This vessel, a two-masted iron steamship of 5,000 tons, was used by the United States in the Spanish-American War as a collier. During the month of May, 1898, the Spanish fleet under Admiral Cervera took refuge in the harbor of Santiago. The city of Santiago is well located within the harbor, about five miles from the ocean proper. The channel leading from the harbor out to the ocean is at certain points quite narrow and comparatively easy to obstruct. This channel was well covered by Spanish batteries on shore, so that it was deemed unwise on the part of the American officers to attempt to enter the harbor with war ships. The American commander decided to attempt to block the channel, and for this purpose concluded to sink the *Merrimac* at a narrow point. It follows necessarily that such an undertaking would be exceedingly dangerous to those who were to steer the unarmed vessel within the channel, and then at the proper moment sink it and endeavor to escape by swimming ashore or attempting to reach a lifeboat.

Assistant Naval Constructor Richmond P. Hobson was chosen at his own request to execute the hazardous undertaking. Volunteers were called for to accompany and assist him. Fifteen hundred officers and men responded, gallantly tendering services, and begged that they be accepted. Six only were accepted, whose names are Daniel Montague, chief master-at-arms of the *New York;* George Charette, gunner's mate of the *New York;* John Murphy, cockswain of the *Iowa;* Francis Kelly, water tender; George F. Phillips, machinist, and Cockswain O. W. Deignan, the last three of the *Merrimac.* Randolph Clousen, cockswain of the *New York,* was during the delay of one day added to the company. On the morning of June 3, 1898, at about half past three o'clock, Hobson steered straight into the channel under a heavy fire from Spanish guns on both sides. As the *Merrimac* reached the spot that had been picked out for her sinking he gave orders to explode the torpedoes. Two of them only exploded. Amid the tremendous fire from the shore batteries, the firing of 8 electric mines in the channel, and torpedoes from two Spanish vessels, the collier sank, her masts and smokestack showing above the water, obstructing but not blocking the fairway. As the ship went down the Spaniards sent up a cheer, believing they had sunk some large war vessel. Hobson and his men held on to a catamaran belonging to their sunken ship for about an hour. Just after sunrise a steam launch came down the harbor with Admiral Cervera on board. Hobson and his men were taken on board the launch, were courteously treated by their captors, and placed in prison. They were all exchanged July 6.

The sinking of the *Merrimac* was an act of heroism which challenged the admiration of the world. The President, in a message to Congress, speaking of the incident, said: "This enterprise, demanding coolness, judgment, and bravery amounting to heroism, was carried into successful execution in the face of a persistent fire from the hostile fleet as well as from the fortifications on shore" (6305). Rear-Admiral Sampson said: "I cannot myself too earnestly express my appreciation of the conduct of Mr. Hobson and his gallant crew. I venture

to say that a more brave and daring thing has not been done since Cushing blew up the *Albemarle"* (6306). The President recommended that a vote of thanks be given Hobson by Congress. He and his crew were subsequently promoted.

Merrimac, The (United States collier), sinking of, in Santiago Harbor, Cuba, by Lieut. Richmond P. Hobson, 6305, 6316.
Naval Cadet Powell to be made ensign for attempting to rescue force of, 6306.
Thanks of Congress to Lieut. Hobson and promotion of, recommended 6306.

Merryman Case.—Merryman, a citizen of Maryland, was arrested at his home in 1861 by order of an officer of the United States Army, and charged with treason. He was imprisoned in Fort McHenry. Chief Justice Taney granted a writ of habeas corpus, which the officer in charge of the prisoner refused to execute on the ground that the President had suspended the writ. The case was taken before the Supreme Court, which decided that the power to suspend the writ of habeas corpus was not vested in the President, Congress alone having that privilege, and that a military officer has no right to arrest a person not subject to the rules and articles of war, except in aid of judicial authority. (See also Habeas Corpus and Milligan Case.)

Mesa Verde National Park. (See Parks, National.)

Messages and Papers of the Presidents, resolution authorizing compilation of, and requesting Hon. James D. Richardson to take charge of the work of preparing the same. (See Prefatory note of first volume.)

Messages, Presidential.—A written communication by the President to Congress At the beginning of each session an annual message is transmitted, going into details of our standing as a Nation and recommending such action as may be deemed necessary to the progress of the country or the correction of abuses. Special messages are sent from time to time to either or both Houses, submitting treaties or correspondence, or in answer to a request from either branch for particular information, or to recommend specific or immediate legislation. Veto messages are sent with the returned bills which the President disapproves, in which he states his reasons for such disapproval. After pointing out wherein a bill fails to meet the requirements of the case he usually suggests the way to an effective measure that may receive Executive sanction. Article II., section 3, of the Constitution declares that the President "shall from time to time give to the Congress information of the state of the Union and recommend to their consideration such measures as he shall judge necessary and expedient." Washington and John Adams read their annual messages to Congress. Jefferson inaugurated the custom, long followed by his successors, of sending messages in writing to Congress (313). They were carried by the private secretary of the President, who is received at the door of the Senate or House, and whose presence is formally announced by an officer of the body, whereupon he delivers the message to the clerks.

President Wilson in 1913 revived the custom of Washington and Adams of orally addressing Congress.

Messages, Presidential. (See Annual Messages; Special session messages; Veto messages, under the several Presidents.)

Metals and Mining—

Metallic Elements and Mining.—Chemically considered, a metal is an element which has the power to replace the hydrogen of acids and form salt; in other words, it forms a base by combining with a hydroxyl group or groups. It is usually hard, heavy, lustrous, malleable, ductile, tenacious, and a good conductor of heat and electricity. Only six or seven metals were known to ancient alchemists, whereas under the modern definition quoted above some forty-five elements are properly called metals. No sharp line can be drawn between metals and non-metals, however, since some of the elements belong to both classes. Though weight is one of the most common properties of metals, a few such as lithium, sodium, potassium, etc., are lighter than water. Metals are distinguished from minerals in that the latter are either the uncombined elements in a native state, or compounds of these elements formed in accordance with chemical laws, and have, therefore, a definite chemical composition and molecular structure. Rocks are commonly referred to as minerals, and the process of extraction from the earth, mining.

The principal metals mined in the United States are, in the order of their importance: Iron, gold, copper, silver, lead, ferromanganese, zinc, aluminum, quicksilver, antimony, molybdenum, tungsten, ferromolybdenum, ferrotungsten, platinum. The principal minerals in the order of their importance are: Coal, bituminous and cannel, clay products, coal (anthracite), petroleum, iron ore, natural gas, cement (Portland

METALLIC

Product	Quantity	Value
Aluminum (consumpt'n)..lbs.	79,129,000	$14,522,700
Antimonial lead (a).....s. t.	16,667	1,572,167
Antimony (b)...........s. t.	(b)2,705	(b)576,501
Bauxite..............l. t.	219,318	1,069,194
Chromic iron ore.......l. t.	591	8,715
Copper, value at New York City (c).............lbs.	1,150,137,192	152,968,246
Ferro-alloys...........l. t.	255,524	9,350,245
Gold (d)..........troy oz.	4,572,976	94,531,800
Iron/Ore (e)..........l. t.	39,714,280	(e)71,905,079
Pig..............l. t.	22,263,263	298,777,429
Lead (refined), value at New York City (c)........	512,794	39,997,932
Manganese ore.........l. t.	2,635	27,377
Manganiferous ore (r)...l. t.	98,265	218,497
Nickel, value at New York City (g)............lbs.	845,334	313,000
Platinum and allied metals, value at N. Y. City,troy oz.	6,324	280,885
Quicksilver, value at S. Francisco...flasks (75 lbs., net)	16,548	811,680
Silver............troy oz.	72,455,100	40,067,700
Tin (metallic equivalent) lbs.	208,000	66,560
Titanium ore (rutile)....s. t.	94	11,280
Tungsten ore (60% concentrates).............s. t.	990	435,000
Uranium and vanadium minerals (h)........s. t.	(h)	(h)941,300
Zinc, value at St. Louis (c)s.t.	343,418	35,028,636
Total value of metallic products.................		$691,000,343

Product	Quantity	Value
Arsenious oxide.........s. t.	4,670	$ 313,147
Asbestos...............s. t.	1,247	18,965
Asphalt...............s. t.	438,271	3,647,592
Barytes (crude).........s. t.	51,547	153,715
Borax (crude).........s. t.	62,400	1,464,400
Bromine................lbs.	576,991	203,094
Calcium chloride........s. t.	19,403	121,766
Cement, barrels (380 lbs. net)	87,257,552	80,533,203
Clay/Products............		164,986,983
Raw (e)...........s. t.	2,209,860	(e)3,756,568
Coal/Bituminous (i)....s. t.	422,703,970	493,309,244
Penna. anthracite..l. t.	81,090,631	188,181,399
Cobalt oxide............lbs.		
Coke (e)..............s. t.	34,555,914	(e)88,334,217
Diatomaceous (infusorial) earth and tripoli.........		252,327
Emery................s. t.	485	2,425
Feldspar..............s. t.	135,419	629,873
Fluorspar.............s. t.	95,116	570,041
Fullers' earth.........s. t.	40,981	403,646
Garnet for abrasive purposes.............s. t.	4,231	145,510
Gems and precious stones...		124,651
Graphite/Amorphous....s. t.	1,725	38,750
Crystalline....lbs.	5,220,539	285,368
Grindstones and pulpstones..		689,344
Gypsum...............s. t.	2,476,465	6,895,989
Lime.................s. t.	3,380,928	13,247,676
Lithium minerals.......s. t.	(j)	(j)
Magnesite (crude)......s. t.	11,293	124,223
Marls................s. t.	(j)	(j)
Mica/Scrap...........s. t.	3,730	51,416
Sheet..........lbs.	556,933	278,540
Millstones.............		43,316
Mineral/Natural pigments (k).......s. t.	66,766	473,036
Paints/Zinc-lead pigments (k).......s. t.	106,791	9,978,710
Mineral waters....gals. sold	54,358,466	4,892,328
Natural gas............		94,115,524
Oilstones, etc..........		167,948
Peat...................		309,692
Petroleum..barrels (42 gals.)	265,762,535	214,125,215
Phosphate rock.........l. t.	2,734,043	9,608,041
Pumice...............s. t.	27,591	59,172
Pyrite...............l. t.	336,662	1,283,346
Salt....barrels (280 lbs., net)	34,804,683	10,271,358
Sand/Glass...........s. t.	1,619,649	1,568,030
Moulding, building, etc., and gravel..s. t.	77,662,086	22,278,969
Sand-lime-brick........		1,058,512
Silica (quartz).........s. t.	153,401	360,502
Slate.................		5,706,787
Stone.................		77,412,292
Sulphur...............l. t.	327,634	5,954,236
Sulphuric acid (60° Baume) from copper and zinc smelters.................s. t.	760,638	5,190,293
Talc and soapstone (exclusive of fibrous talc)......s. t.	86,221	1,043,801
Talc, fibrous.........s. t.	86,075	821,286
Thorium minerals (monazite) and zircon...........lbs.		
Total value of non-metallic products.............		$1,423,395,681
Total value of metallic products.............		691,300,343
Unspecified, metallic and nonmetallic (estimated)......		550,000
Grand total.............		$2,114,946,024

(a) From both foreign and domestic sources. 1914: Domestic, 15,475 tons, $1,462,051; foreign, 1,192 tons, $110,116. (b) Antimony contained in antimonial lead and antimony saved in copper refining. Value of former included in antimonial lead value, and value of latter in "Unspecified." (c) Product from domestic ores only. (d) Value, $20.671834625323 an ounce. (e) Value not included in total value. (f) Exclusive of those ores from Lake Superior district running so low in manganese as to be classed with iron ore. (g) By-product in electrolytic copper refining. (h) 1913: Consists of 2,269 tons of uranium ore and natural), salt phosphate rock, calcium borate, copper sulphate, limestone, zinc white, silica, sand, ochre, pyrites, and talc.

The whole number of mines and quarries in the United States, including the territories of Alaska, Hawaii and Porto Rico was reported by the census of 1910 to be 27,260. To this may be added 166,448 petroleum and gas wells, as the other statistics of mines and mining do not separate oil and gas wells from solid mining. As there are always some of the enterprises non-productive, the following figures relate only to those in operation at the time the enumeration was made. The amount of capital employed in the industry was $3,-380,525,841; there were 1,139,332 persons engaged, and they received $640,167,630 for their services. The value of the aggregate product was $1,238,410,322. Coal led in the value of products with $577,142,935, or 46.6 per cent. of the total. Next in value came petroleum and natural gas with 15 per cent. of the whole value, or $185,-416,684. Copper led the metals with $134,-616,987, nearly 11 per cent. of the whole amount. The only other product of the mines that exceeded $100.000,000 in value was iron, which yielded $106,947,082. The precious metals and structural materials made up the balance.

Meteorological Observatory, establishment of, at Fort Myer, Va., recommended, 4792.

Mettakahtla Indians. (See Indian Tribes.)

Mexican Boundary Commission. (See Mexico.)

Mexican Cotton-boll Weevil, report on, 7079.

Mexican War.—The Mexican War grew out of the annexation of Texas by the United States. March 2, 1836, Texas seceded from Mexico and declared her independence, which she maintained by the defeat of Santa Anna in the battle of San Jacinto, April 21, 1836. The United States, England, France, and Belgium recognized the new Government as independent. Dec. 29, 1845, Texas was annexed to the United States. A dispute as to the boundary induced President Polk to order Gen. Taylor to take a position in the disputed territory on the left bank of the Rio Grande. Here (near Matamoras) he was attacked April 23, 1846, by Mexicans under Arista, and a portion of his army was captured. Taylor advanced into the north of Mexico, leaving garrisons at Corpus Christi and at Fort Brown, opposite Matamoros, and after the battles of Palo Alto (May 8, 1846), Resaca de la Palma (May 9, 1846), Buena Vista (Feb. 22, 23, 1847), and a number of lesser fights, in which the Mexicans were defeated, he obtained control of all northern Mexico. Gen. Scott, landing at Vera Cruz, advanced to the City of Mexico, defeating Santa Anna at Cerro Gordo (April 17, 18, 1847), Contreras (Aug.

(carnotite); 10.5 grams of radium, not isolated, and 432 tons of vanadium in roscoelite and carnotite ores with an arbitrarily assigned value. 1914: 4,294 tons of uranium dre (carnotite), valued at $441,300, including the value of o2.3 grams of radium, not isolated, and 452 tons of vana-2ium in roscoelite and carnotite ores with an arbitrarily assigned value of $500,000. (i) Includes brown coal and lignite, and anthracite mined elsewhere than in Pennsylvania. (j) Value included under "Unspecified." (k) Natural pigments: Ochre, umber, sienna, metallic paint, mortar colors, and ground slate and shale; zinc-lead pigments: Sublimed blue lead, sublimed white lead, leaded zinc oxide, and zinc oxide. l. t., long tons; s. t., short tons.

19, 20, 1847), Churubusco (Aug. 20, 1847), and Molino del Rey (Sept. 7, 8, 1847), causing the surrender of the capital and the termination of the war Sept. 14, 1847. During these operations in Mexico Gen. Kearny and Lieut. Frémont occupied California and New Mexico with American troops. Under the treaty of peace signed at Guadalupe Hidalgo (2423), Mexico, upon the payment by the United States of $15,000,000 and of private claims which amounted to $3,250,000, ceded to the latter the territory now comprising Nevada, Utah, most of Arizona, a large part of New Mexico, portions of Colorado and Wyoming, and all of California (2437).

Mexican War:

American blood shed on American soil, 2292.

American forces—

Gallantry of, referred to, 2490.

General officer to take command of, required, 2358.

Increase in, recommended, 2358.

Kind of money paid to, inquired into, 2360.

Movement of, referred to, 2290, 2334.

Return of, to United States, 2440.

American territory invaded by Mexican forces, 2292.

Ample cause of war against Mexico asserted, 2329, 2383.

Appropriation by Congress, for prosecuting, referred to, 2387.

Armistice, referred to, 2424.

Battle of—

Buena Vista, 2385.

Cerro Gordo, 2386.

Churubusco, 2386.

City of Mexico, 2391.

Contreras, 2386.

Monterey, 2342.

Palo Alto, 2295, 2300, 2342.

Resaca de la Palma, 2295, 2300, 2342.

Vera Cruz, 2385.

Bounty lands for soldiers in, recommended, 2365.

Charge that American army invaded territory of Mexico refuted, 2332.

Discussed, 2287, 2295, 2300, 2306, 2321, 2363, 2383, 2415, 2437, 2481.

Executive orders concerning, 2233, 2373.

Existence of, proclaimed by—

Mexico, 2292.

United States, 2320.

Referred to, 2384.

Expenses of conducting, 2301, 2347, 2365, 2386, 2441, 2555.

Loan necessary to meet, 2347, 2555.

Mexico should be held responsible for, 2348, 2373, 2387.

Forces of United States in, 2490.

Increase of, recommended, 2358.

Gen. Arista in command of Mexican forces, 2291.

Gen. Scott in command of American troops, 2298.
Assignment of command to, discussed, 2298.
Correspondence with, referred to, 2298.
Recall of, referred to, 2299, 2431.
Gen. Taylor in command of American troops, 2291.
Assignment of command to, referred to, 2299.
Brevet rank of major-general conferred upon, referred to, 2299.
Referred to, 2369, 2415, 2418, 2419.
General officer to take command of American forces required, 2358.
Government established in Mexico by American army officers discussed, 2356.
Illustrations of, 2105, 2121, 2153, 2392, 2408, 2440, 2456.
Imposition of duties as war measure proposed, 2352, 2366.
Increase in army recommended by President Polk, 2358.
Invasion threatened by Mexico because of annexation of Texas, 2290, 2292.
Letters of marque and reprisal against Mexican vessels recommended, 2346.
Liberal provision for sustaining military forces recommended, 2293.
Means of transmitting letters to and from American army in Mexico, 2359.
Measure for raising additional force recommended, 2354.
Mexican general considers hostilities begun, 2291.
Military contribution levied upon Mexico. (See Mexico.)
Not provoked by United States, 2322.
Operations of American army near Matamoros referred to, 2293.
Peace concluded, 2437.
Pirates commissioned by Mexico, 2345.
Ports of Mexico in possession of American forces ordered to be opened, 2373, 2379.
Proclamations concerning, 2319, 2371, 2477, 2539.
Proclaimed by—
Mexico, 2292.
United States, 2320.
Referred to, 2384.
Public debt of United States increased in consequence of, 2441.
Recognition of, by Congress recommended, 2293.
Results of, respecting military strength of United States discussed, 2481.
Success of American troops referred to, 2295, 2300, 2342, 2384, 2391.

Suspension of hostilities after battles of Contreras and Churubusco referred to, 2419.
Termination of, 2437.
Threatening aspect of, 2113.
Treaty negotiations discussed, 2306, 2343, 2385, 2419, 2422, 2423, 2424, 2529. (See also California; New Mexico.)
Treaty of Peace—
Proclaimed, 2477.
Transmitted, 2437.
Volunteer force discussed, 2293, 2365.
Increase in, recommended, 2399.
Promptness of, in rushing to the field, 2323.
Report regarding, transmitted, 2359.

Mexico.—Mexico occupies the southern portion of the North American Continent, and extends between 15°-32° 30′ N. latitude and 87°-117° W. longitude. The United States forms a northern boundary, while its territories touch Guatemala and British Honduras in the south; on the east it is bounded by the Gulf of Mexico and the Caribbean Sea, and on the west by the Pacific Ocean.

Physical Features.—The two great ranges of North America, the Sierra Nevada and Rocky Mountains, are prolonged from the north to a convergence towards the narrowing Isthmus of Tehuantepec, their course being parallel with the west and east coasts. The surface of the interior consists of an elevated plateau between the two ranges, with steep slopes both to the Pacific and Atlantic (Gulf of Mexico). In the west is the Peninsula of California, with a mountainous surface, separated from the mainland by the Gulf of California. The Sierra Nevada, known in Mexico as the Sierra Madre, terminates in a transverse series of volcanic peaks, from Colima on the west side to Citlaltepete on the east, the intermediate and highest peaks being Ixtaccihuatl (17,879 feet) and Popocatepetl (19,784 feet). The low-lying lands of the coasts form the Tierra Caliente, or tropical regions (below 3,000 feet), the higher levels form the Tierra Templada, or temperate region (from 3,000 to 5,000 feet), and the summit of the plateau with its peaks is known as Tierra Fria, or cold region (above 5,000 feet).

The only considerable rivers are the Rio Grande del Norte, which forms part of the northern boundary, and is navigable for about seventy miles from its mouth in the Gulf of Mexico, and the Rio Grande de Santiago, which runs from Lake Chapala to the Pacific. The remaining streams are governed by the formation of the land, and run in mountain torrents between deep-cut cañons or "barrancas." The largest fresh-water lakes are Chapala, some fifty miles in length, and Patzcuaro and Xochimilco. In the northwest are saline lakes amid bare and dry regions.

The climate of Mexico varies according to the altitude. Yellow fever sometimes occurs at Merida, Yucatan.

History.—The earliest invaders, or Toltecs, gave place in the thirteenth century to the Aztecs, who were conquered in the sixteenth century by Spanish adventurers under Hernando Cortes. Spanish rule was established at Tenochtitland, a fourteenth century Aztec city (now Mexico), and Mexico remained a Spanish dominion until its freedom was asserted by a revolutionary war, 1810 to 1827. From 1837 to 1848 the province of Texas gave rise to hostilities with the United States, terminating in a three years' war and a cession of the disputed territory to the victorious northern states. In 1810 a Republic was proclaimed, but Iturbide declared himself Emperor in 1821. He was shot in 1824, and a Republic was again established. In 1862 the French troops came to Mexico, and in 1864 an Empire under Ferdinand Maximilian of Austria was declared. (See illustration opposite 4641.)

In 1867 the downfall of the Empire and the death of the Emperor gave rise to the new Republic, under President Juarez, who, during the whole of these three years, had the seat of the Republican Government in the north of the country, chiefly at Chihuahua. From 1876-1911 (with the exception of four years, 1880-84, when General Manuel Gonzalez was President) the executive power was in the hands of General Porfirio Diaz, who was elected President for eight successive terms of four years. In 1911 a revolutionary war led to the resignation of General Diaz and the accession of President Madero, who was deposed by General Huerta and subsequently shot, while under escort from prison. General Huerta assumed office as President pending an election, but the voting was insufficient, and the election was declared to be void. Governor Carranza, of Coahuila, refused adherence to the Huerta administration, and was followed by other states, notably Chihuahua, Nueva Leone, San Luis Potosi, Sinaloa, Puebla, Vera Cruz and Zacatecas. The war was carried on in a most barbarous and cruel manner. Property of Americans and other foreigners was seized, and the owners were insulted, threatened, abused, imprisoned, and in several instances actually met death at the hands of one or the other of the warring factions. Gradually Generals Carranza and Villa came into control of most of the northern states. President Wilson increased the regular troops at the border posts and sent naval vessels to the Mexican seaports to protect the lives and property of Americans and citizens of foreign countries.

On the 9th of April, 1914, a paymaster of the U. S. S. *Dolphin* landed at Iturbide bridge, Tampico, with a whaleboat and boat's crew to take off supplies. The men were unarmed and the boat carried, both at her bow and at her stern, the flag of the United States. The men were arrested, but later released, and an apology was made, but Admiral Mayo demanded that the flag of the United States be saluted with special ceremony. This was refused by Huerta. Citing this and a number of similar insults preceding it, President Wilson, April 20, 1914, asked Congress to approve the use of the land and naval forces of the country to enforce the fullest recognition of the rights and dignity of the United States. This was granted and Vera Cruz was occupied by the American forces. In the three days of fighting seventeen sailors and marines were killed and fifty wounded. The naval occupation was followed by a brigade of the regular army under Gen. Funston. Before attempting an advance into the interior, operations were halted by an offer of mediation between the United States and Mexico made by the diplomatic representatives of Argentina, Brazil and Chile. These met in Niagara Falls, Canada, in May. (See A. B. C. Arbitrators.) By June 12, the mediators had agreed upon a plan for a provisional government for Mexico to consist of a president and a cabinet of four lead-

ing Mexicans who should have been neutral during the revolution. President Wilson demanded that the provisional president should be a constitutionalist, but the mediators refused to sanction this. Meanwhile the military operations of the rebels, or constitutionalists, had brought them close to Mexico City, and Carranza was invited to participate in the deliberations of the mediators, on condition that he agree to an armistice. His successful progress toward Mexico City marred only by a misunderstanding with Villa, his leading general, caused him to refuse anything short of complete surrender of the capital.

June 22, 1914, peace protocols were signed by the mediators at Niagara Falls, Canada, whereby the United States abandoned its claim for a salute to the flag, and waived the question of a war indemnity from Mexico, as well as claims for damages due American citizens, with the understanding that these would be taken up by the provisional government.

At a federal election held July 5, Huerta was elected President and Señor Blanquet Vice-President. Few of the populace participated in the voting and ten days later Huerta resigned and boarded the German cruiser *Dresden* at Vera Cruz for Jamaica, after appointing Francisco Carbajal as provisional president. July 22, an armistice was signed by Carbajal and Carranza.

Carranza and Villa refused to be reconciled to the new provisional government, and threatened to prolong the revolution. Carbajal resigned in favor of Gen. Eulalio Gutierrez, but Carranza refused to recognize the new president, and demanded that the American forces be withdrawn from Vera Cruz. This was complied with and Carranza, on Nov. 26, 1914, occupied the city and proclaimed it the capital of Mexico. Villa and many of the leading generals entered Mexico and installed a government of their own. The United States and several South American republics recognized the Carranza government Oct. 20, 1915.

Carranza's entry into Mexico was followed by dispute with Villa, field marshal of the Constitutionalists. Carranza agreed to turn over the government to a council of constitutionalist military leaders until an election to be held between Oct. 1 and Dec. 31.

The first fight in a second revolution took place Sept. 25, 1914. Carranza changed the capital of Mexico from Mexico City to Querétaro.

The murder of a party of Americans by Mexican bandits, again brought the question of Mexican intervention to the front in 1916. There were heated debates in Congress and a telegram demanding the punishment of the murderers was dispatched to Carranza. As Carranza agreed to this, the affairs was left in his hands. About the middle of the month, a bandit, charged with responsibility for the firing of the Cumbre tunnel, was arrested at Juarez. Later in the month the execution of two Mexicans for the murder of a Texas rancher caused indignation and led to counter accusations on the part of Mexicans. Toward the end of the month, the "invasion" of Mexico by a rescue party threatened international complications.

Even before the murders there had been dissatisfaction in Congress over the Mexican situation, full information from the President as to the course of affairs with Mexico having been demanded by the Senate, without a division, after Senator Stone, chairman of the Committee on Foreign Relations, had announced that there was no objection to it.

On Jan. 10, C. R. Watson, chairman of the Mine and Smelters Operators' Association of Chihuahua and general manager of the Cusihuiriachic Mining Company, with fifteen of his associates, all representative Americans, and one Canadian, while en route from Chihuahua to their mines at Cusihuiriachic, were taken off the train forty miles west of Chihuahua City by bands commanded by Gen. Lopez and Gen. Reyna, operating under the direction of General Villa, stripped naked, and deliberately shot and killed.

It was stated that these men were murdered because they were Americans, and they were killed in accordance with the general policy publicly announced recently by Villa. This act occurred in territory announced to be in control of the Carranza forces.

Thomas A. Holmes, the only member of the mining party to escape, brought the first news of the murders. The bodies were recovered and brought to El Paso, Tex.

The United States government acted quickly through Sec. Lansing, who, Jan. 12, telegraphed a demand on General Carranza for the immediate pursuit, capture, and punishment of the bandits.

At the same time Sec. Lansing, while announcing that every step would be taken to see that the perpetrators of the crime were apprehended and punished, denied published statements that the Watson party has returned to Mexico with the assent of the United States Government. He explained that the State Department never had revoked its repeated warning to Americans to leave and remain out of Mexico on account of unsettled conditions there.

Gen. José Rodriguez, Gen Almeida, and several other Villa chieftains were captured, Jan. 12, by Maximo Marquez, commanding the garrison at the town of Madera, and a small force of Americans who were guarding property at Madera. Almeida was shot immediately. Rodriguez was made prisoner, and his summary execution ordered by Gen. Gavira. About 40 of Rodriguez's men were said to have been killed.

Eliseo Arredondo, Ambassador designate of the de facto government of Mexico, assured Sec. Lansing, Jan. 13, that Carranza troops had been dispatched to western Chihuahua with orders to kill or capture all the bandits concerned in the slaying of American citizens.

Despite the outburst of indignation in Congress over the killing of Americans in Chihuahua, and the demand made in Congressional resolutions for armed intervention in Mexico for the protection of Americans and other foreigners, President Wilson did not change his Mexican policy and was still opposed to armed intervention.

At the request of the United States a number of American mining companies ordered their employees to leave the country.

Gen. Carranza, under date of Jan. 14, published a decree empowering any citizen of Mexico to kill on sight Gen. Villa, Rafel, Castro and Pablo Lopez, murderers of Americans at Santa Ysabel.

Colonel Miguel Baca-Valles, a Villa bandit leader, was put to death in public at Juarez, Jan. 18, and his body was placed on exhibition upon the station platform beside that of Gen. José Rodriguez, another Villa chieftain.

Manuel Gutierrez, an alleged bandit, was arrested at Juarez, Jan. 17, and charged with having been primarily responsible for the firing of Cumbre tunnel, on the Mexican Northwestern Railroad, between Casas Grandes and Pearson, Chihuahua, where twenty-one Americans aboard a train lost their lives on Feb. 4, 1914.

It was alleged that Guitierrez was an offi-

cer of the band led by Maximo Castillo, who was freed Jan. 17 by the Federal authorities in El Paso. Gutierrez had affiliated himself with Villa, and with the disintegration of Villa's forces made overtures to Carranza officials who invited him to Juarez. On his arrival he was arrested. He was supposed to have robbed E. P. Fuller, a ranchman, near Villa Ahumada. Castillo and Jesus San Martin, also accused in affidavits in connection with the tunnel fire, left El Paso for New Orleans, Jan. 17, to take a ship for Cuba.

Bert Akers, a Texas ranchman, was killed at San Lorenzo, near Juarez, Jan. 21, by Bernardo and Federico Duran, Mexican cattle thieves. The men confessed, Jan. 22, and were executed by a Mexican firing squad at Juarez, Jan. 23. The bodies were exhumed, the same day, for identification by a delegation from Texas so that a report might be made officially to Washington. The affair aroused anger in Mexico, and representations were made, Jan. 24, by Andres Garcia, Mexican consul, to the Department of State at Washington, through the Collector of Customs, Z. L. Cobb, that Americans living along the border were stealing cattle in Mexico and smuggling them across the border. Demand was made that the United States stop Americans from stealing Mexican cattle and punish the offenders.

The charge was said to be based on the crossing of the border at several places by Americans to recover on the Mexican side cattle that had been stolen on the Texas side and driven into Mexico.

Two American soldiers swam the Rio Grande, at Progresso, Tex., Jan. 26, and were captured by Mexicans. Comrades of the men, led by three officers, invaded Mexican territory in an attempt to rescue them. Four were believed to have been drowned after a skirmish. Upon a protest from Carranza, the United States sent word that the three officers involved had been placed under arrest awaiting court martial. Efforts of Consul Garza, Carranza's representative, led to the final rescue of the two troopers by Carranza soldiers and their return to Texas.

Looting and killing of unoffending citizens continued during 1916, by all three of the Mexican factions. President Wilson's response to the Fall resolution was made public and there were reports of an attempt to blow up the U. S. battleship *Kentucky* in Vera Cruz harbor and charges were made that the International Harvester Company had financed the Yucatan rebellion aaginst Carranza in 1915.

In Chihuahua City and Bellaza Carranza troops killed many unoffending citizens.

In Oaxca Zapata's men put to death a Catholic parish priest for having associated with rebels. Gen. Villa held up a passenger train near Chihuahua City and superintended the killing of Gen. Gavira, Mexican commander at Juarez.

At the request of the American Government, Villa's brother, Hipolito, was arrested in Havana and was held for extradition. At El Paso he was indicted for sending men to wreck a train in Texas that was carrying Carranza soldiers to the relief of Agua Prieta, some months before. The capital was still suffering from the typhus epidemic, and in Tampico hundreds were dying of smallpox.

President Wilson sent to the Senate his response to the Fall resolution requesting him to report on facts leading up to recognition by the United States of the Carranza government. It was in the form of a letter from Sec. Lansing, summarizing the events which preceded recognition, and transmitting a great volume of data, including a list of all Americans killed in Mexico and along the border during six years.

The President declined to comply with that part of the Fall resolution asking for diplomatic and consular reports on political conditions, as "it was not compatible with public interests to furnish this correspondence, which was of a highly confidential nature, and submitted by consular officers of the United States, by diplomatic or consular officers of other governments and by other persons residing in Mexico."

Mr. Lansing said that under all the circumstances, the de facto government, which at the time of recognition controlled more than 75 per cent. of Mexico's territory, was affording "reasonable adequate protection to the lives and property of American citizens."

The data disclosed that 76 Americans were killed in Mexico in the years 1914, 1913 and 1915, as compared with 47 in the three years preceding, and that twenty civilian Americans and sixteen soldiers were killed on American soil in the past three years as a result of Mexican troubles.

Carranza officials informed the State Department Feb. 15, that they had heard reports of a plot to blow up the battleship *Kentucky* in Vera Cruz harbor in which Consul Canada was alleged to be involved, the object being to force American intervention. The State Department regarded the report as a continuation of the fire the Consul had been under for months from Carranza officials, who charged him with antagonism to their government. When Consul Canada was home on a leave of absence, the State Department, after investigating various statements about his conduct, sent him back to his post.

Charges were made Feb. 18, before the Senate Agricultural Committee by Levy Mayer of Chicago, representative of the American bankers who financed Yucatan sisal planters, that the International Harvester Company had financed the Ortez-Argmedo revolution in Yucatan against Carranza in 1915. The charge was made in connection with the committee's investigation into the alleged monopoly to control the price of hemp.

Mayer told the committee that he was prepared to produce invoices to show that part of a draft for $480,000 had been paid to American munition factories for arms and ammunition. This statement Walter L. Fisher, representing the Harvester Company, denied, saying that the money from the draft was given to Yucatan growers for sisal.

It was charged, Feb. 19, that the International Harvester Company tried to prevent loans to Yucatan planters by American bankers, and, Feb. 29, that part of a $480,000 letter of credit from the Harvester Company was spent for a gunboat and munitions for the revolution.

Border troubles culminated in March, in an unprovoked attack on a U. S. border town by Gen. Villa and a band of desperados. With the consent of Gen. Carranza, an expedition into Mexico was undertaken by the United States to capture the raiders.

At 4:30 o'clock on the morning of March 9, a band of 1500 Mexicans under Gen. Villa, crossed the border and attacked the town of Columbus, New Mexico, and the camp where the Thirteenth U. S. Cavalry was stationed. The Mexican raiders crept past the camp without being discovered and had looted the post office and several stores, set fire to several houses and shot a number of civilians before our troops got into action. After two hours looting, the raiders withdrew across the Mexican border leaving 11 civilians and 8 U. S. soldiers dead as well as 27 of their own men.

The U. S. troops pursued Villa across the border where more fighting took place in which some forty Villistas were killed.

On the following day President Wilson and his cabinet decided to send a punitive expedition into Mexico.

A note from Gen. Carranza was presented to the State Department, March 11, "requesting the necessary permission for Mexican forces to cross into American territory in pursuit of those bandits, acknowledging due reciprocity in regard to forces of the United States crossing into Mexican territory if the raid effected at Columbus should unfortunately be repeated at any other points of the border." Carranza also issued a manifesto, March 12, to the effect that he would forbid the pursuit of Villa on Mexican soil unless the reciprocal right should be granted to Mexico. President Wilson, March 12, agreed to Carranza's terms.

The punitive expedition, reported to number about 6000, entered Mexico, March 15, in two columns. Brig. Gen. John J. Pershing with about 4000 men crossed the border south of Columbus, while Col. George A. Dodd, heading a smaller column, crossed some distance west of Columbus, near Hachita.

Col. Dodd's column reached Casas Grandes, March 17, having penetrated 60 miles into Mexico in two days.

Major Gen. Funston, March 17, asked Washington to secure Carranza's permission to ship in supplies to the punitive expedition over Mexican railroads.

Aeroplanes were sent out to scout for Villa.

The detachment that headed south from Casas Grandes on the road along which Villa was reported to be advancing was one of three subdivisions operating south of Casas Grandes. One column was sent toward Lake Babricora, seventy miles south of Casas Grandes and somewhat to the west. The two other detachments moved as one to Galena, south and east of Casas Grandes, and there separated, one continuing in a more easterly direction toward Carmen, sixty-five miles from Casas Grandes, and the other south toward Cruces, fifty miles from Casas Grandes, which now became the advanced base of the expeditionary forces.

Gen. Funston, March 21, at Gen. Pershing's suggestion appealed to the War Department for more troops, and the 5th Cavalry was ordered to Mexico to protect the one hundred mile line of communications. On March 24, two columns of Gen. Pershing's force were reported 120 miles southeast of Casas Grandes.

President Wilson appealed to the country March 25, for aid in thwarting a conspiracy which he declared had been organized to plunge the United States into war with Mexico. In a formal statement issued at the White House the President charged that a campaign of falsehood was being carried on through the newspapers of the country "for the purpose of bringing about intervention in the interest of certain American owners of Mexican property."

President Wilson expressed the hope that the people of the United States would be on their guard against crediting any story coming from the border and he entreated the editors of newspapers that they "make it a matter of patriotism and conscience to test the source and authenticity of every report they receive from that quarter."

Villa was checked near Namiquipa by Mexican troops but escaped March 26.

The bandit and his men headed into the Madera Valley, which runs south from the

Namiquipa country toward Guerrero. The Americans were 250 miles below the border and as far south as Chihuahua City.

Col. Dodd's column was shifted, March 28, from the eastern slope of the Sierra Madre to the Pacific slope and began to operate out of Madera as a base in Santa Catherina cañon, the "Seven Hills" district, and Babricora.

March 29, Gen. Carranza granted the renewed request of the State Department for permission to use the Mexico Northwestern Railroad in carrying out the pursuit. Gen. Carranza received the new request that morning. His answer was in Washington before dark.

He agreed to permit the use of Mexican railroads for the transportation of supplies, but refused to allow guards on the trains and provided that the supplies must be shipped from one American to another, neither of whom should be directly connected with the army.

With a single dissenting vote in the House, and none in the Senate, Congress, March 28, passed and sent to the White House for the President's signature the urgent deficiency bill, appropriating $8,611,-502 for expenses in connection with the army's punitive expedition into Mexico and the recruiting of the additional 20,000 men to bring the regulars up to maximum strength.

Three hundred and seventy-five Democrats and Republicans in the House voted for the bill, and Representative Meyer London, Socialist, of New York, voted against it, when Representative Mann, the minority leader, asked for a roll call to demonstrate that there was no difference of opinion on the question of national defense or the protection of the troops.

Villa attacked the town of Guerrero, March 27, put to death 172 men in the garrison and held others under guard intending to kill them. During the engagement Villa was shot through the leg but escaped. Two days later he was surprised at Guerrero, in an attack by a flying detachment of American cavalry under Col. Dodd. He was badly defeated, and seriously wounded, and fled to the mountains with Colonel Dodd's men in hot pursuit. His chief military commander, General Eliseo Hernandez, was killed in the fight.

The attack was a surprise. The Villa troops were driven in a ten-mile running fight into the mountains northwest of the railroad where they separated into small bands. Large numbers of Carrancista prisoners who were being held for execution were liberated during the fight. In order to reach Guerrero, Dodd marched fifty-five miles in seventeen hours, and carried on fight for five hours.

General Carranza, March 1, named Juan Sanchez Azcona to be Envoy Extraordinary and Minister Plenipotentiary to Europe with diplomatic jurisdiction over Great Britain, Belgium, France, Switzerland, Italy, Spain and Portugal. Señor Azcona was formerly private secretary to the late President Madero, and for many years was a leading Liberal and a well known editor.

An attack on American troops by a party of Carrancistas and the demand that the United States Army be withdrawn threatened to bring about a crisis in April, which, however, was averted by a conference on the border between representatives of both countries.

After the fight at Guerrero, March 26, in which some 60 Villistas were killed, all trace of Villa was lost, and though it was frequently reported that he was hemmed in and every point of escape carefully guarded

he successfully eluded capture. One of the smaller bands into which the Villa force scattered was struck by Colonel Cano on March 29, and Manuel Boco, the leader, was killed. Boco, one of Villa's chief lieutenants, was said to have ordered the killing of five Mexican employees at the Corralitos ranch March 10, by a band of Villistas on their retreat from Columbus.

Sec. Lansing made a positive denial April 6 of reports that American troops might be withdrawn from Mexico soon, inasmuch as the Villa band had been scattered. On the other hand, it was disclosed that Maj. Gen. Frederick Funston, commanding the Mexican border patrol, had that day recommended to the War Department that some 4000 recruits enlisted for the United States army under authority of the Hay emergency resolution be sent to the border as fast as obtained so that they might be utilized in strengthening the border forces.

A serious Mexican crisis was reached April 13, when the Carranza government requested the immediate withdrawal of the American punitive expedition from Mexico.

The note was a sharp challenge to the legality of the expedition, and asserted that the American troops were in Mexico "without warrant," that they were sent into Mexico by the Wilson Administration under a "false interpretation" and without the Washington Government having "thoroughly comprehended" the Carranza Government's proposal of March 10 for a reciprocal agreement between the two governments under which their forces might cross the border in pursuit of raiders.

The Carranza communication told the United States Government that "it is now time to treat with the Government of the United States upon the subject of the withdrawal of its forces from Mexican territory for these reasons:

"First—The American expedition was sent against Villa without warrant, because there was no previous formal or definite understanding.

"Second—Because the expedition was not fulfilling its object and could not do so, because 'the band headed by Villa has already been dispersed.'

"Third—Because there were 'sufficient Mexican troops to pursue Villa.'"

On the heels of this notice came the disclosure that a band of 100 American troopers, under Major Tompkins, who entered Parral April 12, in alleged violation of "instructions" not to occupy towns, were attacked by a force of Carranza soldiers and obliged to withdraw.

The Major stated that he had entered the town on the invitation of an officer of the Parral garrison. He stated that the officer met him ten miles from Parral, introduced himself, and urged him to accept the hospitality of the military and civil authorities and to discuss a camp site.

Major Tompkins was preparing to move out to the designated camp when soldiers and civilians began to throw stones and shoot at the Americans.

Forty of the Mexican soldiers, including one Major, besides a civilian, were killed by the retreating Americans. The American casualties were two killed and six wounded, including Major Tompkins. His wound was slight.

Sec. Baker, April 19, dispatched Major Gen. Hugh L. Scott, Chief of Staff, to the border as his personal representative to make a complete report on the military problems confronting General Funston.

President Wilson, April 23, approved a recommendation made by Major Gen. Funston for a redisposition of the forces composing the American punitive expedition. The purpose of this redisposition of the forces was to enable the expedition to recuperate and strengthen itself. It thus became evident that there was no intention for the present to withdraw our forces from Mexican soil.

The seven Villa followers who were captured after the raid on Columbus, N. M., were convicted of murder in the first degree, at Deming, N. M., April 24, and sentenced to die May 19.

The Carranza Government, April 24, accepted a proposal from the United States for a conference on the international border between General Alvaro Obregon, Minister of War in the Cabinet of General Carranza, and Major Gen. Hugh L. Scott, to discuss the military aspects of the American punitive expedition into Mexico and the de facto Government's attitude toward the project for the capture of Villa.

It was announced officially, April 25, that the conference between Major Gen. Scott and Gen. Obregon would be held in El Paso, and would start as soon as Gen. Obregon reached the border.

Gen. Carranza, in an official statement, declared he had fully approved the plan for having the meeting at El Paso, and announced that he was especially pleased at the assurances given by Gen. Bell and the announcement that Gen. Scott would call on Gen. Obregon in Juarez first.

The first conference between the representatives of the United States and Mexico began at five o'clock on the afternoon of April 29 in the Mexican Customs House in Juarez, and at seven o'clock the four American Army officers and six Mexican representatives left the building. The result of the conference was not made public.

Another raid into the United States, futile conferences at the border, and a new demand on the part of Carranza for the immediate withdrawal of the United States troops from Mexico were the principal developments of the month of May.

Through two channels the United States notified Gen. Carranza, May 1, that it did not desire at that time to discuss the question of withdrawing the American forces from Mexico. At the direction of President Wilson Sec. Baker so advised Gen. Scott, who, with Gen. Funston, was conferring with Gen. Obregon on the border. After consultation with Sec. Baker and Counsellor Polk, Sec. Lansing later in the day informed Eliseo Arredondo, the Mexican Ambassador Designate, in response to a pressing inquiry from the latter, that the American Government would not be in position to answer Gen. Carranza's formal request for the withdrawal of the troops until the conclusion of the Scott-Obregon conferences.

During these conferences desultory fighting continued. A full squadron of 230 men of the 11th Cavalry surprised and routed a much larger force of Villa bandits at Ojo-Azules, June 4. The American commander under Maj. Robert L. Howze had been pursuing bandits under Gens. Cruz Dominguez and Julio Acosta for several days when they encountered the men camped in the huddled adobe huts of Ojo-Azules. The band, which was the largest remaining under the Villa standard, was believed to be the same as that defeated at Temochic, April 22, by Col. George A. Dodd's command.

The Howze column, consisting of six picked troops and one machine gun detachment, struck the band of Mexicans after an all-night cross-country ride of 36 miles.

Howze attacked without resting either men or horses. Forty-two Mexicans were killed, including Gen. Antonio Angeles, a relative of Filipe Angeles, the former confidant of Villa, and a number wounded. There were no American casualties. More than 50 of the fugitives were rounded up by Americans after the engagement and pursuit of the scattered remnants was continued. In the meanwhile, farther to the east, Mexicans, whether Villa or Carranza forces were not known, again raided Texas, May 5. The bandits' foray, carried them through the southern limits of Brewster County in the Big Bend district of Texas, and taking in three little settlements near the border— Glenn Springs, Boquillas and Deemer.

Three American soldiers and a 10-year-old boy were killed and two American citizens, Jesse Deemer and C. G. Compton, were kidnapped and carried south of the international border.

Within an hour after the news reached El Paso preparations had been begun for adequate action. Maj.-Gen. Frederick Funston ordered that in all, four troops of cavalry should proceed to the raided section to reinforce small detachments already on their way to the scene from Presido, Alpine and other points. Col. Frederick Sibley, of the 14th Cavalry, was placed in charge.

Major George T. Langhorne made a dash across the border in pursuit of the raiders, but halted some 50 miles south of the Mexican border from Boquillas to await the arrival of Col. Sibley and reinforcements. The Federal Government, also, was stirred to action. President Wilson, May 9, ordered out the State militia of Texas, Arizona and New Mexico to patrol the Mexican border, and in addition the War Department directed that three more regiments of the regular infantry be dispatched to the border and placed under General Funston's command. The addition of these troops raised the American ranks by about 7000 men.

On the following day American consuls throughout Mexico were instructed again to call attention of Americans to the State Department's repeated warnings that this government regarded their presence there as undesirable. The last census of Americans in Mexico, taken by the State Department six weeks before, showed less than 3000 throughout the country. Most of them were near Mexico City and the extreme east and west coasts, few remaining in Chihuahua and Sonora.

While military events were developing with such rapidity, the conference over the co-operation of American and Mexican soldiers in Mexico came to an abrupt halt May 11. No agreement was signed, but it was believed that the net result of the conferences was as follows:

First—General Scott was convinced that the Carranza de facto Government understood that the purpose of the United States in sending troops into Mexico was not aggression or armed intervention.

Second—General Obregon had agreed to send 10,000 picked troops into the Big Bend and Parral regions of Mexico to stamp out bandits.

Third—General Obregon had given orders to General Trevino to endeavor to head off the bandits who raided Glenn Springs and Boquillas.

Fourth—The United States troops were to remain in Mexico until the Carranza Government demonstrated that it had power to control the situation in Northern Mexico and where the United States Government had no troops.

Fifth—General Obregon also gave assurances that the Carranza forces would not move from Sonora through Pulpito Pass to operate in the rear of General Pershing's column and would not attack American troops.

Sixth—Every effort should be made by Carranzistas to free the Americans whom the Big Bend bandits kidnapped.

The rescue of Jesse Deemer was effected, May 13, by Troop A and B of Langhorne's 8th Cavalry at Santa Fe Del Pino, ninety miles south of the Rio Grande. Five bandits were killed and 3 taken prisoners on the 15th in a skirmish in the neighborhood.

The State Department, May 18, issued orders to American consuls and vice-consuls at Chihuahua, Juarez, Nogales, Durango, Aguascalientes and Monterey to report to El Paso for a conference with Gen. Funston. The consuls and vice-consuls included in the order were Marion Letcher, at Chihauhau; Thomas D. Edwards, at Juarez; Frederick Simpich, at Nogales; Homer C. Coen, vice-consul at Durango; Gaston Schmutz, at Aguascalientes; and Philip C. Hanna, consul-general at Monterey.

After the conference, one of the consuls was to proceed to Washington to confer with the officials of the State Department.

Official figures of dead, wounded and missing, both soldier and civilian, that marked the progress of the American expedition in Mexico from the time of the Columbus, N. M., raid, showed the following total casualties to May 20:

Killed—United States soldiers, 30; civilians, 24; Mexican soldiers, 301.

Wounded—United States officers, 6; soldiers, 76; civilians, 71; Mexican soldiers, 97.

Candelario Cervantes, second in command to Villa among the Mexican bandits, was shot and killed with Jose Bencomo, another Villista chief, near Cruces, May 26, by United States troops. One American soldier was killed and two were wounded.

The Carranza de facto government, May 31, delivered to the United States government a new and sharp note, bristling with what amounted to charges of bad faith against President Wilson and insisting upon the immediate withdrawal of the American military forces from Mexican soil, or a frank declaration by the American government in explanation of its purpose in retaining them there "idle and inactive."

The note did not fix any time limit within which the American forces should be withdrawn, but asserted that should the American government refuse to comply with these requirements the de facto government might conclude that the expedition was being maintained on Mexican soil for occult reasons and as a precautionary measure in anticipation of a clash with Mexico.

The Mexican situation became increasingly strained during June. Several border raids followed by punitive expeditions, the Mexican threat of attack if United States troops moved south, and the battle at Carrizal resulted in mobilization of state militia and a forcible answer to Carranza's manifesto of May 22.

On June 11 Mexicans raided an American ranch near Laredo, Tex., with the result that 1600 American regulars were drawn from the Engineers Corps of the Coast Artillery to reinforce the border defenses. One of the bandits it was said wore a uniform bearing the insignia of a Carranza lieutenant colonel.

Mexicans attacked the border patrol at San Ignacio June 15 with the result that three American soldiers were killed and six wounded, eight Mexicans were reported killed, a number wounded and several captured. A third punitive expedition followed the bandits into Mexico. A fourth punitive chase crossed the line June 16 and dispersed bandits who had been discovered near San Benito, Tex. The raids resulted in President Wilson's summons to all state militia not already on the field to mobilize. Sixteen warships were sent to watch Mexican ports.

General Trevino on June 15 advised General Pershing that any movement of American troops in Mexico to the south, east, or west would be considered a hostile act and a signal to commence warfare.

On June 20 the President's reply to Carranza's demand of May 22 for the withdrawal of our troops was issued. The note refused the demand and declared the intention of the United States to keep troops in Mexico to protect our citizens in that country and on the border until the *de facto* Government showed that it was willing and able to protect them.

A battle took place June 21 at Carrizal between two troops of American cavalry and seven or eight hundred of the Carranzista forces. The Americans, eighty-four in number, were overwhelmed and defeated; thirteen were killed, twenty-three taken prisoners, fifteen reported missing. Responsibility for the attack was assumed by Carranza in a statement sent to the American government. The Government replied with a sharp note June 24 demanding the release of prisoners taken in the encounter. The prisoners were returned June 28.

Modesto C. Rolland, former Mexican Consul General in New York, left June 24, for El Paso to confer with Dr. Alt, editor of a Mexico City weekly, and Luis Manuel Rojas, director of the Biblioteca Nacional, in Mexico City, representing Mexico and David Starr Jordan, Frank P. Walsh, and William Jennings Bryan, representing the United States. The commission was unofficial and planned to work for a peaceful understanding between the two countries.

Pablo Lopez, Villa's chief lieutenant in the Columbus raid was shot June 6 at Chihuahua City. Four Columbus raiders were hanged at Deming N. M., on June 9, two on June 30. One raider was sentenced to life imprisonment.

Anti-American demonstrations in northern Mexico throughout June indicated a growing restlessness over the continued presence of American troops. On June 7 and 8 mobs attacked the American consulate, the Foreign Club and American residences in Chihuahua City. The consulate was burned. Three mob leaders were reported killed by an American in defense of his house.

Great Britain and the Latin countries of South America had shown concern over the Mexican situation, and offered friendly aid to prevent armed intervention.

Joint Commission.—A joint committee was appointed during August to settle the differences between the United States and Mexico. Toward the end of the month 15,000 National Guardsmen were ordered home from the border.

It was officially announced at the Mexican Foreign Office, August 3, that Luis Cabrera, Ignacio Bonillas and Alberto Pani had been selected as the commissioners to negotiate with the United States commissioners regarding the questions at issue between Mexico and the United States.

Secretary Lansing, August 22d, announced the names of the three American members of the commission. They were: Franklin K. Lane, Secretary of the Interior; George Gray, of Wilmington, Del., former member of the Federal Judiciary, and until recently Judge of the Third Judicial Circuit; Dr. John R. Mott, of New York, who has been General Secretary of the World's Student Christian Federation since 1895, and is General Secretary of the International Committee of Young Men's Christian Associations.

21

The commission met in New London, Conn., and devoted itself September 11 to determining the extent of the control exercised in Mexico by the de facto government. The Mexican commissioners stated that the government roads were being operated with a large degree of regularity, Carranza being in control of the entire 8,000 miles of the Government lines and of about 2,000 miles belonging to private companies. The decrees issued by Carranza bearing on foreign owned property were also discussed.

The commission dealt September 13 wholly with questions raised by taxation decrees issued by General Carranza.

The September 14 session was devoted to an informal interchange of views on the enforcement of law in Mexico.

At the request of the Mexican commissioners, the discussion September 18 was centered on the problem of border control, and a new "policy of equal rights." It was explained officially that the Carranza idea is to put both Mexican and foreign interests upon the same footing, allowing preference to neither.

The attention of the Mexican commissioners was called to instances in which military commanders had, through decrees, threatened with the death penalty any persons who refused to accept paper currency at its par value, and for a similar offense had also threatened merchants with the confiscation of their property. In dealing with these matters the Mexican commissioners pointed out that in so vast a country it was humanly impossible to guard against all abuses, but they laid emphasis on the fact that while such extreme decrees had been issued by subordinate military commanders, the national Government had constantly urged moderation upon the State Governors, and that they had no record of a single instance in which any of these extreme penalties had been inflicted.

Efforts to thwart the commission in its endeavor to adjust border problems were alleged in information laid before the members. United States Secret Service agents began investigating what was said to be a surreptitious campaign led by Americans and designed first to bring about the Villa raid on Chihuahua City, and second, to get it exaggerated in the official military reports, with the object of impeding the work of the commission. The reports of the Chihuahua battle, which were transmitted by Washington and by Mexico City to the Joint Commission, contradicted the statements in the account of Brig.-Gen. George Bell, Jr. It was regarded as established by the State Department that Villa was not with the raiders and had no directing hand in the fight; that no ammunition was captured and carried off by the raiders; that none or very few of the Carranzistas deserted, and that many of the prisoners, who were freed and taken away to become anti-Carranzista soldiers, have been drifting back to Chihuahua City.

The commerce of the United States with Mexico in the fiscal year 1916 was the largest in the history of trade with that country, according to figures made public early in September by the foreign trade department of the National City Bank.

The silver imports from Mexico in 1916 were approximately $19,000,000; in 1915, $16,802,000; in 1913, $25,570,000, and in 1912, $28,147,000. The gold imports from Mexico were in 1915, a little over $6,000,000; in 1914, $11,000,000; in 1913, $20,000,000, and in 1911, $30,000,000.

The chief growth occurred on the import side. The value of imports from that country into the United States increased from $28,646,000 in 1900 to $97,616,000 in 1916,

while exports to Mexico increased from $34,975,000 in 1900 to $61,282,000 in the high record year 1911, but fell to $48,308,000 in 1916.

AREA AND POPULATION

States and Territories	Area in English Sq. Miles	Population, 1910
Aguas Calientes	2,969	118,978
Campeche	18,086	85,795
Chiapas	27,222	436,817
Chihuahua	89,974	405,265
Coahuila	63,728	367,652
Colima	2,273	77,704
Durango	42,265	436,147
Guanajuato	10,948	1,075,270
Guerrero	24,996	605,437
Hidalgo	8,575	641,895
Jalisco	33,486	1,202,802
Mexico	8,949	975,019
Michoacan	22,656	991,649
Morelos	2,734	179,814
Nuevo Leon	23,679	368,929
Oaxaca	35,383	1,041,035
Puebla	12,204	1,092,456
Queretaro	4,492	243,515
San Luis Potosi	24,000	624,748
Sinaloa	27,553	323,499
Sonora	76,619	262,545
Tabasco	10,072	183,708
Tamaulipas	32,268	249,253
Tepic (Ter.)	10,951	171,837
Tlaxcala	1,595	183,805
Vera Cruz	29,283	1,124,368
Yucatan	18,565	337,020
Zacatecas	24,467	475,863
L. California (Ter.)	58,328	52,244
Federal District	579	719,052
Quintana Roo	16,638	9,086
Total	765,535	15,063,207

Railways.—There were 15,804 miles of railway open on Sept. 16, 1912. The "Mexican Central" joins El Paso (Texas) with the city of Mexico, by which passengers can travel in five days from New York. Railway The National via Laredo takes four days to New York, and there is a third route via Eagle Pass (International Railway).

Posts and Telegraph.—There were 2,748 post offices in 1912, dealing (in 1911) with 205,000,000 packets, etc., and 526 telegraph offices (with ten wireless stations), the telegraph lines having a total length of 40,687 miles.

Shipping.—The mercantile marine in 1911 consisted of forty-one steamers (28,737 tons) and sixteen sailing vessels (3,878 tons), a total of fifty-seven vessels (32,615 tons). In 1909-1910 3,613 vessels (6,726,111 tons) entered and cleared at Mexican ports. Acapulco, Manzanillo, Mazatlan, Salina Cruz, and Guaymas are the chief ports on the Pacific, and Vera Cruz, Tampico, Progreso, and Puerto Mexico on the Atlantic or Gulf of Mexico.

The revenue for the year 1909-1910, before the outbreak of the revolution, was $106,328,485, and the expenditure, $95,028,651. The national debt was stated at $438,648,528 in 1910, the year before the rebellion. The unit of value, the peso, is equal to $0.49.8 United States money.

Cities.—Capital, City of Mexico. Population (1910) 470,659. Other towns exceeding 20,000 inhabitants were: Guadalajara, Puebla, San Luis Potosi, Monterey, Merida, León, Vera Cruz, Aguascalientes, Morelia, Chihuahua, Pachuca, Oaxaca, Orizaba, Tacubaya, Guanajuato, Saltillo, Durango, Toluca, Zacatecas, Jalapa, Celaya and Irapuato.

Trade with the United States.—The value of merchandise imported into Mexico from the United States for the year 1913 was

$54,383,424, and goods to the value of $77,-543,842 were sent thither—a balance of $23,160,418 in favor of Mexico.

See illustrations opposite 7920, 7936, 7952.

Mexico:

Affairs of, referred to, 3278, 3411, 3725, 7884, 7907, 7929, 7934.

Agent sent to, referred to, 3114, 8265.

American citizens in—

Captured by army of, 1944, 2010.

Liberated, 2050.

Expelled from jurisdiction of, 2180, 2198, 3044, 3120.

Forbidden to sell goods, 2115.

Murdered, 3096, 3176.

Outrages on, and injuries sustained by, 2207, 2287, 2323, 2383, 2494, 2869, 3043, 3094, 4143, 4358.

Property of, seized or destroyed by, 2323, 3044, 3096, 3120.

American flag insulted by, 2323, 8314.

American troops—

Occupying territory of, referred to, 3657, 3660.

Sent to, for protection of citizens from Indians, 1457.

Should not be considered as encroachment rights upon of,1457.

Referred to, 1646.

To be sent to, for protection of citizens of United States in, recommendation regarding, 3097, 3176, 7934.

Transit of, through territory of, in 1861 referred to, 3574.

Ample cause of war against, asserted, 2269, 2383, 7934.

Apology by commander for arrest of United States sailors in, 7934.

Arbitration of boundary question with Chamizal not satisfactory, 7658.

Arbitration with, at The Hague, 6717, 6731.

Armies of, in Texas defeated, 1487.

Armistice between United States and, referred to, 2424.

Arrest of United States sailors at Tampico, 7934.

Austin-Topolovampo Railroad survey across northern States of, referred to, 4475.

Austrian troops dispatched to, referred to, 3588, 3589.

Blockade of coast of, referred to, 1733.

Blockade of ports of, by France and injurious effect of, on United States discussed, 1705.

Boundary dispute with Guatemala, 4627, 4716, 4802.

Arbitration of, submitted to United States minister to, 6066.

Boundary line with United States—

Adjustment of, chief obstacle in settling difficulties, 2306, 2309.

Appropriation for expenses of commission recommended, 2551, 2709, 4802.

Commission engaged in marking, referred to, 2551, 2665, 2709, 2719, 2813, 2915.

Commissioners appointed, 1318, 2494.

Convention regarding, 4698, 4716, 4760, 4841, 4951, 4957, 5397, 5400, 5622.

Matias Romero's note regarding, referred to, 4957.

Proposed, 4686.

Discussed, 1245, 1370, 4686, 4716, 4918, 5368, 5751.

International boundary commission discussed, 5622, 5870, 6066.

Proclamation regarding, 2926.

Proposition regarding, submitted by United States commissioner unauthorized, 2419.

Recommendation that Executive be given power to advance money for settlement of, 2306, 2309, 2345, 2388.

Referred to, 1245, 1588, 2693, 2900, 4757, 6294.

Settlement of, proclaimed, 2926.

Treaty regarding, transmitted and discussed, 1130, 1370, 1406, 2332, 2743, 4686, 5622.

Legislative provision for execution of, recommended, 1445, 1457, 4825.

Referred to, 1245, 4757.

Water-Boundary Commission discussed, 6334, 6374, 6432.

Cession of California and New Mexico to United States by—

Area and value of, discussed, 2449, 2484.

Discussed and recommendations regarding, 2306, 2309, 2344, 2356, 2386, 2426, 2437, 2444, 2484.

Treaty for, transmitted, 2437.

Cession of territory to United States—

Report on, transmitted, 1588.

Treaty regarding, 2762.

Charge that American army invaded territory of, refuted, 2332.

Chief of, captured, 1487.

Chinese entering United States through, discussed, 5632.

Civil authority of, in Texas expelled, 1487.

Civil dissensions in, 1245.

Civil government established in portions of, held by American army discussed, 2356, 2444.

Civil war in. (See Wars in, *post.*)

Claims of—

Against United States, 2636, 2769, 4244, 4358.

Commission to settle, extension of time of, recommended, 4244.

Referred to, 2770.

Export of arms and ammunition to, 7929, 8089, 8090.

Free Zone—
Discussed, 4055, 4100, 4295, 4806, 6334.
Referred to, 5195.

French troops in, referred to, 3571.
Contraband articles for use of, referred to, 3351.
Evacuation of, by—
Discussed and referred to, 3582, 3653, 3662, 3718.
Indicated and Gen. Grant sent to communicate with American minister, 3641.
Gen. Grant relieved and Gen. Sherman assigned, 3641.
Negroes used by, referred to, 3355.

Fugitive criminals, convention with, for surrender of, 2602, 3264, 4867.
Demands made under, 4791, 6333.
Extension of time for ratification of, recommended, 3274.
Questions arising under, discussed, 5086, 6333.
Report of Secretary of State regarding, 2690.
Termination of, notice of, given by, 6334.

Fur trade with, persons killed while engaged in, 1128.

Government established in, by American army officers, discussed, 2356, 2444.

Government of, overthrow of, 3094, 3175.

Government of, Paredes, referred to, 2341.

Hostile attitude of, toward United States, discussed, 2238.

Hostile Indians in, discussed, 3045.

Hostile interference of foreign powers with, not to be permitted by United States, 3043, 3177.

Huerta's authority in, usurped, 7907.

Immigration of dissatisfied citizens of United States into. (See Immigration.)

Imprisonment of American citizens by authorities of, 2720, 2834, 2837, 4376, 4672, 4678, 4692, 4696, 4852, 4991, 5106.

Indemnity paid to, by United States, referred to, 2636, 2677, 2679, 2705, 2900, 2940.

Independence of, first recognized by United States, 2241, 2323.

Indians of United States on frontier of, referred to, 2580, 2630, 2664, 2714.

Incursions of, discussed, 2666, 2710, 3045.

Inhuman treatment of captives by, 2207.

Insurrection in, United States army and navy forces mobilized on borders of, to guard American interests, 8038. (See also Wars in, *post*.)

Interference of citizens of United States in war of, with Texas, complained of, 2051.

International exhibition to be held in, 4449.

Intervention of foreign powers in affairs of, referred to, 3260.

Invasion of, by—
Spain, discussed, 1009.
Squadron under command of Capt. Thomas Jones, discussed, 2080.

Jurisdiction claimed by, over foreigners committing offenses against Mexicans, discussed, 5087.

Kidnapping of American child in, referred to, 3572.

La Abra Mining Company, award against, 6677.

Language used by, offensive to United States, 2206.

Loan of United States to, discussed, 3264, 3282.

Maximilian—
Capture and execution of, referred to, 3725.
Decree of, declaring blockade of ports proclaimed void, 3631.
Decree of, reestablishing slavery in, referred to, 3569.
Organization for purpose of avenging death of, referred to, 3780.

Military contributions to be levied upon, 2373, 2379.
Amount collected referred to, 2398, 2501, 2528.
Authority for collecting, discussed, 2420, 2522.
Contribution levied discussed, 2374.
Recommendations regarding collection of, 2380, 2381.
Referred to, 2418.

Military posts in, establishment of, recommended, 3045, 3099.

Minister of, to United States, 2051, 2480.
Mission of, terminated, 1456.
Passports demanded by, 2238.
Received, 1595, 4718.

Minister of United States, 808, 1009, 1537, 2219, 2241, 2480.
Assemblage of ministers in, 935.
Postponed, 951.
Correspondence with, referred to, 3723.
Gen. Grant sent to communicate with, 3641.
Referred to, 3654.
Relieved and duties assigned to Gen. Sherman, 3641.
Interference of, in favor of the French, referred to, 3348, 3351.
Passports demanded by, 2289, 2340.

Mexico, City of, Surrender of.—After a series of brilliant operations the United States invaders had overcome three times their own number and were in possession of the capital of Mexico. Before daylight of Sept. 14, 1847, the city council had waited upon Gen. Scott, the American commander, and demanded terms of surrender. He replied that the city had come into his power the night before and that the terms accorded would be imposed by the American army. At 7 o'clock the United States flag was hoisted on the top of the National Palace, and at 9 o'clock Gen. Scott rode into the plaza, escorted by the Second United States Dragoons. Soon after taking possession of the city a fire was opened upon the American soldiers from the roofs of houses, from windows, and street corners by about 2,000 convicts who had been liberated the night before by the fleeing Government. These were joined by as many soldiers, who had disbanded themselves and assumed the garb of citizens. This firing was kept up in a desultory way for 24 hours, and many soldiers were killed or wounded.

Mexico, City of:
Capture of, by American troops, discussed, 2391.
Cemetery at, appropriation for, recommended, 2683.
Referred to, 4149.

Mexico, Treaties with.—The treaty of peace, friendship, limits, and settlement, known as the Guadalupe Hidalgo Treaty, was concluded in 1848, and closed the Mexican War. After a declaration of peace between the two nations, the treaty provided for the appointment of a commission to arrange a provisional peace and restore constitutional government so far as military occupation would permit.

Boundary.—The boundary line between the two republics was defined by this treaty, but modified by the Gadsden Treaty of 1853. Mexicans, who by the change of boundary should pass from the jurisdiction of Mexico, were to be incorporated as citizens of the United States with all reasonable ease and expediency. For the boundary extension the United States agreed to pay to Mexico the sum of $15,000,000 in gold or silver coins of Mexico; $3,000,000 to be paid at the city of Mexico immediately after ratification, and the remaining $12,000,000 in annual installments of $3,000,000 each, with interest at the rate of six per cent. per annum. The United States agreed to the payment of all claims due and to become due, so that Mexico should be free from all expense of any kind in connection with them. The Mexican government was discharged from all claims of United States citizens which arose prior to the signing of this treaty; and the United States agreed to pay the same in a sum not to exceed $3,250,000.

Fortifications.—The privilege of fortifying any point within its own territories was reserved by both nations. Supplies necessary to the support of United States troops within the territories of Mexico prior to evacuation, to be admitted duty free.

Customs Duties.—Until the rehabilitation of the custom house in Mexico, goods arriving shall be exempt from confiscation if dutiable. Disputes arising in regard to matter not covered clearly by this treaty are to be arranged amicably by the parties; failing such amicable arrangement, then they are to be submitted to arbitration of commissioners or of a friendly power. Provision was made for the possible outbreak of war between the two nations.

Gadsden Treaty.—The treaty of 1853, known as the Gadsden Treaty, transferred to the United States the territory out of which Nevada, Utah, California, and parts of Arizona, New Mexico, Colorado, and Wyoming were erected, comprising 45,535 square miles, and relinquishing claims against the United States for damages caused by Indian depredations amounting to between fifteen millions and thirty millions of dollars. In return, the United States paid the sum of $10,000,000, $7,000,000 at the time of signing the treaty, and $3,000,000 on the completion of the survey. No opposition to passage on the plank and rail road across the Isthmus of Tehuantepec, of which the government of Mexico had pledged its support, was to be offered by either party. The privilege of carrying United States mail over the road was accorded without liability of duty charges on such parts of the mail as were not intended for distribution en route.

Boundary Commission.—The boundary convention of 1882 provided for the establishment of an International Boundary Commission for the replacing of such monuments as should be deemed necessary to clearly define the boundary between the two republics. The powers of the commission, the sort of monuments to be used, the cost thereof, and the expenses of the commission, were all clearly detailed in the treaty. Penalties were also agreed upon for destruction or removal of such monuments.

The boundary convention of 1884 established and more clearly defined the boundary of the Rio Grande and the Rio Colorado than did the treaty of 1848 and the treaty of 1853. Several boundary conventions were concluded at later dates to extend the time allowed to the commission for the completion of their work. By a boundary convention of 1889 a boundary commission was established for the determination of the boundary line consequent upon the changes in the courses of the Rio Grande and the Rio Colorado. (For the extradition treaties of 1899 and 1902, see Extradition Treaties.) An arbitration convention was signed in 1908. (See A. B. C. Arbitration.)

The question as to whether the Chamizal tract at El Paso belongs to the United States or Mexico was submitted to arbitration in 1910, but the result proved unsatisfactory. (See page 7658.)

Mexico also became a party to the convention between the United States and the several republics of South and Central America for the arbitration of pecuniary claims and the protection of inventions, etc., which was signed in Buenos Aires in 1910 and proclaimed in Washington July 29, 1914. (See South and Central America, Treaties with.)

Mexico, Gulf of:

Miami Indians. (See Indian Tribes, and Indian Wars.)

Miami, Battle of. (See 194.)

Michigamia Indians. (See Indian Tribes.)

Michigan.—One of the western group of states; nickname, "The Wolverine State"; motto, "Si quæris peninsulam amœnam, circumspice" ("If you seek a delightful peninsula, look about you"). It consists of two peninsulas, which extend from lat. 41° 45' to 47° 30' north and from long. 82° 25' to 90° 30' west. The southern peninsula is bounded on the east by Lakes Huron, St. Clair, and Erie and by Canada (separated by the St. Clair and Detroit rivers), on the south by Indiana and Ohio, and on the west by Lake Michigan. The upper peninsula (separated from the southern by the Strait of Mackinaw) lies between Lake Superior on the north and Lakes Huron and Michigan and the State of Wisconsin on the south and west, and has an area of 58,980 square miles. The State is noted for its great mineral wealth. Its chief industries are the production of copper, salt, lumber, wool, and iron, and in the manufacture of furniture it is one of the most prominent states in the Union. The lumbering industry, in which it formerly led the country, has declined, owing to misuse of the forest, although the industry is still considerable.

Michigan was first settled by the French at Sault Ste. Marie in 1668. It was ceded to Great Britain in 1763, was formally surrendered to the United States in 1796, formed part of the Northwestern Territory and later of Indiana Territory, and was constituted Michigan Territory in 1805. Detroit was taken by the British in 1812, but was recovered by the United States in 1813. Michigan was admitted to the Union in 1837.

Statistics of agriculture collected for the last Federal census placed the number of farms in the State at 206,960, comprising 18,940,614 acres, valued, with stock and improvements, at $1,088,858,379. The average value of farm land was $32.48. The value of domestic animals, poultry, etc., was $137,803,795, including 1,497,823 cattle, valued at $40,500,318; 610,033 horses, $71,312,474; 3,700 mules, $493,825; 1,245,-833 swine, $9,755,042; 2,306,476 sheep, $9,646,595; poultry, $5,610,958. The yield and value of field crops for 1911 is given as follows: corn, 1,690,000 acres, 55,770,-000 bushels, $36,250,000; wheat, 1,025,000 acres, 18,450,000 bushels $16,236,000; oats, 1,500,000 acres, 42,900,000 bushels, $19,-734,000; rye, 400,000 acres, 5,840,000 bushels, $4,964,000; potatoes, 330,000 acres, 31,020,000 bushels, $22,024,000; hay, 2,-411,000 acres, 2,797,000 tons, $47,549,000. The mineral products of the State consist largely of copper and iron, though coal, building stone, sand, gravel, cement, etc., are taken out in paying quantities. The State ranks second in the production of iron ore. In 1910 there were mined 13,303,906 long tons, valued at $41,393,585. The Marquette range, wholly in the State, and the Menominee and Gogebic, extending into Wisconsin, are rich mineral ledges. The State is one of the three largest producers of copper, being surpassed only by Arizona and Montana. The output in 1909 was 227,005,923 pounds, the largest in the history of the industry, valued at $30,-267,456; in 1910, only 219,000,000 pounds was produced, and in 1911 there was a further curtailment of about 5,000,000 pounds on account of the low price of the metal and the general condition of the market.

The manufacturing business is concerned chiefly with lumber, agricultural products, metals and mining.

The number of manufacturing establishments in Michigan having an annual output valued at $500 or more at the beginning of 1915 was 8,724. The amount of capital invested was $869,043, giving employment to 320,611 persons, using material valued at $592,801,000, and turning out finished goods worth $1,086,162,000. Salaries and wages paid amounted to $250,525,000.

Michigan:

Admission of, into Union—
Application for, referred to, 1405.
Conventions held in regard to, 1489.
State government formed by inhabitants of, 1405.
Appropriation for, 382.
Approval of bill providing for road limited to, explained, 1046.
Boundary of—
Controversy with Ohio regarding, 1404, 1407.
With Wisconsin, referred to, 1846.
Governor of, report of, 379.
Homestead entries in Marquette district in, confirmation of, referred to, 4665.
Lands in—
Ceded to United States by Indians, 1257.
Promised to soldiers, not fit for cultivation, recommendations regarding, 555.

Laws of, transmitted, 400, 6257.
Recovery of, from British forces, referred to, 520, 527.
Revenue District established within the State of, 6586.
Supplies furnished citizens of, 527.
Support of, referred to, 382.

Middle Creek (Ky.), Battle of.—Jan. 9, 1862, Col. James A. Garfield broke up his camp at Muddy Creek, Ky., and advanced with 1,800 men to attack Gen. Humphrey Marshall, who had some 2,500 troops, in Johnson County. Marshall, being advised of Garfield's approach, took up a position on the heights of Middle Creek, about two miles from Prestonburg. On the morning of the 10th Garfield began the attack. The battle lasted all day. Marshall retired from the field in the evening upon the arrival of Federal reenforcements and burned his stores to prevent their falling into Federal hands. Seventy-five of the Confederate dead were picked up on the field. The Union loss was less than 30, according to Federal accounts.

Middle States, armed neutrality in, discussed, 3225.

Midnight Appointments.—During the last days of his presidential term John Adams, piqued at the success of Jefferson, whom he bitterly opposed for the presidency, made a number of Federal appointments, in every instance of men opposed to Jefferson and his principles. Among the appointments were sixteen circuit judges. Some of the commissions of these appointees were signed just before midnight of March 3, 1801, and were called "midnight appointments."

"Midnight Ride of Paul Revere."—The ride by Paul Revere from Boston to Lexington, in 1775, to call the "Minute Men" to emergency service; immortalized by Longfellow in his *Midnight Ride of Paul Revere.*

Midway Island, referred to, 5187.

Milan Decree.—Nov. 11, 1807, France and England being then at war, the King of Great Britain and his privy council issued a decree forbidding trade between the United States and any European country under Napoleon's power. Napoleon thereupon, in retaliation, on Dec. 7, 1807, issued the Milan Decree, in which he declared "denationalized," whether found in continental ports or on the high seas, any vessel which should submit to search by a British vessel or should touch at or set sail to or from Great Britain or her Colonies. (See also Berlin Decree; Embargo; Orders in Council.)

Milan and Berlin Decrees:

Discussed and referred to by President—
Jefferson, 409, 415, 430, 432, 434, 441, 446.
Madison, 467, 474, 476, 503, 513, 522.
Proclamations regarding, issued by Jefferson and Madison, 457, 466.

Milan, Italy. Beneficence Congress at, 4626.

Mileage.—Compensation for traveling expenses at a certain rate per mile. The First Congress passed a law allowing each member $6 for every twenty miles traveled in going to and from Congress. In 1818 this was raised to $8, and in 1856 mileage was limited to two sessions. Railway transportation having cheapened traveling expenses, Congress in 1866 reduced the mileage to 20 cents a mile each way.

Miles, The, claims of owners of, against Portugal, 2453.

Militarism.—The term is hard to define, but may be considered as a state of national psychology which exalts military ideals, not only above, but also instead of civil ideals; and which in any country basis its hopes for the greatness of that country upon the development and utilization of its military forces. A necessary concomitant of militarism is the division of the social life of the country along the lines of military caste. It must be pointed out that the mere presence of a large army, or of a system of universal military training, does not imply militarism. France, usually considered one of the most democratic countries, and one peculiarly free from militarism, has had universal military training and an army proportionately almost as large as the army of Germany, which is usually considered the greatest exponent of the ideal of militarism in present times; whereas peaceful Switzerland has the largest army in Europe in proportion to its population. Although militarism was supreme in ancient and feudal times, modern militarism dates from the Napoleonic Wars; and the present German system is the direct result of the organization of Marshal von Moltke, assisted by Bismarck; and is exemplified in the military writings of von Bernhardi and Treitske, and in the philosophy of Neitsche. (See Chauvinism.)

Militarist.—One addicted to militarism (q. v.).

Military Academy.—As early as 1770 the idea of a National Military Academy had been advanced. A committee of the Continental Congress was appointed to "prepare and bring in a plan of a military academy of the army." Washington called the attention of Congress to the matter in 1793, and in 1796 recommended the institution of a military academy (page 194). March 16, 1802, Congress passed the law founding the Academy. On June 20, 1801, the Secretary of War directed that all cadets of the corps of artillerists should report at West Point, on the Hudson River, for instruction, and on Sept. 1, 1801, the school was opened, with four army officers and one civilian as administrators and instructors. (See illustration opposite 1757.)

The general commanding the army has under the War Department, supervision of the Academy. The immediate government consists of a Superintendent, commandant of cadets, and seven commissioned professors. The act of Congress of June 6, 1900, provided that the corps of cadets shall consist of one from each Congressional district, one from each Territory, one from the District of Columbia, two from each state at large, and thirty from the United States at large. The act approved June 28, 1902, provided that the number of cadets to be appointed from the United States at large is not at any one time to exceed forty. An additional appointment of one cadet from Puerto Rico was authorized by a provision in the act of March 3, 1903.

By a law passed April 17, 1916, Representatives may appoint two cadets instead of one. Senators four instead of two and the President eighty, instead of forty.

With each candidate appointed two alternatives are also named. The act of June 11, 1878, had provided that the number of cadets at large should not exceed ten, and this number had been increased to twenty by an act of March 2, 1899. The cadets are appointed by the President, those from the Congressional districts being recommended by a Congressman from the respective districts, and those from the states at large being recommended by the Senators of the respective states. Those from the United States at large and from the District of Columbia are appointed directly by the President. With the exception of those appointed from the United States at large, applicants must be actual residents of the Congressional or Territorial districts or of the states respectively from which they are appointed. Except in cases of unexpected vacancies appointments must be made one year in advance of the date of admission.

Appointees to the Military Academy must be between seventeen and twenty-two years of age, free from any infirmity which may render them unfit for military service, and able to pass a careful examination in English grammar, English composition, English literature, algebra through quadratic equations, plane geometry, descriptive geography and the elements of physical geography, especially the geography of the United States, United States history, the outlines of general history.

The Secretary of War is authorized to permit not exceeding four Filipinos, to be designated, one for each class, by the Philippine Commission, to receive instruction at the United States Military Academy at West Point; Provided, That the Filipinos undergoing instruction shall receive the same pay, allowances, and emoluments as are authorized by law for cadets at the Military Academy appointed from the United States, to be paid out of the same appropriations; And provided further, That said Filipinos undergoing instruction on graduation shall be eligible only to commissions in the Philippine Scouts. Serve for eight years, unless sooner discharged.

The course of instruction, which is quite thorough, requires four years, and is largely mathematical and professional. The principal subjects taught are mathematics, English, French, drawing, drill regulations of all arms of the service, natural and experimental philosophy, chemistry, chemical physics, mineralogy, geology, electricity, history, international, constitutional, and military law, Spanish, civil and military engineering, art and science of war, and ordnance and gunnery. About one-fourth of those appointed usually fail to pass the preliminary examinations, and but little over one-half of the remainder are finally graduated. The discipline is very strict—even more so than in the army—and the enforcement of penalties for offences is inflexible rather than severe. Academic duties begin September 1 and continue until June 4. Examinations are held in each December and June, and cadets found proficient in studies and correct in conduct are given the particular standing in their class to which their merits entitle them, while those cadets deficient in either conduct or studies are discharged.

From about the middle of June to the end of August cadets live in camp, engaged only in military duties and receiving practical military instruction. Cadets are allowed but one leave of absence during the four years' course, and this is granted at the expiration of the first two years. The pay of a cadet is $709.50 per year, and, with proper economy, is sufficient for his support. The number of students at the

Academy is usually about five hundred and fifty.

Upon graduating cadets are commissioned as second lieutenants in the United States Army. The whole number of graduates from 1802 to 1916, inclusive, has been 5,601. It is without exception necessary for a person seeking an appointment to apply to his Senator of Member of Congress. The appointments by the President are usually restricted to sons of officers of the army and navy, who, by reason of their shifting residence, find it next to impossible to obtain an appointment otherwise. The Superintendent in 1917 was Colonel John Biddle, Corps of Engineers, U. S. Army. During 1916, the disbursements of the Academy from government appropriations were $240,-000. On Sept. 1, 1916, the number of students at the Academy was 769 and the corps of instructors numbered 128.

Military Academy:

Appropriation for, recommended, 955, 983.

Bequest of George W. Callum for erection of memorial hall on grounds of, 5674.

Cadets in—

Enlistment of, time of, should be extended, 1607.

Increase in corps of, recommended, 3249.

Promotion of, referred to, 2422.

Discussed, 757, 781, 872, 983, 1019, 4248, 4934, 5879.

Enlargement of, necessary, 433, 471, 551.

Establishment of, recommended, 194, 197, 878.

Expenditures of, 4934.

Extending time for enlistment of cadets in, recommended, 1607.

Government of, rules for, 621.

Improvement in, recommended, 4148.

Military education in, recommendations regarding, 1389.

Regulations for, amended, 4713.

Removal of, suggested, 433.

Rules for government of, 621.

View of, in 1840, 1757.

Military Asylum. (See Soldiers' Home.)

Military Code. (See Code.)

Military Commanders (see also Military Districts and Divisions):

Anonymous letter filed with correspondence of, return of, requested, 3999.

Not vested with authority to interfere with contracts between individuals, order regarding, 3548.

Military Commissions to Cuba, Puerto Rico, and adjacent islands, 6322.

Military Contributions to be levied upon Mexico, 2373, 2379.

Military Control over Railroads, suggested, 8184.

Military Courts and Commissions (see also Lincoln, Abraham; Military Commission, etc.):

Order—

In relation to trials by, 3638.

Sentences of imprisonment remitted, 3537.

Military Divisions and Departments:

Northeastern Department. — Embraces Maine, New Hampshire, Vermont, Massachusetts, Rhode Island, Connecticut. Headquarters at Boston, Mass.

Eastern Department. — Embraces New York, New Jersey, Delaware, Pennsylvania, Maryland, Virginia, District of Columbia, Canal Zone, Porto Rico, with the islands and keys thereto adjacent. Headquarters, Governor's Island, N. Y.

Southeastern Department. — Embraces Tennessee, North Carolina, South Carolina, Georgia, Florida, Alabama, Mississippi, Louisiana, Arkansas, with the coast defenses of Galveston. Headquarters, Charlestown, S. C.

Central Department.—Embraces the states of Ohio, Indiana, Illinois, Wisconsin, Michigan, West Virginia, Kentucky, Minnesota, North Dakota, South Dakota, Iowa, Kansas, Missouri, Nebraska, Colorado. Headquarters, Chicago, Ill.

Southern Department.—Embraces Texas (except coast defenses of Galveston), New Mexico, Oklahoma, Arizona. Headquarters, Fort Sam Houston, Tex.

Western Department.—Embraces Washington, Oregon, California, Nevada, Utah, Montana, Idaho, Wyoming, Alaska. Headquarters, San Francisco, Cal.

Philippine Department.—Embraces all the islands of the Philippine Archipelago. It is sub-divided into the District of Luzon and the District of Mindanao. Headquarters, Manila, P. I.

Hawaiian Department.—Embraces the Hawaiian Islands and their dependencies. Headquarters, Honolulu, H. T.

Military Districts and Divisions:

Assignments to, 3749, 3750, 3754, 3755, 3859, 3860, 3861, 3862, 3863, 3864, 3866, 3869, 3973, 3975, 3976, 4047, 4048, 4753.

Orders regarding, rescinded, 3976, 4048.

Creation of, 3860.

Authority for, referred to, 3830.

Dissolution of, 4048, 4049.

First, fourth and fifth districts dissolved, 4048, 4049.

Instructions relating to third district referred to, 3826.

Plans, etc., for barracks and quarters in Military Division of Potomac, 4666.

Reports and recommendations of commanders of, 3994, 3999.

Military Drafts. (See Drafts, Military.)

Military Education.—The military educational system of the United States, exclusive of the Military Academy at West Point, comprises the following:

I. *The Army War College,* Washington, D. C., under the management of a president and directors detailed from officers of the army. The course of instruction is for one year, beginning September 1. A limited number of officers not below the rank of captain, selected on account of exceptional efficiency and fitness, are detailed annually for instruction. The purpose of the college is to make practical application of knowledge already acquired, not to impart academic instruction.

II. *The Army Service Schools.* The group of schools established at Fort Leavenworth, Kansas, consisting of the Army School of the Line as the basic school, the Army Staff College, the Army Signal School, the Army Field Engineer School, and the Army Field Service and Correspondence School for Medical Officers as special affiliated schools, are designated the Army Service Schools, and are under the direction of a Commandant not of lower grade than that of a Brigadier-General.

The course of instruction at the schools, except as otherwise stated, is included in one term from September 1 to June 30 of the following year.

1. The Army School of the Line. The object of this school is the instruction of selected officers from the line of the army in the leading and care of troops in time of war and their training in time of peace. The Assistant Commandant of the Army Service Schools is also the Director of the School of the Line.

Upon graduation, the student classes are graded, in order of merit, as "honor graduates," "distinguished graduates," and "graduates," respectively.

2. The Army Staff College, for the instruction of officers detailed annually from the highest graduates of the latest class of the School of the Line, recommended by the Academic Board of that school. The object of this college is to impart instruction to officers in the duties of the general staff of an army ; to prepare them for the Army War College and to investigate military inventions, discoveries and developments.

The Commandant, Assistant Commandant, Secretary and Senior Instructors of the School of the Line hold corresponding positions in the Staff College.

3. The Army Signal School, for instruction of officers of the Signal Corps in their duties, including aeronautics ; for instruction of officers of the line, who are designated therefor, in signal duties, and to make research and experiments in subjects pertaining to the work of the Signal Corps. The school is under the general direction of the Commandant of the Army School of the Line.

4. The Army Field Engineer School, for the instruction of officers of the Engineer Corps, not exceeding ten, and engineer officers of the National Guard.

5. The Army Field Service and Correspondence School for Medical Officers, for the instruction of officers of the Medical Corps and of the National Guard. Part one of this school requires attendance in person for a graded course of study, and part two for a course by correspondence. The course of instruction is eight weeks, from April 1 of each year. Students who complete the course satisfactorily receive certificates of proficiency.

III. *The Army Medical School,* Washington, D. C., for the instruction of medical officers of the army, candidates for appointment in the Medical Corps, and medical officers of the National Guard. The faculty consists of a president and instructors. The course of instruction is for eight months, from October 1 each year. Graduates receive diplomas.

IV. *The Coast Artillery School,* Fort Monroe, Virginia. The object of this school is to enlarge the field of instruction of the garrison schools for Coast Artillery officers by advanced courses of study and practical training in technical duties ; to prepare specially selected officers for the more important positions in the Coast Artillery ;

also to educate and train selected enlisted men for the higher non-commissioned staff grades in the Coast Artillery. The courses of instruction for officers and enlisted men are each comprised in one school year, from January 3 to December 1. Special courses in ballistics are also provided.

Officers who are graduated are furnished with diplomas, as "honor graduates," "distinguished graduates," or "graduates," according to their standing.

V. *The Engineer School,* Washington Barracks, D. C. This school is under the control of the Chief of Engineers. Its object is to prepare junior officers of engineers for the active duties of their corps ; to make experiments and recommendations, and to give instruction pertaining to the civil engineering work of the army. The course of instruction is one year, beginning September 1. Diplomas are given to students who successfully complete the course.

VI. *The Mounted Service School,* Fort Riley, Kansas, is under the command of a general officer, who also commands the post of Fort Riley. The object of the school is to give practical instruction to field and company officers of cavalry and field artillery, and to farriers and horseshoers. The courses for field officers begin April 1 and October 10 ; the course for company officers is from September 25 to June 30, following ; and for farriers and horseshoers two courses of four months each. Company officers who are graduated receive diplomas.

VII. *The School of Fire for Field Artillery,* Fort Sill, Oklahoma, for practical instruction in field artillery firing. Courses of instruction are prescribed : A, for captains and lieutenants ; B, for field officers of field artillery ; C, for non-commissioned officers, and D, for officers of the militia. Officers and enlisted men who complete any course satisfactorily receive certificates of proficiency.

VIII. *School of Musketry,* Fort Sill, Oklahoma, for instruction in small-arms firing.

IX. *Garrison Schools,* one at each military post, for the instruction of officers of the army and the National Guard, in subjects pertaining to their ordinary duties. The course covers three years and the annual terms five months each, from November 1st. Certificates of proficiency in each subject of study are given to those who pass the prescribed examination therein.

X. *Post Schools for Instruction of Enlisted Men* in the common branches of education and military subjects.

XI. *Schools for Bakers and Cooks,* at San Francisco, California, Washington, D. C., and Fort Riley, Kansas, for the instruction of selected enlisted men.

XII. *Signal Corps Aviation School,* the object of which is the training of men and officers in military aviation matters.

Officers of the National Guard are admitted to most of the Army Schools, under the Militia law of January 21, 1903, and regulations prescribed by the War Department. They must be nominated by the governors of their states. Those admitted to any of the schools receive mileage and money commutations for subsistence, quarters, etc. A considerable number of militia officers enter these schools, notably the garrison schools, annually.

Military Establishment (see also Army):

Proposition of Czar of Russia for reduction of, discussed, 6335.

Military Expeditions. (See Expeditions Against Foreign Powers.)

Military Governors. (See Provisional Governors.)

Military Information, Bureau of:

Discussed, 5879.

Reorganization of, 5755.

Military Justice, Bureau of, recommendations regarding, 4570.

Military Order of Foreign Wars.—The Military Order of Foreign Wars of the United States was instituted in the City of New York, Dec. 27, 1894, by veterans and descendants of veterans of one or more of the five foreign wars which the United States had been engaged in, to wit: the War of the Revolution, the War with Tripoli, the War of 1812, the Mexican War, and the War with Spain, "to perpetuate the names and memory of brave and loyal men who took part in establishing and maintaining the principles of the Government" in said wars, and "to preserve records and documents relating to said wars, and to celebrate the anniversaries of historic events connected therewith." Since the establishment of the order the United States has fought its fifth foreign war. By an amendment to the constitution all American officers who participate in the war with Spain, or any future foreign campaign recognized by the United States Government as "war," are rendered eligible to membership as veteran companions.

The National Commandery was instituted March 11, 1896, by the officers of the New York, Pennsylvania, and Connecticut commanderies. Present membership, over 1,-800 companions. There are Vice-Commanders-General representing each state commandery.

Military Park. (See Chickamauga and Chattanooga National Military Park.)

Military Peace Establishment. (See Army.)

Military Posts. (See also Forts.)

Disposition of abandoned, recommended, 4524, 4569.

Establishment of—

Lands donated by Indians for, 436.

Recommended, 831, 1475, 1940, 2111, 2190.

Estimates, plans, etc., for, 4666, 4670, 4674, 4677, 4680, 4687.

Military Reservations:

Additional land for Fort Preble, Me., recommended, 4777.

Indian school at, establishment of, recommended, 4683.

Legislation to provide for disposal of, recommended, 4660, 4690, 4737, 4740, 4782, 4783.

Military Schools and Colleges.—Besides the United States Military Academy (q. v.) at West Point there are the following schools and colleges making up a system of advanced instruction in the science and art military education: The War College, for

of war, at Washington, D. C.; the General Service and Staff College, at Fort Leavenworth, Kansas; the Artillery School, at Fort Monroe, Virginia; the School of Submarine Defense, at Fort Totten, New York; the Engineer School of Application, at Washington, D. C.; the School of Application for Cavalry and Field Artillery, at Fort Riley, Kansas, and the Army Medical School, at Washington, D. C.

Military Stores, provisions for—

Discussed, 416.

Recommended, 317.

Military Training in the Schools.—During the Civil War, the passage of the Morrell Act provided financial aid from the Government to colleges with compulsory military drill for all students. It is estimated that by 1917 over 30,000 college students were receiving such military training. In 1895, an unsuccessful attempt was made in Congress to establish a Bureau of Military Education, and to provide for the establishment of uniform military drilling in the public schools of the United States. Many states, notably Wyoming, have provisions for voluntary military drill, and Boston for many years has had such drill in its public high schools. The existence of a belief in the efficacy and the benefits of military training has led to the establishment of private military schools all over the United States.

In 1914, however, the movement for military training in the public schools was resurrected by the outbreak of the Great European War. Opinion in the country was sharply divided on the issue. Military men were almost unanimous in their approval of the measure, as were most of the advocates of what came to be called "Preparedness" (q. v.); but the movement was opposed strongly by organizations of the working-classes and by pacifists (q. v.), while educational and physical training experts differed in their opinions. Many of the proposals for military training in the schools were modeled after the Swiss system (q. v.). In Germany, the school children are given physical training adaptable to military purposes, which, however, is itself given outside the schools. New York state created much interest by passing in 1916 a law for universal military training in the schools. The training is under the supervision of a Military Training Commission of Three, appointed by the Governor. The law applies to boys between the ages of 16 and 19, except those actively employed; and prescribes that not more than three hours a week during the school year may be devoted to this purpose. (See also Australian System of Military Training.)

The practice of twenty countries with respect to military training in the schools is as follows:

Argentina—Obligatory military training in the last two years of secondary schools. Specially trained instructors.

Australia—Military instruction compulsory for all boys from twelve to eighteen years.

Austria — Voluntary organizations for military training of pupils of secondary schools, under government protectorate. Optional rifle practice in the last two years of secondary schools.

Bolivia—Simple drill in connection with gymnastics.

Canada—Military instruction carried on in voluntary cadet corps.

France—Prescribed military instruction without arms, and rifle practice in elementary and higher elementary schools. Ages nine to thirteen years; rifle practice limited to boys over ten years of age. Specially trained instructors. Strong organizations carry on the work of military preparation among older boys.

Germany—Voluntary organizations of older public school pupils and students of secondary schools. Training without arms. Decrees issued during the war provide for preparatory military training of all boys over sixteen years of age.

Great Britain—Strictly voluntary work carried on by private agencies.

Greece—Very intensive military instruction is given in gymnasia, under the patronage of the King. Simple drill obtains in all public schools in connection with physical training.

Hungary—Voluntary organizations in elementary, secondary, and higher schools. In many districts military instruction is obligatory in secondary schools.

Italy—Military training given as obligatory subject in "national colleges." Private agencies provide for simple military drill for younger boys.

Japan—Military gymnastics obligatory in elementary, secondary, and normal schools.

Mexico—Obligatory military drill with arms in all primary and secondary schools. Regulated by state laws.

Netherlands—Military training given in voluntary organizations for boys over fifteen years of age.

New Zealand—Military instruction compulsory for boys over fourteen years.

Norway—Voluntary rifle practice.

Portugal—No military training is given in schools. The subject of "physical culture," which is taught generally, includes simple drill without arms. Boy Scout organizations are numerous.

Russia—Prescribed military gymnastics in elementary and secondary schools.

Spain—No distinct military training is given. Some simple drill is included in the program of physical training.

Sweden—Compulsory rifle practice in public secondary schools for boys from fifteen to eighteen years of age. Given by special instructors.

Switzerland—Instruction in military gymnastics in elementary schools obligatory throughout the school age. Conducted by specially trained instructors. Voluntary rifle practice and military drill both with and without arms.

Military Tribunals. (See Military Courts and Commissions.)

Militia.—Citizens of a state enrolled as soldiers for training and discipline, but called into active service only in emergencies, as distinguished from the regular soldiers, who are in constant service. The Constitution empowers Congress "to provide for calling forth the militia to execute the laws of the Union, suppress insurrections, and repel invasions." In 1792 an act was passed to provide for the national defense by establishing a uniform militia throughout the United States by the enrollment of every free able-bodied white male citizen between the ages of eighteen and forty-five. (See Army.) An act of March 2, 1867, permitted the enrollment of negroes.

The militia was called out by Federal authorities in 1794 to quell the Whisky Rebellion in western Pennsylvania, during the War of 1812, and in 1861, during the Civil War.

The law of Jan. 21, 1903, provided for the better equipment of this service and supplied an organic connection between the National Guard and the Regular Army, the purpose being to create a National Volunteer Reserve that could be called upon whenever needed by the general Government. This law provides that the militia shall consist of every available male citizen in the respective states, territories, and the District of Columbia, and every available male of foreign birth who had declared his intention to become a citizen, the entire militia body being divided into two classes: (1) the Organized Militia, to be known as the National Guard of the State, Territory, or District of Columbia, or by such other designation as may be given them by the laws of the respective states or territories; and (2) the remainder, to be known as the Reserve Militia.

The organized militia of those state and territorial organizations that have in the past or shall in the future participate in the annual appropriation made by Congress for the militia, and the organization, armament, and discipline of the organized militia is the same as that prescribed for the regular and volunteer army.

The act of Jan. 21, 1903, and the laws antecedent thereto restricted the use of the organized militia when called forth by the President in time of emergency to service in the United States and to a period of nine months. The act approved May 27, 1908, removes these two restrictions and makes the organized militia of the several states available for service during the period of commission of the officers or enlistment of the men, and within or without the boundaries of the United States. The call of the President will, therefore, of itself accomplish the transfer of the organized militia specified in his call from state relations to Federal relations. The militia so called forth becomes at once a part of the Army of the United States, and the President becomes its Commander-in-Chief; it is therefore as completely under the orders of the President and as completely serviceable, both as to time and place, as the regular army.

Assuming that all male citizens 18 to 45 years of age are available for military duty the total number of citizen soldiers, eliminating Chinese, Japanese and alien whites, based on the census of 1910, with 10 per cent. added for estimated increase to 1916, the following table compiled by the Census Bureau places the military strength of the United States as 21,071,076, divided among the states as follows:

STATE	NUMBER	STATE	NUMBER
Maine.........	156,449	North Carolina..	401,917
New Hampshire.	93,321	South Carolina..	283,490
Vermont.......	76,017	Georgia........	507,688
Massachusetts..	785,581	Florida.........	177,152
Rhode Island...	129,131	Kentucky......	469,711
Connecticut....	266,697	Tennessee......	434,641
New York......	2,223,633	Alabama......	414,454
New Jersey.....	617,013	Mississippi....	354,133
Pennsylvania...	1,842,266	Arkansas......	321,924
Ohio..........	1,107,888	Louisiana......	347,518
Indiana........	596,682	Oklahoma......	366,339
Illinois.........	1,369,910	Texas..........	828,756
Michigan......	634,518	Montana.......	126,862
Wisconsin......	512,261	Idaho..........	88,839
Minnesota......	505,187	Wyoming......	55,886
Iowa..........	489,829	Colorado......	210,637
Missouri.......	741,180	New Mexico....	75,371
North Dakota...	148,920	Arizona.......	60,915
South Dakota...	143,895	Utah..........	86,590
Nebraska.......	274,507	Nevada........	30,489
Kansas........	379,730	Washington....	350,746
Delaware......	46,139	Oregon........	196,165
Maryland......	279,818	California.....	687,822
Dist. Columbia..	80,858		
Virginia........	410,422	Total for United	
West Virginia...	281,179	States........	21,071,076

Among other important provisions of the new militia act may be mentioned, fixing the organization, armament and discipline of the organize ' militia after Jan. 21, 1910, the same as that of the Regular Army: providing that the organized militia shall be called in time of emergency into the service of the United States in advance of any volunteer force.

The Secretary of War issues without cost to the states or territories all arms and equipment necessary to supply all of the organized militia. The Secretary of War is also authorized to provide for the preparation of the organized militia for the encampment manœuvers and field manœuvers of the regular army in which the militia receives the same pay, subsistence and transportation as the regular army. Upon the requisition of the Governor of any state or territory having militia organized under this law, the Secretary of War may assign one or more officers of the regular army for service in the militia of the state or territory. Alaska has no militia. Guam and Samoa have small provisional forces used for police purposes. The Philippines have a constabulary force for police or regular military service. Puerto Rico has a provisional force under the command of a Lieutenant-Colonel of the United States Army.

Congress annually appropriates $2,000,-000 for the support of the militia, apportioned among the various states according to the strength of their organizations. In 1909, $492,502.25 was devoted to the promotion of rifle practice, and $1,477,497 for arms, equipment and camp purposes. (See Army, *Training Camps.*)

In May, 1917, President Wilson ordered the mobilization of the militia of all the states, and before the end of August the entire militia of the United States was organized in the Federal service. The strength of the national guard toward the end of 1916 was as follows, but it must be remembered that this number was increased by the time that the militia was drafted into federal service. (In spite of the fact that married men with dependents had been mustered out of the militia before the summer, the enlistments had increased the total number of the members; any vacancies were filled from the selective draft):—

Alabama ...	4,604	Montana ...	1,049
Arizona	863	Nebraska ...	1,718
Arkansas ...	1,229	N. Ha'pshire	1,413
California ..	3,592	New Jersey.	4,135
Colorado ...	943	New Mexico.	957
Connecticut .	2,921	New York...	17,852
Delaware ..	575	N. Carolina.	1,309
District of		N. Dakota...	993
Columbia ..	2,125	Ohio	7,413
Florida	1,225	Oklahoma ..	1,268
Georgia	3,918	Oregon	318
Idaho	1,178	Pennsylvania	13,745
Illinois	8,497	Rhode Island	644
Indiana	3,182	S. Carolina..	2,271
Iowa	4,323	S. Dakota...	966
Kansas ...	2,069	Tennessee ..	2,644
Kentucky ..	2,259	Texas	4,563
Louisiana ..	483	Utah	781
Maine	983	Vermont ..	959
Maryland ..	3,156	Virginia ...	2,910
Massachu'tts	7,967	Washington..	1,730
Michigan ...	4,239	W. Virginia.	1,156
Minnesota ..	4,019	Wisconsin ..	4,125
Mississippi ..	1,308	Wyoming ..	498
Missouri ...	2,629		

Total 143,704

The location of the cantonments where the National Guards of the various states were trained for service abroad in the European War will be found under the heading Cantonments.

The Chief of Coast Artillery has indicated that about 20,000 of the organized militia will be required for the coast artillery reserves and approximately the same number for coast artillery supports. These troops would be required for service in the immediate vicinity of the fortifications, and would not be available for use with the mobile army until all question of sea power along the coast had been settled favorably. (See also Army; War, Department of; Artillery; Arms and Ammunition; Naval Militia.)

The Militia law of Jan. 21, 1903, as amended by the act of May 27, 1908, provides: "That the militia shall consist of every able-bodied male citizen of the respective states and every able-bodied male of foreign birth who has declared his intention to become a citizen, who is more than eighteen and less than forty-five years of age, and shall be divided into two classes—the organized militia, to be known as the National Guard (or by such other designations as may be given them by the laws of the respective states or territories), the remainder to be known as the reserve militia."

Militia:

Arming and equipping of, recommended, 4724, 4768, 6159.

Artillery tactics for use of, prepared, 927.

Called into national service in war against Germany, 8306.

Called out to prevent British invasion from Canada, 1618.

Cavalry tactics for use of, prepared, 927.

Discharge of, directed, 455.

Discussed by President—
  Adams, J. Q., 869, 958, 995.
  Arthur, 4768.
  Cleveland, 5877, 5968, 6159.
  Jackson, 1166, 1389, 1474.
  Jefferson, 317, 333, 373, 394.
  Lincoln, 3249.
  McKinley, 6385.
  Madison, 461, 463, 471, 479, 534, 551, 561.
  Monroe, 758, 781.
  Polk, 2481.
  Roosevelt, 6672, 6805, 7236.
  Taft, 7799.
  Tyler, 1902, 2121.
  Van Buren, 1754.
  Washington, 57, 59, 78, 99, 132, 159, 161, 176, 196.

Dispatched to Mexican border, 8130.

Distribution of arms, ordnance, stores, etc., to District of Columbia and Territories, regulations regarding, 5159, 5462.

Encampment of, in coast works, urged, 5476.

Encouragement of, 5550.

Guard, National, referred to, 5476.

Increase in, recommended, 429.

Indian wars, campaigns of, in. (See Indian Wars.)

Insurrections suppressed by. (See Illegal Combinations.)

Militia Bureau, War Department.—By act of June 3, 1916, the Division of Militia Affairs, which had been a subdivision of the War Department under the Chief of Staff (q. v.), became a separate division of the department, under the direct supervision of the Secretary of War. The act of June 3, 1916 was intended to fulfill the federalization of the National Guard up to constitutional limitations, and the passage of the act abolished the National Militia Board. The act provided for the organization, arming, and disciplining of the National Guard, "reserving to states * * * the training of the Militia according to discipline prescribed by Congress." (See Militia; Army; War Department.)

Mill Springs (Ky.), Battle of.—Early in the winter of 1861-62 the Confederate General Felix K. Zollicoffer, with a force of about 5,000 men, intrenched himself at Mill Springs, on the Cumberland River in Wayne County, Ky. Jan. 17, 1862, Gen. George H. Thomas, with 8,000 Union troops, advanced to dislodge him. The Confederates set out to meet Thomas, and on Jan. 19, 1862, an engagement took place, begun by the advance guard of both armies. The Confederates were driven back to their camp, which they abandoned during the night. Twelve pieces of artillery, 156 wagons, 1,000 horses and mules, as well as large quantities of small arms, ammunition, and stores fell into the hands of the Union army. Crossing the Cumberland River, the retreating army burned their boats to prevent pursuit. The loss on the Confederate side was 350. The Unionists lost 246. Gen. Zollicoffer was among the Confederate dead.

Mill Springs, Ky., battle of, discussed, 3301.

Milligan Case.—A United States Supreme Court case involving the right of the President to suspend the rights of citizens under *habeas corpus* proceedings. Oct. 5, 1864, during the Civil War, Milligan was arrested by order of Gen. Hovey, and on Oct. 21 was brought before a military commission convened at Indianapolis, Ind.,

by the same officer. He was tried, found guilty, and sentenced to be hanged for participating in rebellious schemes. By the *habeas corpus* act of Congress in 1863 lists were to be furnished in each State of persons suspected of violating national law. But any such persons arrested against whom no indictments should be found by the circuit court or district court were to be freed on petition verified by oath. The Milligan indictment was not found by the circuit or district court. He objected to the authority of the military commission and sued for a writ of *hab.as corpus* in the circuit court. The case coming before the Supreme Court in 1866, it was decided, Justice Davis reading the opinion, that the writ should be issued and the prisoner discharged. The court held that the power of erecting military jurisdiction in a State not invaded and not in rebellion was not vested in Congress and that it could not be exercised in this particular case; that the prisoner, a civilian, was exempt from the laws of war and could only be tried by a jury; that the writ of *habeas corpus* could not be suspended constitutionally, though the privilege of that writ might be. The Chief Justice and Justices Wayne, Swayne, and Miller, while concurring in the judgment, made through the first named a separate statement of reasons. The decision expressly stated that conspiracies to aid rebellion were enormous crimes and that Congress was obliged to enact severe laws to meet the crisis. (See also Habeas Corpus; Marryman Case.)

Milwaukee, Wis., proclamation granting privileges of other ports to, 2859.

Mineral Lands. (See Lands, Mineral.)

Miners, act for protection of, in Territories, discussed and recommendations regarding, 5663.

Mines.—Submarine mines were first used extensively by the Confederate forces in the Civil War, 90% of these being of the self-acting variety. Other varieties of mines are fired by electricity from points on shore or on ships when the target has arrived over the mine. The Hague Conference of 1907 forbade the use of unanchored mines, the regulations to that effect to remain in force for seven years from that date. Mines are often rendered useless by being exploded by counter-mining, a new set of mines being exploded in their vicinity, and the reverberations of the explosions discharging the originally-laid mines. Another method widely used in the Great European War consisted of sweeping a mine area clear of these engines of destruction by grappling irons or wire nets stretched between two or more vessels drawing little water. (See Submarines.)

Mines (see also Lands, Mineral):

Bureau of, advocated, 7484.

Gold, discovered, 3451.

In Black Hills, 4306, 4355.

In California, 2486.

Mines, Bureau of.—Chapter 240 of the acts of the second session of the 61st Congress to establish in the Department of the Interior a Bureau of Mines was approved May 16, 1910. The act provided for the establishment of said bureau and a director "who shall be thoroughly equipped for the duties of said office by technical education and experience," with an annual salary of $6,000. Transfer to the bureau was provided for the investigations of the analyzing and testing of coals, lignites and other mineral fuel substances, and the investigation as to the cause of mine explosions, from the United States Geological Survey. The duties of the bureau were prescribed as follows: "It shall be the province and duty of said bureau and its director, under the direction of the Secretary of the Interior, to make diligent investigation of the methods of mining, especially in relation to the safety of miners, and the appliances best adapted to prevent accidents, the possible improvement of conditions under which mining operations are carried on, the treatment of ores and other mineral substances, the use of explosives and electricity, the prevention of accidents, and other inquiries and technologic investigations pertinent to said industries, and from time to time make such public reports of the work, investigations and information obtained as the Secretary of said department may direct, with the recommendations of such bureau." (See also Interior, Department of.)

The scope of the Bureau was broadened by act of Congress approved February 25, 1913. Included in the recent activities of the Bureau have been the maintenance of an extensive chief experimental station in Pittsburgh, Pa., the formation of first aid and rescue corps in most of the mines of the country, and the dispatch of a train carrying an elaborate exhibit of first aid to the largest mining centers of the country.

Minister.—1. In political parlance, a representative of one government in the territory of another government, lower in rank than ambassador. *Minister extraordinary*—a personal representative of the chief executive of one nation to a foreign country with specific duties to perform. *Minister plenipotentiary*—a personal representative of the chief executive with full power to conclude a specific negotiation in accordance with the minister's own judgment. (See Ambassador and Consul.) 2. In foreign countries, particularly in Great Britain, the term is used in much the same sense as "secretary" in the President's Cabinet, e. g., the Minister of Foreign Affairs, corresponding to the American Secretary of State.

Ministers of United States (see also Consular and Diplomatic Service; the several powers):

Assurances of respect to, 256, 269.

Assemblage of, in Tacubaya, Mexico, for concluding treaties at Panama, to promote friendliness and good will with South American Republics, 935.

Congress indefinitely postponed, 951.

Instructions to, 997.

Correspondence between, effects of publication of, 385.

Elevation of, missions and title of ambassador conferred, 5874, 6335.

Interfered with by French commander, 780.

List of—

Chargés d'affaires, secretaries, and, transmitted, 2830.

Money appropriated for, rights of, regarding, referred to, 912.

Must have assurances that they will be respected, 256, 269.

Official residences for, recommended, 6072, 6155.

Peace between Great Britain and United States, treaty of, received from, 537.

Presents—

From foreign States not to be accepted by, 1256.

Given to, deposited in State Department, 1256, 1258, 1260.

Previously given to, should be returned, 1257.

Salary of, discussed, 103, 1910, 1953.

Increase in salary of commissioner to China recommended, 2658.

Sent to Congress of Nations. (See under Panama, Isthmus of.)

Ministers to United States. (See the several powers.)

Minnesota.—One of the western group of states; nickname, "The Gopher State"; motto, "L'étoile du nord" ("The North Star"). It extends from lat. 43° 30′ to 49° 25′ north and from long. 89° 29′ to 97° 5′ west. It is bounded on the north by British America, on the east by Lake Superior and Wisconsin, on the south by Iowa, and on the west by the Dakotas, and has an area of 84,682 square miles. The chief industries are wheat growing, lumbering, and flour and grist milling, and in the products of this latter industry the State has the largest output in the country. The manufacture of lumber and timber products is a rapidly progressing industry. Minnesota is one of the leading wheat-producing states of the Union. The region was first explored by the French near the close of the seventeenth century, the first settlement being made at Duluth in 1678. In 1763 France ceded the territory east of the Mississippi to England, by whom it was ceded to the United States in 1783. It formed part of the Northwest Territory organized in 1787, and was successively included in the Territories of Indiana, Michigan, and Wisconsin. The lands west of the Mississippi form part of the Louisiana Purchase, and were included successively in the Territories of Upper Louisiana, Arkansas, Missouri, and Iowa. March 3, 1849, Congress passed an act creating Minnesota Territory. In 1851, 21,000,000 acres of land were acquired of the Dakotas by the treaty of Traverse de Sioux. May 11, 1858, Minnesota became a State.

Statistics of agriculture collected for the last Federal census place the number of farms in the State at 155,759, comprising 27,623,000 acres, valued, with the buildings thereon, at $1,259,510,000, and the implements and machinery used in farming are worth $52,243,000. The number and value of the principal domestic animals was: horses, 767,000, valued at $85,137,-000; mules, 9,000, $1,026,000; milch cows, 1,125,000, $37,125,000; other cattle, 1,288,-000, $17,560,000; sheep, 482,000, $1,928,-000; swine, 1,003,000, $11,534,000. The yield and value of field crops for 1911 is given as follows: corn, 2,200,000 acres, 74,-140,000 bushels, $39,294,000; wheat, 4,350,-000 acres, 43,935,000 bushels, $40,420,000; oats, 2,948,000 acres, 67,214,000 bushels, $26,886,000; rye, 240,000 acres, 4,488,000 bushels, $3,501,000; potatoes, 225,000 acres, 25,875,000 bushels, $15,008,000; hay, 799,-000 acres, 799,000 tons, $9,508,000.

Minnesota far outranks all other states in the mining of iron ore, and during the last four years has contributed both in quantity and value considerably more than half the iron ore produced and marketed in the United States, according to the United States Geological Survey. In 1913 the total marketed production of iron ore in this country was 59,643,098 long tons, valued at $130,905,558, of which Minnesota contributed 36,603,331 tons, valued at $80,789,025. In 1912 Minnesota produced 34,249,813 long tons of iron ore, valued at $61,805,017. Because of its great wealth in iron ores and of their extended development, Minnesota ranks ninth among all the states in the total value of its mineral production. The value of the iron ore produced in the state represents considerably more than ninety per cent of the total output. The chief sources of supply are the Mesabi and Vermilion ranges.

The report of the State treasurer showed a balance on hand Aug. 1, 1910, of $4,261,-231; receipts during the year, $15,612,048, and expenditures, $16,364,789; cash balance July 31, 1911, $3,508,491. The bonded debt at the end of the fiscal year was $1,518,000.

There were in 1906, 8,223 miles of steam railway in the State and 538 miles of electric line. From St. Paul ten railways radiate with a total length of 60,000 miles. The Great Northern owns a line of steamers which run between Puget Sound and China, Japan and the Philippines. The population of the state in 1910 was 2,075,708.

The number of manufacturing establishments in Minnesota having an annual output valued at $500 or more at the beginning of 1915 was 5,974. The amount of capital invested was $354,434,000, giving employment to 115,690 persons, using material valued at $336,849,000, and turning out finished goods worth $493,354,000. Salaries and wages paid amounted to $80,-591,000.

Minnesota:

Admission of, into Union—
Discussion and territory outside of, referred to, 3121.
Taking of census in accordance with act providing for, referred to, 3002.
Constitution of, transmitted, 3000.
Indian massacres in, and persons sentenced to be hanged, discussed, 3345.
Public building to be erected in, referred to, 2682.
Public lands in, to be surveyed, 2838.

Minnesota and Northwestern Railroad Co., suit instituted against, in name of United States referred to, 2830.

Minnetaree Indians. (See Indian Tribes.)

Mint.—By an act of Congress passed April 2, 1792, the first United States mint was established at Philadelphia. The first machinery and first metal used were imported, and copper cents were coined the following year. In 1794 silver dollars were made, and the suceeding year gold eagles. In 1835 branch mints were established in New Orleans, La., at Charlotte, N. C., and at Dahlonega, Ga.; in 1852, at San Francisco, Cal.; in 1864, at Dallas City, Oreg., and in 1870, at Carson City, Nev. The mints at Charlotte and Dahlonega were suspended in 1861, that at Dallas in 1875, that at Carson City in 1885, and that at

New Orleans from 1860 to 1879. Assay offices, considered branches of the mint, were established at New York in 1854, Denver, Col., in 1864, Boisé City, Idaho, in 1872, and at other places at later dates. The mints as at present established are situated at Philadelphia, San Francisco and New Orleans; those at Carson City and Denver are equipped as assay offices, and no coins are made at either. (See also Currency; Coinage Laws.)

Mint:

Abuses of, discussed, 177.
Artists from abroad engaged in, 120.
Branch of—
At Columbus, Ohio, referred to, 4311.
At New Orleans, statement of, transmitted, 6299.
At New York recommended, 2352, 2407, 2500.
Establishment of, recommended and referred to, 75, 1432, 4310,
In California recommended, 2486, 2557, 2621.
Referred to, 2747.
In North Carolina, Georgia, and Louisiana, referred to, 1383, 1495.
Buildings and grounds at Columbus, Ohio, offered to United States for, by F. Michel, 4311.
Coinage at, referred to, 2407.
Proclamation regarding, 239.
Defective coins lodged in, 160.
Medals made in, for army and navy officers, 1845.
Opening of more mints, with authority to coin for foreign nations, recommended, 4201.
At New York, 2352, 2407, 2500.
In California, 2486, 2557, 2621.
In North Carolina, Georgia, and Louisiana, 1383, 1495.
Referred to, 99, 141, 177.
Seizure of, at New Orleans by authorities of Louisiana, referred to, 3199.

Mint, Director of, reports of, transmitted, 303, 305.

Minutemen.—At a session of the provincial congress of Massachusetts, Nov. 23, 1774, it was voted to enroll 12,000 minutemen. They were to be organized as militia and hold themselves ready for service at a minute's notice.

Miraflores Island, San Juan Harbor, Puerto Rico, referred to, 6708.

Miranda Plot.—A joint scheme of citizens of the United States and Great Britain whereby through the agitation of one Miranda, a citizen of Caracas, Venezuela, dissatisfaction was to be spread among the Spanish and French provinces. During the revolutions which it was hoped would ensue Great Britain was to obtain the West Indies and the United States, Florida and Louisiana east of the Mississippi.

Mirboha, The:

Capture of, by the *Philadelphia* near Gibraltar in 1803, 352.

Indemnification to captors of, and of the *Mishouda* for the public accommodation, recommended, 354.

Miscellaneous Transportation. (See Division of Miscellaneous Transportation.)

Misdemeanors. (See Crimes and Misdemeanors.)

Misfeasance.—The use of official power for a wrongful purpose. The act may not be wrongful for a private individual;—the crime consists of the use or influence of the office to further an end not contemplated by the office.

Misfeasance of Office. (See Misfeasance.)

Mishouda, The, indemnification to captors of, recommended, 354.

Misprision of Treason.—Concealment on the part of a citizen of treasonable acts known to him, or neglect to report such knowledge promptly to the proper authorities. The penalty consists of not more than 7 years in prison, and of a fine of not more than $1,000. (See Treason.)

Mission Commission, recommendation of, referred to, 5661.

Mission Indians. (See Indian Tribes.)

Missionaries, American, treatment of, in Turkey discussed, 4627, 5090, 5872, 5962, 6069, 6147.

Missionary Ridge, or Chattanooga (Tenn.), Battle of.—After retiring from Lookout Mountain, Bragg's army concentrated on Missionary Ridge, across the Chattanooga Valley and southeast of the city. On the morning of Nov. 25, 1863, Sherman assailed the Confederate right wing at the extreme north end of the ridge. Hooker advanced from Lookout Mountain across the valley and attacked the left. The battle raged all day, but the Confederates held the position until late in the afternoon, when the center was weakened by withdrawals to support the left and right. It was then that Grant, watching the progress of the fight from Orchard Knob, ordered forward the Army of the Cumberland, under Thomas. Wood's and Sheridan's divisions charged the Confederate center. The brigades of Hazen and Willich were in advance. Darkness came on, when the Confederates retreated. Pursuit was stopped when the ridge was won. The Confederates lost more than 9,000, including 6,000 prisoners. Forty pieces of artillery and 7,000 stand of small arms fell into the hands of the victors. The Federal casualties in the Chattanooga campaign between Nov. 24 and Nov. 29 were 753 killed, 4,722 wounded, and 349 missing—a total of 5,824.

Missions Boundary Dispute, evidence presented to President of United States as arbitrator by Argentine Republic and Brazil, 5867. Award of, discussed, 6058.

Mississippi.—One of the southern group of states; nickname, "The Bayou State." It is named for the river of that name and extends from lat. 30° 10′ to 35° north and from long. 88° 5′ to 91° 40′ west. It is bounded on the north by Tennessee, on the east by Alabama, on the south by the Gulf of Mexico and Louisiana, and on the west by Louisiana and Arkansas (separated by the Mississippi River), and has an area of 46,865 square miles.

The region was visited by De Soto in 1540, and a settlement was attempted by the French under Iberville at Biloxi in 1699. The territory was ceded by France to Great Britain in 1763. Part was ceded to the United States in 1783 and the remainder was acquired in 1803. The Territory of Mississippi was organized in 1798 and admitted as a State in 1817. It seceded Jan. 9, 1861, and was readmitted Feb. 17, 1870. The State has a semi-tropical climate and rich soil.

Statistics of agriculture collected for the last Federal census place the number of farms in the State at 274,382, comprising 18,557,553 acres, valued, with stock and improvements, at $426,314,634. The average value of land per acre was $13.69, an increase from $6.30 in 1900. The value of domestic animals, poultry, etc., was $75,-247,033.

There are 3,975 miles of steam railway and 79 miles of electric line. The Mississippi River and the Gulf Coast provide natural facilities for transit. The population in 1910 was 1,797,114.

The number of manufacturing establishments in Mississippi having an annual output valued at $500 or more at the beginning of 1915 was 2,209. The amount of capital invested was $81,005,000, giving employment to 52,277 persons, using material valued at $41,340,000, and turning out finished goods worth $79,550,000. Salaries and wages paid amounted to $23,008,000.

Mississippi (see Confederate States):

Aaron Burr surrenders to officers in Territory of, 409.

Act endowing church in, vetoed, 475.

Act to authorize special term of circuit court of United States in, to be held in Scranton, vetoed, 4440.

Citizens of Territory of, must be protected, 372.

Combinations, unlawful in, proclamation against, 4276.

Consolidation of Territory of, discussed, 426.

Elections in, and complications growing out of, proclamation regarding, 4276.

Fifteenth amendment, action of, on, referred to, 4001.

Lands granted to, in aid of railroads referred to, 3580.

Lands in Territory of, claimed by Great Britain, 438.

Laws of Territory of, referred to, 292, 303.

Legislative council for—
Dissolved by governor of, 445.
Nomination of, 445.

Memorial from, regarding alleged violation of treaty by United States transmitted, 2003.

Nomination for council of, 445.

Offices in, President Jackson refuses to make further nominations for, 1199.

Provisional governor for, appointed and restoration of, into Union discussed, 3512.

Reconstruction of—
Recommendations regarding, 3965.
Referred to, 4000.
Time for submitting constitution to voters proclaimed, 3970.
Referred to, 3983.
Survey of towns in, referred to, 597.
Unlawful combinations in, proclamation against, 4276.

Mississippi Bubble.—The gigantic commercial scheme commonly known by this name was projected in France by the celebrated financier, John Law, of Edinburgh, in 1717, and collapsed in 1720. Its primary object was to develop the resources of the Province of Louisiana and the country bordering on the Mississippi, a tract at that time believed to abound in the precious metals. The company was incorporated in August, 1717, under the title of "The Company of the West," and started with a capital of 200,000 shares of 500 livres each. They obtained the exclusive privilege of trading to the Mississippi, farming the taxes and coining money. The prospectus was so inviting that shares were eagerly bought, and when, in 1719, the company obtained the monopoly of trading to the East Indies, China and the South Seas, and all the possessions of the French East India Company, the brilliant vision opened up to the public gaze was irresistible. The "Company of the Indies," as it was now called, created 50,000 additional shares; but a rage for speculation had seized all classes, and there were at least 300,000 applicants for the new shares, which consequently rose to an enormous premium. Law, as director-general, promised an annual dividend of 200 livres per share, which, as the shares were paid for in the depreciated *billets d'état*, amounted to an annual return of 120 per cent. The public enthusiasm now rose to an absolute frenzy, and Law's house and the street in front of it were daily crowded by applicants of both sexes and of all ranks, who were content to wait for hours—nay, for days together—in order to obtain an interview with the modern Plutus. While confidence lasted a factitious impulse was given to trade in Paris, the value of manufactures was increased fourfold, and the demand far exceeded the supply. The population is said to have been increased by hundreds of thousands, many of whom were glad to take shelter in garrets, kitchens and stables. But the Regent had meanwhile caused the paper circulation of the National Bank to be increased as the Mississippi scheme stock rose in value, and many wary speculators, foreseeing a crisis, had secretly converted their paper and shares into gold, which they transmitted to England or Belgium for safety. The increasing scarcity of gold and silver becoming felt, a general run was made on the bank. The Mississippi stock now fell considerably, and despite all efforts continued to fall steadily and rapidly. In 1720 the National Bank and the Company of the Indies were amalgamated, but, though this gave an upward turn to the share market, it failed to put the public credit on a sound basis. The crisis came at last. In July, 1720, the bank stopped payment, and Law was compelled to flee the country. The French government was very nearly overturned and widespread financial distress and bankruptcy followed.

Mississippi River:
Act to remove obstructions to navigation in mouth of, vetoed, 2919.

Appropriations for, 768, 934, 2124.
Breakwater near mouth of, referred to, 988.
Bridge over, at Rock Island, Ill., and La Crosse, Wis., 4148.
Channel at mouth of, to be deepened, 3019.
Condition of, near Vicksburg, Miss., referred to, 4082.
Defense of, provision for, recommended, 394.
Delta of, surveys of, referred to, 2666.
Exploration of country west of, referred to, 2261.
Grants to James B. Eads for construction of jetties in, order regarding, 4282.
Improvements of, recommendations regarding, 4571, 4647, 4682, 4784.
Appropriation for, 768, 934, 2124.
Improvement of South Pass of, discussed, 4362, 4524, 4638.
Levees of, preservation of, recommendations regarding, 3652, 4682, 4797.
Mail route from California to, recommended, 2992.
Navigation on—
Appropriation for improving, 934, 2124.
Treaty with Spain, regarding, 106, 110, 164.
Plan for reclamation of alluvial basin of, subject to inundation, 4257, 4272.
Railroad from Pacific Ocean to, recommended, 2714, 2754.
Referred to, 1104, 1196.
Resolution in relation to removal of obstructions to navigation in, reasons for applying pocket veto to, 3138.
Survey of—
Appropriation for, 768.
Near completion of, referred to, 677.
Surveys of mouth of, 1500.

Mississippi River Commission:
Appropriation for protection of levees recommended by, 4682, 4797.
Report of, discussed, 4784.

Missouri.—One of the central western group of states; nickname, "Bullion State;" motto, "Salus populi suprema lex esto" ("Let the people's safety be the supreme law"). It takes its name from the Missouri River, which in turn is named after a tribe of Indians belonging to the Siouan family. The State is included between lat. 36° and 40° 30′ north and long. 89° 2′ and 95° 44′ west. It is bounded on the north by Iowa, on the east by Illinois, Kentucky, and Tennessee (separated by the Mississippi), on the south by Arkansas, and on the west by the Indian Territory, Kansas, and Nebraska (separated in part by the Missouri River), and has an area of 69,420 square miles.

Slaughtering and meat-packing are the most important industries, the manufacture of tobacco ranking second.

The territory was first settled at St. Genevieve by the French in 1755, was ceded to Spain in 1763, ceded back to France in 1800, and was ceded by France to the United States in 1803, forming part of the Louisiana Purchase. Missouri Territory was formed in 1812 and admitted to the Union as a State in 1821.

Statistics of agriculture collected for the last Federal census place the number of farms in the State at 277,244, comprising 34,591,248 acres, valued, with stock and improvements, at $2,052,917,488. The average value of land per acre was $41.80, an increase from $20.46 in 1900. The value of domestic animals, poultry, etc., was $285,839,108, including 2,561,482 cattle, valued at $72,883,664; 1,073,387 horses, $113,976,563; 342,700 mules, $43,438,702; 4,438,194 swine, $31,937,573; 1,811,268 sheep, $7,888,828; poultry, 20,897,208, valued at $11,870,972. The yield and value of the principal field crops for 1911 was: corn, 7,400,000 acres, 192,400,000 bushels, $115,400,000; wheat, 2,300,000 acres, 36,-110,000 bushels, $31,777,000; oats, 1,200,-000 acres, 17,760,000 bushels, $7,992,000; potatoes, 95,000 acres, 2,565,000 bushels, $2,616,000; hay, 2,430,000 acres, 1,458,000 tons, $19,391,000; tobacco, 6,000 acres, 4,-800,000 pounds, $576,000.

Missouri leads all the other states in the production of two important metals, lead and zinc, and in the production of two relatively unimportant minerals, barytes and tripoli, according to a statement made public by the United States Geological Survey in cooperation with the Missouri State Survey. The state also ranks second in the production of mineral paints. The mining and marketing of lead and zinc ores in Missouri is of a character peculiar to the state, in that the ores themselves, or rather the concentrates, are marketed products, and strictly speaking the basis of production is the output and value of the concentrates, as that is the condition in which the product is first sold. In most of the metal-producing states, however, the only method of determining the value is on the metals themselves, principally because of the complex character of the ores, which carry two or more of the metals, these being separated in the smelting and refining process. The lead ores of Missouri and of the other states of the Mississippi Valley carry so little silver that it is disregarded in the assay and sale of concentrate, and the lead produced from them is known to the trade as "soft lead." The total value of the lead and zinc concentrates sold in 1913 was $21,-109,358, against $24,937,161 in 1912. Based on the metallic content the total production of lead and zinc in Missouri in 1913 was valued at $29,494,064, against $34,820,248 in 1912. The decrease in 1913 was almost entirely due to a smaller output of zinc ores, with a marked decline in price.

Third in importance among Missouri's mineral industries is the mining of coal, the production of which decreased slightly, from 4,339,856 short tons, valued at $7,-633,864, in 1912, to $4,318,125 tons, valued at $7,468,308, in 1913.

The report of the State treasurer showed receipts for the year 1910 of $10,-005,610; balance on hand Jan. 1, 1911, $200,557. Cobalt, nickel and barytes are also produced. There are 27,480 acres of land in the State unreserved and unappropriated. The United States land office is at Springfield.

The number of manufacturing establish-ments in Missouri having an annual output valued at $500 or more at the beginning of 1915 was 8,386. The amount of capital invested was $522,548,000, giving employment to 188,266 persons, using material valued at $388,715,000, and turning out finished goods worth $637,952,000. Salaries and wages paid amounted to $126,495,000.

St. Louis and Kansas City are important centers of traffic in live stock and grain. The State has 8,066 miles of steam railroads and 1,129 miles of electric lines. The population in 1910 was 3,293,335.

Missouri (see also Springfield):

Admission of, into Union, proclaimed, 664.

Bank of. (See Bank of Missouri.)

Boundaries of, extended, 1493.

Boundary line with Iowa, dispute respecting, 1175, 1777, 1788.

Defalcation of officers in, 941, 970.

Indian titles to lands in, extinguished, 769, 1538.

Joint resolution placing troops of, on footing with others as to bounties, reasons for applying pocket veto to, 3733.

Judicial districts of, 6733.

Lead mines in, 711, 931.

Military forces to be raised by governor of, for suppression of rebellion in, 3241.

Order regarding, 3243.

Railroads in, to be made available for military uses of Government, 3317.

Security of trade with Mexico, discussed, 1036.

Troops of, orders respecting inspection of records of, 3433.

Missouri, The, loss of, by fire, referred to, 2122.

Aid rendered, by British authorities at Gibraltar, 2123.

Missouri Compromise.—An agreement relative to the question of slavery embodied in a bill passed by Congress March 2, 1820, and in the act admitting Missouri, Feb. 28, 1821. Upon the introduction into Congress during the session of 1818-19 of a bill providing for the admission of Missouri as a state, but prohibiting slavery therein, the opposition on the part of the Southern members became violent and threatening, and after long and brilliant debates a compromise was effected, chiefly through the efforts of Henry Clay. Representative Tallmadge, of New York, in February, 1819, proposed an amendment declaring all children born after the admission of the state to be free. This was modified to make all children born slaves free at twenty-five. The House passed the bill with this amendment, but the Senate refused to concur. Next year the bill passed the House again in the same form. The Senate voted to admit Maine provided Missouri was admitted as a slave state. The House rejected the proposal. Representative Thomas, of Illinois, proposed as a compromise the admission of Missouri as a slave state provided that in future slavery should be prohibited in all the territory forming part of the Louisiana Purchase north of 36° 30′, the southern boundary of the new state. This was agreed to. On the question as to when the compromise was abandoned, whether before or at the passage of the Kansas-Ne-braska bill in 1854, parties and sections have been divided. When Missouri's constitution was laid before Congress it was found that it contained clauses excluding free negroes from the state. The House therefore refused to admit Missouri. Clay effected a further compromise whereby Missouri agreed not to deprive of his rights any citizen of another state.

Missouri Compromise, discussed, 2457, 2491, 2878.

Missouri River, exploration of, 386, 396.

Missouria Indians. (See Indian Tribes.)

Mobile, Alabama; population (1900), 38,469.

> Achievements of Federal forces in harbor of, and orders respecting celebration of, 3439.

> Collection district of, established, 357.

> Object of, misunderstood by Spain, 358.

Mobile and Dauphin Island Railroad and Harbor Co., act regarding grant of right to, to construct trestle between Cedar Point and Dauphin Island, returned, 5784.

Mobile Bay (Ala.), Battle of.—Aug. 5, 1864, Rear-Admiral Farragut, lashed to the rigging of the flagship *Hartford*, passed the forts and obstructions at the entrance to Mobile Bay and captured the Confederate ram *Tennessee*. Mobile Bay was defended by Fort Gaines, on the eastern end of Dauphin Island, Fort Morgan, on the western extremity of Mobile Point, east of the channel, and Fort Powell, situated on a small island west of Dauphin. Forts Gaines and Morgan commanded the main channel, the former mounting 21 guns and the latter 48.

In the bay were the iron-clad ram *Tennessee* and the gunboats *Gaines, Morgan,* and *Selma* under the command of Admiral Buchanan. The *Tennessee* was built on the plan of the *Merrimac.* Her armament consisted of 6 rifles—2 pivots of 7 1-8 inches bore and 4 six-inch broadsides. Obstructions and defense of all kinds had been placed around the harbor and 30 torpedoes were strung across the channel. Farragut's fleet consisted of 14 wooden ships and 4 monitors. Gen. Gordon Granger had landed 4,000 Federal troops on Dauphin Island, in the rear of Fort Gaines, to cooperate with the fleet. The fleet got under way early in the morning and before 7 o'clock the engagement became general. The monitor *Tecumseh* fired the first shot, and shortly afterward struck a torpedo and sunk, with her commander, Capt. Craven, and most of her crew. Within an hour the other vessels had passed the forts and met the gunboats and ram inside the harbor. After a severe contest the *Tennessee* surrendered at 10 o'clock. Farragut's loss was 165 killed and drowned (113 of whom went down on board the *Tecumseh*) and 170 wounded. The Confederate loss was 8 or 10 killed and wounded and 170 surrendered. Of the other three Confederate vessels, the *Morgan* escaped up the bay, the *Gaines* was disabled, and the *Selma* was captured with her crew of 90 officers and men.

The night after the battle Fort Powell was abandoned and blown up. Next day Fort Gaines was shelled by the *Chickasaw* and surrendered with 800 prisoners. Granger's troops were transferred to the rear of

Fort Morgan. Aug. 22 it was bombarded and on the 23d it surrendered. With the defenses of Mobile there were taken 104 guns and 1,464 men. Operations against the city of Mobile were begun March 20, 1865. Two forts protected the city after the passage into the harbor had been made. April 4 these were bombarded. Four days later another bombardment was begun, followed in the evening by an assault. The outer works were carried during the night and preparations made to complete the conquest next day, but at 1 o'clock on the morning of April 9 the garrison surrendered.

Mobile Point, Ala., fortifications at, recommended, 691.

> Referred to, 695.

Mobile River:

> Commerce passing through, obstructed by arbitrary duties and vexatious researches; armed resistance authorized, 372.

Modoc Indians. (See Indian Tribes.)

Modus Vivendi.—Literally, a mode of living. The term is used in diplomatic relations to describe a tentative understanding before a final treaty is concluded; for example see 5581.

Mohawk, The, capture of the *Wildfire* with cargo of slaves, by, 3124.

Mohawk Indians. (See Indian Tribes.)

Mohican Indians. (See Indian Tribes.)

Mo-lal-la-las Indians. (See Indian Tribes.)

Mo-lel Indians. (See Indian Tribes.)

Molino del Rey (Mexico), Battle of.— When the fortifications of Contreras and Churubusco had been passed, Gen. Scott took up his headquarters at Tacubaya, the bishop's castle, overlooking the western approaches to the City of Mexico, and two and one-half miles distant. The first formidable obstruction was El Molino del Rey ("The King's Mill"). Gen. Worth's division of 3,100 men was detailed for attack upon this and its supporting fortifications, Casa de Mata. These were stone buildings, strongly fortified and ably defended, the Mexicans contesting every foot of the ground. The attack was made on the morning of Sept. 8, 1847. After two hours' hard fighting the works were carried and the army of Santa Anna, 14,000 strong, driven back. The Mexican loss was 2,200 killed and wounded (among the former being Generals Valdarez and Leon) and more than 800 prisoners, including 52 commissioned officers. The American loss was 116 (including 9 officers) killed, 665 (including 49 officers) wounded and 18 missing. The magazine of Casa de Mata was blown up, and Worth returned to Tacubaya.

Monaco.—Monaco is a sovereign Principality on the coast of the Mediterranean, nine miles east of Nice, and is enclosed on three sides by the Alpes Maritimes department of France. Its total length is 2¼ miles and its width varies from 165 to 1,100 yards, the total area being 0.579 English square miles or 370.56 English statute acres. The Principality includes the towns of Monaco, Condamine and Monte Carlo, and had a population (in 1908) of 19,121, of whom 635 were native-born Monégasques, 847 naturalized, and the remainder foreigners. There is a large floating population, estimated at 50,000, and the day visitors exceeded 1,500,000 in 1910. The land is divided among 1,300 owners, of whom 300 were Monégasques. The total estimated value of the land (exclusive of the private estate of the Prince) was 227,000,000 francs in 1912.

History.—The Principality has been in the possession of the noble Genoese family of Grimaldi (now Goyon de Matignon-Grimaldi) since the tenth century, with a short break from 1793-1814. In 1814 independence was again secured under the protection of Sardinia. In 1848 the towns of Mentone and Roccabruna were annexed to Sardinia, and in 1860 the protection was transferred to France.

Government.—The Prince was an absolute ruler until the promulgation of a Constitution in 1911. The throne is hereditary in the male line (and afterwards in the female line) of the reigning house by primogeniture, and the daughter of the Heir-Apparent has been recognized as capable of succession falling other issue. Ruler: His Serene Highness Albert Honoré Charles, Prince of Monaco, Duke of Valentinois, Marquis des Baux, born Nov. 13, 1848; succeeded his father Sept. 10, 1889.

By the Constitution of Jan. 8, 1911, parliamentary representation and complete civil liberty were established. There is a Council of State and a National Council of twenty-one members, elected by indirect vote for four years.

The Communes have each a Municipal Council elected by voters of both sexes. Order is maintained by a local police force of about 150 men. There are no taxes and rents are high, the product of the gaming tables (to which none of the inhabitants are allowed access) providing the cost of public works and police.

Towns.—Capital, Monaco. Population, 3,292. La Condamine (6,218) and Monte Carlo (3,794). The gaming establishment is at the last-named, the concessionaire (a joint stock company) having paid 25,000,-000 francs (10,000,000 paid in 1899 and 15,000,000 in 1913) for the concession, and a yearly tribute increasing by 250,000 francs every ten years to a maximum of 2,500,000 per annum in 1937. The concession expires in 1947. At the capital, which occupies the rocky summit of a headland, is the Palace, and an Oceanographical Museum, built by the Prince to accommodate a collection made during thirty years of research.

Monandry.—Having no more than one husband.

Monetary Commission, appointment of, discussed, 6250.

Monetary Convention of Latin Union, Belgium declares its adhesion to, 4957.

Monetary Union, American. (See International American Monetary Union.)

Money, Continental. (See Continental Money.)

Money Order System, discussed, 985, 4639, 4937, 5377, 5756, 5881, 5971.

Money Orders. (See Division of Money Orders.)

Money Orders, International, discussed, 5881, 5971.

Money, Public. (See Revenue, Public.)

Monitor, The. (See Hampton Roads, (Va.), Battle of.)

Monitor, The, engagement with the *Merrimac,* discussed, 3313.

Monmouth (N. J.), Battle of.—An important conflict of the Revolutionary War, fought during the afternoon of June 28, 1778, at Wenrock Creek, Monmouth County, N. J., Gen. Washington in command of the Americans and Sir Henry Clinton commanding the British. June 18 Clinton left Philadelphia for New York with 11,000 men and a large supply train. Washington pursued him with about 20,000 men. After some preliminary skirmishing, in which the Americans, led by Gen. Charles Lee, second in command, retreated, a general battle occurred. The British were defeated and drew off under cover of night, leaving about 300 dead on the field. The Americans lost 288, less than 70 of whom were killed. An incident of the battle was Washington's severe reprimand of Gen. Charles Lee, which resulted in the latter's final dismissal. Lee had opposed bringing on the battle, but when his advice was respected in the council of war, asked and obtained the right to lead off in the engagement.

Monocacy (Md.), Battle of.—Gen. Hunter succeeded Gen. Sigel in command of the Federal forces in the Shenandoah Valley in June, 1864. Ben. Early was detached from Lee's army at Richmond and sent to reenforce Gen. Breckinridge, who commanded the Confederate forces in the valley. Hunter retired westward across the mountains, leaving Washington unprotected. Lee thereupon reenforced Early, increasing his strength to 20,000, and ordered him to threaten Washington, in the hope of compelling Grant to withdraw some of the troops before Richmond and Petersburg. The Sixth Corps, under Wright, was sent to defend Washington, with the Nineteenth Corps, which arrived from Hampton Roads. July 6 Early reached Hagerstown and moved a strong column toward Frederick, whereupon Gen. Lew Wallace advanced from Baltimore with a force of 6,000 men. He encountered Early on the 9th at Monocacy, Md., and for eight hours resisted his advance, but was finally defeated, with a loss of 98 killed, 579 wounded, and 1,282 missing. The Confederate loss was stated by Gen. Early at from 600 to 700, including the cavalry.

Monogamist.—1. A person who has but one wife. (See Bigamy and Polygamy.) 2. A person opposed to more than one marriage.

Monopolies, evils of trusts and, discussed and recommendations regarding, 5358, 5478, 6176.

Monroe, James.—1817-1825.

(FIRST TERM, 1817-1821.)

Eighth Administration—Democratic-Republican.

Vice-President—Daniel D. Tompkins.
Secretary of State—
  John Quincy Adams.
Secretary of the Treasury—
  William H. Crawford.
Secretary of War—
  George Graham.
  John C. Calhoun.
Secretary of the Navy—
  B. W. Crowninshield (continued).
  Smith Thompson.
Attorney-General—
  Richard Rush (continued).
  William Wirt.
Postmaster-General—
  Return J. Meigs.

Nomination.—James Monroe was elected by the Republican party in 1816 and 1820. In the election of 1816 Monroe and Daniel D. Tompkins were the nominees of the Republican Congressional caucus. The Federalists supported Rufus King for President, with no Vice-Presidential candidate.

Vote.—The election took place Nov. 5. The electoral vote, counted Feb. 12, 1817, gave Monroe 183 and King 34; Tompkins received 183 votes for Vice-President, and Howard, 22. Nineteen states took part in this election, Indiana for the first time. King's vote was received from the New England States, where the electors were chosen by the legislatures. Had the people voted there, it is more than probable that they would have expressed approval of the course of the administration in the War of 1812, which the Federalists opposed.

Party Affiliation.—In the Virginia contest over the adoption of the Constitution, Monroe stood beside Henry in opposition, and consented to the ratification only upon the adoption of certain amendments. In the Senate he was a prominent Anti-Federalist and a most determined opponent of the Washington administration. On the publication of Monroe's pamphlet, "A View of the Conduct of the Executive," in 1796, he became the hero of the Anti-Federalists and was made governor of Virginia (1799-1802). Eventually, by his great popularity, he came to fill almost every exalted station to which a politician might aspire.

Political Complexion of Congress.—In the Fifteenth Congress (1817-1819) the Senate, of 44 members, was made up of 10 Federalists and 34 Democrats; and the House, of 185 members, was made up of 57 Federalists and 128 Democrats. In the Sixteenth Congress (1819-1821) the Senate, of 46 members, was made up of 10 Federalists and 36 Democrats; and the House, of 187 members, was made up of 42 Federalists and 145 Democrats. In the Seventeenth Congress (1821-1823) the Senate, of 48 members, was made up of 7 Federalists and 41 Democrats; and the House, of 187 members, was made up of 58 Federalists and 129 Democrats. In the Eighteenth Congress (1823-1825) the Senate, of 48 members, was made up of 40 Democrats and 8 Whigs; and the House, of 213 members, was made up of 72 Federalists and 141 Democrats.

(SECOND TERM, 1821-1825.)

Ninth Administration—Democratic-Republican.

Vice-President—Daniel D. Tompkins.
Secretary of State—
John Quincy Adams (continued).
Secretary of the Treasury—
William H. Crawford (continued).
Secretary of War—
John C. Calhoun (continued).
Secretary of the Navy—
Smith Thompson (continued).
John Rogers (President of Navy Committee Sept. 1-Sept. 16, 1823).
Samuel J. Southard.
Attorney-General—
William Wirt (continued).
Postmaster-General—
Return J. Meigs (continued).
John McLean.

SECOND TERM.—In the election of 1820, no candidates were chosen by Congressional caucus, as there was no opposition to Monroe and Tompkins.

Vote.—The election was held Nov. 7. The electoral vote, counted Feb. 14, 1821, gave Monroe all of the votes but one. It is said that the opposing vote was cast by a New Hampshire elector for John Quincy Adams, in order that Washington alone might have the glory of a unanimous election. Twenty-four states took part in this election—Mississippi, Illinois, Alabama, Maine, and Missouri having been recently added to the Union.

Internal Improvements.—On this question the attitude of Monroe was the same as that of Jefferson and Madison. He held that there was no doubt of the desirability and necessity of contributions from the Federal Government to works of this nature; but that the Constitution did not confer upon the Federal Government the right of making them (pages 587 and 759) without an amendment to the Constitution, which he favored. On this ground, while appreciating the need of the work, he vetoed the bill making appropriations to the improvement of the Cumberland road in 1822.

Public Debt.—The public debt of the United States during the administration of Monroe stood as follows: Jan. 1, 1818, $103,466,633.83; 1819, $95,529,648.28; 1820, $91,015,566.15; 1821, $89,987,427.66; 1822, $93,546,676.98; 1823, $90,875,877.28; 1824, $90,269,777.77; 1825, $83,788,432.71.

Tariff.—The act of April 20, 1818, "to increase the duties on certain manufactured articles imported into the United States" affected such articles as are manufactured from copper or in which copper is the article of greatest value, silver-plated harness, coach and harness furniture, cut glass, tacks, brads, springs, and brown and white Russia sheeting. Another act, on the same day, increased the duties on iron in bars and bolts, iron in pigs, castings, nails, and alum. An act of March 3, 1819, regulated the duties on certain wines. In his Fifth Annual Message (page 675) President Monroe says: "It may be fairly presumed that under the protection given to domestic manufactures by the existing laws we shall become at no distant period a manufacturing country on an extensive scale. Possessing as we do the raw materials in such vast amount, with a capacity to augment them to an indefinite extent; rising within the country aliment of every kind to an amount far exceeding the demand for home consumption, even in the most unfavorable years, and to be obtained always at a very moderate price; skilled also as our people are in the mechanic arts and in every improvement calculated to lessen the demand for and the price of labor, it is manifest that their success in every branch of domestic industry may and will be carried, under the encouragement given by the present duties, to an extent to meet any demand which under a fair competition may be made upon it." In his Sixth Annual Message (page 760) he says: ". . . it appears that our manufactures, though depressed immediately after the peace, have considerably increased, and are still increasing, under the encouragement given them by the tariff of 1816 and by subsequent laws. Satisfied I am . . . that there are other strong reasons applicable to our situation and relations with other countries which impose on us the obligation to cherish and sustain our manufactures. Satisfied, however, I likewise am that the interest of every part of the Union, even of those most benefited by manufactures, requires that this subject should be touched with the greatest caution, and a critical knowledge of the effect to be produced by the slightest change." Again, in his Seventh Annual Message (page 784) he reiterates his views and adds: ". . . I recommend a review of

EXTENT OF THE UNITED STATES DURING THE ADMINISTRATION OF PRESIDENT MONROE, 1817-1825.

(NOT INCLUDING TERRITORIES)

FLAG OF 1825

MISSOURI 1821
LOUISIANA 1812
MISSISSIPPI 1817
ILLINOIS 1818
ALABAMA 1819
TENNESSEE 1796
INDIANA 1816
KENTUCKY 1792
GEORGIA 1788
OHIO 1803
SOUTH CAROLINA 1788
NORTH CAROLINA 1789
VIRGINIA 1788
PENNSYLVANIA 1787
MD. 1788
NEW YORK 1788
DEL. 1787
N.J. 1787
VT. 1791
CONN. 1788
MASS. 1788
N.H. 1788
MAINE 1820

the tariff for the purpose of affording such additional protection to those articles which we are prepared to manufacture, or which are more immediately connected with the defense and independence of the country."

Foreign Policy.—The foreign policy of the Monroe administration has become famous under the name of the Monroe Doctrine. This attitude toward foreign interference in the Western Hemisphere is contained in two paragraphs in the Seventh Annual Message (page 787) sent to Congress Dec. 2, 1823. Very similar sentiments were expressed by President Madison in a message to Congress in 1811 (page 473); and John Quincy Adams, a member of Monroe's Cabinet, and with whom Monroe consulted, is also credited with originating these views. In its practical application, the policy upholds opposition from the United States against foreign conquest of any part of America.

Regarding the relations of the United States with Europe, President Monroe says in his First Annual Message (page 584): "A strong hope is entertained that by adhering to the maxims of a just, a candid, and friendly policy, we may long preserve amicable relations, with all of the powers of Europe on conditions advantageous and honorable to our country."

Commerce.—The commercial status of the United States during the administration of President Monroe may be shown by statistics for the year 1820, here given: Area, 2,059,043 sq. miles; population, 9,638,453; population per sq. mile, 4.68; total money in circulation, $67,100,000; imports, $74,450,000; exports, $69,691,-669; ships built, 51,394 tons; vessels in deep sea trade, 619,048 tons; vessels in coastwise trade, 660,065 tons; post-offices, 4,500.

Slavery.—In his Third Annual Message (page 631) President Monroe, in describing the means taken to put down the slave trade, says: "It is hoped that these vigorous measures, supported by like acts by other nations, will soon terminate a commerce so disgraceful to the civilized world." In a special message (page 632) he recommends that slaves taken from the cargoes of slavers be sent back to Africa and not retained in the United States.

Monroe, James:

Accounts and claims of, discussed by, 846.

Referred to, 889.

Annual messages of, 580, 608, 623, 642, 667, 754, 776, 817.

Biographical sketch of, 572.

Constitutional amendment regarding, internal improvements recommended by, 587, 759.

Correspondence and manuscripts of, unpublished, purchase of, referred to, 5671.

Discretionary power of President over nominations, removals, and other acts discussed by, 847.

Finances discussed by, 584, 613, 629, 646, 675, 756, 761, 780, 785, 822.

Foreign policy discussed by, 573, 582, 624, 627, 639, 672, 685, 762, 787, 791, 817, 829.

Inaugural address of—

First, 573.

Second, 655.

Internal improvements discussed by, 587, 711, 713, 759.

Minister to—

France, nomination of, 148.

Negotiate treaty with Spain, nomination of, 339.

Settled differences with Great Britain, nomination of, 390.

Monroe Doctrine. (See Monroe Doctrine.)

Oath of office, notifies Congress of, time and place of taking, 573.

Portrait of, 571.

Power of legislation in District of Columbia should be taken from Congress and vested in people, 616.

Powers of Federal and State Governments discussed by, 587, 711, 713.

Proclamations of—

Admission of Missouri, 664.

Agreement with Great Britain for force on Great Lakes, 605.

Discriminating duties suspended on vessels of—

Bremen, 606.

France, 752.

Hamburg, 607.

Lubeck, 642.

Norway, 665.

Oldenburg, 666.

Extraordinary session of Senate, 856.

Importation of plaster of Paris, restrictions on, removed, 603, 605.

Lands, sale of, 580.

Ports opened to vessels of Great Britain, 753.

Reward for murder of William Seaver, 663.

Reduction in peace establishment discussed by, 698.

Request of House for documents concerning public officers, refused by, 698.

Secretary of State, 476.

South American Provinces, message of, regarding independence of, 685.

State of Union discussed by, 623, 642, 667, 776, 791, 817.

Tariff discussed by, 675, 760, 784.

Veto message of, regarding repair of Cumberland road, 711.

Monroe Doctrine.—After the overthrow of Napoleon, France, Russia, Prussia and Austria formed the so-called Holy Alliance in September, 1815, for the suppression of revolutions within each other's dominions and for perpetuating peace. The Spanish colonies in America having revolted, it was rumored that this alliance contemplated their subjugation, although the United States had acknowledged their independence. George Canning, English Secretary of State, proposed that England and America unite to oppose such intervention. On consultation with Jefferson, Madison, John Quincy Adams, and Calhoun, Monroe, in his annual message to Congress in 1823 (page 787), embodied the conclusions of these deliberations in what has since been known as the Monroe Doctrine.

Referring to the threatened intervention of the powers, the message declares: "We owe it, therefore, to candor and to the amicable relations existing between the United States and those powers to declare that we should consider any attempt on their part to extend their system to any portion of this hemisphere as dangerous to our peace and safety. With the existing colonies or dependencies of any European power we have not interfered and shall not interfere. But with the Government who have declared their independence, and maintained it, and whose independence we have, on great consideration and on just principles, acknowledged, we could not view any interposition for the purpose of oppressing them, or controlling in any other manner their destiny, by any European power in any other light than as the manifestation of an unfriendly disposition toward the United States." The promulgation of this doctrine is accredited to Mr. Monroe, but Jan. 3, 1811, the principle was substantially enunciated by Mr. Madison. In a message to Congress on that date (page 473), while discussing a threat of Great Britain to take possession of a portion of Florida claimed by Spain, he used these words: "I recommend to the consideration of Congress the seasonableness of a declaration that the United States could not see, without serious inquietude, any part of a neighboring territory in which they have in different respects so deep and so just a concern pass from the hands of Spain into those of any other foreign power."

The practical application of this doctrine goes no further than to place the United States in opposition to any possible attempt of any European power to subjugate or take possession in whole or in part of any American country. The principle involved was clearly set forth by Secretary of State Richard Olney in his dispatch of July 20, 1895, on the Venezuelan Boundary dispute. He stated that the Monroe Doctrine "does not establish any general protectorate by the United States over other American states. It does not relieve any American state from its obligations as fixed by international law, nor prevent any European power directly interested from enforcing such obligations or from inflicting merited punishment for the breach of them."

This interpretation of the Monroe Doctrine has been upheld in the most emphatic manner by President Roosevelt in many of his public speeches and his messages to Congress in which he states that any well-merited punishment inflicted by a European power upon an American state does not violate the Monroe Doctrine, provided that such punishment does not involve any occupation, either permanent or temporary, of American territory.

Monroe Doctrine, 473, 787, 829.

Armed force necessary to maintain, 6664.

A guarantee of peace, 6994.

Explained by Secretary Root to Conference of American Republics at Rio Janeiro, 7059.

Facsimile, opposite 791.

Reasserted by President—
Buchanan, 3043, 3177.
Cleveland, 6064, 6087.
Grant, 4015, 4054, 4083.

Polk, 2248, 2390, 2432.
Roosevelt, 6664, 6666, 6996.
Taft, 7415.
Tyler, 2065.
Referred to, 907.
Territorial aggression by U. S. not covered by, 6995.

Montana.—One of the western group of states; nickname, "Mountain State;" motto, "Oro y plata" (Gold and Silver"). It is included between lat. 45° and 49° north and long. 104° and 116° west. It is bounded on the north by British America, on the east by the Dakotas, on the south by Wyoming and Idaho, and on the west by Idaho, and has an area of 146,997 square miles. Gold, silver and copper are extensively mined and stock raising is an important occupation.

Montana was first entered in 1743 by the Chevalier de la Verendrye who discovered the Rocky Mountains, but no attempt was made at a settlement. Montana formed part of the Louisiana Purchase, and the greater part of it was included in the Nebraska Territory. Montana Territory was organized in 1864 and admitted as a State in 1889.

Statistics of agriculture collected for the last Federal census place the number of farms in the State at 26,214, comprising 13,545,603 acres, valued, with stock and improvements, at $347,828,770. The value of domestic animals, poultry, etc., was $85,-663,187, including 943,147 cattle, valued at $27,474,122; 315,956 horses, $27,115,764; 4,174 mules, $445,278; 99,261 swine, $858,-829; 5,380,746 sheep, $29,028,069. The yield and value of the principal field crops for 1911 is given as follows: Corn, 20,000 acres, 530,000 bushels, $424,000; wheat, 429,000 acres, 12,299,000 bushels, $9,470,-000; oats 425,000 acres, 21,165,000 bushels, $8,466,000; rye, 8,000 acres, 184,-000 bushels, $132,000; potatoes, 27,000 acres, 4,050,000 bushels, $2,997,000; hay, 612,000 acres, 1,224,000 tons, $12,240,000. The mineral products of the State in 1910 were valued at $54,388,117; of this, copper represented $35,950,966; gold, $3,720,400; silver, $6,632,700; coal, $5,329,322; lead, $147,520; zinc, $1,340,064. The State ranks second in the production of copper, being surpassed only by Arizona, and second only to Utah in the production of silver. The copper production in 1911 fell about 10,000,-000 tons short of the output of 1910, due to the policy of curtailment of the companies of the Butte district. The largest number of persons employed in any single manufacturing industry in the State is 3,106, engaged in the lumber and timber production. The total number of persons engaged in manufacture in the State in 1910 was 13,694, and the capital invested was $44,558,000.

Montana has vast undeveloped agricultural and mineral resources and good opportunities are open to prospective settlers. There are within the State 46,532,440 acres of land unappropriated and unreserved, which can be obtained under the General Land Laws of the United States upon application to the land offices in Billings, Bozeman, Glasgow, Great Falls, Helena, Kalispell, Lewistown, Miles City, or Missoula. Most of the land is valueless for agricultural purposes without irrigation, but large irrigation plans are being successfully carried on by the Government and by private enterprise. Under the federal reclamation act more than 471,000 acres of the lands of the State have been irrigated.

The most important industries of the State are smelting and refining copper, and three of the five establishments are worked by one company, which withholds details. Including these there were in 1905, 382 establishments, with a capital of $52,589,-810, employing 9,862 operatives whose wages aggregated $8,652,217, and who transformed $40,930,060 worth of raw material into copper ingots, lumber and building material, flour, beer, and cars, to the value of $66,415,452. In 1906 there were reported 3,300 miles of steam railway and 75 miles of electric street or elevated railway. The length of the telegraph lines was 9,556 miles, and of telephone, 5,384 miles. The population, by the census of 1910, was 376,053.

Montana:

Act—

Erecting Territory of, into surveying district, etc., vetoed, 3624.

Granting right of way to railroads through Indian reservations in, vetoed, 5057.

Admission of, into Union, proclaimed, 5459.

Discussed, 5485.

Lands in—

Opened to settlement by proclamation, 5727.

Set apart as public reservation by proclamation, 6213, 6222, 6227.

Partial organization of, referred to, 3451.

Unlawful combinations in, proclamation against, 5932.

Montauk Point, Long Island, lands lying on, referred to, 139.

Montenegro.—Montenegro is situated in the northwest of the Balkan Peninsula, between 42° 5'-43° 35' N. lat. and 18° 30'-20° 50' E. long. The kingdom is bounded on the northeast by Servia, on the southeast and east by Albania, and on the north and west by Bosnia and Herzegovina and Austrian Dalmatia. The area of the country is 5,800 square miles.

Physical Features.—The country is generally mountainous. The valleys between the various ranges contain fertile and well-watered plains, and in the northwest are rich, grassy uplands and finely wooded slopes.

The principal rivers are the Zeta-Moratcha and the Tara-Piva. The Zeta is remarkable for its disappearance in a subterranean passage beneath a mountain range, and its reappearance, several miles further south, on the other side of the range. The western half of Lake Scutari is within the boundaries of Montenegro, and there are many small lakes in the northern mountains.

History.—Montenegro was a province of the old Servian Empire, which came to an end after the battle of Kossovo (1389), since which date the country has always claimed to be independent, a claim which was successfully defended against the Turks for nearly six centuries. In 1878 the Treaty of Berlin recognized the independence of the Principality, and on October 15-28, 1910, the National Skupshtina (or Parliament) celebrated the fiftieth anniversary of the accession of Nicholas I. by proclaiming the country a kingdom. The crown is hereditary in the male line of the house of Petrovitch Niégoch, and the government is that of a constitutional monarchy. In October, 1912, Montenegro declared war against Turkey, and conducted a vigorous campaign in the northwestern Albania, in conjunction with Servia, Bulgaria and Greece; the second war of 1913 left her recent acquisitions unchanged.

Government.—His Majesty Nicholas I. (Petrovitch Niégoch), King of Montenegro, born Sept. 25 (Oct. 8), 1841, succeeded his uncle (Prince Danilo) Aug. 15 (28), 1860.

The single chamber legislature, or Skupshtina, consists of 62 Deputies, elected by universal suffrage for four years, and 12 official and nominated members, meets annually on Oct. 31 (Nov. 13).

The Kingdom is divided into 5 departments, each under a prefect, and 56 districts, each under a kapetan. Rural communes have an elected mayor.

Ethnography.—The bulk of the population (which is about 500,000) is of a Serbo-Croatian branch of the Slavonic race with Albanians and nomadic gypsies in the acquired region. The Montenegrin language is Serbo-Croatian, with adopted words of Turkish and Italian.

Army.—All able-bodied Montenegrins between the ages of 18 and 62 (except Muhammadan subjects, who pay a fine in lieu of service) are liable for service in the National Militia, which possesses a permanent staff of trained officers. The war effective is about 30,000 of all ranks, and it is estimated that 20,000 well-armed troops could be mobilized within forty-eight hours. There is no cavalry owing to the nature of the country.

Education.—Primary education is compulsory and free, and there are about 120 primary schools with 10,000 pupils. The government also supports itinerant lecturers who instruct the peasants in agriculture and veterinary science, etc. There is no University.

Finance.—The revenue for 1912 was 3,-609,000 kronen and the expenditures, 4,187,-126 kronen. The public debt was stated in 1913 at 9,000,000 kronen. The unit of value is the Austrian krone (crown) equal to $0.20,3, United States money. It is called perper in Montenegro.

The capital is Cettinje.

The exports include cattle, castradina, cheese, raw hides, tobacco, and wool, the imports being mainly manufactured articles and arms and ammunition. The import duties are heavy.

Monterey (Mexico), Battle of. — The Mexican army under Arista, driven across the Rio Grande, took refuge in Matamoras. Taylor receiving reenforcements, demanded the surrender of that city. Arista, unable to hold the place, abandoned it and retreated to Monterey, 180 miles from the Rio Grande and 700 miles from the City of Mexico. Aug. 18, 1846, Taylor, with a force of 6,600 men, began the long march toward Monterey, on the way to the enemy's capital, having established a depot for supplies at Camargo, at the head of steam navigation of the Rio Grande. Sept. 19 the American army encamped in sight of Monterey, in the beautiful valley of San Juan, almost encircled by the Sierra Madre Mountains. The city is the capital of the Province of Nuevo Leon and the seat of the Catholic bishop of the diocese. It was strongly fortified and garrisoned by 10,000 men, mostly regulars, under Gen. Ampudia. The attack was begun by the Americans on Sept. 21 and on the following morning the bishop's palace was taken by assault. The city was then forced, the Mexicans stubbornly retreating from square to square. The fighting continued during the 22d and 23d, and on the morning of the

24th of September an armistice was agreed upon. Gen. Ampudia surrendered the place and was allowed to retire with his army. The American loss was slight.

Monterey, Mexico, battle of, referred to, 2342.

Montgomery, Ala., government of Confederate States first located at, 3225.

Transferred to Richmond, Va., 3225.

Montijo, The, seizure and detention of, by United States of Colombia, 4289.

Claims arising out of, paid, 4358.

Montreal (Canada), Capture and Loss of.—After the taking of Ticonderoga and Crown Point, Ethan Allen, Philip Schuyler, Benedict Arnold, and other Americans were anxious to invade Canada and secure the cooperation of the Canadians with the colonists. In June, 1775, the Continental Congress gave Gen. Schuyler discretionary power to proceed against Montreal. He sent Gen. Montgomery with 3,000 men down Lake Champlain. Gen. Carleton, with 500 British, was forced to surrender on the 13th of November. Eleven vessels also fell into Montgomery's hands. Carleton escaped to Quebec. Benedict Arnold, with 1,200 men, had been ordered to proceed by way of the Kennebec and Chaudière rivers and cooperate with Montgomery before Quebec. The expedition to the latter city proved disastrous. Three brigades of infantry, besides artillery, stores, and ammunition, having arrived from England, the Americans were forced to retire to Lake Champlain. (See also Quebec (Canada), Battle of.)

Monuments. (See Statues and Monuments.)

Morey Letter, The.—A letter published in 1880 during the Presidential campaign, addressed to H. L. Morey, and alleged to have been signed by James A. Garfield, advocating the use of Chinese cheap labor in the United States. The letter was a crude forgery, and Morey a fictitious name.

Morgan's Raid.—In the summer of 1863 the Confederate General Buckner was in East Tennessee, near the borders of Kentucky, preparing for an expedition against Louisville. Gen. John H. Morgan was sent ahead with 2,460 cavalry to pave the way. He crossed the Cumberland River, and having been joined by about 1,000 Kentuckians, passed over the Ohio River into Indiana. The advance of Rosecrans's army prevented Buckner from joining him. Morgan rode through southern Indiana toward Cincinnati, burning bridges, tearing up railroads, and fighting home guards. The whole State of Ohio became alarmed, and a strong Union force was soon in pursuit. Others were advancing upon his flanks, and gunboats were patrolling the Ohio River to prevent his recrossing into Kentucky. Passing around Cincinnati, he reached the river at Buffington's Ford July 19. After a severe battle with various installments of Federal troops which had hotly pursued him, about 800 of the command surrendered, but Morgan, with the remainder, proceeded up the river to Belleville. About 300 succeeded in crossing the river here before the arrival of the gunboats. Many were drowned or shot in attempting to cross, and Morgan, with about 200 of his men, retreated farther up the river to New Lisbon, where he was surrounded and forced to surrender. In his raid Morgan traveled about 350 miles through Indiana and Ohio, making sometimes 50 miles a day. The amount of property destroyed scarcely exceeded $50,000. More than 2,000 of his men were killed or captured. Morgan and some of his officers were sent to Columbus and confined in the penitentiary, from which he and six others escaped. Immediately after his escape he planned another raid into the Union lines in Tennessee, but was surrounded and killed by Union troops under Gen. Gillem, near Greenville, Tenn.

Mormon Church (see also Polygamy):

Commissioners appointed under act in reference to polygamy, etc., referred to, 4678, 4731, 4771, 4801, 4837, 4946.

Manifesto of president of, advising Mormons to refrain from contracting marriages forbidden by laws of the land, 5553, 5803, 5942.

Suit instituted by Government for disincorporation of, discussed, 5379.

Mormon State.—A nickname for Utah (q. v.). (See also States); sometimes also nicknamed Desert State.

Mormons.—A religious body more correctly known as the Church of Jesus Christ of Latter-day Saints. They came into prominence largely because of their practice and advocacy of plural marriage, as a principle of their religion. The church was founded by Joseph Smith in 1830, on what is claimed to have been a divine revelation. The Mormons organized in the State of New York, and migrated successively to Ohio, Missouri and Illinois. These removals were caused by religious and political differences, culminating in the murder of Joseph and Hyrum Smith, the Prophet and Patriarch of the Church, at Carthage, Illinois, June 27, 1844. In July, 1847, the Mormons entered Salt Lake Valley, where they founded their first settlement in the Rocky Mountain region. It was then Mexican soil.

Misunderstandings as to acts and motives caused many difficulties between the Mormons and Federal representatives sent to govern them and administer the laws. In 1856-1857, the Mormons were charged with rebellion against the Government, and an army was sent to suppress the alleged uprising. While there had been trouble between individuals representing both sides, no rebellion existed, and the United States Court records, which the Mormons were accused of having destroyed, were found intact and so reported by Honorable Alfred Cumming, Brigham Young's successor as Governor of Utah. Pending the peaceful adjustment of the difficulty, the territorial militia, under orders from Governor Young, opposed the entrance of the Government troops into Salt Lake Valley.

Special laws bearing upon the Mormons and their institutions were enacted by Congress in 1862, 1882 and 1887. These laws forbade polygamy (marrying of plural wives) and unlawful cohabitation (living in such relations), and provided for their punishment by heavy fines and imprisonment; they also disincorporated the church and confiscated its property. The Mormons having submitted to the laws enacted by Congress against polygamous practices, the confiscated property was returned.

In 1898, B. H. Roberts was nominated for Congress by the Democratic Party in the State of Utah, and was elected, but owing to a charge that he was still living in polygamy, he was not allowed to take his seat. In 1903 Reed Smoot, a Republican, was elected to the Senate and an agitation was immediately set on foot to unseat him, on the ground that, being an official of the Mormon Church, he countenanced polygamy. The agitation was unsuccessful. It was shown that the church, since the Manifesto of 1890, officially discountenancing the further practice of polygamy, had not sanctioned any plural marriages. In 1910, the Mormon Church counted 624 church edifices in its possession, with a membership of 215,796 members. (See illustration opposite 3033.)

Mormons, laws to prevent importation of, recommended, 4947.

Morning Light, The, seizure of the *Jorgen Lorenzen* by, 3271.

Morocco.—Morocco, the largest of the Barbary States, called by the Moors El Maghrib el Aksa, "The Farthest West" (of the Muhammadan World), is situate in the northwest of the African Continent, between 27°-36° N. lat. and 1°-11° 40′ W. long. Included in this area are the Kingdoms of Fez and Morocco, to the north of the Atlas Mountains, and other districts to the south. The northern boundary is the Mediterranean, and the western coast is washed by the Atlantic. The eastern boundary with Algeria has been settled by treaty with France, and meets the southern boundary at the 30th parallel of north latitude, but the remaining southern boundary is indeterminate and irregular to the southwest, where it descends to 26° N. lat. on the Atlantic coast, an approximate area of 314,000 square miles.

Physical Features.—Morocco is traversed from the Atlantic coast in the southwest to the Algerian frontier in the northeast by five parallel ranges, known generally as the Atlas Mountains. Between the various ranges lie well-watered and fertile plains, the lower slopes of the northern flanks of the mountains being well-wooded, while the southern slopes are exposed to the dry winds of the desert and are generally arid and desolate.

Along the Mediterranean coast the Rif Mountains overlook the sea from Melilla to Ceuta. The Bay of Tangier contains the best harbor in Morocco. The most northerly point of Morocco is the peninsula of Ceuta, which is separated from the continent of Europe by the narrow Strait of Gibraltar. The Jebel Musa dominates the promontory, and with the rocky eminence of Gibraltar was known to the ancients as The Pillars of Hercules, the western gateway of the Mediterranean.

The climate is generally good and undoubtedly healthy, especially on the Atlantic coast, the country being sheltered by the Atlas Mountains from the hot winds of the Sahara. The Mediterranean coast is drier and less temperate, but not unhealthy, while the plains of the interior are intensely hot.

History.—From the end of the eighth century A. D. until the year 1912 Morocco was ruled by a despotic Amir or Sultan of various dynasties, that of Filali having reigned since 1649. The imperial umbrella (the symbol of sovereignty) was passed on by nomination, and the rule was arbitrary and unchecked by any civil limits. The country was subject to European intervention at many periods, and during the closing years of the nineteenth century the dominant power in the country was France, whose Algerian territory formed the eastern boundary. By the Anglo-French Convention of 1904 Great Britain had recognized the

predominance of French rights, but in 1905 Germany exhibited an interest in Moroccan affairs, and at the Algeciras Conference in January, 1906, an attempt was made by the Powers to define the various interests, and to establish order in the country by means of an organized police force. Between 1906 and 1911 there were frequent conflicts between French troops and Moroccan tribesmen, and in 1908 internal dissensions led to the defeat and deposition of the Sultan Abd el Aziz IV. by his brother Hafid, who eventually triumphed and was recognized by the Powers in 1909. In 1911 a German gunboat anchored in the harbor of Agadir on the Atlantic coast, and after protracted negotiations Germany abandoned this port, and relinquished all claims to the country under a Franco-German treaty, which secured compensation from France in the Congo region. In 1912 Sultan Hafid abdicated and accepted a pension from France, and was succeeded by his brother Moulai Yusef.

Government.—France is the paramount power in Morocco, and the Government of the country is administered by the French Republic, which is recognized as the "protecting power." In addition to France, the kingdom of Spain has had relations with Morocco for many centuries. Ceuta has been a Spanish possession since the close of the sixteenth century, and forms part of the administrative province of Cadiz, and there are several presidios along the Mediterranean (or Rif) coast, while the adjacent Alhucema and Zaffarin islands are Spanish possessions. The Franco-Spanish treaty of Nov. 27, 1912, regulates the protectorate of Spain over a portion of Morocco, and lays down the boundaries, Tangier (with a small district adjacent) being declared international by treaty between Great Britain, France and Spain.

Ethnography.—There are five distinct racial elements in the population (which numbers between four million and five million), of which three are native, viz.: Berbers, Arabs and Jews, the fourth element are Negroes from the Sudan, the fifth being various colonies of Europeans settled at the ports. The Berbers are the aboriginal inhabitants of the mountainous districts. The Arabs were introduced in the eleventh and twelfth centuries A. D., and inhabit the plains. Many of the inhabitants of the plains are of mixed Berber-Arab descent, and constitute the race known to Europeans as Moors. The Negroes have been imported as slaves from the western Sudan, and there are many mulattoes.

With the exception of the Jews, who number about 300,000, and the 25,000 Europeans, the 65,000 French troops in the French zone, the population is entirely Muhammadan. The language of the country is Arabic.

Production and Industry.—Parts of the cultivable land are entirely neglected and the area under crops is cultivated in the most primitive manner. Among the agricultural products are wheat, barley, maize, beans, peas, birdseed, linseed, coriander, cummin, fenugreek, esparto and hemp, and many fruits, principally figs, almonds, pomegranates, lemons, olives, oranges and dates, the latter growing also on the southern slopes and in the plains. The live stock includes large quantities of horses, cattle, sheep and goats, while the poultry and egg industry is of increasing importance.

Antimony, iron, coal, copper, lead and tin (the last three in considerable quantities) are known to exist, and gold and silver are also found. Rock salt and brine are exported in large quantities. The iron mines of the Atlas are of great antiquity, but have long been abandoned.

The leather industry, which was once of great importance, is greatly reduced, and the native manufactures of woolens, silks and embroideries suffer from the competition of inferior but cheaper articles from Europe. Carpets and rugs are still produced for export and slippers and shawls for the home market and the Levant.

The articles exported are: Hides and skins, wool, oxen, eggs, slippers, almonds, barley, olive oil, beans, wheat, fenugreek, linseed, gums, cummin, coriander, beeswax, canary seed, maize and chick peas.

The imports are: Cottons, sugar, tea, machinery and hardware, flour and semolina, candles, tobacco, wines, spirits, beer, etc., groceries and provisions, oils, vegetables, woolen goods, soap, vegetables and fruit (fresh and preserved), coffee, silk (raw), silk (manufactured).

Cities.—The principal harbors are Tetuan, Tangier, El Araish, Rabat, Casablanca, Mazagan, Saffi, Mehedia, and Mogador. Capital, Fez. Population, about 120,000.

The French have built some narrow gauge military railways from Casablanca to Rabat, to Kinitra and Mequinez, and to Settet, while the Franco-Spanish treaty provides for a line from Tangier to Fez. Telegraphic communication is established by submarine cables from Tangier to Cadiz, Tarifa and Oran, and there are wireless stations at Tangier, Rabat, Casablanca, and Mogador. Roads have also been constructed in the French zone.

Morocco:

Algeciras convention urged upon Congress, 7062.

Consuls of United States in, 169.

Presents given to. (See Consuls.)

Differences with United States, communication from Commodore Morgan relative to adjustment of, referred to, 2063.

Emperor of—

Death of, 169.

Lion and horses presented to the United States by, 1256.

Legation of United States in, premises for, presented by Sultan of, 4823, 4923.

Moors in, conference regarding protection for, 4561.

Relations with, 2081.

Treaty regarding exercise of right of protection in, 4580.

Treaty with, transmitted and discussed, 90, 140, 174, 178, 181, 363, 1458, 1484, 1498, 3582, 7062.

Expiration of first year at hand, 1318.

Vessels of United States seized or interfered with by, 352, 353.

Morocco, Treaties with.—The treaty of peace and friendship of 1787 was superseded by that of 1836. It provided for neutrality of the one power if the other should be at war with a third; and that the subjects of the one power taken in such war on prize vessels should be at once set free and their effects restored to them. Examination and search of vessels of the contracting parties are to be conducted with all possible ease and freedom from embarrassment. Humane treatment of vessels in distress and shipwrecked crews is provided for. If a vessel of an enemy of one of the contracting powers be in a port of the other power at the same time that a vessel of the contracting power leaves the port, the vessel of the enemy shall be detained there for a period of twenty-four hours after the departure of the former.

Freedom of commercial intercourse is extended to vessels and individuals in the dominions of the two nations. Disputes are to be settled by consular officers. Justice is to be impartially dispensed toward the peoples of both nations. The consul may act as executor of estates. The rights, privileges, and powers of consuls are defined as in consular conventions.

The treaty of 1865 provided for the support and maintenance of the lighthouse at Cape Spartel by the United States and such powers of Europe as were contracting parties. The lighthouse was built by the Sultan of Morocco, who, having no navy or merchant marine, gave the support of the light into the hands of the contracting powers without encroachment or loss of rights therein. The Sultan agreed to furnish a guard for the defence of the light, while all other expenses were to be borne by the powers.

The convention as to protection of 1880 was entered into with the United States and several of the powers of Europe, to establish protection on a uniform basis to the representatives of the several nations in Morocco.

Moros, referred to, 6690, 6692, 6720.

Morris, The, referred to, 1030, 2116, 2173, 2206.

Mosquito Indian Strip, Nicaragua:

American citizens in—

Murdered, 5960.

Rights, etc., of, inquired into, 5991.

British troops landed at Bluefields, referred to, 5908.

Claims of Great Britain upon Nicaragua respecting treatment of citizens in, and action of United States, 6066.

Correspondence regarding, 2569.

Insurrection in, and treatment of American citizens, discussed, 5960, 6365, 6433.

Jurisdictional questions regarding, discussed, 5959, 6066.

Mosquito Indians. (See Indian Tribes.)

Mosquitos, Kingdom of. (See Mosquito Indian Strip.)

Mother of Presidents.—Alternative nickname for Virginia. (See Old Dominion State.)

Mother of States.—Alternative nickname for Virginia. (See Old Dominion State.)

Mothers' Pensions.—In connection with country-wide discussion of the education and best development of the child has come within the past few years many definite steps for preserving to the child the benefits gained only from proper home influences. In the belief that separation of mother and child necessarily works to the detriment of the child's development, many states have enacted legislation that will enable mothers too poor to maintain their children, to keep them at home instead of placing them in various institutions. This is being done through a pension or allowance system. Thirteen State Legislatures have passed these so-called "widows' pension" laws, the greater part of them within the last year. A number of cities have provided similar aid by municipal ordinances. The first bill introduced in the New York State Legislature passed the lower house, but failed in the Senate.

Mound Builders.—A prehistoric race of Americans who inhabited the valleys of the Ohio and Mississippi rivers. They are so named because the only traces of their existence are found in mounds of earth formed in regular geometrical shapes containing ashes, stone and bronze implements and weapons. Some of these mounds seem to have been simply places of sepulture, while others show unmistakable evidences of having been erected as fortifications. The race probably became extinct only a few generations before the discovery of America, as De Soto found tribes of Southern Indians who built mounds and possessed other characteristics of the extinct race. They belonged distinctly to the Indian race and to the Stone Age. The mounds range from 2 or 3 feet in height to 132 feet high and 188 feet long, the latter being the dimensions of one at Marietta, Ohio, while one at Grave Creek, W. Va., measures 70 feet in height and 900 feet in circumference.

Mount McGregor Cottage. (See illustration opposite 4927.)

Mount Rainier Forest Reserve, Wash., establishment of, by proclamation, 6209.

Mount Rainier National Park. (See Parks, National.)

Mount Vernon.—The Washington estate originated in 1674 with the grant by Lord Culpeper to John Washington and Nicholas Spencer of 5,000 acres of land on the west bank of the Potomac River, beginning about four miles south of Jones' Point (the original southwest boundary of the District of Columbia). One-half of this estate was inherited by Lawrence Washington, who, in 1743, built his residence there, and named the place Mount Vernon, in honor of the British admiral under whom he had served. At his death, in 1752, title to the property passed to his half brother, George Washington.

During his residence of more than half a century on the estate George Washington increased his holdings to about 7,600 acres, which he divided into five main farms, the survey of which, by the General himself, is preserved in the Library of Congress. He also turned his attention to the enlargement of the mansion and adornment of the grounds. The plans and specifications of the mansion house as it stands today were his personal work, and the neatness and simple beauty so admirably adjusted to harmonize with the landscape surroundings proclaim its architect a person of refined taste and artistic judgment.

Washington described his home as being situated in a high, healthy country ; in a latitude between the extremes of heat and cold ; on one of the finest rivers of the world—a river well stocked with various kinds of fish at all seasons of the year. "It is more than possible," says a recent writer, "that without Mount Vernon Washington himself might not have been precisely what he was. That unique balance of power that differentiates him from all

other men of all times might not have existed but for the conditions in which it had its growth and ultimate maturity. In all the years of his activity, so fateful to mankind, beginning, as it were, with his very boyhood, who may tell what part in the mighty result was due to the simplicity, quietude and dignity of this country place, so persuasive of reflection and so inspiring to high thought, seated as it is on the bluff overlooking the broad and tranquil river with its ever-changing face and its never-changing flow !"

In his will Washington bequeathed the estate to his nephew, Judge Bushrod Washington, of the United States Supreme Court. Later it passed to Bushrod's nephew, John Augustine Washington, whose son, John Augustine, Jr., upon coming into possession through inheritance, offered to sell the entire estate to the nation. The proposition was not accepted, but a part of the property, including the mansion, was purchased by the Mount Vernon Ladies' Association. (See article following.) Several attempts have later been made to have Congress purchase the entire estate and preserve it as a national memorial park. Since the purchase made by the ladies' association the remainder of the estate has been divided and sub-divided and come into the possession of various owners. Many beautiful suburban homes now adorn the spot and the National Government has contributed largely toward its attractiveness by constructing a fine automobile boulevard connecting it with Washington city, which is expected to be completed in 1916.

Mount Vernon Ladies' Association.— A national organization of public spirited American women formed to purchase and maintain as a patriotic shrine the home of George Washington at Mount Vernon, Va. Miss Ann Pamela Cunningham, of South Carolina, founded the society in 1856 and became its first Regent. Edward Everett, of Massachusetts, through his lectures and writings, contributed $70,000, and with other funds aggregating $200,000 raised by popular subscription 200 of the nearly 8,000 acres, including the house owned by Washington, were purchased and turned over to the ladies' association. Their object is to preserve and carry out the landscape features of the estate, care for the house and perpetuate Washington's idea of a model American home. It is stated that 125,000 Americans visit the spot each year.

A council of the association is held annually in Mount Vernon, presided over by the Regent (1915 -Miss Harriet Clayton Comegys, of Delaware). Thirty-two States are represented by Vice Regents.

Mountain Meadow (Utah) Massacre.— Efforts of the Federal Government to enforce the laws against polygamy incited the Mormons to bitter hatred of all opposed to their religion. Brigham Young made threats of turning the Indians loose upon west-bound immigrants unless what he considered the Mormons' rights were respected. Sept. 7, 1857, about 30 miles southwest of Cedar City, a body of about 120 non-Mormon immigrants were attacked by Indians and Mormons under the leadership of John D. Lee, and after a siege of four days were induced to surrender under promise of protection, but all were massacred except 17 children under 7 years of age.

Mountain Meadow Massacre, referred to, 3123.

Mountain State.—A nickname for Montana (q. v.). (See also States.)

Moving Pictures.—This rapidly developed industry consists of the representation upon a screen magnified and illuminated, of a series of photographs in such rapid succession that the impression of one is not effaced from the eye until it is succeeded by another view of the same object in another position, taken at an interval n longer separated from its predecessor than the duration of an impression upon the retina of the eye. The illusion of motion is caused by the fact that an impression made upon the eye lasts for a short time after the object causing it has disappeared. This short time is known as the period of persistence of vision, and its duration varies from one-tenth to one-fiftieth of a second. Pictures, therefore, to convey the illusion of motion must follow each other on the retina at a speed of from ten to fifty per second. Actual experience has shown that a rate of sixteen to twenty per second obviates the flicker caused by a slower rate and the indistinctness due to greater speed.

Early forms of the illusion were the stroboscope and zoetrope, popular toys, wherein a series of pictures were viewed through slits cut in discs or cylinders which were caused to revolve rapidly between the eye and the pictures. These toys grew out of the discoveries of M. Plateau, a blind scientist, of Ghent, Belgium, in 1833. Eadweard Muybridge, in 1877, obtained pictures of running horses, springing animals and climbing men by setting a number of cameras in a row and arranging their shutters to be opened and closed automatically as the objects passed before them. The results of Muybridge's experiments were published in folio form by the University of Pennsylvania. The discovery of instantaneous photography by the German, Auschuetz, the invention of the dry plate process in 1878, and the celluloid roll film, first used by Marey in 1888, combined to bring motion pictures nearer to perfection. Then came the snap-shot camera of Friese-Greene and Evans, which took ten pictures a second. Edison produced sensitized films of celluloid in 1893 and devised the sprocket wheel to carry them across the focal plane of the camera and expose them intermittently, the images being thus successively projected through an object lens upon a distant screen. The Brothers Lumière, of Lyons, France, in 1895, brought out a machine which took the pictures and projected them as well. Some idea of development of the industry may be gained from the fact that the first patent for a motion picture machine was granted Nov. 3, 1857, and by Feb. 17, 1914, there were 479.

Many inventors have essayed machines for connecting moving picture projectors with talking machines, and though some of these have been exhibited, the results have been unsatisfactory because perfect synchronism and the reproduction of the perfect tones of the voice in their original quality and sufficiently loud to be heard in every part of a theatre are difficult to obtain.

The first moving pictures were mere reproductions from scenes of nature, but soon the public became weary of these, and it hence occurred to the early producers to tell stories by means of the film. Naturally enough, the first attempts in this field were comedies, of a crude and superficial nature; and the traditions of the regular stage were followed as faithfully as possible. The art of motion picture acting in these early days was still the art of the old pantomimes, although the actors and producers were aided by the possibility of inserting explanatory legends on the screen as the play developed, to this extent overcoming one of the pantomime difficulties.

It was not until the close of the first decade and the beginning of the second decade of the twentieth century that motion pictures developed a technique of their own. To-day, the producers and actor have evolved an art of their own, irrespective of the regular stage, and by no means inferior to it. Indeed, the motion picture art is well termed to-day the art of the silent drama, and its proponents hail it as an art more difficult and even more significant than the regular dramatic art.

Certainly, aside from artistic considerations, the motion picture has had a social significance which the regular stage could not have. Because of the cheapness of the entertainment provided, much of the problem of wholesome recreation for the great masses of the population was solved. To give only one example of the ramifications of the services rendered by the motion picture film, social workers in immigrant neighborhoods announce that it has provided a new and in some cases the only point of contact between the foreign-born parent and his American child.

To judge from the calibre of the plays produced upon the regular stage since it has been subject to the competition of the "movies," the latter have had a most beneficial effect upon the spoken and acted drama.

Surveys recently made in Washington, D. C., and in other cities indicate that the average daily attendance at moving pictures amounts to one-seventh of the population. Using these figures as a basis, remembering that the rural and sparsely settled districts do not have the same opportunity for attendance as do the urban and more thickly settled districts, it may be said that the average daily attendance in the United States is 12,000,000.

In 1916 there were produced about 4,250 different subjects and in 1917 about 3,200. In 1915, the average number of reels to a subject was 1.75; in 1916, 2.23; in 1917, 2.77; and in January, 1918, 3.30. It is estimated that separate reproductions from the original film average 35 in number. Between one-half and three-fourths of all pictures in the United States are produced in California.

It is estimated that one-fourth of all pictures are broad comedy and travel and news scenes.

In 1916, the exports of films, mostly for Great Britain, amounted to 43,000 miles, valued at $10,000,000; and the imports to 7,000 miles, valued at $1,000,000. Of the exported films, about 75% had already been exposed, and were ready for use.

In 1917, about 375,000,000 feet of film pictures were produced in the United States, according to latest estimates.

Kansas, Pennsylvania, Ohio and Maryland are the only states with official boards of censorship possessing legal powers. Practically every film produced in this country, however, is passed upon by the National Board of Censorship, which is a voluntary organization, but one which in practice has binding power and authority.

In 1918 there were 17,383 moving picture theatres in the United States and 836 in Canada. The Western states have more theatres of this nature in proportion to the population than other sections of the country, the ratio being for Montana, 1 to 2,562 persons; for Arizona, 1 to 2,792 persons; for Nevada, 1 to 2,788 persons; for Idaho, 1 to 2,972 persons. The Southern states have the lowest ratio. Mississippi having 1 to 18,706 persons; South Carolina, 1 to 15,867 persons; Georgia, 1 to 15,546 persons; Alabama, 1 to 15,550 persons. The states with many large cities have a low ratio because of the fact that many of their moving picture theatres have a capacity equal to five times the capacity of the usual moving picture theatre. The ratio in New York is 1 to 7,062 persons; in Massachusetts, 1 to 8,129; in Pennsylvania, 1 to 5,813; in Ohio, 1 to 5,095; in Illinois, 1 to 4,521; in California, 1 to 4,032 persons; in Maine and New Hampshire, 1 to 3,693 persons; in Iowa, 1 to 3,099 persons; and in Kansas, 1 to 4,174 persons. The ratio for the entire United States is 1 to 5,900 persons.

Muck-Raker.—The term was first used by Bunyan in his "Pilgrim's Progress," and came into political use during President Roosevelt's administration, contemptuously characterizing reformers (q. v.), especially writers, who insisted upon stirring up fraudulent and questionable practices among the industrial enterprises of the country, not so much to accomplish improvements as merely to rake up the unpleasant.

Mulligan Letters.—A bookkeeper by the name of Mulligan, in the office of Warren Fisher of Boston, wrote certain letters calculated to implicate James G. Blaine in improper transactions with Fisher in connection with the Little Rock and Fort Smith Railroad. These letters were used as a basis for attacks on Blaine in the nominating convention of 1876, and in the convention and campaign of 1884. Blaine's denial and corroborative evidence in connection with the letters fully satisfied his friends of his innocence.

Mugwump.—A corruption of the Algonquian Indian word "mugquomp," which signifies a chief, ruler, or a person of importance. After long use in local politics the word came into national use in the Presidential campaign of 1884. The newspapers applied the term to those Republicans who refused to support James G. Blaine, the regular party nominee, and it has since been used to designate any person of independent politics or who is supposed to be lacking in loyalty to his political party.

Mumfordville (Ky.), Battle of.—Here on Sept. 17, 1862, the Confederate army under Gen. Bragg attacked the Federals under Gen. J. T. Wilder. The post surrendered to the Confederates, the number of captured being about 4,000.

Munich, Bavaria.—Third International Exhibition of Fine Arts to be held at, 5193.

Municipal Government, District of Columbia should be model of, 6728.

Municipal Ownership.—In its strict sense, the term applies to the ownership by municipalities of public utilities, but it is generally used to describe not only ownership of certain forms of municipal activities, but also management and operation of them, by the municipalities. In the United States, because of the traditional feeling for individualism and private enterprise, and because of its rapid economic development, the movement has not been so pronounced as in Europe, where Germany and Great Britain in particular represent notable achievements in the field of municipal ownership. Nevertheless, as described below, there is a considerable and

an increasing amount of municipal ownership in the United States.

In Germany in 1906, of 1,279 towns of all sizes in Prussia, 561 had municipal ownership in waterworks, 440 in gas works, 201 in electricity plants, 426 in abattoirs and stockyards, 370 in bathing establishments, 42 in quarries, etc., 17 in breweries, 104 in restaurants, 45 in brickyards, and 23 in mills.

In 1908, public utilities were under municipalities in Germany as follows:—Of 2,309 towns, 1,238 had municipal ownership in their waterworks, 709 in their gas works, 413 in their electricity plants, 79 in their street railways, and 814 in their abattoirs. The movement was especially strong in the larger cities, as may be seen from the fact that of the 41 above cities with a population above 100,000, 38 owned their waterworks, 33 their gas works, 33 their electricity plants, 18 their street railways, and 39 their abattoirs.

In 1911, of 41 German cities with a population between 50,000 and 100,000, 29 owned their gas works; of 23 cities with a population between 100,000 and 200,000, 14 owned them, and of 23 cities with a population above 200,000, 16 owned the gas works.

In 1894, there were 64 miles of municipal street railways in Germany; in 1911, 2,700 miles. In 1912, there were 132 such municipal enterprises, of which 95 were in Prussia. Most of the large towns have also their municipal baths, savings banks and pawnshops.

In Great Britain in 1908, cities had outstanding loans approximating $1,000,000,000 for municipal enterprises, chiefly waterworks, which represented 46% of such loans. Harbors and docks accounted for 8% of such loans, street railways for 20% of them, electric plants for 11%, and gas works for 9% of them. There was also a considerable amount of municipal housing enterprise for the poorer working classes.

In 1909, of 451 electricity plants investigated in Great Britain, 249 were under municipal ownership. In all of Great Britain figures indicate that 326 such plants are municipal, with only 151 under private management.

In 1909, of 300 street railways, 176 were municipal and 124 were private. The expenditures on capital account of the former were 49,570,000 pounds; of the latter, 23,373,000 pounds.

In 1905, Great Britain possessed 1,142 municipal waterworks, with a capital of 128,819,000 pounds; and 231 private waterworks, with a capital of 18,718,000 pounds. In 1908, there were 103 municipal harbor and dock undertakings.

In the United States, in 1916, of the 195 cities with a population above 30,000, 150 owned and operated their waterworks. In the same year, there were 1,455 municipal electric light and power plants; 125 municipal gas plants; and 20 municipal asphalt paving plants.

In 1899, 63% of the waterworks of the country were under municipal ownership. In 1912, 48 of the 56 cities with a population above 100,000 owned their waterworks, and in 1915, 155 of the cities with a population above 30,000.

In 1902, 815 of the 3,620 (22%) electric light plants of the United States were municipal; in 1907, 1,252 of the 4,714 (27%); in 1912, 1,562 of the 5,221 (30%). This development, however, has been almost entirely in cities with a population below 30,000.

In 1899, 14 of the 965 gas works of the country, or 1½%, were municipal. In 1914, there were 125 such, of a total of 2,109, or 6%. 112 of the 195 cities with a population above 30,000 have municipal markets.

Other forms of municipal ownership in the United States are scattered, although the movement was strengthened by the general increase in public control due to the war in Europe. In Canada, 75% of the waterworks are municipal.

Munitions.—All physical objects, aside from equipment, used in war, therefore powder, shells and other war materials.

Munitions, sale of, to belligerents during European War, question of, discussed, 8289.

Munitions Board.—A board created by and under the Council of National Defense (q. v.) to control so far as possible under the existing law the production and distribution of munitions in the United States for the use of both that country and of her allies in the European War.

Munitions of War. (See Arms and Ammunition.)

Munn vs. Illinois.—One of the "elevator cases" decided by the Supreme Court of the United States. In 1872 Munn and another were found guilty of violating an article of the Illinois constitution in regard to grain warehouses. They had failed to take out a license and give bond and were charging higher rates for storage than the law allowed. The offenders were fined, and the supreme court of the State affirmed the action of the criminal court. The case was then appealed to the United States Supreme Court. That body affirmed the judgment on the ground that the act of the Illinois legislature was not repugnant to the Constitution of the United States, and that a State could lawfully determine how a man might use his own property when the good of other citizens was involved.

Munsee Indians. (See Indian Tribes.)

Murfreesboro (Tenn.), Battle of, fought Dec. 31, 1862, and Jan. 2, 1863, between forces of General Rosecrans and General Bragg. (See Stone River (Tenn.), Battle of.)

Muscat; seaport on Gulf of Oman:
Presents offered President Van Buren by Imaum of, declined, 1809.
Offered United States, recommendations regarding, 1809, 2169.
Treaty with, 1272, 1457, 1593, 5195.

Muscle Shoals, Ala., mentioned, 6777.

Museum, National, appropriation for, recommended, 4431, 4458.

Musical Instruments.—(From a Report issued by the Census Bureau, August 1, 1913.) The establishments engaged primarily in the manufacture of pianos in 1909 turned out products to the value of $66,569,273, or 74.1 per cent. of the total value of products of the three branches of the industry combined. The value of the products reported by the establishments engaged chiefly in the manufacture of organs ($4,745,655) represented 5.3 per cent of the total for all three branches; and the value of the products reported by the establishments engaged chiefly in the manufacture of piano and organ parts and materials ($18,474,616) represented 20.6 per

cent of the total value of products for the three branches.

The establishments in the three branches of the industry combined (pianos, organs and piano and organ parts and materials) gave employment to 41,882 persons, of whom 38,020 were wage-earners, and paid out $28,313,754 in salaries and wages.

The manufacture of pianos and organs has had an uninterrupted development since 1869, when products to the value of $11,-886,444 were reported. In 1909 the value of products was more than seven times as great, $89,789,544. The largest increases are shown for the decade from 1899 to 1909, when the number of persons engaged in the industry increased 80.4 per cent and the value of products 118.9 per cent. The large piano and organ factories are of comparatively recent development. In 1869 the average establishment gave employment to only twenty-four wage-earners and the average value of products was $46,797; in 1909 the average number of wage-earners was seventy-five and the value of products $177,100.

In 1909, of the total number of reed and pipe organs reported, 1.9 per cent were pipe organs, but of the combined value 51.1 per cent was contributed by pipe organs. In the number of reed organs there was a decrease during the decade 1899-1909 of 39.9 per cent. For pipe organs there was an increase of 117 per cent in number and 130.5 per cent in value. In the manufacture of reed organs, Illinois was the leading state in 1909.

Each census since 1899 has shown an increase in the manufacture of phonographs and graphophones, but by far the greater development occurred during the five-year period 1899-1904, when there was an increase of 2,525, or 178.4 per cent, in the number of persons engaged in the industry, and of $7,990,801, or 355.7 per cent, in the value of products. In 1909, 16 of the 18 establishments were operated by corporations. New Jersey is by far the leading state in the industry, as measured by value of products, followed by Connecticut and New York in the order named.

Of the total value of products reported for the industry in 1909, $11,725,996, the value of complete instruments formed $5,-406,684, or 46.1 per cent, and that of records and blanks $5,007,104, or 42.7 per cent. The remainder, 1,312,208, or 11.2 per cent, represented for the most part horns, needles, matrices and other supplies used in the manufacture or operation of the instruments.

Muskogee Indians. (See Indian Tribes.)

Muster.—The marshaling of troops for military duty. *Muster-out,*—the dismissal of troops when their military services are no longer required.

Muster-Day.—A day for taking the census of all soldiers and military bodies.

Muster-Roll.—A roster for checking up or "calling the roll" of troops to determine who are present for parade or other military duty.

Mutineer.—One who joins in a plot to thwart military or naval authority, especially at sea.

Mutiny.—Concerted action by some of the members of a naval crew or a military body, to oppose and to overthrow the constituted authority thereof.

Naples, Italy:

Claims against, by—

Merchants of United States, 598, 1112.

United States, 556, 598, 867, 1109, 1112, 1157.

Extension of time allowed commissioners for settlement of, recommended, 1267.

Minister of United States to, 557.

Treaty with, referred to, 1195.

Narragansett Indians. (See **Indian Tribes.**)

Nashville Convention.—The Mississippi State convention of 1849 suggested to other Southern States the feasibility of holding conventions to make some public expression on the slavery question and the encroachments of Northern anti-slavery men. Accordingly, a convention was called in Nashville, Tenn., in June, 1850, composed of delegates from all the Southern States. The Wilmot Proviso and the Missouri Compromise were disapproved of by this meeting. Delegates from Texas, Mississippi, and South Carolina advocated open resistance to Federal authority, but more conservative action prevailed. The convention met again in November, but only moderate resolutions were passed.

Nashville (Tenn.), Battle of.—After the battle of Franklin, Nov. 30, 1864, Gen. Schofield retreated to Nashville, closely followed by Hood, who formed his lines near that city Dec. 4. Reenforcements were sent to Thomas at Nashville, swelling his forces to 56,000 men. Dec. 15 Thomas's army advanced against Hood. The day was consumed in manœuvering and skirmishing. There were not many killed or wounded, but the results of the day's operations were the driving of the Confederates from every position held by them and the capture of 16 guns, 1,200 prisoners, 40 wagons, and several hundred stand of small arms. The Union forces bivouacked on the field and renewed the attack the next morning. By 4 o'clock in the afternoon the Confederates were in retreat toward Franklin. They were pursued until Dec. 28, when Hood crossed the Tennessee with the remnants of his army. The loss in killed and wounded was comparatively light, but 53 guns and 4,875 Confederate prisoners were captured.

Nashville, The, mentioned, 6765, 6766, 6767, 6768, 6769, 6836, 6838.

Nassau, Duchy of:

Convention with, 2303.

Exequatur issued consul of, revoked, 3709.

Natchez:

Commissioners of United States assemble in, 186, 192, 236.

Government in, establishment of, recommended, 236.

Natchez, The. (See *General Urrea,* The.)

National Academy of Sciences.—The National Academy of Sciences was incorporated under an act of Congress approved March 3, 1863. It was self-created and retains autonomous powers, but derives national character from the provision in the article of incorporation that "the academy shall, whenever called upon by any depart-

ment of the government, investigate, examine, experiment and report upon any subject of science of art, the actual expense of such investigations, examinations, experiments and reports to be paid from appropriations which may be made for the purpose; but the academy shall receive no compensation whatever for any services to the Government of the United States." The first meeting was held April 22, 1863, and Alexander D. Bache was elected president. Originally the membership was limited to fifty. This limit was removed in 1870, but the policy remained exclusive, election being regarded as a dignity conferred in recognition of special scientific work and only five names are considered for each year's election. A stated session is held annually in Washington on the third Tuesday in April, and another is commonly held elsewhere during each autumn. The membership (at present 96 members and 43 foreign associates) comprises many of the leading scientific specialists of the United States who are grouped into committees on (1) mathematics and astronomy, (2) physics and engineering, (3) chemistry, (4) geology and paleontology, (5) biology, and (6) anthropology. There are in addition a number of foreign associates distinguished for scientific attainment. The president is Dr. W. H. Welch of Johns Hopkins University, and Dr. A. L. Day is the Home Secretary.

National Academy of Sciences, commission from membership of, to formulate plans for forestry system, 6167.

National Air.—The tune, or song, adopted, usually by custom, as a musical symbol of the country; as, in England, "God Save the King"; in France, "The Marseillaise"; in the United States, "The Star Spangled Banner." (See Star Spangled Banner.)

In all public assemblages it is a custom, amounting to an unwritten law, for all persons to stand when the national air is played or sung; likewise it is the custom, under similar circumstances for all men, when out of doors to uncover. This mark of respect is held so sacred that any one violating it is apt to be roughly treated. This is especially true when the martial spirit prevails. Foreigners, even though not in sympathy with the air being played, are expected to obey this custom as a matter of "courtesy to the host."

National Anti-Imperialistic League. (See Imperialism.)

National Anti-Slavery Party.—A party organized in 1833 for united opposition to slavery. It merged into the Liberty Party (q. v.), and finally into the Abolition Party (q. v.).

National Army.—The term applied to the first draft army of 500,000 called to the colors in the war with Germany. (See Army.)

National Association of Naval Veterans.—Organized 1887; 6,000 members; 1,500 contributing members; 30 associations in all the principal cities of the United States.

National Bank Circulation:

Act to fix amount of United States notes and, vetoed, 4222.

Discussed by President—

Arthur, 4720, 4766, 4832.

Cleveland, 4926, 5876, 5966, 5986, 6074, 6157, 6175.

Harrison, Benj., 5474.

Johnson, 3563, 3769.

Roosevelt, 7050.

National Bank Examiners, reports of, referred to, 4655.

National Banks. (See Banks, National.)

National Board of Health.—By act of Congress approved March 3, 1879, a National Board of Health was established, consisting of 7 civilian physicians, 1 army surgeon, 1 navy surgeon, 1 surgeon of the Marine-Hospital Service, and 1 officer of the Department of Justice. This board was abolished by law. A national quarantine law was passed June 3, 1879.

National Board of Health:

Establishment of—

Discussed, 4631.

Recommended, 5983.

Report of, transmitted, 4857, 4972.

National Cemeteries. (See Cemeteries, National.)

Establishment of, and number of Union soldiers buried in, discussed, 3649.

National Committee of Patriotic and Defence Societies. (See Preparedness Societies.)

National Conference of Electricians at Philadelphia referred to, 4956.

National Conservation Association. (See Conservation Commission.)

National Debt. (See Debt, Public.)

National Defense:

Discussed by President—

Wilson, 8020.

National Defense Act.—The name of the act of Congress of June 3, 1916, providing for increases in the provisions for the United States Army. (See Army.)

National Food Board.—This was an organization created by and under the Council of National Defence (q. v.), in order to handle as well as possible the problems arising from the food situation of the country, until Congress passed legislation requested by the President in order to make food regulation efficient and official.

National Forests.—President Cleveland, in his fourth annual message, Dec. 7, 1896 (page 6167), reported that the commission appointed from the membership of the National Academy of Sciences to formulate plans for a national forestry system would soon be prepared to present the result of a thorough and intelligent examination of the preservation of the growing timber of the country. McKinley, in his second annual message, Dec. 5, 1898, reported that up to the previous June 30th, thirty forest reservations had been created by executive proclamations (page 6346). These embraced an estimated area of 40,719,474 acres. By the next year he was able to report the addition of some five million acres to the national forest reserves. (Page 6390.) President Roosevelt discusses at length the importance of the preservation of forests and water supply in his first message after assuming the presidency. (Page 6653.) Mr. Roosevelt's strongest plea for the preservation of our forests is found in his message of Dec. 8, 1908. (Page 7218.)

The great areas contained in the national forests have now been brought to a condition where they are beginning to serve the purposes of the West. The conservation of timber and forage through wise use, and the protection of stream flow, are the means of sustaining many industries which have contributed materially to the prosperity of the country. At the head of the Forest Service are the Forester and the Associate Forester.

The 163 national forests are distributed in six districts, with a District Forester in charge of each, and headquarters as follows: District 1 (Montana, northeastern Washington, northern Idaho, northwestern South Dakota, northern Michigan, northern Minnesota and southwestern North Dakota), Missoula, Mont.; District 2 (Colorado, Wyoming, the remainder of South Dakota, Nebraska and western Kansas), Denver, Col.; District 3 (most of Arizona, Arkansas, Florida, New Mexico and Oklahoma), Albuquerque, N. Mex.; District 4 (Utah, southern Idaho, western Wyoming, eastern and central Nevada and a small portion of northwestern Arizona), Ogden, Utah; District 5 (California and southwestern Nevada), San Francisco, Cal., and District 6 (Washington, Oregon and Alaska), Portland, Ore.

On July 1, 1913, the force employed by the Forest Service numbered 3,791. Of these 3,068 were employed upon the national forests and 723 were engaged in administrative, scientific and clerical work at the Washington and district headquarters. Of the employees on the national forests the force engaged principally in protective work numbered 2,302 men, as follows: Forest Rangers, 359; Assistant Forest Rangers, 888; Forest Guards, 1,053; Game Wardens, 2. The protective force was therefore about one man for every 80,000 acres, or 125 square miles. (Prussia has one man for every 1,700 acres, and Baden one for every 750.)

The branch of silviculture directs the management of the national forests as regards both the systems of cutting mature timber and the work of forest planting; supervises their protection; co-operates with states in developing forest policies adapted to their requirements; co-operates with private forest owners who desire to practice forestry on their lands; and carries on silvicultural investigations of the important species of the United States. In planting within the national forests the primary object is to produce commercial timber, although in a number of cases planting has been done chiefly with the view of reforesting denuded watersheds in order to control and regulate the flow of streams directly supplying cities and towns. During the year ending June 30, 1913, about 30,000 acres in national forests were sown or planted to trees, chiefly Douglas fir, a Western yellow pine, Austrian pine and Engelmann spruce. There are forty Government nurseries which supply the national forests. In the East, forest planting has been done mainly in connection with states and private owners. At the request of the states the Forest Service makes examinations of their forest conditions and conducts other studies needed to serve as a basis for forest legislation and formulation by each state of a forest policy adapted to its special requirements. The service co-operates with private owners, especially small owners, in states which have no State Forester.

The branch of grazing supervises the

grazing of live stock upon the national forests, the principal lines of work being the allotment of grazing privileges. The number of stock grazed during the past season (1913), under permit, was 1,557,118 head of cattle, horses and swine, and 7,867,-851 head of sheep and goats. The annual productive value of this number of stock is more than $20,000,000. The number of persons holding permits to graze live stock during the past year was in excess of 27,000. About 15 per cent of all the sheep in the United States are grazed in the national forests.

The branch of products carries on studies, tests and demonstrations to further the more complete utilization of the products of the forest. A forest products laboratory is operated at Madison, Wis., in co-operation with the University of Wisconsin. In the Western States all products work centres in the district offices at Denver, San Francisco and Portland.

The act of March 1, 1911, commonly known as the Weeks law, provides for the acquisition of forest lands on the watersheds of navigable streams. Its purpose is to promote and protect the navigability of the streams by preserving the forest on the upland portions of their watersheds. Through this act means are afforded of extending the national forest system to regions where the Government has hitherto owned no forest lands and taken no direct part in forest preservation. July 1, 1905, all matters relating to forest reserves passed to the Department of Agriculture.

The original appropriation was $2,000,-000 per year for five and one-half years, beginning with the last half of the fiscal year, 1911. The Agricultural Appropriation bill for the fiscal year, 1913, made the appropriation for 1912 and subsequent years available until expended. Up to July 1, 1913, 5,833,103 acres were reported upon favorably by the Geological Survey. No unfavorable reports have been made.

New York has purchased and set aside 1,642,000 acres in the Adirondack and Catskill Mountains as forest preserves, under the control of the Conservation Commission of the state. These lands and private lands in the preserve counties are protected from fire by an adequate system of rangers.

Pennsylvania has purchased more than 920,000 acres of land for state forest preserves, and the Forestry Commission has the right to purchase additional forest lands at a price not to exceed $5 an acre. The preserves are situated chiefly on the mountains of the central part of the state and located with special references to protecting the water supply at the sources of rivers.

Minnesota, Wisconsin and Michigan have well organized state forest departments. Minnesota has 51,000 acres reserved, Wisconsin 385,000 acres and Michigan 232,000. These are protected from fire and the open land is being planted and the mature timber cut and sold. Kansas, Connecticut, Ohio, New Hampshire and Vermont also distribute planting material to private owners and give them advice in regard to methods of forest management. The following states have forestry departments which seek to protect from fire by means of an organized warden system all of the greater portion of the forest lands in the state: Maine, New Hampshire, Vermont, Massachusetts, Rhode Island, Colorado, Montana, Idaho, Connecticut, New Jersey, Maryland, West Virginia, Kentucky, Tennessee, Alabama, Oregon, Washington and California.

The following table shows the Timber Disposed of, Quantity, Price, and Number of Users, Revenue Under

Specified Heads, and Details of Grazing Privileges, Year Ended June 30, 1915.

(From Reports of the Forest Service, Department of Agriculture.)

Free timber given:	
Number of users	40 040
Timber cut, M ft	123,259
Value, dollars	206,597
Timber sales:	
Number	10,905
Quantity, M ft	1,093,589
Price per M ft. (average), dollars	2.44
Grazing:	
Area of ranges, acres	110,000,000
Kinds of stock—	
Cattle No	1,627,321
Goats, No	51,409
Hogs, No	2,792
Horses, No	96,933
Sheep, No	7,232,276
Total, No	**9,010,731**
Revenue:	
From—	
Timber sales, dollars	1,164,008.29
Timber settlements, dollars	3,180.89
Penalties for timber trespass, dollars	7,284.17
Turpentine sales, dollars	8,832.64
Fire trespass, dollars	660.60
Special uses, dollars	167,007.76
Grazing fees, dollars	1,124,677.44
Grazing trespass, dollars	5,817.56
Total revenue, dollars	**2,481,469.35**

National Forests:

Combining Manzano and Zuni in Arizona and New Mexico, 7987.

National Foundry, erection of, recommended, 1607, 1714.

National Guard.—The enrolled militia of the States is known collectively as the National Guard. (See Militia.)

Encampment of, in coast works recommended, 5476.

Encouragement of, 5550.

Reorganization of, 6672, 6805, 7236.

National Incorporation Act, suggested, 7074, 7455, 7456, 7457, 7458.

National Intelligencer, publication in, of proceedings of President and Cabinet respecting interpretation of reconstruction acts discussed, 3725.

National Monuments.—(See also Statues and Monuments.) By act approved June 8, 1906, the President is authorized to set apart, as National Monuments, certain portions of the land, or landmarks on the land owned and administered by the Government, which may be of historic or scenic interest. There are thirty such monuments which have been set aside for preservation by Presidential order, of which number nineteen are administered by the Interior Department. The Interior Department also administers the more than eighty bird preserves of the Government. (See Interior Department.)

National Museum.—The National Museum is an offshoot of the Smithsonian Institution at Washington, and was organized under the provisions of the act of 1846 creating the parent institution. It is a museum of record, research and education, and the legal depository of all national collections. It is especially rich in American archæology and natural history, but contains specimens from all over the world. The new building was completed in 1910 at a cost of $3,500,000. It contains the specimens collected by the scientific expedition into Africa conducted by Ex-President Roosevelt. Through the beneficence of this private enterprise the museum was enriched by specimens of African mammals superior to that of any other museum in the world. The series of birds, reptiles and plants is also of great importance. The additions to the museum consisted of 4,897 mammals, 4,000 birds, 2,000 reptiles and batrachians and 500 fishes, a total of about 11,397. (See illustration, frontispiece, Vol. VIII.)

National Museum, appropriation for, recommended, 4431, 4458.
Referred to, 6676.

National Parks, should be placed under Department of Agriculture, 7604. (See Chickamauga and Chattanooga National Military Park.)

National Parks and Reservations. (See Parks, National.)

National Party.—In 1900 the National Party was organized as the result of defection from the First Liberty Congress (q. v.). Donelson Caffery was nominated for President and M. Howe for Vice President. The platform declared against expansion, but in favor of the Gold Standard, and it was decided that one elector of the National Party should be voted for at the head of either the Republican or Democratic ticket.

National Prison Congress at Baltimore referred to, 4162. (See also International Prison Congress.)

National Republican Party.—After the defeat of John Quincy Adams by Jackson in 1828 the broad-construction wing of the Democratic-Republican party organized and came out with a platform directly opposed to Jackson on the question of the tariff and the United States Bank. They opposed the spoils system in the public service, favored internal improvements at national expense, a bank of the United States, and a division of the proceeds of land sales among the States. In 1832 they supported Henry Clay for the Presidency and advocated a protective tariff. Clay was defeated, receiving but 49 electoral votes, and in 1835 the party, reenforced by other elements, took the name of Whig.

National Rivers and Harbors Congress.—This body consisted of about three thousand delegates, representing nearly all the states and territories. Processions were held in Washington for a period of three days in the latter part of 1908.

National Security League. (See Preparedness Societies.)

National Shipping Board. (See United States Shipping Board.)

National Silver Party.—O r g a n i z e d in 1896 ; nominated William Jennings Bryan for President and Arthur Sewell for Vice President (the candidates on the Democratic ticket). The platform adopted followed generally the lines of the Democratic platform.

National University.—Washington strongly disapproved of foreign education for American youth and early conceived the idea of establishing a national university

in the central part of the United States. He bequeathed fifty shares of the Potomac Company toward the endowment of such an institution in the District of Columbia, but ultimately the stock of the company proved valueless. Several of the presidents from time to time in their messages recommended the establishment of a national university or universities, or, as they sometimes called them, "seminaries of learning."

National University (see also Education; Seminaries of Learning):
Establishment of, recommended, 58, 194, 197, 398, 470, 553, 878, 4208.
Lands, donation of, to, recommended, 398, 470, 4208.

National Waterways Commission.—A special commission created by Congress in 1909, and the membership of which was drawn entirely from Congress, to make an investigation of transportation by water, and to make recommendations to Congress. It was largely the result of the Lake-to-the-Gulf Deep Waterway Association (q. v.), and of the National Rivers and Harbors Congress (q. v.).

National Zoological Park referred to, 6674.

Nationality.—Federal and not state law determines the status of the nationality of persons in the United States. Until the adoption of the Fourteenth Amendment, the Constitution established no rules regarding the loss or acquisition of nationality. Birth in the country is, as a rule, the test, but not all persons born in the United States are considered as endowed with nationality. The naturalization act of 1790 extended nationality to children born to American parents beyond the sea. In 1855 an act passed restricting this to children whose fathers were citizens. The Civil-Rights Act (q. v.) of 1866 declared "all persons born in the United States and not subject to any foreign power" to be citizens of the United States. The Fourteenth Amendment defines citizens as "all persons born or naturalized in the United States and subject to the jurisdiction thereof." The citizens of Hawaii became citizens of the United States by virtue of annexation, it being so stated in the act of Congress of 1900 which made Hawaii a Territory. The inhabitants of the Philippine Islands and Puerto Rico are entitled to the protection of the Constitution but cannot enjoy the privileges of citizenship until Congress admits their countries to the Union as states or organizes them as territories.

Nations, Congress of. (See under Panama, Isthmus of.)

Nations, Foreign. (See Powers, Foreign; the several powers.)

Native Birds, reservation established for, on Smith Island, 7959.

Natural Rights.—The rights which by nature inhere in man (as distinguished from the rights given by law) such as life, liberty and the pursuit of happiness. (See Declaration of Independence, Volume I, page 1.) The right to these blessings does not carry with it the power to secure them, but government must be formed to establish guarantees of natural rights by the enactment of positive law.

Naturalization.—The investment of an alien with the rights and privileges of citizenship. Section 8 of Article I. of the

Constitution empowered Congress "to establish a uniform rule of naturalization." Naturalization laws were passed by the colonial legislatures of Maryland, Virginia, New York, South Carolina and Massachusetts between 1666 and 1715. In 1740 the British Parliament enacted a law regulating colonial naturalization. In 1790 Congress legislated for the first time so as to provide for uniformity of naturalization under the Constitution. The conditions of this law were that any free white alien might be admitted to citizenship by any court of record of the state in which he has resided for one year, having been a resident of the United States two years. An act of 1795 required five years' residence and application three years prior to naturalization; that of 1798 required fourteen years' residence and application five years prior to naturalization. The act of April 14, 1802, restored the conditions of the act of 1795 and required a proof of five years' residence in the United States and one in the state, good character, an oath of allegiance, and a renunciation of titles and prior allegiance. No alien may be naturalized if his country is at war with the United States. Conditions and procedure in naturalizing an alien are prescribed by sections 2166-2174 of the Revised Statutes of the United States. Naturalization of Chinese is prohibited by section 14, chapter 126, laws of 1882; and of anarchists by the immigration act of 1903. Naturalized citizens of the United States receive the same protection when abroad as native-born citizens. (See also Expatriation.)

The following paraphrase and condensation of the naturalization laws of the United States have been revised by the Commissioner of Naturalization of the Department of Labor, and includes such minor changes in the law as were provided by the recent amendments embodied in the act of Congress, approved June 25, 1910.

The following courts alone have the power to naturalize aliens: United States District Courts now existing, or which may hereafter be established by Congress in any state, United States District Courts for the Territories of Hawaii and Alaska, also all courts of record in any state or territory now existing, or which may hereafter be created, having a seal, a clerk and jurisdiction in actions at law or equity, or law and equity, in which the amount in controversy is unlimited.

The power to naturalize, conferred upon the above mentioned courts, is limited to persons residing within the geographical limits over which their respective jurisdiction extends.

Any alien who is a white person, or of African nativity or African descent, is required, if he desires to become naturalized, to file a declaration of intention in the clerk's office of any court having jurisdiction over the place in which he lives, and such declaration may not be filed until the alien has reached the age of eighteen years. This declaration must contain information as to the name, age, occupation, time and place of arrival in the United States, and must further show that it is the declarant's *bona fide* intention to become a citizen of the United States and to renounce forever all allegiance and fidelity to any foreign prince, potentate, state or sovereignty, and particularly to the one of which he may be at the time a citizen or subject.

Any alien, of the age of twenty-one years and upward, who has served five consecutive years in the United States navy or one enlistment in the United States marine corps, may be admitted to citizenship without any previous declaration of intention.

The widow and children who are under age at the time that an alien who has made his declaration of intention has died, without having secured a certificate of naturalization, are also exempted from the necessity of filing a declaration of intention.

By act of June 25, 1910, any person who on May 1, 1905, was an inhabitant for five years and qualified to become a citizen of the United States and who for the five years preceding May 1, 1910, had resided in the United States continuously and who, because of misinformation in regard to his citizenship, had in good faith exercised the rights and duties of a citizen of the United States because of wrongful information and belief, may, upon proof of these facts satisfactory to a court having jurisdiction to naturalize aliens, petition for naturalization without filing the required declaration of intention upon compliance with the other requirements of the law.

Not less than two years after an alien has filed his declaration of intention, and after not less than five years' continuous residence in the United States, he may file a petition for citizenship in any one of the courts above stated which has jurisdiction over the place in which he resides, provided he has lived at least one year continuously, immediately prior to the filing of such petition, in the state or territory in which such place is located. This petition must be signed by the petitioner in his own handwriting and shall give his full name, place of residence, occupation, place of birth and the date thereof, the place from which he emigrated, and the date and place of his arrival in the United States. If such arrival occurred subsequent to the passage of the act of June 29, 1906, he must secure a certificate from the Department of Labor showing the fact of such arrival and the date and place thereof, for filing with the clerk of the court to be attached to his petition. If he is married he must state the name of his wife and, if possible, the country of her nativity and her place of residence at the time of the filing of his petition, and, if he has children, the name, date and place of birth and present place of residence of each living child. The petition must set forth that he is not a believer in or opposed to organized government, or a member of or affiliated with any organization or body of persons teaching disbelief in or opposition to organized government; that he is not a polygamist or a believer in the practice of polygamy, and that he absolutely and forever renounces all allegiance and fidelity to any foreign country of which he may, at the time of filing such petition, be a citizen or subject. This petition must be verified at the time it is filed by the affidavit of two credible witnesses, who are citizens of the United States and who shall state that they have known the petitioner during his entire residence in the state in which the petition is filed, which must be not less than one year, and that they have known him to be a resident of the United States continuously during the five years immediately preceding the filing of the petition; that during such time he acted as a man of good moral character, attached to the principles of the Constitution of the United States and well disposed to the good order and happiness of the same. If a portion of the five years has been passed by the petitioner in some other state than that in which he resides at the time of filing his petition the affidavit of the witness may verify so much of the petitioner's residence as has been passed in the state, and the portion of said five years' residence out of the state may be shown by depositions at the time of hearing on the petition,

No petition may be heard until the expiration of at least ninety days after it is filed nor within thirty days preceding a general election. At the hearing upon a petition, which shall be a date fixed by order of the court, the witnesses are required to again attend and testify in open court so that the judge or judges thereof may be satisfied that the petitioner is qualified and that he has complied with all the requirements of the law.

An alien who has borne a hereditary title or been a member of an order or nobility must renounce such title or position expressly before becoming naturalized. No alien may become naturalized, if physically capable, who does not speak the English language.

Aliens who are admitted to citizenship by order in open court will be required to take the oath of allegiance and thereafter will be entitled to a certificate of naturalization.

The law also provides as to those persons who, though not citizens, owe permanent allegiance to the United States, and who may become citizens of any state or organized territory of the United States, that they may be naturalized upon compliance with all the requirements of the law, except that they will not be called upon to renounce allegiance to any foreign sovereignty.

At the time of filing his declaration of intention an alien is required to pay to the clerk of the court a fee of one dollar. At the time of filing a petition for naturalization a petitioner is required to pay to the clerk of the court a fee of four dollars.

The naturalization of Chinamen is expressly prohibited by Sec. 14, Chap. 126, Laws of 1882.

Naturalization:

Act on subject of uniform rule of, vetoed, 508.

Discussed by President—
Adams, John, 248.
Arthur, 4715, 4828.
Buchanan, 3171.
Cleveland, 4921, 5090, 5366, 5370.
Grant, 3990, 4193, 4245, 4299, 4359.
Harrison, Benj., 5472, 5478, 5551.
Jefferson, 319.
Johnson, 3715, 3778.
Lincoln, 3381.
Madison, 508, 559.
Roosevelt, 6788, 6790, 6915, 6917, 6935, 7002, 7003, 7055.
Taft, 7372, 7543, 7689.
Washington, 58.

Frauds in, 4245, 4299, 4359, 6916.
Germany, 4419, 4520, 4625, 4916, 5084, 5471, 5869.
Russia, 5961.
Switzerland, 4715, 6337.
Turkey, 4920, 5089, 5872, 5962, 6337.

Treaty regarding, with—
Austria-Hungary, 4069, 4098, 4142.
Bavaria, 3888.
Belgium, 3892.
Denmark, 4160, 4193.
Ecuador, 4119, 4193.
Germany, 3828, 3829, 3830, 3888.
Questions arising under, referred to, 4419, 4520, 4625, 4916, 5084, 5471, 5869.

Great Britain, 3894, 3956, 4014, 4056, 4077.
Prussia, 3827.
Sweden and Norway, 4033, 4142.
Turkey, 4258, 5398.
Question arising out of, 4920, 5089, 5878, 5962, 6337.
Württemberg, 3997.

Naturalization, Federal Bureau of, recommended, 7002.

Naturalization Laws:

Laws regarding expatriation and election of nationality, discussed, 3656, 3778, 4193, 4245, 4300, 4359, 4921. (See also Impressment; Naturalized Citizens.)

Revision of, recommended, 58, 60, 248, 319, 508, 559, 4359, 4828, 4921, 5090, 5370, 5478, 6240, 6789, 6790, 6916, 6917, 6935, 7002, 7003, 7055.

Naturalization of Filipinos, 7689.

Naturalized Citizens (see also Aliens):

Address to, 8066.

Allegiance of, to native government discussed, 3778.

Bureau of registration of. (See Registration Bureau.)

Distinctions not to be recognized between native citizens and, 3172.

Duties of citizenship evaded by, discussed, 5370.

Impressed into military service of foreign countries, 3121, 3656, 6425.

By France, discussed and referred to, 3171, 3715, 5199, 5366.
Italy, referred to, 5673.
Prussia, discussed and referred to, 3120, 3123, 3715, 3778.

Returning to native country and claiming citizenship in United States, discussed, 3381, 3990, 4193, 4245, 4299.

Nautical Almanac.—The Ephemeral and Nautical Almanac of the United States Navy Department was first published in 1853. It contains tables indicating the rising and the setting of the sun, moon and stars, with various astronomical observations of importance to mariners, including announcements of eclipses. It contains data for finding latitude and longitude, and its ephemerides are calculated for both the meridian of Washington and the meredian of Greenwich. It is published three years in advance of the year with which it deals, so that all the information it contains may be used on the longest voyages. (See Navigation.)

Navajo Indians. (See Indian Tribes.)

Naval Academy. (See Navy, Department of.)

Naval Academy.—An institution for the training of naval officers, founded at Annapolis, Md., in 1845, through the efforts of George Bancroft, then Secretary of the Navy. The Academy was not established by formal legislation of Congress, but was opened in October, 1845, under orders from the Secretary of the Navy. It was not until Aug. 10, 1846, that Congress took any action toward the encouragement of the enterprise. At that time $28,000 was appropriated for repairs, improvement and instruction, and the following year a like sum was appropriated. In 1850 the school was reorganized and the name changed to the United States Naval Academy. At the outbreak of the Civil War the Academy was removed to Newport, R. I., where it remained until the summer of 1865, when it was re-established at Annapolis.

The Naval Academy is under the jurisdiction of the Bureau of Navigation of the Navy Department and in the immediate control of an academic board, consisting of a superintendent, who is a naval officer; a commandant of cadets, and the heads of the different departments of study, who are, with one exception, naval officers.

The students of the Naval Academy are called Midshipmen. Two Midshipmen are allowed for each Senator, Representative and Delegate in Congress, two for the District of Columbia, and five each year from the United States at large. The appointments from the District of Columbia and five each year at large are made by the President. One Midshipman is allowed from Porto Rico, who must be a native of that island. The appointment is made by the President, on the recommendation of the Governor of Porto Rico. The Congressional appointments are equitably distributed, so that as soon as practicable each Senator, Representative and Delegate in Congress may appoint one Midshipman during each Congress.

The course for Midshipmen is four years at the Academy, when the succeeding appointment is made, and the examination for graduation takes place. Midshipmen who pass the examination for graduation are appointed to fill vacancies in the lower grade of the Line of the Navy, in the order of merit as determined by the Academic Board of the Naval Academy.

The act of June 29, 1906, prescribes that the Secretary of the Navy shall, as soon as possible after June 1 of each year preceding the graduation of Midshipmen in the succeeding year, notify in writing each Senator, Representative and Delegate in Congress of any vacancy that will exist at the Naval Academy because of such graduation, and which he shall be entitled to fill by nomination of a candidate and one or more alternates therefor. The nomination of candidate and alternate or alternates to fill said vacancy shall be made upon the recommendation of the Senator, Representative or Delegate, if such recommendation is made by March 4th of the year following that in which said notice in writing is given, but if it is not made by that time the Secretary of the Navy shall fill the vacancy by appointment of an actual resident of the State, Congressional District or Territory, as the case may be, in which the vacancy will exist, who shall have been for at least two years immediately preceding the date of his appointment an actual and bona fide resident of the State, Congressional District or Territory in which the vacancy will exist, and of the legal qualification under the law as now provided.

Candidates allowed for Congressional Districts, for Territories, and for the District of Columbia must be actual residents. Candidates at the time of their examination must be physically sound, well formed and of robust constitution. Attention will also be paid to the stature of the candidate, and no one manifestly under size for his age will be received at the Academy. The height of candidates for admission shall

not be less than 5 feet 2 inches between the ages of 16 and 18 years, and not less than 5 feet 4 inches between the ages of 18 and 20 years; and the minimum weight at 16 years of age shall be 100 pounds, with an increase of not less than 5 pounds for each additional year or fraction of a year over one-half. Any marked deviation in the relative height and weight to the age of a candidate will add materially to the consideration for rejection. Candidates must be unmarried, and any Midshipman who shall marry, or who shall be found to be married, before his graduation, shall be dismissed from the service. All candidates must, at the time of their examination for admission, be between the ages of 16 and 20 years. The pay of a Midshipman is $600, beginning at the date of admission. The regulations regarding places and times of examinations and subjects of examinations may be obtained by addressing the Chief of the Bureau of Navigation, Navy Department, Washington.

The Sixty-third Congress, upon the recommendation of the Navy Department, continued the law which had expired by limitation providing for the appointment of two midshipmen by each member of Congress, and the Sixty-fourth Congress, as the first act in larger preparedness, passed the bill giving three appointments to each Senator or Representative. This made possible an increase of 531 midshipmen in a year.

President Wilson signed, Feb. 16, the first of the national defense bills. One increased the entrance class at the Naval Academy.

Naval Academy:

Address to class of 1914 by President Wilson, 7949.

Appropriation for paving sidewalk at, recommended, 4671.

Board of Visitors to, report of, referred to, 3587.

Discussed, 2669, 3386.

Establishment of, recommended, 876.

Instruction at, should be more practical, 7117.

Removal of, discussed, 3561.

Reorganization of, discussed, 2713.

Naval Aeronautics.—The d i v i s i o n of Naval Aeronautics in the Navy Department investigates and develops in particular the use of air-craft from the decks of vessels and from the surface of the seas. (See Aeronautics; Navy; Navy Department.)

Naval Auxiliary Reserve. (See Naval Reserve.)

Naval Coast Defence Reserve. (See Naval Reserve.)

Naval Code. (See Code.)

Naval Code, revision of, 2625.

Naval Communications Service. (See Radio Service.)

Naval Consulting Board.—The Naval Consulting Board was organized in July, 1915, by Secretary of Navy Josephus Daniels. It is composed of members selected by the leading scientific societies of the United States, and it is headed and directed by Thomas A. Edison. Although it advises the Navy Department on all matters of importance in the development of the Navy, it is concerned especially with new inventions, which it investigates and on which it reports, and with plans for industrial preparation for naval purposes, in which work it is assisted by branch committees in all the states of the Union. It also conducts a laboratory in experimental and research work, in order to study all new developments in naval warfare. The personnel of the Board at its organization was as follows: Thomas A. Edison, Lawrence Addicks, A. L. H. Baekeland, H. E. Coffin, Alfred Craven, W. L. Emmett, Cooper Hewitt, A. M. Hunt, B. G. Lamme, Hudson Maxim, Spencer Miller, J. W. Richards, A. L. Riker, Thomas Robins, W. L. Saunders, M. B. Sellers, E. A. Sperry, F. J. Sprague, B. B. Thayer, A. G. Webster, W. R. Whitney, H. A. W. Wood, R. S. Woodward. (See Navy; Navy Department.)

Naval Courts of Inquiry, 892.

Naval Expeditions. (See Arctic Expeditions; Exploring Expeditions.)

Naval Militia.—In 1888 Congress passed an act authorizing the maritime states to organize a naval reserve, to be trained and fitted for operating the coast and harbor defense vessels, etc., in time of war, thus liberating the regular naval force to man the heavy seagoing war ships, etc. Massachusetts was the first state to pass laws providing for such organization. New York took similar action, and by 1898 most of the maritime states had regularly organized naval militia. The first appropriation for the equipment of the force was $25,-000, made by Congress in 1891. The naval militia is now organized in twenty-two states and in the District of Columbia.

The reported strength in 1913 was 586 commissioned officers, 32 warrant officers, 1,639 petty officers and 5,269 enlisted men, a total of 7,526.

All matters relating to the Naval Militia come under the cognizance of the Assistant Secretary of the Navy, who transacts all business with the Naval Militia through the Governors and Adjutants-General (or Quartermasters-General) of the states. The officer in the Navy Department, Washington, having charge of Naval Militia matters is Commander F. B. Bassett, Jr., U. S. N.

Naval Militia, development of, discussed, 5759, 6166, 6669.

Naval Observatory.—A division of the Bureau of Equipment of the Navy Department. Its functions are to determine accurately the positions of the sun, moon, planets and the earth for use in preparing the *Nautical Almanac;* to test chronometers and to issue correct time daily; to distribute to vessels of the navy instruments of precision for navigating purposes; to conduct astronomical investigations of general and special scientific interest, and, since 1894, to publish the *Nautical Almanac.*

In 1830 the Navy Department established a depot of charts and instruments in charge of Lieutenant L. M. Goldsborough, and he mounted a 3-inch transit instrument. In 1833 Lieutenant Wilkes moved the depot to a site on Capitol Hill, and at his own expense built an observatory containing a transit instrument of 3¾ inches aperture and 63 inches focal length; a Borda's circle; a 3½-foot achromatic portable telescope; a portable transit instrument; and a sidereal clock. In 1838 the Secretary of the Navy granted authority for the purchase of all necessary supplies for making a constant series of observations in astronomy, magnetism and meteorology, and detailed naval officers to the work under the instructions of Lieut. J. M. Gilliss.

The new equipment then installed consisted of a sidereal clock and a mean time clock; a meridian circle of 5.5 inches aperture furnished with a circle 30 inches in diameter; a portable achromatic telescope of 3¼ inches aperture and 42 inches focal length. Berlin, Paris, Greenwich and Vienna presented some 200 rare volumes of the highest standard as the nucleus for an astronomical library. The work done at Capitol Hill between 1838 and 1842 was published as *Astronomical Observations Made at the Naval Observatory,* being the first American work of this nature.

In 1842 Congress, through the efforts of Lieut. Gilliss, authorized the erection of a new observatory. Lieut. Maury was placed in charge of the new establishment and gained an international reputation through his studies of ocean currents and other hydrographic and nautical subjects. He was succeeded in 1861 by Lieut. Gilliss and later by Charles H. Davis and John Rodgers.

Among the earliest scientific achievements of the new observatory were the observations of the planet Neptune, secured in 1846, immediately after its discovery, which enabled Sears C. Walker, by identifying two older foreign observations, to discuss the elements of Neptune during his short connection with the observatory. The adaptation of electricity to record observations by Prof. John Locke, formerly lieutenant in the navy, resulted in the installation of the first practical chronograph at the observatory in 1849. With the 9.6-inch equatorial Assistant Astronomer James Ferguson discovered several planetoids between 1854 and 1860. With the 26-inch refractor (made by Alvan Clark), at that time the largest telescope in the world, Prof. Asaph Hall discovered the moons of Mars in 1877. This instrument was set in place in time to observe the transit of Venus in 1874.

The present observatory buildings on the more favorable site of Georgetown Heights were completed in 1893. They comprise a commodious office building occupied by the astronomical, nautical instrument, time service and *Nautical Almanac* departments, while the 26-inch equatorial, a 9-inch and a 6-inch transit circle, and a 5-inch prime vertical instrument are placed in suitable dome and houses to the south, east, west and north of a clock house, the longitude of which is 5h. 8m. 15.78s. west and the latitude 38° 55' 14" north. Besides the above-named instruments there are a 12-inch equatorial, a 6-inch altazimuth, a 5-inch transit, a 5-inch photoheliograph.

Although one of the youngest among the great astronomical institutions, it has developed in a short time to a rank with those at Greenwich and Pulkowa. Its object is rather the development and application of the known facts of astronomy than the making of further discoveries. Professors Newcomb and Hall, of the older scientific staff of the institution, have recently been succeeded by Professors Skinner, See, Updegraph, Eichelberger, Littell and Harschmann. The library now contains some 22,-000 volumes and stands second to Pulkowa only.

Naval Observatory:

Estimates for observation of transit of Venus, referred to, 4668.

Appropriation for, recommended, 4688.

Referred to, 4249.

Removal of, recommended, 5158.

(See also Navy, Department of.)

Naval Officers. (See Navy.)

Naval Order of the United States.—
Composed of a General Commandery and
commanderies in the States of Massachusetts, Pennsylvania, New York, California
and Illinois, and in the District of Columbia. The General Commandery meets triennially on Oct. 5th, and the State Commanderies meet annually in the month of
November. The Massachusetts Commandery
is the parent Commandery, and was organized at Boston on July 4, 1890. The General Commandery was established three
years later, on June 19, 1893. The Companies of the Order are officers and the
descendants of officers who served in the
navy and marine corps in any war or in
any battle in which the said naval forces
of the United States have participated.
The membership clause, as adopted at the
triennial congress held at Boston, Oct. 5,
1895, provides for two classes of members:
First, veteran officers and their male descendants; and, second, enlisted men who
have received the United States naval medal
of honor for bravery in the face of the
enemy.

Naval Parade, to be held in New York
Harbor, 5760.

Naval Peace Establishment. (See Navy.)

Naval Pension Fund. (See Pensions.)

Naval Reserve.—By act of Congress, approved August 29, 1916, provision was made
for the establishment of a naval reserve in
the United States Navy. Under this head,
the act created six classes of service: Fleet
Naval Reserve, Naval Reserve, Naval Auxiliary Reserve, Naval Coast Defence Reserve,
Volunteer Naval Reserve, and Naval Reserve Flying Corps. The same act also
provided for the establishment of a Marine
Corps Reserve. The legislation provides for
a naval reserve force embracing all former
officers and men of the navy now in civil
life, the officers and men of the merchant
marine, and civilians capable of serving the
navy in connection with the defense of the
coasts. After 16 or 20 years of service,
enlisted men may transfer from the active
list to the Naval Reserve. It is estimated
that at the time of the passage of the act,
it provided for a reserve force of 20,000
men, and that after a few years that number
will have increased to 30,000 men.

*Pay.—*In the Fleet Naval Reserve, officers
receive 2 months' base pay of their rank;
and men of 4 years' service, $50 a year;
men of 8 years' service, $72 a year; and
men of 12 years' service, $100 a year. Pay
is increased 25% for each enlistment. In
the Naval Auxiliary Reserve, officers receive
1 month's base pay of their rank, and
men 2 months' base pay of their rating,
with a 25% increase for each enrollment.
Men in the Volunteer Naval Reserve receive
no pay. In all other classes, officers and
men receive 2 months' base pay of their
rank or rating. Enlisted men who transfer
to the Naval Reserve after 16 or 20 years'
service receive between $40 and $60 per
month.

*Service.—*Members of the Naval Reserve
may be ordered into actual service in the
Navy by the President in time of war or
national emergency. Enrollment and re-
enrollment are for terms of four years, but
in times of peace or of no national emergency
members of the Naval Reserve shall be discharged at their request, provided that they
reimburse the Government for any clothing
gratuities which may have been furnished
them during their enrollment. Members
upon enlisting are assigned ranks according

to their qualifications for service, which are
determined by examinations. In time of
actual service, all members of the Naval
Reserve shall be subject to the same regulations as apply to the enlisted men in the
Navy, and their pay during time of actual
service shall be equal to that of enlisted
men and officers in the regular service of
the Navy of corresponding grade.

*Divisions.—*In the Fleet Naval Reserve,
all former officers, including midshipmen, of
the Naval Service, who have been honorably
discharged after not less than one four-year
term of enlistment, are eligible. In the
Naval Reserve, men between the ages of
eighteen and thirty-five who have followed
the sea-going profession are eligible. In the
Naval Auxiliary Reserve, those eligible are
men who have been or who are engaged on
vessels of the American merchant marine
which have been listed by the Navy Department as suitable for service in time of war.
The Naval Coast Defence Reserve is reserved for those citizens who may be of
especial value to the Navy Department in
connection with the defense of the coasts.
Those citizens who are willing to serve in
the Naval Reserve without retainer pay and
uniform gratuity in time of peace are eligible
to the Volunteer Naval Reserve. The Naval
Reserve Flying Corps is composed of those
persons who are skilled in the designing,
building, or operating of aircraft. The
Marine Corps Reserve is divided into classes
corresponding to the first five classes listed
above.

Naval Reserve Flying Corps. (See
Naval Reserve.)

Naval Reserve, National, establishment
recommended, 6669.

Naval Stations.—Naval bases or shore
stations are ports on home or foreign
shores owned or leased by the government,
where fuel and supplies are stored, and
which are regularly visited by vessels on
cruise. Recruiting and instruction are also
carried on at these stations, and they form
the bases for sea manœuvres. Following
are the locations of the permanent stations
at home and abroad:

Annapolis, Md. (naval academy); Balti-
more, Md. (recruiting station); Boston,
Mass. (yard and recruiting station);
Charleston, S. C. (yard and barracks);
Great Lakes, Ill. (training station); Indian
Head (proving ground); Key West, Fla.;
Las Animas, Colo. (hospital); Mare Island,
Cal. (yard, barracks, prison, iron works);
Narragansett Bay, R. I. (training station);
New York, N. Y. (Brooklyn yard); Nor-
folk, Va. (Newport News yard); Philippine
Islands (Olongapo, Cavite, Canacao);
Panama (Canal Zone); Pensacola, Fla.;
Philadelphia, Pa. (recruiting station, home,
hospital, etc.); Port Royal, S. C. (dis-
ciplinary barracks); Portsmouth, N. H.
(yard, iron works, hospital, etc.); Puget
Sound (Bremerton, Wash., dock, etc.); San
Francisco, Cal.; Washington, D. C. (ad-
ministrative dept.); Guam; Guantanamo,
Cuba; Hawaii, H. I.; Tutuila, Samoa;
Yokohama, Japan.

Naval Stations:

Establishment of—

Discussed, 4573, 4586.

In West Indies, recommended, 3777.

Lands for. (See Lands, Public.)

Survey for, mentioned, 1038.

(See also Navy Yards and Docks.)

Naval War College.—A course of lectures on and instruction in the manipula-

tion of torpedoes established by the Government at Coasters Harbor Island, Newport, R. I., in 1889. The class consists chiefly of officers and men in the torpedo service, but lectures are delivered on all branches of naval improvements and progress. The course continues three months in each year.

Naval War College, discussed, 6166.
(See also Navy, Department of.)

Navassa Island, West Indies:
Occupation of, by American citizens, referred to, 3120.
Recognition of, as appertaining to United States, referred to, 5625.
Trial of laborers in, charged with killing agents of Navassa Phosphate Co., discussed, 5625.

Navassa Phosphate Co., trial of laborers charged with killing agents of, in Navassa Island, discussed, 5625.

Navies of the World.—Compiled from the latest available data.

Laws of, having tendency to prolong War of 1812, should be revised, 525.
Prosperous condition of, 2404.
Referred to, 74, 77, 78, 81, 95, 227, 318, 346, 470, 480, 559, 2571.
Treaty with Spain regarding, 106, 110, 164.
Utility of canal, explained, 482, 785.

Navigation Act.—An important move in England's struggle with the Dutch for possession of the carrying trade of the world. The act was first promulgated in 1645, amplified in 1650, and renewed with a few changes by Charles II. in 1660. It related to five subjects—coasting trade, fisheries, commerce with the colonies, commerce with European countries, and commerce with Asia, Africa and America. The clauses of importance to American history were those providing that all colonial trade should be carried on in ships built and owned in England and the colonies and that in the case of many specified goods trade should

Powers	Modern Battleships	Cruiser Battleships	Older Battleships	First-Class Cruisers	Second-Class Cruisers	Third-Class Cruisers	Gunboats	Monitors	Destroyers	Torpedo Boats	Submarines	Personnel Officers and Men
Great Britain	29	10	38	42	37	33	10	..	227	58	85	*137,500
Germany a	19	7	20	9	6	39	7	..	141	47	30	‡66,783
United States	14	..	25	5	5	15	28	9	62	27	50	†64,780
France	17	..	15	18	4	9	6	..	87	173	15	60,621
Japan	9	5	13	12	10	9	5	..	60	54	15	**51,054
Russia	9	4	8	6	6	3	8	..	105	23	48	52,463
Italy	8	..	8	7	3	10	5	..	35	73	20	33,095
Austria-Hungary	4	..	9	3	2	7	3	..	18	53	15	17,581
Brazil	2	..	1	..	5	2	19	..	10	4	3	8,000
Argentina	2	..	..	4	3	1	4	..	10	8	..	9,836
Sweden	..	..	..	1	..	..	9	..	8	51	7	5,715
Netherlands	..	..	6	..	9	2	4	..	8	33	8	11,164
Norway	..	..	..	1	4	..	16	2	3	26	5	1,003
Chile	2	..	1	..	1	2	2	..	13	6	2	10,000
Denmark	..	..	1	..	1	..	4	3	..	15	3	4,000
Spain	3	..	1	..	1	8	..	..	7	26	..	10,165
Portugal	..	..	1	..	..	6	19	..	2	7	2	6,000
Greece	..	1	3	..	..	..	8	3	12	10	2	4,000
Turkey	2	1	3	2	2	1	2	2	10	8	..	30,000
China	..	..	..	..	..	1	..	..	..	10	..	..
Mexico	..	..	..	5	..	..	..	..	2	..	..	1,200
Siam	..	..	1	..	..	..	..	..	..	..	..	5,100

* Naval Reserve seamen, 26,200. † Naval militia, 7,526 men. ‡ Reserve of 110,000 men. ** Reserve of 114,000 men. a The Imperial German Navy is the second in respect of tonnage and armament, and is only exceeded by the British Navy, the additions made from time to time, under a settled plan of development, actually exceeding, in some years, those made by the United Kingdom (1909, German warships launched amounted to 83,184 tons; British, 92,957 tons; 1910, German, 101,830 tons; British, 176,582 tons)

Navigation:
Accidents in, resulting from criminal negligence in use of steam power, discussed, 1253.
Advancement in science of nautical affairs, 2670.
Appropriation for improvement of, recommended, 2666.
Bridges so constructed over waters as to obstruct, discussed, 4934.
Depressed state of, 559.
Extension of laws of, etc., referred to, 2544.

be confined to English markets. The former clause acted as a powerful stimulant to colonial shipbuilding. The act was rendered largely inoperative by the prevalence of smuggling, and the efforts of Great Britain to enforce it were among the leading causes of the Revolution.

Navigation, Bureau of, Navy Department. (See Bureau of Navigation.)

Navigation Laws.—The Constitution gives Congress power to pass navigation laws in accordance with the principles of international law. By act of 1789 a tonnage tax of 6 cents per ton was levied on all American vessels and one of 50 cents a ton on all vessels built and owned in foreign countries and entering American ports, which practically gave a monopoly of American trade to American bottoms. In 1792 the act requiring American registration was passed. In 1793 the coasting trade was closed to foreign vessels. In 1816, 1817 and 1820 the American navigation laws were remodeled and made to correspond closely to those of Great Britain. Tonnage taxes, which had been abolished, were renewed at the outbreak of the Civil War. With the advent of iron vessels came the decrease in American shipbuilding and the decrease in the American marine was further due to the law forbidding any but American-built ships to fly the American flag. This restriction was, however, modified by the act of 1892. The act of 1886 reduced the tonnage rates considerably. (See Seamen's Act.)

Navigators Islands. (See Samoan Islands.)

Navy.—During the Revolution this country had practically no navy. In September, 1775, the British troops, closely environed in Boston, could receive supplies only by water. To intercept these Washington detailed certain of his officers and men who were familiar with nautical matters to patrol Boston Harbor in small armed cruisers. Some of the states had already constructed vessels at public expense to protect their coast line. New England seamen cruised with such effect in Massachusetts Bay as not only to deprive the British garrisoned in Boston of their necessary supplies, but also to add to the resources of the Continental Army by the capture of numerous prizes. At the end of 1775 the Continental Congress began the construction of a navy by ordering thirteen frigates to be built. These performed some service, but most of the achievements of the war were by privateers. By 1781 all of the thirteen Federal vessels had been either captured or destroyed.

In 1797 and 1798, in anticipation of war with France, Congress authorized the construction of the *Constitution, United States,* and *Constellation* and the purchase of twenty-four other vessels. Hostilities with France having been averted, the newly acquired navy was used with good effect in resisting the Barbary States. At the outbreak of the War of 1812 the United States had about a score of vessels, three of them being first-class frigates—the *Constitution*, the *President*, and the *United States*—as against England's 830. The brilliant achievements of American vessels in that war secured increased appropriations. In 1816 $1,000,000 annually for eight years was appropriated.

By the law of 1819 the Navy was largely increased and a resolution provided for naming ships of the line after the states, frigates after the rivers of the United States, and sloop of war after the chief cities and towns. The vessels were divided among four squadrons and stationed in the Mediterranean, the Pacific, the West Indies, and on the coast of Brazil, and in 1841 an additional squadron was ordered to cruise along the coast of the United States. During the Mexican War the Gulf Squadron blockaded Vera Cruz and bombarded the fort of San Juan de Ulloa into submission, while the Pacific Squadron seized Monterey and Los Angeles, Cal.

At the outbreak of the Civil War the United States had only about forty vessels in commission. The character of naval warfare at this time had been changed by improved armament. The old wooden

vessels were useless when opposed by the Whitworth and other modern guns of long range and heavy caliber. The turreted ironclad was born of the emergency. A new navy had to be constructed in order to maintain the blockade of Southern ports, and by Jan. 1, 1864, the National Government had over 600 vessels, seventy-five of them ironclads, with more than 4,600 guns and 35,000 men. After the war the Navy was reduced. Notwithstanding the appropriation of large sums of money, 1882 found the United States in possession of only 140 vessels, and more than 100 of these were incapable of sea service.

Soon after this date a new policy regarding the Navy was inaugurated and has since been pursued with credit and honor to the nation.

The most important navy yard is at Brooklyn, on the East River, where there are four dry docks, a clothing factory where naval uniforms are made for enlisted men, and other adjuncts. (See Navy Yards and Naval Stations.)

The officers of the navy are trained for their profession at the United States Naval Academy at Annapolis (which see).

Target Practice.—So necessary is target practice considered for the efficiency of the United States Navy that there exists a separate division of Target Practice in the Navy Department (q. v.). Up to 1903, target practice in the Navy was at the short range of about a mile, as naval experts were almost unanimous in the opinion that naval battles could never be fought at distances greater than two or three miles. The range of target practice was gradually increased until the outbreak of the European War showed that naval battles could be fought at great distances, and in recent target practices of the United States Navy the range has been thousands of yards. In the practices off Guantanamo in February, 1916, the ships of the Navy averaged 11% of hits at battle distance. Ships of the dreadnaught class, aiming at screen targets 90 feet long and 30 feet high, made 7% of hits at long battle distance and 21% of hits at mean battle distance. Secretary of the Navy Daniels reports that these records are believed not only to have equalled, but even to have bettered the best records made in the European War.

Salutes.—It is the custom of foreign ships of war entering the harbor, or in passing in the vicinity of a fort, to hoist at the fore the flag of the country in whose waters they are and salute it; on the completion of the salute to the flag, a salute (of twenty-one guns) is returned as soon as possible by the nearest fort or battery; if there are several forts or batteries in sight, or within the radius of six miles, the principal fort returns the salute. The Presidential salute of twenty-one guns was adopted that a uniformity in national salutes might be maintained, it being the same number of guns as the royal salute of England. The reason why twenty-one should have been selected as the number of guns has been a source of search and guess, with no satisfactory results. Of the many surmises, the two carrying the most weight of opinion are: First, that twenty-one was the same number of years fixed by English law as the age of majority; the second, that seven was the original salute, and three times seven would signify one seven for each of the divisions, England and Wales, Scotland, and Ireland. It is also asserted that the United States adopted this salute to signify to the mother country that her child had reached its majority, and was prepared, in law, to

INSIGNIA OF RANK OF OFFICERS OF THE U. S. NAVY

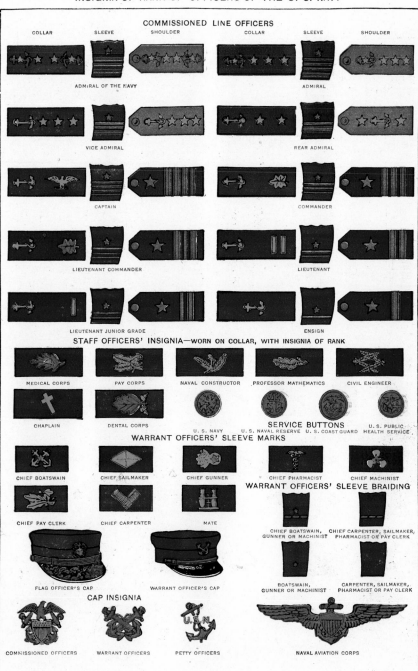

COMMISSIONED LINE OFFICERS

COLLAR   SLEEVE   SHOULDER   COLLAR   SLEEVE   SHOULDER

ADMIRAL OF THE NAVY   ADMIRAL

VICE ADMIRAL   REAR ADMIRAL

CAPTAIN   COMMANDER

LIEUTENANT COMMANDER   LIEUTENANT

LIEUTENANT JUNIOR GRADE   ENSIGN

STAFF OFFICERS' INSIGNIA—WORN ON COLLAR, WITH INSIGNIA OF RANK

MEDICAL CORPS   PAY CORPS   NAVAL CONSTRUCTOR   PROFESSOR MATHEMATICS   CIVIL ENGINEER

CHAPLAIN   DENTAL CORPS

SERVICE BUTTONS

U. S. NAVY   U. S. NAVAL RESERVE   U. S. COAST GUARD   U. S. PUBLIC HEALTH SERVICE

WARRANT OFFICERS' SLEEVE MARKS

CHIEF BOATSWAIN   CHIEF SAILMAKER   CHIEF GUNNER   CHIEF PHARMACIST   CHIEF MACHINIST

CHIEF PAY CLERK   CHIEF CARPENTER   MATE

WARRANT OFFICERS' SLEEVE BRAIDING

CHIEF BOATSWAIN, GUNNER OR MACHINIST   CHIEF CARPENTER, SAILMAKER, PHARMACIST OR PAY CLERK

FLAG OFFICER'S CAP   WARRANT OFFICER'S CAP

BOATSWAIN, GUNNER OR MACHINIST   CARPENTER, SAILMAKER, PHARMACIST OR PAY CLERK

CAP INSIGNIA

COMMISSIONED OFFICERS   WARRANT OFFICERS   PETTY OFFICERS

NAVAL AVIATION CORPS

PETTY OFFICERS' RATING BADGES AND SPECIALTY MARKS

WORN ON SLEEVES OF COATS, OVERSHIRTS AND JUMPERS

THE NUMBER OF CHEVRONS INDICATE THE CLASS OF PETTY OFFICER. THE DISTINGUISHING MARK ABOVE THE CHEVRONS INDICATES THE PARTICULAR BRANCH TO WHICH THE PETTY OFFICER BELONGS

CHIEF MASTER-AT-ARMS

BOATSWAIN'S MATE, FIRST CLASS

GUNNER'S MATE, SECOND CLASS

QUARTERMASTER, THIRD CLASS

MASTER-AT-ARMS | BOATSWAIN'S MATE | QUARTERMASTER | BLACKSMITH | TURRET CAPT. | CARPENTER'S MATE | GUNNER'S MATE | STOREKEEPER

YEOMAN | SAILMAKER'S MATE | PRINTER | ELECTRICIAN | MACHINIST'S MATE | HOSPITAL CORPS | MUSICIAN | COMMISSARY STEWARD

SEAMAN GUNNER | RADIO OPERATOR | GUN CAPTAIN | GUN POINTER, U. S. M. C. | TORPEDOMAN | COOK | EX-APPRENTICE

GUN POINTER, FIRST CLASS | NAVY E | GUN POINTER | BUGLER | EXPERT RIFLEMAN | ENLISTED MEN, NAVAL MILITIA | QUARTERMASTER AVIATION CORPS

CARPENTER, AVIATION CORPS | DRUMMER, U. S. M. C. | MACHINIST, AVIATION CORPS

MISCELLANEOUS INSIGNIA

U. S. NAVAL MILITIA | MIDSHIPMEN | U. S. COAST GUARD

COMMANDER | FIRST CLASS | SECOND CLASS | THIRD CLASS | FOURTH CLASS | SENIOR CAPTAIN

U. S. MARINE CORPS | LIGHTHOUSE SERVICE | COAST AND GEODETIC SURVEY | PUBLIC HEALTH SERVICE

MAJOR GENERAL COMMANDANT | MAJOR | FIRST LIEUTENANT | CHIEF ENGINEER | GRADE 2 | GRADE 1 | SURGEON GENERAL | SURGEON

MISCELLANEOUS CAP DEVICES

COAST GUARD | MARINE CORPS | LIGHTHOUSE SERVICE | COAST AND GEODETIC SURVEY | PUBLIC HEALTH SERVICE | RED CROSS

AIR PLANE DISTINGUISHING MARKS

Y. M. C. A. SLEEVE MARK | UNITED STATES | GREAT BRITAIN | FRANCE | KNIGHTS OF COLUMBUS SLEEVE MARK inherit the land; and to this end fired the "gun of 1776," the figures of which year added together equal twenty-one. The salutes given in addition to the Presidential salute are as follows: To the Vice-President of the United States and the President of the Senate, 19 guns; members of Cabinet, Chief Justice of United States, Speaker of the House of Representatives, 17 guns; rear-admiral, 13 guns; commodore, 11 guns; captain, 9 guns; to a sovereign or chief magistrate of any foreign country, 21 guns; to the heir apparent or consort of a reigning sovereign, 21 guns. A salute in accordance with their rank is also given to the viceroy, governor-general or governors of provinces belonging to foreign states, to ambassadors extraordinary and plenipotentiary, to envoys extraordinary and plenipotentiary, to ministers resident accredited to the United States, to chargés d'affaires in charge of any missions in the United States, to consuls-general accredited to the United States, and to officers of foreign services.

The war with Spain brought the importance of the navy into prominence, and resulted in a general desire for its enlargement, for it became evident that if this country should be attacked by a foreign power, that attack would be by sea; and the true method of defense would be by means of a navy that could meet the enemy, pursue and destroy them on the seas, not by means of mere harbor defenses. The rapidity of this enlargement can be judged by the comparative expenses. For the year ending June 30, 1897, the year before the war with Spain, the cost of the navy was $34,561,546; and for the year 1904 the cost was $102,956,102.

All officers paid under this table, below the rank of Rear-Admiral, are entitled to 10 per cent. increase upon the full yearly pay of their grades for each and every period of five years' service as "longevity pay," computed upon their total actual service in the Navy or Marine Corps, provided that the total amount of such increase shall not exceed 40 per cent. upon the full yearly pay of their grade.

All officers on sea duty and all officers on shore duty beyond the continental limits of the United States shall while so serving receive ten per centum additional of their salaries and increase as above provided, and such increase shall commence from reporting for duty on board ship or the date of sailing from the United States for shore duty beyond seas or to join a ship in foreign waters.

Warrant officers (boatswains, gunners, carpenters, sailmakers, pharmacists, machinists and pay clerks) are paid from $1,125 to $2,250 a year.

Commandants' clerks receive from $1,000 to $1,800 a year.

The present status of the vessels of the Navy is given in the following table:

SHIPS OF THE UNITED STATES NAVY—VESSELS BUILT.

BATTLESHIPS—FIRST LINE.

| Name | Displacement | Net tonnage for Suez Canal | Dimensions | | | Speed (trial) | Guns of 4 inches and over | Guns under 4 inches | Coal capacity bunkers (maximum), 42 cubic feet per ton | Date authorized |
			Length on L. W. L.	Beam on L. W. L.	Draft aft at designed full load					
	Tons	Tons	Ft. In.	Ft. In.	Ft. In.	Knots			Tons	
Arkansas	26,000		554 0	93 2½	29 7	21.05	33	4	2,754	Mar. 09
Delaware	20,000		510 0	85 2½	28 10	21.56	24	4	2,732	June 06
Florida	21,825		510 0	88 2½	30 1	22.08	26	4	2,560	May 08
New York	27,000		565 0	95 2½	29 7	21.47	31	4	2,918	June 10
North Dakota	20,000		510 0	85 2½	28 10	21.01	24	4	2,740	Mar. 07
Texas	27,000		565 0	95 2½	29 7	21.05	31	4	2,960	June 10
Utah	21,825		510 0	88 2½	30 1	21.04	26	4	2,581	May 08
Wyoming	26,000		554 0	93 2½	29 7	21.22	33	4	2,704	Mar. 09

BATTLESHIPS—SECOND LINE.

Name	Displacement	Net tonnage for Suez Canal	Length on L. W. L.	Beam on L. W. L.	Draft aft at designed full load	Speed (trial)	Guns of 4 inches and over	Guns under 4 inches	Coal capacity	Date authorized
Alabama	11,552	4,228	368 0	72 2½	24 9	17.01	18	8	1,481	June 92
Connecticut	16,000	5,877	450 0	76 10	26 8	18.78	24	22	2,510	July 09
Georgia	14,948	5,316	435 0	76 2½	25 10	19.26	24	16	2,014	Mar. 92
Illinois	11,552	4,270	368 0	72 2½	24 9	17.45	18	8	1,522	June 96
Indiana	10,288	3,204	348 0	69 3	26 5	15.55	12	16	1,535	June 96
Iowa	11,346	3,806	360 0	72 2½	27 4	17.09	22	4	1,682	July 90
Kansas	16,000	5,899	450 0	76 10	26 8	18.09	24	22	2,445	Mar. 03
Kearsarge	11,520	4,205	368 0	72 2½	24 11	16.82	26	4	1,679	Mar. 95
Kentucky	11,520	4,209	368 0	72 2½	24 11	16.90	26	4	1,658	Mar. 95
Louisiana	16,000	5,866	450 0	76 10	26 8	18.82	24	22	2,446	July 02
Maine	12,500	4,660	388 0	72 2½	25 6	18.00	20	10	1,908	May 98
Massachusetts	10,288	3,204	348 0	69 3	26 5	16.21	12	16	1,526	June 90
Michigan	16,000		450 0	80 2½	27 1	18.79	8	26	2,437	Mar. 05
Minnesota	16,000	5,882	450 0	76 10	26 8	18.85	24	22	2,420	Mar. 03
Missouri	12,500	4,460	388 0	72 2½	25 8	18.15	20	10	1,932	May 98
Nebraska	14,948	5,305	435 0	76 2½	25 10	19.06	24	16	1,969	Mar. 99
New Hampshire	16,000	5,738	450 0	76 10	27 0	18.16	24	22	2,653	Apr. 04
New Jersey	14,948	5,252	435 0	76 2½	25 10	19.18	24	15	1,993	June 00
Ohio	12,500	4,810	388 0	72 2½	25 4	17.82	20	10	2,331	May 98
Oregon	10,288	3,354	348 0	69 3	26 5	16.79	12	16	1,460	June 90
Rhode Island	14,948	5,252	435 0	76 2½	25 10	19.01	24	16	2,031	June 00
South Carolina	16,000		450 0	80 2½	27 1	18.86	8	26	2,433	Mar. 05
Vermont	16,000	5,861	450 0	76 10	26 8	18.33	24	22	2,486	Mar. 03
Virginia	14,948	5,272	435 0	76 2½	25 10	19.01	24	16	1,970	Mar. 99
Wisconsin	11,552	4,257	368 0	72 2½	24 9	17.17	18	8	1,447	June 96

SHIPS OF THE UNITED STATES NAVY—VESSELS BUILT—*Continued.*

Name	Dis-place-ment	Net tonnage for Suez Canal	Dimensions: Length on L. W. L.	Dimensions: Beam on L. W. L.	Dimensions: Draft aft at designed full load	Speed (trial)	Guns of 4 inches and over	Guns under 4 inches	Coal cap. bunker (maximum), 42 cubic feet per ton	Date authorized
	Tons	Tons	Ft. In.	Ft. In.	Ft. In.	Knots			Tons	
ARMORED CRUISERS										
Colorado	13,680	4,000	502 0	69 6½	26 1	22.24	18	22	1,976	June 00
Maryland	13,680	3,953	502 0	69 6½	26 1	22.41	18	22	2,098	June 00
Montana	14,500	4,509	502 0	72 10½	26 11	22.26	20	26	2,164	Apr. 04
North Carolina	14,500	4,509	502 0	72 10½	26 11	21.91	20	26	2,164	Apr. 04
Pittsburgh	13,680	4,000	502 0	69 6½	26 1	22.44	18	22	1,992	Mar. 99
San Diego	13,680	4,050	502 0	69 6½	26 1	22.20	18	22	2,233	Mar. 99
South Dakota	13,680	4,050	502 0	69 6½	26 1	22.24	18	22	2,233	June 00
Tennessee[2]	14,500	....	502 0	72 10½	26 11	22.16	20	26	2,084	July 02
Washington	14,500	....	502 0	72 10½	26 11	22.27	20	26	2,062	July 02
West Virginia	13,680	3,953	502 0	69 6½	26 1	22.15	18	22	2,098	Mar. 99
CRUISERS, FIRST CLASS										
Brooklyn	9,215	3,368	400 6	64 8	26 6	21.91	20	4	1,449	July 92
Charleston	9,700	....	424 0	66 0	24 10	22.04	14	22	1,818	June 00
Milwaukee	9,700	3,401	424 0	66 0	24 10	22.22	14	22	1,744	June 00
Saratoga	8,150	2,838	380 6	64 10	26 4	21.00	14	12	1,100	Sept. 88
St. Louis	9,700	....	424 0	66 0	24 10	22.13	14	22	1,793	June 00
CRUISERS, SECOND CLASS										
Chicago	4,500	1,560	325 0	48 2½	22 0	18.00	19	11	870	Mar. 83
Columbia	7,350	2,536	411 7	58 2	24 6	22.80	11	2	1,561	June 90
Minneapolis	7,350	2,537	411 7	58 2	24 6	23.07	11	2	1,433	Mar. 91
Olympia	5,865	1,896	340 0	53 0½	25 0	21.69	12	4	1,024	Sept. 88
CRUISERS, THIRD CLASS										
Albany	3,430	1,121	346 0	43 9	19 1	20.52	10	2	782	....
Birmingham	3,750	....	420 0	47 1	18 9	24.33	2	8	1,433	Apr. 04
Boston	3,000	1,280	277 5	42 2	20 10	15.60	6	6	438	Mar. 83
Chattanooga	3,200	....	292 0	44 0	17 0	16.65	10	8	739	Mar. 99
Chester	3,750	....	420 0	47 1	18 9	26.52	2	8	1,408	Apr. 04
Cincinnati	3,183	934	300 0	42 0	19 6	19.91	11	6	727	Sept. 88
Cleveland	3,200	....	292 0	44 0	17 0	16.45	10	8	737	Mar. 99
Denver	3,200	1,566	292 0	44 0	17 0	16.75	10	8	727	Mar. 99
Des Moines	3,200	....	292 0	44 0	17 0	16.65	10	8	705	Mar. 99
Galveston	3,200	....	292 0	44 0	17 0	16.41	10	8	741	Mar. 99
Marblehead	2,072	626	257 0	37 0	16 3	18.44	10	6	354	Sept. 88
Montgomery	2,072	587	257 0	37 0	16 3	19.06	7	2	271	Sept. 88
New Orleans	3.430	1,130	346 0	43 9	19 1	20.00	10	2	768	....
Raleigh	3,183	934	300 0	42 0	19 6	21.12	11	6	713	Sept. 88
Salem	3,750	....	420 0	47 1	18 9	24.72	2	8	1,433	Apr. 04
Tacoma	3,200	1,554	292 0	44 0	17 0	16.58	10	8	727	Mar. 99
MONITORS										
Amphitrite	3,990	....	259 3	55 4	14 8	10.50	6	2	277	Aug. 86
Cheyenne	3,225	....	252 0	50 0	13 3	11.80	6	2	132	May 98
Monadnock	3,990	988	258 6	55 5	14 8	11.63	6	5	395	Aug. 86
Monterey	4,084	822	256 0	59 0½	15 4	13.60	4	6	211	Mar. 87
Ozark	3,225	....	252 0	50 0	13 3	12.03	6	2	352	May 98
Tallahassee	3,225	....	252 0	50 0	13 3	12.40	6	3	363	May 98
Tonopah	3,225	....	252 0	50 0	13 3	13.04	6	2	346	May 98
DESTROYERS										
Ammen	742	....	289 0	26 1½	9 5	30.48	3	5	67,855	Mar. 09
Aylwin	1,036	....	300 0	30 4	10 6	29.60	4	4	92,273	Mar. 11
Balch	1,036	....	300 0	30 4	10 6	29.62	4	4	92,273	Mar. 11
Beale	742	....	289 0	26 1½	9 5	29.65	3	5	68,012	June 10
Benham	1,036	....	300 0	30 4	10 6	29.59	4	4	92,273	Mar. 11
Burrows	742	....	289 0	26 1½	9 5	30.67	3	5	70,176	May 08
Cassin	1,020	....	300 0	30 4	10 3	30.14	4	4	98,280	Mar. 11
Cummings	1,020	....	300 0	30 4	10 3	30.57	4	4	98,280	Mar. 11
Cushing	1,050	....	300 3¼	30 4½	10 9½	29.18	......	......	92,393	Aug. 12
Downes	1,072	....	300 0	30 6	10 9½	29.07	......	......	91,854	Mar. 11
Drayton	742	....	289 0	26 1½	9 6	30.83	3	5	70,580	May 08
Duncan	1,014	....	300 0	30 4	10 6	29.14	4	4	91,284	Mar. 11
Ericsson	1,090	....	300 0	30 6	10 8½	29.29	......	......	92,393	Aug. 12
Fanning	742	....	289 0	26 1½	9 5	29.99	3	5	67,342	June 10
Flusser	700	....	289 0	26 0	10 0	30.41	3	5	324	May 07
Henley	742	....	289 0	26 1½	9 5	30.32	3	5	74,287	June 10
Jarvis	742	....	289 0	26 1½	9 5	30.01	3	5	66,707	June 10
Jenkins	742	....	289 0	26 1½	9 5	31.27	3	5	66,471	June 10
Jouett	742	....	289 0	26 1½	9 5	32.27	3	5	67,420	June 10
Lamson	700	....	289 0	26 0	10 7	28.61	3	5	291	June 06
Mayrant	742	....	289 0	26 1½	9 5	30.22	3	5	73,583	May 08
McCall	742	....	289 0	26 1½	9 5	30.66	3	5	70,575	May 08
McDougal	1,020	....	300 0	30 6	9 8	30.70	4	4	97,980	Aug. 12
Monaghan	742	....	289 0	26 1½	9 5	30.45	3	5	70,074	May 09
Nicholson	1,050	....	300 0	30 4	10 5½	29.08	......	......	92,393	Aug. 12

[2]Now called Memphis

SHIPS OF THE UNITED STATES NAVY—VESSELS BUILT—*Continued.*
DESTROYERS—*Continued.*

Name	Dis-place-ment	Net tonnage for Suez Canal	Length on L. W. L.	Beam on L. W. L.	Draft aft at de-signed full load	Speed (trial)	Guns of 4 inches and over	Guns under 4 inches	Coal capacity bunk-ers (maximum), 42 cubic feet per ton	Date author-ized
	Tons	Tons	Ft. In.	Ft. In.	Ft. In.	Knots			Tons	
O'Brien	1,050		300 0	30 4	10 5½	29.05	.....	.....	92,393	Aug. 12
Parker	1,036		300 0	30 4	10 6	29.55	4	4	92,273	Mar. 11
Patterson	742		289 0	26 1½	9 5	29.69	3	5	70,701	Mar. 09
Paulding	742		289 0	26 1½	9 6	32.80	3	5	70,580	May 08
Perkins	742		289 0	26 1½	10 1	29.76	3	5	73,815	May 08
Preston	700		289 0	26 0	10 11	29.18	3	5	290	June 06
Reid	700		289 0	26 0	10 0	31.82	3	5	324	Mar. 07
Roe	742		289 0	26 1½	10 11	29.60	3	5	70,074	May 08
Smith	700		289 0	26 0	10 7	28.35	3	5	305	June 06
Steret	742		289 0	26 1½	10 1	30.37	3	5	73,815	May 08
Terry	742		289 0	26 1½	10 11	30.24	3	5	70,074	May 08
Trippe	742		289 0	26 1½	9 5	30.89	3	5	69,824	Mar. 09
Wadsworth	1,060		310 0	29 10	10 0	30.67	.....	.....	86,768	Mar. 13
Walke	742		289 0	26 1½	9 5	29.78	3	5	73,815	Mar. 09
Warrington	742		289 0	26 1½	9 5	30.12	3	5	73,583	May 08
Winslow	1,050		300 0	30 4	10 5½	29.05	.....	.....	92,393	Aug. 12

COAST TORPEDO VESSELS. Destroyers. (Not serviceable for duty with fleet.)

Name	Dis-place-ment	Net tonnage for Suez Canal	Length	Beam	Draft	Speed	Guns 4 and over	Guns under 4	Coal	Date
Bainbridge	420	229	245 0	23 1	9 4	28.45	2	7	216	May 98
Barry	420	229	245 0	23 1	9 4	28.13	2	7	183	May 98
Chauncey	420	229	245 0	23 1	9 4	28.64	2	7	216	May 98
Dale	420	229	245 0	23 1	9 4	28.00	2	7	211	May 98
Decatur	420	229	245 0	23 1	9 4	28.10	2	7	209	May 98
Hopkins	408		238 9	23 1½	10 5	29.02	2	8	157	May 98
Hull	408		238 9	23 1½	10 3	28.04	2	8	159	May 98
Lawrence	400		240 7	22 2½	9 5	28.41	2	7	125	May 98
Macdonough	400		240 7	22 2½	9 5	28.03	2	7	119	May 98
Paul Jones	420	229	245 0	23 1	8 11	28.91	2	7	185	May 98
Perry	420	229	245 0	23 1	8 11	28.32	2	7	183	May 98
Preble	420	229	245 0	23 1	8 11	28.03	2	7	183	May 98
Stewart	420		245 0	23 1	9 2	29.69	2	7	194	May 98
Truxtun	433		248 0	22 3½	9 10	29.58	2	8	177	May 98
Whipple	433		248 0	22 3½	9 10	28.24	2	8	179	May 98
Worden	433		248 0	22 3½	9 10	29.86	2	8	188	May 98

TORPEDO BOATS

Name	Dis-place-ment	Net tonnage	Length	Beam	Draft	Speed	Guns 4 and over	Guns under 4	Coal	Date
Bagley	175	68	157 0	17 7½	4 11	29.15	3	3	44	May 98
Bailey	280		205 0	19 3	6 10	30.20	2	4	101	Mar. 97
Barney	175	68	157 0	17 7½	4 11	29.04	3	3	44	May 98
Biddle	175	68	157 0	17 7½	4 11	28.57	3	3	44	May 98
Blakely	196		175 1	17 9	5 11	25.58	3	4	74	May 98
Dahlgren	146		147 0	16 4½	4 7	30.00	3	4	33	June 96
De Long	196		175 1	17 9	5 11	25.52	3	3	74	May 98
Dupont	165		175 0	17 8½	4 8	28.58	3	4	78	Mar. 95
Farragut	279	160	213 6	20 8	6 0	30.13	2	4	97	June 96
Foote	142		160 0	16 1	5 0	24.53	2	3	45	July 94
Fox	154		146 0	15 4	5 10	23.13	3	3	41	June 96
Goldsborough	255		198 0	20 7	6 10	27.40	2	4	91	Mar. 97
Mackenzie	65		99 3	12 9	4 3	20.11	2	1	15	June 96
Morris	105		138 3	15 6	4 1	24.00	3	3	27	......
Rodgers	142		160 0	16 1	5 0	24.49	3	3	45	July 94
Shubrick	200	104	175 0	17 6	5 2	26.07	3	3	84	May 98
Somers	150		149 4	17 6	5 10	15.00	.....	.....	38	......
Thornton	200	104	175 0	17 6	5 2	24.88	3	3	87	May 98
Tingey	165	103	175 0	17 6	4 8	24.94	3	3	75	May 98

TENDERS TO TORPEDO VESSELS

Name	Dis-place-ment	Net tonnage for Suez Canal	Length on L. W. L.	Beam, ex-treme	Mean draft	Speed (trial)	Guns of 4 inches and over	Guns under 4 inches	Coal capacity bunkers (maxi-mum) 42 cubic feet per ton
	Tons	Tons	Ft. In.	Ft. In.	Ft. In.	Knots			Tons
Alert	1,110	713	177 4	32 0	13 0	10.00	......	4	202
Bushnell	3,580		300 0	45 8	15 0	14.14	......	......	197,479[1]
Dixie	6,114	3,074	391 1	48 3	19 11	14.50	......	12	1,100
Fulton	1,408				13 0	12.34	......	2	234
Iris	6,100	1,923	130 6	39 0	24 0	10.00	......	4	307
Melville	7,150	3,941	400 0	54 5½	20 0	15.09	......	......	269,280[1]
Panther	3,380	1,912	304 8	40 8	15 9	13.50	......	......	691
Pompey	3,085		234 0	33 6	15 10	10.50	......	......	205

[1] Gallons fuel oil.

SHIPS OF THE UNITED STATES NAVY—VESSELS BUILT—*Continued.*

GUNBOATS

Name	Displacement	Net tonnage for Suez Canal	Length on L. W. L.	Beam	Draft aft at designed full load	Speed	Guns of 4 inches and over	Guns under 4 inches	Coal capacity bunkers
	Tons	Tons	Ft. In.	Ft. In.	Ft. In.	Knots			Tons
Annapolis	1,010	560	168 0	36 0	12 9	13.17	6	6	235
Callao	243	....	115 3	17 10	7 6	10.00	......	4	34
Castine	1,177	398	204 0	32 1½	12 0	16.03	2	6	215
Dolphin	1,486	447	240 0	32 0	17 0	15.50	......	6	271
Don Juan de Austria	1,132	366	210 0	32 0	15 8	12.20	2	10	209
Dubuque	1,085	568	174 0	35 0	13 4	12.90	6	6	252
Elcano	620	....	157 11	26 0	12 0	11.00	4	4	96
Helena	1,392	921	250 9	39 8	10 0	15.50	8	4	307
Isla de Luzon	1,030	314	192 8	30 1½	12 0	11.23	4	4	163
Machias	1,177	398	204 0	32 1½	13 7	15.46	4	2	267
Marietta	990	532	174 0	34 0	12 10	13.02	6	6	234
Monocacy	190	....	160 0	24 6	2 5	13.25	......	8	13
Nashville	1,371	756	220 0	38 1½	12 7	16.30	8	6	372
Newport	1,010	560	168 0	36 0	12 9	12.29	8	......	229
Paducah	1,085	....	174 0	35 0	13 4	12.85	4	6	242
Palos	190	....	160 0	24 6	2 5	13.25	......	8	13
Pampanga	243	568	115 3	17 10	7 6	10.00	......	6	34
Petrel	890	....	181 4	31 0	12 10	11.40	4	4	198
Princeton	1,010	362	168 0	36 0	12 9	10.64	6	6	231
Quiros	350	560	137 9	22 9	9 3	11.00	......	4	80
Ranger	1,261	....	177 4	32 0	......	10.00	......	......	182
Sacramento	1,425	....	210 0	40 10½	11 6	12.78	3	2	424
Samar	243	....	115 3	17 10	7 6	10.50	......	6	34
Sandoval	100	....	110 0	15 6	5 10	8.00	......	4	16
Vicksburg	1,010	560	168 0	36 0	12 9	12.71	6	6	240
Villalobos	370	....	148 0	23 0	9 0	11.00	......	6	67
Wheeling	990	518	174 0	34 0	12 10	12.88	6	6	256
Wilmington	1,392	921	250 9	39 8	10 0	15.08	8	4	307
Yorktown	1,710	482	230 0	36 0	16 3	16.14	6	8	349

TRANSPORTS

Name	Displacement	Net tonnage for Suez Canal	Length on L. W. L.	Beam	Mean draft	Speed	Guns of 4 inches and over	Guns under 4 inches	Coal capacity bunkers (maximum) 42 cubic feet per ton	Carrying capacity Officers	Carrying capacity Enlisted Men
	Tons	Tons	Ft. In.	Ft. In.	Ft. In.	Knots			Tons		
Buffalo	6,000	....	391 1	48 3	19 5	14.5	6	4	1,408	29	800
General Alava	1,115	....	212 6	29 9	11 0	10.5	......	2	246	15	200
Hancock	8,500	....	450 2	45 4	24 3	......	......	8	900	......	192
Prairie	6,620	....	391 6	48 3	20 9	14.5	......	15	1,330	23	750

SUPPLY SHIPS.

Name	Displacement	Net tonnage for Suez Canal	Length on L. W. L.	Beam	Mean draft	Speed	Guns under 4 inches	Coal capacity bunkers (maximum) 42 cubic feet per ton	Cargo capacity
	Tons	Tons	Ft. In.	Ft. In.	Ft. In.	Knots		Tons	Tons
Celtic	6,750	....	369 8	44 7	21 0	10.5	4	757	....
Culgoa	6,000	2,483	334 4	43 0	21 9	13.25	4	980	....
Glacier	8,325	....	353 0	46 1	25 4	12.3	4	939	....
Supply	4,325	2,692	342 7	43 4	19 5	9.66	6	1,054	....

HOSPITAL SHIP

Name	Displacement	Net tonnage for Suez Canal	Length on L. W. L.	Beam	Mean draft	Speed	Coal capacity bunkers (maximum)	Capacity for patients Officers	Capacity for patients Men
	Tons	Tons	Ft. In.	Ft. In.	Ft. In.	Knots	Tons		
Solace	5,700	....	361 2	44 0	22 0	15.0	1,024	9	234

SHIPS OF THE UNITED STATES NAVY—VESSELS BUILT—*Continued.*

FUEL SHIPS

Name	Displacement	Net tonnage for Suez Canal	Dimensions			Speed		Coal capacity	
			Length over all	Beam	Mean draft, loaded	Loaded	Light	Bunker, 42 cubic feet per ton	Cargo
	Tons	Tons	Ft. In.	Ft. In.	Ft. In.	Knots	Knots	Tons	Tons
Abarenda	6,705	2,133	325 6	42 0½	22 10	9.00	....	832	3,400
Ajax	9,250	3,320	387 6	46 6	24 8	10.00	11.00	512	5,000
Arethusa	6,159		343 6	42 2	20 11	10.00		685	
Brutus	6,600	2,314	332 6	41 6	23 1	10.00		560	4,000
Caesar	5,920	2,072	322 1	43 11	19 7	10.00	11.00	779	3,156
Cyclops	19,360	7,055	542 0	65 0	27 8	14.61		2,286	10,457
Hector	11,230	3,902	403 0	53 0	24 8	12.87		837	8,128
Jason	19,132		536 0	65 0	27 8	14.32		2,048	10,500
Jupiter	19,360		542 0	65 0	27 8	14.00		2,092	10,457
Kanawha	14,500		475 7	56 0	26 2	14.00		1,584	7,539
Mars	11,230	3,902	403 0	53 0	24 8	12.65		837	8,128
Nanshan	4,830		300 0	39 0	20 9	10.5	11.00	437	2,782
Neptune	19,375		542 0	65 0	27 7	12.93		2,048	10,500
Nereus	19,000		522 0	62 0	27 8	14.58		2,048	10,500
Nero	6,360	2,204	323 5	41 0	22 0	9.00		307	3,500
Orion	19,132		536 0	65 0	27 8	14.47		2,048	10,500
Proteus	19,000		522 0	62 0	27 8	14.67		2,048	10,500
Saturn	4,842		297 1	40 5	21 3	11.00		395	2,495
Sterling	5,663		284 0	37 0	22 6	11.00	11.00	469	2,672
Vulcan	11,230	3,092	403 0	53 0	24 8	12.82		837	8,128

CONVERTED YACHTS

Name	Displacement	Dimensions			Speed	Guns of 4 inches and over	Guns untler 4 inches	Coal capacity bunkers (maximum), 42 cubic feet per ton.
		Length	Beam.	Mean draft				
	Tons.	Ft. in.	Ft. in.	Ft. in.	Knots.			Tons.
Aileen	192	120 0	20 0	8 0	14.0	....	3	46
Dorothea	594	182 4	23 5	11 5	14.0		2	80
Eagle	434	155 6	24 0	11 6	12.50		2	68
Elfrida	164	101 6	18 0½	7 9	10.5		1	24
Gloucester	786	204 0	27 2	12 0	17.0		7	123
Hawk	375	145 0	22 0	11 6	14.5		1	72
Huntress	82	97 0	16 0	7 3	14.0		2	17
Mayflower	2,690	273 0	36 0	17 4	14.50		6	538
Scorpion	775	212 9	28 1	11 0	17.85		4	136
Sylph	152	123 8	20 0	7 6	15.0		....	48
Sylvia	302	130 0	18 6	10 0	9.0		4	61
Vixen	806	182 3	28 0	12 8	16.0		6	195
Wasp	630	180 0	23 0	12 0	16.5		2	81
Yankton	975	185 0	27 6	13 10	14.0		2	174

SPECIAL TYPES

Name	Displacement	Type	Dimensions.			Speed.	Guns of 4 inches and over.	Guns under 4 inches	Coal capacity of bunkers
			Length.	Beam.	Mean draft.				
	Tons.		Ft. in.	Ft. in.	Ft. in.	Knots.			Tons.
Baltimore	4,413	Mine depot ship	327 6	48 7½	19 6	20.10	4	4	1,092
Hannibal	4,000	Surveying ship	263 4	39 3	17 7	10.0			4,800
Lebanon	3,285	Ammunition ship	249 0	37 4½	17 3	10.0	4	4	192
Leonidas	4,023	Surveying ship	263 3	39 2½	17 7	9.5			200
Prometheus	12,585	Repair ship	450 0	60 1	26 0	16.0	4		1,614
San Francisco	4,083	Mine depot ship	310 0	49 2	18 9	19.52	8	4	640
Vestal	12,585	Repair ship	450 0	60 0	26 0	16.0	4		1,422
Vesuvius	930	Torpedo practice ship	252 4	26 6½	10 7	21.65		1	135

SHIPS OF THE UNITED STATES NAVY—VESSELS BUILT—*Continued.*
Tugs

| Name | Displacement. | Dimensions. | | | Indicated. horsepower. | Speed. | Coal capacity, 42 cubic feet per ton. |
		Length.	Beam.	Mean draft.			
	Tons.	Ft. in.	Ft. in.	Ft. in.		Knots.	Tons.
Accomac	187	81 5	18 10½	8 5	320	10.0	34
Active	296	107 0	22 6	10 0	600	12.0	82
Alice	318	101 9	25 6	8 0	250	10.0	15
Apache	650	141 6	29 0	10 0	550	10.0	120
Arapaho	548	122 6	24 0	12 10	800	10.76	52,624¹
Choctaw	274	91 5	21 0	10 0	550	10.0	72
Fortune	450	137 0	26 0	9 6	334	10.0	111
Hercules	198	101 6	20 6	9 0	350	12.0	41
Iroquois	702	152 0	26 0	13 6	1,000	13.25	210
Iwana	192	92 6	20 11½	8 0	350	11.58	36
Massasoit	202	89 5	19 0	8 6	150	9.0	35
Modoc	241	96 9	20 10	9 3	175	10.0	41
Mohave	548	122 6	24 0	12 10	800	11.11	52,624¹
Mohawk	368	104 0	24 0	11 0	400	12.0	33
Narkeeta	192	92 6	20 11½	8 0	300	11.22	36
Navajo	800	141 4	27 6	14 1	935	12.0	....
Ontario	1,120	175 0	34 0	12 6	1,517	13.23	445
Osceola	571	125 5	26 3	14 0	800	14.0	154
Patapsco	755	148 0	29 0½	12 3	1,160	13.0	324
Patuxent	755	148 0	29 0½	12 3	1,160	13.0	324
Pawnee	275	112 0	27 3	7 0	250	10.0	17
Pawtucket	225	92 6	21 1	8 9	450	12.2	31
Penacook	230	92 6	21 1	9 0	450	12.0	29
Pentucket	230	92 6	21 1	9 0	450	12.0	29
Peoria	487	131 0	25 0	10 6	270	9.0	70
Piscataqua	854	149 0	28 7	12 0	2,000	16.0	242
Pontiac	401	124 4	27 0	9 6	425	10.5	46
Potomac	785	138 9	28 6	12 0	2,000	16.0	205
Powhatan	194	101 0	21 0	10 0	397	13.0	58
Rapido	186	96 0	16 4	7 6	125	10.0	14
Rocket	270	93 0	28 0	9 0	450	8.0	34
Samoset	225	92 6	21 0	8 9	450	12.0	31
Sebago	243	99 0	21 0	8 0	450	12.0	31
Sioux	155	84 6	19 0	8 0	290	10.0	46
Sonoma	1,120	175 0	34 0	12 6	1,506	13.08	445
Sotoyomo	230	92 6	21 1	9 0	506	11.10	29
Standish	450	137 0	26 0	9 6	400	10.0	82
Tecumseh	221	88 6	21 6	9 3	540	11.0	41
Tillamook	548	122 6	24 0	12 10	800	10.84	52,624¹
Traffic	280	106 0	29 4	9 0	240	10.0	....
Transfer	684	110 0	30 0	10 0	....		
Triton	212	96 9	20 9	9 0	300	13.0	46
Unadilla	355	110 0	25 0	9 11	500	12.0	7,885
Uncas	441	119 3	25 0	12 0	750	12.0	123
Vigilant	300	116 0	21 0	9 0	450	12.0	77
Waban	150	85 0	17 6½	8 0	450	13.0	31
Wahneta	152	92 0	20 11½	8 0	300	11.58	36
Wompatuck	462	117 6	25 6	12 0	650	13.0	133

Pay.—All commissioned officers of the active list of the Navy receive the same pay according to rank and the term of service, the annual base pay of each grade being as follows:

Admiral (in command of fleet) $10,000
Vice Admiral (second in command) . 9,000
Rear Admiral (upper half) 8,000
Rear Admiral (lower half) 6,000
Commodore 6,000
Captain 4,000
Commander 3,500
Lieutenant Commander 3,000
Lieutenant 2,400
Lieutenant (junior grade) 2,000
Ensign 1,700

To each commissioned officer below the rank of rear admiral is allowed 10% of his yearly base pay for each five years of service in the Army, Navy or Marine Corps, but not exceeding in all 40%. Additional provision is made by law that the pay of a captain shall not exceed $5,000; of a commander, $4,500; and of a lieutenant commander, $4,000 yearly. All officers on sea or shore duty beyond the continental limits of the United States receive while so serving 10% additional of pay.

An officer on shore duty where no Government living quarters are furnished is paid an additional $12 monthly for each room to which he is entitled by his rank, as follows:—Rear admirals, 9 and 8 rooms; Captains, 7 rooms; Commander, 6; Lieutenant Commander, 5; Lieutenant, 4 and 3; Ensign, warrant officer and nurse, 2. There are also additional allowances for heat and light, depending upon the month and the place of duty.

Officers of the Navy appointed student naval aviators while detailed for duty involving actual flying in aircraft receive 35% additional pay of their rank; and those who qualified while so detailed receive an additional 50%.

Warrant officers are boatswains, gunners, pay clerks, machinists, carpenters, sailmakers, and pharmacists, and are paid during their first three years' service, $1,500 yearly if at sea; $1,125 if on shore; and $875 while waiting for orders. During the second three years' service, the pay is increased $125 yearly from the above amounts. During the third three years' service, there is an additional $125 yearly from the second three years' service, except in the case of being on shore, when the increase is

$375. During the fourth three years' service, the increase is $250 while at sea, and $125 while on shore or while waiting for orders. After twelve years' service, the additional pay above the last figures is $250, the totals then for three classes being respectively $2,250, $2,000, and $1,500.

After six years from date of warrant, duly qualified warrant officers are commissioned chief warrant officers and receive the pay and allowances of ensigns. After six years from date of commission each commissioned warrant officer may be given the pay and allowance of a lieutenant of the junior grade, and twelve years after the date of commission the pay and allowance of a lieutenant.

While warrant officers are attached to a sea-going ship they are paid a ration allowance of $.40 daily.

All officers in the regular Navy must provide their own uniforms and pay for their subsistence both afloat and ashore.

Pay for the Enlisted Personnel.—The enlisted personnel of the Navy is of extremely complicated and lengthy classification, according to the duties assigned; and pay is according to classification, even within the separate groups.

Chief petty officers average a monthly pay of $68.85, but all chief petty officers who have served as such for one year with credit are given a permanent appointment at $83.00 monthly.

Petty officers of the first class receive, on the average, the monthly pay of $56.42.

Petty officers of the second class receive an average monthly pay of $48.11.

Petty officers of the third class average a monthly pay of $41.00.

Seamen of the first class average monthly pay of $40.76.

Seamen of the second class average monthly pay of $38.38.

Seamen of the third class average monthly pay of $33.80.

Messmen average monthly pay of $49.75.

Additional monthly amounts are paid as follows: $1.50 for each successive reenlistment within four months of date of honorable discharge from previous enlistment. $5.50 for first reenlistment and $3.30 for each subsequent reenlistment if a citizen of the United States and completed previous enlistment. $1.20 per hour spent under water for divers. $5.00 per month for submarine service. There are also many other additional increases for various forms of special or trained work.

A man detained beyond the expiration of his enlistment receives one-fourth of all pay in addition while so detained.

A man receives a gratuity of four months' pay if he reenlists within four months of and presents an honorable discharge from his last enlistment.

Clothing and small stores are furnished free of charge to all enlisted men on their first enlistment. Afterwards articles drawn are furnished at cost price.

Subsistence is furnished enlisted men by the Government. Men on detached duty are furnished money in place of subsistence. Transportation to their homes is furnished men discharged.

Retired List.—Officers on the retired list receive three-fourths of their active duty pay. Enlisted men are retired after 30 years' service, and receive three-fourths of the total pay and allowances they received at date of retirement and cash in lieu of quarters and subsistence.

When first called into active service in time of war or national emergency a uniform gratuity of $150 is allowed each officer of the Naval Reserve and $60 each enlisted man.

Dependents.—All enlisted men must contribute to the support of their immediate families not more than 50% of their pay and not less than $15 monthly. On application, the Government will add to this allotment an allowance of its own of from $5 to $50 per month, according to the size of the family. The amount thus given by the government is fixed by law as follows: $15 for a wife, $25 for a wife and child, $32.50 for a wife and two children, with $5 for each additional child. The sums are monthly. The enlisted men must contribute an amount equal to the government allowance unless such contribution would exceed 50% of their pay.

See also Soldiers' and Sailors' Insurance.

Insignia.—The personnel of our Navy (excepting aviators) wear blue or white uniforms, Aviators wear "khaki" or "Olive-drab." Insignia denoting rank of officers of the Naval Service consist of cap, shoulder, collar and sleeve devices, and specialty marks. (See colored plate: Insignia of Rank U. S. Navy.)

Roosevelt was the most insistent of all Presidents in urging naval efficiency. In his first annual message to Congress he says (pages 6665, 6666): "The work of upbuilding the Navy must be steadily continued. It is not possible to improvise a navy after war breaks out. No one point of our policy, foreign or domestic, is more important than this to the honor and material welfare, and above all to the peace, of our nation in the future. Whether we desire it or not, we must henceforth recognize that we have international duties no less than international rights. * * * The Navy offers us the only means of making our insistence upon the Monroe Doctrine anything but a subject of derision to whatever nation chooses to disregard it. We desire the peace which comes as a right to the just man armed; not the peace granted on terms of ignominy to the craven and the weakling." This attitude was maintained throughout his administration.

Navy:

Admiral of, revival of grade of, recommended, 6345.

Amalgamation of staff corps recommended, 7696.

Appointments in, referred to, 2129, 2134.

Apprentices, corps of, recommended, 2713.

Appropriations for. (See Navy Department.)

Army and, forces mobilized on borders of Mexico to protect interests of citizens of United States during uprising, 7658.

Auxiliary in Spanish-American War, 6313.

Award of medals in, 6927.

Base in Philippines advocated, 6880.

Boys, enlistment of, in, recommended, 1392, 1476, 2713.

Bureau of Navigation, report of chief of, 6294.

Classifying and rating of officers and men, 6602.

Classifying and manning vessels of, 6613.

Code of, revision of, recommended, 2625.

Navy, Department of.—The Continental Navy was under the direction of various committees, boards and agents; the first committee, being one of three members, was appointed on Oct. 13, 1775. In 1781, the Board of Admiralty then acting was replaced by the Secretary of Marine, whose duties correspond with those of the present Secretary of the Navy; but before the end of that year the duties of the office were transferred to the Treasury Department.

Upon the adoption of the Constitution, in 1789, naval matters were placed under the jurisdiction of the War Department and so remained until April 30, 1798, when in consequence of depredations of French cruisers, twelve new ships were added to the fleet; and the modern Department of the Navy was organized with a Secretary at its head. In 1815 a board of three "Navy Commissioners" was created which was charged with the duty of procuring naval stores, of constructing and equipping vessels and of superintending the navy yards; the order creating these Commissioners expressly provides that they should not interfere with the powers of the Secretary of the Navy Department.

In 1842 five bureaus, namely, Navy Yards and Docks, Construction, Equipment and Repairs, Clothing and Provisions, Ordnance and Hydrography, and Medicine and Surgery took the place of the Commissioners. Another reorganization took place in 1862 which placed the Department substantially upon its present basis. The Hydrographic Office was then established and the office of Judge-Advocate-General, created in 1865, was reorganized in 1880. Although assistants to the Secretary had been from time to time appointed before that date, it was not till 1890 that the office of Assistant Secretary was established.

The Secretary of the Navy has the general supervision of the work of the Department, and, although under the Constitution the President is Commander-in-chief of the Navy, the official acts of the Secretary are final. The details of the Secretary's duties are carried out by eight Bureaus, each presided over by a naval officer having the actual or nominal rank of Rear-Admiral. The Bureau of Navigation attends to the promulgation and enforcement of the Secretary's orders; the education of

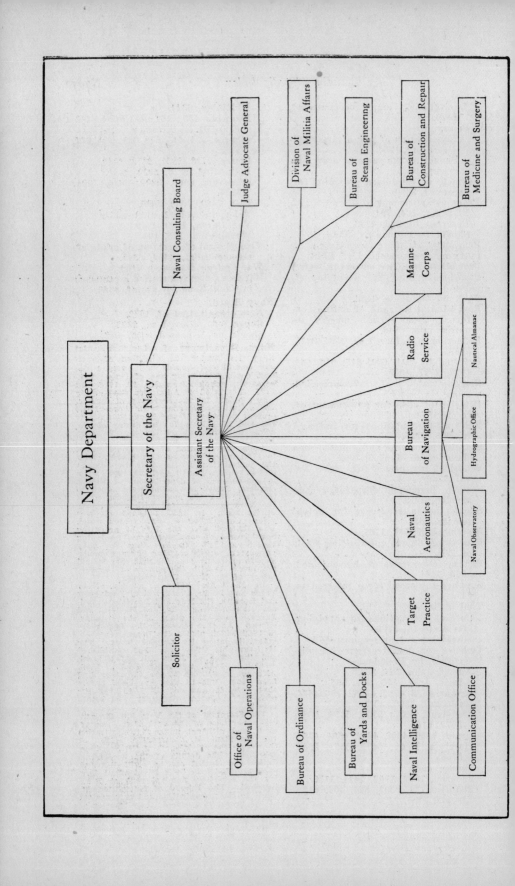

officers (see Naval Academy); the enlistment and education of enlisted men; keeps their records and preserves the Naval Register; and directs the enforcement of all regulations. The Bureau of Yards and Docks attends to the construction, equipment and maintenance of all Docks and Navy Yards. The Bureau of Equipment furnishes all supplies to the ships, directs the Naval Observatory (q. v.) and prepares the *Nautical Almanac*; the Hydrographic Office, whose duties relate to the preparation of charts and gathering information on all kinds of nautical subjects, is a branch of this Bureau. The Bureau of Ordnance supervises the manufacture of offensive and defensive armor and apparatus, and, in connection with the Bureau of Construction and Repairs, their installation on the ships. The Bureau of Construction and Repairs designs and constructs war-ships, has charge of the docking of the ships and repairing all permanent fixtures. The Bureau of Steam-Engineering constructs and repairs all steam machinery. The Bureau of Medicine and Surgery has charge of and furnishes supplies to the Medical Department and all naval hospitals. The Bureau of Supplies and Accounts furnishes all the general supplies and keeps all naval accounts.

In addition to these Bureaus, the offices of the Judge-Advocate-General form the law department of the Navy. The Commandant of Marines is the head of the Marine Corps (q. v.). The General Board, composed of naval officers of various grades, advises the Secretary on technical matters and submits plans for naval manœuvres, etc.

Building Programme.—The Secretary of the Navy in his annual report for 1913, recommended the authorization by Congress of a building programme which should include two dreadnaughts, eight destroyers and three submarines annually.

Naval Schools.—There was established on board the *Des Moines*, in 1913, a school for academic, vocational and technical instruction of enlisted men. The experiment met with such success that it was proposed to install the school generally upon the ships and at the shore stations of the navy. Four schools are now maintained for training recruits—at Newport, Norfolk, Chicago and San Francisco.

Enlistments.—The policy recently adopted by the department of raising the standard for admission to the navy has increased the number as well as bettered the character of the men entering the service. There is now a rigid exclusion of those not morally or physically fit.

For more detailed information as to the scope and activities of the Navy Department consult the index references to the Presidents' Messages and Encyclopedic articles under the following headings:

Bureau of Construction and Repair.	Marine Insurance.
Bureau of Medicine and Surgery.	Marine, Secretary of.
Bureau of Navigation.	Nautical Almanac.
Bureau of Ordnance.	Naval Academy.
Bureau of Steam Engineering.	Naval Consulting Board.
Bureau of Yards and Docks.	Naval Militia.
Hydrographic office.	Naval Observatory.
Judge Advocate General.	Naval Reserve.
Marine Corps.	Naval War College.
	Navigation Act.
	Navigation Laws.
	Navy Yards.
	Office naval operations.

Following is a list of the secretaries of the Navy and the Presidents under whom they served:

President	Secretary of the Navy	Appointed
Adams....	George Cabot, Massachusetts..	1798
"	Benjamin Stoddert, Maryland.	1798
Jefferson...	" "	1801
"	Robert Smith, Maryland....	1801
"	Jacob Crowninshield, Mass....	1805
Madison..	Paul Hamilton, South Carolina..	1809
"	William Jones, Pennsylvania..	1813
"	B. W. Crowninshield, Mass....	1814
Monroe....	" "	1817
"	Smith Thompson, New York...	1818
"	Samuel L. Southard, New Jersey	1823
J.Q.Adams.	" "	1825
Jackson....	John Branch, North Carolina..	1829
"	Levi Woodbury, New Hampshire	1831
"	Mahlon Dickerson, New Jersey..	1834
Van Buren.	" "	1837
"	James K. Paulding, New York..	1838
Harrison...	George E. Badger, N. Carolina..	1841
Tyler....	" "	1841
"	Abel P. Upshur, Virginia......	1841
"	David Henshaw, Massachusetts.	1843
"	Thomas W. Gilmer, Virginia....	1844
"	John Y. Mason, Virginia......	1844
Polk......	George Bancroft, Massachusetts.	1845
"	John Y. Mason, Virginia......	1846
Taylor....	William B. Preston, Virginia....	1849
Fillmore..	William A. Graham, N. Carolina	1850
"	John P. Kennedy, Maryland....	1852
Pierce.....	James C. Dobbin, N. Carolina..	1853
Buchanan	Isaac Toucey, Connecticut......	1857
Lincoln....	Gideon Welles, Connecticut....	1861
Johnson...	" "	1865
Grant.....	Adolph E. Borie, Pennsylvania..	1869
"	George M. Robeson, New Jersey.	1869
Hayes......	Richard W. Thompson, Indiana..	1877
"	Nathan Goff, Jr., West Virginia.	1881
Garfield...	William H. Hunt, Louisiana....	1881
Arthur....	Wm. E. Chander, N. Hampshire.	1882
Cleveland..	William C. Whitney, New York..	1885
B. Harrison	Benjamin F. Tracy, New York..	1889
Cleveland..	Hilary A. Herbert, Alabama....	1893
McKinley..	John D. Long, Massachusetts..	1897
Roosevelt..	" "	1901
" ..	William H. Moody, Mass......	1902
" ..	Paul Morton, Illinois..........	1904
" ..	C. J. Bonaparte, Maryland....	1905
" ..	Victor H. Metcalf, California....	1907
" ..	Truman H. Newberry, Michigan	1908
Taft......	George von L. Meyer, Mass....	1909
Wilson....	Josephus Daniels, N. Carolina..	1913

Navy Department:

Accounts of, in Fourth Auditor's Office referred to, 1096.

Amount charged to State Department for services rendered by naval vessels referred to, 3660.

Appointments in, referred to, 1965.

Appropriations for, 927, 4426.

Diverted to survey of Isthmus of Darien referred to, 4000.

Necessary to render efficient, 1444.

Recommended, 955, 1168, 1475, 2055, 2872, 4405, 4674, 4796.

Referred to, 4407.

Transfer of, referred to, 1818, 2122.

Act authorizing, approved, 2131.

Appropriations for docks, etc., should be separated from those for naval service, 2625, 2670.

Board of Commissioners for, referred to, 603, 631.

Clerks in, referred to, 3585.

Deficiencies in, referred to, 4407.

Expenditures of, 335, 800, 2055, 2064, 2625, 2670, 3450, 3650, 3775, 3882, 4062, 4407, 4425, 4452, 4525, 4573, 5376, 5972.

Fireproof building for, recommended, 2281, 2704.

Land reserved for use of, 6703, 6706.

Navy Board—

New organization of, 1252.

Report of, referred to, 2308.

Should be dispensed with, 1023.

Persons employed in, without express provisions of law, 1964, 2174.

Transfer of—

Coasts, Survey to, recommended, 4727, 4932, 5973.

Light-House Service to, recommended, 4727.

Payment of naval pensions to, recommended, 4060.

Navy League. (See Preparedness Societies.)

Navy List.—A complete account of the ships, personnel, and general organization of the Navy Department of the United States, similar to the Army List (q. v.).

Navy Medical Department, relative rank of officers of, 7000.

Navy, Secretary of:

Letter of Boynton and Fisher to, referred to, 3669.

Report of, 3236, 6294.

Discussed. (See Navy discussed.)

Transmitted, 335, 845, 994, 1097, 1444, 2064.

Navy Yards.—Yards, docks, and shops for construction and repair of vessels, and stations for coaling, storing supplies, and as bases for operation are maintained by the Navy Department as follows:

1. New York Navy Yard, Brooklyn, N. Y.
2. Boston Navy Yard, Boston, Mass.
3. Norfolk Navy Yard, near Norfolk, Va.
4. Portsmouth Navy Yard, Portsmouth, N. H.
5. Philadelphia Navy Yard, Philadelphia, Pa.
6. Mare Island Navy Yard, near San Francisco, Cal.
7. Washington Navy Yard, Washington, D. C.
8. Puget Sound Navy Yard, Bremerton, Wash.
9. Charleston Navy Yard, Charleston, S. C.

Navy Yards:

At Boston, machinery at, for preserving wood, referred to, 4676.

Title of United States to land occupied as, referred to, 4698.

At New York, new boiler shop at, recommended, 4681.

At Norfolk, employment at, referred to, 3660.

At Washington, manufacture of guns at, discussed, 5973.

Civil service in connection with, discussed, 5974.

Order regarding, 6146.

Defense of, demands attention of Congress, 1754.

Discontinuance of, on Atlantic seaboard referred to, 2958.

Establishment of—

At Memphis referred to, 2202, 2829.

On Atlantic seaboard recommended, 3385, 3450.

Mississippi River recommended, 2132.

San Francisco Bay recommended, 2669.

Western river recommended, 3385.

Recommended, 3561.

Improvements in, recommended, 4062.

Labor at, secured through boards of labor, employment, discussed, 6166.

List of. (See Encyclopedic Index article on the Navy.)

Officers and men in, referred to, 765, 3660.

Referred to, 6255.

Near East, and Europe, political conditions in, 7667.

Near East, commerce with, 7667.

Near Eastern Division, State Department.—This division was organized in 1909 by Secretary of State Knox. It falls under the supervision of the third assistant secretary of state (q. v.) ; and it has charge of matters other than administrative in Germany, Austria-Hungary, Russia, Roumania, Servia, Bulgaria, Montenegro, Turkey, Greece, Italy, Abyssinia, Persia, Egypt and the colonies of these countries. (See State Department.)

Nebraska.—One of the western group of states; nickname, "Black Water State." Motto, "Equality before the law." It extends from lat. 40° to 43° north and from long. 95° 25' to 104° west. It is bounded on the north by South Dakota (partly separated by the Missouri River), on the east by Iowa and Missouri (separated from both by the Missouri River), on the south by Kansas and Colorado, and on the west by Colorado and Wyoming, and has an area of 77,520 square miles.

Nebraska originally formed part of the Louisiana Purchase and was later made a part of the Territory of Missouri. It was made a Territory in 1854, and included portions of the Dakotas, Montana, Wyoming and Colorado. Nebraska was admitted to the Union in 1867. The State takes its name from the river. It was first permanently settled at Bellevue in 1847.

The State is one of the first in the production of corn, being extremely fertile in the eastern part and along the Platte River. Its principal industries are agriculture and stock raising, slaughtering and meat packing, South Omaha being one of the great cattle markets of the world. Butter, cheese, condensed milk and kindred dairy products are the chief manufactured products.

The Federal irrigation scheme, completed in 1911, includes the watering of 110,000 acres of Nebraska and Wyoming. There are 3,074,658 acres of land in the State unreserved and unappropriated. Land offices are located at Alliance, Broken Bow, Lincoln, North Platte, O'Neill and Valentine.

Statistics of agriculture collected for the last Federal census place the number of farms in the State at 129,678, comprising 38,622,021 acres, valued, with stock and improvements, at $2,079,817,647. The average value of land per acre was $41.80, an increase from $16.27 in 1900. The value of domestic animals, poultry, etc., was $222,-222,004, including 2,932,350 cattle, valued at $73,074,057; 1,008,378 horses, $102,804,-907; 83,405 mules, $10,374,076; 3,435,734 swine, $29,649,482; 293,500 sheep, $1,486,-948. The yield and value of field crops for 1911 is given as: Corn, 7,425,000 acres, 155,925,000 bushels, $85,759,000; wheat, 3,098,000 acres, 41,594,000 bushels, $36,-169,000; oats, 2,500,000 acres, 34,750,000 bushels, $14,942,000; rye, 52,000 acres, 676,000 bushels, $507,000; potatoes, 116,000 acres, 6,032,000 bushels, $5,549,000; hay, 1,350,000 acres, 1,148,000 tons, $11,-136,000.

While not noted as a manufacturing state, Nebraska has 2,500 establishments, employing 32,000 persons, and capitalized at about $100,000. These are engaged in slaughtering and meat packing, manufacturing flour and meal and dairy products for shipment, and minor industries incidental to local needs. The value of the output of the manufactories in 1911 was about $200,-000,000. There are no mines in the State. The receipts at the State Treasury for the biennial period ending Nov. 30, 1910, were $10,960,919, and the disbursements $10,-744,066; balance on hand, $601,290. School, college and university trust funds of the State amounted to $8,863,690.

The number of manufacturing establishments in Nebraska having an annual output valued at $500 or more at the beginning of 1915 was 2,493. The amount of capital invested was $121,020,000, giving employment to 33,695 persons, using material valued at $174,114,000, and turning out finished goods worth $221,616,000. Salaries and wages paid amounted to $24,011,000.

Nebraska (see also Omaha):

Act—

Extending time of payment to purchasers of Indian lands in, vetoed, 5525.

For admission of, into Union, vetoed, 3687.

For sale of Indian reservation in, 4656.

To provide for lease of Fort Omaha Military Reservation to, vetoed, 6119.

Admission of, into Union, proclaimed, 3714.

Indian lands in, titles to, extinguished, proclaimed, 5535.

Memorial from citizens of, regarding creation of new Territory, 3111.

Military forces sent to and reasons therefor, discussed, 4673.

Public lands in, survey of, referred to, 4959.

Red Cloud Agency in, deficiency in supplies at, 4312, 4313.

Supplies issued, suffering people in, referred to, 4272.

Survey-general in, recommendations for discontinuance of office of, 4959.

Negotiations, Diplomatic, Breaking of. (See Diplomatic Negotiations, Breaking of.)

Negro Plot.—An alleged attempt on the part of certain negroes, incited and assisted by whites, to burn New York City. March 18, 1741, a fire occurred in the chapel and barracks of Fort George. It was at first thought to be accidental, but eight other fires of unaccountable origin within a month strengthened the allegation of one Mary Burton, a servant in the employ of John Hughson, that a number of negroes and sailors were implicated in a plot to destroy the town. It was charged that the Spanish were inciting plots among the negroes. Twenty whites and more than 160 negro slaves were imprisoned. Four whites and 18 negroes were hanged and 13 others were burned at the stake before the excitement abated.

Negro Troops.—In early Revolutionary days and in the first two years of the Civil War negro troops were employed to a limited extent. In July, 1863, a general provision was made for their enlistment in the Union Army and numbers were in service. Since the Civil War there have always been negro troops in the regular army. They served in the war with Spain in 1898, and proved to be less subject to the prevailing fever and the enervating effects of heat than white soldiers.

Negroes.—According to the census of 1900 there were in the United States 9,192,389 colored inhabitants. Of these, 119,050 were Chinese, 85,986 Japanese, and 266,760 Indians, leaving 8,621,493 negroes, or about one-ninth the entire population.

Negroes (see also Freedmen; Liberia):

Colonization of—

Discussed, 3255, 3328, 3341, 3401, 3588.

In Mexico, and action taken by United States for relief of, discussed, 6066, 6096.

Vessels to bring back, 3433.

Education and industrial training, recommended, 7032.

Emigration of—

Agreement with Bernard Koch for, canceled, 3368.

Discussed, 3653.

Exposition to commemorate achievements of, 8064.

Lynching of, discussed, 5767, 7030.

Recruiting of, in War between the States, order regarding, 6335.

Sale of, taken from United States by British forces, referred to, 6278.

To be employed for military purposes in war between the States, order regarding, 3318.

Welfare of, discussed by President Taft, 7376.

Nepal.—Nepal lies between 26° 20'-30° 10' N. lat. and 80° 15'-88° 14' E. long., with an extreme breadth from west to east of 520 miles, and a mean of 150 miles from north to south. The State is bounded on the north by Tibet; on the east by Sikkim; on the south by Bengal and Bihar and Orissa; and on the southwest and west by Agra and Oudh. The area is 54,000 square miles. The dominant race is the Gurkhali, or Gurkha, descendants of Brahmans and Rajputs who retreated from India during the Muhammadan invasions of the fourteenth, fifteenth and sixteenth centuries, and conquered the country in the eighteenth century A. D. The inhabitants are almost entirely Buddhists, but their languages differ according to racial distinctions, the Gurkha dialect being of Sanskrit origin, and the remaining dialects akin to Tibetan. The population is estimated at 5,000,000.

Physical Features.—The Himalayas traverse the centre of western Nepal, and extend along the northern boundary of the eastern division, where the highest peak of the whole range, Mount Everest, rises to 29,002 feet above sea level, the greatest land altitude yet ascertained.

Western Nepal contains many fertile valleys north and south of the range, and the southern portion of eastern Nepal contains low-lying alluvial land known as the tarai.

The rivers of Nepal flow from the Himalayas with a general southward course to the Ganges, their tributaries flowing through the valleys between parallel ranges of lower elevation than the Himalayas. The valley of Nepal and the southern plains have a rainy season from June to October, winter from October to March, and a hot season from April to June. The climate of the mountains and higher valleys depends on latitude as well as altitude, and varies from tropical to alpine conditions.

History.—The conquest of Nepal by the Gurkhas was completed in 1765, since which date the whole country has been under the hereditary rule of the Sahi dynasty. Since 1816 the actual power has been in the hands of successive Prime Ministers. The southern trend of the Gurkha conquests led to a war with the British Government of India in 1814-1816, since which time a British resident has been accepted at Katmandu.

Government.—Internal affairs are unfettered, but foreign relations are controlled by the Government of India, and by arrangement with Nepal, India obtains many fine recruits for its Gurkha regiments.

The public laws have been greatly modified since the first visit of the Nepalese Prime Minister to England in 1851, and the death penalty is now confined to murder and the killing of cows, manslaughter and cattle maiming being punished by imprisonment for life. The private code, especially caste law, is somewhat rigorous, and slavery is a recognized institution.

Ruler: Maharajadhiraja Tribhubana Bir Bikram Jang Bahadur Shah Bahadur Shumshere Jung, born June 30, 1906, succeeded his father, Dec. 11, 1911.

Almost every male Gurkha is a soldier, and there is a standing army of 30,000 infantry and mountain artillery, with a reserve of about 30,000. In addition some 20,000 Gurkhas are in the service of the Government of India in ten rifle regiments.

Education.—Education is provided by the State free of cost in a central college at the capital, with branch schools in the surrounding district. Instruction is given in Sanskrit, Urdu, and English, and there is a considerable sprinkling of English-speaking Nepalese.

Finance.—The revenue, is derived from land rents, forests, customs duties, mining royalties and monopolies, and exceeds $5,-000,000. The trade with India bears a duty each way of about 12 per cent.

Production and Industry.—Every available acre is cultivated for the production of grain, fruit and foodstuffs, and the live stock (which consists only of a few sheep and cattle) is grazed in the jungles or stall-fed. The principal crop is rice, and wheat, pulse, maize and other grains are grown, while fruit, flowers and vegetables are freely cultivated. In the hills tea, cotton and tobacco are grown, and hemp, dye plants and medicinal herbs are obtained.

Gold, silver, lignite and coal have been found, and iron, copper, zinc, lead and sulphur are plentiful. Limestone and marbles abound in central Nepal, and there are numerous mineral springs.

Coarse cottons, paper, bells, brass and iron metal work, weapons, and gold and silver ornaments are the principal manufactures. The dominant Gurkha race despises trade and peaceful industries, which are in the hands of the Newars, a subject Mongol race.

Commerce.—The chief trade route is between Katmandu and the Bengal frontier (76 miles). This road traverses the valley of Nepal, and is the only practicable means of access from India. Two routes lead to Tibet over the Himalayas, near the northwestern and northeastern boundaries, but in each case there is accommodation for pedestrians only in the passes, where goods are carried on men's backs. Three-quarters of the trade is with British India.

Nesqually Indians. (See Indian Tribes.)

Nesqually, Wash., proclaimed port of delivery, **2588.**

Netherlands.—The kingdom of the Netherlands is a maritime country of northwest Europe, extending from 53° 32' 21" to 50° 45' 49" N. lat., and from 3° 23' 27" to 7° 12' 20" E. long. The greatest length from north to south is 164 miles, and the greatest breadth is 123 miles. The kingdom is bounded on the east by Germany, and on the south by Belgium, the northern and western boundaries being the North Sea. At the northeastern extremity the boundary crosses the Dollart, a basin at the mouth of the river Ems.

Physical Features.—The coast of the southwest provinces of Zeeland and South Holland, and of the northern provinces of Friesland and Groningen is broken in many places, and groups of islands have been formed by the inroads of the sea. For nearly 200 miles, however, the western coast consists of unbroken sand dunes, protected from the sea by breakwaters, and on the landward side by plantations. The southern archipelago lies between the estuaries of the Meuse and Scheldt, and north of the Meuse estuary is an irregular land formation known as the Hook of Holland; the northern archipelago extends in a semi-circle from the Texel Gat to the Ems basin. Behind the chain of northern islands or Frisian archipelago, are the great gulf or inland sea, known as the Zuyder Zee, or South Sea, to distinguish it from the external North Sea, the northeastern Shallows or Wadden, and the inundated Ems basin, or Dollart, all of which were formed during the thirteenth century by inroads through the original coast line, now marked by the chain of Frisian islands. The area of the Zuyder Zee and Wadden extends 2,000 English square miles, and the Netherlands portion of the Dollart twenty-three square miles, giving a total area for the kingdom of the Netherlands of close on 14,800 English square miles.

As the name implies, the Netherlands are generally low-lying and flat. Of the total land area, 12,761 square miles, nearly 5,000 square miles would be submerged at high water but for the protecting barriers of sand dunes, dikes and dams, the latter accounting for many of the place names in the country.

The principal rivers are the Rhine (Riju) and the Meuse (Maas), the former crossing the eastern border from Germany and flowing in several branches to the North Sea and Zuyder Zee, and the latter traversing the province of Limburg and flowing to the North Sea. The estuaries of the Scheldt (Schelde) are also in Netherlands territory. The country is also intersected with lesser streams, and these are turned to account for the purposes of navigation, irrigation and land drainage, and are connected by numerous artificial canals, or grachts, lined with trees and studded with windmills. The intervening land often consists of drained morasses, or polders, transformed into fertile agricultural or grazing land. In addition to the communicating canals there are many ship canals, the largest being the New Waterway from Rotterdam to the Hook of Holland, and the North Sea Canal from Amsterdam and the Zuyder Zee, along the bed of the river Y to Ymuiden on the North Sea coast. There are many inland lakes, or meers, particularly in the northeast, of much importance to the fishing industry, but the principal hydrographical feature is the Zuyder Zee, a land-locked inlet about eighty-four miles from north to south, and forty-five miles from east to west at its widest part. The mean depth is between 11 and 12 English feet, and the nature of much of the bed has prompted several drainage projects, the reclaimed soil being capable of practical cultivation. The present Government are preparing fresh proposals for the reclamation of large portions of the Zuyder Zee.

History.—The territory now known as the Netherlands was incorporated as a Province of the Roman Empire in the first century, A. D., being at that time peopled by various Germanic tribes, the names of the Batavi and the Frisii being still preserved in the kingdom. As the Roman empire crumbled to pieces, the south Netherlands became part of the Frankish dominions, and the inhabitants were converted to Christianity, but the Frisians of the north retained their independence and heathendom until the eighth century, when they were subdued and converted by Charlemagne, himself a Netherlander by descent. The twelfth century witnessed the rise of the towns, but by the fifteenth century the lordship of these towns had passed with that of most of the feudal states to the rulers of Burgundy, and the overlordship passed successively to France and Austria and so to the head of the Holy Roman empire, and at the abdication of Charles V. to his son Philip II., King of Spain. The sixteenth and seventeenth centuries witnessed the beginnings of the Reformation and the rise of the Dutch Republic. The religious dissensions had divided the country into a Protestant Northern Netherlands and Catholic Southern Netherlands, the latter forming the country now known as Belgium. The Netherlands were acknowledged to be independent by the Treaty of Münster (1648), and in 1688 their Stadtholder, William, Prince of Orange, who had married the daughter of the Duke of York (James II.), became King William III. of Great Britain. From 1700-1713 the Netherlands were the scene of many battles of the War of the Spanish Succession, and at the close of the eighteenth century the people threw over their Stadtholder (whose office had been declared hereditary in 1747) and the Batavian Republic was set up under the protection of the French Republic, but in 1806 Louis Bonaparte, brother of the Emperor Napoleon, was crowned King of Holland. By the Treaty of London (June 14, 1814) the Northern and Southern Netherlands (the Dutch and Belgian provinces) were united and formed into the Kingdom of the Netherlands, under the Prince of Orange-Nassau, a descendant of the house which had taken a leading part in the destiny of the nation since the thirteenth century. This prince was crowned in 1815 as King William I., but the artificial union of Protestant and Catholic countries broke down in 1830-1831, when the Belgian Provinces revolted, and became an independent kingdom.

Government.—The crown is hereditary in the male (and eventually in the female) line of the House of Orange-Nassau, and Kings William I. (1815-1840), William II. (1840-1849) and William III. (1849-1890) were followed in 1890 by the only surviving child of the last-named sovereign.

Present Ruler: Her Majesty Wilhelmina Helena Pauline Maria, Queen of the Netherlands, Princess of Orange-Nassau, Duchess of Mecklenburg, born at The Hague, Aug. 31, 1880; succeeded her father Nov. 23, 1890; assumed the government (which had been carried on by the Queen-Mother, as Regent) Aug. 31, 1898; married at The Hague, Feb. 7, 1901, to His Royal Highness Prince Henry, Prince of the Netherlands and Duke of Mecklenburg.

The States General consists of two chambers. The First Chamber contains 50 members, elected for 9 years (and renewable as to one-third every 3 years) by the Provincial Legislature. The Second Chamber consists of 100 members elected for 4 years by the direct vote of registered male electors. Electors are not registered until the age of 25, and 64 per cent. of the male population of that age are on the register.

Justice is administered in 101 Cantonal Courts, 23 district tribunals which also act as courts of appeal from the cantonal courts. There are 5 higher Courts of Appeal and a Court of Cassation (Hooge Raad) at The Hague.

Each of the 11 Provinces has a legislature elected for 6 years.

AREA AND POPULATION

Provinces	Area in English Sq. Miles	Population 1909
Drenthe	1,027	173,318
Friesland	1,278	359,552
Groningen	909	328,045
Gelderland	1,965	639,602
Limburg	1,977	332,007
North Brabant	851	626,079
North Holland	1,078	1,107,693
Overyssel	1,291	382,880
South Holland	1,162	1,390,744
Utrecht	531	288,514
Zeeland	692	232,515
Total	12,761	5,858,175

The estimated population on Dec. 31, 1912, was 6,102,399.

Education.—The educational system is peculiar, in that primary instructional establishments are encouraged by State aid, while public institutions are provided (where private enterprise is lacking) by local taxation. Primary education is compulsory between the ages of 7-13, the average attendance being 95 per cent. of the enrolment. Technical education is highly efficient, horticulture and agriculture being a feature of special schools. There are State Universities at Leiden (founded in 1575), Groningen (1585), and Utrecht (1634), and a municipal University at Amsterdam (1877), attended by 4,000 students (700 women), and a Technical University at Delft (1864) attended by 1,200 students.

Finance.—The average revenue for five years including 1914 was 212,445,116 florins and the average expenditure for the same period was 224,574,919 florins. The funded debt Jan. 1, 1914, was 1,148,379,900 florins, the cost of which for interest and sinking fund was 38,505;204 florins. The florin or gulden, the unit of value, is equal to $0.40,2 United States money.

Towns.—Capitals, Court: The Hague; Commercial: Amsterdam and Rotterdam. In 1913 there were 10 communes with a population exceeding 50,000, 11 others exceeding 30,000, and 10 more over 20,000. The chief ports are Amsterdam, Rotterdam, Flushing, Terneuzen, Harlingen, Delfzyl, Dordrecht, Zaandam and Schiedam.

Canals.—The total length of the various canals is stated to exceed 1,500 miles, including the great ship canals, and the network of auxiliary canals connecting the various natural waterways. In 1911 there were 3,190 kilometres of railway open for traffic.

Shipping.—The mercantile marine consisted on Dec. 31, 1911, of 428 sailing ships and 347 steamships.

Production and Industry.—Of the total area (8,038,000 English statute acres) 5,-308,450 acres were under crops and grass, 2,141,930 acres were arable land, and 641,-449 acres were woods and forests in 1909.

At the Census of 1910 there were 1,068,-361 cows, and 958,582 other cattle, 889,-036 sheep and lambs, 224,231 goats, 1,-259,844 pigs, and 327,377 horses.

In 1910 over 20,000 persons were employed in the North Sea fisheries, the herring catch of that year being valued at close on £1,000,000.

The mineral resources of the Netherlands are confined to coal, which is mined in Limburg, and to stone, clay, and other non-metallic minerals, used in the sea defences and for industrial purposes.

The cotton industry is in an increasingly flourishing condition, woolens and linens being manufactured at Tilburg, Leiden, Utrecht, and Eindhoven, and carpets at Deventer. Spirits, liqueurs, and beer, leather, paper making, earthenware, chocolate, diamond cutting, tobacco and shipbuilding, are also important industries.

Trade with the United States.—The value of merchandise imported into Netherlands from the United States for the year 1913 was $125,909,862, and goods to the value of $38,180,967 were sent thither—a balance of $87,728,895 in favor of the United States.

NETHERLAND INDIA.—Lies between 6° N. and 11° S. lat. and 95°-141° E. long., and is divided into two administrations, Java (with Madura) and the "Outposts," under a Governor-General.

DUTCH WEST INDIES.—The possessions in the West Indies are divided into two administrative areas, Surinam (Netherland Guiana) on the mainland of South America, and the island of Curaçao with its dependencies.

Surinam is situated between British and French Guiana, on the northeast coast of South America, and contains an area estimated at 49,845 square miles, with a population (1912) of 95,099. About 50,000 acres are cultivated, the principal products being sugar, cacao, bananas, maize, coffee and rice. Gold is found and exported, and also balata.

Curaçao is an island in the West Indies, about forty miles north of Venezuela. Salt, phosphates, cattle and straw hats are exported, together with the Curaçao orange, with which the celebrated liqueur is flavored.

War with Acheen, neutrality of United States in, 4192.

Netherlands, Treaties with.—The treaty of commerce and navigation of 1839 was in part superseded by the treaty of commerce and navigation of 1852. Together they provide for equitable imposition of duties of import and export, together with the extension to one of the contracting parties of such additional rights, privileges, or exemptions as may hereafter be granted by either of them to a third power. The reciprocal equality of the flags is recognized in home ports and in the colonial possessions. The coasting trade is exempted from the provisions of the treaty. Holland does not relinquish her right of imposing discriminating duties on trade between the home ports of Holland and her colonies; nor does the United States relinquish her right to sustain her discriminating duties on coffee and tea. But in the event of the abolition of these discriminating duties by the one power, the other shall reciprocate. International arbitration was agreed to by a convention signed in Washington May 2, 1908. (For the consular convention of 1878, see Consular Conventions; for the terms of the extradition treaty of 1887, see Extradition Treaties.)

Neutral Rights.—The most recent definition of the rights and duties of neutral powers and persons during war is set forth in a convention concluded Oct. 18, 1907, at The Hague; ratification advised by the Senate of the United States March 10, 1908; ratified by the President Feb. 23, 1909, and the ratification deposited with the Netherlands government Nov. 27, 1909; proclaimed Feb. 28, 1910. Ratifications were deposited at The Hague Nov. 27, 1909, by Germany, United States, Austria-Hungary, Denmark, Mexico, the Netherlands, Russia, Sweden, Bolivia and Salvador.

His Majesty the German Emperor, King of Prussia; the President of the United States of America; the President of the Argentine Republic; His Majesty the Emperor of Austria, King of Bohemia, etc., and Apostolic King of Hungary; His Majesty the King of the Belgians; the President of the Republic of Bolivia; the President of the Republic of the United States of Brazil; His Royal Highness the Prince of Bulgaria; the President of the Republic of Chile; the President of the Republic of Colombia; the Provisional Governor of the Republic of Cuba; His Majesty the King of Denmark; the President of the Dominican Republic; the President of the Republic of Ecuador; His Majesty the King of Spain; the President of the French Republic; His Majesty the King of the United Kingdom of Great Britain and Ireland and of the British Dominions beyond the Seas, Emperor of India; His Majesty the King of the Hellenes; the President of the Republic of Guatemala; the President of the Republic of Haiti; His Majesty the King of Italy; His Majesty the Emperor of Japan; His Royal Highness the Grand Duke of Luxemburg, Duke of Nassau; the President of the United States of Mexico; His Royal Highness the Prince of Montenegro; His Majesty the King of Norway; the President of the Republic of Panama; the President of the Republic of Paraguay; Her Majesty the Queen of the Netherlands; the President of the Republic of Peru; His Imperial Majesty the Shah of Persia; His Majesty the King of Portugal and of the Algarves, etc.; His Majesty the King of Roumania; His Majesty the Emperor of All the Russias; the President of the Republic of Salvador; His Majesty the King of Servia; His Majesty the King of Siam; His Majesty the King of Sweden; the Swiss Federal Council; His Majesty the Emperor of the Ottomans; the President of the Oriental Republic of Uruguay; the President of the United States of Venezuela.

With a view to laying down more clearly the rights and duties of neutral Powers in case of war on land and regulating the position of the belligerents who have taken refuge in neutral territory;

Being likewise desirous of defining the meaning of the term "neutral," pending the possibility of settling, in its entirety, the position of neutral individuals in their relations with the belligerents;

Have resolved to conclude a Convention to this effect:

The territory of neutral powers is inviolable.

Belligerents are forbidden to move troops or convoys of either munitions of war or supplies across the territory of a neutral power.

Belligerents are likewise forbidden to erect on the territory of a neutral power a wireless telegraphy station or other apparatus for the purpose of communicating with belligerent forces on land or sea; or to use any installation of this kind established by them before the war on the territory of a neutral power for purely military purposes, and which has not been opened for the service of public messages.

Corps of combatants cannot be formed nor recruiting agencies opened on the territory of a neutral power to assist the belligerents.

A neutral power must not allow any of the acts referred to in preceding paragraphs to occur on its territory.

It is not called upon to punish acts in violation of its neutrality unless the said acts have been committed on its own territory.

The responsibility of a neutral power is not engaged by the fact of persons crossing the frontier separating to offer their services to one of the belligerents.

A neutral power is not called upon to prevent the export or transport, on behalf of one or other of the belligerents, of arms, munitions of war, or, in general, of anything which can be of use to an army or a fleet.

A neutral power is not called upon to forbid or restrict the use on behalf of the belligerents of telegraph or telephone cables or of wireless telegraphy apparatus belonging to it or to companies or private individuals.

Every measure of restriction or prohibition taken by a neutral power in regard to transportation and communication must be impartially applied by it to both belligerents.

A neutral power must see to the same obligation being observed by companies or private individuals owning telegraph or telephone cables or wireless telegraphy apparatus.

The fact of a neutral power resisting, even by force, attempts to violate its neutrality cannot be regarded as a hostile act.

A neutral power which receives on its territory troops belonging to the belligerent armies shall intern them, as far as possible, at a distance from the theater of war.

It may keep them in camps and even confine them in fortresses or in places set apart for this purpose.

It shall decide whether officers can be left at liberty on giving their parole not to leave the neutral territory without permission.

In the absence of a special convention to the contrary, the neutral power shall supply the interned with the food, clothing, and relief required by humanity.

At the conclusion of peace the expenses caused by the internment shall be made good.

A neutral power which receives escaped prisoners of war shall leave them at liberty. If it allows them to remain in its territory it may assign them a place of residence.

The same rule applies to prisoners of war brought by troops taking refuge in the territory of a neutral power.

A neutral power may authorize the passage into its territory of the sick and wounded belonging to the belligerent armies, on condition that the trains bringing them shall carry neither personnel nor war material. In such a case, the neutral power is bound to take whatever measures of safety and control are necessary for the purpose.

The sick or wounded brought under these conditions into neutral territory by one of the belligerents, and belonging to the hostile party, must be guarded by the neutral power so as to ensure their not taking part again in the military operations. The same duty shall devolve on the neutral state with regard to wounded or sick of the other army who may be committed to its care.

The Geneva Convention applies to sick and wounded interned in neutral territory.

The nationals of a state which is not taking part in the war are considered as neutrals.

A neutral cannot avail himself of his neutrality: If he commits hostile acts against a belligerent: if he commits acts in favor of a belligerent, particularly if he voluntarily enlists in the ranks of the armed force of one of the parties. In such a case, the neutral shall not be more severely treated by the belligerent as against whom he has abandoned his neutrality than a national of the other belligerent state could be for the same act.

The following acts shall not be considered as committed in favor of one belligerent in the sense of the above paragraph: Supplies furnished or loans made to one of the belligerents, provided that the person who furnishes the supplies or who makes the loans lives neither in the territory of the other party nor in the territory occupied by him, and that the supplies do not come from these territories; services rendered in matters of police or civil administration.

Railway material coming from the territory of neutral powers, whether it be the property of the said powers or of companies or private persons, and recognizable as such, shall not be requisitioned or utilized by a belligerent except where and to the extent that it is absolutely necessary. It shall be sent back as soon as possible to the country of origin.

A neutral power may likewise, in case of necessity, retain and utilize to an equal extent material coming from the territory of the belligerent power.

Compensation shall be paid by one party or the other in proportion to the material used, and to the period of usage.

The provisions of the present Convention do not apply except between contracting powers, and then only if all the belligerents are parties to the Convention.

Forty-four countries became parties to this Convention, as follows:

United States,
Argentina,
Austria-Hungary,
Belgium,
Bolivia,
Brazil,
Bulgaria,
Chile,
China,
Colombia,
Cuba,
Denmark,
Ecuador,
France,
Germany,
Great Britain (with reservations),
Greece,
Guatemala,
Haiti,
Italy,
Japan,
Luxembourg,
Mexico,
Montenegro,
Netherlands,
Nicaragua,
Norway,
Panama,
Paraguay,
Peru,
Persia,
Portugal,
Roumania,
Russia,
Salvador,
Santo Domingo,
Servia,
Siam,
Spain,
Sweden,
Switzerland,
Turkey,
Uruguay,
Venezuela.

Washington, 131, 148.
  In address of House, 136.
Wilson, 7888, 7998.
Maintained by United States in—
Insurrection in Cuba, 6023, 6068,
  6126.
Revolution in Brazil, 5867, 5956.
Schleswig-Holstein war, 2548.
War between—
  Acheen and Netherlands, 4192.
  France and allied powers, 148.
  France and Germany, 4050.
    Proclaimed, 4040, 4043, 4045.
  Great Britain and France and
    China, 3037, 3089, 3174.
  Great Britain and Russia, 2864.
  Italy and Austria-Hungary, 8065.
  Mexico and Texas, 1370.
  Russia and Turkey, 4418.
  Spain and her colonies, 582, 627,
    639, 657, 685, 762.
War in—
  Canada, 1702, 1748.
    Proclaimed, 1698, 1699.
  Europe. (See Proclamations be-
    low.)
  Japan, 3888.
    Proclaimed, 3712.
  Mexico, 3444, 3581.
  South Africa, 6371, 6407, 6429.
Of Panama Canal Zone, 8008.
Powers to be invited to accede to
  rules of, in treaty of May 8, 1871,
  4462.
Preserved by foreign powers in Span-
  ish-American War, 6312.
Proclamation of in war between:
  Austria-Hungary and Servia; Ger-
    many and Russia, and Germany
    and France, 7969.
  Austria-Hungary and Russia, 7974.
  Belgium and Germany, 7976.
  Belgium and Austria-Hungary,
    7977.
  France and Austria-Hungary, 7975.
  Germany and Great Britain, 7974.
  Great Britain and Austria-Hungary,
    7975.
  Japan and Austria-Hungary, 7975.
  Japan and Germany, 7976.
  Turkey and Great Britain, 8014.
Protection of neutrals, 3377.
Recommendations respecting, 4828.
United States preserves strict, in
  Boer War, 6371, 6407, 6429.
Violation of—
  By army on Rio Grande, 3574.
  In Department of Texas, action
    of Government regarding, dis-
    cussed, 5877.
Wireless stations ordered to observe,
  7962.

Neutrality, Armed. (See Armed Neutrality)

23

Neutrality, Proclamation of.—Neutrality,
in international law, is the attitude and
conditions of a nation or state which does
not take part directly or indirectly in a
war between other states, but maintains relations of friendship with all the
contending parties. In ancient times war
between any two nations was likely to
involve any other, either through sympathy
or by its being drawn unwillingly into the
controversy on accusation of favoring one
or the other of the belligerents. Modern
civilization has made it possible for a peace-
fully inclined nation to avoid entanglements
in quarrels not of its own making. The
position which a state intends to take in
case of war between its neighbors should
be clearly defined. It is customary, therefore, on the breaking out of hostilities for
every nation not participating therein to
declare its position with reference to the
belligerents. This is usually done by a
proclamation by the chief ruler of a state
proclaiming its neutrality and calling upon
its citizens to refrain from any acts of
hostility or special favor toward either of
the parties to the strife. It is also customary for every nation to put on its statute
books general laws regulating the acts of
its citizens with reference to foreign wars.
Upon the declaration of war between France
and Great Britain in 1793 it was decided
unanimously by Washington and his Cabinet that a proclamation of neutrality
should issue and that a French minister
should be received. The proclamation was
drafted by John Jay and declared the
intention of the United States to pursue a
policy of friendship toward both nations,
and enjoined upon all citizens to avoid a
contravention of that disposition upon pain
of prosecution. It is a curious fact that
the word "neutrality" was omitted from
this proclamation, but it was enforced with
fairness. President Roosevelt on Feb. 11,
1904, issued a proclamation declaring the
neutrality of this country in the Russo-
Japanese War. With the outbreak of the
European war of 1914 President Wilson
issued a number of proclamations all of the
same general tenor. (See pages 7969 et seq.)

Nevada.—One of the western group of
states; nickname, "The Sage Brush State";
motto, "All for our country." Nevada
extends from lat. 35° to 42° north and from
long. 114° to 120° west. It is bounded on
the north by Oregon and Idaho, on the east
by Utah and Arizona, and on the west
and southwest by California, and has an
area of 110,690 square miles. The State
is rich in precious metals, the principal
products being silver and gold. The territory was ceded by Mexico in 1848. and the
first settlements were made in 1848 and
1850. Silver was discovered in 1859. Nevada Territory was organized in 1861 and
was admitted to statehood in 1864.
Nevada is a Spanish word meaning
"snowy" or "white as snow," and the name
of the State was derived from the Sierra
Nevada. The State ranks sixth in size in
the Union. Its length from north to south
is 484 miles, its width 321 miles, and its
area 109,821 square miles.
The history of Nevada is chiefly the history of her mines. Since the discovery of
the Comstock lode and other famous ore
bodies periods of activity and prosperity
have alternated with periods of depression.
Each discovery of high-grade ore in noteworthy quantity has been followed by rapid
settlement in that locality and the establishment of one or more towns. In 1890-
1893 a sharp decline in the price of silver
initiated or accompanied a period of depression in Nevada's mining and general indus-

trial prosperity. Silver is so important a resource of the State that to a large extent even now her prosperity depends upon the market for that metal. Of late years, however, an increased production of gold, copper, and recently of platinum has accompanied a gradual and, it is hoped, substantial industrial progress. Permanent towns have grown up and agriculture and related pursuits are becoming firmly established.

There are within the State 61,177,050 acres of unappropriated and unreserved lands, which can be entered at the United States land office at Carson City. Agriculture is retarded by lack of transportation facilities.

There are 160,000 acres within the State subject to the Federal irrigation project. The farm area consists of nearly 3,000,000 acres, of which about one-third is improved land. The farm animals reported Jan. 1, 1910, were 98,000 horses, valued at $7,644,000; 4,000 mules, $316,000; 19,000 milch cows, $836,000; 404,000 other cattle, $8,363,000; 1,585,000 sheep, $5,864,000. The yield and value of field crops for 1911 is given as follows: Corn, 1,000 acres, 30,000 bushels, $27,000; wheat, 36,000 acres, 1,018,000 bushels, $968,000; oats, 8,000 acres, 360,000 bushels, $223,000; potatoes, 8,000 acres, 1,280,000 bushels, $1,197,000; hay, 254,000 acres, 864,000 tons, $8,208,000. The State is one of the leading producers of gold and silver. The output of gold in 1911 was 917,605 fine ounces, worth $18,968,578; the silver output was 10,651,571 fine ounces, valued at $5,858,364. While theretofore ranking first in the production of silver, Nevada in 1911 took third place, being surpassed by both Utah and Montana. The Ely district, in White Pine County, produced 64,494,640 pounds of copper in 1910, and has increased since. The receipts by the State Treasurer for the fiscal year of 1911 were $994,882, and the disbursements, $1,128,347; balance on hand Jan. 1, 1911, $655,531.

In 1905 there were 115 manufacturing establishments, with a capital of $2,891,997, employing 908 persons, who converted $1,627,776 worth of raw material into finished goods worth $3,096,274.

In 1906 there were 1,440 miles of steam railway in the State and five miles of electric line. The population in 1910 was 81,875.

New England.—A name applied to the northeastern section of the United States by Capt. John Smith in his map of the New World published in 1616. Though composed of separate Colonies, there was always a similarity in the customs and habits of the people. New England formed part of North Virginia, granted to the Plymouth Company by James I. in 1606. In 1643 most of the New England Colonies were united for defensive purposes in the New England Confederation. New England is now applied collectively to the States of Maine, New Hampshire, Vermont, Massachusetts, Rhode Island, and Connecticut.

New England Emigrant Company.—The passage of the Kansas-Nebraska law in 1854 made the institution of slavery in Kansas dependent upon the will of the majority of the people of the state. Pro-slavery advocates in Missouri set to work to establish slavery by assisting in the emigration of Southern families. In 1855 an association was formed in Boston to offset this movement by assisting New England farmers to establish homes in the debatable territory. This organization was known as the New England Emigrant Company, and did much toward making Kansas a free state.

New England Shilling.—The general court of Massachusetts on May 27, 1652, established a mint at Boston and installed John Hull as mint master. The first coins which were struck were but rude planchets stamped "N. E.," near the border on the obverse and the denomination mark (XII) on the reverse, signifying the value of 12d. This was known as the New England shilling and was valued at 18¼ cents.

New France.—A French expedition under Verrazano formed a settlement in America as early as 1524, on land discovered by John and Sebastian Cabot in 1497. In 1535 Jacques Cartier ascended the St. Lawrence River as far as the site of Montreal. The first permanent settlement in New France was founded at Quebec by Champlain in 1608. The colonists cultivated friendly relations with the Indians, and Jesuit missionaries extended the French influence through the region of the Great Lakes to the headwaters of the Mississippi and down that stream to the French possessions in the South. The country was conquered by the English in 1629 and restored in 1632. At the beginning of the Seven Years' War New France was made the scene of a part of the struggle between France and England. By 1750 New France, with Louisiana added, comprised the St. Lawrence and Great Lakes basins and the Mississippi basin, though the settlements were scattered. In 1759 Canada was reconquered by the English and its possessions confirmed to them by the treaty of Paris, Feb. 10, 1763. The result of this treaty was the cession of all the country east of the Mississippi to England and that west to Spain. The French laws were continued in force and religious liberty was extended to Roman Catholics.

New Granada.—A name by which that part of South America now called Colombia was known. (See Colombia.)

Mail transported across Isthmus of Panama, complaints regarding, 2552.

Minister of United States to, reasons for not presenting credentials discussed, 3348.

Postal convention with, 2168.

Relations with, discussed, 2978.

Tonnage duties levied on American vessels by, in contravention of treaty discussed, 2948, 3049.

Treaty with, transmitted and discussed, 2217, 2359, 2361, 2576, 2577, 2581, 2582, 2902, 3063, 3122, 3174, 3349.

　Contravention of, by New Granada, 2948, 3049.

　Provisions of, discussed, 2361.

　Regarding Panama Canal. (See Panama Canal.)

　Right of passage over Isthmus of Panama guaranteed by, 2361, 2555, 2902, 3048, 6807.

Wars in, discussed, 3349.

New Hampshire.—One of the thirteen original states; nickname, "The Granite State." It extends from lat. 42° 40′ to 45° 18′ north and from long. 70° 43′ to 72° 33′ west. It is bounded on the north by the Province of Quebec (Canada), on the east by Maine and the Atlantic Ocean, on the south by Massachusetts and on the west by Vermont (separated by the Connecticut River) and Quebec. New Hampshire is called the "Switzerland of America," being noted for the grandeur of its mountain scenery and the beauty of its lakes. It has an area of 9,341 square miles. It is one of the leading states in the manufacture of boots and shoes, and produces also cotton, woolen, and worsted goods, lumber and timber products, hosiery, and foundry and machine shop products.

New Hampshire was visited by Pring in 1603 and by Capt. John Smith in 1614. It formed part of the territory granted to Gorges in 1621. It was settled by the English at Portsmouth and Dover in 1623. Between 1641 and 1679, and at various times thereafter, was a part of Massachusetts. Its final separation was in 1741. Vermont was claimed as part of New Hampshire until 1764.

About three-fifths of the area of the State consists of forests.

Statistics of agriculture collected for the last Federal census, place the number of farms in the State at 27,053, comprising 3,249,438 acres, valued, with stock and improvements, at $103,704,196. The average value of farm land per acre was $13.70, an increase of $9.83 in 1900. The value of domestic animals, poultry, etc., was $11,-910.478, including 167,831 cattle, valued at $5,240,122 : 46,229 horses, $5,266,389 ; 195 mules, $29,681 ; 45,237 swine, $504,174, and 43,772 sheep, $192,346. The yield and value of field crops for 1911 was: Corn, 23,000 acres, 1,035,000 bushels, $849,000 ; oats, 12,000 acres, 406,000 bushels, $248,-000 ; potatoes, 17,000 acres, 2,125,000 bushels, $1,849,000 ; hay, 640,000 acres, 672,000 tons, $11,558,000 ; tobacco, 100 acres, 170,000 pounds, $27,200. The manufacturing business of the State employs 84,-191 persons and $139,990,000 capital, and turns out $164,581,000 worth of goods annually. The leading industry is the manufacture of boots and shoes and next is

cotton goods, followed by woolen goods, lumber and paper. The indebtedness of the State at the end of the fiscal year 1911 was $463,867. Receipts were $2,612,077, and disbursements, $2,707,535.

The mountain and lake regions of the State afford delightful summer resorts. There are 1,276 miles of steam railways in the State, and 292 miles of electric line. The population in 1910 was 430,572.

The number of manufacturing establishments in New Hampshire having an annual output valued at $500 or more at the beginning of 1915 was 1,736. The amount of capital invested was $156,749,000, giving employment to 85,013 persons, using material valued at $114,993,000, and turning out finished goods worth $182,844,000. Salaries and wages paid amounted to $46,524,-000.

New Hampshire:

　Claims of for maintaining jurisdiction over Indian stream, 269.

　Referred to, 1498.

　Constitution of United States, evidence of ratification of amendments to, by, 65, 107.

　Light-Houses ceded to United States by, 102.

　Northeastern boundary, correspondence regarding. (See Northeastern Boundary.)

New Hope Church, or Pumpkin Vine Creek (Ga.), Battle of.—When Gen. Johnston withdrew the Confederate forces from Resaca, Ga., May 16, 1864, he retired by way of Cassville across the Etowah and occupied a strong position commanding the Allatoona Pass. May 23 Sherman crossed the Etowah and moved towards Dallas. Hooker, with the Twentieth Army Corps, moving from Burnt Hickory toward Dallas, May 25 encountered a force of Confederate cavalry at Pumpkin Vine Creek. They were driven across the stream, and about two miles to the eastward the Federals encountered Johnston's entire army. Here a severe battle took place. The Confederates retired and occupied a strong position from Dallas to Marietta. The losses of each army in these operations were about 2,500 men killed and wounded.

New Ireland.—Jan. 12, 1779, Capt. Mowatt, with three British sloops of war, landed Gen. McLane and 900 troops on the peninsula of Biguyduce (now Castine), on the south coast of Maine. On the 25th of the following July an expedition of nineteen armed vessels and twenty-four transports under Gurdon Saltonstall, a Connecticut sea captain, and 1,500 men from Massachusetts under Gen. Lovell, arrived at Penobscott for the purpose of dislodging the British. They delayed making the attack, however, and the arrival of five British ships from New York on the 13th of August forced them to burn their ships and disperse. As a result of their success the British during the next year attempted to erect Maine into a province under the name of New Ireland.

New Jersey.—One of the thirteen original states. It extends from lat. 38° 56′ to 41° 21′ north and from long. 73° 54′ to 75° 33′ west. It is bounded on the north by New York, on the east by New York (separated by the Hudson River, New York Bay and Staten Island Sound) and the Atlantic Ocean, on the south by Delaware Bay and on the west by Pennsylvania and Delaware (both separated by the Delaware

River.) It has an area of 8,224 square miles.

New Jersey was first settled by the Dutch at Bergen, probably about 1617. There were succeeding colonies there of Swedes, Finns, and English. In 1664 it was granted by the Duke of York to Sir George Carteret, lieutenant-governor of the Isle of Jersey, to be a perpetual inheritance and to be called New Jersey. It was reconquered by the Dutch in 1673 and restored to England in 1674, and sold to the Quakers. Proprietary government ceased in 1702 and New Jersey was made a royal province. It was under the same governor as New York until 1738.

Statistics of agriculture collected for the last Federal census, place the number of farms in the State at 33,487, comprising 2,573,857 acres, valued, with stock and improvements, at $254,832,665. The average value of land per acre was $48.23. The value of domestic animals and poultry, etc , was $24,558,639, including 222,999 cattle, valued at $8,393,117; 88,922 horses, $12,-012,512; 4,041 mules, $621,774; 147,005 swine, $1,127,040; 30,683 sheep, $161,138; poultry, $2,221,610. The yield and value of field crops for 1911 is given as follows: Corn, 270,000 acres, 9,936,000 bushels, $7,-055,000; wheat, 84,000 acres, 1,462,000 bushels, $1,404,000; oats, 71,000 acres, 2,-024,000 bushels, $1,012,000; rye, 72,000 acres, 1,181,000 bushels, $980,000; potatoes, 84,000 acres, 6,132,000 bushels, $6,-439,000; hay, 428,000 acres, 449,000 tons, $9,878,000. Some iron and zinc is mined in the State. The Mine Hill mines, in Sussex County, produced, in 1910, 308,353 short tons of zinc, besides 67,324 tons of crude oil. The receipts by the State Treasurer for the fiscal year 1911 were $8,014,-876, and the disbursements were $9,250,-283; balance on hand Oct. 31, 1911, $3,-301,781.

In 1905 the manufacturing establishments of the State had a capital of $715,-060,174 and employed 289,532 operatives, who converted $470,440,176 worth of raw material into silks, cotton and woolen goods, worsteds, hats, hosiery, ironware, leather, beer, breadstuffs, chemicals, pottery, refined petroleum, etc., to the amount of $774,369,025.

There are 2,297 miles of steam railway within the State and 1,198 miles of electric line. The population in 1910 was 2,537,167.

The number of manufacturing establishments in New Jersey having an annual output valued at $500 or more at the beginning of 1915 was 9,742. The amount of capital invested was $1,352,382,000, giving employment to 431,003 persons, using material valued at $883,465,000, and turning out finished goods worth $1,406,633,000. Salaries and wages paid amounted to $280,984,000.

New Jersey:
Boundary line with New York, 1268.
Ratification of—
Amendment to Federal Constitution by, referred to, 70, 249.
Fifteenth amendment by, 4081.
Fourteenth amendment by, discussed, 3836.
Request from the governor of, that Congress consent to an agreement made with New York State regarding boundary, 1268.

New Jersey, The, interference by American minister to France in case of, 387.

New Jersey Plan.—At the convention held in Philadelphia in 1787 to amend the Articles of Confederation William Paterson, of New Jersey, proposed a constitution providing for a single house of Congress, with power to regulate taxation and commerce and choose the President; that requisitions from states should be continued as under the Articles of Confederation; that a judiciary should be established; that the executive should coerce refractory states or individuals, and other matters of general but minor interest. The plan was unfavorably reported. The convention accepted the Virginia plan with extensive modifications.

New London (Conn.), Capture of.—Sept. 6, 1781, Benedict Arnold's expedition against Connecticut arrived in the harbor of New London. The only defense of the town was the unfinished Fort Trumbull, manned by about 25 or 30 State militia under Capt. Shopley. About a third of these were lost while escaping in boats to Fort Griswold after firing one volley, disabling 4 or 5 of their assailants.

New Madrid (Mo.), Battle of.—On the surrender of Fort Donelson to Grant the Confederates abandoned Columbus, Ky., on the Mississippi, and fell back to New Madrid, Mo., about eighty miles below Cairo. It was defended by Fort Thompson and several batteries and by 6 gunboats mounting heavy guns under Commodore Hollins. March 4, 1862, Gen. Pope appeared before New Madrid with an army of 20,000, which he had been commanding in eastern Missouri. On the 14th, having received heavy guns from Cairo, he gave the place a severe cannonading, disabling several of the gunboats. Gen. McCown, unable to hold New Madrid, removed his garrison during the night and in the midst of a thunderstorm to Island No. 10. Pope lost 51 men killed and wounded.

New Mexico.—One of the southwestern group of states; nickname, "Adobe State;" motto, "Crescit eundo" ("It increases as it goes"). It extends from lat. 40° 20' to 37° north and from long. 103° 2' to 109° 2' west. It is bounded on the north by Colorado, on the east by Texas and Oklahoma, on the south by Texas and Mexico, and on the west by Arizona.

New Mexico was visited by Niza in 1539, and Francisco Vasquez de Coronado conducted an expedition consisting of 400 Spanish and 800 Indians as far north as the present city of Santa Fé in 1540. Near the close of the sixteenth century Spanish missionaries made settlements about the head waters of the Rio Grande, and in 1605 Santa Fé was founded. The Spanish were temporarily expelled by the Indians in 1680. In 1846 the region was conquered by the Americans under General Kearny, who proclaimed himself provisional governor. By the treaty of Guadalupe Hidalgo, proclaimed in 1848, New Mexico became a part of the United States. A territorial government was established by act of Congress approved Sept. 9, 1850. In 1853 a part of the Gadsden Purchase was added to New Mexico, making the present area 122,634 square miles. It was admitted to the Union June 20, 1910.

The industries of New Mexico are mostly confined to mining and stock-raising. Some cereals, vegetables, fruit and cotton are raised. With the extension of irrigation more attention is being given both to agriculture and stock-raising. In 1900 the irrigated area covered 203,893 acres, exclusive of lands in Indian reserves. The area to be reclaimed under the Federal reclamation act includes 40,000 acres in New Mexico. The Rio Grande project provides for reservoir construction for the irrigation of 180,-000 acres in New Mexico and Texas. Private enterprise is also devoted largely to reservoir and canal construction. The forest area covers more than 8,300,000 acres. There are 44,777,905 acres of public lands in the territory unreserved and unappropriated. The land offices are at Clayton, Las Cruces, Roswell, and Santa Fé.

The agricultural development of New Mexico has been promoted by irrigation, both public and private. From less than 400,000 acres of fertile soil in 1900, the farm lands have increased to 2,000,000 acres actually producing through irrigation and dry farming, and it is believed that 3,000,000 acres additional may be reclaimed by storage and diversion of water. The Las Vegas irrigation project just completed will deliver water to 18,000 acres; by diversion of water from the Pecos River, Guadaloupe County, 16,000 acres have been reclaimed; the central pumping station in Portales, Roosevelt County, furnishes water for 10,000 acres. During the fiscal year ending in 1910, the irrigation department received 158 applications to appropriate water to 617,816 acres of land. During the year ended June 30, 1910, 299,255 cattle and 10,988 horses were shipped, at prices ranging from $18 to $28. Sheep to the number of 719,444 were shipped. In the spring of 1910 there were 3,500,000 sheep in pasture in the State. Wild game and fish are abundant.

The copper production of 1910 was 3,-784,609 pounds, while 5,031,136 pounds was produced the preceding year. In 1911 the output was increased and the cost of production decreased. Companies whose finished product cost 15 cents per pound in 1907, sold in 1911 at 12.7 cents and made a profit. The Chino Copper Company, with mills in the Santa Rita district, is the latest important producer. The gold produced in 1911 was worth $639,897, and the silver was valued at $628,282.

In 1906 there were 2,795 miles of steam railway and 14 miles of electric line in the territory. The population in 1910 was 327,-301.

New Mexico:

Abduction of citizens from, referred to, 2643.

Admission of, into Union, discussed, 2556, 7020, 7229.

Admission to Union, Act providing for, vetoed, 7636.

Appropriations for, requested, 3666.

Approval of constitution recommended, 7598.

Boundaries of, discussed, 2446.

Boundary line with Texas, 2566, 2568, 2586, 2587, 2601, 2628.

Proposition of United States regarding establishment of, accepted, 2630.

Proclamation regarding, 2643.

Views of President Fillmore on settlement of, 2603, 2630.

Capitol at Santa Fé, appropriation for completion of, recommended, 4737.

Cession of California and, to United States by Mexico—

Area and value of, discussed, 2449, 2484.

Discussed and recommendations regarding, 2306, 2309, 2344, 2356, 2386, 2426, 2437, 2444, 2484.

Treaty for, transmitted, 2437.

Claims of Texas to portion of. (See Boundary line, *ante*.)

Condition of, discussed, 444.

Constitution adopted by, transmitted, 2611.

Forces to be employed in, 2454.

Government of, discussed, 2557, 2564.

Indian hostilities in, discussed, 4528.

Indians in—

Enslaved, discussed and orders regarding, 3540.

Hostilities of, referred to, 3121.

Number of, 2453.

Land laws, extension of, over; recommended, 2623.

Lands granted to, in aid of colleges accepted, 3358.

Lands in—

Claims under Spanish and Mexican grants, discussed, 5484, 5510, 5561.

Records of Mexican Government regarding, 4257.

Set apart as public reservation by proclamation, 5686, 6872.

Legislative sessions of—

Law providing for time for commencement of, referred to, 4675.

Recommendation by territorial governor for holding, 4736.

Mines in, referred to, 2493.

Officer commanding in, 2587.

Proclamation of, referred to, 2601.

Persons convicted of treason in, referred to, 2448.

Prohibition by authorities of Spain to land American cargoes at, 334.

Revenue laws over, recommended, 2493.

Slavery in, right to introduce, discussed, 2490. (See also Slavery.)

Surveyor-General's office in, recommended, 2493.

Territorial government over—

Deemed inexpedient, 2567.

Difficulties in organizing, 2663.

Proposition and proclamation regarding, 2630, 2643.

Recommended, 2392, 2439, 2488.

Unlawful combinations in, proclamations against, 4441, 5932.

New Netherlands.—The second in order of settlement of the thirteen Colonies. It was the name of the region lying between the Delaware and Connecticut rivers. It was claimed by the Dutch by virtue of its discovery by Henry Hudson, an English navigator in charge of a Dutch expedition, in 1609. A trading post, the germ of a colony, was established, 1613-14, and maintained. In 1614 the States-General of the Netherlands granted the exclusive privilege of trading in New Netherlands to the explorers. In 1615 the New Netherlands Company was formed to trade in furs, but little attempt was made to settle families before 1621. In 1623 the new country was made a province of Holland and granted the armorial distinction of a count. Charles II. of England in 1664 granted the country to his brother, the Duke of York, and the garrison of the little block-house at New Amsterdam, being menaced by six times its number, was compelled to surrender. The place was recovered by the Dutch in 1673, but restored the following year. In 1674 the name was changed to New York. The question of the priority of the settlement of New York by the Dutch to that of Plymouth by the expatriated English Pilgrims, fresh from Holland, is one that still divides the historians. Dr. Brodhead, on the authority of Holland documents, seems, however, to have shown that the early trading post set up by the Dutch in 1613 was never abandoned and was really a settlement before the date of the Plymouth colonization. A similar post was established, 1614, near the present site of Albany.

New Orleans, La.; population (1900),
287,104.

Alarm excited at, over report that Aaron Burr would assemble armies in, 403.

Blockade of port of, removed by proclamation, 3290.

Branch mint at—
Seizure of, by authorities of Louisiana, referred to, 3199.

Capture of, referred to, 3315.

Cincinnati and Louisville expositions, 4819.

Defense of, should engage attention of Congress, 394, 447, 688.

Investigations of Gen. Smith and James T. Brady at, referred to, 3683.

Italians lynched in, discussed, 5617.
Indemnity for, paid by United States, 5751.

Memorial from, regarding irregularity in mail service, 2883.

Rights of deposit at port of, suspended, 338.
Restored, 346.

Riot at, referred to, 3662.

Spanish subjects in, assaulted, 2654.
Claims arising out of, discussed, 2688.

Title to lots in, referred to, 430.

Vessels bound for, for military necessities allowed to enter port of, 3378.

World's Industrial and Cotton Centennial Exposition at, discussed and recommendations regarding, 4773, 4802, 4804, 4863, 4923.

Board on behalf of Executive Departments designated, 4815, 4817.

Also placed in charge of Cincinnati and Louisville expositions, 4819.

Instructions to, 4819, 4820.

Proclamation regarding, 4746.

Report of board of management transmitted, 4953.

New Orleans (La.), Battle of.—Within a week after the battle of Rodriguez Canal both Jackson and Sir Edward Pakenham received reenforcements. Jackson's whole force on the New Orleans side of the river on Jan. 8, 1815, was about 5,000, of which only 2,200 were at the front. Only 800 of the latter were regulars. On the opposite side of the river was Gen. Morgan with 800 militia. This force of 5,800, indifferently armed and disciplined, was confronted by 10,000 of the finest soldiers in the world, most of them fresh from the continental campaign under Wellington. The Americans were intrenched behind their fortifications, which the British were compelled to approach across an open plain. In the conflict 2,600 were lost to the British, of whom 700 were killed, 1,400 wounded, and 500 taken prisoners. The Americans lost only 8 killed and 13 wounded. Probably no other battle in history presents this disparity in the number lost. The battle was fought after peace was proclaimed, but before this news reached New Orleans. (See illustration opposite.)

New Orleans (La.), Capture of.—Feb. 20, 1862, Commodore Farragut, with his flagship, the sloop of war *Hartford*, arrived at Ship Island, 100 miles north-northeast of the mouth of the Mississippi. He was in command of the Western Coast Blockading Squadron, with directions to take possession of New Orleans. A military force to cooperate with Farragut arrived at Ship Island March 25, under Gen. B. F. Butler. The defenses of New Orleans were Fort Jackson, on the right bank or south side of the river, near its last great bend before it separates into the Delta, and Fort St. Philip, a little farther upstream on the opposite side. The former, with its water battery, mounted 75 guns; the latter 40. Just above the forts was a fleet of 15 vessels, including the ironclad ram *Manassas* and a floating battery, covered with railroad iron, called the *Louisiana*. These were in command of Commodore J. K. Mitchell. A heavy chain was also stretched across the river below Fort Jackson. Farragut's fleet consisted of 6 sloops of war, 16 gunboats, 21 schooners, each carrying a 13-inch mortar, and 5 other vessels. The fleet carried more than 200 guns.

Farragut bombarded the forts for six days with his mortar boats without much effect. The Confederate loss was 14 killed and 39 wounded. It was then decided to run by the forts. The obstructions were opened in the face of a heavy fire, and the fleet formed in three divisions and awaited the signal. It was given at half past 3 o'clock on the morning of April 24, 1862. Capt. Bailey led off with his division of 8 vessels. Under the storm of shot and shell they passed the obstructions and ran by the forts against the current in a stream less than half a mile wide, escaping the blazing rafts only to be met at the end of their journey by the Confederate gunboats eager to begin the fight. The second division of the fleet was led through the fiery gauntlet by the *Hartford*, with Farragut on board. The *Sciota*, carrying Fleet Captain Bell, led the third division. The *Kennebec, Itasca,* and *Winona* failed to pass the forts, becoming entangled in the rafts and floating débris and delayed beyond the dawn. The latter lost all but one man of her rifled-gun crew. Having passed the forts the fleet savagely attacked the small Confederate gunboats beyond and their destruction was speedily accomplished. May 1 New Orleans was formally occupied by the United States troops. The Federals lost in the taking of New Orleans 37 killed and 147 wounded. The Confederate loss was stated as only 40 killed and wounded.

New Orleans Massacre.—On M a r c h 15, 1891, a mob broke into the jail at New Orleans and killed a number of Italians, who were held charged with the murder of Mayor Hennessey. (The Mayor had been active in investigating a secret society of Sicilian origin, called "Mafiosi.") Secretary of State Blaine immediately urged the Governor of Louisiana to proceed against the guilty parties. The Italian Premier, through diplomatic correspondence, urged punishment of the members of the mob and indemnity for the death of the Italians. Blaine insisted that the United States was without authority to act, and that the State of Louisiana had full power. Thereupon the Italian Minister at Washington, Baron Fava, quit his post, thus substantially cutting off diplomatic relations. President Harrison restored friendly relations with Italy by reversing Blaine's position and by offering, in the name of the United States, to pay the indemnity demanded, which amounted to something over $24,000.

New Panama Canal Company, treatment of, by Colombia, 6922.

New South Wales, Australia:
International exhibition at Melbourne to celebrate founding of, discussed, 5176.
Postal convention with, 4882.

New York.—One of the thirteen original states; nickname, "The Empire State"; motto, "Excelsior." It extends from lat. 40° 30′ to 45° 1′ north and from long. 71° 51′ to 79° 46′ west. It is bounded on the north and northwest by Ontario, Canada (separated for the most part by Lake Ontario and the St. Lawrence River) ; on the east by Vermont (partly separated by Lake Champlain), Massachusetts, and Connecticut ; on the south by the Atlantic Ocean, New York Bay, New Jersey and Pennsylvania (partly separated by the Delaware River), and on the west by Pennsylvania and Ontario (separated by Lake Erie and the Niagara River). Long Island, Staten Island, and several small islands are included in the State. The area is 49,204 square miles. It is mountainous in the eastern part, along the Hudson River. A beautiful rolling country constitutes the watershed separating the north and south drainage of the western and central parts of the State. To the north the surface descends in undulating terraces toward Lake Ontario. To the south the country is higher, in places reaching an altitude of 2,000 to 2,500 feet. The valley of the Mohawk extends westward from the Hudson for nearly 150 miles. New York is the first state of the Union in commerce, manufactures, population, and estimated value of property, and the second state in value of farms.

Statistics of agriculture collected for the last Federal census, place the number of farms in the State at 215,597, comprising 22,030,367 acres, valued, with stock and improvements, at $1,451,481,495. The average value of land per acre was $32.13, against $24.34 in 1900. The value of domestic animals, poultry. etc., was $183,090,-844, including 2,423,003 cattle, valued at

$83,062,242 ; 59,008 horses, $80,043,312 ; 4,052 mules, $650,497 ; 666,179 swine, $5,-905,272 ; 930,300 sheep, $4,839,651, and poultry, $7,879,388. The yield and value of field crops for 1911 was : Corn, 530,000 acres, 20,405,000 bushels, $15,712,000 ; wheat, 345,000 acres, 6,728,000 bushels, $6,392,000 ; oats, 1,310,000 acres, 38,645,-000 bushels, $19,709,000 ; rye, 135,000 acres, 2,254,000 bushels, $2,006,000 ; potatoes, 375,000 acres, 27,750,000 bushels, $24,975,000 ; hay, 4,763,000 acres, 4,858,-000 tons, $86,958,000 ; tobacco, 3,800 acres, 5,054,000 pounds, $525,616. The State ranks fourth in the production of iron ore, the output for 1910 being 1,287,209 tons, valued at $3,848,683.

In 1906 the output of talc was 67,800 tons, worth $626,000, and 9,642,178 barrels of salt, worth $2,335,150. In 1907, 1,375,-020 tons of iron ore, valued at $2,820,135, mostly magnetite, were mined. The yield of crude petroleum was valued at $2,127,-748, the natural gas at $766,157, the mineral water at $686,574, and the building stone, cement, clay products, etc., at $21,-917,152.

The number of manufacturing establishments in New York having an annual output valued at $500 or more at the beginning of 1915 was 48,203. The amount of capital invested was $3,334,278,000, giving employment to 1,289,099 persons, using material valued at $2,108,607,000, and turning out finished goods worth $3,814,661,000. Salaries and wages paid amounted to $873,771,-000. Preeminent among the industries of the State is the manufacture of clothing. This factory industry originated in the State about 1835, and by 1880 it was first among the industries of the State. In 1905 New York was first in the production of clothing.

The sugar-refining business, though conducted in only eight establishments, turned out $116,438,838 worth of finished goods. Next in importance to sugar comes the manufacture of iron ware and machinery. Printing and the manufacture of liquors, bread, tobacco, meats and flour follow in importance in the order named. Dairying is carried on in 1,766 establishments, with a capital of $9,066,426, and the annual output exceeds $31,000,000. The textile industries turned out $114,371,226 worth of cotton and woolen goods, silks, carpets, hosiery and knit goods in 1905. In 1906 the flour and grist mills made $54,546,435 worth of breadstuffs. The issues from the printing presses brought $137,985,751, nearly half of which was from periodical papers, printed in English, French, German, Italian, Spanish, Hebrew, Scandinavian, Polish, Bohemian, Chinese, Japanese, Arabic, Greek, Hungarian, and twenty-six other languages.

New York City is the third shipping port of the world, London and Liverpool taking precedence. The imports for 1907-08 amounted to $688,215,938, and the exports to $701,062,913 ; the tonnage of foreign trade was : entered, 12,154,780 tons; cleared, 11,939,964 tons.

In 1906 there were 8,336 miles of steam railway and 3,304 miles of electric line. The population in 1910 was 9,113,279.

New York (see also Hudson; New York City):
Boundary line with **New Jersey,** referred to, 1268.
Branch mint in, recommended, 2352.
Canadian outrages on frontier of, discussed, 1618, 1676, 1695, 1840.
Canals in. recommendations regarding, 3334.

New Zealand.—The Dominion of New Zealand is distant about 1,200 miles southeast of the mainland of Australia, and consists of three main islands in the South Pacific Ocean, known as the North, South, and Stewart Islands, between 33°-53° S. latitude and 162° E.-172° W. longitude, with several groups of smaller islands lying at some distance from the principal group.

Physical Features.—A mountain chain traverses the west side of the South Island, culminating in Mount Cook, 12,349 feet in height. The North Island is less generally elevated. The North Island has a large central lake (Taupo) 36 miles long, from which the river Waikato flows northwest to the sea. The celebrated "pink terraces" of Rotomahana, formed by the deposit of silica tinted with oxide of iron, were destroyed by volcanic action in 1886, but are again in process of formation. The South Island has many Alpine lakes of great depth.

The extremes of daily temperature vary throughout the year only by an average of 20°. The mean annual temperature of the whole Dominion for the different seasons is: Spring, 55°; summer, 63°; autumn, 57°; and winter, 48°.

AREA AND POPULATION

Islands	Area in English Sq. Miles	European Population Census of 1911
North Island	44,673	563,729
South Island	57,923	444,120
Stewart Island	665	357
Chatham Islands	375	258
Auckland, Campbell, Antipodes, Bounty, Kermadec, Cook, and other Islands	720	12,598
Maori Population	....	49,844
Total	104,356	1,070,910

History.—The west coast of the South Island of New Zealand was discovered by Abel Jansen Tasman, the navigator (voyaging under the direction of the Netherlands' East India Company), on December 13, 1642. The islands were visited in 1769 by Captain Cook, who returned to them in 1773, 1774, and 1777. In 1793 the Government of New South Wales despatched H.M.S. *Daedalus* to the islands on a diplomatic mission. The first settlement of Europeans was made in 1814, but no colonization took place until 1825. In 1840 British sovereignty was proclaimed, and on May 3, 1841, New Zealand was, by letters patent, erected into a separate colony distinct from New South Wales.

Government.—The Constitution rests upon the Act of 1852, under which the executive authority is entrusted to a Governor appointed by the Crown and aided by a Council of Ministers, with a Legislature of two houses.

Parliament consists of a Legislative Council appointed by the Governor (prior to 1891 the appointments were for life; since that date for 7 years only), at present consisting of 42 members; and a House of Representatives, consisting of 80 members elected for 3 years. Four of the members are Maoris elected by the natives. Women are entitled to register as electors and to vote at the elections for Members of the House of Representatives, but are not qualified for election or for appointment to the Legislative Council. The capital is Wellington.

Army.—The New Zealand Defence Forces consist of the N. Z. Staff Corps (Officers), the Permanent Staff, and the Royal New Zealand Artillery.

Military training is compulsory on all male citizens between the ages of 12 and 25. The Peace Effective is about 30,000 of all ranks. The material from which the Australian and New Zealand armies are being constructed is the finest in the world.

Navy.—The Dominion possesses the super-dreadnought battle cruiser *New Zealand* (18,800 tons), which has been placed at the disposal of H. M. Admiralty, and torpedo-boats and submarine-mining steamers; the Calliope Dock, capable of docking two warships, was subsidized by the Imperial Government in 1898.

Finance.—The annual revenues amount to nearly £12,000,000, and the expenditures are about the same amount. The debt was stated in 1913 as £90,000,000. The British system of money is in use.

Education.—The State system of education is free, secular, and compulsory; there are also 310 private schools, with 20,238 scholars, and in addition, 104 village schools for the Maoris. The higher education of boys and girls in the cities and large towns is carried on in 32 endowed colleges and grammar schools.

Production and Industry.—The area of the two main islands is 65,440,815 acres, and the total extent of land under all kinds of crop, and of land broken up but not under crop, is 1,729,504 acres, while there are 14,214,741 acres of land in sown grass, of which 9,214,515 acres had not been previously ploughed. Amongst the forest productions are the Kauri pine (found only at the northern extremity of the islands), much valued for shipbuilding and for its resin (Kauri gum). New Zealand flax is used for the manufacture of ropes and twine.

Live Stock.—The cattle in 1911 numbered 2,020,171; sheep, 23,750,153 (in April, 1912); pigs, 348,754; and horses, mules and asses, 404,688. The pastures of the South Island produce the celebrated sheep of the Canterbury Plain.

Minerals.—Coal-mining is one of the largest industries. Gold-mining, both alluvial and quartz, is an important industry in many districts, and rich iron ore, in the form of iron sand, has been found in Taranaki, and in the form of brown hæmatite at Parapara; copper is also found.

Dependencies of New Zealand.—Antipodes Group, Auckland Islands, Bounty Islands and Campbell Islands, all uninhabited. Chatham Islands and Cook Islands. The Cook and other islands, annexed to the British Empire in October, 1900, and included in the boundaries of New Zealand since June, 1901, consist of the islands of Rarotonga, Aitutaki, Mangaia, Atiu, Mauke, Mitiaro, The Herveys and Takutea.

New Zealand:

Sequestration of lands in, claimed by William Webster, referred to, 4327.

Titles to lands in, claimed by American citizens, referred to, 5179.

Newbern (N. C.), Capture of.—After securing Roanoke Island Burnside proceeded to the execution of another clause of his orders by advancing upon Newbern. March 14, 1862, he landed a force of men on the banks of the Neuse River, eighteen miles below the city. They advanced within five miles of the place where they encountered a redoubt, which was taken by assault. The bridge over the Trent, a tributary of the Neuse, was burned by the Confederates as they retreated. With the capture of Newbern 46 heavy guns, 3 batteries of light artillery, and a large amount of stores fell into Burnside's hands. The Federal loss was 90 killed and 466 wounded. The Confederate loss was 23 killed, 58 wounded, and about 2,500 prisoners.

Newburg Addresses.—There were many things to criticise and much to complain of in the conduct of the Revolutionary War, but heroic achievement and devotion to the cause of freedom, as a rule, overshadowed the jealousies of officers and the complaints of men. Gen. Horatio Gates had always been a rival of Washington for command of the army, and frequently conspired against the latter's popularity. In 1783, while Washington's army was encamped at Newburg, two anonymous appeals were issued to the officers, urging them to hold a meeting to consider the question of the money due them by Congress. The appeals were written by Capt. Armstrong, of Pennsylvania, and were supposed to have been instigated by the Gates faction. Washington immediately denounced the meeting as subversive of discipline and called a regular meeting of the officers to consider the matter. Gates was placed in the chair. Washington's friends carried motions characterizing as "infamous proposals" the suggestions of the Newburg addresses, and furthermore declaring their unshaken confidence in Congress.

Newfoundland.—The Island of Newfoundland is situated between 46° 37′-57° 39′ N. latitude and 52° 35′-59° 25′ W. longitude, on the northeast side of the Gulf St. Lawrence, and is separated from the North American Continent by the Straits of Belle Isle. The island is about 317 miles long and 316 miles broad, and is triangular in shape. with Cape Bauld north, Cape Race southeast, and Cape Ray southwest at the angles.

Physical Features.—The coast is extremely rugged, and the coastal regions are mountainous, the north and east being excessively cold owing to the quantities of ice brought down from the Greenland seas. The interior is undulating and is covered with tolts (round hills) interspersed with lakes, rivers, and swamps, but containing many fertile valleys, where the climate is favorable to agriculture, and a great wealth of forests, mainly of pine and birch. The climate is salubrious, and the people are a strong, healthy, hardy, industrious race. The thermometer seldom falls below zero in winter, and ranges in the shade in summer from 70° to 80°.

History.—Newfoundland is the oldest English colony in America, for it was discovered by John Cabot on June 24, 1497; the first land seen was hailed as Prima Vista—the present Cape Bonavista. The island was afterwards visited (1500) by the Portuguese navigator, Gaspar de Cortereal, and soon became the centre of an extensive fishing industry, with settlements of Portuguese, Biscayans, and French. In August, 1583, the island was formally occupied by Sir Humphrey Gilbert, in the name of Queen Elizabeth, and by the Treaty of Utrecht (1713) the whole island was acknowledged to be British. A Governor was first appointed in 1728, and in 1885 "Responsible government" was accorded to the island.

Government.—The executive is entrusted to a Governor appointed by the Crown, aided by an Executive Council, with a Legislature of two houses.

AREA AND POPULATION.

	Area in English Sq. Miles	Population 1911
Newfoundland	42,750	238,670
Labrador Coast	120,000	3,949
Total	162,750	242,619

Production and Industry.—The inhabitants are chiefly located on the coast-line of the shore and bays, and for the greater part are engaged in fishing—for cod in summer, and seal fishing in winter and spring; agriculture, mining, and lumbering are also engaging attention, while large pulp and paper mills have been erected. The larger portion of the interior is practically in a state of nature; but their railways have opened up large tracts of rich agricultural, mineral, and timber lands hitherto of small value. There were 770 miles of railway open in 1911.

Shipping.—On Dec. 31, 1910, the Mercantile Marine of Newfoundland consisted of 3,318 sailing vessels of 132,510 tons, and 68 steam vessels of 14,041 tons.

The Capital, St. John's (population 32,-292), contains two cathedrals, several banks, and numerous public buildings.

LABRADOR, a dependency of Newfoundland, forms the most easterly part of America, and extends from Blanc Sablon, in the Straits of Belle Isle, on the south, to Cape Chudleigh, at the entrance to Hudson's Straits (or to Cape Wolstenholme), on the north; the boundaries between Quebec and Labrador being a matter of keen controversy which is expected to come up for settlement before the Judicial Committee of the Privy Council. Labrador possesses valuable cod, herring, trout, and salmon fisheries. One of the grandest spectacles in the universe is provided by the Great Falls of Labrador, on the Hamilton River. The inhabitants of this 850 miles of coastal America are mainly Eskimos, engaged in fishing and hunting. There are no towns, but there are Moravian mission stations at Maggovik, Hopedale, Nain, Okak, Hebron and Killinek. Pulp and paper mills have been founded at Sandwich Bay and Hamilton Inlet, to deal with the almost inexhaustible supply of timber.

Trade with the United States.—The value of merchandise imported from the United States into Newfoundland and Labrador for the year 1913 was $4,888,618, and goods to the value of $1,151,875 were sent thither—a balance of $3,736,743 in favor of the United States.

Newfoundland:
Certain articles of treaty at Washington extended to, 4227, 4243.
Commercial intercourse with, referred to, 2867.
Importations from, proclamation removing duties on, 2922.
Postal convention with, 4203.
Reciprocity with, 6717.

Newport, Vt., privileges of other ports granted to, by proclamation, 3428.

Newspapers, transportation of:
Referred to, 120, 124.
Repeal tax on, recommended, 134.

Nez Percé Indians. (See Indian Tribes.)

Nez Percé War. (See Indian Wars.)

Niagara, The, employed to return negroes to Africa, 3058.

Niagara Falls:
American victory on Canadian side of, 533.
Attack of American forces upon British troops near, unsuccessful, 501.
Ship canal around, discussed, 4150.

Nicaragua.—Nicaragua is the largest of the Central American Republics and is situated between 10° 45'-15° N. lat. and 83° 40'-87° 38' W. long. It is bounded on the north by Honduras and on the south by Costa Rica, the Atlantic and Pacific Oceans washing the east and west coasts. The Atlantic (Caribbean or Mosquito) coast of about 300 miles is low and swampy, with numerous lagoons and estuaries, with harbors at Gracis á Dios, in the extreme northeast, Bluefields, and San Juan del Norte or Greytown in the extreme south. The Pacific Coast of about 200 miles is rocky and elevated, but possesses good harbors in Fonseca, Corinto, Brito and San Juan del Sur. The area is 51,600 square miles.

Physical Features.—A mountain range known in the southeast as the Cordillera de Yolaina runs from the Caribbean coast to the northwestern boundary. Parallel with this range and close to the Pacific is a range of volcanic peaks, of which several are liable to eruption. Between these ranges are low-lying plains and the Lakes of Nicaragua and Managua and east of the main range the country slopes gradually to the low-lying Mosquito Coast.

The principal rivers are the Wanks or Cocos or Segovia, which forms part of the northern boundary with Honduras; the Rio Grande, with its tributary, the Tuma; the San Juan, which forms part of the southern boundary with Costa Rica and flows from Lake Nicaragua to the Caribbean at San Juan del Norte. The main hydrographical features of the country are the vast lakes, Nicaragua and Managua. Lake Nicaragua has total area of almost 3,000 square miles and a total length of over 100 miles. The lake contains numerous islands and islets, the largest containing the two volcanic peaks of Ometepe and Madera. Lake Managua is about thirty miles long and has a total area of 580 square miles. The Paneloya channel connects the two lakes, but the higher level of Managua presents a navigable connection between the two lakes.

History.—Nicaragua was discovered by Columbus in 1502 and was overrun by the Spaniards under Davila in the first quarter of the sixteenth century, and formed part of the Spanish Captaincy-General of Guatemala until the revolt of the Spanish Colonies. In 1821 Nicaragua declared its independence of Spain and from 1823-1839 formed part of the Federation of Central American States, but since 1839 the Republic has been independent.

Government.—The Constitution rests on the fundamental law of Nov. 10, 1911 (as amended in 1913), and is that of a centralized republic. The President is elected by direct suffrage for four years. President of Nicaragua, until Dec. 31, 1916, Adolfo Diaz.

Congress consists of a Senate of 13 members and a Chamber of 40 deputies, elected in both instances for 4 years and renewable as to one half biennially.

There is a supreme court at the Capital, and courts of appeal at Leon, Masaya and Bluefields, with courts of first instance in all centres of population.

Service in the Army is compulsory and universal between the ages of 17 and 55.

Ethnography.—On the east coast are many uncivilized tribal Indians known as Mosquitos, their numbers being estimated at 30,000, while pure-blooded Indians are still living in the central districts. There is also a sprinkling of Europeans and their descendants, the greater number being Spanish and German. The total population is about 600,000.

Production and Industry.—The principal agricultural product is coffee, which is grown, principally in the department of Matagalpa, under German management and exported to Hamburg. Bananas are also grown in the eastern districts and on the Mosquito coast. Rice, beans, sugar, cocoa, and tobacco are also cultivated, but large quantities of foodstuffs are imported. The live stock includes cattle, horses, and pigs. The forest products are important, mahogany and rubber being exported.

Gold and silver, copper, coal petroleum, and precious stones are found, the gold export in 1910 exceeding £200,000. The mines are not fully developed.

Manufactures.—Leather and furniture, beer and spirits, tobacco, candles and soap are among the principal industries, those connected with cattle raising being the most important. The imports are principally cottons and other manufactured goods from the United States.

Foreign Trade.—Of the imports 50 per cent are from the United States and 15 per cent from Germany; the exports, 40 per cent to the United States, 15 per cent to Germany, and 12 per cent to France.

Railways.—A line, 172 miles in length, runs from the principal port of Corinto to Leon Managua and Granada on the lakes, whence a line of steamers runs at regular intervals to the southern shores. Many lines are projected, including a trans-isthmus system to Monkey Point, on the Caribbean.

Posts and Telegraphs.—In 1908 there were 135 post offices and 130 telegraph offices, with 1,591 miles of line, the Republic being linked up with the Pacific cable from Mexico to Peru.

Shipping.—In 1908 the ports were visited by 804 vessels, mainly United States and German. The Pacific harbors are the most frequented, Corinto being the chief commercial port.

Debt.—In May, 1909, the Nicaraguan Government obtained a foreign loan of £1,250,000, issuing gold bonds with interest at 6 per cent. The product of the sale of these bonds was to pay off the British loan of 1886 (£245,000), and the United States loan of 1904 ($1,000,000), while $2,175,000 was set aside for the construction of a new

railroad from Lake Nicaragua to Monkey Point on the Atlantic seaboard. The 1911 government entered into negotiations for a $20,000,000 gold loan in the United States. In June, 1912, the government defaulted in the payment of interest on the 6 per cent bonds, and entered into an agreement with the bondholders for the substitution of other securities with a scheme of payments. Up to September, 1913, the American bankers had advanced only $1,000,000, while they hold as security all the revenues (including customs and railways) and practically control the Banco Nacional.

Cities.—Capital, Managua. Population, 35,000. Others are Leon (65,000), Granada (20,000), Matagalpa, Masaya, Jinotega, Chinandega, Esteli, Boaco, Jinotepe, and Greytown.

The unit of value is the gold *codoba* of 100 centavos, worth $1 in United States currency, the paper peso fluctuating, and being worth about 8 cents. In conjunction with the United States loan scheme a monetary reform has been introduced. Token money of the standard value of the United States dollar is issued by the Banco Nacional, and the paper pesos are convertible at the rate of 12.50 per cordoba.

Trade with the United States.—The value of merchandise imported into Nicaragua from the United States for the year 1913 was $2,925,807, and goods to the value of $1,437,939 were sent thither—a balance of $1,487,868 in favor of the United States.

Nicaragua, Treaty with.—The treaty of friendship, commerce, navigation, and as to isthmian transit, was denounced by Nicaragua to take effect in 1902. The extradition treaty of 1870 was also denounced by Nicaragua to take effect in the same year. The protocol with Nicaragua of 1900 for the construction of an interoceanic canal provided that the President of the United States is empowered to acquire control of such portion of the territory of Nicaragua as may be necessary or advisable to construct a ship canal from a point near San Juan del Norte on the Caribbean Sea, through Lake Nicaragua to Brite, on the Pacific Ocean. As a preliminary to negotiations it is agreed that the details of the canal construction be the same as those contained in a treaty with Great Britain pending decision of the Senate of the United States. (See Extradition Treaties.)

Nicaragua also became a party to the convention between the United States and the several republics of South and Central America for the arbitration of pecuniary claims and the protection of inventions, etc., which was signed in Buenos Aires in 1910 and proclaimed in Washington July 29, 1914. (See South and Central America, Treaties with.)

Nicaragua Canal.—A proposed ship canal across the Republic of Nicaragua to connect the Atlantic and Pacific oceans. As early as 1522 Lake Nicaragua was entered from the western coast and explored by Spanish navigators. In 1550 Antonio Galvao, a Portuguese, proposed four routes for a ship canal across the Isthmus, one by way of Lake Nicaragua and the San Juan River. Later surveys were made by the Spanish and Central American governments. In 1850 Col. O. W. Childs surveyed a canal route from Lake Nicaragua to the Pacific. More complete surveys were made for the United States in 1872-1873 and 1885, and the cost of construction was variously estimated at from $40,-000,000 to $140,000,000. The Nicaraguan Government made concessions to Americans for constructing a canal in 1849 and 1880 and to a Frenchman in 1858, but they all lapsed without results. In 1884 a treaty was signed for the construction of a canal by the United States, but the Senate refused to ratify it. In 1887 a new concession was granted by Nicaragua and confirmed by Costa Rica. A company was immediately formed and chartered by the United States, work was begun, but ceased in 1892 for lack of funds, and finally in 1893 the company was placed in the hands of a receiver. President McKinley in 1899 appointed a commission to report on the question of the best route for an interocean canal and in 1901 a report was presented advising the Nicaragua route, mainly on the ground of the difficulty of acquiring rights and control in Panama. In 1900 the House passed a bill providing for the construction of a Nicaragua Canal but the Senate refused to pass it. Another bill of a similar character passed the House in January, 1902, but before it went to the Senate, a report was received from the Canal Commission recommending the Panama route. The construction of the Panama Canal settles the question of the isthmian route.

Nicaragua Canal (see also Panama Canal):

Clayton-Bulwer treaty for protection of, discussed, 2580, 2617, 2903, 2943, 3117.

Construction of, referred to, 5120, 5544, 5623.

Importance of, discussed, but Government aid to, not recommended, 2553.

Report on, transmitted, 6097.

Contract of Interoceanic Canal Co. discussed, 5470.

Control of, should not be held by one nation alone, 2554.

Correspondence regarding, referred to, 5120.

Discussed by President—
Arthur, 4843.
Buchanan, 3116.
Cleveland, 5870.
Fillmore, 2617.
Harrison, Benj., 5470, 5544, 5623, 5752.
Hayes, 4521.
McKinley, 6265, 6326, 6366, 6433.
Pierce, 2901.
Taylor, 2553, 2571, 2580.

Forfeiture of Nicaraguan concessions to, referred to, 5960.

Government aid to, recommended, 5624, 5752.

Report on, transmitted, 6185.

Right of way for, referred to, 2569.

Should be accomplished under American auspices, 5870.

Treaty regarding, with—
Great Britain, discussed, 2580, 2617, 2943, 3117.
Nicaragua (see also Nicaragua)—
Discussed, 2571, 2601, 4825, 4843.
Withdrawn, 4888, 4912.

Nicaragua Canal Commission discussed, 6326, 6366.

Nicaragua, The, indemnity to owners of, 6826.

Ninety-Six (S. C.), Siege of.—Immediately after the surrender of Charleston (May 12, 1780) Clinton sent Lieut. Conger up the Saluda to Ninety-Six, a village in South Carolina, about seventy-five miles from Columbia. May 21, 1781, a part of Gen. Greene's army laid siege to the place. Kosciusko planned the approaches and the condition of the garrison had become critical, when, on June 20, the siege was raised on the approach of Lord Rawdon with the flank companies of three regiments.

Nipsic, The, disabled at Samoan Islands, 5479.

Niter, appropriation for improvement in manufacture of, recommended, 2957.

No Man's Land.—A small island three miles southwest of Martha's Vineyard, Mass., to which it belongs.

The term was also applied to a strip of land ceded by Texas to the United States in 1850. It lies between lat. 36° 30′ and 37° north and long. 100° and 103° west. It was not included under any government, though often called part of the Indian Territory. The name originally proposed for the district was Cimarron. In 1890 it became part of Oklahoma, and is now known as Beaver County.

Nobel Prize.—The Swedish scientist, Alfred B. Nobel, the inventor of dynamite, died in 1896, bequeathing his fortune, estimated at $9,000,000, to the founding of a fund, the interest of which should yearly be distributed to those who had mostly contributed to "the good of humanity." The interest is divided in five equal shares, given away, "One to the person who in the domain of physics has made the most important discovery or invention, one to the person who has made the most important chemical discovery or invention, one to the person who has made the most important discovery in the domain of medicine or physiology, one to the person who in literature has provided the most excellent work of an idealistic tendency, and one to the person who has worked most or best for the fraternization of nations, and the abolition or reduction of standing armies, and the calling in and propagating of peace congresses."

A committee of the Norwegian Storthing awarded the prize for the promotion of peace between nations to President Roosevelt in 1906. The money value of the prize was about $40,000, and the President devoted it to the Foundation for the Promotion of Industrial Peace at home. In accordance with his wishes, Congress passed an act creating a board of trustees, consisting of the Chief Justice of the United States, the Secretaries of Agriculture and Commerce and Labor, a representative each of labor and capital, and two persons representing the general public, to administer the fund. An industrial peace committee of nine members was authorized to meet in Washington each year during the sessions of Congress to discuss differences arising between capital and labor. (See Industrial Peace Committee.)

Nominations. (See Executive Nominations.)

Nominating Convention. (See Conventions, Nominating.)

Nonimportation Agreement.—In 1765 the merchants of New York and Boston unanimously agreed to order no new merchandise from England, and to countermand old orders. This was done in retaliation for the passage of the Stamp Act by Parliament. The agreement was strictly observed until 1770, when only tea was prohibited. The members of the Continental Congress signed a nonimportation agreement in 1775.

Nonintercourse Act.—In consequence of the interference with American commerce by vessels of France and England, who were then at war, Congress in 1807 passed the embargo act prohibiting foreign commerce. This was found to work unnecessary injury to American shipping interests, and in 1809 it was repealed and the nonintercourse act substituted. It forbade the entrance to American ports of public or private British or French vessels, all commercial intercourse with France or Great Britain, and the importation after May 20, 1809, of all goods grown or manufactured in the two countries or their colonies. The act was to continue until the next session of Congress, but was revived by acts of June 28, 1809, May 1, 1810, and March 2, 1811.

Non-Partisan League— An organization of the farmers of the Northwest, formed as an alliance against the business conditions and the economic system which sustained the evils of which the farmers complained. The program of the League is largely that of agricultural co-operation, but the organization does not represent a new political party. It rather captures the machinery of one of the old parties, and utilizes its capture for its own purposes. The League was formed in 1914 and by 1917 comprised practically all of the farmers of North Dakota, and was gaining remarkable influence in adjacent states. In 1916, it elected by an overwhelming vote its candidate for governor for North Dakota, 81 of 113 members of the State House of Representatives, 18 of 25 state senators, three members of the state Supreme Court, and at the only Congressional by-election in its vicinity in 1917 elected its candidate, Baer, to Congress.

Its immediate program has been the development of state-owned terminal elevators, cold-storage warehouses, flour mills; the exemption of farm improvements from taxations and other planks of the single tax platform; the general elimination of the middleman in marketing the products of the farmers and other methods of making farm product retail prices correspond more closely to the price the farmer is paid for them; and the general reorganization of the industrial, economic, and educational life of the state to meet the needs of the agricultural population. The President and moving force in the League is A. C. Townley, and many of its leaders are Socialists.

Norfolk, Va.:

Blockade of port of, removed by proclamation, 3431.

Referred to, 3446.

British officers treated at hospital at, 3404.

Surrender of, referred to, 3313, 3315.

Vessels entering and leaving port of, order regarding, 3225.

Norfolk (Va.), Burning of.—Lord Dunmore, the royal governor of Virginia, assumed military control of Norfolk in November, 1775. He was defeated in an effort to dislodge some Virginia and Maryland militia who had taken up a position near the town. He thereupon embarked in a British vessel which lay in the Elizabeth River. Col. Woodford, with the Second Virginia Militia, and Col. Howe, with one regiment from North Carolina and two companies of Maryland militia, occupied the town. On Jan. 1, 1776, Dunmore began a bombardment, and sent ashore a party who set fire to the town. Its destruction was completed by the Americans to prevent its becoming a shelter for the British.

Norfolk (Va.), Surrender of.—The movement of the Federal Army up the peninsula of Virginia, in May, 1862, led to the withdrawal of the Confederate force from Norfolk and to the destruction of the ironclad *Merrimac.* This left the James River open to navigation. An expedition was sent out from the Fortress Monroe, under Gen. Wool, May 10, to take possession of Norfolk. It was turned over by the mayor without a struggle.

Norsemen.—In the sagas or accounts of Scandinavian heroes the vikings of Norway are represented as having visited the coast of America as early as 861 A. D. The narratives of the early voyages of the Northmen to America are more or less intermingled with fiction. Enough has been verified, however, to warrant some reliable historians giving credence to the more likely part of their claims. We are told that Norsemen had established a settlement in America in 875 A. D. (probably in Iceland, visited by Nadodd twelve to fifteen years previously), and that Gunbiorn, a Norse navigator, sighted land farther west.

Eric the Red discovered and named Greenland in 982, and three years later made a second voyage to the new country. During the same year an expedition under Bjarni sailed from Iceland to Greenland, but was driven south by a storm and sighted land at Newfoundland and at Cape Cod or Nantucket. Thence he returned to Greenland. In the year 1000 Leif, son of Eric the Red, sailed with one ship and thirty-five men in search of the land seen by Bjarni. He touched on the coast of Labrador and, journeying southward, stopped for the winter near the site of the present city of Boston. Leif called the place Vinland, from the abundance of grapes found. This seems to be the earliest authentic account of Norse discoveries in America.

Thorvald, Leif's brother, visited Vinland in 1002, wintered near Mount Hope Bay, R. I., and in the spring of 1003 sent a party of his men to explore the coast, probably as far south as Cape May. In 1004 Thorvald was killed near Boston by Skrelings (the Icelandic name for the aboriginal Americans), and his companions returned to Greenland. About 1007 or 1008 Thorfinn Karlsefne sailed from Greenland with three ships and 160 persons. He landed at Rhode Island and spent three years in Vinland. The latest tidings of Vinland were received in 1347, and communication with Greenland ceased about 1400. Before Columbus was born European navigators had journeyed westward and touched land, and several maps of the Atlantic Ocean had been made. Prior to 1470 Columbus had visited Iceland, and it has been suggested that he there learned of the Western Continent from the Norse navigators.

North America.—The area of North America, including Mexico, is about 7,200,000 square miles, a little less than twice that of Europe. Its extreme longitudes extend from a little west of 170° W. to 52½° W. in the east of Newfoundland, and its extreme latitudes from about 80° N. latitude to 15° N. latitude in the south of Mexico. It is surrounded by seas on all sides, except in the south, where it joins the Isthmian States of Central America.

The nations of North America, with the form of government and capital of each follow:

Canada (Dominion), Ottawa.
Mexico (Republic), Mexico City.

Newfoundland (British), St. John's.
United States (Republic), Washington.
Alaska (United States), Juneau.

Three main divisions can be made in the relief of North America. The Eastern Mountains, the Great Plains, and the Western Mountains. The Eastern Mountains extend from Labrador to Alabama. The Great Plains form a comparatively level and continuous surface from the Arctic Ocean and the shores of Hudson Bay to the Gulf of Mexico. This is broken in only three places by elevations of importance—the Ozark Mountains, the Lake Plateau (on which stand Lakes Superior, Michigan and Huron) and the Black Hills of South Dakota. A distinction must be made between the Prairies, which are open plains with few trees, rising to about 800 feet in Minnesota at the watershed between Hudson Bay and the Gulf of Mexico and the high plains to the west, which are far dryer and less fertile than the prairie wheat lands. In parts these rise to over 6,000 feet, and are much higher than the Appalachians. In Canada these high plains form the ranching lands of Alberta. In the Arctic plains there are many marshes and lakes. The Western Mountains consist, in the United States, of the Rockies, with summits exceeding 14,000 feet, among which Pike's Peak forms a conspicuous dome, the Sierra Nevada, the highest point of which is Mount Whitney (14,522 feet) and the Cascade range, with Mount Rainier (14,525 feet) and Mount Shasta, and the Coast ranges, which reach 7,500 feet in the densely forested Olympic Mountains of Puget Sound.

Between the Rockies and the Sierra Nevada is the Great Basin traversed by ridges, which rise to no great elevation above the plateau. There is little rainfall, and there are numerous salt lakes, of which the Great Salt Lake in Utah is the most important. The Death Valley in California is several hundred feet below sea-level. The Valley of California is a depression between the Sierra Nevada and Cascade ranges and the Coast ranges. The Western Coast ranges rise to great elevations in Alaska, where Mount St. Elias and Mount McKinley, over 20,000 feet, are the most prominent summits.

Mexico is a tableland, generally above 6,000 feet, which is bounded by two escarpments, the Eastern Sierra Madre, not a distinct mountain range but the margin of the plateau, and the Western Sierra Madre, which is from 8,000 to 12,000 feet and falls steeply to the Pacific. Here is a broad volcanic zone in which Orizaba, 18,252 feet, Popocatepetl, 17,250 feet, and Ixtachihuatl, 16,960 feet, are the highest summits. Colima is the only active volcano. The rivers are mostly short and torrential. The peninsula of Yucatan is a low limestone plateau flat and treeless with few running streams.

Five drainage areas may be distinguished, the Arctic, the Atlantic, the Gulf, Inland and the Pacific. In the Arctic Basin the Mackenzie is the only large river. The Atlantic Basin contains the St. Lawrence draining the Great Lakes and the Hudson. The Delaware, Susquehanna and Potomac cut deeply into the northern Alleghanies, but south of Chesapeake Bay the rivers rise on the eastern margin. The Alabama and Tennessee form longitudinal valleys in the southern Alleghanies. The Mississippi occupies the southern portion of the Great Plains. It has numerous large tributaries, the Ohio on the east, and the Missouri, Platte, Kansas, Arkansas and Red River on the west. The Rio Grande del Norte rises in the San Juan mountains. On the Pacific Coast the Colorado rises in the Rockies and flows in deep cañons through the Arizona deserts. Use has been made of its water to irrigate the Salton depression to the northwest of its mouth. From the Colorado to the Columbia there are no large rivers except in the valley of California, where the Sacramento and San Joaquin are invaluable for irrigation. The Snake tributary of the Columbia River rises in the Yellowstone National Park, and cuts great cañons through a lava plateau. The Frazer, like the Columbia, has a long north and south valley. The Yukon rises not far from the coast in the northwest, and flows into Bering Sea. The Inland Basin, between the Rockies and the Sierra Nevada, has no large rivers.

North Ann Crossing (Va.), Battle of.—Proceeding southward after the battle of Spottsylvania, Grant's army arrived at the North Ann River May 23, 1864. Warren, whose corps was on the right, crossed the river at Jericho, Hancock at a point four miles below, and the Sixth Corps at Jericho. Lee meantime had retired to a position south of the North Ann, and his left wing rested on the river at a point between the two sections of Grant's army. Burnside's corps was unable to cross the river. Lee's position was impregnable and Grant was compelled to withdraw his army to the north side of the river after a loss of 1,607 in killed and wounded. May 27, having been rejoined by Sheridan, the Army of the Potomac moved toward the Pamunky River.

North Carolina.—One of the thirteen original states; nicknames, "The Tar State," "The Tar-Heel State," and the "Old North State;" motto, "Esse quam videri" ("To be rather than to seem"). It extends from lat. 33° 50' to 36° 33' north and from long. 75° 27' to 84° 20' west. It is bounded on the north by Virginia, on the east and southeast by the Atlantic Ocean, on the south by South Carolina and Georgia, and on the west by Tennessee (separated by the Smoky and other ranges of mountains). It has an area of 52,426 square miles. The surface is mountainous in the west, rolling or gently undulating in the center, and toward the eastern coast or lands bordering on the Albemarle and Pamlico Sounds generally level.

Unsuccessful attempts at colonization were made by Sir Walter Raleigh in 1518-1587. Scattering settlements were made prior to 1663, probably as early as 1653. The territory was granted to proprietors in 1663 by Charles II. The first two colonies are known in history as the Albemarle and the Clarendon. In 1669 a constitution was introduced modeled by the philosopher, John Locke, upon principles of a landed aristocracy and feudal service. The constitution was not a success and was abandoned after twenty-five years. Citizens of North Carolina passed a set of resolutions in 1775 similar to the Declaration of Independence. (See Mecklenburg Declaration.) It was the first colony to instruct its delegates in Congress to vote for independence. The State seceded from the Union May 20, 1861, and was readmitted by act of Congress June 25, 1868.

Statistics of agriculture collected for the last Federal census, place the number of farms in the State at 253,725, comprising 22,439,129 acres, valued, with stock and improvements, at $375,716,210. The average value of land per acre was $15.29, as against $6.24 in 1900. The value of domestic animals, poultry, etc., was $62,649,-984, including 700,861 cattle, valued at $12,550,054; 166,151 horses, $18,428,134;

174,711 mules, \$23,669,687; 1,227,625 swine, \$4,628,046; 214,473 sheep, \$559,217, and poultry, \$2,212,570. The value of field crops in the State in a recent year was placed by the census bureau in excess of \$125,000,000.

North Carolina is the leader among the Eastern states in the production of gold, the output for 1910 being 3,291 fine ounces, worth \$68,045. The silver production was 9,053 fine ounces, valued at \$4,620. Iron and copper are also produced. Vegetable raising for early northern markets is a growing industry, as well as dairying.

The manufactures of the State are those of cotton, lumber and tobacco. The total output for 1905 was \$142,520,776, of which \$51,002,843 was cotton goods, oil and cake; \$28,087,969 tobacco, and \$15,731,379 lumber and timber. In 1906 the State contained 4,409 miles of steam railway and 107 miles of electric line. The population in 1910 was 2,206,287.

The number of manufacturing establishments in North Carolina having an annual output valued at \$500 or more at the beginning of 1915 was 5,507. The amount of capital invested was \$253,842,000, giving employment to 151,333 persons, using material valued at \$169,942,000, and turning out finished goods worth \$289,412,000. Salaries and wages paid amounted to \$56,283,000.

North Carolina (see also Confederate States):

Admission of, into United States referred to, 57, 59, 61.

Branch mint in, referred to, 1383, 1495.

Ceding of jurisdiction of lands to the United States by, 64, 105, 167.

Clerks of Federal courts and United States marshal in, referred to, 3661.

Constitution of, referred to, 3831.

Constitution of United States—

Evidence of ratification of, amendment to, by, 62, 68, 182.

Fourteenth amendment to, ratified by, proclamation announcing, 3854.

Governor of, referred to, 64.

Jails in, use of, granted to United States, 103.

Judges, United States, in, opinion of, regarding pensions, 125.

Lands ceded to United States by, referred to, 64, 105, 167. (See also Enc. Art., Franklin.)

Light-house—

Lands ceded to United States for erection of, 103.

Lands, jurisdiction of, for, ceded to United States, 182.

Military governor of, referred to, 3281.

Obstruction to laws in, proclamation regarding, 3743.

Copies of, for executive clerks, 3756.

Provisional governor for, appointed and restoration of, into Union discussed, 3510.

Survey of coast of, 636, 680.

Unlawful combination in, discussed, 4071, 4072.

North Carolina, The:

Seizure and imprisonment of crew of, by Spanish authorities referred to, 2761.

Sent to Mediterranean Sea, 826.

North Dakota.—One of the western group of states; nickname, "Cyclone State;" motto, "Liberty and Union now and forever, one and inseparable." It extends from lat. 46° to 49° north and from long. 96° 30′ to 104° 5′ west. It is bounded on the north by the Dominion of Canada, on the east by Minnesota, on the south by South Dakota, and on the west by Montana. Its area is 70,837 square miles. Its surface is generally undulating and level.

Dakota was first settled at Pembina by French traders in 1780. The territory of Dakota, comprising the present States of North and South Dakota, was organized from Nebraska Territory by act of March 2, 1861. It was divided on the forty-sixth parallel and the upper portion admitted to the Union Nov. 2, 1889 (5455).

Under the Federal reclamation act much improved farm land is subject to irrigation. The tillable area of the State is more than 15,000,000 acres, of which 10,000,000 is improved. The live stock reported Jan. 1, 1910, was 712,000 horses, valued at \$81,-168,000; 8,000 mules, \$1,040,000; 270,000 milch cows, \$8,373,000; 616,000 other cattle, \$12,628,000; 621,000 sheep, \$2,484,-000; 206,000 swine, \$2,266,000; the wool production was 715,000 pounds scoured. The yield and value of field crops in 1911 was: Corn, 290,000 acres, 7,250,000 bushels, \$4,350,000; wheat, 9,150,000 acres, 73,-200,000 bushels, \$65,148,000; oats, 2,180,-000 acres, 51,230,000 bushels, \$21,004,000; rye, 36,000 acres, 598,000 bushels, \$454,-000; potatoes, 42,000 acres, 5,040,000 bushels, \$2,772,000; hay, 192,000 acres, 211,-000 tons, \$1,477,000; flaxseed, of which the production was the largest of any state in the Union in 1910, was 5,778,000 bushels on 1,605,000 acres, and sold for \$13,-578,000. There were 399,041 tons of lignite coal produced in the state in 1910, worth \$595,139. The total mineral output of the State was \$738,818. There were 753 manufacturing establishments in the State, with an aggregate capital of \$11,594,000, paying \$2,422,000 in wages and producing \$19,-150,000 in finished products.

There are within the State 1,300,333 acres of public land unreserved and unappropriated. United States land offices are located at Bismarck, Devil's Lake, Dickinson, Fargo, Minot, and Williston.

In 1906 there were 3,761 miles of steam railway and 16 miles of electric line within the State. The Federal census of 1910 gave the population as 577,056.

North Dakota:

Admission of, into Union—

Discussed, 5485.

Proclaimed, 5455.

Lands in—

Open to settlement by proclamation, 5707.

Set apart as public reservation by proclamation, 5579.

Lottery in, efforts to secure charter for, discussed, 5515.

Unlawful combinations in, proclamation against, 5485.

North Point (Md.), Battle of.—After burning Washington in 1814 Gen. Ross withdrew to Admiral Cockburn's fleet and the invaders ran up the Chesapeake Bay to the mouth of the Patapsco River. On the morning of Sept. 12, 1814, the British forces 9,000 strong were landed at North Point, twelve miles from Baltimore, with provisions for three days and eighty rounds of ammunition per man. Baltimore was defended by about the same number of troops under Gen. Samuel Smith. Hearing of the landing of the British, he sent Gen. Stricker with 3,200 men to oppose their advance. Gen. Ross was killed in a preliminary skirmish. The battle was carried on for four hours, when the Americans fell back toward the city and the British bivouacked on the field.

North Polar Regions.—The arctic Ocean consists of a deep sea over 2,000 fathoms, on the southern margin of which there is a broad continental shelf with numerous islands. Into this deeper sea there is only one broad channel, about 700 miles, between Greenland and Scandinavia. Bering Strait is only 49 miles wide and 27 fathoms deep. The southern boundary of the Arctic Ocean is the Wyville-Thomson and Faeroe-Icelandic submarine ridge, which separates the North Atlantic from the Norwegian and Greenland seas. Most of the icebergs are formed on the east and west coasts of Greenland and are carried south by the Polar currents. The lowest temperature observed is -63° in 85° N. latitude, a good deal less than that of Verkhoyansk (-90°, the least recorded temperature of the globe). Forests of pine and larch reach 73°, N. in Siberia, and to the north of this are dwarf birches, willows, mosses and lichens. There is sufficient vegetation to the north of Greenland to support rodents and ruminants. Among sea animals are the right whale and the narwhal, which is found further north than any other species, and the walrus. The right whale is now almost extinct. Numerous seals are found on the Arctic margin. Numerous races are found along the fringe of the Arctic. The Lapps are the original inhabitants of Arctic Norway; there are wandering tribes of Samoyedes, Tunguses and Yakuts; the Chukches of Bering Peninsula are more numerous than most of the nomadic tribes. The most northerly of the polar peoples are the Eskimo. Peary owed the success of his expedition to the North Pole largely to the help of these tribes, who were called the Arctic Highlanders by Sir J. Ross.

Exploration.—The first discoveries in the Arctic were made by the Norsemen, Iceland being reached in 861 A. D. and Greenland before 1,000 A. D. Newfoundland and Nova Scotia were visited from the settlements made in Greenland. Modern Arctic exploration may be said to commence with the search for the Northwest Passage. In 1496 John Cabot and his son Sebastian reached 58° N. latitude. In 1527 Robert Thorne, of Bristol, actually set out for the North Pole, but the records of his voyage are unsatisfactory. The first attempt on the Northeast Passage was made by Sir Hugh Willoughby and Richard Chancellor. The latter succeeded in reaching the north coast of Russia at a point which afterwards became the port of Archangel, and in opening up trade with that country. The second expedition in this direction was made by Stephen Burrough, who discovered Novaya Zemlya. In 1576 Martin Frobisher sailed for the Northwest Passage and discovered Frobisher and Hudson Straits.

In 1585 John Davis made the most important series of early voyages. He reached 75° N. latitude as a result of three expeditions, but was unable to make the passage round North America to the west. He demonstrated, however, the commercial importance of the Arctic in whales, seal and deer skins. In 1580 an expedition reached the Kara Sea under the auspices of the Muscovy Company, who in 1594 and 1596 again fitted out ships for the exploration of the Northeast Passage. The Pilot, William Barent, was the first Arctic explorer known to pass a winter in the Polar ice.

In 1607 Henry Hudson began his remarkable voyages. His first two expeditions, in which he reached 80° 23' N. latitude, were to the northeast. His last voyage in 1610 was again directed toward the Northwest Passage. The *Discovery* was ice bound in Hudson Bay, and Hudson was deserted by his crew, who mutinied in the ensuing summer, and nothing is known of his fate. In 1615 William Baffin was appointed pilot to the *Discovery* and sent out by the Merchant Adventurers to search for the Northwest Passage. In 1616 he penetrated north along the west coast of Greenland to latitude 77° 45', a record not afterwards passed for two centuries.

In 1725 Russian exploration began, and between that date and 1760 Bering mapped a large part of the northeast coast of Asia and opened up the fur trade. In 1773 another strictly Polar expedition was planned, and John Phipps reached 80° 40' N. latitude, to the north of Spitzbergen. In 1817 two expeditions were sent out with geographical and scientific aims, under Buchan and Franklin, and under Ross and Parry. In 1821 Parry made an attempt to the south of Lancaster Sound. A further voyage in 1823 was also unsuccessful. Meanwhile Franklin made an overland journey to the mouth of the Coppermine River, where a canoe voyage was undertaken to Point Turnagain, 68° 18' N. and 109° 25' W. longitude. Franklin's second overland journey (1825-1827) resulted in further exploration on the Arctic coast of North America. Parry's last Arctic voyage in 1827 was an attempt to reach the Pole by sledge boats. From the north of Spitzbergen, traveling for the first time by night alone, he reached latitude 82° 45'. In 1829 Ross made another attempt on the Northwest Passage in the *Victory*, and reached Bellot Strait, the real channel leading to the Arctic Sea, but failed to recognize it as a passage, and returned without success after spending four winters in the ice. In the course of these voyages he attained the Magnetic Pole. The anxiety at Ross's long absence led to Black's relief voyage in the *Terror*. The *Erebus* and *Terror*, which had returned from the Antarctic, were fitted out with steam, and Franklin was commissioned in 1845 to attempt the entrance to Lancaster Sound. The two ships were last sighted near this point by a whaler, but were never seen again. In 1847 relief expeditions were sent out from the east through Lancaster Sound, from the west through Bering Strait, and from the south to the Arctic shores of North America.

The final result of these search expeditions was the completion of the Northwest Passage by M'Clure, who returned home in 1854. The first authoritative news of the fate of Franklin was obtained by Rae in his exploration of the west coast of Boothia. In 1857 Lady Franklin fitted out a last search expedition, which was commanded by M'Clintock, and finally Franklin's last record was found on the east coast of

King William's Land. From this it was learned that his ship had been caught in the ice and never released. Till 1874 further Polar exploration was left to American, German, and Austrian explorers.

The Northeast Passage was discovered by Nordenskiöld, who reached the mouth of the Yenisei in two successive years, and attained the East Cape in 1879, after a winter in the ice not far from Bering Strait.

The first crossing of the lofty ice-covered plateau of Greenland was accomplished by Nansen in 1888. Another remarkable journey over the inland ice was carried through by Peary, who proved the insular character of Greenland. In 1892 Nansen attempted to reach the Pole by a novel method. His plan was to follow the course taken by the ill-fated *Jeannette*, which had been caught in the ice near Wrangel Land, and had drifted to New Siberia. The *Fram* was constructed to withstand enormous ice pressure, and preparations were made for drifting across the Polar Basin in the hope that the currents would bring the ship close to the Pole. Finding that the ship's track did not approach sufficiently near to the Pole, Nansen and Johannsen left the ship in 1895 with dogs and sledges, and reached N. latitude 86° 14′, the farthest point attained up to that time. The *Fram*, under the command of Otto Sverdrup, finally reached Norway in safety, after drifting to nearly as high a latitude as that attained by Nansen.

In 1896 an attempt to reach the North Pole by balloon was made by Andree, but the expedition was never seen again. In 1909 the Duke of the Abruzzi made an expedition in the *Stella Polare*, and Captain Cagni succeeded in reaching latitude 86° 32′, a little north of Nansen's record, by a sledge journey over the ice.

The honor of first reaching the Pole was reserved for Commander Robert Edwin Peary, of the United States Navy, who finally, after many voyages in the north of Greenland, attained success by a remarkable sledge journey during the winter night, reaching the North Pole on April 6, 1909. (See Article Explorations.)

North Star, The. (See *Rodgers*, The.)

North Star State.—Alternative nickname for Minnesota. (See Gopher State.)

Northeastern Boundary.—By the treaty of 1783 the northeastern boundary of the United States was defined as extending from the source of the St. Croix River due north to the highlands or watershed between the Atlantic and St. Lawrence systems, thence along those highlands to the northwesternmost head of the Connecticut River. There was a continual dispute over this boundary, and the claims of Americans and Canadians were pressed so vigorously as to lead to preparation for hostilities. The matter was referred to arbitration. In 1831 the King of the Netherlands, as arbitrator, made an award which neither Great Britain nor the United States would accept. Finally by the Webster-Ashburton treaty of 1842 the present boundary was agreed upon, not far from that suggested by the Dutch King. The United States secured about seven-twelfths of the disputed territory and Great Britain five-twelfths.

Northeastern Boundary between United States and Great Britain:
Amicable settlement of, discussed, 1747, 1811, 1820.

Appropriation for survey of, necessary, 1845.

Arbitration committed to citizens of Maine, 1007.

Ashburton treaty discussed. (See Ashburton Treaty.)

Commissioners appointed to fix, 188, 191, 242, 264, 1821.

Convention with Great Britain regarding, 347, 351, 958.

Conventional agreement to be arranged, 1811.

Correspondence in regard to, 1564, 1622, 1648, 1687, 1738, 1785, 1791, 1798, 1812, 1945, 1965, 2023.
Referred to, 1448, 1784, 2278.

Depredations committed on disputed territory, 1733.
Correspondence regarding, 1738, 1785, 1791.

Disagreement in decision of, 819, 947.
Report of, 1846, 1945, 1965, 2024, 2087.

Discussed, 64, 65, 191, 242, 264, 268, 1156, 1239, 1316, 1368, 1455, 1591, 1820, 1931, 2047.

Excitement growing out of, partially subsided, 1820.

Imprisonment of American citizens charged with trespassing, 963, 969, 990, 1123.
Release of, 1110.

Joint commission for survey of—
Appointment of, referred to, 1702.
Report of, 2024.

King of Netherlands selected as arbitrator, 974.
Award of, referred to, 1110, 1122, 1123, 1126.
Great Britain agrees to, 1123.
Protest of United States minister against, 1122.

Maps regarding transmitted, 960.

Proposition of United States for settlement of—
Declined by Great Britain, 1368.
To be acceded to by Great Britain, 1811.

Referred to, 922, 946, 1070, 1133, 1156, 1200, 1346, 1448, 1697, 1729, 1784, 1796, 1805, 1954.

Reports of commissioners on, 1846, 1945, 1965, 2024, 2087.

Resolutions of Maine legislature regarding, 1126.

Survey of, referred to, 1845, 1931, 1945.

Treaty regarding, discussed, 2015, 2047.

Northern Cheyenne Indians. (See Indian Tribes.)

Northwest Territory.—The portion of the United States known in history as the Northwest Territory comprises all the country lying between the Ohio River, the Mississippi River and the Great Lakes, immediately west of the original states, and now forming the states of Ohio, Indiana, Illinois, Michigan, and Wisconsin. The original states severally laid claim to this territory by their charters, which granted possession from ocean to ocean. New York ceded her claims to this region to the General Government in 1782, and was followed by Virginia in 1784, Massachusetts in 1785, and Connecticut in 1786. The latter state, however, retained a small tract as the foundation for her school fund. This became known as the Western Reserve.

Congress in July, 1787, passed an ordinance for the government of this territory, and to the wise measures incorporated into that law the states formed from the territory are indebted for much that is wise and judicious in their constitutions. It is claimed by some that the foundations for future national greatness were laid by the manner in which Congress dealt with the question of territorial government at this time. A clause forbidding slavery after 1800 was at first voted down, but afterwards was adopted. The ordinance provided that no land should be taken up until it had been purchased from the Indians and offered for sale by the United States; no property qualification was to be required of electors or elected; a temporary government might be established until the male population of the territory reached 5,000, then a permanent representative government would be permitted, with a Representative in Congress entitled to debate but not to vote. When the inhabitants of any one of the five divisions of the territory reached 60,000 it should be admitted as a state, these states to remain forever a part of the United States, pay their portion of the Federal debt, and in their government uphold republican forms and prohibit slavery; but fugitive slaves were to be surrendered. Arthur St. Clair was governor from 1788 to 1802.

Northwest Territory:

Government established in, and recommendations made to enable the governor and secretary to visit the posts in, 190.

Northwestern Boundary.—The territory bounded on the north by lat. 54° 40′, on the east by the Rocky Mountains, on the south by lat. 42°, and on the west by the Pacific Ocean, has been variously claimed by Russia, Spain, Great Britain, and the United States. Russia's claim rested for the most part upon occupation by fur traders, and was settled by a treaty of Jan. 11, 1825, under the terms of which the United States were to make no settlements north of lat. 54° 40′ and Russia none south of that latitude. England made a treaty with Russia on the same terms. By the treaty which ceded Florida in 1819 the Spanish claims were confined to the south of lat. 42°. This left the territory between 42° and 54° 40′ to the Americans and English. Great Britain had no claim by discovery. The claim of the United States rested upon the voyage of Gray up the Columbia River in 1792 and the explorations of Lewis and Clark through the Rocky Mountains and the Oregon country in 1805 and 1806 under the orders of Jefferson. By the treaty of Oct. 20, 1818, the entire country west of the Rocky Mountains was to be opened to both countries for ten years, and at the end of this period joint occupation for an indefinite time was agreed upon. This arrangement produced much dissatisfaction and was made a political issue in the United States in 1844. (See "Fifty-four Forty or Fight.") After considerable negotiation lat. 49° was agreed upon (in 1846) as the boundary from the Rocky Mountains to the channel between Vancouver Island and the mainland. (See also San Juan de Fuca explorations.)

Northwestern Boundary between United States and Great Britain.

Commission for settlement of, recommended and referred to, 2810, 2866, 3989, 4056.

Convention for adjustment of, 958, 2243, 2299, 3380.

Concluded and signed, 2302.

Exchange of ratifications referred to, 2307.

Correspondence regarding, 890.

Referred to, 2127.

Discussed, 705, 922, 946, 956, 1133, 1614, 1615, 1684, 2049, 2063, 2110, 2127 2180, 2190, 2214, 2242, 2277, 2484, 3092, 3197, 3894, 3899.

Emperor of Germany chosen as arbitrator, 4097.

Award of, 4139.

Thanks of United States tendered, 4140.

Final settlement of, 4357, 4382.

Joint commission for marking, 4141.

Report of, 4191.

Marking and tracing of, recommended, 2655, 2741.

Settlement of—

By arbitration, 4139.

Recommended, 3198, 3213.

Proposition regarding, by—

Great Britain—

Declined, 2243.

Referred to, 2305.

Submitted, 2299.

Accepted, 2302.

Ratification of, referred to, 2307.

United States declined, 2111, 2243.

Referred to, 2305.

Referred to, 2484.

Treaty regarding, 3894, 3956.

Warlike preparations made by Great Britain on account of, 2277.

Norwalk Harbor, Conn., survey of, referred to, 1043.

Norway.—Norway occupies the west and north of the Scandinavian peninsula, between 57° 58′-71″ 11′ N. latitude and 4° 30′ 31° 11′ E. longitude. Within these limits lie the mainland and a multitude of islands and inlets, estimated at 150,000 in all. The boundaries on the north, west, and south are the Arctic and Atlantic Oceans and the North Sea, and the southeast coast is washed by the Skager Rack, which separates the kingdom from the Danish promontory of Jutland. The Swedish frontier forms the eastern boundary, but beyond this frontier to the northeast the Norwegian Amt of Finmarken extends along the boundary of the Russian Grand Duchy of Finland.

Physical Features and Climate.—The coast is extremely rugged, broken by inlets or fjords, and studded with islands. The fjords run inland for a great distance, with precipitous cliffs on either side, and down many of them the mountain torrents find their way to the sea in picturesque, elevated waterfalls.

The coast is fringed with a "fence of islands" (skjærgaard), almost throughout its length from southeast to northeast. In the extreme north is the large island of Magerö, which contains, in North Cape, the most northerly point of Norway and of the continent of Europe.

Norway consists of an almost continuous plateau, with frequent peaks and valleys. In addition to the fjords there are countless inland lakes, the largest being Mjösen, sixty miles in length. The principal river of Norway is the Glommen. Many of the rivers run in precipitous beds, and magnificent waterfalls occur in the course of many of them, the most famous being Sarpsfos on the Glommen, Rjukanfos, or "Smoking Fall." on the Maan, Lotefos and Espelandsfos, which discharge into Hardanger Fjord, and Vöringsfos, on the Bjoreia River.

The climate of Norway is in no way typical of the latitudes in which the kingdom is situated, for although a great part of the land lies within the Arctic Circle, the coast is kept free of ice by the prevailing southwest winds and the Gulf Stream drift of warm waters from the Atlantic Ocean. The direction of the Gulf Stream is not only along the west, but round the north and northeast coast, and the most northerly point of the kingdom is thus kept free from the icy currents which cause many lands in lower latitudes to be ice-bound; in fact, the Skager Rack of the south is liable to be closed by ice although the seas of northernmost Norway, 1,000 miles nearer the North Pole, are free all the year round. The highest mean annual temperature is 45° Fahrenheit on the southwest coast, and the lowest mean is 1° above freezing in the extreme north, when the summer average is as high as 53° Fahrenheit, as against 62°, the summer mean at the capital.

The Midnight Sun.—Owing to the geographical position of Norway, the country generally experiences a phenomenon known as "The Midnight Sun," the sun being above the horizon continuously from May to July, at North Cape, and even in the extreme south there is no darkness from April to August. Conversely, there is no sun at North Cape from November to January, but this absence of sunlight does not prevail further south.

History.—The Kingdom of Norway had been established for some centuries and Christianity had been introduced about 150 years when King Harald III. fell at Stamford Bridge in England (1066 A. D.), and from 1389-1521 the kingdom formed part of the tripartite League of Kalmar (see Denmark), by which Norway, Sweden and Denmark were united under King Eric (1389-1397). In 1521, the secession of Sweden left Norway in union with Denmark, and in 1814, by the Treaty of Kiel (Jan. 14, 1814) this union was dissolved, and the kingdoms of Norway and Sweden were united under one crown. In 1905 the Norwegian Storting adopted a resolution dissolving the union with Sweden (June 7), and later in the same year a referendum resulted in an overwhelming majority (368,211 votes to 184) in favor of the dissolution of the union. Negotiations between representatives of Norway and Sweden settled the terms of the sever-

ance, which was ratified by the Norwegian Storting and the Swedish Riksdag on Oct. 9. On Oct. 27 King Oscar of Sweden and Norway issued a proclamation relinquishing the crown of Norway, and a Norwegian referendum authorized the Storting to offer the crown to Prince Charles of Denmark, who entered the Norwegian capital with his consort on Nov. 25, and was crowned in Trondhjem Cathedral in 1906, as King Haakon VII., the first of that name (Haakon the Good), having reigned over Norway from 935-961 A. D.

Government.—Haakon VII., King of Norway, born at Charlottenlund, Aug. 3, 1872 (son of the late King Frederick III. of Denmark); elected King of Norway and accepted the throne Nov. 18, 1905. The Legislature, or Storting, consists of 123 members, elected for three years by universal suffrage of Norwegians of both sexes, aged twenty-five years, paying a certain minimum of taxation. The Storting meets annually and elects one-quarter of its members to form the Lagting, the remaining three-quarters forming the Odelsting.

There are separate courts for civil and criminal cases. Civil cases are generally brought before a court of mediation (forlikskommission) from which appeals may be brought to local court or to the three superior courts of appeal (overretter) at Christiania, Bergen and Trondhjem. Criminal cases are tried by jury courts or at assizes. The final court of the Kingdom is the Supreme Court at Christiania.

AREA AND POPULATION

Governments	Area in English Sq. Miles	Population 1910
Akershus	2,054	128,042
Bergen	5	76,867
Bergenhus, Nordre	7,130	90,040
Bergenhus, Söndre	6,025	146,006
Bratsberg	5,863	108,084
Buskerud	5,790	123,643
Christiania	6	241,834
Christians	9,790	119,236
Finmarken	18,291	38,065
Hedemarken	10,618	134,555
Jarlsberg and Larvik	896	109,076
Lister and Mandal	2,804	82,067
Nedenes	3,609	76,456
Nordland	14,513	164,687
Romsdal	5,786	144,622
Smaalenene	1,598	152,306
Stavanger	3,531	141,040
Tromsö	8,789	81,902
Trondhjem, Nordre	7,182	84,948
Trondhjem, Söndre	10,131	148,306
Total	124,411	2,391,782

Army.—Service in the National Militia is universal and compulsory. (For the Army, see Armies of the World.)

Navy.—The maritime population is universally liable for service in the Navy between the ages of twenty-two and forty-one, with active training of six months. (For the naval strength, see Navies of the World.)

Production and Industry.—The total land area is estimated at 76,518,000 English acres, of which 17,071,158 acres were (1910) woods and forests, 2,746,514 acres cultivated land, and 57,048,849 acres permanent grass, marsh land and uncultivated. The chief crops were wheat, barley, oats, rye, corn, potatoes and hay. The live stock included cattle, sheep, goats, horses and reindeer.

The chief articles of export are timber, woodwork, wood pulp and matches, fish oil and other products of the fisheries. paper, skins and furs, nails, minerals, stone, ice, saltpetre, cyanide, ferro-silicum, zinc, aluminium, calcium carbide, condensed milk, butter, margarine and tinned goods. The chief imports are cereals, groceries and clothing, coal, hides and skins, cotton and wool, oil, machinery, steamships and metal goods.

Education.—Primary education is compulsory and free between the ages of seven and fourteen, schools being maintained by local taxation with State grants in aid. The attendance is very high, the pupils numbering 376,723 in 1910. The University of Christiania was founded in 1812, and was attended in 1912 by 1,500 students.

Finance. — The budget for 1913-1914 called for an expenditure of 142,020,000 kroner, in anticipation of a revenue of 159,702,000 kroner. The public debt amounts to 362,805,563 kroner, which cost in 1914 17,730,900 kroner in interest and sinking fund. The unit of value, the krone, is equivalent to $0.26,8 United States money.

Railways.—In 1913 there were 1,946 miles of railway open for traffic, 282 miles being private and the remainder State owned. The receipts of the State lines in 1912 were 22,671,596 kroner and the expenses 17,275,549 kroner.

Shipping.—The mercantile marine of Norway is exceeded as to tonnage by only three nations (United Kingdom, United States, and Germany), and amounted in January 1, 1913, to 3,232 vessels (2,488,-582 gross tons), of which 2,126 (1,800,614 gross tons) were steamers and motor boats, and 1,106 (687,968 gross tons) sailing vessels.

Cities.—Capital, Christiania, on the southeast coast at the head of Christiania Fjord. Population (1910), 241,834. There are fourteen other cities having a population of between 10,000 and 100,000.

There are many reasons why Americans should be interested in Norway and in the development of our trade with that rugged and northerly country. There are certainly half as many Norwegians here as there are in the Fatherland and they own six times as much farming land. It is estimated that the property owned by Norwegians in this country is equal in value to the total wealth of Norway. This in itself is an excellent reason for further developing the trade relations between this great part of our population and Norway. And in considering how we may most effectively build up our trade we should consider carefully not only what we may sell to Norway, but what Norway has to sell that we can buy.

The commerce of Norway has increased rapidly in the last few years. In 1901 the exports amounted to $44,248,000; in 1912, the latest year for which statistics are available, they had reached just a little less than $100,000,000. The imports in 1901 were valued at $76,981,000; in 1912 they were valued at just a little more than $150,000,-000. A large part of this trade is in the hands of Germany and England. Of the imports the United States furnish only a paltry 6 per cent. and of the exports we take about 9 per cent. These figures indicate the possibility of extending the commerce between Norway and the United States. The principal Norwegian exports are fish and fish products, wood and wood pulp, paper, oil, hides and skins, sulphur, calcium carbide, condensed milk, and matches. The principal imports are coal and coke, iron and steel wares, rye and rye meal, machinery and locomotives, iron wrought and unwrought, wool and wool manufactures, cotton and cotton manufactures, hides and skins, coffee, sugar, wheat and wheat meal, barley, petroleum, tobacco, and bacon and lard.

N'Quentl-má-mish Indians. (See Indian Tribes.)

Nuestra Senora, The, seizure of, and claims arising out of, discussed, 3795.

Nullification.—The general meaning of nullification is the act of invalidating or making void. In American politics it is almost exclusively applied to the doctrine set forth by John C. Calhoun and his friends in the South Carolina controversy with the Federal Government, 1828-1833. This doctrine asserted the right of any state to declare the unconstitutionality of any United States law, though it should have been enacted in the proper manner and held to be constitutional by the Supreme Court of the United States. It was further claimed that any attempt to enforce such law in a state which had refused to acknowledge its validity would justify it in at once leaving the Union. The immediate cause of this declaration of principles was that the existing tariff law bore unjustly, so it was claimed, on the non-manufacturing and raw-material-producing states of the south. The arguments in favor of nullification were mainly based upon language used by Jefferson and Madison in the Kentucky and Virginia resolutions of 1798 and 1799 in regard to the alien and sedition laws. Here it was asserted that the General Government was not "the final or exclusive judge of the powers delegated to itself, but that, as in all other cases of compact among powers having no common judge, each party has an equal right to judge for itself, as well of infractions as of the mode and measure of redress." Senator Hayne, of South Carolina, was the first to advocate this doctrine in Congress. On the advice of Calhoun the governor of South Carolina called a convention, and an ordinance of nullification was passed on Nov. 19, 1832. This ordinance declared the Federal tariff law "null and void" and authorized the citizens to refuse payment of duties under it. It also denied the right of the Supreme Court of the United States to pass upon the nullification ordinance. The legislature was on the point of enacting a bill in accordance with this ordinance when the necessity was partly obviated by the passage of Clay's compromise measures (c. v., in 1833). The attempt to interfere with the execution of Federal laws was met by President Jackson's prompt instructions to the revenue officers at Charleston, his proclamation of Dec. 10, 1832 (1203), and his special message to Congress on the subject (1173). March 3, 1833, a new tariff bill was passed which gave satisfaction to the nullifiers, and on March 16 a state convention of South Carolina repealed the ordinance of nullification.

Nullification:

Message regarding, 1173.
Proclamation regarding, 1203.
Referred to, 1185, 1197.

Nutmeg State.—A nickname given to the State of Connecticut in facetious reference to the story that wooden nutmegs were manufactured in the state.

Nutrias, The, seizure of, and claims, arising out of, 4114, 5198, 5547, 5673, 5873, 5962.
Award in case of, 6070.

Oath.—A solemn appeal to the Supreme Being in attestation of the truth of some statement or the binding character of some covenant, undertaking, or promise. In point of law an oath is a solemn declaration which is necessary as a condition to the filling of some office more or less public or of giving evidence in a court of justice. The Constitution requires that before the President shall "enter on the execution of his office he shall take the following oath or affirmation : 'I do solemnly swear (or affirm) that I will faithfully execute the office of President of the United States, and will to the best of my ability preserve, protect and defend the Constitution of the United States.' " The first act of Congress provided for oaths of office. An oath similar to the foregoing is required of all officers of the executive, legislative, and judicial departments of states and the nation.

Congress in June, 1778, directed Washington to administer the following oath of allegiance to the officers of the Army before leaving Valley Forge : "I, [name of office] in the armies of the United States of America, do acknowledge the United States of America to be free, independent, and sovereign states, and declare that the people thereof owe no allegiance or obedience to George III, King of Great Britain, and I renounce, refuse, and abjure any allegiance or obedience to him ; and I do—that I will to the utmost of my power support, maintain, and defend the United States against the said King George III, his heirs and successors, and his or their abettors, assistants, and adherents, and will serve the said United States in the office of—— which I now hold, with fidelity according to the best of my skill and understanding." By an act of Congress of Aug. 3, 1861, the oath of allegiance for the cadets at West Point was amended so as to abjure all allegiance, sovereignty, or fealty to any state, county or country whatsoever and to require unqualified support of the Constitution and the National Government. In 1865 oaths of allegiance were required as a condition of pardon of persons who had participated in the rebellion. The oath required of persons appointed to office from the southern states, declaring that they had in no way aided or abetted the rebellion, was called the "iron clad oath," and was modified as soon as all apprehension of further difficulty with the south had passed away.

The oath administered to jurors entering upon their duties is substantially as follows : "You shall well and truly try the issue between the parties and a true verdict give according to the evidence, so help you God" : and the juror sometimes kisses the New Testament. Witnesses must be sworn in a similar manner, the word being, "The evidence you shall give shall be the truth, the whole truth, and nothing but the truth, so help you God." Witnesses must have sufficient understanding to know the nature of an oath, and on this ground young children are excluded as witnesses. A religious belief was formerly required before an oath could be considered as binding. Several statutes of Congress permit a simple affirmation in lieu of an appeal to the Almighty. Any person having conscientious scruples against oaths now makes a solemn affirmation. Jews are sworn on the Pentateuch, keep on their hats, and conclude their oaths with the words "so help me Jehovah." A Mohammedan is sworn on the Koran. A Chinaman is sworn by breaking a dish on the witness box or beheading a fowl. The form of taking an oath is immaterial, the essential thing being that the witness acknowledge some binding effect derived from his sense of moral obligation to tell the truth. (See also Perjury.)

Oath of Allegiance, army officers directed to subscribe, anew, 3219.
　Taken by insurgents in the Philippines, 6692.

Oath of Office:
　Act prescribing, for participants in War between the States discussed, 4076.
　Modification of, recommended, 3580.

Observatories. (See Meteorological Observatory; Naval Observatory.)

Obtrusive Partizanship.— An expression often incorrectly quoted as "Offensive Partizanship" (used by Grover Cleveland, 5079). In the same message he used the term "Pernicious Activity." Both these expressions referred to efforts on the part of office-holders to influence voting, and became very popular.

Ocean Cables:
　Amount expended for telegraphing by, referred to, 4123.
　Atlantic telegraph referred to, 3329, 3382, 3445, 3653.
　Between France and America to be landed on Massachusetts coast discussed, 4519.
　Communication recommended with—
　　Australia, 4567.
　　Guam, Island of, 6354.
　　Hawaiian Islands, 4565, 5086, 5368, 5761, 6354.
　　　Surveys for, in progress, 5623, 5663, 5679.
　　Japan, 4565.
　　Philippine Islands, 6354.
　Concessions to companies and rights of United States regarding, discussed, 3989, 4297, 4519.
　Convention regarding, 5119, 5176.
　Corporate company proposing to operate cable between France and America discussed, 3989, 4297, 4519.
　International agreement regarding interchange of messages recommended, 6401.
　International convention at Paris for protection of, in—
　　1880, 4714.
　　1884, 4799.
　　　Declaration of, transmitted to Senate, 5117, 5187.
　　　Discussed, 5084.
　　　Legislation to carry into effect recommended, 5180.
　Landing of, on American shores referred to, 4853, 5124.
　Legislation for protection of, recommended, 4864.
　Plan for connecting American and European telegraph lines by, referred to, 2952.

Rate charges imposed upon American corporation, questions with Argentine Republic regarding, 6323.

Recommendations of International American Conference regarding, referred to, 5511.

Stipulations with French Cable Co. referred to, 4738, 4744.

Oceania.—One of the geographical divisions of the globe. It embraces the Continent of Australia and the islands of the Pacific Ocean east to Easter Island (109° W.). The islands generally are grouped in two divisions—Australasia and Polynesia.

Australasia is subdivided into Australia proper and Melanesia, "islands of the blacks." The latter includes New Guinea, Bismarck Archipelago, New Caledonia Island, and Solomon, Santa Cruz, New Hebrides, and Loyalty groups. The Fiji Islands (Polynesia), are usually treated with Australia, as are New Zealand and Tasmania.

Polynesia comprises Polynesia proper—Ellice, Samoan, Phœnix, Palmyra, Society, and Tuamotu Islands—and Micronesia, "the little islands." The latter embraces the remaining islands of the Pacific, including Marianne and Caroline west and Hawaiian east. Land area of Oceania, 3,460,000 square miles—more than three-fourths belonging to Australia. (See Australia.)

For the Oceanic possessions of the United States see Hawaii and the islands of Wake and Guam.

British Possessions.—Besides the islands constituting Australasia, the principal groups, and isolated islands belonging to Great Britain are Cook Islands, Manihiki, Tokelau and Phœnix groups, Ellice Islands, Gilbert Islands, Santa Cruz Islands, British Solomon Islands, and the Islands of Pitcairn, Fanning, Malden, and Christmas The New Hebrides Islands are jointly protected by Great Britain and France.

French Possessions.—New Caledonia and dependencies, and the Society Islands, the Marquesas, Tuamotu, Gambier, and Tubuai groups, and the Island of Rapa.

German Possessions.—The northeastern portion of New Guinea (Kaiser Wilhelm' Land), Bismarck Archipelago, the north erly part of the Solomon group, Marshall Islands, the Marianne or Ladrone Islands (exclusive of Guam), the Caroline Islands and Pelew Islands.

New Guinea.—Discovered by Portuguese in 1511; named Papua in 1526; New Guinea in 1545. Visited by Dutch 1676. Circumnavigated by Dampier 1699. The Dutch took possession of the country west of 141° E. in 1828. The southeastern portion became a British protectorate in 1884; a Crown Colony in 1888. A German protectorate was established in the northeast in 1884. Total area about 312,000 square miles. Interior wide plains and lofty mountains; greatest elevation 16,000 feet. The chief rivers are the Kaiserin Augusta and the Fly. The coast line is deeply indented and has fine harbors. The forests contain cedar, sandalwood, ebony, India rubber, areca and sago palms, bamboos, etc. The soil is adapted to tobacco, rice, tea, sugar cane, coffee, cotton, fruits, etc. The German have established cotton and tobacco plantations. The chief industries are wood carving and manufacture of rope and pottery. Leading exports—copra, pearl shell, trepang, gold, pearls, and sandalwood. Gold, coal, and plumbago are found. The population is about 1,800,000. Area of Papua (British), 90,540 square miles; population 270,000. The govern-

ment is administered by a Lieutenant-Governor. New South Wales, Victoria, and Queensland furnish funds and have a voice in its affairs. Port Moresby is the capital; population 1,500. Kaiser Wilhelm's Land —German New Guinea—area 70,000 square miles; population about 300,000. In hands of German New Guinea Company. Friedrich Wilhelmshafen most important harbor.

Samoan Islands.—First explored by Bougainville in 1768; Christianity was introduced in 1830. Neutrality and independence was guaranteed by Great Britain, United States, and Germany in 1889. The islands were divided between Germany and United States in 1899. They are situated in the middle of the Pacific about 400 miles northeast of Fiji; the largest, Savaii and Upolu, belong to Germany. Tutuila and adjacent islands to United States. Total area 1,701 square miles. Chief products are sugar, coffee, cotton, maize, and tropical fruits. Apia is the chief trading center; population 3,742. Pago-pago, Tutuila, is a fine natural harbor. The natives are Christians. (See also Samoan Islands and Tutuila.)

New Hebrides.—Discovered by Spanish in 1606; explored and named by Cook in 1774. The group is northeast of New Caledonia and stretches northwest and southeast 500 miles. Area, 5,700 square miles. Cocoanuts (for copra), maize, millet, coffee, and bananas are grown. Population about 80,000. Jointly administered by France and England.

Solomon Islands.—Discovered by Mendana in 1567-1568; rediscovered by Bougainville 1768. An archipelago in Melanesia, 500 miles east of New Guinea. Area 16,950 square miles, in large part covered with thick forests. Chief commercial products tortoise shell, copra, ivory nuts, and sandalwood. Germany has Bougainville and dependencies in the north; the southern portion of group is under British rule; Choiseul and Isabel were ceded to Great Britain by Germany in 1899.

Trade with the United States.—The value of merchandise imported into Oceania from the United States (including the Philippine Islands) for the year 1912 was $79,-102,845, and goods to the value of $37,-543,441 were sent thither—a balance of $41,559,404 in favor of the United States.

Ocean Mail Post-Office, establishment of, discussed, 5633.

Ocean Mail Service. (See Postal Service, steamship.)

Offenses on High Seas, acts to provide for punishment of, returned, 5769.

Officers, Public (see also the several officers.)

Act regulating tenure of certain civil officers vetoed. (See Tenure-of-Office Act.)

Application of public money by, for private uses should be made a felony, 1709.

Appointment of. (See Executive Nominations.)

Availing themselves of benefits of insolvent-debtors act must be dismissed, 1107.

Bonding system of, discussed, 1611.

Books of, should be carefully inspected, 1709.

Breach of duty in publishing Senate executive business discussed, 2691.

Official Etiquette.—As state social functions in America are not hedged about by the privileges and prerogatives to which rank, station and birth alone entitle the holder in monarchical courts, American ceremonies, observances and ritual are, in comparison, simple and meagre. No special lessons are required nor are rehearsals needed to carry off with proper dignity any of the observances of state courtesy. Nevertheless, although there is an absence of that ostentatious display which marks the ceremonies of the courts of Europe, official etiquette in America is prescribed by a rigid code established by the highest authorities, which is not disregarded.

It is only natural that state receptions should be governed by more arbitrary rules than those which direct purely social intercourse. It must be remembered that when an official reception is held, it is always an official duty that is being performed. The state forms and ceremonies which have obtained in America have varied from time to time according to the usages of the day and the taste of the national hostess. They have, at times, been further modified by periods of national calamity, war and the death of immediate relatives, but through all this variation and modification there has run the golden thread of democratic simplicity so dear to the national heart.

The period of Washington's administration must be regarded as a time of transition. Nor is there cause for wonder that much formality and stateliness marked the dispensation of national hospitality in the beginning of the nation's development. The term "colonial" is today associated in our minds with a courtly, stately conventionality peculiarly its own. Men and women of that time, who, either at first hand or through their mothers and fathers, had received their education in courtesy, grace and proper behavior from the customs of England, could not easily shake off their second nature; and no doubt fretted over the meagre means of gratifying their wishes; but as soon as they were cut off by their own desire from this influence and became self-dependent, that pure simplicity nurtured by individual worth became evident. It is not surprising that in the earliest period the Executive Mansion was a place of stately and continuous reception, and that Martha Washington is famous for the dignity, grace and splendor of her social reign; but, on the other hand, the simplicity of Jefferson's time has passed into a proverb, and was such as to excite comment even abroad. The youth, gaiety and impetuous brilliancy of "Dolly Madison" contributed largely to the breaking down of much of the severity and conventionality which preceded her time.

The President is the leader of social as well as of official life. Although he is accessible to all to the extent that all may call upon him, he is not expected to return any visits. He, of course, has the privilege of calling upon a friend. The same is equally true of the wife of the President. He is always addressed as "Mr. President." He does not leave the country, as a rule, and in this respect is under greater restrictions than any of the crowned heads of Europe. Under this "unwritten law" a foreign legation in Washington is construed as being foreign ground and may not be entered by the President. Neither may he set foot upon a foreign vessel. The only formal calls that he may make are those upon a President-elect, an ex-President, or a President or reigning monarch of a foreign state visiting Washington. He carries no personal card, but one reading simply "The President." He may not accept valuable gifts; and if such are tendered, they are usually placed in the National Museum.

The Chief Justice of the Supreme Court ranks next to the President socially. Below him in turn socially come the Vice-President, the Speaker of the House, the General of the Army and the Admiral of the Navy. It is considered one of the first duties of the Members of the House of Representatives to call upon these when coming to Washington. The social rank of women is decided by that of the husband or father.

The Inaugural Ball, held upon the evening of the day of inauguration, was the first social event in the life of the newly inaugurated President, until it was abolished by President Wilson. It partook more of the nature of a reception than a ball, for it was so largely attended that dancing was an impossibility. It was usually held in one of the departmental buildings. For several days after the President's inauguration, public informal receptions follow and a week or more is consumed in receptions during the day and dinners at night. These latter are classified, to a certain extent, so that all branches of the official service are formally recognized. Saturday is the official reception day at the White House. The public receptions which are held from the first of January until the beginning of Lent were inaugurated by President Jackson. The guests assemble in the East Room and as quickly as this is filled the President greets them as they pass out. The formal receptions are not held so frequently as previously, on account of the great increase in the number of Senators and Representatives. This is compensated for by inviting some Members of Congress to state dinners and entertaining others with less ceremony.

The scene at a formal or official reception is a brilliant one. The Government officials, the officers of the Army and Navy, and the foreign legations mingle in uniform, and the ladies are not in full dress, but in reception toilettes. Diplomats and attachés wear their court costumes. The President stands at the head of the line, next to him his wife, who invites several prominent ladies to assist her in receiving. As the guests enter, they pass down the receiving line until they have greeted all of the ladies of the receiving party. The daughters of the household of a state official are not invited to state dinners unless the daughter is the female representative of the family.

The general conduct of, and the social observances at these several ceremonies are the same as those which direct social observances elsewhere in good society. The cards of invitation and responses to the ordinary receptions do not differ from those in other American homes; but at the state dinners and official receptions, which are to be regarded in some sense as an interchange of international courtesy, the rules of attendance are very strict and no one would think of neglecting to attend without an eminently satisfactory excuse.

Official Publications. (See Records and Documents.)

Official Register. (See Biennial Register.)

Officialism.—The perfunctory performance of duties in office merely for pay or glory, without genuine display of public interest.

Ogallala Indians. (See Indian Tribes.)

Ogden vs. Saunders.—An important United States Supreme Court case limiting the operation of State bankruptcy laws. Ogden, of Louisiana, declared upon certain bills of exchange drawn in 1806 upon the defendant Saunders, a citizen of Kentucky, but then living in New York. Saunders pleaded a certificate of discharge under the act of the New York legislature of 1801 for the relief of insolvent debtors. The district court of Louisiana gave judgment for the plaintiff. On a writ of error the case was taken before the Supreme Court of the United States, which decided in 1827 that the power to pass bankruptcy laws did not belong exclusively to the United States, and that the fair and ordinary exercise of that power by the States need not involve a violation of the obligation of contracts, but that State law could not discharge a debt due to a citizen of another State. Justice Johnson delivered the opinion, in which concurred Chief Justice Marshall and Justices Duval and Story.

Ogden, Utah, bill to authorize city of, to assume increased indebtedness vetoed, 5518.

Ogdensburg (N. Y.), Capture of.—In September, 1812, Gen. Brown was sent to Ogdensburg, N. Y., at the mouth of the Oswegatchie River, to garrison Fort Presentation and attempt the capture of some British stores that were reported as being on the way up the St. Lawrence River. Oct. 2, about forty British bateaux, escorted by a gunboat, were seen approaching. On the 4th two gunboats and twenty-five bateaux, containing 750 men, started for Ogdensburg. The American force amounted to about 1,200 effective men. After two hours of firing the invaders withdrew with a slight loss. No one was injured on the American side. Later Maj. Forsyth was placed in command of the garrison at Ogdensburg. With a party of citizens and militia he crossed over to Elizabethtown, Canada, Feb. 6, 1813, and rescued a number of prisoners held there. In retaliation for this exploit Lieut.-Col. McDouell, with about 800 men, crossed the river on the ice Feb. 22, 1813, and after a short engagement gained possession of the town, which they gave over to plunderers.

Ohio.—One of the central western group of states; nickname, "The Buckeye State." Ohio extends from lat. 38° 24′ to 41° 57′ north and from long. 80° 34′ to 84° 49′ west. It is bounded on the north by Michigan and Lake Erie, on the east by Pennsylvania and West Virginia (separated by the Ohio River), on the south by Kentucky (separated by the Ohio River), and on the west by Indiana, and has an area of 41,040 square miles.

Ohio was first visited by the French under La Salle at the end of the seventeenth century. It was claimed by both the French and English. It was ceded to Great Britain in 1763 and to the United States in 1783. In 1787 it became part of the Northwest Territory. The first settlement was made at Marietta in 1788. The State was admitted to the Union in 1802.

Statistics of agriculture collected for the last Federal Census, place the number of farms in the State at 272,545, comprising 24,105,708 acres, with stock and improvements, valued at $1,902,694,589. The average value of farm land per acre was $53.34, an increase from $33.35 in 1900. The value of the domestic animals poultry, etc., was $197,332,112, including 1,837,607 cattle, valued at $51,403,344; 910,224 horses, $93,910,638; 22,850 mules, $2,775,-831; 3,105,627 swine, $19,412,730; 3,909,-162 sheep, $14,941,381; poultry, $9,532,672. The yield and value of field crops for 1911 was: Corn, 3,900,000 acres, 150,540,000 bushels, $87,313,000; wheat, 2,265,000 acres, 36,240,000 bushels, $32,987,000; oats, 1,700,000 acres, 54,570,000 bushels, $24,-556,000; rye, 60,000 acres, 930,000 bushels, $790,000; potatoes, 190,000 acres, 12,350,-000 bushels, $10,374,000; hay, 2,556,000 acres, 2,505,000 tons, $47,344,000; tobacco, 88,000 acres, 81,400,000 pounds, $6,186,400.

Ohio ranks fourth among the states in the value of its mineral production, according to the United States Geological Survey. The total value of the mineral production of the state increased from $111,-229,656 in 1912 to $121,690,661 in 1913. It is the premier state in the value of clay products and in the manufacture of grindstones and pulpstones. It is second in the production of bromine and lime, third in the output of calcium chloride, natural gas, salt, sand and gravel, and gypsum, fourth in the production of coal, oilstones, scythestones, and stone, and seventh in quantity and sixth in value in the production of petroleum. Ohio ranks next to Pennsylvania and second in the country in the manufacture of pig iron, and if pig iron rather than iron ore were taken as the measure of iron production, Ohio would rank second in the total value of its mineral products, which would be increased in 1913 by nearly ninety per cent over the value obtained if pig iron is excluded. Practically all the pig iron produced in Ohio, however, is made from Lake Superior ores and the iron production is credited to the state in which the iron ore was mined.

The two leading products of Ohio are coal and clay products, coal having slightly the better of it in 1912 and 1913, whereas in 1911 the value of the clay products exceeded that of coal. The production of coal in 1913 amounted to 36,200,527 short tons, valued at $39,948,058, the output both in quantity and value being the maximum record for the state. The production of petroleum, which stands third among the state's mineral industries and in which Ohio ranks sixth, value considered, among all the states, decreased slightly in quantity, from 8,969,007 barrels in 1912 to 8,781,468 barrels in 1913, while the value increased about 45 per cent over the previous year, from $12,085,998 to $17,538,452. The value of the natural gas produced in 1913 was $10,416,699 in 1913, against $11,891,299 in 1912.

The number of manufacturing establishments in Ohio having an annual output valued at $500 or more at the beginning of 1915 was 15,658. The amount of capital invested was $1,677,552,000, giving employment to 606,807 persons, using material valued at $1,020,782,000, and turning out finished goods worth $1,782,808,000. Salaries and wages paid amounted to $424,189,000.

Ohio (see also Columbus; Dayton; Portsmouth):
Boundary of—
　Act respecting, executed, 637.
　Controversy with Michigan, regarding, 1404, 1407.
　Referred to, 1173.
Lands in—
　Referred to, 833.
Title of United Brethren to, 801.
Michigan boundary line dispute with, and the necessity of an early settlement of, by Congress, 178.
National Guard of, expiration of enlistment of, referred to and thanks of President tendered, 3440.
Ratification of fourteenth amendment withdrawn by, 3836.

Ohio Companies.—In 1749 George II. granted to a band of wealthy citizens of Virginia and Maryland, calling themselves the Ohio Company, a tract of land containing 500,000 acres, lying in the Ohio Valley south of the Ohio River. Thomas Lee was the projector of the company, but it was later conducted by Lawrence Washington. The terms of the grant required that 100 families should be established upon the tract, a fort should be built, and a garrison maintained. A number of storehouses were also established. In 1783 the territory east of the Missis-

sippi, north of the Ohio River, and west of Pennsylvania, which before the Revolution had been part of the Province of Quebec and afterwards had been claimed by Virginia, was ceded to the United States, with the proviso that it was to be settled and formed into states. March 1, 1786, Rufus Putnam suggested a second Ohio company, and two days later he and Messrs. Cutler, Brooks, Sargent, and Cushing formed an association and issued 1,000 shares at $1,000 each in Continental certificates or $125 in gold. A year afterwards Congress granted certain lots free of charge, and an enormous tract was bought at about eight or nine cents per acre in specie. Colonization was immediately begun. Slavery was prohibited. This company had large influence in shaping the ordinance for the government of the Northwest Territory, of which it became a part.

Ohio River:
Canal from Chesapeake Bay to. (See Chesapeake and Ohio Canal.)
Navigation on, 824, 909.
　Appropriation for, 934.
　Mode of improving, referred to, 1196, 2685.
Referred to, 1104, 1491.
Ship canal around fall of, 3819.
Survey of, appropriation for, 768.

Ojibwa Indians. (See Indian Tribes.)

Oklahoma.—One of the southern group of states formed in 1907 by the Union of Oklahoma with the Indian Territory. Nickname, "Boomer State." Motto, "Labor omnia vincit," (Labor conquers everything). It extends from latitude 33° 35' to 37° north and from longitude 94° 20' to 103° west. It is bounded on the north by Kansas and Colorado, on the east by Arkansas and Missouri, on the south by Texas (separated by the Red River) and on the west by Texas and New Mexico. It has an area of 70,057 square miles.

Oklahoma Territory was formed in 1890 from the western part of Indian Territory and the public strip called No Man's Land (q. v.). Invasions of the Indian Territory took place in 1879 but the settlers were ordered out by proclamations of President Hayes (pages 4499, 4550). Several subsequent invasions of the Territory were made in defiance of Federal law, but all expeditions of settlers were arrested and their towns broken up. Finally delegates of the Creek Nation met at Washington and sold the western half of their domain to the United States Government for $2,280,857. Congress ratified this agreement March 1, 1889. By proclamation of President Harrison (5450) Oklahoma was opened to settlement at noon April 22, 1889, and during the afternoon of that day 50,000 settlers, who had been encamped on the border, rushed into the territory, formed a provincial government, and laid out town sites. In 1893 the Cherokee strip was ceded by the Indians to the Government for $8,300,000. Agriculture and stock-raising are the principal industries. Salt is the only mineral now mined, but in the future mining promises to be the chief industry of Oklahoma, as gold, silver, lead, zinc and gypsum are known to exist in many places.

Statistics of agriculture collected for the last Federal census, place the number of farms in the state at 1,908,192, comprising 28,859,353 acres, valued, with stock and improvements, at $918,198,882. The average value of land per acre was $22.49, an increase from $6.50 in 1900. The value of domestic animals, poultry, etc., was $152,-432,792, including 1,953,560 cattle, valued at $43,187,601 ; 742,959 horses, $63,651,631 : 257,076 mules, $28,618,224 ; 1,839,030 swine, $11,997,641 ; 62,472 sheep, $253,864 ; poultry, $3,713,943. The yield and value of the field crops for 1911 was : Corn, 5,-675,000 acres, 36,888,000 bushels, $25,822,-000 ; wheat 1,122,000 acres, 8,976,000 bushels, $8,258,000, oats, 909,000 acres, 8,181,-000 bushels, $3,927,000 ; rye, 4,000 acres, 38,000 bushels, $40,000 ; potatoes, 30,000 acres, 540,000 bushels, $670,000 ; hay, 810,-000 acres, 648,000 tons, $5,184,000, and cotton, 915,000 bales. In the production of petroleum Oklahoma now ranks second, having been surpassed only by California in 1910. The production that year was 52,-028,718 barrels. Some gold and silver also are produced.

The number of manufacturing establishments in Oklahoma having an annual output valued at $500 or more at the beginning of 1915 was 2,518. The amount of capital invested was $65,478,000, giving employment to 22,700 persons, using material valued at $70,970,000, and turning out finished goods worth $102,006,000. Salaries and wages paid amounted to $14,213,000.

The Federal census of 1910 gave the population as 1,657,155.

Oklahoma:

Appropriation for settlement under treaties of freedom, etc., upon lands in, recommended, 4785.

Admission to Union discussed, 7020.

Boundary line with Colorado, 6937.

Lands in—
Agreement for cession of, 5648, 5649, 5768.
Opened to settlement by proclamation, 5450, 5591, 5710, 5838, 6020, 6695.
Referred to, 5637.
Reservation of, 6695, 6889.

Laws of Nebraska in force in, continuation of, recommended, 5566.

Memorial from Wichita and Caddo Indians regarding claims to lands in, 5671.

Organization of, discussed, 5393.
Act regarding returned, 5503.

Reservations in, ceded to United States, 5591.

Suffering among settlers in, recommendations regarding, 5516.
Memorial from legislature asking for relief, 5567.

Unauthorized occupancy of, 4832, 4943.

Proclamations against, 4811, 4888.

Oklahoma Central Railroad, act to authorize construction and operation of railway by, through Territories, vetoed, 6014.

Oklahoma City, Okla., act authorizing issuance of bonds by, to provide the right of way for railroad, vetoed, 5571.

Old Bay State.—A nickname for Massachusetts (q. v.). (See also States.)

Old Colony.—A popular name for Plymouth County, Mass. The territory was formerly included in the Plymouth Colony, but, being unable to obtain a charter from the British Crown on account of its outspoken opposition to the established church, was in 1691 absorbed into Massachusetts Bay Colony.

Old Dominion.—A name popularly applied to the State of Virginia. In colonial documents Virginia is frequently referred to as "His Majesty's Dominion of Virginia."

Old Dominion State.—A nickname for Virginia (q. v.), (See also States) ; sometimes also nicknamed Mother of States and Mother of Presidents.

Old Hickory.— An affectionate nickname given to Andrew Jackson in 1813 when, disregarding the order of the Secretary of War to disband his troops, he assumed the responsibility of marching them in a body from Natchez, at his own expense. The Government afterwards approved Jackson's disobedience, and reimbursed him. The nickname stuck to him even through his Presidency, and to his grave.

Old Line State.—A nickname for Maryland (q. v.). (See also States.)

Office of Exhibits. (See Exhibits, Office of.)

Office of Farm Management. (See Farm Management, Office of.)

Office of Indian Affairs. (See Department of the Interior.)

Office of Inspection. (See Inspection, Office of.)

Office of Public Roads and Rural Engineering. (See Public Roads and Rural Engineering, Office of.)

Old North State. — Alternative nickname for North Carolina. (See Tar Heel State.)

Old Point Comfort, Va., school for artillery instruction at, 824.

Old-Settlers' Meeting.—A gala day or picnic occasion, especially in rural sections, where the countryside gathers to do homage to the fathers and mothers who settled in and developed the neighborhood. (See Settler and Pioneer.)

Old Winnebago Reservation, Dakota, restoration of, to public domain, order regarding, declared void, 4890.
Discussed, 4943.

Oldenburg:
Commercial relations with, 820.
Exequatur issued consul of, revoked, 3710.
Referred to, 3720.
Treaty with, 2479.
Vessels of, discriminating duties on, suspended, 666, 1059.

Oleomargarine, act defining butter and imposing tax on, approved and discussed, 4992.

Oligarchy.—Government by a few officials, —derived from the Greek words meaning "few rule."

Olive Branch, The, condemnation of, indemnification asked for, 1268.

Olmstead et al. vs. Rittenhouse's Executrixes.—In 1778 Olmstead and other citizens of Connecticut were pressed into the service of the British aboard the sloop *Active*. They revolted and took possession of the vessel, and were in turn captured by the Pennsylvania armed brig *Convention*. The State court of admiralty of Pennsylvania adjudged the *Active* lawful prize and awarded the proceeds of her sale to the State, officers and crew of the *Convention*, and the owners, officers, and crew of *Le Gerard*, a privateer, which assisted in the capture. Olmstead and the others claimed the whole prize, but were awarded only one-fourth. They then appealed to the Federal commissioners of appeals and received a favorable verdict. The State court of admiralty of Pennsylvania set aside this verdict and ordered that the money be brought into court. May 1, 1779, the loan certificates for the prize money were deposited with State Treasurer Rittenhouse. In 1803 the district court of the United States for the State of Pennsylvania entered a final decree that the money be paid over to the libellants. The case having come before the United States Supreme Court, March, 1808, that court ordered a mandamus as against the district judge, and in 1809 judgment was executed in favor of the plaintiffs in spite of violent opposition from Pennsylvania, which opposition had prevented Judge Peters from carrying out his decree. The facts in the matter are all given in the Peters case. (See also 456, Peters *vs.* United States.)

Olustee (Fla.), Battle of.—In February. 1864, a Federal expedition was sent to Florida from Port Royal under command of Gen. Seymour. It was composed of twenty steamers, eight schooners and about 5,000 troops. Feb. 7 the land forces occupied Jacksonville. On the 18th they marched inland, encountering the Confederates on the 20th at Olustee, a railroad station about fifty miles west of Jacksonville. The battle was unexpected and was fiercely fought from 2 o'clock till dark, when the vanquished Federals retired twenty miles to Barbers. Seymour lost nearly 2,000 men, as well as five pieces of artillery, in this disastrous fight, and the expedition returned to Hilton Head.

Olympia, The, mentioned, 6297.

Omaha, The. (See Ikisima Island.)

Omaha Indians. (See Indian Tribes.)

Omaha, Nebr., act to extend privileges to port of, vetoed, 4999.

Oman.—Oman is an independent sultanate of southeast Arabia, with a Muhammadan population that is mainly Arab, but contains many foreign elements, including Indians, Persians, Baluchis, and Swahili negroes. The territory of the sultanate extends from the peninsula of El Katar, on the Persian Gulf, to the promontory of Ras Sair, on the Arabian Sea, a total length of coast of close on 1,500 miles. The northwest extremity is in 51° 30' E. longitude, and Oman extends to the easternmost point of Arabia in 59° 48' E. longitude, and thence southwest to a point about 54° 28' E. longitude and 16° 50' N. latitude. The most northerly point is Ras Musandum in 26° 30' N. latitude. The area is 81,000 square miles.

Physical Features.—The northwest and southwest extremities are in the form of a horse-shoe, the intervening land being the arid and sandy desert of central and southern Arabia, the great Ruba el Khali, or Dahna Desert, which covers the peninsula, from Oman in the east to Yemen in the west. The northern coast of Oman is washed by the Persian Gulf; the Cape of Ras Musandum reaches to the narrow Strait of Ormuz; the eastern coast is washed by the Gulf of Oman, and the southeastern coast by the Arabian Sea. The promontory (Ras Jebel) which terminates in Ras Musandum is formed by the western horn of a range of mountains, which stretches across northeastern Oman, from Musandum to El Hadd, and shuts out the coastal districts from the interior. The west coast of the Ras Jebel promontory, known as the Pirate Coast, and the remainder of the Persian Gulf littoral, are low lying and sandy, and many rocky islets lie close inshore.

History.—Oman was established as an independent sultanate in 1741 by Ahmed ben Said, an imam (or sultan) of Yemen, who consolidated his power at the expense of the Ottoman empire In the earlier years of the nineteenth century Oman was the most powerful state in Arabia, and the rule of the Sultan was extended over the Makran coast of the Arabian Sea and over parts of East Africa, including Socotra and Zanzibar. In 1856 the sultanate was divided by the two sons of Sultan Seyyid, and Zanzibar was formed into a separate sultanate.

Government.—The government is absolute and is hereditary in the descendants of Ahmed ben Said. At the present time the authority of the Sultan is effective only in the capital and the neighboring territory, for although the Bedouin Arabs recognize his superiority, the rule is only nominal in the interior, and trade is hampered by tribal warfare and robbery of caravans, which are forced to proceed with strong escorts through the various passes over the mountains, some of which are guarded by friendly chiefs. Since 1798 the relations between Muscat and England have been friendly, and many conventions and treaties have been made. British warships have upheld the authority of the Sultan against rebellious tribes. The Sultan is in treaty relations with the Government of India and receives annually a subsidy, while a British agent resides at the capital. A joint Anglo-French declaration of 1862 guarantees his independence, and the Sultan is pledged not to cede territory to any Power but the British Government. His Highness Seyyid Taimar bin Turki; born 1886, succeeded his father as Sultan in 1913.

Cities.—Capital, Muscat, the principal seaport, on the east coast. Population about 25,000. Other towns and ports are Matrah, about five miles north of the capital (population 10,000, Barkha and Sohar, on the east coast; and Sharkah on the Pirate Coast. The principal inland towns are Nizwa in the "Garden of Oman," and Bereima in the northwest.

Production and Industry.—Communication is carried on by pack animals (chiefly dromedaries) under strong escort, and there is a much frequented route from the Turkish territory in the northwest to the town of Bereima. From Bereima the route leads southward to Nizwa and the Garden of Oman, thus connecting the northwest with the eastern ports. There is a pilgrimage route of twenty-one days across the Arabian Desert, from the Garden of Oman to Mecca, in the Turking-Arabian vilayet of Hedjaz.

The trade of Oman is considerable, the seaboard trade of Muscat and Matrah exceeding $3,450,000 in 1912-1913. The chief export is dates, the principal imports being rice, arms and ammunition, coffee, cotton and silk goods. There is an import duty of 5 per cent *ad valorem*, which forms the principal source of revenue, but exports are free.

Omnibus Bill.—Early in the first session of the Thirty-first Congress Henry Clay introduced a series of six resolutions as a basis for the compromise of the slavery question. These resolutions provided for the admission of California as a free state; territorial governments for New Mexico and Utah without conditions as to slavery; a territorial boundary line between Texas and New Mexico favorable to the former; payment of the Texas debt; suppression of the slave trade in the District of Columbia; a more effective fugitive slave law, and a denial of the power of Congress to interfere with the slave trade between the slave states.

On Feb. 5 and 6, 1850, Clay ably advocated the passage of his resolutions by the Senate. That body was strongly Democratic, though the administration was Whig. Debate on Clay's resolutions lasted two months and was participated in by Webster (Mass.), Calhoun (S. C.), Benton (Mo.), King (Ala.), Davis and Foote (Miss.), Hamlin (Me.), Cass (Mich.), Seward and Dickinson (N. Y.), Chase and Corwin (Ohio), Douglass (Ill.), Frémont (Cal.), Soulé (La.), Hale (N. H.), Mangum (N. C.), Hunter and Mason (Va.), Bell (Tenn.), and others of note. On April 19 the resolutions were referred to a committee of thirteen, with Clay as chairman, and consisting of six other Whigs and six Democrats. On May 8 this committee submitted an elaborate series of bills embodying the substance of Clay's resolutions. These several bills were known collectively as the "Omnibus bill," and the last was passed on Sept. 20. (See also Compromise of 1850.)

Oneida, The. (See *Aroostook*, The.)

Oneida Indians. (See Indian Tribes.)

Oneota, The, purchased for Peru, detention of, 3831, 3835.

Onondaga Indians. (See Indian Tribes.)

Ontario, Lake. (See Lake Ontario.)

Open Door in China.—With China foreign commerce is a matter of modern history. As early as 1516 the Portuguese had established a trading port in China and, together with the Dutch, English and Americans, who followed them, carried on an irregular and unsatisfactory trade for a hundred years without government protection or favor besides being looked upon with suspicion and hatred, as barbarians. From 1664 to 1834 England's China trade was in the hands of the East India Company, whose monopoly came to an end in the latter year. The opium trade, worth $5,000,000 to $8,000,000 annually to the government of British India, had long been illegal, and China, in 1837, decided to suppress it. England's refusal to make traffic in opium a crime punishable with death brought on a war in 1840. This was concluded by a treaty which opened to British trade the five ports of Canton, Amoy, Fu-Chow, Ning-Po, and Shanghai.

Caleb Cushing, heading an embassy from the United States, negotiated a similar treaty in 1844. By its terms a customs duty was established and in consideration of a transit duty, goods were given free conveyance to all places in China.

In 1856 England again found a pretext for war with China, and was joined by France in 1857. This was terminated in 1858 by the treaty of Tien-Tsin, which granted toleration to the Christian missionaries in China, and freedom of Chinese rivers to English and French merchant vessels. At the same time Russia signed a treaty by which she acquired the Amur territory.

While these powers were gaining concessions in China, President Buchanan sent William B. Reed to open negotiations on behalf of the United States. The result of Mr. Reed's efforts was a treaty of amity and commerce, guaranteeing that no American vessel should engage in contraband trade with China.

Anson Burlingame, United States minister to China from 1861 to 1867, won the confidence of the Orientals and secured a treaty granting further concessions. Burlingame later headed a Chinese embassy accredited to eleven different nations. In June, 1873, the Chinese Emperor for the first time gave personal audience to the ministers of the United States, Russia, Great Britain, France, Germany, Holland, and Japan. By the war with Japan, in 1894-1895 China was forced to concede the independence of Korea, and cede to Japan the island of Formosa, the Liaotung peninsula and the Pescadore Islands and an indemnity in money.

While China was thus embarrassed Russia, through France, advanced a loan of $77,290,000 to help pay the Japanese indemnity. In 1896 American and German capitalists loaned $80,000,000 and in 1898 another $80,000,000 was advanced by the English and German banks. In return for these loans valuable railway and trading concessions were exacted with a view to establishing spheres of influence which would serve as an excuse for military occupation.

Until 1904 only twenty-one ports had been opened to foreign trade. In that year three others were opened, and in 1906 sixteen more allowed the ships of the western world to enter. The opening of these ports was looked upon by China as a great concession wrung from her by the overpowering military strength of the allied commercial world. The agreements of 1897-1898 provide that "the administration of the Imperial Maritime Customs Service shall be conducted by representatives of foreign powers until 1943."

An outbreak of the anti-foreign feeling in China, directed against Americans in particular, on account of the Chinese exclusion laws of this country, was shown in the boycott against American goods which began in the southern provinces in 1905. This was entirely dispelled by the wise policy of the Roosevelt administration, carried into execution by Secretaries John Hay and Elihu Root.

William H. Taft, when Secretary of War, declared in a speech made in China that the United States would actively interfere whenever necessary to preserve the open door in all parts of the Chinese empire. Further acts of friendship on the part of the United States were the remission of a part of the Boxer indemnity, upon recommendation of President Roosevelt, and the liberal contributions, under Presidential patronage, to the famine fund in 1908.

Open Door, in the Orient, policy of the United States to be firm in controversies, 6797.

Open Shop.—A term used to describe the conditions of employment in an establishment where men are and may be employed irrespective of their membership or nonmembership in a trade union or other labor organization. (See Trade Unions, Closed Shop.)

Orange River Colony.—A British colony in South Africa. It was formerly an independent republic known as the Orange Free State, and was founded by the Boers in 1836 and recognized by Great Britain ten years later. In consequence of the part taken in the Boer War it was annexed to the British Crown in 1900. Area, 48,326 square miles; population in 1890 (estimated), 77,716 white and 129,787 blacks, natives of the country.

Order of Indian Wars of the United States.—This order was organized at Chicago Ill., June 10, 1896, and received its charter from the State of Illinois. The order consists of two classes of companions: First, commissioned officers of the army, navy, and marine corps, and of state and territorial organizations, which have been, or may hereafter be, engaged in conflicts, battles or actual field service against hostile Indians in the United States; second, sons of living members of the first class. The object of the Association is to perpetuate the history of the services rendered by the American military forces in their conflicts and wars within the territory of the United States, and to collect and secure for publication historical data relating to the instances of brave deeds and personal devotion by which Indian warfare has been illustrated.

Order of the Founders and Patriots of America.—This order was founded in 1896, its object being "to bring together and associate congenial men whose ancestors struggled together for life and liberty, home and happiness, in the land when it was a new and unknown country and their patriot descendants; from them came thorough patriots who sustained the Colonies in the struggle for independence in the Revolutionary War; to teach reverent regard for the names and history, character and perseverance, deeds and heroism of the founders of this country and their patriot descendants; to teach that the purpose of the founders could have had no lasting result but for their patriot sons; to inculcate patriotism; to discover, collect, and preserve records, documents, manuscripts, monuments, and history relating to the first colonists and their ancestors and their descendants, and to commemorate and celebrate events in the history of the Colonies and the Republic." Eligibility—Any man above the age of twenty-one years, of good moral character and reputation, and a citizen of the United States, who is lineally descended in the male line of either parent from an ancestor who settled in any of the Colonies now included in the United States of America prior to May 13, 1657, and whose intermediate ancestors in the same line during the Revolutionary period adhered as patriots to the cause of the Colonies, shall be eligible for membership. There are state societies in New York, Connecticut, New Jersey and Pennsylvania.

Orders in Council.—As the sovereigns of Great Britain can act only through privy councilors or upon their advice, the more formal acts of the administration must proceed from the authority of the sovereign in council, and their execution is directed at a meeting of the privy council, and laid before Parliament within thirty days if in session, and if not in session within thirty days after assembling. Those of most interest in the United States were issued in 1793 and 1794, prohibiting trade with France and directing the seizure of neutral ships engaged in such traffic. In 1806 an order was issued declaring the whole coast of Europe from the Elbe to Brest, France, under blockade. The specific order which caused the greatest indignation in America and provoked retaliatory measures by both France and the United States was that of 1807, which prohibited neutral trade directly with France or her allies. All goods were ordered to be landed in England, to pay duties there, and to be reexported under British regulations. (See also Berlin Decree; Embargo; Milan Decree.)

Oregon.—One of the Pacific coast states; motto, "The Union;" nickname, "Webfoot country," from the excessive rainfall. It extends from lat. 42° to 46° 15′ north and from long. 116° 40′ to 124° 32′ west. It is bounded on the north by Washington (partly separated by the Columbia River), on the east by Idaho (partly separated by the Snake River), on the south by Nevada and California, and on the west by the Pacific Ocean. It has an area of 96,699 square miles. Oregon is traversed by the Coast Range and Cascade and Blue Mountains, which run parallel to the coast in the eastern portion of the state. It is drained largely by the Columbia, though there is a large inland basin in the southeast. The chief industries are fishing and agriculture.

The mouth of the Columbia River was discovered by Capt. Gray, an American, in 1792. The river was partly explored by Lewis and Clark in 1804-5. A trading post was founded at Astoria in 1811. The territory, long in dispute, was finally made part of the United States by the treaty with Great Britain in 1846. It was organized as a territory in 1848 and was admitted to the Union in 1859.

Statistics of agriculture collected for the last Federal census, place the number of farms in the state at 45,502, comprising 11,685,110 acres, valued, with stock and improvements, at $528,243,782. The value of domestic animals, poultry, etc., was $59,-461,828, including 725,255 cattle, valued at $17,570,685; 271,708 horses, $25,181,143; 9,927 mules, $185,788; 217,577 swine, $1,-570,949; 2,699,135 sheep, $12,213,942; poultry, $1,067,743. The yield and value of field crops for 1911 was: Corn, 20,000 acres, 570,000 bushels, $456,000; wheat, 796,000 acres, 16,726,000 bushels, $12,545,-000; oats, 359,000 acres, 12,457,000 bushels, $5,481,000; rye, 18,000 acres, 351,000 bushels, $316,000; potatoes, 46,000 acres, 5,980,000 bushels, $4,007,000; hay, 452,-000 acres, 949,000 tons, $9,110,000. The mineral production of the state is inconsiderable, the coal output having been curtailed by the use of petroleum from California for fuel for railroads and in manufactures. The lumber cut has grown steadily for many years, until lumbering has taken first rank in the state's industries. Oregon has one-sixth of the standing timber of the United States. In 1909 there were 1,-468,155 thousand feet cut, which sold for $18,010,588, mostly fir, spruce and cedar. The salmon catch on the Oregon side of the Columbia River in 1908 was 18,464,000 pounds, and on the coast streams 6,423,000 pounds. Nearly five thousand men are engaged in the Columbia River fisheries. The state has of late years become noted for its innovations in government. In the general election of 1910 the voters enacted under the initiative four important measures. They were: Presidential preference, giving to each voter the opportunity of expressing in primary elections his choice for president and vice-president of the United States. The single tax, which authorizes each county in the state to prescribe its own method of taxation; an employers' liability law, prepared and submitted to the people by organized labor, after a less objectionable bill had met defeat in the legislature; the three-fourths jury verdict, which has reduced the number of mistrials and relieved the badly congested condition of the courts. A constitutional amendment extending the right of suffrage to women was submitted to the voters in Nov., 1912. This has been defeated three times with increasing majorities. (See Initiative, Referendum and Recall.)

Sugar, beets and hops are also important crops. Apples and plums are raised in great abundance and shipped to all leading markets. West of the Cascade Mountains almost every crop common to the temperate zone is grown, but east of the mountains the country is arid. The Federal irrigation plan, now in operation, contemplates the reclamation of 254,000 acres in Oregon. Private irrigation schemes will add 267,000 acres more. There are 6,072,550 acres of forest reservation in the state. July 1, 1908, there remained unreserved and unappropriated, 16,957,913 acres of land. The United States land offices are located at Burns, LaGrande, Lakeview, Portland, Roseberg and The Dalles.

The mineral output of 1907 was valued at $2,638,587, and consisted of gold, silver, copper, coal, nickel, cobalt, lead and gypsum. Garnets and opals are found.

The number of manufacturing establishments in Oregon having an annual output valued at $500 or more at the beginning of 1915 was 2,320. The amount of capital invested was $139,500,000, giving employment to 35,449 persons, using material valued at $63,258,000, and turning out finished goods worth $109,762,000. Salaries and wages paid amounted to $26,614,000.

Large ocean-going vessels navigate the Columbia River as far as Portland. The railway mileage in 1907 was 2,031 miles of steam road and 286 miles of electric lines. The population in 1910 was 672,765.

Oregon:

Lands in—

Granted for construction of wagon roads, frauds in, 5195.

Granted to, for Willamette Valley and Cascade Mountain Wagon Road Co., 4665.

Granted to Hudsons Bay Co. by Great Britain, 2073.

Grants of, to settlers, recommended, 2308.

Opened to settlement by proclamation, 6018.

Referred to, 2662.

Set apart as public reservations by proclamation, 5719, 5859, 5864.

Light-houses to be erected in, 2557, 3902.

Mail facilities to, recommended, 2247, 2307, 2354, 2489, 2560.

Provisions for, 2409.

Military posts in, recommended, 2190.

National rights in, must be maintained, 2247.

Officers of, referred to, 2494.

Overland mail route, recommended, 2247, 2354.

Population of, 2435.

Referred to, 2272, 2305.

Report on, by Lieut. Wilkes, referred to, 2013.

Seat of government of—

Conflict of opinion respecting establishment of, and recommendations regarding, 2685.

Correspondence with Governor Gaines relative to, 2684.

Territorial government over, recommended, 2307, 2354, 2408, 2434.

Approval of act to establish, and reasons therefor, 2456.

Oregon, The—

Mentioned, 6317.

Voyage and arrival of, from San Francisco, discussed, 6316.

Oregon Boundary. (See Northwestern Boundary.)

Oregon Indians. (See Indian Tribes.)

Organized Labor. (See Trade Unions.)

Original Package.—In the enforcement of the prohibitory liquor law in the State of Iowa the officers were frequently charged with exceeding the limits of the state's jurisdiction in interfering with the traffic in spirits. State officers seized and confiscated liquors which it was claimed by the owners were sent into the state for reshipment to points outside the jurisdiction of the state courts. State officers defended themselves under the prohibition amendment to the constitution. In 1890 the Supreme Court of the United States, in the case of Leisy & Co. *vs.* Hardin, held that the plaintiffs, brewers in Illinois, had the right to carry liquors into any state and sell them in the original package without reference to local prohibitory or restrictive laws. The decision of the Court rested on the right of Congress to have exclusive control of interstate commerce. Congress thereupon passed a law giving states control of

the liquors so imported, although in the original package.

Oriskany (N. Y.), Battle of.—In August, 1777, Gen. Burgoyne sent a detachment of his army, consisting of 200 regulars, Sir John Johnson's Royal Greens, and some Canadian rangers and Indians, under Col. St. Leger, to operate in western and central New York and ultimately to join the main army under Howe at New York. St. Leger proceeded by way of the St. Lawrence River, Lake Ontario, and the Oswego and Oneida rivers to within a few miles of Fort Stanwix (now Schuyler, near the present city of Rome, on the Mohawk River. The post was garrisoned by less than 1,000 men, under Colonels Gansevoort and Willet. Gen. Herkimer collected the militia of Tryon County and advanced to the assistance of the fort. On Aug. 6 when about six miles from the post, near Oriskany, he fell into an ambush and was fiercely assailed by the British and the Indians under Brant. By reason of a successful sally by Willet the assailants were repulsed, but not without the loss of 400, including many of the leading patriots of that region. St. Leger made no official report of his loss except that of his Indian allies. The fight lasted several hours and was one of the most fiercely contested conflicts of the war. St. Leger, deserted by his Indian allies, retired precipitately to Canada.

Orleans, Territory of.—The old name for the present State of Louisiana. In March, 1804, after the purchase of Louisiana from France, Congress divided the territory, cutting off that portion between Texas and the Mississippi River and from the Gulf of Mexico north to the parallel of lat. 33° north and establishing it as a territory, with William C. C. Claiborne as governor. In 1810 the citizens of Baton Rouge, territory of St. Francisville, overcame the local Spanish garrison, shot the Spanish governor and established the Territory of West Florida. After the people of West Florida had elected a governor and framed a constitution President Madison issued a proclamation (465) directing Governor Claiborne, of the Territory of Orleans, to take possession of West Florida and annex it to Orleans. In February, 1811, an act was passed "to enable the people of the Territory of Orleans to form a constitution and state government." April 12, 1812, an act was passed for the admission of the State of Louisiana into the Union, extending the limits to include all between the Mississippi and Pearl Rivers south of lat. 31° north.

Orleans Territory:

Admission into Union applied for by, 483.

Citizens of, must be protected, 372.

Indians inhabiting, 386.

Territory south of Mississippi Territory and eastward of Mississippi River, added to, 465, 469.

Expenses incurred incident thereto, 482.

Osage Indians. (See Indian Tribes.)

Payment of interest due, referred to, 4058.

Treaty with, 464, 474, 554, 614, 616, 767, 883, 889, 912, 1040, 3393, 3578, 3833, 3843.

Osborn vs. United States Bank, Ohio.—A leading case in the Supreme Court, September term, 1819, involving the right of a State to tax United States property. Osborn, auditor of the State of Ohio, through his deputy, forcibly took from the United States Bank at Chillicothe $100,-000 and delivered it to the State treasurer as payment to the State under the act which was passed by the legislature Feb. 8, 1819, levying taxes upon banks doing business in the State without authorization of the State law. The United States circuit court of Ohio decreed that a restitution be made with interest. The Supreme Court of the United States, having been appealed to, affirmed the decision of the circuit court, but gave no interest. The opinion was delivered by Chief Justice Marshall and was very elaborate. Justice Johnson dissented on the point of jurisdiction. Clay, Webster, and Sergeant argued for the right of the bank to sue in the circuit court of the United States. (See also McCulloch *vs.* Maryland.)

Osette Indians. (See Indian Tribes.)

Ostend Manifesto.—In 1852 France and England, fearful of the filibustering expeditions against Cuba and the possible future favor of the United States toward such expeditions, suggested a tripartite convention in which each nation should disclaim all intention to obtain possession of Cuba and should discountenance such possession by another power. With a view to promoting negotiation with Spain for the purchase of Cuba by the United States, Pierre Soulé, American minister to Spain (empowered to negotiate for the purchase of Cuba), John Y. Mason, minister to France, and James Buchanan, minister to Great Britain, met at Ostend, Belgium Oct. 9, 1854, and after three days' session adjourned to meet at Aix-la-Chapelle. They wrote to the United States Government their views of the policy the Administration should pursue. Their message or communication is known as the Ostend Manifesto. It declared that, as Spanish oppression in Cuba was such that the island would speedily resort to arms to free herself, the United States should offer Spain a sum not to exceed $120,000,000 for Cuba, and in the event of Spain's refusal to sell, the United States would be justified in taking forcible possession of Cuba rather than see it Africanized, like Santo Domingo. President Pierce did not think it prudent to act upon this suggestion, and Soulé, disgusted, resigned soon afterwards and returned home.

Oswego (N. Y.), Capture of.—May 5, 1814, the British squadron commanded by Sir James Yeo, and consisting of 8 vessels, aggregating 222 pieces of ordnance, besides several gunboats and other small craft, moved toward Oswego, N. Y., at the mouth of the Oswego River. The squadron carried more than 1,200 troops, under Lieut.-Col. Drummond. Oswego was protected by Fort Ontario, mounting six old guns, and a garrison of less than 300 men, under Lieut.-Col. Mitchell. These repulsed a landing party sent ashore and the fleet put to sea. It returned the next day and landed the greater portion of the force, which ascended a long, steep hill to the fort in the face of a heavy fire from the Americans. Overwhelming numbers finally compelled Mitchell to fall back. The American loss was 69, including among the killed Lieut. Blaney. The British lost 94, among the wounded

being Capt. Mulcaster, of the *Princess Charlotte,* and Capt. Popham, of the *Montreal.*

Otoe and Missouria Reservation, Nebr.:
Right of way for railroad through, referred to, 4681.
Sale of, bill for, 4656.

Otoe Indians. (See Indian Tribes.)

Ottawa Indians.. (See Indian Tribes.)

Ottoman Empire.. (See Turkey.)

Ottoman Empire, Treaties with.—A treaty of commerce and navigation was concluded in 1830. The text of the treaty was in the Turkish language, and by reason of the difficulty of exact translation, much diplomatic correspondence has resulted without reaching an accord. By its terms equitable imposition of taxes and duties is agreed upon in the case of merchants of the Sublime Porte traveling in the possessions of the United States and upon citizens of the United States traveling in the countries and ports of the Sublime Porte; and conditions of trade shall be conducted in all cases upon the terms of the most favored nation. Appointment of consular officers is agreed upon in the dominions of both parties upon the terms usual in consular conventions. Brokers may be employed to assist in the conduct of business; and vessels coming to the several ports in both countries shall proceed upon the same conditions of charges as the most favored nation.

In case of litigation between subjects of the Sublime Porte and citizens of the United States, no decision shall be made or verdict reached unless the American dragoman be present; and citizens of the United States peaceably and lawfully follow their avocation shall not be molested. When an offence has been committed such citizens shall be tried before their own consul and punished by his sentence or decision. American vessels may safely go under their own flag, but must not take the flag of another country nor lend their flag. Merchant vessels may pass the royal residence and come and go in the Black Sea. The vessels of either country may not be taken by force and be compelled to engage in war service. The customary humane regulations are made regarding shipwreck. (For the extradition treaty of 1874, see Extradition Treaties.)

Ounalaska, The, condemned by Salvador and subsequently presented to United States, recommendations regarding, 4988.

Outlawry.—1. A state of society dominated by individuals, or groups of individuals, who treat the law with contempt, or take the law into their own hands. 2. A form of punishment which deprives a person from the benefits or protection of the law.

Outrages on American Citizens. (See Central America; Costa Rica; Mexico; New Granada; Puerto Rico; the several powers.)

Overt Act. (See Act of Hostility.)

Ozania River, building of bridge over, at Santo Domingo City by American citizens, 5784.

Pacific **Forest Reserve**, Washington.
(See Mount Ranier Forest Reserve.)
Pacific **Highways.** (See Transcontinental Highways.)
Pacific **Ocean:**
Claims of foreign powers to territory on. (See Northwestern Boundary.)
Commerce on, force should be employed to maintain, 827, 928, 1115.
Harbor and breakwater on coast of, recommended, 4572.
Junction between Atlantic and—
Desired, 2813, 2988.
Referred to, 2128, 2676.
Railroad from Mississippi River to, recommended, 2714, 2754.
Vessels to examine harbors in, 984.
War on, referred to, 4667.
Pacific **Ocean Exploring Expedition,** expenses of, referred to, 994.
Pacific **Railroads.**—In 1848 Asa Whitney, a New York merchant, zealously advocated the building of a railroad by the Federal Government to the Pacific Ocean from some point on the Missouri or Mississippi River. A bill providing for such a road was introduced in the Senate. It was opposed by Thomas H. Benton and finally tabled by a vote of twenty-seven to twenty-one. The next year Benton introduced a Pacific railroad measure of his own. In March, 1853, an act was passed providing for surveys. By 1855 Government surveyors had ascertained practicable passes through the Rocky Mountains. The rapid growth of the Pacific States in consequence of the "gold fever" and the difficulty of communication between the East and the West, on account of the vast extent of intervening plains made railroad communication more and more desirable. The hopelessness of undertaking so stupendous a work with private capital led many who otherwise were opposed to the principle of Federal aid to internal improvements to advocate the building of the Pacific railroads under Government subsidies. In 1860 both the leading political parties in their platforms declared in favor of building a road under national supervision. The outbreak of the Civil War and the necessity for closer military communication aided the movement.

The bill providing for the Union Pacific and Central Pacific roads was approved July 2, 1862, and granted as subsidies 6 per cent gold bonds of the United States. It gave to the Union Pacific $16,000 per mile for the great plain west from Omaha, Nebraska, $48,000 per mile for 150 miles over the Rocky Mountains, and $32,000 per mile for the remainder—in all, 1,034 miles, $27,236,512; to the Central Pacific $16,000, $32,000, and $48,000 per mile—in all, 883 miles, $27,855,562. Each company also received 12,800 acres of land per mile of road—25,000,000 acres in all—by a subsequent act July 1, 1864. The companies were allowed to issue an equal amount of their own bonds, which were to be a first lien on the road, the Government bonds the second. The time fixed for opening was set at July 1, 1876, and the road was actually opened May 10, 1869. The two lines were joined, with impressive ceremonies, at Promontory Point, Utah. The last tie, of laurel wood, with a plate of silver upon it, was laid, and the last spike, made of iron, silver and gold, was driven in the presence of distinguished men. The officers of the road and a large concourse of visitors from East and West were present. Telegraph wires were attached to the last rail, and the last blows were signaled upon bells in Washington and other large cities. In many places large crowds had gathered to receive the first intimation, conveyed almost instantaneously over the electric wires, that the great work was complete. When the signal was received in San Francisco and elsewhere all the church bells were rung, and cannons were fired. The general direction is nearly east and west on or about the fortieth degree of latitude. The total length of the road built by the two companies from Omaha to San Francisco is 1,917 miles. July 2, 1864, a charter with subsidies was granted to the Northern Pacific from Lake Superior to Puget Sound, a distance of 1,800 miles, and thence to the Columbia River, 200 miles. The land granted to this road amounted to 47,000,000 acres, or 73,000 sq. miles. The road was commenced in 1870 and was to have been finished in 1879, but in 1873 the company became embarrassed and ceased work. In 1875 the company was reorganized and the time for construction extended. On Sept. 9, 1883, the last spike was driven at a point fifty miles west of Helena, Mont. The Great Northern extension from Pacific Junction, Mont., to Lowell, on Puget Sound, was completed Jan. 6, 1893.

July 27, 1866, the Atlantic and Pacific road was chartered to run from Springfield, Mo., to the Pacific on or near the thirty-fifth parallel of latitude, a distance of 2,000 miles, and subsidized with 42,000,000 acres of land. March 3, 1871, the Southern Pacific road was chartered to run from Marshall to El Paso, Tex., thence through New Mexico and Arizona to Los Angeles, Cal., along the thirty-second parallel of latitude. The act granted the same amount of land per mile as the others had received.

In May, 1878, an act, known as the Thurman Act, was passed, prescribing more stringent terms for the repayment of government advance. In addition to the amounts retained out of sums due for government service, the Act of 1862 provided for the payment of five per cent of the net earnings of the company. The Act of 1878 retained the entire amount due to the companies for government service, one-half to be applied to interest payments, one-half to form a sinking fund for the principal, and it required, moreov r, the annual payment of a fixed sum ($850,000 for the Union Pacific and $1,200,000 for the Central Pacific), or so much thereof as might be necessary to make the total obtained by adding the five per cent of net earnings and the whole of the compensation retained, equal to twenty-five per cent of the net earnings. The method of computing the net earnings was prescribed, and it was provided that the additional payments thus required were not to be exacted unless the net earnings were sufficient to meet the interest on the bonds prior in lien to the government mortgage.

From a memorandum issued by Secretary of the Treasury, McAdoo, Sept. 30, 1914, the Central Branch Union Pacific Railroad is still indebted to the United States $3,618,779.72, of which $1,600,000 is principal and $2,018,779.72 is interest.

Pacific **Railroads:**
Condition and obligations of, discussed, 6169.
Construction of, discussed by President—
Buchanan, 2988, 3057, 3103, 3181.
Fillmore, 2622.
Johnson, 3560, 3651.

Lincoln, 3333, 3388, 3451.

Taylor, 2558.

Funding of debt of, recommended, 4837.

Government aid to, recommended, 2988, 3057, 3103, 3181.

Indebtedness of—

Change of plan for payment of, suggested, 5111.

Commission to report plan for settlement of, recommended, 5640.

Commission to settle, 6343, 6389.

Discussed, 6169.

Order regarding, 6233.

Report of Commissioner of Railroads on, discussed, 5640.

Reports of commissioners on, discussed, 5181, 5384.

Lands granted in aid of, discussed, 2823, 3651, 4065, 4944, 5384.

Forfeiture of, discussed, 4837, 5379.

Revocation of withdrawal of, referred to, 5197.

Kansas Pacific, sale of, discussed, 6342, 6390.

Northern Pacific agreements with Indians for sale of lands for use of, 4657, 4740, 4779, 4864, 4954, 5178.

Southern Pacific, contracts and leases of, referred to, 4958.

Union Pacific—

Bonds issued to, referred to, 3794.

Completion of section of, extension of time for, recommended, 3582.

Construction of—

Discussed by President—
Johnson, 3560, 3651.
Lincoln, 3333, 3388, 3451.
Referred to, 3891, 4003.

Discussed by President—
Cleveland, 6169.
Johnson, 3881.

Injunction restraining election of officers of, referred to, 3963.

Location of, referred to, 3578.

Points of commencement of, discussed and order regarding, 3401, 3435.

Reorganization of, recommended, 5969.

Report of Attorney-General regarding, referred to, 4434.

Report of Government directors of, referred to, 4661, 4745, 4789, 4850, 4958, 4959.

Sale of, discussed, 6273, 6342, 6389.

Subscriptions to capital stock of, order designating place for receiving, 3476.

Pacific Squadron. (See Manila Harbor (Philippine Islands), Battle of.)

Pacific Telegraph, referred to, 3329, 3382, 3445, 3564, 3643.

Pacifist.—The term arose during the Great European War, and is applied to those persons who are opposed to war; evidently the word was coined in order to displace the more awkward "pacificator." Although the word is loosely applied to those who are sympathizers with or workers in the cause of international peace, it is more correctly applied to those persons who are opposed to war under any conditions, non-resistants, sometimes described as believers in peace-at-any-price. In the days preceding the entrance of the United States into the war the word sprang into great prominence, and became applied indiscriminately to all those persons who opposed war with the Central Powers. Although there had been many peace societies active in the United States in the past few decades, yet most of these did not oppose the war with Germany, and hence were not considered "pacifist" organizations, —for instance, the Carnegie Foundation for the Advancement of Peace, the American Peace Society, the World Court League, the League to Enforce Peace. The two pacifist organizations most prominent in the days before President Wilson's announcement of a state of war were the American Union against Militarism and the Emergency Peace Federation, each of them newly organized bodies. The Woman's Peace Party, founded by Jane Addams, was not prominently active in the period preceding the war, nor was Henry Ford, the instigator and backer of the so-called Ford Peace Expedition (q. v., under European War). The American Federation of Labor was definitely anti-pacifist, and Socialists in the United States divided sharply on the issue. (See Peace Societies.)

Pactole, The, referred to, 1172.

Padroni System, discussed, 6065.

Painting presented to Congress, Lincoln and Cabinet at reading of Emancipation Proclamation, 4435.

Paintings of Presidents.—Official portraits of the presidents as they hang in the White House have been selected as the best work of contemporary artists. Most of them have been painted by order of Congress. They are:

George Washington	Gilbert Charles Stuart
John Adams	George P. A. Healy
Thomas Jefferson	Eliphalet F. Andrews
James Madison	Unknown
James Monroe	Unknown
John Quincy Adams	George P. A. Healy
Andrew Jackson	Eliphalet F. Andrews
Martin Van Buren	George P. A. Healy
W. H. Harrison	Eliphalet F. Andrews
John Tyler	George P. A. Healy
James K. Polk	George P. A. Healy
Zachary Taylor	Eliphalet F. Andrews
Millard Fillmore	George P. A. Healy
Franklin Pierce	George P. A. Healy
James Buchanan	Eliphalet F. Andrews
Abraham Lincoln	Unknown
Andrew Johnson	Unknown
U. S. Grant	Thomas LeClear
R. B. Hayes	Daniel Huntington
James A. Garfield	Eliphalet F. Andrews
Chester A. Arthur	Daniel Huntington
Grover Cleveland	S. Frost Johnson
Benjamin Harrison	S. Frost Johnson
William McKinley	Joel Benziger
Theodore Roosevelt	John S. Sargent
William Howard Taft	Max Zorn

Paints, Oils and Varnishes.—As early as 1795 the use of paint for houses was common in the United States. In cities and towns the inside of the house, at least, was painted, and in all but the cheaper wooden buildings the outside carried a coat of paint. The white house with green window blinds, was for many years of our early history the typical American dwelling.

A small mill for making linseed oil was started in New York City in 1715, and in 1718 John Prout, Jr., erected a linseed oil mill in Connecticut. In 1786 four oil mills were in operation in Lancaster County, Pa. These greatly stimulated the use of paints, and in 1804 Samuel Wetherill made the first successful attempt to manufacture white lead. Red lead, as well as white, was made by him of as good a quality as that imported.

In 1806 experiments in color making were carried on by Anthony Tiemann, and within the year he began the regular manufacture of paints. His first productions were rose pink, Dutch pink, French green and blue. The manufacture of Prussian blues was begun in 1809, and in 1820 chrome yellow was added to the products of this establishment. By 1811 Philadelphia mills were turning out twenty-two different colors of paint, and three small red-lead factories at Pittsburg (the first west of the Alleghanies), were making an annual product of $13,000. Chrome paints of first quality in the early days of the industry commanded as much as $3 a pound, and the business was profitable. Extensive deposits of chromic iron, discovered in Chester County, Pa., gave an added impetus to paint grinding, and its growth was strong and steady. The succeeding decade saw the industry firmly established in New York. By 1820 there were extensive works in Brooklyn and New York, producing red and white leads, chrome and other colors, while a factory in Rensselaer County, N. Y., was turning out annually $4,500 worth of Prussian blue extracted from the by-product of a tannery.

Before 1828 all the varnish used in this country was imported. Its use, while less general than that of paint, was common enough to recommend it to manufacturers as a profitable business, and the first establishment for its manufacture was founded by P. B. Smith in New York City in 1828. Tilden & Hurlburt, the first permanent concern in the business, was established in 1830. This firm made the first importations of gum copal from Zanzibar and the west coast of Africa, and was the first to export American varnish, consigning a quantity to Mexico and South America in 1836. The quality of the American goods proved so exceptional that they not only competed with, but in a great measure supplanted, the exportations of the European manufacturers. The stimulation of a heavy foreign demand added to increased domestic consumption so swelled the business that the matter of obtaining supplies of the gums used became of serious importance. In 1857 such quantities of these raw materials were used that the manufacturers were obliged to establish a system of direct trade with the west coast of Africa.

The growth of the paint and varnish business had in the meantime affected the oil mills. Up to 1836 these mills had used only home grown seed, and a capacity of fifty bushels a day was a fair average output. With the growing use of linseed oil new methods were found necessary, and the firm of J. & L. K. Bridge, of Brooklyn, in that year imported the first cargo of flaxseed from Sicily. Odessa, Alexandria and Calcutta, were successively opened as supply points of this rapidly increasing trade.

In 1850 the paint industry entered upon a new era. The zinc deposits of New Jersey, opened in that year, gave an adequate and cheaply worked supply of ore from which the oxide could easily be reduced. This zinc oxide, in the form of white powder, had long been recognized as a valuable substitute for white lead as a body for

paints. It had up to this time, however, received little attention owing to the small amount available for the market. The new and abundant supply turned the attention of manufacturers to experiments in this direction, and its use has since become general. Several mines were opened and soon were placing the white powdery zinc oxide on the market.

Mineral paints, made from different earths, came into prominence about this time, under strong claims of being fireproof and indestructible. Ready mixed paints were introduced to the trade in 1852. About 1857 D. F. Tiemann & Co. made carmine from cochineal, a monopoly theretofore held by France. In 1860 they made a blue, soluble in water, for laundry use, and free from acid. They also established the manufacture of quicksilver vermilion, previously monopolized by England.

The National Lead Company, which controls the greater part of the output of white lead in this country, includes and operates its own oil and paint grinding mills, as well as the lead factories proper, and with a capitalization of about $30,000,000, is the largest concern in the paint business.

Reports were received from 855 establishments engaged in the paint and varnish industry in 1914, the total products of which for the year were valued at $149,049,820. Of these 855 establishments, the principal business of 799 was the manufacture of paints or varnishes, and 56 were engaged primarily in other industries but produced paints or varnishes to the value of $3,507,-182 as subsidiary products.

The products in 1914 comprised colors or pigments valued at $17,407,955 ; oil paints, $70,582,461 ; water paints and kalsomine, $2,202,281 ; varnishes and japans, $36,061,-203 ; fillers, including putty, $3,239,174 ; bleached shellac, $1,806,802 ; and other products to the value of $17,749,944.

The more important materials used in the manufacture of paint and varnish are lead in the form of pig lead or as oxides and white lead, zinc white, iron oxides and other earth colors, barytes, dry colors, gums, and solvents or vehicles such as linseed oil, turpentine, benzine, and wood and grain alcohol.

Returns were received from 108 establishments engaged in the production of essential oils in 1914, the total products of which for the year were valued at $2,565,361.

Including the by-products and the essential oils distilled for others, the total production in 1914 comprised 363,991 pounds of peppermint, valued at $601,617 ; 94,209 pounds of spearmint, valued at $238,074 ; 41,178 pounds of black birch, valued at $67,691 ; 6,000 pounds of wintergreen, valued at $24,538 ; 4,702 pounds of wormwood, valued at $9,040 ; and oils of camphor, cedar, cloves, lemon, parsley, patchouli, pennyroyal, sandalwood, sassafras, tansy, etc., to the value of $348,522.

Petroleum Refining.—Petroleum or rock oil was first found in the United States in 1635, in what is now southwestern New York or northwestern Pennsylvania. A well in Kentucky in 1829 yielded such great quantities that it was drained into the Cumberland River or burned. It was only used to a small extent for lighting and in medicine. The petroleum districts of the United States are western Pennsylvania, Ohio, Indiana, West Virginia, Kentucky, Tennessee, Texas, California, Oklahoma, and in smaller quantities in other western states. The refining of petroleum is based upon the separation of the component hydrocarbons by a process of fractional distillation.

The method of mining or drilling for petroleum is the same as that used in sinking gas or artesian water wells. Cheap and rapid transportation is secured by means of a series of tanks about thirty miles apart, connected by underground pipes, and the oil is forced from one set of tanks to another by means of pumps. Pennsylvania has about 25,000 miles of such pipe line.

The growth of the petroleum industry in the United States is shown by the following table, which gives the annual production at five-year intervals since 1859:

Year	Barrels	Year	Barrels
1859	2,000	1890	45,823,572
1860	500,000	1895	52,892,276
1865	2,497,700	1900	63,620,529
1870	5,260,745	1905	134,717,580
1875	10,926,945	1910	236,997,659
1880	26,286,123	1915	290,312,535
1885	21,858,785		

Crude Petroleum Production, 1914.—(United States Geological Survey.)

	Barrels (42 gallons)
California	99,775,327
Mid-Continent (Kansas, Oklahoma, etc.)	97,995,400
Pennsylvania grade (Appalachian)	24,101,048
Illinois	21,919,749
Gulf	13,117,528
Lima-Indiana	5,062,543
Colorado, Wyoming, and other fields	3,790,940
Total production	265,762,535

Reports were received from 176 establishments operating refineries, the products of which for the year 1914 were valued at $396,361,405. They used 191,262,724 barrels of crude petroleum.

The production of naphthas and lighter products, chiefly gasoline, increased from 10,806,550 barrels in 1909 to 29,200,764 barrels in 1914, or by 170.2 per cent, while the value increased from $39,771,959 to $121,919,307.

Of the 176 refineries in 1914, 48 were in Pennsylvania, 38 in California, 23 in Oklahoma, 13 in Kansas, 9 in Texas, 9 in Illinois, 8 in New Jersey, 7 in Ohio, 6 in New York, 4 in Colorado, 3 in Maryland, 3 in West Virginia, 2 in Wyoming, and one each in Indiana, Louisiana, and Missouri.

Palestine, outrages committed on American citizens in, 3015.

Palisades Interstate Park.—The State of New York possesses several forest reservations and also several parks. One, the Niagara reservation, comprises the land about the great cataract, purchased at a cost of $1,000,000. The State Forest Preserve in the Adirondack region on Oct. 1, 1913, contained 1,495,257.29¼ acres, and the Catskill Forest Preserve on the same day contained 112,750.15 acres. There are also Letchworth Park, about the falls of the Genesee River; John Boyd Thatcher Park, about the Indian Ladder, in Albany County, and islands in the St. Lawrence river.

Lastly, there is the Palisades Interstate Park, partly in the state of New Jersey and partly in the state of New York, extending along the Hudson river in its Palisades region, and extending north so as to include Bear mountain. The development of this park to its present great dimensions began in 1910, when Mary D. Harriman, widow of the late Edward H. Harriman, informed Governor Hughes of New York that, following the wishes of her husband, she was willing to convey 10,000 acres of land in the counties of Orange and Rockland to be used as a park, and also give $1,000,000 toward the park project.

The Palisades Park Commission had the same year collected $1,625,000 for the same

purpose. Previously the commission had acquired by gift of land and of money to the amount of $300,000, a contribution of $400,000 from the state of New York, and $50,000 from the state of New Jersey, the face of the Palisades from Piermont to Fort Lee. It was also proposed in 1910 that the state of New York should appropriate $2,500,000 for a further purchase of land for the Palisades Interstate Park. Subsequently, in 1910, this proposal was ratified by the voters, and consequently the Palisades Interstate Park, which will cost nearly $6,000,000, was authorized.

The commissioners of the Palisades Interstate Park since 1910 have been busily engaged in developing the park. The state of New York is preparing to build the last end of Route 3, north of the New Jersey state line, so that ultimately there will be a state highway from the state boundary line of New Jersey and New York along the west shore of the Hudson river north to Newburgh. The commissioners have also co-operated with the state of New York and Orange county, N. Y., in securing the construction of Route 3 of the New York state highway system along the Hudson river through the United States Reservation at West Point and around Storm King mountain. The park roads, when built, are to connect with the main state highways of New York and New Jersey. There is a "Henry Hudson Drive" under the Palisades and a road from Bear mountain on the Hudson river, to Southfields, both of which are on park properties. The commission is advancing the Englewood approach to the Henry Hudson drive. The drive, when completed, will be located under the Palisades in the state of New Jersey, with a number of approaches or spurs connecting the drive with the roads on top of the cliff.

A camp has been established at Blauvelt for the use of working girls, which is used by girls of all nationalities and religions.

Palmetto State.—A nickname for South Carolina (q. v.). (See also States.)

Palo Alto (Mexico), Battle of.—May 7, 1846, Gen. Taylor started from Point Isabel, with a force of 2,288 men, to relieve Fort Brown, twenty-seven miles away. At noon on the following day, when about half way between Point Isabel and Fort Brown, Taylor's army sighted the enemy at the water hole of Palo Alto. The regular Mexican force under Arista numbered 6,000 men, and there were some irregular troops and twelve pieces of artillery. Battle was immediately begun and fiercely fought until sunset. By the light of the moon and the burning prairie grass the belligerents buried their dead. The Mexicans lost 200 killed and 400 wounded. The American loss was only 4 killed and 40 wounded.

Palo Alto, Mexico, Battle of, referred to, 2295, 2300, 2342.

Pan-American Congress. (See International American Conference.)

Pan-American Exposition.—To illustrate the progress of civilization in the western hemisphere during the nineteenth century, there was held at Buffalo, N. Y., from May 1 to Nov. 2, 1901, an International American Fair, participated in officially by the various states of the Union, by Canada, and the South and Central American countries. The site covered an area of 350 acres and the buildings were artistically designed and arranged so as to present an allegorical study of man's struggle with the elements and his final triumph. The color scheme, as well as the artistic beauty, gained for the grounds the name of the Rainbow City. The total attendance was 8,179,674. The cost of the exposition was $8,860,757, and the receipts $5,534,643, a deficit of $3,326,-114. President McKinley was shot by an assassin in the Temple of Music while holding a reception there Sept. 6, 1901, and died eight days later at the home of the president of the Exposition.

Pan-American Exposition, referred to, 6675.

Pan-American Railroad, discussed, 6864.

Pan-American Union.—The Pan-American Union (the new name given to the International Bureau of American Republics by the Fourth International American Conference, which met at Buenos Aires in July and August, 1910) was established under the recommendation of the First Pan-American Conference, held in the City of Washington in 1889-90 for the purpose of developing and maintaining closer relations of commerce and friendship between the twenty-one Republics of the Western Hemisphere. Its first report was transmitted to Congress in 1891 (5647). It was reorganized by the Third and Fourth Pan-American Conferences, held in Rio de Janeiro in 1906, and in Buenos Aires in 1910, respectively, and its scope widened by imposing many new and important duties. The Pan-American Union regularly communicates with these governments, and furnishes such information as it possesses or can obtain on a great variety of subjects to all of the Republics and to their officials and citizens. It is the custodian of the archives of the Pan-American Conferences, and is especially charged with the performance of duties imposed upon it by these conferences. The Pan-American Union is sustained by contributions from the American Republics in proportion to their population and is governed by a board composed of their diplomatic representatives at Washington, and the Secretary of State of the United States, who is ex-officio its chairman. It is therefore strictly an international institution and not a subordinate bureau of any one government. Its chief executive officer is the Director-General, elected by this governing board. It publishes a monthly bulletin containing the latest information respecting the resources, commerce, and general progress of the American Republics, as well as maps and geographical sketches of these countries, handbooks of trade, travel, and description, and special reports on commerce, tariffs, improvements, concessions, new laws, etc. It also conducts a large correspondence not only with manufacturers and merchants in all countries looking to the extension of Pan-American trade, but with writers, travelers, scientists, students, and specialists, for the purpose of promoting general Pan-American intercourse. Another and practical feature of the Pan-American Union is the Columbus Memorial Library and reading room, which contains 22,000 volumes relating to the American Republics. (See also International American Conference and American Republics, Bureau of.)

See illustration opposite 7156.

Pan-American Union:

Financial conference, 8071.

Practical work of, 7415.

Panama.—The Republic of Panama occupies the Isthmus which connects the continent of North and South America, and lies between Costa Rica and Colombia, having formed a department of the latter Republic until Nov. 4, 1903. The isthmus of

Panama lies between 7° 15'-9° 39' N. latitude and 77° 15'-83° 30' W. longitude, and has an area of 32,380 square miles. The northern coast is washed by the Caribbean Sea (Atlantic) and the southern coast by the Pacific Ocean.

Physical Features.—The country is everywhere mountainous, with a ridge, more or less defined, extending from the western to the eastern boundary, and consists of a succession of hills and valleys with little open plain. The Cordilleras of Chiriqui and Veraguas of the west are continued eastward by the Cordilleras of Panama and Darien.

The largest rivers are the Tuira, or Rio Darien, of the eastern province, rising close to the Caribbean shore and flowing into the Pacific in the Gulf of San Miguel; the Chepo, or Bayano, with a similar course to the Bay of Panama; and the Chagres which flows northward through Gatun Lake to the Caribbean, part of its course being utilized for the Panama Canal. The only lake is that of Gatun, which has been formed by the construction of a dam in order to raise the water level of the Canal.

Although lying within the tropics the climate is not unhealthy, and the mean temperature varies little throughout the republic, being about 80° Fahrenheit. The wet season lasts from April to December, and the dry season is bracing with dry northeast winds from the Caribbean.

History.—Panama formed a department of the Republic of Colombia from 1855 until its secession in 1903. On Jan. 4, 1904, a constitutional assembly was elected and a constitution was adopted, under which a centralized republic was inaugurated.

Government.—The President is elected by the votes of all adult male citizens for the term of four years and is ineligible for a successive term of office, unless he retires from office eighteen months before the elections. There is no Vice-President, but the assembly elects three designados to provide a head for the State in case of the death of the President. President (1912-1916, elected Oct. 1, 1912): Dr. Belisario Porras.

The executive power is vested in the President, who appoints ministers, judges of the Supreme Court, diplomatic representatives, and provisional governors.

The National Assembly consists of a single chamber of twenty-eight members, elected for four years by direct adult male suffrage, and meets biennially on Sept. 1. The President has a veto on legislation, but the Assembly can pass the same bill a second time and the President must then sign it, if the Supreme Court declares it to be within the constitutional limits.

The Supreme Court consists of five judges, appointed by the President, and there are superior courts and circuit courts, and justices of municipal courts appointed by the five judges of the first-named tribunal.

Each of the seven provinces is under a governor, appointed by the President, and possesses municipal districts with elective legislatures, and an alcalde appointed by the governor. Under the treaty by which the Panama Canal Zone was ceded to the United States, the municipalities of Colon and Panama within the ceded area, were expressly excluded from the zone.

There is no standing army, but the integrity of the republic has been guaranteed by the United States. Order is maintained by a small national police force.

Education.—Primary education is free and compulsory, 294 primary schools being maintained by the State, the pupils numbering nearly 20,000. There are also secondary and special schools, for the training of teachers, and a university has been opened at the capital, with a competent staff of professors, both native and foreign.

Finance.—The assembly meets biennially, and votes a provision for two financial years. The finances of the Republic at the present time show a surplus in the treasury with no debts of $500,000. In addition the United States Government paid the first instalment of $250,000 per annum for rental of the Canal Zone, which sum is on deposit in the United States as well as $6,000,000 gold, portion of the $10,-000,000 paid for the Canal Zone Concession. Moreover the government has nearly $1,000,000 gold invested in the National Bank in Panama and as a guarantee for the parity of the silver currency with gold (balboa=$1 United States money).

	1912.	1913.
Revenue	$3,455,287	$3,842,214
Expenditure	3,402,504	3,842,214

There is a small local debt of about $500,000. The Government has $6,300,-000 invested in the United States, and $750,000 in the National Bank.

Production and Industry.—The soil is extremely fertile, but there is little cultivation, and nearly one-half the land is unoccupied. The greater part of the cultivated portion is under bananas, other crops including coffee, tobacco and cereals, while cacao grows wild in the northwestern province of Bocas del Toro. The forest-clad hills provide valuable medicinal plants and dyestuffs, India rubber, mahogany and other timber and cabinet woods. The live stock is being greatly improved and there are excellent grazing grounds. Immigration is encouraged by the grant of small farms to likely settlers on favorable terms. The fisheries are important, and the pearl industry is being largely exploited with profitable results. Gold is mined in the eastern provinces, and copper is found in the west, where also valuable coal deposits exist and await development. Iron is also found, and there are productive salt mines on Parita Bay, while mineral springs abound.

Chocolate factories and soap works have been established in the capital, and sugar refineries are projected. The tobacco and salt industries are government monopolies.

The principal exports are bananas, rubber, raw cocoa, vegetable ivory, mother-of-pearl, cabinet woods and medicinal plants; the imports are almost entirely manufactured goods and foodstuffs. Customs duties (15 per cent *ad valorem*, except on flour, rice, corn and a few prime necessities which are 10 per cent *ad valorem*), are levied at all ports, including those of the Canal Zone, the latter being paid over to the Panama government by the officials of the United States, but supplies for the canal are exempt from duty.

Transportation.—The only railway runs along the canal route from Colon (or Aspinwall) to Panama and was included in the purchase by the United States. This interoceanic line is fifty miles in length and was built by United States capitalists in 1855. In the province of Bocas del Toro the United Fruit Company (American) have constructed about 150 miles of railway (including spurs) on their banana plantations, which cover an area of 35,000 acres. This line is being extended toward Port Limon (Costa Rica), and only twenty miles separates the terminal from that port.

In 1910 there were ninety-six post-offices and thirty-seven telegraph offices, with one wireless station. There is a wireless station at Colon, and another with radius of 260 miles at Balboa. A high power station to communicate 3,000 miles or more is being erected in the Canal Zone.

Cities.—Capital, Panama, on the south coast, the Pacific terminus of the interoceanic line from Colon (Atlantic) and within the Canal Zone, but expressly reserved to the Republic. Population (1911), 37,505. Other towns are Colon (17,748), David (10,000), Los Santos, Santiago, Las Tablas, Bocas del Toro.

Trade with the United States.— The value of merchandise imported into Panama from the United States for the year 1913 was $24,562,247, and goods to the value of $4,234,010 were sent thither—a balance of $20,328,237 in favor of the United States.

Panama:

Consul of United States in, absence of referred to, 3844.

Dispute with Costa Rica settled by arbitration, 7657.

Federal district created in, 5083.

Independence gained, 6741, 6771, 6787, 6809, 6814, 6833.

Our relations with, 7664.

Revolts against Colombia, details of, 6810, 6811, 6832, 6833.

Treaty with, for canal, 6816, 6823, 7020.

United States grants $10,000,000 to, 6855.

United States minister to, status of, 6938.

United States removes discriminating tonnage duties against, 6954.

Vessels from, duties on, suspended by proclamation, 4871.

Panama, Treaties with.—By The treaty concluded in 1903 for the construction of a ship canal, it was agreed that the United States guarantees and will maintain the independence of Panama. The United States receives in perpetuity the use, occupation, and control of a zone of land for the construction, maintenance and protection of a canal; said zone to be ten miles in width and extending five miles in width on both sides of the central line of the path of the canal, and three marine miles at each end out to sea. Grant is also made of other parts of territory adjacent which may be necessary for the construction and maintenance of the canal. This grant includes the islands of Perico, Naos, Culebra, and Flamenco. The rights, power, and authority of the United States within the zone shall be the same as though the territory were an integral part of the United States. The use of rivers, streams and bodies of water is included in the grant.

The Republic af Panama acknowledges a monopoly to the United States of the construction of the canal within the limits of its possessions. At the same time the grants hereby conveyed do not in any degree invalidate the claims of private landholders within the area; nor does the grant interfere with the rights of the public to roads and means of conveyance within the territory. Damages arising from the occupancy by the United States are to be appraised by a joint commission of Panama and the United States and awards for damages resulting from the construction of the canal shall be paid solely by the United States.

The United States has the power to make such alterations in the sanitary arrangements of the cities of Panama and Colon as it may deem desirable for the supply of water and the distribution of sewage; and for such improvements made at the cost of the United States, that government has the authority to impose reasonable taxes upon the inhabitants of the cities.

Authority is granted to the United States to adopt the measures necessary for the maintenance of law and order within the limits of these cities. The Republic of Panama transfers to the United States all rights of sovereignty over the canal, the New Panama Canal Company, and the Panama Railroad Company which it has inherited from the Republic of Colombia, and authorizes the United States to exercise all such rights and privileges in the construction of the canal.

The only charges, imposts, and duties which are to be levied by the United States at the entrance to the canal and by the Republic of Panama shall be the ordinary charges of toll for the use of the canal and the imposition of customs duties upon such merchandise as is destined to be consumed within the Republic of Panama. No national, state, or municipal taxes shall be imposed upon the canal or upon any machinery, or material of construction, or auxiliaries and accessories of all kinds. The telegraph and telephone lines within the zone shall be at the service of the government of the Republic of Panama for the transmission of official messages at the customary and usual rates. There shall be free and safe access permitted by Panama to the immigration to the zone by persons of all classes and nationalities.

The United States agrees to pay to Panama for the rights, privileges and concessions herein granted ten millions of dollars in gold on ratification of this treaty and an annual sum of two hundred and fifty thousand dollars, beginning nine years after ratification.

The canal shall be neutral in perpetuity and shall be opened in accordance with the treaty between the United States and Great Britain on this subject. Free transportation of vessels, troops, and munitions of war is granted to Panama. If any terms or conditions of this treaty shall prove incompatible with later terms or conditions granted to a third power, the Republic of Panama agrees to waive its rights on such points. No anterior pledges, debts, liens, trusts, or liabilities granted by the Republic of Panama shall operate to the detriment of the United States and any damages resulting therefrom shall be liquidated by Panama.

All claims for remuneration in connection with the canal construction which have been arranged for or any profits which might accrue to the advantage of Panama are hereby renounced by that power.

The United States has full power to police, fortify, and station troops to preserve order or maintain safety in the canal zone. The rights hereby granted to the United States shall not be lessened or impaired by any changes in the laws or in the political integrity of Panama. Naval or coaling stations will be conveyed by Panama to the United States by sale upon terms to be agreed upon should such become necessary for the better maintenance or preservation of the canal.

An extradition treaty was signed in 1904, the terms of which will be found in the Encyclopedic article, Extradition Treaties. Panama also became a party to the convention between the United States and the several republics of South and Central America for the arbitration of pecuniary claims and the protection of inventions, etc., which was signed in Buenos Aires in 1910 and proclaimed in Washington July 29, 1914. (See South and Central America, Treaties with.)

Panama Canal.—The idea of constructing a ship canal between the Atlantic and Pacific oceans occurred to navigators as soon as the form of the continents of North and South America became known. As early as 1527 H. de la Serna surveyed a canal route from Chagres to Panama. Lopez de Gomarfa in 1551 proposed to the Spanish Government the building of a canal. In 1698, when William Paterson, an adventurous Scot, had established an English colony on the Isthmus of Darien which he called New Caledonia, he advocated constructing a canal across the narrow strip of land separating the two great oceans. Many surveys have been made of the Isthmus with the view of piercing it with an artificial waterway. The United States obtained some very complete maps of the country by the explorations of Col. Hughes in 1849, Lieut. Strain in 1854, Lieut. Michler in 1858, and Commodores Selfridge and Tull in 1870 and 1875. (See opposite 3882.) In 1869 a treaty was signed by representatives of the United States of Colombia and the United States, providing for the construction of a canal by the latter nation, but there was so much delay and the treaty was so amended by the Colombian Congress that the matter was temporarily dropped by the United States. In 1877 the Colombian Government granted a concession to a Frenchman named Wyse for constructing a canal giving him "exclusive privilege for the excavating of a canal between the two oceans," the terminal ports and waters to be neutral.

At the invitation of Ferdinand de Lesseps, an International Scientific Congress met at Paris in 1879 and hastily decided upon the Panama route for a canal, the American members of the congress refraining from voting. The Panama Canal Company was then formed, with De Lesseps as president, and the Wyse concession was purchased for 10,000,000 francs. The route selected was close to the present line of the Panama Railroad, crossed the Chagres River six times and contemplated a long and deep cut through the Cordillera. The cost had been estimated at $169,000,000, and shares of the company had been taken by French citizens, many of them of the middle class, to the amount of $260,000,-000. Work was begun in 1881, but the affairs of the company were conducted with so great corruption, that it became bankrupt in 1889, and a year later suspended work. In 1892, after an investigation of the affairs of the company, De Lesseps, his son, the contractor Eiffel and others in public life were arrested on charges of fraud in the management of the funds intrusted to them for use in the construction of the canal, and in March of the following year, the New Panama Canal Company was formed, with renewed concessions to terminate in April, 1910.

In the meantime American interest in an interoceanic canal had revived, and there was much discussion of a route across the territory of Nicaragua. The Nicaragua Canal Association obtained concessions from Nicaragua and carried on work of construction from 1889 until 1893, when it became bankrupt. In 1899 a commission was appointed by Congress to determine the most feasible route for an isthmian canal. It reported that if the rights and property of the New Panama Canal Company could be purchased for a reasonable price a canal across Panama could be built more economically than one across the territory of Nicaragua, and recommended the Panama route. In order that the United States might have exclusive control over the proposed canal the Clayton-Bulwer Treaty (q. v.), between Great Britain and the United States, was superseded by the Hay-Pauncefote Treaty on Dec. 17, 1901. In 1902, in accordance with the report of its commission appointed in 1899, Congress passed an act (approved June 28), authorizing the President to secure for the United States the property of the New Panama Canal Company, at a cost of $40,000,000. It was further provided in the act, that "should the President be unable to obtain for the United States a satisfactory title to the property of the New Panama Canal Company and the control over the necessary territory of the Republic of Colombia * * * within a reasonable time and upon reasonable terms, then the President should endeavor to provide for a canal by the Nicaragua route." The Colombian Government, however, on Aug. 12, 1903, rejected the Hay-Herran Treaty, which had been negotiated between it and the United States, thereby refusing the United States' final offer of $10,000,000 down and $250,000 annually for the Panama concession. (See Hay-Herran Treaty, page 6828.)

On Nov. 3, 1903, the Department of Panama proclaimed its independence of Colombia, and having been recognized as an independent republic by the United States, on Nov. 18, the Isthmian Canal Treaty between the United States and the Republic of Panama was signed at Washington.

According to this treaty the Republic of Panama granted to the United States the perpetual use, occupation and control of a zone of land ten miles wide (five miles on each side of the central line of the route of the canal) across the Isthmus, complete sovereignty to which was to pass to the United States. The price paid the Republic of Panama by the United States was $10,-000,000 down and $250,000 annually as long as the convention should continue, beginning nine years after the date of ratification. The United States also guaranteed the neutrality of the canal and the independence of the Republic of Panama. Ratifications of the treaty were exchanged at Washington on Feb. 26, 1904. According to an act of Congress approved April 28, 1904, the President took possession of the Canal Zone, and organized its government. The President also appointed an Isthmian Canal Commission of seven members, and directed that the War Department, through this Commission, should undertake the supervision of the construction of the canal and the government of the Canal Zone. On April 4, 1905, this Commission was dismissed and a second appointed, the responsibility being placed chiefly upon the executive committee of three members.

The present composition of the Isthmian Canal Commission is as follows: Chairman and Chief Engineer, Col. George W. Goethals; Assistant Chief Engineer, Col. H. F. Hodges, Civil Engineer, U. S. N.; assistant to the Chief Engineer, H. H. Rousseau; Division Engineer, Central Division, Lieut.-Col. D. D. Gaillard; Division Engineer, Atlantic Division, Lieut.-Col. William L. Sibert; Chief Quartermaster, Lieut.-Col. C. A. Devol; Chief Sanitary Officer, Col. W. C. Gorgas; Hon. Maurise H. Thatcher, in charge of the Department of Civil Administration.

A proposed expression of regret from the United States Government for its recognition of the Republic of Panama raises the question whether the secession of Panama from Colombia was or was not a legal action.

The federation of the United States of Colombia was formed Dec. 17, 1819, and its Constitution promulgated July 12, 1820. At that time the Isthmus of Panama, a separate Spanish administrative department, was still under Spanish control.

In November, 1821, the Isthmus of Panama revolted, expelled the Spanish garrison and set up an independent state. In so doing it received no Colombian assistance. Subsequently, of its own volition, and reserving its sovereign rights, it federated with the States of Colombia. In 1830 Panama warned the Colombian Government that the illegal assumption of autocratic power by Bolivar would force it to resume its separate existence, and this decision was only modified by Bolivar's resignation of the presidency in that year. In 1841, after five years of civil war, an Isthmian Convention met at Panama and voted to separate from the federation and to resume their independent sovereign rights. Under this resolution the Isthmus remained independent for about a year, when it rejoined the federation on the promise of promulgation of a new Constitution that should recognize its rights.

Two Constitutions adopted in 1843 and 1853 were unsatisfactory and caused continuous insurrection on the Isthmus. Finally, by an amendment to the Constitution of New Granada in 1855, Panama was recognized as a sovereign state, while all the other provinces remained in direct control of the central Government. In 1858 this amendment was confirmed by the promulgation of a new Constitution creating the Granadan Confederation, and constituting a group of sovereign states federated for limited purposes, but otherwise independent and possessing at all times the rights of nullification and secession. In 1860 several of the states in this federation, including Panama, adopted ordinances of secession and the president of the republic recognized their right to do so in addressing the President of the State of Panama as follows:

"I trust that in reply to this letter you will advise me that the State of Panama is still in union with the others, and that you will send your plenipotentiary to take his seat in the Congress, the convocation of which I have communicated to you."

In September, 1861, a new agreement of federation, signed by the President of the State of Panama and the commissioner plenipotentiary of the United States of New Granada, contained the following specific reservations:

Article 1. The sovereign State of Panama shall be incorporated into the new national entity which is called the United States of New Granada, and shall continue in consequence to form one of the federal sovereign states which compose that association * * * with the specific reservation and conditions expressed in the following article.

Article 2. * * * the said state to be hereby incorporated with the United States above mentioned, but this state, in exercise of its sovereignty, reserves to itself the right to refuse its approval to the said new pact, and to the Constitution which may be drawn up, whenever, in its judgment, it may violate the autonomy of the state.

And this agreement was ratified by the Legislative Assembly of Panama, Oct. 15, 1861, with the following stipulation:

The president of the state is hereby authorized, in order to reconstitute the republic, to incorporate the said state therein, always provided that it shall be accorded the same concessions as set forth in the agreement of Sept. 6 last.

The rights of nullification and secession recognized in the constitutional amendment of 1855, the Constitution of 1858, and the agreement of 1861 were never relinquished by the citizens of Panama, and the terms of this agreement of 1861 were included in the Colombian Constitution of 1863. But notwithstanding this fact, a new Constitution promulgated in 1885, by executive decree, and in violation of the procedure of amendment defined in previous Constitutions, purported to terminate those rights and to reduce the Isthmus of Panama to the status of a crown colony without representation in the national Congress; and it was held in involuntary subjection by overpowering garrisons of the national army stationed in the Isthmian cities by order of the executive at Bogota.

The act of secession adopted by the citizens of Panama in popular assembly Nov. 3, 1903, was, therefore, a reassertion of legal rights maintained since the independence of Panama was achieved by its citizens in 1821, and in the meantime on numerous occasions asserted by Panama, acknowledged by the Colombian Government and never relinquished by the citizens of Panama; and the recognition of the independence of the Republic of Panama was, as Secretary Root wrote to Colombian Minister Mendoza in 1906, "a recognition of the just rights of the people of Panama."

It would appear that the recognition of the Republic of Panama was an act for which the United States should take credit to itself in espousing the cause of an oppressed people, and for which it owes the Government of Colombia no apology or reparation.

The canal is about fifty miles in length from deep water in the Caribbean Sea (Limon Bay) to deep water in the Pacific Ocean. The minimum width is 500 feet and the depth is forty-one feet. Vessels entering the canal from the north, or Caribbean, end pass through a sea level channel for about seven miles to the Gatun dam and locks, where, by a series of three lifts, they are raised to eighty-five feet above sea level.

The Gatun dam, which is the largest ever built crosses the Chagres River where it flows between two hills. It is 8,000 feet long across the top and 2,100 feet thick at its greatest width at the base. Its crest is 115 feet above sea level, or thirty feet above the level of Gatun Lake. The dam expands the waters of the river and lake into one continuous body of water 164 square miles in area, backing them through the Culebra cut thirty-one miles to Pedro Miguel lock. A spillway 285 feet wide carved 1,200 feet through solid rock carries off the surplus water.

The Culebra cut, which ranks with the Gatun dam as one of the engineering wonders of the age, pierces the highest part of the mountain range on the isthmus. Gold Hill, 330 feet high, had to be cut down to within forty feet of sea level, necessitating the removal of nearly a hundred million cubic yards of earth. The cut is 300 feet wide at the bottom and nine miles long.

After reaching this elevation through the locks at Gatun, vessels proceed thirty-one miles to Pedro Miguel lock and are lowered thirty feet to Miraflores Lake, whence, by two more locks, they are lowered to the level of the Pacific Ocean, eight miles from deep water.

There is a 1,000-foot dry dock at the Pacific side, and the locks are each 1,000 feet long and double. The time of transit through the canal of an ordinary ocean-going vessel is from nine to eleven hours. Passage through the locks is aided by electric "mules" or locomotives on tracks at each side, and vessels may proceed under their own steam at the entrances and through Gatun Lake.

The toll rate is $1.20 per net ton, about the same as the charges for passage through the Suez canal (8146, 8148).

The canal puts the United States on an equal footing with Europe in trading with Australia, New Zealand, China, Japan, Hawaii and the Philippines. A ten-knot ship can now run by way of the canal from New York to Yokohama in fifteen days less than it takes to go by the Suez route, bringing the Japanese city nearer to New York than Liverpool by 1,805 miles.

From New York to all Pacific American ports north of Panama, there will be a uniform reduction by way of the canal of 8,415 miles and to such ports south of Panama a uniform reduction of about 5,000 miles. Between New York and Hawaii or Manila the saving is about 5,800 miles. Distances from Liverpool and Antwerp to points on the Pacific coasts of North and South America are shortened about 6,000 and 2,600 miles, respectively. Wellington, New Zealand, by canal is 2,542 miles nearer New York, and the distance between them 2,759 miles less than between Wellington and Liverpool.

The chief engineer in charge of the work was Col. George W. Goethals, U. S. A. The construction of the canal was made possible largely through the sanitation work of Gen. W. C. Gorgas, U. S. A., under whose supervision the fever germs and disease breeding mosquitoes were eliminated at a cost to the government of more than twenty million dollars. The number of men on the work reached the maximum in March, 1913, when 44,733 were employed, of whom between 5,000 and 6,000 were Americans. From that date the number began to decrease. Work was begun in February, 1910. The official opening was set for Jan. 1, 1915, but work progressed so far beyond expectations that vessels and cargoes passed through six months earlier.

Early in May, 1914, cargoes of sugar from Hawaii were transferred to barges and towed through the canal, reloaded and landed in New York May 27th. June 8th, the *Alliance*, 4,000 tons, was towed through the locks. The question of the exemption of American coastwise vessels from payment of tolls is discussed by Presidents Wilson and Taft. (See also Hay-Pauncefote Treaty.)

The total cost of the work is about $375,-000,000. To pay three per cent interest on cost, one per cent for sinking fund and to provide for maintenance, operation and government of the zone and payments to Panama will require a revenue of nearly $20,000,000. It is estimated that 10,000,-000 tons of freight will pass through the canal the first year, one-fifth between American ports. (See also Suez Canal.)

The Canal toll earnings up to April 1, 1915, totaled $2,894,300. The total cost of operation and maintenance during the same period was $3,020,000, a deficit of $125,700. See illustrations opposite 7092, 7108, 7140, 7172, 7236, 7268.

Panama Canal:

American control of, to encourage coastwise trade, 7761.

Belligerent vessels, rules for use of, by, 8008.

Board of Engineers, pay of, 6970.

British protest against tolls, 7760.

Canal Zone—
　Executive Orders—
　　Establishing permanent government for, 7920.
　　Fixing interest rates in, 7905.
　　Forbidding corrupting employees in, 7918.
　　Providing conditions of employment in, 7923.
　　Regulating bearing of arms in, 7903.
　　Regulating hunting in, 7919.
　Extent and population of, 7687.
　Government for, discussed, 7687.
　Military government for, suggested, 7687.

Neutrality of, proclaimed, 8008.

Clayton-Bulwer treaty for protection of, discussed, 2580, 2617, 2903, 2943, 3117, 4628.

Commission, expenses of, 6730.

Committee created to open, 7944.

Compensation for employees injured on, 7990.

Construction, progress of—
　Earthquake, 7278.
　Engineers' report, 7269.
　Gatun dam, 7269.
　Lock system, 7268.
　Organization, 7275.
　Rock excavation, 7278.
　Type of, 7277.
　Water supply, 7279.

Control and supervision of, 4713.

Controlled and owned by United States, 7759.

Control of—
　Compared with Suez Canal, 7758, 7759.
　Discriminates only in favor of coastwise trade, 7761.

Discussed by President—
　Arthur, 4628, 4713.
　Buchanan, 3048, 3116.
　Cleveland, 4888, 4912.
　Grant, 3987.
　Hayes, 4474, 4537, 4562.
　Jackson, 1491.
　Johnson, 3663, 3885.
　Pierce, 2901, 2943.
　Polk, 2361.
　Roosevelt, 6663, 6718, 6806, 6827-6857, 7020, 7022, 7100, 7229, 7268, 7287, 7348.
　Taft, 7374, 7518, 7686, 7758.
　Taylor, 2554, 2580.
　Wilson, 7920, 7923, 7930, 7933.

Dock facilities, supplies and repairs furnished by Government, 7688.

Employees on, compensation for, when injured, 7990.

Establishing permanent government of, 7920.

Establishing Washington Office for, 7930.

Exemption of coastwise shipping from tolls, or refund, 7758.

Exemption of tolls amounts to subsidy, 7761.

Extension of favors not contrary to Hay-Pauncefote treaty, 7760.

Fixing interest rates in Zone, 7905.

Forbidding corrupt influencing of Canal Zone employees, 7918.

Form of government for Zone, 7687, 7920, 7930.

Fortification of necessary, 7519.

Great Britain protests against remission of tolls, 7758, 7933.

Hay-Pauncefote treaty invoked in opposition to control of, 7758, 7933.

Legislation for maintenance and control, 7687, 7903, 7905, 7918, 7920.

Maintenance and management by government, 7521.

Memorandum to accompany signature of act for control of, 7758.

Neutralization of, 7759.

Pictures of, 7092, 7108, 7140, 7172, 7236, 7268.

President Roosevelt's policy, regarding, 6827-6857.

Progress of work on, and early completion promised, 7686.

Protest against remission of tolls absurd, 7760.

Protest by British Government against tolls on, 7758.

Providing conditions of employment in Canal Zone, 7923.

Question of control could be decided by Supreme Court, 7763.

Railroad companies forbidden to own and operate ships using, 7521, 7962.

Referred to, 1647.

Regulating bearing of arms in the Canal Zone, 7903.

Regulating hunting in Zone, 7919.

Repeal of exemption from tolls clause of law asked, 7933.

Sanitation of Canal Zone, 7021.

Ships owned by railroads forbid use of, 7762.

Tolls—
　Remission of, to American shipping, 7688.
　Rates proclaimed, 7766, 7806.
　Should be fixed by President, 7688.
　Tonnage estimated, 7519.

Treaty regarding, with—
　Colombia, 3900, 4011, 4068.
　　Discussed, 6740, 6816, 6828, 6829.
　Great Britain, 2580, 2617, 2903, 2943, 3117, 7933.

The industrial buildings and other temporary structures will be placed on the bay shore overlooking the entrance to the harbor. The citizens of San Francisco have subscribed $7,000,000, the state legislature has authorized an appropriation of $5,000,-000 and the municipality one of $5,000,-000 for the exposition. The various commercial and industrial bodies of San Francisco have interested themselves in the enterprise and numerous plans have been considered to make the occasion of the exposition attractive to the visitors who may be expected to come in throngs from all parts of the world, not only to witness the wonderful uprising of San Francisco from its desolation by fire, but to view the scenic splendors of the Pacific Coast region.

Panchita, The, seizure of, on African coast, 3017.

Panhandle State.—A nickname for West Virginia (q. v.). (See also States.)

Panics.—A word formed from the name of the Greek god of shepherds, who is said to have had the power of inspiring sudden fright without apparent cause. It is now commonly used to describe a state of fear bordering on frenzy, from whatever cause induced. In history great commercial crises are spoken of as panics. England, Holland and France have experienced them, and the United States has passed through several notable ones. Those most disastrous have usually followed general injudicious speculation in lands or inflated securities. The crisis of 1816-1819 in the United States, it is claimed, was due to the speculation and disorder following the War of 1812. The next occurred in 1825. A very memorable panic was that of 1837. The few years preceding had been marked by extraordinary speculation, carried on with an unsound banking system. Jackson's "specie circular" caused many banks to suspend, and credit was generally impaired throughout the country. Governmental aid was invoked by many financial institutions, but without avail, as Van Buren, who had succeeded to the Presidency, insisted upon individuals righting their own affairs. In 1857 another period of inflation was followed by another panic. Again in 1873 there was a severe monetary crisis. Just twenty years later occurred the last panic from which the country has suffered. (See also Black Friday.)

The crisis of 1873 is usually dated from the failure of Jay Cooke & Co., Sept. 18th. The New York Stock Exchange closed on the 20th and was not reopened until the end of the month. Clearing House loan certificates were issued in large quantities, the last of which were redeemed Jan. 14, 1874. There had been certain premonitory symptoms of the approaching collapse, and there followed a long period of depression, which did not reach its lowest point until three years later. The number of business failures reported by commercial agents in 1872 was 4,069, and by 1876, the year of the deepest depression, the number had steadily increased to 9,084.

The depression of 1893 was preceded by reckless investments in foreign securities and was brought on by the shipments of gold to Europe caused by the operation of the act of Congress of July 14, 1890, which required the purchase by the United States Treasury of 4,500,000 ounces of silver per month. When the gold reserve held in the Treasury for the redemption of United States notes fell to near $100,000,-000, panic seized the business centers of the country. Bank reserves in New York fell from $25,439,925 in May to $5,481,975 in June. The financial tension was rendered more acute by the news that the Indian government had suspended the public coinage of silver. This caused insistent demands for the repeal of the silver purchase law. President Cleveland called an extra session of Congress and the vicious measure was repealed, whereupon recovery was rapid, aided materially by imports of gold and easier money.

Renewed activity in all lines of manufacture and commerce succeeded the panic of 1893 and the year 1906 witnessed the culmination of the remarkable industrial expansion. In 1907 many great railway and industrial enterprises endeavored to sell securities to augment their working capital, with the result that the stock markets felt the oversupply and prices fell with a crash; bank loans were called in and debtors failing to respond were sold out. The crisis was accentuated by the efforts of a few men to corner certain stocks, and their failure caused the suspension of banks which held their securities as collateral for loans. It transpired that the market manipulators were in some instances officers of the banks making the loans, and criminal indictments were secured against them. This panic was relieved by J. Pierpont Morgan, who formed a pool of $25,-000,000 to lend on approved security. (See Currency Laws.)

Panics:

Bank of United States attempts to bring about, 1250.

Derangement in moneyed institutions, 623.

Failures frequent in large cities, 630.

Labor, fall in price of, 630.

Pecuniary embarrassments existing in Union, 629.

Prostrations of business, discussed by President—

Buchanan, 2968, 3051.

Cleveland, 5833.

Grant, 4189, 4197, 4238.

Hayes, 4397.

Roosevelt, 7040, 7050.

Tyler, 2057.

Van Buren, 1541.

Paoli (Pa.) Massacre.—After the retreat from Brandywine Washington moved out on the Lancaster road as far as Warren's Tavern. Finding that Howe did not contemplate an attack upon Reading, Washington stationed Gen. Anthony Wayne with 1,500 men at Paoli, a retired and well-chosen position, to be ready to fall upon the rear of Howe's army. On the night of Sept. 20, 1777, Wayne was surprised, through the treachery of the people of the country, and 300 of his men were killed, wounded, or captured, with a loss of only an inconsiderable number of the enemy. Wayne saved his artillery and most of his baggage.

Papago Reservation. (See Gila Bend Reservation, Ariz.)

Papal States.—A former dominion of Italy, comprising the Romagna, the Marches, Umbria, and the present province of Rome, and governed directly by the Papal See. It was bounded on the north by the Lombardo-Venetian Kingdom, on the east by the Adriatic Sea, on the southeast by the Kingdom of Naples, on the southwest by the Mediterranean Sea, and on the west by Tuscany and the Duchy of Modena. In 1860 the larger part was annexed to Italy, and the remainder in 1870.

Papal States (see also Italy):

Annexation of, to Italy, referred to, 4098.

Outrages on American citizens in, 3110.

Revolutions in, 2551.

Vessels of, discriminating duties on, suspended by proclamation, 942, 3022.

Paper and Wood Pulp Industry.—Returns were received by the Department of Commerce from 727 establishments engaged in the paper and wood pulp industry in 1914. Of the total number, 503 establishments manufactured paper only, 63 wood pulp only, and 161 both paper and wood pulp.

The production of wood pulp in 1914 amounted to 2,894,650 tons, as compared with 2,498,955 tons in 1909, the increase being 15.8 per cent. In addition to the domestic production there were used 534,395 tons of imported pulp in 1914 and 301,392 tons in 1909, the increase for this item being 77.3 per cent.

The total value of the paper produced in 1914 was $294,355,875, as compared with $235,242,437 in 1909, the increase being 25.1 per cent.

The production of news paper in 1914 amounted to 1,313,284 tons, valued at $52,942,774, as compared with 1,175,554 tons, valued at $46,855,560, in 1909, the increase in quantity being 11.7 per cent., and in value, 13 per cent. There were manufactured in the later year 934,979 tons of book paper, valued at $73,499,514, and in the earlier, 694,905 tons, valued at $54,798,-840, the increase in quantity being 34.5 per cent., and in value, 34.1 per cent.

The production of fine paper amounted to 247,728 tons, valued at $34,054,918, in 1914, and to 198,213 tons, valued at $29,-076,638, in 1909, the increase in quantity being 25 per cent. and in value, 17.1 per cent.

The production of wrapping paper was 881,799 tons, valued at $49,372,753, in 1914, and 766,760 tons, valued at $42,456,-427, in 1909, the increases being 15 per cent. in quantity and 16.3 per cent. in value.

COMPARATIVE SUMMARY OF THE MANUFACTURE OF PAPER AND WOOD PULP.

| | Census | | Per cent of increase(*), 1909-1914. |
	1914	1909	
Number of establishments........	718	777	7.6*
Persons engaged in manufacture.....	95,516	81,473	17.2
Proprietors and firm members	221	250	11.6*
Salaried employees......	6,838	5,245	30.4
Wage earners	88,457	75,978	16.4
Primary horsepower	1,613,916	1,304,265	23.7
Capital............	$534,625,000	$409,349,000	30.6
Services...........	66,164,000	50,315,000	31.5
Salaries........	12,918,000	9,510,000	35.8
Wages.........	53,246,000	40,805,000	30.5
Materials...........	213,181,000	165,442,000	28.9
Value of products..	332,147,000	267,657,000	24.1
Value added by manufacture.....	118,966,000	102,215,000	16.4

* Decrease.

Location of Establishments.—Of the 727 establishments reported in 1914, 152 were located in New York, 86 in Massachusetts, 59 in Wisconsin, 54 in Pennsylvania, 48 in Ohio, 44 in Connecticut, 39 in Michigan, 38 in Maine, 34 in New Jersey, 31 in New Hampshire, 24 in Indiana, 23 in Vermont, 22 in Illinois, 13 in Maryland, 8 each in Minnesota, Virginia, and West Virginia, 7 in Delaware, 5 each in California and Oregon, 3 each in Iowa, Kansas, North Carolina, and Washington, 2 in Texas, and 1 each in the District of Columbia, Georgia, Mississippi, Rhode Island, South Carolina.

History.—Paper was manufactured in this country near Philadelphia as early as 1690. The growth of the industry, however, was slow until within the last forty years, during which time the introduction of improved machinery and the use of wood fibre as a material have brought about a remarkable growth in the industry. In the decade 1899-1909 the value of products increased $140,330,802 or 110.2 per cent, this percentage being higher than that for any other decade since 1869. Some part of this increase, however, was due to advance in prices, particularly during the first half of the decade.

Up to 1899 native spruce and poplar were used almost exclusively for pulp wood. Since that time, however, the advancing price of the native stock has led to the increased importation of these woods from Canada and to the use of other and cheaper native woods.

Paper Currency. (See Currency; Finances discussed.)

Paraguay.—Paraguay proper is an inland state of South America, lying between the rivers Paraguay and Alto Paraná, and bounded on the north by the Brazilian province of Matto Grosso, while the Chaco territory lying between the rivers Paraguay and Pilcomayo (and bounded on the north by Bolivia), is also claimed to be Paraguayan, but forms the subject of a long-standing dispute between Paraguay and Bolivia. The whole country may be said to be bounded on the north by Bolivia and Brazil, on the east by Brazil and Argentina, and on the south and west by Argentina. The area is given as 172,000 square miles.

Physical Features.—The country consists of a series of plateaus. The Paraguay and Alto Paraná Rivers are navigable at all seasons. The Pilcomayo River is navigable for 180 miles from Asuncion. The plateaus are covered with grassy plains and dense forest. The Chaco is practically a dead level, pierced by great rivers; it suffers much from floods and still more from drought.

History.—Paraguay was visited in 1527 by Sebastian Cabot, and in 1535 was settled as a Spanish possession. From that date to 1776 the country formed part of the vice-royalty of Peru, from which it was separated in 1776 and made an adjunct of the vice-royalty of Buenos Aires. In 1811 Paraguay declared its independence of Spain, and from 1814-1840 was governed by Francia, a Paraguayan despot, who was succeeded by Lopez, 1840-1862. In 1862 Francisco Solano Lopez succeeded his father, and in 1864 declared war against Brazil, Argentina and Uruguay being involved in the struggle. Against these three nations Lopez conducted a five years' war, which terminated in his defeat and death at the Battle of Cerro Corá, March 1, 1870. This dogged struggle reduced the country to complete prostration, and the population, which was 800,-000 in 1857, is alleged to have fallen in

1870 to 250,000, of whom barely 30,000 were men.

Government.—The present constitution was adopted at the close of the war, and under its provisions the head of the executive is the President, elected by an electoral college for four years and ineligible for office for eight consecutive years after the expiration of his term. A Vice-President is similarly elected, and succeeds automatically in case of the death, expulsion or absence of the President. There is a Cabinet of five members. The republic is subject to frequent revolutions, of which those of 1911 and 1912 were exceptionally fierce and sanguinary. President (Aug. 15, 1912-1916) : Eduardo Schaerer.

Congress consists of two houses. The Senate is composed of thirteen members, elected by direct vote for six years, one-third renewable every two years ; the Chamber of Deputies contains twenty-six members, elected by direct vote for four years and renewable as to one-half every two years.

There is a supreme court at the capital with three judges, two courts of appeal, a court of jurymen, and nine judges of first instance.

Population.—The inhabitants of Paraguay are mainly of Guarani Indian descent. The old Spanish stock has, to a large extent, become mixed with the primitive inhabitants, but during the last fifty years a considerable number of Europeans have settled in the country. The Paraguayan Chaco is only partially explored and is inhabited almost entirely by tribes of nomadic Indians, estimated at 100,000. The population of Paraguay proper includes about 50,000 uncivilized Indians, and 20,000 to 30,000 foreigners, of whom about 10,000 are from Argentina, 10,000 to 15,000 are Italian, 3,000 German, 1,500 Brazilian, 1,000 Spanish, 750 French, 600 Uruguayan, and 400 to 500 British. Immigration is encouraged, but has fallen to about 500 yearly since 1909. The official language is Spanish, but Guarani is general, and little else is spoken away from the towns.

Production and Industry.—The chief natural products are timber and yerba maté (Paraguayan tea). Tobacco and fruit, chiefly oranges, are grown for export, sugar cane, roots and grain for home consumption. The chief industry is stock raising. The primitive conditions of the country and the scarcity of labor appear to be, at present, unfavorable to agriculture. The soil and climatic conditions, however, are said to be exceptionally promising.

Marble, lime and salt are found and worked in small quantities. Iron ore is said to exist in large quantities, but coal has not been found. Copper manganese and other minerals exist, but the mineral resources are practically unexplored.

The principal exports are oranges, hides, tobacco, yerba maté, timber, dried meat, meat extracts, and quebracho extract. The imports are textiles, hardware, wines, foodstuffs, fancy goods, drugs and clothing. The principal sources of revenue are import and export duties, land tax, stamps, stamped paper and sundry internal taxes.

Finance.—The revenue of the country varies widely between 500,000 and 3,000,000 pesos, and the expenditures, while nearer constant, vary from 600,000 to 1,000,000 pesos. The gold peso, the standard of value, is equivalent to the dollar of the United States, the silver peso to $0.43,5, and the current paper pesos of the country, of which 65,000,000 are in circulation, has depreciated to almost nothing. There is a debt of something over $10,000,000.

Railways.—A railway (Paraguay Central) has been built and extended from Asuncion, the capital, to Encarnacion, a total distance of 232 miles. There is a through train service from Asuncion to Buenos Aires, the coaches being conveyed across the intervening rivers by means of train ferries. The rolling stock is up-to-date and the sleeping and restaurant cars similar to those of European main lines. Under normal conditions vessels drawing ten feet can reach Asuncion.

Trade with the United States.—The value of merchandise imported into Paraguay from the United States for the year 1912 was $187,867, and goods to the value of $58,285 were sent thither—a balance of $129,582 in favor of the United States.

Paraguay:

Affairs in, referred to, 4069.

Boundary question with Argentine Republic, submission of arbitration of, to President of United States, referred to, 4449.

Claims of United States against, 2980, 3050, 3091, 3114, 3195, 3270, 3281.

Commissioners appointed to adjust, 3050.

Convention regarding, 3108.

Naval force sent to, to await contingencies, discussed, 3050, 3091.

Satisfactorily settled, 3091.

Convention with, award of commissioners under, discussed, 3195, 3268.

Imprisonment of American citizens in, 3884, 3898.

Minister of United States to—

Controversy with President of, discussed, 3883.

Difficulties, referred to, 3890, 3898, 3899.

Withdrawn, 3987.

Questions with, regarding right of asylum discussed and referred to, 3883, 3890, 3898, 3899.

Treaty with, 2759, 2813, 3091, 3108, 3114.

Ratification of—

Delayed, 2914.

Refused, 2980.

Vessels of United States seized or interfered with by, 2952, 3046, 3091, 3195.

War with Brazil—

Good offices of United States tendered, 3776, 3883.

Referred to, 4078.

Paraguay Expedition. (See illustration opposite 2817.)

Paraguay, Treaties with.—A treaty of friendship, commerce, and navigation was concluded in 1859. Concessions to the United States include free navigation of the Paraguay River as far as the boundaries of Brazil and of the right side of the Parana in the dominions of Paraguay on like terms as are conferred upon other nations ; vessels may discharge all or part of the cargo at the ports of Pilar or may proceed to Asuncion. Rights and concessions enjoyed by other nations are conferred and shall accrue to the United States. Equitable imposition of charges, tolls, and fees; freedom of importation and exportation is equally enjoyed by the United States and Paraguayan vessels.

The rights of citizens of the United States to conduct trade, commerce, and to follow trades, vocations, and professions, in Paraguay are equal to those of subjects of Paraguay. The transfer and holding of property, succession to real or personal property by will or otherwise and free and open access to courts of justice are secured to citizens of the United States. The consular office may act as executors or administrators of estates.

No military exactions of service or forced loans or contributions other than those to which all subjects of Paraguay are lawfully subject shall be imposed. Consular appointment is provided for as in consular conventions. In the event of war it is agreed that citizens of each country residing or doing business within the confines of the other shall suffer no injustice, persecution, or spoliation and shall be free to continue in business or to close out as they may elect; nor shall debts, stocks, or interest be sequestered or detained. Religious freedom is secured to citizens or subjects in the dominions of the other contracting party.

International arbitration on the lines laid down by The Hague Convention of 1899 was agreed to by a treaty signed at Asuncion March 13, 1909.

Paraguay also became a party to the convention between the United States and the several republics of South and Central America for the arbitration of pecuniary claims and the protection of inventions, etc., which was signed in Buenos Aires in 1910 and proclaimed in Washington July 29, 1914. (See South and Central America, Treaties with.)

Parcel Post.—The agitation for a parcel post in the United States dates back to 1875 at least, and during the following thirty-five years (to quote Postmaster-General Wanamaker), only four objections have been raised against it, namely, the United States, the Wells Fargo, the American, and the Adams express companies.

In 1907 Postmaster-General Meyer advocated the establishment of a general and a local parcel post system. His plan for the general parcel post he described as follows: "The present rate for the transmission of fourth-class matter through the mails is 16 cents a pound, and the limit of weight is four pounds. Under our postal treaties the rate from any American post office to 29 foreign countries is 12 cents a pound, and the limit of weight to twenty-four of these countries is eleven pounds. The Department has simply recommended that our citizens be permitted to dispatch parcels to each other, in our own country, at as liberal a rate as that at which they are allowed to send them to a foreign country.

"The general parcels post system is in operation in Great Britain, New Zealand, Australia, Germany, Austria, France, Belgium, Italy, Holland, Chile and Cuba. The weight limit in each case (with the exceptions of Austria and Belgium) is eleven pounds. In England 26 cents will mail an eleven-pound package, the rate being 6 cents for the first pound and 2 cents for each additional pound. Germany has scheduled its rates by zones; thus all packages conveyed not more than 10 miles are charged 6 cents, and for greater distances they are charged 13 cents, and when the parcels exceed 12 pounds, the rates are

for each additional 2 pounds carried 10 miles, 2 cents; 20 miles, 3 cents; 50 miles, 5 cents; 100 miles, 8 cents. The weight limits in Austria and Belgium are, respectively, 143 and 132 pounds."

As to the cost of a general parcel post system in the United States, Mr. Meyer, using the cost of handling fourth-class matter as a basis, estimated it as follows:

Revenue from postage	$240.00
Expenditures:	
R. R. charge per ton $29.70	
Labor charge per ton 103.87	
Other conveyances 15.70	149.27
Excess of receipts over expenditures	$90.73

The above figures being based on the average haul (540 miles), Mr. Meyer pointed out that $90.73 excess would cover the transportation by rail of the entire ton over an additional 1,640 miles.

"This recommendation is founded upon the broad ground of the ability of the Government to render the service at a profit, yet with great advantage to the farmer, the retail merchant, and other patrons of the rural routes. The necessary machinery is at hand."

Postmaster-General Hitchcock, in December, 1910, recommended the establishment of a general parcel post throughout the country "as soon as the postal savings system is thoroughly organized." As the preliminary step he hoped that Congress would authorize the local parcel post, which, he said, would entail little if any additional expense, and which, if successful, might lead to the general one. However, he urged Congress to appropriate a fund for further investigation of the cost and possibilities of the general system at the time when it authorizes the local parcel post.

In accordance with an act of the Sixty-second Congress a parcel post system was inaugurated Jan. 1, 1913.

The limit of weight for parcels of fourth-class matter for delivery within the first and second zones was extended by act of Dec. 6, 1913, to fifty pounds, and delivery in other than the first and second zones is twenty pounds.

Parcels weighing four ounces or less are mailable at the rate of one cent for each ounce or fraction of an ounce, regardless of distance. Parcels weighing more than four ounces are mailable at the pound rates shown in the table on the following page, a fraction of a pound being considered a full pound.

The rate on parcels for Alaska, the Hawaiian Islands, the Philippine Islands, Guam, the United States Postal Agency at Shanghai (China), Tutuila (Samoa), and the Canal Zone (except for parcels weighing four ounces or less, on which the rate is one cent for each ounce or fraction thereof), is twelve cents per pound or fraction thereof.

Third-class matter can not be sent by parcel post. (See Postal Rates.)

Seeds, cuttings, bulbs, roots, scions and plants are matter of the fourth class, but are chargeable with the special rate of postage of one cent for each two ounces or fraction thereof, regardless of distance. Ordinary or parcel post stamps are valid for postage and for insurance and collect on delivery fees on fourth-class mail.

Packages mailed as first-class matter should be sealed. Fourth-class parcels must not be sealed.

Boxes to which the lids are nailed or screwed may be accepted for mailing at the fourth-class rates of postage, if, with reasonable effort, the lids can be removed for the purpose of permitting examination of the contents.

Parcels in bags or cloth so stitched that the necessary examination can not be made will be regarded as closed against inspection.

In addition to the name and address of the sender which is required, it is permissible to write or print on the covering of a parcel, or on a tag or label attached to it, the occupation of the sender, and to indicate in a small space by means of marks, letters, numbers, names or other brief description, the character of the parcel, but ample space must be left on the address side for the full address in legible characters and for the necessary postage stamps. Inscriptions such as "Merry Christmas," "Please do not open until Christmas," "Happy New Year," "With best wishes," and the like, may be placed on the covering of the parcel in such manner as not to interfere with the address.

Parcels may be remailed or forwarded on the payment of additional postage at the rate which would be chargeable if they were originally mailed at the forwarding office, in which case the necessary stamps shall be affixed by the forwarding postmaster. Payment must be made every time the parcel is forwarded.

A mailable parcel on which the postage is fully prepaid may be insured against loss in an amount equivalent to its actual value, but not to exceed $25, on payment of a fee of five cents, and in an amount equivalent to its actual value in excess of $25, but not to exceed $50, on payment of a fee of ten cents in stamps, such stamps

Weight in pounds	Local *	ZONES							
		1st Up to 50 miles	2d 50 to 150 miles	3d 150 to 300 miles	4th 300 to 600 miles	5th 600 to 1,000 miles	6th 1,000 to 1,400 miles	7th 1,400 to 1,800 miles	8th Over 1,800 miles
1	$0.05	$0.05	$0.05	$0.06	$0.07	$0.08	$0.09	$0.11	$0.12
2	.06	.06	.06	.08	.11	.14	.17	.21	.24
3	.06	.07	.07	.10	.15	.20	.25	.31	.36
4	.07	.08	.08	.12	.19	.26	.33	.41	.48
5	.07	.09	.09	.14	.23	.32	.41	.51	.60
6	.08	.10	.10	.16	.27	.38	.49	.61	.72
7	.08	.11	.11	.18	.31	.44	.57	.71	.84
8	.09	.12	.12	.20	.35	.50	.65	.81	.96
9	.09	.13	.13	.22	.39	.56	.73	.91	1.08
10	.10	.14	.14	.24	.43	.62	.81	1.01	1.20
11	.10	.15	.15	.26	.47	.68	.89	1.11	1.32
12	.11	.16	.16	.28	.51	.74	.97	1.21	1.44
13	.11	.17	.17	.30	.55	.80	1.05	1.31	1.56
14	.12	.18	.18	.32	.59	.86	1.13	1.41	1.68
15	.12	.19	.19	.34	.63	.92	1.21	1.51	1.80
16	.13	.20	.20	.36	.67	.98	1.29	1.61	1.92
17	.13	.21	.21	.38	.71	1.04	1.37	1.71	2.04
18	.14	.22	.22	.40	.75	1.10	1.45	1.81	2.16
19	.14	.23	.23	.42	.79	1.16	1.53	1.91	2.28
20	.15	.24	.24	.44	.83	1.22	1.61	2.01	2.40
21	.15	.25	.25	....	....	....	....	....	....
22	.16	.26	.26	....	....	....	....	....	....
23	.16	.27	.27	....	....	....	....	....	....
24	.17	.28	.28	....	....	....	....	....	....
25	.17	.29	.29	....	....	....	....	....	....
26	.18	.30	.30	....	....	....	....	....	....
27	.18	.31	.31	....	....	....	....	....	....
28	.19	.32	.32	....	....	....	....	....	....
29	.19	.33	.33	....	....	....	....	....	....
30	.20	.34	.34	....	....	....	....	....	....
31	.20	.35	.35	....	....	....	....	....	....
32	.21	.36	.36	....	....	....	....	....	....
33	.21	.37	.37	....	....	....	....	....	....
34	.22	.38	.38	....	....	....	....	....	....
35	.22	.39	.39	....	....	....	....	....	....
36	.23	.40	.40	....	....	....	....	....	....
37	.23	.41	.41	....	....	....	....	....	....
38	.24	.42	.42	....	....	....	....	....	....
39	.24	.43	.43	....	....	....	....	....	....
40	.25	.44	.44	....	....	....	....	....	....
41	.25	.45	.45	....	....	....	....	....	....
42	.26	.46	.46	....	....	....	....	....	....
43	.26	.47	.47	....	....	....	....	....	....
44	.27	.48	.48	....	....	....	....	....	....
45	.27	.49	.49	....	....	....	....	....	....
46	.28	.50	.50	....	....	....	....	....	....
47	.28	.51	.51	....	....	....	....	....	....
48	.29	.52	.52	....	....	....	....	....	....
49	.29	.53	.53	....	....	....	....	....	....
50	.30	.54	.54	....	....	....	....	....	....

* The local rate applies to parcels mailed under the following conditions: 1. At any post office for local delivery at such office. 2. At any city letter carrier office, or at any point within its delivery limits, for delivery by carriers from that office. 3. At any post office from which a rural route starts, for delivery on such route, or when mailed at any point on a rural route for delivery at any other point thereon, or at the office from which the route starts, or for delivery on any other rural route starting from the same office.

to be affixed. The amount of the insurance fee shall be placed on the receipt given the sender and on the coupon retained at the mailing office.

The sender of a mailable parcel on which the postage is fully prepaid may have the price of the article and the charges thereon collected from the addresses on payment of a fee of ten cents in stamps affixed, provided the amount to be collected does not exceed $100. Such a parcel will be insured against loss without additional charge in an amount equivalent to its actual value, but not to exceed $50.

Matter manifestly obscene, lewd, lascivious, or immoral is unmailable, also spirituous, vinous, malted, fermented, or other intoxicating liquors, or odorous, inflammable or otherwise dangerous substances.

Parcel Post, extension of, recommended, 7102, 7227, 7694.

Pardons:
Amnesty proclamation of President Lincoln, 3414.
  Discussed, 3390, 3455.
  Persons entitled to benefits of, defined, 3419.
  Referred to, 3508.
Amnesty proclamations of President Johnson, 3508, 3745, 3853, 3906.
  Authority for, discussed, 3895.
  Circular regarding, 3539.
  Persons worth more than $20,000 to whom special pardons issued, referred to, 3583.
  Referred to, 3659, 3669, 3722, 3779.
General amnesty and removal of political disabilities recommended, 4107, 4209.
Granted—
  American citizens by Queen of Spain, 2689, 2692.
  Counterfeiters, forgers, etc., referred to, 3818.
  Deserters from Army, 413, 497, 499, 528, 1062, 3364, 3479, 4189.
    Act authorizing, 3365.
  Foreigners on condition of emigration to United States discussed, 3653.
  Insurgents in Pennsylvania, 173, 293.
    Referred to, 176.
  Persons carrying on lawless trade, but who aided in defense of New Orleans, 543.
  Persons guilty of unlawful cohabitation under color of polygamous marriage, 5803, 5942.
Political disabilities, removal of, recommended, 4107, 4209.
Queen of Spain grants, to American citizens, 2689, 2692.
Sentences of deserters condemned to death commuted, 3434.

Paris, The, mentioned, 6313.

Paris, Declaration of.—In the treaty of Paris, which was concluded March 30, 1856, between Russia and Turkey, Great Britain, France, and Sardinia, the following declarations with regard to the conduct of war were subscribed to by all the parties to the treaty and have since been accepted by nearly all civilized nations: First, Privateering is and remains abolished. Second, Neutral goods in enemies' ships, enemies' goods in neutral ships, except contraband of war, are not liable to capture. Third, Paper blockades are unlawful. The United States refused to agree to this declaration on account of the clause doing away with privateers, as the country was compelled to rely largely upon such service in naval warfare. This refusal cost it heavily in the Civil War, although it was willing to subscribe to the declaration in 1861. In 1871 the declaration was censured by the British Parliament.

Paris, France:
International Congress of Electricians at, 4581, 4625, 4714. (See also National Conference of Electricians.)
International convention at—
  For protection of—
    Industrial property, 4560, 4794, 4857, 5118.
    Ocean cables—
      In 1880, 4714.
      In 1884, 4799.
      Declaration of, transmitted to Senate, 5117.
      Discussed, 5084.
  On the subject of trade-marks, 4714.
International exhibition at—
  In 1878, 4405, 4419, 4447.
  In 1889, 5181, 5471.
International Monetary Conference at—
  In 1867, 3776, 3792.
    Report of S. B. Ruggles on, referred to, 4013.
  In 1878, 4447, 4464, 4474, 4510.
  In 1881, 4625.
  In 1882, 4697.
International Postal Congress at, discussed, 3387.
  New convention adopted by, 4453.
Official publications, a g r e e m e n t reached for interchange of, 4718.
Spanish-American Peace Commission at, 6321, 6322.
Universal exposition at—
  In 1867, 3569, 3592, 3660, 3776.
    Commissioners of United States to, 3798, 3828.
    Correspondence regarding, 3668.
    Memorial to Congress concerning, 3668.
  To be held in 1900, 6061.
    Representation of United States at, discussed, 6247, 6267, 6275, 6329, 6368, 6411, 6427, 6461.

Paris, Monetary Conferences at.—There have been three important international monetary conferences held in Paris. The first assembled June 17, 1867, at the solicitation of France, to "consider the question of uniformity of coinage and seek for the basis of ulterior negotiations."

The United States sent representatives, as did also nearly every European nation. The conference adjourned after about a month without having arrived at any definite conclusion.

August 16, 1878, a second international monetary conference convened at Paris, this time at the instance of the United States, "to adopt a common ratio between gold and silver for the purpose of establishing internationally the use of bimetallic money and securing fixity of relative value between those metals." The collective decision of the European delegates was that this would be impossible, monetary questions being governed by the special situation of each State or group of States. With this as the final conclusion the conference adjourned August 29.

The conference of April 8, 1881, assembled at the call of France and the United States to adopt a permanent relative value between gold and silver, but adjourned July 8 without arriving at any agreement. (See also Brussels, Belgium; Paris, France.)

Paris, Treaties of.—Paris has been the scene of numerous important diplomatic conferences, both between France and other powers and between neighboring nations, who found hospitable neutral ground of the French capital.

Among the most important of treaties of Paris is that of Feb. 10, 1763, between Great Britain on one side, and France, Spain, and Portugal on the other. France ceded to Great Britain Canada, Prince Edward Island, Cape Breton, Mobile, all the territory east of the Mississippi, Dominica, Tobago, St. Vincent and Granada. England restored to France Guadeloupe, Martinique, St. Pierre, Miquelon and Pondicherry, and ceded St. Lucia to her. Spain ceded Florida to Great Britain, England restored Havana to Spain, and France ceded Louisiana to Spain.

The treaty of Paris of 1782-83 between Great Britain on one side and France, Spain, and the United States on the other, was arranged in 1782 and formally ratified Sept. 3, 1783. John Jay, John Adams, Benjamin Franklin, and Henry Laurens formed the American commission. The absolute independence of the United States was recognized; Florida and Minorca were returned to Spain; navigation of the Mississippi was made free to both Spain and the United States; the Americans relinquished their pretensions to the territory north of Lake Erie; the St. Lawrence River system from the western end of Lake Superior to the forty-fifth parallel was made the boundary between the United States and the British possessions (from the forty-fifth parallel to the sea the boundary followed the highlands after an uncertain fashion and was long a matter of dispute); loyalists and tories were to be protected in America; English troops were to be withdrawn without destroying any property or taking away any negro slaves belonging to Americans; the right of fishing on the Canadian and Newfoundland coasts was granted to Americans. The portion of the treaty which directly affected America was signed at Paris, but that between Great Britain, France, and Spain was signed at Versailles, by which name the entire treaty is sometimes called.

At Versailles the region of Senegal was granted to France and neutral restitution of conquests in the West Indies was made.

In 1908 commissioners were appointed by the Governments of the United States and Spain to meet at Paris and frame a treaty of peace in accordance with the terms of the protocol signed Aug. 12, 1898.

The commissioners began their sessions Oct. 1 and ended with the signing of a treaty of peace, Dec. 10. (See also Treaties with the various countries.)

Paris Tribunal of Arbitration:

Acts to give effect to award of, proclaimed, 5926, 6123.

Award of, discussed, recommendations regarding, 5958, 6062.

Case of United States at, prepared by John W. Foster, 5748.

Convention for settlement of claims under, 6097.

Discussed, 5869.

Enforcement of regulations in accordance with decision of, referred to, 6000.

Failure of negotiations of, to protect fur seals of Alaska, 6182.

Reports of agent of United States to, transmitted, 5909.

Parks, National.—Congress has on several occasions set aside and exempted from sale certain territory because of its picturesque character or historic interest. The principal tracts thus appropriated to the use of all the people up to the present time are the Yellowstone National Park and the Yosemite National Park, which was made a national park by act of Congress passed June 30, 1864, and ordered to include the Mariposa Big Tree Grove. This park was granted by Congress to the State of California, conditional upon its being forever set aside as a place of public resort and recreation. It is about 155 miles from San Francisco, is six miles long by about a mile in width, and its perpendicular depth below the surrounding country is about a mile, though it lies 4,000 feet above the level of the sea. Yellowstone Park was created by an act approved March 1, 1872, which dedicated it as a pleasure ground for the benefit and enjoyment of the people. Its general elevation is about 6,000 feet, though mountains 10,000 and 12,000 feet high rise on every side. The region abounds in scenery of unparalleled grandeur. Tall columns of basalt rise to 1,000 feet in height; waters of different degrees of temperature and of untold therapeutic properties are met on every hand; acres of miniature volcanoes sputter and fume; giant geysers intermittently spurt columns of hot water and steam hundreds of feet into the air from basins of all sizes and most fantastic shapes and vivid colorings, while the Gardiner River plunges through a forbidding black hole into the Grand Canyon, whose precipitous walls of 2,000 feet in height have never been explored, and emerges, with an abrupt descent of 350 feet, to pursue its tranquil course over a fertile rolling prairie.

In 1890 three sections of land in Tulare County, Cal., containing giant trees, were reserved for a national park. In 1890 Congress provided for a park of 1,500 acres on Rock Creek, District of Columbia, half the cost ($1,200,000) being paid by the people of Washington and half by the United States. Later Congress reserved the battle grounds of Chickamauga, Shiloh, Vicksburg, and others as public parks. The total area of the national parks amounts to 3,883,196 acres.

The national parks and reservations mentioned below are under the supervision of the Secretary of the Interior. General in formation, the annual administrative reports, copies of the rules and regulations, and compilations of the laws relating to the parks may be obtained from the Secretary of the Interior or from the superintendents of the parks.

Yellowstone National Park is in Wyoming, Montana, and Idaho, and has an area of 2,142,720 acres. The superintendent's address is Yellowstone Park, Wyoming. The park can be reached by the following railroads : Northern Pacific Railroad to Gardiner, the northern entrance, via Livingston, Mont. ; Oregon Short Line Railroad to Yellowstone, Mont., the western entrance ; Chicago, Burlington and Quincy Railroad to Cody, Wyo., from which the eastern entrance to the park is accessible. Stage and private transportation connections for the reservation are made at all these points. The tourist season extends from June 1 to Sept. 15, but accommodations are furnished at Mammoth Hot Springs the entire year.

Yosemite National Park, California, including the Yosemite Valley and Mariposa Big Tree Grove, embraces an area of 719,-622 acres. The superintendent's address is Yosemite, Cal. The park can be reached from Merced on the Atchison, Topeka and Santa Fé and the Southern Pacific railroads, by way of Yosemite Valley Railroad, which runs to the western boundary, and by connections of the same roads to Raymond, on the southwest ; stage lines run from the terminus of the Yosemite Valley Railroad and from Raymond to Yosemite Valley within the park.

Glacier National Park, Montana, has an area of approximately 915,000 acres, of which 15,000 acres have been surveyed. Within the limits stated there are 250 lakes, ranging from ten miles to a few hundred feet in extent. There are more than sixty glaciers between five square miles and a few acres in area. There are wild animals, plants, and rocks in numbers and quantity to satisfy the most ardent student, and views of great variety, beauty and grandeur to gratify the artist and the lover of nature. The park can be reached via the Great Northern Railway.

Mount Rainier National Park, Washington, has an area of 207,360 acres. The superintendent's address is Ashford, Wash. The park is reached by stage or private transportation from Ashford, Wash., on the Tacoma Eastern Railroad, and by trail from Fairfax, on the Northern Pacific Railroad. The tourist season extends from June 15 to Sept. 15.

Sequoia National Park, California, has an area of 161,597 acres. The address of the superintendent is Ranger, Cal., during the tourist months (June 1 to Sept. 15) and Three Rivers, Cal., the balance of the year. This park may be reached from Visalia, on the Southern Pacific and the Atchison, Topeka and Santa Fé railroads by way of the Visalia Electric Railroad Company to Lemon Cove, thence by stage or private conveyance.

General Grant National Park, California, has an area of 2,536 acres. This reservation is administered jointly with Sequoia National Park, and the tourist season extends from June 1 to Sept. 15. The address of the superintendent is given above. The park may be reached by stage and private conveyance from Sanger, on the Southern Pacific Railroad.

Crater Lake National Park, Oregon, has an area of 159,360 acres. The address of the superintendent during the tourist months (June 15 to Sept. 30) is Crater Lake, Ore., and during the balance of the year Klamath Falls, Ore. This park may be reached by steamer line and stage from Klamath Falls, Ore, or by private conveyance from Medford, on the Southern Pacific.

Wind Cave National Park, South Dakota, contains 10,522 acres. The superintendent's address is Wind Cave, S. Dak. This park may be reached by private conveyance from Hot Springs, on the Chicago, Burlington and Quincy and the Chicago and Northwestern railroads, or by similar conveyance from Custer, on the Chicago, Burlington and Quincy Railroad. The reservation is open to tourists the entire year.

Sullys Hill Park, North Dakota, on the shore of Devil's Lake, has an area of 780 acres. The address of the superintendent is Fort Totten, N. Dak. Devil's Lake, Narrows, and Tokio, on the Great Northern Railroad, are close to the park, and from these points the reservation can be approached by wagon, or by boat (private conveyance).

Platt National Park, at Sulphur, Oklahoma, has an area of 848.22 acres. Sulphur is the post-office address of the superintendent. The town is accessible by the Atchison, Topeka and Santa Fé and the St. Louis and San Francisco railroads. The park, which is open to tourists the entire year, is within walking or riding distance of the railroads.

Mesa Verde National Park, Colorado, has an area of 42,376 acres, and the five-mile strip under the park jurisdiction for the protection of ruins, which abuts the park, contains 175,360 acres. The address of the superintendent is Mancos, Col., the nearest railroad station, on the Rio Grande Southern Railroad. This station is about twenty-five miles from the ruins, which may be reached only by horseback or afoot.

Casa Grande Ruin, Arizona, a reservation, has an area of 480 acres. The nearest railroad station is Casa Grande, on the Southern Pacific Railroad. It may also be reached by private conveyance from Florence, Ariz., on the Phœnix and Eastern Railroad. The address of the custodian is Florence. The Mesa Verde National Park and the Casa Grande Reservation were set aside to protect the instructive prehistoric ruins and other objects of antiquity which they contain. These ruins are being excavated and repaired and are open for the inspection of visitors. Reports on the repair of such ruins have been issued by the Department of the Interior, and more detailed accounts are distributed by the Bureau of American Ethnology, Smithsonian Institution.

Hot Springs Reservation, Arkansas (the permanent reservation), has an area of 911.63 acres. Eleven bathhouses on the reservation and thirteen in the city of Hot Springs, as well as several hotels operated in connection with bathhouses, receive hot water from the springs, under lease with the Secretary of the Interior. The address of the superintendent is Hot Springs, Ark.

Rocky Mountain National Park, created by the act of Jan. 26, 1915, is in Colorado, about 45 miles in an air line northwest of Denver. It has an area of approximately 229,000 acres, and is on both sides of the Continental Divide in the neighborhood of Long's Peak. The park may be reached from Lyons, on the Chicago, Burlington and Quincy Railroad ; from Loveland, on the Colorado and Southern Railroad, and from Granby, on the Denver and Salt Lake Railroad.

Lassen Volcanic National Park, the bill creating which President Wilson signed in August, 1916, is California's fourth national park. Lassen Peak, which showed volcanic activity only a few years ago, was set apart as a national monument in 1906. Cinder Cone, in its immediate neighborhood was also thus distinguished at the same time. The new national park includes both of these remarkable volcanic monuments within its area of 82,880 acres.

Parks, National, establishment of Bureau of, recommended, 7724.

Parley.—In military parlance, a conference between army officers of belligerents.

Parliamentary.—In accordance with the rules laid down for the guidance of assembly deliberations; originally in accordance with the rules laid down for the guidance of Parliament.

Parliamentary Law. (See Parliamentary.)

Parole.—To permit or grant leave of absence, especially to a soldier.

Partizan (or Partisan).
ing to a political party, or to a political principle; especially a blind follower of such party or principle.

Party.—In political parlance, a body of persons working together for the same political ends. (See Political Parties.)

Passamaquoddy Bay, between Maine and New Brunswick, commissioners to mark international boundary in, referred to, 6063.

Passport.—A document issued by competent civil authority, granting permission to the person specified in it to travel or authenticating his right to protection. In some nations no person is allowed to leave the country without a passport from his government; but the regulations of the different jurisdictions regarding the use of passports have greatly varied and of late years have exhibited a tendency toward a relaxation of stringency, extending in many countries to their total abolition. Passports of the United States, which are given under the seal of the Secretary of State, request that the person named therein be permitted to pass freely and safely, and in case of need that aid and protection be afforded him.

The extent to which an American passport held by a naturalized citizen of this country is recognized in his native land, depends principally upon whether that country has concluded a treaty of naturalization with the United States, although, under the law of this country, no distinction is made between native and naturalized American citizens so far as their right to protection is concerned. The United States has treaties of naturalization with the following European countries: Austria-Hungary, Belgium, Denmark, the German States, Great Britain, Norway, and Sweden.

Passports:

Abolishing fees for and providing for certification of, 7968.

Authentication of, denial of, by Russian consuls to Jews, discussed, 6067.

Charge for, for citizens visiting foreign countries, referred to, 4985.

Issue of, extended to residents of United States insular possessions, 6747.

Laws regarding issue of, revision of, recommended, 5370.

Order amending rules governing granting of, 7966.

Order regarding, rescinded, 3537.

Persons not permitted to enter United States without, 3475.

Order modifying, as to Canada, 3483.

Regulations of foreign powers regarding, printing of reports on, recommended, 6181.

Patagonian Boundary, between Chile and Argentine Republic, referred to, 4629.

Patapsco River, Maryland, act for improvement of, vetoed, 2921.

Patent Congress, International, at Vienna, 4215.

Patent Law. (See Patent Office.)

Patent Medicines. (See Medicines, Patent.)

Patent Office. (See Patents and Interior Department.)

Patent Office:

Accounts of, deficiency in, 1031.

Analytical digest of patents recommended, 2708.

Appropriations, estimates for, 4676.

Building for, recommended, 1133.

Deficiency appropriation for payment of salaries in, recommended, 4668.

Discussed by President—
- Cleveland, 4945, 5110.
  Grant, 3995, 4065, 4155, 4206, 4306.
  Harrison, Benj., 5553.
  Jackson, 1096.
  Johnson, 3652, 3774, 3880.
  Lincoln, 3253.
  McKinley, 6345, 6388, 6453.
  Pierce, 2750.

Establishment of, recommended, 556.

Fire in, referred to and recommendations regarding, 4405, 4407.

Inventions—

Examination of, to prevent explosions, referred to, 1726.

Referred to, 1728, 1732.

Protection to American inventors in Europe secured, 4190.

Should be encouraged, 58, 60, 2750.

Laws relating to improvement of, recommended, 881, 1120, 2750.

Receipts and expenditures of. (See discussed, *ante*.)

Reciprocity with foreign countries in relation to patents, recommended, 6802.

Reorganization of—
Discussed, 4155.

Recommendation regarding, 4115.

Separation of, from Interior Department, recommended, 4155, 4206.

Transfer of, from State Department to Attorney-General, recommended, 2265.

Patents.—Literally, open letters. In England the word is applied to all licenses and authorities granted by the Crown. Patents for titles of nobility were first granted by Edward III. in 1334. The earliest patent for the exclusive privilege of printing books was granted in 1591. The property right of inventors and discoverers to their arts and manufactures was first secured by letters patent by an act passed in 1623. In the United States a patent is generally understood to mean the right to the exclusive use for a limited number of years, of a new or useful invention or discovery by the inventor or discoverer or his heirs or assigns. A few patents had been issued by the states. In 1790 the first patent law was passed by the General Government, and granted letters patent for fourteen years to both citizens and foreigners. Application had formerly to be made to the Secretaries of War and State and the Attorney-General. In 1793 an act was passed permitting the issue of patents to citizens only and requiring a fee of $30. The states were not permitted to issue patents. This was decided in the case of Gibbons *vs.* Ogden (q. v.), from New York. In 1836 the patent laws were revised and the present patent system in this country may be said to date from that year. One of the most important changes then introduced was the regulation requiring a preliminary examination of the novelty and patentability of an invention. In 1839 an inventor was given the right to use his invention before applying for a patent, but such use was limited to two years. Under the law of 1842 patents were granted for a term of seven years; the term was subsequently extended to fourteen years, and finally in 1861 the present seventeen-year term was granted. The patent laws were revised in 1870 and patents were allowed to all persons, both citizens and foreigners, who could prove the novelty and usefulness of their inventions. The salient features of the patent laws of to-day, however, are still those of the law of 1836. The number of patents granted annually is about 30,000. Since the year 1836, no less than 885,635 patents have been issued by the United States, while the combined total of foreign countries amounts to 1,863,836. (See also Department of the Interior.)

Patents are issued in the name of the United States, and under the seal of the Patent Office, to any person who has invented or discovered any new and useful art, machine, manufacture, or composition of matter or any new and useful improvement thereof, or any new original and ornamental design for an article of manufacture, not known or used by others in this country before his invention or discovery thereof, and not patented or described in any printed publication in this or any foreign country, before his invention or discovery thereof or more than two years prior to his application, and not in public use or on sale in the United States for more than two years prior to his application, unless the same is proved to have been abandoned, upon payment of the fees required by law and other due proceedings had.

Every patent contains a grant to the patentee, his heirs or assigns, for the term of seventeen years, except in the case of design patents, of the exclusive right to make, use, and vend the invention or discovery throughout the United States and the territories, referring to the specification for the particulars thereof.

If it appear that the inventor, at the time of making his application, believed himself to be the first inventor or discoverer, a patent will not be refused on account of the invention or discovery, or any part thereof, having been known or used in any foreign country before his invention or discovery

thereof, if it had not been before patented or described in any printed publication.

Joint inventors are entitled to a joint patent; neither can claim one separately. Independent inventors of distinct and independent improvements in the same machine cannot obtain a joint patent for their separate inventions; nor does the fact that one furnishes the capital and another makes the invention entitle them to make application as joint inventors; but in such case they may become joint patentees by means of a deed of assignment.

No person otherwise entitled thereto will be debarred from receiving a patent for his invention or discovery, by reason of its having been first patented or caused to be patented by the inventor or his legal representatives or assigns in a foreign country, unless the application for said foreign patent was filed more than twelve months prior to the filing of the application in this country, and four months in cases of designs, in which case no patent shall be granted in this country.

If an inventor wishes to file an application for patent, a copy of the Rules of Practice, containing forms and instructions, will be sent upon request. It is advisable, in every case, that the services of a competent registered patent attorney be secured, as the value of patents depends largely upon the skilful preparation of the specification and claims.

Applications for a patent must be made in writing to the Commissioner of Patents. The applicant must also file in the Patent Office a written description of the invention or discovery, and of the manner and process of making, constructing, compounding, and using it, in such full, clear, concise, and exact terms as to enable any person skilled in the art or science to which it appertains, or with which it is most nearly connected, to make, construct, compound, and use the same; and in case of a machine, he must explain the principle thereof, and the best mode in which he has contemplated, applying that principle, so as to distinguish it from other inventions, and particularly point out and distinctly claim the part, improvement, or combination which he claims as his invention or discovery. The specification and claim must be signed by the inventor and attested by two witnesses.

When the nature of the case admits of drawings, the applicant must furnish a drawing of the required size, signed by the inventor or his attorney in fact, and attested by two witnesses. The applicant, if required by the Patent Office, shall furnish a model of convenient size to exhibit advantageously the several parts of his invention or discovery, but a model should not be sent unless first called for by the Patent Office.

The applicant shall make oath that he verily believes himself to be the original and first inventor or discoverer of the art, machine, manufacture, composition, or improvement for which he solicits a patent; that he does not know and does not believe that the same was ever before known or used, and shall state of what country he is a citizen and where he resides, and whether he is the sole or joint inventor of the invention claimed in his application. In every original application the applicant must distinctly state under oath that the invention has not been patented to himself or to others with his knowledge or consent in this or any foreign country for more than two years prior to his application, or on an application for a patent filed in any foreign country by himself or his legal representatives or assigns more than twelve months prior to his application in this country, or four months in cases of designs. If any application for patent has been filed in any foreign country by the applicant in this country or by his legal representatives or assigns, prior to his application in this country, he shall state the country or countries in which such application has been filed, giving the date of such application, and shall also state that no application has been filed in any other country or countries than those mentioned; that to the best of his knowledge and belief the invention has not been in public use or on sale in the United States nor described in any printed publication or patent in this or any foreign country for more than two years prior to his application in this country.

Every patent or any interest therein shall be assignable in law by an instrument in writing; and the patentee or his assigns or legal representatives may, in like manner, grant and convey an exclusive right under his patent to the whole or any specified part of the United States.

A reissue is granted to the original patentee, his legal representatives, or the assignees of the entire interest when, by reason of a defective or insufficient specification, or by reason of the patentee claiming as his invention or discovery more than he had a right to claim as new, the original patent is inoperative or invalid, provided the error has arisen from inadvertence, accident, or mistake, and without any fraudulent or deceptive intention. Reissue applications must be made and the specifications sworn to by the inventors, if they be living.

Fees must be paid in advance, and are as follows: On filing each original application for a patent, $15. On issuing each original patent, $20. In design cases: For three years and six months, $10; for seven years, $15; for fourteen years, $30. On every application for the reissue of a patent, $30. On filing each disclaimer, $10. For certified copies of patents and other papers in manuscript, ten cents per hundred words and twenty-five cents for the certificate; for certified copies of printed patents, eighty cents. For uncertified printed copies of specifications and drawings of patents, five cents each. For recording every assignment, agreement, power of attorney, or other paper, of three hundred words or under, $1; of over three hundred and under one thousand words, $2; for each additional thousand words, or fraction thereof, $1. For copies of drawings, the reasonable cost of making them. The Patent Office is prepared to furnish positive photographic copies of the drawings of pending patented or abandoned cases, in sizes and at rates as follows: Large size, 10x15 inches, twenty-five cents; medium size, 8x12½ inches, fifteen cents. Negative photographic copies of specifications and drawings of foreign patents, or of any page or part of page of any printed publication in the possession of the office, will be furnished on paper 7x11 inches, for fifteen cents per sheet. Fee for examining and registering trade-mark, $10, which includes certificate. Stamps cannot be accepted by the Patent Office in payment of fees.

The receipts of the Patent Office during the year ending December 31, 1912, were $2,118,158.30, and expenditures, $2,022,-066.11. Receipts over expenditures, $96,-092.19. Total net surplus to December 31, 1912, $7,160,017.95. The number of new patents issued during 1912 was 37,573.

The total number of applications filed at the Patent Office in seventy-five years, 1837-1912, was 1,926,009; number of original patents, including designs and reissues issued, 1,106,235.

There is now no law permitting the filing of a caveat, the old law having been repealed July 1, 1910. Patent No. 1,000,000 was granted August 8, 1911, to F. H. Holton, of Akron, O., for an automobile tire.

Patents:

Commissioner of recommendations of, referred to, 4115.

Protection of in South and Central America, 7984.

Patriotic Societies, National (see Encyclopedic Index articles on following subjects):

American Continentals.
American Cross of Honor.
American Flag Association.
American National Red Cross Association.
Anti-Saloon League.
Army and Navy Union.
Aztec Club of 1847.
Carnegie Hero Fund.
Cincinnati, Society of.
Colonial Dames of America.
Colonial Society of America.
Dames of the Revolution.
Daughters of the American Revolution.
Daughters of the Revolution.
Grand Army of the Republic.
Huguenot Society of America.
Interstate National Guard Association.
Loyal Legion, Military Order of.
Medal of Honor Legion.
Mayflower Descendants.
Military Order of Foreign Wars.
Mount Vernon Ladies' Association.
National Association of Naval Veterans.
Naval Order of the United States.
Navy League of the United States.
Order of Indian Wars of the United States.
Order of the Founders and Patriots.
Purity Federation.
Regular U. S. Army and Navy Union.
Societies of Spanish War Veterans.
Societies of the Union Army of 1861-65.
Society of the Army and Navy of the Confederate States.
Societies of the War of 1812.
Society of Colonial Wars.
Sons of the American Revolution.
Sons of the Revolution.
Sons of Veterans, U. S. A.
Tammany Society.
Union Veteran Legion.
United Confederate Veterans.
United Daughters of the Confederacy.
United Sons of Confederate Veterans.
United States Daughters of 1812.
Veterans of Indian Wars.
Washington Headquarters Association.
Woman's Relief Corps.

Patriotism:—Ardent devotion to the cause and purposes of one's country, usually accompanied by willingness to fight for that country.

Patrol.—A soldier who guards life or property. (See Picket, Sentry and Sentinel.)

Patrons of Husbandry.—A secret society organized for the purpose of establishing cooperation among farmers. In 1876 it took the name "Grangers" (q. v.).

Paul vs. Virginia.—An important case before the United States Supreme Court. The statutes of Virginia required the deposit in the State treasury of certain moneys in State bonds by insurance companies not incorporated under the State laws in return for licenses to do business in the State. This law was enacted Feb. 3, 1866, and later in the month a supplemental act was passed. In the same year Samuel Paul, a citizen of Virginia, acting as agent for a New York insurance company, was indicted before the Circuit Court of Petersburg and sentenced to pay a fine of $50 for refusing to comply with the above law. The court of appeals of Virginia affirmed the decree of the Circuit Court, and, the case having been taken to the Supreme Court of the United States, that tribunal affirmed the judgment of the State court of appeals on the ground that the State law in question did not conflict with that clause of the National Constitution which declares that "the citizens of each State shall be entitled to all privileges and immunities of citizens in the several States," nor with the power of Congress to "regulate commerce with foreign nations and among the several States." Justice Field, for the court, held that issuing a policy of insurance is not a transaction of commerce. The policies are local transactions and are governed by the local law. Justice Field stated that corporations are not citizens within the meaning of the Constitution.

Paulus Hook (N. J.), Capture of.—In the summer of 1779 the British had a garrison of 383 men stationed at Paulus Hock, N. J., opposite New York City. At 3 o'clock on the morning of Aug. 19, Maj. Harry Lee, with a force of 300 picked men, made a descent upon the fort and in a short engagement killed 30 men and took 160 prisoners. The British having retired to a small circular redoubt too strong for Lee's men, he returned to camp with his prisoners. Congress rewarded Lee with thanks and a gold medal.

Paupers, Foreign:
Introduction of, into United States, 1686, 2368.

Legislation respecting, recommended, 4757.

Request of President to withdraw articles regarding, from consideration of House, 1692.

Involuntary deportation of convicts, idiots, insane persons, and, to United States, referred to, 4219, 4588.

Pawnee Indians. (See Indian Tribes.)

Pawnee Reservation, Ind. Ter., enlargement of, bill for, 4695.

Paymaster General. (See War Department and Army.)

Payson Forest Reserve, Utah, proclaimed, 6849, 7273.

Pea Patch Island, Delaware River:
Fortifications for, 1038, 1725.

Jurisdiction of, should be secured by Government, 1725.

Private claims to, 695, 799.

Proceedings to try title to, referred to, 1809.

Pea Ridge (Ark.), Battle of.—Called by the Confederates the battle of Elk Horn. In December, 1861, Gen. Samuel R. Curtis took command of the 12,000 Federal troops at Rolla, Mo., and advanced against Gen. Sterling Price, who retreated before him into Arkansas. Gen. Price was joined by Gen. Ben. McCulloch. In January Gen. Earl Van Dorn assumed command of the combined Confederate forces, estimated at 16,000, including some 5,000 Cherokee Indians recruited for the service by Albert Pike. Curtis had about 10,000 men in line and forty-eight pieces of artillery. March 7, 1862, Van Dorn attacked Curtis in his position on Pea Ridge, a line of bluffs along Sugar Creek, in Benton County, Ark. Skillful manipulation of the artillery in Sigel's division did much toward determining the result. Fighting continued all day, and during the night both armies changed positions. The battle was renewed at sunrise on the 8th, and after two hours Van Dorn's forces retreated. The Confederate Generals McCulloch and McIntosh were killed and Price and Slack were wounded. The Confederate losses were about 1,300. The Union army lost 1,351 in killed, wounded, and missing.

Peace Commission:
In 1867, treaties concluded by, 4005.
Spanish-American, at Paris, 6321, 6322.

Peace Congress, International, at Washington, 4684, 4717.
Invitation extended, American nations to attend, 4685.
Postponement of, referred to, 4717.

Peace Establishment of Navy. (See Navy.)

Peace, International.—The most powerful factors in the bringing about of universal peace have been democracy and education. The one has taken the powers of peace and war from sovereigns and ruling classes and has placed them in the custody of those on whose shoulders the scourge of war must inevitably fall—the masses. The other has dissipated the racial and religious bigotry bred by ignorance and instilled a wholesome broadness of view and charity for all men into the minds of the young of successive generations, so that, in the occidental world, there remains to-day scarcely a vestige of the old national antipathies.

Viewing the movement for international peace thus—as a movement in which the working masses of all races and all nations are interested—it is peculiarly pleasant to note that the first important instance of arbitration was afforded by the world's foremost popular governments, Great Britain and the United States. The story is told in the article entitled "Alabama Claims."

Since that glorious achievement the movement for arbitration, for universal peace, and for disarmament has progressed rapidly. The article, "Hague Peace Conference," describes a recent achievement of the propaganda.

The longest step forward was taken in August, 1911, when President Taft negotiated with Great Britain and France (see p. 7997) treaties contemplating the arbitrament of *all* questions. They differed from previous pacts having for their purpose the arbitration of international controversies by frankly including in the differences susceptible of adjudication even questions involving national honor, theretofore the most elastic pretexts of war. An idea of the character of the treaties (which were the same in each case) may best be obtained by following the steps provided for therein in a supositious case of an act contrary to the Monroe Doctrine on the part of Great Britain. Even though such an injury to our national pride aroused a fervor throughout the country as passionate as the popular sentiment that forced the government to declare war in 1898, and even though public opinion and the administration were united in the belief that the question was not properly subject to arbitration, yet would we be bound by the treaty to request Great Britain, through diplomatic channels, to appoint three members to constitute with three American members the Joint High Commission of Inquiry provided for by the treaty. Either party might, according to the treaty, postpone convening the Commission until one year from the date of our request, thus affording opportunity for warlike preparations, for diplomatic negotiations, or for moderate counsels, as the case might be; but if neither party desires such postponement the Commission would convene immediately. The six Joint High Commissioners would hear the two sides of the controversy, subpœna and administer oaths to witnesses, and make a report which should elucidate the facts, define the issues, and contain such recommendations as it may deem appropriate. This report would not be considered as a decision on the facts or the law, and, if five or all of the six Commissioners considered the matter properly subject to adjudication, the controversy would, under the treaty, go to some arbitral tribunal like that at The Hague for settlement, no matter whether or not the people of both countries were unanimous in demanding war or not.

Peace Note:

From President Wilson to Belligerent Nations, 8190.

Belgian Reply to, 8196.

Entente Allies' Reply to, 8195.

Germany's Reply to, 8193.

Peace Societies. (See Pacifist.)—Among the prominent peace societies in the United States may be mentioned the American Union Against Militarism; the Emergency Peace Federation (organized Feb. 7, 1917); the Women's Peace Party; the American Peace Society; the World Court League, which aims for the establishment of an international Supreme Court; the Carnegie Peace Foundation, which seeks to prepare the way for perpetual peace by education; and the League to Enforce Peace (q. v.). Of these, the only ones actively to oppose the entrance of the United States into the European War were the first two mentioned, which, after the declaration of war, devoted themselves to opposing such war measures as censorship and conscription. The American Committee on War Finance was a committee growing out of the American Union Against Militarism, and agitated for an increase in taxation which would enable the war to be met by the present, instead of by future generations. After war was declared, the Emergency Peace Federation called a Conference for discussing terms of peace on May 30, 1917. The Religious Society of Friends, who refuse to participate in war, also had their peace committees active during the war agitation.

Peace Treaties.—When William Jennings Bryan was appointed Secretary of State by President Wilson in 1913, he conceived a plan for the advancement of the cause of peace throughout the world by means of treaties pledging all nations to submit their grievances with other nations to representatives of disinterested nations for adjustment instead of resorting to war. They were on the same plan but on a broader scale than President Taft's treaties with Great Britain and France. These provided for a year's delay on request of either party before resort to arms, and in the meantime a joint high commission of three to investigate the dispute. The senate eliminated so much of the Taft treaties as to make them valueless and they were never signed.

Bryan's idea was not so much arbitration as delay for a year, or at least six months, during which time investigations should be made and neither nation should increase its army or navy. It was informally advanced at a grapejuice banquet given to some forty members of the diplomatic corps in Washington in April, 1913. President Wilson acquiesced in the movement, and thirty-nine treaties were prepared. The text of the original treaties follows:

Article I.—The high contracting parties agree that all disputes between them, of every nature whatsoever, which diplomacy shall fail to adjust, shall be submitted for investigation and report to an International Commission, to be constituted in the manner prescribed in the next succeeding Article; and they agree not to declare war or begin hostilities during such investigation and report.

Article II.—The International Commission shall be composed of five members, to be appointed as follows: One member shall be chosen from each country, by the Government thereof; one member shall be chosen by each Government from some third country; the fifth member shall be chosen by common agreement between the two Governments. The expenses of the Commission shall be paid by the two Governments in equal proportion.

The International Commission shall be appointed within four months after the exchange of the ratifications of this treaty; and vacancies shall be filled according to the manner of the original appointment.

Article III.—In case the high contracting parties shall have failed to adjust a dispute by diplomatic methods, they shall at once refer it to the International Commission for investigation and report. The International Commission may, however, act upon its own initiative, and in such case it shall notify both Governments and request their cooperation in the investigation.

The report of the International Commission shall be completed within one year after the date on which it shall declare its investigation to have begun, unless the high contracting parties shall extend the time by mutual agreement. The report shall be prepared in triplicate; one copy shall be presented to each Government, and the third retained by the Commission for its files.

The high contracting parties reserve the right to act independently on the subject-matter of the dispute after the report of the Commission shall have been submitted.

* Article IV.—Pending the investigation and report of the International Commission, the high contracting parties agree not to increase their military or naval programs, unless danger from a third power should compel such increase, in which case the party feeling itself menaced shall confidentially communicate the fact in writing to the other contracting party, whereupon the latter shall also be released from its obligation to maintain its military and naval status quo.

Article V.—The present treaty shall be ratified by the President of the United States of America, by and with the advice and consent of the Senate thereof; and by the President of the Republic of Guatemala, with the approval of the Congress thereof; and the ratifications shall be

* Article IV was eliminated by most of the signatories.

exchanged as soon as possible. It shall take effect immediately after the exchange of ratification, and shall continue in force for a period of five years; and it shall thereafter remain in force until twelve months after one of the high contracting parties has given notice to the other of an intention to terminate it.

In witness whereof the respective plenipotentiaries have signed the present treaty and have affixed thereunto their seals.

Done in Washington on the twentieth day of September, in the year of our Lord nineteen hundred and thirteen.

After the elimination of Article IV and some other changes in phraseology thirty of the thirty-nine governments to which it had been submitted indicated tentative acceptance of the proposal. Of the nine which refused two later signed. By the time the European war was well under way, peace treaties had been signed by Italy, Argentina, Bolivia, Brazil, Russia, Norway, Persia, Portugal, Denmark, Chile, Costa Rica, Honduras, Nicaragua, The Netherlands, Switzerland, Salvador, Guatemala, Panama, Uruguay and Venezuela.

Peace Without Victory Address, President Wilson's, 8199.

Peach Tree Creek (Ga.), Battle of.— July 17, 1864, Sherman's army advanced across the Chattahoochee River and Johnston fell back toward Atlanta. Just at this time Johnston was superseded in command of the Southern army by Gen. John B. Hood. Before the Federal forces could be brought into line of battle before Atlanta they were attacked by Hood's army near Peach Tree Creek, July 20, 1864. The attack fell mainly upon Newton's division of the Fourth Corps, the Twentieth Corps, and Johnston's division of the Fourteenth Corps. After a severe battle the Confederates retired into their intrenchments, leaving upon the field 500 dead, 1,000 wounded, 7 stand of colors, and many prisoners. The Federal loss in killed, wounded, and missing was 1,500. Gen. Hood censured Hardee for the reverse.

Peacock, The.—A United States sloop of war, carrying eighteen guns, commanded by Capt. Lewis Warrington. On April 29, 1814, when off the coast of Florida, this vessel attacked the British brig *Epervier*, also mounting eighteen guns. After a battle lasting forty minutes, in which 22 of her men were killed or wounded, the *Epervier* surrendered. It proved a rich prize, as it had on board $118,000 in specie. On June 30, 1815, the *Peacock* attacked and captured the *Nautilus*, of fourteen guns. This capture took place after the treaty of peace. Next day, on ascertaining this fact Capt. Warrington released the *Nautilus*, and returned home.

Pearl Harbor, Hawaii, improvement and fortification recommended, 7484.

Pearl River, Hawaiian Islands, improvement of harbor of, and establishment of naval station at, recommended, 5623.

Pelican State.—A nickname for Louisiana (q. v.). (See also States); sometimes also nicknamed the Creole State.

Pembina, Minn., proclamation granting privileges of other ports to, 2859.

Penitentiaries.—The first penitentiary in the United States was founded in Philadelphia in 1786 through the influence of the Society of Friends. This was followed soon afterwards by the New York prisons at Sing Sing and Auburn. Sept. 23, 1789, Congress recommended to the several states to make it the duty of keepers of jails to receive prisoners committed under authority of the United States. In 1790 the legislature of Pennsylvania passed a law to try the system of solitary confinement of prisoners at hard labor as a reformatory measure. A society for the improvement of prison discipline and for the reformation of juvenile offenders was established in Boston in 1815, and in 1825 the House of Refuge on Blackwell's Island, N. Y., the first institution in the United States for reforming juvenile delinquents, was opened. The contract system of leasing prisoners to private parties began with the Mississippi penitentiary Feb. 21, 1867.

*Federal Penitentiaries.—*All territorial penitentiaries were placed under control of United States marshals and the Attorney-General was authorized to prescribe rules for their government by act of Congress of June 10, 1871. In 1874 the United States Military Prison was established at Fort Leavenworth. In 1886 a United States jail was located at Fort Smith, Ark. In 1891 Congress authorized three United States prisons, there being now, besides those mentioned above, a United States penitentiary at Atlanta, Ga., one on McNeil's Island, State of Washington, a United States jail in the District of Columbia, and a Territorial prison at Yuma, Arizona. There is also one penitentiary in Hawaii, and in the Philippine Islands two such institutions for the confinement of offenders against the civil law. In the several states, under state jurisdiction, there are altogether fifty-six prisons and penitentiaries. United States prisoners not confined in Federal institutions are kept in those of the various states.

Penitentiaries:

State laws regulating, discussed, 5755.

Uniform credit for good behavior in, recommended, 5755.

Penitentiaries, Government:

Erection of, recommended, 4836, 5102, 5363, 5880, 5969, 6161.

Military prison at Fort Leavenworth, use of, as discussed, 6161.

Recommended, 5969.

Penitentiary Congress, International, at London, 4162.

Pennant.—A streamer-like pointed flag.

Penn Yan, N. Y., special agent to take charge of post-office in, referred to, 3799.

Pennamite War. (See Wyoming Controversy.)

Pennsylvania.—One of the thirteen original states; nickname, "The Keystone State"; motto, "Virtue, Liberty and Independence." It extends from lat. 39° 43' to 42° 15' north and from long. 74° 40' to 80° 34' west. It is bounded on the north by Lake Erie and New York, on the east by New York and New Jersey (separated from both by the Delaware River), on the south by Delaware, Maryland and West Virginia, and on the west by Ohio and West Virginia. It has an area of 45,126 square miles. Pennsylvania was originally named Sylvania ("forest country"). In 1681 William Penn obtained a grant of 40,000 square miles of land from Charles II in payment of a debt of £16,000 due Penn's father, an admiral in the English navy. The King gave the territory the name of Pennsylvania in honor of Penn. In 1682 the city of Philadelphia was laid out on plans drawn in England. Penn established a popular form of proprietary government and offered inducements to immigrants by his wise administration and honorable dealings with the Indians. His rights passed to 'his heirs, from whom they were purchased by the state in 1776. Pennsylvania had been settled by a colony of Swedes in 1638, prior to the grant of the territory to Penn. The United States Constitution was ratified by a state convention Dec. 12, 1787. A new state constitution was made in 1790, another in 1838, and the present in 1873.

The state is traversed from northeast to southwest by low parallel ranges of the Alleghanies, and is drained by the Ohio, Susquehanna, and Delaware Rivers. It is the first state in the production of petroleum and the manufacture of iron and second in general manufactures.

Pennsylvania so far exceeds all the rest of the states in the value of its mineral products as to stand almost alone. Exclusive of the value of pig iron, coke, and other derived or secondary products not included in the total, the value of Pennsylvania's mineral production is nearly one-fourth that of the entire country; and in 1913, according to figures of the United States Geological Survey computed in co-operation with the Pennsylvania Topographic and Geologic Survey Commission, it equaled the combined value of the production of West Virginia, Illinois, Ohio, and California, the next four states in the value of their mineral products.

Pennsylvania derives its mineral wealth almost entirely from nonmetalliferous mining operations. Except for a small amount of copper it produces none of the precious or semiprecious metals, and the only other metal which figures in the total production of the state is iron, of which a small quantity (less than 500,000 tons of ore in 1913) is mined. In addition, however, to being the premier state in the production of coal, Pennsylvania leads also in the manufacture of cement, the burning of lime, and the production of mineral paints, sand, slate, and stone. It is second in the value of clay products and natural gas, and sixth in the production of petroleum.

Although not an iron-ore state, Pennsylvania is by far the leading producer of pig iron, which is obtained from the Lake Superior ores. The production in 1913 was 12,871,349 long tons, valued at $197,726,-314. If the value of the pig iron made in Pennsylvania were added to the value of the other products of the state, the total values for 1913 would have exceeded $700,-000,000, which is more than one-fourth of the value of the total mineral production of the United States.

The production of coal in Pennsylvania in 1912 amounted to 246,227,086 short tons, valued at $346,993,123; in 1913 the value was $388,220,933, an increase of $41,227,-810, or 12 per cent, over 1912.

Second in importance among Pennsylvania's mineral industries is the manufacture of Portland cement, closely followed by the clay-working industry. The production of cement in 1913 was 28,060,495 barrels, valued at $24,268,800, against 27,-625,340 barrels, valued at $18,945,835, in 1912. The value of the clay products, exclusive of raw clay mined and sold, increased from $21,537,221 in 1912 to $24,-231,482 in 1913. Although ranking second in the total value of its clay products, Pennsylvania is first in the production of brick and tile. A large part of the fire clay is mined in connection with coal min-

ing and becomes in reality a by-product of that industry.

Fourth in importance among Pennsylvania's mineral products is natural gas, in the production of which Pennsylvania was the leading state until 1910. In 1910 West Virginia attained first place in the production of this fuel, and she has continued to hold it, but Pennsylvania continues to rank first in its consumption, making up for the shortage in its own production by bringing in gas from West Virginia. The value of the natural gas produced in Pennsylvania increased from $18,539,672 in 1912 to $21,-695,845 in 1913.

Up to 1894 Pennsylvania was the leading state in the production of petroleum, but in 1895 it was exceeded by Ohio, the production of Pennsylvania having begun to decline in 1891, while Ohio was approaching its maximum, which was attained in 1896. In more recent years West Virginia, Texas, California, Illinois, and Oklahoma have all risen rapidly and passed Pennsylvania in the production of petroleum. On account of the higher grade of Pennsylvania's oil, however, it still ranks fifth in value of production. The output of petroleum in Pennsylvania increased slightly in quantity, from 7,837,948 barrels in 1912 to 7,963,282 barrels in 1913, with an increase of over 50 per cent in value, from $12,886,752 to $19,805,452.

The number of manufacturing establishments in Pennsylvania having an annual output valued at $500 or more at the beginning of 1915 was 27,521. The amount of capital invested was $3,149,411,000, giving employment to 1,060,562 persons, using material valued at $1,688,921,000, and turning out finished goods worth $2,832,349,000. Salaries and wages paid amounted to $672,563,000.

May 9, 1900, with the exception that the requirements as to dependence are eliminated. This act therefore supersedes the act of June 27, 1890, in so far as the claims of widows are concerned, and pensions are not now being granted to widows under the act of 1890 upon applications executed and filed on or after April 19, 1908.

There is no law granting service pensions to any person for service rendered since 1858, aside from the allowances made under the provisions of sections 4756 and 4757, Revised Statutes, for twenty years' and ten years' service, respectively, in the United States Navy or Marine Corps.

There were added to the rolls during the year ended June 30, 1911, the names of 26,200 new pensioners. The number of pensioners lost from the rolls during the year was 55,185, showing a decrease of 28,985 on the rolls, as compared with the close of the fiscal year 1910. There were 892,098 pensioners on the rolls June 30, 1911. The pension disbursements for the fiscal year ending June 30, 1914, were 172,·417,546.

The dollar-a-day pension law of May 11, 1912, provides that any person who served ninety days or more in the military or naval service of the United States during the late Civil War, and who has been honorably discharged therefrom, and who has reached the age of sixty-two years or over, on making proof of such facts is entitled to receive a pension as follows: Age sixty-two years—For a service of ninety days, $13.00 per month; six months, $13.50; one year, $14.00; one and one-half years, $14.50; two years, $15.00; two and one-half years, $15.50; and three years and more, $16.00. Age sixty-six years—For a service of ninety days, $15.00 per month; six months, $15.50; one year, $16.00; one and one-half years, $16.50; two years, $17.00; two and one-half years, $18.00, and three years and more, $19.00. Age seventy years—For a service of ninety days, $18.00 per month; six months, $19.00; one year, $20.00; one and one-half years, $21.50; two years, $23.00; two and one-half years, $24.00, and three years and more, $25.00. Age seventy-five years—For a service of ninety days, $21.00 per month; six months, $22.50; one year, $24.00; one and one-half years, $27.00, and two years and more, $30.00. And such pension shall commence from the date of filing the application in the Bureau of Pensions. Any person who served sixty days or more in the war with Mexico, and who received an honorable discharge, is entitled to $30.00 per month. Any person who was wounded in battle or in line of duty in the Civil War, and is now unfit for manual labor by reason thereof, or who from disease or other causes incurred in line of duty resulting in his disability, is now unable to perform manual labor, is entitled to $30.00 per month.

The following are the rates for total disability from causes incident to the service:

Army.—Lieutenant-colonel and all officers of higher rank, $30; major, surgeon, and paymaster, $25; captain, provost marshal, and chaplain, $20; first lieutenant, assistant surgeon, and deputy provost marshal, $17; second lieutenant and enrolling officer, $15; enlisted men, $8.

Navy.—Captain and officers of higher rank, commander, lieutenant commanding and master commanding, surgeon, paymaster, and chief engineer, respectively ranking with commander by law, $30; lieutenant, surgeon, paymaster, and chief engineer, respectively ranking with lieutenant by law, and passed assistant surgeon, $25; master,

professor of mathematics, assistant surgeon, assistant paymaster and chaplain, $20; first assistant engineer, ensign, and pilot, $15; cadet midshipman, passed midshipman, midshipman, clerks of admirals, paymasters, or other officers commanding vessels, second and third assistant engineers, master's mate, and warrant officers, $10; enlisted men, $8.

Civil Service.—President Taft on several occasions advocated pensions for civil employees of the government, which should be provided by a fund jointly accumulated by the government and the employees. (See pages 7551, 7697 and 7754.) His argument was based on the grounds of justice to the employee and improvement of service. A bill was introduced to that effect, but failed of passage.

Marine Corps.—Lieutenant-colonel and officers of higher rank, $30; major, $25; captain, $20; first lieutenant, $17; second lieutenant, $15; enlisted men, $8.

The number of pensioners and the amounts paid each year from 1869 to the fiscal year ended June 30, 1916, as reported by the Commissioner of Pensions, follows:

Year	Number of Pensioners on the Rolls			Paid as Pensions
	Invalids	Widows, etc.	Total	
1870	87,521	111,165	198,686	$29,351,488.78
1871	93,394	114,101	207,495	28,518,792.62
1872	113,954	118,275	232,229	29,752,746.81
1873	119,500	118,911	238,411	26,982,063.89
1874	121,628	114,613	227,241	30,206,778.99
1875	122,989	111,832	234,821	29,270,404.76
1876	124,239	107,898	232,137	27,936,209.53
1877	128,723	103,381	232,104	28,182,821.72
1878	131,649	92,349	223,998	26,786,009.44
1879	138,615	104,140	242,755	33,664,428.92
1880	145,410	105,392	250,802	56,689,229.08
1881	164,110	104,720	268,830	50,583,405.35
1882	182,633	103,064	285,697	54,313,172.05
1883	206,042	97,616	303,658	60,427,573.81
1884	225,470	97,286	322,756	57,912,387.47
1885	247,146	97,979	345,125	65,171,937.12
1886	270,346	95,437	365,783	64,091,142.90
1887	306,298	99,709	406,007	73,752,997.08
1888	343,701	108,856	452,557	78,950,501.67
1889	373,699	116,026	489,725	88,842,720.58
1890	415,654	122,290	537,944	106,093,850.39
1891	536,821	139,339	676,160	117,312,690.50
1892	703,242	172,826	876,068	139,394,147.11
1893	759,706	206,306	966,012	156,906,637.94
1894	754,382	215,162	969,544	139,986,726.17
1895	751,456	219,068	970,524	139,812,294.30
1896	748,514	222,164	970,678	138,220,704.46
1897	747,492	228,522	976,014	139,949,717.35
1898	758,511	235,203	993,714	144,651,879.80
1899	754,104	237,415	991,519	138,355,052.95
1900	752,510	241,019	993,529	138,462,130.65
1901	748,649	249,086	997,735	138,531,483.84
1902	739,443	260,003	999,446	137,504,267.99
1903	729,356	267,189	996,545	137,759,653.71
1904	720,921	273,841	994,762	141,093,571.49
1905	717,761	280,680	998,441	141,142,861.33
1906	701,483	284,488	985,971	139,000,288.25
1907	679,937	287,434	967,371	138,155,412.46
1908	658,071	293,616	951,687	153,093,086.27
1909	632,557	313,637	946,194	161,973,703.77
1910	602,180	318,903	921,083	159,974,056.08
1911	570,050	322,048	892,098	157,325,160.35
1912	538,000	322,294	860,294	152,986,433.72
1913	503,633	316,567	820,200	174,171,660.80
1914	470,331	314,908	785,239	172,417,546.26
1915	437,723	310,424	748,147	165,518,266
1916	403,120	296,089	709,572	159,155,090.

The amounts that have been paid for pensions to soldiers, sailors, and marines, their widows, minor children, and dependent relatives on account of military and naval service in the several wars and in the regular service since the foundation of the government to June 30, 1915, are as follows:

Revolutionary War (estimate)$ 70,000,000
War of 1812
(Service pension) 45,991,743
Indian Wars (Service pension) 13,790,299
War with Mexico (Service). 50,422,229
Civil War 4,765,075,020
War with Spain and insurrection in the Philippine Islands 53,744,668
Regular establishment 39,098,319
Unclassified 16,508,449
                          ───────────
Total $5,054,630,727

Pensions:

Act—

For relief of dependent parents and honorably discharged soldiers and sailors now disabled and dependent, vetoed, 5134.

To allow pension of $37 per month to soldiers losing arm and leg, returned for amendment, 4382.

To provide for settlement of claims barred by limitations, opinions regarding, referred to, 115, 125.

Acts granting, vetoed. (See Cleveland, Grover; Grant, Ulysses S.)

Army officers not allowed, except in certain cases, 1005.

Civil retirement and contributory pension system, 7697.

Civil Service, for age and disability, approved, 7754.

Disability, pension act dismissed, 5552, 5762, 5883, 5977.

Discussed by President—

Adams, J. Q., 874, 927, 958.

Arthur, 4645.

Cleveland, 4945, 5108, 5382, 5883, 5977, 6168.

Grant, 3995, 4066, 4156, 4207, 4254, 4307.

Harrison, Benj., 5484, 5550, 5552, 5639, 5762.

Jackson, 1019.

Johnson, 3560, 3650, 3652, 3774, 3880.

Lincoln, 3253, 3452.

McKinley, 6345, 6388, 6452.

Madison, 482.

Monroe, 588.

Roosevelt, 6803.

Taft, 7697, 7754.

Tyler, 1902.

Expenditures for. (See Discussed, *ante*.)

Foreign pensioners, provision for payment of expenses of obtaining evidence regarding, recommended, 4668.

Frauds discussed. (See Pension Laws.)

Laws in regard to. (See Pension Laws.)

Names and ages of pensioners should be taken with census, 1744.

Naval pensioners and pension fund referred to, 1810, 1837, 4408, 6283.

Transfer of payment of, to Navy Department recommended, 4060.

Pension obtained by fraud. (See Pension Laws.)

Payments to invalids, order regarding, 6308.

Pensioners entering Confederate army should be stricken from rolls, 3253.

Pensioners in Southern States, recommendations regarding restoration of certain, 4254.

Report regarding, transmitted, 3061, 4408.

Revolutionary War—

Amount paid pensioners of, referred to, 602, 927.

Compensation to agents in paying, referred to, 2354.

Sums paid to, and residences of pensioners referred to, 602.

Pensions, Bureau of.—Up to 1833 the disbursement of pensions had been under the supervision of the Secretary of War and the Secretary of the Navy. In that year Congress established the Pension Bureau and placed J. L. Edwards in charge. He immediately assumed the business theretofore under the War Department, and in 1840 the pension affairs of the Navy Department were transferred to this Bureau. In 1849, when the Department of the Interior was created, the Pension Bureau was placed under its jurisdiction. The chief officer of this Bureau is called the Commissioner of Pensions.

Pensions, Bureau of:

Expenditures of. (See Pensions discussed.)

Good work of, 6803.

Increase in clerical force of, 5552. Recommended, 4673.

Transfer of, from Interior Department to War Department recommended, 4060.

Pensions, Commissioner of, provision for continuance of, recommended, 1789.

Peoples Party. (See Populist or Peoples Party.)

Peoria Indians. (See Indian Tribes.)

"Perdicaris Alive or Raizuli Dead."—In 1904, Ion H. Perdicaris, an American citizen, was held for ransom by Raizuli, a bandit in Morocco. After mild negotiations had failed to obtain the release of Perdicaris, John Hay, then Secretary of State, by direction of President Roosevelt sent to Mr. Gummere, the American Consul at Tangier, the famous ultimatum cablegram: "We want Perdicaris alive or Raizuli dead." The result was the immediate release of Perdicaris.

Perjury.—In law the willful giving, under oath lawfully administered in a judicial proceeding, of false testimony in regard to a matter or thing material to the issue or point of inquiry. The early Romans threw perjurers from the Tarpeian Rock. The Greeks branded them with a mark of infamy. After the Empire became Christianized any person who swore falsely upon the Gospels was sentenced to have his tongue cut out. The canons of the early church imposed eleven years' penance. In some countries the perjurer was liable to any punishment to which his false testimony had exposed an innocent person. In England perjury was punished by fine, the pillory, and imprisonment. It is now in both England and America a statutory offense, punishable by fine or imprisonment, or both.

Permanent Taxation. (See Revenue, Public; Taxation.)

Pernicious Activity.—A phrase contained in an Executive order of President Cleveland. It occurred in the following sentence: "Individual interest and activity in political affairs are by no means condemned. Officeholders are neither disfranchised nor forbidden the exercise of political privileges, but their privileges are not enlarged nor is their duty to party increased to pernicious activity by officeholding." (5079.) (See Obtrusive Partisanship.)

Perpetual Emigrating Fund Co., suit instituted by Government for termination of, discussed, 5379.

Perry's Victory Exposition.—The one hundredth anniversary of the victory of Commodore Oliver Hazard Perry over the British fleet under command of Captain Barclay in the battle of Lake Erie, Sept. 10, 1813, was celebrated by an historical and educational exposition at Put-in-Bay Island during the summer of 1913 and a dedication of a national memorial to Commodore Perry and the American seamen who perished in that conflict, the remains of many of whom have reposed in unmarked graves on Put-in-Bay Island for nearly a hundred years. The memorial cost more than a million dollars. Congress has appropriated $250,000.

The State of Ohio took the initiative in the project by necessary legislation providing for the appointment of commissioners to carry forward such plans as they deemed advisable, and since that time Pennsylvania, Michigan, Illinois, Wisconsin and other states, nine in all, by legislation and the appointment of commissioners, joined in the enterprise.

The officers of the Ohio Commission were: President, William H. Reinhart, Sandusky; Vice-President, George H. Worthingham, Cleveland; Secretary, Webster P. Huntington, Columbus; Treasurer, S. M. Johannsen, Put-In-Bay. Among the other members of the commission were Lieut-Gen. Nelson A. Miles, Rear-Admiral Charles E. Clark, Col. Henry Watterson, Myron T. Herrick and Richmond P. Hobson.

The exposition opened July 4, 1913, and closed Sept 10. Its historical and educational interests were under the direction of the historical societies and the universities and colleges of the states participating. The only industrial feature related to an exhibit for the promotion of the shipping interests of the great lakes. In conjunction with the permanent memorial to Commodore Perry the exposition commemorated the one hundredth anniversay of Gen. William Henry Harrison's northwestern campaign.

Perryville (Ky.), Battle of.—Oct. 1, 1862, the Confederate forces under Bragg and Kirby Smith having united at Frankfort, Ky., Bragg issued a proclamation calling the people of Kentucky to his assistance. He inaugurated a provisional government at Frankfort, with Richard Hawes as governor. Buell's army, divided into three corps, under McCook, Gilbert, and Crittenden, advanced against the Confederates by way of Louisville. Oct. 8, McCook's corps was attacked near Perryville, and after a fight lasting all day Bragg's army was repulsed. The engagement, while not general all day, was severe. During the night the Confederates retired, and later retreated to Cumberland Gap, leaving 1,200 wounded and sick behind. The Federal losses were 916 killed (including Generals Jackson and Terrell), 2,943 wounded, and 489 missing—a total of 4,348. The Confederates lost 510 killed, 2,635 wounded and 251 missing—a total of 3,396.

Persia.—Persia is a kingdom in the west of the continent of Asia, and is bounded on the north by Russian Transcaucasia, the Caspian Sea, and Russian Transcaspia, on the east by Afghanistan and British Baluchistan; on the south by the Arabian Sea and the Persian Gulf; and on the west by Asiatic Turkey. The territory thus defined lies, approximately, between 44°-63° E. longitude, and between 25°-39° 45' N. latitude, an area of 630,000 square miles. It is called Iran by the natives, and is referred to in the Bible as Elam.

Physical Features.—The kingdom occupies the western and greater portion of the Iranian Plateau (which extends between the valleys of the Indus and the Tigris), and consists of a series of plateaus. The coast of the Caspian is low lying and forest clad; the shores of the Persian Gulf and Arabian Sea are low and sandy, but elsewhere the country between the mountain ranges is elevated. In the southeast are two volcanoes, Kuh i Basman (dormant), about 12,000 feet in height, and Kuh i Nushadar (active), a triple-peaked cone of 12,681 feet. The Kizil Uzain, the Herhaz, the Gurgan and the Atrek rivers flow into the Caspian Sea. Many rivers into the Persian Gulf and Arabian Sea. The salt swamps of the depressions of the interior are watered by many streams, which soon lose themselves in the saline swamps or dry salt area. There are many lakes, the largest being Lake Urmia, about 4,000 feet above sea level, its area being close on 1,000 square miles and its waters so salt that fish cannot live therein.

History.—The country now known as Persia formed part, at various times, of a much greater kingdom, and under Cyrus (560-528 B.C.) was included in a mighty empire extending from Asia Minor and Syria to the Indies. Attempts at a westward extension under Darius (521-485 B.C.) and Xerxes (485-465 B.C.) were checked by the victories of the Greeks at the battles of Marathon (490), Thermopylæ (480), Salamis (480) and Platæ (479 B.C.). Under a later dynasty (226-651 A.D.), known as the Sassanians (Assassins or Isma'ilites), the Persian empire was extended once again, to be consolidated by Chosroes (or Khosra), over an area from the Red Sea to the Indus, and from Arabia into the heart of Central Asia. From the eighth to the tenth centuries A.D. Persia fell under Moslem rule, and with a short interval of independence was afterwards overrun by the Mongols from the northeast, forming part of the territories of Jenghiz Khan at his death in 1272. A further period of independence was interrupted by the conquest of Persia by Timur (Tamburlane the Great), from whose death (1405) to the present time the kingdom has been independent, under the rule of a Shah, the reign of Nadir Shah (1736-1747) being the most brilliant in the annals of modern Persia. After the death of Nadir, Afghanistan asserted its independence, and the nineteenth century witnessed the gradual decay of the kingdom. The rule of the Shah was absolute and despotic from the earliest times, but many internal dissensions, culminating in the revolution of 1905-1906, have marked the later years of Persian history and have further weakened the powers of resistance to external forces. Owing to increasing popular discontent with a corrupt and incompetent administration and an extravagant Court, a nationalist movement began in December, 1905. Owing to the vacillation of the Shah and the anarchical state of affairs, England and Russia made strong representations in favor of the restoration of a constitutional régime. A Russian force eventually crossed the frontier, while the revolutionary bands concentrated on Teheran, which was occupied without much fighting on July 13, 1909. The Shah was deposed by the National Council, and his son, aged eleven years, appointed to succeed him. It declared its intention of strengthening the army, punishing disorders, reforming the police and law courts, improving education and provincial administration, and employing foreign advisers in certain offices. In October, 1910, England demanded the restoration within three months of security on the southern trade routes, failing which she would take over the policing of the Bushire-Isfahan route. In 1911 the ex-Shah invaded Persia from Russian territory, but after he was defeated and driven out, his followers continued the struggle. Russia and England despatched further troops; and while the Russian troops remain in the country, the British troops were withdrawn, as Great Britain preferred to give the Persian Government time to restore order themselves, and, with that view, strongly support the gendarmerie being formed under Swedish officers.

Government.—In August, 1906, the Shah, admitting the need for reforms, granted a Constitution. The first elections for the Mejliss (National Council or Consultative Assembly) were held in October, 1906. A Cabinet of eight responsible Ministers was formed in September, 1907. In October, 1907, the Shah signed a new Constitution limiting the sovereign prerogatives and ecclesiastical authority, and granting liberty of conscience of the person, of education, of the press, of association, and of speech. But he broke his pledges and violently dissolved the Mejliss. A fresh nationalist movement sprang up, Tabriz being the centre of revolt. Ruler: Sultan Ahmed Mirza, Shah in Shah (King of Kings); born at Tabriz, Jan. 20, 1898; succeeded to the throne July 17, 1909. Regent: Aboul Kassim Khan, Nazer-ul-Mulk; appointed Sept. 25, 1910. The young King was crowned at Teheran July 21, 1914. The Executive government is entrusted to a cabinet of seven ministers.

Under the constitution outlined in the rescript of Shah Muhammad Ali (who abdicated on July 16, 1909, and was succeeded by his son, the present ruler), issued on August 5, 1906, a legislature (mejliss) was to be inaugurated, consisting of an upper house, or Senate, of sixty members (thirty appointed and thirty elected), and of a National Council of 156 members elected for two years and meeting annually on October 8.

The administration of justice is entrusted to co-ordinate authorities, offences under the written or religious law being dealt with by the Sheikhs-ul-Islam and subordinate priests, and those against customary law by the governors, lieutenant-governors and their subordinates.

By the Anglo-Russian Convention of Aug. 31, 1907, Great Britain and Russia mutually engaged to respect the integrity and independence of Persia, while marking out certain regions in southeastern and northern Persia, in which each had, for geographical and economic reasons, special interests. Russia engaged not to seek political or commercial concessions (for railways, mines, etc.) beyond a line running from the Afghan frontier via Gazik, Birjand and Kerman, to Bunder Abbas, while Great Britain made a like engagement as regards a line running from Kasr-i-Shirin via Isfahan, Yezd and Kakhh, to the point of intersection of the Russian and Afghan frontiers. In the so-called Neutral Zone either of the contracting parties is at liberty to obtain concessions. This includes the provinces of Arabistan and Fars, an area of 200,000 square miles, containing a million and a half of population. The Russian sphere covers 300,000 square miles, and includes the provinces of Ardalan, Astrabad, Azerbaijan, Gilan, Hamadan, Irak Ajmi, Isfahan, Karmanshah, Kasvin, Khamseh, Khorasan, Luristan, Mazandaran, Teheran and Yezd. Karman is solely British and Kuhistan is jointly British and Russian.

The debt consists of Russian and British loans to the amount of some $36,000,000. The capital is Teheran.

Persia:

Persia, Treaties with.—A treaty of friendship and commerce was concluded in 1856. Provision is made for the reception and protection of ambassadors and diplomatic agents on terms of the most favored nation; freedom of travel is secured to all citizens, and of trade in conformity with the laws of the country in which such is carried on. Such privileges as may at any time be conferred upon other powers are to be enjoyed by citizens and subjects of the two contracting powers. No exceptional or discriminating tax upon import or export is to be charged. Suits and disputes are to be tried before the proper Persian officer in the presence of the consul or of his agent or representative at the place of consular residence. Disputes between citizens of the United States are to be settled by and before the consul.

Disputes between citizens of the United States and subjects of other powers in Persia are to be settled by their consuls. The goods and effects of a citizen or subject dying in the country of the other shall be delivered to his heirs or successors; when such are not represented, the effects shall be delivered to the consul for disposition. Each country shall appoint a diplomatic agent to reside at the seat of government of the other, and three consuls, those of the United States to reside at Teheran, Bender Bushir, and Tauris; those of Persia at Washington, New York, and New Orleans. No greater number of domestics may be retained by the diplomatic agent in Persia than are allowed to Russia by treaty.

Personal-Liberty Laws.—A name given to laws passed by some of the northern states for the purpose of impeding the operations of "fugitive-slave laws." In 1840 and the years immediately prior and subsequent thereto most of the northern states enacted statutes for the protection of negroes within their borders. Indiana and Connecticut had previously provided that fugitive slaves might have trial by jury. After the Prigg decision many of the states forbade the use of their jails for the detention of fugitives. The bitter opposition in the north to the fugitive-slave law of 1850 induced many of the state legislatures to enact personal-liberty laws. Besides prohibiting the use of state jails, these laws forbade state judges and officers to assist claimants or issue writs. Trial was to be given all alleged fugitives. Such acts were passed by Vermont, Connecticut, Rhode Island, Massachusetts, Maine, Michigan, Wisconsin, Kansas, Ohio, and Pennsylvania, and heavy penalties were provided for their violation. New Jersey and California alone of the northern states sanctioned the return of fugitives. It was claimed by the people of the South that these laws were in violation of Article IV., section 2, of the Constitution, which reads as follows: "No person held to service or labor in one state, under the laws thereof, escaping into another, shall, in consequence of any law or regulation therein, be discharged from such service or labor, but shall be delivered up on claim of the party to whom such service or labor may be due."

Perthshire, The, appropriation to owners for detention of, recommended, 3247.

Peru.—Peru is a maritime country on the northwest of the South American Continent, between 1° 31'-17° 47' S. latitude (the territory between 17° 47'-19° 13' being the department of Tacna, occupied by Chile), with a coast-line on the Pacific of about 1,200 miles. It is bounded on the north by Ecuador and Colombia, on the east by Bolivia and Brazil, and on the south by Chile.

Physical Features.—The country is traversed throughout its length by the Andes, running parallel to the Pacific coast, the highest points being Huascaran (22,050 feet), Huandoy (21,100 feet), Arequipa (or Misti) volcano (20,013 feet), Hualcan (20,000 feet), and Lirima, Tocora, and Sarasara, all over 19,000 feet. There are four distinct regions, the costa, west of the Andes, a low arid desert except where watered by transverse mountain streams, but capable of irrigation; the sierra or western slopes of the Andes, the punas or mountainous wastes below the region of perpetual snow, and the inward slopes and boundless forests of the Amazonian basin.

History.—Peru was conquered in the sixteenth century by Francisco Pizarro, who subjugated the Incas (a tribe of the Quichua Indians), who had invaded the country some 500 years earlier, and for nearly three centuries Peru remained under the Spanish rule. A revolutionary

war of 1821-1824 established its independence, declared on July 28, 1821.

AREA AND POPULATION

Departments	Area in English Sq. Miles	Estimated Population 1906
Amazonas	13,941	53,000
Ancachs	16,659	317,000
Apurimac	8,186	133,000
Arequipa	21,947	172,000
Ayacucho	18,188	227,000
Cajamarca	12,545	333,000
Callao	14	34,000
Cuzco	131,305	313,000
Huancavelica	9,264	168,000
Huanuco	13,896	109,000
Ica	8,685	68,000
Junin	23,314	306,000
Lambayeque	4,593	93,000
Liberdad	10,190	188,000
Lima	13,278	250,000
Loreto	254,507	120,000
Madre de Dios	24,645	16,000
Moquegua	5,714	32,000
Piura	14,822	154,000
Puno	41,000	403,000
San Martin	31,243	33,000
Tacna	12,590	39,961
Tumbez	1,930	8,000
Total	692,616	3,569,961

If the total may be assumed at 3,500,000 the races may be approximately stated at: Whites, 480,000; Indians (Quichua and Aymará tribes and "wild" Indians of the forests of the eastern interior), 2,000,000; Half-castes (Cholos or Spanish Indian and Zambos or Spanish Negro), 875,000; Negroes, 87,500; and Asiatics (mainly Chinese), 60,000.

Government.—The constitution rests upon the fundamental law of Oct. 18, 1856 (amended Nov. 25, 1860), and is that of a democratic Republic. The President and two Vice-Presidents are elected for four years by direct vote of the people, and are ineligible for a succeeding term of office. President (1912-1916): Señor Guillero Billinghurst, installed Sept. 25, 1912, for four years.

Congress consists of a Senate and Chamber of Deputies, and meets annually on Independence Day (July 28) for ninety days. The Senate is composed of fifty-two members, the Chamber of 116 members, in each case elected by the direct vote of all male citizens aged twenty-one who can read and write or possess a small property or tax-paying qualification.

There is a Supreme Court at Lima, the members of which are appointed by Congress, and Superior Courts at Arequipa, Ayacucho, Cajamarca, Cuzco, Huaraz, Piura, Puno, and Truxillo.

The twenty Departments and three Provinces are subdivided into Provinces (110 in all), which again are parcelled out into 850 districts. At the head of the Department is a Prefect, with a sub-Prefect over each Province.

Army.—By a law of Dec. 27, 1898, service in the Army is compulsory for all citizens. (For the Army, see Armies of the World.)

Navy.—The Peruvian Navy consists of 2 modern protected cruisers (Almirante Grau and Coronel Bolognesi), one modernized cruiser (Lima), and two submarines; with certain miscellaneous craft, school ships, sailing vessels, etc.

Production and Industry.—The eastern provinces are of vast extent and fertility with a tropical climate, while the valleys running from the Andes to the coast are very fertile and are capable of development by irrigation. The staple agricultural product is sugar, while cotton is grown in large and increasing quantities. The medicinal products of the eastern provinces are valuable, and include cinchona (Peruvian bark), sarsaparilla, copaiba, cocaine, etc. India rubber is a product of the Amazonian basin, and coffee and cocoa are increasingly grown, while the sugar plantations are mainly in the costa west of the Andes. The Live Stock includes herds of guanaco, llama, and alpaca, the wool being a valuable item of the export trade. Guano is brought from the Lobos and other islands on the Pacific coast.

The mountains are rich in minerals, among which silver, quicksilver, copper and coal (of inferior quality) are conspicuous; while in the department of Tumbez, in the northwest, there are important beds of petroleum. Gold is found in many districts, but especially in the province of Carabaya, where mining on an important scale is carried on. An American syndicate has bought four-fifths of the whole mineral zone of Cerro de Pasco and many others in neighboring mining districts, and has constructed a railway from Oroya to Cerro de Pasco.

There is a lack of industrial development, but many openings exist for capital so soon as the rich land on the inward slopes of the Andes is taken up by suitable colonists.

The principal imports are coal, cotton, woollen, linen, and silk goods, drugs, earthen and stone wares, machinery, explosives, metals and manufactures thereof, oils, stationery, paper manufactures, timber, and wheat. The chief exports are sugar, copper and other ores, guano, gold, silver, cotton, llama and alpaca wool, rubber, and cocaine.

Finance.—The average revenue for four recent years was 3,164,954 libra, and the expenditures for the same time average 3,201,372 libra. The libra, the unit of value, is equivalent to the English pound or $4.8665 of United States money.

During September, 1916, the Congress of Peru had under consideration the proposed budget for the fiscal year 1917. The proposed appropriations for the various branches of the government were as follows, the amounts being in Peruvian libra, which are now quoted at par, $4.8665: Ministry of Fomento, £198,736; Foreign Relations, £58.667; Government, £553,749; Justice, £554,565; Legislative, £108,322; Treasury, £1,296,589; War and Marine, £641,609; total expenditures, £3,412,237.

The estimated revenues are based on the actual receipts during the first half of the present fiscal year, with the exception of revenues provided for in recent laws, such as the taxes on inheritances and mineral export duties. No revenue is estimated from the opium monopoly this year, as it is the desire of the executive to prohibit the sale of this drug except for medicinal purposes. The estimated revenues were as follows: Maritime customs duties, £852,680; fluvial duties, £66,000; export duties on agricultural and mineral products, £296,890; taxes, £812,587; monopolies, £774,500; postoffice, £105,100; telegraph, £32,000; wireless, £1,500; impost on circular checks, £23,000; education funds, £161,500; various revenues, £286,480; total revenues, £3,412,237.

Cities.—Capital, Lima, on the mountain stream Rimac, with a magnificent cathedral founded by Pizarro in 1540. Population (1908) 143,500. Other towns are Callao (34,346), Arequipa (40,000), Cuzco, the ancient capital of the Incas, Ayacucho and Iquitos.

Peru (see also Peru-Bolivian Confederation):

Alleged agreement between ministers of United States, Great Britain, France, and Italy in, 4745.

Claims against, of—
Members of Hydrographic Commission of the Amazon, 6099.
United States, 1594, 2193, 4463, 4919, 5988, 6092, 6335.
Arbitration of, 6335.
Convention for adjustment of, referred to, 1933, 1944, 2135, 2193, 2294, 2400, 2586, 3353, 3381, 3396, 3893, 3987, 5088.
Amendment to, recommended, 3553.
Indemnity paid, 2400.
Indemnity stipulated to be paid, 2586.
Payment of mutual claims, 3445.

Claims of, against United States (see also *Georgiana*, The; *Lizzie Thompson*, The)—
Appropriation for, 4013.
Convention for adjustment of, 3893, 4013.

Commercial relations with, 1159, 2745.

Domestic disturbances in, 5960.

Earthquakes in, 3885.

Fugitive criminals, convention with, for surrender of, 4068, 4247.

Termination of, referred to, 4919.

Government in, restored, 5088.

Guano imported from. (See Guano.)

Gunboats constructed by Spain in and near New York to operate against, discussed, 3987.

Imprisonment of American citizens by, and claims arising out of, 5988, 6092, 6335.

Lobos Islands, discussed. (See Lobos Islands.)

Naval force of United States on shores of, 875.

Neutral rights, treaty with, regarding, 2953.

Proceeds of cargo of the *Macedonian* seized in, by authorities of Chile. (See *Macedonian*, The.)

Railroads operated by American citizens in, questions affecting American interests in connection with, 5470.

Relations of, with Chile, referred to. 4662, 4673.

Treaty with, transmitted and discussed by President—
Buchanan, 3001
Cleveland, 5179, 5369,
Fillmore, 2600, 2680.
Grant, 4068, 4212, 4247.
Pierce, 2952.
Polk, 2422, 2475.
Tyler, 1944, 2116, 2135.

Termination of—
  Notification of, given by Peru, 6335.
  Referred to, 4919.
Vessels purchased for, from United States, detained, 3831, 3835.
Vice-President of, refuge given to, by the *St. Louis,* 1133.
War between Chile, Bolivia, and, 4522, 4563, 4628, 4717.
  Claims of United States arising out of, 4913, 5083, 5369, 5514.
  Conditions of peace proposed by Chile, discussed, 4662, 4717, 4760.
  Efforts of United States to bring about peace, discussed, 4522, 4563, 4582, 4662, 4717.
  Stable government restored in Peru, 5088.
  Terminated, 4822.
  Treaty of peace, discussed, 4760.

Peru, Treaties with.—A convention declaring the rights of neutrals at sea was concluded in 1856. Both parties recognize the principle that free ships make free goods and that the property of neutrals on an enemy's vessel is not subject to detention or confiscation unless contraband of war. The rights resulting from a formal recognition of these principles shall be conferred upon all other countries who desire to accede. Arbitration and naturalization conventions are also in force. (For extradition terms of 1899, see Extradition Treaties.)

Peru also became a party to the convention between the United States and the several republics of South and Central America for the arbitration of pecuniary claims and the protection of inventions, etc., which was signed in Buenos Aires in 1910 and proclaimed in Washington July 29, 1914. (See South and Central America, Treaties with.)

Peru-Bolivian Confederation (see also Bolivia; Peru):
  Dissolution of, referred to, 1751.
  Treaty with, 1563, 1694, 1706.

Pet Banks. (See Banks, Pet.)

Petersburg, Va., explosion of mine in front of, referred to, 3471.

Petersburg (Va.), Siege of.—When Grant crossed the Rapidan, May 4, 1864, with the Army of the Potomac to operate against Lee, he ordered Ben. Butler, with the Army of the James, to proceed up the James River toward Richmond. Butler's army consisted of the Tenth and Eighteenth army corps, under Generals Gillmore and W. F. Smith, and numbered 38,648 officers and men and ninety guns. May 5, he occupied City Point and Bermuda Hundred, eighteen miles southeast of Richmond. On the evening of May 13 and the morning of the 14th he carried a portion of the first line of defenses of Richmond at Fort Darling, on Drury's Bluff. On the 16th Butler was attacked and driven back to Bermuda Hundred. June 10 he sent a force under Gillmore and Kautz against Petersburg. The cavalry entered the town, but were driven back, and the expedition returned to Bermuda Hundred. June 15, after a march of fifty-five miles from Cold Harbor in two days, Grant was ready to cross the James. The army of 130,000 men crossed by pontoon bridge in three days. The two armies were now united and pre-

pared for final operations against Richmond. The first step toward taking Richmond seemed to be the occupation of Petersburg, twenty-two miles to the south, on the Richmond and Petersburg Railroad. June 16, 1864, after the junction of the Army of the James and the Army of the Potomac, an attack was made on Petersburg by W. F. Smith's corps. The assaults were continued for four days. Reenforcements were sent from Richmond to defend the place, and the attempts cost Grant 7,881 men.

During parts of June and July a powder mine was dug beneath portions of the Petersburg intrenchments. It was intended to explode this and make an assault through the breach thus made. The mine, known as "the Crater," was charged with 8,000 pounds of powder, and at 4 o'clock A. M., July 30, 1864, was exploded. A Confederate battery and most of a regiment were blown up. The assault, which was made by 50,-000 men under Burnside, Warren, and Ord, was a total failure, and 4,000 men were lost in it. Gen. Mahone commanded the Confederate force that recovered the line broken by the explosion. During this siege a number of brilliant sorties were made. The losses in Lee's army are not fully reported. Elliott's brigade lost 677 men. Petersburg was not surrendered until April 3, 1865, nearly a year afterward.

Petition.—The Constitution prohibits Congress from making any law to abridge "the right of the people peaceably to assemble and to petition the Government for a redress of grievances." Feb. 11, 1790, a petition signed by Benjamin Franklin was offered to Congress, praying for the abolition of slavery, but no notice was taken of it. Between 1830 and 1844 numerous petitions from Abolitionists poured into Congress. May 26, 1836, the House resolved, by a vote of 117 to 68, that "all petitions, memorials, resolutions, propositions, or papers relating in any way to the subject of slavery or the abolition of slavery shall, without being printed or referred, be laid on the table, and that no further action be taken thereon." This was the first of the famous "gag rules" of Congress. John Quincy Adams championed the cause of the Abolitionists and opposed the gag rules for ten years, finally securing their repeal. In 1837 he presented a petition to Congress purporting to come from slaves. This was the first of the kind ever offered, though in 1800 Congress was thrown into an uproar of debate by a petition from freed negroes.

In his annual message to Congress, Dec. 2, 1835, President Jackson asserted that publications addressed to the passions of slaves and stimulating them to insurrection were being circulated through the mails, and suggested laws to prohibit, under severe penalties, such circulation (1394). One of the most noted laws under this recommendation was the Atherton gag, introduced by K. G. Atherton, of New Hampshire. It was rescinded in 1845. The rules of Congress now provide that petitions, when presented, shall be indorsed with the name of the member presenting them and the committee to which they were referred. They are entered by the Clerk on the Journal and then transmitted to the proper committee.

Petrel, The, mentioned, 6297.

Petroleum. (See Paints, Oils, etc.)

Petroleum, taxation of, in Holland, etc., referred to, 4979, 4986.

Pettaquamscut Purchasers.—In 1660 John Hull, who had become well known through his coinage of pine-tree money

Philippines.—The Philippine group, lying off the southern coast of Asia, extending almost due north and south from Formosa to Borneo and the Moluccas, between longitude 116° 40'-126° 34' and latitude 4° 40'-21° 10', approximately numbers about 3,141 islands and islets, of which 1,668 are listed by name, while 1,473 are, so far as known, without names. The actual land area is about 115,026 square miles. The six New England States, New York, and New Jersey have about an equal area. The island of Luzon, on which the capital city (Manila) is situated, is the largest, most populous, and wealthiest member of the group, being about the size of the State of New York. Mindanao is nearly as large, but its population is very much smaller. There are two islands with areas exceeding 10,000 square miles each, namely, Luzon with 40,969, and Mindanao with 36,292. There are nine islands each of which has an area of more than 1,000 square miles and less than 10,000. There are twenty between 100 and 1,000 square miles, seventy-three between 10 and 100 square miles, and two hundred and sixty-two between 1 and 10 square miles. The remaining number, 2,775, or seven-eighths of all, have areas less than a square mile each.

The area of the larger islands with population ascertained by the latest United States census follows:

Island	Area	Population 1903
Luzon	40,969	3,798,507
Mindanao	36,292	499,634
Samar	5,031	222,690
Panay	4,611	743,646
Mindoro	3,851	......
Leyte	2,722	357,641
Negros	4,881	460,776
Cebu	1,762	562,247
Bohol	1,441	243,148

The capital of the Archipelago is Manila, with 234,409 inhabitants. Other towns are: In Luzon, Bauan (39,094), Lipa (37,-934), Laoag (34,454), Batangas (33,131), San Carlos (27,166), Tobacco (21,946); in Samar, Calbayog (15,895); in Panay, Janiuay (20,738), Miagao (20,656), Hoilo (19,-054); in Cebú, Argao (35,448), Cebú (31,-079), Barili (31,617), Carcar (31,895), Sibonga (25,848); in Leyte, Baybay (22,-990), Ormoc (16,128).

A census of the Philippines was taken in 1903 under the auspices of the Census Office. The population returned was 7,635,426. Of this number about seven millions are more or less civilized. The wild tribes form about 9 per cent. of the entire population. Racially the inhabitants are principally Malays. The civilized tribes are practically all adherents of the Catholic Church, the religion being that introduced into the country by the Spaniards when they took possession of the islands in 1565. The Church has since then been a strong ruling power and the priesthood is numerous. The Moros are Mohammedans.

The density of population in the Philippines is 67 per square mile. In Continental United States it is 26 per square mile. Foreigners number about 50,000, of whom nearly three-fourths are Chinese. Exclusive of the army there are 8,135 Americans in the islands, nearly one-half being located in the city of Manila. There are about twenty-five different tribes in the islands, speaking fifteen or sixteen distinct dialects, the largest tribe being the Visayans, who form nearly one-fourth of the entire civilized population (3,219,030). The Tagalogs, occupying the provinces in the vicinity of Manila (1,469,695), rank second in number and the Ilocanos (803,-942) the third.

Education has been practically reorganized by the Americans. The total annual enrolment is 440,050. Seven thousand six hundred and seventy-one teachers are employed, of whom 658 are Americans and 7,013 Filipinos. English is very generally taught, and the next generation of Filipinos will probably speak that tongue. Pauperism is almost unknown in the islands. In 1902 there were only 1,668 paupers maintained at public charge. Vital statistics are as yet restricted to Manila. The death rate in the city of Manila is 24.20 per thousand. The birth rate is 36.51 per thousand.

In 1912 there were 70 newspapers and periodicals published in the islands, 19 being in English, 16 in Spanish, 15 in native dialects, 7 in Spanish and English, 11 in Spanish and native dialects and 2 in Spanish, English, and native dialects. The assessed real estate property value in 1912 was 484,037,327.10 pesos. The reported value of church buildings, mostly Catholic, is 41,698,710 pesos.

The climate is one of the best in the tropics. The thermometer during July and August rarely goes below 79° or above 85°. The extreme ranges in a year are said to be 61° and 97°, and the annual mean 81°.

Although agriculture is the chief occupation of the Filipinos, yet only one-ninth of the surface is under cultivation. The soil is very fertile, and even after deducting the mountainous areas it is probable that the area of cultivation can be very largely extended and that the islands can support population equal to that of Japan (42,000,000).

The chief products are hemp, rice, corn, sugar, tobacco, cocoanuts, and cacao, hemp being the most important commercial product and constituting 43 per cent. of the value of all exports. Coffee and cotton were formerly produced in large quantities —the former for export and the latter for home consumption; but the coffee plant has been almost exterminated by insects and the home-made cotton cloths have been driven out by the competition of those imported from England. The rice and corn are principally produced in Luzon and Mindoro and are consumed in the islands. The cacao is raised in the southern islands, the best quality of it at Mindanao. The sugar cane is raised in the Visayas. The hemp is produced in Southern Luzon, Mindaro, the Visayas, and Mindanao. It is nearly all exported in bales. Tobacco is raised in many of the islands, especially Luzon and Negros.

In the year ending June 30, 1913, the exports of domestic merchandise from the United States to the Philippines were $25,-360,646, and the total imports from the Philippines for the same period were $21,-010,248.

The imports of merchandise from foreign countries, year ending June 30, 1913, were $30,948,498, and the exports were $33,-834,438. The principal foreign countries trading with the Philippines are Great Britain, French East Indies, China, and Spain.

On July 1, 1902, Congress passed (chapter 1369) "An act temporarily to provide for the administration of the affairs of civil government in the Philippine Islands." Under this act complete civil government was established in the Archipelago, except that portion inhabited by Moros, comprising part of Mindanao and the Sulu Islands, and the office of Military Governor was terminated. Wm. H. Taft was appointed Civil Governor by the President, the title being subsequently changed to that of Governor-General. Governor Taft was succeeded by Luke E. Wright in December, 1903, by Henry Clay Ide in 1905, James F. Smith in 1906, W. Cameron Forbes in 1909, and Francis Burton Harrison in 1913. The government was composed of a Civil Governor and seven commissioners, of whom four were Americans and three Filipinos. By act of Congress, approved May 11, 1908, the commission was increased by one member, to be appointed by the President, making the commission nine members in all, including the Governor-General, who is President of the Philippine Commission. There are four executive departments—Interior, Finance and Justice, Commercial and Police, and Public Instruction. There are thirty-eight provinces, each with a Governor, a Treasurer, and prosecuting attorney (provincial fiscal). Local governments have been established in about 725 towns. The officials consist of a President, Vice-President, and Councilmen (the latter varying in number according to the population) and are elected by the qualified voters of the municipality and serve for four years. The Judiciary consists of a Supreme Court, with seven Judges; Courts of First Instance, Justice of the Peace Courts, and a Court of Land Registration. There are seventeen Judicial Districts. In each province there is a Court of First Instance and a Court of the Justice of the Peace in each organized municipality in every province where there is a Court of First Instance. Two resident commissioners are elected to represent the islands in the House of Representatives at Washington. The Presidential appointees are members of the Commission.

In March, 1907, the President, in accordance with the act of Congress, directed the Commission to call a general election of delegates to a Philippine Assembly. The new Assembly was chosen July 30, and was opened October 16 by Secretary of War Taft. The total vote recorded at the election for delegates was 104,000, which is only 1.4 per cent. of the population. The second election was held on November 2.

1909. The number of persons registered was 208,845 and the number of votes cast 192,975, which is 2.81 per cent of the population. The third election was held on June 4, 1912. Incomplete returns showed 248,154 registered voters and 235,786 votes cast. By act of February 15, 1911, the members of the Philippine Assembly are elected for four years from the 16th day of October following their election, and the resident commissioners for four years, their term of office beginning on March 4 following their election. The next election will take place about June 1, 1916.

At the first session of the Sixty-first Congress an act was passed and approved August 5, 1909, readjusting the custom duties on imports from all countries, including the United States, on the basis generally of reductions. By act of Congress approved March 23, 1912, the act of July 1, 1902, to provide for the administration of the affairs of civil government in the Philippine Islands, was amended to read :—"That all inhabitants of the Philippine Islands continuing to reside therein who were Spanish subjects on the eleventh day of April, eighteen hundred and ninety-nine, and then resided in said islands, and their children born subsequent thereto, shall be deemed and held to be citizens of the Philippine Islands and as such entitled to the protection of the United States, except such as shall have elected to preserve their allegiance to the Crown of Spain. *Provided,* That the Philippine Legislature is authorized to provide by law for the acquisition of Philippine citizenship by those natives of the Philippine Islands who do not come within the foregoing provisions, the natives of other insular possessions of the United States, and such other persons residing in the Philippine Islands who could become citizens of the United States, under the laws of the United States if residing therein.

The Philippine Constabulary, which is distributed throughout the Archipelago in 119 stations, consists of 323 officers and 4,157 enlisted men.

There are in operation 587 post-offices, free delivery municipal letter-carrier service in 397 municipalities, 253 money-order offices, and 47 postal-savings banks, with 35,802 accounts. Of the 35,751 depositors, 29,555 are Filipinos.

The total kilometreage of telegraph and cable lines on June 30, 1912, was 9,010.84, and the number of telegraph offices 267. There are also four wireless stations operated. The total kilometreage of railroads in operation is 1,014.3.

Of the legislation enacted by the legislative authority in the islands during the last two years might be mentioned that fixing the gold-standard fund at a sum equal to 35 per cent of the money of the Government of the Philippine Islands in circulation and available for that purpose, exclusive of the silver certificates in circulation protected by gold reserve ; that providing for the apportionment between the insular, provincial, and municipal governments of taxes paid by grantees or franchises ; that embodying certain provisions concerning the building and operation of railroads, and that providing for the establishment of an irrigation system.

The Philippine Islands came into the possession of the United States as a result of the war with Spain through the treaty of Paris, Dec. 10, 1898. Two days before the ratification of the treaty the Filipinos, under Aguinaldo, attacked the American soldiery in Manila and an insurrection was set on foot which lasted for two years.

Philippine Independence.—The Philippine bill as reported from conference, with the Clarke amendment providing for independence of the islands within four years eliminated, but containing a promise of freedom whenever the Filipinos have demonstrated their ability to maintain a stable government, finally was approved by the Senate August 16 and passed the House August 18, 1916. The vote was 37 to 22 in the Senate. All those who voted for the measure were Democrats and twenty-one of the twenty-two Senators who opposed the bill were Republicans. The only Democrat to vote against the bill was Senator Lane of Oregon. The Philippine Commission, which had been in charge of the islands' affairs since their annexation, was dissolved by the bill. In its place was set up in general legislative control of the Philippine legislature of two houses—both elected by the native people. Twenty-four of the twenty-six members of the upper house, or Senate, are now chosen by the electorate. All were formerly appointed by the Governor-General. In accordance with the doctrine of offering as wide an opportunity as possible for self-education in government, the electoral franchise was also extended to include all those who speak and write a native dialect. Formerly property ownership or the ability to speak and write English or Spanish were the requirements. The change increased the electorate from 250,000 to approximately 800,000 or 900,000 voters. The executive departments, with the exception of that of Public Instruction, were placed entirely in the hands of the new Legislature. The Vice-Governor is to be head of that department. He, with the Governor-General, an auditor, assistant auditor, and the justices of the Supreme Court, will be the only officers appointed by the President of the United States. The Governor-General has the same veto power over the native Legislature as that enjoyed by the Executive in the American form of government, and all acts of the Philippine Government are subject to the jurisdiction of the President, Congress, and Supreme Court of the United States. Americans on the islands are required to give up American citizenship before voting there. President Wilson signed the bill August 29.

Trade with the United States.—The value of merchandise imported into the Philippine Islands from the United States for the year 1913 was $25,384,793, and goods to the value of $21,010,248 were sent thither—a balance of $4,374,545 in favor of the United States.

Philippine Islands:

Administration of, 6661, 6663, 6800.

Amnesty proclaimed for insurgents, 6690.

Army of United States in, 6694, 6720, 6947.

Cable communications with, recommended, 6348.

Cattle plague in, 7015.

Civil and military government in, 6692, 6720, 6740, 6815, 6861, 6886.

Commissioners to, and duties of, set forth by President, 6584.

Contributions to be levied upon. (See Military occupation of, *post.*)

Cruelty by soldiers in, 6720.

Disasters to agriculture in, 7015.

Distress in, 6732, 6738.

Expeditions to, under command of Gen. Merritt, 6315.

Education in, 7015.

Eulogy of civil servants in, 6229.

Extension of debt limit recommended, 7689.

Force, etc., suggestions from commanders regarding, requested by President, 6580.

Free trade with, proposed, 7017, 7050, 7374.

Friars' lands, disposition of, 7689.

Gen. Otis directed to avoid conflict with insurgents in, 6584.

Government for. (See Military occupation of, *post.*)

Grants of public or corporate rights in, order regarding, 6583.

Military occupation of, by United States and government for, or ders regarding, 6569, 6571, 6572, 6581.

Joint occupation with insurgents not to be permitted, 6579.

Naturalization of natives recommended, 7689.

Naval base in, proposed, 6806.

Oath of allegiance to United States taken by insurgents, 6692.

Peace in, 6692, 6720, 7015.

Progress of, 6928, 7015, 7017, 7051, 7232.

Proposed scientific surveys in, 6944.

Revenue of, 7015.

Self-government of, 6929, 7911, 8017.

Tariff in, 6738, 7050, 7374, 7380, 7406, 7516.

Troops to Iloilo, order to send, 6583.

Value of, 6928.

Vessels of Spain from, discriminating duties on, suspended by proclamation, 5155.

Victory of—

American squadron over Spanish fleet in bay of Manila discussed, 6297, 6315.

Commander of American squadron—

Appointed acting rear-admiral, 6297, 6568.

Sword to be presented to, and medals to men under, 6302.

Thanks of Congress to, and men under, 6298.

Recommended, 6297.

Reply of, 6302.

Thanks of President tendered, 6568.

Referred to, 6297.

Commander of the *Hugh McCulloch*, in recognition of services of, recommended, 6305.

American squadron and land forces at Manila discussed, 6319.

Thanks of President tendered commanders and men, 6579.

Phœnix, Arizona, office of Surveyor-General located at, 6704.

Phonograph.—The word phonograph is indiscriminately applied to all talking machines or instruments used for the reproduction of previously recorded sounds, whether of the voice or of musical instruments. A pencil attached to one prong of a tuning fork and passed lightly over a sheet of paper while the fork vibrated produced the first recorded sound. The earliest device for registering speech was made by Leon Scott in 1855. He called his machine the phonautograph. It consisted of a sort of cone, the larger end of which was open to receive the sound. From the smaller enclosed end, projected a tube, across which was stretched a flexible membrane. To this membrane was attached a bristle which moved in consonance with the slightest motion of the membrane. In front of the membrane was a horizontal cylinder or roll of paper covered with lampblack, against which the bristle touched lightly. Sound waves entering the open end of the cone were transmitted to the bristle by the vibrations of the membrane, and as the blackened cylinder was made to revolve and advance slowly the faintly moving bristle cut through the lampblack, leaving a white wavy line which was an exact graphic record of the sounds entering the cone.

In 1877 Edison constructed a form of this machine, substituting a metal diaphragm for the membrane, a sharp metallic point for the bristle and a wax or tin-foil-covered cylinder for the lampblack coated paper. In this machine the microscopic sound waves were indented instead of traced on the surface of the cylinder.

By reversing the machine and causing the metal point to retrace the indentations previously made in the cylinder the original sound was reproduced by the diaphragm.

Charles S. Tainter and C. A. Bell in 1885 substituted a wax cylinder for the tin-foil, and an up and down line was cut rather than indented in the wax.

In 1887 Emil Berliner, a German-American of Philadelphia, patented the gramophone, wherein the sound waves of a diaphragm are recorded on a disk as a wavy line in a horizontal plane, instead of as a vertical cut in a cylinder. As this line is cut in a continuous spiral, no feed screw is necessary to propel the metal point or the recorded sound waves, only a clock spring being necessary to rotate the disk. This was incorporated in the machine by Eldridge R. Johnson. With the expiration of the Tainter and Bell patents on wax records the etching process was abandoned for the wax cutting process, which now became common property, but horizontal recording was retained. Berliner made electrotyped reverses of these wax records, and from the plates so obtained duplicate copies of the records may be turned out like printed sheets from the printing press. The records, formerly stamped in celluloid or vulcanized rubber, are now printed on light fibrous compositions similar to paper pulp coated with shellac.

The manufacture of disk records began in 1897, and soon became recognized as an important industry. The cylinder machines remained in use under the names dictaphone and dictograph, and are used for recording conversation for future reproduction, such as testimony, instruction, commercial correspondence, etc., and the reproductions have been accepted as legal evidence by judges of criminal courts.

Opera singers, orators, musicians, orchestras, bands, and other entertainers were soon in demand for making records for reproduction, and the voice that once enthralled a contemporaneous audience but a

brief hour may now become immortal and
be heard by millions after life has left the
human tones. The field thus widened has
afforded new and increased popularity and
earning power for all who sing or talk or
play an instrument for hire. Some of the
favorite singing artists are paid outright
for the records of their voices, while others
receive a percentage of the price of every
record sold. An idea of the extent of the
business may be had from the statement
that the royalties of an individual singer
have exceeded $100,000.

In 1889 there were but two establishments in the country making records and
reproducing instruments. In ten years the
number had increased to eleven, with a
capital of $3,348,282, and a yearly output
valued at $2,246,274. In 1909 there were
18 establishments with a total capital of
$14,363,361, and an output valued at $11,-
725,996. In 1914 the eighteen establishments turned out products which they valued at $27,115,916, an increase of 139.7
per cent. in five years. Although the number of records and blanks increased but one-
tenth of 1 per cent. in the five years the
declared value of the goods increased from
$5,007,104 to $11,111,418, an increase of
121.9 per cent. This is said to be due to
the increased price obtained for disk records
over cylinders.

Phosphates discovered on coast of Brazil, 4795.

Piankeshaw Indians. (See Indian
Tribes.)

Pichon, Citizen, letter of Charles M.
Talleyrand to, regarding United
States ministers to France, 273.

Picket.—1. A soldier placed on guard to
discover the movements of the enemy, and
to give warning in case an enemy approaches.
2. A small number of soldiers sent out after
comrades who have over-stayed their leave
of absence. 3. A small force of soldiers kept
ready, under arms, to meet a surprise attack by the enemy. 4. A selected member of
a labor union organization sent out to reason with non-union workers or strike-break-
ers, or to intimidate them, in the effort to
prevent them from working under non-union
conditions. 5. A selected member of the
National Woman's Party (see Woman Suffrage) detailed in 1917 to guard the entrances to the White House for the purpose
of impressing the President with the seri-
ousness of their intentions. (See Patrol,
Sentinel and Sentry.)

Piegan Indians. (See Indian Tribes.)

Pierce, Franklin.—1853-1857.
Seventeenth Administration—Democratic.
Vice-President—William R. King.
Secretary of State—
William L. Marcy.
Secretary of the Treasury—
James Guthrie.
Secretary of War—
Jefferson Davis.
Secretary of the Navy—
James C. Dobbin.
Secretary of the Interior—
Robert McClellan.
Postmaster-General—
James Campbell.
Attorney-General—
Caleb Cushing.
Nomination.—Pierce was elected as a
Democrat. At the national convention
which met at Baltimore in June, 1852, thir-
ty-five ballots were taken for a Presiden-
tial candidate without a choice being
reached and without mention of Pierce's

name. Up to that point Lewis Cass and
James Buchanan were leaders in the bal-
loting. Virginia then presented Pierce's
name and he was chosen on the forty-
ninth ballot.

Platform.—The platform of the Democratic party commended rigid economy in
public expenditure and a tariff for revenue
and for the gradual payment of the public debt; opposed the national banking system as being unconstitutional; favored
free immigration and ease of naturalization; deprecated Federal interference in
domestic affairs, and especially in imposing
restrictions upon slave-holding; supported
the Fugitive Slave Act; characterized the
war with Mexico as just and necessary;
and condemned monopolies and exclusive
legislation for the benefit of the few.

Opposition.—The Whig National Convention at Baltimore, in June, 1852, nominated
General Winfield Scott on the fifty-third
ballot, over Millard Fillmore and Daniel
Webster. The party stood upon a platform embodying strict construction of the
Constitution; freedom from entangling alliances with foreign countries; a tariff for
revenue and for the encouragement of
American industry; internal improvements,
and support of the Fugitive Slave Act.
The Free-Soil Democrats met at Pittsburg
in August, 1852, and nominated John P.
Hale, on a platform setting forth strict
construction of the Constitution; "no more
slave states, no slave territory, no nation-
alized slavery, and no national legislation
for the extradition of slaves"; the abolition of slavery; the repugnance of the
Fugitive Slave Act to the Constitution; the
inconsistence with Democracy of the Compromise Measures of 1850; the natural
right of all men to the soil; the holding in
trust of the public lands for the landless
settlers; the keeping of government funds
separate from banking institutions; the
provision by Congress of internal improvements; the hostility of the Free Democratic party to both the Whigs and the
Democrats; and embodying the principles
of the party in the phrase "Free Soil, Free
Speech, Free Labor, and Free Men."

Vote.—The popular vote in thirty-one
states—California participating for the
first time—gave Pierce, 1,601,274; Scott,
1,386,580; and Hale, 155,825. The electoral vote, counted on Feb. 9, 1853, gave
Pierce 254 votes, and Scott 42.

Party Affiliation.—Pierce gave his earliest
political allegiance to the cause of General
Jackson, whom he supported throughout.
In Congress he opposed the abolition of
slavery within the District of Columbia,
and the policy of internal improvements.
When he left Congress and retired temporarily to private life, he favored the annexation of Texas; and led the Democrats
of his state in the memorable struggle
against John P. Hale. In 1850, he reluc-
tantly supported the several compromise
measures, including the Fugitive Slave Act
and the admission of California as a free
state. He was thus in hearty accord with
the principles enunciated by his party when
elected to the Presidency.

Political Complexion of Congress.—In the
Thirty-third Congress the Senate was composed of 62 members, of whom 38 were
Democrats, 22 Whigs, and 2 Free-Soil.
The House was composed of 234 members, of whom 159 were Democrats, 71
Whigs, and 4 Free-Soil. In the Thirty-
fourth Congress the Senate, of 62 members,
was made up of 42 Democrats, 15 Republicans, and 5 Americans. The House, of 234
members, was divided as follows: 83 Democrats, 108 Republicans, and 43 Americans.
Finance.—The platform of the Democratic

party upon which Pierce was elected committed the administration to a policy of rigid economy in the expenditure of the public funds. The practice of this economy, and opposition to internal improvements, curtailed the expenditure and left a surplus in the Treasury, which was applied to the reduction of the public debt, and made the subject of an argument in favor oi a reduction in the tariff. The condition of the public finances is referred to and discussed in each of the annual messages, but as the statements cover dissimilar periods, the following table will better show the financial status of the country during the administration at the end of each fiscal year :—

Year.	Public Debt, Less Cash, in Treasury.	Receipts, Total Net, Ordinary.
1853	$59,803,117.70	$61,587,032.00
1854	42,242,222.42	73,800,341.00
1855	35,586,956.56	65,350,575.00
1856	10,965,953.01	74,056,699.00

Year.	Expenditures, Total Net, Ordinary.	Total Money in Circulation.
1853	$44,078,156.00	$402,238,107.00
1854	51,967,528.00	425,551,240.00
1855	56,316,198.00	418,020,247.00
1856	66,772,528.00	425,846,625.00

Foreign Policy.—In his Inaugural Address (page 2730) President Pierce advocated the cultivation of peace with the nations of the world. He said : "The rights, security and repose of this Confederacy reject the idea of interference or colonization on this side of the ocean by any foreign power beyond present jurisdiction as utterly inadmissible." During this administration, no fewer than twenty-eight treaties with foreign powers were signed. Among the most important of them was that with Japan by Commodore Perry ; the settlement with Great Britain of the fisheries rights in Canada, and the free navigation of the St. Lawrence, and the Gadsden Treaty with Mexico. Complications with Nicaragua caused the bombardment of Greytown in the spring of 1854, by the United States vessel *Cyane*, in retaliation for property stolen from Americans ; and in 1856, William Walker conducted a filibustering expedition against Nicaragua with such temporary success that President Pierce recognized the Minister sent by him to the United States. The British Minister and the Consuls at New York, Philadelphia, and Cincinnati were dismissed by President Pierce for complicity in recruiting in the United States for the Crimean War, in 1854 and 1855. Bills for the reorganization of the diplomatic and consular systems were signed by the President in 1855. The attempts to gain Cuba from Spain, in which the Ostend Manifesto (*q. v.*) was an incident, in 1854, proved abortive by reason of the unfriendly attitude of European powers and the excitement at home over the Kansas-Nebraska Bill. In his Fourth Annual Address he said (page 2950) : "In foreign relations we have to attemper our power to the less happy condition of other Republics in America and to place ourselves in the calmness and conscious dignity of right by the side of the greatest and the wealthiest of the Empires of Europe."

Slavery.—In his Inaugural Address (page 2730) the President set forth his conviction that slavery was constitutional, as was also the Fugitive Slave Act, and denounced slavery agitation. "Such," he says, "have been, and are, my convictions,

and upon them I shall act. I fervently hope that the question is at rest, and that no sectional or ambitious or fanatical excitement may again threaten the durability of our institutions or obscure the light of our prosperity." Doubtless he was sincere in his hopes and wishes, but the enforcement of his policies was fraught with tremendous and lasting results. The two most important pre-slavery measures supported by the Pierce administration were the Ostend Manifesto and the Kansas-Nebraska Bill. President Pierce reviews the historical and constitutional aspects of slavery in his Third Annual Message (page 2860), and, in concluding his denunciation of abolitionist reformers, says : "I know that the Union is a thousand times stronger than all the wild and chimerical schemes of social change which are generated one after another in the unstable minds of visionary sophists and interested agitators."

In his Fourth Annual Message (page 2930) he is especially severe in his arraignment of the slavery reformers, of whom he said : "They are perfectly aware that the change in the relative conditions of the white and black races in the slave-holding states which they would promote is beyond their lawful authority ; that to them it is a foreign object ; that it cannot be effected by any peaceful instrumentality of theirs ; that for them and the states of which they are citizens the only path to its accomplishment is through burning cities, and ravaged fields, and slaughtering populations, and all there is most terrible in foreign, complicated with civil and servile, war ; and that the first step in the attempt is the forcible disruption of a country embracing in its broad bosom a degree of liberty and an amount of individual and public prosperity to which there is no parallel in history, and substituting in its place hostile governments, driven at once and inevitably into mutual devastation and fratricidal carnage, transforming the new peaceful and felicitous brotherhood into a vast permanent camp of armed men, like the rival monarchies of Europe and Asia."

But for the wanton opening of the slavery question, Pierce's administration would have been one of the most creditable in the nation's history. But for the repeal of the Missouri Compromise and the popular excitement attending the whole question of slavery the defection from the Democratic party and the formation of the Republican party in 1856 would have been at least longer delayed.

Internal Improvements.—In his First Annual Message (page 2751) President Pierce declares that the subject of internal improvements "has stood as a deep graven line of division between statesmen of eminent ability and patriotism" ; refers to President Jackson's message of May 27, 1830, on the subject ; and asks Congress for a reconsideration of the subject, with a view to adopting a settled standard of action. In vetoing certain bills making appropriations for works coming under this head (page 2790), the President fully discusses the several phases of the question and clearly defines his opposing attitude, summing up with these words : "On the other hand, so long as these improvements are carried on by appropriations from the Treasury the benefits will continue to inure to those alone who enjoy the facilities afforded, while the expenditure will be a burden upon the whole country and the discrimination a double injury to places equally requiring improvement, but not equally favored by appropriations." He

EXTENT OF THE UNITED STATES DURING THE ADMINISTRATION OF PRESIDENT PIERCE, 1853-1857.

(NOT INCLUDING TERRITORIES)

MAINE 1820

VT. 1791

N. H. 1788

CONN. 1788

R. I. 1790

N. J. 1787

DEL. 1787

MD. 1788

NEW YORK 1788

PENNSYLVANIA 1787

VIRGINIA 1788

NORTH CAROLINA 1789

SOUTH CAROLINA 1788

GEORGIA 1788

FLORIDA 1845

MICHIGAN 1837

OHIO 1803

INDIANA 1816

KENTUCKY 1792

TENNESSEE 1796

ALABAMA 1819

MISSISSIPPI 1817

WISCONSIN 1848

ILLINOIS 1818

MISSOURI 1821

ARKANSAS 1836

LOUISIANA 1812

IOWA 1846

TEXAS 1845

CALIFORNIA 1850

FLAG OF 1857

seeks to illustrate the difficulty of knowing what improvements may properly be provided by the national government and what should be left to individual or state enterprise, by concrete examples of railroads and harbor improvements. Again, in 1856, several bills of the same nature were vetoed by the President. In fact, nearly all of the vetoed measures during this administration were bills of this nature.

Commerce.—In his Second Annual Message (page 2808) President Pierce was able to say: "Our foreign commerce has reached a magnitude and extent nearly equal to that of the first maritime power of the earth, and exceeding that of any other." Especial emphasis was laid in this message upon the necessity of securing by treaty with the other world powers a recognition of the rights of neutrals in time of war as the best means of conserving the commercial interests and safety of the country. Great progress was made by the administration in securing from European nations a treaty agreement to the principle that free ships make free goods, except in the case of articles contraband of war, and that neutral property other than contraband, though on board enemy's ships, shall be exempt from confiscation. The condition of the commercial aspects of the country during the four years' administration is presented in the following table:

	1853	1854
Imports	$263,777,265	$297,803,794
Exports	203,489,282	237,043,764
Miles of Railway	15,360	16,720
Tons of Vessels Built	427,494	536,046
No. of Immigrants	368,645	427,833

	1855	1856
Imports	$257,808,708	$310,432,310
Exports	218,909,503	281,219,423
Miles of Railway	18,374	22,016
Tons of Vessels Built	583,450	469,293
No. of Immigrants	200,877	195,857

Tariff.—In his First Annual Message, President Pierce (page 2747) asks the attention of Congress to the consideration of a decrease in duties, in view of the surplus in the Treasury. Again, in his Third Annual Message he says (page 2871): "The conspicuous fact that the annual revenue from all sources exceeds by many millions of dollars the amount needed for a prudent and economical administration of public affairs, can not fail to suggest the propriety of an early revision and reduction of the tariff of duties on imports." In his Fourth Annual Message (page 2941) he urges a reduction so that the revenue from customs should not exceed forty-eight or fifty millions. Congress accordingly passed the act of March 3, 1857, "reducing the duty on imports, and for other purposes."

Army.—In his Second Annual Message President Pierce (page 2819) urges that the forces be increased to prevent the Indian atrocities on the frontier, and adds: "Without increase of the military force these scenes will be repeated, it is to be feared, on a larger scale and with more disastrous consequences." At the previous session of Congress a bill was passed increasing the pay of the rank and file of the Army, which the President reports "has had beneficial results, not only in facilitating enlistments, but in obvious improvement in the class of men who enter the service." He regrets that the increase had not been extended to the officers. To meet the present needs of the nation, he asks for four new regiments, two of infantry and two of cavalry. Several suggestions are made in this message to re-

form the Army organization, especially in the direction of the creation of a retired list in order to provide for officers who, having rendered distinguished or even meritorious service, would, by the standard of seniority be promoted to posts which impairment by age would render them unfit to fill. He asks that a test of one year be made of the efficacy of the plan proposed. The organization of the artillery is subjected to criticism because the force as then organized required infantry duty from the force, because of its arrangement in regiments instead of batteries.

In his Fourth Annual Message (page 2941) he commends the work of the Army in suppressing the hostile demonstrations of the Indians and reiterates his recommendation for the adoption of measures of reform in the organization and in the increase of the force which "during the past year has been so constantly employed against the hostile Indians in various quarters that it can scarcely be said to have been a peace establishment."

Navy.—The Navy was substantially increased during this administration by the addition of six new steam frigates, of which the President says (page 2942): "The condition of the Navy is not merely satisfactory but exhibits the most gratifying evidences of increased vigor. . . . The new frigates ordered by Congress are now (1856) afloat and two of them are in active service. They are superior models of naval architecture and with their formidable battery add largely to public strength and security."

Among the reforms in the organization of the Navy carried through by this administration were the apprentice system by which boys were trained for service on a three years' cruise in national vessels, the permission granted to honorably discharged seamen to enlist after a few months without cessation of pay, and the law for the promotion of discipline in the naval force.

Pierce, Franklin:

Annual messages of, 2740, 2806, 2860, 2930.

Biographical sketch of, 2728.

Death of, announced and honors to be paid memory of, 3979.

Domestic relations discussed by, 2874, 2930, 2950.

Exequaturs granted consuls of Great Britain revoked by, 2924, 2925.

Finances discussed by, 2746, 2817, 2870, 2940.

Foreign policy discussed by, 2731, 2745, 2807, 2864, 2904.

Inaugural addresses of, 2730.

Intercourse with British minister terminated by, 2908.

Internal dissensions discouraged by, 2755, 2930.

Internal improvements discussed by, 2751, 2789, 2790, 2919, 2920, 2921.

Large standing army unnecessary in time of peace, 2733.

Portrait of, 2227.

Powers of Federal and State Governments discussed by, 2751, 2755, 2780, 2789, 2790, 2855, 2874, 2919, 2920, 2921, 2930.

Proclamations of—

Boundary line with Mexico, 2926.

Pilgrim Fathers.—A name given by William Bradford in his journal to certain emigrants under the leadership of Bradford, Brewster, Cushman, Carver, and Miles Standish, who came to New England early in the seventeenth century on account of religious differences in England and founded the colony of Plymouth. Those who came in the first three ships are also called "old comers" or "forefathers." The first ship, the *Mayflower,* arrived on the coast in December, 1620, and had on board 108 souls. The *Fortune* came in November, 1621, with twenty-nine, and the *Anne* and *Little James* came in August, 1623, bringing forty-six persons. In religion the Pilgrims were Separatists or Independents, while the settlers of Massachusetts Bay were Puritan, who at first adhered to the Church of England and endeavored to purify it.

Pillage.—Plunder, especially that captured from the enemy in war. (See Plunder.)

Pinchot-Ballinger Controversy. — James R. Garfield, Secretary of the Interior under Roosevelt, and Gifford Pinchot, Chief Forester, attacked the policy and conduct of Mr. R. A. Ballinger, Secretary of the Interior under President Taft, in the matter of the conservation of the natural resources in the public domain, using as their principal text the course of Mr. Ballinger with reference to the coal lands in Alaska. The principal items in the indictment of Mr. Ballinger were as follows:

(1) That, in 1907, as Land Commissioner under President Roosevelt, he ordered the so-called Cunningham claims prepared for patent, though to his knowledge there were on file three reports by field agents that these claims were fraudulent, and that shortly thereafter he urged a Congressional Committee to favor a law which would have validated the claims.

(2) That he violated a statute by aiding in the prosecution of a claim which was pending while he was Land Commissioner within two years after leaving that office.

(3) That, by unwise administration, Mr. Ballinger caused the nation the loss of valuable water-power sites on the public domain.

Congress, in January, 1910, appointed a committee consisting of six members from each house to investigate the charges. In September the four Democratic members and one "insurgent" Republican met in Minneapolis, and drafted a report recommending the dismissal of Mr. Ballinger. The seven "regular" Republican members issued a majority report, Dec. 7, 1910, in which it was declared that the evidence did not exhibit Mr. Ballinger as being anything but a competent and honorable gentleman, honestly and faithfully performing the duties of his high office with an eye single to the public interest. The most important finding of the committee was that coal mines on the public land should be leased, not sold, by the Government.

Pine-Tree Money.—On May 27, 1652, the general court of Massachusetts passed an act establishing a mint at Boston. John Hull was appointed mint master, and he began the coinage of shillings, 6d. pieces, and 3d. pieces. This was called pine-tree money from a design on the obverse of a pine-tree encircled by a grained ring, with the legend "Masathusets. In." The coinage was discontinued on the death of the mint master, Oct. 1, 1683.

Pine Tree State.—A nickname for Maine (q. v.), (See also States); sometimes also nicknamed Down East State and Lumber State.

Pines, Isle of, Cuba, referred to, 6739.

Pioneer.—One who blazes the way for a new settlement or movement. He may or may not become a permanent fixture. In the development of America, pioneers have played a tremendously important role, going into new sections of the country and risking their lives among savages, wild animals, and expansive woods or prairies, with nothing but faith to assure safety. The development of the great West has been due in large measure to intrepid pioneers. (See Explorer.)

Pioneering. (See illustration opposite 2929, and description on back.)

Piracy.—Robbery on the high seas. In the law of nations the essential element of piracy is the intention of preying indiscriminately on the human race, and not a desire to interfere with the trade of some distinct power. As the high seas are not under the jurisdiction of any one state, the crime of piracy is triable in any court. The difference between a pirate and a privateer consists in these facts, that whereas the former is a sea rover who preys on the vessels and goods of any nation he may chance to run across, or who makes descents upon land for purposes of plunder, a privateer, on the other hand, has for his purpose the preying upon the commerce of a hostile nation only; he is under bond to the state whose flag he flies and of which he carries the commission or letter of marque granting him a share in the prizes taken. A privateer exceeding his commission might not be considered a pirate, but one with commissions from two opposite belligerents would be, for it would be apparent that his motive would be plunder of both. A vessel of a part of a country organized for rebellion has been held to be piratical because, although it may have a commission, such commission issued by an unknown and unrecognized power can not be admitted as valid, as it offers no guaranty of legal belligerent behavior. Piracy in the international sense of the word, however, is a crime against all nations; but any nation may class other crimes under this head.

The United States in 1820 made the slave-trade piracy for any of its citizens on any ship and for persons not citizens on any of its vessels. Notwithstanding this law passed by the United States, slave trading was not piracy in the international sense of the word. Search of a vessel by a public ship of another state is a war right only, but the right to search on suspicion of piracy exists at all times. The usual penalty for piracy is the confiscation of the vessel and hanging of the crew, while the penalty for privateering is at most imprisonment. (See also Privateering.)

Piracy:

Cuba, piracies from, suppressed, 782.

Gulf of Mexico, force employed in, for suppression of, 826.

Mediterranean Sea infested with piracies, 929.

Practice of—

Death penalty for, discussed, 2202.

Must be suppressed, 848.

Prizes captured by pirates, recommendations regarding recapture of, 3248.

Puerto Rico, piracies from, suppressed, 783.

Sumatra, American vessels attacked by pirates on coast of, 1159.

Vessels instructed to defend themselves against, 3248.

West Indies, 758, 765, 984.

Suppression of, in, 929.

Pittsburg Landing (Tenn.), Battle of. (See Shiloh (Tenn.), Battle of.)

Pi-Ute Indians. (See Indian Tribes.)

Plague, The (see also Contagious Diseases; International Sanitary Conference; Quarantine Regulations):

Regulations to prevent introduction of, into United States, 4501.

Revoked, 4509.

Plant Industry, Bureau of.—This bureau of the Department of Agriculture conducts experiments in economic botany, physiology, and diseases of plants and forest trees; plant breeding; soil bacteriology; biophysics; acclimatization and adaptation of plants. It also studies farm management; demonstration work with farmers in improved farm practice; conditions of agriculture under dry land, irrigation and other special conditions. It also collects and tests seeds and plants from foreign countries. It engages in the purchase and distribution of seeds, largely through members of Congress; makes tests of imported and domestic seeds, and establishes standard grades of grain and cotton. It takes care of department parks and conservatories, and manages the Arlington Experimental farm.

There are more than 6,300,000 farms in the United States. The primary function of this bureau is to assist the farmer to increase the output per acre and at the same time to build up and maintain the fertility of the soil.

Study of the diseases of forest trees, plants, fruit, potatoes, cotton and truck crops engage the attention of the bureau. In one recent year $2,730,892 was expended in fighting diseases of plants. Standard grades of cotton and corn have been established by the bureau and enacted into law by Congress to the advantage of both buyer and seller.

Plaster of Paris, restriction on importation of, removed by proclamation, 603, 605.

Platforms.—In politics the platform of a party is the public declaration of the principles that the party represents. In May, 1832, a national assembly of young men was held in Washington, D. C., to indorse the nomination of Henry Clay by the National Republican party. They agreed to the first platform ever adopted by a national convention. In 1844 both the Whigs and Democrats drew up platforms, but in 1848 the Whigs refused to commit themselves by a platform. After this time the adoption of party platforms by national conventions became general.

Platt Amendment. (See Cuba.)

Platt National Park. (See Parks, National.)

Plattsburg, The, surrender of persons charged with murder on board of, referred to, 1808.

Plattsburg (N. Y.), Battle of.—The overthrow of Napoleon by the allied powers in 1814 released many British soldiers from service in Europe, and several thousand of them were sent to reenforce the little army in Canada. By Aug. 1, Governor-General Prevost had 15,000 troops under his command at Quebec, most of them hardened veterans from the Peninsula. One brigade was sent west. The remainder were held for a contemplated invasion of New York. Wilkinson and Hampton had been retired from the American Army and Gen. George Izard was placed in command of the right wing of the Army of the North, May 4, 1814, with headquarters at Plattsburg, N. Y., near the head of Lake Champlain. Notwithstanding it was evident that the British contemplated a descent upon New York by way of Lake Champlain and the Hudson, Izard was detached from his command and sent with 4,000 men to the Niagara frontier, leaving Gen. Macomb in command with about 3,500 men. Sept. 6, 1814, the British army, fully 14,000 strong, already upon American soil, marched toward Plattsburg. Maj. Wool, with a body of about 300 regulars, met the invading army at Beekmantown, about four miles north of Plattsburg, and subjected it to a harassing fire all the way to the Saranac River. Wool's retreating column crossed the stream to South Plattsburg and destroyed the bridges. Though in overwhelming force, the British army was checked, with a loss in killed and wounded of more than 200 men. The American loss was 45.

From Sept. 7 to 11, Prevost's army rested, preparatory to acting in conjunction with the fleet on Lake Champlain. On the 11th, while the forces of Macomb and Prevost contended on land, a desperate naval battle was fought on Lake Champlain between the American and British fleets, the former under Macdonough and the latter under Downie. This battle lasted for two hours, resulting in victory for the Americans. The British lost 200 men and the commodore of the fleet. The news of the naval victory reached the contending armies at a critical point of the battle and turned the tide in favor of the Americans. Prevost fled with his army to Champlain, leaving behind his sick and wounded and large quantities of stores. Sept. 24 the British returned to Canada, having lost in the expedition about 2,000 men. (See Lake Champlain, Battle of.)

See illustration opposite 583.

Plattsburg, N. Y., battle of, British troops defeated in, 534.

Plattsburg Training Camp—The wave of Preparedness (q. v.) which swept over the country in 1914, 1915, and 1916, was responsible for the establishment of a training camp for college graduates and business and professional men at Plattsburg, N. Y., in 1915. The camp was under the direction of the United States Regular Army, and directly under Major-General Leonard Wood, commander of the Department of the East. The camp was so successful and attracted so much attention that other similar camps were established in different parts of the country during the following year. The Plattsburg camp was held again in 1916, and in 1917 was used as a training center for officers volunteering for service in the European War. Attendance at the camp was voluntary, and did not increase the attendant's military obligations to the Government; and the camp was established primarily for those men who wished to increase their potential military effectiveness for the country, but who were unable to assume service in the National Guard.

Pleasant Hill (La.), Battle of.—After the defeat of the Federal army under Gen. Banks at Sabine Cross Roads, April 8, 1864, it retreated by way of Pleasant Grove to Pleasant Hill, about eighteen miles south, where Banks was joined by Gen. A. J. Smith with 10,000 men. Occupying a strong position here, the Federals awaited the pursuing force under Kirby Smith and Dick Taylor. April 9, about 4 o'clock in the afternoon, the Confederates came up and began the attack. In the battle which ensued they were checked and some of the guns they had taken the day before at Sabine Cross Roads were retaken. Banks now returned to the Red River at Grand Ecore, having lost in the campaign 18 guns, 5,000 men, 130 wagons, 1,200 horses, and many small arms.

Pleuro-Pneumonia among cattle, discussed, 4578, 4508, 4771, 5112, 5383, 5764, 5887.

Plumed Knight of Maine.—A soubriquet given to James G. Blaine.

Plunder.—In military parlance, belongings taken by force, usually those of a non-military character. (See Pillage.)

Plurality.—The excess in votes obtained by the winning candidate over the votes obtained by the second best candidate when there are more than two candidates in the field; same as majority in case of two candidates.

Plutocracy.—Government controlled by the people of wealth; also applied to characterize the wealthy classes generally.

Plymouth Colony.—The earliest settlement in Massachusetts. It was founded by a party of English Separatists who arrived in this country Dec. 21, 1620, and landed for permanent settlement in the following January. These Separatists were dissenters from the Church of England. Unlike the Puritans, who sought to purify the church, they regarded such purification as hopeless, and therefore advocated and practiced separation. The Plymouth colonists came to America from Delft, Holland, whither they had emigrated from Plymouth, England. One of the chief objects in coming to America was to enjoy their religion without molestation. The company named their settlement Plymouth, partly because it had been so called by Capt. John Smith, who had previously surveyed the harbor, and partly because the people of Plymouth, England, had treated them kindly. Miles Standish was made captain, with military authority, soon after landing, and John Carver was chosen the first governor of the colony. They entered into a treaty with Massasoit, chief of the Wampanoags, which was faithfully kept for fifty-five years. No royal charter was ever granted. With the arrival of the ship *Fortune* and twenty-nine immigrants in 1621 came a land patent from the Council for New England. The patent did not fix territorial limits, but allowed 100 acres of land to each immigrant and 1,500 for public buildings, and empowered the grantees to make laws and set up a government. After enduring many hardships and privations the first colonists were joined by others from England and material prosperity followed. Plymouth Colony became a member of the New England Confederation in 1643. By the Massachusetts charter of 1691 it was united with the Colony of Massachusetts Bay.

Plymouth Company.—In 1606 a company of merchants of Bristol and Plymouth, England, were incorporated under a charter granted by James I. and called the North Virginia Company. They became a rival of the London Company. In 1607, having obtained a grant of land between Long Island and Passamaquoddy Bay, they sent out two ships carrying a company of colonists commanded by George Popham. A settlement was attempted on the Kennebec, but Popham died and the other colonists returned home. The company continued to exist till 1620, when it was reorganized as the New England Company or Council for New England.

Plymouth, N. C., capture of, referred to, 3458.

Pocket, The, convention with Texas, for adjustment of claims in case of, 1686.

Pocket-Borough.—An opprobrious term referring to a political division supposed to be completely controlled by a leader or boss;

especially with the implication that it is controlled by the use of money from his pocket.

Pocket Vetoes. (See the several Presidents; the several messages.)

Point Barrow, Alaska, refuge station established at, 5476.

Poland.—A country of northeastern Europe bounded by Russia, Prussia and Austria. It is said to have become a duchy under Lechus or Lesko I, 550; and a kingdom under Boleslas, about 992; the natives belong to the great Slavonic family. The word Pole is not older than the 10th century. This kingdom in its best days embraced a territory of about 284,000 sq. miles, and extended 713 miles north and south and 693 east and west.

Its destruction as a separate nationality and the absorption of its territory by Austria, Prussia, and Russia, commencing in 1772 (when it embraced an area of about 282,000 sq. miles, with a population of not far from 12,000,000) and finished in 1795, the aid of Poland herself, and while sympathy is aroused at the needless destruction could not have been accomplished without of a nation, still it was due (1) to the inveterate jealousy and feuds of the Polish nobility among themselves; (2) the absence of a middle or national class, which the nobles made impossible; (3) the intolerance of the Jesuitical Romish party; (4) total incapacity of its later rulers; (5) no natural frontier boundaries. Its history as a nation ceased in 1795 with Stanislas II, when Courland was annexed to Russia and the King resigned his crown at Grodno. This followed the suppression, by the Russians, of an insurrection of Poles under Kosciusko, after his return from America, where he took part in the Revolution. Napoleon I wintered his army in Warsaw, the ancient capital, in 1806-7. The central provinces were constituted a kingdom under Alexander of Russia in 1815. In 1831 another revolution broke out, and after its suppression the Polish language was prohibited in the courts of law and in public places. In 1841 Poland was declared a Russian province.

During the European war beginning in 1914 Warsaw was occupied by the Germans and the Russians were expelled from the province. November 5, 1916, a joint proclamation by the Emperor of Germany and the Emperor of Austria established the Polish districts and provinces into a national state with a hereditary monarchy and a constitutional government. The exact delimitation of the frontiers of the revived kingdom were left to the future for decision, as was also the question of who should be placed upon the throne.

Polar Congress, International, at Hamburg, Germany, 4535.

Policy, Foreign. (See Foregin Policy.)

Poliomyelitis. (Infantile Paralysis.)—
So far as can be discovered, this disease is of recent origin. At least, the first serious poliomyelitis outbreak occurred in New York in 1907. The disease, which is acutely infectious, is caused by a strong virus which distributes itself generally throughout the body, but attacks in particular the brain and the spinal cord. Infection may be either direct, as from the nose or mouth of a person suffering from the disease or carrying the virus without injury to himself; or indirect, as from the use of a towel or drinking glass after such a person. The name of infantile paralysis, generally used to de-

scribe the disease, owes its origin to the fact that the disease usually attacks young children, especially those under five; and to the fact that paralysis, complete, partial, or slight, often is an after-result. However, so many cases of infantile paralysis pass unnoticed because of the absence of evil aftereffects that it has been estimated that paralysis does not occur in the majority of cases, although it may well occur in the majority of those cases where the infection is strong enough to make its presence evident. The most frequent symptoms are fever, stiffness of the neck, digestive disturbances, and vomiting. If paralysis is to develop, it usually occurs from 2 to 8 days after the illness of the patient has become pronounced.

The most severe epidemic of poliomyelitis in the world occurred in New York City in the summer of 1916, and to a lesser extent in different parts of the country. It is estimated that 12,000 cases broke out in that period, of which almost 25% were fatal. All efforts to find a cure proved futile—drugs being useless and the best results being obtained by injecting into the spinal canal of the patient a blood serum from a person who had had the disease some years previously. The best treatment would seem to be scientific after-care, and convalescence should last for from one to two years after the disease has departed.

Political Economy. (See Economics.)

Political Expenses, appropriation for, suggested, 7106.

Contributions from corporations should be prohibited, 7370.

Political Parties.—The following is a list of the principal political parties extant and heretofore existent in the United States. (See respective names): Abolition, American, Anti-Federalists, Anti-Masonic, Democratic, Democratic-Republican, Federalists, Free Soil, Greenback, Independence, Independent National, Liberal Republicans, Liberty, National, National Anti-Slavery Society, National Republican, National Silver, Patrons of Husbandry, People's Progressive, Prohibition, Populist, Populist or People's, Republican, Social-Democrat, Socialist, Socialist Labor, Sound Money Democrats, Strong Government Men, Tory, Whig.

Political Prisoners. (See Civil War.)

Politician.—A person, in or out of office, who helps to direct political affairs; especially one who helps another person as a candidate in an effort to secure office for himself either by election or appointment.

Polk, James K.—1845-1849.

Fifteenth Administration—Democratic.
Vice-President—George M. Dallas.
Secretary of State—
James Buchanan.
Secretary of the Treasury—
Robert J. Walker.
Secretary of War—
William L. Marcy.
Secretary of the Navy—
George Bancroft.
John Y. Mason.
Postmaster-General—
Cave Johnson.
Attorney-General—
John Y. Mason.
Nathan Clifford.
Isaac Toucey.

Polk was elected by the Democratic party, Nov. 5, 1844. He was the first "dark-horse" candidate ever nominated by a prominent party. At the Democratic National Convention held in Baltimore, May 27-29, 1844,

EXTENT OF THE UNITED STATES DURING THE ADMINISTRATION OF PRESIDENT POLK, 1845-1849.

(NOT INCLUDING TERRITORIES)

MAINE 1820

VT. 1791

N. H. 1788

MASS. 1788

CONN. 1788

R. I. 1790

N. J. 1787

DEL. 1787

MD. 1788

NEW YORK 1788

PENNSYLVANIA 1787

VIRGINIA 1788

NORTH CAROLINA 1789

SOUTH CAROLINA 1788

GEORGIA 1788

FLORIDA 1845

MICHIGAN 1837

OHIO 1803

INDIANA 1816

KENTUCKY 1792

TENNESSEE 1796

ALABAMA 1819

WISCONSIN 1848

ILLINOIS 1818

MISSISSIPPI 1817

IOWA 1846

MISSOURI 1821

ARKANSAS 1836

LOUISIANA 1812

TEXAS 1845

FLAG OF 1849

Van Buren and Cass were the leaders in the first eight ballots. On the ninth ballot, Polk's vote rose from 44 in the eighth to 233, sufficient for the nomination.

Platform.—The platform of the party reaffirmed the nine sections of the platform of 1840 and added three more sections. These specified that the public lands should be held as the Constitution provides, and that proceeds from the sale should not be distributed among States; that the veto power of the President should in no wise be curtailed; and that all of Oregon belonged to the United States, and that Texas should be reannexed as soon as practicable.

Opposition.—At the Whig National Convention held at Baltimore in May, 1844, Henry Clay was endorsed for the Presidency, and the first Whig national platform was formulated. It advocated a well-regulated currency, tariff for revenue and protection, distribution of the money derived from sales of public lands, a single term for the Presidency, curtailing of Executive Power, and an effective, careful, and economical government. The Liberty party met at Buffalo in convention on Aug. 30, 1843, and nominated James G. Birney for the Presidency. The platform adopted at that convention announced belief in human brotherhood, the abolition of slavery.

Vote.—The popular vote cast by twenty-six States gave Polk, 1,337,243; Clay, 1,-299,068; and Birney, 62,300. The electoral vote, counted on Feb. 12, 1845, gave Polk 170 and Clay 105.

Party Affiliation.—Polk was brought up a Jeffersonian in politics and, during the whole period of Jackson's administration, he was a leading supporter of his policies. As Speaker of the House (1835-1839) he supported Van Buren's administration. His opposition to the reforms advocated by the anti-slavery party was firm but not rabid. As Governor of Tennessee (1839-1841) he opposed the national bank, Federal taxation for revenue surplus, and the policies of the Abolitionists. He strongly favored the reannexation of Texas, and it was upon this issue that he was elected President.

Political Complexion of Congress.—In the Twenty-ninth Congress (1845-1847) the Senate, of 56 members, was composed of 30 Democrats, 25 Whigs, and 1 vacancy; and the House, of 225 members, was made up of 141 Democrats, 78 Whigs, and 6 Americans. In the Thirtieth Congress (1847-1849) the Senate, of 58 members, was composed of 37 Democrats and 21 Whigs; and the House, of 227 members, was made up of 108 Democrats, 115 Whigs, and 4 Independents.

Public Debt.—The public debt of the United States during the years of Polk's administration stood as follows: 1846, $15,-550,202.97; 1847, $38,826,534.77; 1848, $47,044,862,23; 1849, $63,061,858.69.

In his First Annual Message (page 2252) President Polk referred to the total extinguishment of the public debt by a previous administration and cherished the hope that, by especial effort, his administration might bring about the same most desirable result. But the expenses due to the wars in which the country became involved soon dispelled all hope of accomplishing his purpose.

Tariff.—In his First Annual Message (page 2253) President Polk discusses the tariff in theory and the scale of the tariff of 1842 specifically. He points out the difference between the revenue standard and the protection standard, and says: "It does not follow that Congress should levy the highest duty on all articles of import which they will bear within the revenue standard, for such rates would probably produce a much larger amount than the economical administration of the Government

would require." Such incidental protection as a tariff for revenue carries with it should in his opinion be so regulated that the tax may be made to bear equally upon consumers, and should be so arranged as to justly protect all industries alike. He refers to the fact that the tariff of 1842 was passed by a majority of only one vote in the Senate and two in the House (page 2255). He recommends a reduction in the tariff and prefers the *ad valorem* to the specific duty. "Such a system, when once firmly established, would be permanent, and not be subject to the constant complaints, agitations, and changes, which must ever occur when duties are not laid for revenue, but for the protection merely of a favored interest."

In a special message of June 16, 1846, the President presents a plan from the Secretary of the Treasury for the modification of the duties. He says (page 2301): "The high duties at present levied on many articles totally exclude them from importation, whilst the quantity and the amount of others which are imported are greatly diminished. By reducing these duties to a revenue standard, it is not doubted that a large amount of the articles on which they are imposed would be imported, and a corresponding amount of revenue be received at the Treasury from this source." On July 30, 1846 Congress passed an act "reducing the duty on imports, and for other purposes." This act went into effect on Dec. 1, 1846. In his Third Annual Message the President (page 2403) reports the satisfactory working of this act in its first year, and says: "All the beneficial effects which were anticipated from its operation have been fully realized." The revenue for the year was increased over $8,000,000. "While the repeal of the prohibitory and restrictive duties of the act of 1842 and the substitution in their place of reasonable revenue rates levied on articles imported according to their actual value has increased the revenue and augmented our foreign trade, all the great interests of the country have been advanced and promoted." These results are reported as continuing during the following year (page 2497). The President's attitude on the question of protection is fully enunciated in his discussion of the American System in his Fourth Annual Message (page 2504).

Foreign Policy.—On the annexation of Texas and the possible interference by foreign powers, the President said in his Inaugural Address (page 2230): "I regard the question of annexation as belonging exclusively to the United States and Texas. They are independent powers competent to contract, and foreign powers have no right to interfere with them or to take exceptions to their reunion. Foreign powers do not seem to appreciate the true character of our government. . . . Foreign powers should therefore look on the annexation of Texas to the United States not as the conquest of a nation seeking to extend her dominions by arms and violence, but as the peaceful acquisition of a territory once her own, by adding another member to our confederation, with the consent of that member, thereby diminishing the chances of war and opening to them new and ever-increasing markets for their products." In his First Annual Message (page 2237) the President, in referring to the same subject, said: "We may rejoice that the tranquil and pervading influence of the American principle of self-government was sufficient to defeat the purposes of British and French interference, and that the almost unanimous voice of the people of Texas has given to that interference a peaceful and effective rebuke. From this example, European governments may learn how vain diplomatic arts and intrigues must ever prove upon this continent against the system of self-government which seems natural to our soil, and which will ever resist foreign interference." In the same message he reviews the conditions of the war with Mexico.

War with Mexico.—The proclamation of war against Mexico (page 2320) was issued by President Polk on May 13, 1846. In his Second Annual Message (page 2321) the President goes fully into the Mexican War history.

In his Third Annual Message, in speaking of the Mexican War (page 2394), he says: "I am persuaded that the best means of vindicating the national honor and interest and of bringing the war to an honorable close will be to prosecute it with increased energy and power in the vital parts of the enemy's country." In his Fourth Annual Message (page 2481), in speaking of the effects of the Mexican War, the President says: "One of the most important results of the war into which we were recently forced with a neighboring nation is the demonstration it has afforded of the military strength of our country. . . . The great results which have developed and been brought to light by this war will be of immeasurable importance in the future progress of our country. They will tend powerfully to preserve us from foreign collisions, and enable us to pursue uninterruptedly our cherished policy of 'peace with all nations, entangling alliances with none.'"

Panama.—A special message (page 2361) accompanies the treaty with Granada, which by its thirty-fifth article confers upon the United States the right of passage across the Isthmus of Panama. The President says: "The importance of this concession to the commercial and political interests of the United States can not be easily overrated. The route by the Isthmus of Panama is the shortest between the two oceans, and from the information herewith communicated it would seem to be the most practicable for a railroad or a canal."

Slavery.—In his Fourth Annual Message President Polk gives his views on slavery (page 2491) in these words: ". . . No duty imposed on Congress by the Constitution requires that they should legislate on the subject of slavery, while their power to do so is not only seriously questioned but denied by many of the soundest expounders of that instrument. Whether Congress shall legislate or not, the people of the acquired territories, when assembled in convention to form State constitutions will possess the sole and exclusive power to determine for themselves whether slavery shall or shall not exist within their limits. . . . Any and all of the states possess this right, and Congress can not deprive them of it. The people of Georgia might if they chose so alter their Constitution as to abolish slavery within its limits, and the people of Vermont might so alter their Constitution as to admit slavery within its limits."

Polk, James K.:

Acquisition of Yucatan, discussed by, 2431.

Advice of Senate desired by, 2299.

American system, discussed by, 2504.

Annexation of Texas, discussed by, (See Texas.)

Annual messages of, 2235, 2321, 2382, 2479.

Biographical sketch of, 2221.

Cession of California and New Mexico, discussed by. (See California or New Mexico.)

Constitutional treasury recommended by, 2256.

Successful operation of, discussed by, 2406, 2498.

Death of announced and honors to be paid memory of, 2546.

Declaration of war against Mexico, facsimile of, opposite 2312.

Discretionary power of President over nominations, removals, and other acts, discussed by, 2232, 2281, 2416, 2452, 2529.

Finances discussed by, 2252, 2346, 2401, 2406, 2496.

Foreign policy discussed by, 2229, 2236, 2248, 2276, 2322, 2337, 2361, 2386, 2431, 2437, 2444, 2480.

Geographical distinctions in country, discouraged by, 2413.

Inaugural address of, 2223.

Internal improvements, discussed by, 2310, 2460, 2506.

Large standing army unnecessary in time of peace, 2263.

Mexican War discussed by, 2287, 2295, 2300, 2306, 2321, 2363, 2383, 2415, 2437, 2481.

Monroe Doctrine, reasserted by, 2248, 2390, 2432.

National banks, discussed by, 2504.

Pocket veto of, 2460.

Portrait of, 2220.

Powers of Federal and State Governments, discussed by, 2310, 2456, 2460, 2490, 2506.

Principles of laws of war, discussed by, 2444.

Proclamations of—

Discriminating duties suspended on vessels of—

Brazil, 2372.

France, 2371.

Existence of war between United States and Mexico, 2320.

Extraordinary session of Senate, 2539.

Privileges of other ports granted Lewiston, N. Y., 2319.

Retrocession of Alexander County to Virginia, 2320.

Treaty with Mexico, 2477.

Request of House for—

Account of expense for foreign intercourse refused, 2281.

Information regarding foreign intercourse refused by, 2416, 2452.

Referred to, 2529.

Request of Senate for information regarding annexation of Texas refused by, 2232.

Slavery discussed by, 2490.

State of the Union discussed by, 2321, 2382, 2479.

Tariff discussed by, 2253, 2301, 2348, 2366, 2403, 2497, 2506.

Texas, relations with, discussed by. (See Texas.)

To cultivate peace and good will with all nations, policy of American people, 2383.

Veto messages of—
Continuing works in Wisconsin, reasons for applying pocket veto, 2460.
French spoliation claims, 2316.
Improvement of rivers and harbors, 2310.

Veto power of President discussed by, 2512.

Warehousing system, discussed by, 2405.

Poll.—(a) The receiving and counting of votes, or the act of voting. (b) The place where votes are cast and received.

Poll Tax.—An individual or head tax levied upon the male citizens of some foreign countries and a portion of the United States. The Federal Government has the power to levy such a tax in proportion to the census (20) but has never exercised it. Before the Revolution the Colonies levied poll taxes at various times. In 1898 twenty-seven states and territories levied and collected a poll tax. Some states, as South Carolina, have constitutional provisions for levying the poll tax. In Ohio and some other states any tax on polls is prohibited by the constitution. In others, as in Massachusetts and Tennessee, its payment is made a qualification for voting. Many of the states devote their revenue from poll taxes to free schools.

Pollock vs. Farmers' Loan and Trust Co. (See Income Tax Cases.)

Polyandry.—Having more than one husband;—the antithesis of Monandry (q. v.).

Polygamy (see also Mormons):
Discussed by President—
Arthur, 4644, 4731, 4771, 4837.
Buchanan, 2985.
Cleveland, 4946, 5379.
Garfield, 4601.
Grant, 4105, 4157, 4309, 4310.
Harrison, Benj., 5553, 5641.
Hayes, 4511, 4557.
Roosevelt, 7428.
Pardons granted persons guilty of unlawful cohabitation under color of polygamous marriage, 5803, 5942.

Ponca Commission, appointment and report of, discussed, 4582.

Ponca Indians. (See Indian Tribes.)

Poncarar Indians. (See Indian Tribes.)

Pontiac's War.—A war between the English garrisons and settlers on the western frontier and a confederacy of the Delaware, Shawnee, Mingo, Ottawa, Chippewa, and other Indian tribes, led by Pontiac, an Ottawa chief. Pontiac assembled a great council of Indians near Detroit April 27, 1763, and unfolded his plans for retarding or preventing white settlers locating west of Pittsburg. To capture Detroit was Pontiac's special task, and May 7 was the date selected, but the commander of the post was warned of the plot by an Indian girl, and the attempt was not made. The town was surrounded, however, and July 31 the garrison made a night attack on the Indians in which 59 English were killed or wounded. Oct. 12 Pontiac raised the siege and retired. Forts Sandusky, St. Joseph, Miami, Ouatanon, Mackinaw, Presque Isle, Le Bœuf, and Venango were taken and their garrisons massacred by the Indians in this war. A treaty of peace was made in 1766. Pontiac was murdered by a Kaskaskia Indian in 1769.

Pontifical States. (See Italy; Papal States.)

Pontoon-Bridge.—A bridge for small bodies, as the support of a flooring or road.

Poor Richard's Almanac.—In 1732 Benjamin Franklin began the publication of Poor Richard's Almanac. It contained many homely but very striking maxims, and for this reason became famous.

Pope of Rome, sentiments of regard for President, conveyed, referred to, 2761.

Popular Vote.—Vote of the people. The popular vote has been gradually extended, and by the XVII Amendment provision was made for the election of United States Senators by direct popular vote. (See Amendments.)

Population.—The first United States census having been taken in 1790, all population figures previous to that date are based upon estimates.

Early estimates, of somewhat doubtful accuracy, give the following population figures for the colonies and states since incorporated into the Union:

1688...... 200,000	1760......1,695,000	
1714...... 434,000	1770......2,312,000	
1750......1,260,000	1780......2,945,000	

The number of immigrants added to the population was estimated for different periods as follows:

From 1654 to 1701......... 134,000
From 1702 to 1800......... 492,000
From 1801 to 1820......... 178,000
From 1821 to 1890.........15,000,000

The people of New England were almost purely English; those of New York largely Dutch, Pennsylvania and the countries to the southward attracted many Germans, Scotch, Irish, and Huguenot immigrants, the latter settling largely in South Carolina and Georgia.

Population, Center of.—(See Center of Population.)

Population of the United States from 1790 to 1917. (See table on following page.)

Populist or People's Party.—In December, 1889, a meeting of the Farmers' and Laborers' Union of America was held at St. Louis, Mo., for the purpose of consolidating the various bodies of organized farmers which had been formed at different times and places in the United States since 1867, and which were known

POPULATION OF THE UNITED STATES AT TEN-YEAR INTERVALS BETWEEN 1790 AND 1910, AS SHOWN BY THE FEDERAL CENSUS, TOGETHER WITH ESTIMATES FOR JULY 1, 1915, AND 1917, BASED ON INCREASES SHOWN FROM 1900 TO 1910.

States and Territories	1790	1800	1810	1820	1830	1840	1850	1860	1870	1880	1890	1900	1910	1915	1917
Alabama				127,901	309,527	590,756	771,623	964,201	996,992	1,262,505	1,513,017	1,828,697	2,138,093	2,301,277	2,348,273
Alaska Territory												63,592	64,356	64,356	64,873
Arizona									9,658	40,440	59,620	122,931	204,354	247,299	259,666
Arkansas				14,273	30,388	97,574	209,897	435,450	484,471	802,525	1,128,179	1,311,564	1,574,449	1,807,229	1,853,665
California							92,597	379,994	560,247	864,694	1,208,130	1,485,053	2,377,549	2,843,275	2,983,843
Colorado								34,277	39,864	194,327	419,198	539,700	799,024	935,799	975,190
Connecticut	237,946	251,002	261,942	275,248	297,675	309,978	370,792	460,147	537,454	622,700	746,258	908,420	1,114,756	1,223,583	1,254,926
Dakota								4,837	14,181	135,177	Divided into North and South Dakota.				
Delaware	59,096	64,273	72,674	72,749	76,748	78,085	91,532	112,216	125,015	146,608	168,493	184,735	202,322	211,598	214,270
District of Columbia		14,093	24,023	33,039	39,834	43,712	51,687	75,080	131,700	177,624	230,392	278,718	331,069	358,679	366,631
Florida					34,730	54,477	87,445	140,424	187,748	269,493	391,422	528,542	751,139	870,802	904,839
Georgia	82,548	162,686	252,433	340,989	516,823	691,392	906,185	1,057,286	1,184,109	1,542,180	1,837,353	2,216,331	2,609,121	2,816,289	2,875,953
Hawaii Territory												154,001	191,909	211,909	217,660
Idaho									14,999	32,610	84,385	161,772	325,594	411,996	436,881
Illinois			12,282	55,211	157,445	476,183	851,470	1,711,951	2,539,891	3,077,871	3,826,351	4,821,550	5,638,591	6,069,519	6,193,626
Indiana		5,641	24,520	147,178	343,031	685,866	988,416	1,350,428	1,680,637	1,978,301	2,192,404	2,516,462	2,700,876	2,798,142	2,826,154
Indian Territory												Merged into Oklahoma 1a.			
Iowa						43,112	192,214	674,913	1,194,020	1,624,615	1,911,896	2,231,853	2,224,771	2,220,771	2,224,771
Kansas								107,206	364,399	996,096	1,427,096	1,470,495	1,690,949	1,807,228	1,824,771
Kentucky	73,677	220,955	406,511	564,317	687,917	779,828	982,405	1,155,684	1,321,011	1,648,690	1,858,635	2,147,174	2,289,905	2,365,185	2,386,866
Louisiana			76,556	153,407	215,739	352,411	517,762	708,002	726,915	939,946	1,118,587	1,381,625	1,656,388	1,801,306	1,843,042
Maine	96,540	151,719	228,705	298,335	399,455	501,793	583,169	628,279	626,915	648,936	661,086	694,466	742,371	767,638	774,914
Maryland	319,728	341,548	380,546	407,350	447,040	470,019	583,034	687,049	780,894	934,943	1,042,390	1,188,044	1,295,346	1,351,941	1,368,240
Massachusetts	378,787	422,845	472,040	523,287	610,408	737,699	994,514	1,231,066	1,457,351	1,783,085	2,238,943	2,805,346	3,366,416	3,662,339	3,744,564
Michigan		8,850	4,762	8,896	31,639	212,267	397,654	749,113	1,184,059	1,636,937	2,093,889	2,420,982	2,810,173	3,015,442	3,074,560
Minnesota							6,077	172,023	439,706	780,773	1,301,826	1,751,394	2,075,708	2,246,761	2,296,024
Mississippi		8,850	40,352	75,448	136,621	375,651	606,526	791,305	827,922	1,131,597	1,289,600	1,551,270	1,797,114	1,926,778	1,964,122
Missouri			19,783	66,586	140,455	383,702	682,044	1,182,012	1,721,295	2,168,380	2,679,184	3,106,665	3,293,335	3,391,789	3,420,143
Montana									20,595	39,159	132,159	243,329	376,053	446,054	466,214
Nebraska									122,993	452,402	1,058,910	1,066,300	1,192,214	1,258,624	1,277,750
Nevada								6,857	42,491	62,266	45,761	42,335	81,875	108,736	108,736
New Hampshire	141,885	183,858	214,460	244,161	269,328	284,574	317,976	326,073	318,300	346,991	376,530	411,588	430,572	435,575	442,530
New Jersey	184,139	211,149	245,562	277,575	320,823	373,306	489,555	672,035	906,096	1,131,116	1,444,933	1,883,669	2,537,167	2,881,840	2,936,467
New Mexico									91,874	119,565	153,593	195,310	327,301	396,917	416,066
New York	340,120	589,051	959,049	1,372,812	1,918,608	2,428,921	3,097,394	3,880,735	4,382,759	5,082,871	5,997,853	7,268,894	9,113,279	10,086,568	10,366,778
North Carolina	393,751	478,103	555,500	638,829	737,987	753,419	869,039	992,622	1,071,361	1,399,750	1,617,947	1,893,810	2,206,287	2,371,095	2,418,559
North Dakota											182,719	319,146	577,056	713,083	752,260
Ohio		45,365	230,760	581,434	937,903	1,519,467	1,980,329	2,339,511	2,665,260	3,198,062	3,672,316	4,157,545	4,767,155	5,088,627	5,181,220
Oklahoma												398,331	1,657,155	2,114,307	2,245,968
Oregon							13,294	52,465	90,923	174,768	313,767	413,536	672,765	809,490	848,806
Pennsylvania	434,373	602,365	810,091	1,049,458	1,348,233	1,724,033	2,311,786	2,906,215	3,521,951	4,282,891	5,258,014	6,302,115	7,665,111	8,383,992	8,591,029
Rhode Island	68,825	69,122	76,931	83,059	97,199	108,830	147,545	174,620	217,353	276,531	345,506	428,556	542,610	602,765	620,090
South Carolina	249,073	345,591	415,115	502,741	581,185	594,398	668,507	703,708	705,606	995,577	1,151,149	1,340,316	1,515,400	1,607,745	1,634,340
South Dakota											328,808	401,570	583,888	680,046	707,740
Tennessee	35,691	105,602	261,727	422,823	681,904	829,210	1,002,717	1,109,801	1,258,520	1,542,359	1,767,518	2,020,616	2,184,789	2,271,379	2,296,316
Texas							212,592	604,215	818,579	1,591,749	2,235,523	3,048,710	3,896,542	4,293,310	4,472,494
Utah							11,380	40,273	86,786	143,963	207,905	276,749	373,351	423,300	438,974
Vermont	85,425	154,465	217,895	235,981	280,652	291,948	314,120	315,098	330,551	332,286	332,422	343,641	355,956	362,452	364,974
Virginia	747,610	880,200	974,600	1,065,366	1,211,405	1,239,797	1,421,661	1,596,318	1,225,163	1,512,565	1,655,980	1,854,184	2,061,612	2,171,014	2,205,522
Washington									23,955	75,116	349,390	518,103	1,141,990	1,471,043	1,565,810
West Virginia								11,594	442,014	618,457	762,704	958,800	1,221,119	1,359,474	1,399,320
Wisconsin			40,352			30,945	305,391	775,881	1,054,670	1,315,497	1,686,880	2,069,042	2,333,860	2,473,533	2,513,758
Wyoming									9,118	20,789	92,531	60,705	145,965	174,148	182,264
Total	3,929,214	5,308,483	7,239,881	9,638,453	12,866,020	17,069,453	23,191,876	31,443,321	38,558,371	50,155,783	62,622,250	75,994,575	91,972,266	100,399,318	102,826,309

Unorganized Non-Contiguous Territory.—Panama Canal Zone, 61,279; Philippine Islands, 8,643,302; Porto Rico, 1,183,173; Tutuila Group and Guam, 19,491; Total, 9,907,245.

under the general name of Grangers (q. v.). The consolidated body was called the Farmers' Alliance and Industrial Union. On Dec. 2, 1890, a national convention was held at Ocala, Fla. Thirty-five States and Territories were represented by 163 delegates. Independent political action was decided upon, and a platform was adopted advocating free silver, the sub-treasury plan, equal taxation, a graduated income tax, election of President, Vice-President, and Senators by direct vote, and prohibition of alien ownership of land.

The second convention was held at Cin-cinnati, Ohio, May 19, 1891. Thirty States and Territories were represented by 1,418 delegates. At this convention the Ocala platform was heartily indorsed and the name People's party was adopted. A third national meeting was held at St. Louis, Mo., in February, 1892. It was decided to put in the field candidates for President and Vice-President, and on July 2, 1892, a national body of delegates met at Omaha, Nebr., and nominated Gen. James B. Weav-er, of Iowa, for President, and James G. Field, of Virginia, for Vice-President. Weaver obtained a popular vote of 1,041,-028 and an electoral vote of 22.

In 1896 the People's party met at St. Louis, Mo., and nominated for President William J. Bryan of Nebraska, and for Vice-President Thomas E. Watson, of Georgia. Mr. Bryan had been previously nominated for the Presidency by the Demo-cratic party. In the popular vote the Bryan and Watson ticket (straight Popu-list) received 245,728 votes, and Bryan and Sewall ticket (Democratic and straight fusion ticket) 6,257,198 votes. In the electoral college McKinley and Hobart (Re-publican candidates) received 271 votes. Bryan, 176, Sewall 149, and Watson 27. On May 10, 1900, a convention of the fusion wing of the party met at Sioux Falls, S. D., and nominated William J. Bryan for President and Charles A. Town for Vice-President. Mr. Town withdrew in favor of Adlai Stevenson, the Demo-cratic candidate, and on Aug. 28th the ex-ecutive committee nominated Mr. Steven-son. The anti-fusion wing of the party met at Cincinnati on May 10th and nomi-nated Wharton Barker for President and Ignatius Donnelly for Vice-President. The Democratic and fusion nominees received 6,374,397 popular votes and 155 electoral votes. The anti-fusion (middle of the road) wing of the People's party received 50,373 popular votes. In 1904 the People's party nominated Thomas E. Watson for President and Thomas H. Tibbles for Vice-President and they received 120,903 votes. In 1908 Watson and Samuel Williams of Indiana were nominated to head the ticket. The vote this year fell to 33,871.

Pork-Barrel.—A term applied, in compara-tively recent years, to the Congressional ap-propriations for local improvements, with the insinuation that they are not vital to the cause of the country, but that they are obtained as a result of "log-rolling" (q. v.) and favoritism, and for the purpose of im-pressing constituents with the importance of their Congressmen or Senators,—such as appropriations for rivers and harbors, post-office buildings, etc.

Pork Products. (See Animals and Ani-mal Products.)

Port Gibson (Miss.), Battle of.—On the night of April 16, 1863, the Federal gun-boats under Admiral Porter succeeded in running past the batteries at Vicksburg. Grant ordered Sherman to make a feint on the Confederate batteries at Haines Bluff,

above Vicksburg, while Porter covered the landing of McClernand's and McPherson's corps at Bruinsburg, a few miles below Grand Gulf. Immediately upon landing Mc-Clernand pushed forward toward Port Gib-son. A march of eight miles brought him in sight of the Confederates, whom he forced back until dark. The next day (May 2) the Confederates held a strong position, which they stubbornly defended. That night the troops slept on their arms. During the night the Confederate forces retired across the Bayou Pierre, pursued next day by Mc-Pherson's corps. The Federal loss was 131 killed, 719 wounded, and 25 missing—a total of 875. One thousand prisoners and 5 cannon were taken from the Confederates.

Port Hudson (La), Surrender of.—As early as August, 1862, Confederates began to fortify Port Hudson, a point on the Mis-sissippi River in Louisiana, at the terminus of the Clinton and Port Hudson Railroad, twenty-five miles above Baton Rouge and one hundred and forty-seven miles above New Or-leans. Dec. 14, 1862, Maj.-Gen. N. P. Banks took command of the Department of the Gulf, and in March, 1863, made a demon-stration against Port Hudson while Farra-gut's fleet attempted to run the batteries to assist Porter in the naval investment of Vicksburg. The attempt was a failure. May 26, 1863, Banks again invested Port Hud-son, and was reenforced by Maj.-Gen. Au-gur, Brig.-Gen. T. W. Sherman, and Gen. Weitzel, increasing his forces to 12,000 men. An unsuccessful assault was made on the 27th, which showed the place to be strongly fortified. Banks lost 2,000 men in the as-sault. June 14 a second assault was made after a bombardment of several days by Far-ragut's fleet. This was also repulsed, with a loss of 700 killed and wounded. Banks now invested the place by a series of ap-proaches. July 6 the news of the surrender of Vicksburg reached Port Hudson, and three days later Gardner surrendered, with 6,340 men and 51 guns. Besides, the gar-rison lost about 500 prisoners or deserters before the surrender, and about 700 killed and wounded.

Port Republic (Va.), Battle of.—June 9, 1862, the morning after the skirmish be-tween the forces of Ewell and Frémont at Cross Keys, Jackson drew in Ewell, crossed the branch of the Shenandoah, and destroy-ing the bridges cut off two brigades of Shields's advance from Frémont, defeated them in battle, and captured some 450 pris-oners and 800 muskets.

Port Royal (S. C.), Expedition to.—Oct. 29, 1861, a strong naval and military ex-pedition left Hampton Roads under com-mand of Commodore Samuel F. Du Pont and Gen. Thomas W. Sherman. The first was composed of the steam frigate *Wabash*, fourteen gunboats, twenty-two first-class and twelve smaller steamers, and twenty-six sail-ing vessels. The land forces under Sherman consisted of thirteen regiments of volun-teers, forming three brigades and numbering 10,000 men. After a tempestuous voyage the fleet arrived off Port Royal, S. C., Nov. 3. Upon each side of the mouth of the Broad River is an island on which the Confederates had built forts. On Bay Point Fort Beaure-gard mounted twenty-three guns, and on Hil-ton Head, opposite, Fort Walker had six, some of them of the largest caliber. A fleet of eight steamers lay inside the har-bor. The guns of the fort were fully manned by 1,700 South Carolinians, and a field battery with 500 men supported one of them. On the 7th Du Pont brought his gun-boats into action. He manœuvred his fleet in a circle around the harbor between the forts, firing broadsides as he passed the Confederate batteries. His shells wrought havoc in the works, but the moving ships were little damaged. For four hours the battle raged, when the garrison retreated leaving everything behind. Forty-three guns were captured. Hilton Head was made the center of later naval operations.

Porto Rico.—The island of Porto Rico, over which the flag of the United States was raised in token of formal possession on October 18, 1898, is the most eastern of the Great Antilles in the West Indies and is separated on the east from the Danish island of St. Thomas by a distance of about fifty miles, and from Haiti on the west by the Mona passage, seventy miles wide. Distances from San Juan, the capital, to important points are as follows: New York, 1,411 miles; Charleston, S. C., 1,200 miles; Key West, Fla., 1,050 miles; Havana, 1,000 miles.

The island is a parallelogram in general outline, 108 miles from the east to the west and from 37 to 43 miles across, the area being about 3,600 square miles, or somewhat less than half that of the State of New Jersey (Delaware has 2,050 square miles and Connecticut 4,990 square miles). The population according to an enumeration made by the United States Government in 1900 showed a population of 953,243, of whom 589,426 are white and 363,817 are colored. The density was 260 to the square mile in 1900; 83.2 per cent of the population could not read. The population in 1910 is reported as 1,118,012.

Porto Rico is unusually fertile, and its dominant industries are agriculture and lumbering. In elevated regions the vegetation of the temperate zone is not unknown. There are more than 500 varieties of trees found in the forests, and the plains are full of palm, orange, and other trees. The principal crops are sugar, coffee, tobacco, and maize, but oranges, bananas, rice, pineapples, and many other fruits are important products. The largest article of export from Porto Rico is sugar. The next is tobacco. Other exports in order of amount are coffee, fruits, molasses, cattle, timber, and hides.

The principal minerals found in Porto Rico are gold, carbonates, and sulphides of copper and magnetic oxide of iron in large quantities. Lignite is found at Utuado and Moca, and also yellow amber. A large variety of marbles, limestones, and other building stones are deposited on the island, but these resources are very undeveloped. There are salt works at Guanica and Salina on the south coast, and at Cape Rojo on the west, and these constitute the principal mineral industry in Porto Rico.

The principal cities are Mayaguez, with 16,939, Ponce, 35,027 inhabitants; and San Juan, the capital, with 48,716. The shipments of domestic merchandise from the United States to Porto Rico, year ending June 30, 1913, were $32,223,191. The exports of domestic merchandise to the United States were $40,529,665. The foreign trade, year ending June 30, 1913, was: Imports, $3,745,057; exports, $8,564,942.

An act providing for a civil government for Porto Rico was passed by the Fifty-sixth Congress and received the assent of the President April 12, 1900 (page 6678). Under this act a civil government was established which went into effect May 1, 1900. There are two legislative chambers, the Executive Council, or "upper house," composed of the Government Secretary, Attorney-General, Treasurer, Auditor, Commissioner of the Interior, and Commissioner of Education, and five citizens appointed by the President, and the House of Delegates, or "lower house," consisting of thirty-five members, elected by the people. The island is represented in the Congress of the United States by a Resident Commissioner.

President Roosevelt in messages to Congress Dec. 5, 1905 (page 7018), Dec. 3, 1906 (page 7051), Dec. 3, 1907 (page 7104) and Dec. 8, 1908 (page 7233) recommended the granting of United States citizenship to the Porto Ricans, and a bill was introduced in the Sixty-second Congress providing for the same, but failed to reach a final vote.

The Legislature of 1912 enacted a sanitation law establishing an insular board of health, and a general sanitary organization, provided a bureau of labor, and authorized investment by the treasurer of $200,000 in first mortgage bonds of a corporation to be organized for the construction of a modern hotel in San Juan. It also authorized a bond issue of $500,000 in connection with port improvement at San Juan. The Legislature of 1913 provided for the retirement on three-quarter pay of the Justices of the Supreme Court of the island after ten years' service, and upon reaching sixty-five years of age, and ordered the establishment of an insular hospital in each of the seven districts in which the island is divided, for those suffering from transmissible and contagious diseases.

Sanitary problems connected with, referred to, 6341.

Slavery in, discussed, 4100.

Release of persons held in, discussed, 4194.

Tariff laws of, evidence of modifications of, proclaimed, 5583.

Referred to, 5615, 5747.

Telephones in, 6732.

Vessels from certain ports of, duties on, suspended by proclamation, 4871.

Vessels of Spain from, discriminating duties on, suspended by proclamation, 4810, 5075, 5155.

Discussed, 5089.

Suspension revoked, 5074.

Vessels of United States, discriminating duties and fines on, in, 4626, 4714, 4763, 4786, 4788, 5961.

Abolished, 4810, 5155.

Retaliatory measures, discussed, 4763.

Visit of American naval officer to, referred to, 845.

Ports. (See Rivers and Harbors.)

Portsmouth, N. H., dry dock at, about completed, 2669.

Site for, 934.

Portsmouth, Ohio, act to erect public building at, vetoed, 5152.

Portsmouth, Treaty of.—A treaty of peace between Russia and Japan, at Portsmouth, N. H., Sept. 5, 1905, bringing to a close the war that had been waged between those two countries since Feb. 11, 1904.

Shortly after the battle of the Japan Sea, May 27-29, 1905 (see Japan), President Roosevelt, after conference with the Russian Ambassador and the Japanese Minister, sent identical notes to the Governments of the two countries, urging them to begin direct peace negotiations with each other, and offering the services of the United States in bringing their envoys together. Japan accepted the proposition two days later, and Russia within a week. Various places were proposed for the meeting: Paris. The Hague, Chefoo, Geneva, and Washington. As the summer heat made the latter place unsuitable, the United States Government offered the use of a building at the United States Navy Yard, at Portsmouth, N. H., and the offer was accepted. The envoys appointed were, on the part of Japan, Baron Komura, Minister of Foreign Affairs, and Kogoro Takahira, Minister to the United States; and on the part of Russia, Count Sergius Witte and Baron Rosen, Ambassador to the United States.

On Aug. 5 the envoys assembled on the United States cruiser, *Mayflower,* near Oyster Bay, L. I., and were introduced by President Roosevelt. The sessions of the conference began Aug. 9, when the Japanese presented their terms: I. Recognition by Russia of the preponderating influence of Japan in Korea; II. Simultaneous evacuation of Manchuria by Russia and Japan; III. Transfer to Japan of the Russian leases of Port Arthur and Dalny; IV. The return of Manchuria to China according to the previous agreement between Russia and China; V. The cession of Sakhalin Island to Japan; VI. The transfer to Japan of all public property in Port Arthur and Dalny, rights of private property to be respected; VII. The transfer to Japan of the Manchurian railroad between Port Arthur and Dalny and Harbin; VIII. Russia to retain the main line in Vladivostok; IX. The reimbursement of Japan for the expenses of the war; X. The surrender to Japan of the Russian warships interned at neutral ports; XI. Limitation of Russia's naval strength in the Pacific; XII. Fishing rights for citizens of Japan in Russian waters.

To some of these Russia agreed at once; but the questions of indemnity and the cession of the Island of Sakhalin still remained open, and by the 19th of August the negotiations seemed certain to end in failure. The pressure of neutral nations, brought to bear on both parties, and especially the influence of President Roosevelt, led to a compromise. Japan waived the question of indemnity, and withdrew her demand for the interned warships; while Russia consented to the surrender of the southern half of the island of Sakhalin. Each nation agreed to pay the cost of the maintenance of its prisoners of war, an arrangement much to the advantage of Japan. An agreement was reached August 29, and the formal treaty was signed Sept. 5, 1905. Ratifications of the treaty were exchanged on Oct. 14, 1905. (See also Japan.)

Portugal.—Continental Portugal occupies part of the maritime district of the Iberian Peninsula, between 6° 15'-9° 30' W. longitude, and 37°-42° 8' N. latitude, and is bounded on the north and east by Spain, and on the south and west by the Atlantic Ocean. The Azores and Madeira Islands form an integral part of Portugal for administrative purposes.

Physical Features.—Portugal is generally hilly, but with no great heights, and there are many plains. The principal rivers are Douro, Tagus, Guadiana and Minho. The climate is equable and temperate, the southwestern winds bringing an abundant rainfall. Lisbon has an annual mean temperature of 61° F., but there is a difference of 50° F. in the extremes.

History.—From the close of the eleventh century until the revolution of 1910 the government of Portugal was a monarchy, and in the year 1500 the King of Portugal was "Lord of the conquest, navigation, and commerce of India, Ethiopia, Arabia and Persia," the territories of the Empire including also the Vice-Royalty of Brazil, which declared its independence in 1822 (see Brazil). In 1910 an armed rising drove the King and the Royal family into exile, effected a separation of Church and State and set up a Republic.

Government.—The National Assembly of Aug. 21, 1911, sanctioned the Republic and adopted a Constitution, with a President elected by Congress for four years, a Congress of two Chambers, and an Executive appointed by the President but responsible to the Legislature. The Republic was formally recognized by the Powers on Sept. 11, 1911. President of the Republic (Aug. 24, 1911-1915), Dr. Manoel d'Arriaga. There is a Congress of two houses, the Senate and the Chamber of Deputies. The Senate consists of seventy-one members, elected by the Municipal Councils of the Republic for six years, one-half renewable every three years. The Chamber of Deputies (or National Council) consists of 164 members, elected by direct vote for three years.

There are Courts of first instance in each

of the 193 judicial districts or comarcas, with Courts of Appeal (tribunaes de relação) at Lisbon and Oporto and at Ponta Delgada in the Azores. There is a Supreme Court of Appeal at Lisbon.

The Republic is divided into twenty-one Districts (Continental Portugal seventeen, Azores three, Madeira one), governed by an appointed Governor, a District Auditor and an elective council of three members.

AREA AND POPULATION

Districts	Area in English Sq. Miles	Population Census 1911
Aveiro	1,064	336,243
Azores	922	242,560
Beja	3,958	192,499
Braga	1,041	382,276
Bragança	2,512	192,024
Castello Branco	2,581	241,184
Coimbra	1,507	359,387
Evora	2,856	148,295
Faro	1,937	272,861
Guarda	2,114	271,616
Leiria	1,316	262,632
Lisboa	3,085	852,854
Madeira	314	169,783
Portalegre	2,404	141,481
Porto	892	679,540
Santarem	2,554	325,775
Vianna do Castello	857	227,250
Villa Real	1,649	245,547
Vizeu	1,937	416,744
Total Portugal	35,500	5,960,056
Portuguese Colonies	804,841	9,675,000
Grand Total	840,341	15,635,056

In 1911 there were 41,197 foreigners resident in Portugal, of whom 20,517 were Spanish, 12,143 Brazilians, 2,516 British, 1,832 French, 1,645 Americans.

For the army see Armies of the World and for the navy see Navies of the World.

Production and Industry.—The principal products are wheat, barley, oats, maize, flax and hemp, while the vine is extensively cultivated, the best wine being produced in the elevated tracts, and the commoner kinds in the low-lying country. In the plains and lowlands rice, olives, oranges, lemons, citrons, figs, and almonds are abundantly grown. The vine and the olive are the chief branches of industry, the rich red wine known as "port" being grown in the Paiz do Vinho and carried down the Douro partly in sailing vessels but mainly by rail, for shipment at Oporto. The Live Stock (1910) included cattle, sheep, pigs, and horses.

There are extensive forests of oak, chestnut, seapine, and cork, covering nearly 27 per cent of the cultivated area of the country, and cork products are largely manufactured for export, while the wine trade requires much timber for the numerous cooperages, much of which, however, is imported from abroad.

The value of the fish landed annually is about 6,000,000 milreis, including tunny fish and sardines and fresh water salmon, 8,298 vessels employing 26,892 men, are engaged in the deep-sea and coast fisheries.

Education.—Primary is free and nominally compulsory between the ages of seven and fifteen, but attendances are not strictly enforced, and over 75 per cent of the population above seven years old are illiterate. The University of Coimbra (founded in 1291 at Lisbon and transferred to Coimbra in 1527) has a library of 150,000 volumes. In 1910 there were 1,100 matriculated students at the University.

Finance.—The average annual revenue for the five years ending with 1913 was 72,-000,000 escudos, and the expenditure for the same time averaged 76,000,000 escudos. The escudo, the unit of value, is the ancient milreis, and is equivalent to $1.08 United States money. The debt was stated on Jan. 1, 1913, at $64,018,000, with carrying charges of $21,701,000.

Railways, etc.—In 1910 there were 1,760 miles of railway open and working, of which 680 miles were State owned. The principal lines cross the Spanish border to the ports of Lisbon and Oporto, and a coastal system runs from the northern boundary to Faro on the south coast. The principal waterways are the Lower Tagus and the Douro, the latter traversing the wine district, which provides most of the traffic.

Cities.—Capital, Lisbon, on the Tagus. Population (1911) 435,359. Oporto had a population (1911) of 194,664. There are no other large cities.

Trade with the United States.—The value of merchandise imported into Portugal from the United States for the year 1913 was $4,167 158, and goods to the value of $6,-870,223 were sent thither—a balance of $2,703,065 in favor of Portugal.

PORTUGUESE INDIA has an area of 1,470 square miles, with an estimated population of 605,000. The Portuguese dominions consist of Goa on the western coast of India, about 265 miles southeast of Bombay; Damão, on the east side of the Gulf of Cambay, and of Diu, a town and fort on an island on the west side of the same gulf. These settlements form a single administrative province under a Governor-General.

MACAO is a settlement on the western side of the estuary of the Canton River, occupied by the Portuguese in the sixteenth century, and finally ceded by China in 1887.

PORTUGUESE TIMOR consists of the northern portion of Timor, a large island in the Malay Archipelago, of an enclave on the northwest coast of the island, and of the neighboring island of Pulo Cambing, with area of 7,450 square miles, and an estimated population of 300,000.

CAPE VERDE ISLANDS are an archipelago of the west African coast, between 14° 47'-17° 13' N. latitude and 22° 40'-25° 22' W. longitude, consisting of twelve islands. They were settled by the Portuguese, who imported negroes from the African coast to work the plantations, slavery being finally abolished in 1876. The inhabitants are mainly negroes and mulattoes, who speak a debased form of Portuguese, and belong to the Roman Catholic Church. Coffee is the principal product, maize, millet, sugar cane, manioc, oranges, tobacco and cotton being also grown. The exports are coffee, physic-nuts, millet, sugar, spirits, salt, live animals, skins and fish; the imports being coal, textiles, food stuffs, wine, metals, tobacco, pottery, machinery and vegetables.

PORTUGUESE GUINEA extends along the west coast of Africa between the Casamanci district of Senegal (French) and French Guinea. The settlement includes also Orango, Bolama, Bissao and other islands, and has a total area of about 14,000 square miles, with an estimated population of 300,-000 to 500,000, of various negro tribes. The interior is dense forest with palms, ebony and mahogany.

SÃO THOMÉ and *PRINCIPÉ* are two islands in the Gulf of Guinea. The principal product of both islands is cocoa, the exports of which were about one-sixth of the world's supply in 1907. Exaggerated reports as to the conditions of indentured laborers stopped the cocoa exports from 1909-1910, but the conditions have now been radically altered.

ANGOLA lies south of the Kongo River in West Africa and extends eastward as far as Rhodesia. The northern boundary is that of the Belgian Kongo, and the southern boundary is conterminous with German Southwest Africa.

PORTUGUESE EAST AFRICA lies between German East Africa on the north and Natal on the south. The area is estimated as 300,000 square miles, with population not exceeding 3,200,000, of whom about 10,000 are Europeans. Of the natives, 90 per cent are Bantu negroes. The Province of Moçambique is administered by a Governor-General, with headquarters at Lourenço Marques. Large portions of the territory are leased to the Companhia de Moçambique (headquarters, Beira), the Companhia di Zambezia (Quelimane), and the Companhia do Nyasa (Porto Amelia). The mineral resources include coal and ironstone, malachite, copper, gold, petroleum and bitumen. The agricultural products are wheat and other cereals, sugar-cane, rice, groundnuts, coffee and tobacco. The exports are principally rubber, sugar, coal, beeswax, coco-nuts, copra and mangrove bark, ivory, cattle, skins and hides, ground-nuts, cotton, tobacco and gold; the imports being cotton goods, hardware and foodstuffs. The special trade of the Province is about 30,000,-000 escudos annually, the transit trade being of approximately the same value, on the way to and from the Transvaal (via Lourenço Marques and Beira).

Portugal (see also Lisbon; Oporto):

Blockade established by, claims of United States growing out of, 1098, 1113, 1243.

Brazil, questions with respecting escape of insurgent Admiral Da Gama, 5956.

Citizens of, effort made to improve condition of, 762, 786.

Claims of United States against, 1071, 1113, 1157, 1243, 1317, 2268, 2453, 2550, 2618, 2680, 2759. (See also *General Armstrong*, The; *Miles*, The.)

Admitted, but payment of, delayed, 1456.

Convention for adjustment of, referred to, 2618, 2642, 2655.

Payment of, 1157, 1243, 1368, 1749, 2655.

Commercial relations with, 811.

Vessels sent to protect American interests, 1099.

Copyright privilege extended, by proclamation, 5830.

Cotton culture in African possessions of, referred to, 3267.

Diplomatic relations with, resumed, 1008.

Duties on rice reduced by, 1243.

Friendly disposition of, toward United States, 919.

Government of, removed to Lisbon, 674.

Internal tranquility restored to, 1317.

Minister of United States in, 90.

Salary of, referred to, 3667.

Railroad in, operated by American citizens, seized by Government of, 5470.

Claim regarding, submitted to arbitration, 5546.

Relations with, 89, 168, 820.

Republic of, recognized, 8049.

Revenue laws of United States, complaints of, against, referred to, 1956.

Slavery in colonies of, abolition of, discussed, 4289.

Treaty with, referred to, 1821, 1839, 1894, 2127.

Vessels of—

Discriminating duties on, suspended by proclamation, 4080.

Report regarding, 1135, 1443.

Requested by Portugal, 1442.

Duties on, 1135.

Proclamation levying duties on, 1589.

Referred to, 1592.

Vessels of United States seized or interfered with by, 1070, 1098, 1113, 1243.

Vice-consul of, to United States, exequatur of, revoked, 4038.

Wines of, duties on, referred to, 2127, 2250.

Portugal, Treaty with.—A reciprocal commercial arrangement was made with Portugal in 1900. It provides for a preferential tariff on goods (chiefly wines, their products, and works of art) coming into the United States; and on certain classes of goods (chiefly food-stuffs, machinery, oils, tar, and pitch) entering Portugal, the Azores, and Madeiras from the United States. Should the United States at any time impose high duties on crude cork and coffee from Portugal, that country reserves the right to arrest the operation of this convention on three months' notice. Arbitration, extradition and naturalization conventions are also in force.

Post-Office. (See Post-Office Department.)

Post-Offices.—First-class post-offices are those in which the postmaster receives a salary of more than $3,000 yearly; second class, those in which the postmasters' salaries are between $3,000 and $2,000 yearly; third class, those in which the postmasters' salaries are between $2,000 and $1,000 yearly; and fourth-class, those in which the postmasters' salaries are below $1,000 yearly. The salaries of postmasters in the first three classes depend upon the gross receipts of their offices, although third-class postmasters receive an additional three cents for each money order they issue. Fourth-class postmasters receive a commission on the cancellation of stamps in their offices. The scale provides that fourth-class postmasters receive the full amount of their cancellation up to $50 quarterly, with sliding scales between this amount and cancellation up to $250 quarterly, and in addition they receive rents of boxes in their offices. (See Post-Office Department.)

Post-Office Building:

Destruction of, by fire referred to, 1483.

Erection of—

Appropriation for, recommended, 1483, 1911.

Recommended, 1477, 1720.

Erection of, for joint use of Washington City post-office and Post-Office Department recommended, 5479.

Extension of, referred to, 2915, 2917.

Heating and ventilating of, referred to, 3110, 3112.

Illustration, frontispiece, Vol. IV.

Referred to, 1798.

Uniform standard in amount of gross receipts to fix right of community to, recommendations regarding, 5377.

Post-Office Department.—This department of the executive branch of the federal government was established under the Constitution Sept. 26, 1789, but the work then officially taken up by it had been in continuous operation from early colonial times. Up to 1693 the postal service was entirely carried on by the towns and villages. From that year until 1707 it was administered under the patent granted Thomas Neale by the King in 1691, Andrew Hamilton having been appointed Postmaster-General of America. He established a weekly service from Portsmouth, N. H., to Virginia, and so successful was his administration that he has been called "The Father of American posts." He was succeeded by his son, John Hamilton, in 1703.

On Dec. 25, 1774, Postmaster-General Foxcroft announced the end of the British postal system in North America, and on July 26, 1775, nearly a year before political independence was declared, the Continental Congress appointed Benjamin Franklin Postmaster-General of the Colonies. When Franklin was sent to Europe in 1776, Richard Bache, his son-in-law, was was Postmaster-General. In the passage of the postal ordinance of Oct. 18, 1782, which unified all previous postal acts, Congress required the payment of postage in silver or

its equivalent, and newspapers were admitted to transportation in the mails. The rates were fixed at 7.4 cents for single letters carried less than sixty miles; 11.1 cents for distances between sixty and a hundred miles and three cents for each additional hundred miles. It was in this year that the Post-Office Department, in distinction from the postal service, was practically created, and from this time the modern American post-office dates its origin. In the same year Ebenezer Hazard was appointed Postmaster-General. Under his administration an American Atlantic service was established and the domestic service perfected and extended, until, at the end of his term, 1789, there were eighty-five post-offices in the country and 2,399 miles of post-roads, the volume of business being about 300,000 letters a year.

Up to this time the means of transportation had been almost entirely by horseback, but an act of Congress of Sept. 6, 1785, gave the Postmaster-General power to make contracts for the transmission of mail by stage-coach. After the establishment of the Constitution, in 1789, the postal service was for a time carried on under the direction of the Treasury Department, although the postal ordinance of 1782 remained in force until 1792, when a new postal law reforming the postage tariff was passed.

The law permanently and definitely establishing the Department was passed May 8, 1799. In 1810 the office of Second Assistant Postmaster-General was created, a new postage tariff (8 to 25 cents, according to distances for single letters, and one cent each for newspapers not going beyond the State of publication) was established, and the various post-routes connected in one system. In 1811 the Department established a service between Baltimore and Philadelphia in coaches owned by the Government, and two years later the Postmaster-General was authorized to make use of steamboats in the transportation of mail.

The organic law of the Department was again changed in 1825, provision being made for the building of a General Post-Office at the seat of Government, and the Postmaster-General being given great powers in the conduct and development of the service. In 1827 the salary of the Postmaster-General was made $6,000 a year, the same as that of heads of the other Executive Departments, and two years later he was called to a seat in the Cabinet.

The present extent and recent growth of the service is shown in the following table:

FISCAL YEARS	Number of Post-Offices	Revenue of the Department	Expenditure of the Department	AMOUNT PAID FOR—	
				Compensation to Postmasters	Transportation of the Mail
1900	76,688	$102,354,579	$107,740,268	$19,112,097	$56,374,206
1901	76,945	111,631,193	115,554,920	19,949,514	58,264,040
1902	75,924	121,848,047	124,785,697	20,783,919	61,153,775
1903	74,169	134,224,443	138,784,488	21,631,724	65,321,711
1904	71,131	143,582,624	152,362,117	22,273,344	69,820,732
1905	68,131	152,826,585	167,399,169	22,743,342	72,862,605
1906	65,600	167,932,782	178,449,778	23,544,585	76,174,945
1907	62,659	183,585,005	190,238,288	24,575,696	81,090,849
1908	61,158	191,478,663	208,351,886	25,599,397	81,381,421
1909	60,144	203,562,383	221,004,102	26,569,892	84,052,596
1910	59,580	224,128,657	229,977,224	27,521,013	85,259,102
1911	59,237	237,879,823	237,648,926	28,284,964	88,058,922
1912	58,729	246,744,015	248,525,450	28,467,726	89,154,811
1913	58,020	266,619,525	262,067,541	29,162,662	92,278,517
1914	56,810	287,934,565	283,543,769	29,968,515	98,002,421
1915	56,380	287,248,165	298,546,026	30,400,145	104,701,200
1916	55,935	312,057,688	306,204,033	31,135,230	102,189,229

Of the whole number of post-offices at the close of the fiscal year, June 30, 1915, 8,920 were Presidential offices and 47,460 were fourth-class offices.

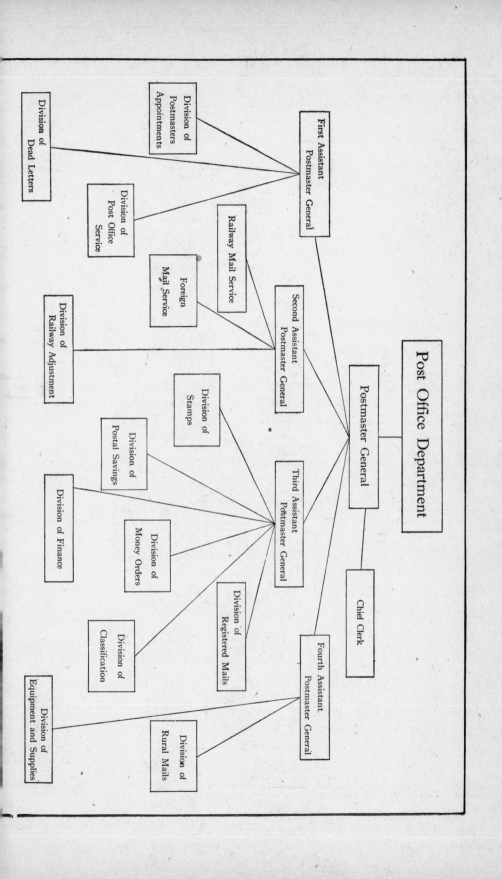

Post Office Department

Postmaster General

Chief Clerk

First Assistant Postmaster General
- Division of Postmasters Appointments
- Division of Dead Letters
- Division of Post Office Service

Second Assistant Postmaster General
- Railway Mail Service
- Foreign Mail Service
- Division of Railway Adjustment

Third Assistant Postmaster General
- Division of Stamps
- Division of Postal Savings
- Division of Finance
- Division of Money Orders
- Division of Registered Mails
- Division of Classification

Fourth Assistant Postmaster General
- Division of Equipment and Supplies
- Division of Rural Mails

Following is a list of the Postmasters-General and the Presidents under whom they served :*

PRESIDENT	Postmaster-General	Appointed
Washington	Samuel Osgood, Massachusetts...	1789
"	Timothy Pickering, Mass......	1791
"	Joseph Habersham, Georgia.....	1795
Adams....	" "	1897
Jefferson...	" "	1801
" ...	Gideon Granger, Connecticut....	1801
Madison...	" "	1809
" ...	Return J. Meigs, Jr., Ohio......	1814
Monroe....	" "	1817
"	John McLean, Ohio............	1823
J.Q. Adams	" "	1825
Jackson....	William T. Barry, Kentucky....	1829
" ...	Amos Kendall, Kentucky........	1835
Van Buren.	" "	1837
"	John M. Niles, Connecticut....	1840
Harrison...	Francis Granger, New York·.....	1841
Tyler......	" "	1841
"	Charles A. Wickliffe, Kentucky...	1841
Polk.....	Cave Johnson, Tennessee.......	1845
Taylor....	Jacob Collamer, Vermont.......	1849
Fillmore...	Nathan K. Hall, New York.....	1850
" ...	S. D. Hubbard, Connecticut....	1852
Pierce.....	James Campbell, Pennsylvania...	1853
Buchanan..	Aaron V. Brown, Tennessee.....	1857
" ...	Joseph Holt, Kentucky.........	1859
" ...	Horatio King, Maine..........	1861
Lincoln....	Montgomery Blair, Maryland...	1861
"	William Dennison, Ohio........	1864
Johnson...	" "	1865
" ...	Alex. W. Randall, Wisconsin....	1866
Grant.....	John A. J. Cresswell, Maryland...	1869
"	James W. Marshall, Virginia...	1874
"	Marshall Jewell, Connecticut....	1874
"	James N. Tyner, Indiana....●..	1876
Hayes.....	David McK. Key, Tennessee.....	1877
" ...	Horace Maynard, Tennessee....	1880
Garfield..	Thomas L. James, New York.....	1881
Arthur...	Timothy O. Howe, Wisconsin...	1881
"	Walter Q. Gresham, Indiana.....	1883
"	Frank Hatton, Iowa..........	1884
Cleveland..	William F. Vilas, Wisconsin.....	1885
" ...	Don M. Dickinson, Michigan....	1888
B. Harrison	John Wanamaker, Pennsylvania..	1889
Cleveland..	Wilson S. Bissell, New York.....	1893
" ...	William L. Wilson, West Virginia................	1895
McKinley..	James A. Gary, Maryland......	1897
" ...	Charles Emory Smith, Penn...	1898
Roosevelt..	" " ...	1901
" ...	Henry C. Payne, Wisconsin.....	1901
" ...	Robert J. Wynne, Pennsylvania...	1904
" ...	George B. Cortelyou, New York..	1905
" ...	George von L. Meyer, Mass....	1907
Taft......	Frank H. Hitchcock, Mass......	1909
Wilson....	Albert S. Burleson, Texas.......	1913

* The Postmaster-General was not considered a Cabinet officer until 1829.

By the act of July 2, 1836 the accounting was transferred to the Auditor of the Treasury for the Post-Office Department, and it was required that all revenues of the Department be paid into the United States Treasury. Until the passage of this act all postmasters had been appointed by the Postmaster-General, but from this time those whose commissions amounted to $1,000 or more a year were to be appointed by the President, with the advice and consent of the Senate, for a term of four years. The four assistants are appointed in the same way.

Railway mail service was authorized in 1838.

Postage rates were fixed on a weight basis in 1845, but with distance limitation (half ounce 300 miles, five cents).

Stamps were authorized in 1847. (See Postage, Postage Stamps, Postage Rates).

Postal Savings Banks were authorized by act of June 25, 1910, and the Parcel Post began operations Jan. 1, 1913.

The money-order system was established on May 17, 1864 ; and the special-delivery system on Oct. 1, 1883.

The free rural-delivery system was begun in 1897, and two years later the registry system was extended in cities so that letters might be registered at the home of the sender.

For more detailed information as to the scope and activities of the Post-Office Department consult the Index references to the Presidents' Messages and Encyclopedic articles under the following headings :

Assistant Postmasters-General.
City Delivery, Division of.
Civil Service.
Division of Dead Letters.
Division of Finance.
Division of Miscellaneous Transportation.
Division of Money Orders.
Division of Railway Adjustment.
Division of Registered Mails.

Division of Rural Mails.
Division of Stamps.
Foreign Mail Service.
Mail Matter.
Parcel Post.
Postage Stamps.
Postal Conventions.
Postal Currency.
Postal Rates.
Postal Savings.
Postal Service.
Postmaster-General.
Post-Offices.
Railway Mail Service.
Star Routes.

Post-Office Department:

Act regarding post-office, vetoed, 4339.

Assistant in, recommended, 4938, 5102.

Building for. (See Post-Office Building.)

Clerks in, referred to, 3585.

Discussed. (See Postal Service discussed.)

Funds of, deficit in, 1335, 2943, 3107.

Issuance of commissions to officials by Postmaster-General, recommended, 4063, 4193.

Laws of, recommendations regarding, 784.

Reforms in, recommended, 6163.

Revenues and expenditures of—
Appropriation for, 2202, 2992.
Bill providing for, failure of, to pass, 3102.
Deficit turned into surplus in two years, 7693.

Discussed by President—
Adams, J. Q., 877, 929, 956, 985.
Arthur, 4639, 4728, 4769.
Buchanan, 2992, 3054, 3056, 3107.
Cleveland, 4937, 6101, 5377, 5880, 5969, 6161.
Fillmore, 2625, 2670.
Grant, 3994, 4151, 4203, 4250, 4363.
Harrison, Benj., 5551, 5633, 5756.
Hayes, 4426, 4452, 4526, 4574.
Jackson, 1023, 1090, 1253, 1335, 1393, 1476.
Johnson, 3561, 3650, 3775, 3882.
Lincoln, 3252, 3332, 3386, 3450.
McKinley, 6335.
Monroe, 784, 827.
Pierce, 2748, 2822, 2872, 2943.

Polk, 2264, 2355, 2502.
Roosevelt, 6675, 6677, 6723, 6798, 6913, 7102.
Taft, 7433, 7525, 7693, 7732, 7733, 7814.
Tyler, 1902, 2056, 2202.
Van Buren, 1610, 1719, 1755, 1836.
Second class mail matter, report of commission on, 7733.
Treasurer for, should be appointed, 1336.

Post-Offices:

Classification of fourth-class, recommended, 6172.
Clerks in, legislation regarding classification of, recommended, 5378.
Consolidation of, 6164, 6172.
Number of, 784, 6344.
Increase in, 877, 933, 956, 985, 1610, 1719, 1755, 2355, 2625, 2670, 2992, 4203, 4574, 4769, 5376, 5756, 5881, 5971.

Post Roads. (See Mail Routes.)

Postage.—The price established by law to be paid for the conveyance of a letter or other mailable matter by a public post. Rates of postage were fixed by the Continental Congress in 1789 as follows: Single letters under 60 miles, 7.4 cents; between 60 and 100 miles, 11.1 cents; between 100 and 200 miles, 14.8 cents, and 3.4 cents for each additional 100 miles. As early as 1794 a delivery system was inaugurated, a fee of 2 cents being required for each letter delivered. In 1814 the rates of postage were increased by 50 per cent, but the old rate was restored in 1816. Mails were first carried on horseback, later by stage coach, and in 1834 by railway. July 7, 1838, Congress declared every railroad to be a mail route.

The free-delivery system was established in 1872 in cities of 50,000 population or over, and in 1887 the system was extended. *Rural Free Delivery.*—In 1896 the experiment of free delivery in rural districts was tried and proved to be a success; since that date the principle has been adopted and is being extended all over the country. (See also Post-Office Department.)

The following table exhibits the growth of the rural delivery service from 1898 to 1915:

Year	Carriers (Number)	Daily Mileage	Annual Cost
1898..........	148	2,960	$50,241
1900..........	1,276	28,685	420,433
1901..........	4,301	100,299	1,750,321
1903..........	15,119	332,618	8,051,599
1904..........	24,566	552,725	12,645,275
1905..........	32,055	721,237	20,864,885
1906..........	35,318	820,318	25,011,625
1907..........	37,582	883,117	26,661,555
1908..........	39,143	891,432	34,371,939
1909..........	40,499	979,541	35,661,034
1910..........	40,997	993,068	36,914,769
1911..........	41,559	1,007,772	37,125,630
1912..........	42,199	1,021,492	41,859,422
1913..........	42,805	1,028,603	45,642,766
1914..........	43,652	1,050,266	47,377,070
1915..........	43,710	1,073,099	50,000,000

The maximum salary of rural carriers was increased July 1, 1914, from $1,100 to $1,200.

Postage (see also Franking Privilege):
Census papers discussed, 654.
Increase in, recommended, 3056.
On census papers discussed, 654.
Reduction in—
Discussed, 2202, 2264, 2412, 2560, 2671, 2713, 2943, 4835, 4937, 5101.
Recommended, 1476, 1836, 2503, 2560, 2625, 4728, 4769, 4836.
Revenue derived from. (See Post-Office Department, revenues, etc., of.)

Postage Stamps.—An official mark or stamp affixed to or embossed on letters sent through the mails as evidence of the prepayment of postage. Adhesive stamps were made as an experiment by James Chalmers in his printing office in Dundee in 1834, but they were not made public till November, 1837. In February, 1837, Sir Rowland Hill proposed a postage stamp for prepayment of letter postage. In 1840 Mulready's envelope was introduced, bearing an allegorical design of England attracting the commerce of the world, but this was soon superseded by the adhesive stamp. Local stamps were in use in various cities in the United States as early as 1842—in New York, St. Louis, Baltimore, and Brattleboro. By act of May 3, 1847, the use of postage stamps was authorized, and issues of 5 and 10 cent stamps were made by the Government bearing, respectively, designs of the heads of Franklin and Washington. In 1851 three new values were added—1, 3, and 12 cents. From this time till 1860 a complete series was issued in values from 5 to 90 cents. In 1869 a new series was brought out in various designs, such as a horseman, a locomotive, eagle, steamship, landing of Columbus, Declaration of Independence, heads of Franklin, Washington, and Lincoln. The series of 1870-72 bore heads of Franklin, after Rupricht's bust; Jackson, after Powers; Washington, after the bust by Houdon; Lincoln, after Volk; Stanton, from a photograph; Jefferson, after Powers's statue; Clay, after the bust by Hart; Webster, after the Clevenger bust; Scott, after the bust by Coffee; Hamilton, after Cerrachi; and Perry, from Wolcott's statue.

At the International Postal Conference held at Berne, Switzerland, in 1874, the Universal Postal Union was formed, with rates of 5 cents per half ounce on all letters passing between the countries composing the union. In 1875 a 5-cent stamp was issued for this foreign service, bearing the head of Jackson, taken from a photograph, and in 1882 another of the same value with the head of Garfield. Stamped envelopes were issued in 1852 and postal cards in 1872.

Postal Congress, International, at—
Berne, 4250.
Lisbon, 4938.
Paris, 3387.
New convention adopted by, 4453.
Washington, 6164.

Postal Conventions.—At the instance of Montgomery Blair, Postmaster-General of the United States, an international conference of postal delegates was held at Paris, in May and June, 1863. Hon. John A. Kasson represented the United States. The objects of the conference were to facilitate postal intercourse between nations and t inaugurate a general system of uniform international charges at reduced rates of postage and to form the basis of future conferences. President Johnson, in his third annual message of Dec. 3, 1867 (page 3775), reported the ratification of postal conventions with Great Britain, Belgium, the Netherlands, Switzerland, the North German Union, Italy, and the colonial government of Hong Kong, largely reducing the rates of ocean and land postage to and from and within those countries.

In October, 1874, the general postal union at Berne, Switzerland, reduced international letter postage generally to five cents per half ounce. A third convention for a Universal Postal Union was signed at Paris, June 1, 1878, by John N. Tyner and Joseph H. Blackfan on behalf of the United States. The postal congress at Lisbon in April, 1886, confirmed the international rate of five cents per half ounce for prepaid letters and two cents for postal cards. The next congress was held at Vienna in 1891. President Hayes gave a good idea of the extent of the Postal Convention in his second annual message of Dec. 2, 1878 (page 4453). The rate of postage or letters to foreign countries now is five cents for the first ounce or less (each additional ounce three cents), except Great Britain, Germany, Canada, Cuba and Mexico, where the rate is two cents.

Postal Conventions:

Discussed, 3387, 4152, 4938.

Embarrassment arising under, referred to, 4453.

With—

Bahama Islands, 5377.

Barbados, 5377.

Belgium, 3775, 3883, 4203.

Canada, 4836, 5377.

China, 4775.

Costa Rica, 3284.

France, 4250.

Germany, 3775, 3883, 4203.

Great Britain, 2528, 2560, 2724, 3650, 3775, 3833, 3883.

Honduras, 5377.

Italy, 3775, 3883.

Japan, 4203.

Mexico, 3235, 3264, 5377.

   Ratification of, referred to, 3274.

Netherlands, 3775, 3883.

New South Wales, 4882.

Newfoundland, 4203.

Sweden and Norway, 4203.

Switzerland, 3775, 3883, 4250.

Postal Crimes:

Act relating to, etc., returned, 5204.

In Canal Zone, order relating to, 7964.

Postal Currency.—During the Civil War, when silver became very scarce, a substitute for fractional currency was invented by Gen. Spinner, United States Treasurer under President Lincoln. It consisted of postage stamps pasted upon paper used for Government securities and representing different sums. These pieces of paper were circulated among the clerks of the Department and became for a while the medium of exchange in a small way.

Postal Matter, abuse of classification of, 6675.

Postal Notes. (See Money-Order System.)

Postal Savings Banks. — To encourage people of small means to deposit their savings where they would be immediately available in emergency, and at the same time be secure from misappropriation while earning a small interest, postal savings banks have been established in most other progressive countries, and in the United States the question was long discussed before being put in operation.

Post-office savings banks were established in England in 1861 to meet the growing wants of the people for a secure and convenient place of deposit for savings.

President Roosevelt said, in his Seventh Annual Address, Dec. 3, 1907 (page 7102) : "I commend to the favorable consideration of the Congress a postal savings bank system, as recommended by the Postmaster-General. The primary object is to encourage among our people economy and thrift and by the use of postal savings banks to give them an opportunity to husband their resources, particularly those who have not the facilities at hand for depositing their money in savings banks. Viewed, however, from the experience of the past few weeks, it is evident that the advantages of such an institution are still more far-reaching. Timid depositors have withdrawn their savings for the time being from national banks, trust companies, and savings banks ; individuals have hoarded their cash and the workingmen their earnings ; all of which money has been withheld and kept in hiding or in safe-deposit box to the detriment of prosperity. Through the agency of the postal savings banks such money would be restored to the channels of trade, to the mutual benefit of capital and labor."

In continuation of Mr. Roosevelt's policy and in accordance with the declarations of the platform on which he was elected, Mr. Taft, in his Inaugural Address, March 4, 1909, said (page 7373) : "The incoming Congress should promptly fulfill the promise of the Republican platform and pass a proper postal savings bank bill. It will not be unwise or excessive paternalism. The promise to repay by the Government will furnish an inducement of savings deposits which private enterprise cannot supply and at such a low rate of interest as not to withdraw custom from existing banks. It will substantially increase the funds available for investment as capital in useful enterprises. It will furnish absolute security which makes the proposed scheme of government guaranty of deposits so alluring, without its pernicious results."

Congress appropriated $100,000, June 25, 1910, to start the postal savings system, and named as trustees the Postmaster-General, the Secretary of the Treasury, and the Attorney-General. On Jan. 2, 1911, a selected post-office in each of the forty-eight states was prepared to accept deposits. (See Banks, Postal Savings.)

An act of Congress approved June 25, 1910, authorized the establishment of postal savings depositary offices, created a board of trustees, consisting of the Postmaster-General, the Secretary of the Treasury, and the Attorney-General, with power to designate such post offices as they may select to be postal savings depositary offices. Accounts may be opened by the deposit of a dollar or a larger sum in multiples of a dollar, or by purchasing a postal savings card for ten cents and affixing thereto, at convenience, nine specially prepared postal savings stamps costing ten cents each. The holder, on presenting the card, is entitled to open an account with one dollar to his credit. Additional deposits may be made in like manner, but no person may deposit more than $100 in any one month, and the balance to the credit of any person shall never exceed $500, exclusive of accumulated interest. The Treasurer of the United States is treasurer of the Board of Trustees, and five per cent of the deposits are to be deposited with him as a reserve. The funds received at any depositary are to be deposited in any local bank willing to receive the same under the terms of the act and pay 2½ per cent interest thereon. The Government pays the depositor 2 per cent on all sums on deposit for one year, computed monthly, and it is assumed that the ½ per cent difference between the amount paid the depositor and the 2½ per cent paid by the bank will pay the cost of administering the law. Provision is also made for converting deposits in postal savings banks, in amounts of $20 or multiples thereof, into United States bonds bearing interest at 2½ per cent, payable semi-annually. The board may at any time withdraw 30 per cent of the funds and purchase bonds or other securities of the United States, and, under direction of the President, may withdraw the other 65 per cent and similarly invest the amount. At first only one post office in each state was designated as a depositary. On Nov. 1, 1911, 4,747 banks had been established. The postal savings banks have done even better than had been expected. Their record is said to surpass even that of the postal savings banks of Great Britain following their opening. Two predictions of their advocates have been fulfilled. First it has encouraged thrift among the young, many children becoming depositors; and, second, it has checked the outflow of money to Europe by foreigners who are suspicious of privately conducted savings banks.

The law of June 24, 1910, was amended on May 18, 1916, to allow deposits up to $1,000 deposited at any time and in any amount. Government bonds at 2½% purchased with postal savings are not counted toward the limit of $1,000. On June 30, 1916, postal savings deposits amounted to $86,619,885, representing 602,937 depositors, with an average deposit of $142.67. At that time there were provisions for receiving postal savings in 8,421 depositories, including 854 fourth-class post-offices, and 5,634 banks were also authorized to receive postal savings. The postal savings system is under the supervision of the third assistant postmaster-general (q. v.). (See Post-Office Department; Postal Service.)

At the close of the year 1911, there were 5,185 post-offices accepting deposits, and these showed a balance on hand of $10,-614,676. At the end of the next year the report showed 12,177 post-offices accepting deposits, and the total deposits had reached $28,057,059.

Balance to the credit of depositors June 30, 1914, $43,444,271; deposits during fiscal year, $70,314,858; deposits withdrawn during the fiscal year, $48,074,421; balance to credit of depositors June 30, 1915, $65,684,-708; balances on deposit in banks June 30, 1915, $60,086,318.94.

Postal Savings Banks:

Recommended by President—

Arthur, 4639.

Grant, 4152, 4204.

Hayes, 4574.

Roosevelt, 7102, 7226.

Taft, 7373, 7434, 7525.

Three months of experiment, 8073.

Postal Service.—The first mention of a postal service in the United States is that of the General Court of Massachusetts in 1639: "It is ordered that notice be given that Richard Fairbanks, his house in Boston

is the place appointed for all letters which are brought from beyond the seas, or are to be sent thither to be left with him, and he is to take care that they are to be delivered or sent according to the direction. And he is allowed for every letter a penny, and must answer all miscarriages through his own neglect in this kind." Out of this humble beginning grew the present post-office department, with nearly sixty thousand offices, earning a revenue of $266,-619,525 for the past year.

Postal Service:

Abuses of, discussed, 4640, 4730, 5970, 6162.

Civil Service in, discussed, 5972, 6172. (See also Railway Mail Service.)

Communication with Santiago, Cuba, order regarding, 6577.

Consolidation of post-offices recommended, 6164, 6172.

Correspondence with foreign countries, security required in, 1477.

Discussed by President—

Adams, J. Q., 877, 929, 956, 985.

Arthur, 4639, 4728, 4769, 4835.

Buchanan, 2992, 3056, 3101, 3107, 3184.

Cleveland, 4937, 5100, 5376, 5880, 5970, 6161.

Fillmore, 2625, 2670, 2713.

Grant, 3994, 4063, 4103, 4151, 4203, 4250, 4305, 4363.

Harrison, Benj., 5478, 5551, 5559, 5633, 5756.

Hayes, 4426, 4452, 4526, 4573.

Jackson, 1023, 1089, 1168, 1252, 1335, 1393, 1476.

Johnson, 3561, 3650, 3775, 3882.

Lincoln, 3252, 3332, 3386, 3450.

McKinley, 6344, 6386.

Monroe, 784, 824.

Pierce, 2748, 2822, 2872, 2943.

Polk, 2264, 2355, 2412, 2502.

Roosevelt, 6677, 6723, 6798, 6913, 7102.

Taft, 7433, 7525, 7693, 7732, 7733, 7814.

Taylor, 2559.

Tyler, 1902, 1941, 2056, 2123, 2202.

Van Buren, 1610, 1719, 1755, 1835.

Washington, 58, 75, 99, 120, 124.

Employees in, number of, 6344.

Expenditures for. (See Post-Office Department.)

Foreign postal arrangements and routes referred to, 2175, 2411, 2413, 2428, 2502, 2560, 2697, 2724, 3332, 3565, 3586, 3650, 3883, 4151, 4203, 4522, 4640, 4938, 5101, 5559, 5634.

Franking privilege discussed. (See Franking Privilege.)

Frauds in, discussed, 4640, 4730.

Free-delivery System—

Discussed and recommendations regarding, 4204, 4769, 4836, 4937, 5103, 5376, 5756, 5881, 5971, 6451.

Unit of weight in rating first-class matter discussed, 4836.

Unlawful publications, prohibited from using, 1394.

Postal Treaties. (See Postal Conventions.)

Postal Union, International (see also Postal Congress, International): Convention for establishment of, 4250.

Postal Union, Universal, discussed, 4574, 4640, 5971, 6164.

Postmaster-General.—The head of the Post-Office Department, and as such the director of the entire postal service of the country. The postmaster-general has been a member of the Cabinet since 1829, and his salary is $12,000 a year. By act of June 8, 1872, his tenure of office is during the term of the President by whom he is appointed and for one month thereafter, unless removed with the advice and consent of the Senate. His powers over his department are particularly untramelled and broad. He appoints all the important officers in his department, except the assistant postmasters-general (q. v.) and the purchasing agent, who are appointed by the President. He makes the contracts with railroad lines, steamship companies and other agents of transportation for the conveyance of the mails; and concludes postal contracts with other countries, although these latter must receive the approval of the President. He adds new post-offices to the list and abandons old ones, according to his judgment; and his discretion is the sole factor in enlarging or contracting the postal system in its various details. (See Post-Office Department.)

Postmaster-General:

Disclaims any intended disrespect in communication to Senate, 1745.

Post-office building report of, recommending erection of, 1483.

Postmasters appointed by, referred to, 2571.

Report of, recommending erection of new post-office building, 1483.

Report for year ended June 30, 1911, 7731.

Postmasters:

Amount due from, 784.

Appointment of, by Postmaster-General, referred to, 2571.

Appointments of, referred to, 2008.

Assistants more efficient in classified service, 7732.

Inclusion in classified service recommended, 7732.

Classification of fourth-class, discussed and recommendations regarding, 6172, 7102.

Compensation to, discussed, 784, 2943, 4363, 5377.

Interference with, discussed, 4363, 5550.

Relative merit of, plan to indicate, recommended, 5479, 5489.

Potato.—The so-called Irish potato is native to the west coast of South America, and is said to have been introduced into Ireland by Sir Walter Raleigh, who grew the roots on his large estate in County Cork. Though now so universal an article of food it was scarcely known prior to the 17th century, and was not generally cultivated until the middle of the 18th.

Potato Crop.—Estimated acreage, production, and value, 1907 to 1914, and in 1915 by states.* (Source: Reports of the Department of Agriculture.)

Year	Acreage	Total Farm Value, Dec. 1
1907	3,128,000	$184,184,000
1908	3,257,000	197,039,000
1909	3,525,000	206,545,000
1910	3,720,000	194,566,000
1911	3,619,000	233,778,000
1912	3,711,000	212,550,000
1913	3,668,000	227,903,000
1914	3,708,000	198,609,000
State.		
Alabama	20,000	1,440,000
Arizona	1,000	95,000
Arkansas	28,000	1,915,000
California	78,000	7,605,000
Colorado	53,000	3,935,000
Connecticut	24,000	2,189,000
Delaware	11,000	784,000
Florida	12,000	1,104,000
Georgia	16,000	1,030,000
Idaho	28,000	1,960,000
Illinois	126,000	8,177,000
Indiana	75,000	3,990,000
Iowa	148,000	8,392,000
Kansas	71,000	4,361,000
Kentucky	51,000	3,534,000
Louisiana	28,000	1,357,000
Maine	142,000	15,407,000
Maryland	44,000	2,646,000
Massachusetts	26,000	2,933,000
Michigan	355,000	11,729,000
Minnesota	285,000	11,782,000
Mississippi	13,000	983,000
Missouri	90,000	5,292,000
Montana	39,000	3,022,000
Nebraska	110,000	4,851,000
Nevada	13,000	1,565,000
New Hampshire	16,000	1,444,000
New Jersey	93,000	9,068,000
New Mexico	8,000	760,000
New York	355,000	18,048,000
North Carolina	35,000	2,300,000
North Dakota	80,000	2,952,000
Ohio	153,000	8,782,000
Oklahoma	35,000	2,499,000
Oregon	48,000	3,312,000
Pennsylvania	280,000	15,120,000
Rhode Island	5,000	506,000
South Carolina	11,000	1,012,000
South Dakota	68,000	2,737,000
Tennessee	36,000	1,996,000
Texas	42,000	2,866,000
Utah	20,000	1,575,000
Vermont	24,000	2,100,000
Virginia	140,000	10,675,000
Washington	61,000	4,365,000
West Virginia	50,000	3,802,000
Wisconsin	298,000	11,667,000
Wyoming	16,000	1,440,000
Total, 1915	3,761,000	$221,104,000

* Does not include sweet potatoes.

Potomac, The, instructions given commander of, at Sumatra, 1138.

Potomac River:

Bridges over, in District of Columbia. (See District of Columbia.)

Improvement of, recommended, 4430, 4458, 4532, 4579, 4651.

Bill for, submitted, 4533.

Lands lying on, referred to, 128.

Prairie Grove (Ark.), Battle of.—Sept. 19, 1862, President Lincoln directed that Missouri, Arkansas, Kansas, and the eastern portion of Indian Territory should constitute the Department of the Missouri, to be commanded by Brig.-Gen. Samuel R. Curtis. The only important engagement that occurred in this department while Curtis was in command was at Prairie Grove, Ark. The Confederate General Thomas C. Hindman was on his way north into Missouri with a large force when, on Dec. 7, 1862, he encountered the united forces of Generals James G. Blunt and Francis J. Herron. During the engagement which ensued the Federals lost 1,148 and the Confederates, 1,317. The latter retired during the night.

Prairie State.—A nickname for Illinois (q. v.), (See also States) ; sometimes also nicknamed Sucker State.

Prayer, special day of, set apart for nations engaged in war, 8007.

Preachers of Discontent, discussed by President Roosevelt, 7033.

Preemption Laws.—The first law regulating the preemption of and payment for public lands was passed March 3, 1801. It was a special act affecting the Symmes colonization scheme on the Miami River. A number of preemption laws were passed, most of them of a more or less special nature. The first general law was passed in 1830. The law of 1841 granted, in consideration of residence and improvement, freedom of entry upon 160 acres of public lands to any person over twenty-one years of age; twelve to thirty-three months were allowed for payment, and the amount to be paid varied with the situation and value of the tract preempted. (See Lands, Public.)

Preemption Laws:

Discussed, 1713, 1753, 3651, 4064, 5484.

Recommended, 1606, 2259.

Amendments to law recommended, 2408, 2500.

Repeal of preemption act recommended, 4770, 4837, 5107.

Preparedness.—Few movements in all our history have so gripped the minds and hearts of the American people as the movement for adequate preparation on land and sea, either for aggressive or defensive purposes in case of war. The Preparedness movement cannot be said to have originated among those men in the public eye who for years had been urging the need for a larger army and navy. It originated rather among citizens who formerly had been deaf or antagonistic to the cry for increased appropriations for war purposes; and it originated as a direct result of the European War. For the supreme lesson in military tactics taught by that vast conflict was the impossibility of preparing adequately on short notice, and the necessity for carefully-planned and matured preparations for any new forces which a nation might need at any given time. Preparedness was brought home to America also as a fact, and not a theory, by diplomatic differences between the United States and the belligerent European countries, especially Germany, when the entrance of the United States into the struggle became no longer debatable, and passed from a probability to a certainty.

For the position which the United States occupied among the nations of the world in respect to military strength, see the articles Armies of the World and Navies of the World. From these tables, it will be understood that the first direction taken by the Preparedness movement was inevitably towards an extensive increase in our land forces. The unwieldiness and the lack of centralized authority in the National Guard, so far as availability for Federal purposes was concerned, were well revealed by the mobilization of troops on the Mexican border in 1916. (See Mexico.) The smashing victories of the Teutonic armies early in the European War could be explained only by the attention long paid military preparedness by Germany, while the same explanation arose for the sturdy resistance of the French and the immediate and complete domination of the English Navy over all the seas. On the other hand, the length of time taken by England to get her land fighting-machine under way, despite the most earnest efforts, proved the weakness of a country which waited until the declaration of war in order to prepare. Accordingly, along with the Preparedness movement went a movement for universal military service and for military training in the public schools. (See Compulsory Military Service and Military Training in the Schools.)

As the danger of America being plunged into the European vortex daily became more acute, the Preparedness movement also devoted itself largely to the question of making our Navy better available for service. The prominent part played by submarines and aeroplanes in the European War had almost revolutionized naval tactics, and grave doubts arose whether our navy, despite its strength, was sufficiently prepared in the newer fields of naval activities.

Preparedness became almost the leading subject of discussion in private so well as in public gatherings all over the United States. The resignation of Secretary of War Garrison on Feb. 10, 1916, because of a difference of opinion with President Wilson concerning the federalization of the National Guard, created intense excitement; and the country was virtually divided into two camps on the issue involved. Many new organizations such as the National Security League and National Defense Society were created in order to assist the preparedness movement, while organizations like the Navy League redoubled their efforts for naval Preparedness. Mass-meetings and parades were held all over the United States in support of Preparedness, and there were few meetings of public or semi-public bodies in which the subject was not discussed. An idea of the amount of interest involved may be gathered from the fact that the great Preparedness Parade held in New York on May 13, 1916 took 12 hours to pass a given point, and consisted of no less than 125,683 men and women marching in support of the cause. Preparedness became a political event of the first magnitude, not only in the national election of 1916, but also in state and municipal elections. One result of the agitation arose in the establishment of a large training camp for volunteers at Plattsburg, N. Y. (q. v.). The motto of the movement was early "In times of peace, prepare for war;" but as the sinking of American vessels by German submarines seemed to many persons to constitute acts of actual warfare, the motto became "In times of war, prepare for war."

On the other hand, the opponents of Preparedness were by no means few or inactive. To some extent, the opposition came from citizens and non-citizens of Teutonic descent, called in this crisis, fairly or unfairly, German-Americans (q. v.); but the majority of the opponents, although not necessarily those most active in the propaganda against Preparedness, were Americans sincerely convinced that Perparedness was the first step towards a war which they wished to avoid. The Women's Peace Party, the Emergency Peace Federation, and the Union Against Militarism were particularly active. The position taken by them and by their supporters was that the European conflict arose from the fact that the countries of Europe had been prepared for it. They asserted furthermore that by resorting to Preparedness America was betraying the interests of peace, and was abandoning the position which would logically accrue to her after the war was over as the nation which had shown by her record that she, and she alone, could be entrusted to lead the warring nations to a new and perpetual peace. It was claimed, in addition, that America was geographically not involved in a European quarrel, and that her geographical position made aggression against her an impossibility.

On October 6, 1915, in a speech in New York, President Wilson definitely committed himself to the Preparedness program; and his administration devoted itself to having enacted many measures carrying out the Preparedness idea. The army re-organization act, approved on June 3, 1916, made new and elaborate increases in the army of the United States (q. v.), nor could it be said that the Administration neglected the navy of the United States (q. v.). Many administrative changes in behalf of preparedness, such as the organization of new boards for industrial and scientific integration and preparedness, were made; but even with all this preparation, when the United States finally entered the conflict on April 6, 1917, she was still only partially prepared to assume her burden of the conflict; and many months elapsed in the formation and completion of the plans necessary to place a strong American army on the battlefields of Europe.

Preparedness Means Peace. — A catch-phrase much used during the European War, and prior to the President's message of April 2, 1917, asking Congress to declare the existence of a state of war.

Preparedness Societies. — (See Preparedness.) Among the many societies called into existence by or aiding in the Preparedness movement in this country may be mentioned the following: The Navy League, the first preparedness society, with 330,000 members in 1917, which was organized in 1902, to assist in the enactment of laws constantly making for the increased efficiency of the Navy, until it becomes the greatest navy in the world; The Army League, which is organized to promote interest in and legislation for the increased efficiency of the Army; The Universal Military Training League, organized for the establishment of Compulsory Military Service (q. v.) and of a National Defense Commission: the National Security League, which was organized on Dec. 1, 1917, and has an enrollment of 100,-000 members in its program for increased military preparation for the United States; the American Rights Committee, organized to end the violation of American rights on the high seas. All these bodies are represented on the National Committee of Patriotic and Defense Societies. (See Preparedness.)

President, The.—Previous to the War of 1812 American commerce had suffered considerably at the hands of British cruisers, which hovered about our coasts and captured many United States vessels bound for France. These cruisers also made many impressments of sailors. In May, 1811, Commodore John Rodgers, commanding the American frigate *President* was ordered to put to sea from Chesapeake Bay and protect our commerce. When thirty miles off Cape Charles, May 16, Rodgers gave chase to the *Little Belt*, a British frigate. The latter fired upon the *President*, attempted flight, and failed to show her colors. The fire was returned by the *President*, and in eighteen minutes the *Little Belt* was disabled. A dispute arose as to which of the commanders was at fault, but it was never decided, as the discussion was dropped by mutual agreement. In September, 1814, the *President*, under Decatur, was captured by the *Endymion*, and other British vessels.

President of a State.—Some of the earlier organized states provided for a president as the executive head. To avoid misunderstanding and confusion, this was afterwards changed to governor. The first constitutions of Pennsylvania and New Hampshire, adopted in 1776, provided for an executive council of which one member was president. Delaware, South Carolina and the New Hampshire constitution of 1784 provided for a single head, but called him

president. South Carolina in 1778, Pennsylvania in 1790, and Delaware and New Hampshire in 1792 altered the title to governor.

President of United States.—The title of the Chief Executive of the United States. In 1696 William Penn proposed a plan for a general government for the Colonies in America. The plan comprehended a chief executive with the title of president. The Albany Convention proposed that of president-general. The Continental Congress had its president. In the Convention of 1787 it was decided that there should be a single executive to whom the title of president was given. In order to be eligible, the president must be thirty-five years of age, a native-born citizen of the United States, and a resident within the United States for fourteen years. He is elected for a term of four years by electors chosen by the different states. These electors are chosen by direct vote of the people, on ballot tickets usually headed by the names of the candidates voted for as president and vice-president, followed by the names of the electors, who are pledged to vote for these candidates only. (See Electoral Colleges.)

The president's duties and powers under the Constitution are to approve or veto bills; to grant reprieves and pardons for offenses against the United States, except in case of impeachment; to make treaties; to nominate ambassadors and other public ministers, consuls, judges of the Federal courts, etc., and, by and with the consent of the Senate appoint such officers; to fill vacancies that may occur during the recess of the Senate by granting commissions which shall expire at the end of the next session; to convene one or both Houses of Congress, and to adjourn Congress to such a time as he may deem proper in case it can not agree upon an adjournment. He is also commander-in-chief of the army and navy and of the militia of the several states when called into the service of the United States. He is required to give information to Congress from time to time regarding the state of the Union and recommend to its consideration such measures as he shall judge necessary and expedient; receive ambassadors and other public ministers; see that the laws are faithfully executed, etc. He receives a salary of $75,000 per annum. Up to the time of the ratification of the twelfth amendment (1804) the president and vice-president were not separately voted for, but the candidate for president who received next to the highest number of votes was made vice-president. Jefferson and J. Q. Adams were elected by the House of Representatives, as provided by the Constitution, neither presidential candidate having a majority of the electoral vote.

Title and Term of the President.—The address of the president is simply "The President of the United States." In the First Congress, there was debate over a title and it was proposed by some members that he be addressed as "His Excellency" and by others as "His Highness," but a committee reported that "it is not proper to annex any style or title other than that expressed in the Constitution." In the Constitutional Convention the first report fixed the term of office at seven years without eligibility to re-election. In debate various periods from "during good behavior" to twenty years were favored. The limit to four years was finally adopted in grand committee and ratified by the convention.

Presidential Flag.—It is usual in other countries to have a special ensign to designate the presence on a vessel of the ruler of the nation. It was not until lately that the United States had such a flag. President Arthur suggested it in the early part of 1882, and, as his Cabinet concurred in his suggestion, decided on the design of a blue ground with the arms of the United States in the center. The Navy Department ordered that this flag should be displayed at the mainmast of any vessel that bore the president. Arthur first used it in 1883.

The theoretical model for the President of the United States was the King of England, but the practical model used by the framers of the Constitution was a composite of the colonial governors and the executive heads of states already formed. Popular confidence in Washington was all that prevented further limitation of the powers of the Chief Executive. The ultimate position of the American President was not determined until the end of Jackson's administration. Washington established and maintained the office upon a broad national basis, but even he could not render it strictly nonpartisan. Jefferson first exemplified the methods of a brilliant statesman and a successful party leader. Under the weaker partisanship of his immediate successors the congressional caucus usurped many of the prerogatives of the Executive.

The strong will and determined character of Jackson soon restored the presidency to a position equal to if not superior in power to the legislative and judicial branches of the government. It was during his administration that the congressional caucus declined before the growing power of the national convention, and the development of party machinery based upon executive patronage. This national party machinery later became a source of weakness by securing the election of second-rate party men over first-rate statesmen of unavowed party loyalty.

The arbitrary military powers of the President reached their highest development under Lincoln. As commander in chief of the land and naval forces he declared the existence of insurrection, suspended the civil law and denied the writ of habeas corpus to prisoners hundreds of miles from the scene of the disorder.

The Constitution requires the President to execute the laws and vests in him the power of appointment of executive officers and consequently the power of removal. These, with the veto power, in the hands of a judicious leader give him more power than is wielded by most constitutional monarchs of Europe.

Although the Constitution requires all treaties with foreign powers to be concluded "with the advice and consent of the senate," the President may direct the writing of treaties, and if amended by the Senate against his wishes he need not submit them to the diplomats of other nations. He has the power to recognize the independence of a revolutionary faction in a foreign country and thus establish or destroy a nation.

President of United States (see also the several Presidents):

Act—
Fixing salary of, vetoed, 4334.
Of Congress approved but not signed, whether in force discussed, 856.
Of Congress duly certified and approved which had not passed discussed, 1353.
Providing for performance of duties of, in case of death, etc., of

Vice-President and, returned, 5674.
Appointing power of. (See Executive Nominations.)
Appointment of members of House by, in whose election they have been officially concerned discussed, 1011, 1120.
Appointments of, referred to, 1965.
Arbitration of boundary dispute between Brazil and Argentine Republic submitted to. (See Cleveland, Grover.)
Arbitrator of claim of Italy against Colombia. (See Cleveland, Grover.)
Bills considered by, time allowed for, discussed, 2993, 3060.
Cabinet of. (See Cabinet.)
Civil service extended over employees in office of, 6232.
Communications of, to Congress not to be questioned by foreign power, 1397.
Compensation due, referred to, 889.
Conduct of public officers, request of House for documents concerning, declined, 847.
Constitutional amendment—
Designating officer to succeed, in event of vacancy in Presidency and Vice - Presidency recommended, 3837, 3889. (See also Successor to, *post*.)
Regarding election of, recommended, 1010, 1081, 1120, 1168, 1253, 1336, 1395, 1478, 3838, 3889, 4196, 4397.
Regarding selection of electors recommended, 5644.
Relative to approval of separate items of bill and veto of others recommended, 4196, 4725, 4774, 4840.
Constitutional function as commander of Army, act interfering with, discussed, 3670.
Repeal of, recommended, 3871.
Constitutional meaning of "inability to discharge powers and duties of office of," discussed and recommendations regarding, 4652, 4734, 4774, 4840.
Death of. (See Garfield; Harrison, W. H.; Lincoln; Taylor.)
Discretionary authority of, to—
Invite nations to conference on subject of coinage recommended, 5877.
Retaliate in cases of discriminating duties levied on American vessels recommended, 4763, 5205.
Send delegates to foreign conventions, recommendations regarding, 4714, 4763, 4827, 5546, 6325.

Presidential Elections.—The record of any popular vote for electors prior to 1828 is so meagre and imperfect that a compilation would be useless. In most of the states, for more than a quarter century following the establishment of the Government, the State Legislatures "appointed" the Presidential electors, and the people therefore voted only indirectly for them, their choice being expressed by their votes for members of the Legislature.

1789.—Previous to 1804, each elector voted for two candidates for President. The one who received the largest number of votes was declared President, and the one who received the next largest number of votes was declared Vice-President. The electoral votes for the first President of the United States were: George Washington, 69; John Adams, of Massachusetts, 34; John Jay, of New York, 9; R. H. Harrison, of Maryland, 6; John Rutledge, of South Carolina, 6; John Hancock, of Massachusetts, 4; George Clinton, of New York, 3; Samuel Huntingdon, of Connecticut, 2; John Milton, of Georgia, 2; James Armstrong, of Georgia; Benjamin Lincoln,

ELECTORAL AND POPULAR VOTES FOR PRESIDENT AND VICE-PRESIDENT

Year of Election	Candidates for President	Popular Vote	Plurality	Electoral Vote	Candidates for Vice-President	Electoral Vote
1828	Andrew Jackson,* Tenn. (Dem.)	647,231	138,134	178	John C. Calhoun,* S. C. (Dem.)	171
	John Q. Adams, Mass. (Nat. R.)	509,097	....	83	Richard Rush, Pa. (Nat. R.)	83
					William Smith, S. C. (Dem.)	7
1832	Andrew Jackson,* Tenn. (Dem.)	687,502	157,313	219	M. Van Buren,* N. Y. (Dem.)	189
	Henry Clay, Ky. (Nat. R.)	530,189	....	49	John Sergeant, Pa. (Nat. R.)	49
	John Floyd, Ga. (Ind.)	} 33,108	{........	11	Henry Lee, Mass. (Ind.)	11
	William Wirt (c), Md. (Anti-M.)			7	Amos Ellmaker (c), Pa. (Anti-M.)	7
					Wm. Wilkins, Pa. (Dem.)	30
1836	Martin Van Buren,* N. Y. (Dem.)	761,549	24,893	170	R. M. Johnson (d)* Ky. (Dem.)	147
	W. H. Harrison, Ohio (Whig)			73	Francis Granger, N. Y. (Whig)	77
	Hugh L. White, Tenn. (Whig)	} 736,656	{	26	John Tyler, Va. (Whig)	47
	Daniel Webster, Mass. (Whig)			14	William Smith, Ala. (Dem.)	23
	Willie P. Mangum, N. C. (Whig)			11		
1840	W. H. Harrison,* Ohio (Whig)	1,275,017	146,315	234	John Tyler,* Va. (Whig)	234
	Martin Van Buren, N. Y. (Dem.)	1,128,702	....	60	R. M. Johnson, Ky. (Dem.)	48
	James G. Birney, N. Y. (Lib.)	7,059			L. W. Tazewell, Va. (Dem.)	11
					James K. Polk, Tenn. (Dem.)	1
					Thomas Earle, Pa. (Lib.)	.....
1844	James K. Polk,* Tenn. (Dem.)	1,337,243	38,175	170	George M. Dallas,* Pa. (Dem.)	170
	Henry Clay, Ky. (Whig)	1,299,068	....	105	T. Frelinghuysen, N. J. (Whig)	105
	James G. Birney, N. Y. (Lib.)	62,300		.....	Thomas Morris, Ohio (Lib.)	.....
1848	Zachary Taylor,* La. (Whig)	1,360,101	139,557	163	Millard Fillmore,* N. Y. (Whig)	163
	Lewis Cass, Mich. (Dem.)	1,220,544	....	127	William O. Butler, Ky. (Dem.)	127
	Martin Van Buren, N. Y. (F. Soil)	291,263		.....	Charles F. Adams, Mass. (F. Soil)	.....
1852	Franklin Pierce,* N. H. (Dem.)	1,601,474	220,896	254	William R. King,* Ala. (Dem.)	254
	Winfield Scott, N. J. (Whig)	1,380,576	....	42	William A. Graham, N. C. (Whig)	42
	John P. Hale, N. H. (F. Soil) (i)	156,149		.....	George W. Julian, Ind. (F. Soil)	.....
	Daniel Webster (k), Mass. (Whig)	1,670				
1856	James Buchanan,* Pa. (Dem.)	1,838,169	496,905	174	J. C. Breckinridge,* Ky. (Dem.)	174
	John C. Fremont, Cal. (Rep.)	1,341,264	....	114	William L. Dayton, N. J. (Rep.)	114
	Millard Fillmore, N. Y. (Amer.)	874,538	....	8	A. J. Donelson, Tenn. (Amer.)	8
1860	Abraham Lincoln,* Ill. (Rep.)	1,866,352	491,195	180	Hannibal Hamlin,* Me. (Rep.)	180
	Stephen A. Douglas, Ill. (Dem.)	1,375,157	....	12	H. V. Johnson, Ga. (Dem.)	12
	J. C. Breckinridge, Ky. (Dem.)	845,763	....	72	Joseph Lane, Ore. (Dem.)	72
	John Bell, Tenn. (Union)	589,581	....	39	Edward Everett, Mass. (Union)	39
1864	Abraham Lincoln,* Ill. (Rep.)	2,216,067	407,342	e 212	Andrew Johnson,* Tenn. (Rep.)	212
	George B. McClellan, N. J. (Dem.)	1,808,725	....	21	George H. Pendleton, Ohio (Dem.)	21
1868	Ulysses S. Grant,* Ill. (Rep.)	3,015,071	305,456	f 214	Schuyler Colfax,* Ind. (Rep.)	214
	Horatio Seymour, N. Y. (Dem.)	2,709,615	....	80	F. P. Blair, Jr., Mo. (Dem.)	80
1872	Ulysses S. Grant,* Ill. (Rep.)	3,597,070	762,991	286	Henry Wilson,* Mass. (Rep.)	286
	Horace Greeley, N. Y. (D. & L.)	2,834,079	....	g ...	B. Gratz Brown, Mo. (D. & L.)	47
	Charles O'Conor, N. Y. (Dem.)	29,408			John Q. Adams, Mass. (Dem.)	.....
	James Black, Pa. (Temp.)	5,608			John Russell, Mich. (Temp.)	.....
	Thomas A. Hendricks, Ind. (Dem.)			42	George W. Julian, Ind. (Lib.)	5
	B. Gratz Brown, Mo. (Dem.)			18	A. H. Colquitt, Ga. (Dem.)	5
	Charles J. Jenkins, Ga. (Dem.)			2	John M. Palmer, Ill. (Dem.)	3
	David Davis, Ill. (Ind.)			1	T. E. Bramlette, Ky. (Dem.)	3
					W. S. Groesbeck, Ohio (Dem.)	1
					Willis B. Machen, Ky. (Dem.)	1
					N. P. Banks, Mass. (Lib.)	1
1876	Samuel J. Tilden, N. Y. (Dem.)	4,284,885	250,935	184	T. A. Hendricks, Ind. (Dem.)	184
	Rutherford B. Hayes,* Ohio (Rep.)	4,033,950	....	h 185	William A. Wheeler,* N. Y. (Rep.)	185
	Peter Cooper, N. Y. (Gre'nb)	81,740		.....	Samuel F. Cary, Ohio (Gre'nb)	.....
	Green Clay Smith, Ky. (Proh.)	9,522			Gideon T. Stewart, Ohio (Proh)	.....
	James B. Walker, Ill. (Amer.)	2,636			D. Kirkpatrick, N. Y. (Amer.)	.....

* Elected. (a) The first Republican Party is claimed by the present Democratic Party as its progenitor. (b) No candidate having a majority of the electoral vote, the House of Representatives elected Adams. (c) Candidate of the Anti-Masonic Party. (d) There being no choice, the Senate elected Johnson. (e) Eleven Southern States, being within the belligerent territory, did not vote. (f) Three Southern States disfranchised. (g) Horace Greeley died after election, and Democratic electors scattered their votes. (h) There being a dispute over the electoral vote of Florida, Louisiana, Oregon, and South Carolina, they were referred by Congress to an electoral commission composed of eight Republicans and seven Democrats, which, by a strict party vote, awarded 185 electoral votes to Hayes and 184 to Tilden. (i) Free Soil.

ELECTORAL AND POPULAR VOTES FOR PRESIDENT AND VICE-PRESIDENT—*Continued.*

Year of Election	Candidates for President	Popular Vote	Plurality	Electoral Vote	Candidates for Vice-President	Electoral Vote
1880	James A. Garfield,* Ohio (Rep.)	4,449,053	7,018	214	Chester A. Arthur,* N. Y. (Rep.)	214
	W. S. Hancock, Pa. (Dem.)	4,442,035		155	William H. English, Ind. (Dem.)	155
	James B. Weaver, Iowa (Gre'nb)	307,306			B. J. Chambers, Tex. (Gre'nb)	
	Neal Dow, Me. (Proh.)	10,305			H. A. Thompson, Ohio (Proh.)	
	John W. Phelps, Vt. (Amer.)	707			S. C. Pomeroy, Kan. (Amer.)	
1884	Grover Cleveland,* N. Y. (Dem.)	4,911,017	62,683	219	T. A. Hendricks,* Ind. (Dem.)	219
	James G. Blaine, N. Y. (Rep.)	4,848,334		182	John A. Logan, Ill. (Rep.)	182
	John P. St. John, Kan. (Proh.)	151,809			William Daniel, Md. (Proh.)	
	Benjamin F. Butler, Mass. (Gre'nb)	133,825			A. M. West, Miss. (Gre'nb)	
	P. D. Wigginton, Cal. (Amer.)					
1888	Grover Cleveland, N. Y. (Dem.)	5,538,233	98,017	168	Allen G. Thurman, Ohio (Dem.)	168
	Benjamin Harrison,* Ind. (Rep.)	5,440,216		233	Levi P. Morton,* N. Y. (Rep.)	233
	Clinton B. Fisk, N. J. (Proh.)	249,907			John A Brooks, Mo. (Proh.)	
	Alson J. Streeter, Ill. (U. L.)	148,105			C. E. Cunningham, Ark. (U. L.)	
	R. H. Cowdry, Ill. (U'd L.)	2,808			W. H. T. Wakefield, Kan. (U'd L.)	
	James L. Curtis, N. Y. (Amer.)	1,591			James B. Greer, Tenn. (Amer.)	
1892	Grover Cleveland,* N. Y. (Dem.)	5,556,918	380,810	277	Adlai E. Stevenson,* Ill. (Dem.)	277
	Benjamin Harrison, Ind. (Rep.)	5,176,108		145	Whitelaw Reid, N. Y. (Rep.)	145
	James B. Weaver, Iowa (Peop.)	1,041,028		22	James G. Field, Va. (Peop.)	22
	John Bidwell, Cal. (Proh.)	264,133			James B. Cranfill, Tex. (Proh.)	
	Simon Wing, Mass. (Soc. L.)	21,164			Charles H. Matchett, N. Y. (Soc. L.)	
1896	William McKinley,* Ohio (Rep.)	7,104,779	601,854	271	Garret A. Hobart, N. J. (Rep.)	271
	William J. Bryan, Neb. (Dem.)	} 6,502,925	{	176	Arthur Sewall, (Dem.)	149
	William J. Bryan, Neb. (Peop.)				Thomas E. Watson, Ga. (Peop.)	27
	Joshua Levering, Md. (Proh.)	231,007			Hale Johnson, Ill. (Proh.)	
	John M. Palmer, Ill. (N. Dem.)	133,148			Simon B. Buckner, Ky. (N. Dem.)	
	Charles H. Matchett, N. Y. (Soc. L.)	36,274			Matthew Maguire, N. J. (Soc. L.)	
	Charley E. Bentley, Neb. (Nat. (j))	13,969			James H. Southgate, N. C. (Nat. (j))	
1900	William McKinley,* Ohio (Rep.)	7,207,923	849,790	292	Theodore Roosevelt,* N. Y. (Rep.)	292
	William J. Bryan, Neb. (Dem. P.)	6,358,133		155	Adlai E. Stevenson, Ill. (Dem. P.)	155
	John G. Woolley, Ill. (Proh.)	208,914			Henry B. Metcalf, Ohio (Proh.)	
	Wharton Barker, Pa. (MP(m))	50,373			Ignatius Donnelly, Minn. (MP(m))	
	Eugene V. Debs, Ind. (Soc. D.)	87,814			Job Harriman, Cal. (Soc. D.)	
	Jos. F. Malloney, Mass. (Soc. L.(k))	39,739			Valentine Remmel, Pa. (Soc. L.)	
	J. F. R. Leonard, Ia. (U. C (n))	1,059			John G. Woolley, Ill. (U. C. (n))	
	Seth H. Ellis, Ohio (U. R. (o))	5,698			Samuel T. Nicholson, Pa. U. R. (o)	
1904	Theodore Roosevelt,* N. Y. (Rep.)	7,623,486	2,545,515	336	Charles W. Fairbanks,* Ind. (Rep.)	316
	Alton B. Parker, N. Y. (Dem.)	5,077,911		140	Henry G. Davis, W. Va. (Dem.)	403
	Eugene V. Debs, Ind. (Soc.)	402,283			Benjamin Hanford, N. Y. (Soc.)	
	Silas C. Swallow, Pa. (Proh.)	258,536			George W. Carroll, Tex. (Proh.)	
	Thomas E. Watson, Ga. (Peop.)	117,183			Thomas H. Tibbles, Neb. (Peop.)	
	Charles H. Corrigan, N. Y. (Soc. L.)	31,249			William W. Cox, Ill. (Soc. L.)	
1908	William H. Taft,* Ohio (Rep.)	7,678,908	1,269,804	321	James S. Sherman,* N. Y. (Rep.)	321
	William J. Bryan, Neb. (Dem.)	6,409,104		162	John W. Kern, Ind. (Dem.)	162
	Eugene V. Debs, Ind. (Soc.)	420,793			Benjamin Hanford, N. Y. (Soc.)	
	Eugene W. Chafin, Ariz. (Proh.)	253,840			Aaron S. Watkins, Ohio (Proh.)	
	Thomas E. Watson, Ga. (Peop.)	29,100			Samuel Williams, Ind. (Peop.)	
	August Gillhaus, N. Y. (Soc. L.)	13,825			Donald L. Munroe, Va. (Soc. L.)	
	Thos. L. Hisgen, Mass. (Ind.)	82,872			John Temple Graves, Ga. (Ind.)	
1912	Woodrow Wilson,* N. J. (Dem.)	6,296,019	2,173,512	435	Thomas R. Marshall,* Ind. (Dem.)	435
	William H. Taft, Ohio (Rep.)	3,484,956		8	Herbert S. Hadley, Mo. (Rep.)	8
	Theodore Roosevelt, N. Y. (Prog.)	4,119,507		88	Hiram W. Johnson, Cal. (Prog.)	88
	Eugene V. Debs, Ind. (Soc.)	901,873			Emil Seidel, Wis. (Soc.)	
	Eugene W. Chafin, Ariz. (Proh.)	207,928			Aaron S. Watkins, Ohio (Proh.)	
	Arthur E. Reimer, Mass. (Soc. L.)	22599			August Gilhaus, N. Y. (Soc. L.)	
1916	Woodrow Wilson,* N. J. (Dem.)	9,116,296	568,822	276	Thomas R. Marshall, Ind.* (Dem.)	276
	Charles E. Hughes, N. Y. (Rep.)	8,547,474		255	Charles W. Fairbanks, Ind. (Rep.)	255
	J. Frank Hanly, (Proh.)	225,101			Ira Lambrith, (Proh.)	
	Allan L. Benson, (Soc.)	750,000			George R. Kirkpatrick, (Soc.)	
	Arthur E. Reimer, Mass. (Soc. L.)	11,470			Caleb Harrison, (Soc. L.)	

* Elected. (j) Free Silver Prohibition Party. (k) In Massachusetts. There was also a Native American ticket in that State, which received 184 votes. (m) Middle of the Road or Anti-Fusion Party. (n) United Christian Party (o) Union Reform Party. *See N. Y. American, Dec. 17th, 1916.

of Massachusetts, and Edward Telfair, of Georgia, 1 vote each. Vacancies (votes not cast), 4. George Washington was chosen President and John Adams Vice-President.
1792.—George Washington, Federalist, received 132 votes; John Adams, Federal-ist, 77; George Clinton, of New York, Republican (a), 50; Thomas Jefferson, of Virginia, Republican, 4; Aaron Burr, of New York, Republican, 1 vote. Vacancies, 3. George Washington was chosen President and John Adams Vice-President.

ELECTORAL VOTE FOR PRESIDENT, BY PRINCIPAL POLITICAL PARTIES AND BY STATES, 1900 TO 1916

State	1900			1904			1908			1912				1916		
	Republican	Democratic	Total	Republican	Democratic	Total	Republican	Democratic	Total	Republican	Democratic	Progressive	Total	Republican	Democratic	Total
Alabama		11	11		11	11		11	11		12		12		12	12
Arizona											3		3		3	3
Arkansas		8	8		9	9		9	9		9		9		9	9
California	9		9	10		10	10		10	2		11	13		13	13
Colorado		4	4	5		5		5	5		6		6		6	6
Connecticut	6		6	7		7	7		7	7			7	7		7
Delaware	3		3	3		3	3		3		3		3	3		3
Florida		4	4		5	5		5	5		6		6		6	6
Georgia		13	13		13	13		13	13		14		14		14	14
Idaho		3	3	3		3	3		3		4		4		4	4
Illinois	24		24	27		27	27		27		29		29	29		29
Indiana	15		15	15		15	15		15		15		15	15		15
Iowa	13		13	13		13	13		13		13		13	13		13
Kansas	10		10	10		10	10		10		10		10		10	10
Kentucky		13	13	13		13		13	13		13		13		13	13
Louisiana		8	8		9	9		9	9		10		10		10	10
Maine	6		6	6		6	6		6		6		6	6		6
Maryland	8		8	1	7	8	2	6	8		8		8		8	8
Massachusetts	15		15	16		16	16		16		18		18	18		18
Michigan	14		14	14		14	14		14			15	15	15		15
Minnesota	9		9	11		11	11		11			12	12	12		12
Mississippi		9	9		10	10		10	10		10		10		10	10
Missouri		17	17	18		18	18		18		18		18		18	18
Montana		3	3	3		3	3		3		4		4		4	4
Nebraska	8		8	8		8		8	8		8		8		8	8
Nevada		3	3	3		3		3	3		3		3		3	3
New Hampshire	4		4	4		4	4		4		4		4	4		4
New Jersey	10		10	12		12	12		12		14		14	14		14
New Mexico											3		3		3	3
New York	36		36	39		39	39		39		45		45	45		45
North Carolina		11	11		12	12		12	12		12		12		12	12
North Dakota	3		3	4		4	4		4		5		5		5	5
Ohio	23		23	23		23	23		23		24		24		24	24
Oklahoma								7	7		10		10		10	10
Oregon	4		4	4		4	4		4	5			5	5		5
Pennsylvania	32		32	34		34	34		34			38	38	38		38
Rhode Island	4		4	4		4	4		4		5		5	5		5
South Carolina		9	9		9	9		9	9		9		9		9	9
South Dakota	4		4	4		4	4		4			5	5	5		5
Tennessee		12	12		12	12		12	12		12		12		12	12
Texas		15	15		18	18		18	18		20		20		20	20
Utah	3		3	3		3	3		3	4			4		4	4
Vermont	4		4	4		4	4		4	4			4	4		4
Virginia		12	12		12	12		12	12		12		12		12	12
Washington	4		4	5		5	5		5			7	7	7		7
West Virginia	6		6	7		7	7		7		8		8	8		8
Wisconsin	12		12	13		13	13		13		13		13	13		13
Wyoming	3		3	3		3	3		3		3		3		3	3
Total	292	155	447	336	140	476	321	162	483	8	435	88	531	255	276	531
Plurality	137			196			159			347				21		

1796.—John Adams, Federalist, 71; Thomas Jefferson, Republican, 68; Thomas Pinckney, of South Carolina, Federalist, 59; Aaron Burr, of New York, Republican, 30; Samuel Adams, of Massachusetts, Republican, 15; Oliver Ellsworth, of Connecticut, Independent, 11; George Clinton, of New York, Republican, 7; John Jay, of New York, Federalist, 5; James Iredell, of North Carolina, Federalist, 3; George Washington, of Virginia; John Henry, of Maryland, and S. Johnson, of North Carolina, all Federalists, 2 votes each; Charles Cotesworth Pinckney, of South Carolina, Federalist, 1 vote. John Adams was chosen President and Thomas Jefferson Vice-President. (b)

1800.—Thomas Jefferson, Republican, 73; Aaron Burr, Republican, 73; John Adams, Federalist, 65; Charles C. Pinckney, Federalist, 64; John Jay, Federalist, 1 vote. There being a tie vote for Jefferson and Burr, the choice devolved upon the House of Representatives. Jefferson received the votes of ten states, which being the largest vote cast for a candidate, elected him President. Burr received the votes of four States, which being the next largest vote, elected him Vice-President. There were 2 blank votes.

1804—The Constitution having been amended, the electors at this election voted for a President and a Vice-President, instead of for two candidates for President. The result was as follows: For President, Thomas Jefferson, Republican, 162; Charles C. Pinckney, Federalist, 14. For Vice-President, George Clinton, Republican, 162; Rufus King, of New York, Federalist, 14. Jefferson was chosen President and Clinton Vice-President.

1808—For President, James Madison, of Virginia, Republican, 122; Charles C. Pinckney, of South Carolina, Federalist, 47; George Clinton, of New York; Republican, 6. For Vice-President, George Clinton, Republican, 113; Rufus King, of New York, Federalist, 47; John Langdon, of New Hampshire, 9; James Madison, 3; James Monroe, 3. Vacancy, 1. Madison was chosen President and Clinton Vice-President.

1812.—For President, James Madison, Republican, 128; De Witt Clinton, of New York, Federalist, 89. For Vice-President, Elbridge Gerry, of Massachusetts, 131; Jared Ingersoll, of Pennsylvania, Federalist, 86. Vacancy, 1. Madison was chosen President and Gerry Vice-President.

1816.—For President, James Monroe, of Virginia, Republican, 183; Rufus King, of New York, Federalist, 34. For Vice-President, Daniel D. Tompkins, of New York, Republican, 183; John Eager Howard, of Maryland, Federalist, 22; James Ross, of Pennsylvania, 5; John Marshall, of Virginia, 4; Robert G. Harper, of Maryland, 3. Vacancies, 4. Monroe was chosen President and Tompkins Vice-President.

1820.—For President James Monroe, of Virginia, Republican, 231; John Q. Adams, of Massachusetts, Republican, 1. For Vice-President, Daniel D. Tompkins, Republican, 218; Richard Stockton, of New Jersey, 8; Daniel Rodney, of Delaware, 4; Robert G. Harper, of Maryland, and Richard Rush, of Pennsylvania, 1 vote each. Vacancies, 3. James Monroe was chosen President and Daniel D. Tompkins Vice-President.

1824.—For President, Andrew Jackson, of Tennessee, Republican, 99; John Quincy Adams, of Massachusetts, Republican, 84; Henry Clay, of Kentucky, Republican, 37; William H. Crawford, of Georgia, Republican, 41. No candidate having a majority of the electoral vote, John Quincy Adams was elected by the House of Representatives. For Vice-President, John C. Calhoun, of South Carolina, Republican, 182; Nathan Sanford, of New York, Republican, 30; Nathaniel Macon, of North Carolina, Republican, 24; Andrew Jackson, of Tennessee, Republican, 13; Martin Van Buren, of New York, Republican, 9; Henry Clay, of Kentucky, Republican, 2; Calhoun was chosen Vice-President.

Presidential Electors.—Persons chosen by the people of the several states to elect the President and Vice President. As a matter of custom, though not of legal requirement, the electors exercise the choice in accordance with the expressed wish of the voters at the polls.

Presidential Electors:
  Constitutional amendment regarding selection of, recommended, 5644.
  Method of appointment of, and effect of gerrymander discussed, 5643.
  (See Electors; Electoral Colleges).

Presidential Primaries.—The presidential primary is a device to enable the voters at large to record their choice for candidates for the presidency. It was little heard of previous to 1911, but in that year it became a leading topic of political discussion. Provisions for the presidential primary exist as statutes in six States—New Jersey, Wisconsin, Nebraska, North Dakota, Oregon, and California. The California law, which is typical of the others, provides that the name of any person may be put upon the ballot at the presidential primary election to be held in May, preceding an election for president, through the filing of a petition signed by one per cent of any party in each Congress district. The chief merit of such a primary, in the opinion of those who support it, would be the practical elimination of the national nominating conventions and the opportunity given the people at large of recording their choice for the presidency. The main objections urged by the opponents of the

presidential primary are that it would intensify factional bitterness and add to the expense of elections. The presidential primary had its chief supporters in 1911 among the members of the progressive wings of both Democratic and Republican parties. An attempt was made to indorse the idea at the meeting of the National Republican Committee held in Washington in December, 1911, but it failed. In addition to the states which have provided for presidential primaries by statute South Carolina and Louisiana observe them as party rules, and some other states have what is equivalent. Pennsylvania delegates to the National Conventions are elected by direct primaries and candidates for delegate are permitted to print on the ballot the name of the candidate for the presidency they wish to support.

Presidential primaries or some equivalent expression of opinion were held in 1912 in California, Illinois, Maryland, Massachusetts, Nebraska, New Hampshire, New Jersey, North Dakota, Ohio, Oregon, Pennsylvania, South Dakota and Wisconsin, and upon the results in these states Mr. Roosevelt based his assertion that he was the people's choice, but it was found that only two-thirds of the voters expressed their choice.

Presidential Succession.—The Constitution provides for the succession of the vice-president in case of the death, removal, resignation, or disability of the president, and gives Congress power to provide what officer shall succeed in case of the death, removal, etc., of the vice-president. In 1793 Congress enacted that in such case the president of the Senate should succeed, and then the speaker of the House of Representatives. This was attended with some inconvenience and danger and there was some doubt of its constitutionality. An act of Congress, approved Jan. 19, 1886, provided that the succession should pass to the members of the Cabinet in the following order: Secretary of State, Secretary of the Treasury, Secretary of War, Attorney-General, Postmaster-General, Secretary of the Navy, and Secretary of the Interior. The Secretaries of the Department of Agriculture, and of the Department of Commerce and Labor, whose offices have been created since the passage of the Succession Act, are not eligible for presidential succession. The following Vice-Presidents have succeeded to the Presidency on account of the death of the President: John Tyler, Millard Fillmore, Andrew Johnson, Chester A. Arthur, and Theodore Roosevelt. (See Vice-Presidents, and Cabinet, also Atchison, D. R., in Index.)

Presiding Ladies of the White House. (See biographies and portraits in text volumes at the beginning of the administrations of the respective Presidents.)

Presque Isle, Pa.:
  Obstructions to entrance of harbor of port of, 786.
  Title to, proffered by marine hospital of Pennsylvania, 4735.

Press, Freedom of.—The first amendment to the Constitution, introduced in the First Congress, established freedom of speech, religion, and the press. Though the Federal Constitution was originally silent upon the subject, nearly all of the states inserted in their constitutions clauses permitting freedom of speech and publication to every citizen. Abuses of this liberty were punishable under the common law. New York and New Jersey made no provision in their first constitutions, but clauses were later embodied insuring the widest liberty of expression. During British rule of the Colonies this freedom was much restricted by the star chamber press censorship regulation of 1637, which was confirmed by Parliament in 1643.

Pretoria, Republic of, joint resolution relating to congratulations from, vetoed, 4384.

Primaries. (See Presidental Primaries.)

Prince of Wales, visit of, to United States, 3171.

Prince of Wales Island, Alaska, referred to, 6697.

Princeton (N. J.), Battle of.—The beginning of the year 1777 found the British army of 7,000 or 8,000 men encamped at Princeton, N. J. On Christmas night, 1776, Washington had turned back his retreating army, recrossed the Delaware, overcome the Hessians at Trenton, and again crossed the Delaware into Pennsylvania. To relieve Cadwalader he again crossed the river and was ready to march upon Princeton. Cornwallis, who had been sent by Howe from New York, advanced to meet him with most of his army. Washington skilfully passed around the left wing of Cornwallis's army, and on Jan. 3, 1777, encountered the British rear guard, consisting of three regiments and three troops. These were scattered, with the loss of about 500. The American loss was 25 or 30, besides officers. Cornwallis retreated to New Brunswick and Washington occupied a strong position at Morristown, remaining there until the latter part of May.

Princeton, The, construction of, referred to, 2130.

Printing and Engraving. (See Engraving and Printing, Bureau of.)

Printing and Publishing.—At the close of the Revolutionary war the printing trade was carried on almost exclusively in the Atlantic coast cities. The earliest establishments set up in inland cities were at Lexington, Ky., Pittsburg, Pa., and Cincinnati, Ohio. The main printing centers have always been New York, Philadelphia, Chicago and Boston.

The growth of the business has been accelerated by the invention of electrotyping, stereotyping, type-setting machines, the cylinder press and the web press (printing from a continuous roll of paper, instead of separate sheets.) The manufacture of wood-pulp paper cheaply in large quantities has also been an important factor. Governmental encouragement, in the form of special rates of transportation by the Postoffice, has always been a large asset of the publishing business.

According to the census of 1910 there were 31,445 establishments engaged in printing books, periodicals, newspapers, music and job work in the United States. These were capitalized at $588,345,708, and gave employment to 388,466 persons, paying them in wages and salaries an aggregate of $268,086,431. The value of the output is placed at $737,876,087.

Printing has been the most generous contributor to human progress, and perhaps the most powerful factor in making the nineteenth century the leader of all centuries in genius and invention. The construction of the 10-cylinder press by Robert Hoe in 1853 was considered one of the greatest steps forward recently made in printing. The first practical improvement upon typesetting was made by Mergenthaler with his linotype machine, by which a row of brass matrices assembled in a line of desired length by means of a keyboard became the mould in which the writer's words were cast in softer metal ready for the ink and press. Other type-composing machines were invented, and new methods of cutting and casting ornamental styles and sizes of display type gave artistic tone to the printed page.

The greatest advances in press building since 1880 have been made in perfecting presses. These machines are now constructed of such enormous size and with such great capacity that it is possible to obtain at short notice a newspaper press which will produce 100,000 impressions per hour printed in twelve colors.

In 1862 the kind of news paper ordinarily used was made of cotton rags. It was imperfect, poor in color and made in the crudest manner. The price was 24 cents a pound. At present wood pulp paper of uniform quality can be bought for two cents per pound.

The volume of advertising circulars, booklets and pamphlet literature was never before so large or of such mechanical excellence as during the last decade.

Machinery for folding printed sheets, gathering, stitching and building them into book form has been so perfected that the costliest literary treasures of the past generation may be reproduced and placed in the reader's hands today at trifling cost.

A notable feature of the printing industry of the past decade has been the growth of monthly magazines. By sensational articles on timely subjects, wide circulation and enormous sales have been secured. This brought increased advertising, and the transportation of this class of merchandise through the mails at reduced rates granted for the purpose of disseminating learning caused President Taft to call attention to the propriety of increasing the rates to offset a deficit in the Postoffice Department. (See pages 7433, 7528, 7733.)

According to the census classification the printing and publishing industry is made up of three branches, comprising: (1) establishments whose chief business is book and job printing, book printing and publishing, or book publishing only; (2) establishments whose sole or chief business is music printing, or music printing and publishing, or music publishing only; and (3) establishments which are engaged in the printing and publishing, or in the publishing only, of newspapers and periodicals, some of the first-named doing job work also. The number of establishments in this industry in 1914 aggregated 31,612, and the total value of their products amounted to $810,508,111. Of the 31,612 establishments canvassed for 1914, those engaged in the printing and publishing or in the publishing only of newspapers and periodicals numbered 19,317. Those engaged chiefly in the printing and publishing of books and pamphlets or in job printing, or both, numbered 12,115, and the number engaged solely or chiefly in music printing, or music printing and publishing, or music publishing only, numbered 180. The total value of products reported for 1914, of establishments printing and publishing newspapers and periodicals, was $495,905,984. The value of products of establishments engaged chiefly in book and job work of all kinds aggregated $307,330,861 in 1914. The value of products of establishments engaged chiefly in music printing and publishing in 1914 aggregated $7,271,266. The value of products of the newspaper and periodical branch of the industry formed 61.2 per cent of the total in 1914; of the book and job branch, 37.9 per cent; and of the music printing and publishing branch, nine-tenths of 1 per cent. The daily newspaper, according to the census definition, is a publication issued on each of the secular days of the week, Sunday editions being excluded. A morning and an evening paper issued by the same plant are counted as two papers. A total of 2,580 dailies was reported for 1914. The aggregate circulation of the dailies in 1914 was 28,436,030. The number of Sunday papers published in the United States in 1914 was 570, as compared with 520 in 1909; and their combined circulation in the later year, 16,445,820, represented an increase of 23.2 per cent as compared with the corresponding figure for the earlier year. The number of weekly newspapers and periodicals reported for 1914, 15,166, shows a slight increase as compared with the corresponding number in 1909, 15,097. The 1914 circulation of such publications was 50,454,738, an increase of 23.6 per cent as compared with 1909.

Printing executed by authority of the several Departments referred to, 2911.

Printing Office, Government. (See Government Printing Office.)

Prison Congress, International, at—
St. Petersburg, 5117.
Stockholm, 4406, 4464.

Prison Congress, National, at Baltimore, 4162.

Prisoners. (See Imprisonment.)

Prisoners of War. (See Civil War; War of 1812.)

Prisons. (See Penitentiaries.)

Private.—In the army, a soldier's rank, as distinguished from an officer's.

Private Armed Vessels:
Depredations of, must be checked, 358.
Instructions were issued May 28, 1798, to commanders of armed vessels of United States to seize foreign vessels attacking those of the United States, especially those sailing under the flag of the French Republic.
Issuance of commissions to, discussed, 779.
Referred to, 2774.
Proposition to forego resort to, in case of war discussed, 2809, 2945.

Private Claims against United States:
Amount paid on, referred to, 1778, 1783.
Proceedings under act for payment of, suspended, 565.
Report of commissioners referred to, 566.
Settlement of, by commission recommended, 2627, 2673, 2714.

Private Land Claims. (See Court of Private Land Claims.)

Private Property:
Right to capture, at sea in time of war, 6795, 6796.
Seizure and confiscation of, referred to, 3831.
Shall not be taken for public use without just compensation, 435.

Privateering:
Abolition of, discussed, 2945.
Issuance of commissions to vessels for, discussed, 779, 2774.
Not to be resorted to by—
France in war with Spain, 779.
United States in war with Spain, 6474.
Referred to, 6312.
Proposition to forego resort to, in case of war discussed, 2809, 2945.
Referred to, 2909.

Privateers.—Armed vessels owned and officered by private persons, but acting under commissions from the government known as letters of marque. It was formerly the custom of all nations in time of war to legalize private vessels to assist the regular navy in blockading the ports of an enemy, intercepting supplies, and capturing prizes. Vessels so employed are called privateers and are supplied with letters of marque on condition of their conforming to the rules and usages of war. Herein lies the difference between privateers and pirates (q. v.). These vessels and crews may be hired or impressed by the government or they may be owned, officered, and sent to sea at private expense under government commission. The latter has been a favorite way of employing sailors and merchant ships when commerce has been hampered by war, and to a nation with a small navy it affords protection against formidable naval foes.

The practice of privateering has long been looked upon as an evil by the most advanced nations. At the Declaration of Paris in 1856 (q. v.) one of the rules of warfare subscribed to was that "privateering is and remains abolished." The United States refused to agree to this clause of the declaration on the ground that without privateers it would have no adequate sea force in time of war. As the agreement was only binding on parties thereto, American commerce was left a prey to the ships of all other nations. In 1861 Secretary Seward, on behalf of the United States, made an offer to England and France to come under the operation of the rules of war subscribed to in the Declaration of Paris, but the offer was refused on the ground that it would impose an international rule of warfare upon the Confederate States then in rebellion. In the colonial wars Great Britain derived much support from colonial privateers. Upward of 400 were fitted out and ravaged the French West Indies and made numerous captures along the coast of France.

In March, 1776, the Continental Congress accorded permission to citizens to fit out privateers against the British. During that year 342 British vessels fell a prey to privateers fitted out at Salem, Cape Ann, Newburyport, Bristol, and other seaports. This sort of warfare became so lucrative that sailors could hardly be induced to enter the regular service. Jan. 28, 1778, an American privateer surprised and captured the British fort of New Providence, in the Bahamas, and a 16-gun man-of-war. During the War of 1812 some 500 privateers were fitted out. They were mostly schooners or brigs of 200 or 300 tons and carried from 80 to 100 men. Of 400 British vessels captured in 1813 four-fifths were taken by privateers. Later in this war larger vessels like the *Reindeer, Avon,* and *Blakeley* were built. They did not confine themselves to merchant vessels, but attacked and frequently captured British war ships. They hung about the coasts of Great Britain, Ireland, and the Canary and West Indian Islands, and greatly aided the American cause.

Prize Agents, accounts of, referred to, 773, 816.

Prize Court (International), ratified by United States, 7670.

Prize Courts.—Courts which adjudicate the property in vessels captured at sea from a belligerent. The general rule is that when a captor brings home a prize the tribunal of his own country has sole jurisdiction over it and the decision rendered is binding everywhere. A prize court differs from other courts in that the property of foreigners is brought within its jurisdiction, not voluntarily, as in ordinary courts, but by force. During the colonial wars prize cases were adjudged by the admiralty courts held by colonial governors as vice-admirals, or by judges whom they appointed, with appeal to commissioners in England. With the outbreak of the Revolution the states established admiralty courts to hear prize cases. The Continental Congress established a court of appeals for such cases when in dispute between the states. Under the judiciary act of 1789 the United States district courts were made prize courts, with appeal to the Supreme Court.

Prize Money.—A dividend from the proceeds of a captured vessel and her cargo, etc., paid to the captors. Prior to March 3, 1899, prize money in the United States was distributed according to an act of June 30, 1864. If the prize was equal or superior to the captor, it became the sole property of the latter. If inferior, the United States took half and the captors divided the remainder. Privateers with letters of marque kept the whole of the prize unless otherwise stipulated in their commissions. By the Navy personnel act of March 3, 1899, the law authorizing the distribution of prize money among the captors of vessels was repealed.

Prize Money referred to, 2570.

Pro-Ally.—Favoring the Entente Allies (q. v.) in the European War, or a person favoring them.

Pro-German.—Favoring Germany in the European War; a person who favors Germany in the European War.

Pro-Teuton.—Favoring the Teutonic powers in the European War as against the Allies (q. v.); pro-German (q. v.).

Proclamations. (See the several Presidents or the several subjects.)

Products. (See Agricultural Products; Animals and Animal Products.)

Progressive Labor Party.—At the annual session of the United Labor party held at Syracuse, N. Y., Aug. 19, 1886, the radical or socialistic element withdrew and formed the Progressive Labor party. They advocated a common inheritance of land, wealth, and industries and upheld all the tenets of extreme socialism.

Progressive Party.—Theodore Roosevelt having been defeated for the Republican nomination for President at the hands of the National Convention in June, 1912, called a convention of his own followers and people in general who were dissatisfied with the Republican party and its managers to meet in convention in Chicago in August, 1912. This convention formed the Progressive party and nominated Mr. Roosevelt for President and Hiram W. Johnson, of California, for Vice-President.

They adopted a platform declaring in favor of direct primaries; nation-wide Presidential preference primaries; direct election of United States Senators; the short ballot and the initiative, referendum, and recall in the States; a more easy and expeditious method of amending the Federal Constitution; the bringing under effective National jurisdiction of those problems which expand beyond the reach of the individual States; equal suffrage for men and women; limitation of campaign contributions and expenditures, and publicity before as well as after primaries and elections; laws requiring the registration of lobbyists, publicity of committee hearings, and recording of all votes in committee; prohibiting Federal appointees from taking part in political organizations and political conventions.

Popular review of judicial decisions on laws for securing social justice; the review by the Supreme Court of the United States of decisions of State courts declaring legislative acts unconstitutional; the reform of legal procedure and judicial methods; the prohibition of the issuance of injunctions in labor disputes when such injunctions would not apply if no labor dispute existed, and jury trial for contempt in labor disputes except when the contempt was committed in the presence of the court; effective legislation looking to the prevention of industrial accidents, occupational diseases, overwork, involuntary unemployment, and other injurious effects incident to modern industry; the fixing of minimum safety and health standards for the various occupations and the exercise of the public authority to maintain such standards; the prohibition of child labor; minimum wage standards for workingwomen, to provide a "living wage" in all industrial occupations; the general prohibition of night work for women and the establishment of an eight-hour day for women and young persons.

One day's rest in seven for all wage-workers; the eight-hour day in continuous twenty-four-hour industries; the abolition of the convict contract labor system; substituting a system of prison production for governmental consumption only, and the application of prisoners' earnings to the support of their dependent families; publicity as to wages, hours, and conditions of labor; full reports upon industrial accidents and diseases, and the opening to public inspection of all tallies, weights, measures, and check systems on labor products; standards of compensation for death by industrial accident and injury and trade disease which will transfer the burden of lost earnings from the families of working people to the industry, and thus to the community; the protection of home life against the hazards of sickness, irregular employment, and old age, through the adoption of a system of social insurance adapted to American use; the establishment of continuation schools for industrial education; industrial research laboratories; a Department of Labor; the development of agricultural credit and cooperation; the encouragement of agricultural education; the establishment of a Country Life Commission; full and immediate inquiry into the high cost of living, and immediate action dealing with every need disclosed thereby.

A National Health Service; establishment of a strong Federal administrative commission to maintain permanent active supervision over industrial corporations, as the Government now does over National banks and, through the Interstate Commerce Commission, over railways; the strengthening of the Sherman Law by specific prohibitions; the enactment of a patent law to prevent the suppression or the misuse of patents in the interest of injurious monopolies; giving the Interstate Commerce Commission the power to value the physical property of railways; the abolition of the Commerce Court; prompt legislation for the improvement of the National currency system which shall give the Government full control over the issue of currency notes; the appointment of diplomatic and consular officers solely for fitness and not for political expediency; the retention of forest, coal, and oil lands, water and other natural resources in the ownership of the Nation; a vigorous good roads campaign through the construction of National highways; the extension of the rural free delivery service.

The retention of the natural resources of Alaska in ownership by the Nation, and their prompt opening to use upon liberal terms requiring immediate development; for Alaska the same measure of local self-government that has been given to other American territories; the comprehensive development of waterways; the operation of the Panama Canal so as to break the transportation monopolies now held and misused by transcontinental railways; a protective tariff which shall equalize conditions of competition between the United States and foreign countries both for the farmer and the manufacturer, and which shall maintain for labor an adequate standard of living; an immediate downward revision of the tariff; a non-partisan, scientific tariff commission; a graduated inheritance tax.

The ratification of the Amendment of the Constitution giving the Government power to levy an income tax; introduction of judicial and other peaceful means of settling international differences; an international agreement for the limitation of naval forces, and, pending such an agreement, the maintenance of the policy of building two battleships a year; protection of the rights of American citizenship at home and abroad; governmental action to encourage the distribution of immigrants, and to supervise all agencies dealing with them, and to supervise and promote their education and advancement; a wise and just policy of pensioning American soldiers and sailors; a parcel post, with rates proportionately to distance and service; the rigid enforcement and extension of the Civil Service Act; a readjustment of the business methods of the National Government, and a proper coordination of the Federal bureaus; governmental supervision for the protection of the public from fraudulent stock issues.

At the presidential election the following November the party polled a popular vote of more than 4,119,507 votes, carrying the States of Michigan, Minnesota, Pennsylvania, California, South Dakota and Washington, thus winning 88 electoral votes. This split of the Republican vote resulted in the election of Wilson, the Democratic candidate, to the presidency.

No presidential candidate was nominated in 1916.

During July the greater part of the Progressive party followed the lead of Col. Roosevelt and the national committee in endorsing Hughes for the presidency. Local organizations in several states, however, refused to be reconciled. John M. Parker, vice-presidential nominee of the Progressive convention held in Chicago in June, issued a call for a new Progressive ticket July 15, to be drawn up at a convention scheduled to open in Chicago Aug. 5. He declared:

"The Bull Moose led his loyal followers into the wilderness—and there deserted them. Let us eternally bury their emblem, and adopt as the new emblem of the progressive party the national bird, the American eagle, which will always be a patriotic inspiration to look upward, and a constant reminder to be true to those sterling principles which have made America great, and brought to this country the bravest and most adventurous spirits of the Old World. These, and their descendants, are truly loyal and patriotic Americans."

The insurgent element was successful at the Syracuse meeting of the New York state committee, July 22, and managed to prevent an endorsement of Hughes. The insurgents then made preparations for a second Bull Moose National Convention in Chicago on August 5.

Plans for the reorganization and perpetuation of the Progressive Party as a national political organization were adopted at Indianapolis, August 3, at a conference of Progressive representatives. The conference decided against reassembling the party for a national convention to fill the vacancy on the national ticket, caused by Theodore Roosevelt's declining the nomination for President. Instead, the organization decided to put up an electoral ticket in every State where there is the nucleus of an organization left, bearing the name of John M. Parker of Louisiana, nominee for Vice-President, in the hope of perhaps electing enough presidential electors, who might prove the balance of power in the event of a close contest between the two parties. The indorsement of Hughes was severely criticized by the party leaders.

Prohibition, National.—Prohibition first appeared as a national political issue in 1869, and since 1872 the Prohibition party has placed presidential tickets in the field. The party candidates since 1872 with the popular vote polled have been as follows:

1872—James Black, Pennsylvania.. 5,608
1876—Green Clay Smith, Kentucky. 9,522
1880—Neal Dow, Maine.......... 10,305
1884—John P. St. John, Kansas...150,369
1888—Clinton B. Fiske, New York..249,506
1892—John Bidwell, California.....255,841
1896—Joshua Levering, Maryland..131,312
1900—John G. Woolley, Illinois....208,555
1904—Silas C. Swallow, Pennsylvania 258,838
1908—Eugene W. Chafin, Illinois...241,252
1912—Eugene W. Chafin, Arizona..207,928
1916—J. Frank Hanly, Indiana....225,101

In 1896 the party split on the silver question, those favoring the free coinage of silver at the ratio of 16 to 1, forming the National party and nominating Charles E. Bentley, who received 13,968 votes.

Prohibition, State.—The prohibition of the manufacture and sale of alcoholic drinks has long been a subject of political discussion in America. Long before the Revolution the liquor traffic was taxed, and the Continental Congress advised the states to pass laws prohibiting the distillation of grain. Prohibition became a purely state political issue first in the Maine legislature in 1837, when a prohibitory bill was introduced and defeated. In 1846 a bill with the same purpose became a law, but did not serve the purpose and was succeeded in 1851 by a more effective measure drafted by Neal Dow. This law provided for search and seizure, but the Prohibitionists lost their majority and the law was repealed. Later a second law was passed which was made a part of the state constitution in 1884 and is still in force.

Between 1849 and 1856 prohibitory laws were passed in the following states and were repealed or made inoperative as indicated below: Illinois repealed in 1853; Rhode Island repealed in 1863; Pennsylvania repealed in 1866; Delaware repealed in 1867; Massachusetts repealed in 1868; Connecticut repealed in 1872; Michigan repealed in 1875; New York declared unconstitutional; Iowa amended in 1894 so as to be ineffective; Vermont repealed in 1902; New Hampshire repealed in 1903.

Including those States which decided at the election of 1916 to prohibit the manufacture and sale of intoxicating liquors, twenty-three are now denominated "dry." The strictly prohibition States are: Alabama, Arizona, Arkansas, Colorado, Georgia, Idaho, Iowa, Kansas, Maine, Michigan, Mississippi, Montana, Nebraska, North Carolina, North Dakota, Oklahoma, Oregon, South Carolina, South Dakota, Tennessee, Washington, West Virginia, Virginia.

Besides these, Florida and Utah in 1916 elected Governors pledged to enforce prohibitory liquor laws. Including those states made partially dry under local option, more than 60 per cent of the people of the country and 85 per cent of the area are under prohibition. The popular vote of Alaska in 1916 favored abolition of the liquor traffic.

The Prohibition National Convention of 1916 was held at St. Paul, Minn., July 19-21. J. Frank Hanly, former governor of Indiana, was nominated for president by a vote of 440 to 181 for William Sulzer, former governor of New York, his nearest competitor. Dr. Ira D. Landrith, of Nashville, Tenn., was nominated for vice-president.

The platform expressed opposition to the "wasteful military programs of the Democratic and Republican parties," but favored "preparedness for peace." It suggested a "compact among nations to dismantle navies and disband armies," but until "such court and compact are established we pledge ourselves to maintain an effective army and navy and to provide coast defenses entirely adequate for national protection."

It also favored legislation to encourage the establishment of an adequate fleet of American merchant ships. It opposed war with Mexico, pledged aid to the protection of American lives, and favored use of force when necessary.

Projectile.—A shell or other missile to be thrown into the ranks of the enemy, usually by the use of cannon, but sometimes by hand.

Proletariat.—Used by the Romans to designate the lower classes, or plebeians, as distinguished from the patricians. It is now generally used, especially in the philosophy of Socialism (q. v.), to designate the industrious poor.

Prometheus, The, firing into and seizure of, by British vessel, 2675, 2680.

Property at Sea:
International agreement to regard, as exempt from capture by belligerent powers, recommended, 6338.

International conference at Washington for security of life and, 5468, 5493, 5498.

Maritime powers invited to attend, 5370.

Recommended, 5180.

Treaty with Italy regarding, 4098.

Property, Captured:
Cotton captured and forfeited referred to, 3666.

Should not be adjudged without regular investigation, 485.

Property, Industrial, international convention at Paris for protection of, 4560, 4794, 4857, 5118.

Property, Private:
Seizure and confiscation of, referred to, 3831.

Shall not be taken for public use without just compensation, 435.

Proprietaries.—American territory was parceled out by the various crowned heads of Europe to personal friends or favorites or in recognition of some useful service to the sovereign. Persons to whom these grants were made established what were known as proprietary governments. The proprietor appointed the governor, and in general performed all those acts of government which are usually the prerogative of the Crown. New York, New Jersey, Pennsylvania, the Carolinas, Delaware, and Maryland were proprietary governments. The laws of Pennsylvania and Delaware were subject to the supervision of the Crown, but those of Maryland were not.

Prosperity.—A condition where there is abundant fulfilment of all desires, including work at good wages,—as distinguished from hard times, where so many people are out of employment that charity has to be widely extended to ameliorate the suffering. The word "prosperity" is much played upon in political campaigns, as it is the most alluring condition which can be promised constituents.

Prosperity, National, discussed, 6709, 6710, 6894, 6973.

Protection.—In political economy the principle or system of imposing such duties on imported goods as will protect or foster domestic industries. Tariffs are either chiefly to produce revenue or to afford protection. Nearly all American tariffs previous to that of 1824 come under the former head. But the preamble of the first tariff act of 1789 declared that one of its objects was "the encouragement and protection of manufactures," and the principle of protection was ably advocated by Secretary Hamilton, in his elaborate report on manufactures, in 1791, and by many members of Congress from that time to the present. The tariff of 1816 was claimed as protective and proposed as such by northern members, while Calhoun and other southerners advocated it. Later the relative views of north and south were radically changed, and the north became protectionist, while southern members (except Clay and his Whig followers) were for a low tariff for revenue only. The tariff bill introduced in the House of Representatives in 1820 by Representative Baldwin, of Pennsylvania, from the Committee on Manufactures was frankly stated to be a protective measure, and at that time the question of a protective duty was first suggested to be unconstitutional. This bill did not pass, but in 1824 a tariff bill became a law with average duties of 37 per cent. The protectionists claimed that many of the duties were too low for effective protection, and in 1828, after a prolonged commercial depression, a congress opposed to protection passed a high protective tariff, which satisfied neither party, and was denounced as "a bill of abominations." The failure of another act, passed in 1832, to sufficiently reduce the rates of the tariff of 1828 was the chief cause of the nullification movement (q. v.). The Clay-Calhoun tariff of 1833, known as the "Compromise of 1833," gradually reduced duties to a revenue basis. The act of 1842 was protective; that of 1846 (the Walker tariff) was strictly a revenue tariff. The Morrill tariff of 1861 and all subsequent tariff acts have been protective. The duties have been high, running from an average of 18 per cent to 48 per cent ad valorem on all dutiable articles.

In 1908, President Taft was elected on a platform which advocated a revision of the Dingley Tariff. Immediately after his election he called an extra session of Congress (7379) and recommended a reduction of duties. Congress, after deliberating nearly all summer, passed a tariff law, taking away all protection from hides, and making reductions of 10 to 15 per cent on leather, lumber, paper, coal, iron and steel sheets, and chemicals. The principle of protection was abandoned in the Democratic tariff law of 1913. (See Tariff; Import Duties.)

Protection of Industrial Property Union, acts of international conference, 7671.

Protective Tariff. (See Protection and Import Duties discussed.)

Protestant Church at American embassy at Rome, removal of, referred to, 3662, 3717.

Protestant Episcopal Church in Alexandria, Va., act incorporating, vetoed, 474.

Protests.—The official papers of the Presidents as they are sent to Congress are properly designated "messages," but on several occasions the Chief Executives have sent papers known as "protests." They are sent in the customary message form, but contain the formal protest of the President against the actions of Congress as a whole or of one or the other of the two Houses.

Protests of President—
Buchanan to proceedings of House, 3145, 3150.
Jackson to resolutions of Senate charging him with violating Constitution and laws, 1288.
Additional statement regarding, 1312.
Johnson to act depriving him of command of Army, 3670.
Tyler to action of House in adopting report assailing his official conduct, 2043.

Proteus, The.—The vessel in which Gen. Adolphus W. Greely, with twenty-four men, sailed from St. Johns, Newfoundland, July 7, 1881, and reached Discovery Harbor (lat. 81° 44' north, long. 64° 45' west), Aug. 12, 1881, where he established his station. The *Proteus* was lost in Smith Sound, midway between Cape Sabine and Cape Albert, July 23, 1883, while attempting to reach Lady Franklin Bay with a relief party for Greely.

Proteus, The, loss of, and court of inquiry regarding, 4790.

Protocol.—A preliminary agreement between countries or other conflicting forces,—reached by diplomatic negotiation, and executed by the signatory powers,—upon which to base a permanent treaty or contract.

Providence Plantations.—In 1636 Róger Williams and his followers, who advocated complete separation of church and state and toleration for all creeds, were banished from Massachusetts Bay Colony. They journeyed southward and founded Providence. Two years later the followers of Anne Hutchinson founded Portsmouth, and in 1639 Newport was settled. In 1644 Williams obtained from the parliamentary commissioners a patent which associated the three towns in one community. Both Plymouth and Massachusetts claimed the territory, but failed to make their claims good. In 1663 a new charter was granted, which united Rhode Island to the Providence Plantations and remained substantially the fundamental law until 1842.

Providence Plantations. (See Rhode Island.)

Providencia, The, appropriation for seizure of, by American steamer recommended, 3263.

Provincial.—Peculiar to a confined section,—usually a rural section. (See Provincialism.)

Provincialism.—A state of mind, expression, or manners peculiar to a confined section, especially a province or rural district.

Provisional Courts in Louisiana, order regarding, 3323.

Provisional Governors (see also Reconstruction; Restoration):
Appointment of, and restoration into Union of—
Alabama, 3521.
Florida, 3527.
Georgia, 3516.
Mississippi, 3512.
North Carolina, 3510.
South Carolina, 3524.
Texas, 3519.
Referred to, 3577, 3643.
Restoration referred to—
Arkansas, 3423, 3452.
Louisiana, 3423, 3452.

Provisions, importation of, into foreign countries and rates of duty on, referred to, 5503.

Prussia.—A Kingdom of northern Germany. It is bounded on the north by the North Sea, Denmark, Oldenburg, and the Baltic, on the east by Russia, on the south by Austria, Saxony, etc., and on the west by Luxemburg, Belgium, and the Netherlands. In the northern and eastern portions the country is generally level, but in the south and southwest it is hilly or mountainous. The chief agricultural products are rye, wheat, oats, potatoes, barley, millet, fruit, beet root, tobacco, and maize. Prussia is very largely engaged in manufacturing. The government is a hereditary constitutional monarchy administered by a King and a Landtag consisting of two chambers.

Prussia is the principal State of the German Empire. It has seventeen votes in the Bundesrath and 236 members in the Reichstag. Hanover, Frankfort, Nassau and some other states were acquired by Prussia in 1866. This resulted in forming the North German Confederation. As a result of the war between France and Germany, 1870-71, the German Empire was formed, with the crown hereditary in the Prussian dynasty.

The agricultural area of Prussia is 28,-479,739 hectares, divided, in 1905, into 3,-308,651 separate holdings or farms, about two-thirds of which were of less than ten hectares (twenty-five acres) in area. These farms supported a population of 10,948,476. The chief crops were rye, hay, oats, potatoes, wheat and barley. There were vineyards of 18,033 hectares, yielding 370,107 hectolitres of wine.

In 1905-6, 286 establishments consumed 12,596,787 metric tons of beet root in the manufacture of 1,861,970 metric tons of raw sugar and 260,859 metric tons of molasses ; 4,326 breweries made 33,600,000 hectolitres of beer—ninety litres per head for the population ; 6,404 distilleries produced 3,722,032 hectolitres of alcohol.

Prussia yields about half the world's zinc ; copper, lead and coal are also mined. During 1910 there were 663,534 persons employed in the mines and their wages were 800,392,890 marks. (German mark = 23.8 cents.)

The area of Prussia is 135,134 square miles, and the population (1910), 40,165,-210.

Prussia: (See also German Empire.)
American citizens in—
Expelled from, 3123.
Impressed into military service of. (See Naturalized Citizens.)
Commercial relations with, 820.
Confederate envoys sent to Great Britain and France referred to. (See Mason and Slidell.)
Friendly disposition of, toward United States, 919.
Fugitive criminals, convention with, for surrender of, 2267, 2689, 2719.
Ratification of, referred to, 2450.
Immigration treaty with, 3827.
Imprisonment of American citizens by, 1136.
Naturalization treaty with, 3827.
Treaty with, transmitted and discussed, 287, 296, 968, 1002, 2267, 2689, 2719, 3827.
Impressment of American citizens into military service, violating treaty with, 3827.
Violation of, by United States complained of, 2249.
Vessels of—
Application for rights regarding, 621.
Suspension of discriminating duties on, recommended, 969.
Vessels of United States, discriminating duties on, abolished by, 969.

Prussia, Treaties with.—Of the treaty of 1785 the only article that has survived is that on the neutrality of vessels. The treaty of amity and commerce of 1799 contained many articles which expired by limitation in 1810, and some others were revived by treaty of 1828. Contraband goods may be detained ; ves-

sels are to be distinctively marked for recognition in time of war by passport and other specified documents. The examination and search of vessels in time of war is to be conducted with ease, freedom from embarrassment and annoyance, according to specified methods. Vessels taken by an enemy and recaptured by one of the parties thereto are to be restored to the other of these parties. Humane treatment is to be extended in cases of distress on shipboard and in wrecks. Citizens of the one party are not to act offensively against the other when at war with a third party. The neutrality of vessels and the principle that free ships make free goods are fully recognized. In case of war between the parties thereto, citizens of the one in the country of the other shall be fully protected in life, property and business. Prisoners of war are not to be sent to unsafe or unhealthy localities but are to be cared for humanely and with regard to safety of life and health.

The treaty of commerce and navigation of 1828 extended freedom of trade without discrimination in shipping charges or import duties by reason of the nationality of the carrying vessels. The coastwise trade is excepted from provisions. All commercial privileges are upon the basis of the most favored nation. The establishment of consuls and consular agents is permitted and prescribed with full powers regarding the arrest and detention of deserters and the administration of the affairs of deceased persons. (For extradition terms, see Extradition treaties.)

Prussianism.—A term applied to the militarism (q. v.) which many observers characterize as the prevailing spirit of the German Empire, of which the foundation is Prussia (q. v.).

Public Accounts. (See Accounts, Public.)

Public Acts. (See Acts, Public; Bills and Acts.)

Public Archives, building for, recommended, 7728.

Public Buildings. (See Buildings, Public.)

Public Buildings, Commissioner of. (See Buildings, Public, Commissioner of.)

Public Buildings, Surveyor of. (See Buildings, Public, Surveyor of.)

Public Credit. (See Credit, Public.)

Public Debt. (See Debt, Public.)

Public Defenses. (See Defenses, Public.)

Public Deposits. (See Deposits, Public.)

Public Documents. (See Records and Documents.)

Public Domain:
Classification of, suggested, 7719.
In Alaska, 7719.
Mineral lands, leasing of, suggested, 7719.
Reclamation act, amendments suggested, 7719.

Public Health (see also Quarantine Regulations):
Federal aid for State and City health boards recommended, 7104.

Placing Federal bureaus of, under one department recommended, 7229.

Public Health and Marine Hospital Service, United States:
Land reserved for, in Puerto Rico, 6708.

Public Health Service. (See Health Service.)

Public Information Committee.—By order of President Wilson on April 13, 1917, a committee on Public Information was created. The committee is composed of the Secretaries of War, Navy and State, with a civilian director. The appointment of civilian director went to Mr. George Creel, formerly Director of Public Safety in Denver, Colorado, and later a writer of prominence on political and social questions. Secretary of State Lansing announced, on May 8, 1917, that all further news from the State Department would be given out through the newly-created Bureau of Intelligence within that department, and that all employees of the Department were forbidden to give out to any one information of any character. (See Censorship.)

Public Lands Division, Justice Department.—This bureau enforces the laws respecting the public lands (q. v.). (See also Justice Department.)

Public Land Laws. (See Lands, Public.)

Public Land Offices. (See Land Offices, Public.)

Public Lands. (See Lands, Public.)

Public Lands Commission, report of, referred to, 4535, 6863, 6947.

Public Libraries, discussed, 6676.

Public Money. (See Revenue, Public.)

Public Officers. (See Officers, Public.)

Public Printer.—The officer in charge of the printing of Government documents, etc. (See Government Printing Office.)

Public Records. (See Records and Documents.)

Public Reservations. (See Reservations, Public.)

Public Revenue. (See Revenue, Public.)

Public Roads. (See Agriculture, Department of, also Mail Routes.)

Public Statutes of United States. (See Revised Statutes.)

Public Supplies. (See Supplies, Public.)

Public Works. (See Internal Improvements.)

Publications, Division of, Agriculture Department.—An office in the Department of Agriculture to which is entrusted the editing of agricultural publications, particularly the *Year Book* of the department. This office also has charge of all the printing and illustrating done for the Department of Agriculture, as well as the distribution of the documents after they are printed. The publications include regular "Farmers' Bulletins," "Experiment Station Record," "Month-

ly Weather Review," and "Crop Reporter," also works of more special character. These are given free to scientific institutions and to collaborators of the department, libraries, colleges and experiment stations. The expenditures of the bureau in this line amount to about $4,500,000 per year.

Publications, Official. (See Records and Documents.)

Puebla (Mexico), Battle of.—After Gen. Scott had proceeded on his march to the City of Mexico, Gen. Rea, a guerrilla chief, was joined by Santa Anna. Col. Childs, commandant of the Puebla garrison left by Scott, sent Capt. Blanchard with thirty-three men to capture a band of guerrillas. Blanchard and twenty-two men were ambuscaded and killed the latter part of August, 1847. Sept. 25 Santa Anna demanded the surrender of the forts at Puebla. Childs, who had only about 360 men, refused and maintained his position in spite of an almost continuous fire of the Mexicans, until relieved by reenforcements under Gen. Lane, on Oct. 12.

Puget Sound.—An arm of the Pacific extending into the State of Washington southward from the Strait of San Juan de Fuca, by which it is connected with the Pacific. The sound is divided into two parts—Puget Sound proper and Admiralty Inlet. The latter is to the north and the former to the south. Fine harbors are found along the sound, the water generally being quite deep. It is about eighty miles long.

Puget Sound Agricultural Co.:
Claims of, against United States, referred to, 3888.
Treaty with Great Britain regarding, 3395, 3401.
Commissioners appointed under, 3447.
Award of, and appropriation for, recommended, 3989.
Value of possessory rights of, referred to, 2866.

Pumpkin Vine Creek (Ga.), Battle of—
(See New Hope Church (Ga.), Battle of.)

Puritan, The, mentioned, 6318.

Pure Food Act. (See Food and Drugs Act.)

Purity Federation.—The object of this Federation is to unite in national co-operation all those forces in America that are striving to promote purity in the life of the individual and in social relations through preventive educational, reformatory, rescue, law enforcement, legislative and sanitary lines of effort. It is in every sense non-sectarian, and is open to all who are sincerely and seriously striving to promote its object. Many of the leaders in religious, philanthropic and reform movements in the United States are officially connected with this Federation. Each year a largely attended national purity congress is held under the auspices of the Federation.

Puyallup Commission, report of, transmitted, 5663.

Puyallup Indians. (See Indian Tribes.)

Pyramid Lake Reservation, Nev., agreement for cession of portion of, 5649.

Quadruple Alliance. (See Central Powers.)

Quallah Battoo, Sumatra, American citizens murdered in, 1138.

Quapaw Indians. (See Indian Tribes.)

Quarantine.—A term derived from the French word "quarantaine" (m. Lat. quarantena), meaning "forty days." Passengers on vessels arriving at Venice from the Levant were formerly required to remain forty days in the House of St. Lazarus or Lazaretto. This regulation was afterwards adopted by other ports in southern Europe, and, with various changes in the period of detention, extended to travelers from all ports whence contagion might be carried. In the United States quarantine enactments were passed by the colonial legislatures and subsequently for many years by the states. The first national quarantine act was passed Feb. 23, 1799, and required Federal officers to aid in the execution of state or municipal quarantine regulations. In 1878, however, a national quarantine law was passed authorizing the establishment, in certain contingencies, of national quarantines. In March, 1883, $100,000 was appropriated by the Federal Government for maintaining quarantine stations along the coasts, and the authority for declaring quarantine was conferred upon the President. Most of the quarantine stations are under state supervision. The mode of procedure is as follows: On the arrival of a vessel she is visited by the health officer, who examines her bill of health, musters the passengers and crew, and inspects the vessel in every part. If free from contagious disease, and if she does not hail from an infected port, she is allowed to proceed without further detention. If she hails from an infected port, she is detained until the expiration of the period of incubation of the disease prevalent at the port whence she sailed. If disease is found on board, or if the vessel is in an unsanitary condition, the diseased persons are removed to a quarantine hospital and the vessel allowed to proceed after a thorough purification.

Quarantine Regulations (see also Contagious Diseases; International Sanitary Conference):

For Canal Zone, 7966.

Proclamation regarding, 4812.

Referred to, 4840.

Recommendations regarding, by President—

Adams, John, 261.

Arthur, 4622, 4840.

Cleveland, 5877.

Harrison, Benj., 3765.

Hayes, 4444.

Jefferson, 371.

Monroe, 854.

Roosevelt, 6914, 6948, 7104, 7228.

Quarter-Deck.—The deck used for promenade by officers of a war vessel.

Quarter Dollar.—In 1786 the Continental Congress decided upon certain coins. Among these was a quarter dollar, to be made of silver. The United States Mint was established in 1792 and began coinage in 1793. It was not until 1796, however, that the silver quarter was issued. Its weight was fixed at 104 grains. It was reduced to 93 grains in 1853, and by the coinage act of 1873 was raised to 96.45 grains, or 0.200 of an ounce, the present weight, and 900 fine. The coin is legal tender to the amount of $10. The quarter dollar of 1827 is one of the rare coins of the United States. There were no issues of this coin during the years 1798 to 1803, 1808 to 1815, nor during 1817, 1824, 1826, and 1830.

Quarter Eagle.—A gold coin of the United States authorized in 1792 and first coined in 1796. It is legal tender in any sum. The present weight of the coin is 0.134 ounce, or 64.5 grains, and the fineness 900. It is coined under an act of Congress of June 28, 1834.

Quartering Acts.—Certain acts of the British Parliament distasteful to the American colonists. The first was passed in 1765 and compelled the Colonies to provide the garrisons in America with fire, candles, vinegar, salt, bedding, cooking utensils, and liquors. This was the first act requiring the colonists to tax themselves for imperial object. In 1774 an act was passed legalizing the quartering of imperial troops in Boston.

Quartermaster-General. (See War Department and Army.)

Quartermaster-General of Army, fireproof building for records in office of, recommended, 4524.

Quebec (Canada), Battle of.—After taking Montreal Gen. Montgomery proceeded down the St. Lawrence River to Quebec, where on December 5, 1775, he joined the expedition which had been sent by way of the Kennebec and Chaudière rivers under Benedict Arnold. Their combined forces amounted to about 3,000 men, supported by about a dozen light guns. Carleton had for the defense of Quebec one company of regulars, a sloop of war, and a few marines, together with as many of the citizens as could be induced to enlist—in all something like 1,600 men. On the night of Dec. 31 the city was attacked. Montgomery was killed, Arnold was wounded, and the troops retired in confusion. Three thousand troops were sent to reenforce Arnold, and 4,000 occupied Montreal, St. Johns and Chambly. May 6, 1776, three brigades of infantry, besides artillery, stores, ammunitions, transports, and men-of-war, arrived from England and the Americans retired, leaving Canada as it was before the invasion. (See also Montreal (Canada), Capture and Loss of.)

Queen Anne's War.—The name of which the War of the Spanish Succession was known in America. It broke out in 1702 and was ended with the treaty of Utrecht in 1713. The New England Colonies suffered from frequent inroads of French and Indians from Canada, but the New York Colony was protected by the barrier of the Six Nations of Indians, then at peace with the English. Aug. 10, 1703, Indians under French leaders attacked Wells, Cape Porpoise, Saco, Casco, Scarboro, Spurwink, and Purpooduck, completely destroying the last two. In 1704 and 1705 James Moore, of South Carolina, with 50 whites and about 1,000 Creek Indians, attacked and destroyed several Spanish settlements in Florida. Col. Church organized an expedition in Maine in 1704 and proceeded up the coast as far as the Bay of Fundy, destroying all the settlements and taking 106 prisoners, with the loss of only 6 men. Feb. 28, 1704, about 350 French-Canadians and Indians burned the town of Deerfield, Mass., massacring 40 persons and taking 100 prisoners. After three attempts by the New England troops Acadia was finally captured. July 30, 1711, Gen. Nicholson left Albany with an army of 4,000 men and Hovenden Walker sailed from Boston with a fleet and 7,000 men, as well as a fine train of artillery, to attack Quebec and Montreal. The fleet was driven upon the rocks at the mouth of the St. Lawrence. losing eight transports and more than 1,000 men. The survivors sailed for England and the army disbanded.

Queenston Heights (Canada), Battle of. —Early in October, 1812, Ben. Van Rensselaer resolved to invade Canada from western New York. His headquarters were at Lewiston, opposite Queenston, Canada. The American army consisted of 3,650 regulars and 2,650 militia. The British force on the western bank of the Niagara River numbered 1,500, including about 250 Indians under John Brandt. Maj. Ben. Brock, who had taken Detroit in August, had returned to the east and established his headquarters at Fort George. He posted batteries every mile along the river from there to Queenston. On the morning of Oct. 13, 1812, the invasion was begun prematurely, insufficient boats having been provided for transportation. Reenforcements came so slowly that the advance guard was forced to surrender. Gen. Brock was mortally wounded. Van Rensselaer was disabled and the American command fell upon Captain Wool. British reenforcements and Indians pressing hard upon the Americans, they were forced to surrender. About 900 Americans were taken prisoners, 90 were killed, and about 100 wounded. The British lost in killed, wounded, and captured about 130. The number of Indians killed is not known.

Querétaro, Treaty of. (See Guadalupe Hidalgo, Treaty of.)

Quids.—A name applied to the anti-Madison faction of the Republican party, led by John Randolph from 1805 to 1811. Jefferson strongly favored the succession of Madison and the Quids declared war upon the administration, charging "backstairs" influence. They opposed the restrictive system and nominated Monroe in 1808.

Quint.—One of the silver coins presented by Robert Morris to the Continental Congress in 1783 for consideration as a national coin. It weighed 5 pennyweights and 15 grains and was equal to about 35 cents. On the obverse was an eye, 13 points crossing (equidistant) a circle of as many stars, and the legend "Nova Constellantio"; on the reverse, "U. S. 500," surrounded by a wreath and the legend, "Libertas Justitia." This coin was not accepted and afterwards, with the mark, became known as the Nova Constellatio coinage.

Qui-nai-elt Indians. (See Indian Tribes.)

Quil-leh-ute Indians. (See Indian Tribes.)

Quo Warranto.—The legal writ served upon public officers calling upon them to show cause why they should not perform certain duties, or why they should not be removed from office, whether they have acquired the office legally or illegally.

Quorum.—A word adopted from the Latin, meaning in the original tongue "of whom." Legally it denotes a certain specified number out of a large number necessary to act for certain purposes. Business in charge of trustees or committees might often be retarded on account of the absence of one or more members if the actions of a quorum were not legal. Unless otherwise stipulated, a majority of the members of any body is considered a quorum. In parliamentary usage a quorum is the number that must be present in order that business may be transacted. It is sometimes less than 1 per cent of the members, as in the case of the British House of Lords, where 3 out of 450 members constitute a quorum. According to the Constitution, a majority of either branch of Congress constitutes a quorum. For the first fifty Congresses the presence of a constitutional quorum in the House was determined by a count of votes. No matter how many members were present, unless a majority voted it was considered there was not a quorum present. This sometimes led to obstructive tactics. In 1890, during the first session of the Fifty-first Congress the Speaker of the House ruled that a quorum was present when enough members were visible to constitute a quorum, whether they voted or not. The Senate enforces the rule which requires a majority of the body to vote in order that a quorum may be counted.

Radical.—In politics, a person who advocates extreme doctrines,—the antithesis of conservative; in the plural a group, or party, urging extreme reforms.

Radio. (See Wireless Telegraph.)

Radio Service, Navy Department.—The name of this service has recently been changed to the "Naval Communications Service." It is in charge of the Government Radio Service, and of all telegraph, telephone, and cable communications connected with the naval service. It also maintains a censorship over all radio stations in time of war, and in time of peace it maintains such a censorship to the point of enforcing the neutrality (q. v.) of the United States. There are 51 radio stations in service, which are operated both on shore and on light vessels. There is an extensive radio system operated from various points on the coasts in order to control the movements of the United States fleet, and the Navy Department is connected at all times with all its naval stations, navy yards, and radio stations in the United States by means of telephone, telegraph and cable connections. In 1916, the naval communications service carried 628,997 official messages and 97,084 commercial messages. By act of Congress approved August 13, 1912, radio stations within the jurisdiction of the United States may be taken over by the Government for use in naval communications, to the exclusion of other control and use; and all radio stations not necessary to Naval communications may be closed for radio communication. By order of April 6, 1917, President Wilson issued an order to this effect, to be operative during the war with Germany.

Railroads and Equipment.—The first railway in the United States is said to have been the three-mile private tramway running from the Quincy (Mass.) granite quarries to tidewater at Neponset, over which was hauled the stone to build Bunker Hill monument. The road was completed in 1826 at a cost of $34,000 and the cars were drawn by horses. This was followed chronologically by the Mauch Chunk (Pa.) switchback in 1827. The first railroad, however, on which cars were actually drawn by a locomotive was the Carbondale Railroad, built in 1828, by the Delaware and Hudson Canal Company from their coal mines to Honesdale, Pa., a distance of sixteen miles. In 1829 a locomotive named the "Stourbridge Lion," built in England from plans of Horatio Allen, an American engineer, was brought over and began running regularly on this road. Within the year the multi-tubular boiler engine, which succeeded the Allen type, was perfected by Robert Stephenson, an English miner. It was this locomotive, named the "Rocket," that made the present day railroad possible.

The first American locomotive to run over an American railroad was the "Tom Thumb," invented and built by Peter Cooper and driven by him over the Baltimore and Ohio Railroad in 1830. This locomotive was defeated by a horse on one of its earliest trial trips, much to the humiliation of its inventor.

The regular motive force of the Baltimore and Ohio Railroad at that time was horse power, and for some miles the stage route ran alongside the tracks. While making an exhibition run in the "Tom Thumb," Mr. Cooper encountered the proprietor of the stage route at the point where the two roads became parallel. The latter had been awaiting an opportunity with one of his fleetest horses, and entered upon the race with a determination to show the superiority of horseflesh over steam. Mr. Cooper fired up his little furnace to its fullest capacity and the "Tom Thumb" whirled along exceeding the speed limit of those days, if they had one. He was showing a bright pair of wheels to the ambitious stage driver when suddenly the belt which passed over one of the wheels of the carriage and worked a pair of bellows to blow the fire, broke, the fire blackened and died down and the stage coach driver drew ahead in triumph.

The second American locomotive was built at the West Point foundry, near Cold Spring, N. Y., (where the Parrott guns were cast during the Civil war) after plans by E. L. Miller, and was equipped with a common vertical boiler. It attained a speed, unattached, of thirty to thirty-five miles an hour; and, with a train of five cars, fifteen to twenty miles an hour. This locomotive named the "Best Friend" was built for the South Carolina Railroad, which ran between Charleston and Hamburg.

The bursting of the boiler of the "Best Friend" caused the introduction of the "barrier car" on this road. This was a car loaded with bales of cotton coupled between the locomotive and the passenger coaches, to protect the travellers from being scalded by steam in case of an explosion.

Among other very early American railroads were the Baltimore and Susquehanna, dating from 1830; the little four-and-a-half mile line between New Orleans and Lake Pontchartrain, starting the same year; the Boston and Lowell, incorporated in 1830; the Boston and Providence, and Boston and Worcester, incorporated in 1831; and the Mohawk and Hudson, which commenced running in September, 1831. See illustration opposite 1295.

The possibilities of the railway were at once recognized by the rival seaports of the Atlantic—New York, Boston, Philadelphia and Baltimore. The Erie Canal penetrating to the interior of the continent on the line of least elevation above tidewater, had made New York the national port of entry and chief center of distribution. Even New Orleans, with the Mississippi River as a feeder, felt the diversion of trade through the Erie Canal. It was the effort to recover this trade that caused the Baltimore and Ohio Railway to be projected. Philadelphia, too, began reaching toward the west with a railway, and the Boston and Worcester penetrated the Berkshire hills toward Albany. New York capitalists, to maintain the supremacy of the seaport, supplemented the Erie Canal with the Erie Railroad. The New York Central Railway was formed in 1853 by the consolidation of five small railways. The rapid increase of railway mileage from 1830 is shown in tabular form as follows:

1830	23	1870	52,922
1835	1,098	1880	93,296
1840	2,818	1890	166,706
1845	4,633	1900	194,262
1850	9,021	1910	243,107
1855	18,374	1915	246,816
1860	30,626		

Prior to 1850 there were few railroads west of the Alleghanies. The first to be built in the Mississippi Valley were the Clinton and Port Hudson, incorporated, in 1833, and the Bayou Sara and Woodville road, incorporated in Louisiana in 1831, as the West Feliciana Railroad. These pioneer railroads of the South have been operating continuously since 1840. A system of land grants did much to foster railroad building in the West. The general government allotted certain alternate sections of public lands to the several States in the West and these States ceded them under conditions, in the nature of a subsidy, to the railroads. The Illinois Central and the Mobile and Ohio were the first to obtain these advantages. During the Civil war railway building was impeded but the westward stride was resumed in 1865, and only fell off during the financial panic of 1873. Adverse legislation checked the extension of railways between 1911 and 1915.

Transcontinental Lines.—April 1, 1850, a meeting was called in Philadelphia to discuss the feasibility of a railroad to the Pacific coast. The discovery of gold in California turned all Eastern eyes on the newly acquired territory won from Mexico. From a little known region where traders bartered for hides with the indolent Mexicans the Pacific coast became the El Dorado where the Eastern thousands longed to go; and venturesome miners early on the spot clamored for supplies the East was anxious to exchange for Western gold. The only communication between the Atlantic and Pacific was around Cape Horn, across the Isthmus of Panama, or over land across the plains and mountains, beset by hostile Indians, hunger, thirst, and the parching sun of the intervening prairies. The Philadelphia meeting was twenty years ahead of its time. The second step toward transcontinental railways was taken during the administration of President Pierce, when Jefferson Davis, Secretary of War, organized and carried out a great survey, laying out several routes across the continent. See illustration opposite 3658.

In response to the repeated demands Congress July 1, 1862, incorporated the Union Pacific, which, in its junction, seven years later, with the Central Pacific near Ogden, Utah, completed the first transcontinental line. (See Pacific Railroads.)

Railroad statistics for 1911 as presented by Poor's Manual are as follows:

Cost of roads and equipment	$15,872,462,792
Number of miles operated	246,655
Passengers carried one mile	33,565,339,282
Tons of freight moved one mile	258,599,943,687
Revenue from earnings, etc.	$1,085,951,595
Paid in taxes, dividends, interest, etc.	957,829,732
Surplus for the year	128,121,863
Capital stock	8,582,463,256
Bonded debt	10,989,608,551

Reports to the Interstate Commerce Commission for the fiscal year ending June 30, 1913, by roads having gross operating revenues of $100,000 or more for the year showed 244,418 miles of single track in use. Of the total number (63,378) of locomotives 14,396 were passenger and 37,924 freight. The number of cars was 2,445,508, of which 51,700 were passenger, and 2,273,-564 freight.

The average rate of interest on railroad bonds has been steadily declining from 4.94 in 1883 to 3.74 in 1911. The average dividend rate declined from 2.76 in 1883 to 1.51 in 1897, and then advanced to 3.64 in 1911.

Equipment.—In 1831 Matthias W. Baldwin, a maker of bookbinders' tools in Philadelphia, was engaged to build a model locomotive for exhibition in a local museum. The success of this model resulted in Mr. Baldwin being engaged to construct a locomotive for the Philadelphia, Germantown and Norristown Railway Company. This engine, "Old Ironsides," attained a speed of thirty miles an hour with train, and, detached, is said to have made sixty miles. This was the pioneer of the Baldwin Locomotive Works, later owned by Burnham, Williams & Co. The Rogers Locomotive

Works were established in Paterson, N. J., in 1836, and the Schenectady works in 1848. After the war the Pittsburg works, those at Providence, R. I., the Brooks shops at Dunkirk, N. Y., and the Richmond, Va., works were established. The total number of locomotives in use on the railways of the United States, Canada and Mexico in 1894 was given by Poor's Manual as 35,813. The number of establishments engaged in the manufacture was thirteen.

The real progress in locomotive building has been increasing the weight of trains which can be hauled with certainty at rates of speed previously regarded as phenomenal. September 11, 1895, a locomotive of the New York Central hauled the Empire State Express from New York to East Buffalo, 436 1-2 miles, in 407 2-3 minutes, an average speed of 64.26 miles an hour.

The Erie Railroad conducted a test at Binghamton, N. Y., on July 24, 1914, of the pulling power of the new Centipede locomotive, which weighs 410 tons and has 24 driving wheels. The officials in charge kept adding car after car of coal to the train until it consisted of 250 fully loaded steel cars, with a total weight of 21,000 tons. The locomotive pulled this train 40 miles at the rate of 15 miles an hour.

In 1857 Thomas Hall, of Boston, constructed and exhibited a small electric locomotive, which took its current from a stationary battery by means of the rails and wheels. Electrical locomotives were tried on the New York elevated railroad in 1886. After 1890 electric locomotives were common, especially on suburban lines.

The first passenger coach, used in Pennsylvania in 1832, was a stage coach slightly enlarged. With the increased speed of the locomotive attention was drawn to the wheels, and Messrs. Knight, Edgar, Winans and Davis of Baltimore developed and improved the flange. The sleeping car had its origin as early as 1838. In 1858 two sleeping cars were run between Cleveland and Buffalo, but they were not popular. It was while riding in one of these that George M. Pullman designed the improvements which have revolutionized railway travel. His first car, the "Pioneer," was built in 1863. This car was used to convey President Lincoln's body from Chicago to Springfield, Ill., for interment, and shortly afterward by General Grant to go from Detroit to Galena, Ill.

In the winter of 1868-69 the first Westinghouse air brake was used on the Steubenville accommodation train running on the Pittsburg, Cincinnati & St. Louis Railroad.

The transportation of various kinds of products, such as live stock, coal, dressed meat, oil, and timber, has called into being cars especially adapted to each class of freight, and steel is gradually supplanting wood in the construction of all cars.

Speed Records.—The fastest single mile on record for a railway train was 32 seconds, made by the Empire State Express on the New York Central Road, at Crittenden, N. Y., in May, 1893, which was at the rate of 112.5 miles per hour. Numerous instances are recorded of short runs (five miles or less) at a rate of more than a hundred miles an hour. The best record for the longest distance was made by the Chicago, Burlington & Quincy train in running from Chicago to Denver, 1,025 miles, in 18 hours and 52 seconds, a rate of 58.74 miles an hour, in February, 1897. The New York Central trains have repeatedly made the distance between New York and Chicago, 960 miles, at an average speed of more than 60 miles an hour.

Among the fastest regular trains in the United States are believed to be the New

York Central "Empire State Express," between New York and Albany, 143 miles in 175 minutes, and the "Congressional Limited," on the Pennsylvania Railroad, which makes the run from Jersey City to Washington in 4 hours and 46 minutes, a distance of 227 miles. The "Pennsylvania Special," over P. R. R., which runs from Jersey City to North Philadelphia, 84 miles in 83 minutes; from Jersey City to Harrisburg, Pa., 194 miles in 196 minutes. The Royal Blue Line from New York to Philadelphia (Reading Terminal), 91.1 miles, in 1 hour, 50 minutes. On November 25, 1913, a special train, consisting of a locomotive and two cars, ran from Washington, D. C., to Jersey City, 227 miles, in 4 hours, the fastest trip ever made between the two cities.

In October, 1905, the "Harriman Special" made the run from Oakland to Jersey City (3,239 miles) in 73 hours, 12 minutes, or 44.30 miles per hour. In May, 1906, the "Harriman Special" made the run from Oakland, Cal., to New York City in 71 hours, 27 minutes. The "Scott Special" left Los Angeles, Cal., July 9, 1905, and arrived in Chicago (2,415.5 miles) July 11, having made the run in 44 hours, 54 minutes, maintaining an average speed while in motion of 51 miles an hour.

The Jarrett and Palmer special theatrical train, Jersey City to Oakland (San Francisco), 3,311 miles, June, 1876, 83 hours, 45 minutes; average speed, 39.53 miles per hour.

On November 15, 1907, at Clayton, N. J., in a trial test on Pennsylvania R. R. between steam and electric locomotives, the steam engine made 93.6 miles an hour on a specially built seven mile curved track, while the electric locomotive made but 90 miles an hour.

Returns for 1914 were received from 242 establishments which manufactured 138,178 steam and electric cars, valued at $165,071,-427. These totals include figures for 118 railroad repair shops which reported the construction of 11,049 new cars, valued at $12,811,087, and 7 establishments engaged primarily in other lines of manufacture but which produced 4,481 railway cars, valued at $3,178,677, as subsidiary products.

In 1914 there were built 135,357 steam-railway cars, valued at $155,029,539. The number of steam passenger cars built in 1914 was 3,558, and their value was $45,-027,083. Of freight and other cars for use on steam railroads, the output in 1914 was 131,799, valued at $110,002,456.

The number of electric cars manufactured in 1914 was 2,821, and their value was $10,041,888. The output of electric cars in 1914 comprised 2,583 passenger cars, 110 freight cars, and 128 other cars.

Eight Hour Day.—A strike vote among the 300,000 members of the four-train service brotherhoods on the question of an eight-hour day and time and a half for overtime was taken during July. The vote followed the failure of the conference in June with the representatives of the railroads of the United States.

The National Conference Committee of the railways made public, July 25, a summary of findings on wages paid by the roads, together with the conclusion that their employees constitute one of the highest paid groups of workers. Railroad accountants had been examining the payrolls of every road in the country for six months. The purpose of the railway managers was to combat the effort of the four brotherhoods to obtain raises in pay. They held that the men were paid sufficiently high not to need an increase in wages.

The average yearly wage payments to all Eastern train employees (including those who worked only part of the year), as shown by the 1915 payrolls, were:

	Passenger.	Freight.	Yard.
Engineers	$1796	$1546	$1384
Conductors	1724	1404	1238
Firemen	1033	903	844
Brakemen	1018	858	990

Three-quarters of these men (including all those who put in a full year's service) earned these wages:

Engineers (road), $1585 to $3224; (yard), $1303 to $2178.

Conductors (road), $1552 to $3004; (yard), $1145 to $1991.

Firemen (road), $933 to $1762; (yard), $752 to $1633.

Brakemen (road), $862 to $1707; (yard), $834 to $1635.

For the whole country, the average wages of three-quarters of the employees were:

	Passenger.	Freight.	Yard.
Engineers	$2067	$1892	$1526
Conductors	1850	1719	1310
Firemen	1203	1117	924
Brakemen	1095	1013	1076

Declaring a break inevitable unless some strong measures of intervention were speedily introduced, an appeal was made to President Wilson August 2, to take action in the matter of the threatened railroad strike. It was backed by as large a number of business men as had ever been heard on a single subject. The spokesman was Harry A. Wheeler, of Chicago, chairman of the committee on the railroad situation of the Chamber of Commerce of the United States.

On the 3d, the President designated G. W. W. Hanger, assistant commissioner of mediation and conciliation, to be a member of the United States Board of Mediation and Conciliation. This filled the one vacancy on the board and placed it in a position to take up the railroad matter just as soon as the trouble should come to a crisis.

Ninety-four per cent of the 400,000 railway workers voted for a strike if the carriers should fail to grant their demands at a conference in New York August 8. The vote was as follows, in favor of a strike:

Locomotive engineers—	Per cent
Southern District	98.72
Western District	90.35
Eastern District	94.54
Firemen and enginemen	98.10
Railway trainmen	97.00
Railway conductors—	
Western District	84.03
Eastern District	84.08
Southern District	93.04
General officers	85.00

The services of the Federal Mediation Board were accepted by both sides August 9, and conferences were arranged at once, but by the 13th the Federal Mediators announced the failure of their efforts. President Wilson then proposed several White House conferences, after which he submitted, on the 16th, the following proposals:

"Acceptance by the railroad managers of the eight hour day.

"Abandonment by the employees of their demands for time and one-half for overtime, and the acceptance of pro rata for overtime.

"Abandonment by the railroad managers of their contention that the entire controversy be submitted to arbitration either by the Board of Mediation or a board appointed by the President.

"Appointment of a commission to investigate the operation of the eight hour day, to determine its cost to the railroads, and to make recommendations concerning the collateral problems involved and the payment of time and one-half for overtime."

These proposals were rejected by the Managers' Committee the next day, whereupon President Wilson summoned the railroad presidents, who, on the 18th, failed to accept the settlement plan. The plan was formally accepted by the four railway brotherhoods. A delegation of railroad executives went to the White House August 22, and discussed with President Wilson a modified acceptance of his proposals.

It was learned that the President told the railroad presidents that he would not act as mediator between the brotherhoods and the railroads beyond the proposal for settlement he had made and which had been accepted by the brotherhoods.

The special committee of railroad executives drew a compromise proposal, August 24, which provided:

"The eight-hour basic day should be granted to the trainmen.

"The administration should make every effort to obtain a freight rate increase for the roads.

"Congress should be asked to enact legislation to insure settlement of future labor disputes through an investigating commission."

After lengthy conferences President Wilson announced, August 28, that he would go before Congress to ask for legislation to stop the impending strike. He appealed to the brotherhood heads to have the strike order for Labor Day rescinded, but was told that the order was beyond recall. His appeal to Congress was made August 29. He upheld the Brotherhoods' attitude, placed blame on the railway managers and suggested the following six propositions:

"1. Enlarge the membership of the Interstate Commerce Commission from seven to nine, as provided for in the Adamson bill, which passed the House some time ago.

"2. Establish an eight-hour day as a basis for wage and work on all interstate carriers.

"3. Appoint a small commission to observe the results of the eight-hour day and report to Congress without recommendation.

"4. That Congress signify its approval of an increase in freight rates as a basis of compensating the railroads for the extra cost of the eight-hour day.

"5. That the powers of the Board of Mediation and Conciliation be increased so as to give it authority to investigate labor troubles and to make a report thereon, in the meantime making it unlawful for a strike or lockout to occur while this work is going on.

"6. Give the President authority to use the military forces of the Government to keep the roads running in case of a strike and give the President power to draft men into the military service for this purpose."

Measures taken by Congress Aug. 31, with the active assistance of President Wilson, insured the passage of both houses of a bill that would satisfy the brotherhoods.

The impending railroad strike was averted, Sept. 2, by the passage of the Adamson eight-hour bill.

Railroad officials declared that the action of Congress would cost them $60,000,000 a year in increased wages to the trainmen. Brotherhood officials, however, said the enactment would mean not more than an annual increase of $20,000,000.

The Adamson eight-hour bill passed the House, Sept. 1, by a vote of 239 to 56, and the Senate on the following day by a vote of 43 to 28—almost a strict party vote. The bill was passed without amendments amid stirring scenes, after many Senators, Democrats and Republicans, had fought desperately to amend the measure by provisions designed to prevent industrial disasters in the future. Some Senators, thoroughly aroused, declared Congress was being coerced

into enactment of legislation which it did not desire and which it knew would return to plague it in the future.

In both Houses the measure was signed within few minutes after the final vote in the Senate, and it was sent at once to the White House, where President Wilson signed it at 7:30 o'clock Sunday morning. That there might be no question as to the legality of the measure as a result of its having been signed on Sunday, the President also affixed his signature upon his return to Washington on the following Tuesday.

Three hours after the measure passed the Senate, the heads of the four great railroad employees' brotherhood canceled the strike orders which were to have taken effect on Sept. 4.

The bill provided that after Jan. 1, 1917, eight hours should be regarded as a basis of reckoning for a day's pay of men engaged in the operation of railroad trains in interstate commerce (excepting roads less than 100 miles long and electric lines), that they should receive pro rata pay for work in excess of eight hours, and that their rate of compensation should not be changed pending an investigation for from six to nine months of the effect of the eight-hour day upon the railroads by a commission to be appointed by the President.

"*Adamson Law*—Section 1. That beginning Jan. 1, 1917, eight hours shall, in contracts for labor and service, be deemed a day's work, and the measure or standard of a day's work for the purpose of reckoning the compensation for service of all employees who are now or may hereafter be employed by any railroad which is subject to the provisions of the act of Feb. 1, 1887, "An act to regulate commerce," as amended, and who are now, or may hereafter be actually engaged in any capacity in the operation of trains used for the transportation of persons or property, on railways from any state or territory of the United States or the District of Columbia to any other state or territory of the United States or the District of Columbia, or from one place in a territory to another place in the same territory, or from any place in the United States to an adjacent foreign country, or from any place in the United States through a foreign country to any other place in the United States.

"Section 2. That the president shall appoint a commission of three, which shall observe the operation and effects of the institution of the eight-hour standard workday as above defined, and the facts and conditions affecting the relations between such common carriers and employees during a period of not less than six months nor more than nine months, in the discretion of the commission, and within 30 days thereafter such commission shall report its findings to the president and Congress. That each member of the commission created under the provisions of this act shall receive such compensation as may be fixed by the president. That the sum of $25,000, or so much thereof as may be necessary, be and hereby is appropriated out of any money in the United States treasury not otherwise appropriated to be immediately available and to continue available until the close of the fiscal year ending June 30, 1917, for the necessary and proper expenses incurred in connection with the work of such commission, including salaries per diem, traveling expenses of members and employees and return, furniture, office fixtures and supplies, books, salaries and other necessary expenses, the same to be approved by the chairman of said commission and audited by the proper accounting officers of the treasury.

"Section 3. That pending the report of the

commission herein provided for, and for a period of 30 days thereafter, the compensation of railway employees subject to this act for a standard eight-hour workday shall not be reduced below the present standard day's wage, and for all necessary time in excess of eight hours such employees shall be paid at a rate not less than the pro rata rate for such standard eight-hour workday.

"Section 4. That any persons violating any provision of this act shall be guilty of a misdemeanor and upon conviction shall be fined not less than one hundred dollars and not more than one thousand dollars, or imprisonment not to exceed one year, or both."

The determination of the railroads to oppose the 8-hour law is consistent with their opposition to all regulation of their affairs by federal laws. They opposed the creation of the Interstate Commerce Commission and the extension of its authority to regulate rates. They declared the Hepburn law confiscatory and therefore unconstitutional.

Effect of the Adamson Eight-Hour Law.— George W. Goethals, E. E. Clark and George Rublee were appointed in 1916 a committee to observe and report on the operation and effect of the Adamson Law. Their report was made in January, 1918; and comprised the following findings:

The eight-hour day has become an accomplished fact for the measure of a day's work for certain classes of railroad employees. The employees recognized by the railroads as entitled to the eight-hour basis under the law, are as follows: Engineers, firemen, conductors and assistant conductors, baggagemen, brakemen, and flagmen, in road and yard service, and generally also hostlers. The average number of these employees in 1916 was 308,373, or about 17% of the total number of railroad employees.

As actually applied in practice, the eight-hour standard observed is the so-called speed basis of 12¼ miles per hour. That is to say, on a run of 100 miles or less, overtime begins after 8 hours, while on a 125 mile run it begins after 10 hours. Although there has been general permission for overtime, yet the law has had some effect in reducing the actual hours of work, but chiefly in yard service. Between March and October, 1917, over 11,000 yard crews were placed on eight-hour shifts.

In road service, the decrease in working hours has been slight, the law having had the effect chiefly of increasing wages. The annual increase to the railroads' payroll from this source is estimated at $61,000,-000. The passenger service is but slightly affected by the law, but in road freight service the increase in wages has averaged 15% and in yard service the increase has been about 25%.

A detailed study of the payrolls indicates that 12½% of the employees named above as coming under the law received no increase in pay in January, 1917, as a result of the eight-hour law; 30% received less than $10 per month increase; 23% received between $10 and $20 increase; and 34½% received monthly increases in pay of more than $20.

In the eastern district on slow freight service the actual time during which engineers are on duty is from 12 to 13 hours per run. In the local freight service, the hours are from 11 to 12 per run in all districts. In slow freight service in the southern and western districts, the figures are considerably lower than in the eastern district.

For the year ending January 1, 1918, railroad statistics for roads with operating expenses above $1,000,000 were as follows:

Average number of miles operated..231,155
Revenues:

Freight	$2,829,246,769
Passenger	825,496,365
Mail	58,681,549
Express	106,895,282
Miscellaneous	223,913,186

Total operating revenues.$4,041,014,239

Expenses:

Maintenance of way and structures	$ 444,458,855
Maintenance of equipment.	691,025,391
Traffic	64,966,241
Transportation	1,529,800,773
Miscellaneous	138,253,598

Total operating expenses.$2,852,880,196

Net revenue from operations.$1,188,134,043

Tax accruals and uncollectible revenues ....$ 220,865,520

Operating income ....$ 967,268,523

The growth in railroading in 1916-1917 is seen in the following compilation of the Interstate Commerce Commission from the reports of 178 railroads for the month of May:—

	May, 1917	May, 1916
Average number of miles operated	227,514	227,109
Operating revenues	$337,869,250	$294,517,994
Operating expenses	233,147,873	193,348,746
Net revenue from operating	$104,721,377	$101,169,248
Revenues per mile	$1,485	$1,297
Expenses per mile	1,025	851
Net revenue per mile	$ 460	$ 446

The above figures may be contrasted with the figures for 1915 as follows:—

Cost of roads and equipment	$17,247,101,881
Number of miles operated..	257,569
Passengers carried one mile	32,384,247,563
Tons of freight moved one mile	276,830,302,723
Capital stock	$8,994,894,721
Bonded debt	$12,133,064,357
Average rate of dividend...	3.80%
Locomotives	65,099
Passenger cars (exclusive of Pullmans)	55,705
Freight cars	2,356,338
Company cars	95,934

Federal Control.—The circumstances leading up to federal control of the transportation systems of the country are adequately described by President Wilson himself on pages 8409 to 8413 and 8418 to 8421. There remain to be added only the facts that much of the inability of private management to handle the railroads of the country satisfactorily under war conditions was due to priority orders for munitions, steel, food and fuel, etc., and that private control was unable to provide for new equipment to the extent made possible by federal control because of various legal restrictions and because of the abnormal condition of the money and security markets.

A law enacted by Congress and approved by the President on March 21, 1918, provided for the operation of the railroads under federal control and for the compensation of their owners, etc. During the period of federal control each carrier is to receive annually a sum equal to its average annual operating income for the three years ending June 30, 1917. Any income above that amount remains the property of the United States, the figures to be obtained by the Interstate Commerce Commission.

War taxes for the period beginning with January 1, 1918, and all taxes prior thereto must be paid by the carrier from its own funds, later taxes being paid out of revenues derived by the government under federal control. The government shall consider as part of the expenses of operation the cost of maintenance, repair, and depreciation and the creation of reserves, etc., necessary to return the roads to the owners at the end of federal control in the same condition as when acquired. Wherever it is apparent to the President that abnormal conditions in 1914-7 make the above remuneration unfair, he may make with the carriers concerned such other agreement as seems to him just and fair.

Street and interurban electric lines, however, are excluded from the provisions of the Act.

All claims for compensation not adjusted as provided above and below may be submitted to boards appointed by the Interstate Commerce Commission.

Dividends paid by carriers under federal control must not be beyond those paid in 1914-7, except with the approval of the President.

Five hundred million dollars is appropriated for the expenses of government control. The President may order carriers to make improvements, etc., to be paid for from this fund.

The carriers may issue securities during federal control, with the approval of the President, and the latter may, out of the fund above-mentioned, buy such at a price not above par and may sell them not below the cost thereof. The President may delegate the powers granted him by the Bill, but no government official may receive extra compensation for additional duties thus performed.

All carriers are subject to all laws and suits, etc., as before federal control, except that no process, final or mesne, may be filed against a property under federal control. The President is given authority over fares and rates, etc., subject, however, to the veto of the Interstate Commerce Commission after hearing and investigation in the case of rates concerning which complaint has been made.

All property and moneys derived from operation under federal control become the property of the United States, but in the custody of the same officers as before federal control. Expenditures follow a similar course. Federal control must end twenty-one months after the end of the war, but the President may relinquish his authority over all or any of the carriers previously to that time. Nothing in the Act may be construed as affecting the powers of the several states over the carriers, except where the transportation of troops and war materials or the issue of stocks and bonds are concerned; nor to indicate nor to express the post-war attitude of the government toward the railroads.

The average net income of the railroads for 1914-7 was the highest in the history of the railroads of the country, as indicated by the following figures:

1915 .... $ 728,212,079
1916 1,043,839,822
1917 1,069,750,514
Average 947,267,472

On May 26, 1918, Director-general of Railroads McAdoo announced wage increases of more than $300,000,000, retroactive to January 1, 1918, and affecting nearly 2,000,000 employees. The wages policy of the Federal Administration was announced as based on the need for a decent standard of living, rather than on the law of supply and demand for labor; on equal pay for similar work; on the eight-hour day as a basis of wages computation in all railroad work; on equal pay for men and women, and for negroes and whites for identical or similar work. A standing wage board consisting of three representatives of the employees and three of the employers was established to adjust problems in the development of the Government's wages policy. Simultaneously a general increase of approximately 25% in both passenger and freight rates was announced, in order to meet these and other increases in the operating expenses of the railroads.

In connection with the Federal Railroad Administration, the great express companies of the nation were combined in one body under government control in June, 1918.

Appointed and powers outlined, 8410.

Discriminations by, in coal and oil, 7287.

Disputes on, failure of arbitration in, 8145, 8184.

Eight-hour working day on, 8144, 8183.

Employees of, character of, 6980.

Employers' Liability Law needed on, 7912.

Executives of, praised for cooperation with Government, 8412, 8418.

Freight rates, establishment of maximum and minimum, 6977.

From—
Atlantic to Pacific States recommended, 2988.
Missouri River to Pacific Ocean, uniform gauge for, 3361.
Omaha, Nebr., to Sacramento, Cal., discussed, 3881.

Government aid to, under Constitution discussed, 2753.

Government control over, urged, 6978, 7074, 7087, 7200, 8117.

Government operation of—
Address of President Wilson to Congress concerning, 8418.
Assumed, 8409.
Benefits of, 8412, 8419.
Explained, 8412.
Returns to private investors from, suggested, 8420.

Government ownership of, discussed, 6981.

Grant to American citizens for lines of, through Mexico, 3665.

Hours of employees on, 6982, 7035.

In Europe, 3270.

Interownership between competing, prohibition of, 7447, 7552.

Investors in securities of, to be safeguarded, 8413, 8419.

Lands granted in aid of, discussed, 2749, 2823, 3580, 3651, 4065, 4944, 5384.
Forfeiture of, discussed, 4837, 5379.
Provocation of withdrawal of, referred to, 5197.

Military control over, suggested, 8184.

Military possession of, taken by United States, 3314, 3379.

National inspection and control of, recommended, 6978, 7074, 7087.

N. Y., N. H. & H. R. R. Co., dissolution of, directed, 8023.

Publicity of accounts of, 6978.

Rates—
Agreements concerning, approved by Interstate Commerce Commission, legalization of, urged, 7444, 7552.

Discussed, 7128.

Equality of, desirable, 6655.

Freight, increase in, suggested, 8148.

Governmental control of, 7038.

Increases in, attempted, withdrawal of, under injunction, 7487.

Maximum and minimum, 6977.

Regulation and revision of, 6902, 6977, 7079.

Rebates of—
Evils of, 6977, 7025.
New York Central case of, 7025.

Rebates, Federal abolition of, recommended, 6900, 6901, 6976, 6977, 7024, 7025, 7026.

Referred to, 3479.

Right of way for, through reservations. (See Indian Reservations.)

Safety-Appliance law, 6803, 6897.

Safety appliances urged for, 6982.

Securities of—
Authority of Interstate Commerce Commission over, 7342, 7368, 7447, 7552.
Holders of, to be protected under Government operation, 8413, 8419.

Shipments by, abuses in, 6901.

Strikes discussed. (See **Strike Commission**.)

Subsidies to—
Discussed, 4064.
Information regarding, transmitted, 4958.
System of, condemned by President Wilson, 8018.

Survey for, across continent discussed, 2753.
Recommended, 2558.

Taxation of, discussed, 4730.

Total mileage of, discussed, 5741.

Traffic agreements on, need of, 7342.

Transportation rates. (See **Railroad Transportation**.)

Travel on, increased safety for, 6897.

Valuation of, by Interstate Commerce Commission, request for appropriation for, 7553.

Railroads, Commissioner of, report of, discussed, 5640, 5763.

Railway Adjustment. (See **Division of** Railway Adjustment.)

Railway Mail Service:
Classification of employees in, 5429.
Amendments to rules regarding, 5465, 5466, 5542, 5610, 5948, 5954, 5955, 6040.
Discussed, 5882.
Recommended, 4527.
Time for, extended, **5462**.
Discussed, 5488.
Discussed, 5882.

Railway Mail Service, Division of.—An act of Congress of September 6, 1785, authorized the Postmaster-general to contract for the delivery of mail by stage-coach. In 1811, the Post-Office Department established a system of mail service between Baltimore and Washington in stage-coaches owned by the Government, and in 1813 the Postmaster-general was authorized to use sailing vessels in the transportation of mail. The first railway post-office was established in 1862 and the first definite railway mail service was inaugurated in 1864, although railway post-offices had been suggested to the Postmaster-general by assistant postmaster-general Hobbie, as early as 1847. The present service is in operation over 217,462 miles of railroad, and covers 327,069,708 miles of actual service. It is estimated that 15,000,000,000 pieces of matter are transported and assorted by the railway mail service in the course of a year. The appropriations for this branch of the post-office service in 1917 were $31,931,669, and the estimate for 1918 is $31,108,410. The service is administered under the second assistont postmaster-general (q. v.), and comprises 34 officers, 114 chief clerks, and 18,-649 permanent railway postal clerks. The special cars used in the service are virtually traveling post-offices, and although they are furnished by the railroads, they are manned by the Government postal service. In addition to transportation by railroad, mail is transported by the Department by wagon, by special messenger, by electric car, by steamship lines, by dog sled. by motor vehicles, by pneumatic tubes, and by aeroplane. (See Post-Office Department, Postal Service.)

Railway Postal Service. (See Postal Service; Railway Mail Service.)

Rain-Getter Dyrenforth. (See Rain-Maker.)

Rain-Maker.—In ancient times a priest or sorcerer who claimed the power to bring rain by prayer or incantations. During the years of the intensified settlement of the then arid states of Kansas and Nebraska, the United States Government tried out the experiment of causing the condensation of moisture, with consequent rain-fall, by the use of explosives. R. G. Dyrenforth was the leader of the movement for this experiment, and thus acquired a sobriquet derived from his initials, Rain-Getter Dyrenforth.

Raizuli. (See ''Perdicaris alive or Raizuli dead.'')

Raleigh, The, mentioned, 6297.

Rally.—A large gathering of people, especially in political campaigns, for the purpose of arousing or rallying enthusiasm for a political or other cause, or for the success of party candidates. In certain sections party leaders frequently organize rallies in the nature of picnic parties, accommodating their followers with boat or other transportation to the rallying place, and there serving a feast, accompanied by music and speech-making.

Rambouillet Decree.—March 23, 1810, after the American Congress had repealed the non-intercourse act of March 1, 1810, Napoleon ordered the immediate seizure and sale of all American vessels in the ports of France or the ports of her territories occupied by French armies. In this decree

Napoleon avowed his determination to prohibit any commercial intercourse with the enemies of France which was not enjoyed by that country also. Under this decree 132 vessels, with their cargoes, valued at $8,000,000 were ordered sold. (See also Berlin Decree; Embargo; Milan Decree; Nonintercourse Acts.)

Rampart.—A breastwork of earth or other substance, thrown up around a fort, as protection against the shells of the enemy.

Ramsey & Carmick, claims of, referred to, 3065.

Ranger, The, referred to, 1030.

Raritan, The, postponement of sailing of, referred to, 2129.

Ratification of Constitution.—The Constitution, by its terms, was not to become binding until ratified by nine of the thirteen states. It was signed by the delegates in convention Sept. 17, 1787, and by them submitted to Congress. Congress immediately ordered copies sent to all the states. Hamilton, Jay and Madison took leading parts in bringing about the ratification by the states. Gen. Washington's great influence was also thrown into the scale. The commercial classes in most of the states favored its adoption, but there was much opposition to it on all sides. Delaware was the first state to ratify the new document, taking favorable action thereon Dec. 7, 1787. It was then ratified by the other states in the following order: Pennsylvania, Dec. 12; New Jersey, Dec. 18; Georgia, Jan. 2, 1788; Connecticut, Jan. 9; Massachusetts, Feb. 6; Maryland, April 28; South Carolina, May 23; New Hampshire, June 21; Virginia, June 25; New York, July 26; North Carolina, Nov. 21, 1789. and Rhode Island, May 29, 1790. The Constitution went into effect March 4, 1789, before North Carolina and Rhode Island had ratified it.

Ration.—(Usually in the plural.) The food served in specified quantities to soldiers and other persons under military government. In times of military stress and scarcity of rations, soldiers are permitted to forage. (See Forage.)

Ratification of Constitution. (See Constitution; Admission of States.)

Raymond (Miss.), Battle of.—May 7, 1863, Sherman effected a junction with Grant, swelling the force about to proceed to the siege of Vicksburg to 50,000 men, including infantry, cavalry, and artillery. Grant immediately ordered a general movement on two parallel roads on the southeast of the Big Black River. McPherson, advancing on the road nearest the river, met two brigades of the enemy, under Gregg and Walker, at Raymond, fifteen miles southwest of Jackson, on May 12, and after a sharp engagement defeated them. The Confederate loss was 103 killed and 720 wounded and missing. McPherson lost 69 killed, 341 wounded, and 32 missing.

Reaction.—In political parlance, the political tendency after progress to become conservative to the extent of retiring from advanced theories and to go back to original conditions.

Reactionary.—A victim of reaction (q. v.); one opposing progress.

Rear-Admiral.—This is a naval grade created by act of Congress in 1862. This grade in the Navy ranks with that of major-general in the Army. Until the special acts creating the grades of admiral and vice-admiral, that of rear-admiral was the highest naval office. There are now fifteen rear-admirals ranking with major-generals in the Army, and nine rear-admirals ranking with brigadier-generals.

Rear-Admiral, rank of acting, conferred upon certain officers inquired into, 4848.

Rebates, apparent conflict of decisions by district judges concerning, 7024.

New York Central and Hudson River R. R. convicted for giving, 7026.

Holt (Judge), opinion and sentence quoted, 7025.

Letter showing illegal payment in California, 7135.

Rebecca, The, seizure and sale of, at Tampico, 5123, 5502.

Rebel.—One who resists government or other authority, often with force.

Rebellion.—Forcible antagonism to the organized government or other authority,—in military parlance amounting to an incipient or full-fledged war.

Rebellion Records. (See War of Rebellion, Official Records of.)

Rebellion, War of. (See Civil War.)

Rebellions. (See Illegal Combinations.)

Reciprocal Trade Agreements. (See Foreign Import Duties.)

Reciprocity.—Reciprocity is the granting by one nation of certain commercial privileges to another, whereby the citizens of both are placed upon an equal basis in certain branches of commerce. A reciprocity agreement between the United States and Canada was concluded in 1854 and terminated in 1866. A similar one was made with Hawaii in 1875. Other treaty arrangements of a reciprocal character were made from time to time. The subject derived the greatest interest from attention directed to it in 1888 and the final incorporation of the principal in the tariff of 1890. For many years previous to this time the anti-protection or tariff-reform party had attacked the existing tariff regulations on the ground that by levying high duties on the products of South American Republics those countries had not only to send their products elsewhere for sale, but as a natural consequence, to purchase their goods in other markets than those of the United States; in other words that a vast trade was diverted from us to Europe because of the restrictions imposed upon commerce by our tariff.

This discussion led to the adoption of a reciprocity arrangement with Central and South American countries. The first step toward this end was the calling of the Pan-American Congress (q. v.). Among the numerous subjects of mutual interest discussed at this congress was a recommendation for reciprocity treaties. In June, 1890, the Secretary of State, James G. Blaine, sent a letter to the President for transmission to Congress, calling attention to the proposed scheme. He suggested a practical and prompt test of the reciprocity principle by an amendment to the McKinley tariff bill, then pending (see Tariff), authorizing the President to declare the ports of the United States free to all the products of any nation of the American hemisphere upon which no export duties are imposed whenever and so long as such nation shall admit to its ports, free of all national, provincial, municipal, and other taxes, certain specified articles from the United States. The "reciprocity section" was incorporated in the tariff law approved Oct. 1, 1890. This clause was held to be constitutional by the Supreme Court, and the first treaty negotiated under it was with Brazil, Feb. 5, 1891. Treaties were also negotiated with Spain (for Cuba and Puerto Rico); with England (for some of her West Indian possessions); with Santo Domingo, Guatemala, Salvador, Costa Rica, Honduras, Nicaragua, Germany, Austria-Hungary.

These treaties were abrogated by the passage of the Wilson bill (see Tariff) in 1894. The Dingley law of 1897 provided for reciprocity treaties, to be made by the President, with regard to a limited number of articles; and for broader treaties to be negotiated by the President, subject to the ratification of the Senate. Of the first class, agreements were made with France, Italy and Switzerland; of the second class treaties were negotiated with France, Great Britain (for Jamaica, Turks and Caicos islands, Barbados, and British Guiana), Denmark (for the Danish West Indies), San Domingo, Nicaragua, Ecuador and the Argentine Republic, but none of them secured the ratification of the Senate. A reciprocity treaty with Cuba was ratified by the Senate in March, 1903, and the additional legislation necessary to put it in force was passed in December of the same year.

The tariff law passed in 1909 contained the maximum and minimum feature, which prescribed certain rates to be enforced for one year, at the end of which time 25 per cent ad valorem was to be added as the maximum duty. The President is then authorized to apply the minimum rates to the imports from a country which gives its best rates to the products of the United States, and which accords to the United States treatment which he considers reciprocal and equivalent. (See Tariff.)

On Jan. 26, 1911, President Taft sent to Congress a special message transmitting an agreement between the Department of State and the Canadian Government, obligating both parties to attempt to secure legislation which will reciprocally lower tariff rates on about six hundred items. (See p. 7961.) In urging the passage of the treaty, the President recalled Canada's neighborliness and friendship as shown in the settlement of all disputes and in the co-operation between the boards of railway control on both sides the border, dwelt upon the necessity of conserving our own resources by buying those of our neighbor, pointed out the similarity in labor and transportation conditions here and there, mentioned the harm to Americans which will accrue if the "imperial preference" doctrine becomes a tenet of Canadian political faith, maintained that the accession of a new supply of raw materials would inure to the benefit of all sections and, in prophetic vein, characterized the agreement as a step toward closer friendship between peoples related by blood, common sympathies and identical moral and social ideas. Animals, poultry, food stuffs, products of farm, garden and dairy, fruits, fish, oysters, salt, mineral waters, lumber, machinery, minor metal manufactures, coal, meats, flour, meal, farming utensils, fruit trees and Portland cement are the articles on which the tax is to be lowered or entirely removed. The effect of the proposed treaty, according to 1910 figures, would be to decrease the revenue of the United States by $4,849,933, and that of Canada by $2,-560,579. On July 26, 1911, the reciprocity measure, having been passed by both Houses, was signed by the President and became law. Sept. 1, 1911, the Canadian Parliament had not yet ratified the agreement. (See Reciprocity.)

Reciprocity, maximum and minimum feature of, expected to remove European discriminations, 7668.

Agreement with Germany discussed, 7502.

With Netherlands, 6961.

With Spain, 6966.

(See Canada, Reciprocity with.)

Reclamation Service, Interior Department.—The Reclamation Service was established by act approved June 17, 1909, in order to redeem arid lands by irrigation (q. v.). The act created a Reclamation Fund from the sale of certain public lands. In 1914, 761,271 acres were irrigated, and plans made for the irrigation of 500,000 more acres. The average crop value on the land thus newly redeemed for profitable cultivation was $23.50 per acre. (See Interior Department.)

Reclamation Service, discussed, 6801, 6908. (See Irrigation.)

Reconcentrados.—The name given the agricultural inhabitants of Cuba who were by the edict of Feb. 16, 1896, of Captain-General Weyler concentrated within the lines of the Spanish armies and cities of that island. This resulted in great suffering to the persons thus herded together, many of them dying of disease and from starvation. The mortality was so frightful and their suffering so intense that their condition excited universal pity. On the suggestion of the President of the United States, Congress made an appropriation for their relief.

Reconcentrados:

Appropriation for, recommended, 6292.

Policy of Gen. Weyler regarding, discussed, 6256, 6283, 6284, 6308.

Revoked, 6285.

Reconstruction.—In American politics a term signifying, the restoration of those states which had seceded of local self-government and normal relations with the Union. The period of reconstruction embraced the Administrations of Johnson and Grant and presented some perplexing problems to the statesmen of the reunited country: Were the states still in the Union, with no other disability than that of having no legal governments, or had their act of secession reduced them to the condition of territories subject to the Union? Did reconstruction mean their erection into new states or their restoration with their old names and boundaries? Did the power to reconstruct lie in the states themselves or in the General Government; and if in the General Government, did it lie with Congress or with the Executive? If it lay with the people of the disorganized state, who or what defined that people and decided who might and might not vote in the reorganization? If it lay with Congress, could the Executive, without the authority of Congress, proceed to reconstruct, simply leaving it to Congress to accept or reject the states so reconstructed? President Lincoln had proceeded upon the

theory that nothing more was necessary than that a sufficient number of loyal citizens should form a state government of which the officials were loyally desirous of maintaining constitutional relations with the Union (3423). President Johnson proceeded upon nearly the same theory.

The view held by the majority in Congress was that the southern states could be readmitted only on such terms as that body should impose. The ground taken in support of this view was that the substantial results of the war respecting the civil rights of the negro could not be secured in any other way, because of the reluctance of some legislatures to accept these results. Before Congress met in December, 1865, President Johnson had recognized provisional governments in all the southern states except one, on their acceptance of the thirteenth amendment. Congress then proposed the fourteenth amendment and insisted upon its acceptance as a prerequisite to readmission to the Union. The same body on March 2, 1867, passed over President Johnson's veto, the military reconstruction bill introduced in the House by Thaddeus Stevens. Under this law the south was divided into five military districts under the command of the generals of the Army, who were to effect a registration of voters, including negroes and excluding those persons who had been disqualified by the fourteenth amendment. These voters were to make and ratify a constitution and submit it to Congress, and if it was acceptable the state should be reinstated whenever its legislature had ratified the fourteenth amendment. (See illustration opposite 3754.)

Tennessee was readmitted to the Union in 1866, Alabama, Arkansas, Florida, Georgia, Louisiana, North Carolina, and South Carolina in 1868, and Mississippi, Texas and Virginia in 1870. (See also Restoration.)

Reconstruction Acts:

Interpretation of, 3750.

Proceedings of President and Cabinet regarding, as set forth in *National Intelligencer*, discussed, 3725.

Repeal of, recommended, 3760, 3870.

Vetoed. (See Reconstruction.)

Reconstruction of Southern States (see also Restoration):

Act providing for more efficient government or rebel States vetoed, 3696.

Acts supplementary to, vetoed, 3729, 3734.

Assignments under, 3749, 3750, 3754, 3755, 3859, 3860, 3861, 3862, 3863, 3864, 3866, 3869.

Expenses of carrying act into effect discussed, 3719, 3725, 3764.

Joint resolution to carry act into effect approved and reasons therefor, 3719.

Joint resolutions to carry acts into effect vetoed, 3743.

Acts to admit certain Southern States into Union vetoed, 3846, 3848.

Discussed by President—

Grant, 3965, 3982, 4050.

Referred to, 4354.

Hayes, 4394, 4410, 4445.

Johnson. (See Restoration.)

Government for Tennessee, more efficient for, and other rebel states vetoed, 3696.

Ratification of fourteenth amendment proclaimed—

Alabama, 3857.

Georgia, 3858

Louisiana, 3856.

North Carolina, 3854.

South Carolina, 3855.

Record, Congressional. (See Congressional Record.)

Records and Documents (see also Exchanges for Official Documents; International Bureau of Exchanges):

Building for, 4452, 4781, 6456.

Documents in care of legations referred to, 4070.

Laws for punishing persons abstracting or mutilating, recommended, 2683, 2713, 3940.

Recruit.—One who enlists for service, especially in the Army or Navy. (See Army and Navy.)

Red Book.—The official publication of the Austria-Hungarian government, giving its side of the diplomatic negotiations which preceded the European War.

Red Cloud Agency, Nebr., deficiency in supplies at, 4312, 4313.

Red Cross, American National.—The Red Cross is "a confederation of societies in different countries for the amelioration of the condition of wounded soldiers in the armies, in campaigns on land or sea." It carries on its work under the sign of a red cross on a white ground used as a flag, always with the national flag, or as an arm badge. By Article 7 of the Geneva Convention this sign protects its wearers as neutral. The society originated with Henri Dunant after the battle of Solferino in 1859, Gustave Moynier of Geneva, president of the "Society of Public Utility of Switzerland," called a meeting "to consider the formation of permanent societies for the relief of wounded soldiers." This was held Feb. 9, 1863, and resulted in an international meeting Oct. 26, following, and a treaty between twelve European governments, assuring neutrality and protection to all working under the Red Cross. This treaty was concluded at Geneva, Aug. 22, 1864. It was adopted by Great Britain, Feb. 18, 1865; Prussia, June 22, 1865: Turkey, July 5, 1865; and Russia, May 22. 1867. The United States Senate acceded to it, March 16, 1882, and it was proclaimed by President Arthur, July 26, 1882. The treaty is now generally observed by civilized governments of the world.

The American National Association of the Red Cross was organized at Washington, D. C., May 21, 1881, and was incorporated for twenty years. July 1, 1881. Miss Clara Barton was elected first president. It was reincorporated April 17, 1893, for the relief of suffering by war, pestilence, famine, flood, fires, and other calamities of sufficient magnitude to be deemed national in extent. The officers of the American organization are: Board of Consultation—The President of the United States and Members of the Cabinet. The association was reorganized and incorporated by Congress, 1905. National Headquarters, Room 341, War Department, Washington, D. C. President—Woodrow Wilson. Treasurer—Sherman Allen. Secretary—Charles L. Magee. Chairman of Central Committee—Maj.-Gen. Geo. W. Davis. National Director—Ernest P. Bicknell. Executive Committee—Miss Mabel T. Boardman, James Tanner, Charles Nagle, Huntington Wilson, Brig.-Gen. George H. Torney, U. S. A.; Surg.-Gen. Chas. F. Stokes, U. S. N. Associate societies in the various states have done noble work in aiding sufferers by calamity from forest fires, floods, fevers, etc.

On Jan. 1, 1917, the number of chapters was 250 and the number of members, 286,-400. The cash receipts for the previous eleven months were $1,544,245.43 and the total disbursements, $1,352,100. 30% of the receipts were devoted to the European War Relief and 16% to the Preparedness Fund. The membership of the official magazine had reached 230,000.

With the entrance of the United States into the European War, the Red Cross naturally both altered and broadened its organization. President Wilson placed in general charge of its activities Mr. H. P. Davidson, a New York financier, who inaugurated and completed before the beginning of the summer of 1917 a campaign for contributions for war purposes to the amount of $100,000,000. On September 10, 1917, Mr. Davidson made public an account of the activities of the Red Cross since the announcement of war on April 6, 1917, as follows:

Along the route followed by the troops the Red Cross has established infirmaries and rest stations, each in charge of an American trained nurse with an American man to assist her.

Additional infirmaries and rest stations will be established in the near future, and adequate buildings are also being erected wherever needed.

Canteens are being established by the Red Cross at railway stations where American soldiers on reserve duty or on leave, and those returning to or from duty, may find rest and refreshment. Baths, food, games, and other comforts will be made available at these canteens.

The war council has appropriated $100,-000 for medical research work in France.

To be able to do its work without delay, the Red Cross is establishing warehouses at different points of importance in the French theater of war. An appropriation of $500,-000 has been voted to establish this service and provide its first stock of supplies.

In response to a cable from the commission in France, the war council appropriated $1,500,000 to purchase foodstuffs to be sent to France.

It has also appropriated $1,000,000 for the purchase of supplies in France, all for use in the hospital supply service.

At the military railroad stops the Red Cross is establishing shower baths, laundries, and mending and disinfecting rooms. Then there will be rest rooms, with books, writing materials, and games. Some of the stations will have dormitories and lunch rooms.

Near the firing line the Red Cross is establishing field canteens. Extending the work already begun by the French Red Cross, it will provide one of these canteens for every corps of the French Army and as well as later for the American Army.

To carry out these plans the war council has made appropriations of about $700,000, which will establish the canteens and maintain them for about three months.

A Red Cross transportation service through the cooperation of the French, British, and Italian Governments, the United States Shipping Board, and the leading steamship and railroad companies has been established to handle the vast quantities of medical and relief supplies now being shipped almost daily to France, Belgium, Serbia, Russia, and other belligerent countries.

The Red Cross will have cargo space on every steamer chartered by the United States Shipping Board. Army transports also will carry Red Cross supplies.

The French railroads are overtaxed, and their facilities must be available for the military needs of the army. The Red Cross has accordingly determined to develop its own motor transport service.

The first unit of trucks has been forwarded.

In advance of the fighting forces the United States sent to the European battle fields six base hospitals organized during the last year by the Red Cross—the first United States Army organization sent to Europe. These were sent at the request of the British commission.

More than a dozen base hospitals organized by the American Red Cross are now seeing active service in France, and others are rapidly being made ready for foreign service.

It is estimated that some 500,000 persons are afflicted with tuberculosis as the direct result of the war. Scientific efforts to control the spread of the malady are not only of supreme concern to France herself, but they are of great importance in making France healthy for our own troops.

All work is being done under the general administration of the French Government, and by French people.

The American Red Cross has appropriated $1,000,000 for the relief of sick and wounded French soldiers and their families.

The Red Cross plans to be able to take care temporarily of these returning populations.

It is not the policy of the Red Cross to rebuild the villages of France, but it is our hope to be able to give a new start in life to a large number of persons who have been left destitute by the ravages of the German army.

The Red Cross has accordingly appropriated $40,090 for a provisional experiment in this direction, the plans for the experiment having been worked out in France by Mr. Homer Folks.

Most of those in charge for the Red Cross of the work in France are giving their own time and paying their own expenses.

The appropriations made for use in Europe outside of France, covering drugs and medical supplies, relief funds, and expenses, are as follows:

For Russia	$322,780.87
For Roumania	247,000.00
For Italy	210,000.00
For Serbia	222,500.00
For England	8,800.00
For Armenia	600,000.00
Other appropriations	36,000.00

The total appropriations by the war council for Red Cross work in Europe are as follows:

In France	$10,692,601.00
Outside of France	1,647,080.87
Grand total	$12,339,681.87

Some of the European appropriations are to cover a full year, but the greater part will have been spent by November of the current year.

By Nov. 1, 1917, the Red Cross was prosecuting in Europe the following endeavors:

Needful gifts and pensions to sick and wounded French soldiers and to French families in distress.

Twenty dispensaries for both resident civilians and for better health conditions in the war zones to be occupied by the American soldiers.

A dental ambulance and a nurses' service for American soldiers.

A distributing service supplying 3,423 French military hospitals; a surgical dressings service supplying 2,000 French hospitals; and an extensive service preparing for all future American hospital needs.

Ten canteens operated at the French front, with provision for 20 more. Similar canteens for soldiers coming and going in Paris. Twelve rest stations and a number of recuperation stations for American soldiers.

An artificial limb factory near Paris, and special plants for the manufacture of splints and nitrous oxide gas.

Recreation in connection with hospitals and diet kitchens; a movable hospital in four units accommodating 1,000 men; a casualty service for gathering information regarding wounded and missing.

A medical research bureau.

A children's refuge and hospital within the war zone; a medical centre and travelling hospital in wrecked villages, accommodating 1,200 children; medical work along extensive lines for re-patrie children returned (about 500 daily) from points within the German lines; a hospital and convalescent home for such children and an ambulance service for other repatries.

Infant welfare stations in connection with each dispensary along the national lines planned by the Rockefeller Foundation.

Extensive tuberculosis endeavors, including the work previously done along these lines by volunteer Americans. Completion of an unfinished tuberculosis sanitarium near Paris, and extensions to the barracks erected by the city of Paris. A comprehensive health centre in a large French Department.

Elaborate arrangements for helping refugee families during the winter with clothing, beds and shelter. For this work, the entire devastated district of France was divided into six districts, with large warehouses in each. In this connection, four devastated villages are being repaired so as to permit families to live in them during the winter. A number of portable houses are also furnished.

Barracks for training disabled soldiers, and experimental agricultural stations for them.

Extensive Belgian relief work, with preparations for helping all those Belgians liberated by each change in the battle-line. Transportation of many Belgian children into places in France where they may be cared for.

By November 1, 1917, 15,000 nurses had been enrolled in the Red Cross, many of them volunteering their services. Of this number, 2,000 had already been sent abroad. It was estimated that the 15,000 nurses were sufficient to care for an army of 11,500,000 men.

From the entrance of the United States into the European War on April 6, 1917, to Nov. 1, 1917, there had been collected in the war fund $79,895,355, of which $9,129,389 was reserved for return to the various chapters for Red Cross work. The total appropriations from the amount col-

lected were $40,851,259, of which $26,934,-416 was for foreign relief as follows:
France, $19,581,240; Belgium, $720,-001; Russia, $1,428,041; Serbia, $493,204; Roumania, $1,518,399; Italy, $214,000; Great Britain, $1,066,520; Armenian and Syrian Relief, $1,800,000; Miscellaneous, $113,012.

United States items were as follows: Supplies to forces, $3,448,729; hospital work, $379,500; sanitary work around cantonments, $183,500; miscellaneous, $108,-488—a total of $4,120,217. Appropriations for re-sale, mostly for materials to be worked into garments, were $7,659,000. This sum will eventually be refunded to the War Fund.

In addition there was appropriated $1,-417,626 from the funds given by donors for especially stated purposes.

Red Cross, American National:

Aid furnished Cubans by, discussed, 6284, 6308.

School children urged to enroll in, 8358.

Work accomplished by, in Spanish-American War, discussed, 6320.

Red Cross Association, international conference of:

Held at Karlsruhe, Baden, referred to, 5205.

Report of, referred to, 4856.

Red Cross, Foreign, report on, 6863.

Red Cross, International, proposition of Switzerland to extend compact of, in Spanish-American War, discussed, 6336.

Listing of alien enemies for, 8274.

Red Cross Week, proclaimed, 8264.

Red-Line Map.—An early map of part of North America, discovered by Jared Sparks in the archives of Paris and sent to Daniel Webster during treaty negotiations with Great Britain over che northeastern boundary question. It had been executed in 1746 by D'Anville, and later (1782) sent to the French minister, Vergennes, by Franklin. A strong red line drawn near the ridge in which the Kennebec and Penobscot rivers rise more than favored the English claims respecting the northeastern boundary of the United States. The map was displayed in a secret session of the Senate and before the Maine commissioners, and was, in part at least, the ground on which the Webster-Ashburton treaty was signed.

Red Mud State.—A nickname for New Jersey (q. v.), (See also States); Dominion State was formerly used as a nickname for New Jersey.

Red River:

Exploration of, 386.

Unsuccessful, 396.

Improvement of, progress made in, 1442.

Red, White and Blue Book: 8282.

Redemptioners.—A name applied to a class of indentured servants who came to the American Colonies under bond for a certain number of years in payment for their passage hither. Many were kidnapped and placed in forced slavery for a term of years. They usually served from four to seven years. On their release these redemptioners were awarded fifty acres of

land and became free citizens. The system was introduced into Virginia with the first colony in 1607, and in Massachusetts in 1631. It obtained also in Maryland, New York, Connecticut, and Pennsylvania, but was discontinued in 1750.

Redress of Grievances, right of the people to petition for, shall not be abridged, 28.

Referee Board of Consulting Scientific Experts, Agriculture Department.—This is a Federal board under the jurisdiction of the Department of Agriculture which makes researches on scientific questions involved in the food and drug inspection.

Feb. 20, 1908, the Secretary of Agriculture appointed Dr. Ira Remsen, president of Johns Hopkins University; Dr. Russell H. Chittenden, dean of the Sheffield Scientific School, Yale University; Dr. John H. Long of Northwestern University; Dr. Alonzo Taylor, of the University of California; and Dr. Christian A. Herter, of Columbia University, consulting scientific experts of the Department of Agriculture, and four days later organized them into what is known as the Referee Board. This board was appointed in response to a request made to President Roosevelt by a number of manufacturers of articles of food. These manufacturers assured the President that they would discontinue the use of sulphur dioxide, saccharin, and benzoate of soda in food if such a board found them harmful.

It was made the duty of this board to submit to the Secretary of Agriculture opinions independent of those expressed by the Bureau of Chemistry in cases where a great number of food manufacturers of the country claim that the opinions of the Bureau of Chemistry are at variance with the scientific knowledge of the present day.

Questions as to the harmfulness of the use in foods of the following substances were referred to the Referee Board: Benzoate of soda, saccharin, sulphate of copper, sulpuhur dioxide, and alum. The report of this board led the Secretary of Agriculture to the decision that benzoate of soda may be used in the preservation of food, provided the amount used is clearly stated upon the package of food containing it.

As to saccharin, the board reported that the use in small quantities (0.3 gram per day, or less) added to food is without deleterious or poisonous action, while taken in larger quantities, especially exceeding a grain a day is liable to induce disturbance of digestion. Its substitution for cane or other sugar, must be regarded as substitution.

Conclusions reached in regard to copper salts used as coloring matter for vegetables were that the quality or strength of the food were not injuriously affected. A daily dose of 100 grams of coppered peas or beans would not contain more than 100 or 150 milligrams of copper. Such a bulk of vegetables is so large, however, that it would not likely be maintained as a diet for many days in succession.

Referendum. (See Initiative, Referendum and Recall.)

Reforestation, urged on government land and navigable streams, 7465, 7538.

Reform Schools. (See District of Columbia.)

Reformer.—A person who endeavors, either by speech or action, to bring about in civilization certain reforms which seem to him to be needful.

Refunding.—The process of substituting a series of low-interest-bearing bonds for those of a higher rate or for a floating debt not funded. Aug. 31, 1865, the debt of the United States amounted to $2,845,907,626, of which sum only $1,109,568,192 was funded. By December, 1867, the floating debt, compound-interest notes, seven-thirties, and United States notes had been converted into a funded debt of nearly $700,000,000. The refunding act of 1870 authorized the issue of a certain amount of 5, 4½, and 4 per cent bonds to take the place of the existing bonds, most of which were bearing 6 per cent interest. During the next ten years this substitution was carried to an extent that decreased the annual interest charges from $82,000,000 to $62,000,000. In 1881 the annual interest was decreased nearly $20,000,000 more by the Windom refunding scheme, which converted $460,000,000 5 and 6 per cent bonds into bonds bearing 3 and 3½ per cent interest.

Regiment. (See Army and Navy.)

Register of Debates.—A record of the Congressional debates and proceedings from December, 1824, to October, 1837. It was a continuation of the Annals of Congress and contains many valuable state papers as well as the routine Congressional work. The Register of Debates was succeeded by the Congressional Globe. (See also Annals of Congress; Congressional Globe; Congressional Record.)

Register of the Treasury. (See Treasury Department.)

Registered Mails. (See Division of Registered Mails.)

Registration.—A precaution taken in certain states to prevent frauds in elections. It consists of the preparation of lists of the electors of every precinct, voters being required to present themselves before the registrar on specified days prior to election to have their names recorded and to answer questions as to their qualifications as electors. These lists are open to inspection and scrutiny by the public.

Registration Bureau of naturalized citizens, recommended, 4828, 4921, 5090, 5370.

Registration for Draft. (See Draft.)

Registry, American, repeal of law denying, to ships built abroad and owned by Americans, recommended, 5985.

Foreign built ships admitted to, 8006.

Repeal of law, denying to ships built abroad and owned by Americans, recommended, 5985.

Regular U. S. Army and Navy Union.—A patriotic, fraternal, and beneficial organization, chartered under act of Congress, for soldiers' and sailors' rights and benefits. Headquarters, 4 Warder Street, N. W., Washington, D. C. Membership is confined to regulars of the United States Army, Navy, or Marine Corps, whether discharged, retired, or in the service.

Regulators.—In 1768 the people of Orange County, N. C., oppressed by the unjust acts of Edmund Fanning, clerk of the court of Orange, formed an association, headed by Herman Husbands and William Hunter, for regulating public grievances and abuse of power. They sent messengers to the governor with a statement of their grievances. The governor and council decided that the course of the Regulators tended to high treason, and on their reassembling in July to hear the report of the messengers, the governor, at the head of a body of troops, compelled them to take the oath of allegiance to the Crown and disperse. Some of the leaders of the Regulators were held to answer in the courts for their actions. The following year another petition was rejected. The Regulators offered an organized resistance to the troops, under Governor Tryon, and at Almance, on the Haw River, they were routed by the governor and their leaders arrested. Some of these leaders were executed. Martin, the next governor, compromised with the Regulators.

Relations, Foreign. (See the several powers.)

Relief Party.—A political faction in Kentucky politics between 1820 and 1826. The party was composed of debtors and included a majority of the voters. It advocated relief of delinquent debtors and disputed the constitutionality of the replevin act. In 1823 the Supreme Court decided the replevin act to be unconstitutional and in 1824 the legislature of the state repealed the court of appeals act and organized a new court. The Relief party then became known as the New Court party. The Anti-Relief or Old Court party, securing a majority in the legislature in 1827, restored the old court, and the issue was not renewed.

Religion—

And morality the foundation of the state, 212.

Establishment of, no law respecting shall be made, 28.

Free exercise of, shall never be prohibited, 28.

Test of, shall not be applied as qualification for any office or position of trust, 26.

Religions in the United States.—The following table represents a careful estimate of the religious communicants of the United States:

Adventists	107,000
Baptists:	6,375,000
North	1,255,000
South	2,700,000
Colored	2,018,000
Brethren, Dunkards and Plymouth	135,000
Catholic, Eastern Orthodox	467,000
Catholics, Western	14,100,000
Christians	115,000
Christian Scientists	100,000
Congregationalists	775,000
Disciples of Christ	1,525,000
Evangelical	205,000
Friends	120,000
German Evangelical	265,000
Jews	2,350,000
Latter-Day Saints (Mormons)	400,000
Lutherans	2,435,000
Methodists	7,475,000
Meth. Epis.	3,660,000
African M. E.	620,000
African M. E. Zion	570,000
M. E., South	2,075,000
Presbyterians	2,110,000
Protestant Episcopal	1,050,000
Reformed	505,000
Salvation Army	27,500
Spiritualists	200,000
United Brethren	260,000
Unitarians	70,000
Universalists	55,000

The total number of communicants is 40,000,000, with 181,000 ministers and 225,000 churches.

Of the population of the world, Christians number about 565,000,000; Confucianists and Taoists, 300,000,000; Hindoos, 210,-000,000; Mohammedans, 225,000,000; Buddhists, 140,000,000; Jews, 13,500,000; with some 200,000,000 heathen. Of Christians, 293,000,000 are Catholics and 172,000,000 are Protestants.

Religious Establishments:

Baptist church in Mississippi Territory, act for relief of, vetoed, 475.

Protestant church at American embassy at Rome, removal of, referred to, 3662, 3717.

Protestant Episcopal church in Alexandria, Va., act incorporating, vetoed, 474.

Separation of church and state, recommendation to declare, 4310.

Value of church property, discussed and taxation of, recommended, 4288, 4310.

Religious Freedom.—The First Amendment to the Constitution of the United States (q. v.) requires that "Congress shall make no law respecting the establishment of religion, or prohibiting the free exercise thereof." Religious freedom doubtless had its greatest inspiration from James Madison while he was in the Virginia Legislature. An attempt was made to levy a tax upon the people of that state "for the support of teachers of the Christian religion." Madison wrote what he called a "Memorial and Remonstrance," in which he appealed to the people against the evil tendency of such a precedent, and which convinced people that Madison was right. A bill was passed providing "that no man shall be compelled to frequent or support any religious worship, place, or ministry whatsoever * * * nor shall suffer on account of his religious opinions or belief; but that all men shall be free to profess, and, by argument, maintain their opinions in matters of religion, and that the same shall in nowise diminish, enlarge, or affect their civil capacities." The religious tests to which many of the states put their office-holders were gradually abandoned, and the final separation of church and state in America came in 1833, when Massachusetts discontinued the custom of paying preachers.

Religious Test. (See Religious Freedom.)

Remonetization.—Legally to re-establish as legal tender anything of value used as money.

Removals from Office.—The Constitution gives the President power to make appointments to civil office by and with the advice and consent of the Senate, but is silent on the subject of removals. Debate on this point arose in Congress in 1789, and it was concluded to allow the power of removal to rest with the President alone. This continued to be the policy of the Government until 1867. In this year charges were preferred in the House of Representatives against President Johnson, alleging corrupt use of the appointing, pardon-ing, and veto powers, corrupt disposition of public property, and interference in elections. The charges were referred to the Judiciary Committee and a bill was prepared and passed over the President's veto providing that, with certain exceptions, every officer appointed by the President with the concurrence of the Senate should retain his office until a successor should in like manner be appointed. This is known as the Tenure-of-Office Act (q. v.). Johnson's suspension of Secretary Stanton in violation of this act led to his impeachment in 1868. The law was repealed in 1887.

Removals from Office (see also Executive Nominations):

Act regulating tenure of certain civil offices, vetoed. (See Tenure-of-Office Act.)

Discretionary authority of President regarding, discussed by President—

Cleveland, 4960.

Grant, 3992.

Jackson, 1351.

Johnson, 3690, 3767, 3820.

Tyler, 1905, 1941.

For partisan purposes, discouraged, 1941.

Partisan interference in elections cause of removal, 1905.

Referred to, 1796, 1911, 1912.

Resolution of Senate regarding, and reply of President Hayes, 4433.

Reno, Jesse L., major-general in Army, nominations of, and reasons therefor, 3362.

Repatriation.—Again to become a citizen after expatriation (q. v.).

Repeal.—To make null, by legislative action, a law previously enacted.

Repeater.—In politics, a person who casts, or undertakes to cast, more than one vote for a given measure, a given candidate, or a set of candidates. Repeating is made a penal offense by state laws.

Representatives.—The constitutional designation of the members of the House of Representatives. They are elected by direct vote of the people, in representative districts fixed by state law, according to the apportionment made every ten years by Congress as to the quota of each state. Representatives must be at least twenty-five years of age, residents of the state in which chosen, and citizens of the United States for seven years previous to their election. (See also Congress; Apportionment; and House of Representatives.)

Representatives:

Appointment of, by President in whose election they have been officially concerned, discussed, 1011, 1120.

Appointments office, relation to of, to. (See Executive Nominations.)

Apportionment of—

According to census of 1890 necessary, 5553.

Representatives-at-Large. — Representatives in Congress elected on general tickets, as distinguished from those elected on district tickets, in cases where the state has failed to redistrict after it has become entitled to additional representation in Congress. (See Apportionment; House of Representatives.)

Representatives, House of. (See Congress.)

Republic, Grand Army of the. (See Grand Army of the Republic.)

Republican Party.—In the early days of the Republic Thomas Jefferson became the leader of a party opposed to the monarchical ideas of the Federalists. This party was first known as the Democratic-Republican, and the adherents were called both Democrats and Republicans, usually the latter, until the Jackson-Adams contest.

The Republican party of later days was formed in 1854, with opposition to slavery as its chief tenet. The compromise of 1850 (q. v.) had disrupted the Whig party. The passage of the Kansas-Nebraska act materially influenced the general coalition that followed of Whigs, Free-Soilers, Abolitionists, and Know-Nothings. They assumed the name of Republicans and at once won a plurality in the House of Representatives. They held their first national convention in Philadelphia in 1856, and nominated Fremont and Dayton for President and Vice-President. At the election which followed they were defeated, but in 1859 again came into control of the House.

In 1860 they elected Mr. Lincoln to the Presidency. For the next fourteen years the party was supreme. It enlarged the powers of Congress by a broad construction of the Constitution, carried on the Civil War, abolished slavery, reconstructed the governments of the seceding states, maintained a protective tariff, and refunded the national debt. The party nominees during this period were: 1860, Abraham Lincoln, of Illinois, and Hannibal Hamlin, of Maine; 1864, Abraham Lincoln, of Illinois, and Andrew Johnson, of Tennessee (Johnson becoming President on the death of Lincoln); 1868, Ulysses S. Grant, of Illinois, and Schuyler Colfax, of Indiana; 1872, Ulysses S. Grant, of Illinois, and Henry Wilson, of Massachusetts.

In 1872 those who opposed General Grant's administration left the party and formed the Liberal Republican party (q. v.). In 1874 the party lost control of the House of Representatives and did not regain it until 1880. In 1876 it elected Rutherford B. Hayes, of Ohio, and William A.

Wheeler, of New York (see Electoral Commission). In 1880 James A. Garfield, of Ohio, and Chester A. Arthur, of New York, were elected (Arthur becoming President on the death of Garfield), but the party lost control of the House in 1882.

In 1884 James G. Blaine, of Maine, and John A. Logan, of Illinois, were defeated, but the party retained control of the Senate. In 1888 Benjamin Harrison, of Indiana, and Levi P. Morton, of New York, were the candidates and were successful on a tariff issue. The party also regained control of the House in that year. Dissatisfaction with the McKinley tariff law led to the loss of the House by the Republicans in 1890, and in the Presidential campaign of 1892 President Harrison (Whitelaw Reid, of New York, being the Vice-Presidential candidate) was defeated for re-election, and the party lost control of the Senate. In 1894 the Republicans again regained control of the House.

In 1890 the free coinage of silver appeared as an issue and the platform of the Republican convention at St. Louis declared against free coinage "except by international agreement with the leading commercial nations of the world" and favored the gold standard "until such agreement could be obtained." As a result of this opposition to the gold standard many western Republicans left the party and supported William J. Bryan, the Democratic candidate. The Republicans were successful, however, William McKinley, of Ohio, and Garret A. Hobart, of New Jersey, being elected, their popular vote being 7,111,607 and the electoral vote 271.

In 1900 the issues were "imperialism" (defined by the Democrats as the tendency of the Republic, under Republican rule, to move away from the old democratic practices and beliefs), silver, the tariff and trusts. The Republicans were again successful, William McKinley, of Ohio, and Theodore Roosevelt, of New York, being elected, receiving 7,208,244 popular votes and 292 electoral votes. President McKinley was assassinated Sept. 6, 1901, and died on the 14th of that month. Theodore Roosevelt then succeeded to the Presidency.

During the administration of McKinley and Roosevelt the party passed the Dingley tariff law on protective lines (see Tariff); the Spanish War was carried to a successful conclusion; the rebellion in the Philippines extinguished and the islands given a stable civil government; Hawaii was annexed; and a currency bill establishing the gold standard was passed. During this administration also our new possessions in the far East brought the United States into the group of world powers.

In 1904 there were no well defined issues, the silver and tariff questions being in abeyance. The Republican candidates, Theodore Roosevelt, of New York, and Charles W. Fairbanks, of Indiana, were successful, the popular vote being 7,624,982 and the electoral vote 336.

Besides the suppression of slavery the Republican party has favored full citizenship to emancipated slaves, prompt payment of the national debt, tariff for protection as well as revenue, free ballot, generous pension legislation, increase of the Navy and the strengthening of the coast defenses, a system of national bank currency based on United States bonds deposited with the Secretary of the Treasury, a national circulating medium based on a gold standard, a vigorous foreign policy, a liberal interpretation of the Monroe Doctrine, national protection of timber, encouragement of irrigation, and the building of the Panama Canal by the United States.

In 1908 the National convention was held at Chicago, June 16 to 19. William H. Taft, of Ohio, was nominated for President, and James S. Sherman, of New York, for Vice-President. The platform adopted declared in favor of equality of opportunity; revision of the tariff; a more elastic currency; the establishment of postal savings banks; an employers' liability law; amending the rules of procedure in Federal courts; conserving the natural resources of the country; the extension of foreign commerce, etc. Taft and Sherman received a plurality of 1,233,494 of the popular vote and a majority in the electoral college of 269.

The national convention of the party met in Chicago in June, 1912, and nominated President Taft for President and James S. Sherman for Vice-President. The platform adopted declared in favor of upholding the courts, for sound banking laws and the usual declaration in favor of the tariff. By the defection of ex-President Roosevelt and his followers, who formed the Progressive party, the Republican ticket was defeated in 1912, and a Democratic President and Congress were elected. The popular vote for President was: Taft, 3,484,956; Roosevelt, 4,119,507; Wilson, Dem., 6,293,019. The electoral vote stood: Wilson, 435; Roosevelt, 88; Taft. 8.

The 1916 convention met in Chicago in June, and after conferences with the Progressive party, which met at the same time in the same city, Mr. Roosevelt's name was rejected and Supreme Court Justice Charles E. Hughes was nominated to head the national ticket, and Charles W. Fairbanks was named for vice president. The platform advocated woman suffrage as a measure of justice to one-half the adult people of the country. At the election in the following November, Mr. Hughes was defeated by President Wilson by a popular vote of approximately 9,120,700 to 8,539,000.

Republican River, bridge over, reconstruction of, recommended, 4777.

Republican Valley Railroad, right of way across Otoe and Missouria Reservation, Nebr., for, bill for, 4681.

Repudiation.—The refusal of a state or government to pay or to be bound by debts contracted by a previous administration. In 1790 the debts of all the states of the Union were assumed by the National Government, partly on the ground of justice, because they had been contracted in the prosecution of the Revolutionary War, and partly on the ground of expediency, as this action tended to strengthen the credit of the states. For forty years thereafter the states remained almost free from debt. Bonds of the several states were easily disposed of abroad, and by 1840 an aggregate of $200,000,000 had been sold. In that year Indiana found it impossible to pay the interest on her outstanding bonds, and it was only by strong efforts that Ohio managed to meet her obligations. In 1842 the Bank of Pennsylvania failed, and soon afterwards Pennsylvania, Maryland, Mississippi, Michigan, Louisiana, Indiana, and Illinois found themselves almost bankrupt. They all suspended payment of interest on their debts, but Mississippi, Michigan, Louisiana, and North Carolina felt constrained to repudiate the capital as well as interest.

It was in Mississippi that the word "repudiation" originated in this connection. Governor McNutt, in a message to the legislature, suggested a plan for "repudiating

the sale of certain of the state bonds on account of fraud and illegality." The bonds fell into default and an appropriation for their payment was overwhelmingly defeated at the polls in 1852. Michigan repudiated certain canal bonds. The southern states came out of the Civil War with heavy indebtedness and diminished resources, and were in some instances almost bankrupt. In the years immediately following the close of the Civil War most of the southern states compromised or readjusted their bonded indebtedness, and in some states the legislature declared certain bonds fraudulent, illegal, and void. During the depression following the panic of 1873 some cities, towns, and countries endeavored to repudiate their bonds, but the Supreme Court of the United States gave judgments against them.

The eleventh amendment forbids suits against the states. In 1903 certain of the repudiated bonds of North Carolina came into the possession of the State of North Dakota, and North Carolina was sued in the Supreme Court by the latter State for payment. The Supreme Court, by a decision of Feb. 1, 1904, held that North Carolina was liable for and must pay both principal and interest on the bonds in question. Some European countries have also at times repudiated their obligations.

Requisitions.—Under the Articles of Confederation the Continental Congress had only one means of raising money—by requisitions upon the states. Between 1782 and 1786 requisitions amounting to more than $6,000,000 had been made. Only one-sixth of this had been paid by March, 1787. Under the Constitution the President may make requisitions upon the state for men to assist the National Government in time of war, but there is no provision for requisitions of money. Instead that instrument provides for the expenditures of the Government by duties on imports and taxes collected from the citizens.

Resaca (Ga.), Battle of.—March 14, 1864, Gen. Sherman was placed in command of the military Division of the Mississippi, which was composed of the Army of the Cumberland, under Maj.-Gen. Thomas; the Army of the Tennessee, under Maj.-Gen. McPherson, and the Army of the Ohio, under Maj.-Gen. Schofield, and numbered a total of 98,797 men and 254 guns. The Confederate forces under Gen. Johnston were estimated at 60,000. After the battle of Chattanooga the Confederates had retreated to Dalton, Ga., thirty-nine miles southeast of Chattanooga and ninety-nine miles northwest of Atlanta. May 4, Sherman made a demonstration in front of the Confederate position on Rocky Face Mountain, northeast of Dalton, while McPherson, with some 40,000 men, attempted to turn the Confederate left and occupy Resaca. Johnston thereupon, on May 13, evacuated Dalton and fell back upon Resaca. Polk was posted on Johnston's left, resting on the Oostanaula River, Hardee in the center, and Hood on the right. Sherman laid a pontoon bridge across the Oostanaula and sent a division across to threaten Johnston's connections with Rome, while the main body of the army pressed Resaca in front. May 14 an attack by a portion of Sherman's force was repulsed with a loss of 1,000 men. Johnston attempted to turn Sherman's left flank, which gave McPherson a good position, to recover which the Confederates fought stubbornly till 10 o'clock at night. Skirmishing was renewed the next morning and continued all day. During the night of the 15th Johnston again retreated. Sherman's losses during the two days were between 4,000 and 5,000 in killed and wounded and missing. Johnston's losses aggregated 2,500.

Resaca de la Palma (Tex.), Battle of.—
On May 9, 1846, the day following the battle of Palo Alto, Gen. Taylor's army of 2,200 proceeded on the way toward Fort Brown. When about three miles from the Rio Grande River, Arista's army of 5,000, which had been slowly retreating before the advancing Americans, halted in the valley of Resaca de la Palma (dry river bed of the palm) and prepared to give battle. At 3 o'clock in the afternoon the action began. Before dark the Mexicans were completely routed. They fled in disorder across the river to Matamoras. Eight pieces of artillery, large quantities of ammunition, 3 standards, and about 100 prisoners, including Gen. La Vega and other officers, fell into the hands of the Americans. The total casualties in the Mexican army were 755. The American loss was 107.

Resaca de la Palma, Tex., battle of, referred to, 2295, 2300, 2342.

Reservations. (See Indian Reservations; Lands, Indian; Military Reservations; Reservations, Public; Washington City.)

Reservation, Public:
Discussed 6346.
Lands set apart as, by proclamation of President—
Cleveland, 5859, 5864, 6122, 6205, 6207, 6209, 6211, 6213, 6215, 6216, 6218, 6219, 6221, 6222, 6225, 6227.
Harrison, Benj., 5577, 5590, 5595, 5686, 5695, 5705, 5719, 5722, 5786, 5792, 5795, 5797, 5804, 5810, 5811, 5814, 5815.

Reserve Bank. (See Currency Law.)

Reserve Banking System.—The banking and currency law, known as Federal Reserve act, was passed Dec. 23, 1913.

Under the system known as the National banking system, which was inaugurated at the latter end of the civil war, the National banknote currency was based upon Government bonds deposited in the Treasury, and the currency thus issued has been classed by economists as bond-secured currency. This plan was evolved not only to nationalize and unify the currency, which had theretofore consisted of notes issued by State banks, but as well to create a market for United States bonds, and in this way to sustain their value. It was entirely successful for the latter purpose, but has outworn its usefulness as a banking system because of its entire want of elasticity.

The Federal Reserve act is the result of a long discussion by statesmen, financiers, economists and bankers, and is a constructive measure based upon and growing out of many bills which have been introduced within the past twenty years. Under it twelve cities, known as Federal Reserve cities, are established, and the (continental) United States is divided into twelve geographical districts, each district containing one of the reserve cities. The twelve districts and their respective reserve cities are as follows:

Federal Reserve Districts.—No. 1.—Maine, New Hampshire, Vermont, Massachusetts, Rhode Island, and Connecticut. Federal Reserve City, Boston, Mass.

No. 2.—The State of New York. Federal Reserve City, New York.

No. 3.—New Jersey and Delaware; all that part of Pennsylvania east of the western boundary of McKean, Elk, Clearfield, Cambria, and Bedford Counties. Federal Reserve City, Philadelphia, Pa.

No. 4.—Ohio; all that part of Pennsylvania west of district No. 3; Marshall, Ohio, Brooke, and Hancock Counties, W. Va.; all that part of Kentucky east of the western boundary of Boone, Grant, Scott, Woodford, Jessamine, Garrard, Lincoln, Pulaski, and McCreary Counties. Federal Reserve City, Cleveland, Ohio.

No. 5.—District of Columbia, Maryland, Virginia, North Carolina, and South Carolina; all of West Virginia except Marshall, Ohio, Brooke, and Hancock Counties. Federal Reserve City, Richmond, Va.

No. 6.—Alabama, Georgia, and Florida; all that part of Tennessee east of the western boundary of Stewart, Houston, Wayne, Humphreys, and Perry Counties; all that part of Mississippi south of the northern boundary of Issaquena, Sharkey, Yazoo, Kemper, Madison, Leake, and Neshoba Counties; all of the southeastern part of Louisiana east of the western boundary of Pointe Coupee, Iberville, Assumption, and Terrebonne Parishes. Federal Reserve City, Atlanta, Ga.

No. 7.—Iowa; all that part of Wisconsin south of the northern boundary of Vernon, Sauk, Columbia, Dodge, Washington, and Ozaukee Counties; all of the southern peninsula of Michigan, viz., that part east of Lake Michigan; all that part of Illinois north of the southern boundary of Hancock, Schuyler, Cass, Sangamon, Christian, Shelby, Cumberland, and Clark Counties; all that part of Indiana north of the southern boundary of Vigo, Clay, Owen, Monroe, Brown, Bartholomew, Jennings, Ripley, and Ohio Counties. Federal Reserve City, Chicago, Ill.

No. 8.—Arkansas; all that part of Missouri east of the western boundary of Harrison, Daviess, Caldwell, Ray, Lafayette, Johnson, Henry, St. Clair, Cedar, Dade, Lawrence, and Barry Counties; all that part of Illinois and Indiana not included in district No. 7; all that part of Kentucky not included in district No. 4; all that part of Tennessee and Mississippi not included in district No. 6. Federal Reserve City, St. Louis, Mo.

No. 9.—Montana, North Dakota, South Dakota, and Minnesota; all that part of Wisconsin and Michigan not included in district No. 7. Federal Reserve City, Minneapolis, Minn.

No. 10.—Kansas, Nebraska, Colorado, and Wyoming; all that part of Missouri not included in district No. 8; all that part of Oklahoma north of the southern boundary of Ellis, Dewey, Blaine, Canadian, Cleveland, Pottawatomie, Seminole, Okfuskee, McIntosh, Muskogee, and Sequoyah Counties; all that part of New Mexico north of the southern boundary of McKinley, Sandoval, Santa Fe, San Miguel, and Union Counties. Federal Reserve City, Kansas City, Mo.

No. 11.—Texas; all that part of New Mexico and Oklahoma not included in district No. 10; all that part of Louisiana not included in district No. 6; and Pima Graham, Greenlee, Cochise, and Santa Cruz Counties, Ariz. Federal Reserve City, Dallas, Tex.

No. 12.—California, Washington, Oregon, Idaho, Nevada, and Utah; all that part of Arizona not included in district No. 11. Federal Reserve City, San Francisco, Cal.

Every National bank is required to become a stockholder in the Federal Reserve bank of the district in which it is situated, and any state bank or trust company which complies with certain specified requirements is permitted to become a member bank. There are at the present time approximately 7,500 National banks in the United States which have thus been required to become member banks.

The largest district, in respect to number of member banks—the seventh or Chicago district—has 952 member banks. The smallest district—the sixth or Atlanta district—has 372 member banks. The number of member banks may largely increase in the near future from the addition of State banks and trust companies as member banks.

Each member bank is required to subscribe to the stock of the Federal Reserve bank of its district in the amount equal to 6 per centum of its paid-up capital stock and surplus. The Federal Reserve bank does not do business with the public in the sense that banks usually do; it may better be described as a bank of banks. It is made a depository for a certain proportion of the reserve of all the member banks, and in addition may also be a depository for Government funds. An important function is as a bank of issue and redemption of currency, for it may secure from the Treasury Government notes known as Federal Reserve notes, which it is authorized to issue against commercial paper with a minimum gold reserve of 40 per centum. Besides this, Federal Reserve banks are granted certain powers in the matter of operations in the open market, such as the purchase of commercial paper, foreign exchange, etc., and in a general way are expected to perform important functions as clearing houses between their member banks.

Each Federal Reserve bank has nine directors, three of whom represent the member banks, three represent commercial, agricultural or other industrial pursuit (these six being chosen by the member banks), and finally three Government directors chosen by the Federal Reserve Board. These nine directors are charged with the duty of appointing all necessary officers, including the active manager of the bank, who is designated as its President or Governor.

Under the act the whole system is under the supervision of a central board in Washington, known as the Federal Reserve Board, consisting of the Secretary of the Treasury and the Comptroller of the Currency acting ex-officio, and five members named by the President with the approval of the Senate. The five members first selected (who took oath of office August 10, 1914) are as follows:

Charles S. Hamlin, Governor, term of office, 2 years.

Frederic A. Delano, Vice-Governor, term of office, 6 years.

Paul M. Warburg, term of office, 4 years.

W. P. G. Harding, term of office, 8 years.

A. C. Miller, term of office, 10 years.

At the termination of the term of office of these five members all subsequent appointees will be named for ten-year terms, except, of course, those who may be selected to fill unexpired terms.

The salary of the members of this board is $12,000 per annum each, which salaries, together with all other expenses of operating the system, are assessed against the Federal Reserve banks in proportion to their capital stock and surplus. Secretary to the board, H. Parker Willis; Assistant Secretary, Sherman Allen. Headquarters, Washington, D. C.

When organized, the capital of the Reserve banks of the system was as follows:

Dist. No. 1 (Boston)	....	$9,924,543
Dist. No. 2 (New York)	....	20,687,606
Dist. No. 3 (Philadelphia)	.....	12,500,738
Dist. No. 4 (Cleveland)	....	12,100,384
Dist. No. 5 (Richmond)	....	6,542,713
Dist. No. 6 (Atlanta)	....	4,702,558
Dist. No. 7 (Chicago)	....	12,967,701
Dist. No. 8 (St. Louis)	....	6,367,006
Dist. No. 9 (Minneapolis)	.....	4,702,925
Dist. No. 10 (Kansas City)	......	5,600,977
Dist. No. 11 (Dallas)	....	5,653,924
Dist. No. 12 (San Francisco)	...	8,115,494

Resolute, The, restoration of, to British Government, discussed, 2953.

Restoration of Southern States (see also Reconstruction):

Acts regarding, vetoed. (See Reconstruction.)

Discussed by President Johnson, 3551, 3570, 3593, 3643, 3696, 3729, 3734, 3756, 3781, 3846, 3848, 3870.

Provisional governor appointed for—
Alabama, 3521.
Florida, 3527.
Georgia, 3516.
Mississippi, 3512.
North Carolina, 3510.
South Carolina, 3524.
Texas, 3519.

Restraint of Trade.—Conduct in the industrial or commercial world which is calculated to diminish the sum-total of trade, or to prevent freedom of trade by all persons desiring to engage in it. The restraint is effected by monopoly or by action tending to monopoly. (See Anti-Trust Law and Sherman Act.)

Resumption. (See Specie Payments.)

Retroactive.—Imposing a punishment for an act performed prior to the passage of the law. A retroactive law, while permissible as to civil conduct, is inhibited by the Constitution as to criminal conduct. (See Ex Post Facto.)

Returning Boards.—Boards established in certain states for the purpose of canvassing the returns of an election. The reconstructed state governments of South Carolina, Florida, and Louisiana, created by statute returning boards to canvass and certify to the returns of elections held in those states. In violation of the generally accepted principle of state government, these returning boards were clothed with judicial as well as ministerial powers. This subject is of interest chiefly in relation to the Presidential election of 1876, in which the result depended upon the action of these boards.

Revenue Cutter.—A small armed vessel owned and used by the Government to enforce customs regulations.

Revenue-Cutter Service.—The Revenue-Cutter Service is a military arm of the Government attached to and under the direction of the Treasury Department. The Service was organized in 1790 and constituted the original naval force of the country. There being at that time no Navy Department, the Service was placed under the Treasury Department, where it has remained ever since. It is charged with the enforcement of the navigation and customs laws of the United States, the assistance of vessels in distress, the protection of the sealing industry in Alaska, the enforcement of the quarantine laws, the destruction of derelicts and other floating dangers to navigation, and numerous other duties appropriate to its class of vessels. Each winter, by direction of the president, a number of the cutters patrol the coast for the special purpose of assisting vessels in distress. The Service cooperates with the Navy when directed by the president and has so cooperated in every war in which the United States has been engaged.

The officers of the Service are commissioned by the president and hold rank by law with officers of the Army and Navy as follows: Captain-Commandant with Colonel in the Army and Captain in the Navy; Senior Captains and Engineer-in-Chief with Lieutenant-Colonels in the Army and Commanders in the Navy; Captains with Majors in the Army and Lieutenant-Commanders in the Navy; First Lieutenants with Captains in the Army and Lieutenants in the Navy; Second Lieutenants with First Lieutenants in the Army and Lieutenants (Junior Grade) in the Navy; Third Lieutenants with Second Lieutenants in the Army and Ensigns in the Navy.

There are now in the Service 228 commissioned officers and cadets on the active list, and 1,500 petty officers and enlisted men. Commissioned officers of the line are appointed from Cadet graduates of the School of Instruction at New London, Ct. The Cadet course covers three years and embraces profession and academic subjects. Cadets are appointed after competitive examinations, conducted by boards of commissioned officers of the Revenue-Cutter Service.

Appointments to the Engineer Corps are made after competitive examination, and successful candidates are appointed Cadet Engineers for a period of six months prior to being commissioned Third Lieutenants of Engineers in the Service. Candidates for the Engineer Corps must be not less than twenty-one nor more than twenty-six years of age.

In January, 1915, the Revenue Cutter Service was combined with the Life-Saving Service to form the Coast Guards. (See Coast Guards.)

Revenue-Cutter Service:

Act relating to revenue cutters and steamers vetoed, 2219.

Land reserved for use of, 6701.

Organization of, 1088.

Retirement of officers in, 6708.

Steam vessels in, employment of, recommended, 1121.

(See also Treasury Department of.)

Revenue Flag.—The last act of the Fourth Congress, March 2, 1799, was to pass a law to regulate the collection of duties and tonnage and to establish ports of entry. In order that the vessels of the collection officers might be easily recognized, Congress ordered that vessels in the revenue service carry a flag of sixteen perpendicular stripes, alternate red and white, the union of the ensign bearing the arms of the United States in dark blue on a white field beneath a semicircle of thirteen blue stars.

Revenue Inspectors, salary of, 127.

Revenue Officers, official conduct of, referred to, 912.

Revenue, Public.—In a political sense the revenue of a state is the annual income derived from taxation, customs, and other sources, to be appropriated to governmental expenditures. The principal sources of revenue of the United States are customs, internal revenue, sale of public lands, and miscellaneous receipts. Customs receipts have always formed the bulk of the revenue. In 1789 the total revenues of the Government amounted to $4,410,000. This total gradually swelled to $56,000,000 in 1860. Then the increased duties of all kinds, imposed as war measures, augmented the revenues to hundreds of millions, reaching the maximum of $520,000,000 in 1866. Then it declined to an average of about $350,000,000 between 1878 and 1898. In 1901 the revenue, increased by a Spanish-American War tax, was $587,685,338.

The income tax law of 1913, during the first year of its operation, yielded but $28,253,000 in revenue, a little more than half the amount estimated by Treasury officials. It was disclosed upon analysis that nearly 58 per cent of the total was paid by residents of three States—New York, New Jersey and Pennsylvania.

The corporation excise tax of 1909, modified in 1913, produced for the fiscal year 1913-14 a total of $43,127,000.

The decline in customs duties consequent upon the European war in 1914 caused Congress to enact, upon the urgent recommendation of President Wilson (page 7980), a special war revenue tax, to be in effect for one year.

ORDINARY RECEIPTS BY FISCAL YEARS

Years Ending June 30	Customs	Internal Revenue	Miscellaneous Items	Total Ordinary Receipts
1903..	$284,479,582	$230,810,124	$45,106,968	$560,396,674
1904..	261,274,565	232,904,120	45,538,229	539,716,914
1905..	261,798,857	234,095,741	48,712,161	544,606,759
1906..	300,251,878	249,150,213	45,315,851	594,717,942
1907..	332,233,363	269,666,773	61,225,524	663,125,660
1908..	286,113,130	251,711,127	63,236,466	601,060,723
1909..	300,711,934	246,212,644	56,664,912	603,589,490
1910..	333,683,445	289,933,519	51,894,751	675,511,715
1911..	314,497,071	322,529,201	64,346,103	701,372,375
1912..	311,321,672	321,612,200	58,844,593	691,778,465
1913..	318,891,396	344,416,966	60,802,868	724,111,230
1914..	292,320,015	380,041,007	62,312,145	734,673,167
1915..	209,786,672	415,069,646	72,454,509	637,910,828
1916..	213,185,845	512,702,029	53,776,678	779,664,552

Revenue, Public (see also Tariff; Finances; Import Duties; Taxation):

Act—

Designating and limiting funds receivable for, reasons for applying pocket veto to, 1501.

To provide for collection, safekeeping, and distribution of, by fiscal corporation vetoed, 1921.

Additional $100,000,000 to be raised through internal taxes urged, 8361.

By direct taxation, 265, 268.

Collection and disbursement of, free from defalcation, discussed, 5542, 5746.

Custody and distribution of, discussed by President—

Polk, 2352, 2406, 2498.

Tyler, 1896, 1937.

Van Buren, 1541, 1596, 1707, **1757**, 1827.

Deposits of, in banks referred to, 1916.

Derived from public lands. (See Lands, Public.)

Diminution of, 461, 480, 675, 923.

Disbursements of, referred to, 1810.

Discussed. (See Finances Discussed.)

Duties for raising. (See Import Duties.)

Embezzlement of, referred to, 2212. (See also Defalcation.)

Expenses incurred in collection of, referred to, 2563.

Frauds in, discussed, 989, 4797.

Insufficient for authorized expenditures, 7370, 7379.

Laws for raising. (See also Import Duties.)

Abuses of, referred to, 1016.

Alterations in, 142, 8111.

Codification of, recommended, 4201.

Complaints of Spain and Portugal against, referred to, 1956.

Improvement in, recommended, 925, 1016, 8111.

Judicial construction of, injurious, 1788.

Opposition to, from—

Pennsylvania. (See Pennsylvania.)

South Carolina. (See South Carolina.)

Southern States. (See Civil War.)

Revision of, recommended, 3773.

System of, satisfactory, 75, 79.

Measures to provide additional, urged, 7980, 8111.

Only enough should be collected to meet wants of Government, 1464.

Per centum allowed public officers for disbursement of, referred to, 1727.

Policy of Mexico in exempting from duty imports into territory on borders of United States. (See Zona Libre.)

Referred to, 3903.

Suits growing out of, discussed and recommendations regarding, 5098.

Surplus of—

Application of, to—

Educational purposes and internal improvements recommended, 397, 444.

Navy and national works recommended, 1380.

Purchase of Government bonds recommended, 3985.

Apportionment of, among States. (See States of the Union.)

Discussed by President—

Arthur, 4635, 4721.

Cleveland, 5093, 5165, 5361, 5372.

Fillmore, 2660, 2714.

Grant, 3985.

Harrison, Benj., 5473, 5549, 5630.

Jackson, 1014, 1077, 1380, 1458.

Jefferson, 397, 444.

Pierce, 2747, 2818.

Van Buren, 1707.

Joint resolution directing payment of Treasury surplus on public Debt, reasons for applying pocket veto to, 5073.

Proposition to deposit in banks throughout country discussed, 5168.

System of—

Changes made in, productive of good results, 1247.

Evil effects of, discussed, 1459.

Tariff for raising. (See Import Duties.)

Revere's Ride, Paul. (See "Midnight Ride of Paul Revere.")

Revised Statutes:

Appointment of commission to prepare, recommended, 2671, 2714.

Preparation of, and recommendations regarding, 3250.

Referred to, 4687.

Revolution.—The overthrow of an established political system or a radical change of government effected by extra legal means is known as a political revolution. Among the most important revolutions of modern history are the English Revolution of 1642-1649, which culminated in the execution of Charles I and the establishment of the Protectorate under Cromwell; the second English Revolution, resulting from the Stuart tyranny after the Restoration known as the "Glorious Revolution of 1688," which, under William III, firmly established the principles of free constitutional government in Great Britain; the American Revolution which resulted in the establishment of the Republic of the United States in 1776; the French Revolution, which broke out in Paris in 1789 and was followed by a reign of blood and terror, terminating with the execution of Robespierre in 1794; the French Revolution of 1830, which exiled Charles X and elevated Louis Philippe to the throne; the uprising of the French people in 1848, which deposed Louis; the Italian Revolution of 1859-60, whereby the various minor sovereigns of the peninsula were driven into exile and the whole territory came under the dominion of King Victor Emmanuel; the insurrections which established the third French Republic in 1870 and the Republic of Brazil in 1889.

Revolutionary Convention. (See Convention, Revolutionary.)

Revolutionary Pensions. (See Pensions.)

Revolutionary War.—The war for redress of grievances, and later for independence, waged by the thirteen American Colonies against the mother country, Great Britain. The Revolution had several causes. Increase in population in America naturally caused a desire for independence, especially after the expulsion of the French. In 1763 the Government of George III resolved to enforce more strictly the navigation act and other laws restricting American trade in the interest of England, to station garrisons in America, and to pay a part of the expense by a stamp tax. The Stamp Act aroused violent opposition, expressed through the Stamp Act Congress of 1765. Taxation without representation in Parliament was declared illegal and tyrannous. The British Government persisted in the principle, taxing various imports from 1767 to 1770 and tea thereafter. The Boston Tea Party led Parliament to pass acts retaliating on that city and altering the charter of Massachusetts. The Colonies were by this time united, through their committees of correspondence, in opposition to the Crown. Sept. 5, 1774, the First Continental Congress was convened in Philadelphia. It published a declaration of rights, protested to the King and Parliament, and entered into a non-importation agreement. April 19, 1775, Gen. Gage, the British commander in Boston, met with the first armed resistance at Lexington and Concord, and war was begun. The Colonists were assisted by France, Spain, and in the later years of the struggle, by the Netherlands.

Following are the principal events of the Revolution: Boston Massacre, March 5, 1770; Boston Tea Party, Dec. 16, 1773; First Continental Congress, Sept. 5, 1774; battles of Lexington and Concord, April 19, 1775; meeting of the Second Continental Congress and capture of Ticonderoga, May 10; Mecklenburg Declaration of Independence, May 20; battle of Bunker Hill, June 16 and 17; evacuation of Boston, March 17, 1776; British repulse off Charleston, June 28; Declaration of Independence, July 4; battle of Long Island, Aug. 27; battle of White Plains, Oct. 28; loss of Forts Washington and Lee, retreat through New Jersey and battle of Trenton, end of 1776; battle of Princeton, Jan. 3, 1777; battle of Bennington, Aug. 16; battle of Brandywine, Sept. 11; battle of Stillwater, Sept. 19; battle of Germantown, Oct. 4; battle of Saratoga, Oct. 7; Burgoyne's surrender, Oct. 17; adoption of the Articles of Confederation, Nov. 15; treaty with France, Feb. 6, 1778; battle of Monmouth, June 28; storming of Stony Point, July 16, 1779; victory of Paul Jones, Sept. 23; British capture Charleston, May 12, 1780; battle of Camden, Aug. 16; Arnold's treachery exposed, Sept. 23; battle of King's Mountain, Oct. 7; battle of the Cowpens, Jan. 17, 1781; Articles of Confederation ratified by the last of the States, March 1; battle of Guilford Court-House, March 15; battle of Eutaw, Sept. 8; surrender of Cornwallis at Yorktown, Oct. 19; peace of Paris, Sept. 3, 1783; evacuation of New York, Nov. 25, 1783. The United States then comprised the territory from Canada to Florida and from the Atlantic Ocean to the Mississippi River. The total number of enlistments in the American army during the war was 368,410; the total cost was $135,193,703.

Revolutionary War:

Allowances to officers in, referred to, 906.

Pensioners of. (See Pensions.)

Referred to, 2755.

Soldiers of, land warrants issued to, 889.

Revolutions. (See Illegal Combinations; the several powers.)

Reward offered for arrest of—

Alleged instigators of assassination of President Lincoln, 3505.

Distribution of, referred to, 3577.

Persons claiming, directed to file claims, 3551.

Revoked as to certain persons, 3551.

Persons from foreign countries commiting depredations in United States, 3484.

Willis Anderson, 943.

Rhine, The, French steamer, referred to, 3460.

Rhode Island.—One of the thirteen original states of the Union and the smallest of the United States; nicknamed, "Little Rhody;" motto, "Hope." It lies between lat. 41° 18′ and 42° 1′ north (not including Block Island) and long. 71° 8′ and 71° 53′ west. It is bounded on the north and east by Massachusetts, on the south by the Atlantic Ocean, and on the west by Connecticut, and has an area of 1,248 square miles. It is an important manufacturing state, being first in proportion to its population in the manufacture of cotton, woolen, worsteds, etc., and second only to Massachusetts in the production of cotton goods.

Rhode Island was visited by Verrazano in 1524 and probably by Norse navigators in the twelfth century. Roger Williams made the first permanent settlement at Providence in 1636. The first charter was granted in 1643 and a more liberal one in 1663. Rhode Island ratified the Federal Constitution in 1790. The official name of the state is "The State of Rhode Island, and Providence Plantations."

Statistics of agriculture collected for the last Federal census place the number of farms in the state at 5,292, comprising 443,308 acres, valued, with stock and improvements, at $32,990,739. The value of domestic animals, poultry, etc., was $3,276,472, including 34,148 cattle, valued at $1,309,088; 9,547 horses, $1,424,177; 14,038 swine, $123,647; 6,789 sheep, $32,637; poultry, $368,018. The yield and value of field crops in 1911 was: Corn, 11,000 acres, 495,000 bushels, $470,000; oats, 2,000 acres, 58,000 bushels, $34,000; potatoes, 5,000 acres, 550,000 bushels, $583,000; hay, 61,000 acres, 61,000 tons, $1,470,000. Stone is the principal mineral product of the state. Manufacturing made great progress during the decade ending in 1910 when the last census was taken. At the end of this period there were 1,944 establishments, with an aggregate capital of $289,416,000; consuming raw materials which cost $158,652,000, paying wages totaling $18,130,000 to 112,565 employees, and selling the output for $279,438,000. The leading industry is cotton spinning, 2,055,912 spindles, capitalized at $43,527,584, producing an output of $30,628,843. In worsted goods manufacture $38,789,543 was invested, which produced $44,477,596. Foundries capitalized at $23,728,205 produced a finished product valued at $13,959,283. The dyeing and finishing industry, closely allied with the textile manufactories, involved $16,969,936 capital and added $9,981,457 to the value of goods. Jewelry manufacture is capitalized at $11,199,233, and produces an output selling at $14,431,756. The manufacture of silverware is capitalized at $8,552,489, and produces $5,323,264. The latest industry to take on large proportions is the manufacture of rubber goods. The bonded debt of the state in 1910 was $4,800,000. The real and personal property was valued at $511,960,122. The receipts and expenditures of the State Treasurer each vary between $2,000,000 and $2,500,000. The population according to the Federal census of 1910 was 542,610. (See also Providence Plantations.)

Rhode Island:

Accession of, to Union, 67.

Constitution in, attempts of people to establish free. (See Dorr's Rebellion.)

Constitution of United States—

Convention for consideration of, 64.

Evidence of ratification of amendments to, 68, 182.

Dorr's Rebellion in—

Correspondence regarding, 2139.

Discussed, 2136.

Free constitution in, attempts of people to establish. (See Dorr's Rebellion.)

Lands in, United States empowered to hold, 146.

Union, accession of and Providence Plantations to, 67.

Ricara Indians. (See Indian Tribes.)

Rice. (See Agricultural Products.)

Rich Mountain (W. Va.), Battle of.— Soon after the ordinance of secession had been ratified by the State of Virginia, Maj.-Gen. George B. McClellan, who had been assigned to the command of the Federal forces in the Department of the Ohio, issued an address to the loyal citizens of western Virginia. Many enlistments from that State followed, and he determined to occupy at least part of it with Federal troops. Accordingly, May 23, 1861, the First Virginia Regiment, 1,100 strong, which had been organized in Cincinnati by Virginians, crossed the Ohio with the Fourteenth and Sixteenth Ohio regiments and took possession of Parkersburg. The Confederates, commanded by Governor Wise under the immediate direction of Col. Porterfield, retired after several skirmishes to the base of Rich Mountain, near Beverly, in Randolph County. McClellan's forces in the neighborhood amounted to more than 30,000 men on July 4, while the Confederates could scarcely muster 10,000. July 11, Gen. Rosecrans made a detour of the mountain and forced the surrender of 600 men under Col. Pegram, and Gen. McClellan defeated the main body of the Confederates under Gen. Garnett. The Union losses in the actions at Rich Mountain were 11 killed and 35 wounded. The loss to the Confederates was 200 killed and 1,000 prisoners. Seven pieces of artillery also fell into the hands of the Union forces.

Richmond (Ky.), Battle of.—After the Confederates had evacuated Corinth, Miss., in the summer of 1862, they began to concentrate in the vicinity of Chattanooga, Tenn. By the middle of August they had collected an army estimated at from 55,-000 to 65,000 under Gen. Braxton Bragg. Gen. E. Kirby Smith, with about 20,000 men, passed up the Cumberland Mountains on the east, and, going through the gaps, invaded Kentucky. At Richmond he encountered Gen. Manson (Aug. 30), who was defending the place with a garrison of Buell's army. Mason was defeated and Smith proceeded to Frankfort. Loss about 5,000 on each side.

Richmond, Va., Government of Confederate States transferred to, 3225.

Riders.—Objectionable legislative measures likely to be vetoed if passed as separate bills, but which are made part of important bills, such as appropriations for current expenses, etc., in order to insure Executive sanction. The rider is an encroachment on the independence of the Executive. In many of the states a rider has been made an impossibility by confining each bill to a single subject or by permitting the veto of single clauses of appropriation bills. It has never been prohibited in Congress. Riders were numerous during the anti-slavery contest, the Civil War, and the conflict with President Johnson. A number of important bills have been passed as riders, among them the bill increasing salaries in 1873. The first use of the rider of national importance was the joining in 1820 of the bill for the admission of Maine to that permitting slavery in Missouri, so as to compel the acceptance of both or neither. These were afterwards separated. The Army appropriation bill of 1856 as sent from the House to the Senate had a rider prohibiting the employment of Federal troops for the enforcement of Territorial law in Kansas. Riders were added to all appropriation bills by the Democratic majority in the House during the first session of the Forty-seventh Congress in 1879; but all these bills were vetoed by the president and were finally passed without riders. The Platt Amendment (see Cuba) was a rider to the Army Appropriation Bill of 1901.

Rifle Clubs in South Carolina, proclamation against, 4350. (See also Ku-Klux Klans.)

Rifle, Magazine, for use of infantry service, selected, 5878.

Rifle Practice, commended to attention of soldiers and civilians, 7070, 7236.

Right of Asylum, discussed by President—

Cleveland, 5961.

Johnson, 3883.

Right of Search.—Great Britain has always claimed the right to search vessels of other powers upon the high seas for deserting English sailors and for contraband goods in time of war. This has not been exercised with regard to the vessels of the United States since the War of 1812, though nothing was said in the treaty of Ghent about search and impressment of sailors. Before that war this right was exercised and search was made for English sailors, and many American seamen were impressed as deserters from the English navy, and search was made for such goods as were declared subject to confiscation in accordance with the paper blockade of the continent and the orders in council. This was one of the grievances that brought on the War of 1812. The right of search for the purpose of suppressing the slave trade was carefully regulated by several treaties between Great Britain and the United States.

Right of Search:

Discussed by President—

Buchanan, 3038, 3170.

Madison, 484, 505.

Tyler, 1930, 2048, 2082.

Proposition regarding, mutual, referred to, 2626.

Questions regarding, with—
   Cuba, 3986.
   Great Britain, 484, 505, 1930, 2048, 2082.
      Claim of Great Britain abandoned, 3038, 3171.
      Mutual right of search, referred to, 1943.
      Referred to, 2286, 2297.
Right of Suffrage. (See Elective Franchise.)
Right of Way. (See Indian Reservations.)
Rights. (See Bill of Rights and Natural Rights.)
Rights, Bill of. (See Bill of Rights.)
Rights of Federal and State Governments. (See Powers of Federal and State Governments.)
Rights of Man.—A pamphlet by Thomas Paine, published in England in 1791. Its radical appeal was so strong that Paine was outlawed.
Rio Grande River:
   Construction of dams in, opposite El Paso, Tex., referred to, 5400.
   Disorders on, discussed by President—
      Arthur, 4627, 4716.
      Buchanan, 3113, 3115.
      Fillmore, 2688.
      Grant, 4143, 4161, 4220, 4244, 4295, 4358.
      Harrison, Benj., 5751.
      Hayes, 4407, 4424, 4449, 4521.
      Neutrality violated by army on, referred to, 3574.
      Report upon state of, 2777.
      Storage and use of waters of, for irrigation, discussed, 5959, 6281.
Riots at Chicago, proclamation regarding, 5931.
Riparian Rights.—Rights to the usage of water-front for various purposes.
River and Harbor Bills.—There has always been some objection to appropriations for the improvement of rivers and harbors on the ground that the benefits, while mostly local, are paid for out of the general Treasury. The first bill for harbor improvements in the United States was passed March 3, 1823. Since 1854, appropriations for the improvement of rivers and harbors were frequently inserted in the regular appropriation bill. Separate bills for this purpose were vetoed by Presidents Tyler (2183), Polk (2310), Pierce (2789), and Grant (4336). In 1870 a $2,000,000 appropriation was made. This was the largest up to that time. After this they gradually increased until they reached nearly $19,-000,000 in 1882-83. President Arthur vetoed the bill carrying this appropriation (4707), but it was passed over his veto. Biennial appropriations have since been the rule. The appropriation for 1891 was $25,-000,000. The expenditures of 1896, including the direct appropriations of about $30,-000,000 and the contracts for future expenditures, amounted to a total of about $80,000,000. The bill carrying this amount was vetoed by President Cleveland (6109), but was passed over his veto. River and harbor bills have since been passed in 1899, 1900, and 1902, and 1905.
River Crow Indians. (See Indian Tribes.)
River Raisin (Mich.), Battle of.—After Col. Lewis had occupied Frenchtown, Mich., Jan. 18, 1813, with 650 men, he was reenforced by Gen. Winchester with about 300 from the latter's camp on the Maumee River. These were stationed along the river outside the town. Before daylight on the morning of Jan. 22 they were attacked by 500 British under Col. Proctor, and 600 Indians under Round Head and Walk-in-the-Water. Some 200 Americans were killed or wounded in battle or massacred after their surrender and Winchester and 700 men were made prisoners. Only 33 of Winchester's detachment which arrived at Frenchtown are known to have escaped. The British lost 24 killed and 158 wounded.
Rivers and Harbors (see also Internal Improvements):
   Act for improvement of—
      Reasons for applying pocket veto to, 1201.
      Vetoed by President—
         Arthur, 4707.
            Discussed by, 4724.
         Cleveland, 6109.
         Polk, 2310.
         Tyler, 2183.
   Appropriations for, 416.
   Bill making, approval and reasons therefor, 4331.
   Discussed, 4362, 4833.
   Expenditures of, referred to, 4371.
   Recommended, 2558, 2666, 2711, 3993, 5477.
   Should only be made after surveys, 2204.
   Breakwater near mouth of Mississippi River, referred to, 988.
   Breakwaters for, referred to, 1126.
   Deepening of channels of, at Federal expense, recommended, 7489.
   Expenditures for, referred to, 4788.
      Discussed, 4197.
   Foreign powers, if friendly, should be allowed use of, 523.
   Fortifications for, recommended, 230, 297, 318, 442, 447, 455, 477, 2055.
   Fortifications in, completed, 461.
   Improvement of, referred to, 1785.
      Recommended, 7690.
   Opened to British vessels, 753.
      Closed, 941.
   Survey of, referred to, 1490.
   Waterway from the Lakes to the Gulf recommended, 7690.
Roads, Post. (See Mail Routes and Transcontinental Highways.)
Roads, Public.—The Sixty-second Congress made an initial appropriation of $500,000 to aid the state in improving public high-

ways and an additional sum of $25,000 was voted for a committee to investigate the subject of federal aid in state road-building.

History.—The majority of the main Roman highways were built at public expense. They were maintained in part by the labor of soldiers and convicts or slaves, or by enforced service, which, in some instances, took the form of taxation. But in whatever form the maintenance, it was at the expense of the district through which the road passed. Tolls as a means of repairing highways were unknown to the Romans. The supervision of the roads was intrusted to men of the highest rank. Augustus himself seems to have made those about Rome his special care. Cross roads were placed in charge of the local magistrates, although occasionally a portion of a road was assigned to some landowner to maintain at his own cost.

The present road system of France was founded by Napoleon. He built many roads through the empire, among them the road over the Simplon Pass, which was commenced in 1800 and required six years for completion. It was under him that the work was systematized and placed in the hands of a permanent body of engineers.

In 1775 Tresaguet, a French engineer, published a treatise on broken stone roads. His work preceded that of Macadam and Telford by about forty years.

The first record of road legislation in England goes back as far as 1285, and it provides that the trees and bushes on both sides of all roads for a distance of 200 feet shall be cut away to prevent robbers from lurking therein and rushing upon victims unawares.

In 1346 Edward III. authorized the first toll to be levied for the repair of roads. This commission was granted to the master of the Hospital of St. Giles and to John Holborn, authorizing them to levy toll on vehicles passing on the roads leading from the hospital to the old Temple of London, and also on an adjoining road called the Portal. In 1523 Parliament passed its first act relative to the repair of roads.

State Highway Construction and state aid for local highway improvements are being carried on by a number of states on a large scale. Massachusetts and New Jersey, which began state aid for work in the early nineties, continue to improve, while New York, Pennsylvania, Maryland and California are carrying on extensive operations, and altogether more than half the states of the Union have taken up highway improvement in some form. At the beginning of 1912 Massachusetts had built more than 880 miles of road at a cost of about $9,000 per mile. In Delaware a state highway has been laid out from a point on the southern boundary to a point near Wilmington in the north, about a hundred miles. This road is to be built under the direction and at the expense of General Coleman Du Pont. New York State in 1912 voted an appropriation of $50,000,000 for the purpose of road building.

Federal Aid.—President Wilson, July 11, 1916, signed a bill, authorizing an expenditure of $85,000,000 in five years by the Federal government on condition that the states should expend amounts similar to those apportioned to them: $75,000,000 was for rural post roads, and $10,000,000 for roads and trails in national forests.

The Office of Public Roads in the Department of Agriculture issued a bulletin in 1909 showing the mileage of public roads in the United States as follows:

Total mileage of stone roads in United States............................ 59,237

Total mileage of gravel roads in United States............................ 102,870
Total mileage of sand-clay, brick, bituminous-macadam and other improved roads in U. S........................ 28,372
Total mileage of all public roads in United States...................... 2,199,645
Total mileage of all improved roads in United States..................... 190,476
Percentage of all roads improved....... 8.66

The same document gives the road mileage of the leading states as follows:

Indiana........	24,955	Washington....	4,520
Ohio...........	24,106	Missouri.......	4,755
New York......	12,787	South Carolina.	3,534
Wisconsin......	10,167	Alabama.......	3,263
Kentucky......	10,114	Pennsylvania...	3,364
Illinois.........	8,914	Tennessee......	5,353
California......	8,587	New Jersey.....	3,377
Massachusetts..	8,463	Florida........	1,752
Georgia........	5,978	Maryland......	2,142

(See also Transcontinental Highways.)

Roads, Public and Rural Engineering, Office of, Agriculture Department.—This is a bureau of the Department of Agriculture devoted to the collection and dissemination of information regarding road management; experiments in road making and road improvement; and scientific tests of road materials. The office lends its aid to local organizations having for their object the improvement of public roads by supplying, upon request, drafts of tentative constitutions and by-laws and outlines of a working policy. The advice given depends largely upon the objects for which the association is formed and the prevailing local conditions. The advice given through correspondence is supplemented by the distribution of various publications on road-making and maintenance; and where the movement is of sufficient magnitude to warrant it, representatives of the Office of Public Roads and Rural Engineering are sent to address the local organizations and point out ways and means by which they can accomplish the best results.

Roanoke Island (N. C.), Expedition to. —Butler's Hatteras expedition of Aug. 26, 1861, had opened Pamlico Sound and the Confederates had retired to Roanoke Island. This island is about ten miles long and was the key to all the rear defenses of Norfolk. Four-fifths of the supplies for Norfolk passed its guns. It was defended by Ben. Wise with 3,000 men. Jan. 7, 1862, Gen. Burnside was ordered to unite with Flag Officer Goldsborough, in command of the fleet at Fortress Monroe, capture Newbern, reduce Fort Macon, and seize the Wilmington and Weldon railroad. On the night of Jan. 11 the expedition arrived off Hatteras and encountered a terrific storm. Several transports were lost and the *City of New York*, with her cargo, worth a quarter of a million dollars, went to pieces. By Feb. 7 the remainder of the expedition had crossed the bar and proceeded up Croatan Channel. The Confederate fleet was driven up the channel. Their flagship—the *Curlew*—was set on fire by a shell and Burnside landed 10,000 men on Roanoke Island. The garrison of 2,675 officers and men was captured and the Confederate fleet pursued to Elizabeth City and destroyed. Burnside lost 250 men.

Roanoke Island, N. C., thanks of President to forces capturing, 3305.

Robert College, establishment of, at Constantinople referred to, 3900.

Rock Creek, D. C., construction of bridge over, referred to, 1844.

Rock Island, Ill., bridge over Mississippi River at, 4148.

Rock Island Arsenal, Ill., appropriation for, recommended, 4680, 4738.

Rocky Mount (S. C.), Assault on.—July 13, 1780, Thomas Sumter, with about 75 men, made an attack upon the British post at Rocky Mount, thirty miles northwest of Camden, under command of Lieut.-Col. Turnbull. The post consisted of two log houses perforated for small arms. Three unsuccessful assaults were made. The Americans finally withdrew after a loss of 13 killed and wounded, including Col. Reed. The British loss was about the same.

Rodgers, The, dispatched for relief of Jeannette Polar Expedition, 4726.

Rogatory Letters, report regarding execution of, transmitted, 5570.

Rogue River Indians. (See Indian Tribes.)

Rome, Italy:

American college at, threatened confiscation of, 4801.

Occupation of, by King of Italy, 4085.

Protestants removed from, referred to, 3662, 3717.

Sanitary conference at, 4918.

Proclamation regarding, 4898.

Roorback.—A general term for political forgery, or a fictitious report for political purposes, generally promulgated before an election. The name comes from a certain political story circulated in 1844 as an extract from Baron Roorback's Tour Through the Western and Southern States.

Roosevelt, Theodore.—Sept. 14, 1901, to March 4, 1909.

(FIRST TERM, SEPT. 14, 1901-MARCH 4, 1905.)

Twenty-ninth Administration (continued) Republican.

Roosevelt became President on the death of President McKinley, and took the oath of office Sept. 14, 1901. McKinley's appointees were continued at the head of the executive departments for a time, the first change being the appointment of Leslie M. Shaw to succeed Lyman J. Gage as Secretary of the Treasury and Henry C. Payne to succeed Charles E. Smith as Postmaster-General, Jan. 8, 1902.

Vice-President.—At the Republican National Convention, at Philadelphia, in 1900, President McKinley received the whole 730 votes in nomination for President, and Roosevelt received 729 for Vice-President (he not voting). Roosevelt was the fifth Vice-President to succeed to the Presidency by the death of the President in office, and the third to succeed by the death of the President by assassination.

Thirtieth Administration—Republican.

(SECOND TERM, MARCH 4, 1905 - MARCH 4, 1909.)

Vice-President—Charles W. Fairbanks.

Secretary of State—
John Hay (continued).

Secretary of the Treasury—
Leslie M. Shaw (continued).

Secretary of War—
William H. Taft (continued).

Attorney-General—
William H. Moody (continued).

Postmaster-General—
Henry C. Payne, from Jan. 8, 1902.
Robert J. Wynne, from Oct. 10, 1904.
George B. Cortelyou, from March 6, 1905.
Charles J. Bonaparte from July 1, 1905.

Secretary of the Navy—
William H. Moody.
Paul Morton (continued).

Secretary of the Interior—
Ethan A. Hitchcock (continued).

Secretary of Agriculture—
James Wilson (continued).

Secretary of Commerce and Labor—
George B. Cortelyou.
Victor H. Metcalf (continued).

SECOND TERM—Nomination.—The Republican party in National Convention at Chicago, June 22, 1904, nominated President Roosevelt by acclamation. The platform of 1904 rehearsed the recent performances of the Republican administrations, the gold standard established, the results in the Philippines, the beginning of the Panama Canal, irrigation of arid lands, increase of the navy; pledged the enforcement of anti-trust laws; reaffirmed protection; favored extension of reciprocity; upheld the gold standard; urged the increase of the merchant marine; declared for a larger navy; endorsed the exclusion of Chinese labor; declared for civil service reform; favored international arbitration; urged inquiry into the constitutionality of negro enfranchisement; advocated equal laws for labor and capital; paid a tribute to the memory of President McKinley; and eulogized President Roosevelt.

Opposition.—The Democratic National Convention at St. Louis, July 9, nominated Alton B. Parker on the first ballot over William R. Hearst. The Prohibition party, at Indianapolis, June 30, nominated Silas C. Swallow by acclamation. The People's party, at Springfield, Ill., nominated Thomas E. Watson by acclamation. The Socialist party, at Chicago, May 5, nominated Eugene Debs by acclamation. The Socialist Labor party, at New York, July 4, nominated Charles H. Corrigan by acclamation. The United Christian party, at St. Louis, May 2; the Continental party, at Chicago, Sept. 1; and the National Liberty (Negro) party, at St. Louis, July 7, placed candidates in the field.

Party Affiliation.—President Roosevelt from his earliest connection with politics was attached to the Republican party. In his earliest days, as a representative to the State legislature of New York, he maintained a large degree of independence; yet he was chosen a delegate to the National Republican Convention in 1884, and was chairman of the delegation. He was an independent Republican in 1886, as a candidate for the mayoralty of the City of New York. His identity with the Republican party became very close during the Harrison administration and as Assistant Secretary of the Navy under McKinley in 1897. In 1898 he was the Republican Governor of the State of New York.

Vote.—The popular vote ran: Roosevelt, 7,623,486; Parker, 5,077,971; Debs, 402,-283; Swallow, 258,536; Watson, 117,183; and Corrigan, 31,249. The electoral vote gave Roosevelt 336 and Parker 140.

Political Complexion of Congress.—In the Fifty-seventh Congress (1901-1903) the Senate, of 91 members, was composed of 29 Democrats, 56 Republicans, 1 Populist, 1 Silver party, 1 Fusionist, and 2 vacancies; and the House, of 357 members, was made up of 153 Democrats, 198 Republicans, 3 Populists, 1 Silver party, 1 Fusionist, with 2 vacancies. In the Fifty-eighth Congress

(1903-1905) the Senate, of 90 members, was composed of 32 Democrats and 58 Republicans, and the House, of 382 members, was composed of 174 Democrats, 206 Republicans, 2 Union Labor, with 2 vacancies. In the Fifty-ninth Congress (1905-1907) the Senate, of 90 members, was composed of 32 Democrats and 58 Republicans; and the House, of 386 members, was made up of 136 Democrats and 250 Republicans. In the Sixtieth Congress (1907-1909) the Senate, of 92 members, was composed of 31 Democrats and 61 Republicans; and the House, of 386 members, was made up of 164 Democrats and 222 Republicans.

Tariff.—President Roosevelt in his First Annual Message (page 6650) said: "There is general acquiescence in our present tariff system as a national policy. The first requisite to our prosperity is the continuity and stability of this economic policy. . . . . Our experience in the past has shown that sweeping revisions of the tariff are apt to produce conditions closely approaching panic in the business world. . . . Reciprocity must be treated as the hand-maiden of protection. Our first duty is to see that the protection granted by the tariff in every case where it is needed is maintained, and that reciprocity be sought for so far as it can safely be done without injury to our home industries." In his Second Annual Message (page 6712) the President seeks to refute the argument that a reduction of the tariff would curb trusts. He says: "Many of the largest corporations, many of these which should certainly be included in any proper scheme of regulation, would not be affected in the slightest degree by a change in the tariff save as such change interfered with the general prosperity of the country. The only relation of the tariff to big corporations as a whole is that the tariff makes manufactures profitable, and the tariff remedy proposed would be in effect simply to make manufactures unprofitable. To remove the tariff as a punitive measure directed against trusts would inevitably result in ruin to the weaker competitors who are struggling against them." As a corrective to conditions, the President advises the extension of reciprocity treaties. "Wherever the tariff conditions," he says, "are such that a needed change can not with advantage be made by the application of the reciprocity idea, then it can be made outright by a lowering of the duties on a certain product." In his Special Session Message of Nov. 10, 1903, the President discusses the proposed reciprocity treaty with Cuba. In his Sixth Annual Message (page 7050) the President says: "I most earnestly hope that the bill to provide a lower tariff for or else absolute free trade in Philippine products will become a law. No harm will come to any American industry; and while there will be some small but real material benefit to the Philippines, the main benefit will come by the showing made as to our purpose to do all in our power for their welfare." In his Seventh Annual Message (page 7083) on tariff revision, the President says: "This country is definitely committed to the protective system and any effort to uproot it could not but cause widespread industrial disaster. . . . But in a country of such phenomenal growth as ours it is probably well that every dozen years or so the tariff laws should be carefully scrutinized so as to see that no excessive or improper benefits are conferred thereby, that proper revenue is provided, and that our foreign trade is encouraged. . . . This means that the subject can not with wisdom be dealt with in the year preceding a Presidential election, because, as a matter of fact, experience has conclusively shown that at such a time it is impossible to get men to treat it from the standpoint of public good. In my judgment the wise time to deal with the matter is immediately after such election." In the same message the President favored the incorporation of both income tax and inheritance tax as a part of the system of Federal taxation. On page 7099, the President says: "There should be no tariff on any forest product grown in this country, and in especial there should be no tariff on wood pulp."

Civil Service.—In his First Annual Message President Roosevelt (page 6673) urged appointment in all possible cases upon the merit system, which he maintained was the only fair test of fitness; "all applicants should have a fair field and no favor, each standing on his merits as he is able to show them by practical test. In my judgment," he says, "all laws providing for the temporary employment of clerks should hereafter contain a provision that they be selected under the Civil Service law." In his Third Annual Message (page 6803) the merit system is reported as working most satisfactorily: "The completion of the reform of the civil service is recognized by good citizens everywhere as a matter of the highest importance, and the success of the merit system largely depends upon the effectiveness of the rules and the machinery provided for their enforcement." In his Fifth Annual Message (page 7011) the President says: "The question of politics in the appointment and retention of the men engaged in merely ministerial work has been practically eliminated in almost the entire field of Government employment covered by the civil service law." In a veto message of Feb. 5, 1909 (page 7176), the President urges that the employees engaged in the work of taking the thirteenth census be brought into the classified service and quotes Hon. Carroll D. Wright, who had charge of the census after 1890, as estimating that more than $2,000,000 and over a year's time would have been saved had the force been so regulated.

Public Debt.—The public debt of the United States during the years of President Roosevelt's administration proper stood as follows: July 1, 1905, $989,866,772.00; 1906, $964,435,686.79; 1907, $858,685,510; Nov. 1, 1908, $897,253,990.00.

Commerce.—In his Gubernatorial Message to the legislature of New York, in 1899, Governor Roosevelt took his stand upon the principle of taxing and regulating corporations and others who enjoyed franchises. To properly adjust taxation and to apply effective restriction were to be attained by investigation of conditions. "The first essential," he said, "is knowledge of the facts —publicity." This sentiment led to the desire expressed in his First Annual Message (page 6649) for the appointment of a Secretary of Commerce and Labor. "It should be his province to deal," he said, "with commerce in its broadest sense; including among many other things, whatever concerns labor and all matters affecting the great business corporations and our merchant marine." In his Second Annual Message (page 6712) he said: "I believe that monopolies, unjust discriminations, which prevent or cripple competition, fraudulent over-capitalization, and other evils in trust organizations and practices which injuriously affect interstate trade, can be prevented under the power of Congress to 'regulate commerce with foreign nations and among the several States' through regulations and requirements operating directly upon such commerce, the instrumentalities thereof, and those engaged therein." In speaking of the working of the Department

EXTENT OF THE UNITED STATES DURING THE ADMINISTRATION OF PRESIDENT ROOSEVELT, 1901-1909.

(NOT INCLUDING TERRITORIES)

MAINE 1820

N. H. 1788

VT. 1791

MASS. 1788

CONN. 1788

R. I. 1790

N. Y. 1788 · NEW YORK 1788

N. J. 1787

PENNSYLVANIA 1787

DEL. 1787

MD. 1788

WEST VIRGINIA 1863

VIRGINIA 1788

NORTH CAROLINA 1789

SOUTH CAROLINA 1788

GEORGIA 1788

FLORIDA 1845

OHIO 1803

KENTUCKY 1792

TENNESSEE 1796

ALABAMA 1819

MISSISSIPPI 1817

MICHIGAN 1837

INDIANA 1816

ILLINOIS 1818

MISSOURI 1821

ARKANSAS 1836

LOUISIANA 1812

WISCONSIN 1848

IOWA 1846

OKLAHOMA 1907

TEXAS 1845

MINNESOTA 1858

NEBRASKA 1867

KANSAS 1861

NORTH DAKOTA 1889

SOUTH DAKOTA 1889

COLORADO 1876

WYOMING 1890

MONTANA 1889

UTAH 1896

IDAHO 1890

NEVADA 1864

WASHINGTON 1889

OREGON 1859

CALIFORNIA 1850

FLAG OF 1909

of Commerce and Labor, the President said in his Third Annual Message (page 6785): "Publicity in corporate affairs will tend to do away with ignorance and will afford facts upon which intelligent action may be taken. Systematic, intelligent investigation is already developing facts the knowledge of which is essential to a right understanding of the needs and duties of the business world. The Department of Commerce will be not only the clearing house for information regarding the business transactions of the Nation, but the executive arm of the Government to aid in strengthening our domestic and foreign markets, in perfecting our transportation facilities, in building up our merchant marine, in preventing the entrance of undesirable immigrants, in improving commercial and other industrial conditions and in bringing together on common ground those necessary partners in his Fourth Annual Message (page 6901) he industrial progress—capital and labor." In said: "Above all else we must strive to keep the highways of commerce open to all on equal terms; and to do this it is necessary to put a complete stop to all rebates." In his Fifth Annual Message (page 6974) the President said: "I am in no sense hostile to corporations. This is an age of combination, and any effort to prevent all combination will be not only useless, but in the end vicious, because of the contempt for law which the failure to enforce law inevitably produces. . . . The corporation has come to stay, just as the trade union has come to stay. Each can do and has done great good. Each should be favored so long as it does good. But each should be sharply checked where it acts against law and justice." The President's Special Message of May 4, 1906, explicitly sets forth the conditions of the Standard Oil Company and the railroads as they appear to the Bureau of Corporations. Stock Yard and Packing House abuses are dealt with in his message of June 4, 1906.

In his Sixth Annual Message (page 7078) the President said: "Among the points to be aimed at should be the prohibition of unhealthy competition, such as by rendering service at an actual loss for the purpose of crushing out competition, the prevention of inflation of capital, and the prohibition of a corporation's making exclusive trade with itself a condition of having any trade with itself."

Roosevelt, Theodore:
Accident compensation for workmen discussed, 7087.
Addresses—
Detroit, to Spanish War veterans, 6699.
Luther Church memorial at Washington, 6972.
White House, to Interparliamentary Union, 6891.
Admission of states, 7020.
Adulterated foods, regulation of interstate traffic in, 7012.
Agricultural experiment stations, report on, 6733, 6861.
Agriculture, Department of—
Activities of, 6655, 6905.
Importance of, 7091.
Secretary of, authority of, to check spread of contagious diseases among animals, 6948.
Urgent need for improvement in, 7257.

Alaska—
Alexander Archipelago Forest Reserve set apart in, 6697.
Boundary line, location of, 6792.
Boundary tribunal, members of, 6793.
Report of, 6826.
Delegate in Congress, recommended, 6920, 7019.
Development of, discussed, 6793, 6799, 6920.
Forest Reserve established in, 6697.
Fur seal service, supervision of by Bureau of Fisheries, 7230.
Government of, discussed, 7052, 7103.
Government railroad for, 6920, 7019.
Government roads and railway for, 6920.
Harbor Island (Sitka) reserved for Revenue Cutter Service, 6701.
Legislation needed for, 6725, 6799, 6919.
Local government for, 7103.
Needs of the people of, 6920, 6941, 7103.
Resources of, 6913.
Salmon commission, report of, 6860.
Alaskan Indians, character of, 7020.
Alaska-Yukon Pacific Exposition, object of, 7052, 7103.
Alcohol, denatured, freedom from tax, 7224.
Alexander Archipelago Forest Reserve set apart in Alaska, 6697.
Algeciras Convention, commercial rights under, 7062.
Aliens, naturalization of, report on, 6935.
Rights of, under treaties, enforcement of, 7055.
Amendment to Constitution—
Needed to impose income tax, 7044.
Relating to marriage and divorce, suggested, 7048.
Suggested, to authorize control of corporations, 6649.
America's attitude toward the world, 7059.
Place among great nations, 6709.
American citizens detained as British prisoners of war, 6681.
American Republics—
Attitude toward, 6923.
Bureau of, work of, 7125, 7231.
Conference of, 7057.
International union of, proposed building for, 6824.
Mediation in war between, 7062.
Sanitary convention of, report of, 6737, 6823.
Americanism, definition of, 6915.

Beet Sugar, progress of industry in United States, 6865, 6947.

Big business, benefits of government supervision of, 7079.

Biographical sketch of, 6637.

Biological Survey, services rendered by, 7106.

Birth rate, alarming decrease in, 7048.

Black Mesa Forest Reserve, part of, restored to public domain, 6700.

Boll weevil—
Attention called to, 6802.
Report on, 6949.

Bookbinder (W. A. Miller) restored to service in Government Printing Office, 6783.

Boston agreement, combination of corporations in, 7195.

Brazil, courtesies extended by, 7060.

Bribery, crime of, should be made extraditable, 6791.

British schooner Lillie, damages for, 6730, 6824.

British steamship Eastry, damages for, 6734, 6859, 7365.

British steamship Lindisfarne, damages for, 6934.

Brownsville, discharge of colored troops at, 7329.
Report on disorder at, 7347.

Buffalo, Pan-American exposition creditable to, 6675.

Buffalo, preservation of herds, 7013.

Bureaus, redistribution of, 7229.

·Business prosperity, effect of laws on, 6645.

Cabinet officer to deal with commerce and labor, 6649.

Cabinet, secretary of commerce, with seat in, asked, 6716.

Cable, need for, to Hawaii and Philippines, thence to Asia, 6663, 6718.

Cable, Pacific, provided for, 6719.

Cables damaged during Spanish War, claims for, 6824.

Calaveras big tree grove, preservation of, 6859.

California, land reserved in, for lighthouse sites, 6701, 6702, 6705.

Campaign contributions, publication of, 7105.

Canal Zone, report of visit to, 7305.

Capital and Labor. (See Labor.)

Capital, combinations of, 6790.
Organized, problem of control of, 6895.

Captains of industry, achievements of, 6646.

Census—
Act to provide for, 7178.
Clerks and employees, civil service rules to apply to, 7176, 7228.
Office should be permanent bureau, 6676.
Thirteenth, preparation for, 7104.

Central American Republics. (See American Republics.)

Charleston Exposition, commended, 6675.

Cheyenne Indian lands disposed of, 6873.

Chicago customs service, examiners of tea and tobacco added to, 6971.

Child Labor—
Investigation of conditions of urged, 6898, 6983.
Prohibition of, throughout the nation, 7342.

Child Labor Law—
Model, for District of Columbia, 7036, 7090, 7342.
Probable enactment of, 7189.

Children, dependent, conference on care of, 7358.

China—
Agent appointed to rearrange tariff duties with, 6700.
Agreement with the powers, 6678.
American trade in, plans for extension of, 6915.
Boycott of American goods in, 7010.
Commercial treaty with, 6797.
Consular service in, should be more adequate, 7009.
Defenselessness evils shown by example of, 7149.
Friendship for United States, 7124.
Open door in, advocated, 6679.
Preparedness, need for, shown by, 7149.

China and Korea, extraterritorial system in, 6939.

China and Mexico, fixed ratio for gold and silver money for, 6735, 6787, 6825, 6941.

Chinese immigration discussed, 6650, 7009.

Chinese indemnity, remission of, 7123.

Cities, plan to make Washington model for, 6902.

Citizenship, laws relating to, defective, 6917.

Civil Service—
Commission and heads of departments to appoint unclassified laborers, 6707.
Examinations—
Instruction in, by government employees forbidden, 6970.
Questions, sources of, 7010.
Extension of classified service to District of Columbia, 6673.
Laws extended to employees—
In Executive Department, 6893.
In Government Printing Office, 6893.
In Philippines, 6892.
Of Isthmian Canal Commission, 6893.

Holding company rights of, discussed, 7079.

International importance of, 6646.

Legislation governing—
Character of, 6785.
Discussed, 7190.

Overcapitalization of, discussed, 6647, 6712, 6976, 7039, 7077, 7130, 7132, 7139.

Political contributions from, 7023.

Power of State to regulate, address of Governor Fort, of New Jersey, 7135.

Publicity of accounts of, 7199.

Publicity of methods, 6648.

Securities of, investors in, protection for, 7079.

State regulation of, inadequate, 6975, 7073.

Tariff does not control, 6712.

Corrupt leaders, types of, 7034.

Country life, report of commission on, 7253.

Courts, delays in, remedies for, 7209.

Creek Indians, agreement with, 6696.

Criminal action against evil-doers, 7024.

Criminal laws, revision of, urged, 6918, 7003.

Cuba—
Commercial reciprocity treaty with, 6740, 6741.
Copyright law extended to, 6781.
Duties on vessels and cargoes from, suspended, 6690.
Independence of, 6660.
Insurrection in, 7056.
Markets of, controlled by American producers, 6683.
Peace restored under provisional government, 7121.
Policy of United States toward, 6682, 7057.
Prosperity of, under occupation, 7234.
Provisional Government for, 7056.
Reciprocity Treaty with, 6660, 6682, 6717.
United States Naval Stations in, 6742.

Culebra Island placed under jurisdiction of Navy Department, 6703.

Currency—
Elasticity in, urged, 6654, 6715, 6914, 6989, 7080, 7082, 7198.
Emergency, recommended, 7080.
Integrity of, 6787.
Legislation needed to secure stability in, 7049.

Custom House, site at Ft. Yuma, Ariz., reserved, 6705.

Dams in navigable streams, conditions of grants for, 7166.

Davidson, Francis S., bill for relief of returned, 6736, 6773.

Debts, public, compulsory collection of, by foreign nations, 7060.

Department methods, economy in, 7105.

Desert Lands. (See Lands, Desert.)

Disarmament, result of, forecast, 6922, 6993.

Discontent, preachers of, harm wrought by, 7033.

Dishonest business methods denounced, 7140.

District of Columbia—
Alleys of, 6650.
Charities, Board of, 6804.
Child Labor Law for, urged, 7036.
Enactment of, probable, 7189.
Classified service in, urged, 6673.
Corporation laws of, weak, 6943.
Employers' Liability Law for, urged, 6728, 6896, 6982.
Factory Laws for, 6650.
Industrial training in schools of, 7045.
Model Laws for, 6983.
Municipal government ideal should be reflected in, 6728.
Needs of, 7356.
Orphans in, care of, 7361.
Truant Court for, 7035.

Divorce. (See Marriage and Divorce.)

Dominican Republic, export of arms and ammunition to, forbidden, 6968.

Drago Doctrine, statement of, 7061.

Eastry, British steamship, damages to owners of, 6734, 6859, 7365.

Economic policy, prosperity dependent upon, 6652.

Education, National Bureau of, purpose of, 7227.

Eight-hour day in Government service, 7035, 7208.

Eight-hour law, extension of to all Government contracts, 7088.

Elections—
Bribery and corruption in, 6990.
Federal, Law to punish fraud in, 6917.

Employers' Liability Law—
Constitutionality of, 7087.
For District of Columbia, 6982.
General aspects of, discussed, 7206, 7208.
Judges, opinions of, 7216.
New enactment of, 7189.
Re-enactment in constitutional form urged, 7126.
Re-enactment of, 7342.
Shortcomings of, 7036.
Urged, 6728, 6896.

Endicott Board, Report of, 7284.

European war command not to be given, 8260.

Forbidden to give instruction in civil service examinations, 6970.
Half holidays for, 7208.
Service expected from, 6650.
Government printing office, civil service laws extended to employees of, 6893.
Government publications discussed, 6728.
Government right of appeal in criminal cases, 7023.
Government service—
Merit system in, 6728.
Union labor in, 6897.
Grain, standard for grades of, suggested, 7093.
Grazing homesteads, size of, 7004.
Grazing lands, extent of, 7096.
Great Britain and United States, convention between, 6736.
Guatemala, Salvador and Honduras, war between, 7061.
Gun-foundry board, purpose of, 7284.
Hague Peace Conference—
First—
Monroe Doctrine supported by, 6664.
Unsettled problems after, 6991.
Second—
Calling of, 6923, 6991.
Discussed, 7117, 7120.
Preliminaries to, 7065.
Third, provisions for, 7120.
Hague Permanent Court of Arbitration—
Discussed, 6993.
Report of case of United States vs. Mexico, 6731.
United States and Mexico first case to be considered, 6718.
Venezuelan claims before, 6794, 6941.
Half holidays for government employees, 7208.
Harbor Island, Alaska, reserved for revenue cutter service, 6701.
Hawaii—
Cable to, need for, 6663.
Condition and aims of, 7051.
Development of, discussed, 7018, 7232.
Fortification of, recommended, 7017.
Legislation for, aim of, 6660.
Leprosy in, study of, recommended, 6921.
Light-house in, 6799.
Taken over, 6867.
Needs of, 6921.
Steamer connection with, 7104.
Health—
Bureau of, legislation to strengthen, 7104.
Public, protection of, 7228.
Hepburn law, money needed to enforce, 7190.

"Hermitage," the home of Andrew Jackson, funds for upkeep recommended, 7104.
Homestead lands, manner of drawing for, described, 6878, 6885.
Homesteads, Uintah Indian lands allotted for, 6956.
Honduras, Guatemala and Salvador, war between, 7061.
Honolulu Harbor, dredging needed for, 6921.
Hospital corps, reorganization of needed, 7000.
Humphreys, Judge, comments on decision of, in case of beef-packers, 7291.
Immigrants—
Character of, desired, 6651, 6916.
Chinese, discussed, 7009.
Educational and physical tests for, 6651.
Exclusion of immoral and anarchistic, 6651, 7007.
Question of, discussed, 6788, 7007.
Steamship companies promote coming of, 7006.
Immigration laws discussed, 6651, 6715.
Inaugural address, as—
President, 6930.
Vice President, 6638.
Inauguration, illustration of, opposite 6932.
Income taxes—
Constitutionality of, 7044.
Urged, 7042, 7083.
Indian agents, qualifications for, 6802.
Report of investigation of, 6864.
Indian lands opened to settlement, 6687, 6702, 6873, 6875, 6882, 6956.
Indian service, physicians in, allowed private practice, 6893.
Removal from politics, 7225.
Indian Territory and Oklahoma, admission as one state, 7020.
Indians—
Absorption of, into body politic, 6674, 6726.
Citizen, needs of, 7014.
Citizens of United States, 6674.
Education of, 6802.
Liquors should be denied, 6675.
Tribal funds of, allotment of, 6674.
Welfare of, 6674, 6911.
Industrial accidents, deaths due to, 7110.
Industrial and technical education discussed, 7045.
Industrial disputes, compulsory government investigation of, 7089.
Industrialism the dominant note in modern life, 6895.

Labor attacks on, discussed, 7209, 7211.

Laws made by, 7213.

Judgments, setting aside of, on technicalities, 7025.

Judicial opinions of—
Employers' Liability Law, 7216.
Interstate Commerce Law, 7217.

Justice, miscarriage of, in case of beef-packers, 7291.
Obstructions to, in case of offenders against the Republic, 6918, 7003.

Kansas, land districts in, consolidated, 6706.

Korea and China, extraterritorial system in, 6939.

Kosciusko, statue of, to be erected in Washington by Polish citizens, 6860.

Labor and Commerce, Cabinet Officer to deal with, 6649.

Labor—
And Capital, problem of, 6715, 6899, 7090.
Bureau, work of, 6898.
Commissioner of, report of Colorado disturbance, 6942.
Conditions for, 6650.
Contract, convict, should be done away with, 6650.
Demands of, for judiciary legislation, 7209.
Disputes—
Effect of investigation of, 7036.
Injunctions in, discussed, 6983.
Successive steps for settlement of, 7089.
Disturbance in Colorado, report on, 6942.
Eight-hour day for, recommended, 6650.
Hours of, on railroads, 6982.
Law, child, for District of Columbia, urged, 7036.
Leadership of, discussed, 6973, 7071.
Of women and children, investigation of, 7035.
Organized—
Attacks on judges by, 7209.
Problem of control of, 6895.
Organizations, exemption of, from anti-trust law, discussed, 7194.
Protection of, by tariff, from foreign competitors, 6649.
Union, in government service, 6897.
Welfare of, discussed, 7205.

Laborers, Chinese, exclusion of, recommended, 6650.
Exclusion of foreign contract, 6649.
(Unclassified) to be appointed by heads of departments and Civil Service Commission, 6707, 6780.

Land Laws—
Changes needed in, 6800, 7004, 7302.
Commission to investigate, 6801.
Report of, 6863.
Fraud under, 7302.

Land Office, receipts of, 6800.

Lands—
Arid, reclamation and irrigation of, 6658, 6724, 6801, 6908, 7004.
Coal—
Government ownership of, 7038, 7100.
Leasing of, 7303.
Desert, frauds committed under, 7302.
Districts in Kansas consolidated, 6706.
Executive department holdings of, 6739.
For townsites, reservation of, 6874.
Fraud in, 7096.
Grazing, control of, 7304.
Grazing, illegal fences on, 7096.
Mineral and coal claims, 7302.
Dishonestly acquired, 6790.
Philippine, disposition of, 6815.
Public—
Classification of, 7266.
Commission to revise, creation of, urged, 6725.
Report of, 6911, 6947.
Home builders to possess, 6725, 6800.
Indian. (See Indian Lands.)
Railroad grants, timber on, 7303.
Timber and stone act, harm done by, 7302.
Tree-planting, set apart, 6709.

Latin American Republics, importance of, 7231.

Law enforcement, appropriation needed for, 6790.

Laws' delay, consequence of, 7029.

Legislation, ill-considered and vicious, 7216.

Leprosy, study of, in Hawaiian Islands, recommended, 6921.

Levees, Mississippi, government support of, 7005.

Lewis and Clark Exposition proposed, 6798.

Library of Congress, scope of activities, 6676.

Life-saving efforts, recognition of, 6896.

Life-Saving Service, pensions for, recommended, 7013.

Light-house reservation in—
San Bernardino, Cal., 6701, 6705.
St. Nicholas Island, Cal., 6702.

Light-houses in—
Alaska, 6799.
Hawaii, taken over, 6867.

Naval armaments, limitation of, hopeless, 7113.

Naval base needed in Philippines, 6806.

Naval cadet, title should be abolished and midshipman restored, 6667.

Naval Militia, should be encouraged, 6669.

Naval reserve needed as auxiliary, 6669.

Naval Station, land in Luzon, P. I., reserved for, 6701.

Navy—
Battleship fleet cruise around the world, 7237.
Battleships for, four needed yearly, 7147, 7236.
Colombian activities of, 6741.
Cruise of battleship fleet around the world, 7237.
Desertion from, denounced, 6684.
Discharges from, 6707.
Efficiency of—
Credit for, 6667.
Maintenance of, 7000, 7067.
Peace assured by, 6666, 7117.
General staff recommended for, 6806, 7237.
Good conduct pay, 6702.
Gunnery practice in, should be unceasing, 6668.
Hospital ships for, 7237.
Increase of, urged upon Congress, 6722, 7148.
Lessons for, taught by recent history, 7001.
Manoeuvres and marksmanship, 6722.
Mess attendants, classification and pay of, 6702.
Midshipmen, oversupply of, 7116.
Monroe Doctrine needs strong, 6666, 6805.
Offensive nature of, 7114.
Officers' grades in, 7115.
Pay fixed in certain branches of, 6700, 6702, 6708.
Personnel of—
Discussed, 6722.
Efficiency of, 7115.
Improvement in, 7068.
Increase needed in, 7002.
Undesirable, discussed, 6684, 6773.
Reserve force composition, 6669.
Squadron sent to Turkey, 6796.
Target range, land for, reserved in Washington, 6706.
War requirements of, 7114.
Worn-out vessels of, 7001.

Navy Department, Culebra Island placed under jurisdiction of, 6703.

Negro, education of, benefit to whites, 7032.

Netherlands, reciprocal tariff concessions granted, 6961.
Text of commercial agreement with, 6962.

Neutrality—
Enjoined upon Government officials during Russo-Japanese War, 6892.
Proclaimed in Russo-Japanese War, 6868.

Neutrals, rights and duties of, defined at Hague, 7120.

Newfoundland, reciprocity treaty with, 6717.

New Mexico and Arizona, statehood for, 7020, 7229.

New Mexico and Oklahoma, boundary between Colorado and, 6937.

New York Central Railroad, conviction and fine of, 7026.

Nicaragua, Norwegian steamer, claims of, 6826.

North Dakota, Indian lands in, opened to settlement, 6882.

Norway, copyright privileges extended to, 6954.

Norwegian steamer, Nicaragua, claims of, 6826.

Ocean Mail—
Extension of act for, recommended, 7108.
Lines, establishment of, 7231.
Service, 6788.

Offenders against government, difficulties of prosecution of, 6918, 7003.

Offices, unnecessary, abolition of, 6988.

Oil industry, freight rates in connection with, 7293.
Investigation of, urged, 7288.

Oil lands, leasing of, 7303.

Oklahoma and Indian Territory, admission as one state, 7020.

Oklahoma and New Mexico, boundary between Colorado and, 6937.

Oklahoma, Fort Sill reservation restored to public domain, 6695.

Oklahoma, statehood for, 7103.

Old age pensions, suggested, 7206.

Ordnance Department, claim of Lieut. Col. Scott against, for use of his sighting system, 6826.

Orient—
Importance of, for United States trade, 6914.
Trade with, 7362.

Overcapitalization—
Evils of, discussed, 6647, 6712, 6976, 7039, 7077, 7130, 7132, 7139.
Power of Congress to regulate, 6647, 6712.

Pacific trade, possibilities of discussed, 7052.

Panama—
Convention with for construction of canal, 6816.

Miraflores Island in, reserved for quarantine, 6708.
Needs of the Island, 7051.
Ponce harbor, pier for, 6733.
Railway and light company ordinances, 6730, 6825, 6932, 6934.
Telephone line for, 6732.
Visit to, report of, 7299.
Welfare of, under United States, 6660, 6720, 7018.
Portrait of, 6636.
Postal Savings Bank system recommended, 7102, 7226, 7346.
Postal service discussed, 6677, 6913. (See also Mail.)
Postmasters, fourth-class, protection of, civil service laws for, 7102.
Post Office Department, revenue of, 6723.
Predatory wealth, acts of representatives of, 7135.
Pribilof Islands, destruction of seals on, 7063.
Prince Henry of Prussia, committee to entertain, 6703.
Printing, government—
Cost of, 6728.
Extravagance in, 6914, 6988.
Printing Office, supervision of, by executive department, 7229.
Prize Courts, International, established, 7120.
Prosperity of United States discussed, 6646, 6652, 6710, 6894.
Protective system discussed, 7083.
Public Lands Commission, report of, 7096.
Publicity in corporation management discussed, 6648, 6711.
Pure Food legislation—
Benefits of, 7225.
Government control exemplified by, 7080.
National, need of, 7038.
Quarantine law, national, need for, 6914.
Quarantine, Miraflores Island, Porto Rico, reserved for, 6708.
Queen Victoria, sorrow expressed for death of, 6680.
Race hatred, discussed, 7031.
Race suicide discussed, 7048.
Railroad land grants, timber on, 7303.
Railroads—
Accidents on, discussed, 7086.
Agreements, lawful, among, 7130, 7342.
Block signals for, urged, 6982.
Control of, by Interstate Commerce Commission, 7190, 7200. (See also Rates and Securities.)
Criminal acts of, 7025.
Discriminations in coal and oil, 7287.

Employees of, hours of, 6982, 7035.
Federal inspection of, suggested, 7086.
Government ownership of, discussed, 6981.
Personnel on, discussed, 6980.
Rates—
Equality of, desirable, 6655.
Government control of, 7038.
Maximum and minimum, 6977.
Rebate system of, denounced, 7025.
Regulation of, by Interstate Commerce Commission, 6902, 6977, 7079.
Safety appliances for, urged, 6982.
Safety on, 6897.
Securities, control of, by Interstate Commerce Commission, 7200, 7342.
Shipments, abuses in, 6901.
Receivers of common carriers, Attorney General to appoint, 7342.
Reciprocity arrangements—
Discussed, 6652.
Urged, 6682, 6714.
With—
Cuba, 6682, 6717, 6740, 6743.
Germany, 7283.
Netherlands, 6961.
Newfoundland, 6717.
Spain, 6966.
Reclamation (See also Irrigation)—
Arid lands, importance of, 6658.
Policy of, outlined, 6660.
Service—
Organization of, 6801.
Purpose of, 7095.
Work of, 6908.
Red Cross Societies in foreign countries, report on, 6863.
Revenue Cutter Service—
Island in Sitka Harbor, Alaska, reserved for, 6701.
Retirement from granted, 6708.
Revenues and expenditures—
Discussed, 6654, 6787.
Readjustment needed, 6988.
Record of, during six years, 7082.
Rifle practice, National Board for promotion of, 7070.
Rio Grande, distribution of waters of, 6737.
Root, Secretary, address before third conference of American Republics, 7059.
Rosecrans, Major Gen. W. S., Federal employees excused from duty to attend funeral of, 6706.
Rural Free Delivery discussed, 6724, 6798.
Russo-Japanese War, neutrality proclaimed in, and enjoined, 6868, 6892.

Rubber Industry.—Crude rubber is prepared from a milky sap (latex) of certain plants found between the latitude of 30° north latitude and 30° south. In other words, the plants which give rubber are found only in tropical or semi-tropical climates. Crude rubber is produced in South America, Central America, Asia and Africa, and on many tropical islands, but the best rubber comes from the valley of the Amazon, of which the seaport is Para.

The first importation of rubber into the United States was regarded as a curiosity, and no commercial value was placed upon it. It could be bought for about five cents a pound. Around 1825 some hundred pairs of rubber shoes were brought in and sold, however. In 1833 the Roxbury India Rubber Company was formed to make rubber varnish, but failed several years later when its rubber varnish was found impracticable.

The history of the rubber industry in its modern aspects begins with the invention of the vulcanizing process around 1840 by Goodyear and Hancock, although methods of utilizing soft rubber had been perfected several years previously. However, many difficulties were encountered in transmitting the vulcanizing process to the various methods of manufacturing various articles, so that many branches of the rubber industry did not become stable until many years after 1840. For instance, it was not until 1860 that the manufacture of various druggists' sundries made of rubber became established on a firm basis.

In 1877, the first solid rubber tires were manufactured, followed shortly by the pneumatic tires. Soon the demand for tires became greater than the demand for other rubber goods, and the adjoining figures will show the predominating position played in the rubber industry by the production of tires. Indeed, it was the great demand for tires which stimulated so tremendously the cost of rubber which has characterized the industry of late years, although to some extent the prices have advanced because of wasteful methods of collecting rubber and because insufficient rubber acreage has been planted to atone for the acreage destroyed.

There have been many attempts to manufacture artificial or synthetic rubber, but up to the present time none of them has succeeded, although many other substances today are used as admixtures in the rubber industry.

A special report of the Census Bureau gives complete statistics of the rubber industry in the United States. The report covers twelve months just before the relations of the United States with the war in Europe upset the equilibrium of all industries, and hence gives a true picture of the

In studying the adjoining figures, it must be remembered that in recent years the value of all commodities increased and consequently the value of the dollar decreased comparatively.

The Census report covers establishments manufacturing chiefly rubber belting and hose, those producing chiefly rubber boots and shoes, and establishments producing other rubber goods, especially rubber tires, rubber clothing, druggists' and stationers' sundries, etc. It does not include establishments manufacturing chiefly elastic woven goods. The findings of the report for that year will be found in an adjoining table.

Of the wage-earners engaged in the industry in the census year, 80% were male and 20% female, as compared with 76% male in 1909 and 24% female.

In the report year, there were 87 proprietors and firm members, as compared with 103 in 1909; 514 salaried officers, as compared with 348 in 1909; 998 superintendents and managers, as compared with 667 in 1909; and 13,200 clerks and other subordinate officials (in 1909, 5,677).

The greatest number of wage-earners are employed in the spring and early summer.

In the belting and hose section, the leading state was New Jersey, where 2,239 of the 5,515 wage-earners in this section were employed.

In the boot and shoe section, the leading state was Massachusetts, where 8,087 of the 18,687 wage-earners in this section were employed.

The leading state in the general section was Ohio, where more than half of the 50,220 wage-earners in this section were employed, followed by New Jersey (6,316), Massachusetts, New York, Pennsylvania, and Connecticut.

The greatest number of wage-earners in the rubber industry were employed where the hours of work were 54-60 in number (31,739); 23,969 were employed where the weekly hours were 54; 9,959 where the hours were 48-54; 4,750, where the hours were 60; 3,216 where the hours were 48 or less; and 389 where the hours were more than 60.

In the report year, 12% of the establishments were owned by individuals (in 1909, 16%); 83% by corporations (73% in 1909); 5% by others (11% in 1909).

	Total	Establishments Producing Chiefly—		
		Belting and Hose	Boots and Shoes	Others
No. Establishments	342	18	23	301
Persons Engaged	88,821	6,205	20,359	62,257
Capital	$267,671,422	$22,436,922	$46,051,464	$199,183,036
Salaries and Wages	60,445,980	4,595,615	11,944,733	43,905,632
Rent and Taxes	2,226,322	164,958	345,678	1,715,686
Cost of Materials	163,034,713	12,967,004	23,956,036	126,111,673
Value of Products	300,993,796	23,560,089	53,822,123	223,610,784

The following figures reveal the growth of the rubber industry in the United States in recent years:—

	Report Year	1909	1899	1889
No. Establishments	342	267	301	167
Persons Engaged	88,821	56,059	(1)	(1)
Capital	$267,671,422	$162,144,564	$78,463,771	$36,764,825
Salaries and Wages	60,445,980	32,977,676	18,575,728	9,526,909
Cost of Materials	163,034,713	122,745,102	60,240,559	26,243,853
Value of Products	300,993,796	197,394,638	99,880,693	42,853,817

(1) Figures not available.

99% of the wage-earners were employed by the corporations, who produced goods to the value of 99% of the whole.

83% of the value of the products were manufactured in establishments where the production was valued at more than $1,000,000 annually.

Rum, Romanism and Rebellion.—At a meeting of clergymen of all denominations held in the Fifth Avenue Hotel, New York, during the Presidential campaign of 1884, Rev. Samuel D. Burchard, in an address favoring the election of the Republican candidate, described the Democrats as the party of Rum, Romanism and Rebellion. The phrase was immediately taken up and used to alienate many persons otherwise friendly to the Republican party, and as the party in that year suffered defeat by a very small margin many attributed it to the utterance of this alliterative phrase.

Rumania.—Rumania is situated in southeastern Europe, northeast of the Balkan Peninsula, and consists of the eastern territory of Dobrudja, on the Black Sea, the northern territory of Moldavia between the Carpathians and the river Pruth, and the southern territory of Walachia, between the Transylvanian Alps and the river Danube. These territories lie between 43° 25'-48° 15' N. latitude and extend from 22° 25'-29° 40' E. longitude. The political neighbors of Rumania are Russia (Bessarabia) on the east, Hungary on the northwest and north, Servia on the west, and Bulgaria on the south.

Physical Features.—The country lies mainly in the basin of the Danube, the plain consisting of rich pasture and agricultural land, the intermediate region of the vineyard and fruit districts and the higher slopes and valleys of birch, larch and pine forests.

The Danube enters the country at the junction of the Hungarian-Servian-Rumanian boundary in the extreme west, through the Iron Gates between the Balkans and Carpathians (Transylvanian Alps), and forms the southwestern boundary with Servia and the southern boundary with Bulgaria for nearly 300 miles. The "Iron Gates," so called from the numerous rocks in the waterway, have been rendered navigable by blowing up the principal obstructions (see European Commission of the Danube post). The Danube flows northeast and north, and effects a confluence with the Sereth and Pruth before reaching the Black Sea through the delta of north-eastern Dobrudja. Many tributaries join the Danube from the foothills of the northern mountains across the Walachian Plain.

The Danube is frozen over every winter, in some years for three months. The climate of Rumania is extreme, with intense cold and fierce summer heat.

History.—The Kingdom of Rumania has its origin in the union of the Danubian Principalities of Walachia and Moldavia and the addition thereto of a strip of southern Bessarabia, under the Treaty of Paris in 1856. The principalities were an integral part of the Turkish Dominions, but for many years a spirit of independence has been exhibited, although tribute was paid to the Sultan. In 1859 the Conventions of the two principalities met at Bucharest and Jassy and elected Prince Alexander John Cuza as ruler, under the suzerainty of the Porte. Prince Cuza reigned from 1859-1866, in which year he abdicated, and Prince Charles Antony of Hohenzollern-Sigmaringen was elected in his stead. By the Treaty of Berlin, July 13, 1878, the new Principality was recognized as an independent State, and the territory of the Dobrudja was recognized as part of the Principality. Rumania was forced into the Balkan war of 1913, and at its conclusion acquired further territory from Bulgaria. King Charles died in November, 1914, and was succeeded by his nephew, Ferdinand.

Government.—On March 14 (27), 1881, Rumania was raised to a Kingdom, and recognized as such by all the Great Powers, the Prince being crowned at Bucharest on May 9 (22), 1881. The crown is hereditary in the male line of the house of Hohenzollern-Sigmaringen, and by a law of March 14 (27), 1889, Prince Ferdinand of Hohenzollern, nephew of the King, was declared heir-presumptive to the throne. Rumania is not a Balkan State and took no part in the war against Turkey in 1912-1913, but secured a readjustment of her southeastern frontier while Bulgaria was at war with Greece and Servia in 1913.

Under the Constitution there is a parliament of two houses. The Senate consists of the Heir-Apparent, the two Archbishops and six Bishops, and the Rectors of the Universities of Bucharest and Jassy, with 109 senators, elected for four years by electoral colleges in each constituency. The Chamber of Deputies consists of 183 members, elected by three colleges, the first and second composed of direct electors on a property and educational franchise, the third being formed of the remaining tax-payers, of whom the illiterate vote indirectly, the remainder being direct voters with the other colleges.

The law is based principally upon the Code Napoléon, and the courts consist of communal and circuit courts with appeals to the sessional courts.

The kingdom is divided into thirty-three departments governed by Prefects, and are subdivided into sub-prefectures and communes.

Population.—The population may be estimated at 7,250,000 in 1913 (including the population of the territory ceded by Bulgaria), and of this total over 6,000,000 are Rumanians (Vlachs), the remainder being Jews, Armenians, Gipsies, Greeks. Germans, Turks, Tartars, Magyars, Servians and Bulgarians. The Jews and Armenians increase more rapidly than the Vlach or other racial elements. The Rumanian language is of Latin origin, with many borrowed words from Magyar or Greek sources. For the army see Armies of the World.

Navy.—The Navy consists (1913) of thirty vessels on the Black Sea and the Danube, and includes one cruiser of 5,000 tons and six gunboats; four torpedo-boat destroyers are being built in Italy. The Navy is manned by 140 officers and 2,200 seamen.

Finance.—The budget for 1914-1915 provided for an expenditure of the equivalent of $91,877,000, in anticipation of a revenue of $94,062,000. The debt in 1913 was stated at 1,814,991,615 leu, the leu, the unit of value, being equivalent to $0.19.3 United States money.

Production and Industry.—The soil of the Walachian Plain, and of the lower districts of Moldavia, is among the most fertile in the world, and the productive vineyards (176,452 acres) had an output of 21,855,614 gallons of wine in 1911. There are close on 1,000,000 acres of meadow land for hay. The Live Stock includes cattle and buffaloes, sheep, goats, pigs, horses, mules and asses. Since 1886 State control has prevented the further depletion of the forest area, which lies principally in the mountain valleys of northwest Moldavia. Petroleum, salt, lignite and brown coal are found and largely worked, salt being a Government monopoly, while iron, copper, lead, mercury, cinnabar, cobalt, nickel, sulphur, arsenic, and china clay also occur. The petroleum (and ozokerite) industry is reviving, and now assumes first-class importance. Stone, granite, and marble are now largely worked, and amber is found in valuable quantities. There are many mineral springs, and some of the State-supported spas are much frequented, Baltzateshte in particular being a favorite resort for invalids from eastern Europe.

Railways.—In 1910 there were 3,755 kilometers of line open for traffic, almost the entire system being State owned. There are five lines from the northern to the southern boundaries and there are east-west lines through the capital.

An International Commission was created by the Treaty of Paris (1856) with enlarged powers under the Treaty of Berlin (1878) for the control of the navigation of the Danube. The Commission exercises sovereign powers over the navigation of the river, the headquarters being at Galatz. The cost of administration is met by dues and amounts to about £60,000 annually. A large dock has been opened (1892) at Braila, and the Iron Gates were rendered navigable in 1896 by the destruction of the dangerous rocks in the waterway.

Entrance into European War.—The question of Rumania's entry into the war was settled Aug. 28, 1916, when a note declaring that Rumania from 9 o'clock on the evening of Aug. 27, considered herself in a state of war with Austria-Hungary was presented to the Austro-Hungarian Foreign Minister by the Rumanian Minister at Vienna.

According to the note the persecution of Rumanians by Austro-Hungarian officials was alleged, and it was charged that agreements which existed between Rumania and the former members of the Triple Alliance had been broken in letter and spirit from the time Germany and Austria entered the war. Italy, the declaration said, was obliged to detach herself from Austria and Germany.

In conclusion, the communication set forth as follows the motives in compelling Rumania to enter the war:

First—The Rumanian population in Austrian territories is exposed to the hazards of war and of invasion.

Second—Rumania believes that by intervening she can shorten the world war.

Third—Rumania places herself on the side of those Powers which she believes can assist her most efficaciously in realizing her national ideal.

An official statement issued in Berlin said: "After Rumania, as already reported, disgracefully broke treaties concluded with Austria-Hungary and Germany she declared war yesterday against our ally. The Imperial German Minister to Rumania has received instructions to request his passports and to declare to the Rumanian Government that Germany now likewise considers herself at war with Rumania."

The entrance of Rumania into the European War turned out to be one of the most pathetic tragedies of the conflict. Facing the German charge of treachery but a feeble resistance was made to the advancing Teuton armies, and within six months the entire country was in the hands of the victorious Central powers.

Trade with the United States.—The value of merchandise imported into Rumania from the United States for the year 1913 was $2,417,591, and goods to the value of $348,481 were sent thither—a balance of $2,069,110 in favor of the United States.

Rumania:

Consular convention with, 4622, 4627. Referred to, 4757.

Diplomatic relations with, 3989, 3994.

Independence of, announced, 4562.

Persecution of Israelites in, 4017, 4121, 4122.

Trade-marks, treaty regarding, 4667.

Treaty with, 4658.

Rumania, Treaties with. (For details of the consular convention of 1881 see Consular Conventions.)

Rump Convention.—A name designating a meeting of the minority members of a party convention who secede from the convention, and declare for a different policy or different candidates. One of the most notable instances of rump conventions occurred when Senator Teller of Colorado, aided by Senator Cannon of Utah, led a party of Free Silver advocates out of the Republican Convention in 1896, and virtually delivered them to the Democratic party, because the Republican platform declared for the Gold Standard.

Rural Credits. (See Farm Loan Act.) Bill for creation of, deferred, 8018. System of, recommended, 7908.

Rural Delivery. (See Division of Rural Delivery.)

Rural Free Delivery. (See Postoffice.)

Russia.—The Russian Empire, which covers nearly eight and a half million square miles of the land surface of the globe, extends from the west limits of Poland, in 17° E. longitude, to East Cape, the extremity of the Continent of Asia, in 191° E. (169° W.) longitude, and from Cape Chelyuskin, in the Taimyr Peninsula (77° 40' N. latitude), to the frontier of Afghanistan, 35° N. latitude. Of this vast area Russia in Europe is bounded on the north by the Barents Sea; on the west by Scandinavia, the Gulf of Bothnia and the Baltic Sea, and by the German and Austro-Hungarian Empires and Rumania; on the south by the Black Sea and the Caucasus; and on the east by the Caspian Sea and the Ural Mountains.

European Russia has an area exceeding 2,000,000 square miles, and is 1,700 miles from north to south, and 1,400 miles from east to west. Asiatic Russia has an area of close on 6,500,000 square miles, and is 4,000 miles from east to west, and 2,400 miles from north to south (from the Kara Sea to the Pamir boundary).

In the Gulf of Bothnia are the Karlo, East Kvarken and Aland Islands of Finland; Dagö and Osel in the Baltic; Novaya Zemlya, Koiguyev and Vaigach, in the Barents Sea; the New Siberian Islands, Bear Islands, and Wrangel Land, in the Arctic Ocean; the Commander Islands off Kamchatka; and the Shantar Islands and the northern part af Sakhalin, in the Sea of Okhotsk.

Physical Features.—European Russia consists of a vast plain, the eastern Lowland of Europe, between the Ural Mountains and the Caucasus of the east and south and the Carpathians of the southwest. The Ural Mountains, which divide the Continents of Europe and Asia, and extend from the Kara Sea to the Caspian, culminate in Tóllposs-is (5,400 feet), but the Caucasus, which run from the Black Sea to the Caspian, reach to 18,526 feet in Mount Elburz and 16,546 feet in Mount Kazbek.

Asiatic Russia is enclosed by mountain ranges within which lie the Plains of Turkestan and Siberia. The principal rivers of European Russia are the Volga, Don, Dnieper, Bug and Dniester, the Vistula, Niemen and Duna, the Neva, Onega, Dvina and Mezen, and the Pechora. Asiatic Russia contains the four great rivers, Ob, Yenisei, Lena, and Amur. Finland and the Baltic provinces contain innumerable lakes, Ladoga being the largest lake of Europe.

The climate of European Russia is typical of the most extreme Continental conditions, Moscow having a winter temperature of 12° F., while the summer temperature of the eastern portion is above 68° F. At Verkhoyansk the soil has been found to be permanently frozen to a depth of nearly 400 feet, although the summer mean temperature is higher than that of Paris.

History.—The vast Russian Empire is the outcome of the Tsardom of Muscovy, founded in the latter part of the fifteenth century by Ivan the Great, of the house of Rurik, who reigned from 1462 to 1505, and enlarged the Principality of Moscow into an autocratic kingdom over a wide territory. In 1613 the throne passed to a collateral branch of the house, Michael Romanov (1613-1645) being elected Tsar by the National Assembly. Since the accession of the Romanovs the boundaries of the Empire have been constantly extended. Little Russia, or the Ukraine, was annexed in 1667, and under Peter the Great (1689-1725) an outlet was acquired on the Black Sea by the capture of Azov from the Turks, and the Baltic Provinces and part of Finland were captured from the Swedes. The capital was transferred from Moscow to St. Petersburg (now Petrograd) in 1711, and Peter the Great was proclaimed Emperor of All Russia. At the close of the eighteenth century the Empire extended from Courland to the Urals, and from the Arctic to the Black Sea. In the nineteenth century Russian rule was extended over the basin of the Amur and from the Caspian Sea to Chinese Turkestan, and at the beginning of the twentieth century the present limits from the Baltic to the Pacific, and from the Arctic to the Asiatic Plateau, were prevented from spreading to the Yellow Sea by the Russo-Japanese War of 1904-1905.

(See also European War of 1914, and Russian Revolution, below.)

Government.—From the establishment of the Principality of Moscow, which became the dominant force in Russian affairs at the downfall of the Tartar rule (1238-1462), until the beginning of the present century the government of Russia was an unlimited autocracy. Certain reforms were introduced from time to time. Serfdom was abolished in 1861, and elective provincial and municipal assemblies were created in 1864-1870, while the legal system was purged of many of its gravest abuses. The unsuccessful termination of the Russo-Japanese War of 1904-1905 led to the expression of a national feeling in favor of representative institutions, and on October 17 (30), 1905, the Tsar issued a manifesto promising a constitution. In 1906 the "Imperial Duma" was opened by the Tsar, but its demands were regarded as excessive, and it was dissolved. The second Duma (1907) met with a similar fate, and before the third Duma was elected the franchise and methods of representation were modified. The third Duma was elected on Nov. 1 (14), 1907, for five years, and has proved to be less revolutionary in character than its predecessors.

The crown is hereditary in the house of Romanov-Holstein-Gottorp. The Emperor must belong to the Orthodox Church, and must not wear a crown involving residence outside the boundaries of the Empire. But the Imperial theory that limits set to the power of the crown by imperial concession may be revoked by imperial decree scarcely justifies the term "Constitutional Monarchy." Many topics are withheld from discussion by the legislature, so that parliamentary government is far from complete, while the franchise is highly restricted, elections to the Duma are indirect, and ministers are responsible not to the legislature but to the Tsar. Ruler: Nicholas II. Alexandrovitch, Emperor and Autocrat of all the Russias, Tsar of Moscow, Kiev, Vladimir, Novgorod, Kazan, Astrakhan, Poland, Siberia, Tauric Chersonese, and of Georgia, Lord of Pskov, Grand Duke of Smolensk, Lithuania, Volhynia, Podolia and Finland, etc.; born at Petrograd, May 6 (19), 1868; came to the throne Oct. 20 (Nov. 2), 1894.

By Imperial rescript of Oct. 17 (30), 1905, the Emperor declared his intention of sharing the legislative power with an elected national assembly, or Imperial Duma, and by a proclamation of Feb. 20 (March 5), 1906, the Council of the Empire was associated with the Duma, as an Upper Chamber. The Council of the Empire consists of ninety-eight members appointed by the Emperor, and ninety-eight members elected by various bodies for nine years and one-third renewable triennially (six are elected by orthodox clergy, forty by provincial assemblies, sixteen by landowners, eighteen by the nobility, six by the Academy of Sciences and the universities, and twelve by commercial and industrial corporations). The judicial system consists of four sets of tribunals and a supreme court. (For the army see Armies of the World and for the navy see Navies of the World.)

Russian Revolution, 1917.—The entire civilized world was thrilled by news from Petrograd (the name of the Russian capital since the outbreak of the Great European War—the old name, St. Petersburg, being discarded because of its German form) on March 16, 1917, announcing the destruction of the Russian autocracy and the establishment of a democratic form of government in Russia. For years and years, liberals, radicals, and revolutionists in the Tsar's empire had planned to overthrow the ruling dynasty, only to be crushed so mercilessly and thwarted so effectively that the days of democratic government in the largest of the countries of Europe had seemed to belong to the dim and distant future. The announcement of the complete overthrow of the Tsar's government was particularly timely in that it came but three weeks before the United States allied herself with Russia as the opponent of the Imperial German Government in the European War. Because of the fact that the new democratic form of government in Russia took long firmly to establish itself, and because of the difficulty of complete communication between Russia and America during the war, the facts of the revolution are not matters of definite general knowledge. The following statements, however, seem to be warranted:

Despite the thoroughness of the revolution, it was accomplished quietly, and with comparatively little bloodshed. Indeed, only the small number of persons possessing intimate knowledge of factors working below the surface in Russia were aware that any comprehensive steps toward revolution were being taken. In these respects, the Rusian revolution furnishes a great contrast to the French Revolution. For the primary cause of the revolution, one must turn to the rise of the Duma in Russia, (See Russia—History), with the constant attempt of the Tsar and of the Russian oligarchy to limit its power. With the beginning of the European War, liberals and radicals in Russia temporarily abandoned their efforts for the democratization of the government, but soon were aroused again to active opposition to the forces in power because of the lack of vigor with which the Government was prosecuting the war. Not only was there inefficiency, but there was also every indication that the entire administration of the Russian army was overrun with graft and lack of patriotism, so that the sacrifices of the Russian people in both life and money were being made in vain. The army, disgusted with oligarchy, had become imbued with an intense longing for democracy. The strength of German influence at court also soon made itself felt. Two premiers appointed by the Tsar, who was considered a weak pawn in the hands of the unscrupulous nobility in power, were known to be pro-Teuton in their sympathies, and fears were freely expressed that a separate peace with Germany would be negotiated. A coarse but shrewd Russian priest, Gregory Rasputin, had achieved marvelous power at court, and it was known that his influence was being used for German purposes; and other ministers appointed to power were reactionaries whom the liberals had long fought to discredit—notably the universally-hated Protopopoff.

Efficient and liberal forces in the Duma accordingly were moved to agitate for reforms, only to be met with absolute denial of their requests. By February, 1917, the maladministration and dishonesty of the Government had served to bring on a famine. Food was almost unobtainable and the people became desperate. In the

meantime, the army had seen itself rendered ineffective, and lent itself readily to the seeds of revolt sown quietly and effectively in its ranks—probably under the direction particularly of the premier of the new government soon to be established, Lvoff. Rasputin was assassinated. Early in March strikes and protest meetings sprang out everywhere in Petrograd, and the army openly sympathized with them. The police were unable to subdue the rioters, and on March 4, the troops were ordered to patrol the streets and the city was placed under martial law. But the troops soon sided with the strikers against the police. Finally, on March 9, 1917, the Duma, under the leadership of its president, Rodzianko, formally renounced allegiance to the Government.

The Tsar replied by dissolving the Duma, but the Duma refused to be dissolved, and appealed to the army and to the people for support. Hunger parades and democratic demonstrations filled the streets of Petrograd. The Tsar turned to his army for help, but the army itself had become transformed by the new spirit, and allied itself with the Duma. All over Russia, the mass of the peasants rose in support of the revolution, and in the Russian armies at the front and in the Russian navies on the seas the representatives of the old order were stripped of their authority practically overnight. Statements have been made that the revolt in the army and navy was accomplished quietly, but later reports seem to indicate that the old officers of the Tsar were not displaced without bloodshed. In Petrograd itself, however, the revolution was met with only weak resistance. Even the planners of the revolution seem to have been surprised at the strength it displayed, and at the weakness of the opposition of the autocracy, formerly believed almost impregnable in its strength. The part played by the Church is not clear. By March 11, the revolution was an accomplished fact. Nicholas II abdicated the throne for himself and for his son, thus ending the three hundred years' rule of the Romanov dynasty. Other members of the royal family were dispossessed and imprisoned. Grand Duke Nicholas was removed as commander-in-chief of the army, to be succeeded by General Alexeff. The red flag of Socialism was adopted as the official flag of Russia, although the Government so far established seems to be along the lines of representative democracy, with Socialistic proposals held, temporarily at least, in the background. Indeed, the moderation which the new government has shown has dissatisfied the more extreme elements in Russia, and the latter were responsible for an unsuccessful demonstration against the new ministry on May 3 and 4, 1917, led by the Socialistic Council of Workmen's and Soldiers' Delegates, representing more radical forces in Russia, who desire peace, although not a separate peace, and more radical reforms in the new government.

The Premier of the new cabinet is Lvoff, who more than any one man, seems to have been responsible for the revolution. The controlling forces in the new government, however, would seem to be Professor Paul Miliukoff, Minister of Foreign Affairs, who would be called in America a liberal, and the more radical Socialist, Kerensky, Minister of Justice. Soon after the revolution, the throne of Russia was offered to Grand Duke Michael, but he refused to accept the offer unless the Russian people should elect him by universal suffrage. On assuming power, the new government announced that it would prosecute the war against the Central Powers with increased energy. Complete amnesty for all political and religious offenses, universal manhood suffrage (with the status of woman suffrage in doubt), and a constitutional assembly similar to the American Congress have been proclaimed. All social and religious restrictions, especially all restrictions upon the Jews, have been abolished, all political prisoners have been released from Siberia, including many whose earlier but unsuccsessful efforts made the present revolution possible, complete liberty of speech and press have been assured, and all workingmen are to have the right to organize themselves into workingmen's associations. The police are to be abolished, their places to be filled by a new militia answerable to the Government. And every effort is to be made to remove the economic distress from which the Russians have so long suffered, and to establish social and legislative reforms which will parallel the steps towards social justice being taken by all the other great countries of Europe and America.

Early in May, 1917, it was announced that commissions from Russia and the United States would exchange visits, both to consult about the prosecution of the European War, and also to give and receive advice on the perpetuation of the Russian Revolution. It was announced that the chairman of the American commission would be Elihu Root, former Secretary of State; the other members to be: Charles R. Crane, of Chicago, manufacturer; John R. Mott, of New York, International Secretary of the Young Men's Christian Association; Cyrus McCormick, of Chicago, President of the International Harvester Company; Samuel R. Bertron, of New York, banker; James Duncan, vice president of the American Federation of Labor; Charles Edward Russell, of New York, writer and Socialist; Major-General Hugh L. Scott, chief of staff, United States Army; Rear-Admiral James H. Glennon, United States Navy.

In the several months following the revolution, dissension broke out between the conservative element in control of the new ministry, and the radical and Socialistic element represented by the Council of Soldiers' and Workmen's delegates. The latter insisted that the Government put into effect more radical social and economic reforms than it had been considering, and also that announcement be made that Russia, although she would not consider separate peace with Germany, was anxious for and would work towards a universal peace with no annexations and no indemnities. Minister Miliukoff had created much dissatisfaction by his earlier announcement that Russia was supporting all the aims of the Entente Allies in the war, and on May 16, Miliukoff resigned, after Minister of War Guchkoff had tendered his resignation. The Ministry was willing to abdicate its position, and turn over the reins of government to the Council; but the latter did not feel itself prepared to accept them, although it succeeded in having passed its resolution for an immediate and universal peace without indemnities and annexations. For a time, it appeared as though the effects of the revolution would disappear in anarchy, but on May 17, it was announced that the Ministry and the Council had agreed upon a coalition government. Lvoff remained as premier, Tereschenko succeeded Miliukoff as foreign minister, Kerensky became minister of war, and new vacancies in the Cabinet were recruited largely from the ranks of the Socialists.

For some time, Germany made no attack upon the new republic, confining her efforts to wide-spread and insidious propaganda for a separate peace. When this propaganda proved unsuccessful, however, German armies delivered crashing blows against Russia, who was unable to withstand them. The need for a strong hand in power was increasingly evident, and Kerensky replaced Lvoff as premier in July, 1917, with almost dictatorial powers. General Alexieff was succeeded in complete command of the Russian armies by General Brusiloff, who was in turn succeeded in August by General Korniloff. The latter headed a revolt in September, but was unsuccessful, and was replaced.

Years of inefficiency and distrust by the all-powerful Socialists of the non-Socialistic allies of Russia, however, rendered the Russian military strength almost non-existent. On all parts of the battle-front, the soldiers interposed little or no resistance to the oncoming Germans, in many cases deserting in large numbers or deliberately laying down their arms. Premier Kerensky re-established the death penalty in the army, which had been abolished with the success of the Revolution, and thereby created the first open split between himself and the more radical powers in control of the Council of Soldiers' and Workmen's delegates. The split constantly widened— the issue being between the Government, which wanted to establish a Socialist regime slowly and deliberately, and those, of whom Tseretelli and Tseidse were leaders, who demanded that a Socialistic state be established in short order.

During the months of August and September, the government made every effort to render the army potent again, but the task was too herculean to be accomplished quickly, and the German offensive swept onward with little opposition, until Riga, little more than 300 miles from Petrograd itself, was occupied on September 3.

In September, 1917, Russia was proclaimed a republic.

From the days of the Russian advance upon Riga, the situation in Russia became more and more chaotic; and as communication with Petrograd was often not available, it became difficult for the outside world to understand the exact significance of new developments. One fact, however, stands out clearly. The sentiment for immediate general peace negotiations gained steadily. There was practically no element favoring a separate peace with Germany; but the majority of the Russians seem to have been won over to the position that further prosecution of the war was criminal for all the belligerents concerned. This creed was led by the Bolsheviki, or the Socialistic element inclined more to internationalism than to national patriotism; and the person who crystallized the Bolshevik sentiment was Nicholas Lenine. Indeed, the Bolsheviki became so powerful in the early days of November, 1917, that they compelled Kerensky to abandon the government and to flee from Moscow. Kerensky went to the army for support, and returned to Petrograd with a military backing.

Whether the two elements could arrange a compromise without civil war was problematical; but there was no denial that the result hastened the concrete statement of war aims and peace terms from Russia, and the offer of an armistice leading to a general democratic peace.

From all reports reaching America, the mass of the Russian people was concerned more with the economic and agricultural problems confronting the country than with the international and military problems. Throughout all the civil strife, the Council of Workmen continued its session; and this body in the last analysis represented the government rather than the administration and the Cabinet ministers.

In the large cities, the philosophy of Syndicalism (q. v.) was being put into practise in many instances, and to this extent a reaction from the Socialist conception of a powerful centralized state was yielding to the theory of more freedom for industry in and of itself. The land throughout Russia was being distributed according to the needs of the peasants; and the internal governmental disorder was reflected only slightly in the daily lives of the people. Indeed, through the stormiest days of the Revolution the crowds were orderly and restrained, and there was practically no looting.

Education—There are universities at Petrograd (with 9,000 students) and at Moscow, with the modern Shaniavski University of Moscow, and at Kasan, Kiev, Kharkov, Odessa, Saratov, Tomsk, Warsaw, and Yuriev, with a total of about 41,000 students.

AREA AND POPULATION

Divisions	Area in English Sq. Miles	Population Jan. 1 (14) 1912
European Russia (the 50 Provinces)	1,862,524	122,550,700
Poland	49,018	12,776,100
Finland	144,178	3,140,100
Caucasia	180,703	12,288,100
Central Asia	1,325,530	10,727,000
Siberia	4,786,730	9,577,900
Inland Seas and Lakes	317,468	......
Khiva (Khiva)	26,028	800,000
Bokhara (Bokhara)	78,524	1,500,000
Total	8,770,703	173,359,900

The total population was estimated in 1914 as 178,380,000. More than 90% of the people are Slavs. The rural population is about 6 times as great as the urban population. The population of Petrograd in 1915 was estimated at 2,140,000; of Moscow, at 1,815,000; of Odessa, at 640,000; of Kiev, at 630,000; and of Riga, at 560,000. Warsaw in Poland has a population of about 800,000. In European Russia there are 20 towns with more than 100,000 inhabitants, and five in Asiatic Russia; and 130 with a population between 30,000 and 100,000.

Production and Industry.—The land area of the Russian Empire is estimated at 5,300,000,000 English statute acres, of which about 70 per cent is unfit for cultivation, 20 per cent is covered with forests, and 10 per cent is cultivated land. The total area under cereals, potatoes, etc., in 1912 was 361,045,636 acres. The number of live stock in 1912 was: Cattle, 48,896,000; sheep and lambs, and goats, 74,066,000; pigs, 13,508,000; horses, 33,169,000. The area of woods and forests is estimated at close on 1,000,000,000 acres. Of the total area about 60,000,000 acres are under exploitation, yielding a net profit to the State in 1909 of 46,000,000 roubles. The fisheries are an important industry, on account of the numerous fast days in the Orthodox Church calendar.

The Obdorsk and Ural Mountains contain great mineral riches, and are the principal seat of the mining and metallic industries, producing gold, platinum, copper and iron of very superior quality. Silver, gold and lead are also obtained in large quantities from the mines in the Altai Mountains. Among the non-metallic minerals are petroleum, coal, rock-salt, marble and kaolin or china clay. Russia is now the largest producer of petroleum in the world, the output amounting to 530,000,000 poods (of thirty-six pounds) in 1910 and

to 515,620,000 poods in 1911. An immense bed of coal, both steam and anthracite, and apparently inexhaustible, has been discovered in the basin of the Donetz (between the rivers Donetz and Dnieper). The coal output for the whole of Russia in 1911 was 1,420,160,000 poods (62 = 1 ton). Other mineral products in 1910 were gold ore (schlich), producing 3,606 poods of pure gold, platinum 335 poods, pig iron (171,000,000 poods in 1908), steel and rails (2,000,000 tons in 1906), copper (14,401,000 poods in 1907), and quicksilver (325 tons in 1904).

In 1912, there were produced 58,500 kilograms of gold, 5,525 kilograms of platinum, 18,000 kilograms of silver, 4,200,000 metric tons of pig iron, 3,700,000 metric tons of iron and steel, 31,000,000 metric tons of coal, 9,250,000 metric tons of naphtha, and 2,000,000 metric tons of salt.

In 1916, it was estimated that in European Rusia only there had been produced 162,000,000 quintals of wheat. In the middle of 1916, there were stored in elevators, warehouses. etc., 3,125,000 quintals of wheat and 1,150,000 quintals of flour.

In 1910 the number of factories and works of all kinds open was 32,503, employing 2,080,896 hands. The principal manufactures are cottons, flax and silk, sugar, distilling (a Government monopoly) and brewing, tanning, shoes and gloves, furniture, paper, flour, tobacco and hemp. Other carving, metalwork, etc., and agricultural machinery is now manufactured on a large scale. The imports consist principally of raw materials and machinery; the exports are mainly food products and minerals. Home manufactures are protected by prohibitive duties on manufactured articles, but their development awaits cheaper fuel and improved transport services.

In 1915, the number of factories under state supervision was estimated at 14,060, employing 2,000,000 persons.

A great deal of the internal trade is carried on by itinerant vendors, but the principal agency is the fair, over 16,000 fairs being held annually, of which 85 per cent are in European Russia. The largest and most famous is that of Nijni-Novgorod, with a turnover of some 200,000,000 roubles, other large fairs being held at Irbit, Kharkov, and Menzelinsk in European Russia, and at Omsk and Ishim in Siberia.

In 1915, the imports were valued at 1,114,000,000 rubles and the exports at 392,000,000 rubles. The value of the chief articles of imports was: Chemical products, 54,119,000 rubles; metals, 73,825,000 rubles; paper, 47,500,000 rubles; machinery, 45,500,000 rubles; hides, 44,425,000 rubles; cotton, 42,750,000 rubles. The value of the chief articles of export was: Cereals and flour, 68,000,000 rubles; butter, 62,225,000 rubles; flax and tow, 38,745,000 rubles; and timber, 27,300,000 rubles.

In 1914, imports from Germany amounted to 418,000,000 rubles and exports to 250,000,000 rubles; imports from the United Kingdom to 167,350,000 rubles and exports to 190,000,000 rubles; imports from the United States to 77,000,000 rubles and exports to 23,350,000 American dollars; imports from France to 43,000,000 rubles and exports to 55,600,000 rubles; imports from the Netherlands to 19,435,000 rubles and exports to 95,000,000 rubles.

Finance.—The budget for 1914 called for an expenditure of 3,558,261,499 roubles. The national debt of the empire was stated on Jan. 1, 1914, as 8,811,380,139 roubles. The amount of gold held by the Bank of Russia was 1,673,577,241 roubles. The free balance in the Treasury Jan. 1, 1913, was 434,000,000 roubles. The rouble, the unit of value, consists of 100 kopecks, and is equivalent to $0.31,5 United States money.

Railways.—The total length of lines open for regular traffic on Jan. 1, 1913, was 46,-839 miles (Russian Government 29,316 miles, private companies 14,096 miles, Finland 2,347 miles, Eastern China Railway 1,079 miles). Exclusive of Finland (*q. v.*) there are in European Russia about 150,000 miles of navigable rivers and canals and lakes. In Asiatic Russia there are 85,000 miles of waterway, of which 20,000 miles are navigable. Some 175,000 persons are engaged in the traffic.

Shipping.—The sea-going Mercantile Marine on Jan. 1, 1913, consisted of 716 steamers (790,075 tons) and 500 sailing vessels (184,105 tons), the steam fleet being valued at £15,300,000 and the sailing fleet at £1,700,000. Steam fleet was manned by 17,157 persons, the sailing ships by 12,-333 persons.

Cities.—Capital, St. Petersburg (name ordered changed to Petrograd during the war with Germany in 1914), on the Neva. Estimated population (1913), 2,018,596. In 1910 there were in the Russian Empire 25 towns with a population exceeding 100,-000 (European Russia 20, Asiatic Russia 5), 59 with a population between 50,000 and 100,000 (European Russia 46, Asiatic Russia 13), and 63 with a population between 30,000 and 50,000.

Trade with the United States.—The value of merchandise imported into Russia from the United States for the year 1913 was $25,363,795, and goods to the value of $26,-958,690 were sent thither—a balance of $1,-594,895 in favor of Russia.

In 1916, the United States imported from Russia goods to the value of $5,917,000 and exported thither goods to the value of $313,-515,000.

FINLAND.—The Grand Duchy of Finland, on the Gulf of Finland and Bothnia, was conquered by Russia from Sweden, and finally annexed in 1809. The country was formerly governed by the Imperial Finnish Senate, of twenty-two members, with a Diet of four estates elected by the people. This form of government gave way on Jan. 1, 1907, to a new Constitution involving a single Chamber elected by universal suffrage of both sexes. Women are likewise eligible for election to the Chamber. Finland is thus the first country to concede woman suffrage and representation, and it is noteworthy that it has been gained without agitation.

Education in Finland is on a very different footing from the remainder of the Russian Empire. Primary education is compulsory and free between the ages of seven to fifteen, and the schools are well attended. Special schools make a feature of cattle farming, dairying, and agricultural instruction. The University of Helsingfors has about 3,000 students.

BOKHARA is a vassal state of the Russian Empire in Central Asia, and lies between 37°-41° N. latitude and 62°-72° E. longitude. Rice, wheat and other cereals, and tobacco, flax, fruits and hemp are grown, and large quantities of cotton are produced in the irrigated western plain. Silk is also a flourishing industry, cottons, silks and woolens are manufactured in addition to leather and saddlery, and salt is produced in considerable quantities. The exports are mainly to Russia, and consist of raw cotton and silk, skins and hides, and carpets: the imports are principally manufactured goods and sugar from Russia, and cotton goods, tea, shawls, and indigo from British India. Trade is carried on mainly by camels and pack animals.

Russia:

Aid furnished Greeks by. (See Greece.)

American insurance companies, treatment of, in, discussed, 5961.

Bering Sea fisheries discussed. (See Bering Sea Fisheries.)

Claims of, against United States, payment of, recommended, 6336.

Claims of United States against, 3826, 6336.

Confederate envoys sent to Great Britain and France referred to. (See Mason and Slidell.)

Conference with in relation to treaty of 1832, 7669.

Consuls of, in United States, authentication of passports to Jews denied by, discussed, 6067.

Czar of—

Assassination of, resolutions of condolence on, 4626.

Coronation of, at Moscow discussed, 4758, 6067.

Proposition of, for reduction of military establishment discussed, and action of United States regarding, 6335.

Emperor of—

Accepts umpirage of first article of treaty of Ghent, 645, 672.

Decision of, 756.

Ratification of, 767.

Accession of, to throne, 950.

Assassination of, attempted, referred to, 3653, 3658, 3669.

Death of, discussed, 916.

Intervention of, regarding independence of South American provinces, 892.

Meditation of, for peace between United States and Great Britain offered, 511.

Accepted by United States, 511.

Declined by Great Britain, 519, 532.

Son of, visits United States, 4099.

South American Independence, 892.

Famine in, recommendations regarding supplies to be sent, 5648.

Fugitive criminals, convention with, for surrender of, 5398, 5871.

Grand Duke of, visits America, 4099.

Imprisonment of American citizens by, 4162, 4789, 4793.

Israelites in—

Condition of, referred to, 4690, 4714.

Measures enforced against, and subsequent banishment of, discussed, 5623.

Proscriptive edicts against, 5518.

Jeannette Polar Expedition, survivors of, aided by subjects of. (See Jeannette Polar Expedition.)

Minister of, to United States—

Appointed, 950.

Russia, Treaties with.—The convention as to the Pacific Ocean and the northwest coast of America was concluded in 1824. Free and unmolested fishing and trading rights in those parts of the Pacific Ocean as yet unoccupied are to be mutually enjoyed by both nations. Where stations are located, citizens of the one country may not resort for trade or fishing to the establishments of the other without express permission. Citizens of the United States may not erect any establishment on the northwest coast of America to the north of, nor shall Russia to the south of fifty-four degrees and forty minutes of north latitude. Spirituous liquors and firearms and other munitions of war are declared to be prohibited articles of sale to the natives or to others within the territory covered by this convention. Punishment for infraction of this article to be at the discretion of the contracting powers or their officers.

The treaty of commerce and navigation of 1832 conferred freedom of commerce, reciprocal treatment of vessels without discriminating duties by reason of the nationality of the carrying vessel, freedom of export and import (excepting the coastwise trade), the appointment of consular officers in terms of the usual consular conventions, with powers over deserters from ships and in the administration of affairs of deceased citizens, and, in general, the extension of large commercial privileges upon the most favored-nation terms. The conditions of the treaty were applicable to Poland in so far as possible.

As certain especial privileges had been extended to Sweden and Norway in regard to Poland and Finland, it is specified that such preferential conditions shall not extend to the United States.

The treaty of 1854 established the rights of neutrals at sea on the principle that free ships make free goods and that the property of neutrals on board an enemy's vessel shall not be subject to confiscation. The provisions of this treaty are to be extended to all powers formally recognizing the principles and expressing a desire to accede to the treaty.

Alaska Cession.—The treaty of 1867 ceded Alaska to the United States. The details of the boundaries contained in the first article gave rise to the long disputes between the United States and Canada over the location of the boundaries which were the subject of later treaties with Great Britain. With the territory, Russia ceded all public property in Alaska with the records and archives of the government pertaining to affairs in Alaska, but reserved the right to make exact copies of them at any time. Citizens of Alaska who desired to retain their allegiance to Russia might return to that country within three years from the date of cession. The native tribes were to be subjected to such laws as the United States might in their interests and its own discretion make for their government. In consideration of the cession of territory and rights over it, the United States agreed to pay within ten months after ratification the sum of seven million two hundred thousand dollars in gold to Russia, at Washington. (For extradition agreements, see Extradition Treaties.)

In 1894 a *modus vivendi* was arranged in relation to the fur-seal fisheries in Bering Sea and the North Pacific Ocean, by which it was agreed that citizens of the United States might not fish within a zone of ten nautical miles from the shores of Russian possessions in Bering Sea and the Pacific Ocean, nor within thirty nautical miles of the Commander Islands and Robben Island. Vessels of the United States so infringing are to be seized by duly qualified Russian officers and handed over as soon as practicable to the United States authorities, who shall cause the cases to be tried by the ordinary courts. The Russian government agreed to limit the seal catch for the year 1894 in the vicinity of the islands named to thirty thousand head. The provisions of this treaty are in nowise retroactive.

Oct. 22, 1911, Russia became a party to the convention for the preservation of fur seals by signing the agreement with Great Britain, Japan and the United States.

In June, 1904, it was agreed that corporations having a legal existence in either country should be recognized in the other, and in 1906 an agreement for the protection of trade-marks was effected.

Russian America. (See Alaska.)

Russian Colony, desire of representatives of, to emigrate to United States discussed, 4207.

Russian Revolution, 1917. (See Russia.)

Russian Revolution, praised and discussed, 8263, 8299.

Russo-Japanese War.—Russia's occupation of Manchuria after the uprising of the Boxers (q. v.) was a matter of vital importance to Japan, as it endangered the independence of Korea, and brought Russia into dangerous proximity to Japan on the shores of the China and Japan seas. In April, 1902, Russia had promised to withdraw from Manchuria in eighteen months, but in September, 1903, she informed the Powers that it would be impossible for her to withdraw at the time specified.

In June, 1904, the Japanese Government opened negotiations with Russia, looking to the latter's withdrawal from Manchuria; but, losing patience at what she regarded as the dilatory tactics of the Russian officials, on Feb. 6, 1904, Japan broke off diplomatic relations with Russia, and four days later attacked the Russian fleet at Port Arthur, damaging several ships and driving the Russians into the harbor.

From that time until the fall of the port, Jan. 2, 1904, the Japanese fleet under Admiral Togo blockaded and bombarded Port Arthur, losing two battleships and several smaller vessels, but inflicting still more damage on the Russians.

Japan formally declared war on Feb. 11, 1904, and China and the United States issued proclamations of neutrality. Japanese troops at once occupied Korea, and on May 1 forced the passage of the Yalu River. Three days later the Japanese began to land troops on the Liao Tung Peninsula, north of Port Arthur, and moving down the peninsula defeated the Russians at Nanshan Hill and Kinchau, seizing Dalny at the end of the month. A Russian force from the north under Stackelberg, attempting a diversion in favor of Port Arthur, was decisively defeated at Vafangow, June 15, and while Generals Kuroki and Oku followed up the retreating Russians, General Nogi after driving General Stoessel, the Russian commander, from his outlying positions, laid siege to Port Arthur at the end of July. On Aug. 10, the Russian fleet in the harbor of Port Arthur, finding its position desperate, attempted to break out, a part of the vessels succeeding in reaching neutral ports, but the greater number being driven back

into the port. Four days later the Russian squadron from Vladivostok, which had been making desultory raids on Japanese commerce, was defeated by a Japanese fleet, under Admiral Kamimura, one Russian vessel being sunk and the rest badly damaged. On Aug. 16, General Nogi demanded the surrender of Port Arthur, and, on General Stoessel's refusal, began an unsuccessful general assault which cost the Japanese 14,000 men. While Nogi's forces pressed the siege of the fortress the Japanese armies in the north, under the command of Marshal Oyama, the Japanese commander-in-chief, drove the Russians under Kuropatkin from Liao-Yang (Sept. 4), and checked a last attempt to relieve the city by repulsing a Russian advance over the Sha River (Oct. 14). By assaults and siege operations the Japanese steadily advanced upon Port Arthur, the capture of 203-meter Hill (Nov. 30) enabling them to bombard the fleet in the harbor, and on Dec. 31 they broke through the inner line of defenses. On Jan. 2, 1905, General Stoessel surrendered the city with 47,000 men. The Japanese loss during the siege was 50,000; the Russian not less than 20,000. The fall of Port Arthur left Nogi's forces free to join the army of the north under Oyama. After repulsing a Russian forward movement at the Hun River (Jan. 28), the Japanese assumed the offensive and again defeated Kuropatkin in a fifteen days' battle (Feb. 23-March 10) near Mukden, the ancient capital of Manchuria, and entered the city. About 750,000 men were engaged in this battle, operating on a front eighty miles long. The Russian loss was 90,000 killed and wounded, and 40,000 prisoners, the Japanese loss being less than half that of the Russian.

Meanwhile the Russian Baltic fleet, under Admiral Rogestvensky—their last naval resource, for the Black Sea fleet was confined within the Dardanelles by treaty stipulations, and demoralized by a mutiny of its sailors—had sailed from Libau (October, 1904), and was making its way to the East in several divisions by way of the Suez Canal and Cape of Good Hope. An attack on an English fishing fleet in the North Sea (Oct. 21)—the Russians mistaking the fishing boats for Japanese torpedo boats—nearly involved Russia in war with England, the affair being finally settled by arbitration; and the prolonged stay of the Russians off Madagascar and in Kamranh Bay, Saigon, led to a protest from Japan to the French Government.

On May 27 the Russian fleet encountered the Japanese under Admiral Togo, at the entrance to the Sea of Japan, and was practically annihilated, only 1 cruiser escaping to Vladivostok, and 3 to Manila, where they were interned. Six battleships, a coast defense battleship, and 4 cruisers were sunk; 2 battleships and 2 coast defense battleships surrendered; many torpedo boats and smaller vessels were sunk or captured; Admirals Rogestvensky and Nebotatoff were taken, with 3,000 of their men; and 14,000 Russians perished. The Japanese losses were inconsiderable. Shortly after the battle a Japanese force occupied the Island of Sakhalin.

On June 11, President Roosevelt, after conference with the Japanese minister and the Russian ambassador, sent to Tokyo and St. Petersburg identical notes, urging the two governments to open direct peace negotiations with each other. This action resulted in the ending of the war by the Treaty of Portsmouth (q. v.). Dissatisfaction with the result of the negotiations led to some rioting in Japanese cities. (See illustrations opposite 6836, 6886, 6948, 7028.)

Sabina, The, American seamen rescued by, compensation for, requested by owners of, 2005.

Sabine Cross-Roads (La.), Battle of.— Gen. N. P. Banks's army, which had been concentrated at Alexandria, La., advanced up the Red River March 25, 1864, by way of Natchitoches, Pleasant Hill, and Mansfield, toward Shreveport. April 8, arriving at Sabine Cross-Roads, on the Sabine River, the Federals encountered a part of the Confederate army under Gen. Kirby Smith, commanded by Gen. Richard Taylor. The Confederates attacked and Banks was badly defeated, losing 3,000 in killed, wounded, and missing. The Confederates captured 19 guns and an immense amount of ammunition and stores. The Confederate loss was reported by Gen. E. Kirby Smith as over 2,000 killed and wounded.

Sabotage. (See Socialism.)

Sac and Fox Reservation, Okla.:
Cession of portion of, to United States proclaimed, 5591.
Sale of—
Bill providing for, 4959.
Referred to, 4972.

Sac Indians (see Indian Tribes):
Treaty with, 4001.
War with. (See Indian Wars.)

Sacketts Harbor (N. Y.), Attack on.— May 29, 1813, a British force of 1,000 or 1,200 regulars and a large body of Indians was convoyed from Kingston, Canada, to Sacketts Harbor, N. Y., by a squadron under Sir James Yeo, the whole expedition being under the command of Sir George Prevost, Governor-General of Canada. The Americans, mostly raw militia, were at first forced back, but later rallied and the British were driven to their boats, leaving their dead upon the field.

Sacketts Harbor, N. Y.:
Barracks built at, 653.
British attack on, repulsed, 524.

Sackville-West Affair.— Lord Sackville, the British Minister to the United States from 1881 to 1888, wrote a letter during the Presidential campaign of 1888 in which he advised an alleged naturalized citizen, of English birth, by the name of West, to vote the Democratic ticket, on the ground that the success of the Democratic party, with its free trade policies, would be beneficial to Great Britain. President Cleveland promptly rebuked Lord Sackville for his conduct, and in December handed him his passports. See 5365, 5396.

Sacramento Pass (N. Mex.), Battle of. —When Gen. Kearny had established the supremacy of the United States authority at Santa Fé he dispatched Col. Doniphan with 800 men to join Wool in an expedition against Chihuahua. Dec. 27, 1846, Doniphan reached El Paso del Norte, a town of about 5,000 inhabitants on the road to Chihuahua, at one of the principal crossings of the Rio Grande. Here he was joined by Wightman's artillery, consisting of 100 men. He then proceeded toward the Sacramento River. Where the road to Chihuahua crosses the river the Mexican General Heredia was posted with 1,575 men. Feb. 28, 1847, he was attacked by the Americans and driven from his position with a loss of 110 pieces of artillery. Col. Doniphan and his little army entered the city of Chihuahua March 1 and 2.

"Safe and Sane Fourth." (See Fourth of July Accidents.)

Safety-Appliance Law:
Judgment of Supreme Court on, 6982.
Discussed, 6803, 6897.
Government inspectors under, 6982.

Safety at Sea:
Confirmation of convention for, 6982.

Safety Fund.— Owing to the unstable character of the currency issued and the insecurity of deposits of State banks, the New York legislature in 1829, upon the suggestion of Martin Van Buren, passed a law known as the safety-fund act. Under the provisions of this law banks chartered by the state were required to pay into the state treasury a certain percentage of their capital stock to serve as a fund out of which the liabilities of any of them that might fail should be made good. This was the beginning of reform in the banking system. Under this law there were ten bank failures, resulting in a loss of all their capital, amounting to $2,500,000, which proved conclusively the inadequacy of the safety fund. In 1838 the free-banking system was adopted.

Sag Harbor, N. Y., survey of, referred to, 1043.

Saganaw Indians. (See Indian Tribes.)

Sage-Brush State.— A nickname for Nevada (q. v.). (See also States) ; sometimes also nicknamed the Battle State and Silver State.

Saginaw, Mich., bill to provide for purchase of site and erection of public buildings at, returned, 5571.

Sa-heh-wamish Indians. (See Indian Tribes.)

Sah-ku-méhu Indians. (See Indian Tribes.)

Sailors Creek (Va.), Battle of.— After the Confederate defeat at Five Forks and the retreat of Lee's army from Richmond and Petersburg, Lee made his way due west and reached the Danville Railroad at Amelia Court-House on April 4, 1865. Sheridan passed him and reached the railroad at Jetersville, 7 miles southwest. Lee, finding retreat cut off in this direction, moved westward toward Farmville. At Sailors Creek, April 6, Custer, joined by Crook and Devin, succeeded in piercing the Confederate column, took 16 guns, 400 wagons, and many prisoners. Ewell's corps and part of Pickett's division were thus cut off. The cavalry detained this force of between 6,000 and 8,000 until, having been surrounded by Wright with the Sixth Corps, Ewell surrendered. Five generals, more than 7,000 prisoners, several hundred wagons, and many guns were taken.

St. Albans, Vt., privileges of other ports granted, by proclamation, 2473.

St. Augustine, Fla., harbor of, referred to, 1040.

St. Bartholomews, unlawful expedition planned in, 769.

St. Clair Flats, acts making appropriations for deepening channel over, vetoed, 2919, 3130.

St. Domingo. (See Santo Domingo.)

St. Elizabeth's Hospital. (See Government Hospital for Insane.)

St. John Island, treaty concluded with Denmark for cession of, to United States transmitted and discussed, 3777, 3779, 3796, 3886.

St. John River, navigation of, referred to, 2273, 2675.

St. Lawrence River, navigation of:
Correspondence with Great Britain regarding, 960.
Referred to, 2675.
Right to exclude American citizens from, claim of, by Canada discussed, 4058.

St. Louis, The:
Mentioned, 6313.
Refuge given Gen. Miller and Vice-President of Peru by, 1133.

St. Louis and San Francisco Railway Co., application of, for right of way across Indian Territory, 4653.
Bill granting, referred to, 4655.

St. Louis Harbor, survey of, referred to, 2135.

St. Marys Falls Canal, toll imposed upon vessels passing through, by United States as retaliatory measure, proclaimed, 5725.
Referred to, 5749.
Revoked by proclamation, 5812.

St. Marys River:
Act making appropriation for deepening channel over flats of, in the State of Michigan vetoed, 2920.

St. Paul, The, mentioned, 6391.

St. Petersburg, Russia:
Fourth International Prison Congress at, discussed and recommendations regarding, 5117.
International Statistical Congress in, 4221.

St. Pierre, destruction of city of, 6680.

St. Regis, Capture of.—At the outbreak of the War of 1812 it was agreed between the British and Americans that the village of St. Regis, on the boundary line between Canada and New York, occupied by Christian Indians, should remain neutral. In violation of this agreement the Canadian commander-in-chief put a garrison in the place and many of the Indians were induced to join the British army. On the morning of Oct. 22, 1812, Maj. Young, with about 200 men, surprised this garrison and took 40 prisoners, some muskets, and a quantity of blankets, after killing 7 men. None of the American force was injured.

St. Regis Indians. (See Indian Tribes.)

St. Thomas Island, treaty with Denmark for cession of, to United States transmitted and discussed, 3777, 3779, 3796, 3886.

Salaries, Congressional.—Under the Articles of Confederation each state paid its own members of Congress, but the Convention of 1787 made the members independent of the states in this respect. The first clause of Article I., section 6, of the Constitution provides that "the Senators and Representatives shall receive a compensation for their services, to be ascertained by law and paid out of the Treasury of the United States." Members of the First Congress were paid $6 per day and $6 for each twenty miles of travel going and coming. The salaries have frequently been changed. From 1789 to 1815 they were $6 per day; from 1815 to 1817, $1,500 per year; from 1817 to 1855, $8 per day; from 1855 to 1865, $3,000 per year; from 1865 to 1871. $5,000 per year; from 1871 to 1874, $7,500 per year; from 1874 to 1908, $5,000 per year. A mileage of twenty cents is allowed both ways. Senators and representatives have received the same salaries except during 1795, when senators received $7 per day while members received but $6. At present members of both houses receive $7,500 per annum. The speaker of the House receives $12,000 per year.

Salaries, Division of Postmasters', in Post-Office Department.—This division falls under the supervision of the First Assistant Postmaster-General (q. v.). (See Post-Office Department; Division of City Delivery; Civil Service; Division of Rural Delivery.)

Salaries, Executive.—Sept. 24, 1789, Congress fixed the salary of the President of the United States at $25,000 per annum, at which figure it remained until 1873, when it was increased to $50,000. The Constitution provides that the salary of the President shall not be diminished during his term of office, and for this reason that part of the "salary-grab" act of 1873 which increased his salary was not repealed in 1874 with the other provisions of that act. The salary of the Vice-President, placed at $5,000 in 1789, was raised to $8,000 in 1853, to $10,000 in 1873, reduced to $8,000 in 1874, and in 1908 increased to $12,000, and the President's salary was fixed at $75,000.

Of the Cabinet officers the Secretaries of State and the Treasury received in 1789 salaries of $3,500 each, the Secretary of War $3,000, the Attorney-General $1,500, and the Postmaster-General $2,000. In 1819 the pay of the four Secretaries (State, Treasury, War, and Navy) was made $6,000, that of the Postmaster-General $4,000, and that of the Attorney-General $3,500. The Cabinet officers and Vice-President now receive $12,000 per year. Washington at first declined to receive any pecuniary compensation as President. He asked that the estimates for his station be limited to such actual expenditures as the public good might be thought to require (page 45).

Salaries, Judicial.—In 1789, when the United States courts were organized, the Chief Justice of the Supreme Court was paid $4,000 and the associate justices $3,500 each. The district judges received from $1,000 to $1,800. These salaries have been increased from time to time. At the present time (1914) the Chief Justice of the Supreme Court receives $15,000, the associate justices $14,500, the circuit court judges $7,000, and the district court judges $6,000. The Chief Justice of the United States Court of Claims receives $6,500 and the four associate judges $6,000 each. The Constitution provides that the salaries of Federal judges may not be diminished during their continuance in office.

Salaries of Public Officers (see also the several officers):
Commissions claimed by, referred to, 1730.

Fee system, abolition of, as applicable to certain officials discussed, 6161.

Recommended, 4939, 5879, 5968.

Fixed salaries recommended, 1387, 4718, 4838, 4922, 4939, 5879, 5968.

Increase for head of Secret Service recommended, 7253.

Increase in, recommended, 4107.

Mode of paying, referred to, 1954.

Recommendations regarding, 195, 198, 4107.

Referred to, 1807.

Tariff of fees for clerks, marshals, etc., recommended, 2666, 2714, 4770, 4836, 4939, 5103.

Salary Grab.—A popular name for the act of March 3, 1873, whereby the salaries of the President and Vice-President, members of Congress, justices of the Supreme Court and other Federal officials were materially increased. The provisions for the increase were introduced by Benjamin F. Butler, of Massachusetts, and made a rider to the appropriation bill. By this law the President's salary was increased from $25,000 to $50,000 per year; that of the Chief Justice from $8,500 to $10,500; those of the Vice-President, Cabinet officers, associate justices, and Speaker of the House from $8,000 to $10,000, and of Senators and Representatives from $5,000 to $7,500. Another act, passed the next day, made that part of the law relating to salaries of members of Congress retroactive, thus giving themselves $7,500 instead of $5,000 a year from March 4, 1871, to March 4, 1873. and following years. This excited the indignation of the people to such an extent that the laws were repealed the following year, except such provisions as related to the President and justices of the Supreme Court.

Salt, duties on, discussed, 397, 1470.

Salt Springs:

Cession of, to United States, 342.

Referred to, 803, 892.

Salt Works in Kentucky, act for relief of owners of, vetoed, 4170.

Salvador.—Salvador occupies part of the south coast of Central America, between Guatemala and Nicaragua (Gulf of Fonseca), the northern boundary being conterminous with the Republic of Honduras, and the southern boundary being the Pacific Ocean. It is situated approximately between 13°-14° 20′ N. latitude and 87° 45′-90° W. longitude, and is about 140 miles from east to west, and about 60 miles from north to south. The area is about 7,225 square miles.

Physical Features.—There are distinct areas in the low alluvial plains of the coast and the interior plateau, with a mean elevation of about 2,000 feet, broken in many places by volcanic cones, of which the highest are Santa Ana (8,300 feet) and San Miguel (7,120 feet). The lowlands are generally hot and unhealthy, but the climate of the plateau and mountain slopes is temperate and healthy. There is a wet season from May to October, and a dry season from November to April.

Hydrography.—The principal river is the Lempa, which rises in Guatemala and flows into the Pacific, being navigable for most of its course by small steamers. In the eastern districts the Rio San Miguel rises near the Honduras boundary and flows into the Bay of Fonseca, and in the center of the Republic is the large volcanic lake Ilopango.

History.—Salvador was conquered in 1526 by Pedro de Alvarado, and formed part of the Spanish viceroyalty of Guatemala until 1821. In 1840 the Republic broke away from the federation of Central American States.

Government.—The constitution rests upon the fundamental law of 1864 (revised in 1886), the President and Vice-President being elected for four years by direct vote of the people, the President being ineligible for a successive term in either office. President (Feb. 9, 1913-1915), Carlos Melendez, born Feb. 1, 1861.

The National Assembly, consisting of a single chamber of forty-two Deputies (three for each Department) elected for one year by the direct vote of all adult male Salvadorians, meets annually from February to May, and elects a President and Vice-President for each session.

There are local courts of first instance, district courts, and a supreme court at the capital. Each of the fourteen Departments has a governor appointed by the central executive, but the municipalities have elective magistrates and officials.

For the army see Armies of the World.

Population.—There are fourteen departments with an estimated population of 1,200,000. Of the total population about 10 per cent are creoles and foreigners, 50 per cent half-castes, and 40 per cent Indians, the negro element being negligible. The language of the country is Spanish.

Production and Industry.—The principal products are coffee, sugar, indigo, "Peruvian" balsam (grown in Salvador, but formerly shipped from Callao in Peru), tobacco, cocoa, rice, cereals, and fruits. Cotton is being grown under a Government subsidy.

Gold, silver, copper, mercury, and lead are found, and there are indications of coal and iron, but only gold and silver are systematically worked, mainly in the department of Morazan.

Finance.—The average annual expenditure for the five years ending with 1913 were 13,230,002 pesos and the average revenue for the same period was 13,575,217 pesos. The national debt was stated on June 1, 1913, as $6,917,000. The peso, the unit of value, is worth $0.40 in United States money.

The capital is San Salvador, with a population of 60,000.

Trade with the United States.—The value of merchandise imported into Salvador from the United States for the year 1913 was $2,389,971, and goods to the value of $1,-371,568 were sent thither—a balance of $1,018,403 in favor of the United States.

Salvador:

Commercial relations with, 5663.

Consular convention with, 4070, 4212, 4880.

Difficulties of, with Great Britain, 2643.

Fugitive criminals, convention with, for surrender of, 4033, 4212, 4247.

Questions arising under, discussed, 5961.

Insurrection in, and refuge on board American vessels sought by insurgents discussed, 5961.

President of, confirmed, 5544.

Report of Thomas C. Reynolds on, transmitted, 5116.

Tariff laws of, evidence of modifications of, proclaimed, 5684, 5800. Discussed, 5747.

Treaty with, transmitted and discussed, 2572, 2694, 3280, 4033, 4070, 4212, 4247.

Vessel condemned by, subsequently presented to United States, recommendations regarding, 4988.

War with Guatemala, 5543.

Salvador, Treaties with.—Our earliest treaty with Salvador, then known as the Republic of San Salvador, was a convention of amity, navigation and commerce, which was proclaimed April 18, 1853. This was superseded by the treaty of Dec. 6, 1870, which provided for reciprocal privileges in business, religious freedom, protection of persons and property in each country by the government of the other, consular prerogatives, and the usual restrictions of neutrality in case of war. It also contained the most favored nation clause. On notice given by Salvador this treaty was abrogated May 30, 1893. Dec. 19, 1901, a protocol for the arbitration of certain claims against Salvador by citizens of the United States was signed. Naturalization and arbitration conventions were concluded in 1908. The arbitration convention, which was for five years, was extended in 1914 for another five years. Salvador also became a party to the convention between the United States and the several republics of South and Central America for the arbitration of pecuniary claims and the protection of inventions, etc., which was signed in Buenos Aires in 1910 and proclaimed in Washington, July 29, 1914. (See South and Central America, Treaties with.)

Salvo.—1. The firing of a number of guns at the same time. 2. The striking, at the same time, of several missiles on the enemy's defense. 3. The simultaneous shouting of a body of people.

Sam-ahmish Indians. (See Indian Tribes.)

Samana Bay:

Convention with Dominican Republic for—
Lease of, 3999.
Transfer of, 3799.

Possession of, desired by European powers, 4015.

Proposition of foreign power to purchase right to, referred to, 4017.

Samoan Islands.—A group of fourteen islands in the South Pacific Ocean. The principal islands are Savaii, Upolu, and Tutuila. The United States has a coaling station in the harbor of Pago-Pago, granted in 1872. The neutrality of the islands was guaranteed by the United States, Great Britain, and Germany in 1889 by treaty. This convention of treaty between the three countries provided for a foreign court of justice, a municipal council for the district of Apia, the chief town, with a foreign president thereof, authorized to advise the King; a tribunal for the settlement of native and foreign land titles, and a revenue system for the Kingdom.

In 1899 the kingship was abolished, and by the Anglo-German agreement of Nov. 14, accepted Jan. 14, 1900, by the United States, Great Britain and Germany renounced in favor of the United States all rights in the Island of Tutuila and others of the Samoan group east of 171° east, the islands to the west of that meridian being assigned to Germany. (See also Tutuila.)

Samoan Islands:

Affairs of, and policy of United States regarding—
Discussed by President—
Cleveland, 5088, 5389, 5391, 5397, 5871, 5963, 6067.
Harrison, Benj., 5469, 5545.
McKinley, 6414.

Reports on, transmitted, 5197, 5367, 5385, 5392, 5395, 5397, 5909, 5911, 6001.

Application of inhabitants of, for protection of United States, 4116, 4421, 5089.

Application of Tutuila Island for protection of United States, and offer of naval station by, 4122.

Autonomy and independence of, should be preserved, 5390.

Conference regarding, at—
Berlin discussed, 5391, 5397, 5469, 5871, 5963.
Washington referred to, 5469.

Government of, discussed, 4563, 6336.

Insurrection in, discussed, 5871, 5963, 6375, 6428.

King of, death of, 6336.

Privileges ceded to United States in harbor of Pago-Pago by—
Discussed, 4449, 4522.
Referred to, 5367.

Report on, referred, 4217, 4473.

Settlement of questions regarding, referred to, 5747.

Special agent to, power of, referred to, 4315, 5382.

Treaty between United States, Great Britain, and Germany regarding, 5469, 5545.
Discussed, 5871, 5963, 6067.
Referred to, 6336.

Treaty with, 4433, 4449.

Vessels of United States—
Disabled and destroyed at, 5479.
Sent to, 5390, 5871.

Weakness of, discussed, 5088.

Samoan Islands, Treaties with.—In 1899 a convention was made between the United States, Germany, and Great Britain, relating to settlement of claims of American citizens, German, and British subjects, for damage sustained by unwarranted military action in Samoa. It was agreed that the King of Sweden and Norway should be invited to act as arbitrator therein, and that his decision in the premises be final, and that the three governments be bound to make good the losses in accordance therewith. Oct. 14, 1902, Oscar II., King of Sweden and Norway, as arbitrator, rendered his decision, in which he found the action of the United States culpable in bringing back the Malietoans after deportation, and supplying them with arms and ammunition without the knowledge of the German consul. For this and for other reasons, King Oscar held the British and United States responsible for damages.

The convention of 1899 contained the renunciation by Germany in favor of the United States of all claims and rights in respect to the Island of Tutuila and all other islands of the Samoan group east of longitude 171 degrees west. The United States renounced all claims and rights in favor of Germany of the islands of Upolu, Savaii, and all other islands of the Samoan group west of longitude 171 degress west. The three signatory nations continue to enjoy equal rights in respect of commerce and commercial vessels in the islands. (See also Germany.)

San Carlos Reservation, Ariz., coal lands on, referred to, 4683.

San Domingo. (See Santo Domingo.)

San Fernando, The, seizure of, and claims arising out of, 4114, 5198, 5547, 5673, 5873, 5962.

Award in case of, 6070.

San Francisco, Cal.:

Cable communication between Pacific coast and Hawaiian Islands recommended. (See Ocean Cables.)

Presidio of, appropriations for buildings at, recommended, 4161.

San Francisco Bay, Cal., floating dock to be constructed at, 2669.

San Gabriel (Cal.), Battle of.—Dec. 29, 1846, Gen. Kearny with 500 men left San Diego for Los Angeles, 145 miles away. Jan. 8, 1847, Flores, acting governor and captain-general, with 600 men and 4 pieces of artillery, was encountered on the commanding heights of San Gabriel, prepared to dispute the passage of the Rio de los Angeles by the Americans. The baggage train and artillery crossed under a harassing fire and then the enemy was charged, and in 10 minutes Kearny was master of the field. One seaman, acting as an artilleryman, was killed and 1 volunteer and 8 seamen wounded, 2 mortally.,

San Jacinto, The:

Collision of, with the *Jules et Marie,* appropriation for owners of latter, recommended, 3343.

Removal by, of Confederate envoys from British vessel *Trent.* (See Mason and Slidell.)

San Juan (Cuba), Battle of. (See Santiago (Cuba), Battle of.)

San Juan, Cuba, captured by American troops, 6317.

San Juan Hill, Cuba. (Capture of, illustration opposite 5978.)

San Juan de Fuca Explorations.—Certain explorations on which are based the American claims to possession of territory bordering on the Pacific. The portion of the Pacific Coast between the parallels of lat. 40° and 50° north was visited on behalf of Spain in 1592 by a Greek pilot named De Fuca, in 1640 by Admiral Fonte, and subsequently by other explorers, and maps of the coast line had been made. The treaty of 1790 between Spain and Great Britain only gave the latter fishing and trading rights in the vicinity of Puget Sound. The discovery and exploration of Columbia River by Capt. Gray, an American; the purchase from France in 1803 of the Louisiana territory; the exploration of Columbia River by Lewis and Clark, by order of the United States, in 1804-5, and the treaty of limits concluded with Spain in 1819, by which all the territory north of lat. 42° north was expressly declared to belong to the United States, were held to be sufficient proofs of the latter's title to the territory. Great Britain nevertheless claimed a large portion of the region, while the United States claimed the country to lat. 54° 40' north. In 1846 the boundary was settled at the forty-ninth parallel as far as the channel between Vancouver Island and the mainland, and from that point on a line through the middle of that channel and the Strait of Juan de Fuca to the Pacific. (See Northwestern Boundary.) Navigation of the channel was to be free to both countries. Under this treaty the United States claimed the Canal de Haro as the channel through which the boundary was to run, and Great Britain claimed Rosario Straits. San Juan and other islands were thus in dispute. To avoid conflict, the occupation by both nations of the Island of San Juan at opposite ends was agreed upon. The Emperor of Germany, who was selected as arbitrator of the dispute, decided in favor of the United States in 1872 (4140). (See also "Fifty-four Forty or Fight.")

San Juan Hill, Battle of, referred to, 6637.

San Juan Island:

Conflicting claims of Great Britain and United States to, discussed, 3092, 3171, 3197.

Settlement of, by arbitration, 4139.
Recommended, 3198, 3213.

Gen. Scott sent to, 3094.
Correspondence of, referred to, 3110.

Joint occupancy of, 3659.

Military force placed on, 3093.

Possession of, awarded United States, 4140.

Referred to, 3110, 3171, 3819.

San Juan, Nicaragua:

Bombardment of, 2778.

Military expedition under authority of Great Britain landed at, discussed, 2903.

Transactions between Capt. Hollins and authorities of, 2760.

San Juan, Puerto Rico, shelled by American fleet, 6316.

San Juan Question. (See San Juan de Fuca Explorations.)

San Juan River:

Survey of, to be made, 3444.

Territorial controversies between States bordering on, 2736.

San Nicolas Island, referred to, 6702.

San Salvador. (See Salvador.)

Sanders Creek (S. C.), Battle of.—Generally known as the battle of Camden. In the summer of 1780 Gen. Gates had been appointed to the command of the Southern army, and, reenforced by Baron De Kalb, Armand's Legion, Porterfield's Virginia regiment, and Rutherford's North Carolina militia, his force numbered over 4,000, of whom less than 1,000 were regulars. Cornwallis, with about 2,000 British and Tories, of whom 1,500 were regulars, proposed to surprise Gates's army. Gates had determined to surprise Cornwallis. Both advancing, the two armies unexpectedly met at Sanders Creek, near Camden, S. C., on the night of Aug. 16, 1780. After some skirmishing hostilities were suspended until the morning, when, with the first British attack, the Virginia and South Carolina militia fled, after a feeble resistance, due in part to an imprudent order by Gen. Gates. Baron De Kalb bore the brunt of the battle and fell, being wounded 12 times. The American defeat eventually became a rout. Their loss in killed, wounded, and prisoners was upward of 2,000. The British lost 325 men, 68 of whom were killed. Previous to this action Sumter, with about 400 men, captured a British convoy with stores and 200 prisoners, but was himself surprised the next day by Tarleton, who recaptured the stores, killed 100 men, and took 300 prisoners. The British, in the Camden battle, came into possession of 7 pieces of artillery, 2,000 muskets, the entire baggage train, and nearly 1,000 prisoners, including Generals De Kalb, Gregory, and Rutherford.

Sandusky, Ohio, British attack on, repulsed, 524.

Sandwich Islands. (See Hawaiian Islands.)

Sandy Bay, Mass., harbor of, referred to, 1040.

Sandy Creek (N. Y.), Battle of.—May 19, 1814, while the British squadron on Lake Ontario was blockading Sacketts Harbor, where Commodore Chauncey was fitting out a squadron for active service, certain heavy guns and cables destined for some of the American ships were yet at Oswego Falls. The blockade preventing their being convoyed by water to the harbor, Capt. Woolsey, commander of the *Oneida,* volunteered to transport them by way of the Big Sandy Creek, partly overland, to their destination. Sir James Yeo, of the blockading squadron, sent 2 gunboats, 3 cutters, and a gig to intercept Woolsey. The latter had detailed 130 riflemen and the same number of Oneida Indians to proceed along the banks of the creek to assist in repelling any possible attack. May 30 the British gunboats sighted Woolsey's flotilla and began firing. Within 10 minutes the British squadrons, with officers and men to the number of 170, were prisoners and prizes. Not a single American life was lost. The British loss was 18 killed and 50 wounded. The cannon and cables were safely landed at Sacketts Harbor.

"Sane Fourth." (See Fourth of July Accidents.)

Sanitary Bureau, International, appropriation to, 6823.

Sanitary Conference, International, at— Rome, 4898, 4918. Washington, 4564, 4622, 4631, 6737.

San Marino, the smallest republic in the world, is situated on the Adriatic, 14 miles southwest of Rimini, in northern Italy. It has an area of 2 English square miles.

Population (1910), 10,655. It is named in consequence of its traditional foundation by Saint Marinus, in the reign of the Emperor Diocletian (284-305 A. D.) and possesses a monastery founded in the ninth century. The independence of the republic has survived all attempts at suppression and is secured by a treaty with the King of Italy. The supreme power resides in the Arringo, or general assembly, which meets twice a year at the capital, the executive being entrusted to two *Capitani Reggenti,* selected every six months from the sixty members of the Great Council, who are elected by universal suffrage in three classes (twenty from the nobility, twenty from the landowners and twenty from the people) for nine years, and are renewaoie as to one-third every three years. There is a defence force of about 1,200 men, and all citizens between the ages of sixteen and sixty are liable for service. The revenue in 1909-1910 amounted to 398,900 lire. The exports are wine, cattle and stone. The Capital (San Marino, population 1,500) stands on Mount Titain, and has an impregnable castle.

Santa Fé, N. Mex., capitol at, appropriation for completion of, recommendation regarding, 5872.

Grant of land to, 6872.

Santa Fe Trail.—There is said to be in the ancient palace at Santa Fe a Spanish document proving the existence of a trail in the last quarter of the 18th century from the old French settlements in what is now Illinois, to some of the Spanish towns in New Mexico, and from one of these to California. In 1804 a merchant of Kaskaskia, Ill., dispatched a courier with goods to Santa Fe. In 1822 the Santa Fe trail proper was opened—a wonderful road some 800 miles in length, rising so imperceptibly for three-quarters of its distance as to seem perfectly level, and without a bridge from end to end. The eastern terminus was first at Franklin, Mo., then at Independence, and later at Westport, on the Missouri River. The early traders carried their merchandise on pack horses or mules, and in 1824 the prairie schooner appeared. Along this road General Kearny and Colonel Doniphan led the expedition which annexed the western states to the Union during the Mexican war. The Santa Fe railroad now closely follows the trail, which was the scene of many stagecoach robberies and Indian attacks. Wagon trains bound for the Pacific coast rendezvoused at Emporia, Kan., whence they were escorted by scouts or military guards.

Santa Maria, The, presented to United States by Spain discussed and recommendation regarding, 5872.

Santa Rosa Island (Fla.), Battle of.—Oct. 9, 1861, a force of 1,500 or 2,000 Confederates landed on Santa Rosa Island, Pensacola Harbor, Fla., and surprised the camp of Wilson's Zouaves about a mile from the fort. Maj. Vogdes was sent to the relief of the camp with two companies. He was captured, but the assailants retired to their boats under the heavy fire of the regulars after setting fire to the camp. The Federal loss was 60 killed and wounded. The Confederate loss was not reported.

Santiago, Cuba:

American army under Maj.-Gen. W. R. Shafter lands near, 6317.

American interests in, confided to British consul, 6331.

Movement against and subsequent capitulation of, discussed, 6317.

Thanks of President tendered commander and men, 6574, 6577.

Postal communication with, order regarding, 6577.

Santiago (Cuba), Battle of.—On Monday, June 20, 1898, the American fleet of about 55 ships, including the naval convoy which had left Tampa, Fla., on June 7, came within sight of the town of Daiquiri, about fifteen miles east of Santiago, which was the point selected for the landing. Upon landing at Daiquiri, Gen. Wheeler's command of cavalry was ordered to take position on the road to Siboney. Gen. Young's brigade (about 965 men), during the night of June 23-24, passed Gen. Lawton's division, which was on the road from Siboney to Santiago.

About three miles from the former place, near Las Guasimas, June 24, they encountered the enemy posted in a strong natural position. The Spanish forces occupied a range of hills in the form of obtuse angles, with the salient toward Siboney. The attack, says Gen. Young, of both wings was simultaneous, and the junction of the two lines occurred near the apex of the angle, on the ridge, which had been fortified with stone breastworks flanked by blockhouses. The Spanish were driven from their position and fled precipitately toward Santiago. The American forces numbered about 965, the Spanish 2,000 to 2,500. American losses, 1 officer and 15 men killed; 6 officers and 46 men wounded. Forty-two dead Spanish soldiers were found on the field, while the Santiago (Spanish) papers the day after the battle gave their loss as 77 killed.

After this battle the Spaniards retired to the outer defenses of Santiago. These were the village of El Caney to the northeast, and the San Juan Hill extending south from that village and forming a natural barrier to the eastward of the city. July 1 these defenses were attacked by forces under Gen. Lawton, who was expected to take El Caney and then move toward Santiago and support the attack of Wheeler's and Kent's divisions upon the main Spanish army. The battle began at 6 A. M. and soon became general. The enemy fought with much obstinacy, but were slowly driven back. After Lawton had become well engaged, Grimes's battery, from the heights of El Poso, opened fire on the San Juan blockhouses, and Wheeler's and Kent's divisions moved forward, crossed the river, and formed for an attack on San Juan Hill. During this formation Col. Wikoff was killed. The command of the Second Brigade then devolved upon Lieut.-Col. Worth, who was soon severely wounded, and then upon Lieut.-Col. Liscum, who fell a few minutes later, and Lieut.-Col. Ewers took command. The Spaniards strongly intrenched upon the hills in front of the American forces, San Juan Hill and Fort San Juan, the latter position being a few hundred yards nearer Santiago.

The American forces charged up San Juan Hill in the face of a heavy fire, captured this point, crossed the plain below, and charged Fort San Juan, driving the enemy before them. At midnight of July 1 Gen. Bates arrived with reenforcements, and at daylight on the 2d his brigade was placed on the ridge to the left of the American lines. Gen. Lawton's forces were placed on the right. All day a brisk fire was kept up by the two armies, part of the time in a drenching rain. At nightfall the firing ceased, but at 9 P. M. a vigorous assault was made all along the lines, which was repulsed, the Spaniards retiring to their trenches. The following morning firing was resumed and continued until near noon, when a white flag was displayed by the enemy.

The total losses of the American forces during the three days' fighting (July 1, 2, and 3) were: Officers killed, 13; privates, 87; officers wounded, 36; privates, 561; missing, 62. The entire strength of the command which fought the battle of San Juan was 362 officers and 7,391 privates. The defenses of Santiago were constructed with much engineering skill, as were also the batteries in the harbor. The city was at once surrounded by the American army, so that the Spaniards could not escape. The ridge upon which the Americans were stationed was favorably located and overlooked the city. The fortifications and barbed wire fences could easily be seen. The Spaniards seemed to realize that their condition was hopeless, and on Sunday morning, July 3, their fleet steamed out of the harbor. The destruction of this fleet was complete.

On the 16th Gen. Toral informed the American commander that the Spanish Government at Madrid had authorized the surrender, and thereupon final terms of absolute capitulation were duly signed. The conditions of the surrender included all forces and war material in the division of Santiago. The United States agreed to transport, without unnecessary delay, all the Spanish troops in the district to Spain. Officers were to retain their side arms and officers and men their personal property. The Spanish commander was authorized to take the military archives of the district. The Spanish forces were to march out of Santiago with honors of war and deposit their arms at a point to be mutually agreed upon, to await the disposition of the United States Government, etc. The troops surrendered and returned to Spain were about 24,000.

Santiago Harbor, Cuba:

Forts at mouth of, shelled by American squadron, 6316.

Spanish fleet in, 6316.

Attempting to escape, destroyed by American squadron, 6317. (See also encyclopedic article, Santiago Harbor, Battle of.)

Thanks of President tendered officers and men of American squadron, 6573.

The *Merrimac* sank in, by Lieut. Hobson, 6305, 6316.

Naval Cadet Powell to be made ensign for attempting to rescue force of, 6306.

Thanks of President to Lieut. Hobson and promotion of, recommended, 6306.

Santiago Harbor (Cuba), Battle of.—This engagement, which is also known as the battle of July 3, was the decisive naval combat of the Spanish-American War. For six weeks the Spanish fleet under Rear-Admiral Pascual Cervera had been imprisoned in the harbor of Santiago by the American blockading squadron in command of Acting Rear-Admiral Sampson. On the morning of July 3, 1898, at about 9.30 o'clock, while the men of the American

vessels were at Sunday quarters for inspection, the Spanish fleet, consisting of
the *Infanta Maria Teresa, Vizcaya, Cristo-
bal Colon, Almirante Oquendo, Pluton,* and
Furor, attempted to escape. The ships,
coming out of the harbor at the rate of
eight or ten knots an hour, passed without
difficulty the collier *Merrimac,* which had
been sunk in the channel by Lieut. Hobson.
Signals were at once made from the United
States vessels, "Enemy's ships escaping,"
and general quarters were sounded. Rear-
Admiral Sampson being about seven miles
from the scene of battle, the command of
the American vessels during the engagement devolved upon Commodore Schley.
Under his direction, the squadron closed in
on the fleeing vessels, and in about two
hours the entire Spanish fleet was destroyed. The Spanish losses were 600
killed and about 1,400 prisoners, including
the admiral. The loss on the American
side was 1 killed and 1 wounded, while
not a vessel was materially damaged.
From this crushing defeat Spain was unable to recover, and her effort upon the
ocean ceased. (See illustration opposite
6058.)

Santo Domingo.—The Republic occupies
the eastern part of the island of Haiti, covering 18,045 square miles of its total area
of 28,000 square miles, or rather more than
two-thirds of the whole island, the remainder forming the Republic of Haiti (*q. v.*),
and lies between 17° 37'-20° N. latitude
and 72°-68° 20' W. longitude.

Physical Features and Climate.—Santo Domingo is distinctly mountainous. The highest point in the republic is Loma Tina (10,-
300 feet), an isolated mountain in the
south of the island. Between the Sierra
de Monti Cristi in the north and that of
Cibao in the center is a vast well-watered
plain, known as the Vega Real, from Samaná Bay in the east to Manzanillo Bay
in the west, a distance of close on 150
miles. In the southeast is another great
plain, stretching from Ozanam River to the
east coast, about 100 miles distant.

The principal rivers are the Yaqui del
Norte and the Yaqui del Sur, which rise
on either side of the central range and
flow into the Bays of Manzanillo (northwest) and Neyba (south), and the Yuna,
which drains the Vega Real and flows into
Samaná Bay; the Ozama, upon which the
capital stands, is the most important of
the lesser streams. The republic lies entirely with the tropics, but the climate has
a wide range on account of the diversity of
levels, and the capital, in particular, is
healthy and comparatively cool. Rainfall is
abundant and the wet and dry seasons are
clearly marked. The prevailing wind is
from the east, and the island is generally
free from hurricanes.

History.—The Dominican Republic is the
Spanish portion of the island of Haiti (or
Santo Domingo), which was discovered by
Columbus in 1492 and peopled by the
Spaniards with imported African slaves,
who soon exterminated the Indian tribes.
In 1821 an independent republic was proclaimed and the Spaniards abandoned the
country, but from 1822-1844 the territory
was made part of the neighboring republic
of Haiti.

There are twelve provinces with a total
area of 18,045 square miles and an estimated population of 700,000.

Government.—In 1844 the Dominican Republic was founded, the present constitution
resting upon a fundamental law of Nov. 6,
1844, since modified in many instances.
The President is elected for six years by
indirect vote. Provisional President of the

Republic, José Bordas (elected by Congress,
April, 1913). Up to the close of 1916 he
had been succeeded by Eliado Victoria, Ramon Baez, Juan Isidoro Jiminez, Desiderio
Arias, Jacinto de Castro.

The revolutionary movement under Gen.
Desiderio Arias caused the United States
to intervene in the affairs of the island.
Marines were landed, and a number of cities
and forts occupied.

Congress consists of a Senate and a Chamber of Deputies. The Senate contains one
member from each province, and the
Chamber twice that number, the houses
thus numbering twelve and twenty-four,
elected in each case by indirect vote, Senators for six years, one-third renewable
every two years, Deputies for four years,
one-half so renewable.

Each of the twelve Provinces is administered by a Governor appointed by the
President. The governing classes are mainly white.

There are three main elements in the
population, the most numerous being mulattoes of Spanish-Negro descent, with many
full-blooded negro descendants of slaves
imported by Spain from the sixteenth to
the nineteenth centuries, and native-born
and settled whites, principally Spanish, but
partly French and English, with a few
Turkish Christians from Turkey. The religion of the country is Roman Catholic, but
all creeds are tolerated. Spanish is the language of the Republic, with a sprinkling of
French and English in the towns.

Finance.—In 1907 the Republic ratified a
treaty with the United States, under which
the latter country collects the customs and
acts as an intermediary between the Dominican Republic and its foreign creditors.
The Debt was stated on Jan. 1, 1912, at
$20,000,000.

The revenue and expenditure for the
years 1908-1912 are stated as follows:

Year	Revenue	Expenditure
1908	$3,984,300	$3,990,000
1909	4,520,120	4,530,000
1910	4,700,000	4,650,000
1911	4,860,000	4,806,000
1912	5,809,785	5,845,994

Production and Industry.—The plains of
the Republic and, in particular, the Vega
Real and Santiago valley in the north,
and Los Llanos or the plain of Seybo in
the southeast, are well watered and extraordinarily fertile, and contain the finest
sugar lands in the West India Islands,
while the mountainous districts are especially suited to the culture of coffee, and
tropical fruits may be grown throughout the
Republic with a minimum of attention. The
sugar industry is in a flourishing condition,
and the exports are increasing and cacao is
now the second most important industry;
coffee, cotton, tobacco, and rice are grown
with variable success. The country abounds
in timber, including mahogany and other
cabinet woods and dye-woods, but the industry is undeveloped and transport facilities are lacking. Live Stock.—The treeless
prairies, or savannahs, are capable of supporting large herds of cattle, but they are
mainly in a state of nature.

Gold and silver were formerly exported
in large quantities, and platinum is known
to exist, while iron, copper, tin, antimony,
and manganese are also found; but copper
is the only metal now produced, and one
gold-washing plant is in course of construction. Of the non-metallic minerals the
principal production is salt, of which great
quantities exist in the Neyba district of the
south.

Exports.—The principal exports in 1912 were sugar $5,841,357, cacao $4,248,724, and tobacco $370,637; the principal imports being cottons $1,608,465, breadstuffs, rice and provisions $1,710,892, and iron and steel manufactures $1,626,800. Sixty per cent of the total trade is with the United States, the share of Germany being 16 per cent. While the bulk of the sugar is entered in the Customs statistics as going to the United States, it is nearly all reexported, the United Kingdom receiving about 50 per cent and Canada 25 per cent.

Railways.—There were (1911) about 500 miles of railway open, of which 150 miles are government line, 80 miles belong to an English company and the remainder are private lines on the various plantations.

Shipping.—The mercantile marine consists of a few small sailing vessels and two small coasting steamers. In 1912, 1,076 vessels (783,893 tons) engaged in the foreign trade entered and cleared at the ports of the Republic. There is an excellent roadstead in Samaná Bay on the northeast coast.

The unit of value is the United States gold dollar.

Trade with the United States.—The value of merchandise imported into Santo Domingo from the United States for the year 1913 was $5,802,767, and goods to the value of $3,728,774 were sent thither—a balance of $2,073,993 in favor of the United States.

See illustration opposite 6996.

Santo Domingo:

Annexation of, to United States—
Discussed by President—
Grant, 4006, 4015, 4053, 4082, 4176, 4365.
Johnson, 3886.
Roosevelt, 6997.
Report of Secretary of State on, transmitted, 4072.
Treaty for, submitted, 4000, 4015.
Failure of ratification of, discussed, 4053, 4176, 4365.
President declines to communicate privileges relating to, 4012.
Referred to, 4006, 4082.
Views of Cabral on, communicated to Senate, 4071.
Application of, to United States to exercise protectorate over, referred to, 4193.
Claim of United States against, 6329.
Claims of citizens of United States to guano on Alta Vela Island, 3827.
Colony of negroes on coast of, order regarding return of, 3433.
Commerce with restraints on, removed, 278, 280, 285, 292, 294.
Complaints of France against, 379.
Commercial relations with, 287, 773, 5663.
Condition and resources of, report on, 4009, 4070, 4071.
Customs of, taken over by United States, 7377, 7379.
Diplomatic intercourse with, provision for, recommended, 4083.

Economic condition of, 6997.
Export of coal and arms to, forbidden, 6968.
Fugitive criminals, convention with, for surrender of, 3669.
Imprisonment of American citizens by authorities of, 4004, 4013.
Incorporation of, with Spanish Monarchy referred to, 3233.
Instructions to naval officers in command on coast of, referred to, 4023, 4075.
Minister of United States to, nominated, 2909.
Payment of moneys claimed to be due, from United States referred to, 4382.
Peace concluded between contending parties in, 2658.
Political condition of, referred to, 773.
Proposition of foreign power to purchase, referred to, 4017.
Report of George B. McClellan on, transmitted, 4071.
Revolution in, referred to, 3826, 6427.
Samaná Bay, convention for transfer of. (See Samaná Bay.)
Social condition of, discussed, 3885.
Tariff laws of, evidence of modifications of proclaimed, 5587.
Referred to, 5615, 5747.
Treaty with, transmitted and discussed, 3669, 4826, 4842, 4921, 6950.
Withdrawn, 4888, 4922.
Vessel of United States fired upon at Azua, 6095.
War in, discussed, 2619, 3445, 6365.
Peace concluded, 2658.

Santo Domingo, Treaties with.—A convention of amity, commerce and navigation and for the surrender of fugitive criminals was concluded with the Dominican Republic in 1867. This provided for reciprocal privileges of citizens and the exchange of diplomatic and consular officers, and the extradition of criminals. This convention terminated Jan. 13, 1898, on notice from the Dominican Republic.

In 1903, by an arbitration protocol the claim of the San Domingo Improvement Company of New York was submitted to a board of arbitrators consisting of John G. Carlisle, Manuel de J. Galvan and Judge George Gray. These rendered an award July 14, 1904, providing for the redelivery of the various properties to the Dominican Republic and the payment by the republic of $4,481,250 in monthly installments to the financial agent of the United States and for the security for such payments the customs revenue; and customs houses of Puerto Plata, Sanchez, Samaná and Montecristy, and all other ports of entry or custom houses now existing or as might thereafter be established on the coast or in the interior north of eighteen degrees and forty-five minutes and east of the Haitian boundary, were to be assigned and designated, which custom houses were to be turned over to a financial agent, to be appointed by the United States, who was to have entire charge of such custom houses and of the collection of the revenues therefrom.

Receiver of Customs.—In 1907 a convention was concluded providing for the assistance of the United States in the collection and application of the customs revenues of the republic. In the preamble to this treaty it is stated that owing to the disturbed political conditions of the country, debts and claims had been created to the amount of more than $30,000,000, and that these same conditions had prevented the peaceable and continuous collection of revenue, and that the debts were continually increasing. Fiscal agents of the republic effected a compromise whereby all its foreign creditors agreed to accept $12,407,000 for debts and claims amounting to about $21,184,000 of nominal or face value, and the holders of internal debts or claims of about $2,028,258 nominal or fac value agreed to accept about $645,817 therefor, and the remaining holders of internal debts or claims on the same basis as the assents already given will receive about $2,400,000 therefor, which sum the Dominican Government fixed upon as the amount which it will pay to such remaining internal debt-holders; making the total payments under such adjustment and settlement, including interest as adjusted and claims not yet liquidated, amount to not more than about $17,000,000.

Part of the plan of settlement was the issue and sale of bonds of the Dominican Republic to the amount of $20,000,000, bearing five per cent interest payable in fifty years and redeemable after ten years at 102¼. It was agreed that the President of the United States should appoint a receiver to collect all the customs duties accruing in the several custom houses of the Dominican Republic until the payment and retirement of any and all bonds thus issued. It is also provided that until the whole of the public debt is paid no further obligations shall be incurred and no modification of internal or customs duties shall be made, except with the consent of the President of the United States.

Santo Dominigo also became a party to the convention between the United States and the several republics of South and Central America for the arbitration of pecuniary claims and the protection of inventions, etc., which was signed in Buenos Aires in 1910 and proclaimed in Washington July 29, 1914. (See South and Central America, Treaties with.)

Santo Domingo City, building of Ozama River bridge at, by American citizens, 5784.

Saratoga, Battle. (See Bemis Heights.)

Sardinia:
Commercial relations with, 820.
Treaty with, 1729, 1749, 1916.

Sassacus, The, engagement with the *Albemarle* referred to, 3411.

Sault Ste. Marie Canal, passage of English or Canadian steamer through, referred to, 4014. (See also Canals.)

Savages Station (Va.), Battle of.—One of the Seven Days' Battles before Richmond. June 29, 1862, Sumner and Heintzelman retired from Fair Oaks and took up a position near Savages Station, on the Richmond and York River Railroad. After destroying the supplies there, Heintzelman moved south across the swamp. Magruder, in pursuit, finding Fair Oaks abandoned, advanced to Savages Station and made an attack on Sumner's corps in the afternoon. The latter maintained his ground till dark. During the night he retreated into the White Oak Swamp, leaving 2,500 sick and wounded in the hospital at the station.

Savannah (Ga.), British Occupation of.—Nov. 27, 1778, Commodore Hyde Parker convoyed a fleet of transports to Savannah, which carried about 3,500 British soldiers. The troops landed at Tybee Island, fifteen miles from Savannah, and captured the city Dec. 29. The American force under Gen. Robert Howe consisted of about 800 Continentals and 400 militia. The British loss was officially reported as 3 killed and 10 wounded. Eighty-three American dead and 11 wounded were found on the field. Some 450 were taken prisoners, while the others retreated up the Savannah River and reached South Carolina. Forty-eight cannon, 23 mortars, 94 barrels of powder, and a large quantity of provisions fell into the hands of the British.

Savannah (Ga.), Fall of. (See Fort McAllister, Ga.)

Savannah (Ga.), Siege of.—In 1779 Washington sent Gen. Lincoln to take command of the army in the South, and requested Count d'Estaing, in command of the French fleet in American waters, to coöperate in an effort to retake Savannah, Ga., Sept. 16, 1779; the latter appeared off Savannah with 33 vessels and 6,000 men. After the capture of 2 frigates and 2 storeships a regular siege was commenced by the allies. The city was defended by a force of about 3,000 British troops under Gen. Prevost. On the morning of Oct. 9, 1779, about 3,500 French and 850 Americans advanced to the attack. The fighting was fierce for nearly an hour, when the assailants gave way after a loss of nearly 1,000 men. Count Pulaski was killed and Count d'Estaing was wounded. The loss to the garrison was only 56 in killed and wounded. Next to Bunker Hill this fight was the bloodiest of the war.

Savannah River, survey of, referred to, 1128.

Savings Banks. (See Banks, Savings.)

Saxony.—A Kingdom of the German Empire, bounded on the north and east by Prussia, on the south by Bohemia, and on the west by Saxe-Altenburg, Saxe-Weimar-Eisenach, and Reuss. It is noted for its rich mines of coal, silver, tin, lead, iron, etc. For its size, Saxony is the busiest industrial state in the German Empire. It manufactures extensively machinery, textiles, tools, porcelain, glass, foundry products, beer and spirits. The government is a hereditary constitutional monarchy, administered by a King, an upper chamber, and a lower chamber of eighty-two deputies. Saxony sends four representatives to the Bundesrat and twenty-three to the Reichstag. It entered the North German Confederation in 1866 and became a state of the German Empire in 1871. Area, 5,787 square miles; population (1910), 4,508,601.

Saxony, convention with, 2267.

Saxony, Treaties with.—The convention of 1845 abolished the *droit d'aubaine* and all other taxes on emigration; provided for a period of two years in which an alien may close up the affairs of a legator from whom by alienage he is unable to inherit or hold property; settled questions of the disposal and holding of property by aliens, and the settlement of disputes concerning the same. (See German Empire.)

Scabbard.—A sheath for a sword or similar weapon.

Schedule K. (See Tariff, Wool.)

Scheldt Dues, discussed and treaty regarding, 3381, 3395, 3459.

Schleswig-Holstein War, neutrality of United States in, discussed, 2548.

Schools. (See Education; Indian Schools.)

Schuylkill Arsenal, at Philadelphia, appropriation for, recommended, 4785.

Science and Art:

Promotion of advocated, 58, 60, 61, 194, 878.

Tariff discriminations against foreign works of art, 4794, 4824, 4826, 5091, 6291.

Sciences, National Academy of. (See National Academy of Sciences.)

Scotan Indians. (See Indian Tribes.)

Scout.—A person detailed to obtain information regarding an enemy.

Sea.—A general term referring to all the salt navigable waters. (See Freedom of the Seas.)

Sea Witch, The, wreck of, near Cuba, 2907.

Seacoast Defenses. (See Defenses, Public.)

Seal Fisheries. (See Alaska, Bering Sea Fisheries, Great Britain, claims against, and Russia, claims against.)

Seal of United States.—Immediately after the declaration of independence a committee was appointed to prepare a device for the great seal of the United States. The committee consisted of Benjamin Franklin, John Adams, and Thomas Jefferson. They reported various devices during several years. William Barton, of Philadelphia, was appointed to submit designs. Sir John Prestwich, an English antiquarian, suggested a design to John Adams in 1779. It was not until June 20, 1782, however, that a seal was adopted. This was by the Congress of the Confederation. It was a combination of the various designs of Barton and Prestwich, and consisted of: Arms—Paleways of thirteen pieces argent and gules; a chief azure; the escutcheon on the breast of the American eagle displayed proper, holding in his dexter talon an olive branch and in his sinister a bundle of thirteen arrows, and in his beak a scroll with the motto *E Pluribus Unum* (out of many, one). Crest—A glory *or* (gold) breaking through a cloud proper and surrounding thirteen stars, forming a constellation *argent* (silver) on an azure field. Reverse —A pyramid unfinished, symbolizing the strength and growth of the states; in the zenith an eye in a triangle surrounded with a glory proper; over the eye, around the rim, the words *Annuis cœptis* (God has favored the undertaking); beneath the pyramid MDCCLXXVI and the words *Novus ordo sœclorum* (a new order of things). This seal has never been changed, and is in charge of the Secretary of State.

The seal is stamped upon all signatures of the President, attested by the Secretary of State.

Accompanying the report and adopted by Congress, were the following remarks and explanation: "The escutcheon is composed of the chief and pale, the two most honorable ordinaries. The pieces pales represent the several states all joined in one solid compact entire, supporting a chief which unites the whole and represents Congress. The motto alludes to this union. The pales in the arms are kept closely united by the chief, and the chief depends on that union and the strength resulting from it for its support, to denote the confederacy of the United States of America and the preservation of their union through Congress. The colors of the pales are those used in the flag of the United States of America; white signifies purity and innocence; red, hardiness and valor; and blue, the color of the chief, signifies vigilant perseverance and justice. The olive branch and arrows denote the power of peace and war, which is exclusively vested in Congress. The constellation denotes a new state taking its place and rank among other sovereign powers. The escutcheon is borne on the breast of an American eagle without any other supporters, to denote that the United States of America ought to rely on their own virtue. The pyramid on the reverse signifies strength and duration. The eye over it and the motto allude to the many signal interpositions of Providence in favor of the American cause. The date underneath is that of the Declaration of Independence, and the words under it signify the beginning of the new American era which commences from that date."

Seamen's Act.—The La Follette bill to promote the welfare of American seamen in the merchant marine of the United States was one of the much discussed administration measures of the Sixty-third Congress. It was signed by President Wilson, March 4, 1915.

General provisions fix the percentage of a crew that must be able seamen, the percentage of each department that must understand the language of the officers, and define seamen as men over nineteen years old having had three years' experience of a specified kind.

Perhaps the most important provision in the act imposes upon foreign vessels leaving American ports the same requirements as to life-saving appliances as are demanded of American ships. All ships built after July 1, 1915, must carry life-saving equipment for all persons on board, of which 75 per cent must be regular lifeboats and not more than 25 per cent life rafts or collapsible lifeboats. For the lake and river steamers a distinction is recognized between the excursion season, from May 15 to Sept. 16, when the restrictions are somewhat relaxed.

Another provision affecting foreign as well as American seamen is that providing that seamen reaching American ports may demand and receive half of their pay already earned. If this demand is refused the seaman is freed from his contract and is then entitled to all he has earned up to that time.

Other provisions abolish arrest and imprisonment as a penalty for desertion, and seek to abrogate treaty provisions in relation thereto.

The spirited controversy over navigation laws revealed the fact that not enough was known of the regulations of the principal countries to make an adequate comparison.

For example, emphasis is frequently laid upon the fact that our laws require that American ships be officered by American citizens, and complaint is made that this is unjust and unusual. Upon making a comparison of the laws in the Bureau's report, it is found that the laws of Japan provide that no foreigner may be employed as an officer on a vessel of a subsidized company without Government approval. Norway and Germany do not expressly prohibit the employment of foreign citizens, but the fact that applicants for licenses as officers are required to pass examinations in Norwegian and German, respectively, practically excludes persons of other nationalities.

All the selected countries except Japan have laws requiring adequate quarters for the crew. Germany has since 1905 required 123 cubic feet of air space in the sleeping quarters for each sailor, and France has required the same space since 1908. England fixed its requirement at 120 feet in 1907, and Norway adopted this minimum in 1909. Requirements for American vessels were not raised to 120 feet until 1915.

The provision in the Act of March 4, 1915, for a new class of sailors designated as "certified lifeboat men" has been the subject of much discussion. The Bureau's report brings out the fact that a British Commission appointed especially to investigate the subject of lifeboat equipment recommended as far back as 1912 that two "efficient boathands" should be carried for each lifeboat and that "facilities should be given to enable all hands to prove their competency as efficient boat hands." However, Parliament has not yet adopted this recommendation. A German rule promulgated in March, 1898, requires that emigrant ships shall carry at least two adult persons in the crew for every collapsible boat; at least three for every ordinary rigid boat; and at least four for every regulation life boat.

Seamen, American:
Appropriation for relief of, 472.
Captured by Tripolitans, 356.
Impressment of, by—
  Chile, 2772.
  Great Britain, 383,430, 495,934,2016.
    Account of J. B. Cutting for expenditures incurred in liberating, 108.
  Japan, convention with regarding shipwrecked seamen, 4561.
  Tripolitans captured by captain and crew of the frigate *Philadelphia*, 356.
Maltreatment of, on ships plying between New York and Aspinwall, 3413.
Number of, on vessels, 374.
Outrages committed upon, by pirates in West Indies and Gulf of Mexico, 765.
Pirates, outrages on, 765.
Protection for, measure providing, proposed, 6348.
Relief of—
  Agent appointed for, 192.
  Appropriation for, 472.
  Convention with Japan regarding shipwrecked seamen, 4561.
  Provision for, 343.
  Recommended, 6333.
  When discharged abroad recommended, 331.
Rights of, in foreign ports, 8091.
Shipment and discharge of, 4740.
Welfare act suspended, 8101.

Seamew, The, satisfaction due for detention of, admitted by Great Britain, 2111.

Seaport Towns, protection for. (See Defenses, Public, provision for.)

Search, Right of. (See Right of Search.)

Seat of Government:
Boundaries of, referred to and proclaimed, 86, 192, 194.
Removal of, from Philadelphia to Washington, 281, 295, 298, 299, 300.

Sebois River, referred to, 1128.

Secession.—The act of going aside or withdrawing, as from a religious or political organization. The word has received world-wide notoriety from its use in connection with the secession of certain of the United States from the Union in 1860 and 1861. After the adoption of the Constitution in 1787 the idea of the sovereignty of the individual states remained familiar to the minds of many Americans. The Federalists of New England made threats of secession in 1811 and 1814, and secession was generally looked upon as an available remedy for Federal aggression. This claim has been advanced, directly or indirectly by many of the states in turn and has on such occasions usually been condemned by the others as treasonable. It was involved in or explicitly put forward by the Kentucky Resolutions, the Hartford Convention, and the South Carolina Nullification Ordinance (q. v.). While Jefferson condemned "scission," some of his writings admitted it to be a remedy of the last resort. As agitation against slavery became more intense secession was looked upon as the right and destiny of the southern states. South Carolina was ready to secede in 1850. The Nullification Ordinance of 1832 and other measures passed by that state were early steps in that direction.

Gen. Jackson, then President, felt that such a power lodged in a state would be fatal to the Union and altogether unconstitutional. His emphatic opposition, as expressed in his military preparations, as well as his strong message and proclamation on nullification, in 1833 (1166, 1203), checked this feeling for a time, but the postponement to a final test was perhaps chiefly due to the unpopularity of the nullification doctrine among the states-rights people themselves. Another reason why the South Carolina nullification movement was stopped was the adoption by Congress of the Clay-Calhoun compromise tariff bill, which gave satisfaction to the nullifiers and their states-rights friends in the south who did not accept nullification as a rightful or expedient remedy.

The secession doctrine was revived on the election of Lincoln in 1860. Many of the southern people felt that the triumph of the Republican party meant the adoption of a policy of such interference with the institution of slavery as to make it impossible for the southern states any longer to secure and enjoy their constitutional rights, within the Union.

Accordingly, Dec. 20, 1860, after the election of Lincoln, South Carolina, by convention, passed an ordinance repealing her adoption of the Constitution in 1788, and reviving her independence. Mississippi seceded Jan. 9, 1861; Florida, Jan. 10; Alabama, Jan. 11; Georgia, Jan. 19; Louisiana, Jan. 26; Texas, Feb. 1; Virginia, April 17; Arkansas, May 6; North Carolina, May 20; Tennessee, June 8, all by conventions. Opposition to secession in many states was based rather upon the ground of inexpediency than unconstitutionality. The National Government never recognized the validity of the ordinances of secession adopted by the southern states. (See illustration opposite 3151.)

Secession, right of States regarding, discussed by President—
Buchanan, 3159, 3186.
Lincoln, 3206, 3221.

Second, Assistant Postmaster-General. (See Assistant Postmasters-General.)

Second Assistant Secretary, State Department.—The office of second assistant secretary of state was created in 1866. This officer has charge of certain diplomatic affairs of great importance to the work of the Department of State. He is appointed by the President, by and with the consent of the Senate, and his yearly salary is $4,500. Under his jurisdiction fall the Latin American and Mexican Division (q. v.), the supervision of mail (q. v.), the Diplomatic Bureau (q. v.), and the Citizenship Bureau (q. v.). (See State Department.)

Second Class Mail Matter, Commission on, report of, 7733.

Secret Lodges, proclamation against lawless incursions of, on northern frontier, 1925.

Secret Service.—The Secret Service of the United States is under the Department of the Treasury and is directly under charge of the assistant secretary of the treasury. The first formal appropriation for this service was made in 1865, to the amount of $100,-000 included in the Sundry Civil Appropriation Bill.

The original purpose of the Secret Service organization was that of detecting counterfeiting, but its functions have been enlarged and widened.

The Secret Service force has been called upon to protect the Presidents, especially after the assassination of McKinley; to gather evidence against violators of the Customs Laws and the Excise Laws; to gather evidence against land frauds, resulting in many arrests and convictions, as well as in the recovery to the United States of vast tracts of land illegally acquired by private individuals and public officials; and to gather evidence against violators of the anti-trust laws and generally against violators of any Federal Statutes.

An auxiliary arm of the Secret Service in the Department of Justice, directly under the administrative branch, is the Bureau of Investigation. Another auxiliary force consists of the Post-Office Inspectors, working under the Post-Office Department. Each of the departments can avail itself of the services of the Secret Service Department for detecting criminals.

During the Spanish-American War the confidential agents of Spain were detected by the Secret Service and evidence procured which caused the expulsion from Canada of the Spanish Legation, members of which were acting as spies.

The efficiency of the Secret Service Department as a whole was well illustrated immediately after the declaration of war with Germany in 1917, when the outbreaks caused by German spies and plotters were feared and confidently expected by many American citizens. The Secret Service, however, had thoroughly acquainted itself with all the machinations of the German Spy System; and the Department of Justice, by the aid of the Secret Service, was enabled promptly to make wholesale arrests of the leaders of the German Spy System in America, which had the result of breaking down the German scheme, and of throwing consternation into its leaders. It is generally claimed that the United States has as effective a Secret Service as any country in the world. (See Treasury Department.)

Secret Service:

Amendment to law a benefit to criminals, 7225.

Assertion that Congress did not wish to be investigated by, 7226.

Complaint of amendments to law, 7225.

Defense of use of Secret Service men in discovering land frauds, 7245.

Evidence of land and timber frauds secured by, 7225.

Increase in salary of chief of, recommended, 7253.

Land frauds investigated by, 7249.

Report of special committee on President's message relating to, 7238.

Senator and member of Congress indicted on evidence secured by, 7226.

Secretaries.—By a series of acts passed in the early part of 1781 Congress organized the Government under several Departments, at the head of which were placed secretaries with duties similar to those of the secretaries of the British Government. The Secretary of the Navy was originally the Secretary of Marine. The Secretary of the Treasury was originally the Superintendent of Finance. Now all the heads of Departments, nine in number, are denominated secretaries, except the Attorney-General and the Postmaster-General. (See also Cabinet; Presidential Succession, and Administration.)

Secretary of Agriculture. (See Agriculture, Department of.)

Secretary of Commerce.—The first Secretary of Commerce of the United States was William C. Redfield, who was appointed when the Department was separated from the Department of Commerce and Labor on March 4, 1913. He is ninth in the Presidential succession (q. v.), and his yearly salary is $12,000. He is charged with the general development and encouragement of American commerce, trade, and transportation, through the activities of the Commerce Department (q. v.).

Secretary of the Interior.—The office of Secretary of the Interior was definitely established by act of Congress approved March 14, 1862, but the duties of the office have never been carefully defined. The Secretary of the Interior has assumed the administration of various details of internal administration of the government, such as the administration of Indian affairs; supervision over mines, irrigation, pensions and patents; direction of the educational work of the country; government of the territories, Alaska and Hawaii; the direction of the General Land Office; and the administration of the National Parks. In addition to his administration duties, he renders decisions on laws affecting public lands and pensions, and formulates the policy of the Department of the Interior thereon. (See Interior Department and list of sub-headings at end of article.)

Secretary of the Navy. (See Navy Department.)

Secretary of State. (See State Department.)

Secretary of the Treasury. (See Treasury Department.)

Secretary of War.—The office of Secretary of War was established in 1781, succeeding the Board of War which had been in military charge of the War of the Revolution. The Secretary of War is third in the line of Presidential succession (q. v.), and his yearly salary is $12,000. He prepares estimates for and directs the appropriations and expenditures of the Department of War; and accordingly, although the President is the commander-in-chief of the Army, the Secretary of War and the War Department are responsible at any given time for the efficiency in war of the United States. Besides administration of the war forces of the country, the Secretary of War has supervision over the Military Academy at West Point (q. v.), over the Army War College at Washington, and over bridges across navigable streams and harbors. In addition, he has charge of the publication of the *Official Records of the War of the Rebellion.* (See War Department; Army.)

Sedition Law.—In 1798, when war between the United States and France was imminent, there were in the United States by estimate 30,000 Frenchmen organized into clubs, and 50,000 sympathizers with France, who had been English subjects. Many of the newspapers of the country at the time were controlled by aliens, mostly French, English, Irish, and Scotch refugees. Those alien residents who sympathized with France—the larger number—attacked the Government fiercely through the press for its attitude toward that country. In order to restrain this feeling, which excited bitter animosity among those Americans who resented the French attitude toward the United States, the Federalists in control of Congress passed the famous alien and sedition acts. The sedition act of July 14, 1798, was modeled on two English acts of 1795. It provided heavy fines and imprisonment for any who should combine or conspire against the operations of the Government, or should write, print, or publish any "false, scandalous, and malicious writings" against it or either House of Congress or the President, with intent to bring contempt upon them or to stir up sedition. The penalties imposed were fines of $5,000 and five years' imprisonment, and $2,000 and two years' imprisonment, respectively. This, as well as the alien act, was regarded by the Republican party as unconstitutional and subversive of the liberty of press and speech. They called forth the Virginia and Kentucky resolutions (q. v.). The sedition act expired in 1801. (See also Alien and Sedition Laws.)

Seed Distribution:
Act making special, in draught-stricken counties in Texas, vetoed, 5142.
Recommendations regarding, 5888, 5982, 6171.

Seigniorage:
Act for coinage of, vetoed, 5915. Discussed, 5875.

Seizures. (See Vessels, United States.)

Selden, Withers & Co., reimbursement of Indians on account of failure of, recommended, 2836.

Self-Government.—A democracy or a republican form of government as distinguished from a monarchy, autocracy or oligarchy, for the reason that in a democracy or a republican form of government the people direct the formulation of their own laws, and therefore govern themselves.

Seminaries of Learning (see also Education; National University):
Establishment of, discussed and recommended, 470, 878.
Power to establish should be conferred upon Congress, 587.

Seminole Indians. (See Indian Tribes.)

Seminole Wars.—After the War of 1812 the combined British and Indian stronghold known as the Negro Fort, on the Appalachicola River, was a constant menace to the Georgia settlers. During 1817 there were several massacres of whites. Gen. E. P. Gaines was intrusted with the task of subjugating the Indians. He destroyed an Indian village on the refusal of the inhabitants to surrender certain murderers, and the Indians retaliated by waylaying a boat ascending the Appalachicola with supplies for Fort Scott and killing 34 men and a number of women. Gen. Jackson took the field against the Indians in January, 1818, and in a sharp campaign of six months defeated them completely, destroying their villages and driving them from every stronghold. Among the prisoners taken were two English subjects, Arbuthnot and Ambrister, who were charged with inciting the Indians to hostilities. These were tried by court-martial and hanged.

Jackson pursued the Indians into Florida, which was then Spanish territory, captured Pensacola and St. Marks, deposed the Spanish government, and set up an American administration. This territory was later returned to Spain, but the outgrowth of the incident was the cession of Florida to the United States in satisfaction of the latter's claims, and the payment to Spain besides of $5,000,-000. The second Seminole war was the most stubborn and bloody in all the Indian wars. It originated in the refusal of part of the tribe to cede their lands to the whites and remove to the Indian Territory. Osceola, one of the chiefs opposed to immigration, was placed in irons by Gen. Thompson, an agent of the United States. Osceola regained his liberty, killed Thompson and others at Fort King, and cut to pieces a body of troops. Operations against Osceola and his warriors were conducted with great severity, but with varying success, under Scott, Call, Jesup, Taylor, and others. The Indians were supposed to be subjugated in 1837, but Osceola fled and renewed the struggle. He was taken by strategy in 1842 and the war ended. (See illustration opposite 1929 and description on back.)

Seminole Wars:
American forces in, and officers commanding, discussed, 611, 1472, 1833.

Senate.—The upper branch of the legislature of the United States. The Senate is composed of two representatives from each state, until 1913 chosen by the state legislature for a period of six years; accordingly the membership has varied in number, from time to time, from twenty-two members representing eleven states in the First Congress to ninety-six members representing forty-eight states in the sixty-third Congress. Senators must be thirty years of age, residents of the state they represent, and must have been citizens of the United States for at least nine years; they receive a salary of $7,500 per annum and a small allowance for stationery and mileage. Should a vacancy occur in the Senate during a recess of the state legislature, the governor of the state makes a temporary appointment which is valid until the next meeting of the legislature. The Constitution provides that the terms of Senators shall so overlap that one-third of the members retire every two years. The presiding officer of the Senate is the Vice-President of the United States who votes only in case of the votes being equally divided. Besides the legislative functions, the Senate ratifies or rejects all treaties negotiated by the President; confirms or rejects all appointments to the higher Federal offices; exercises the functions of high-court of impeachment; and in case the electors fail to make a choice, elects the Vice-President of the United States from the two candidates receiving the largest number of electoral votes. The exercise of these wide powers given to it by the Constitution, has rendered the Senate more powerful than the House; the reverse being usually the case with upper houses.

In the Constitution adopted by Virginia in 1776 the name Senate was given to the Virginian upper chamber, but the term was not applied to the upper house of the Federal Congress until Aug. 6, 1787; which up to that time had been known as the "second branch." Since the name has been adopted in the Congress of the United States it has spread to all states whose legislatures are divided into two chambers.

The composition of the Senate is due to one of the most important proposals in the constitutional convention at Philadelphia, known as the "Connecticut Compromise" which was brought forward by Oliver Ellsworth and Roger Sherman. This compromise settled the conflicting claims of the large and small states by providing for equal representation of states in the Senate, the House being chosen on a population basis. The seventeenth amendment to the Constitution, adopted May 31, 1913, provides for the election of senators by direct vote of the people, instead of by the legislatures of the states as formerly. Some of the states had already, before the adoption of this amendment, provided for the election of their senators by direct vote of the people.

See illustration, frontispiece, Vol. XI.

Senatorial Courtesy.—In order that the dignity of the body may be preserved, the Senate gives considerable attention to the personal wishes of its members. In addition to the observance of courteous address, polite language, and the exercise of those acts of kindness which tend to lighten official duties and render social life a pleasure, there is a tacit understanding as to the conventional privileges to be accorded to each in the official deliberations. Should the name of any former member of the Senate be presented to that body by the President for their advice as to his appointment to a Federal office, Senatorial courtesy requires immediate confirmation without reference to a committee. The privileges of speaking as long as he may choose on any question before the Senate is a courtesy granted each Senator, and though it is charged that undue advantage has sometimes been taken of this privilege it was not abridged until on the closing session of the Sixty-fourth Congress on March 5, 1917, a small group of Senators was enabled by employing a filibuster (q. v.) to prevent action upon President Wilson's request for power to use armed neutrality (q. v.). At the President's request, the Senate continued its meetings, and on March 8, by a vote of 76 to 3, adopted a rule whereby closure (q. v.) may be enforced. The rule provides that two days after notice in writing from sixteen Senators the question of closing debate on a particular bill shall be settled without debate, and if settled in the affirmative, by two-thirds, that bill shall be held before the Senate till its final disposition, and each Senator shall be limited to one hour's debate in all on the bill itself, amendments to it and motions arising from it. To prevent endless roll calls the rule further provides that after the two-thirds vote no amendment may be offered without unanimous consent.

Senators of United States:

Seneca Indians. (See Indian Tribes.)

Sentinel.—A soldier placed on watch, especially to give quick warning of probable attack.

Separatist.—Sometimes used as a synonym for secessionist. (See Secession.)

Sequoia National Park. (See Parks, National.)

Serbia. (See Servia.)

Servia.— Servia is situated in the north of the Balkan Peninsula and is bounded on the north by Hungary, on the south by Greece, on the east by Rumania and Bulgaria, and on the west by Bosnia, Montenegro, and Albania.

Physical Features.—The country is generally mountainous, and consists of extensive forest-clad slopes, uncultivated heaths, and fertile meadows and valleys. The

Transylvania Alps, the Balkans and the Rhodope ranges extend from Rumania and Bulgaria into eastern Servia, while outliers of the Bosnian and Albanian highlands cross the western border. In the north the Drina and Save effect a confluence at Belgrade with the Danube, which forms the remainder of the northern (and part of the northeastern) frontier, and is joined in the northeast by the Timok, which is also a frontier river for part of its course. The chief inland river is the Morava, which rises in Bulgaria and flows through Servia, from south to north, into the Danube. The valleys of these rivers contain the most fertile districts of the kingdom. The principal river of Macedonian Servia is the Vardar, which rises in the Shar Mountains on the Albanian frontier and flows southward to the Greek frontier and thence to the Gulf of Salonica. The climate is generally mild, but is subject to the continental extremes.

History.—The earlier Serb kingdom was extinguished by the Turks at the battle of Kossovo in 1389, and from that date until the early years of the nineteenth century the country formed a Turkish pashalik. After heroic struggles the pashalik was recognized as an autonomous principality by the Treaty of Adrianople (1829), and by the Treaties of San Stefano and Berlin (1879) the complete independence of the country was recognized, a kingdom being proclaimed on March 6, 1882. On May 29 (June 11), 1903, the descendant of the Obrenovich dynasty, which had ruled Servia as Princes and Kings since 1830, was assassinated, and a grandson of Karageorge, a national hero of the risings of the early nineteenth century, was elected King by the Skupshtina and Senate, and was crowned in September, 1904.

Oct. 19, 1912, the Balkan League (Bulgaria, Servia, Montenegro and Greece) waged a successful war against the Ottoman Empire; in 1913 Bulgaria was engaged in a war with the other members of the League on a question as to the division of the conquered territories. Servia also became involved in a dispute about her western (Albanian) frontier, but withdrew her claims on the representations of the European powers. By the Treaty of Bucharest the Serbo-Bulgarian boundary was delineated, and agreement was also reached with Greece as to the line of the southern boundary.

July 28, 1914, following the assassination of the Austrian Archduke and his wife by a Bosnian student, said to have been incited by Servian societies and with Servian official connivance, Austria declared war against Servia. The government evacuated Belgrade, which was soon occupied by the Austrians.

During the progress of the war the kingdom was completely overwhelmed by the Teutonic armies. King Peter escaped to France and the shattered armies joined the French at Salonika.

Ethnography.—In 1910 the total population of 2,911,701 was composed of 2,250,-000 Servians (Serbo-Croatian Slavonians), 160,000 Rumanians, 47,000 Gypsies, 8,000 Austro-Hungarians and Germans, and 6,000 Jews. The bulk of the Servians belong to the national (Orthodox Eastern) Church, there being 8,500 Roman Catholics and a small number of Protestant Christians. In the territory acquired in 1913 are large numbers of Mohammedans.

The mineral wealth of Servia awaits development. Gold, silver, antimony, nickel, mercury, manganese, graphite, copper, iron, lead, and zinc are found, and coal, marble,

sulphur and oil are won in small quantities. Mineral springs abound. The industrial population is small, the sixty principal establishments in 1910 employing 5,000 hands.

AREA AND POPULATION

Departments	Area in English Sq. Miles	Population 1910
City of Belgrade	5	89,876
Belgrade	782	155,815
Chachak	1,465	138,922
Kragojevatz	887	189,025
Kraina	1,119	112,142
Krutchevatz	1,046	167,371
Morava	1,117	203,638
Nish	988	198,768
Pirot	933	112,314
Podieravatz	1,606	259,906
Podrinyi	1,293	238,275
Rudnik	606	85,340
Smederevo	493	143,216
Timok	1,235	149,538
Toplitza	1,095	110,218
Ujitsi	1,269	146,763
Valievo	947	157,648
Vranya	1,675	252,937
Conquered Territory (about)	16,000	....
Total	34,561	2,911,701

Railways, etc.—About 580 miles of railway were open for traffic in 1911, the main lines crossing the Danube at Belgrade-Semendria, and uniting in a single route as far as Nish, whence they run via Pirot to the Bulgarian boundary and Sofia, and via Vranya across the Turkish frontier, both lines leading to Constantinople. In the territory acquired in 1913 a line runs along the Vardar valley to Salonica (Greece), with eastern and western branches to Bulgaria and Albania.

Servia:

Consular convention with, 4627, 4658. Referred to, 4757.

Diplomatic relations with, referred to, 4522, 4718.

Neutrality of United States in war with—

Austria-Hungary, 7969.

Treaty with, 4658.

Servia, Treaties with.—The convention of commerce and navigation of 1881 provided for freedom of commerce, navigation, and trade upon full, equitable, and reciprocal bases; established the rights of real and personal property holders; conferred trade privileges; restricted the prohibition of imports; exempted citizens of the one country from enforced military service or contributions in the country of the other; granted terms of the most favored nation in matters of import and export duties; exempted goods from any form of transit duty; goods for the one country to be conveyed over the railroads of the other on terms equal to those of the citizens of the country. (For terms of the consular convention of 1881, see Consular Conventions. For terms of the extradition treaty of 1901, see Extradition Treaties.)

Servitude.—State of being in slavery. (See Slavery.)

Sessions of Congress. (See Extraordinary Sessions of Congress.)

Settlement.—A community of individuals, especially one newly located.

Settlement Worker. (See Social Settlements.)

Settlements. (See Social Settlements.)

Settler.—One who takes up his abode in a new country. By custom the settlers of various communities in the United States have been alluded to by the second generation as Old-Settlers, and holidays have been set apart, or special occasions designated, for Old-Settlers' Days or Meetings. (See Old-Settlers' Meeting and Pioneers.)

Seven Days' Battles.—A series of battles fought in the Peninsular campaign, in the vicinity of Richmond, Va., between the Army of the Potomac, under McClellan, and the Confederate army under Lee. The first conflict occurred on June 25, 1862, and a battle was fought each succeeding day but one to July 1. June 25 McClellan's army before Richmond, numbering 115,102, received orders to advance. Lee's army on both sides of the Chickahominy aggregated 80,835. Hooker advanced beyond Fair Oaks and secured his ground. Meantime the Confederates had placed Richmond in a state of security and determined upon aggressive movements. Lee had succeeded Johnston in command, and it was determined to bring the mass of the army down the Chickahominy and threaten McClellan's communications with the York River. Jackson had moved out of the Shenandoah Valley and was at Hanover Court House, ready to render what assistance might be required. Some Federal historians say that McClellan determined to change his base of operations to the James River, seventeen miles south of Fair Oaks. The writers on the Southern side deny this. The retreat was accomplished with a loss to the Federal army of 15,249 men. The operations of the two armies are described under the headings Mechanicsville, Gaines Mill, Savages Station, Frayser's Farm, and Malvern Hill. A few weeks later the Federal army was withdrawn from the James and the Peninsular campaign was ended.

Seven Nations. (See Indian Tribes.)

Seven Pines and Fair Oaks (Va.), Battle of.—From Williamsburg to Richmond, Va., the distance is about fifty miles. By May 30, 1862, Casey's and Couch's divisions of Keyes's corps of McClellan's army had crossed the Chickahominy and advanced respectively to Fair Oaks and Seven Pines, six and seven miles, respectively, from Richmond. Heintzelman's corps had also crossed and was encamped several miles to the rear of Couch on the Williamsburg road, and Sumner was ready to make the passage of the stream when a heavy rain, which occurred on the night of May 30, rendered this impracticable. Joseph E. Johnston, who was in command of the Confederate forces, sent Generals Longstreet, Huger, D. H. Hill and Gustavus W. Smith to attack this advance guard of the invading army. The fighting began at 1 P. M., May 31. The Federals gradually fell back. At 4:30 the arrival of Sedgwick's division of Sumner's corps turned the tide of battle. At sunset Gen. Johnston was severely wounded by a piece of shell, and the command devolved upon Gen. Smith. In the morning the Confederates renewed the attack. They were finally repulsed about noon. The Confederates lost 4,233. The Federals lost 5,739, of whom 890 were killed. Gen. Lee assumed command of the Confederate army the day following the battle. (See illustration opposite 3277.)

Seven Sisters.—New Jersey had long been known as the "Mother of Trusts" because of the leniency of the state laws regulating combinations of capital. During Woodrow Wilson's term as Governor, and when supported by a Democratic Legislature, he stated in a message: "The laws of New Jersey, as they stand, so far from checking monopoly, actually encourage it. They explicitly permit every corporation formed in New Jersey to purchase, hold and assign the securities of any and all other corporations of this or any other state, and to exercise at pleasure the full rights of ownership in them, including the right to act as stockholders. This is the very method of forming vast combinations and creating monopoly against which the whole country has set its face."

In accordance with the Governor's wishes seven bills were introduced into the Senate Jan. 20, 1913, and, under his personal exhortation, passed in less than a month, and became Chapters 13 to 19, Laws of New Jersey, 1913. Their provisions are briefly as follows:

First.—A trust is defined as a combination or agreement between corporations, firms or persons for the following purposes: (1) creating or carrying out restrictions in trade, or acquiring a monopoly, either in intra-state or inter-state business or commerce; (2) limiting or reducing production and increasing prices; (3) preventing competition in production, transportation or marketing of any commodity; (4) fixing a standard price with a view to controlling the price of any commodity; (5) making any agreement by which, directly or indirectly, free and unrestricted competition among the parties to the agreement is precluded; (6) making any secret or oral agreement or understanding with the object of accomplishing any of the above-mentioned purposes. Violation of these provisions is made a misdemeanor and, in case of a corporation, the offence shall be deemed that of the individual directors, and the charter of the offending company may be revoked.

Second.—All corporations, firms or persons engaged in the production or sale of any commodity are forbidden to discriminate between different persons or sections or to charge one a lower price than another for the same service.

Third.—Corporations may purchase real and personal property and the stock of any corporation necessary for its business, and may issue stock in payment therefor in *bona-fide* transaction, but no fictitious stock can be issued for profits anticipated but not yet earned.

Fourth.—Persons incorporating with fraudulent or unlawful intent or for the purpose of restraining trade or acquiring a monopoly, shall be guilty of a misdemeanor.

Fifth.—In case two or more corporations are merged or consolidated, the consolidated corporation may issue bonds or other obligations "to an amount sufficient with its capital stock to provide for all the payments it will be required to assume in order to effect such merger or consolidation," provided that such bonds shall not bear more than six (6) per cent interest.

Sixth.—No corporation can "hereafter purchase, hold, sell, assign, transfer, mortgage, pledge or otherwise dispose of the shares of the capital stock or securities of any other corporation nor, as owner of such, exercise any of the privileges of ownership or the right to vote thereon. Provision is made that a corporation is not prevented from (1) acquiring the securities created by a non-competing corporation in payment of debt; (2) purchasing, as a temporary investment, out of its surplus earnings, the securities of a non-competing corporation; (3) investing its funds in such securities when held by it for the benefit of its employees or any funds held for insurance, rebuilding or depreciation purposes.

Seventh.—Mergers of corporations shall not impair the rights of any creditor of either of the merged corporations. Approval for a merger of corporations must be obtained from the State Board of Public Utilities Commissioners and filed with the Secretary of State.

Seward's Folly.—The action of William H. Seward, Secretary of State, in negotiating the purchase of Alaska in 1867, was criticised severely by many people, and referred to as Seward's Folly. The value of Alaska to the United States has long since robbed the phrase of any but historical value. (See Alaska.)

Sewells Point, Va., evacuation of batteries on, referred to, 3313.

Shadrach Case.—One of many exciting fugitive slave cases of ante-bellum days. In May, 1850, Frederic Wilkins, a Virginian slave, made his escape and found his way to Boston, where he obtained employment under the name of Shadrach. Subsequently he was arrested and imprisoned in the United States court-house, pending trial. He was liberated by a body of colored people and assisted to Canada. Intense excitement prevailed in Boston, which spread over the entire country when Congress turned its attention to the infringement of the law. Clay introduced a resolution requesting the President to inform Congress of the facts in the case. President Fillmore issued a proclamation (2645) announcing the facts and calling upon the people to prevent future disturbances.

Sharpsburg (Md.), Battle of. (See Antietam (Md.), Battle of.)

Sharp-Shooter.—Term applied especially to a soldier who picks off members of the enemy forces by expert rifle shooting. (See Sniper.)

Shasta Forest Reserve, proclaimed, 7334.

Shawanese Indians. (See Indian Tribes.)

Shawnee Indians. (See Indian Tribes.)

Shays's Rebellion.—An insurrection of some people of western Massachusetts against the state government in 1786-87, under the leadership of Daniel Shays. After the close of the Revolution much discontent and actual want prevailed throughout New England, especially in Massachusetts. The annual state tax amounted to $1,000,000. Riots and armed mobs were frequent. The chief grievances complained of were that the governor's salary was too high; that the senate was aristocratic; that lawyers' fees were extortionate and the taxes burdensome. The relief demanded was the issue by the state of paper money. This was refused. Shays, at the head of 1,000 armed men, took possession of Worcester, Dec. 5, 1786, and prevented the session of the Supreme Court. The court having adjourned to Springfield, the same men attempted to prevent the session there, but were forestalled by the militia. In January, 1787, three bodies of insurgents, under Shays, Luke Day, and Eli Parsons, marched upon Springfield with the purpose of capturing the Continental arsenal. Shays's army, numbering about

1,000, was attacked by about 4,000 militia under Gen. Benjamin Lincoln, and was put to flight with a loss of 3 killed and 1 wounded. Shays and some of his followers joined Parson's force, but were dispersed by the militia at Petersham in February, 1787. Shays escaped, but 150 others were captured and their leaders sentenced to death. All, however, were ultimately pardoned on laying down their arms.

Sheep Husbandry, report of Commissioner of Agriculture on, 4462.

Experiment station established, 8101.

Sheepeater Indians. (See Indian Tribes.)

Shell Castle Island, N. C., beacon to be erected on, 182.

Shenandoah, The.—Notwithstanding the provisions of the British foreign enlistment act of 1819, which forbids the equipment of any land or naval forces within British dominions to operate against any friendly nation, the *Florida*, *Alabama*, *Georgia*, *Shenandoah*, and other Confederate vessels were allowed to escape in spite of the protest of the United States minister. The *Shenandoah* sailed from London as the *Sea King* Oct. 8, 1864, commanded by Capt. James Iredell Waddell, of the Confederate navy. Making for Madeira her name was changed to *Shenandoah*. From Madeira she sailed for Melbourne, destroying a number of United States merchant ships on the way. Thence she went to Bering Sea and did great damage to whaling vessels. At the close of the war the *Shenandoah* was surrendered to the British Government, and later turned over to the United States. The depredations of the *Shenandoah* were made a part of the Alabama claims against Great Britain. (See also Alabama Claims.)

Shenandoah, The (see also Alabama Claims):

Judgments rendered by claims commission on claims arising from captures by, referred to, 4322.

Reported surrender of, referred to, 3575.

Sherman Act.—A compromise financial measure introduced into Congress by Senator John Sherman, of Ohio, and passed July 14, 1890. It repealed the Bland-Allison Act of 1878 and directed the Secretary of the Treasury to purchase silver bullion to the amount of 4,500,000 ounces per month, at the market rate, issuing Treasury notes in payment therefor. These notes were to be redeemed in coin at the Treasury on demand. The act also directed the coinage each month of 2,000,000 ounces of the bullion into standard silver dollars. The repeal of the Sherman Act was frequently urged. In the summer of 1893 the law was claimed to be a leading cause of the business depression, and President Cleveland summoned Congress to meet in special session Aug. 7. Congress, after a long debate, passed Nov. 1 the Voorhees bill, repealing the silver-purchasing clause of the Sherman Act, but affirming bimetallism as a national policy.

Sherman Act:

Discussed, 5548, 5628.

Repeal of purchasing clause of, discussed, 5875, 6073, 6074.

Recommended, 5833.

Sherman's March. (See illustration opposite page 3437.)

Shilling.—The name of a coin in use in several European states, varying in its value. The English shilling is one-twentieth of a pound sterling, the Danish copper shilling is one-ninety-sixth of a rixdaler, and equal to one-fourth of a penny of English money. The Swedish shilling is twice the value of the Danish. In some parts of Germany the shilling is used as a fractional coin of the value of one penny sterling. In America this coin was first issued from the mint at Boston. The first struck were known as the New England shilling, Willow Tree, Oak Tree, and Pine Tree coins. One of the earliest coins used in America was the Bermuda shilling. Lord Baltimore had shillings coined in London for use in Maryland. As money of account the shilling varied greatly in the Colonies.

Shiloh, or Pittsburg Landing (Tenn.), Battle of.—One of the most hotly contested battles of the Civil War. After the first line of Confederate defenses in the West had been broken by Grant, Gen. Beauregard was sent to establish another. He selected the line of the Memphis and Charleston Railroad. The Confederate army to the number of 45,000 was concentrated at Corinth, Miss., under command of Albert Sidney Johnston. Polk, Bragg, Hardee, and Breckinridge were there with their corps, and Van Dorn and Price were on the way from Arkansas with 30,000 more. After taking Fort Donelson, the Federal army under Grant proceeded up the Tennessee River to Pittsburg Landing, a point 219 miles from its mouth, on the west bank, near the intersection of the state lines of Alabama, Mississippi, and Tennessee, and about twenty miles from the Confederate camp at Corinth. Five divisions of Grant's army, under Generals W. T. Sherman, Hurlbut, W. H. L. Wallace, McClernand, and Prentiss, were here encamped, and, including Gen. Lew. Wallace's division, about seven miles down the river, numbered 40,000 men. Buell's army of 40,000 was expected to reenforce them here, and it was the intention upon his arrival to proceed against Johnston at Corinth. The latter, however, without waiting for his own reenforcements, resolved to attack Grant before the arrival of Buell's forces. April 3, 1862, Johnston marched his army from Corinth and on the 6th attacked the Federal army. After a day's hard fighting Grant's army was driven back from the vicinity of Shiloh Church nearly to the river, a distance of three miles. A part of the expected reenforcements arrived just in time to help to check the last charge of the victorious Confederates. The battle was reopened on the morning of the 7th by Buell, who had arrived during the night with 20,000 men. The second day's fighting was as stubborn as the first had been, but the Confederates were outnumbered. At 2 P. M. Beauregard ordered preparations made for the retreat, which by 4 o'clock was under way. He was not pursued. The casualties were: Confederates—killed, 1,728; wounded, 8,012; prisoners, 959; total, 10,699. Federals—killed, 1,735; wounded, 7,882; prisoners, 3,956; total, 13,573. Gen. Albert Sidney Johnston was killed on the first day of the battle and was succeeded by Gen. Beauregard in the command of the Confederate army.

Shimonoseki Indemnity.—Shimonoseki is a seaport of Japan whose forts command a strait of the same name. In 1864 these forts were attacked and destroyed by a squadron of war vessels, representing the United States, England, France and Holland, in retaliation for the firing on merchant vessels of those nations by the forts. The Japanese Government was compelled to pay damages for the injuries inflicted by the forts, besides an indemnity, amounting together to $3,000,000. Our share in this sum was $785,000. Only a small portion of it was needed for damages inflicted, and the remainder lay in our public treasury for some years. It was not applied to any public use, and finally, after repeated attempts to refund the extortionate excess, it was repaid to Japan in 1884.

Shinplasters.—During the war small change disappeared from circulation and the people resorted to postage stamps and private notes. The latter, representing ten, twenty-five and fifty cents, issued by retail dealers to facilitate trade, were of little value beyond the particular locality where they were issued, except as plasters for broken shins, and hence were called "shinplasters." The fractional notes printed by the government under the law of 1863 were also called "shinplasters," but merely because their forerunners had borne that name.

Ship Island, utility of forts on, for protection of Mississippi coast, 2266, 2293.

Shipbuilding.—A summary of the general results of the 1914 census of manufactures for the shipbuilding and boat-building industry, issued by the Bureau of the Census, Department of Commerce, consists of a detailed statement, relating to the United States as a whole and showing, for the years 1909 and 1914, the value of the work done on new vessels, whether launched or not during the census year; the value of repair work done; the kind, number, and tonnage of vessels of 5 gross tons and over which were launched during the year; and the number of power boats of less than 5 tons which were completed during the same period. The statistics relate only to work done in private shipyards and manufacturing establishments.

Reports were received from 1,145 establishments, whose products—that is, construction and repair work done—during the year were valued at $88,682,071.

The total number of vessels of 5 gross tons and over launched during the census year decreased from 1,584 in 1909 to 1,113 in 1914, or by 29.7 per cent, and the gross tonnage decreased from 467,219 in 1909 to 424,660 in 1914, or by 9.1 per cent. Iron and steel vessels launched decreased from 158 in 1909 to 126 in 1914, or by 20.3 per cent, and in tonnage from 254,986 to 242,559, or by 4.9 per cent. The number of wooden vessels launched decreased from 1,426 in 1909 to 987 in 1914, or by 30.8 per cent, and the tonnage from 212,233 to 182,101, or by 14.2 per cent.

Steel merchant vessels building or under contract to be built in private American shipyards on December 1, 1916, according to builders' returns to the Bureau of Navigation, Department of Commerce, numbered 400 of 1,428,003 gross tons. On December 1, 1915, builders' returns of construction or contracts for the construction of steel merchant vessels aggregated 202 vessels of 761,511 gross tons. The tonnage building or ordered on December 1, 1916, however, is less (17 vessels of 51,943 gross tons), than on November 1, 1916. During November American yards finished 22 vessels of 68,922 gross tons, and made new contracts for 7 steel merchant vessels of 18,285 gross tons.

European War Legislation.—In 1917, the Sixty-fourth Congress gave the President authority, in time of war or national emergency occurring before March 1, 1918:

To place an order, to refuse which was made illegal, with any person for any ships or war materials needed by the Government and of the kind and quantity usually produced by such person.

To modify or cancel any existing contract for the production of war materials, as found necessary by the Government. If the person holding such contract refuse to consent to such modification, the President may take over all or a part of his plant and use it as necessary.

To require the owner or occupier of any plants in which war materials or ships are produced to place at the disposal of the Government all or any of his output.

To requisition and take over for Governmental purposes and use any plant of any kind, even without agreement with the owner or occupier.

Just compensation for such action is to be determined by the President. If the person to be compensated is not satisfied with the amount, he shall receive one-half of it and may bring suit for such additional amount as he feels himself entitled to.

In the same year the Sixty-fifth Congress gave the President power to requisition and take over any ship already constructed or in process of construction or thereafter to be constructed, or any part of such ship, including its charter. It authorized the President also to take over any ship within the jurisdiction of the United States which at the time of coming therein was owned in whole or in part by any corporation or subject of any nation with which the United States is at war, or was under the register of such nation, and further provided for a board of survey to determine the value of such vessel, the findings of the board to be competent evidence as to any claim for compensation. (See also United States Shipping Board.)

On April 9, 1918, it was announced by official Washington authority that at that time the United States had 390 vessels, with a total tonnage of 2,762,605 tons, engaged in the transportation of troops and material across the Atlantic. Of the vessels, 322 flew the American flag, with a carrying capacity of 2,365,344 tons, the other 68 vessels being chartered ships of neutral nations. In addition, 471,000 tons of seized Dutch shipping were available for service.

In 1917, the Emergency Fleet Corporation awarded contracts for 411 wooden and composite vessels, of dead weight capacity aggregating 1,460,900 tons. There were awarded also in the same year contracts for 225 steel cargo vessels of 1,663,800 tons dead weight tonnage. By requisition, 403 vessels under construction were obtained, of a dead weight tonnage approximating 2,800,000 tons.

On April 1, 1918, the Shipping Board announced that a total of 182 steel vessels had been launched in American shipyards since the beginning of the war shipbuilding campaign. In addition, 85 requisitioned vessels turned over to the Shipping Board had been finished; 3 contract steel vessels had been finished; 170 requisitioned vessels had been launched; 12 contract steel vessels had been launched, including the 3 completed. The total tonnage of the 170 requisitioned vessels launched was 1,173,-217 tons. The tonnage of the 12 contract vessels was 99,200 tons. The three completed and delivered contract vessels aggregated 26,400 tons and the nine launched but uncompleted contract vessels aggregated 72,800 tons.

From January 1, 1917, to January 1, 1918, the number of shipyards in the United States increased from 66 to 142. A feature of the war shipbuilding accomplishments of the United States was the construction and successful utilization of concrete ships. Among other successes was the development of the so-called fabricated ship, in which much of the shaping of plates, riveting, etc., was done in a fabricating shop rather than in a shop connected with the shipyard.

Shipbuilding:

Consular returns on, in foreign countries, referred to, 2955.

Decline in American, discussed, 4200.

Encouragement to American, recommended, 4060, 4255, 4727, 5984.

Ship-owners impede government by charging high freight rates, 8313.

Shipping, American. (See Commerce discussed.)

Shippers, right to choose transfer routes for goods should be vested in, 7446.

Shipping, importance of, in war against Germany, 8250.

Shipping Board, powers of, 8316

Ship Purchase Law.—The administration's perfected shipping bill was introduced in the House, May 7, 1916, by Chairman Alexander of the Committee on Merchant Marine and Fisheries. It directed the Secretary of the Treasury to sell Panama Canal bonds to obtain the funds necessary to carry out the provisions of those sections of the bill authorizing the construction, equipment, lease or purchase of vessels, or the creating a $50,000,000 shipping corporation, and directed the shipping board to investigate the navigation laws, with a view to their amendment, and the cost of building merchant vessels in the United States and abroad, the encouragement of investments in American shipping and other maritime questions, and report to Congress.

Drastic provisions are included to prevent illegal combinations in the shipping trade. The bill also gives the shipping board sweeping powers over rates and practices and clothes it with authority to require regular and special reports from water carriers engaged in carrying the commerce of the United States. The board is authorized to receive and hear complaints and to enforce reparation to the complainant for injury done. Records of investigations made by the board shall be competent evidence in all courts of the United States. The board is to have authority to compel the production of papers and to hear testimony under oath.

The Attorney-General is authorized to intervene on behalf of the board whenever any of its orders shall have been violated and to apply to the courts for the proper process to put such order into effect.

Democratic Senators in caucus July 8, reached an agreement on the bill, thus ending one of the most serious party divisions that occurred in the Wilson Administration.

The principle for which Chairman Alexander of the House committee fought in conference to have the government-owned ships operated in the coastwise as well as in the foreign trade of the United States met with approval at the hands of the Senate Democrats. The other amendments which the caucus agreed upon were as follows:

The Government shall not purchase ships from any of the belligerent nations, nor any ship already engaged in the American trade unless it is about to be withdrawn from that trade.

No ship shall be acquired by the government which is below 75 per cent of its original efficiency.

The government shall not undertake to operate its ships unless all efforts fail to negotiate satisfactory leases or sales to private corporations for that purpose, the government reserving the right, however, to prescribe conditions under which ships shall be operated and in what service they shall engage.

By a strictly party vote the Senate Commerce Committee, July 18, directed Senator Simmons to report the bill favorably to the Senate with the following amendments:

The Shipping Board shall be limited in jurisdiction to vessels on the high seas and on the Great Lakes.

Ferrying, towing, transfer and lighterage are operations which are not subjected to this regulation.

The Secretary of Commerce and Secretary of the Navy are removed from the Shipping Board.

The government will not purchase any vessel—(a) engaged in American trade; (b) which flies a belligerent flag; (c) which is not adapted to the requirements outlined in the bill, and (d) which is not at least 75 per cent as efficient as when new.

The vessels may engage in the coastwise trade. In other words, the coastwise trade is opened up to foreign built vessels acquired by American citizens under this act.

No American vessel can be sold to a foreigner unless the Shipping Board first has its refusal and gives its permission.

The Shipping Board, though a government corporation, may not operate the government vessels in foreign trade unless it is impossible to lease such ships to private interests.

When in times of war the government commandeers American vessels compensation therefor shall be based upon normal conditions.

The bill passed the Senate Aug. 18, 38 to 21, all in the affirmative being Democrats and all in the negative Republicans. All of the committee amendments were agreed to without a record vote, and other amendments were inserted. One amendment, the so-called anti-blacklist provision authorizing customs officials to withold clearance to any ship refusing American cargo except for the reason of being fully laden, subsequently attracted the attention of the Allied Embassies. The provision was inserted at the last moment because of penalties attached to ships which carry blacklisted cargo. President Wilson signed the bill Sept. 7, 1916. The following were later nominated by the President to be members of the Board: William Denman, of San Francisco; Bernard N. Baker, of Baltimore; John A. Donald, of New York; John Barber White, of Kansas City, Mo., and Theodore Brent, of New Orleans.

Ship Purchase Bill:
Compared to railroad subsidy, 8018.
Urged by Wilson, 8018, 8072.

Ships.—In the fiscal year ending June 30, 1917, there entered ports of the United States American tonnage of 18,724,710 and foreign tonnage of 31,738,569, a total of 50,738,569. During the same twelve months there cleared from ports of the United States American tonnage of 19,-145,754 and foreign tonnage of 32,924,316, a total of 52,072,070.

Ships, Foreign-Built, admitted to American registry, 8006.
Law regarding, suspended, 8354.

Shire.—A division of the Kingdom of Great Britain, dating back to the time of the Saxon invasion. It is now taken to mean almost the same as county, as most of the English county names terminate in the word shire. The shire has been extended to Scotland and Wales. In 1643 the general court of Massachusetts Bay Colony ordered that the whole Colony, which then included the present State of New Hampshire, be divided into four shires—Essex, Middlesex, Suffolk, and Norfolk. The name was used for county in all the Colonies.

Shirt and Collar Industry.—A study of the shirt and collar industry reveals the fact that American manufacturers have the home market pretty much to themselves, as foreign competition in these lines is of very little importance. The largest import of collars and cuffs for any one year was $70,000 in 1913, while the total production of these articles as far back as 1909 was $17,200,000. The present output is much greater, but no statistics are available. The total value of the shirts produced in this country in 1909 was $82,400,000, compared with which the imports are insignificant.

The manufacture of shirts was founded as a systematic industry in 1832 in New York, and in 1909 that city manufactured 27.74 per cent of the total output of the country. Troy and Albany produced 8.85 per cent, Philadelphia 8.68 per cent, Baltimore 8.53 per cent, and St. Louis 4.07 per cent. New York State and Pennsylvania produced more than half the shirts made in the country.

Of the total sales of all of the 42 establishments reporting, 58.87 per cent was made to retailers, 38.76 per cent to jobbers, 0.68 per cent by mail order, and 1.69 per cent was exported. Practically all of the high-grade shirts were sold direct to retailers and that portion of the product which was sold to jobbers consisted of work shirts and other low-priced lines. The total expense of 26 establishments which sold all or the greater part of their product to retailers was 8.88 per cent, which is more than twice as large as the total selling expenses of the 12 establishments selling all or a greater part of their product to jobbers. However, the establishments which sold all or a greater part of their product to retailers had a manufacturing and final profit somewhat larger than the profits shown by the establishments which sold all or a greater part of their product to jobbers.

Shoe-String District.—The Sixth Congressional District of Mississippi, as laid out in 1874, is so called because it consists of a narrow strip extending along the Mississippi River almost the entire length of the state. (See Gerrymander.)

S'Homamish Indians. (See Indian Tribes.)

Shoshone Indians. (See Indian Tribes.)
Treaty with, 3397, 3898.

Shoshone Reservation, Wyo., agreement for cession of portion of, 5649.

Shoulder Strap.—A decorative strap worn over the shoulder as an insignia distinguishing the rank of an officer; also distinguishing one military or naval division from another.

Shrapnel.—A missile loaded with a quantity of smaller missiles, which scatter in the enemy's ranks by automatic explosion at any predetermined range.

Siam.— Siam occupies the central portion of the Indo-Chinese Peninsula, and lies between 4° 20'-20° 15' N. latitude and 96° 30'-106° E. longitude. The area is stated at 195,000 square miles. It is bounded on the north by British India and French Laos, east bv French Laos and Cambodia, south by the Gulf of Siam and the British Malay States, and west by British India. East and west are Spheres of Influence, in which the French and British governments, while disclaiming any intention of annexing territory (Agreement of April, 1904), are entitled to obtain concession from Siam. Between these spheres is a Neutral Zone, which is declared to be inviolable by France and Britain.

Physical Features.—Northern Siam, which is occupied by Laos States under the suzerainty of the King of Siam, contains a series of parallel ranges of no great mean elevation, but with precipitous heights in the extreme north. These hills are covered with forests, from which most of the teak is obtained. Eastern Siam, which also contains Laos States, conquered by Siam about a hundred years ago, consists of a vast river basin encircled by hills, the central portions being sandy desert. Central Siam is also a great plain flanked on the west by high mountains (Mulai 6,886 feet), and contains the richest and most fertile tracts of the kingdom. Southern Siam extends down the Malay Peninsula, which has a broken range of mountains parallel with the coasts, and consists principally of dense and valuable forests.

The principal Siamese river is the Menam (Menam Chao Phaya), which rises in the northern hills and flows into the Gulf of Siam at the port of Bangkok. For six months in every year the river overflows its banks, leaving rich deposits of silt, which provide the most fertile tracts of the kingdom. The wet season lasts from May to October, when the heat is not excessive, and in the dry season the nights are cool.

History.—The Kingdom of Siam is believed to have been founded some time in the sixth century A. D., by a race that had migrated many years earlier from southwest China. The kingdom was extended over the Malay Peninsula toward the close of the twelfth century. Intercourse with Europe was first established at the beginning of the sixteenth century when the Portuguese conquered part of the Malay Peninsula and the French and English have gradually worked their way to the borders of the kingdom, relations with the latter having been always friendly, while the rival claims of France and Siam over the frontiers of Annam led to a Franco-Siamese war in 1893.

Ethnology.—The number of inhabitants in 1912 was 8,149,487. The majority of the population is Siamese and Lao. There is, however, a large number of Chinese and, in the south, Malays. There are no reliable figures showing the proportion of each race. The foreign residents number about 2,000, of whom nearly one-half are British, with 244 Germans, 218 French, 163 Danes, 135 Americans, 123 Italians. The Siamese, Laos and Cambodians, are Buddhists, but the Malays of the peninsula are almost all Muhammadans. The language of the central districts is Siamese ; in the eastern and northern districts the Laos have their own

tongue, and the peninsular montons and states are partly Malay speaking.

Government.—The kingdom is now secured from further aggression by the Anglo-French Convention of 1896, under which Central Siam is declared to be inviolable, and each Power renounces the right to annex territory adjoining its borders, although preserving the right of commercial penetration. The Government is an absolute monarchy, and the sovereign appoints his successor from among the male members of the Royal Family. Ruler : Somdetch Phra Paramendr Maha Vajiravudh Mongkut Klao (King of Northern and Southern Siam and of all its Dependencies, and of the Laos, Malays and Karens), born Jan. 1, 1880 ; succeeded his father King Chulalongkorn, Oct. 23, 1910.

The Kingdom is divided into 17 Provinces or Montons, each under a High Commissioner controlled by the Minister of the Interior. These comprise several sub-provinces, which are subdivided into districts. Sub-divisions of the district are under village headmen. Bangkok is directly governed by the Minister of Local Government.

Recent reforms, including the final abolition of slavery in 1905, have brought into existence an organized system of local and divisional courts, with magistrates trained at a school of law and assisted by European advisers.

Service in the Army is universal and compulsory, and although the law is only partially applied there is a standing army of about 25,000 men.

Education.—Education is generally in the hands of the priests from the Buddhist monasteries scattered all over the country, and scarcely any adult Siamese are illiterate. Government effort is not only co-ordinate but is directed toward a general advance in the system practised by the monasteries. An estimate of the pupils of the various schools states their number at close on 160,000 throughout the Kingdom, exclusive of the capital, while government effort has provided accommodation for some 15,000 others, including secondary, special and technical schools. The English language is very generally taught in the capital and there are three English schools with English masters, while many Siamese are educated in Europe, particularly in England.

Production and Industry.—The principal industry is the cultivation of rice, which is the national food and principal commodity exported. Irrigation is bringing large areas of northern Siam into cultivation, and the standard of cultivation is being systematically raised. Siamese rice is in great demand abroad. Other crops are tobacco, pepper, coco-nuts, cotton and maize, while fruit is abundantly grown. The forests are pre d and the teak industry is maintaining its importance.

Gold, silver, rubies and sapphires are won and exported, and tin, copper, iron, zinc, coal and other minerals are known to exist, the tin exports exceeding 5,000 tons annually, almost entirely from Mouthon Puket. In 1911-1912 export of tin = 5,199 tons.

Finances.—The average annual revenue for the five years ending with 1913 was 61,076,000 ticals. The expenditure for 1913 was 61,581,897 ticals. The national debt consists of an Anglo-French loan of £1,000,-000, an Anglo-French-German loan of £3,-000,000, and a federated Malay States loan of £4,000,000. The tical, the unit of value, is equivalent to $3,708 of United States money.

Railways.—On Nov. 1, 1913, there were 721 miles open for traffic, the principal line running from Bangkok along the Menam to a terminus at Dem Chai, near the town of Phré. A network of railways and canals affords easy communication throughout Central Siam, and the traffic is enormous. Northern and eastern Siam are less favorably situated, but southern Siam is to have a compensating system of railways.

Siam:

American representative at coronation of King of, 7667.

Claim of United States against, 6184.

Adjustment of, 6336.

Diplomatic relations with, 6336.

Appropriation for, recommended, 4799.

Gifts received from, referred to, 3267.

Legation of United States in, premises for, presented by Government of, 4823, 4825, 4923.

Appropriation for erection of building on, recommended, 5494.

Liquor traffic in, agreement with, for regulation of, 4803.

Minister of United States to, mission created, 4718, 4761, 4825.

Treaty with, 1272, 1457, 1593, 2951, 3061, 3834.

Siam, Treaties with.—The convention of amity and commerce of 1833 was modified in some directions by the treaty of 1856. Freedom of commerce was extended to citizens of the United States except in importation of arms and munitions of war, and opium, and in the exportation of rice, which is prohibited. The duties payable on ships, it was agreed, should be those paid by the most favored nation; and should there be in the future any diminution in the same in favor of any foreign nation, the United States should share the favor. Humane treatment of shipwrecked mariners was provided for.

A subject of Siam in debt to a citizen of the United States or a citizen of the United States in debt to a subject of Siam shall be obliged to bring all of his goods for sale and apply the proceeds to the payment thereof; should the proceeds be insufficient, the debtor shall not be liable for the balance. Merchants from the United States may rent houses in Siam, but shall rent the king's factories and pay the usual rent therefor. Goods brought to Siam by merchants shall be reported in detail to the king, but no duty shall be charged thereon. Should any foreign country other than Portugal be privileged to appoint consuls at Siam, that privilege shall also be accorded to the United States.

The treaty of 1856 afforded full protection to merchants of the United States in Siam. As Siam has no ships of war, it was agreed that the vessels of war of the United States meeting a Siamese vessel at sea should render to it all possible aid not in violation of the laws of neutrality; and American consuls in foreign ports out of Siam shall render aid to the captains of Siamese vessels in such ports. Provision is made for the appointment of a consul at Bangkok. (See Consular Conventions.) American merchants may trade freely in any port of Siam, but shall reside permanently at Bangkok, where they may rent land, but may not purchase land within two hundred seng (four English miles) of the city walls until they have lived for ten years in Siam or have permission so to buy. Apart from this, American merchants may buy or rent houses anywhere within twenty-four hours' journey from Siam, measured at the rate of speed at which boats travel. Freedom of conscience is allowed to all.

Vessels of war of the United States may enter the river and anchor at Paknam, but only with special permission may proceed to the docks. On articles of import the duty shall be three per cent, payable either in money or in goods. Unsalable and re-exported goods shall be entitled to a drawback. Opium may be imported free of duty, but may not be sold to the opium farmer or his agents. It may be re-exported without impost or duty levied upon it. In times of threatened scarcity the Siamese government may prohibit the export of salt, rice, and fish, on thirty days' notice.

By an agreement of 1884 it is permitted to sell in Siam liquors of a strength allowed to be manufactured in Siam. Beers and wines may be sold on an import duty not to exceed ten per cent. The strength of liquors shall be tested by a Siamese official. The Siamese government may at any time stop the importation of liquors or spirits which, in their opinion, prove deleterious to the health of the people.

Siberia, survivors of *Jeannette* expedition aided by people of. (See *Jeannette* Polar Expedition.)

Sibyl, The, English schooner, appropriation for, recommended, 3890.

Sicily (see also Italy):

Claims of United States against, 1113.

Act to authorize Secretary of Treasury to compromise, vetoed, 1365.

Commissioner appointed to consider, 1244.

Convention regarding, 1269.

Payment of, 1317, 1368.

Fugitive criminals, convention with, for surrender of, 2870.

Neutral rights, treaty with, regarding, 2836.

Relations opened with United States, 1706.

Treaty with, transmitted and discussed, 1170, 1196, 1244, 2271, 2479, 2836, 2870, 2884.

Sierra Forest Reserve, Cal., mentioned, 7278.

Signal Service:

Building for, recommended, 4657.

Chief Signal Officer. (See Chief Signal Officer.)

Discussed, 4148.

Establishment and organization of, discussed, 4304, 4934.

Reorganization of, recommended, 5487.

Separate organization of, recommended, 4637, 4934.

Services of, in Spanish-American War, discussed, 6314.

Silk and Silk Goods.—For many years after the Revolution premiums and bounties for planting mulberry trees and for producing raw silk were authorized by a number of states, especially in New Jersey, New York, Pennsylvania and the New England States. Dr. Ezra Stiles, president of Yale College, and Benjamin Franklin were among the notable early promoters of the movement. The establishment of the industry in England and France was due to royal patronage and it was considered not inconsistent with public policy here to extend state encouragement to an industry which, when established, would undoubtedly prove profitable. In December, 1825, the subject was introduced into Congress by Mr. Miner, of Pennsylvania, and the Secretary of the Treasury was instructed to prepare a well digested manual on the growth and manufacture of silk. This resulted in the publication by Congress of the document known as the "Rush Letter" of 220 pages, besides illustrations of machinery, and is a carefully executed work.

Sericulture gained the public ear, and for ten years all went well. Silk conventions and meetings were held in many states, and the agricultural literature of the country became suffused with descriptions of the Chinese mulberry tree and the possible profits in raising silk worms. Speculation began and the price of trees advanced far beyond the value of all the silk they could ever raise. Silk culture companies were organized and manufacturers and farmers were induced to invest in them. The bubble burst in 1839. One speculator who had put $80,000 in trees and cuttings vainly offered them to his neighbors for pea brush at $1 a hundred. Notwithstanding the favorable climatic conditions both in France and the United States for the growth of mulberry trees and the rearing of silk worms and cocoons silk culture has dwindled in both countries, because more remunerative occupations are afforded by other lines of industry. In other words, it don't pay. Although in France the raisers of cocoons and reelers of silk are protected by a considerable bounty, payable by the French government to her citizens as against the Italians, that country produces less than 4 per cent. of the world's supply of raw silk. Her silk manufacturers are well content to purchase, as America does, the raw silk from Italy, Japan and China, in all of which countries the ruling rates of wages are much less than in the United States. Both France and the United States pursue the same fiscal policy of admitting raw silk free of duty, and therefore both are on a par in this respect.

Meanwhile, step by step, but slowly, improvements have been effected here in the manufacture of silk goods. The making of sewing silk became a household industry in New England, at first by hand, and later by machinery. The manufacture of silk trimmings of various kinds was commenced in Philadelphia in 1815, and ribbons in Baltimore in 1829. These goods, together with fringes, gimps and tassels, and silk thread, especially suited for use on sewing machines, continued to be the principal products of the silk industry in the United States until the outbreak of the Civil war.

As reasons for the rapid as well as powerful development of the United States silk industry, notwithstanding the competition of well introduced imported goods and the splendid organization of the importers, and in spite of the mistrust which was felt by the consumers for a long time against the domestic goods, we find:

1.—The natural capability of the American merchant and manufacturer, his common sense, enterprise and self-confidence.

2.—The capital which is always ready to support enterprise in this country, in the form of extensive and liberal credits.

3.—The support which is given all these undertakings by the people, by the city and state governments in the form of tax privileges, donations of lots, putting up mill buildings, and renting same at a low rate of interest; even in some cases by subscribing part of the working capital.

4.—The intellectuality of the American technician, who, through his inventions of time-saving machinery, which is simply constructed and easy to handle, is, perhaps, unequalled.

5.—The easy intercourse between manufacturer and dealer, which enables the first to get fully and promptly acquainted with the needs and wants of the consumer.

The American manufacturer is largely his own merchant and distributor. He is in close touch with the dealers and retailers, knows what they want, and manufactures accordingly.

In England the silk industry has suffered a great decline since 1860. In recent years leading manufacturers there have emphasized the importance of specially organized technical schools for the education of artisans and for teaching drawing and designing to selected pupils. In the United States every large silk plant is a school of design, a teacher of scientific and technical education. All such plants have a corps of special designers and many are in touch with artists and establishments abroad, whence is derived the latest information concerning novelties in all lines of manufacture. Skillful chemists are likewise attached to these plants.

The production of raw silk in China is an absolutely unknown quantity. When prices in Europe and America are relatively high the supply increases surprisingly. When prices are normal or low the supply decreases. It is obvious, however, that by closer attention to the United States market China could greatly extend its raw silk trade with this country. The vast amount of capital invested and the large number of operatives employed in the silk industry throughout the world should be a commercial stimulus to China, the greatest producer of raw silk, to perfect its silk reeling processes by the application of skilled labor so as to secure a larger share of the profits of a business in which the country has so many natural advantages.

China now contributes 41.8 per cent. of the world's supply of raw silk; Japan and Italy each 20 per cent.; France, 3.3 per cent. and all other countries 14 per cent.

The silk manufacturing industry includes two classes of establishments: (1) Those for making finished silk products, such as woven fabrics, braids and trimmings, sewing, embroidery, and wash silks; and (2) Those making silk yarn, known technically as organzine, tram, and spun silk. Organzine and tram constitute respectively the warp and woof of silk fabrics, and are made from the best grades of raw material by the process of throwing (doubling, twisting and winding the filaments into yarn.) Spun silk is produced by spinning, in much the same manner as wool fabrics are spun, the short fibered silk from pierced cocoons or from waste silk of any sort which cannot be thrown in the usual manner. The concerns engaged only in the manufacture of organzine and tram are known as throwsters and winders. Few establishments include the entire process of silk making. Including both branches of the industry there were 852 establishments in operation in

1909. These were capitalized at $152,158,-002, and employed 105,238 persons, to whom $46,097,364 was paid in salaries and wages. The total value of the finished product was placed at $196,911,667.

American silk manufacturers, after the sudden outbreak of the European war in 1914, strove to provide against any stoppage of foreign importations of finished goods, raw material or dye stuffs. Commerce was threatened by warships of the hostile powers and insurance rates were high. A record consumption at home and abroad had absorbed reserve stocks, and there was a scarcity of raw material. This caused high premiums to be paid for ready stocks, but some of the mills were forced to suspend operations on account of inability to get orders for the spring trade.

In spite of depressed business conditions fifty-one new silk mills were built in 1914. Of these twelve were for the manufacture of ribbon, twenty-five for broad silk, and the remainder divided between throwing and yarn mills. Of the new mills twenty-one were built in Pennsylvania, and 19 in New Jersey, 13 of the latter in Paterson.

Returns were received from 900 establishments engaged in the industry in 1914, the products of which, for that year, were valued at $253,764,170.

Silkworms, memorial from Count de Bronno Bronski regarding introduction of, into United States, 2584.

Silver.—One of the precious metals and the one most in use during historic times, both in the arts and as a medium of exchange. In the earliest ages, even before there was a record, as in prehistoric Greece and Italy, silver mines were worked, and the refined metal obtained from the ores was employed in ornamental and useful arts. It was not so early used as a money metal, and when finally its use as such was begun it was made into bars or rings and sold by weight. Shekels, or pieces of silver, are alluded to in the book of Genesis. Abraham, in the land of Canaan, bought a field for sepulture and paid for it in silver. But the best authorities state that the first regular coinage of either gold or silver was in Asia Minor, in Phrygia or Lydia. The Egyptians did not have coins in the earliest times, although otherwise their civilization was advanced. In ancient times silver was plentiful in Spain. Hannibal, it is stated, obtained 300 pounds per day from the mines there during the Carthaginian occupation of that country. At a much earlier day the Athenians had valuable silver mines at Laurium, in the territory of Attica. Silver, as well as gold, was employed in the erection of Solomon's Temple at Jerusalem. Silver drinking cups and silver ornaments on horn or ivory drinking cups were in use among the Vikings. In fact, all the civilized and semi-civilized nations and tribes of antiquity made free use of this metal. It was more common even then than gold, and therefore less precious. At a later period the Incas in Peru, the Toltecs and Aztecs in Mexico, and the Mayas in Yucatan employed it for ornamental purposes and for objects of utility, both in their temples and palaces. Among modern civilized and enlightened peoples its use is so common as to require no special remark.

The metal itself is found in almost every part of the globe, usually in combination with other metals. Take the whole historical period and it is found that the South American mines are the richest. Mulhall is authority for the statement that Mexico has produced more silver since 1523

than any other country within the last 500 years. He values the total output there for the period at $3,050,000,000. Mexico has also the largest annual output, producing 60,808,978 oz. fine, valued at $35,269,-200; the United States follows next with 57,682,800 oz. fine, worth $33,456,000. Large masses have been found in nuggets, as one of 370 pounds at La Paz, Bolivia, in 1749; another of 560 pounds at Königsberg, Norway, and still another of 800 pounds at Huantaya, Peru. Sonora, Mexico, however, claims to have extracted a huge lump of silver weighing 2,700 pounds.

The subject has entered into American politics, the Democratic party in 1896 having declared for the free coinage of the metals at the former ratio of 16 to 1. The French ratio was at 15½ to 1. The repeal in 1873 of the law providing for the free and unlimited coinage of silver was the beginning of an agitation for the restoration of bimetallism. (See also Bland-Allison Act; Coinage Laws; Sherman Act.)

SILVER PRODUCTION FROM MINES IN THE UNITED STATES : 1792 TO 1915
(From Reports of the Director of the Mint, Treasury Department)

Calendar Year	Fine Ounces (Troy)	Commercial Value
April 2, 1792–July 31, 1834.		Insignificant
July 31, 1834–Dec. 31, 1855	619,100	$816,000
1856	38,700	52,000
1857	38,700	52,400
1858	38,700	52,000
1859	77,300	105,100
1860	116,000	156,800
1861	1,546,900	2,062,000
1862	3,480,500	4,684,800
1863	6,574,200	8,842,300
1864	8,507,800	11,443,000
1865	8,701,200	11,642,200
1866	7,734,400	10,356,400
1867	10,441,400	13,866,200
1868	9,281,200	12,306,900
1869	9,281,200	12,297,600
1870	12,375,000	16,434,000
1871	17,789,100	23,588,300
1872	22,236,300	29,396,400
1873	27,650,400	35,881,600
1874	28,868,200	36,917,500
1875	24,539,300	30,485,900
1876	29,996,200	34,919,800
1877	30,777,800	36,991,500
1878	35,022,300	40,401,000
1879	31,565,500	35,477,100
1880	30,318,700	34,717,000
1881	33,257,800	37,657,500
1882	36,196,900	41,105,900
1883	35,732,800	39,618,400
1884	37,743,800	41,921,300
1885	39,909,400	42,503,500
1886	39,694,000	39,482,400
1887	41,721,600	40,887,200
1888	45,942,700	43,045,100
1889	50,094,500	46,838,400
1890	54,516,300	57,242,100
1891	58,330,000	57,630,000
1892	63,500,000	55,662,500
1893	60,000,000	46,800,000
1894	49,500,000	31,422,100
1895	55,727,000	36,445,500
1896	58,834,800	39,654,600
1897	53,860,000	32,316,000
1898	54,438,000	32,118,400
1899	54,764,500	32,858,700
1900	57,647,000	35,741,100
1901	55,214,000	33,128,400
1902	55,500,000	29,415,000
1903	54,300,000	29,322,000
1904	57,682,800	33,456,024
1905	56,101,600	34,221,976

1906	56,517,900	38,256,400
1907	56,514,700	37,299,700
1908	52,440,800	28,050,600
1909	54,721,500	28,455,200
1910	57,137,900	30,854,500
1911	60,399,400	32,615,700
1912	63,766,800	39,197,400
1913	67,601,111	40,864,871
1914	72,455,100	40,067,700
1915	74,961,075	37,397,300

PRODUCTION OF SILVER, CALENDAR YEAR 1915

States and Territories	Fine Ounces	Commercial Value
Alaska	1,054,634	$ 526,100
Arizona	5,665,672	2,826,500
California	1,689,924	843,100
Colorado	7,199,745	3,591,900
Georgia	141	100
Idaho	13,042,466	6,506,800
Illinois	3,892	1,900
Michigan	581,874	290,300
Missouri	55,534	27,700
Montana	14,423,173	7,195,600
Nevada	14,453,085	7,210,500
New Mexico	2,337,064	1,165,900
North Carolina	1,496	700
Oregon	125,499	62,600
Philippine Islands	15,148	7,600
South Carolina		
South Dakota	197,569	98,600
Tennessee	99,171	49,500
Texas	724,580	361,500
Utah	13,073,471	6,522,200
Vermont	150	100
Washington	213,877	106,700
Wyoming	2,910	1,400
Total	74,961,075	$37,397,300

The ratio of silver to gold has varied greatly. 1,000 B. C. it was 12 to 1, if the best figures obtainable are to be relied upon. At the Christian era it was 9 to 1. 500 A. D., just twenty-four years after the downfall of the Western Empire of Rome, the ratio was 18 to 1, but in 1100 A. D. it had fallen to 8 to 1. At the close of the seventeeth century it was 10 to 1, and at the end of the last century 15 to 1. In 1850 the ratio was 15.4 to 1; in 1870, 18.40 to 1; in 1893, 26.49; 1909, 35.75. In the coinage of the United States mints the ratio of 15,988 to 1 of gold is maintained.

Silver. (See Gold and Silver.)

Silver Certificates:

Discussed, 5474.

Repeal of act for issuance of, recommended, 4633, 4720.

Suspension of issuance of, recommended, 4830.

Silver Coinage. (See Coins and Coinage.)

Sinews of War.—The term is applied to funds used for war expenses.

Single Standard. (See Monometallism.)

Silver State.—Alternative nickname for Nevada. (See Sage-Brush State.)

Single Tax.—The doctrines of what is today called the single-tax seem to have been suggested first by the group of the French economists known as the Physiocrats, around the year 1775: but these doctrines disappeared n the rise of modern political economy with the publication of Adam Smith's *Wealth of Nations* in 1776. Hence it was Henry George who founded the modern single-tax philos-

ophy in 1879, which is the year when his *Progress and Poverty* was published. George was born in Philadelphia in 1839, and spent his early years as a sailor and printer. As a youth he emigrated to California, where he was engaged in newspaper work from 1858 to 1876. In 1869, he was moved and perplexed by the scenes of vast poverty opened before his eyes in a trip to New York, and during the next ten years he thought unceasingly of the problem of poverty, coming to the conclusion that it was due to the system of private ownership of land. *Progress and Poverty* was published in the midst of extreme poverty, and achieved little notice for several years. But eventually the eloquence and the passionate fervor of the writer would not be denied, and from 1882 to 1887 the book was the most popular book on economics ever written. From 1880 to 1890, George was a propagandist, running unsuccessfully for mayor of New York City in 1886, and dying just before the end of his second campaign for the same office in 1897. His son, Henry George, Jr., was elected to the House of Representatives from 1911 to 1915.

The following statement of the single tax principle was written by Henry George, Sr.: We are in favor of raising all public revenues for national, state, county, and municipal purposes by a single tax upon land values, irrespective of improvements, and all the obligations of all forms of direct and indirect taxation. Since in all our states we now levy some tax on the value of land, the single tax can be instituted by the simple and easy way of abolishing, one after another, all other taxes now levied and commensurately increasing the tax on land values until we draw upon that one source for all expenses of government, the revenue being divided between local governments, state government, and the general government, as the revenue from direct tax is now divided between the local and state governments, or by a direct assessment being made by the general government upon the states and paid by them from revenues collected in this manner. The single tax we propose is not a tax on land, and therefore would not fall on the use of land and become a tax on labor. It is a tax not on land, but on the value of land. Then it would not fall on all land, but only on valuable land, and on that not in proportion to the use made of it, but in proportion to its value—the premium which the user of land must pay to the owner, either in purchase money or rent, for permission to use valuable land. It would thus be a tax not on the use and improvement of land, but on the ownership of land, taking what would otherwise go to the owner as owner, and not as user.

In assessments under the single tax all values created by individual use or improvement would be excluded, and the only value taken into consideration would be the value attaching to the bare land by reason of neighborhood, etc., to be determined by impartial periodical assessments. Thus the farmer would have no more taxes to pay than the speculator who held a similar piece of land idle, and the man who, on a city lot, erected a valuable building, would be taxed no more than the man who held a similar lot vacant. The single tax, in short, would call upon men to contribute to the public revenues not in proportion to what they produce or accumulate, but in proportion to the value of the natural opportunities they hold. It would compel them to pay just as much for holding land idle as for putting it to its fullest use. The single tax, therefore, would: First. Take the weight of taxation off the agricultural districts, where land has little or no value irrespective of improvements, and put it on towns and cities, where bare land rises to a value of millions of dollars per acre. Second. Dispense with a multiplicity of taxes and a horde of tax-gatherers, simplify government, and greatly reduce its cost. Third. Do away with the fraud, corruption, and gross inequality inseparable from our present methods of taxation, which allow the rich to escape while they grind the poor. Land cannot be hid or carried off, and its value can be ascertained with greater ease and certainty than any other. Fourth. Give us with all the world as perfect freedom of trade, as now exists between the states of the Union, thus enabling our people to share through free exchanges in all the advantages which nature has given to other countries, or which the peculiar skill of other peoples has enabled them to attain. It would destroy the trusts, monopolies, and corruptions which are the outgrowths of the tariff. It would do away with the fines and penalties now levied on any one who improves a farm, erects a house, builds a machine, or in any way adds to the general stock of wealth. It would leave every one free to apply labor or expend capital in production or exchange without fine or restriction, and would leave to each the full product of his exertion. Fifth. It would, on the other hand, by taking for public use that value which attaches to land by reason of the growth and improvement of the community, make the holding of land unprofitable to the mere owner and profitable only to the user. It would thus make it impossible for speculators and monopolists to hold natural opportunities unused or only half used, and would throw open to labor the illimitable field of employment which the earth offers to man. It would thus solve the labor problem, do away with involuntary poverty, raise wages in all occupations to the full earnings of labor, make overproduction impossible until all human wants are satisfied, render labor-saving inventions a blessing to all, and cause such an enormous production and such an equitable distribution of wealth as would give to all comfort, leisure, and participation in the advantages of an advancing civilization, in securing to each individual equal right to the use of the earth. It is also a proper function of society to maintain and control all public ways for the transportation of persons and property, and the transmission of intelligence; and also to maintain and control all public ways in cities for furnishing water, gas, and all other things that necessarily require the use of such common ways.

There is no single-tax political party organized in the United States, but many staunch advocates of the single-tax principle have been among our most prominent administrators of public office, including several mayors of large cities and members of the Cabinet. Several countries, notably New Zealand, tax unimproved land in accordance with the single-tax doctrine, and Germany also has levied partial, though not complete taxes upon the "unearned increment" of land value. Provision for this purpose was also made in England in the famous Lloyd-George budget of 1909. There are few political economists who favor the single tax, but many of its upholders have made notable contributions to American political and social science.

Sinking Fund.—An account or fund set aside for the payment of a debt or obligation. It is formed by successively appropriating or setting aside sums for the designated purpose. Alexander Hamilton made an unsuccessful attempt under the Confederation to establish a sinking fund for the liquidation of the national debt. The first national sinking fund in this country was created by act of Congress Aug. 2, 1790. The present sinking fund to retire the national debt was established by an act of Feb. 25, 1862, and amended by later acts. It sets apart annually a special fund for the payment of interest on and for the purchase of a given per cent of the national debt. Bonds so redeemed are to be canceled and deducted from the outstanding indebtedness of the Government. In addition there is to be purchased annually an amount of Government bonds equal to the annual interest on bonds previously bought for the sinking fund. The sinking fund is thus, as far as interest is concerned, in the position of any other holder of the Government's obligations receiving interest on the bonds that have been purchased for its account, except that the bonds belonging to it have been canceled and the debt considered reduced by that amount. An act of April 17, 1876, provides that fractional currency, redeemed by the Treasury, shall constitute a part of the sinking fund.

Sinking Fund, repeal of law recommended, 5754.

Sinn Fein.—The name of an Irish society for Irish independence. The name is Gaelic, and signifies "Ourselves only." The Sinn Fein Society advocates the complete separation of Ireland from English and all other outside influences, not only in governmental but also in economic and literary activities. It stands for the official use of Gaelic in all Irish intercourse, and in other ways declines to be bound in any way with the English. Theoretically the society does not stand for active resistance to the English authorities, but many of its leaders were implicated in the rebellion breaking out in Dublin during the European War. (See Home Rule for Ireland.)

Sioune Indians. (See Indian Tribes.)

Sioux City, Iowa, acts for erection of public building at, vetoed, 5015, 5301.

Sioux Commission:
Discussed, 5480.
Report of, discussed, 5496.

Sioux Indians. (See Indian Tribes.)

Sioux Reservation, Dakota:
Division of portion of, into separate reservations proclaimed, 5529.
Compensation to, for losses sustained in, referred to, 5568.
Lands granted to Chicago, Milwaukee and St. Paul Railway Co., declared forfeited by Proclamation, 5944.
Opened to settlement, 6875, 6882.
Purchase of portion of, recommended, 4837.
Restoration of to public domain, order regarding, declared void, 4890.
Discussed, 4943.
Right of way for railroad through, 4775, 4780.

Sioux State.—Alternative nickname for North Dakota. (See Cyclone State.)

Sioux Wars discussed, 3333, 4360, **5636.**

Sir Robert Pell, The, outrages committed on, 1695.

Sisseton Indians. (See Indian Tribes.)

Sitka, Alaska, port of entry, order regarding, 3865.

Sivewright, Bacon & Co., compensation to, 6734, 6859.

Six Nations of Indians. (See Indian Tribes.)

Sixteen to One. (See Silver.)

Skagit Indians. (See Indian Tribes.)

Skai-wha-mish Indians. (See Indian Tribes.)

Skipwith, Fulwar, consul-general to France, nomination of and reasons therefor, 170.

Skirmish.—A small fight, between military enemies, not of sufficient magnitude or importance to be dignified by the name of battle.

S'Klallams Indians. (See Indian Tribes.)

Skope-áhmish Indians. (See Indian Tribes.)

Sk-táh-le-jum Indians. (See Indian Tribes.)

Sk-táhl-mish Indians. (See Indian Tribes.)

Slackers.—The term, originating in England, but thence spreading to other countries, used to describe those persons who did not volunteer for service in the European War through cowardice, laziness, or selfishness, but not through conscientious scruples. The term is not to be confused with "conscientious objectors" (q. v.).

Slaughterhouse Cases.—A series of five cases bearing upon the creation of monopolies or trusts and defining the scope of the Fourteenth Amendment. The Crescent City Live Stock, Landing and Slaughterhouse Co. was incorporated by the Louisiana legislature March 8, 1869. The Butchers' Development Association protested against this act of the legislature on the ground that it created a monopoly. Suit was brought against the State by Paul Esteben and others on the ground that their business was injured. It was claimed by the plaintiffs that the creation of a monopoly of this sort by the State legislature was in violation of the Fourteenth Amendment to the Constitution which prohibits State legislatures from enforcing laws "which shall abridge the privileges or immunities of the citizens of the United States." The Supreme Court of Louisiana decided that the law did not conflict with the amendment to the Constitution. The Supreme Court of the United States, April 14, 1873, and Jan. 24, 1887, affirmed the decision. In these celebrated cases the Supreme Court likewise decided that the fundamental character of the Government had not been changed in any way by the Civil War. The judgment of the Supreme Court of Louisiana was not entirely affirmed in the last case mentioned, that of the Crescent Live Stock Co. *vs.* Butchers' Union. That part which constituted a judgment against the Crescent City Live Stock Landing and Slaughterhouse Co. solely, for damages for the malicious prosecution, was reversed and the case remanded for further proceedings. In that case Justice Matthews delivered the opinion, and there was no dissenting opinion. In the other cases Justic Miller rendered the court's judgment. Justice Field, for himself, and Justices Swayne and Bradley, delivered a dissenting opinion.

Slave Representation.—One of the most difficult problems encountered by the framers of the Constitution was the representation to be accorded in Congress to those portions of the country whose population consisted partly of slaves. It was contended, on the one hand, that, being persons, they should be represented, and, on the other hand, that, being property, they should be made the object of taxation. A compromise was finally reached providing that for purposes of reckoning a state's proportion of representatives, as well as its direct taxes, its population should be "determined by adding to the whole number of free persons, including those bound to service for a term of years, and excluding Indians not taxed, three-fifths of all other persons"—i. e., slaves. This method of computing population was first suggested in 1783 by the Continental Congress as a basis for the apportionment of contribution from the states, to be agreed upon as an amendment to the Articles of Confederation. It remained in force until the abolition of slavery.

Slave Trade. (See African Slave Trade.)

Slavery.—A slave is defined as a person who is the chattel or property of another and is wholly subject to his will. Slavery probably originated at an early period of the world's history in the accident of capture in war. It existed in all the ancient Oriental nations of which we have any record. In the Homeric poems it was the ordinary destiny of prisoners of war. The prevalence of Christianity tended to ameliorate the condition of the slave. Laws respecting the sale of slaves in England were made by Alfred the Great. The English peasantry were commonly sold for slaves in Saxon and Norman times; children were sold in Bristol market like cattle for exportation, many being sent to Ireland and Scotland. In 1574 Queen Elizabeth ordered her bondsmen in the western countries made free at easy rates, and in 1660 serfdom was finally extinguished in England. By the decision of Lord Mansfield, of the Court of King's bench, in the Sommersett case (q. v.), slavery was declared illegal in England. In Scotland bondage to the soil was not gotten rid of until the close of the last century.

Parliament abolished trade in negro slaves in 1807, and in 1833 an act was passed abolishing, slavery throughout the British colonies. In pursuance of this act 770,280 negroes became free Aug. 1, 1834. About the time of the American Revolution societies of prominent men were formed for the purpose of ameliorating the condition of the negro slaves. Pennsylvania was the first state to organize such a society, in 1787, with Benjamin Franklin as president. New York followed with a similar society, John Jay as its first president and Alexander Hamilton as its second. Immediately after came Rhode Island, and Maryland in 1789, with such members as Samuel Chase and Luther Martin; Delaware, with James A. Bayard and C. A. Rodney; Connecticut, in 1790; Virginia, 1791, and New Jersey, in 1792. The most that was accomplished by these societies was the suppression of the slave trade in 1808. Pennsylvania provided for the gradual emancipation of her slaves in 1780;

Smithsonian Institution.—James Smithson, F. R. S., a natural son of the first Duke of Northumberland, and an eminent English chemist and mineralogist, died in 1829. He bequeathed £105,000 to the Government of the United States in trust to "found at Washington an establishment, under the name of the Smithsonian Institution, for the increase and diffusion of knowledge among men." This bequest became operative in 1835. In 1838 the United States Government received from the court of chancery of Great Britain $515,169, which was increased by investment to $703,000. After the discussion of numerous plans, Congress in 1846 created the present establishment. The Institution has devoted itself to the two lines of work marked out in the terms of the bequest—the prosecution of original research and the publication and distribution of memoirs on subjects relating to science. During its existence it has originated many important scientific undertakings, which have later been taken up by the Government and prosecuted on broader lines under the control of special bureaus, some under the direction of the Institution, others independently. Out of its meteorological service the Weather Bureau has grown; in connection with its work in ichthyology the Fish Commission was established.

Under the direction of the Institution are the National Museum, which is the legal custodian of all government collections, the Bureau of International Exchanges, the Bureau of American Ethnology, the Astro-Physical Observatory, and the Zoological Park. The Institution maintains a table at the biological station at Naples, Italy, to which it sends students to conduct investigations. From time to time the Institution sends scientific expeditions, the most recent being those to Alaska to discover remains of mammoths and other large mammals, and to British Columbia to investigate and explore the glaciers there situated. The Institution has a library of 250,000 volumes. The direction of the affairs of the Institution is vested in a Board of Regents, consisting of the Chief Justice, the Vice-President, three senators, three representatives, and six other citizens, two of whom shall reside in Washington. The President of the United States and his Cabinet are members of the Institution. The secretary is elected by the Board of Regents. Joseph Henry, the first secretary, served from the founding of the Institution in 1846, till his death in 1878; he was succeeded by Spencer F. Baird, and upon the latter's death in 1887, Samuel P. Langley was placed in charge of the work. He was succeeded as secretary by Charles D. Wolcott. The Institution is located in Washington City and occupies an ornate building of Seneca brown stone, situated in a prominent place in the Mall, which extends from the Capitol to the Washington Monument. In 1904, the remains of James Smithson, who so far as it is known, had never visited this country, were brought from Geneva to Washington and placed in the Institution.

The entire consignment of pickled skins of animals killed in Africa by former President Roosevelt and his son, Kermit, was received at the Smithsonian Institution. Among the animals represented in this collection were rhinoceros, wild beeste bush busk, eland, wart hog, water buck, Impali zebra, giraffe, hyena, lion, Grant's gazelle, leopard, cheetah, reed buck, Thompson's gazelle, steinbuck, dik-ack, baboon, klipper springer and jackal.

Smithsonian Institution:

Bequest to United States by James Smithson for founding, 1406.

Fulfillment of objects of, suggested, 1723, 1942, 2124.

Prosecution of claim to, referred to, 1647, 1723.

Referred to, 1490, 6674, 6767, 7044.

Medium for interchange of official publications, 4718.

Organization of, recommended, 2751.

Request of regents of, for appropriation for National Museum commended, 4431, 4458.

Smoke Abatement Exhibition at London referred to, 4695.

Smuggling.—In the United States the offense of smuggling is defined as "the act, with the intent to defraud, of bringing into the United States, or, with like intent, attempting to bring into the United States, dutiable articles without passing the same, or the package containing the same, through the custom-house or submitting them to the officers of the revenue for examination." The penalties which may be enforced are a fine of not less than $50 nor more than $5,000, or imprisonment for not more than two years, or both, seizure and condemnation of the vessel or vehicle used, and various other special penalties. The British navigation laws of the latter part of the seventeenth and first half of the eighteenth centuries induced bold and extensive smuggling into the Colonies. Merchants and prominent public men otherwise respectable felt no hesitation about cheating the revenue by illicit trade with pirates and West Indian merchants. New York was the principal port for smugglers, though Boston, Philadelphia, and Charleston were also enriched by smuggled goods. This led the British Government to enforce the acts of trade which did much to precipitate the Revolution.

Smuggling:

Pernicious practice of, should be prevented, 644.

Practice of, criminal in free governments, 480.

Snake Indians. (See Indian Tribes.)

Sniper.—One who picks off enemy forces, one at a time, by sharp-shooting. (See Sharp-Shooter.)

Sno-ho-mish Indians. (See Indian Tribes.)

Snoquálmoo Indians. (See Indian Tribes.)

Soap.—The manufacture of soap has grown to be one of the hundred million dollar industries in the United States.

Reports were received by the Department of Commerce from 513 establishments that manufactured soap in 1914, the total products of which for the year were valued at $135,340,499. Of these 513 establishments, the principal business of 371 was the manufacture of soap, and 142 were engaged primarily in other industries, such as slaughtering and meat packing and the manufacture of food products, cottonseed products, and patent medicines and compounds, and produced soap as a subsidiary product.

Soc Indians. (See Indian Tribes.)

Social-Democratic Party. (See Socialist Party.)

Social Service.—One of the most illuminating evidences of the awakening of the social conscience in the last one hundred years has been the development in recent years of what is called social service. Social service, or social work, covers efforts being made for the improvement of the conditions of life, especially among those who are in want, suffering, or need of assistance. The term has broadened far beyond the earlier attempts merely to remedy distress by the application of charity or of other relief, and now covers for the greater part efforts being made all over the globe to prevent the existence of social misery. Social service has become a science, if not an exact science; and has its rules and theories applicable to social amelioration hardly less definite than the rules applicable in medicine to the attack on illness. Any attempt to enumerate the number of social service organizations or workers would be fruitless, as there is no sharp line to distinguish social endeavors from other endeavors which are not altogether devoted to the pursuit of private profit in industry. For instance, social service covers such diverse fields of activities as the prevention of prostitution; family rehabilitation; legislation for higher wages and shorter hours; attempts to democratize industry, and to improve the working conditions in mines, factories, and on means of transportation; the acquisition of better mental hygiene; the attack on drunkenness; child labor and minimum wage legislation; the surveys of entire cities to determine the evils existing therein; the advance of a new science of penology; and the general education of the community to the ways in which "the other half lives."

Social Settlements.—Neighborhood centers established by persons anxious to improve conditions in neighborhoods where the inhabitants, either through their own faults or through the press of circumstances, are in need of assistance in order to attain the socialized development possible to them. Settlements aim, not so much to change or to revolutionize the life in the poorer urban sections where they are located as to develop the inherent beneficial qualities of that life to the best advantage. In other words, settlement workers attempt not so much to help others, as would the agents of a charitable institution, as to help others to help themselves. In pursuit of this ideal, many and varied activities are developed in a neighborhood settlement. Educational, literary, dramatic, musical and social clubs are organized and directed; physical training is made available; friendly visits are paid the families in the neighborhood; vocational guidance is provided for the children; free medical and nursing advice is given; and attempts are made to obtain new laws and working conditions which will accrue to the happiness of the poor.

Settlements seem to be developments primarily of the United States and of England, where Arnold Toynbee inaugurated the settlement by going down to live in the slums of Whitechapel, in the parish of Canon Samuel A. Barnett, in 1875. He soon associated with himself a group of other university men, who had also been inspired by the gospel of assistance to the needy as preached by John Ruskin; and Toynbee Hall, the first social settlement, was established by Canon Barnett in 1885. Stanton Coit established in 1887 the University Settlement in the East Side of New York, and his example was followed by Jane Addams, who established in Chicago in 1889 the most famous of all settlements, Hull House. Other well-known settlements in the United States are the Henry Street Settlement in New York, where Lillian Wald inaugurated visiting nursing in the homes of the poor, and the Chicago Commons, where Graham Taylor has wielded a strong intellectual and political influence in the life of all of Chicago. Hardly an American city of size is now without its settlement or settlements.

As originally established, settlements were centers where altruistic persons made their headquarters for their individual friendly work among the poor; but they soon passed from such centers of private influence into large and complex institutions. The way having thus been indicated, municipalities all over the country began to establish public civic and neighborhood centers, usually in the public schools; and the tendency of the settlement movement is hence to resign the institutional work to the public authorities, and go back to the original conception of a center of private influence.

Social Work. (See Social Service.)

Social Worker.—One engaged in social service (q. v.).

Socialism.—Few terms are more difficult to define than Socialism. Not only is the exactness of the word obscured by the fact that Socialism is an international movement, and represents different practises and theories in different countries; but also it must be recorded that the European War greatly altered the status of Socialism along with that of most other comprehensive conceptions. Starting, then, from the negative point of view, Socialism must be sharply differentiated from *Anarchy*, which would restrict the sway of government, whereas Socialism would extend it. Socialism must not be confused again with either vague and unformulated philosophies which are covered by the term *Utopianism*, or with even a radical liberalism which represents a reform rather than a revolutionary movement. Socialism as such must also be distinguished from

State Socialism.—This term again is hard to define, but may be considered as representing a vast and extensive system of social reform in behalf of the masses, carried into execution by a benevolent government under the present organization of society. It differs from Socialism—first, in that Socialism holds that the fundamental necessity for lasting improvement in the body social is the abolition of the present capitalistic organization of society; and secondly, in that Socialism believes that the vital reforms for the masses should be worked out not only for the masses, but also by them. State Socialism would embrace such reforms as old-age pensions; workmen's compensation; state illness, death, accident, and unemployment insurance; limitless educational scholarships; the assumption of governmental responsibility for all the deserving in need of assistance; enactments for minimum wages and minimum hours of employment; state control over, but not ownership of, large industry; stringent child labor regulations; a system of the state as landlord, both of farms and of houses; state artistic and literary subsidization; and similar other measures calculated to improve the social conditions of the mass of the workers in a country. State Socialism is essentially paternalistic. Germany before the war is usually considered the best example of State Socialism in any large modern country. Socialism must also not be confused with

Syndicalism.—Syndicalism, whose upholders are usually called in the United States Industrial Workers of the World (I. W. W.). differs from Socialism in that it is primarily an organization of industrial working-people believing in one universal industrial union, in the accomplishment of which end sabotage is justifiable. *Sabotage*, often called the philosophy of direct action, is the justification and the accomplishment of the destruction of property belonging to the propertied class against whose interests syndicalism is agitating. Syndicalism differs from the usual trade union philosophy as exemplified by the American Federation of Labor (see Trade Unions) in that the latter is organized into a system of individual unions according to craft, obtaining its ends by peaceful and legislative methods, whereas syndicalism believes in only one comprehensive, fighting, international organization. With syndicalism's views concerning the industrial organization of the working-class, Socialism has been in accord to a great extent, but is definitely opposed to sabotage. Socialism must be differentiated also from *Communism*, which in its various phases would provide for equality of income or of use of goods of economic value.

Having thus defined what Socialism is not, we may be in a better position to describe what it is. First, however, it must be pointed out that Socialism is not only a theory, but is a definitely-organized political movement. In this respect, it offers a great contrast to a philosophy like that of the single-tax (q. v.), which has organized no political movement to carry forth its message, and to the prohibition movement (q. v.), most of whose advocates in municipal, state and national elections vote for candidates of one of the two leading political parties, and not for the candidate of the Prohibition Party. And if the political aims of Socialism were to be described in one phrase, that phrase would be "the public ownership and control of all factors of production of social value." In other words, Socialism would do away with the present competitive system of private ownership of industry, and substitute a co-operative system of state production, in which the state would produce and sell all socially-necessary utilities without profit, and, eliminating profit and returns on capital, pay all workers salaries in proportion to services rendered. With this economic program as the keystone of the arch of Socialism, it will be seen that Socialism takes no stand upon questions like divorce, religion, and prohibition, although Socialists as individuals have usually well-defined ideas upon these issues. Indeed, there exists a sect within the Christian Church known as *Christian Socialists*, and a number of ministers of all denominations are members of the Socialist Party.

Among the objections usually offered by opponents of Socialism are the following: By destroying competition, Socialism would destroy incentive. By extending state control, individual freedom would be endangered. By abolishing the law of supply and demand, it would be difficult to substitute a workable basis upon which to determine the payment of salaries of those in industry. Public administration is notoriously corrupt and inefficient. Political economists, in addition, usually question the correctness of the assertion that of land, labor, and capital—the three elements of production—labor alone should receive reward in the shape of wages. To these objections, Socialists in the past have usually replied by asserting that the evils of the present system more than counterbalance the evils imputed to a Socialistic system; and since the outbreak of the European War have pointed to the incursion of Government into practically every field of private endeavor as proving the efficiency and workable value of the Socialist program.

Socialism, moreover, claims for itself the title of a science; and in asserting that its adoption is inevitable in the progress of civilization, bases its argument chiefly upon three creeds: (1) The materialistic interpretation of history, which claims that the course which human development assumes at any particular period is the result of the system of economic production prevalent in that period. This creed is usually accepted even by non-Socialists as sound to a great extent, being supported by many biologists, economists, and historians, and seemingly strengthened by no less an authority than Herbert Spencer. (2) The doctrine of class struggle, which claims that the interests of the workers and of the employers in modern society are diametrically opposed, and that the numerically-larger class of the workers will permanently improve their own conditions only by joining the political party of the workers and thus becoming "Class-conscious." It is usually claimed by opponents of Socialism that this doctrine has degenerated into a doctrine of class-hatred. According to Karl Marx, the class-struggle would eventually divide all people into either an upper or a lower class; but the steady growth of a middle class in modern society, although it would seem to refute Marx's belief, nevertheless has not put a quietus upon the growth of Socialism. (3) The theory of surplus value, which claims that Labor produces more than it receives, and that this surplus goes into the pockets of the owning-class.

Since the Socialist movement is a movement against the capitalistic system which prevails in all modern countries, Socialism is inevitably an International movement. Most Socialists accordingly have claimed in the past that the only war recognized by them as ethical is a struggle between the capitalist class on the one hand, and workers, or "proletariat," on the other hand. Nevertheless, although from this point of view, all struggles between nations as they are constituted at present are essentially civil warfare, nevertheless the various Socialist Congresses in the past have never definitely refused to allow Socialists in a given country to support a war waged by that country in case of invasion, and under certain other conditions. In that connection, the part played by Socialists in the European War was and is of especial interest (see below).

History.—The rise of what we call Socialism dates from the early years of the nineteenth century, as a result of the social misery prevalent at that time. The philosophy of Saint Simon as published in France in 1817 and the co-operative experiments of Robert Owen in England in the same year definitely began the Socialist propaganda, and were supported by the Utopian schemes of Fourier. The term Socialist was first applied in 1835 to the endeavors of Owen; but as then used the term was largely synonomous with the present-day term of "Utopian," as signifying an attitude which was visionary, and at first the term was indignantly repudiated by the founders of modern Socialism. The speculations of Blanc in 1844 in the field of political socialism, and the agitation of Lassalle later in Germany for social reform strengthened the foundation for the later Socialist movement, but the creation of a definite international Socialist movement was due to Karl Marx, assisted by Frederick Engels.

In November, 1847, a group of political refugees, mostly Germans, met in East London, and adopted the famous Communist Manifesto, as prepared by Marx and Engels, as the basis for the Socialist movement. For some years, however, the movement grew slowly. In 1864, the International Workingmen's Association was organized, but after some years of struggle, it died in 1876. During the later seventies, however, the Socialists began to make themselves felt as a political force in Europe. Scattered groups of Socialists became strongly organized—and the doctrine of Socialism began to take root even in countries outside of Europe. On July 14, 1889, the one hundredth anniversary of the fall of the Bastille, the first International Socialist Congress was held in Paris, and was attended by many leaders who were soon to impress the force of Socialism upon the actions of all European governments—Liebknecht, Bebel, Keir Hardie, John Burns, Victor Adler. Since that time, hardly a ministry in Europe has been organized without Socialists in its roster, including three premiers of France—Viviani, Millerand, and Briand, and a present member of the English War Council. Indeed, the governing party in France is called the Socialistic Radicals. The "International," as the International Socialist organization is familiarly called, was formed in 1864, one year after the organization of the Social Democratic Party in Germany, under which name the Socialists are politically organized in that country. German immigrants to the United States began to organize Socialist groups in 1864, and in 1869 sections of the International were formed in different parts of the country. At the present time there would seem to be a large number of Socialists who disavow the teachings of Karl Marx (1818-1883) as the basis of their Socialism, but it is admitted that he was the founder, not only of the Socialist movement, but also of the trend towards a greater social emphasis in modern political economy. At no time does the enrolled membership of the Socialist Party approach the Socialist vote in different countries, but the Socialist organization is on record as asserting that its greatest desire at the present time is the education of the working-class to the particular "class-conscious" doctrine of Socialism.

The voting strength of Socialism is as follows:

	Vote		Percentage Members Congress	
	1914	1904	1914	1904
Austria	1,081,441	780,000	17%	2%
Belgium	483,241	305,361	22%	18%
Finland	310,503	100,000	45%	1%
France	1,106,047	860,827	13%	8%
Germany	4,238,919	3,010,771	28%	20%
Great Britain	529,193	100,000	6%	1%
Italy	822,280	326,016	12%	6%
Russia	300,000		4%	..%
Sweden	172,980	10,000	28%	2%
United States	931,381	441,776	....	....

In Germany.—It is in Germany that Socialism has become strongest, in spite of the fact that Germany before the European War had advanced farther along the lines of state socialism than any of its great rivals in the world. The Social Democratic Party before the war was the largest single political body in the Reichstag; and if the Reichstag were elected by a strictly proportionate, or one-man-one-vote method, there would be 138 Socialist members, or 35%, instead of the present number of 111. In 1914, the enrolled membership of the Party was 1,080,-000, of whom practically 1,000,000 were men. In Hamburg, three-quarters of the voters are Socialists; in the kingdom of Saxony, a majority of the voters; and almost one-half in Berlin itself. Socialism in Germany both before and during the war was one of the strongest factors in the political life of the German people.

In France.—In 1914, in elections later than those given in the preceding table, 101 Socialists were elected to the Chamber of Deputies, or approximately one-sixth of the total membership. Socialism has given rise to many quasi-Socialist parties, such as the Independent Socialists and the Socialistic Radicals, the ruling political party. *In Russia,* determined Governmental opposition succeeded in stamping out Socialism as such, and Socialists, radicals, liberals, and revolutionists have worked together to stamp out autocracy. *In Great Britain,* Socialism as a political unit is very weak, but is well expressed in the British Labor Party, a federation of radical unionists with Socialist organizations. The total membership of this combination in 1914 was 1,895,498; and in it are included men of great influence throughout the land, such as John Burns and Keir Hardie. *In the United States,* the

Soicalist Party as such was not organized until 1900, and represented an amalgamation of the Social Democratic Party and the greater part of the Socialist Labor Party (q. v.). The largest membership ever attained within the Party itself was 117,984, in 1912. The largest individual membership within the Socialist Party, though not the largest vote, in that year was in the State of Pennsylvania. The Presidential election of that year showed that the largest proportion of Socialist votes, in comparison with the total number of votes cast, occurred in Nevada, Alaska and Washington, with the smallest proportion in the Southern States. The largest individual vote was cast in the State of Ohio. For further details, see the article Socialist Party.

United States Platform.—The platform of the Socialist Party in the United States for 1912 is more typical of the Socialist program than the platform of 1916, which was affected greatly by the war situation. The 1912 platform reaffirms allegiance to the Socialist principles explained above, attacks the capitalist system, and declares that the benefits of prosperity accrue to the owning class, not to the workers. Definite proposals are for the collective ownership and democratic management of all transportation, telephone and telegraph, and express lines, and also of the banking system and of all large industry. The platform demands the immediate acquisition of all municipal food-handling agencies, and the addition of all mines, oil-wells and forests to the public domain. It asks immediate relief for unemployment by the extension of public works, the shortening of the working-day, the establishment of at least 1½ days rest in each week for all employed in industry, the prohibition of child labor under the age of 16, the application of the minimum wage, the abolition of official charity for a system of old-age pension and state insurance against illness, death, unemployment, accidents, and industrial diseases. It demands the extension of taxes upon inheritances, incomes, and corporations; and asks for the introduction into American national, state and municipal political life of the initiative, referendum and recall. It demands universal equal suffrage for women; the abolition of the United States Senate, of the veto power of the President, and of the right of the Supreme Court to pass upon the constitutionality of any act passed by the representatives of the people; the ending of the indirect method of Presidential elections; and the changing of the requirement for a three-fourths states' ratification vote to amendments to the Constitution, in favor of a majority vote. It calls for a constitutional convention to revise the Constitution, asks the curbing of the courts' power to issue injunctions, and pleads for the free administration of the law.

Socialists and the War.—The part played by Socialism in the Great European War must remain a matter of conjecture until the end of the war re-establishes free and unbiased communication between the countries of the world. The following description of the situation is merely an attempt to combine various opinions expressed by leading Socialists in America:—Because of the fact that the Socialist movement was the one great International movement which theoretically would refuse to ally itself with a war program, the weakness of the Socialist opposition to the war, especially in Germany, must be admitted. Historically, however, no International Socialist Conference has gone on record flatly against all war, and the anti-war resolution passed at the Stuttgart Conference in 1907 took a compromise position, declaring only against imperialism (q. v.) and militarism (q. v.). At that conference, Bebel, leader of the German Socialists, refused to assert that in the event of war between Germany and France, the German Socialists would not make war against their French comrades. The founders of Socialism were not pacifists (q. v.)—Marx justifying war under certain conditions, and Engels predicting in 1892 that a great European war, fought by the people, would lead to a general revolution in Europe. Socialists had long laid plans to forbid war by inaugurating a general strike, but the plans were not carried out when Germany began her march through Belgium in 1914. The Social Democratic Party of Germany had even voted for the Government's war budget in 1913.

On July 29, 1914, the International Socialist Bureau was meeting in Belgium, and devoted all of its energies to opposing the imminent struggle. On July 30, there were monster demonstrations against war, in which the German Socialists joined, even though Russia had already begun to mobilize. In Berlin itself on July 28 and 29, there were Socialist mass-meetings against war, and the executive committee of the Social Democratic Party opposed war even so late as July 30. On July 31 and on August 1, the latter date being the one on which it is generally agreed war formally began, the Socialist organ, the *Vorwaerts*, came out against war. But there the Socialist opposition ended for some months. On August 4, the 111 delegates of the Social Democratic Party in the Reichstag voted for the war loan of the Government, although in the party caucus held just previously to the vote, 14 of the 111 opposed such action. Even on the second great war credit voted on December 2, 1914, the only Socialist registered in the negative, amid scenes of uproar and even violence, was Karl Liebknecht, who was severely censured by his own party for that independent action. But on the third war loan, passed March 20, 1915, there were 2 Socialist votes recorded in the negative, and 30 Socialists absented themselves from the Reichstag chamber as a protest against the loan. In April, May and June, the Party definitely split on the war question, and no longer acted with unanimity. The majority still supports the Imperial Chancellor, but the minority in opposition to the war is steadily growing in numbers. Liebknecht, who was denied a chance to express himself in the Reichstag until April 8, 1915, was finally expelled from the Party for his stand against the war, and some months later was expelled from the Reichstag on the charge of treason, and in company with the veteran Socialist leader, Rosa Luxembourg, was imprisoned. Haase, formerly the leader of the Party, was expelled in the course of the war, and now heads a party of his own, the leadership of the majority, which still supports the government, but with reservations, falling to Scheidemann. The leader Ledebour is now also definitely with the minority opposing the government. It would seem that the minority is only opposing certain schedules in the program of the Government, and that only a minority of the minority is with Liebknecht in opposition without compromise. The Socialist newspaper, the *Vorwaerts*, is with the majority supporting the Government, but with reservations, while the trenchant opponent of the war, Maximilien Harden, with his paper, the *Zukunft*, can hardly be classed as a Socialist. On the whole then, it would seem that, although the greater number of the Socialists in Germany still are not ready to go so far as to oppose the Government's prosecution of the war, yet the sentiment for peace in the Empire is definitely under the leadership of those Socialists who have broken, both with their own party and with the Government.

The Socialist movement in Austria is also well organized, but very little has escaped the censor concerning the activities of the Socialists in that country. The veteran leader, Victor Adler, was allowed to publish a plea for peace as early as February, 1915; and it may be surmised that the Austrian Socialists as a body are now united against the further participation of their country in the struggle. In France, the Socialists opposed a declaration of war until their country was invaded, since which time there does not seem to have arisen any peace sentiment among them. In Great Britain, the Independent Labor Party defeated a resolution against the further prosecution of the war, as early as April, 1915, by a vote of only 121 to 120. When war was announced, John Burns resigned from the Cabinet, but has never opposed the war; and George Bernard Shaw, a Fabian Socialist (q. v.), has created much opposition by his severe criticisms of England's position in the struggle, although he has not come out openly for England's retirement from it.

In the United States, the war question definitely has split the party into two camps. Even at the election of 1916, the great decrease in the Party vote was unquestionably due to the military question, and when war was declared, many prominent Socialists, with a large following, denounced and refused to be guided by the action of the forces in control of the Party, who at a convention in St. Louis declined to support the United States in its entrance into the struggle. This resolution was later submitted for endorsement to a referendum of the members of the Party, and there were many resignations from the Party membership.

No account played by the Socialists in the European War would be complete without mention of the Russian Revolution of 1917 (q. v.). From the little authentic news of the epochal event which can be gleaned during the war, the planners of the revolution were not prepared for anything more than a change from a reactionary to a liberal monarchy, and the transformation of the revolution into a successful attempt once for all time to abolish monarchy, and to establish in Russia a representative democracy would seem to have been due to the efforts and agitation of the elements in Russia which can be correctly described as Socialistic. (See European War; Socialist Party; Germany; France; England; Russia.)

Guild Socialism.—An offshoot of the Socialist movement representing a reaction against the power of the centralized state and a return to the medieval organization of industry into trade guilds. Guild Socialism would leave the control of each industry to the workers in that industry, although there is no reason why such control should not be guided by a central administrative body where it affected other industries. Reports from Europe during the war indicate that dissatisfaction with the arbitrary nature of much of the state socialism adopted by the belligerent countries stimulated a strong feeling toward guild socialism, especially in Great Britain.

Syndicalism.—Although syndicalism has many features in common with trade unionism and with Socialism, its distinct origin lies in recent years with the French thinker, Georges Sorel. As a matter of fact, the term is derived from the French word for trade union, "syndicat." In the United States, the movement got its first foothold in 1903 in the Colorado strike of that year. The Industrial Workers of the World was formed in 1905 to carry out the syndicalist program, the body representing a federation of the Western Federation of Miners, the United Metal Workers, and the Labor Alliance. It was not long, however, before the Western Federation of Miners withdrew; and the rapidly increasing strength of the Socialist movement in the next ten years served to act as a damper on the growth of the I. W. W. At the present time, they seem to become dangerous only where labor conditions are unusually unfair; and to that extent represent a stronger protest than could be made by the more orderly economic forces of the trade unions or the political action of the Socialists. At different times, the I. W. W. become prominent in certain sections, as is shown by the statement that their activities have been most pronounced in Lawrence, Lowell, Paterson, South Carolina, Montana, and Washington, but seldom contemporaneously. At the present time, there are two distinct branches, one being more radical than the other.

The philosophy of syndicalism distrusts the abolition of the capitalist system by legislation, and bases its hope upon the workers seizing control of industry by direct action. Industry accordingly would be directed by the workers in it, and the activities of the state, as a political organization, would disappear. The general strike of all workers is the means usually proclaimed as the means to gain control over all industry. For the I. W. W. believe that the lot of a worker in one industry cannot be differentiated from the lot of a worker in another industry, and hence insist upon the formation of all workers into one big industrial union, acting homogeneously, instead of into separate craft unions, acting independently, as in the American Federation of Labor. Society at present being a class struggle, the I. W. W. endorse sabotage, or the limitation of output and the destruction of property, if necessary, in the fight against the employing class.

Although syndicalism has had its ups and downs in the United States, there were in France, prior to the war, about 600,000 syndicalists; and the movement was also especially strong among the agricultural classes of Italy.

For a contrast between the syndicalist and the trade union points of view, consult also the article Trade Unions.

Socialist Labor Party.—This party took its name at a convention held at Newark, N. J., in 1877. In 1883 a congress of Socialists met at Baltimore, Md., and formed a national party, but the growth of the organization was retarded by the anarchistic outbreak in Chicago in 1886. The party was reorganized in 1889, formally assuming the name Socialist Labor party, and their first national convention was held in New York City August 28, 1892. Simon Wing, of Massachusetts, was nominated for President, and Charles H. Matchett, of New York, for Vice-President. The platform advocated public ownership of all railroads, telegraphs, and other public utilities, the initiative and referendum, the recall of representatives, and the abolition of the Presidency, Vice-Presidency and Senate. In that year the party polled 21,532 votes.

In 1896 Charles H. Matchett was the candidate for President and Matthew Ma-

guire for Vice-President. The platform advocated state ownership of all means of production. The vote in this year was 36,-274. In 1898 the party in eighteen states cast 82,204 votes. In 1899 the Socialist Labor party split, most of its members going to the Social Democratic party or Social Democracy (now the Socialist party).

Socialist Party.—This party was organized as the Social Democracy in 1897 by Eugene V. Debs, at Chicago. In 1898 the party's candidate polled, chiefly in Massachusetts, 9,545 votes. In 1900 Eugene V. Debs was the party's candidate for President and Job H. Harriman for Vice-President. The platform advocates state ownership of all means of production and distribution, with the public ownership of railways, mines, etc., also the initiative and referendum, and public work for unemployed. In that year the party vote was 84,003, many additions to the party being received from the Socialist Labor party (*q. v.*).

In 1901 at the Indianapolis convention the party formally united with the seceders from the Socialist Labor party, and took the name of Socialist party, except in some states, particularly in New York and Wisconsin, on account of certain provisions in the election laws of those states. In 1902 the party vote was 229,762.

In 1904 Eugene V. Debs and Benjamin Hanford were the Presidential and Vice-Presidential candidates, and received 402,-283 votes. The Socialist party has at times elected local officers in several states, and at one time had representatives in the Massachusetts legislature. In 1908 Debs polled 420,793 votes for President.

Victor Berger, of Wisconsin, became in 1910 the first Socialist Congressman to be elected to the United States House of Representatives, but was defeated for re-election in 1912. In 1914, Meyer M. London, Socialist, was elected to the House from New York City, and was re-elected in 1916. In 1912, Debs, candidate for President, received 901,-873 votes, about 6% of the total vote cast. In 1916, Allen Benson, candidate for President, received 568,377 votes, or slightly above 3% of the total vote cast. In that year Milwaukee elected a Socialist Mayor for the second time and Minneapolis for the first time. In 1914, there were 31 Socialist members of the legislatures of 13 states. (See Socialism.)

Whatever might be the final results of the official antagonism of the Socialist Party to the prosecution of war by the United States against Germany, the effect of that opposition during the war itself was to make tremendous increases in the Socialist Party vote and membership. In the New York mayorality campaign in November, 1917, more than one in every five votes was cast for the Socialist candidate; and in Chicago the Socialist ticket was beaten decisively only by an amalgamation of the Republican and Democratic parties. In New York State, the elections of the same month increased the Socialist representation in the legislature from two to eleven; and in New York City, Socialists were for the first time seated in the Board of Aldermen, seven being elected. The increase in the vote in New York was about 450% over the vote of 1912, and a scarcely lower percentage was maintained in other elections all over the country. Although much of this vote did not represent increased allegiance to Socialist principles—coming from pacifists, pro-Germans, and protestants against the Government's policy of suppressing certain Socialist newspapers and periodicals—yet the increase in the membership of the Party and in the subscription list of Socialist journals was marked. Many men of prominence joined the Party for the first time—offsetting thus to a great extent the defection of many of the intellectual leaders who resigned from the Party because of its attitude toward the war against Germany.

Socialist Party, teachings of, based on class hatred, 7210.

Socialists, used as pawns by German government, 8280.

Society of American Florists, act incorporating, vetoed, 6010.

Society of Army of the Cumberland, statue of Gen. Garfield to be erected in Washington by, 4795.
　Unveiling ceremonies, order regarding, 5162.

Society of Colonial Wars.—Instituted in 1892 to "perpetuate the memory of these events and of the men who, in military, naval, and civil positions of high trust and responsibility, by their acts or counsel assisted in the establishment, defense, and preservation of the American Colonies, and were in truth the founders of the Nation. With this end in view it seeks to collect and preserve manuscripts, rolls, and records; to provide suitable commemorations or memorials relating to the American Colonial period, and to inspire in its members the paternal and patriotic spirit of their forefathers, and in the community respect and reverence for those whose public services made our freedom and unity possible." Eligibility is confined to an adult male descendant of an ancestor who fought in battle under Colonial authority, from the settlement of Jamestown, Va., in 1607, to the battle of Lexington, in 1775, or who served as Governor, Deputy-Governor, Member of the Council, or as a military, naval, or marine officer in the service of the Colonies, or under the banner of Great Britain, or was conspicuous in military, official, or legislative life during that period.

Society of Friends:
　Management of Indians committed to, 3992, 4063, 4106, 4154, 4206, 4254, 4307.
　Paper to President, from, on Indian affairs, referred to, 4075.

Societies of Spanish War Veterans.— Astor Battery Association.—Organized December, 1904. Composed of original members of the Astor Battery, which served in the Philippines campaign of 1898. Meets annually, Aug. 13, anniversay of the capture of Manila, at Reunion-Army of the Philippines, and at the annual national encampment of the United Spanish War Veterans.

　Naval and Military Order of the Spanish-American War.—Instituted Feb. 2, 1899. Membership is composed of persons who served on the active list or performed active duty as commissioned officers, regular or volunteer, during the war with Spain,

or who participated in the war as naval or military cadets. Membership descends to the eldest male descendant in the order of primogeniture.

　Society of the Army of the Philippines. —Composed of American soldiers who fought in any of the campaigns in the Philippine Islands.

　Society of the Army of Santiago de Cuba. —Organized in the Governor's Palace at Santiago de Cuba, July 31, 1898. Annual dues, $1; life membership, $25. No initiation fee. There are branch societies in Massachusetts, New York, Ohio, Michigan, Illinois, California, and the District of Columbia.

　United Spanish War Veterans.—National Encampment United Spanish War Veterans.—Organized April 18, 1904, by the consolidation of the National Army and Navy Spanish War Veterans, National Association of Spanish-American War Veterans, and the Society of the Service Men of the Spanish War. Soldiers and sailors of the regular and volunteer army, navy and marine corps who served honorably during the war with Spain or in the insurrection in the Philippines are eligible to membership.

　United Volunteer Association.—All white soldiers and sailors who served honorably in the military or naval service of the United States during the war with Spain or the incident insurrection in the Philippines are eligible to membership. This society was organized at Chattanooga, Tenn., Aug. 17, 1899, and has a membership (1909) of nearly 38,000. It is national in scope and character.

Society of the Army and Navy of the Confederate States, in the State of Maryland.—Organized in 1871, "to collect and preserve the material for a truthful history of the late war between the Confederate states and the United States of America; to honor the memory of our comrades who have fallen; to cherish the ties of friendship among those who survive, and to fulfil the duties of sacred charity toward those who may stand in need of them." The membership is 925.

Society of the Cincinnati. (See Cincinnati, Society of the.)

Societies of the Union Army of 1861-65.—Society of the Army of the Tennessee.—Organized at Raleigh, N. C., April 14, 1865; the headquarters are at Cincinnati. Army of the Tennessee Association; organized at Washington, D. C., August, 1902; all who served in that army eligible to membership. Society of the Army of the Cumberland; organized in February, 1868, and its present membership is 350. Society of the Army of the Potomac; the Society was organized in 1868; the present membership is over 2,000. Association of the Thirteenth Army Corps; this Association was organized at Milwaukee, August, 1889.

Societies of the War of 1812.—The Veteran Corps of Artillery of the State of New York, Constituting the Military Society of the War of 1812. Instituted as a military society by the officers of the War of 1812, on Jan. 3, 1826, in the City of New York, and incorporated under the laws of the State of New York, by the surviving veteran members, Jan. 8, 1892. Consolidated Jan. 8, 1848, with the Veteran Corps of Artillery (instituted by officers of the Revolutionary War, Nov. 25, 1790). Hiram Cronk, last surviving Veteran member War of 1812, born April 29, 1800, died May 13, 1905. The original members comprise those who actually served in the military or naval forces of the United States during the War of 1812, or on vessels other than merchant ships which sailed under commissions of letters of marque and reprisals from the United States in that war. Eligibility to hereditary membership is confined by law to descendants of those who actually served in the War of 1812, and to descendants of former members.

General Society of the War of 1812.— Is composed of federated state societies, in Pennsylvania, Maryland, Massachusetts, Connecticut, Ohio, Illinois, District of Columbia, New York, New Jersey, and Delaware, the members of each of which state societies are borne upon the membership roll of the general society. Any male person above the age of twenty-one years who participated in, or who is a lineal descendant of one who served during the War of 1812-14 in the army, navy, revenue marine, or privateer service of the United States, offering satisfactory proof to the state society to which he makes application, and is of good moral character and reputation, may become a member. In case of failure of lineal descendants of an actual participant in said war, one collateral representative who is deemed worthy may be admitted to membership.

Sociology.—The status of this science is so vaguely defined that any definition must be a purely individual venture. Perhaps sociology may be described as the science of the relations existing between individuals and society in their social contacts, as distinguished from their economic and individualistic contacts. It may hence not inaccurately be described as the socialized side of economics (q. v.). One tendency of sociology has been to investigate and to deduce laws concerning the origins of society and of modern social organization. Another and later tendency has been to make sociology the theory on which social service (q. v.) must be based. Modern sociology is concerned with such subjects as the origin and basis of family life, the strength of sex appeal, the permanence and power of racial characteristics upon the life of the individual, the reaction of human beings to their environments, the psychological effect of group-consciousness in determining the actions of an individual, and the effects of wages upon crime and immorality. From this list, it may be observed that, however sociologists may differ in the theories and methods they pursue, they all attempt in one way or another to describe the impulses which account for the actions of individuals, groups, and nations.

Sociology is an offspring of the latter half of the nineteenth century. It can not be altogether disassociated from economics, but its founders are often declared to be Comte and Saint-Simon, while the greatest impetus to sociological speculations was given by Herbert Spencer.

Soils, Bureau of.—A bureau of the Department of Agriculture devoted to the investigation, classification, survey and mapping of soils; studies in soil chemistry and physics; soil fertility; explorations to discover the sources of natural fertilizers; studies in the physical and chemical properties of soils and materials and methods of artificial fertilization, with their influence on the original soils. One of the special features of the bureau is the study of tobacco culture, curing, packing and exporting, as well as the introduction of new and improved varieties.

The soil survey is an institution devoted to the accumulation of a well-defined group of facts. These facts have a scientific as well as a practical value. The practical knowledge can be applied in many cases at once, and valuable economic and social results arise from it. This is the value that is usually emphasized—to be able to direct agricultural progress along proper lines, to point out natural adaptabilities of soil, and to suggest improved methods of cultivation based on a knowledge of the soil to be cultivated. These are some of the possibilities and actualities of the soil survey.

Soil Fertility, importance of conserving, 7462.

Soldiers' and Sailors' Insurance.—Not many months after the declaration of war against Germany in 1917, Congress, at the request of President Wilson, made provision for automatic insurance and benefits for death or injury during service in that war, instead of relying upon the old cumbersome and unfair pension scheme. Compensation is payable by the United States without contribution from the person injured or killed in active service. *In addition* to that compensation, a person in service had the option of purchasing additional insurance up to $10,000 at low rates averaging $8.00 per $1,000 at the age of 27. The *additional* income from this latter source for his family in case of death would be $57.50 monthly.

Compensation to Family in Case of Death.—The only persons entitled to receive compensation in case of death are the widow, children and dependent widowed mother of the deceased. The monthly sums payable in each case are as follows, and are not dependent upon the pay of the deceased:

1—For a widow alone, $25.

2—For a widow and one child, $35.

3—For a widow and two children, $47.50 with $5.00 additional for each child up to two.

4—For one child, if there be no widow, $20.

5—For two children, $30.

6—For three children, $40, with $5 for each additional child up to two.

7—For a widowed mother, $20. The amount payable under this sub-division shall not be greater than a sum which, when added to the total amount payable to the widow and children, does not exceed $75.

Compensation to a widow or widowed mother shall continue until death or remarriage.

Compensation to a child shall cease at the age of 18, or at marriage, unless the child is incompetent.

Funeral Allowance.—The United States shall pay funeral expenses, not to exceed $100.

Compensation in Case of Total Disability.—During the continuance of total disability, monthly compensation shall be paid to the injured person.

The amounts payable monthly are as stated, and are not based upon the pay of the injured person.

1—If he has neither wife nor child living, $30.

2—If he has a wife but no child living, $45.

3—If he has a wife and one child living, $55.

4—If he has a wife and two children living, $65.

5—If he has a wife and three or more children living, $75.

6—If he has no wife but one child living, $40, with $10 additional for each child up to two.

7—If he has a widowed mother dependent upon him for support, then in addition to the above amounts, $10.

To an injured person who is totally disabled, and in addition so helpless as to be in constant need of a nurse or attendant, such additional sum shall be paid as shall seem reasonable to the director, but not to exceed $20 monthly.

For certain specified conditions, or if the injured person is permanently bedridden, $100 monthly compensation is provided without an allowance for a nurse.

Compensation in Case of Partial Disability.—The amount of compensation in the case of partial disability is a percentage of the compensation provided in case of total disability.

The percentage is equal to the reduction in earning capacity resulting from similar injuries in civil life.

Attention is called to the very important provision that the United States shall furnish medical, surgical and hospital services, and supplies, in addition to pecuniary compensation.

The men and their dependents are also protected by the automatic insurance granted as follows:

Automatic Insurance.—Any person in active service on or after the sixth of April, 1917, is insured automatically until Feb. 12, 1918, unless he has applied for insurance to take effect at an earlier date.

The protection thus given is against death and against total permanent disability occurring, while in active service, from the above dates.

If the insured person die without having become so disabled during the above period, monthly instalments of $25 *each* will be paid his wife, child or widowed mother. These instalments are payable to the wife during her widowhood, or to the child or widowed mother while they survive him, but not more than 240 such instalments shall be paid.

If the injured person becomes totally and permanently disabled during the period stated above, he will receive an income payable in monthly instalments of $25 each during his disability. If he die, like instalments are payable to the wife during her widowhood, or to the child or widowed mother while they survive him, but not more than 240 such instalments shall be paid, less the number of instalments which may have been paid the insured while disabled.

Soldier.—Any member of a military organization. In the United States soldiers are especially classified as regular soldiers attached to the regular army and volunteer soldiers who proffer their services in emergencies. (See Army and Navy, National Guard and Militia.)

Soldiers' Homes.—*Regular Army*—The National Home for aged and disabled soldiers of the regular army of the United States is situated in Washington, D. C., occupying a beautiful site outside the city limits. It was established in 1851 with money raised by a levy on the City of Mexico during the Mexican War, and is supported by a regular tax on each soldier of the army.

All soldiers who have served twenty years as enlisted men in the army (including volunteer service, if any), or who have served in any war, and all soldiers of less than twenty years' service who have incurred such disability, by wounds, disease, or injuries in the line of duty while in the regular army, as unfits them for further service, are entitled to the benefits of the Home.

A pensioner who enters the Home may assign his pension, or any part of it, to his child, wife, or parent, by filing written notice with the agent who pays him. If not so assigned, it is drawn by the treasurer of the Home and held in trust for the pensioner, to whom it is paid in such sums as the governor of the Home deems proper while he is an inmate of the Home, the balance being paid in full when he takes his discharge and leaves the Home.

Inmates are subject to the Rules and Articles of War, the same as soldiers in the army. They are comfortably lodged, fed, and clothed and receive medical attendance and medicine, all without cost to them. There are 1,453 men (1916) receiving the benefits of the Home.

Applications for admission to the Home may be addressed to the "Board of Commissioners, U. S. Soldiers' Home, War Department, Washington, D. C.," and must give date of enlistment and date of discharge, with letter of company and number of regiment for each and every term of service, and rate of pension, if any, and must be accompanied by a medical certificate showing nature and degree of disability if any exists.

Volunteers.—There are National Homes for disabled volunteer soldiers at Dayton, O.; Milwaukee, Wis.; Togus, Me.; Hampton, Va.; Leavenworth, Kan.; Santa Monica, Cal.; Marion, Ind.; Danville, Ill.; Johnson City, Tenn., and Hot Springs, S. Dak. The aggregate number of members cared for is about 35,000.

The Board of Managers of the National Home for Disabled Volunteer Soldiers informs the disabled soldiers and sailors of the United States that Homes have been established, at the places above named, for all such as are unable to earn a living by labor. All the ordinary comforts of a home are provided—chapels for religious services; halls for concerts, etc.; hospitals, with experienced surgeons and nurses;

libraries and reading rooms; amusement halls; post and telegraph offices; stores, etc. Good behavior insures kind treatment.

Soldiers and sailors are especially informed that the Home is neither a hospital nor almshouse, but a home, where subsistence, quarters, clothing, religious instruction, employment when possible, and amusements are provided by the Government of the United States. The provision is not a charity, but is a reward to the brave and deserving, and is their right, to be forfeited only by bad conduct at the Home or conviction of heinous crimes. A soldier or sailor desiring admission may apply by letter to either of the managers, whereupon a blank application will be sent to him, and if he be found duly qualified, transportation will be furnished, or he can apply personally or by letter at the branch nearest to his place of residence.

President of the Board of Managers, Maj. James W. Wadsworth, 346 Broadway, New York City, N. Y.; Secretary, John M. Holley. Esq., La Crosse, Wis.

The requirements for admission are: (1) An honorable discharge from the United States service during a war in which it was engaged. (2) Disability which prevents the applicant from earning his living by labor. (3) Applicants for admission will be required to stipulate and agree to abide by all the rules and regulations made by the Board of Managers, or by its order; to perform all duties required of them, and to obey all the lawful orders of the officers of the Home. (4) A soldier or sailor must forward with his application for admission his Discharge Paper and when he is a pensioner, his Pension Certificate, which papers will be retained at the branch to which the applicant is admitted, to be kept there for him, and returned to him when he is discharged. This rule is adopted to prevent the loss of such papers and certificates, and to hinder fraudulent practices; and no application will be considered unless these papers are sent with it. If the original discharge does not exist, a copy of discharge, certified by the War or Navy Department, or by the Adjutant-General of the state, must accompany the application.

State Homes for disabled volunteer soldiers are maintained at the following places:

California—Yountville.	New Jersey { Kearny. / Vineland.
Colorado—Monte Vista.	New York { Bath. / Oxford.
Connecticut—Noreton H'ts.	
Idaho—Boise.	
Illinois—Quincy.	North Dakota—Lisbon.
Indiana—Lafayette.	Ohio { Sandusky. / Madison.
Iowa—Marshalltown.	
Kansas—Fort Dodge.	Oregon—Roseburg.
Massachusetts—Chelsea.	Pennsylvania—Erie.
Michigan—Grand Rapids.	Rhode Island—Bristol.
Minnesota—Minnehaha.	South Dakota—Hot Springs.
Missouri—St. James.	Vermont—Bennington.
Montana—Columbus Falls.	Washington { Orting. / Port Orchard.
Nebraska { Grand Island. / Milford.	Wisconsin—Waupaca.
New Hampshire—Tilton.	Wyoming—Cheyenne.

Confederate Soldiers' Homes are maintained at Atlanta, Ga.; Austin, Tex.; Beauvoir, Miss.; Columbia, S. C.; Hermitage, Tenn.; Higginsville, Mo.; Jacksonville, Fla.; Little Rock, Ark.; Mountain Creek, Ala.; New Orleans, La.; Pewee Valley, Ky.; Pikesville, Md.; Raleigh, N. C.; Richmond, Va; Washington, D. C.

Soldiers' Homes:

Erection of, recommended, 2559, 2624.

Recommendations of board of commissioners regarding, 4777.

Should be under jurisdiction of War Department, 7229.

Site for, selected, 2668.

Soldiers, Quartering of, without consent, forbidden in times of peace; in time of war, must follow manner prescribed by law, 29.

Solicitor-General.—The office of solicitor-general was created by the act of June 22, 1870, which created the Department of Justice. The solicitor-general acts as attorney-general whenever the latter is unable to attend to the duties of his office. The position of the Solicitor-General is unique in that he is the "Court Lawyer" for the United States. He prepares and argues cases in which the United States Government is involved, and is assisted by various assistant attorneys-general. He represents the Government in all cases in the Supreme Court of the United States; he determines whether pending cases shall be prosecuted or abandoned, and, in a word, has charge of all Government litigation. He is appointed by the President, and his salary is $10,000 a year. (See Attorney-General, Justice Department.)

Solicitor for the Department of State.—This officer is appointed by the President, by and with the consent of the Senate. His yearly salary is $5,000 and he is assisted by three assistants who are appointed by the Secretary of State at a yearly salary of $3,000 each. The office was created in 1866 with the title of "Examiner of Claims," but in 1891 the title became "Solicitor for the Department of State." The Solicitor is under the jurisdiction of the Justice Department, but he also has duties assigned to him by the Secretary of State. He is the law officer of the State Department, and renders opinions on all matters referred to him. He also has supervision over claims, manages extradition proceedings, and is in charge of the legal aspects of Naturalization. (See State Department; Justice Department; Court of Claims, Extradition; Naturalization; Departmental Solicitors.)

Solicitors, Departmental, Justice Department.—All departments of the Government have solicitors under the supervision of the Attorney-General, except the Departments of War and Navy, whose legal affairs are conducted by their judge advocates-general (q. v.). The departmental solicitors have offices in the buildings of the department to which they are assigned. In the Department of the Interior (q. v.), the assistant attorney-general handles appeals from the decisions of the General Land Office, prepares opinions, etc. The solicitor for the Department of State (q. v.) advises the Secretary of State on matters of law, especially of international law; decides claims of United States citizens against foreign governments and claims of foreigners against the United States; and also is in charge of extradition proceedings. The solicitor for the Treasury Department (q. v.) handles revenue prosecutions, and other legal matters for his department. The solicitor in the Internal Revenue Office (q. v.), the solicitor in the Department of Commerce (q. v.), the solicitor in the Department of Labor (q. v.), all have charge of the legal affairs of their departments. The Post-Office Department (q. v.) also has an assistant attorney-general. The salaries of the departmental solicitors are $5,000 yearly. (See Justice Department; Solicitor-General.)

Solicitor of the Treasury, office of, established, 1090.

Operations of, referred to, 2539.

Sommersett Case.—A negro slave named Sommersett accompanied his master from Boston to London in October, 1769. He became ill and was turned adrift by his master. His condition aroused the compassion of Granville Sharp, who cared for him until he was restored to health. He was then claimed by his master and taken before Lord Mansfield, of the court of King's bench. Here he was discharged on the ground that in England slavery could exist only by positive law, and in the absence of such a law a person could not be deprived of liberty on the ground that he was a slave. This decision determined the future course of England in the delivery of fugitives.

Sons of American Revolution.—A patriotic society composed of lineal descendants of soldiers, sailors, and conspicuous patriots of Revolutionary times. The society was organized in California July 4, 1875. Another society of the same name was organized in New York in 1889 and quickly outrivalled the older society; attempts to unite the two were made unsuccessfully in 1892 and 1897. The Eastern Society has thirty-eight branches in the states and branches in the District of Columbia and Hawaii. The total membership is about 11,000.

Sons of Confederate Veterans. (See Confederate Veterans, United Sons of.)

Sons of Liberty.—A society organized by the younger and more ardent patriots of Connecticut in 1755, to advance colonial liberty. They advocated non-importation, aided in the hanging in effigy of the stamp distributor Oliver in 1765, and in 1774 proposed the organization of a continental congress. The appellation is sometimes applied to the whole body of American patriots. Another organization calling themselves "Sons of Liberty" existed in 1862-1864 in Indiana and other states and actively opposed the efforts of the United States Government in the prosecution of the war for the preservation of the Union, and several leaders were tried and condemned by a military commission. (See also Milligan Case.)

Sons of the Revolution.—A society of the same nature as the Sons of the American Revolution. It was established in New York in 1875, and has now thirty-one state branches. The principal point of difference between the Sons of the Revolution and the Sons of the American Revolution is the matter of eligibility, which in both is

dependent on hereditary descent. In the latter society membership is contingent upon lineal descent from patriots of the Revolution, while in the former it is extended to collaterals.

Sons of Veterans, U. S. A.—Camp No. 1, Sons of Veterans, U. S. A., was organized in the City of Philadelphia, Sept. 29, 1879. The organization is composed of lineal descendants, over eighteen years of age, of honorably discharged soldiers, or marines who served in the late Civil War. There are now about one thousand camps, with a membership of fifty thousand, distributed among twenty-five divisions, corresponding to states, the general society or national body constituting the Commandery-in-Chief. Each camp has its own officers, the head officer being the commander. The principal officer of the division is the division commander. The Sons of Veterans Auxiliary is an association of women auxiliary to the above organization.

Sound Dues. (See Baltic Sea.)

Sound Money Democrats.—A group defecting from the Democratic Party in 1896. In convention they nominated John M. Palmer for President, and General Simon B. Buckner for Vice President; and their platform declared for the gold standard.

Soup-Houses.—Literally meaning houses where free soup is served to hungry and suffering people,—distinguished from breadlines (q. v.) in that soup-houses are resorted to only on occasions of temporary distress due to panic or unemployment, and are utilized by self-respecting, industrious people who would willingly work, but who can find no opportunity; whereas the bread-line is ever present, and usually administers only to the habitually-unemployed element.

South America.—The area is 6,750,000 square miles, a little more than one and three-quarter times that of Europe. The extreme longitudes are Cape Branco 35° W. and Punta Parina 81° W., and the extreme latitudes, Punta Gallinas, 12½° N. and Cape Horn 56° S. South America is surrounded by the ocean, except where it is joined to Central America by the narrow isthmus of Panama.

The independent republics of South America are Argentina, Bolivia, Brazil, Chile, Colombia, Ecuador, Brazil, Peru, Uruguay and Venezuela. Besides these are British, French and Netherlands' Guiana.

Islands adjacent to South America are the Falkland Islands, Galapagos Islands, Graham Land, Sandwich Group, South Georgia, South Orkneys and South Shetlands.

In the south Tierra del Fuego is separated from the mainland by the Straits of Magellan. The physical features consist of a Western Mountain belt and two Upland Plateaus.

The Upper Plateaus consist of the highlands of Brazil and Guiana, between which are the lowlands of the Amazon.

The extensive lowlands of the Orinoco, Amazon, and Paraná-Paraguay system were once inland seas, and afford great areas of level land. Ocean vessels can reach Iquitos on the Amazon, which is 2,300 miles from the ocean in consequence of the small fall of the river.

On the West Coast the rivers are generally too rapid to be navigable, in consequence of the proximity of the mountains to the sea, but they are invaluable in the dry regions for irrigation.

The Amazon has numerous tributaries, which are themselves great rivers, and occupies with its basin a large part of South America. Owing to the melting of the snows in February and the rains which mainly occur at this season on the Andean slopes, it has a marked flood season, reaching its maximum in June, when it overflows its banks.

The Plate Estuary is formed by the junction of the Paraná and Uruguay. A larger amount of water is brought down than by any other river system in the New World excepting the Amazon. The Paraná is navigable for some 1,200 miles by ocean vessels.

Quito, in Ecuador, at over 9,000 feet, and Bogota, in the uplands of Colombia, at a little below 9,000 feet, have temperatures between 55° F. and 58° F. in both summer and winter, while Para, at the mouth of the Amazon, and Iquitos, on the Upper Amazon, are between 78° F. an 79° F. throughout the year. The diminution of temperature with altitude is shown most noticeably on the high Andean plateau, where La Paz, at over 12,000 feet, has a summer temperature of only 52° F., and near the margin of the Tropics, where Sao Paulo, in the coffee-growing uplands of southeast Brazil at about 2,500 feet, is about 9° colder than Rio at sea level. The local influence of the cold current is shown in the difference of temperature between points in the same latitude on the East and West coasts—Bahia, in latitude 12° S. is 10° warmer than Callao.

Outside the Tropics the eastern side of South America has a high summer temperature, above 68° F. to south of 40° S. latitude, as a consequence of which wheat can be grown successfully to the south of Buenos Aires.

cure an appropriation from Congress for sending an accredited minister to Buenos Ayres, which had become a free and independent Republic. Congress, however, refused. March 8, 1822, President Monroe in a special message to Congress (685) recommended the recognition of Buenos Ayres, Chile, Colombia, and other republics, and the establishment of international relations with them. This Congress agreed to. The commercial relations between the United States and these republics have steadily improved since this action. A conference, known as the International American Conference (q. v.), representing the United Sates and these republics, met in Washington in 1889 to encourage closer business relations. This resulted in the establishment of the Bureau of American Republics (q. v.). The latest example of the recognition of a new republic by this country occurred in the year 1903, when the Republic of Panama proclaimed its independence of Colombia on Nov. 4 and received the recognition of the American government two days later.

South and Central American Countries, Treaties with.—At the Fourth International American Conference, held in Buenos Aires in August, 1910, representatives of Argentina, Brazil, Chile, Colombia, Costa Rica, Cuba, Santo Domingo, Ecuador, Guatemala, Haiti, Honduras, Mexico, Nicaragua, Panama, Paraguay, Peru, Salvador, Uruguay and Venezuela agreed upon several important points of international comity, among which was a convention for the submission of pecuniary claims to arbitration whenever such claims are of sufficient importance to warrant the expense of arbitration. They also agreed that decisions of such claims should be rendered in accordance with the principles of international law, and all controversies submitted to The Hague Court of Arbitration. This treaty was signed at Buenos Aires August 11, 1910, ratification advised by the Senate Feb. 1, 1911, ratified by the President of the United States March 21, 1911, and proclaimed by Wilson July 29, 1914.

Another convention between the same republics adopted at the same conference provided for the protection of inventions, patents, designs and industrial models. For the text of these treaties see President Wilson's proclamations, pages 8362 and 8364.

South Carolina.—One of the thirteen original states; nickname, "The Palmetto State;" motto, "Animis opibusque parati" ("Prepared in mind and resources"). It lies between lat. 32° 4′ 30″ and 35° 13′ 2″ north and long. 78° 28′ and 83° 18′ west. It is bounded on the north and northeast by North Carolina, on the southeast by the Atlantic Ocean, and on the southwest and west by Georgia (separated for most part of the distance by the Savannah River). It has an area of 30,989 square miles. The surface is level near the coast, undulating in the interior, and mountainous in the northwest. The state produces gold, porcelain, clay, phosphates, and other minerals, and is especially noted for the production of rice and sea-island cotton.

South Carolina was partially explored by the Spaniards in 1525, who named it Chicora. An unsuccessful attempt to colonize was made by the French under Ribault in 1562. The first permanent settlement was made by the English in 1670. Charleston was founded in 1680. Charles II. gave the territory between lat. 29° and 36° 30′ north, to eight of his favorites in 1663, and two years later he issued a charter placing the control of the colony in their

hands. They employed John Locke, the philosopher, to draw up a constitution which should provide an ideal government. This "grand model" proved to be an attempt to set up the feudal system in America, and was abandoned by the proprietors in 1693. South Carolina became a royal colony in 1729.

The first constitution was adopted in 1776. The Federal Constitution was ratified May 23, 1788. The state seceded on Dec. 20, 1860, and was readmitted by act of Congress June 25, 1868.

Statistics of agriculture collected for the last Federal census, place the number of farms in the state at 176,434, comprising 13,512,028 acres, valued, with stock and improvements, at $392,128,314. The average value of land per acre was $19.89, against $7.14 in 1900. The value of domestic animals, poultry, etc., was $45,131,380, including 389,882 cattle, valued at $7,888,259; 79,847 horses, $10,147,178; 155,471 mules, $23,830,361; 665,211 swine, $2,552,344; 37,559 sheep, $81,362, and poultry, $1,206,615. The yield and value of field crops in 1911 was: Corn 1,790,000 acres, 32,578,000 bushels, $29,646,000; wheat, 83,000 acres, 946,000 bushels, $1,164,000; oats, 345,000 acres 7,038,000 bushels, $5,067,000; rye, 3,000 acres, 30,000 bushels, $44,000; rice, 10,000 acres, 117,000 bushels, $88,000; potatoes, 10,000 acres, 700,000 bushels, $854,000; hay, 64,000 acres, 69,000 tons, $1,173,000; tobacco, 13,600 acres, 11,016,000 pounds, $1,388,016, and cotton, 1,480,000 bales. The report of the State Treasurer for the fiscal year 1911 showed a balance Dec. 31, 1910, of $648,730; receipts for year, $3,208,790; expenditures, $3,132,164; cash balance Dec. 31, 1911, $725,356; public debt, $6,528,485.

The number of manufacturing establishments in South Carolina having an annual output valued at $500 or more at the beginning of 1915 was 1,885. The amount of capital invested was $203,211,000, giving employment to 77,693 persons, using material valued at $91,009,000, and turning out finished goods worth $138,891,000. Salaries and wages paid amounted to $29,052,000.

The turpentine and rosin industries, for which the state was formerly noted, are dying out, because of the exhaustion of the pine forests. The imports at the harbor of Charleston for 1907 were $3,528,553, and the exports $1,082,466. The population, according to the census of 1910, was 1,515,400.

South Carolina (see also Confederate States):

Amendment to Federal Constitution, referred to, 598.

Census of—
　Referred to, 108.
　Return of, delay in, 104.

Claims of, for advances made during War of 1812, 1027.

Commissioners from, to President Buchanan, 3189.

Correspondence on, referred to, 3195.

Constitution of, referred to, 3830.

Delay in return of census of, 104.

Forts and fortifications ceded to United States by, 384.

Fourteenth amendment to Constitution, ratified by, 3837.

Proclaimed, 3855.

South Carolina Inter-State and West Indian Exposition.—An industrial and educational fair, held at Charleston, S. C., from Dec. 1 to June 2, 1902. The site covered an area of 250 acres and the buildings were in the Spanish Renaissance style of architecture, covered with staff, tinted an ivory white. The United States and many of the individual states made exhibits, as well as Cuba, Porto Rico, and Guatemala. Notable original groups of historical statuary exhibited were "The Aztec," "The Negro," and "The Huguenot." The total attendance was 674,806. The cost of the exhibition was $1,250,000, and the receipts $313,000.

South Dakota.—One of the western group of states. Nickname, "Coyote State." Motto, "Under God the people rule." It lies a little north of the center of the continent, between lat. 45° 57′ and 42° 28′ north (extreme southeast point: west of the Missouri the southern boundary is 43° north) and long. 96° 26′ and 104° 3′ west. It is bounded on the north by North Dakota, on the east by Minnesota and Iowa, on the south by Nebraska, and on the west by Montana and Wyoming. It has an area of 77,615 square miles. The Missouri River divides the state into two nearly equal portions. The eastern part is generally smooth and rolling. West of the river the country rises more rapidly and culminates in the Black Hills, an elevated region some 60 by 100 miles in extent, the central point of which is Harney's Peak, 9,700 feet high. The Bad Lands, in the southeastern part, is an interesting geological formation, consisting of a desert region abounding in canyons, depressions, walls, and castles of white earth, rich in soil-making chemicals and interesting fossils.

The early history of the State is identical with that of North Dakota (q. v.), from which it was separated and admitted as a state in 1889. The total land area is 49,-184,000 acres, of which 12,908,977 acres are reserved for the Indians. With the exception of the forests of the Black Hills the State is almost an arid plain. In 1902 about 12,107,114 acres were vacant land. In 1908 there remained unreserved and unappropriated 6,561,295 acres. About 40,-000 acres are irrigated and the Federal plan of irrigation will reclaim 100,000 acres in the Belle Fourche Valley. United States Land offices are located at Aberdeen, Chamberlain, Lemmon, Mitchell, Pierre and Rapid City.

The value of domestic animals, poultry, etc., in 1910 was $128,202,000, including 612,000 horses, valued at $64,260,000; 10,-000 mules, $1,210,000; 656,000 milch cows, $21,648,000; 1,131,000 other cattle, $28,-832,000; 829,000 sheep, $3,316,000; 805,-000 swine, $8,936,000. The yield and value of field crops in 1911 was: Corn, 2,310,000 acres, 50,820,000 bushels, $26,935,000; wheat, 3,700,000 accres, 14,800,000 bushels, $13,468,000; oats, 1,540,000 acres, 11,396,-000 bushels, $4,900,000; rye, 13,000 acres, 130,000 bushels, $99,000; potatoes, 56,000 acres, 4,032,000 bushels, $2,822,000; hay, 459,000 acres, 252,000 tons, $2,142,000. The gold output in 1911 was 359,444 fine ounces, worth $7,430,367, most of which was produced at the Homestake mine, at Lead, in the Black Hills. The silver produced the same year was 206,188 fine ounces, valued at $113,403. Natural gas, lead, stone and clay products are also found. The manufactures of the State are confined mainly to flour, lumber and dairy products. The report of the State Treasurer for the fiscal year ended June 30, 1911, showed receipts for the year, $3,760,213; expenditures, $4,001,626; cash balance, $421,156. The population in 1910 was 583,888.

South Mountain, or Boonsboro (Md.), Battle of.—After driving the Union army back upon the fortifications around Washington, Lee's army crossed the Potomac into Maryland. The Confederate commander issued an address to the people offering them the protection of his government and calling for volunteer soldiers. He sent the greater part of his army, about 25,000 men, under Jackson, to capture the garrison at Harpers Ferry. As soon as it became known at Washington that Lee had crossed into Maryland, McClellan was ordered to follow him with all the troops not needed to defend Washington. Sept. 12, 1862, McClellan reached Frederick with a force estimated at from 80,000 to 90,000 just after it had been evacuated by Lee's army, which had passed west over the Catoctin Mountains toward South Mountain. The road from Frederick to Hagerstown, Md., passes through Turners Gap of this mountain. Here on Sept 14, 1862, Gen. D. H. Hill, with a force of about 6,000 men, successfully resisted repeated assaults from Hooker's and Burnside's corps, fully 30,000 strong. At 3 P. M. Hill was re-enforced with 1,900 men, and later in the day by Longstreet with six brigades, only four of which, numbering 3,000 men, were seriously engaged. The gap was contested from 8 A. M. until after dark. During the night the Confederates retired. Franklin took possession of Crampton's Gap, six miles below, held by the Confederates under Howell Cobb. The Federal loss at Turners Gap, South Mountain, was 328 killed and 1,463 wounded and missing, and at Crampton's Gap 115 killed and 418 missing. The Confederate loss at both aggregated 934.

South Polar Regions.—The A n t a r c t i c Ocean includes much more of the circumpolar ocean than the part south of the Antarctic Circle (66½° S.), as drifting pack ice is carried a long way to the north. Icebergs are often met with north of 45° S. It is now considered that the land which has been sighted at various points forms part of the Antarctic continent, probably loftier than Greenland and larger than Australia. This plateau is covered with a sheet of *névé* and ice which seems to be slowly creeping toward the sea. The icebergs differ completely from those of the Arctic, forming large flat-topped islands with perpendicular sides.

In the interior the plateau rises to over 10,000 feet and is remarkably level. On this some of the peaks exceed 15,000 feet. In Victoria Land there have been great volcanic eruptions in geologically recent epochs. To these are due the conical peaks of Erebus (12,760 feet), which is still active, Terror, Melbourne, and Discovery, and numerous isolated craters.

There are no land animals, but microscopic life has been found in ponds which can endure great extremes of cold and heat.

Exploration.—A southern continent was believed to exist in the sixteenth and seventeenth centuries, but it was not till 1774 that Cook crossed the Antarctic Circle and reached in his voyages 71° 10' S.-106° 54' W. in 1774. This was the furthest point south attained in the eighteenth century. Bellingshausen, in a Russian expedition supplementing Cook's voyages, reached 69° 25' S. and 1° 11' W. in 1819, and in 1821 sighted the first land ever seen within the Antarctic Circle, to which he gave the name of Peter I. Island. In 1823 James Weddell reached 74° 15' S. and 34° 17' W. In 1831-1832 Biscoe discovered Graham Land. In 1835 an attempt was made to reach the Magnetic Pole by a French expedition that met with no success, though land was sighted inside the Antarctic Circle.

In 1839 the *Erebus* and *Terror*, the former commanded by Ross, entered pack ice in 174° E., and succeeded in getting through the ice into open sea to the south. He discovered a chain of mountains south of Cape Adare in 71° S., and the land was taken possession of as Victoria Land. The names of the two ships were given to the volcanoes. In 1842 an attempt was made to pass the Great Ice Barrier on the east, and the land was discovered now known as King Edward's Land.

There was no more exploration till 1874, when the first steamer, the *Challenger*, reached 66° 40' S. and 78° 30' E. In 1894 Borchgrevink, a sailor on board a Norwegian whaler, was one of a party that landed near Cape Adare, the first to set foot on the Antarctic continent. In 1895 interest in Antarctic exploration was aroused by the efforts of Sir Clement Markham, President of the Royal British Geographical Society, and the International Geographic Congress, and the modern era of South Polar discovery was inaugurated.

In 1899 Borchgrevink, in the *Southern Cross*, an expedition equipped by Sir George Newnes, took dogs and sledges to attempt to reach the Magnetic Pole, and landed near Cape Adare. It was found that the ice barrier had receded about 30 miles south since it had been mapped by Ross in 1841.

In 1901-1904 a national Antarctic expedition was organized under Scott. In 1902 Scott, Shackleton, and Wilson reached 82° 17' S. with dog sledges. An elevation of 9,000 feet was attained on the plateau. Nordenskjöld, in the *Antarctic*, and Bruce, in the *Scotia*, added to the knowledge of the South Polar regions. In 1904 Charcot, in the *Français*, and in 1909 in the *Pourquoi Pas*, explored the Bellingshausen Sea. In 1909 Shackleton, in the *Nimrod*, attempted to land a shore party to winter on King Edward's Land but wintered near the base of Mount Erebus, about 20 miles to the north of the *Discovery's* winter quarters. An ascent of Mount Erebus was made. David reached the South Magnetic Pole, and Shackleton with his companions reached the upper plateau at about 10,000 feet, where they were obliged to return in 88° 23' S., 113 miles from the Pole. In 1910 Scott left in the *Terra Nova* for an extended period or scientific exploration. It was expected that he would be the first to reach the Pole, but Captain Amundsen attained the most southerly point on Dec. 16, 1911, after a remarkably rapid journey. He used dogs and skis and relied on depots of seal meat. The mountain range of Victoria Land was reached in about 85° S. and a path to the plateau found by the Devil's Glazier, between elevations of 12,000 to 15,000 feet. The plateau was 10,750 feet at its highest point, and sloped slightly downward to the Pole at 10,500 feet.

Captain Robert Falcon Scott, R. N., was born June 6, 1868, and reached the South Pole on Jan. 18, 1912, with four companions. On the return journey he perished with his party on (or about) March 29, 1912, the bodies being discovered by the relief expedition on Jan. 18, 1913.

Southern States (see also Confederate States; Reconstruction; Secession; Slavery; Civil War):

Acts—

For admission of certain, vetoed, 3846, 3848.

To provide for more efficient government of, vetoed. (See Reconstruction.)

Blockade of ports of. (See Civil War.)

Commercial intercourse with. (See Confederate States.)

Condition of, discussed, 4107.

Courts for, referred to, 3576.

Direct tax to be collected from, referred to, 3589.

Elections in, complications growing out of, and other disturbances discussed, 4071, 4072, 4104, 4117, 4161, 4166, 4218, 4219, 4250, 4259, 4273, 4367, 4372.

Federal interference in, discussed, 4259.

Habeas corpus, writ of, suspended in certain sections, 4090, 4093.

Revoked as to Marion County, S. C., 4092.

Proclamations regarding, 4086, 4088, 4089, 4090, 4092, 4093, 4177, 4226, 4230, 4276, 4350.

Troops stationed at polling places in, referred to, 4367, 4372.

Governments to be reestablished in, proclamations regarding, 3414, 3423.

Act to guarantee to certain States republican form of government, 3424.

Discussed, 3390.

Joint resolution excluding electoral votes of States lately in rebellion vetoed, 3849.

Kidnapping of negroes in, for purpose of selling as slaves in Cuba, 3578.

Modification of oath of office pertaining to efficient administration of revenue and postal laws in, recommended, 3580.

Reconstruction of. (See Reconstruction.)

Report on conditions in, by—

Grant, Ulysses S., 3571.

Schurz, Carl, 3571.

Sherman, William T., 3576.

Truman, Benjamin C., 3584.

Restoration of, into Union. (See Restoration.)

Revenue and postal laws in, referred to, 3580.

Union and Confederate flags, return of, to respective States recommended, 5163.

Proposition withdrawn, 5164.

Unlawful combinations in. (See Elections in, *ante*.)

Southwest Territory.—A region comprising portions of the present States of Tennessee, Kentucky, and Mississippi, together with a strip of land ceded to the General Government by South Carolina. Though never organized under one territorial government, it was known as the Southwest Territory. An unsuccessful attempt was made to organize a portion of this territory into a new state to be called Franklin (q. v.). With the admission of Tennessee and Kentucky and the organization of a Territorial government in Mississippi this territory went out of existence.

Spain.—The Kingdom of Spain occupies the greater portion of the Iberian Peninsula of southwestern Europe, and consists of Continental Spain, occupying eleven-thirteenths of the peninsula (the remainder being occupied by the Republic of Portugal and the British rocky fortress of Gibraltar), the Balearic Islands, the fortified station of Ceuta, and the Canary Islands. The Balearic and Canary Islands and Ceuta form an integral part of the kingdom, which also possesses certain colonies and dependencies. Continental Spain lies between 36°-43° 45' N. latitude and 4° 25' E.-9° 20' W. longitude, and has a total area of 191,893 square miles. The Balearic Islands are an archipelago of four large and eleven small islands in the Mediterranean. Of the four larger islands, Majorca has an area of 430 square miles; Minorca (260 square miles) possesses the magnificent harbor of Port Mahon and a former capital in Ciudadela; Iviza has La Ciudad as capital; and Formentera has an area of 37 square miles. The eleven small islands have an area of 985 square miles—a total for the Archipelago of 1,935 square miles. Ceuta is a fortified post on the Moroccan coast, opposite Gibraltar (the Straits of Gibraltar being 14 miles wide between the two fortresses), and consists of a promontory connected with the mainland by a narrow isthmus. At the seaward end of the promontory is the Monte del Haeko, formerly called Abyla, and one of the "Pillars of Hercules." Ceuta has an area of 5 square miles, with a population of about 13,000. The Canary Islands are an Archipelago in the Atlantic Ocean, about 60 miles from the coast of West Africa. The total area is 2,807 square miles and the population (1910) 419,809. The Archipelago consists of seven islands and six uninhabited islets. Of the seven inhabited islands, Teneriffe has an area of 782 square miles and a population of close on 150,000, its capital, Santa Cruz, having 53,403 inhabitants in 1910, and forming the administrative center of the group. Fuerteventura, Grand Canary, Lanzarote, Palma, Gomera, Hierro are the others.

Physical Features.—Central Spain consists of an extensive tableland, between the Cantabrian Mountains and the Pyrenees in the north and the Sierra Nevada in the south, with the Castilian Divinding Range running almost east and west in the middle of the plateau. Between the plateau and the Pyrenees is the northeastern lowland of the Ebro Valley, and in the southwest is the valley of the Guadalquivir. The principal rivers are the Tagus, Douro, Ebro, Guadiana, and Guadalquivir.

The early inhabitants were Celts and Iberians, with Phoenician colonists.

The climate of the tableland has great extremes, but that of the eastern (Mediterranean) provinces is more equable, while the southern provinces are sub-tropical, with great summer heat and mild winters, vegetation being at its best in midwinter. The north and northwest have a mild and equable climate with abundant rainfall.

History.—Roman Spain was invaded in the fifth century by the Vandals, Visigoths, and Suebi, and early in the eighth century the country was conquered by Moslems from northern Africa, who remained the dominant power for nearly 700 years, but before their expulsion from Spain, at the instigation of the Inquisition in 1502, they had sunk from the position of conquerors to semi-servile trading communities. The greatness of the country began with the reign of Ferdinand and Isabella (1474-1516), under whom the Kingdom was consolidated and its dominions extended by adventurous conquerors, who carried the religion and flag of Spain over a territory many times greater than their native land. Toward the close of the sixteenth century the Netherlands passed to the Spanish crown by inheritance, and the zenith of Spain's grandeur may be said to have been reached. The religious wars in the Low Countries and in France and a war with England, marked by the disastrous expedition of the Great Armada (1588), were the beginnings of the decadence of Spain, which suffered from a century of weak kings, whose line ended in 1700 at the death of Charles II. The succession led to a great European war, which terminated in the Treaty of Utrecht, signed by England and France on April 11 (and by England and Spain on July 13), 1713, by which Gibraltar was ceded to England. At the beginning of the nineteenth century the country was an easy prey to the armies of Napoleon, who placed his brother upon the throne. Napoleon's generals occupied Spain and Portugal in 1812, but within two years the invaders were driven out by the genius of Wellington, and Ferdinand VII. was restored in 1814. The nineteenth century witnessed many upheavals, including the revolution of 1820, the revolt of the South American Colonies, 1821-1823, the Carlist Wars of 1840, 1860, and 1873-1876 (by which the adherents of Don Carlos, brother of Ferdinand VII., endeavored to obtain the throne for their leader and his successors), a revolution of 1868 and the institution of a Republic 1868-1874, the Bourbon restoration of 1874, the Cuban insurrections of 1869 and 1898, and the Spanish-American War of April-December, 1898, terminating in the Treaty of Paris (December 12, 1898), by which Spain renounced the sovereignty of Cuba and ceded Porto Rico, the Philippine Islands and other territory to the United States.

Government.—The government is that of a constitutional monarchy; hereditary in the male (and eventually in the female) line of the house of Bourbon-Anjou, the constitution resting on the fundamental law of June 30, 1876. Ruler: Alfonso XIII, King of Spain, of Castile, Leon, Aragon, the two Sicilies, Jerusalem, Navarre, Grenada, Toledo, Valencia, Galicia, Majorca and Minorca, Seville, Cerdeña, Cordova, Corcega, Murcia, Jaen, Algarva, Algeciras, Canary Islands, etc.; born (posthumously) May 17, 1886; assumed the government May 17, 1902; married May 31, 1906.

The legislative body, or Cortes, is composed of the Senate and the Chamber of Deputies. The Senate contains 360 members, of whom one-half are hereditary official or life members and one-half elective, in three classes: (1) Grandees of Spain, with incomes exceeding 60,000 pesetas, and high officials of the Church, Army, Navy, and judiciary; (2) Life members nominated by the Sovereign; (3) Members elected by the 49 provinces (3 each) and by the academies, universities, dioceses, and State corporations, and renewable as to one-half every five years. The Chamber of Deputies consists of 404 members (1 for every 50,000 of the population) elected by universal suffrage of all male Spaniards aged twenty-five.

The Kingdom is divided into 495 *partidos judiciales*, each containing a court of first instance, from which appeals are heard by 15 *audiencias territoriales*. Criminal causes are determined by quarterly assizes in each of the 49 provinces. There is a Supreme Court of Cassation (with civil and criminal departments) at the capital.

Education.—Primary Education is nominally compulsory and is mainly free. There are universities at Barcelona, Granada, Madrid, Salamanca, Santiago, Saragossa, Seville, Valencia, and Valladolid.

Population.—The census of the forty-nine provinces taken in 1910 gave the population as 19,588,688, in an area of 194,700 square miles. The density of population (100.6 per square mile) bears no true relation to the resources of the Kingdom, which could easily support more than five times the present number of inhabitants. Included in the generic term "Spaniards" are about 500,000 Basques in the northern provinces, Catalans in the northeast and Galicians in the northwest.

Production and Industry.—The total area is estimated at 124,616,000 English statute acres, of which (in 1906) 53,606,114 acres were cultivated.

In 1911 there were 3,245,000 acres of vineyards, which produced 3,019,000 tons of grapes, and 3,587,790 acres of olive trees, which produced 1,729,894 tons of olives. In 1912 there were 525,853 horses, 928,920 mules, 829,410 asses, 2,561,894 cattle, 15,829,954 sheep, 3,116,226 goats, and 2,571,359 pigs. The year 1911 was one of the worst possible from the point of view of breeding. The coast fisheries include sardines, tunny, anchovies, salmon and cod, and employ over 70,000 fishermen, the value of the annual catch being about 50 to 60 million pesetas; the sardine-curing establishments employ a further 16,000 persons.

The mineral resources of the country are only partially exploited, and principally by foreign capital under foreign direction. In the production of copper ore, lead ore, mercury and silver, however, Spain is surpassed by no other European country, and its annual output of salt is exceeded only by that of Austria-Hungary. Coal is very plentiful, but the production is comparatively small, and among the other minerals are manganese, antimony, gold, cobalt, sodic sulphate, barytes, phosphorite, alum, sulphur, china clay, lignite, asphalt and various building stones. Over 150,000 persons are employed in mineral production, and the annual output exceeds 200,000,000 pesetas in value.

Cotton and linen manufactures are the most important industries, and increased efforts are being exerted to supply the home demand since the loss of the former colonial outlets, but the imports are still considerable. Tobacco (a Government monopoly), leather, paper, soap, chocolate, cork, distilling and fruit preserving are also considerable industries.

Finance.—The budget for 1913 provided for an expenditure of 1,146,901,171 pesetas from a revenue of 1,167,436,472 pesetas, leaving a surplus of 20,535,300 pesetas. The national debt was stated Jan. 1, 1913, as 9,407,141,705 pesetas, at 4 and 5 per cent. The unit of value, the peseta, is equivalent to $0.19.3, United States money, the same as the French franc.

Railways.—In 1912 there were 9,161 miles of railway open, all lines being owned by companies with a State guarantee.

Cities.—Capital, Madrid, on the river Manzanares. Population 571,539. At the census of 1910 there were 7 towns with populations exceeding 100,000, 15 others exceeding 50,000 and 13 more above 25,000.

Trade with the United States.—The value of merchandise imported into Spain from the United States for the year of 1913 was $31,471,723, and goods to the value of $23,220,012 were sent thither—a balance of $8,251,711 in favor of the United States.

RIO MUNI (or Spanish Guinea) is a coastal settlement of West Africa between German Cameroon and French Congo, extending about 125 miles inland. The inhabitants are Bantu tribes. Cocoa, coffee, and bananas are cultivated, and rubber, palm-oil, palm-kernels, and other forest produce are exported.

RIO DE ORO is a possession on the northwest coast of Africa, between Cape Bogador and Cape Blanco. The territory is part of the waterless Sahara, with a sparse population of wandering Muhammadan Arabs. There are valuable fisheries off the coast, and cattle, sheep, and camels are bred where vegetation permits.

SPANISH COLONIES (exclusive of Ceuta and the Canary Islands, which form an integral part of Spain) consist of certain settlements and islands of western Africa, with a total area of close on 82,400 English square miles, and a population exceeding 275,000.

FERNANDO PO lies in the Bight of Biafra in 3° 12′ N. latitude and 8° 48′ E. longitude, about 20 miles distant from the west coast of Africa, and is a mountainous island (Pico de Santa Isabel, 10,800 feet), with forests of oil palm, ebony, mahogany, and oak, and sugar cane, cotton, and indigo. Cocoa, coffee, sugar, tobacco, vanilla, and kola nut are cultivated, and large quantities of cocoa and other products are exported. The capital is Basile, and the largest town Port Clarence (1,500 inhabitants). Dependencies of the island of Fernando Po are :—

Annopon Island, in the Gulf of Guinea, in 1° 24′ S. latitude and 50° 35′ E. longitude. The roadstead at the capital (San Antonio de Baia) is much frequented by passing vessels, which also obtain water and vegetables from the islanders.

Corisco Islands, consisting of Corisco, Bana, Elobey Grande and Elobey Chico, lie in Corisco Bay, and export ebony, logwood, and other forest produce.

MOROCCO AND THE SAHARA.—By a treaty signed on Nov. 27, 1912, between France and Spain, the latter acquired a zone or sphere of influence in North Morocco, the capital being Tetuan, where the Sultan's authority is represented by a Khalifa. The limits of the Rio de Oro and Rio Muni were also defined in the treaty with France (see "Morocco").

Melilla is a town on a rocky promontory of the Riff coast, connected with the mainland by a narrow isthmus. The population is about 9,000, and the settlement (which was conquered from the Moors in 1490) exports goatskins, eggs, and beeswax, and imports cotton goods and provisions.

Spain (see also Barcelona; Madrid):

American citizens—
Conspiracies of, against, 146, 394.
Proclamation against, 392, 546.
Property of, destroyed by, 372, 376, 682.
Rescued by vessel of, 1123.
Rights of, violated by authorities of, 2770.

Authority of, in the Floridas almost extinct, 600, 609.
Authority to grant or dispose of lands of, in Louisiana referred to, 651.
Black Hawk seized by and interfered with by Spain. (See *Black Hawk,* Encyclopedic Article on.)
Blockade—
Establishment by, claims of United States growing out of, 1112.
Of Spanish Main referred to, 776.
Boundary line with, and questions regarding, 186, 192, 236, 245, 263, 388, 962, 1038.
Improper advances made by Spain, 388.
Caroline Islands—
Dispute with Germany regarding, 4916.
Questions touching rights of American citizens in, 5622, 5751, 5872.
Civil war in, 1592.
Claims of, against United States (see also *Amistad,* The; East Florida Claims; *Nuestra Senora,* The)—
Discussed, 2461, 2688, 2742, 2977, 3042, 3092.
Payment of, recommended, 2401, 2688, 2742, 2977, 3042, 3092.
Claims of, to lands in Arizona and New Mexico under grants, 5484, 5510, 5561.
Claims of United States against, and relations with, discussed (see also *Black Warrior,* The; *El Dorado,* The; *Virginius,* The)—
Adjusted by arbitration, 4919.
Apportionment of funds received, recommended, 1368.
Awards of commissioners referred to, 4960, 5192.
Commissioners appointed to settle, 674.
Convention regarding, 339, 354, 372, 1269, 1271, 1316, 3124, 3172.
Interest due under, not paid, 1931.
"Cuban Claims" discussed, 3040, 3091, 3172.
Discussed by President—
Adams, John, 242, 264.
Adams, J. Q., 990.
Arthur, 4758.
Buchanan, 2976, 3040, 3091, 3172.
Cleveland, 4919, 5871, 5910, 5962, 5989, 5998, 6069.
Fillmore, 2721.
Grant, 4051, 4099, 4195, 4210.
Harrison, Benj., 5470, 5518, 5677.
Hayes, 4448.
Jackson, 1007, 1069, 1109, 1112, 1156, 1241, 1316, 1364, 1368.

Jefferson, 339, 354, 372, 376.

Madison, 560.

Monroe, 582, 608, 610, 641, 682.

Pierce, 2767.

Van Buren, 1592.

Joint commission referred to, 4535, 4626.

Appropriation for umpires of, recommended, 4801.

Awards of, referred to, 5192.

Payment of, 867, 1316, 2869, 4052, 4290, 4797, 6069.

In coin demanded by claimants, 3777, 4003.

Referred to, 329.

Refused, 372, 376, 582, 2779.

Resulting from Cuban insurrection discussed, 4051, 4099, 4448, 5874, 6180.

Treaty regarding, referred to, 1364.

Combination of sovereigns to assist in subjugating American provinces discussed, 790.

Commercial relations of United States with Cuba and Puerto Rico. (See Cuba; Puerto Rico.)

Commercial relations with, 110, 112, 113, 139, 161, 5089, 5663.

Treaty regarding, discussed, 4919.

Commissioner to, referred to, 3890.

Commissioners arrange treaty of peace with. (See Enc. Art. on Spanish-American War.)

Conspiracy of citizens of United States against, 146, 394.

Proclamation against, 392, 546.

Consul of, in United States exequatur issued, revoked, 2588.

Consul of United States at Cadiz, refusal of to certify invoices of wine, 3667, 4214.

Conventions with. (See Treaty with, *post.*)

Copyright privilege extended, by proclamation, 6024.

Cuban insurrection, discussed. (See Cuba.)

Decree of, regarding introduction of Chinese laborers into Cuba, 4116.

Delivery to, of person charged with crime against, referred to, 3412.

Differences and negotiations with, discussed, 89, 139, 141, 143, 144, 145, 168, 174, 178, 241, 245, 251, 393, 415, 469, 598, 2811, 2840.

Expeditions against territory of, discussed, 146, 394, 582, 590, 592, 601, 609.

Proclamations against, 392, 546.

Florida, cession of, to United States by. (See Florida.)

Force ordered to protect citizens of United States from troops of, 394.

Fugitive criminals, convention with, for surrender of, 4376, 4699, 4738.

Referred to, 4757.

Gunboats constructed by, in and near New York to operate against Peru, discussed, 3987.

Hostile disposition of, toward United States, 376, 393, 611.

Imprisonment of American citizens by, 594, 2643, 4116, 5905. (See also Cuba.)

Pardon of, discussed, 2689, 2692.

Released, 6284.

Indemnity paid by, on account of execution of Gen. Ryan and others, referred to, 4408.

Indians—

Aid furnished by, 611.

Relations with United States regarding, 139.

Interference by, with the commerce of the United States, 329.

Internal contests in, 1368, 1592, 2112, 2811.

Hope expressed that prosperity will return with peace, 1749.

Lands purchased from, by United States, 956, 1029.

Letters regarding treaty of United States with, transmitted, 794.

Louisiana, transfer of, to United States disagreeable to, 376.

Maj.-Gen. Jackson's entrance into Florida not an encroachment upon rights of, 611.

Maritime jurisdiction of, in waters surrounding Cuba, referred to, 3380.

Minister of, to United States—

Withdrawal of, 6296, 6312.

Minister of United States to, 107, 148, 164, 339, 6257, 6284, 6286.

Correspondence with, referred to, 3964.

New minister to be sent to, 2976, 3040.

Recall of, 148.

Requested, 2976, 3040.

Referred to, 2176, 2210.

Withdrawal of, 6312.

Navigation treaty with, 106, 110, 164.

Neutral vessels deemed lawful prize by, 432.

Obstruction of commerce on Mobile River, by, 372, 376.

Orders to the forces to protect citizens of the United States from troops of, 394.

Pacific policy of, toward former colonies, 1009.

Peace conference between South American Republics and, held in Washington, 4052, 4099.

People of, efforts to improve condition of, 762, 786.

Persons claiming American citizenship captured on the *Competitor* by, 6180, 6183.

Vessels being built in New York for Spain forbidden to depart, 3987.

Spanish Provinces. (See Wars, Foreign.)

United States, preparations for, referred to, 376. (See also Spanish-American War.)

Spain, Treaties with.—The treaties with Spain prior to the treaty of Paris were expressly annulled and abrogated in 1902, except the treaty of Feb. 17, 1833, which was continued in force. It provided for the payment of claims of the United States by the issuance by Spain of a series of inscriptions. The commission to determine the claims (appointed by Congress, June 7, 1836) awarded the sum of $549,850.28 to the claimants. The payment of the interest on this sum is made perpetual by the convention.

The treaty of peace of 1898, known as the Treaty of Paris, closed the Spanish-American War. By it Spain relinquished all authority and claim of sovereignty to Cuba and ceded Porto Rico and Guam to the United States. In consideration of the payment by the United States, within three months of the ratification of the treaty, of twenty millions of dollars, Spain ceded to the United States the archipelago known as the Philippines. It was agreed that the United, States should for the space of ten years from the signing of the treaty admit Spanish ships and merchandise to the Philippines on the same terms as United States ships and merchandise. Spanish soldiers taken as prisoners of war at Manila were to be sent back to Spain at the expense of the United States, with their arms restored to them. Spain should evacuate the Philippines as speedily as possible, taking with her, as her property, the movable munitions of war and arms, the larger arms to be left in position and purchased from Spain by the United States upon terms to be agreed upon. All prisoners of war to be released by both parties. No indemnity to be sought by either government from the other. The United States to settle all claims against Spain covered by the relinquishment of this treaty.

Spain relinquished to the United States all wharves, docks, barracks, and similar public property in Cuba, Porto Rico, Guam, and in the Philippines without prejudice to private interests therein. Provision was made for establishing the political status of subjects of Spain electing to remain within the ceded possessions. The right of establishing a consular office by Spain in any of the ceded districts was accorded by the treaty.

In 1900 an additional treaty was made to cover the cession of the outlying islands of the Philippines not specifically included in the treaty of 1898. These were particularly the islands of the Cagayan Sulu and Sibitu, for which cession the United States agreed to pay the sum of one hundred thousand dollars to Spain.

In 1902 a treaty of friendship and general relations was closed with Spain to cover largely the points in the treaties which had been abrogated by war. This treaty covered the points usual in treaties of commerce and navigation, and consular conventions.

An arbitration convention on the lines prescribed by The Hague Convention of 1899 was signed April 30, 1908.

Spanish-American Provinces. (See South American Provinces; South American Republics.)

Spanish-American War.—In February, 1895, the natives of Cuba, after years of oppression by their Spanish rulers, which was in no wise lightened by various unsuccessful revolutions, determined to throw off the yoke of Spain. They took up arms against the mother country, and quickly the entire island was in a state of insurrection. This revolution, like previous outbreaks which had occurred in the island, was not at first considered of sufficient importance to warrant interference or recognition on the part of the United States, although Americans were outspoken in their sympathy for Cuba and indignant at the stories of mistreatment of Cubans at the hands of Spanish governors.

A similar outbreak in the island occurred in 1868, during the Administration of President Grant. In his message to Congress Dec. 6, 1869, President Grant said : "The contest (in the island) has at no time assumed the conditions which amount to a war in the sense of international law, or which would show the existence of a *de facto* political organization of the insurgents sufficient to justify a recognition of belligerency" (page 3985). In a message of June 13, 1870, describing the conditions in the island, he said : "The insurrection itself, although not subdued, exhibits no signs of advance, but seems to be confined to an irregular system of hostilities, carried on by small and illy armed bands of men, roaming without concentration through the woods and the sparsely populated regions of the island, attacking from ambush convoys and small bands of troops, burning plantations and the estates of those not sympathizing with their cause" (page 4018). Again, Dec. 7, 1875, in a message to Congress he used the following language in respect to conditions in the island : "Considered as a question of expediency, I regard the accordance of belligerent rights still to be as unwise and premature as I regard it to be, at present, indefensible as a measure of right" (page 4293).

President Cleveland entertained an opinion in regard to the insurrection in Cuba arising in 1895 similar to those expressed by President Grant in regard to the insurrection of 1868, and in his message of Dec. 2 of that year he said : "Whatever may be the traditional sympathy of our countrymen as individuals with a people who seem to be struggling for larger autonomy and greater freedom, deepened, as such sympathy naturally must be, in behalf of our neighbors, yet the plain duty of their government is to observe in good faith the recognized obligations of international relationship" (page 6068). He insisted that belligerent rights should not be accorded to the insurgents, because of peril and injury to our own interests. He said in his message of Dec. 7, 1896 : "Imperfect and restricted as the Spanish government of the island may be, no other exists there, unless the will of the military officer in temporary command of a particular district can be dignified as a species of government" (page 6151).

The foregoing expressions of opinion prove unmistakably that there was no reaching out on the part of the United States to interfere with the Spanish rule in Cuba. When President McKinley was inaugurated the insurrection described by his immediate predecessor still existed, and the grave questions which had confronted the latter were now presented for his consideration. He declined to interfere in the troubles in the island in any way and expressly refused to recognize the independence of Cuba. He declared Spain should be given reasonable time in which to apply promised reforms. In pursuance of Spain's promise autonomous administrations were established in some of the larger cities, but subsequent developments demonstrated the futility of such action and the failure of the newly formed governments. The revolution dragged on, sapping the substance of the people as it progressed and rendering destitute the poorer classes. Crimes were committed on every hand, while desolation and disorder reigned.

To add to the horrors and atrocities of the struggle, the Captain-General of the island, Valeriano Weyler, Feb. 16, 1896, issued an edict initiating a cruel policy which he called "reconcentration." By Weyler's order the agricultural inhabitants were herded into the cities, their lands laid waste, and their homes destroyed. Crowded within the cities and lines of the Spanish armies, the non-combatant men, women, and children died from disease and starvation in untold numbers. Reports of the conditions in Cuba were from time to time brought to the United States, and the public mind throughout the country was greatly stirred. While this state of affairs existed the second-class battleship *Maine*, which had been dispatched to Cuban waters on a friendly mission, was on the night of Feb. 15, 1898, blown up in the harbor of Havana. In this catastrophe two officers and 258 sailors and marines perished (page 6295). A thorough investigation of this disaster was immediately instituted, and at its close a report was made to the effect that the destruction of the ship had been wrought by an explosion from without, produced by a submarine mine (page 6281).

The tension of the public mind, already great, was increased by this report and by the suspicion in the minds of many as to the cause of the disaster. The people could not much longer be held in check, and to those who were even casually observant it was apparent that a crisis in our affairs with Spain was imminent. Congress was in session and unanimously appropriated $50,000,000 for the national defense. The coasts of the United States were poorly defended, the Navy needed ammunition and supplies and an increase in vessels, while the Army required enlargement in men and munitions. April 6 the continental powers, through their envoys in Washington, gave expression to the hope that an amicable adjustment of the impending troubles might be reached. The President replied to their representations, and with them shared the hope that peace might be preserved. The President in his message of April 11, 1898, announced the failure of diplomacy to bring about a satisfactory settlement of the difficulties and recommended to Congress forcible intervention (page 6281).

April 19, after refusing to recognize the government of Cuba, Congress with much unanimity declared the island independent of Spain and authorized forcible intervention (page 6297). The resolutions met with the approval of the Executive, and he signed them the next day. Spain regarded this act on the part of the United States as "equivalent to an evident declaration of war." The ministers of the two countries were recalled and diplomatic relations terminated. April 22 a blockade of Cuban ports was proclaimed (page 6472), and the following day a call was made for 125,000 volunteers (page 6473). A formal declaration of war was recommended by the Presi-

dent, and April 25 Congress declared the existence of war from and including April 21. Due notification of the existence of war was given to the various governments April 25, nearly all of which immediately responded with proclamations of neutrality.

May 25 there was a second call for volunteers, 75,000 in number (page 6477). Like the initial call for 125,000, this was responded to without delay. The regular army was largely increased, as was the enlisted force of the Navy. More than 100 vessels were added to the Navy by purchase. The coast defenses were rapidly strengthened, additional guns placed in position, and an auxiliary navy was created. About 1,500 submarine mines were placed at the most exposed points on the coast. Cable, telegraph, and telephone lines were constructed in many places. In addition to the national defense fund of $50,000,000, which was expended in large part by the Army and Navy, Congress provided further means for prosecuting hostilities by the war revenue act of June 13, authorizing a 3 per cent popular loan not to exceed $400,000,000 and levying additional imposts and taxes. Of the authorized loan $200,000,000 was offered and promptly taken, the subscriptions far exceeding the call.

The first encounter occurred April 27, when a detachment of the blockading squadron made a reconnaissance in force at Matanzas, Cuba, shelled the harbor forts and demolished several new works in course of construction. The next engagement occurred May 1, at Manila, in the Philippine Islands. The American squadron at Hongkong, under Commodore George Dewey, had been instructed to proceed to the Philippine Islands and to capture or destroy the formidable Spanish fleet assembled at Manila. At daybreak of May 1 Dewey's fleet, successfully passing over the submarine mines, entered Manila Bay and after a few hours' engagement destroyed the entire fleet of ten warships and one transport, captured the naval station and forts at Cavite, and completely controlled the bay of Manila, with the ability to take the city at will. On the American side not a life was lost, the wounded numbering only seven, and not a vessel was materially injured. The Spanish loss in killed and wounded exceeded 400. Thus the first great battle of the war was a victory of the United States, magnificent in effect and extraordinary in detail, standing unequalled in the achievements of naval warfare. The effect of this remarkable victory gave a prestige of invincibility to the United States which, though long deserved, had never been appreciated by the great naval powers of the earth. Reenforcements, under Maj.-Gen. Wesley Merritt, were hurried to the Philippine Islands and firmly established within sight of Manila, which lay helpless before the American guns. The first expedition sailed from San Francisco May 25 and arrived off Manila June 30. Other expeditions seen followed, until the total force landed at Manila consisted of more than 15,000 officers and men.

In the meantime, large forces were assembled at various points along the coast of the United States to invade Cuba and Puerto Rico. San Juan, Puerto Rico, and the forts at the entrance to Santiago Harbor, Cuba, were shelled by the American squadrons, but none of the attacks had any appreciable result. On the night of June 3, in an attempt to blockade the mouth of Santiago Harbor, Assistant Naval Constructor Richmond P. Hobson, accompanied by seven men from the American squadron, sank the collier *Merrimac* across the narrow channel. This unparalleled act of heroism thrilled not only the hearts of the American people, but challenged the admiration of the world. Under the protection of a portion of the American fleet a landing of 600 marines was effected at Guantanamo Bay on June 10. This port was taken and held after severe fighting by the marines, who were the first organized forces of the United States to land in Cuba. By June 16 additional forces had been landed.

June 20 the advance of the American army under Maj.-Gen. William R. Shafter, landed at Daiquiri, about fifteen miles east of Santiago, and the next day began the movement against the city. The first serious engagement in which the American troops lost heavily occurred at Las Guasimas June 24. By nightfall of that day ground within five miles of Santiago was won. (See Santiago, Battle of). The outworks of Santiago were taken July 1 after a severe battle, and on the next day El Caney and San Juan were captured after a desperate struggle. The investment of the city was now complete. The naval forces co-operated, shelling the town and the coast forts.

On the following day, July 3, occurred the decisive naval combat of the war. The Spanish fleet under Rear-Admiral Pascual Cervera, which had been confined in the harbor of Santiago for six weeks by the blockading squadron under acting Rear-Admiral William T. Sampson, attempted to escape. The Spanish vessels were intercepted and utterly destroyed by the American fleet under the immediate direction of Commodore Winfield S. Schley, who assumed command during the temporary absence of Rear-Admiral Sampson. The Spanish loss was 600 killed and about 1,400 prisoners, including the admiral.

Spain was unable to recover from the catastrophe, and her efforts upon the ocean virtually ceased. The capitulation of Santiago, which embraced the entire eastern end of Cuba, soon followed. July 17 the American army occupied the city. The number of Spanish soldiers surrendered was 22,000.

An expedition against Porto Rico, consisting of about 3,500 men, under command of Maj.-Gen. Nelson A. Miles, was immediately fitted out, and landed at Guanica July 25. Gen. Miles's force was subsequently increased to about 17,000. With the exception of a few slight engagements, there was no serious resistance, and the middle of August found much of the island in the possession of the American troops.

As early as July 26 Spain made overtures for peace through M. Jules Cambon, the French ambassador at Washington. August 12 the peace protocol was signed, by which hostilities were brought to an end.

August 15, the news of the signing of the protocol not having reached the Philippines, the battle of Manila was fought, and the last scene of the war was enacted when, after a brief assault by the American land and naval forces, the city was compelled to surrender.

The number of military forces engaged by the United States in the war, as reported to the Commissioner of Pensions, was: Regulars, 57,329; militia and volunteers, 223,235; navy, 31,959—total, 312,523.

The total casualties in killed and wounded during the war were—Army, officers killed, 23; enlisted men killed, 257—total, 280; officers wounded, 113; enlisted men wounded, 1,464—total, 1,577. Navy—killed, 17; wounded, 67; died as result of wounds, 1; invalided from service, 6—total, 91. In the entire campaign by land and sea the United States did not lose a flag,

gun, ship, or transport, and, with the exception of the crew of the *Merrimac*, not a soldier or sailor was taken prisoner.

August 7 the American troops in Cuba began to embark for home, and the entire force was returned to the United States by August 24, after an absence of only two months. A treaty of peace was signed at Paris by the commissioners of the two countries Dec. 10, 1898. It was ratified on the part of the United States Feb. 6, and on the part of Spain March 19, 1899. By the treaty it was provided that Spain relinquish all claim of sovereignty over and title to Cuba; that Puerto Rico and other West Indian islands of Spain, one island in the Ladrones, and the entire Philippine group be ceded to the United States, and that Spain be paid $20,000,000. The ratification of the two Governments were exchanged in Washington April 11, 1899, and on the same day President McKinley issued the following proclamation: "Whereas a treaty of peace between the United States of America and Her Majesty the Queen Regent of Spain, in the name of her august son, Don Alfonso XIII, was concluded and signed by their respective plenipotentiaries at Paris on the 10th day of December, 1898, the original of which, being in the English and Spanish languages, is word for word as follows: [Here the full text of the treaty is inserted.] And whereas the said convention has been duly ratified on both parts and the ratifications of the two Governments were exchanged in the city of Washington on the 11th day of April, 1899: Now, therefore, be it known that I, William McKinley, President of the United States of America, have caused the said convention to be made public, to the end that the same and every article and clause thereof may be observed and fulfilled with good faith by the United States and the citizens thereof."

Spanish-American War:

Treaty of peace proclaimed (see Enc. Art., Spanish-American War), 6356.

Vessels of United States in Great Lakes granted facilities by Canada for returning, 6331.

Volunteers called for by proclamation, 6473, 6477.

Discussed, 6296, 6312, 6313.

Mustered out, referred to, 6322.

To be mustered out, 6342.

Wade, James F., member of military commission, to Cuba, 6322.

War-revenue act discussed, 6314.

Wheeler, Joseph, operations of cavalry division under, around Santiago, discussed, 6317.

Wilmington, attempts of the, to silence batteries at Cardenas, 6302, 6316.

Wilson, John M., Puerto Rican expedition reenforced by division of, 6318.

Winslow disabled in conflict in Cardenas Bay, 6304, 6316.

Rescued by the *Hudson,* 6304.

Thanks of Congress to officers and men of, recommended, 6304.

Woodford, Stewart L., minister to Spain, mentioned, 6257, 6284, 6286.

Withdrawal of, 6312.

Young, Samuel B. M., operations of brigade under, around Santiago discussed, 6317.

Spanish Main, blockade of ports of, referred to, 776.

Spanish Milled Dollars referred to, 239.

Spanish Milled Doubloons referred to, 304.

Spanish West Indies referred to, 4113.

Speaker.—The title of the presiding officer of the House of Representatives. The Constitution provides that "the House of Representatives shall choose their Speaker and other officers." It is doubtful, however, if the framers of the Constitution contemplated vesting the Speaker with the power he now enjoys. The system of legislation by committees which has gradually grown up, carrying with it the prerogative of the Speaker to name them, has greatly extended his influence. The first Speaker of the modern sort—more of a leader of the House than a presiding officer—was Henry Clay. As the representative of the House the Speaker presides over the deliberations of that body, appoints its committees, supervises its journal, certifies to the amount of compensation due its members, signs the bills, resolutions, warrants, subpœnas, etc., and has the right, as a member to participate in debate after calling another member to the chair. The Speaker rarely avails himself of this privilege. He is chosen by the House from among the members.

Following is the list of the Speakers of the House: Frederick A. C. Muhlenberg, Pennsylvania; Jonathan Trumbull, Connecticut; Jonathan Dayton, New Jersey;

Theodore Sedgwick, Massachusetts; Nathaniel Macon, North Carolina; Joseph B. Varnum, Massachusetts; Henry Clay, Kentucky; Langdon Cheves, South Carolina; John W. Taylor, New York; Philip P. Barbour, Virginia; Andrew Stevenson, Virginia; John Bell, Tennessee; James K. Polk, Tennessee; Robert M. T. Hunter, Virginia; John White, Kentucky; John W. Jones, Virginia; John W. Davis, Indiana; Robert C. Winthrop, Massachusetts; Howell Cobb, Georgia; Linn Boyd, Kentucky; Nathaniel P. Banks, Massachusetts; James L. Orr, South Carolina; William Pennington, New Jersey; Galusha A. Grow, Pennsylvania; Schuyler Colfax, Indiana; James G. Blaine, Maine; Michael C. Kerr, Indiana; Samuel J. Randall, Pennsylvania; J. Warren Keifer, Ohio; John G. Carlisle, Kentucky; Thomas B. Reed, Maine; Chas. F. Crisp, Georgia; David B. Henderson, Iowa; Joseph G. Cannon, Illinois; Champ Clark, Missouri.

Special Agents, Treasury Department.—These officials investigate the work of the customs collectors, and make other investigations relative to the customs service of the United States. (See list of references under Customs.)

Special-Delivery Stamps:

Discussed, 4836, 5881, 5971.

Special Session Messages of President—

Adams, John, 223.

Cleveland, 5833.

Hayes, 4404, 4472.

Lincoln, 3221.

McKinley, 6244.

Madison, 453, 511.

Pierce, 2927.

Roosevelt, 6741.

Taft, 7379.

Tyler, 1893.

Van Buren, 1451.

Wilson, 7871.

Specie Circular.—An order drafted by Senator Benton, of Missouri, and issued by the Secretary of the Treasury July 11, 1836, by order of President Jackson (6329). It was designed to check speculative purchases of public lands. In it the officials were directed to receive nothing but gold and silver in payment for public lands. The circular was issued in opposition to the sentiment of Congress, which at the next session passed a bill to rescind the order, but Jackson defeated the bill by a pocket veto. The President's action aroused much indignation and, it is claimed, hastened the panic of 1837.

Specie Payments.—The United States suspended specie payments Jan. 1, 1862, and Congress authorized the issue of large quantities of United States notes to be a legal tender. In this action the Government had been preceded by most of the banks of the country, following the example of the New York banks. Jan. 14, 1875, the act authorizing the resumption of specie payments of Government contracts to begin Jan. 1, 1879, was approved by President Grant in a special message (4268). To this end the purchase of bullion and the manufacture of subsidiary coin was at once begun. The mints were run overtime to supply the demand for specie, and resumption became an accomplished fact.

Specie Payments:

Act providing for resumption of, approved and discussed, 4268.

Banks refused to pay Government demands in specie, 1810.

Discussed by President—

Cleveland, 6073.

Grant, 3983, 4061, 4198, 4239, 4247, 4268, 4301, 4379.

Hayes, 4397, 4413, 4510, 4567.

McKinley, 6253.

Reports on, 1726.

Resumption of—

By Chile discussed, 6059.

Discussed, 3879, 4379, 4510, 4567.

Recommended, 3983, 4061, 4102, 4239, 4247, 4301, 4310, 4413.

Suspension of, by banks discussed, 1541, 1751, 1757, 1777, 1789, 3330.

Specific Duty.—A duty on imported goods, based on the weight or quantity thereof.

Spies.—In war-times, a spy is a person who, in disguise or not wearing distinctive marks of the belligerent with whom he is connected, mingles with the enemy within the enemy's lines of fortifications or other territory in order secretly to procure information for his own country. Because of the fact that the status of spies had long been indefinite and because of the penalty of death involved, a series of regulations drawn up by The Hague tribunal indicates precisely that no person shall be considered a spy who is not wearing a disguise, who is carrying messages openly, or who obtains information concerning the enemy in air-craft. The regulations further provide that to be considered a spy a person must be traveling, (a) under false pretenses, (b) within territory occupied by the enemy, (c) for the proved purpose of obtaining information of use to his own forces. The regulations provide further that no person shall be convicted as a spy without fair trial or after he has rejoined the forces with which he is connected. In times of peace, a spy is a person who secretly endeavors to obtain information concerning the defences, resources, etc., of a country in order to supply another country with such information. (See Espionage Law.)

Spitzbergen Islands, negotiations for adjusting claims in, 7670.

Spy Bill. (See Espionage Law.)

Spoils System.—The policy of bestowing public offices upon members of the party in power as rewards for political services. These official rewards once secured, the beneficiaries found it incumbent upon them to assist in keeping in power the party to which they owed their positions not only by a strict attention to the duties of their offices, but also by making friends and votes for their superior officer. Under the spoils system, it is charged, official duties are often made secondary to partisan obligations. This system is not confined to American politics, but is carried on in England, where Parliament has created a patronage secretary, who takes charge of the apportionment and keeps regular accounts with the members of Parliament of the positions which have been filled upon their recommendation. In the United States the system developed first in New York and Pennsylvania. Tammany Hall made effective use of the system in

its fight against the Clintons in the first quarter of the present century. It was extended to state politics by the "Albany Regency," established by Martin Van Buren in 1818. It was not until Jackson's time, however, that it became a feature of Federal politics. The spoils system derived the name commonly applied to it from a sentence used in a speech made by Senator William L. Marcy, of New York, while urging the Senate to confirm the nomination of Martin Van Buren as minister to England. In defense of the charge against Van Buren that he had introduced the custom of removal from office for opinion's sake, Mr. Marcy, speaking for the Democrats of New York, declared that "they see nothing wrong in the rule that to the victor belongs the spoils of the enemy." It has since been a regular feature of American politics in every Administration, tempered of late by the provisions of the civil-service act of 1883. (See also Civil Service.)

Spoliation Claims (see also France, claims against discussed):

Act providing for—

Ascertainment and satisfaction of, vetoed, 2316.

Ascertainment of, vetoed, 2840.

Spoliations (see also Alabama Claims; the several powers, claims against; Vessels, United States, seized):

Discussed by President—

Adams, John, 237.

Jefferson, 371, 383, 413.

Monroe, 765.

Washington, 138.

Spooner Act, mentioned, 7022.

Spot Resolutions.—When President Polk sent a message to Congress announcing that American citizens had been killed by Mexicans on American soil, and asked for a formal declaration of war, Abraham Lincoln, in the House of Representatives, introduced resolutions requesting the President to indicate the exact spot on American soil where the killing had taken place. Thus the name "Spot Resolutions." The results of Polk's message were negative, for the declaration of war was not voted.

Spottsylvania Court-House (Va.), Battle of.—After 2 days' fighting in the Wilderness, south of the Rapidan River, in Virginia, Grant attempted to turn Lee's right flank and advance toward Richmond by way of Spottsylvania Court-House. This resulted in a series of battles. Lee discovered the movement of Grant's army and reached Spottsylvania first. By May 9, 1864, Grant had his army concentrated near Spottsylvania. Hancock commanded the right, Warren the center, and Sedgwick the left. The latter was killed while placing his artillery on the 9th, and Wright succeeded him in command of the Sixth Army Corps. May 10 and 11 there was desultory fighting, skirmishing, and maneuvering for positions. Grant's losses during the 10th are supposed to have exceeded 10,000 men, and Lee's are also supposed to have been severe. The morning of May 12 opened with an advance by Hancock's column, which surrounded and captured with the salient an entire division (Gen. Edward Johnson's) of 3,000 Confederates, including 2 generals and between 30 and 40 guns. The fighting of this day was as severe as any during the war. Lee made five furious assaults in quick succession, with the view of dislodging Hancock and Wright from the captured salient. From dawn till dusk the battle raged. The Federal assault on the Confederate line was checked. It was renewed without success on the 18th. After several days of maneuvering and having received reenforcements enough to make up for his losses, Grant, on the 20th and 21st of May, moved southward toward the North Anna River. The Federal losses in the battle of Spottsylvania Court-House, including the conflicts at Todd's Tavern, Corbin's Bridge, Alsop's Farm, Laurel Hill, Po River, Ny River, the angle of the salient, Piney Branch Church, Harris's Farm, and Guiney's Station, between May 8 and 21, 1864, were officially reported as 2,725 killed, 13,416 wounded, and 2,258 missing, a total of 18,399. The Confederate losses, only partially reported, were (Ewell's, Johnson's, and McGowan's divisions), 4,001 killed and wounded.

Springfield (N. Y.), Battle of.—June 6. 1780, Generals Sterling, Knyphausen, Mathews, and Tryon left Staten Island with 5,000 men to attack Washington's army at Morristown, N. J. Sterling was killed and Knyphausen took command. He advanced to within half a mile of Springfield, harassed all the way by the settlers and militia. Sir Henry Clinton returned to New York on June 17 from Charleston, S. C., and prepared to join Knyphausen. On June 23 the British advance was made in two columns. The American outposts were forced back upon Springfield, which the British burned, and then retreated to Staten Island. The British loss amounted to about 150, the American to 83.

Springfield, Ohio, act to establish port, of delivery at, vetoed, 5002.

Squadron:

African, instructions to officers of, referred to, 2173, 3071.

Asiatic. (See Manila Harbor, Battle of.)

Home, proposed extension of duties of, referred to, 2129.

Mediterranean, referred to, 1905, 1953.

Pacific. (See Manila Harbor, Battle of.)

Squatter.—One who takes possession of or "squats on" land, especially Government land, without ownership or easement rights. In the interest of public policy, and to encourage settlement, a squatter may acquire permanent ownership of such land if unmolested in its cultivation for the period of statutory limitation. (See Squatter Sovereignty.)

Squatter Sovereignty.—The rule allowed by custom, whereby squatters may acquire ownership to land. (See Squatter.)

Squawksin Indians. (See Indian Tribes.)

Squi-aitl Indians. (See Indian Tribes.)

Squier, E. George, treaties with Nicaragua and San Salvador concluded by, 2572.

Squin-áh-mish Indians. (See Indian Tribes.)

Staff of Army. (See Army.)

Stalwart.—A term embraced by certain members, or groups of members, of the Republican Party toward the latter part of the nineteenth century in the assumption of principles which they believed to be sturdy, or stalwart. Afterwards, in derision, the term was hurled back at them by their opponents as denoting lack of progress. (See Stand-Patters.)

"Stalwarts."—A term applied to the partizans who opposed the "Half-Breeds" (q. v.). The "Stalwarts" were opposed to the withdrawal of troops from the Southern States, and favored the Spoils System (q. v.) as against the Civil Service. When Garfield appointed a Collector of the Port of New York in defiance of the traditional method of first having a recommendation from the Senior Senator of the State of New York, Conkling, the Senior Senator from that state, resigned, as did also Platt, the Junior Senator. The bitterness engendered between the "Stalwarts" and the "Half-Breeds" may have been largely responsible for the assassination of Garfield.

Stamford Harbor, Conn., survey of, referred to, 1043.

Stamp Act.—An act of the British Parliament passed in 1765 and put into effect in the American Colonies Nov. 1 of that year. It levied on British subjects in America specifie sums for each of the common transactions of business. Deeds, bonds, notes of hand, indentures, insurance policies, leases, contracts of sale, etc., were not to be enforced by courts unless written on stamped paper bought of the officers of the Crown. Without stamped wills testamentary dispositions would be void; without stamped receipts debts could not be acquitted; vessels at sea without clearances written on stamped paper were liable to seizure and confiscation if they fell in with one of the King's ships; only stamped newspapers could be exposed for sale; without stamped certificates marriages could not lawfully be contracted; unstamped writs and executions had no force or effect; in short, the American citizen must have been daily paying money into the British treasury at its stamp office or in respect to much of the protection which society undertakes to afford he was an outlaw. Under this act business was suspended. The people absolutely refused to use the stamps. Benjamin Franklin presented a petition of the colonists to the House of Commons, and on March 18, 1766, the stamp act was repealed. The agitation resulting from the act was one of the leading causes in effecting the Revolution.

Stamp-Act Congress.—A body which met at New York Oct. 7, 1765, composed of delegates from all the Colonies except Virginia, North Carolina, New Hampshire, and Georgia. There were 26 members, including 4 from New York, 2 each from Rhode Island and Delaware and 3 each from Massachusetts, Connecticut, New Jersey, Pennsylvania, Maryland and South Carolina. Timothy Ruggles, of Massachusetts, was chosen president. The manifestoes issued by this congress were "A Declaration of the Rights and Grievances of the Colonists of America," an address to the King, a memorial to the House of Lords, and a petition to the House of Commons, all of a loyal and respectful tone. The congress adjourned Oct. 25.

Stamps. (See Division of Stamps.)

Stand-Patters.—A term applied to members of political parties who can not be induced to subscribe to any change of policy or to progress. The term became used especially in the administration of Taft to describe those Republicans who opposed changes in the tariff and in other methods of government which were demanded by the more radical element among the Republicans.

Standard Oil Case.—Charges of dishonesty and unfair business methods have frequently been made against the Standard Oil Company. These were discredited or silenced by technical denials until it was found that the Standard Oil Company was trying to gain possession of the new and rich oil fields of Eastern Kansas and Northern Oklahoma, which had been opened during the winter of 1904-5. Many independent companies had been formed, both for producing oil and refining it, and the savings of thousands of people were invested in the business. It soon became apparent, however, that the Standard Oil Company was endeavoring to control the field. Freight rates were so advanced that it was impossible to ship oil to refineries at Kansas City, and the producers were told that if they sold any oil to independent refiners, the Standard would refuse to take any surplus they might have. This seemed to indicate that the Standard was determined to crush all business rivals, as it was charged with having done in the Eastern oil fields. Congressman Campbell, of Kansas, introduced a resolution on the subject and in February, 1905, an investigation was ordered by the Bureau of Corporations. Commissioner Garfield submitted a report May 17, 1906. This showed that the Standard Oil Company had an advantage over all independent companies in the shipment of oil. The report says: "The Standard Oil Company has habitually received and is now receiving, secret rates and other unjust and illegal discriminations. Many of these discriminations were clearly in violation of the interstate commerce laws, and others, whether technically illegal or not, had the same effect upon competitors. These discriminations have been so long continued, so secret, so ingeniously applied to new conditions of trade, and so large in amount as to make it certain that they were due to concerted action by the Standard Oil Company and the railroads."

A second investigation of the Standard Oil Company was undertaken by the Interstate Commerce Commission at the request of Congress, and their report was submitted Jan. 28, 1907. It stated: "The sworn testimony before us abundantly confirms the conclusions reached by the Commissioner of Corporations. The ruin of competitors has been a distinct part of the policy of the Standard Oil Company in the past, systematically and persistently pursued. It has maintained a system of espionage over the shipments of its rivals; it has ruined competitors by means of local competition, that is by reducing prices in the field of operation of its rivals, while maintaining prices elsewhere; it has pursued the policy of molding public opinion by purchasing space in newspapers and printing innocent looking articles setting forth the benefits conferred by the Standard Oil Company; it has induced the railroads to purchase all their lubricating oil from it at a double price, thus securing a profit very much like a rebate; it has paid employees of its rivals for information, and has sold different grades of oil out of the same barrel."

Herbert Knox Smith, Commissioner of Corporations, presented a report May 20, 1907, dealing mainly with the Standard Oil pipe lines. It showed these lines to consist of 40,000 miles of trunk lines and feeders; and it pointed out that, while the Standard Oil Company had no monopoly in the production of oil, it transported through its pipe lines 90 per cent of the oil from the Pennsylvania, Indiana, and Ohio fields and 98 per cent of that from the Kansas-Oklahoma fields. Its monopoly was also shown to consist in the fact that it refined about 86 per cent of all the oil refined in the United States. The extent of these pipe lines was believed to prevent the construction of rival pipe lines. Commissioner Smith estimated that a charge of 20 cents per barrel would cover the cost of transportation from Lima, Ohio, to the seaboard, and yield 10 per cent on the investment. The actual charge was shown to be 53½ cents per barrel.

Early in 1907 the Attorney-General of the United States brought suit against the Standard Oil Company of Indiana, in the District Court at Chicago, under the Elkins law forbidding discrimination and the giving of rebates by common carriers engaged in interstate traffic. The action was based on the report of Commissioner Garfield, mentioned above, which related to the shipments of oil from the great refineries of Whiting, Indiana, to the southwestern market, by way of East St. Louis, Illinois, where the oil came into competition with the product of the Kansas and Oklahoma fields. This region was reached by three competing railroads, the Chicago and Eastern Illinois, the Chicago, Burlington and Quincy, and the Chicago and Alton. Each road had filed with the Interstate Commerce Commission and kept posted at its freight offices a class rate of 18 cents per 100 pounds, but their books showed that they had given the Standard Oil Company a commodity rate on oil of 6 or 6¼ cents per hundred. Each company had its own methods of concealing the true charge. Commissioner Garfield stated that the "whole scheme of the 6 cent rate, including both the failure to file tariffs with the Interstate Commerce Commission and the secret methods of billing, were devised at the suggestion and with the knowledge of the Standard Oil Company and primarily for the purpose of concealing the extraordinarily low rates from its competitors."

The defense plead that "these rates were not solicited nor accepted knowingly with the intention of violating the law; that the law did not forbid a shipper to take directly from a carrier a rate less than the published rate, the purpose of the law being to prevent indirect methods and secret devices; the company could have secured rates as low as those accepted over the Chicago, Burlington and Quincy or over the Chicago and Eastern Illinois, and that the Elkins law, under which the suit was brought, was nullified by the Hepburn law, subsequently passed." The case was based specifically on the transit of a car of oil from Whiting, Indiana, over the Chicago and Alton Railroad, at the six-per-cent rate. April 13, after deliberating two hours, the jury returned a verdict of guilty on 1,462 counts. Before determining the amount of the fine, Judge Landis demanded evidence of the actual ownership of the Standard Oil Company of Indiana. This was shown to be the Standard Oil Company of New Jersey. Judge Landis then, on August 3, imposed the maximum fine of $20,000 on each count, an aggregate of $29,240,000. The defendant company appealed the case to the Circuit Court of Appeals for the seventh circuit, and on July 22, 1908,

Judge Peter L. Grosscup, of Illinois, two other judges concurring, handed down an opinion reversing the finding of the District Court, holding that the court below erred in its ruling that a shipper may be convicted of re-accepting a concession from the lawful published rate, even though it was not shown that the shipper knew what the lawful published rate was; its ruling that the number of offenses is the number of carloads of property transported, irrespective of the question whether each carload is the whole or only a part of a single transaction; and its ruling that the largeness of the fine imposed was due to the effect to reach and punish a party that was not before the court.

Judge Grosscup declared the fine imposed by Judge Landis "an abuse of judicial discretion." The validity of the courts' reasoning was universally discussed. President Roosevelt pronounced the ruling of Judge Grosscup "a gross miscarriage of justice." The Government applied to the Circuit Court of Appeals for a rehearing, which was denied, and on Nov. 20, 1908, Attorney-General Bonaparte petitioned the United States Supreme Court for a writ of certiorari. This petition was dismissed Jan. 4, 1909, leaving the case to be retried in the District Court.

Judge McCall, in the United States Circuit Court of Jackson, Tenn., Nov. 17, 1910, instructed the jury to bring in a verdict of not guilty.

Standard Oil Corporation, statements made by, declared untruthful, 7133.

Standard Time.—According to the standard time, which was adopted by agreement at 12 o'clock on November 18, 1883, by all the principal railroads of the United States, the continent is divided into five longitudinal belts, and a meridian of time is fixed for each belt. These meridians are fifteen degrees of longitude, or one hour's time apart. The time divisions are called intercolonial time, eastern time, central time, mountain time, and Pacific time. Eastern Maine, New Brunswick and Nova Scotia use the sixth meridian; the Canadas, New England, the Middle States, Virginia and the Carolinas use the seventy-fifth meridian, which is that of Philadelphia; Alabama, Georgia, Florida, Texas, Kansas and the larger part of Nebraska and Dakota use the nineteenth meridian, which is that of New Orleans; the territories to the western border of Arizona and Montana go by the time of the one hundred and fifth meridian, which is that of Denver; and the Pacific States employ the one hundred and twentieth meridian. In passing from one time-belt to another a person's watch will be an hour too fast or too slow, according to the direction in which he is traveling. This new system, which has reduced the time standards from fifty-three to five, was suggested by Professor Abbe, of the Signal Service Bureau at Washington, and was elaborated by Dr. A. P. Barnard, of Columbia University, New York.

Standards, Bureau, of. (See Bureau of Standards.)

Star Chamber.—Used as an adjective before "Proceeding," "Conference," "Deliberation," or the like, the term means that the session is secret and, presumably, for some selfish purpose,—not for the interest of the public.

Star Routes.—Star Routes are those mail routes of the United States Government on which, owing to lack of railroad or steamboat facilities, the mail is carried on horseback or wagons. They are called star routes because in the route books of the Post-Office Department they are marked with three groups of four stars each, the groups being intended to signify "celerity, certainty, and security" in this method of carrying the mail. (See also Postal Service.)

Star Route Trials.—Early in 1881 vague rumors were in circulation of extensive fraud in this service. It was said that there was a "ring" to defraud the government. Included in it were some of the large contractors, the Second Assistant Postmaster-General, Thomas J. Brady, some subordinates in the department, Senator Stephen W. Dorsey, of Arkansas, and others. Brady resigned April 20, 1881. Proceedings in one of the principal cases were begun against the conspirators, but they were dismissed on account of irregularity in the form of the action. Early in 1882 several persons were arrested for furnishing fraudulent bonds on the bids for service, and indictments were found against Brady, Stephen W. Dorsey, John W. Dorsey, John M. Peck and John R. Miner, who had made the bids; H. M. Vaile, a subcontractor; M. C. Rerdell, S. W. Dorsey's secretary; Turner, a clerk in Brady's office; and against one of the principal contractors. The method by which, as charged, the government was defrauded consisted in first obtaining the contracts for the routes, and in subsequently having the payments vastly increased, in compensation for additional mail trips per week, and faster time on each trip. This latter was called "expediting" the route. The Dorsey combination, as the conspirators were popularly called, controlled one hundred and thirty-four Star Routes, on which the original compensation was $143,169. By increasing the number of trips beyond what the locality required, and by "expediting" them, this amount had been increased to $622,808. On one route the compensation had been increased from $398 to $6,133.50; the revenue derived therefrom by the government was $240.

The cases came up for trial in the District of Columbia, June 1, 1882. The government employed special counsel to aid the district attorney, and the defendants, too, were represented by eminent lawyers. After a protracted trial, the case was submitted to the jury on Sept. 8; as they were not able to agree as to all of the defendants, they were kept out until Sept. 11, on which day the presiding judge, Wylie, deeming an agreement on all the defendants unlikely, accepted the verdict. Peck and Turner were found not guilty; Miner and Rerdell, guilty; as to the Dorseys, Vaile and Brady there was a disagreement. Preparations were at once made for a new trial in the cases in which there had been a disagreement and the motions of the counsel of Miner and Rerdell for a new trial were granted. The second trial began in December, 1882. Rerdell, on this trial, pleaded guilty and turned state's evidence. On June 12, 1883, the case was given to the jury, and on the 14th a verdict of not guilty was rendered. In April, 1883, W. P. Kellogg, ex-Senator from Louisiana, and Brady were indicted for receiving money for services in relation to a Star Route contract. The cases never resulted in a conviction.

At the conclusion of the first of these trials charges of attempted bribery of the jury, both on behalf of the government and of the defense, were made. The foreman of the first jury, Dickson, and another juror, claimed to have been approached on behalf of the government, and still another juror on behalf of the defense. Before the first trial had ended Dickson had made a sworn statement of the facts in his case, and it was charged that he had used it in the jury-room for the purpose of influencing the verdict. The Department of Justice investigated the cases, and declared its belief that no government officials were involved; it implied that all the attempts had been for the purposes of the defense. Dickson was subsequently indicted for attempting corruptly to influence the jury.

Star Spangled Banner.—A patriotic song written by Francis Scott Key, of Baltimore (q. v.) on the night of Sept. 13, 1814, during the bombardment of Fort McHenry by the British. Key had gone under a flag of truce to solicit the release of some friends who had been seized by the English Admiral Cochrane during the attack on the city of Washington. Upon Key's arrival the British fleet was about to begin the attack on Fort McHenry, and though his request for the release of his friends was granted, Admiral Cochrane refused to allow him or his friends to leave the ship before the battle. During the excitement of the bombardment Key wrote the famous song on the back of a letter. It was published and sung at the theatres to the tune of "Anacreon in Heaven."

Stars and Bars.—The flag of the Confederate States of America. The first provisional Senate recommended that "the flag of the Confederate States shall consist of a red field with a white space extending horizontally through the center and equal in width to one-third the width of the flag." The Union was a blue square extending across the upper red and the white stripe. In the blue square nine stars were arranged in a circle. The bars were, by their colors, red and white, intended to express the qualities of courage and purity. The blue field of the union expressed fortitude, and the nine stars represented the number of States in the Confederacy. It was first displayed March 4, 1861, simultaneously with the inauguration of Lincoln, being unfurled over the statehouse at Montgomery, Ala. In 1863, the Stars and Bars too closely resembling the Stars and Stripes, the Confederate Congress adopted a white flag with one blue star in the center. Another variation commonly used was a white field with blue diagonal stripes and white stars, and a piece of fringe at the outer edge. Some of the army corps adopted a battle flag with a red ground, blue diagonal cross, and white stars.

Stars and Stripes. (See Flag.)

State Banks. (See Banks, State.)

State Constitutions. (See Constitutions, State.)

State Courts. (See Courts, State.)

State Debts:

Contracted abroad, discussed, 1940.

Guaranty of, by General Government discussed, 2064.

Injure public credit, 2061.

Referred to, 1769.

Repudiation of contracts referred to, 1962.

State, Department of.—This Department of the federal government had its origin in a Committee of Correspondence, which was appointed Nov. 29, 1775, to invoke foreign aid in behalf of the American Colonies.

This committee was succeeded by the Committee of Foreign Affairs, which was created by an act of the Continental Congress, April 17, 1777. "A plan for the Department of Foreign Affairs" was reported to Congress in January, 1781, and the Department was organized Aug. 10 of that year; Robert R. Livingston was made Secretary and he filled the position until June 4, 1783. On the retirement of Livingston the Department of Foreign Affairs practically ceased to exist for about a year, Congress managing the foreign relations of the country through committees. Sept. 21, 1784, John Jay was appointed Secretary and the functions of the office were revived.

After the acceptance of the Constitution Congress passed a law entitled "an act for establishing an Executive Department to be denominated the Department of Foreign Affairs." This became a law on July 27, 1789, and John Jay, being in charge of the old Department, was continued temporarily in charge of the new one. The existence of this Department, however, was destined to be brief, for on Sept. 15 following, an act of Congress was approved which provided that "the Executive Department denominated the Department of Foreign Affairs, shall hereinafter be denominated the Department of State, and the principal officer shall hereafter be called the Secretary of State," and on Sept. 26 Thomas Jefferson was made Secretary.

The Secretary of State is charged, under the direction of the President, with duties appertaining to correspondence with the public ministers and the consuls of the United States, and with the representatives of foreign powers accredited to the United States; and to negotiations of whatever character relating to the foreign affairs of the United States. He is also the medium of correspondence between the President and the chief executives of the several states of the United States; he has the custody of the Great Seal of the United States, and countersigns and affixes such seal to all executive proclamations, to various commissions, and to warrants for the extradition of fugitives from justice. He is also the custodian of the treaties made with foreign States, and of the laws of the United States. He grants and issues passports, and exequaturs to foreign consuls in the United States are issued through his office. He publishes the laws and resolutions of Congress, amendments to the Constitution, and proclamations declaring the admission of new states into the Union.

The scope of the department has been so enlarged that it is now the most important branch of the government, though many of its original functions have been transferred to other departments.

According to the law of April 10, 1790, the Department was given charge of the patent business, which it retained until 1849, when the work was given over to the new Department of the Interior. A law passed May 31, 1790, made the Department of State the repository of maps, charts, and books for which copyright might be granted by United States district courts, but in 1859 these records were turned over to the Department of the Interior and later to the Library of Congress, where the business is now conducted. From 1790 until 1850 the Department also cared for the enumeration of the census, but in the latter year that work was given to the Department of the Interior, from which, in 1903, it was transferred to the Department of Commerce and Labor. Territorial affairs were also under

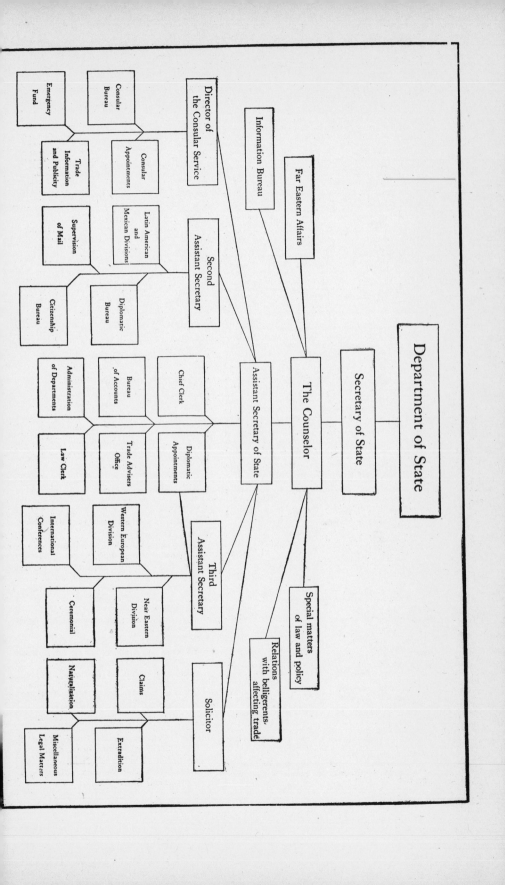

Department of State

Secretary of State

The Counselor

- Special matters of law and policy
- Relations with belligerents affecting trade

Far Eastern Affairs

Information Bureau

Assistant Secretary of State
- Chief Clerk
  - Diplomatic Appointments
- Bureau of Accounts
  - Trade Advisers Office
- Administration of Departments
  - Law Clerk

Second Assistant Secretary
- Latin American and Mexican Divisions
- Diplomatic Bureau
  - Citizenship Bureau
- Supervision of Mail

Director of the Consular Service
- Consular Bureau
  - Emergency Fund
- Consular Appointments
  - Trade Information and Publicity

Third Assistant Secretary
- Western European Division
  - International Conferences
- Near Eastern Division
  - Ceremonial

Solicitor
- Claims
- Naturalization
  - Extradition
  - Miscellaneous Legal Matters

the care of the Department of State until the organization of the Department of the Interior in 1849.

In 1853 an Assistant Secretary of State was provided by law with power to act as Secretary during the latter's absence or during an interregnum. A Second Assistant Secretary was provided for in 1866, and in 1875 the office of Third Assistant Secretary was created.

In 1848 the office of Examiner of Claims was created, whose duties were to examine claims of our citizens against foreign governments and of foreigners against our Government, but when the Department of Justice was formed, in 1870, this office passed under its jurisdiction. In 1891 the title of this office was changed to Solicitor for the Department of State. In 1856 the Statistical Office of the Department of State was established; in 1874 the title was changed to Bureau of Statistics and a year later it was again changed to the Bureau of Foreign Commerce and in 1903 transferred to the Department of Commerce and Labor and made a part of its Bureau of Statistics. The Bureau of Indexes was established in 1870, the Bureau of Accounts in 1873; and the Bureau of Rolls and Library in 1874. Work originally done by the Home Bureau has since been given to the Passport Bureau and the Bureau of Appointments. Other important Bureaus are the Diplomatic Bureau which has charge of all correspondence between the Department and our diplomatic agents abroad and foreign diplomatic agents in the United States, prepares treaties, etc.; and the Consular Bureau. The Bureau of Trade Relations was established in 1903 to manage the work of the consular officials in obtaining reports for the Department of Commerce and Labor. Under this department are also placed the United States Representatives on International Tribunals of Egypt, and the Bureau of American Republics.

For more detailed information of the scope of the activities of the State Department consult the Index references to the Presidents' Messages and Encyclopedic articles under the following headings:

Admission of States.
Ambassadors.
Archives.
Assistant Secretary of State.
Citizenship Bureau.
Claims, Court of.
Commerce Court.
Consular Appointments.
Consular Bureau.
Consular Conventions.
Consular Service.
Consuls.
Copyright.
Counselor, State Department.
Diplomatic and Consular Service.
Diplomatic Appointments.
Diplomatic Bureau.
Director of Consular Service.
Egypt, Tribunals of.
Exequaturs.
Extradition.
Extradition Treaties.
Far Eastern Affairs.
Foreign Relations.

Great Seal of the United States.
Information Bureau.
Latin American and Mexican Divisions.
Library of Congress.
Naturalization.
Near Eastern Division.
Neutral Rights.
Passports.
Patents.
Presidential Succession.
Proclamations.
Second Assistant Secretary of State.
Solicitor for the State Department.
State Rights and State Sovereignty.
Third Assistant Secretary of State.
Trade Adviser.
Trade Information and Publicity.
Treaties.
Western European Division.

Following is a list of the Secretaries of State and the Presidents under whom they served.

President	Secretary of State	Appointed
Washington	Thomas Jefferson, Virginia	1789
"	Edmund Randolph, Virginia	1794
"	Timothy Pickering, Mass	1795
Adams	" "	1797
"	John Marshall, Virginia	1800
Jefferson	James Madison, Virginia	1801
Madison	Robert Smith, Maryland	1809
"	James Monroe, Virginia	1811
Monroe	John Quincy Adams, Mass	1817
J.Q.Adams	Henry Clay, Kentucky	1825
Jackson	Martin Van Buren, New York	1829
"	Edward Livingston, Louisiana	1831
"	Louis McLane, Delaware	1833
"	John Forsyth, Georgia	1834
Van Buren	"	1837
Harrison	Daniel Webster,* Massachusetts	1841
Tyler*	Hugh S. Legare, South Carolina	1843
"	Abel P. Upshur, Virginia	1843
"	John C. Calhoun, S. Carolina	1844
Polk	James Buchanan, Pennsylvania	1845
Taylor	John M. Clayton, Delaware	1849
Fillmore	Daniel Webster, Massachusetts	1850
"	Edward Everett, Massachusetts	1852
Pierce	William L. Marcy, New York	1853
Buchanan	Lewis Cass, Michigan	1857
"	Jeremiah S. Black, Pennsylvania	1860
Lincoln	William H. Seward, New York	1861
Johnson	" "	1865
Grant	Elihu B. Washburn, Illinois	1869
"	Hamilton Fish, New York	1869
Hayes	William M. Evarts, New York	1877
Garfield	James G. Blaine, Maine	1881
Arthur	F. T. Frelinghuysen, New Jersey	1881
Cleveland	Thomas F. Bayard, Delaware	1885
B. Harrison	James G. Blaine, Maine	1889
"	John W. Foster, Indiana	1892
Cleveland	Walter Q. Gresham, Illinois	1893
"	Richard Olney, Massachusetts	1895
McKinley	John Sherman, Ohio	1897
"	William R. Day, Ohio	1897
"	John Hay, Ohio	1898
Roosevelt	" "	1901
"	Elihu Root, New York	1905
"	Robert Bacon, New York	1909
Taft	Philander C. Knox, Penn	1909
Wilson	William J. Bryan, Nebraska	1913
"	Robert Lansing, New York	1915

* Daniel Webster also continued by President Tyler in 1841 until appointment of successor.

State, Department of:
Agents employed by, without express provisions of law, 2004, 2134.
Amount charged to, for service rendered by naval vessels, 3660.
Appropriations and expenditures of, referred to, 4381.
Building for—
Completed and possession taken by, 4301.
Recommended, 2704, 4060.
Change in laws relating to management of, referred to, 4587.
Changes made in force of, referred to, 6178.
Clerks in, referred to, 3585, 3799, 4654.
Contingent fund of bureaus in, estimates for, referred to, 5120.
Historical archives in, 6099.
Historical manuscripts in, plan for publishing, referred to, 5198.
Increase of work of, 7022.
Legal services amount paid for, by, referred to, 3828.

Library in, referred to, 4740.
Officers commissioned by, referred to, 4003.
Officers in, referred to, 4332.
Public records in, means for preservation of, referred to, 4113.
Reorganization of, 7420.
Salaries and expenses of, referred to, 3892.
Substitutes in employment of, referred to, 4975.
Trade factor, 7415, 7502, 7599.
Transfer of—
Patent Office from, to Attorney-General, recommended, 2265.
Portion of business of, recommended, 1024, 2704.
Territorial affairs from, to Interior Department recommended, 4060, 4145.

State of the Union, discussed by President—
Adams, J. Q., 865, 916, 944, 978.
Arthur, 4822.
Buchanan, 2967, 3028, 3051, 3083, 3157, 3191, 3200.
Cleveland, 4909, 5358, 6146.
Fillmore, 2613.
Grant, 3981, 4050, 4107, 4138, 4238, 4259, 4286 4353.
Harrison, Benjamin, 5467, 5542, 5741.
Hayes, 3656, 3690, 3755, 3799.
Jackson, 1005, 1063, 1107, 1154, 1366, 1511.
Jefferson, 316, 344, 349, 373.
Johnson, 3551, 3570, 3589, 3593, 3643, 3756, 3837, 3871.
Lincoln, 3245, 3255, 3334, 3389, 3452.
McKinley, 6307.
Madison, 524, 552, 558.
Monroe, 623, 642, 667, 776, 791, 817.
Pierce, 2740, 2806, 2874, 2930.
Polk, 2321, 2382, 2479.
Roosevelt, 6645, 6709, 6710, 6894, 6973.
Taylor, 2547.
Tyler, 1927, 2047, 2110, 2187.
Van Buren, 1590, 1700, 1746, **1819.**
Washington, 95, 175, 205.

State, Secretary of:
Appointments by, referred to, 1965.
Letter to, regarding Lousiana province, 336.
Report of, 26, 334, 384, 430, 637, 652, 1131, 6346.

State, War, and Navy Building, construction of, discussed, 4301, 4524, 4638.

Staten Island, sale of fortifications on, to United States proposed, 934.

States of the Church. (See Italy; Papal States.)

States of the Union. (See also the several States):
Accounts of the United States with, 133.

Act—
Containing provisions denying certain right to protect themselves with militia, discussed, 3670, 3871.
Granting lands to—
For benefit of insane persons vetoed, 2780.
Reasons for applying pocket veto, 1275.
To provide colleges in, vetoed, 3074.
To pay moneys collected under direct tax of 1861 to Territories, District of Columbia, and, vetoed, 5422.
To settle claims of, reasons for applying pocket veto to, 1200.
Admission of, see article Admission of States.
Admission of, discussed and recommendations regarding, 3033, 3086.
Agitation in, growing out of slavery discussed. (See Slavery.)
Alliances between, discouraged, 209.
Amicable relations between, desired, 2806.
Area of, and extent of public domain in, referred to, 2768.
Commerce between, discussed, 3560.
Constitutional rights of. (See powers of Federal and State Governments.)
Debts contracted by, abroad, discussed, 1940.
Guaranty of, by General Government, discussed, 2064.
Injure public credit, 2061.
Referred to, 1769.
Repudiation of contracts by, referred to, 1962.
Disbursements made within Territories and, 1045.
Education in. (See Education.)
Federal Government in, uniform operation of, suggested, 1024.
Funds deposited with—
May be necessary to use portion of, 1458.
Not intended as a gift, 1458.
Referred to, 1823.
Governments to be reestablished in Southern States. (See Confederate States.)
Indebtedness of, to United States referred to, 379.
Insurrection, existence of, in certain, proclaimed, 3238, 3293, 3366.
Proclamations declaring insurrection at an end, 3515, 3627, 3632.
Tax upon real estate in, declared a lien on same, 3293.
Lands—
Granted to—
For educational purposes, 1029, 1045, 3587, 4206.

States	Admitted to the Union.	Area Square Miles.	Population Jan. 1, 1917 (Estimated)	Nickname.	Flower.
1. Delaware	Dec. 7, 1787	2,370	214,270	Diamond ...	Peach Blossom
2. Pennsylvania .	Dec. 12, 1787	45,126	8,591,029	Keystone ...	
3. New Jersey...	Dec. 18, 1787	8,224	2,981,105	Red Mud ... Empire State of the South	
4. Georgia	Jan. 2, 1788	59,265	2,875,953		
5. Connecticut ..	Jan. 9, 1788	4,965	1,254,926	Nutmeg	Mountain Laurel
6. Massachusetts	Feb. 6, 1788	8,266	3,747,564	Old Bay.....	
7. Maryland	Apr. 28, 1788	12,327	1,368,240	Old Line....	Golden Rod
8. South Carolina	May 23, 1788	30,989	1,634,340	Palmetto ...	
9. New Hampshire	June 21, 1788	9,341	443,467	Granite	
10. Virginia	June 25, 1788	42,627	2,202,522	Old Dominion	
11. New York....	July 26, 1788	49,204	10,366,778	Empire	Rose
12. North Carolina	Nov. 21, 1789	52,426	2,418,559	Tar Heel....	
13. Rhode Island.	May 29, 1790	1,248	620,090	Little Rhody	Violet
14. Vermont	Mar. 4, 1791	9,564	364,322	Green Mountain	Red Clover
15. Kentucky	June 1, 1792	40,598	2,386,866	Corn Cracker	
16. Tennessee ...	June 1, 1796	42,022	2,296,316	Volunteer ..	
17. Ohio	Feb. 19, 1803	41,040	5,181,220	Buckeye	Carnation
18. Louisiana	Apr. 30, 1812	48,506	1,843,042	Pelican	Magnolia
19. Indiana	Dec. 11, 1816	36,354	2,826,154	Hoosier	Corn
20. Mississippi ..	Dec. 10, 1817	46,865	1,964,122	Bayou	Magnolia
21. Illinois	Dec. 3, 1818	56,665	6,193,626	Prairie ..... Land of Flowers	Violet
22. Alabama	Dec. 14, 1819	51,998	2,348,273		Golden Rod
23. Maine	Nov. 15, 1820	33,040	774,614	Pine Tree...	Pine Cone
24. Missouri	Aug. 10, 1821	69,420	3,420,143	Bullion	Golden Rod
25. Arkansas ...	June 15, 1836	53,335	1,753,033	Bear	Apple Blossom
26. Michigan	Jan. 26, 1837	57,890	3,074,560	Wolverine ..	Apple Blossom
27. Florida	Mar. 3, 1845	58,666	904,839	Everglade ..	Orange Blossom
28. Texas	Dec. 29, 1845	265,896	4,472,944	Lone Star...	Blue Bonnet
29. Iowa	Dec. 28, 1846	56,147	2,224,771	Hawkeye ...	Wild Rose
30. Wisconsin ...	May 29, 1848	56,066	2,513,758	Badger	
31. California ...	Sept. 9, 1850	158,297	2,983,843	Golden	California Poppy
32. Minnesota ...	May 11, 1858	84,682	2,296,024	Gopher	Moccasin
33. Oregon	Feb. 14, 1859	96,699	848,866	Web-Foot ...	Oregon Grape
34. Kansas	Jan. 29, 1861	82,158	1,840,707	Garden	Sunflower
35. West Virginia	June 19, 1863	24,170	1,399,320	Panhandle ..	Rhododendron
36. Nevada	Oct. 31, 1864	110,690	108,736	Sage Brush..	
37. Nebraska	Mar. 1, 1867	77,520	1,277,750	Black Water.	Golden Rod
38. Colorado	Aug. 1, 1876	103,948	975,190	Centennial .	Columbine
39. North Dakota.	Nov. 3, 1889	70,837	752,260	Cyclone	Wild Rose
40. South Dakota.	Nov. 3, 1889	77,615	707,740	Coyote	Anemone Patens
41. Montana	Nov. 8, 1889	146,572	466,214	Mountain ...	Bitter Root
42. Washington ..	Nov. 11, 1889	69,127	1,565,810	Chinook	Rhododendron
43. Idaho	July 3, 1890	84,313	436,881	Gem of the Mountains.	Syringa
44. Wyoming	July 10, 1890	97,914	182,264		
45. Utah	Jan. 4, 1896	84,990	438,974	Mormon	Sego Lily
46. Oklahoma	Nov. 16, 1907	70,057	2,245,968	Boomer	Mistletoe
47. New Mexico..	Jan. 6, 1912	122,634	416,966	Adobe	
48. Arizona	Feb. 14, 1912	113,956	259,666		

Funds deposited with, not intended as a gift, 808.

May be necessary to use portion of funds deposited with, 1458.

Table showing distribution of, 1479.

Tide of population flows into new, 2123.

Union and Confederate flags, return of, to respective States recommended, 5163.

Proposition withdrawn, 5164.

Weights and measures, sets of, made for, 1477.

State Rights and State Sovereignty.—
"State rights" is the doctrine that every state is sovereign within the limits of its own sphere of action, made so by the declared will of the nation as expressed in the Constitution; and that the will of the nation, appropriately manifested, as provided in the Constitution, may change that sphere. "State sovereignty" is the doctrine that the states, at the formation of the Union, delegated a portion of their sovereignty to the National government, reserving the right to revoke the agency and to resume the exercise of all the elements of sovereignty at any time by seceding.

In the Constitution, the rights of the National government are distinctly stated; the rights of the state are limited only by the expressly declared national right. Previous to the Civil War the term "state rights" was used to designate the idea of "state sovereignty," and misuse has raised a prejudice in many minds even against the legitimate theory of "state rights" brought forward since that event. The arguments against "state sovereignty" may be summarized as follows: The colonies did not fight each for its own independence, but each for the independence of all, as is shown by their joint action throughout, in military as well as civil matters. The sovereignty acquired in that struggle was never individually exercised, but all remained under the national sovereignty raised by the common fight for liberty. All the elements and insignia of sovereignty were vested in the National government, as the power to declare war and peace and to coin money, and moreover the power to amend the Constitution, except in a very few particulars, was given to three-fourths of the states, and on the theory of state sovereignty this would imply the self-contradictory condition of a sovereign state voluntarily exposing itself to changes in its government without its consent to the change. It may be maintained that secession would afford the needed relief; but if this had been the intention, the consent of all the states to an amendment would have been required, since it must be presumed that the union was intended to endure.

The doctrine of "state sovereignty" was put forward at various times. (See Hartford Convention; Nullification.) Soon after the nullification troubles it became the ally of slavery, and the result of the Civil War put it to rest forever. State sovereignty and secession finally disposed of, the theory of state rights as above outlined could be developed. The danger of extreme particularism had been avoided; extreme centralization during the exercise of war powers by the President and Congress was inevitable. The Supreme Court holds the balance, and its adjudication has, since the war, laid down the relations of the states and the National government as above.

State Socialism. (See Socialism.)

States Relations Service, Agriculture Department.—Under a plan of reorganization of the Department of Agriculture approved by law of May 8, 1914, the States Relations Service was created. It has general charge of the department's business with the State Agricultural Colleges and Experiment Stations, and of certain other related functions. The act provides for a nation-wide system of instruction for the farming population in agriculture and home economics outside of the schools and colleges.

The general lines of the extension system for the whole country have been well marked out, and embrace (1) the county agricultural agents, (2) the boys' and girls' clubs, (3) the movable schools, and (4) the supporting work of the college and department specialists.

The appropriation for this work for the first year of its existence (1914) was $2,280,000. This was met by approximately $2,653,000 from the states.

States Rights. (See Powers of Federal and State Governments.)

Statistical Congress, International:

At St. Petersburg, 4142, 4221.

The Hague, 4082.

Invitation to hold next meeting in United States recommended, 4142.

Statistics, Bureau of.—A Bureau of the Department of Commerce and Labor. It was established in 1866 as a Bureau of the Treasury Department, but on the establishment of the Department of Commerce and Labor, in 1903, it was transferred to that Department. It collects and publishes from time to time statistics of the commerce of the United States with foreign countries, immigration statistics, etc. Its annual statistical Abstract of the United States and reports on commerce and navigation are important documents. (See also Agriculture, Department of, and Crop Estimates, Bureau of.)

Statistics, Bureau of, act to establish, referred to, 4807.

Statuary Hall, formerly the hall of the House of Representatives, was established as Statuary Hall by act of Congress of July 2, 1864. By this legislation a National Hall of Statuary was created, and the President was authorized to invite each state to contribute to the collection to be formed; two statues, in either marble or bronze, of deceased citizens of the state whom "for historic renown or from civil or military services" the state should consider as worthy of commemoration in this National Hall of Statuary.

The following is a list of statues presented by the states:

Alabama—J. L. M. Curry.
Connecticut—Roger Sherman.
Connecticut—Jonathan Trumbull.
Florida—John W. Gorrie.
Idaho—George L. Shoup.
Illinois—James Shields.
Illinois—Frances E. Willard.
Indiana—Oliver P. Morton.
Indiana—Lew Wallace.
Iowa—James Harlan.
Iowa—Samuel J. Kirkwood.
Kansas—John J. Ingalls.

Kansas—George W. Glick.
Maine—William King.
Maryland—Charles Carroll.
Maryland—John Hanson.
Massachusetts—Samuel Adams.
Massachusetts—John Winthrop.
Michigan—Lewis Cass.
Michigan—Zachariah Chandler.
Missouri—Francis P. Blair.
Missouri—Thomas H. Benton.
New Hampshire—John Stark.
New Hampshire—Daniel Webster.
New Jersey—Richard Stockton.
New Jersey—Philip Kearny.
New York—Robert R. Livingston.
New York—George Clinton.
Ohio—James A. Garfield.
Ohio—William Allen.
Pennsylvania—J. P. G. Muhlenberg.
Pennsylvania—Robert Fulton.
Rhode Island—Nathanael Greene.
Rhode Island—Roger Williams.
South Carolina—John C. Calhoun.
Texas—Stephen F. Austin.
Texas—Samuel Houston.
Vermont—Ethan Allen.
Vermont—Jacob Collamer.
Virginia—Washington.
Virginia—R. E. Lee.
West Virginia—John E. Kenna.
West Virginia—Francis H. Pierpont.
Wisconsin—James Marquette.

Works of art in the Capitol Building, Washington, have been acquired by gift from private individuals interested in the preservation of the historical, biographical, or pictorial art of the nation; by the gift from states, as instanced by the statues of distinguished citizens forming the collection in Statuary Hall, and by purchase by the Government. A general supervision of the art works of the Capitol is exercised by the Joint Committee on the Library. This committee also has charge of accessions to the art works of the Capitol Building, except as otherwise provided by law.

Statues and Monuments:

Clinton, George, statue of, presented to Congress by New York, 4214.

Dinosaur proclaimed, 8087.

Garfield, James A., statue of, to be erected in Washington, 4795.
> Unveiling ceremonies, order regarding, 5162.

Liberty Enlightening the World. (See Liberty Enlightening the World.)

Rawlins, John A., statue of, recommendations regarding erection of, 4124.

Thomas, George H., statue of, to be unveiled, 4509.

Washington, George, statue of—
> to be erected at Caracas, Venezuela, 4716.
> To be placed in Capitol, 881, 1170, 1910.

Washington Monument. (See Washington Monument.)

Wooster, David, monument to memory of, information regarding, 801.

Yorktown, Va., monument at, referred to, 4850.

Statute of Limitations should be repealed in criminal cases, 1492.

Statutes of Limitations and Interest Laws.

—The following table gives the legal and contract interest rates in the several States, and the statutes of limitations of notes, judgments and accounts:

STATES AND TERRITORIES.	INTEREST LAWS.		STATUTES OF LIMITATIONS.		
	Legal Rate.	Rate Allowed by Contract.	Judgments.	Notes.	Open Accounts.
	Per ct.	Per ct.	Years	Years	Years
Alabama	8	8	20	6	3
Alaska	8	12	10	6	1
Arkansas	6	10	10	5	3
Arizona	6	10	5	4	3
California	7	Any rate.	5	4	4
Colorado	8	Any rate.	20	6	6
Connecticut	6	6	(o)	(e)	6
Delaware	6	6	10	6‖	3
D. of Columbia	6	10	12	3	3
Florida	8	10	20	5‖	2
Georgia	7	8	7	6‖	4
Hawaii	8	12	20(n)	6	6
Idaho	7	12	6	5	4
Illinois	5	7	20	10	5
Indiana	6	8	20	10	6
Iowa	6	8	20(d)	10	5
Kansas	6	10	5	5	3
Kentucky	6	6	15	15	5(a)
Louisiana	5	8	10	5	3
Maine	6	Any rate.	20	6(c)	6§§
Maryland	6	6	12	3	3
Massachusetts	6	Any rate.	20	6	6
Michigan	5	7	10	6	6
Minnesota	6	10	10	6	6
Mississippi	6	10	7	6	3
Missouri	6	8	10	10	5
Montana	8	Any rate.	10(b)	8	5
Nebraska	7	10	5‡‡	5	4
Nevada	7	Any rate.	6	4	4
N. Hampshire	6	6	20	6	6
New Jersey	6	6	20	6	6
New Mexico	6	12	7	6	4
New York	6	6††	20(n)	6	6§§
North Carolina	6	6	10	3*	3
North Dakota	7	12	10(m)	6	6§§
Ohio	6	8	15(p)	15	6
Oklahoma	6	10	5(h)	5	3
Oregon	6	10	10	6	6
Pennsylvania	6	6	5(f)	6‖	6
Porto Rico	6	12	(q)	(q)	(q)
Rhode Island	6§	Any rate.	20	6	6
South Carolina	7	8	10	6	6
South Dakota	7	12	10(l)	6	6
Tennessee	6	6	10	6	6
Texas	6	10	10‡‡	4	2
Utah	8	12	8	6	4
Vermont	6	6	8	6	6§§
Virginia	6	6	20	5*	2¶
Washington	6	12	6	6	3
West Virginia	6	6	10	10	5
Wisconsin	6	10	20(n)	6	6
Wyoming	8	12	21	5	8

* Under seal, 10 years. § Unless a different rate is expressly stipulated. ‖ Under seal, 20 years. ¶ Store accounts; other accounts 3 years; accounts between merchants 5 years. †† New York has by a recent law legalized any rate of interest on call loans of $5,000 or upward, on collateral security. ‡‡ Becomes dormant, but may be revived. §§ Six years from last item. (a) Accounts between merchants 2 years. (b) In courts not of record 5 years. (c) Witnessed 20 years. (d) Twenty years in Courts of Record; in Justice's Court 10 years. (e) Negotiable notes 6 years, non-negotiable 17 years. (f) Ceases to be a lien after that period, unless revived. (h) On foreign judgments 1 year. (l) Ten years foreign, 20 years domestic. (m) Subject to renewal. (n) Not of record 6 years. (o) No limit. (p) Foreign. Domestic 6 years. (q) Varies from 3 to 30 years.

Penalties for usury differ in the various States. California, Colorado, Maine, Massachusetts (except on loans of less than $1,000). Montana and Nevada have no provisions on the subject. Loss of *principal and interest* is the penalty in Arkansas and New York. Loss of *principal* in Delaware and Oregon.

Statutes of United States. (See Revised Statutes.)

Statutory.—By authority of the statute. Statutory law is law passed by the Legislature either of the nation or state. It is distinguished from common law in that it is interpreted by the judiciary, as nearly as ascertainable, according to the literal meaning intended by the legislators. (See Common Law.)

Steam Boiler Explosions:
Commission to inquire into causes of, 4213, 4434.
Examinations of inventions to prevent, referred to, 1726, 1728, 1732.

Steam Engineering, Bureau of, Navy Department. (See Bureau of Steam Engineering.)

Steam Power:
Accident in navigation resulting from criminal negligence in use of, discussed, 1253.
Use and development of, in naval warfare, discussed, 1901, 2122, 2132.

"Steam Roller" Tactics.—The action of the Republican leaders in the nominating convention of 1912 was characterized by their opponents throughout the campaign as "Steam Roller" Tactics, because it was alleged that the Committee on Credentials had arbitrarily seated contesting delegates regardless of the merits of the cases involved, and by so maneuvering had gained a majority for the platform and the candidates desired by the reactionaries.

Steamboat Inspection Service, Commerce Department. — This service is charged with the inspection of all vessels flying the United States flag which are not directly connected with the Navy Department. In addition to general inspection concerning safety, the Service investigates the serviceability of all vessels for the kind of service they are to render, sees that the accommodations for both passengers and crew are sufficient, and examines the safety of all the equipment, with especial attention to boilers. In 1916, the Service inspected and certificated 7,349 vessels, issued licenses to 18,102 officers and 24,425 seamen, tested and examined 203,017 life preservers, and reported that, on the vessels which are required to report the number of passengers they carry, 317,066,553 persons were carried. (See Commerce Department.)

Steamboat Inspection Service, discussed, 4931.

Steamboats, casualties in, discussed, 1611.

Steamship Mail Service. (See Postal Service.)

Steamships:
Australian line referred to, 4101.
Claims of German lines to interest on dues illegally exacted, 5084, 5367.
Construction of, into war vessels when needed, recommended, 2203.
Line of, between—
Havre and New York referred to, 2011, 2173.

San Francisco and Japan and China, 4101.
Naval reserve of, recommended, 5492.
Proposals for construction of iron steamships for trans-Atlantic service referred to, 4023.
Rapid service of, recommended by International American Conference, 5511.
Recommendations regarding, by President—
Harrison, Benj., 5491, 5559.
McKinley, 6340.

Steel. (See Iron and Steel.)

Ste'h-chass Indians. (See Indian Tribes.)

Steilacoom Indians. (See Indian Tribes.)

St-káh-mish Indians. (See Indian Tribes.)

Stockbridge Indians. (See Indian Tribes.)

Stockholm, Sweden, International Prison Congress to be held in, discussed, 4406.
Proceedings of, referred to, 4464.

Stockton and Stokes, claims of, 1499.
Payment of, referred to, 1720.

Stoluck-whá-mish Indians. (See Indian Tribes.)

Stone, Clay and Cement.—Stone suitable for building purposes is found in nearly all the States. In value of output for general purposes Pennsylvania takes the lead. In the matter of stone for building and monumental uses Vermont heads the list. Marketable grades of stone are really confined to a few states. Granite comes largely from the New England States, but California also ships considerable quantities. Slate is found mainly in Pennsylvania and Vermont. Marble is quarried in Vermont, Tennessee, Georgia, New York and Massachusetts.

In 1785 a marble quarry was opened at Dorset, Vt.; about 1800, marble quarrying and sawing was carried on at Marbledale, Conn., and Stockbridge, Mass. Sandstone, at present largely used for flagging, was first put on the market in the form of grindstones by John Baldwin; the first slate quarry in Vermont was opened in 1845 by Col. Allen and Caleb Ranney at Scotch Hill, Fair Haven. The granite industry had its beginning at Quincy, Mass., about 1820.

The value of the production of stone in the United States in 1914 reached the great total of $77,412,292.

Clay Products.—The clay products industries are divided into two distinct classes: (1) Brick and tile making, including paving brick and sewer pipe; (2) pottery, terra cotta, and fire-clay products, including porcelain ware, earthen and stoneware, china and sanitary ware. There were 5,037 establishments engaged in the two branches of the business when reports were made for the census of 1910. They were capitalized at $316,022,470, and gave employment to 146,786 persons, paying in salaries and wages $78,144,116. More than four-fifths (83.7 per cent.) of these were engaged in making brick and tile.

Pottery.—The art of molding clay into articles for domestic use is one of the old est of handicrafts, and doubtless developed shortly after or coincident with the carving of weapons. Specimens of clay molding carry fragments of the early history of all races. The Mound Builders of prehistoric America had distinctive pottery.

To the Chinese and the Egyptians we are indebted for a later development of earthenware fabrication. Josiah Wedgwood was the pioneer master of the ancient art in England. In 1744, Edward Heylyn, of the Parish of Bow, and Thomas Frye, of the Parish of West Ham, Essex, England, applied for a patent for the manufacture of chinaware, in which they specify that the material used is an earth produced by the Cherokee Indians of America. As early as 1765 South Carolina had a pottery which seriously threatened Wedgwood's American trade. Before 1800 the pottery business was fairly well established in Philadelphia and vicinity. The Jersey Porcelain Company of Jersey City was incorporated in 1825. In 1837 the Indiana Pottery Company was started at Troy, Ind., on the Ohio River. East Liverpool, Ohio, owes its prosperity to the discovery of potter's clay in the neighborhood by James Bennett, an English potter, who erected the first works there in 1839. Trenton, N. J., built its first pottery in 1852. The earliest ware was mostly plain white undecorated or yellow, followed by white, carrying blue designs.

The census of 1910 reported 822 establishments engaged in the manufacture of stoneware, earthenware, white and cream-colored ware, chinaware, delft and belleek-ware, porcelain electrical supplies, architectural terra cotta, fire brick, sewer pipe, etc. These turned out products valued at $76,118,861, and employed 56,168 wage-earners, to whom they paid $29,753,495 for the year.

Cement.—Two classes of cement are generally recognized in this country—hydraulic, or natural rock cement (made from a limestone containing a relatively high proportion of clay, by burning at a low heat, and grinding the product to powder) ; and Portland cement (made from an artificial mixture of carbonate of lime (either chalk, limestone or marl,) with a certain proportion of clay, burning at a white heat and grinding the clinker to powder.)

Common natural rock, or hydraulic cement, is sometimes called Rosendale cement, because it is made in large quantities near Rosendale, Ulster County, N. Y. It is also made in Pennsylvania, Kentucky and Indiana, at several points in Illinois, and around Milwaukee, Wis. Recent annual outputs of these districts were : New York, 2,500,000 barrels ; Indiana and Kentucky, 1,500,000 ; Pennsylvania, 1,340,000 ; Wisconsin, 330,000 barrels.

Portland cement was first made in England in 1824, and derives its name from its resemblance to the limestone of Portland Island, in the English channel. The industry was then taken up in Germany, where the annual output is something like 20,000 barrels, whereas England makes 9,000,000 barrels. Portland cement was first made in the United States at Copley, Pa., in 1878, and since then works have been established in more than a dozen other states.

The growth of the cement industry is one of the marvels of American progress. In 1885 we were able to make about 150,000 barrels. This amount was doubled every five years till 1900 when the demand, public and private, for concrete construction caused the production to jump to more than 11,000,000 barrels ; two years later it exceeded 17,000,000. Today the best grades of American Portland cement are as good as those produced anywhere, and in effective-

ness of equipment, extent of output, and cheapness of production, the leading Portland cement plants of this country are models for the world. Not even in the development of our iron and steel industry have American energy, resourcefulness, and mechanical ability been more strikingly displayed.

Stone River, or Murfreesboro (Tenn.), Battle of.—Oct. 30, 1862, Gen. Buell was succeeded in the command of the Army of the Ohio by Gen. William S. Rosecrans. During December the Federal army of 41,-421 infantry, 3,266 cavalry, and 2,223 artillery, with 150 guns, lay at Nashville, Tenn. The recent invasion of Kentucky by the Confederates under Gen. Bragg having proven unsatisfactory to the Confederate government, he was again ordered to the north soon after he had reached Chattanooga. By Christmas he was posted near Murfreesboro, about thirty miles southeast of Nashville, with an army of 37,000 men. Rosecrans had planned to assail the Confederate right early on the morning of Dec. 31, in front of Murfreesboro. Bragg, anticipating his design, attacked McCook on the Federal right and drove him from his position with considerable loss, including 3,000 prisoners and 28 guns. Some Federal accounts represent the Confederates as repulsed four times after their successful charge. Both armies rested on Jan. 1, 1863. On the 2d Rosecrans resumed his efforts to turn the Confederate right. Some statements are to the effect that Bragg attacked unsuccessfully. The one here followed says the Federals advanced, were forced back across Stone River, but later recovered the ground and threw up breastworks. Bragg retired from his position on the 3d and occupied Murfreesboro, which he evacuated on the 5th. He then fell back about twenty-five miles to Duck River. The Federal loss in the fighting about Murfreesboro was 1,723 killed, 7,245 wounded, and more than 3,000 prisoners—a total of about 12,000. The loss of the Confederates was about 11,000 men in killed, wounded, and missing. This battle is called by the Confederates the battle of Murfreesboro. It was one of the bloodiest of the Civil War.

Stono Ferry (S. C.), Battle of.—In the early summer of 1779 the British under Gen. Prevost advanced upon Charleston and demanded its surrender. They were driven off by the vigorous action of Pulaski, Rutledge, Moultrie, Laurens, and others. In his retreat toward Savannah, Gen. Prevost left a detachment in charge of Stono Ferry, ten miles below Charleston on the Stono River. June 20 these were attacked by Gen. Lincoln. In the absence of concerted action the assault failed and the Americans withdrew after losing 146 in killed and wounded.

Stony Creek (Canada), Battle of.—When the British were driven from Fort George, on the Niagara River, they fled westward under command of Gen. Vincent as far as Stony Creek, six miles southeast of the present city of Hamilton, and about fifty miles from Niagara River. Here they made a stand, having been reenforced by troops from Kingston. They were closely followed by 1,300 Americans under Generals Chandler and Winder. At midnight June 5, 1813, Vincent, with about 800 men, started for the American camp. The attack was made before daylight, and the combatants were unable to distinguish friend from foe. Chandler and Winder were both captured and Vincent was lost

In the woods. The British command then devolved upon Col. Harvey, who, despairing of driving the Americans from their position, withdrew from the attack while it was yet dark. The Americans fled to Forty-Mile Creek, where they were joined by 400 reenforcements. The total casualties of the battle were: Americans, 154; British, 178.

Stony Point (N. Y.), Storming of.— With a view to regaining possession of the Hudson, Gen. Clinton in June, 1779, occupied and fortified Verplanck's Point and Stony Point, garrisoning the latter with 600 men. To circumvent his movements Washington sent for Anthony Wayne and asked him if he could take Stony Point. His reply is said to have been: "I will storm hell if your excellency will plan it." Accordingly, Washington planned the assault, and on the night of July 16, 1779, Wayne, with about 800 men selected from three regiments of infantry, a detachment from West Point, and Col. Lee's light-horse, made a sudden assault upon the fort. The plans were carefully executed, the guns were carried off, and the works destroyed. The British casualties were 20 killed, 74 wounded, 58 missing, and 472 prisoners—a total loss of 624. The total American loss was only 15 killed and 83 wounded. Among the latter was Gen. Wayne. This, the boldest exploit of the Revolution, was initiated by the capture and gagging of a sentinel, the countersign having been obtained by a negro strawberry vender and by him communicated to the Americans. While the negro chatted with the sentry the latter was seized by the American advance party.

Straw Shoe Channel, steamers sailing under American flag prohibited from passing through, referred to, 3896, 3902.

Streight's Raid.— In the spring of 1863, about the time Col. Grierson's flying column of cavalry was organized at Memphis, Tenn., Col. A. D. Streight, of the Fifty-first Indiana, was permitted by Gen. Rosecrans to take a body of 1,800 cavalry from Tuscumbia, Ala., to attempt the destruction of railroads and other property in northern Alabama and Georgia. The raiders started out April 12 and were captured May 3, 1863, near Rome, Ga., having accomplished nothing. The capture was made by Forrest's cavalry.

Strict Constructionist.— In political parlance, a political party or individual insisting upon the precise application of the wording of the Constitution. The Anti-Federalists and their successors, the Democratic-Republicans, and, until very recently, the Democratic party have usually been regarded as strict constructionists.

Strike Commission:
Discussed, 5983, 7037.
Report of, transmitted, 5988.
(See also Arbitration, Labor and Labor Question.)

Strong Government Men.— A party organized in 1783 which favored a strong central government and a loose construction of the Constitution.

Subconstitutional Centennial Commission, memorial of, proposing to celebrate centennial anniversary of framing Constitution, discussed, 5118.

Subjugation.— The act of bringing another under control, usually by force of arms.

Submarine Cables. (See Ocean Cables.)

Submarine Telegraph Company, claim against United States, 6824.

Submarines.— Annalists trace the records of under-sea operations back to the days of Alexander the Great. Systematic study of attack below the water line was made as early as the thirteenth and fourteenth centuries, for several English ships were reported destroyed in 1372 by fire carried under water. The idea certainly is not a novel one, for what more natural suggestion could present itself than a thrust in the rear when a frontal attack fails against a foe. Passing over the earlier accounts of submarine boats for lack of confirmation, we find fairly reliable descriptions of such vessels in 1580, 1605, 1624, 1680, 1747, mostly built and operated in England.

The earliest attempts at submarine naval operations in America were made in 1775 by David Bushnell, who built an iron vessel shaped like a tortoise, water tight and with an air capacity sufficient for one man one hour. This was made to dive under water and propelled forward at a speed of two or three knots an hour by means of screws worked by the hands of the operator. There were automatic air tubes and a depth gauge, as well as an auger for boring holes in the hulls of vessels attacked and attaching torpedoes.

In this submarine, called the *Turtle*, Sergeant Lee was enabled to get beneath the English man-of-war *Eagle* in New York harbor. Lee's attack failed because his auger was not sharp enough to penetrate the copper-covered bottom of the *Eagle*. A later attempt to torpedo the British frigate *Cerberus*, at anchor off New London, was made in 1777, but the torpedo drifted astern and destroyed the schooner *Ramilles* and killed several men on board. This was the first vessel ever destroyed in this manner.

Between 1796 and 1810 Robert Fulton built submarine boats in America and France. On his *Nautilus* he once remained submerged five hours. His *Mute* had an armor plating and was propelled by a noiseless steam engine. Fulton's work was followed by more or less successful efforts in England, France, Germany and Russia; but the civil war in America furnished a notable stimulus to submarine architecture. A partially submerged Confederate vessel attacked the Federal *Ironsides* in 1863, and the same kind of a craft destroyed the *Housatonic* in Charleston harbor in 1864. These Confederate submarines were called "Davids," possibly in the hope that they would vanquish their giant foes of the United States Navy. Between 1878 and 1888 Garrett and Nordenfelt made successful experiments with submersible boats, and one by Gustave Zédé in 1888 was looked upon as a success; it was fifty-six feet long, thirty tons displacement, and had a speed of ten knots. George C. Baker made many submarine trips in Lake Michigan in 1892. Submarines built by Simon Lake in 1894 and 1897 remained submerged more than ten hours, and traveled 200 miles under the waters of Lake Champlain. These vessels were designed more for scientific exploration and the salvage of sunken cargoes than for offense.

Congress appropriated $200,000 in 1892 to enable the Navy Department to build and test a submarine. The plans of J. P. Holland were accepted, and the tenth improvement on this type was ordered in 1900. It is fitted with three torpedo tubes, carries the largest Whitehead tor pedoes, and makes eight to nine knots speed. Eight of these boats were put in commission in 1903. Variations in the types are designated by letters (from A to M) and the number of vessels authorized has reached fifty-nine. (See Navy, Department of.) March 25, 1915, the F-4 was submerged in Honolulu harbor, Hawaii, and her crew of twenty-one men perished.

The Great European War increased so rapidly the power and the scope of the submarine that it is impossible to forecast the limits of its development. The submarine in the war has proved to be one of the determining factors in the conflict, although it has fallen below the expectations of its most ardent panegyrists, for example, Sir Percy Scott, the English naval expert, who predicted in a letter to the London *Times* in 1914 that the under-water boat would drive the above-water boat out of existence. Among the famous exploits of submarines in the war were the sinking of the English armored cruisers *Cressy*, *Hogue*, and *Aboukir*, each above 12,000 tons, by the German U-9 within the space of an hour and a half on September 22, 1914; and the entrance of the English B-11 into the Dardanelles early in 1915, where she sank a Turkish battleship, passing under five rows of submarine mines in her dash into and from the harbor. It was the actions of the German submarines which led to the entrance of the United States into the war, Germany announcing in 1917 that all ships of any country entering the war-zone which Germany had drawn around the British Isles would be sunk on sight after Feb. 1, 1917. Previously, the British liner *Lusitania* (q. v.) had been torpedoed without warning on May 7, 1915, with the loss of over 1,000 lives, 107 of them Americans. After spirited negotiations with the United States, the Imperial German Government had agreed to cease its destruction of ships without warning, and to safeguard lives on such vessels before destroying them; but these assurances, which were never given unqualifiedly, were annulled by the announcement of the campaign beginning February 1, 1917.

The submarine is built roughly in the shape of a cigar. Types constructed in Germany in 1917 are over 300 feet in length, and have accommodations for 60 or more men. Besides being equipped with tubes for the discharge of torpedoes, which, however, seem to be limited by the nature of the submarine's structure to eight in number, most of the larger submarines are armed with a rapidfire gun, of at least 3-inch caliber; carry a wireless apparatus; have equipment for signaling both above and below the surface; and are equipped with more than one periscope. This latter is a tubular-shaped attachment which emerges from the surface when the submarine is submerged, and is fitted with lenses which enables those inside the submarine to sight objects on the surface. The compasses are gyroscope compasses, which enable the boat to be steered in any position. The submarine is submerged either by admitting water into the ballast tanks, or by inclined planes, or by both methods. The air is purified during submersion by oxylithic powder, although the method is constantly subject to change.

The methods used in the European War to foil submarine attacks are still a matter kept in religious secrecy by the various governments; but there seems to be little doubt that a most effective method has been the use of wire netting. The direct enemy most to be feared by submarines would seem to be small and light, but speedy vessels armed with a single 3-inch gun or six-pounder. Because of the extremely fragile nature of the submarine, it cannot withstand attack on the surface from even a lightly-armed vessel; and hence must attack secretly all ships except those carrying no defensive armament. The range of the submarine under the surface extends for hundreds of miles, the German submarine *Deutschland* arriving in Baltimore in July, 1916, after crossing the ocean in sixteen days, partly submerged and partly on the surface. (See *Deutschland*.) A few months later an armed German submarine arrived in New London, Connecticut. According to official tabulations of the State Department at Washington, German submarines from the beginning of the war on August 1, 1914, to a point shortly after the entrance of the United States into the conflict had sunk more than 700 vessels of neutral countries, of which number nineteen were American ships and more than 400 were Norwegian. At that time more than 250 American lives had been lost through submarine attacks upon both belligerent and neutral vessels. (See Mines.)

Subsidies to Railroads:

Subsidies to Steamships:

Subsidy.—Derived from the Latin *subsidium*, originally the troops stationed in reserve in the third line of battle, from *subsidere*, to sit down. In Europe, after the period of its first use, it meant a sum of money paid to an ally to aid in carrying on war. In England it was a special tax levied upon persons and not upon property. It has now come to mean money paid by a government to individuals or companies, such as steamship or railway in excess of the value of services rendered and in aid of individual enterprise. Railways in the United States have been assisted by state and municipal subscriptions to their bonds. National aid to railways, with the exception of the Union and Central Pacific, has been in the form of land grants. In the case of the Pacific roads, in addition to 33,000,000 acres of land, the company was granted a money subsidy of more than $25,000 a mile.

The first subsidized steamships were those of the Cunard Line, which in 1838 were allowed an annual subsidy of £81,-000 by Great Britain. Two years later agitation was begun in the United States to have steamship mail lines established on the subsidy plan, and in 1845 the Postmaster-General was authorized to make contracts for carrying foreign mail in steamships sailing under the American flag. In 1847 an act was passed requiring the Secretary of the Navy to arrange for United States steamships to carry the mail from New York to Liverpool, to the West Indies and Gulf ports, and from Panama up the Pacific coast. By 1852 the Government was paying $2,000,000 a year for foreign mail service, but Congress soon after put an end to all mail subsidies. An act of March 3, 1891, directed the Postmaster-General to pay $4 a mile run for first-class vessels for carrying foreign mails and in consideration of their use as auxiliary naval vessels.

In 1898 Senator Hanna introduced into the Senate a comprehensive bill to provide subsidies for all classes of American shipping. The bill passed the Senate in March, 1902, but failed to pass the House, although several small subsidies have been granted both before and since that date.

Subtreasury System.—The subtreasury system of the United States is an outgrowth of the panic of 1837. In his special session message to Congress that year President Van Buren strongly recommended such a system (1541). Silas Wright, of New York, introduced a bill in Congress in accordance with the President's recommendation. It prohibited Government agents from receiving anything but gold and silver. In 1840 the bill became a law and subtreasuries were established at New York, Boston, Charleston, and St. Louis, the mint at Philadelphia and the branch mint at New Orleans having been also made places of deposit. The law was repealed in 1841, and reenacted in 1846. The subtreasury at Charleston has been suspended, but subtreasuries have been established at Baltimore, Chicago, Cincinnati, and San Francisco.

Subtreasury System:

Condemnation of, referred to, 1898.

Discussed by President—

Taylor, 2556.

Tyler, 1898, 2060.

Van Buren, 1541, 1596, 1706, 1751, 1757, 1827.

Modifications in, recommended, 2556.

Sucker State.—Alternative nickname for Illinois. (See Prairie State.)

Sudan. The Sudan extends from the southern boundary of Egypt, 22° N. latitude, to the northern shore of the Albert Nyanza, 2° 19' N. latitude, and reaches from the French Sahara about 18° 15' E. (at 22° N.) to the northwest boundary of Eritrea in 38° 30' E. (at 18° N.). The greatest length from north to south is approximately 1,400 miles, and from east to west 1,200 miles. The northern boundary is the twenty-second parallel of North latitude; on the east lie the Red Sea, Eritrea and Abyssinia; on the south lie the British Protectorate of Uganda and the Belgian Congo, and on the west the French Congo.

Physical Features.—The greater portion of the region consists of the Nubian Desert on the east and the Libyan Desert on the west, divided by the fertile valley of the Nile, which is nowhere of great width.

The Nile basin covers an area of nearly 1,100,000 square miles, and while part of the basin lies in Abyssinia and Eritrea, its course from the Central African Lakes to the Mediterranean is within the British Protectorate of Uganda and Central Africa, and the Anglo-Egyptian and Egyptian dominions.

From the Ripon Falls (on the northern shore of Victoria Nyanza) to Rosetta (on the Mediterranean) the length of the waterway is stated to be 3,475 miles. Between Khartoum and Wadi Halfa occur five of the six Cataracts, the remaining (first) cataract being in Egypt at Assuan.

The western banks of the White Nile and the interior of Kordofan Province afford pasturage to countless herds of excellent cattle, and the gum forests of the latter province provide one of the principal exports of the Sudan.

Area and Population.—Area 984,520 English square miles. Estimated population 3,000,000. The inhabitants of the Anglo-Egyptian Sudan are partly Arabs, partly Negroes, and partly Nubians of mixed Arab-Negro blood, with a small foreign element, including Europeans.

Government.—The Anglo-Egyptian Sudan is administered by a Governor-General, aided, since 1910, by a Council nominated from among the Officials of the Government. The Sudan does not fall under the jurisdiction of the Mixed Tribunals of Egypt, and has its own Civil and Criminal Codes, based on those of India and Egypt.

Suez Canal.—The idea of connecting the Red Sea with the Mediterranean dates back into remote Egyptian history more than thirteen hundred years before the Christian Era. During the reign of Seti I and Rameses II a canal was dug from the Nile to Lake Timseh and thence to the Red Sea. This became choked up with sand and a new canal was begun by Necho, a son of Psammetichus I, about 600 B. C. and completed by Darius Hystaspis a hundred years later. At the beginning of the Christian Era the canal was no longer navigable, but was probably restored under Trajan. After again becoming impassable the canal was restored during the seventh century by Amru, the Mohammedan conqueror of Egypt. When Napoleon invaded Egypt in 1798-99, he ordered surveys made for a canal, but was forced to abandon the country before its completion. An international commission made preliminary surveys for a canal in 1846, but one of the engineers recommended a railroad across the isthmus and this was built by British capital in 1858.

Under the direction of Ferdinand De Lesseps plans for a canal were drawn in 1855 and submitted to an international commission. A concession was obtained from Said Pasha, Khedive of Egypt, and De Lesseps organized a stock company with £8,000,000 capital to build the canal. Work was begun April 25, 1859, and the canal was opened to traffic Nov. 17, 1869, the entire cost amounting to £16,632,953—about $80,000,000. Under the terms of the concession the Khedive received nearly one-half of the stock issued. Becoming financially embarrassed in 1875, he sold his shares to the British government for $20,-400,000. This interest is now valued at something like $170,000,000, and yields a revenue of some $5,000,000.

The length of the canal from Port Said on the Mediterranean to Port Tewfik on the Gulf of Suez is eighty-seven statute miles—sixty-six actual canal and twenty-one miles of lakes. The original width was 150 to 300 feet at the water level, seventy-two feet at the bottom, and twenty-six feet deep. Successive enlargements have increased the depth to thirty-six feet and the width to from 213 to 262 feet, permitting the passage of 15,000-ton vessels. The net tonnage of the canal during the first year of its operation was 6,576. When the practicability of the Suez route to India became known the tonnage increased by leaps and bounds till in 1911 it reached 18,324,794, more than 11,000,000 of which was British. The toll rates are $1.25 per ton.

Suffrage.—The privilege of participating in the government of a state or nation by voting at an election of officers or on a change in the fundamental law. Suffrage under the Constitution of the United States is exercised by such electors in each state as have the qualifications necessary for elector of the most numerous branch of the state legislature (15). The Constitution does not guarantee the suffrage to any citizen, but by the fourteenth and fifteenth amendments the states are forbidden to abridge the privileges or immunities of United States citizens or to deny or abridge the right of suffrage on account of race, color, or previous condition of servitude. The age of twenty-one is universally fixed upon as that when suffrage may be exercised.

In some states ability to read and write is required, in some a small property qualification or tax is imposed, while in others aliens who have declared their intention to become citizens are allowed to vote. Until the present century suffrage was greatly restricted in America. Massachusetts and New Haven Colonies for a long time allowed none but church members to vote. There have been periods in the history of nearly all the Colonies when only freeholders were allowed to vote. When the states in the Federal Union first framed their constitutions some of them retained the church-membership qualification, while others permitted suffrage to freeholders only. In 1798 Georgia abolished the property qualification, and was followed by Maryland in 1801, Massachusetts and New York in 1821, Delaware in 1831, New Jersey in 1844, Connecticut in 1845, Virginia in 1850, North Carolina in 1854, South Carolina in 1865, and Rhode Island, except in municipal elections, in 1888. The new states have mostly provided for manhood suffrage from the first. Several of the southern states have adopted methods, varying from each other, but all with the single expressed purpose of excluding negroes from the franchise and yet avoiding the constitutional consequences of discriminating "on account of race, color, or previous condition of servitude."

In four states women possess suffrage on equal terms with men, namely, in Wyoming, Colorado, Utah, and Idaho. In Kansas women can vote in school and municipal elections. Women possess school suffrage in seventeen states; namely, in Arizona, Connecticut, Illinois, Massachusetts, Michigan, Minnesota, Nebraska, New Hampshire, New Jersey, New York, North Dakota, Ohio, Oregon, South Dakota, Vermont, Washington, and Wisconsin. In addition to school suffrage Montana and Iowa permit women to vote upon the issuance of municipal bonds; while Louisiana gives to women tax-payers the right to vote on all questions concerning the expenditure of public money. A modified and restricted form of suffrage is also granted in Kentucky and Texas, so that women have either full or partial franchise in twenty-seven states of the Union. (See also Woman Suffrage.)

Suffren, The, French seamen on, accidentally killed by salute from the *United States,* 1273.

Sugar.—The term sugar, strictly applied, means cane sugar, which is manufactured from sugar cane, sugar beats, maple sap and sorghum. Up to about 1840 most of the world's sugar was manufactured from sugar cane. This plant appears to have been a native of India and to have been introduced to the rest of the world by way of China. It was introduced into Santo Domingo soon after the discovery of America, and from there spread to Cuba and was carried to Louisiana by the Jesuits in 1751. Manufacture in the United States began in New Orleans in 1794.

Cane sugar was discovered in the beet root by Andreas Sigismund, Marggraf of the Berlin Academy of Science in 1747, and its extraction was developed by both French and Germans. Experiments in the culture and manufacture of beet sugar were begun in Philadelphia in 1830 but

failed. Successive failures are reported up to 1880, when the industry seems to have been firmly established.

The Census of 1910 reported 233 establishments engaged in the manufacture of sugar, with a capital of $153,167,000, employing 15,658 persons, paying in wages and salaries $9,876,000, converting $247,-583,000 worth of raw material into finished products valued at $279,249,000.

The world's production of cane and beet sugar from 1900 to 1914 in English tons was reported by Willett & Gray of New York as follows:

Years	Cane	Beet	Total
1900....	3,056,294	5,590,992	8,647,286
1901....	3,646,059	6,066,939	9,712,998
1902....	4,079,742	6,913,504	10,993,346
1903....	4,163,941	5,756,720	9,920,661
1904....	4,234,203	6,089,468	10,323,631
1905....	4,594,782	4,918,480	9,513,262
1906....	6,731,165	7,216,060	13,947,225
1907....	7,329,317	7,143,818	14,473,135
1908....	6,917,663	7,002,474	13,920,137
1909....	7,625,639	6,927,875	14,553,514
1910....	8,327,069	6,597,506	14,914,575
1911....	8,422,447	8,560,346	16,982,793
1912....	9,066,030	6,820,266	15,886,296
1913....	9,215,637	8,965,127	18,180,764
1914....	9,865,016	8,908,470	18,773,486

Sugar. (See also Beet Sugar.)

Manufacture of—

Encouragement of, recommended, 4578.

From sorghum and sugar cane, discussed, 5383.

Manufacture of milk, in Switzerland, referred to 4979.

Placed on free list, discussed, 5626.

Probable retaliatory action of foreign governments for proposed imposition of duty on, 5910.

Protest of Germany to discriminating duty on, recommendations regarding, 5957.

Supervision provided by tariff law for domestic production of, transfer of, to Agricultural Department, recommended, 5554.

Sugar-Beet Culture, 4534, 5554, 6347.

Sugar Bounty:

Discussed, 5875, 5964.

Payment of appropriation for, contained in sundry civil bill, referred to, 6095.

Suits Against Government, act regarding bringing of, vetoed, 5682.

Sully's Hill Park. (See Parks, National.)

Sumatra, attack on American vessels by pirates on coast of, 1114, 1159.

Instructions to commander of the *Potomac,* regarding, 1138.

Sumter, Fort, Attack on. (See illustration opposite 3213.)

Sumpter, The, arrest of part of crew of at Morocco, referred to, 3345.

Sunday Laws. (See Blue Laws.)

Sunflower State.—Alternative nickname for Kansas. (See Garden State.)

Municipal Building

Sunset State.—Alternative nickname for Oregon. (See Web-Foot State.)

Superintendent of Finances. (See Finances, Superintendent of.)

Superintendent of Immigration, report of, discussed, 5877.

Superintendent of Life-Saving Service. (See Life-Saving Service.)

Superior, Lake. (See Lake Superior.)

Supervising Architect, Treasury Department.—This officer plans and supervises the construction of all buildings of the United States Government, as well as the repairs therein.

Supervision of Mail, State Department. —The Division of Mail in the Department of State was created in 1873. It has control of a general nature over the official correspondence of the Department and its representatives, and is under the supervision of the second assistant secretary of state (q. v.). (See State Department.)

Supplies, Public:
Distribution of, referred to, 141.
Officer should be placed in charge of, 141.

Supreme Court. (See Court, Supreme.)

Supreme Court Justices. (See also Judiciary.)
Salaries of, increase in, 3996.
Should be exempted from other duties, 830.

Supreme Court Reports.—The opinions and decisions of the Supreme Court are recorded in 214 volumes, including the cases decided up to October, 1908. They comprise its work from its first session in 1790 to the present time. They begin with the volume numbered 2 Dallas and include 3 volumes by Dallas, covering the period between 1790 and 1800; 9 volumes by Cranch, 1800 to 1815; Wheaton, 12 volumes, 1816 to 1827; Peters, 16 volumes, 1828 to 1842; Howard, 24 volumes, 1843 to 1860; Black, 2 volumes, 1861 to 1862; Wallace, 23 volumes, 1863 to 1875. Up to that date the reports had reached 89 volumes by the different compilers. Since 1876 the reports have been styled 90 U. S., 91 U. S., etc.; 90 U. S. was reported by Wallace; 91 to 107 U. S. was reported by William J. Otto, from 1875 to 1882; 108 to 186 U. S., between 1882 and 1902, by J. C. Bancroft Davis, and the remainder by Charles Henry Butler. (See Dallas, in Biographic Index.)

Surgeon General. (See War Department and Army.)

Surgeon General, Public Health. (See Health Service.)

Surgeon-General of Army:
Building for library of, recommended, 4657, 4833.
Ordered to accompany ex-President Jackson home, 1540.

Surplus Revenue, Distribution of.—In his annual message of Dec. 1, 1834 (page 1316), President Jackson announced the extinguishment of the public debt. The compromise tariff measure of 1832, while it made some reduction in the revenue derived from import duties, produced a surplus in the Treasury. Jackson advocated the distribution of this surplus among the states rather than the appropriation of it to other purposes. A bill providing for such disposition of the surplus was attached to the bill regulating public deposits and passed by Congress in 1836. Under this law all the money in excess of $5,000,000 in the Treasury, Jan. 1, 1837, was to be deposited with the state in proportion to their representation in the electoral college, and in four installments. The states were required to give certificates of deposit payable to the Secretary of the Treasury on demand. None of the banks selected by the Government as the custodians of public funds was under any kind of official supervision by the states which chartered them or by the General Government. The sum to be divided was $37,468,859. Three installments of the money were paid to all the states except the few that had refused to accept it on the conditions imposed. The return of these loans of the states has never been demanded.

Surplus Revenue in Treasury. (See Treasury.)

Surtax.—A tax over and above a previous tax already levied against persons or articles of the same class.

Surveyors, Public, punishment of persons interrupting in performance of the trusts confided to them, referred to and recommendation for penalty for the same, 1042.

Surveys, control and supervision of geographical and geological, discussed, 4218. (See also the several surveys.)

Susan B. Anthony Amendment.—The proposed amendment to the Constitution allowing women the same rights of suffrage as men. It has been introduced into all recent Congresses, but has either failed to come to a vote, or else has failed to receive the two-thirds vote of both Senate and House necessary to submit a proposed amendment to the Constitution for ratification by three-fourths of the states. The amendment is named after the founder of the woman suffrage movement in the United States. (See Woman Suffrage.)

Susan Loud, The, seizure of, by Spanish or Cuban authorities referred to, 2679.
Claims arising out of, referred to, 2721, 2900.

Suspension Bridge, N. Y., proclamation granting privileges of other ports to, 2859.

Susquehanna, The, repair of, referred to, 2764.

Susquehanna Company.—An organization, composed mostly of Connecticut farmers, formed in 1754 for the purpose of colonizing the Wyoming country. This was the name given to a strip of land bought by Connecticut from the Plymouth Company in 1631. Under the charter granted by James I. to the Plymouth Company in 1620, their territory extended from the Atlantic to the Pacific and from lat. 40° to 46° north. The grant of Charles II. to William Penn extended to 42° north, thus overlapping the Plymouth grant to more than the extent of the territory sold to Connecticut, which extended to 41° south. In 1754 the Susquehanna Company made a treaty with the Six Nations of Indians, securing the right to settlement upon their purchase. Charles II. confirmed the sale to Connecticut, and Pennsylvania, though disputing the sale, made no effort to prevent a settlement. The first settlers in the disputed territory were driven off by the Indians in 1763. In 1769 some forty more settlers arrived in the Wyoming region and were arrested by Pennsylvania officials. For the next six years a sort of civil warfare was kept up between the settlers of the disputed tract, and only suspended during the Revolution, after which the dispute was arranged between the states and the titles to the land confirmed. (See also Wyoming Controversy.)

Susquehanna, or Conestoga Indians. (See Indian Tribes.)

Sutler.—One who follows the Army and supplies the troops with necessities and luxuries, not as a patriotic service, nor in an official capacity, but purely for gain. (Same as Camp-Follower. Both terms are generally used in derision.)

Sutro Tunnel, referred to, 4148.

Swamp Lands. (See Lands, Swamp.)

Swash-Buckler.—One who struts in braggadocio fashion, especially a soldier who undertakes to intimidate civilians on account of assumed military authority.

Swanton, Vt., proclamation granting privileges of other ports to, 2859.

Sweden.—Sweden occupies the eastern and greater portion of the Scandinavian peninsula of northern Europe, and lies between 69° 3′ 21″-55° 20′ 18″ N. latitude and 11° 6′ 19″-24° 9′ 11″ E. longitude, with an extreme length of close on 1,000 English miles and a greatest breadth of about 250 English miles. The kingdom is bounded on the northeast by the Grand Duchy of Finland, on the east by the Gulf of Bothnia and the Baltic Sea, on the southwest by the Cattegat and Skagerrack, and on the west by the Kingdom of Norway. The coast is fringed with an island fence (skargard), the largest islands of the west coast being Orust and Tjörn, while Oland (519 square miles) and Gotland (1,220 square miles) lie off the southeast coast, in the Baltic Sea.

Physical Features.—The main Scandinavian range, known as the Kölen (keel), forms a natural boundary between Sweden and Norway from the northwestern boundary to the center of the kingdom, the greatest elevations being in the extreme north. Central Sweden consists principally of fertile and wooded plains, and includes the four great lakes of Hjälmaren, Mälaren, Vänern and Vättern. In the extreme south are the plains of Skane, consisting of rich meadow land and occasional woods of beech.

The principal rivers of the north are the Torne, Kalix, Stora and Lilla Lule (on which is the famous cataract, the Harsprang), the Pite, Skellefte, Ume and Vindel, Angerman, Indal and Ljusnan. In the southern portion are the Dal and Klar, while the short Göta contains the celebrated falls of Trollhättan. The surface of the lakes and rivers of Sweden occupies about one-twelfth of the total area of the Kingdom.

About one-seventh of the Kingdom lies within the Arctic Circle, but the country receives a large measure of protection from the western mountain barrier, and the peninsula, as a whole, is warmed by the Atlantic Drift. Compensation for the shortness of the northern summer is afforded by atmospheric refraction, which increases the time of sunshine and light, but from October or November to May or June navigation is impeded, and from December to April the coasts are ice-bound.

History.—In 1319 the Kingdoms of Sweden and Norway were united under one sovereign, but in 1397 the League of Kalmar formed tripartite kingdom under the hegemony of Denmark. Sweden broke from the League in 1523, and in 1814 the crown of Norway was ceded by Denmark to Sweden. In 1905 the King of Sweden renounced the crown of Norway.

Government.—The Government is that of a limited monarchy, hereditary in the male line (by primogeniture) of the House of Bernadotte, Prince of Ponte Corvo, who was elected to the succession by the Riksdag on Aug. 21, 1810, and ascended the throne on Feb. 5, 1818. The constitution rests upon the fundamental law of June 6, 1809, which declares the king to be irresponsible, invests in him the executive authority, and confers initiation and veto of legislation. Ruler: Gustav V., King of Sweden, of the Goths and the Vandals; born June 16, 1858; succeeded December 8, 1907.

The Riksdag consists of two elective Chambers, of which the First Chamber contains 150 members elected by the Landsting, or Councils of the Län (prefectures), on a population basis, and with eligibility confined to those of Swedish birth, aged thirty-five years, who possess real property valued at 50,000 kronor, or annual taxed incomes exceeding 3,000 kronor. The Second Chamber consists of 230 members, and are elected for a maximum of three years by universal manhood suffrage.

The country is divided into 121 judicial districts, each with a court of first instance, consisting of a judge and twelve unpaid jurymen, elected by the inhabitants. There are High Courts at Stockholm, Jönköping and Kristianstad, and a Supreme Court at the capital.

For the army and navy see Armies of the World aᵀ Navies of the World.

Population.—The country is divided into twenty-five prefectures, having a total area of 169,532 square miles. The Swedish people are Scandinavians, but the population includes, in the north, about 20,000 Finns and 7,000 Lapps. More than 99 per cent of the people belong to the Swedish Lutheran Church.

Education.—Primary education is compulsory and free, and is maintained by local taxation with State grants. Illiteracy is very rare, and good attendances at the schools are secured. In 1911 there were 15,200 primary schools, with 792,000 pupils. There are Special schools for technical instruction and navigation, and Universities at Uppsala (2,300 students) and Lund 1,250 students), as well as State and private faculties at Stockholm and Göteborg.

Production and Industry.—The common cereals and potatoes and fruits are grown and the live stock includes horses, cattle, sheep, pigs, reindeer, goats and fowls. The forests cover more than half the area of the kingdom, and consist of pine, birch and fir, producing timber, wood pulp, pitch, tar and fuel. In 1911 nearly 72,000 persons were employed in the various timber, wood work and wood pulp industries, the combined output being valued at close on 331,-000.000 kronor.

The kingdom is rich in minerals, including iron of excellent quality (Dannemora iron being converted into the finest steel) ; gold and silver in small quantities ; copper, lead, nickel, zinc, cobalt, alum, sulphur, porphyry and marble.

In addition to the industries in connection with the production of the forests and mines, there are flour and sugar mills, breweries and distilleries, tanneries and shoe factories, cotton and wool spinning and weaving establishments. The industrial output is considerable, and may be valued at close on 220,000,000 kronor annually.

Railways, Etc.—At the end of 1912 there were 14,300 kilometers of railway open, of which 4,700 kilometers were the property of the State. There were 3,837 postoffices in 1912 and 6,600 miles of telegraph line (exclusive of railway telegraph lines). The Mercantile Marine of Sweden in 1911 consisted of 969 steam vessels of 852,520 tons, and 471 sailing vessels of 118,138 tons.

Finances.—The annual average expenditure for six years ending 1914 was 243,-322,600 kronor, and the revenues for the same time averaged 244,489,000 kronor. The national debt was stated Jan. 1, 1913, as 602,000,000 kronor. Of this total almost the whole was raised for and expended in the construction of railways, which produced a net revenue in 1912 (after providing for working expenses, interest and amortization) of 20,295,000 kronor. The unit of value, the krona, is equivalent to $0.26,8 in United States money.

Cities.—Capital, Stockholm; population (1912) 350,955. In addition to the capital, there were (1912) twenty-nine towns with a population exceeding 10,000.

Trade with the United States.—The value of merchandise imported into Sweden from the United States for the year 1913 was $12,104,366, and goods to the value of $11,-174,419 were sent thither—a balance of $929,947 in favor of the United States.

Sweden and Norway (see also Bergen):

Claims of, against United States, referred to, 1172.

Claims of United States against, 867, 1109.

Payment of, 867, 1112.

Commercial relations with, 820.

Consul of, to United States, exequatur to, revoked, 3626.

Revocation annulled, 3630.

Ericsson, John, restoration of remains of, to Sweden discussed, 5547.

Famine in, referred to, 3799.

Fugitive criminals, convention with, for surrender of, 3114, 5871.

Gothenburg system of regulating liquor traffic in, report on, transmitted, 5785.

Interference with the vessels of the United States. (See *Admiral P. Tordenskiold*, The.)

Minister of United States to—

Nomination of, 318.

Transfer of, to Bogota, referred to, 3665.

Missionaries of Sweden, murder of, in China discussed, 5868.

Naturalization treaty with, 4033, 4142.

Postal convention with, 4203.

Treaty with, transmitted and discussed, 566, 919, 959, 962, 3114, 5871.

Commissioner to negotiate, nominated, 254.

Vessels of, claims of, for reduction in tonnage dues, 5494, 5621.

Vessels of Norway—

Discriminating duties on suspended by proclamation, 665.

Interfered with by United States. (See *Admiral P. Tordenskiold*, The.)

Reciprocal rights for, requested, 671, 707.

Vessels of United States seized or interfered with by. (See Claims against.)

Vice-Consul of, to United States, exequatur of, revoked, 3627.

Revocation annulled, 3630.

Sweden and Norway, Treaties with.—The treaty of amity and commerce of 1783 expired in 1796 by its own limitations. Some of its sections were revived by the treaty of 1816, which, in turn, expired by its own limitations in 1826, and was replaced by the treaty of commerce and navigation of 1827. By it freedom of commerce and trade was accorded to both nations, and for the ships of the island of St. Bartholomew, which was included. Equable imposition of charges, tolls, dues, and imposts was secured for the vessels of both nations; imports were to be taxed without regard to the nationality of the carrying vessel; and the coastwise trade was excluded from the terms of the treaty. The consular office was created and provided for as in consular conventions. Humane provisions were made for the relief of the shipwrecked and for ships in distress. A naturalization convention was concluded in 1869. Upon the dissolution of the union of Norway and Sweden, the Swedish government agreed to continue in force and abide by all treaties with the United States. (For the extradition terms of the treaty of 1893, see Extradition Treaties.)

Swift & Co., vessels purchased for Peru by, from United States detained, 3831.

Swin-á-mish Indians. (See Indian Tribes.)

Swine Products. (See Animals and Animal Products.)

Swiss Confederation. (See Switzerland.)

Swiss System of Military Training.—During the agitation in the United States for universal military training, arising as a result of the European War, much interest was manifested in the system of military training as practised in Switzerland. Switzerland has no standing army, but military training is compulsory upon every citizen. (Switzerland, having no seacoast, has naturally no navy.) Switzerland, of about the same size and population as the State of Massachusetts, by virtue of its present system, completed in the year 1907, can muster almost immediately upon call a half million trained soldiers, with a larger number in reserve.

The Swiss boy begins his training for future service at the age of 8, when he begins a carefully-planned system of gymnastics. At the age of 11, he joins a cadet corps, in which membership is voluntary, but well-nigh universal. In the cadet corps, he receives his first practice in the "setting-up" exercises, and is put through simple drills. Each corps has a uniform of its own design, although the design is usually the same in each particular locality; and the state furnishes assistance only in the shape of the rifle and the ammunition used by the corps. From the age of 16-20, the Swiss youth is a member of a voluntary preparatory military organization, like the cadet corps, except for the fact that the rifle used is the standard army musket and the marksmanship practice becomes serious.

It is at the age of 20 that the Swiss youth enters upon compulsory military service. First, he must pass a physical and literary examination, and if he is rejected as unfit for service, he becomes liable to a rather severe special military tax. He receives his instruction at a field camp something like our own Plattsburg (q. v.), where the recruits are subdivided into the various branches of the service for which they are best qualified. This preliminary training lasts for a period of between 60 and 75 days, according to the branch of service, and during that time the recruit receives all his expenses and a pay of ten cents a day. Until the age of 32, these men are called together for sixteen days' additional training every year or two years, according to the branch of the service for which they have been trained. Between the ages of 32 and 40, the Swiss is a member of the Landwehr, or First Reserve, and after that of the Landsturm, or last reserve. Appointment as officers is open to men in the ranks. (See Compulsory Military Service; Australian System of Military Training; Preparedness.)

Switzerland.—The Federated Cantons of Switzerland lie in Central Europe between 45° 49′ 2″-47° 48′ 32″ N. latitude and 5° 57′ 26″-10° 29′ 40″ E. longitude, and are bounded on the north by the German Empire, on the east by the Austrian Empire and the Principality of Liechtenstein, on the south by the Kingdom of Italy, and on the west by the French Republic. The area is given as 15,950 square miles.

Physical Features.—Switzerland is the most mountainous country in Europe, having the Alps, covered with perennial snow and glaciers, and rising from 5,000 to 15,217 feet above the level of the sea, along the southern and eastern frontiers, and throughout the chief part of the interior, and the Jura Mountains in the northwest. The main chain of the Alps occupies the whole of southern Switzerland, the highest peaks being the Dufourspitze of Monte Rosa (15,217 feet), the Don of the Mischabel range (14,942 feet), and the Finsteraarhorn of Bernese Oberland (14,026 feet). The highest summit of Europe (Mont Blanc, 15,782 feet) is in the Pennine Alps, across the French frontier. The Jura Mountains rise between the valleys of the Rhine and Rhone and form a natural barrier between France and Switzerland, the highest peaks being Mont Tendre (5,512 feet) and the Dôle (5,505 feet); while the highest peak of the range, Crêt de la Neige (5,653 feet), like that of the Alps, is in French territory.

Three great rivers rise in the mountains of Switzerland, the Rhone, Rhine, and Aar, while the Thur is a Swiss tributary of the Rhine. The Lakes of Switzerland include Geneva (225 square miles) in the southwest, and Constance (208 square miles) in the northeast, neither of which is wholly

Swiss; while Neuchâtel (93 square miles) is entirely within Swiss territory; Maggiore is partly Italian; Lucerne and Zurich are entirely Swiss; Lugano is mainly Swiss; Thun and Bienne lie wholly within the Canton of Berne; Zug lies in three of the northern cantons; Brienz, in the Canton of Berne; Morat lies in the Cantons of Fribourg and Vaud; Wallensee is in St. Gall and Glarus · and Sempach in the Canton of Lucerne.

History.—The Swiss Confederation is a collection of free States drawn together for mutual protection and for the preservation of their independence. The States so combined were at one time part of Germany, Italy or Burgundy, and have been in alliance since the thirteenth century; and to that alliance other States have been attracted. In 1291 the league consisted of the present Cantons of Schwyz, Uri and Unterwalden, to which five others were joined between 1332 and 1353. To these eight Cantons five more were added between 1481-1513, six in 1803, and three in 1815, in which year the perpetual neutrality and inviolability of Switzerland were guaranteed by Austria-Hungary, the United Kingdom, Portugal, Prussia and Russia, and a Federal Pact was drawn up at Zurich and confirmed by the Congress of Vienna. This Pact formed the basis of the Federal Constitution until 1848, when a new constitution was adopted by a majority of the Swiss people, and of the Cantons and demi-Cantons, and in the same manner, on May 29, 1874, the present constitution was ratified, since which date there have been fifteen partial revisions of the constitution, similarly ratified.

Ethnography.—The people of Switzerland, numbering 3,753,283, comprise four nationalities, distinguished by their language into German, 71 per cent; French, 21 per cent; Italian, 6 per cent; and Ronmashe (in the Grisons), 2 per cent.

Government.—Under the Constitution the Federal Government is supreme in external affairs, and regulates the army, postal and telegraph systems, the mint and paper currency and the systems of weights and measures, while it provides for a national revenue, regulates the tariff, and has power to legislate in matters of sanitation, citizenship, civil and penal law, copyright, bankruptcy, patents, universities and certain public works, such as the forest service, waterways and railways. The legislative authority is entrusted to a Federal Assembly of two chambers which elects a Federal Council as an executive authority. The Federal Assembly also elects for one year a President of the Swiss Confederation and a Vice-President of the Federal Council. The election takes place annually in December and the President and Vice-President take office on January 1st. The Vice-President is eligible for the office of President and is generally elected in succession. President (Jan. 1-Dec. 31, 1914): M. Motta.

The Bundesversammlung, or Assemblée fédérale, consists of two houses, the Ständerat or Conseil des états and the Nationalrat or Conseil National. The Ständerat consists of forty-four representatives, two from each Canton, chosen by the people in the majority (but by the Cantonal legislature in six) of the Cantons. The Nationalrat contains 189 members elected by the people of each Canton for three years, on a population basis of one for each 20,000 inhabitants. Electors are all adult male citizens, and all electors (except the clergy) are eligible. Parliament meets three or four times annually at the capital, and legislation may proceed in either house, while a referendum to the electors may be secured by the petition of 30,000 electors or upon the request of eight Cantons.

The Bundesversammlung in common session of the two houses elects the Federal Executive (the Bundesrat, or Conseil fédéral), consisting of seven members elected for three years. The President of the Confederation (Bundespräsident) is chosen annually from amongst the seven members of the Federal Council and always holds the portfolio of Foreign Affairs, the remaining portfolios being redistributed annually amongst the remaining members of the Council.

The Federal Supreme Court (Bundesgericht, or Tribunal fédéral) consists of twenty-four full members (and nine substitutes) elected for six years by the two houses of the Federal Parliament, which also elects the President and Vice-President of the Tribunal for terms of two years.

Each of the twenty-two Cantons (Unterwalden, Appenzell and Bâle being subdivided into sub-Cantons, making 25 Canons and sub-Cantons) is divided into administrative districts under prefects appointed by the Cantonal authorities, or by the people of the districts, and each canton has a legislature, executive and judiciary. The cantons are sovereign states (within the restrictions of the Federal Constitution), and federal citizenship can only be obtained by an alien by means of admission to one of the political communes and by the confirmation of such naturalization by the Cantonal authorities and the previous consent of the Federal Council. (For the army, see Armies of the World.)

Education.—Education is controlled by the Cantonal and Communal authorities, and there is no Federal organization. Primary education is free and compulsory, and illiteracy is rare, especially in the Protestant Cantons. The school age varies, but is generally from six to fifteen years. Special schools: There is a Federal technical high school at Zurich of architecture, civil, mechanical and agricultural engineering, chemistry, forestry, mathematics, physics and science, with 1,333 students (466 foreigners) in 1911; and at Lausanne there is a Cantonal school of engineering. There are Universities at Bâle (founded in 1460), Zurich, Berne, Geneva, Fribourg (Catholic), Lausanne, and Neuchâtel, some of these having earlier foundations as académies. There is also a law school at Sion. The matriculated students in 1911 numbered 6,600, of whom 2,000 were women.

Finance.—The average annual expenditure for the five years ending with 1912 was 134,056,373 francs, and the revenues for the same years averaged 134,063,804 francs.

Production and Industry.—The total area of the Confederation is estimated at 9,900,000 English statute acres, of which 5,682,214 acres were cultivated (Census of 1912) and 2,232,359 acres were woods and forests. All the common cereals are produced and the vineyards yielded 16,499,174 gallons of wine in 1911. Horses, cattle, sheep, goats and pigs are raised.

The area of the forests exceeds 2,100,000 acres (more than one-fifth of the area of the country), of which two-thirds are communal and cantonal property and one-third in private ownership. In 1910 nearly 2,000,000 cubic meters of timber were cut, and the industry employed nearly 20,000 persons.

Gold, silver, lead, iron, copper and coal are found, but the only important industries are asphalt in the Val de Travers of Neuchâtel, and the saline works on the Rhine. There are numerous mineral springs. Mining and quarrying employed 13,000 persons in 1910. Textiles, watchmaking, embroidery, machinery, chocolate, shoemaking, straw-plaiting, wood-carving, and various agricultural factories for condensed milk, cheese and soups and preserved meats, in addition to breweries, and distilleries and printing establishments, employed over 250,000 persons in 1910.

Railways.—In 1911 there were 3,154 miles of railway open and working, carrying 17,500,000 tons of goods, and 98,500,000 passengers, the gross receipts being 202,615,000 francs (1910) and the working expenses 136,332,000 francs.

Cities.—Capital of the Swiss Confederation, Berne. Population (1910) 85,650. In 1910 there were twenty-four communes with populations exceeding 10,000.

Trade with the United States.—The value of merchandise imported from the United States into Switzerland for the year 1913 was $826,549, and goods to the value of $23,260,180 were sent thither—a balance of $22,433,631 in favor of Switzerland.

Switzerland (see also Berne):

American citizens of Hebrew persuasion in, discriminated against 3123.

Claims of, against United States, 5199.

Consul of United States in, charges against character of, refuted, 3718.

Consuls of United States requested by, to protect citizens of, in countries where it is not represented, 4627.

Convention with, 1406, 2356, 2414, 2634, 2723.

Discussed, 2634, 2723.

Copyright privilege extended by proclamation, 5582.

Referred to, 5625.

Floods in, referred to, 3885.

Fruits, American, restrictions upon importation of, into, discussed, 6331.

Fugitive criminals, convention with, for surrender of, 2356.

Immigration questions with, 4520, 4627, 4715.

Milk sugar manufactured in, referred to, 4979.

Minister of, to United States, elevated to plenipotentiary mission, 4718.

Naturalization question with, 4715, 6337.

Postal convention with, 3775, 3883, 4250.

President of, member of claims commission between United States and Chile, 5867.

Proposition of, to extend Red Cross compact in Spanish-American War discussed, 6336.

Treaty with—

To be negotiated, 4759.

Transmitted, 2356.

Switzerland, Treaties with.—The convention of friendship, commerce, and extradition of 1850 ran until 1899, when notice was given of intention to terminate some of its provisions. Others were terminated by the treaty of 1900. Those which persist provide for personal and property privileges of the citizens of the one country residing and trading in the country of the other, with all of the rights, privileges, and immunities of the citizens of the country. Freedom of conscience is granted to all; the right to hold, possess, acquire, and to alienate property, immunity from military service, and enforced military contributions, and free and open access to courts of justice are secured.

The taxes upon citizens shall be equitable. Passports shall be supplied in order to establish the character and the citizenship of persons traveling between the two republics. The disposal, acquisition, and inheritance of property shall be free, easy, and unhindered. When an heir to property is disqualified from holding it by reason of his alienage, the heir or other successor shall be granted the time permitted by the canton in which the property is situated to dispose of the same. Consuls shall be appointed under conditions common to consular conventions. (For terms of the extradition treaty of 1900, see Extradition Treaties.)

Arbitration of international differences on the lines laid down by The Hague Convention of 1899 was agreed to by treaty signed at Washington, Feb. 29, 1908.

Sydney, New South Wales, international exhibition in, discussed, 4519, 4559, 4625.

Syndicalism. (See Socialism.)

Tacoma, Wash., act granting use of lands to, for purpose of public park, vetoed, 5282.

Tactics.—In military parlance, the planning of military and naval action, especially that preparatory for battle; the object being to out-general and out-maneuver the enemy, rather than rely wholly upon superior strength and equipment. (See Maneuvering.)

Tacubaya, American ministers assemble in, 935. (See also Panama, Isthmus of.)
Congress indefinitely postponed, 951.
Instructions to, referred to, 997.

Taft, William H.—1909-1913.
Thirty-first Administration—Republican.
Vice-President—James S. Sherman.
Secretary of State—
  Philander C. Knox.
Secretary of the Treasury—
  Franklin MacVeagh.
Secretary of War—
  Henry L. Stimson.
Attorney-General—
  George W. Wickersham
Postmaster-General—
  Frank H. Hitchcock.
Secretary of the Navy—
  George von Lengerke Meyer.
Secretary of the Interior—
  Walter L. Fisher.
Secretary of Agriculture—
  James Wilson.
Secretary of Commerce and Labor—
  Charles Nagel.

Platform.—The platform of the Republican party in the Presidential campaign of 1908 on which Judge Taft based his candidacy declared for a downward revision of the Dingley Tariff Law; for statutory reform in injunction procedure so as to provide notice before the issuance of the writ; for Federal incorporation of interstate commerce corporations; for postal savings banks; for the settling of constitutional questions regarding the income tax; for the encouragement by mail subsidies of Pacific and South American lines; for the regulation of railroad stock and bond issues by the Interstate Commerce Commission, and the incidental physical valuation of railroads; for the legalizing of rate agreements when sanctioned by the Commission; for the reorganization of certain Bureaus so as to facilitate the execution of the Interstate Commerce and Anti-trust Laws; and for the continuance of the Roosevelt policies regarding the conservation of our natural resources. Summarizing his purposes, Judge Taft said: "The practical, constructive and difficult work, therefore, of those who follow Mr. Roosevelt is to devise the ways and means by which the high level of business integrity and obedience to law which he has established may be maintained and departures from it restrained without undue interferences with legitimate business."

Tariff Revision.—The first work to which the new administration addressed itself was tariff revision. Until Aug. 5, 1909, Congress in special session wrestled with its intricacies. The Payne-Aldrich Bill, passed on that date, was a downward revision, though in the President's estimation not sufficiently downward, and by its creation of a Court of Customs appeals and a Tariff Board was a distinctively progressive measure. The provision for an income tax on corporations with its incidental assurance of control and surveillance was the answer to the President's message of June 16, 1909 (page 7389). The attacks on the

measure drew from the President his speech at Winona, Minn. (page 7393), the most careful and thorough discussion of the subject which has appeared. (See Tariff; Income Tax.)

Postal Savings Bank.—The Postal Savings Banks were established, one in each of the forty-eight States, on Jan. 1, 1911, under the law passed June 25, 1910. The success of the plan has led the Postmaster-General to recommend extending the system to five hundred localities. (See Postal Savings Banks.)

Reform in Injunction Procedure.—The President urged upon Congress in his Inaugural Address and in his First and Second Annual Messages the passage of a law which would forbid the issuing of an injunction by any Federal Court without previous notice and hearing of the parties to be enjoined, unless in the Court's discretion the requisite delay would result in irreparable injury to the complainant (pp. 7378, 7431, 7524). (See Injunctions; Boycott.)

Federal Incorporation.—In his Message on the anti-trust law (page 7449), the President discussed the causes of the tendency of modern business to amass in ever-growing units, analyzed the beneficial and baneful effects of such amalgamation, defined direct and indirect restraint of trade, outlined the true intent and scope of the Sherman law as affecting monopolistic combinations, but not those actuated merely by desire to reduce production cost, condemned the Knight Sugar Trust decision, argued against amending the law, mentioned the inquiry into companies suspected of violations of the law which was contemplated by the Department of Justice if funds became available, and recommended the enactment of a law which would provide Federal charters for interstate commerce corporations and assure governmental supervision and control. (See Interstate Commerce.)

The Income Tax.—On the question of the income tax the President in his Message of June 16, 1909 (page 7389), recommended that, though he was convinced of the constitutionality of such a tax, it would be wiser not to contradict the Supreme Court by reenacting a law which in the Pollock case it had declared unconstitutional, but by a two-thirds vote to submit to the States an amendment to the organic law expressly conferring the requisite power. (See Amendments; Income Tax and Income Tax Cases.)

Interstate Commerce Law.—To make the Interstate Commerce Law a "complete and effective measure for securing reasonableness of rates and fairness of practices in the operation of interstate railroads, without undue preference to any individual or class over any others," adequate to "prevent the recurrence of many of the practices which have given rise in the past to so much public inconvenience and loss," the President on Jan. 7, 1910 (page 7441), sent to Congress a special message in which he recommended the creation of a new Court, to be called the United States Court of Commerce and to have jurisdiction over proceedings brought by carriers to nullify orders of the Interstate Commerce Commission. The President pointed out that carriers by injunctions could and did suspend the commission's orders for months and even years, and that few orders of any consequence escaped such tactics. By means of the new Court such proceedings could be promptly and consistently disposed of by Judges deeply versed in the intricacies of the subject. Its decisions were to be final excepting review by the Supreme Court, and even if it appealed from the order could not be stayed except by the Supreme Court. The President recommend-

EXTENT OF THE UNITED STATES DURING THE ADMINISTRATION OF PRESIDENT TAFT, 1909-1913.

(NOT INCLUDING TERRITORIES)

MAINE 1820

VT. 1791

N. H. 1788

MASS. 1788

CONN. 1788

R. I. 1790

NEW YORK 1788

N. J. 1787

DEL. 1787

MD. 1788

PENNSYLVANIA 1787

WEST VIRGINIA 1863

VIRGINIA 1788

NORTH CAROLINA 1789

SOUTH CAROLINA 1788

GEORGIA 1788

FLORIDA 1845

OHIO 1803

KENTUCKY 1792

TENNESSEE 1796

ALABAMA 1819

MICHIGAN 1837

INDIANA 1816

ILLINOIS 1818

MISSISSIPPI 1817

WISCONSIN 1848

MISSOURI 1821

ARKANSAS 1836

LOUISIANA 1812

IOWA 1846

MINNESOTA 1858

KANSAS 1861

OKLAHOMA 1907

TEXAS 1845

NORTH DAKOTA 1889

SOUTH DAKOTA 1889

NEBRASKA 1867

COLORADO 1876

NEW MEXICO 1912

MONTANA 1889

WYOMING 1890

UTAH 1896

ARIZONA 1912

WASHINGTON 1889

IDAHO 1890

OREGON 1859

NEVADA 1864

CALIFORNIA 1850

FLAG OF 1913

MADE BY BUREAU OF NATIONAL LITERATURE (INC.)

ed that the Commission be empowered to commence proceedings on its own initiative; that the law be amended so as to permit the changing of rates only after submission of the schedule to the Commission. in order that, if unsatisfactory, the proposed change might be stayed pending investigation; that its duties be confined to quasi-judicial functions, utilizing the Department of Justice to prosecute and defend suits under the law. By an act passed June 18, 1910, Congress put on the statute books the recommendations above summarized, but rejected two other suggestions of the President, first, that the issue of railroad securities be made subject to the Commission, and second, that rate agreements under certain circumstances be permitted. (See Interstate Commerce; Common Carriers.)

Conservation.—In the President's speech at St. Paul, Minn. (page 7555), he took the high ground that, as the successor to Theodore Roosevelt, he could not be other than an earnest advocate of every measure calculated "to prevent the continuance of the waste which has characterized our phenomenal growth in the past." But "conservation is national. It affects every man of us, every woman, every child. What I can do in the cause I shall do, not as President of a party, but as President of the whole people. Conservation is not a question of politics, or of factions, or of persons. It is a question that affects the vital welfare of all of us, of our children and our children's children." The President's conservation address, like his tariff speech, is replete with definite and detailed recommendations showing a minute study of the subject. The agricultural and mineral land laws should be left unchanged; the funds available for reclamation should be concentrated on selected projects, $20,000,000 in bonds having been authorized for engineering purposes; the states severally must control the handling of the seventy-five per cent of existing forests which is privately owned; withdrawals had been legalized by a definite statute; oil, gas and phosphate lands, and the coal fields of Alaska should be conserved by a leasing system; and water-power sites should be conserved by leasing the Federal Government's riparian rights to users or transferring such rights to the states so as to complete their title to and control of both stream and site. (See Lands, Public; Conservation Commission.)

Ship Subsidy.—In President Taft's Inaugural and two Annual Messages he discussed the question of subsidizing steamship lines to South America under conditions assuring publicity by giving to them the profit on mail carried by them, urging that if action were not immediately taken we would be the only nation unable to avail ourselves of the Panama Canal when completed and that should war come we would find ourselves destitute of sailors and shipping, without which the navy is like arms without a body. The question of the subsidy was vigorously discussed in the last session of the Sixty-first Congress, but no action was taken. (See pp. 7374, 7435, 7503.) (See Subsidy; Merchant Marine.)

Navy Personnel Improved.—In order to match the superb vessels of the navy with efficiency in the personnel, Congress passed measures submitted and urged by President Taft in his Message of Feb. 25, 1910, which will reduce the ages at which line officers become captains and rear-admirals. (See page 7470.) (See Navy; Navy, Dept. of.)

Canadian Reciprocity.—On Jan. 26, 1911, the President sent to Congress a special message transmitting an agreement between the Department of State and the Canadian Government obligating both parties to attempt to secure legislation which will reciprocally lower tariff rates on about six hundred items. (See page 7581.) In urging the passage of the treaty (which, as affecting tariff legislation, will have to pass both Houses) the President recalled Canada's neighborliness and friendship as shown in the settlement of all disputes and in the cooperation between the boards of railway control on both sides the border, dwelt upon the necessity of conserving our own resources by buying those of our neighbor, pointed out the similarity in labor and transportation conditions here and there, mentioned the harm to Americans which will accrue if the "imperial preference" doctrine becomes a tenet of Canadian political faith, maintained that the accession of a new supply of raw materials would inure to the benefit of all sections and, in prophetic vein, characterized the agreement as a step toward closer friendship between peoples related by blood, common sympathies and identical moral and social ideas. Animals, poultry, food stuffs, products of farm, garden and dairy, fruits, fish, oysters, salt, mineral waters, lumber, machinery, minor metal manufactures, coal, meats, flour, meal, farming utensils, fruit trees and Portland cement are the articles on which the tax is to be lowered or entirely removed. The effect of the proposed treaty, according to 1910 figures, would be to decrease the revenue of the United States by $4,849,933, and that of Canada by $2,560,579. (See Reciprocity.)

Turning to matters of administration, Taft took judicial appointments out of politics; made the taking of the thirteenth census non-political (page 7539); recommended and by executive order effected the extension of the civil service (pp. 7424, 7549); instituted a vigorous inquiry into the government service in the interest of economy and efficiency, which resulted in a $52,000,000 saving in the 1911 estimates (pp. 7424, 7550); advocated as an improvement of efficiency the giving of pensions to superannuated clerks (pp. 7425, 7551); and, in his message regarding the rivers and harbors bill of 1910, declared his intention of vetoing any future bill which does not concentrate the moneys thereby provided on a certain few projects which may then be carried to completion instead of diffusing at great cost temporary and futile activity over a multitude of projects (page 7489). President Taft was renominated by his party, but Mr. Roosevelt's candidacy split the party and resulted in the election of Wilson.

Taft, William H.:

Accident pensions. (See Pensions.)

Agricultural credits, European, investigated, 7775, 7819.

Agricultural lands. (See Lands, Public.)

Agriculture, Department of—
  Influence on foreign trade, 7374.
  Operations of, in 1910, 7536.

Agriculture, diversification of, in South, discussed, 7537.

Alaska—
  Coal lands in, acreage, tonnage, value and conservation of, discussed, 7564, 7720.
  Commission government suggested for, 7722.
  Governor and council urged for, 7436, 7535.

Chile, arbitration of American claims against, by Edward VII, 7417.

Cordiality of relations with, 7498.

China—
Civil war in, early end to, urged by United States, 7771.
Currency reform in, 7418, 7497.
Indemnity from, remitted for aid of students, 7419.
Japan not granted mining monopoly by, 7420.
Likin abolished in, 7418.
Loans to, 7497, 7664, 7666.
Open-door principle applied to railroad loan in, 7419, 7496.
Opium evil suppressed in, 7419.
Policy of United States in, 7772.
Railroad loans arranged in, 7419, 7496.
Representative government established in, 7497.
Russo-Japanese alliance's effect on, 7498.
Situation in, discussed, 7784.

Chugach Forest Reserve (Alaska), elimination of 12,800 acres from, explained, 7599.

Civil pensions approved, 7754.

Civil retirement and contributory pension system, 7697.

Civil Service—
Discussed, 7753, 7755.
Economy and efficiency in, 7698.
Pensions for age and disability, 7425, 7551, 7697, 7751, 7754.
Post-offices, local, should be placed under, 7739.

Civil Service Commission—
Oath-administering powers should be conferred on, 7475.
Operation of, in 1910, discussed, 7549.
Quarters for, should be improved, 7439.

Civil Service Law—
Extension of, to Washington offices of five departments, recommended, 7549.
Reclassification of employees under, recommended, 7424.

Claims, Pan-American agreements for arbitration of pecuniary, discussed, 7499.
Payment of, immediately upon decision by Court of Claims, recommended, 7522.

Coal and coal lands. (See Lands, Public.)

Colombia—
Arbitration between Haiti and, 7657.
Relations of United States with, discussed, 7771, 7853.

Colorado River—
Improvements of, 7722, 7780.
Parking of Grand Canyon recommended, 7536.

Works to prevent overflow of, recommended, 7544.

Combinations, monopolistic, failures outweigh successes in attempts to make, 7451.

Commerce and Labor, Department of—
Bureaus consolidated in, 7437.
Foreign trade factor, 7374.
Merit system should be extended to, 7538.
Operation of, in 1910, discussed, 7538.
Reorganization of, recommended, 7368.

Commerce Court—
Decisions sustained by Supreme Court, 7757.
Defended, 7755.
Formation of, to handle certain interstate commerce cases, recommended, 7442.
Jurisdiction and procedure of, outlined, 7443, 7757.

Commerce, foreign—
Chambers of, suggested, 7674.
Need for greater government effort in, 7789

Congo, prospect of reform in, discussed, 7412.
Report on conditions in, transmitted, 7393.

Congress, Cabinet officers should have seats in, 7811.

Congressmen, publicity regarding campaign funds of, recommended, 7439.

Conservation of natural resources, policy of, discussed, 7370, 7436, 7459, 7555, 7573, 7816.

Consular Service—
Legislation needed for, 7421.
Merit system should be extended to, 7504, 7768.

Copyrights, conventions with South American republics for protection of, 7499.

Corporation Tax—
Provided for, 7406, 7510.
Urged, 7391.

Cost of living, international commission on, 7724.

Costa Rica and Panama, arbitration between, 7657.

Council of national defense recommended, 7697.

Courts, Federal, reforms in, discussed, 7430, 7522, 7810.

Crop of 1910, value and effect of, upon business conditions, discussed, 7536.

Cuba, progress of sanitary and other improvements in, 7416.
Termination of provisional government in, 7388.

Grand Canyon of the Colorado, parking of, urged, 7393, 7536.

Great Britain—
Arbitration with—
Canada boundary dispute, 7495.
North Atlantic Fisheries Dispute, 7779.
Pecuniary claims—
Discussed, 7495.
Terminated, 7778.
Treaty of, 7617.
King of, coronation of, 7668.

Great Lakes, State reasons for not constructing gunboat on, transmitted, 7481.

Guantanamo, construction of naval base at, recommended, 7531.

Haiti and Colombia, arbitration between, 7657.

Health, Bureau of, formation of, recommended, 7438, 7543.
Conflict of rival schools regarding, deprecated, 7543.

Honduras—
Financial assistance to, by United States, 7500.
Treaty proposed with, 7663.

Immigration—
Asiatic—
Rigorous enforcement of prohibition against, recommended, 7372.
Diversion of, from New York to South and West, recommended, 7543.
Literacy test for, disapproved, 7847.
Restriction of, urged, 7543.

Imperial Valley, improvement of, 7780.

Inaugural Address, 7368.

Income tax, urged and discussed, 7390.

Incorporation, Federal, of Trusts. (See Trusts.)

Indian Commissioner, increased salary urged for, 7817.

Indians, problem of, discussed, 7817.

Industrial Property Union, protection of, 7671.

Industrial relations, commission on, 7725.

Inheritance tax urged, 7370, 7390.

Injunctions discussed and recommendations concerning procedure governing, 7378, 7431, 7524.

Interior, Department of—
Business of, nearer up to date than ever before, 7533.
Problems of, discussed, 7816.
Provision for review by court, of land decisions of, recommended, 7489, 7531.
Recommendations of (1910), to Congress, partly approved, 7464.
Secretary of, legislation empowering, to withdraw lands from entry, recommended, 7464.

International Congress of School Hygiene, appropriation urged for, 7841.

Interstate Commerce Commission—
Powers of, increase and limitations of, discussed, 7441, 7445, 7552.
Reorganization of, discussed, 7368.

Interstate Commerce Law—
Amendments suggested for, 7444-7448.
Discussed, 7488, 7552.
Message on, 7441.
Referred to generally, 7368, 7432.

Irrigation. (See Reclamation.)

Italy, participation in semi-centennial expositions of, recommended, 7446.

Japan—
Annexation of Korea by, 7498.
Mission of condolence to, 7785.
Relations and treaty with, 7420, 7666.

Jones, John Paul, inhuming of remains of, in crypt at Annapolis, recommended, 7531.

Judges, salaries of, increase urged in, 7525.

Justice, Department of—
Clerks of Federal courts removed, 7691.
French spoliation awards, 7691.
Operations of, in 1910, discussed, 7522.
Reorganization of, 7368.

Knight Sugar Trust decision, effect of, discussed, 7451.

Korea, annexation of, by Japan, 7498.

Labor, Bureau of, conciliatory work of, commended, 7540.

Labor organizations, exemption of, from anti-trust law, disapproved, 7865.

Laborers, act specifying eight-hour day for, on work for government, recommended, 7540.

Lading, bills of, enactment preventing issue of fraudulent, recommended, 7553.

Lake Erie depth regulations, report transmitted on, 7477.

Lands, Public—
Acreage of, original and contemporaneous, 7557.
Agricultural, laws governing disposition of, discussed and commended, 7532, 7557.
Classification of, urged, 7460, 7720.
Coal fields, acreage, classification, valuation, and disposition of, discussed, 7562.
Claims for, discussed, 7566.
Cunningham claims for 5,280 acres of, 7565.
Governmental control of industry made possible by leasing of, 7564, 7566.

Personnel of (See also Officers)—
Laws governing need change, 7470, 7529.
Praised, 7429.
Roosevelt's policy regarding, reiterated, 7371.
Secretary of the, naval aids urged for, 7807.
Staff corps of, amalgamation of, 7696.
Supply fund of, administration of, discussed, 7530.
Yards, reorganization of, 7430, 7529, 7696.
Vice-admiral, creation of grade of, urged, 7472.
Navy Department, estimates of, for 1911-12, discussed, 7530.
Negro—
Centennial celebration of freedom of, 7439.
Patriotism of, recalled and commended, 7377.
Progress of, requisite to progress of South, 7377.
Voting restrictions on, urged, 7376.
New Mexico—
Admission of, to statehood—
Act for, vetoed, 7636.
Recommended, 7435, 7598.
Constitution of—
Approval of, urged, 7598.
Clause of, respecting boundary with Texas, should be annulled, 7576.
Newspapers, American, in foreign lands, urged, 7790.
Nicaragua, crimes and overthrow of Zelaya government in, 7418.
Intervention of United States in, 7773.
Outcome of civil war in, 7500.
Settlement of claim against, 7417.
Treaty with, proposed, 7663.
North Atlantic Fisheries dispute with Great Britain settled, 7779.
Ohio River, canalization of, discussed and recommended, 7465.
Oil lands. (See Lands, Public.)
Oklahoma, report on extent and value of coal lands in, 7475.
Old age pensions. (See Pensions.)
Opium—
Conference at The Hague, discussed, 7781.
International Commission, 7671.
Report of, transmitted, 7469.
Taxes and laws regulatory of, recommended, 7470.
Traffic, suppression of, in United States, recommended, 7419, 7596.
Pacific slope coal supply in Alaska, 7564.

Panama—
Costa Rica and, dispute between, arbitrated, 7657.
Indemnification for United States sailors outraged in, 7417.
Police reform in, under United States guidance, 7416.
Relations with, 7664.
Panama Canal—
British protest against remission of tolls, 7758.
British protest discussed, 7760.
Control of—
Compared with Suez Canal, 7759.
Discriminates only in favor of coastwise trade, 7761.
Forbids use of ships owned by railroads, 7762.
Dock facilities, supplies and repairs furnished through government, 7688.
Fortification of, appropriation urged for, 7483, 7519.
Hay-Pauncefote treaty cannot prevent extension of favors, 7760.
Maintenance of, when complete, discussed, 7520.
Neutralization of, 7759.
Payment for, by bonds, recommended, 7370, 7423.
Progress of work on, 7374, 7518, 7686, 7805.
Railroad-owned vessels, prohibition of, from—
Effected, 7762.
Urged, 7521.
Supplies at, sale of, urged, 7520.
Tolls—
Announced, 7806.
Remission of, to American shipping, 7688, 7758.
To be imposed, discussed, 7519.
Trade factor, 7374, 7520.
Use of—
Denied to owners of vessels violating anti-trust law, 7763.
To be in interest of public, 7762.
Panama-Pacific International Exposition, services of, 7819.
Pan-American Conference (Fourth), 7414.
Pan-American Union, discussed, 7664.
Parcels Post, establishment of, recommended, 7528, 7694, 7732, 7814.
Parties, political, essential to popular government, 7405.
Patents, conventions with South American republics for protection of, 7499.
Peace, international, plans for promotion of, discussed, 7372, 7494.
Pearl Harbor, Hawaii, establishment of naval base at, recommended, 7429.

Republican party, solidarity of, requisite to continuance of Roosevelt policies, 7405.

Revenue Cutter Service organization, abolition of, urged, 7740.

Reviewing inaugural parade, photograph of, opposite 7394.

Rivers and Harbors—
Improvements recommended in, 7690.
Waterway from the lakes to the gulf, recommended, 7690.

Rivers and Harbors Bill of 1910, criticized, and reforms proposed, 7489, 7517.

Roosevelt policies to be furthered and maintained, 7368.

Root, Elihu (Senator), argument by, at Hague in Fisheries Case, praised, 7493.

Russia, treaty of 1832 with, change needed in, 7669.

Safety Appliance Law, discussed, 7378, 7449, 7553.

Seals, fur, preservation and government utilization of, discussed, 7410, 7477, 7540, 7779, 7823.

Seals, fur, treaty with Great Britain, France and Russia concerning, consummated, 7670.

Second-class mail matter rates—
Increase urged in, 7433, 7528.
Report of commission on, 7733.

Service Corps established, 7800.

Sherman, Vice-President, death of, announced, 7764.

Shippers, right to choose transfer routes for goods should be vested in, 7446.

Siam—
Coronation of King of, United States represented at, 7667.
Treaty with, to be revised, 7420.

Soil, importance of conserving fertility of, 7462.

South, formation of opposition party in, desirable, 7375.

South America—
Bank, central, in, 7416.
Steamship lines to, direct, 7374.
Subsidy for, 7374, 7435, 7503.

Spanish battleships, salvage in Cuban waters, 7629.

Spanish Treaty Claims Commission, report of, transmitted, 7486.

Spitzbergen Islands—
Conference on, 7413.
Problem of, discussed, 7782.

State, Department of, as trade factor, 7415, 7502.
Reorganization of, 7420, 7767.

Stone and timber lands. (See Lands, Public.)

Supreme Court, restriction of jurisdiction of, 7431, 7523.
Right of appeal to, discussed, 7523.

Tariff. (See also Customs)—
Act placing articles on free list, vetoed, 7625.
High cost of living not caused by, 7403.
Monopolies created by excessive duties under, 7394.
Principles discussed, 7795.
Rates on iron and steel, and engines and machine tools disapproved, 7749, 7751.
Reduction of duties of, vetoed, 7631.
Revision of—
Discussed and urged, 7369, 7379, 7395, 7511, 7751.
Postponement of, urged, 7408.
Wool (Schedule K), 7677.

Tariff Board—
Appointed, 7676.
Appropriation for, recommended, 7480.
Operation of, discussed, 7422, 7427, 7511.
Report of, submitted in justification of veto of wool tariff bill, 7646.
Work of, commended, 7646.

Tariff of 1909—
Coal schedule of, discussed, 7401.
Cotton schedule of, discussed, 7399.
Crockery schedule of, discussed, 7400.
Defended, 7393.
Iron schedule of, discussed, 7403.
Leather schedule of, discussed, 7401.
Lumber schedule of, discussed, 7401.
Maximum and minimum provision of, discussed, 7406, 7422, 7426, 7479, 7488, 7501, 7777.
Newspaper misrepresentation of, 7395, 7396, 7511.
Philippine free trade, provided by, 7407.
Print paper schedule of, discussed, 7401.
Wool schedule of, condemned, 7402, 7618.

Tariff, wool—
Discussed, 7622, 7676, 7746.
Veto of, 7618, 7745.

Taxation. (See Income Tax; Corporation Tax; Inheritance Tax.)

Telegraph lines, inclusion of, in postal system, opposed, 7732.

Thanksgiving Proclamations, 7392, 7491, 7764.

Trade Commission, establishment of, urged, 7819.

Trade, foreign, discussed, 7374, 7450, 7776.

Tahoe Forest Reserve, proclaimed, 7307.

Talladega (Ala.), Battle of.—After the destruction of Tallasahatchee. Jackson was informed that 160 friendly Creek warriors, with their families, were hemmed in at Talladega, in Lashley's fort, by 1,000 hostile Indians. Nov. 8, 1813, Jackson set out with 1,200 infantry and 800 cavalry to raise the siege. By 4 o'clock the next morning they had surrounded the enemy, who, 1,080 strong, were concealed in the thickets. At daylight the battle began. It resulted in the complete rout of the savages. As many as 290 dead warriors were found and many others doubtless perished in the woods of the surrounding mountains. The number of the wounded could not be ascertained, but was large. The loss to the whites was 15 killed and 85 wounded.

Tallasahatchee (Ala.), Battle of.—The massacre at Fort Mims spread consternation throughout the region inhabited by the Creeks, and hardy volunteers came forward thirsting for vengeance. Gen. Jackson led the Tennessee militia across the line into Alabama. Upon his arrival at the Coosa he was informed that the Creeks were assembled at Tallasahatchee, a town in an open woodland, not far from the present village of Jacksonville, the county seat of Benton County, Ala., on the southeast side of the Tallasahatchee Creek. Jackson sent Gen. Coffee with 1,000 horsemen to destroy the town. Nov. 3, 1813, Coffee's men surrounded the place and the Indians came out to meet them. The battle was short, sharp, and desperate. The victory for the whites was complete. Every warrior was killed. None asked for quarter, and each fought to the death. At the close of the battle 186 bodies were counted on the plain. It is believed that 200 were killed. Eighty-four women and children were made prisoners. The loss to the whites was 5 men killed and 41 wounded.

Tammany.—In 1789 the Columbian Order was organized in New York City by William Mooney, as a counter move against the foundation of the so-called Aristocratic Society of the Cincinnati. In 1805 it was incorporated under the name of Tammany Society. This was in memory of Tammany, an aged, wise and friendly chief of the Delaware Indians. At this time charitable societies were also organized in Philadelphia and other cities and named in his honor. The only one of the number that survives is that in New York. William Mooney was the first grand sachem of Tammany, and was assisted by thirteen sachems, representing the governors of the thirteen states. The members wore Indian insignia. In 1811 the society built the original Tammany Hall, fronting on City Hall Park. Since then a local political party, favored by a majority of the members of the Tammany Society, has always had its headquarters in the house of the society, and has been popularly known as "Tammany Hall." In theory the Tammany Hall general committee has no relation to the Tammany Society save as tenant of the latter's edifice, yet in practice they are coordinate branches of one political system, the society being in effect the citadel of the controlling spirits of the Tammany Hall party. Tammany Hall claims to be the regular Democratic organization of the city and county of New York, though that claim has often been contested. By means of a thoroughly organized system of Tammany clubs and assembly district associations it has usually held a paramount place in city politics.

Taos (N. Mex.), Battle of.—Feb. 3, 1847, Col. Price, with about 400 Americans, arrived at the town of Don Fernando de Taos, on the top of the Taos Mountain, which had been the scene of the murder of Governor Bent and his party. The Mexicans, numbering 600, had taken refuge in a stone church and two other large buildings. They resisted the American assaults during Feb. 4 and on the morning of the 5th surrendered. The American loss was 54 killed and wounded; that of the Mexicans 152 killed and many wounded.

Tar Heel State.—A nickname for North Carolina (q. v.). (See also States); sometimes also nicknamed Old North State.

Target Practice. (See Navy.)

Tariff.—The word "tariff" is generally applied to the customs duties levied by Congress on merchandise imported. Tradition identifies the word with the town of Tarifa, Spain. Here, during the Moorish occupancy of the country about Gibraltar, all vessels passing through the strait were compelled to put in and pay such duties as were demanded by the chiefs in possession. Among the Greeks and Romans a duty similar to the tariff of the present day was known, and in England, as early as 980, during the reign of Ethelred, duties on ships and goods were levied, to be paid at Billingsgate. Charles II. established a regular schedule of rates in 1663. After 1846 England gradually abolished her tariff duties, beginning with the repeal of the corn laws and continuing until 1891-1892, when revenue duties alone were collected, and those upon less than twenty articles.

In the United States the First Congress passed a tariff law levying on an average less than 8 per cent ad valorem on imports. This was approved by Washington July 4, 1789. Madison opened the discussion of this measure in Congress. South Carolina and Georgia favored a rate of 5 per cent, Pennsylvania one of 12 or more, while New England and Virginia succeeded in getting the rate raised a little above what the far south asked for, but placed it lower than the chief manufacturing states desired. The tariff of 1816 imposed duties of about 25 per cent on certain leading manufactures, under protest from the leading agricultural states of the south. In 1824 a new tariff act was passed, increasing among the changes made, duties on metals and agricultural products. Jan. 31, 1828, the "tariff of abominations," as it was named by its enemies, was introduced in the House. It embodied in part the recommendations of a national convention of manufacturers held at Harrisburg, Pa., but satisfied neither the friends nor the opponents of protection. This bill proposed a 41 per cent rate and was favored by Daniel Webster, who reversed his position of 1824. South Carolina protested against the proposed measure as unconstitutional and unjust and oppressive. North Carolina also protested, and Alabama and Georgia denied the power of Congress to lay duties for protection. July 14, 1832, President Jackson approved a bill reducing the tax on iron, increasing that on woolens, making some raw wools free, and leaving cotton unchanged. This bill retained the protective feature of the law of 1828, but reduced the taxes somewhat. South Carolina passed an ordinance nullifying this act (see Nullification), but her ordinance was rescinded after the approval of the compromise tariff of 1833. This measure, introduced by Clay and supported by Cal-

houn, provided for a gradual reduction of duties to a uniform rate, to be reached in 1842. It secured a revenue tariff by successive reductions. In 1842, the Whigs being in a majority, Congress enacted a protective tariff, which President Tyler vetoed (2033).

July 30, 1846, a tariff law was enacted which subordinated the principle of protection to that of revenue. It passed the House by a vote of 114 to 95 and the Senate by the casting vote of Vice-President Dallas. The average rate of duty was fixed at about 25 per cent. This was lowered to about 20 per cent by an act of 1857. In 1861 the principle of protection was reasserted in the Morrill Act, which increased the rates of 1857 about one-third. During the Civil War the tariff rates were repeatedly raised to meet the expenses of Government and stimulate manufacture. These rates were continued long after the cessation of hostilities. In 1882 a tariff commission was appointed to visit different sections of the country in the interest of tariff revision. The commission recommended a reduction of 20 per cent in rates.

President Cleveland, in his message of Dec. 8, 1885 (page 4926), recommended a reduction of the tariff, and his message of Dec. 6, 1887 (page 5165), was devoted exclusively to this topic. From this time on, party lines began to be drawn on the tariff question, most of the Republicans favoring protection and the majority of advocates advocating a revision in the direction of lower duties. The Mills bill, framed largely in accordance with President Cleveland's views, passed the House, but failed in the Senate, where a bill embodying the ideas of the protectionists on tariff revision was substituted for it by the Republican majority. In the Fifty-first Congress, the Republicans being in control, passed the McKinley tariff act of 1890 raising the duties to an average of 48 per cent. By the elections of 1890 and 1892 the Democrats came into power, and in the Fifty-third Congress the House passed the Wilson bill providing for substantial reductions, especially on raw materials. Amendments were added in the Senate which essentially changed its character and the bill became law in 1894 without the President's signature. It provided for an income tax which was, however, declared unconstitutional by the Supreme Court.

The elections of 1894 and 1896 returned the Republicans to power, and in 1897 the Dingley law was passed, which imposed the highest rates of duty ever known in our history. It has been revised so far as concerned the Philippines in 1905, when a lower tariff came into force, and again in 1906, when the islands were given practically free trade with this country; of the few articles excepted, the most important were sugar, coffee, and tobacco.

The revision of the Dingley Tariff in 1909 is discussed by President Taft in his address at Winona (page 7393) which was evoked by the furious storm of criticism to which the tariff and its sponsors were subjected. This discontent produced a rupture in the Republican ranks, "insurgent" Congressmen lining up against "standpatters." The Federal patronage was employed to awaken insurgents to a sense of duty to the party, but without avail. Public sentiment on the question was expressed in the Democratic victory of 1910, the insurgent Republicans being mostly re-elected.

In the 1910 tariff, provision was made for the application of a maximum or minimum schedule of rates to the imports of a foreign country in accordance as it discriminates against or in favor of American goods; for corporation tax of one per cent of net earnings; for a revised tariff establishing free trade with the Philippines; for a Customs Court of Appeals consisting of five judges and six attorneys to prosecute customs cases before the Court; and for a tariff board.

The tariff board was conceded to be an advance, but its best friends were the foremost in terming it ineffectual. The kind of tariff board desired by President Taft is outlined in a bill introduced, Jan. 5, 1911, by Representative Longworth of Ohio, which provides for a permanent commission of five members to be appointed by the President and confirmed by the Senate, who, by the use of $250,000 shall, in sittings here or abroad, investigate the cost of production of tariff-taxed goods, particularly as regards labor, for which purpose they are to be vested with the power of issuing subpœnas, administering oaths, and taking testimony (Congress to act on cases of non-compliance with subpœnas), and, on demand expressed in a joint resolution, they shall report to Congress, or, on his demand, shall report to the President. (Page 7619.) (See also Foreign Import Duties; Import Duties, Tariff of 1913.)

With the election of President Wilson and a Democratic Congress in 1913 a downward revision of the tariff was assured, for Congress had already partially framed the Underwood bill, and President Wilson called an extra session April 8, 1913, and in his address called attention to the duty of the party in power, and urged immediate passage of the Underwood bill. Oct. 3, 1913, the President signed the bill. The main feature of the law was the income tax provision, and the next importance was the removal of all protection from agricultural products and meats. Duties on the manufacture of cotton and woolen goods were cut 10 to 50 per cent. Raw wool was admitted free, and sugar became free after three years. In the article Tariff of 1913 following the rates of the Wilson tariff are compared with those of the Payne-Aldrich act of 1909.

Tariff:

Aldrich-Payne. (See Payne-Aldrich.)

Bill to reduce duty on wool, vetoed by Taft, 7745.

Board—
   Appropriation urged for, 7480.
   Creation and functions of, 8151, 8158.
   Permanent, appointed, 7677.
   Provisions for, in Payne-Aldrich Law, 7407, 7427.
   Temporary, appointment of, 7676.

Coal, anthracite, duties should be removed, 6714.

Concessions, reciprocal, granted to—Netherlands, 6961. Spain, 6966.

Differential principle to govern revision of, 7369, 7511.

Dingley—
   Effect of, on manufactures, 6713.
   General approval of, 6652, 6713.
   Revision needed in, 7369, 7379, 7393.
   Diplomatic negotiations concerning, 7488, 7501.

Discussed by President—
   Roosevelt, 6652, 6713, 7083, 7189, 7346.
   Taft, 7369, 7393, 7399, 7422, 7479, 7501, 7511, 7618, 7631, 7677, 7745, 7777, 7795.
   Wilson, 7869, 7871, 8030 8151, 8158.

Effect of, on industry, 6713, 7747.

Engines and machine tools, reduction of duty on, vetoed, 7625.

Finished articles should not be put on free list when raw materials are dutiable, 7751.

Germany—
   Protest of, against discriminating duty on sugar and recommendations concerning, 5957.
   Reciprocity with, discussed, 7283.
   Relations with, concerning, 7122.

High cost of living not caused by, 7403.

Industry injured by low, 7747.

Investigation of, discussed, 7189.

Iron and steel schedule, discussed and vetoed, 7749.

Low rate on woolen goods would destroy fne goods industry, 7747.

Low rate on tops and yarn would disrupt industry, 7747.

Machine tools, rates on, discussed, 7751.

Minimum and maximum rates, discussed, 7406, 7422, 7426, 7479, 7488, 7501, 7777.

Non-partisanship, should guide rates of, 7751.

Payne-Aldrich—
   Address in defense of, 7393.
   Critics of, within Republican Party, 7404, 7408.
   Downward revision accomplished by, 7399.
   Newspaper misrepresentation of, 7395, 7511.

Philippines—
   Free trade provided for, 7407.
   Urgent necessity of tariff in, 6737.

Principles discussed, 7795.

Reciprocity with—
   Canada. (See Canada, Reciprocity with.)
   Germany, 7283.

Republican Party platform and principles of, discussed, 7083, 7394, 7399.

Revision of—
   Democratic Party principles dominant in, 8151.
   Differential principle to govern, 7369, 7511.
   Downward, accomplished by Payne-Aldrich Law, 7399.
   Need for, discussed by President—
     Roosevelt, 7083.
     Taft, 7369, 7379, 7393, 7511, 7751.
     Wilson, 7871.

Wool, reduction of duty on, recommended, 7677.

Wool (Schedule K), 7677.

Tariff Board.—Section 2 of the Tariff act of 1909 provides that "from and after March 31, 1910, except as otherwise specially provided for in this section, there shall be levied, collected and paid on all articles when imported from any foreign country into the United States or into any of its possessions (except the Philippine Islands, Guam and Tutuila) the rates of duty prescribed by the schedules and paragraphs of the dutiable list of Section 1 of this act, and in addition thereto 25 per centum ad valorem, which rates shall constitute the maximum tariff of the United States. * * * To secure information to assist the President in the discharge of the duties imposed upon him by this section, and the officers of the Government in the administration of the customs laws, the President is hereby authorized to employ such persons as may be required."

Under this authorization President Taft on Sept. 15, 1909, appointed a non-partisan Tariff Board of three Republicans and two Democrats to perform the duties required by the act: Before the work of the board became available to Congress the Democratic party came into control and the Underwood tariff law was passed. (See Tariff of 1913.)

Wilson Tariff Board.—President Wilson expressed himself in favor of an out-and-out independent Tariff Board, Jan. 25, to Representative Claude Kitchin, chairman of the Committee on Ways and Means and chosen floor leader of the House Democrats.

As proposed by the President, such a commission would have specific powers to:

Investigate the administrative and fiscal effects of customs laws now in force or which may be passed in the future;

Determine the relations between rates of duties on raw materials and those on finished or partly finished products;

Investigate the effects of ad valorem and specific duties and of those which are a compound of advalorem and specific;

Examine the arrangement of schedules of duties and the classification of the articles on the several schedules;

Investigate the provisions of law relating to the tariff, the regulations of the Treasury Department applying to invoices and other questions with application to the collection of customs duties;

Determine generally the working of the customs and tariff laws in their economic effects and administrative methods.

Foreign Trade Under the New Tariff.—Secretary Redfield transmitted to the Senate a detailed statement of the results of the Underwood-Simmons tariff act as reflected in the foreign trade of the country up to the time the war started in Europe. The statement was prepared in the Bureau of Foreign and Domestic Commerce in response to a Senate Resolution of Jan. 17, 1916, calling upon the Secretary of Commerce for information in regard to trade under the present tariff.

The report calls particular attention to the import trade for the fiscal year 1914, as that year covers 12 of the 13 months immediately preceding the outbreak of hostilities in Europe and is the period held to indicate most accurately the effect the new tariff has had upon American imports. According to statistics given in the report the increase in imports for 1914 amounted to $81,000,000, or 4.5 per cent, as compared with 1913. This increase, the report states, is only $20,000,000 in excess of the average

annual increase in imports for the 17 years from 1899 to 1915, and is less than the average increase during the last few years of that 17-year period. There was an increase in 12 of the 17 years, varying from $245,000,000 in 1910 to $80,000,000 in 1902.

Free goods, not dutiable goods, are responsible for the increased imports for the fiscal year 1914, the report states. Articles subject to duty, if considered as a single class, decreased perceptibly. Imports free of duty increased from $988,000,000 to $1,128,000,000, whle the imports of dutiable goods fell off from $825,000,000 to $766,000,000. The increase in the total free imports was due largely to the transfer of many important articles from the dutiable list to the free list by the tariff act of 1913. Among the articles so transferred are iron ore, pig iron, Bessemer ingots, steel rails, baling and fencing wire, cotton ties, wool, flax, hemp, burlap, cotton bagging, lumber, chemicals, wood pulp, leather, boots and shoes, agricultural implements, food animals, corn, meat, milk, cream, and, when imported from countries that admit free of duty similar products from the United States, wheat, wheat flour, and potatoes.

The close correspondence between the estimated customs receipts and the actual receipts under the Underwood-Simmons tariff is remarkable, the report shows. It is estimated that the bill as it passed the House of Representatives would produce during its first full year of operation $258,000,000; as it passed the Senate, $248,000,000; and as finally enacted, $249,000,000, or $20,750,000 a month. Since the new rates on sugar and molasses became effective March 1, 1914, the law was in full operation only five months before the outbreak of the war. During the quarter from April 1 to June 30 the duties amounted to $63,600,000, or $21,200,000 a month. The receipts, therefore, exceeded the expected returns by $450,000 a month, or at the rate of $5,000,000 a year.

In comparing the import and export trade of the country, the report says:

"We import more than we export of crude foodstuffs and meat animals and of miscellaneous articles, while we export more than we import of the remaining groups—crude materials for use in manufacturing, foodstuffs partly or wholly manufactured, manufactures for further use in manufacturing, and manufactures ready for consumption. It is of interest to note the chief article of import and of export falling within each of these groups. Of crude materials for use in manufacturing, hides are most largely imported and cotton most largely exported. Of foodstuffs in crude condition, including food animals, coffee represents the largest import and wheat the largest export. Of partly or wholly manufactured foodstuffs, sugar leads in the importation and wheat flour in the exportation. Wood pulp stands first among the imports and copper in pigs and bars first among the exports of manufactures for further use in manufacturing. Of manufactures ready for consumption, manufactures of vegetable fibres other than cotton stand first among the imports and machinery first among the exports. In the miscellaneous group, clover seed is the chief import and horses the chief export. This comparison is based on the fiscal year 1914. The obvious lesson to be drawn from this comparison is the diversity of our import and export trade. Our imports consist largely of articles which for natural reasons can not be produced here or for economic or geographic reasons can be produced more cheaply abroad. The exports from this country represent the articles which, by reason of our agricultural or mineral wealth, or by reason of our industrial organization, we can produce better or more cheaply than the producer in other countries."

The effect of the tariff on wages is one of the much-debated points on which the report touches. It is shown that there is a large number of industries in which, under the present tariff, the average duty collected on imports is greater than the average expenditure for wages by domestic manufacturers. This group includes such diverse lines as flour, sugar, butter, and condensed milk, soap, candles, and glue, hosiery, corsets, and buttons. Even in the case of pottery, where wages constitute nearly 40 per cent of the entire value of the output, the average ad valorem duty on competing products is still higher.

Another group consists of industries in which the payment for wages constitute a larger share of the product than does the import duty in the case of imported goods. This group covers some of our most successful industries. Rubber goods, steel works and rolling mills, carriage factories, bicycles, motor cycles, locomotives, clocks and watches and firearms and ammunition are among the industries in which the domestic producer has to pay proportionately more for wages than his foreign competitor pays in the shape of import duties.

Tariff Board:
Report of, submitted in justification of veto of wool bill, 7746.
Work of, commended by Taft, 7746.
Tariff Commission.—The plea long coming from all classes and parts of the country to "take the tariff out of politics" was finally met in the Tariff Bill passed by Congress on September 8, 1916. That bill provided for a Tariff Commission of 6 members, not more than 3 of whom are to belong to the same political party. The members are appointed by the President, by and with the consent of the Senate, for a period of 12 years' service, and command a yearly salary of $7,500. Provision is made for power to subpoena witnesses, conduct investigations, etc., in order to make the work of the Commission effective. The duties of the Commission are to investigate and to report annually on the effect of the tariff rates to Congress, and at any other time when requested to the President or to the Tariff Committees of the House and the Senate. The members of the first commission appointed under the act of 1916 were: Prof. F. W. Taussig, of Harvard University, Chairman; ex-Congressman David J. Lewis, of Maryland; Edward P. Costigan, of Colorado; ex-Congressman William Kent, of

TABLE OF LEADING ARTICLES IMPORTED INTO THE UNITED STATES OR ANY OF ITS POSSESSIONS (EXCEPT PHILIPPINE ISLANDS, GUAM AND TUTUILA), GIVING RATES AT ENTRY BY THE TARIFF ACT OF 1913 COMPARED WITH THE TARIFF ACT OF 1909.

(The following table covers only the articles of principal importance imported.)   (ad val.—ad valorem; n.s.p.f.—not specially provided for.)

ARTICLES	RATES OF DUTY UNDER	
	Law of 1909	New Law of 1913
Schedule A—Chemicals, Oils and Paints:		
Acids, n.s.p.f.	25 p.c. ad val.	15 p.c. ad val.
Alcoholic compounds, n.s.p.f.	60c. lb. and 25 p.c. ad. val.	10c. lb. and 20 p.c. ad. val. to 40c. lb. and 20 p.c. ad. val.
Alkalies, alkaloids, and all chemical and medicinal compounds, preparations, mixtures and salts, and combinations thereof....	25 p.c. ad val.	15 p.c. ad val.
Ammonia, Carbonite of.	1½c. lb.	¾c. lb.
Drugs.	1¼c. lb. and 10p.c. ad val.	10 p.c. ad val.
Glue, value not above 10c. per pound.	2½c. lb.	1c. lb.
Oil, castor, gals.	35c. gal.	12c. gal.
Oil, olive in bottles, etc., gals.	50c. gal.	30c. gal.
Oil, whale, gals.	8c. gal.	5c. gal.
Opium, crude and not adulterated, containing 9 per cent. and over of morphia, lbs.	$1.50 lb.	$3.00 lb.
Perfumery, cosmetics, containing alcohol.	60c. lb. and 50 p.c. ad val.	40c. lb. and 60 p.c. ad val.
Perfumery, cosmetics, not containing alcohol.	60 p.c. ad val.	60 p.c. ad val.
Soap, Castile.	1¼c. lb.	10 p.c. ad val.
Soap, toilet.	50 p.c. ad val.	30 p.c. ad val.
Soda, bi-carbonate of.	5-8c. lb.	¼c. lb.
Sponges, not advanced in value by chemical processes.	20 p.c. ad val.	10 p.c. ad val.
Schedule B—Earths, Earthenware and Glassware:		
Cement.	8c. 100 lbs.	10 p.c. ad val.
Earthenware, porcelain, decorated.	60 p.c. ad val.	40 p.c. ad val.
Earthenware, common.	25 p.c. ad val.	15 p.c. ad val.
Glassware, plain and cut.	60 p.c. ad val.	45 p.c. ad val.
Marble, manufactures of, except for jewelry.	50 p.c. ad val.	45 p.c. ad val.
Spectacles, eyeglasses, opera and field glasses, and frames for same.	50 p.c. ad val.	35 p.c. ad val.
Schedule C—Metals and Manufactures of:		
Iron, bar.	6-10c. lb.	5 p.c. ad val.
Steel, n.s.p.f. in sec. 112 of act.	Graduated rate	12 p.c. ad val.
Automobile chassis and finished parts of automobiles not including tires.	45 p.c. ad val.	30 p.c. ad val.
Copper plates.	2½c. lb.	5 p.c. ad val.

TABLE OF LEADING ARTICLES IMPORTED INTO THE UNITED STATES—*Continued*

ARTICLES	RATES OF DUTY UNDER	
	Law of 1909	New Law of 1913
Pens, metallic, except gold pens	12c. gross	8c. gross
Table and kitchen utensils, metal	40 p.c. ad val.	25 p.c. ad val.
Tin plates	12-10c. lb.	15 p.c. ad val.
Pins, not jewelry	35 p.c. ad val.	20 p.c. ad val.
Iron beams, girders, joists	Graduated rate	10 p.c. ad val.
Cast iron andirons, plates, stove plates, hollow ware	8-10c lb.	10 p.c. ad val.
Aluminum, and alloys of any kind in which it is the chief component, in crude form	7c. lb.	2c. lb.
Watch movements not jewelled, watch cases	Graduated rate	30 p.c. ad val.
Schedule D—Wood and Manufactures of:		
Briar wood and similar wood unmanufactured	15 p.c. ad val.	10 p.c. ad val.
Paving posts, railroad tires, telephone, trolley and telegraph poles	10 p.c. ad val.	10 p.c. ad val.
House or cabinet furniture, and manufactures of wood or bark, n.s.p.f	35 p.c. ad val.	15 p.c. ad val.
Schedule E—Sugar, Molasses and Manufactures of:		
Sugars and syrups of cane juice	Above 75 degrees polariscope 95-100 of 1c. per lb. and for each additional degree 35-1000 of 1c. per lb.	Not above 75 degrees polariscope 71-100 of 1c. per lb.; for every additional degree 26-1000 of 1c. per lb.
Saccharin	65c. lb.	65c. lb.
Sugar cane in its natural state, or unmanufactured	20 p.c. ad val.	15 p.c. ad val.
Molasses, not above 40 degrees	20 p.c. ad val.	15 p.c. ad val.
Maple sugar and maple syrup	4c. lb.	3c. lb.
Glucose or grape sugar	1½c. lb.	1½c. lb.
Sugar candy, valued more than 15c per pound, and chewing gum	50 p.c. ad val.	25 p.c. ad val.
Schedule F—Tobacco and Manufactures of:		
Tobacco, wrapper, filler, leaf	$1.85 lb. to $2.50 lb.	$1.85 lb. to $2.50 lb.
Snuff	55c. lb.	55c. lb.
Cigars and cigarettes	$4.50 lb. and 25 p.c. ad val.	$4.50 lb. and 25 p.c. ad val.
Schedule G—Agricultural Products and Provisions:		
Horses and mules and all live animals, n.s.p.f	25 p.c. ad val.	10 p.c. ad val.
Barley, bushel of 48 pounds	30c. bushel	15c. bushel
Barley malt, bushel of 34 pounds	45c. bushel	25c. bushel
Oatmeal and rolled oats	1c. lb.	30c. 100 lbs.
Oats, bushel	15c. bushel	6c. bushel
Rice, cleaned	2c. lb.	1c. lb.
Macaroni, vermicelli, and all similar preparations	1½c. lb.	1c. lb.
Butter and substitutes	6c. lb.	2½c. lb.
Cheese and substitutes therefor	6c. lb.	20c. p.c. ad val.
Hay	$4 ton	$2 ton
Honey	20c. gal.	10c. gal.
Hops	16c. lb.	16c. lb.
Seeds, flax seed, linseed and other oil seeds, n.s.p.f	25c. bushel	20c. bushel
Seeds, castor	25c. bushel	15c. bushel
Fish, except shell fish, packed in oil or in oil and other substances	1c. lb.	25 p.c. ad val.
Fruits, apples, peaches, quinces, cherries, plums and pears	25c. bushel	10c. bushel
Fruits, preserved, n.s.p.f	2c. lb.	1c. lb.
Fruits, oranges, grapefruit, lemons and limes in bulk	1c. lb.	½c. lb.
Pineapples, in bulk	$8 per 1,000	$5 per 1,000
Nuts of all kinds, shelled or unshelled, n.s.p.f	1c. lb.	1c. lb.
Spices, unground, n.s.p.f	Free list	1c lb.
Chocolate and cocoa unsweetened, prepared or manufactured, n.s.p.f	Graduated rate	8 p.c. ad val.
Chocolate and cocoa, sweetened, prepared or manufactured, valued at 20c. per pound or less	Graduated rate	2c. lb.
Schedule H—Spirits, Wines and Other Beverages:		
Brandy and other spirits manufactured or distilled from grain or other materials, n.s.p.f	$2.60 gal.	$2.60 gal.
Champagne and all other sparkling wines, quarts	$9.60 per doz.	$9.60 per doz.
Wines, still, in casks, vermuth and similar beverages	45c. gal.	45c. to 60c. gal.
Wines, still, in bottles, quarts	$1.85 per doz.	$1.85 per doz.
Malt liquors, in bottles, jugs, gallons	45c. gal.	45c. gal.
Mineral waters, in bottles, quarts	30c. doz.	20c. doz.
Schedule I—Cotton Manufactures:		
Cotton thread, uncolored, according to numbers	2½c. lb. to 28c. lb.	5 to 25 p.c. ad val.
Cotton thread, colored, bleached, according to numbers	6c. lb. to 67c. lb.	7½ to 27½ p.c. ad val.

TABLE OF LEADING ARTICLES IMPORTED INTO THE UNITED STATES—*Continued*

ARTICLES	RATES OF DUTY UNDER	
	Law of 1909	New Law of 1913
Cotton cloth, uncolored, according to numbers...............	1c. sq. yard to 8c. sq. yard	7½ to 27½ p.c. ad val.
Cotton cloth, colored, bleached, according to numbers..........	Graduated rate	10 to 30 p.c. ad val.
Cotton handkerchiefs or mufflers, hemmed or hemstitched, n.s.p.f.	4¼c. sq. yard and 10 p.c. ad val.	30 p.c. ad val.
Cotton clothing, ready made...............................	50 p.c. ad val.	30 p.c. ad val.
Cotton hosiery, pairs.....................................	70c. doz. to $2 doz. and 15 p.c. ad val.	$1.20 doz. pairs and 30 to 50 p.c. ad val.
Cotton shirts, drawers, and all underwear, n.s.p.f..............	60c. doz and 15 p.c. ad val. to $2.25 doz. and 35 p.c. ad val.	30 p.c. ad val.
Cotton, plushes, velvets, corduroys.........................	9c. sq. yard and 25 p.c. ad val. to 12c. sq. yard and 25 p.c. ad val.	40 p.c. ad val.
Lace manufactures..	60 p.c. ad val.	35 to 45 p.c. ad val.
Schedule J—Flax, Hemp and Jute and Manufactures of:		
Flax hamp or ramie single yarns, finer than 80 lea or number....	35 p.c. ad val.	10 p.c. ad val.
Mattings for floors..	3½c. sq. yard	2½c. sq. yard
Schedule K—Wool and Manufactures of:		
Combed wool or tops, n.s.p.f...............................	Graduated rate	8 p.c. ad val.
Yarns..	Graduated rate	18 p.c. ad val.
Cloths, knit fabrics, felts not woven and all manufactures of every description, wholly or chiefly of wool, n.s.p.f.................	Graduated rate	35 p.c. ad val.
Blankets, n.s.p.f., and flannels.............................	Graduated rate	25 to 30 p.c. ad val.
Dress goods, women's and children's........................	Graduated rate	35 p.c. ad val.
Clothing, ready made and wearing apparel of every description, n.s.p.f...	44c. lb. and 60 p.c. ad val.	35 p.c. ad val.
Carpets, woven whole for rooms, and rugs...................	10c. sq. foot and 40 p.c. ad val.	50 p.c. ad val.
Plushes, velvets and all other pile fabrics, cut or uncut.........	Graduated rate	45 p.c. ad val.
Schedule L—Silk and Silk Goods:		
Silk partially manufactured, or spun silk.....................	35 p.c. ad val.	20c. lb. to 35 p.c. ad val.
Silk, wearing apparel......................................	60 p.c. ad val.	50 p.c. ad val.
Silk, yarns, threads.......................................	45c. lb. to 60c. lb.	35 to 60 p.c. ad val.
Silk, all manufactures of, n.s.p.f...........................	Graduated rate	45 p.c. ad val.
Schedule M—Papers and Books:		
Printing paper, other than paper commercially known as hand-made or machine hand-made, valued above 2½c. per lb., n.s.p.f.	3-10c. lb. to 8-10c. lb.	12 p.c. ad val.
Books, of all kinds, bound or unbound pamphlets, engravings, photographs, n.s.p.f....................................	25 p.c. ad val.	15 p.c. ad val.
Paper, manufactures of, n.s.p.f............................	35 p.c. ad val.	25 p.c. ad val.
Playing cards...	10c. pack and 20 p.c. ad val.	60 p.c. ad val.
Schedule N—Sundries:		
Beads...	35 p.c. ad val.	35 p.c. ad val.
Brushes..	40 p.c. ad val.	35 p.c. ad val.
Bristles..	7½c. lb.	7c. lb.
Diamonds and other precious stones, cut but not set...........	10 p.c. ad val.	20 p.c. ad val.
Feathers...	20 to 60 p.c. ad val.	20 to 60 p.c. ad val.
Furs, dressed...	20 p.c. ad val.	20 p.c. ad val.
Furs, wearing apparel.....................................	50 p.c. ad val.	45 p.c. ad val.
Gloves...	$1.25 doz. to $5.80 doz.	$1 to $3 doz. pair
Gutta Percha...	35 p.c. ad val.	15 p.c. ad val.
Hair, human..	20 p.c. ad val.	20 p.c. ad val.
Leather, manufactures of..................................	15 p.c. ad val.	30 p.c. ad val.
Musical instruments.......................................	45 p.c. ad val.	35 p.c. ad val.
Phonographs, gramophones, graphophones, or parts...........	45 p.c. ad val.	25 p.c. ad val.
Paintings and statuary....................................	15 p.c. ad val.	25 p.c. ad val.
Toys...	35 p.c. ad val.	35 p.c. ad val.
Umbrellas..	50 p.c. ad val.	35 p.c. ad val.

THE FREE LIST (Subject to change by conference committee)

Acids (not provided for in above list under Schedule A).
Aconite.
Agates, unmanufactured.
Agricultural implements.
Albumen, n.s.p.f.
Alcohol.
Ammonia, nitrate and sulphate of.
Animals brought into U. S. temporarily or for breeding purposes.
Animals, wild.
Anthracite coal.
Antixins.
Aromatic (not garden) seeds.
Arrowroot, not manufactured.
Arsenic.
Art, works of.
Articles returned after having been exported.
Asbestos, unmanufactured.
Asphaltum.
Bacon.
Bagging for Cotton, etc.
Barbed fence wire.
Barks, n.s.p.f.
Beans, n.s.p.f.
Beef, fresh.
Beeswax.
Belting leather.
Benzine.
Berries, n.s.p.f.
Bibles.
Birds.
Bismuth.
Bituminous coal.
Boneblack.
Books for the blind and for religious, philosophical scientific or literary purposes, persons or families from foreign countries, professional.
Boots.
Borax, crude.
Brass.
Brimstone.
Briquets.
Broom corn.
Buckwheat.
Bullion, gold or silver.
Burlaps.
Cabinet woods, unmanufactured.
Calcium, n.s.p.f.
Camel's hair.
Carbolic acid.
Cash registers.
Cast-iron pipe.
Cattle.
Cement.
Chalk, crude.
Charts, n.s.p.f.
Citizens of U. S. dying in foreign countries, personal effects of.
Clapboards.
Coal.
Cobalt.
Cocoa, n.s.p.f.
Cocoanuts in the shell.
Cocoons, silk.
Cod liver oil.
Coffee.
Coins, gold, silver and copper.
Composition metal, n.s.p.f.

Copper, in plates, bars, ingots or pigs, n.s.p.f. and ore.
Copperas.
Cork, unmanufactured.
Corn.
Corn-meal.
Cotton and cotton bagging.
Cotton gins.
Cotton waste.
Cottonseed oil.
Cream.
Croton oil.
Curry.
Cyanide of potassium and soda.
Darning needles.
Drawings.
Drugs, not advanced.
Dyeing and tanning materials.
Dyewoods, n.s.p.f.
Engravings, n.s.p.f.
Etchings, n.s.p.f.
Evergreen seedings.
Explosive substances.
Extracts, n.s.p.f.
Fans, common palm leaf.
Fats.
Fencing, barbed and galvanized wire.
Ferro Manganese.
Fibres and grasses.
Films, moving picture.
Firewood.
Flat rails, iron or steel.
Flax.
Flint, flints and flint stones unground.
Flocks.
Flower and grass seeds, n.s.p.f.
Foreign stamps.
Fossils.
Fowls.
Fruit plants, for purpose of propagation or cultivation.
Fruits or berries, n.s.p.f.
Fulminates.
Furniture of persons or families from foreign countries.
Furs, undressed.
Galvanized wire.
Gasoline.
Glass, plates or disks.
Glaziers' diamonds.
Gloves, leather, n.s.p.f.
Glue, stock.
Gold, bullion, metals, ore and sweepings.
Gold, silver, copper or other metal coins.
Grains.
Granite, n.s.p.f.
Grass seed and sisal.
Grasses and fibers.
Guano, manures and all substances used only in manure.
Gunny bags, old and cloth.
Gunpowder.
Gutta-percha, crude.
Hair, n.s.p.f.
Hams.
Handle bolts.
Hand sewing needles.
Harness, saddles and saddlery, or parts thereof.
Harvesters.
Hemlock bark, extract of.

Hemp, n.s.p.f.
Herbs, used as drugs, n.s.p.f.
Hides.
Hones and whetstones.
Hoop iron or steel, coated or not coated with paint.
Hoops, iron or steel, cut to lengths.
Horns and parts of.
Horsehair.
Horseshoe nails.
Horseshoes.
Household effects.
Ice.
India rubber, crude.
Indigo.
Ingots.
Insects' eggs.
Instruments, philosophical and scientifical.
Inventions, models of.
Iodine, crude and resublimed.
Ipecac.
Iron Ore.
Iron or steel bands, cut to lengths and manufactures of.
Iron or steel billets.
Iron or steel nails, rails and scrap.
Junk, old.
Jute.
Kerosene.
Kindling wood.
Lamb.
Lambskin.
Land fowls.
Lard.
Laths.
Leather, boots and shoes, harness, rough, saddles, and saddlery, shoe laces, sole, uppers, vamps.
Leaves used as drugs n.s.p.f.
Leeches.
Lemon and lime juice.
Lemon peel, not preserved.
Libraries.
Lifeboats and life-saving apparatus.
Linotype machines.
Lithographic stones not engraved.
Loadstones.
Logs.
Loops, iron.
Lubricating oils, n.s.p.f.
Lumber, planed or finished, n.s.p.f.
Machines, for spreading tar and oil and for sugar making, linotype, sewing, thrashing, typesetting.
Magnesite, crude or calcined.
Maize.
Manganese, oxide and ore of.
Manila.
Manures.
Manuscripts.
Maps, n.s.p.f.
Marroons.
Marrow.
Marshallow.
Meal, corn.
Meats.
Medals of gold, silver or copper.
Metal composition, n.s.p.f.
Nut oil.

Nux vomica.
Oakum.
Oil cake.
Oils not provided for in list under Schedule A.
Orange juice, peel, not preserved, candied or dried.
Ore, cobalt, copper, emery, gold, iron, manganese, manganiferous iron, nickel, silver, tin, tungsten-bearing.
Paper, printing, n.s.p.f. stock, crude.
Paraffin and paraffin oil.
Parchment.
Paris green.
Pearl, mother of, and pearl shells.
Pebbles, Brazilian.
Periodicals and newspapers issued within 6 months of time of entry.
Personal effects.
Petroleum.
Phosphates, crude.
Phosphorus.
Photographic, and moving picture films not exposed or developed.
Pigs, copper, iron.
Pipe, cast-iron.
Plants, fruits, tropical and semi-tropical, for propagation or cultivation.
Rapeseed.
Rattan.
Reapers.
Reeds, unmanufactured.
Regalia and gens, statuary and casts of sculpture.
Roots, n.s.p.f.
Rye and rye flour.
Saddlery.
Safety lamps.
Sago.
Salt.
Saltpetre, crude.
Scientific apparatus.
Seeds, all flower and grass, n.s.p.f.
Sewing machines.
Sheep.
Shellfish and shells.
Shingles.
Shoddy.
Shoes, leather.
Silk, raw.
Silver, bullion, coins, medals, ore, sweepings.
Sisal grass.
Skins, undressed.
Soda, arseniate, ash, cyanide, nitrite, silicate, sulphate.
Sole leather.
Specimens, botany and mineralogy and natural history not for sale.
Spermaceti oil.
Spikes.
Spirits, turpentine.
Sprigs, cut.
Stamps, foreign.
Statuary.
Thrashing machines.
Timber.
Tin, except plates.
Tobacco stems.
Trophies.
Turpentine.
Twine.
Type, old.
Typesetting machines.

Tariff of 1913.—Shortly after his inauguration in 1913, President Wilson called Congress together in extra session, and in his opening address (page 7871) pointed out the duty laid upon the party by the recent elections, which had given the Democrats control of both branches of Congress and the Executive. The preceding tariff law was accordingly passed.

Tarrateen Indians. (See Indian Tribes.)
Tawakaro Indians. (See Indian Tribes.)
Tax, Income. (See Income Tax.)
Tax, Inheritance. (See Inheritance Tax.)
Tax, Poll. (See Poll Tax.)

Taxation.—The exaction of money from the individual for the use of the state is a function of all forms of government. The generally accepted theory of taxation in America is that money to be used in the service of all the citizens of the state is justly raised by taxation; that a tax which does not bear equally upon all or which, bearing equally upon all, is used only for the benefit of a few is unjust. The direction taken by all efforts at tax reform is toward self-annexation—i. e., the community as a whole to decide what is required of each individual for the public expense. Out of this principle grew the doctrine that no tax can be levied save by the representatives of the people who must pay it. It was in defense of this principle that the American colonists objected to the stamp tax imposed by Parliament and raised the claim that "taxation without representation" is tyranny. The tax levied by a conquering nation upon a vanquished foe is tribute. Direct taxation is authorized by the Constitution in proportion to the population. The first direct tax was for $2,000,000, and was levied pro rata upon the sixteen states existing in 1798. Others have since been levied, notably that of 1861, when $20,000,000 was levied in this manner for prosecuting the war. Three-fourths of this amount was by act of March 2, 1891, refunded to the states. C ngress is forbidden by the Constitution to lay any tax or duty on exports (page 20). States are forbidden to lay duties on either exports or imports, but may resort to direct taxation. Until the Civil War the federal government relied chiefly upon duties upon imports for its revenue, but since that time an internal-revenue tax has been collected. Income taxes have become established and inheritance taxes have been recommended. State taxation is direct and is assessed upon real and personal property, upon privileges, and upon individuals or polls. Before 1800 most of the states passed laws to regulate taxation. All except Delaware levied a tax on land, and nine of the original thirteen states collected a poll tax. The systems of county, state, and municipal taxation are numerous and constantly changing. According to the contention of those who favor the single-tax theory, taxation should be solely upon land values, exclusive of improvements. (See Income Tax; Inheritance Tax; Internal Revenue; Single Tax; Tariff.)

Taxation (see also Import Duties):
Balance due from collectors, 620.
By States upon the franchises of street railway and similar corporations, 7422.
Consular reports on, 5201.
Direct, discussed, 265, 268.
Forms of, discussed, 7422.
Income and inheritance tax recommended, 7423, 7463.
Increase in, 5549.
Recommended, 134, 4247.
Internal-revenue stamps, referred to, 3903.
Joint resolution to correct clerical errors in internal-revenue act, vetoed, 3471.
On capital and deposits of banks, repeal of, recommended, 4636.
Reduction in, 4765.
Recommended, 4102, 4422, 4636, 4721, 4831, 5474.
Repeal of laws regarding, recommended, 316, 589.
Well-digested system of, recommended, 514.

Taxes, Direct.—Section 8 of Article I of the Constitution authorizes Congress to lay and collect taxes. During the history of the Government it has not been deemed necessary to lay direct taxes but five times —in 1798, 1813, 1815, 1816, and 1862. The last time was during the Civil War, when a direct tax of $20,000,000 was levied, to be proportionately assessed against all lots of ground with their improvements and dwelling houses. The operation of the act was suspended July 1, 1872, and by an act of March 2, 1891, $15,000,000 of this amount was refunded to the states. The earlier direct taxes were levied on houses, lands, and slaves. (See also Income Tax; Inheritance Tax.)

Taylor, Zachary.—March 5, 1849-July 9, 1850.
Sixteenth Administration—Whig.
Vice-President—Millard Fillmore.
Secretary of State—
John M. Clayton.

EXTENT OF THE UNITED STATES DURING THE ADMINISTRATION OF PRESIDENT TAYLOR, 1849-1850.

(NOT INCLUDING TERRITORIES)

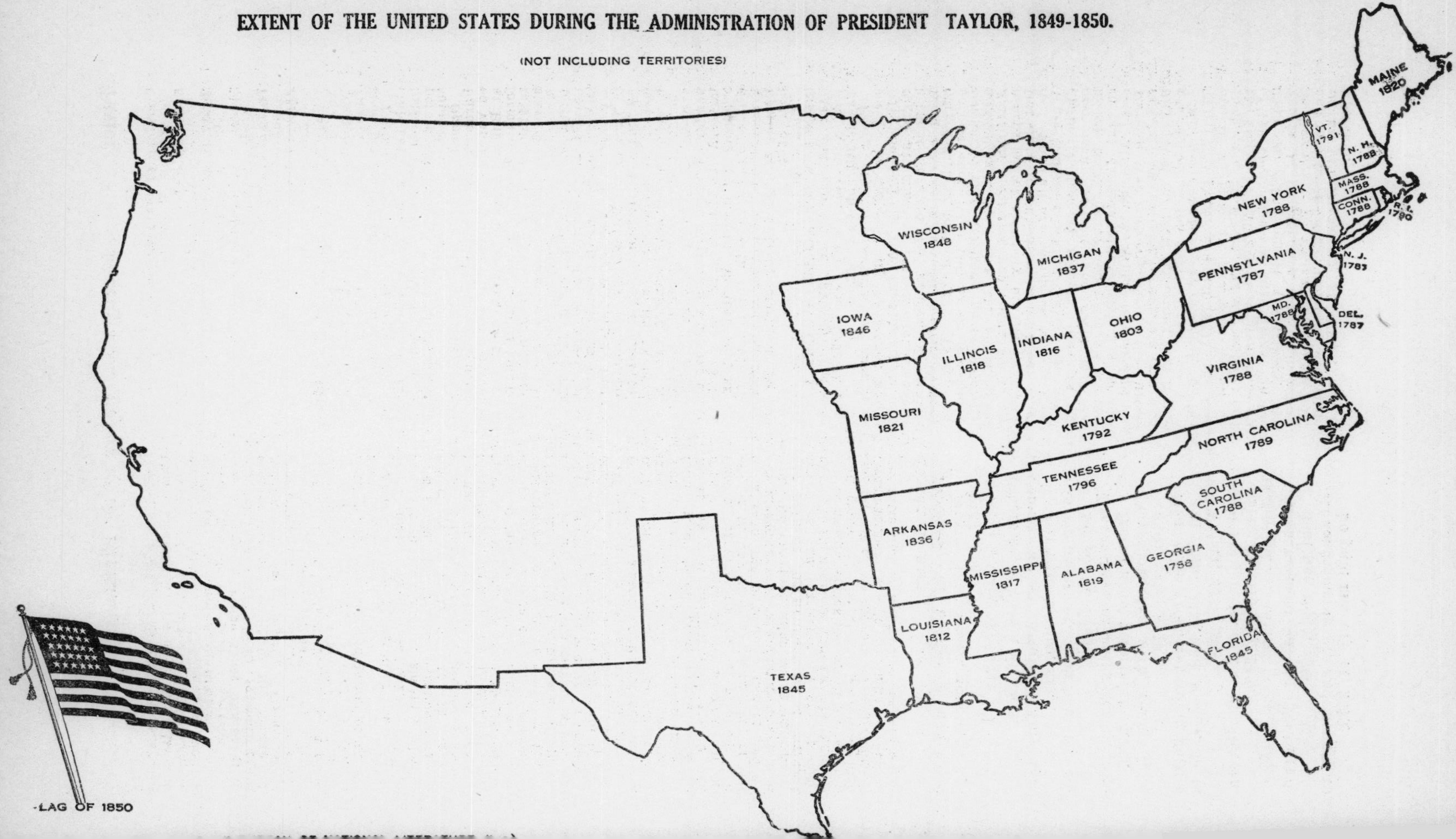

FLAG OF 1850

TEXAS
1845

IOWA
1846

MISSOURI
1821

WISCONSIN
1848

LOUISIANA
1812

ARKANSAS
1836

ILLINOIS
1818

INDIANA
1816

MICHIGAN
1837

MISSISSIPPI
1817

ALABAMA
1819

TENNESSEE
1796

KENTUCKY
1792

OHIO
1803

GEORGIA
1788

SOUTH
CAROLINA
1788

NORTH CAROLINA
1789

VIRGINIA
1788

PENNSYLVANIA
1787

NEW YORK
1788

FLORIDA
1845

MD.
1788

DEL.
1787

N.J.
1787

CONN.
1788

MASS.
1788

N.H.
1788

VT.
1791

MAINE
1820

Secretary of the Treasury—
  William M. Meredith.
Secretary of War—
  George W. Crawford.
Secretary of the Navy—
  William B. Preston.
Secretary of the Interior—
  Thomas Ewing.
Postmaster-General—
  Jacob Collamer.
Attorney-General—
  Reverdy Johnson.

Taylor was elected by the Whig party, Nov. 7, 1848. He was nominated at the Whig National Convention at Philadelphia, June 7 and 8, 1848. Clay was the next most popular candidate for nomination.

Platform.—The platform endorsed General Taylor's candidacy, proclaimed Washington's administration as the model, supported the Mexican War, and solicited the support of the Whig party.

Opposition.—The Free-Soil Convention, or Barnburners, and the Abolitionists supported Van Buren. At the Free-Soil Convention at Buffalo, Aug. 9 and 10, Van Buren was formally nominated on a platform maintaining the rights of free labor against the slave power and the securing of a free soil for a free people, proposing no Federal interference with slavery, citing the Jefferson proviso of 1800 against the extension of slavery, advocating the prohibition of slavery in all new territory, demanding freedom in Oregon, cheap postage, and government retrenchment, supporting internal improvements, recommending free grants of land to settlers, and advising rapid payment of the public debt. The Democratic National Convention at Baltimore, May 22-26, 1848, nominated Lewis Cass on a platform which included the platforms of 1840 and 1844, endorsed and justified the Mexican War, expressed sympathy with the republicans of France, denounced monopolies and exclusive legislation, and heartily endorsed the policies of Polk.

Vote.—The popular vote cast by thirty States gave Taylor, 1,360,601; Cass, 1,220,544; and Van Buren, 291,263. The electoral vote, counted on Feb. 14, 1849, gave Taylor 163 and Cass 127.

Party Affiliation.—Taylor's continuous service in the army of the United States left him entirely free from party or sectional attachments. When his name was brought forward for nomination at the Whig convention, several resolutions were offered seeking to bind Taylor to the support of such Whig policies as the non-extension of slave territory, no more foreign acquisition by conquest, the protection of American industries, and opposition to the usurpation of authority by the Executive. But these resolutions were ruled out of order. Upon all of these questions, and upon Whig policies generally, Taylor had never distinctly declared himself. He was the only man available who could heal the breach in the party and unite all the discordant elements with possible hope of success. Although the Whigs had opposed the Mexican War with vehemence, they nevertheless chose as their candidate a man who had played the most important part in the prosecution of the war.

Political Complexion of Congress.—In the Thirty-first Congress (1849-1851), the Senate, of 62 members, was composed of 35 Democrats, 25 Whigs, and 2 Free-Soil: and the House, of 227 members, was made up of 116 Democrats and 111 Whigs. In the Thirty-second Congress (1851-1853), the Senate, of 62 members, was composed of 36 Democrats, 23 Whigs, and 3 Free-Soil; and the House, of 233 members, was made up of 140 Democrats, 88 Whigs, and 5 Free-Soil.

Foreign Policy.—The ratification of the Clayton-Bulwer Treaty (see Great Britain, Treaties with) took place during the administration of President Taylor. The question of the Panama railway, upon which it bore, was referred to in President Taylor's First Annual Message (page 2555) and again in the massage (page 2580) presenting the Clayton-Bulwer Treaty to the Senate for ratification. In expressing his reasons for the conclusion of this treaty, he says: "At the time negotiations were opened with Nicaragua for the construction of a canal through her territory I found Great Britain in possession of nearly half of Central America, as the ally and protector of the Mosquito king."

Finances.—The public debt on July 1, 1849, amounted to $63,061,858.69. In speaking of the increase, President Taylor said (page 2555): "The extraordinary expenses of the Mexican War and the purchase of California and New Mexico exceed in amount this deficit, together with the loans heretofore made for these objects. I therefore recommend that authority be given to borrow whatever sum may be necessary to cover that deficit. I recommend the observance of strict economy in the appropriation and expenditure of public money." He leaves the matter of the sub-treasury system to the wisdom of Congress, and adds: "If continued, important modifications of it appear to be indispensable."

Tariff.—In his First Annual Message (page 2556) President Taylor advocated a revision of the tariff so as to increase the revenue. He said: "I do not doubt the right or duty of Congress to encourage home industry, which is the great source of national as well as individual wealth and prosperity. I look to the wisdom and patriotism of Congress for the adoption of a system which may place home labor at last on a sure and permanent footing and by due encouragement of manufactures give a new and increased stimulus to agriculture and promote the development of our vast resources and the extension of our commerce." He strongly recommends the placing of specific duties instead of *ad valorem*, and suggested the fixing of duties high enough "to afford substantial and sufficient encouragement to our own industry and at the same time so adjusted as to insure stability."

Communication to Senate from Vice-President, 2590.
Funeral arrangements, 2594.
Referred to, 2613.
Remains of, removal of, referred to, 2611.
Resolutions of—
 Congress on, to be transmitted to Taylor, 2598.
 House and Senate on, 2593.
Special message regarding, 2600.
Exequatur issued consul of Spain revoked by, 2588.
Finances discussed by, 2555.
Foreign policy discussed by, 2548, 2555.
Inaugural address of, 2542.
Mentioned, 681, 2174.
Neutrality laws observed by, 2548.
Portrait of, 2540.
Proclamations of—
 Exequatur issued consul of Spain, revoked, 2588.
 Military expedition against provinces of Mexico, 2545.
Ports of delivery constituted, 2588.
Remains of, removal of, referred to, 2611.
Signature of, 2566.
State of the Union, discussed by, 2547.
Subtreasury system, discussed by, 2556.
Tariff discussed by, 2556.
Veto power of President, discussed by, 2561.

Tea:
Duties on—
 Recommended by President—
 Grant, 4303.
 Hayes, 4422, 4511.
 Polk, 3047, 3086.
 Repeal of, recommended, 4061.
Growth and culture of, recommended, 4578.

Tehuantepec, Isthmus of, transit way across:
Discussed by President—
 Buchanan, 3117.
 Cleveland, 4912, 4956.
 Fillmore, 2617, 2656, 2702.
 Pierce, 2766, 2901.
 Polk, 2388.
 Taylor, 2554, 2580.
Measures for protection of American citizens and property in, recommended, 3048, 3069, 3100.
Referred to, 2693, 3018.
Treaty regarding, with—
 Great Britain, 2580, 2617, 2903, 2943, 3117.
 Mexico, 2642, 2656.
 Ratification of, opposed by President Pierce, 2766.
 Rejection of, by Mexico, discussed, 2702.

Telegraph:
Illustration of first, 2929.
Outrages committed on, 1695.

Telegraph Lines (see also Atlantic Telegraph; International Ocean Telegraph):
Contract for use of, by Post-Office Department recommended, 5562, 5634.
Government control of, discussed by President—
 Arthur, 4728, 4769.
 Grant, 4104, 4152, 4204.
 Harrison, Benj., 5562, 5634.
Inclusion in postal system opposed, 8112.
Military possession of, taken by United States, 3309.
Operation of, discussed, 4297.
Pacific telegraph, referred to, 3329, 3382, 3445.
Proposed overland, between America and Europe, discussed, 3445.
Union of Postal system and, discussed. (See Government Control of, *ante*.)

Telephone. (See illustration opposite 4422.

Ten-Hour System. (See Hours of Labor.)

Tender.—The offer to a creditor of any kind of money which the law defines as legal. (See Legal Tender Cases.)

Tennessee.—One of the southern group of states. Nicknames: "The Volunteer State"; "The Big Bear State"; motto: "Agriculture; Commerce." It lies between lat. 35° and 36° 35′ north and long. 81° 37′ and 90° 15′ west. Tennessee is bounded on the north by Kentucky and Virginia, on the east and southeast by North Carolina (separated by the Great Smoky and Bald ranges of the Alleghanies), on the south by Georgia, Alabama and Mississippi, and on the west by Arkansas and Missouri (separated by the Mississippi River). The area is 42,022 square miles. The eastern portion of the state is mountainous, while the extreme western part, bordering on the Mississippi River, consists of a flat alluvial plain, where vegetation grows with almost tropical luxuriance. Between these two extremes are the valley of the Tennessee in its southern course, an important agricultural region, and the Cumberland Plateau, a table-land with an elevation of 2,000 feet. Extending from this plateau to the Tennessee River in its northern course through the state lies the great central basin, sometimes called the Garden of the State. West of the Tennessee Valley rises another fertile plateau before the descent to the lowlands of the Mississippi. The leading productions are corn, wheat, cotton, and live stock. Tennessee produces some of the finest tobacco grown in the United States. Manufactures of cotton goods and iron have grown up since the Civil War. The capital, Nashville, is one of the greatest educational centers in the South.
The first permanent settlement was made in 1769 at Wautauga by immigrants from North Carolina. When North Carolina proposed to cede this territory to the General Government these settlers objected and organized a state under the name of Franklin

Territorial Expansion:
Annexation discussed. (See Alaska; California; Cuba; Florida; Gadsden Purchase; Hawaiian Islands; Louisiana Purchase; New Mexico; Philippine Islands; Porto Rico; St. John Island; St. Thomas Island; Santo Domingo; Texas; Yucatan.)
Foreign policy discussed by President—
Adams, John, 228.
Adams, J. Q., 862, 868, 884, 895, 903, 922, 950.
Buchanan, 2966, 2998, 3037, 3041, 3066, 3089, 3092, 3173, 3177.
Cleveland, 4912, 5867, 5871, 5873, 5892, 5955, 5963, 6064, 6068, 6087, 6148.
Fillmore, 2614, 2656, 2701, 2715.
Grant, 3985, 4006, 4015, 4018, 4050, 4053, 4082, 4101, 4143, 4176, 4192, 4245, 4290, 4365.
Harrison, Benj., 5445, 5618, 5750, 5783.
Harrison, W. H., 1873.
Hayes, 4418, 4420.
Jackson, 1159, 1222, 1324, 1370, 1378, 1456, 1484, 1500.
Jefferson, 311, 346, 349.
Johnson, 3564, 3581, 3777, 3886, 3888.
Lincoln, 3248, 3255, 3327, 3444.
McKinley, 6248, 6280, 6295, 6307.
Madison, 452, 473.
Monroe, 573, 582, 624, 627, 639, 672, 685, 762, 787, 791, 817, 829.
Pierce, 2731, 2745, 2807, 2864, 2904.
Polk, 2229, 2236, 2248, 2276, 2322, 2337, 2361, 2386, 2431, 2437, 2444, 2480.
Taylor, 2548, 2555.
Tyler, 1890, 2049, 2064, 2160, 2169, 2171, 2176, 2190, 2193, 2206.
Van Buren, 1590, 1702, 1748, 1819.
Washington, 120, 213.

Territories.—At the close of the Revolutionary War several of the states had claims to extensive tracts of land beyond their western borders. The claim was set up that these territories belonged to the United States, as having been won by all in common. Between 1781 and 1802 all these outlying tracts passed by acts of cession under the jurisdiction of the United States. Subsequent additions have been made by purchase or treaty. (See Alaska, California, Florida, Gadsden Purchase, Louisiana Purchase, Oregon, Texas, etc.) The Continental Congress resolved that the western territory to be ceded to the United States "shall be settled and formed into distinct republican states, which shall become members of the Federal Union and have the same rights of sovereignty, freedom, and independence as the other states." The Northwest Territory was organized in 1787, the Southwest in 1790. The Federal District of Columbia is governed directly by Congress, through a commission. An organized territory has a governor, appointed by the President, by and with the advice and consent of the Senate, for four years,

and a legislature composed of a council and a house of representatives chosen every two years by the people. A delegate to Congress, who may speak but not vote, is elected by the people for two years. Territorial legislation is subject to Congressional control. Territorial courts are provided for, the judges of which are appointed by the President for four years, and confirmed by the Senate, and over which the United States Supreme Court has appellate jurisdiction. Alaska has a form of government similar to that originally provided for organized territories, but has no legislature. The only remaining territories are Alaska, District of Columbia and Hawaii, of which Alaska and Hawaii are administered by the Interior Department. In Alaska, the Government is planning extensive railroad construction under its own management. The Interior Department regulates and patrols the fisheries (including the seal hatcheries) of Alaska, conducts two salmon hatcheries, supervises the reindeer industry, and conducts Government agricultural and mine experimental stations. (See Hawaii, Alaska, District of Columbia, Interior Department.)

Territories (see also the several Territories):
Act to pay moneys collected under direct tax of 1861 to States, District of Columbia, and, vetoed, 5422.
Admission of, into Union, discussed and recommendations regarding, 3033, 3086.
Affairs in, discussed by President—
Grant, 4157.
Harrison, Benj., 5640.
Courts of, appeals from, to Supreme Court, recommendations regarding, 4939.
Distribution of arms, ordnance, stores, etc., to District of Columbia and, regulations regarding, 5159, 5462.
Judges in, authority of, as Federal Judges referred to, 2268.
Mineral resources of, discussed, 3330.
Miners in, act for protection of, discussed, and recommendations regarding, 5563.
Northwest of Ohio referred to, 142, 183.
Officers in, absence of, referred to and orders regarding, 3720, 4095.
Power of legislatures of, to authorize corporations to issue bonds referred to, 1757.
Roads within, power to construct, discussed, 2749.
Slavery in, discussed. (See Slavery.)
South of Ohio—
Admission to Union sought by, 189.
Referred to, 183.
Supreme Court decision regarding slavery in. (See Slavery.)
Transfer of affairs of, from State Department to Interior Department recommended, 4060, 4145.

Teton Indians. (See Indian Tribes.)
Texan War. (See Wars, Foreign.)
Texas.—The largest of the United States; nickname, "The Lone Star State." It lies between lat. 25° 51′ and 36° 30′ north

and long. 93° 27′ and 106° 40′ west. It
is bounded on the north by Oklahoma, on
the northeast by Arkansas, on the east by
Arkansas and Louisiana, on the south and
southeast by the Gulf of Mexico, on the
south and southwest by Mexico, and on the
west by New Mexico. It has an area of
265,896 square miles. It consists of a low
coast region in the southeast, west of this
a prairie country, a hilly region, elevated
plains to the north and west, and a mountainous country west of the Pecos River.
It is an important agricultural state, the
leading products being cotton, corn, live
stock, sugar and rice. The manufacture of
lumber and timber products, cotton seed
oil and grist and flour mill products are
the chief industries. The discovery and
development of the oil fields has added to
the wealth and population of the State.

La Salle made a landing at Matagorda
Bay and built a fort in 1685. By the
treaty of 1819-1821 with Spain the United
States surrendered her claim that Texas
was included in the Louisiana Purchase.
Meanwhile Mexico had declared her independence of Spain, and Texas with Coahuila formed a state of the Mexican Republic. Texas seceded from Mexico,
proclaiming her independence March 2,
1836. After the defeat of the Mexican
forces under Santa Anna, by General Houston in the battle of San Jacinto, April 21,
1836, the Republic of Texas was recognized
by England, France, Belgium and the United
States. Annexation was accomplished by a
joint resolution of Congress Dec. 29, 1845.

The dispute over the Western boundary
led to the Mexican War. On March 25,
1850, Texas ceded to the United States all
claims to territory outside her present limits, receiving therefor $10,000,000. An or-
dinance of secession was passed Feb. 1,
1861. The State was readmitted to the
Union March 30, 1870.

In the eastern part of the state are
valuable yellow-pine forests, and there are
oyster and other fisheries on the coast.

Statistics of agriculture collected for the
last Federal census, place the number of
farms in the state at 417,770, comprising
112,435,067 acres, valued, with stock and
improvements, at $2,217,645,164. The aver-
age value of farm land was $14.53 per acre
against $4.70 in 1900. The value of do-
mestic animals, poultry, etc., was $318,646,-
509, including 6,934,586 cattle, valued at
$132,985,879 ; 1,170,068 horses, $84,024,-
635 ; 675,558 mules, $73,979,145 ; 2,336,363
swine, $11,639,366 ; 1,808,709 sheep, $6,301,-
364 ; poultry, $4,806,642. The yield and
value of field crops for 1911 was: Corn,
7,300,000 acres, 69,350,000 bushels, $55,-
480,000 ; wheat, 700,000 acres, 6,580,000
bushels, $6,580,000 ; oats, 737,000 acres,
18,499,000 bushels, $9,989,000 ; rye, 2,000
acres, 20,000 bushels, $21,000 ; rice, 238,300
acres, 8,174,000 bushels, $6,539,000 ; pota-
toes, 50,000 acres, 2,850,000 bushels, $3,-
591,000 ; hay, 606,000 acres, 606,000 tons,
$7,211,000 ; tobacco, 300 acres, 195,000
pounds, $39,000, and cotton, 4,280,000 bales.
Texas ranks first among the states in the
production of cotton. Petroleum to the
extent of about 9,000,000 barrels was produced in 1911, showing a gradual decrease
in the last few years. The coal mined was
1,892,176 short tons, valued at $3,160,965.

The number of manufacturing establishments in Texas having an annual output
valued at $500 or more at the beginning of
1915 was 5,084. The amount of capital
invested was $283,544,000, giving employ-
ment to 91,114 persons, using material
valued at $253,090,000 and turning out fin-
ished goods worth $361,279,000. Salaries
and wages paid amounted to $59,179,000.

Texas (see also Confederate States):
Acquisition of, not attempted by con-
quest, 2337.
Act—
Authorizing special seed distribu-
tion in drought-stricken counties
in, vetoed, 5142.
To constitute new division of judi-
cial district of, etc., vetoed, 6185.
Admission of, into Union—
Constitution adoption by, 2236,
2266.
Discussed. (See Annexation of,
post.)
Foreign interference discussed,
2237.
Withdrawal of application for, re-
ferred to, 1705.
Annexation of, to United States—
Correspondence regarding, referred
to, 2167, 2168.
Desired by, 1456, 1487.
Discussed by President—
Polk, 2229, 2236, 2329, 2337.
Tyler, 2160, 2169, 2171, 2176,
2193, 2206.
Information regarding, desired by
Senate, refused, 2232.
Not an offense to Mexico, 2329.
Protest of Mexico against, referred
to, 2238.
Question of, presented to people of,
2196, 2337.
Immediate annexation favored,
2197, 2337.
Referred to, 1587, 1693, 2210,
2483.
Terms of, accepted by, 2236, 2337.
Annexation treaty with United
States—
Consent of Mexico to, not required,
2171, 2177, 2195.
Debts of, to be assumed by General
Government, 2197.
Discussed and referred to, 2160,
2169, 2171, 2176, 2193, 2206.
Opposition to, discussed, 2171,
2176.
Ratification of, regarded by Mexico
as a declaration of war by United
States, 2170.
Referred to, 2175, 2194.
Rejection of, by Senate, discussed,
2176.
Transmitted, 2160.
Armistice between Mexico and, re-
ferred to, 2172.
Army of United States sent to pro-
tect territory of, from invasion,
2238, 2261.
Boundary dispute regarding Greer
County. (See Greer County.)
Boundary line of, 2166.
Boundary line of, with Louisiana,
960.

Boundary line of, with New Mexico, 2566, 2568, 2586, 2587, 2601, 2609, 2628.
  Proposition of United States regarding establishment of, accepted, 2630.
  Proclamation regarding, 2643.
  Views of President Fillmore on settlement of, 2603, 2630.
Boundary line of United States with—
  Appropriation for expenses of marking, recommended, 2839.
  Convention regarding, 1684, 1705, 1706, 1750, 1822.
    Commissioners appointed under, 1750, 1822, 1932.
    Final decision of, 1944.
  Demarcation of, referred to, 1957, 2003.
  Proposition for establishment of, accepted by, 2630.
  Proclamation regarding, 2643.
  Referred to, 4790.
Brazos Santiago, commerce of, referred to, 2610.
Civil and political condition of, discussed, 1484.
  Referred to, 1449, 1457, 1496.
Civil authority of Mexico in, expelled, 1487.
Claims of, against United States, 2198, 2251.
  Payment of, in stock, discussed, 2661.
Claims of, to portion of New Mexico, discussed. (See Boundary line of, with New Mexico, *ante.*)
Claims of United States against, convention for adjustment of, 1686.
Commercial relations with, 1964.
  Treaty regarding, 2030.
Constitution of, ratification of, referred to, 2236.
  Letter regarding, referred to, 2266.
Correspondence—
  Regarding title to, 2173.
  With Mexico, regarding, 2014.
Debts of—
  Referred to, 2210.
  To be assumed by United States, 2197.
Defense and improvement of coast of, referred to, 2304.
Diplomatic agents of, accredited to United States, 2175.
Disorders on frontier of. (See Rio Grande River.)
Frontiers of, increase of cavalry force on, referred to, 4372.
Government established in, 1487.
Governor of, letter of, regarding extension of civil jurisdiction, discussed, 2603.
  Referred to, 2609.

Independence of—
  Acknowledgment of, by Santa Anna, referred to, 2330.
  Conditional agreement of Mexico to acknowledge, discussed, 2239.
  Discussed by President—
    Jackson, 1484.
      Referred to by President McKinley, 6287.
    Polk, 2330.
    Tyler, 2113.
  Recognized by United States, 1500.
Indians in—
  Assignment of lands to, recommended, 2710.
  Colonization of, referred to, 2833.
Insurrection in, termination of, proclaimed, 3632.
  Correction of date in, by proclamation, 3747.
Invasion of United States frontier by armed force from, 1726.
Judicial authority of, interference of military forces with, referred to, 2568, 2585.
Mexico threatens to renew war with, discussed, 2194, 2206.
Military aid to be furnished to, by United States, referred to, 2174.
Military force on frontier of, referred to, 2173, 4424.
Minister of United States to—
  Nomination of, 1501.
  Referred to, 2175.
Principles of civil liberty destined to flourish in, 3280.
Prisoners rescued from jail in Starr County by Mexicans, referred to, 4408.
Provisional governor for, appointed and restoration of, into Union, discussed, 3519.
  Referred to, 4000.
Reconstruction of—
  Referred to, 4000.
  Time for submitting constitution to voters, proclaimed, 3971.
  Referred to, 3983.
Relations with, 1943, 2014, 2168.
Treaties of, with France and Great Britain, referred to, 2210, 2212, 2297.
Treaty with, 2030, 2160, 2168.
War with Mexico. (See Wars, Foreign.)
Texas, Department of, neutrality laws of United States and Mexico violated in, and action of United States, discussed, 5877.
Texas Fever among cattle, discussed, 5887, 5957.
Texas vs. White et al.—A case before the Supreme Court of the United States in which the acts of secession of the Southern States were declared void and the rights

of a State of the Union held to be unimpaired by the acts of a revolutionary government within the State.

In 1851 the United States issued to the State of Texas 5,000 coupon bonds for $1,000 each, payable to the State of Texas or bearer, with interest at 5 per cent semi-annually, in settlement of certain boundary claims. Some of these bonds were seized by the officers of the State government during the Civil War and sold to White & Chiles and others of New York. The bonds were payable only when indorsed by the governor. The State convention in 1866 passed an ordinance looking to the recovery of these bonds. An act passed in October of that year authorized the governor to proceed in his discretion to carry out this intention. The agent appointed by the executive procured the filing of a bill the same year asking for an injunction and the recovery of the bonds in question. The case came before the Supreme Court of the United States at the December term, 1868, on the original bill. The injunction was granted on the general ground that the action of a revolutionary State government did not affect the right of Texas as a State of the Union having a government acknowledging her obligations to the Federal Constitution. The court pronounced the act of secession void, Chief Justice Chase rendering the opinion. Justice Grier dissented on all the points raised and decided. Justices Swayne and Miller concurred in dissenting on the capacity of the State of Texas, "in her present condition," to waive on an original suit. On the merits of the case they united with the majority.

Further hearing was accorded to certain parties, and both complainant and defendants were granted liberty in the decree to apply for further directions in its execution. In one place in the court's opinion the Chief Justice said it was a historical fact that in 1862 the government of Texas in control was its only actual government, its acts in almost all respects valid, though unlawful and revolutionary as to the United States. December, 1869, the additional part of this celebrated case, known in the reports as Texas *vs.* Hardenberg, arose, the Chief Justice deciding for the court that upon the whole case the decree must be for the complainant as to the bonds claimed by Hardenberg.

Further decisions of the Supreme Court on additional portions of the case are as follows, briefly: December, 1870, *In re* Paschal, Justice Bradley delivering the court's judgment, it was ordered that the motion to compel George W. Paschal to pay to the clerk of the court the money received by him be denied. An order was granted to discharge him as solicitor and counsel for the complainant in the second case. October, 1874, *In re* Chiles, Justice Miller rendering the court's opinion, Justices Field and Hunt dissenting, it was ordered that Chiles pay a fine of $250 and the costs of the proceeding and stand committed to the marshal's custody until the same be paid. This was for contempt in disobeying the court's decree.

Textiles and Glass, report on cost of producing in United States and Europe transmitted, 5674.

Thames (Canada), Battle of.—After Perry's victory over the British fleet on Lake Erie, Gen. Harrison completed his preparations for the invasion of Canada. Sept. 21, 1813, the embarkation of the army on Perry's transports began. On the afternoon of the 27th the Army of the North-

west, consisting of 5,000 men, under the immediate command of Gen. Harrison and Gen. Shelby, governor of Kentucky, landed at Amherstburg (Malden), but found that Proctor's army, about 800 regulars and 1,200 Indians, had fled inland. Harrison started in hot pursuit. In response to the repeated demands of Tecumseh the British made a stand about eight miles north of the river Thames. Here they were attacked on Oct. 5 by about 3,000 Americans. A short but decisive battle took place, in which the British and Indians were completely routed and Chief Tecumseh was killed. The precise number of casualties in this battle is not known. The American loss was probably about 15 killed and twice that number wounded. The British lost about 18 killed, 26 wounded, and 600 taken prisoners, of whom 25 were officers Proctor made his escape. Thirty-three dead Indians were found upon the field after the battle. (See the illustration opposite 569.)

Thanks of Congress:
  Tender of, recommended to—
    Alden, James, 3277.
    Bailey, Theodorus, 3277.
    Baldwin, Charles H., 3277.
    Bell, Henry H., 3277.
    Boggs, Charles S., 3277.
    Breese, K. Randolph, 3277.
    Caldwell, Charles H. B., 3277.
    Craven, Thomas T., 3277.
    Crosby, Pierce, 3277.
    Cushing, William B., 3457.
    Dahlgren, John A., 3284.
    Davis, Charles H., 3284.
    De Camp, John, 3277.
    Dewey, George, etc., 6297.
    Donaldson, Edward, 3277.
    Du Pont, Samuel F., 3265, 3271.
    Farragut, David G., 3276.
    Foote, Andrew H., 3283.
    Goldsborough, Louis M., 3266.
    Guest, John, 3277.
    Harrell, Abram, 3277.
    Harrison, Napoleon, 3277.
    Hobson, Richmond P., 6306.
    Lardner, James L., 3284.
    Lee, Samuel P., 3277.
    Morris, George U., 3345.
    Morris, Henry, 3277.
    Newcomb, Frank H., etc., 6302.
    Nichols, Edward F., 3277.
    Porter, David D., 3277, 3284, 3352.
    Preble, George H., 3277.
    Queen, Walter W., 3277.
    Ransom, George M., 3277.
    Renshaw, William B., 3277.
    Rodgers, John, 3392.
    Rowan, Stephen C., 3284.
    Russell, John H., 3277.
    Smith, Albert N., 3277.
    Smith, Melancton, 3277.
    Smith, Watson, 3277.
    Stringham, Silas H., 3284.
    Swartwout, Samuel, 3277.
    Wainwright, Jonathan M., 3277.
    Wainwright, Richard, 3277.
    Winslow, John A., 3457.

Third Assistant Secretary of State, State Department.—This office was created in 1875, and at the present time carries with it an annual salary of $4,500. The third assistant secretary of state is appointed by the President, by and with the consent of the Senate. Together with the assistant secretary of state, he is in charge of the diplomatic appointments ; and in addition has charge of the Western European Division (q. v.) and the Near Eastern Division (q. v.) of the Department. He attends also to the Departments' representation in International Conferences and to the ceremonial part of the diplomatic service. He is also in charge of the Bureau of Rolls and of the Library of the Department. (See State Department.)

Three-Cent Piece.—A small silver coin authorized by Congress in 1851. It was coined from 1851 to 1873, inclusive, with the exception of the year 1857. Its weight was originally 12,375 grains, but in 1853 this was reduced to 11.52 grains. The three-cent coin was legal tender to the amount of thirty cents. March 3, 1865, Congress authorized another three-cent piece, to be made of an alloy of copper and nickel. With the exception of the year 1877, this piece was coined continuously till 1890. Its weight was thirty grains.

Three-Dollar Piece.—A gold coin of the United States, authorized in 1853. Its coinage was begun the next year and continued till 1890. The weight of the coin was 77.4 grains, and it was legal tender to an unlimited amount.

Ticonderoga (N. Y.), Capture of.—As soon as the events of Lexington and Concord became known it was decided by the Americans to seize the British fort a' Ticonderoga, at the junction of Lakes George and Champlain. The place was garrisoned by 44 men under Capt. Delaplace. On the night of May 10, 1775, Col. Ethan Allen, with other officers and 270 Green Mountain boys, gained an entrance to the fort and Allen demanded its surrender, as traditionally reported, "in the name of the Great Jehovah and the Continental Congress." Finding resistance useless, Delaplace surrendered the garrison and 120 cannon, with muskets, ball, and powder. The surprise was so complete that not a man was lost.

Ticonderoga, The, cruise of, 4693.

Tigre, Island of seizure and occupation of, by Great Britain referred to, 2570, 2601.

Timber-Culture Act.—An act passed by Congress March 3, 1873, for the promotion of forestry. It granted to settlers 160 acres of treeless land on condition that they plant and cultivate a certain number of forest trees.

Timber-Culture Act:
   Act respecting repeal of, returned, 6182.
   Repeal of, recommended, 4770, 4837, 5107.

Timber Lands. (See Lands, Public.)

Time, Regulation of. (See International Meridian Conference.)

Tippecanoe.—A nick-name given to William Henry Harrison on account of his victory at the Battle of Tippecanoe. (See Tippecanoe, Battle of.)

Tippecanoe and Tyler too.— The campaign cry used prior to the election of Harrison and Tyler in 1840, arising from Harrison's success at the Battle of Tippecanoe. (See Tippecanoe, Battle of.)

Tippecanoe, Battle of (Nov. 7, 1811).—In 1806, Tecumseh, chief of the Shawnee Indians, and his brother Elkswatana, called the Prophet, formed a plan for a great confederacy of all the western and southern Indians against the whites. Their doctrine was opposed to tribal rights, and they claimed that no part of the territory could be sold by any tribe to the whites without the consent of all the Indians.

William Henry Harrison, who had been on the staff of General Anthony Wayne at the battle of Maumee Rapids, and Secretary to General Arthur St. Clair, Governor of the Northwest Territory, was appointed in 1801, Governor of the Indiana Territory, from which was later formed the States of Indiana, Illinois, Michigan and Wisconsin. By the close of 1805 Harrison had extinguished Indian titles to 46,000 acres of land in the territory. Sept. 30, 1809, he concluded a treaty by which, for $10,550, he secured nearly 3,000,000 acres along the Wabash and White Rivers. Tecumseh and the Prophet told the Indians they were cheated by the treaties, and appealed to their savage nature to turn against the whites. About 1808 Tecumseh established his council fire on the banks of the Tippecanoe River in Tippecanoe County, Indiana, near the site of the present village of Battle Ground. Harrison was aware of the hostile feeling among the Indians over the treaties of Vincennes and Fort Wayne, which he had negotiated, and began preparations for defense. While building a stockade on the site of the present city of Terre Haute, Oct. 11, 1811, one of the white sentinels was killed by an Indian in ambush. This determined Harrison to march against the camp at Tippecanoe. On the night of Nov. 6, 1811, he encamped within a mile of the Indian village, and the Prophet had agreed to a conference on the following day. Harrison's party consisted of about 800, including 500 Indians and Kentucky militiamen. The hostile Indians were estimated by Harrison at 700. They were under the command of White Loon, Stone Eater, and Winnemac, Tecumseh being then on a mission to the Creeks and Cherokees to induce them to join his confederacy. Without waiting for the promised conference or even the dawn of day, the savages made a furious assault on Harrison's camp, which they maintained with ferocious bravery for two hours. It was after daylight when the last of the Indians were driven from the field, leaving forty of their number dead on the battleground. The loss to the whites was 37 killed and 151 wounded. The entire loss of the Indians was never ascertained. Next day Harrison advanced to the town, found it deserted, destroyed it and returned to Vincennes. This disaster broke the power of Tecumseh. (See illustration opposite 457.)

Titles. (See Lands, Public.)

Tobacco.—A native American plant of the Nightshade family (*Nicotiana tabacum*), the leaves of which have strong narcotic effects. It was named from the Indian tabaco or pipe in which the aborigines smoked the leaves. The word was applied by the Spaniards to the herb itself. Its use was observed in Santo Domingo in 1492. It was introduced into European countries by the early voyagers, and the Virginia settlers made it their chief agricultural product, and even used it as the standard of value. Tobacco was unknown to the civilized world prior to the discovery of America. It is a sedative and narcotic, and is used by more people and among more nations than any similar substance, with perhaps the exception of tea. After its introduction into England in 1585, its habitual use soon spread over Continental Europe and into Asia, notwithstanding the determined efforts of ecclesiastic and civil authorities to prohibit it. When the period of persecution had run its course, it was looked upon as a medicine and was prescribed for all sorts of human ailments. Its habitual use was looked upon as a luxury to be enjoyed only by the well-to-do. From 1619 to 1641 prices in London ranged from three pence to three shillings per pound. During the civil war in the United States, the price ranged from twelve cents to forty-five cents per pound.

Tobacco as a Revenue Producer.—Owing perhaps to its universal use and its general regard as a luxury, tobacco is the most heavily taxed article in the world. In this country the internal revenue tax is six cents per pound for the manufactured product. Cigars, large, are taxed $3 per 1,000; small, and cigarettes, 54 cents per 1,000. The United Kingdom levies a tax of from 77 cents to 85 cents per pound; cigars, $1.21 per pound. Norway taxes manufactured tobacco 22 cents per pound; Sweden, 12 cents; Switzerland, 22 cents; Germany, 9 cents; Holland, 14 cents; Russia, 38 cents. In France, Spain, Italy, Portugal, Austria, Turkey, Rumania the government monopolizes the trade in tobacco. It is also made the object of special excise taxes from time to time.

The production of tobacco in the United States as reported to the Department of Agriculture in the year 1913 was as follows:

States	Acres	Pounds	Farm Value Dec. 1
New Hampshire..	100	177,000	$32,000
Vermont.........	100	170,000	31,000
Massachusetts...	6,600	11,550,000	2,044,000
Connecticut.....	20,200	35,754,000	6,614,000
New York.......	4,600	5,980,000	718,000
Pennsylvania....	33,100	47,995,000	4,080,000
Maryland.......	22,000	17,600,000	1,408,000
Virginia........	175,000	113,750,000	10,238,000
West Virginia...	10,800	8,856,000	974,000
North Carolina...	265,000	172,250,000	19,809,000
South Carolina...	50,000	36,500,000	3,540,000
Georgia.........	1,900	1,900,000	475,000
Florida.........	4,300	4,300,000	1,290,000
Ohio...........	86,800	78,120,000	6,875,000
Indiana.........	13,500	12,150,000	1,094,000
Illinois.........	600	468,000	56,000
Wisconsin......	45,600	53,808,000	5,919,000
Missouri........	4,100	4,920,000	640,000
Kentucky.......	400,000	364,000,000	30,576,000
Tennessee......	77,400	63,468,000	4,760,000
Alabama.......	200	140,000	39,000
Louisiana.......	700	280,000	98,000
Texas..........	200	116,000	24,000
Arkansas.......	700	427,000	77,000
United States..	1,223,500	1,034,679,000	$101,411,000

The following table shows the production, consumption and revenue derived from other countries for the year 1913, as compared with the United States:

Countries	Production	Total Consumption	Total Revenue (Customs and Excise)
	Pounds	Pounds	Dollars
United States..	953,734,000	a550,429,000	106,879,000
Germany......	56,952,951	271,205,899	45,072,123
Russia........	233,451,159	202,503,424	41,140,511
France........	35,780,658	116,364,079	104,840,422
United Kingdom	....	95,983,525	86,804.340
Austria-Hungary	b159,087,904	159,191,240	63,663,744

The revenue receipts from tobacco in the United States in recent years have been as follows:

Fiscal Year	Revenue Receipts	Fiscal Year	Revenue Receipts
1906	...$48,422,997	1912	... 70,590,151
1907	... 51,811,070	1913	... 76,769,424
1908	... 49,862,754	1914	... 79,986,639
1909	... 51,887,178	1915	... 79,957,373
1910	... 58,118,457	1916	... 88,063,947
1911	...$67,005,950	1917	...102,230,205

The detailed statement of manufactured tobacco withdrawn for consumption in 1917 follows:

	Number
Cigars, weighing more than 3 lbs. per thousand	8,266,770,593
Cigars, weighing not more than 3 lbs. per thousand..	950,130,520
Cigarettes, weighing more than 3 lbs. per thousand..	27,458,394
Cigarettes, weighing not more than 3 lbs. per thousand	30,501,735,144

	Pounds
Snuff	35,377,351
Tobacco, chewing and smoking	445,763,206

Statistics of the last census show there were in 1909, 15,822 manufacturing establishments engaged in the tobacco industry. These were owned and operated by 17,634 proprietors or firm members, and employed 197,637 salaried employees and wage-earners, and used a total capital of $245,660,000. These establishments converted $177,186,000 worth of raw material into finished product valued at $416,695,000. They paid in salaries and wages $86,114,000.

Tobago, Island of, duties on vessels from, suspended by proclamation, 5598, 6502.

Toledo, Ohio, proclamation granting privileges of other ports to, 2859.

Toledo War.—A bloodless dispute between Ohio and Michigan in 1835 over the territory which contained the city of Toledo. Just previous to Michigan's making application for admission to the Union, Ohio proposed to assume control of the disputed tract. Michigan passed an ordinance making the occupation of Toledo by Ohio authorities a penal offense and appealed to the Federal Government to sustain the action. The militia were called out on both sides. When armed hostilities became imminent, Michigan was admitted as a State and awarded the Upper Peninsula in exchange for the Toledo tract in dispute.

Toledo War, controversy regarding boundary between Ohio and Michigan known as, 637, 1173, 1404, 1407.

Toll.—A fee collected for a privilege. This form of collecting has been employed as a means for paying the cost of building roads and bridges, usually when a county or other corporate body borrows the money on bonds to pay for the work involved, and then sets up toll gates, where, through a series of years, money is collected from travelers on the road for the redemption of the bonds. Sometimes, however, the building is done by private enterprise and paid for thereafter with tolls collected, both for re-imbursement and for profit. Toll-bridges and toll-roads are now almost extinct, the preferred method being that of taxation.

Tonawanda Indians. (See Indian Tribes.)

Tonga Islands:
Treaty between Germany and Great Britain and, referred to, 5121.
Treaty with, 5121.

Tonga, Treaties with.—The treaty of amity, commerce, and navigation of 1886 provides privileges to the citizens of the one country in that of the other equal to those of the most favored nation. Trade privileges, except in the case of laborers, shall in no case be more restrictive than those granted to others. Shipping charges shall be no higher than those paid by the national ships in home ports.

Ships-of-war of either power shall have free access to any of the ports; and to facilitate repairs the government of Tonga agrees to sell to the United States land on the islands to provide a coaling or other station. Mail steamers from the United States crossing the Pacific Ocean shall have full harbor privileges on payment of one-third the customary shipping charges, so long as the vessels so partaking of this privilege shall carry the Tonga mails free of charge. Whaling and fishing vessels are granted large privileges in the islands free of harbor charges so long as they do not trade or barter spirituous liquors, arms, or ammunition to the Tongas.

No United States citizen residing in Tonga shall be compelled to do military service, or to pay higher or other license fees than do the subjects of Tonga. Deserters are to be apprehended by the local authorities upon application from the consul or, when such is deficient, from the master of the vessel. Consular officers may be appointed in terms customary in consular conventions. Freedom of conscience is extended to all citizens of the United States in Tonga.

Tonkawa Indians. (See Indian Tribes.)

Tonnage Duties. (See Vessels, Foreign.)

Topeka Constitution.—The enactment of the Kansas-Nebraska bill, which, it has been claimed, in effect repealed the Missouri Compromise forbidding slavery north of 36° 30′, left the question of slavery to be decided by the people of the territories before admission. The proslavery and antislavery advocates at once began a struggle for supremacy. Oct. 23, 1855, a constitutional convention representing the anti-slavery population of Kansas met at Topeka. This convention adopted the boundaries set by the Kansas-Nebraska bill, prohibited slavery after July, 1857, and conferred the right of suffrage on "white male citizens" and on "every civilized male Indian who has adopted the habits of the white man." This convention was dispersed by Federal troops. The bill to admit Kansas into the Union under the provisions of the Topeka constitution was introduced in the House of Representatives by Daniel Mace, of Indiana, April 7, 1856, and in the Senate by Lewis Cass, of Michigan, March 24. The bill passed the House, but failed in the Senate. (See also Lecompton Constitution; Wyandotte Constitution.)

Topeka Constitution. (See Kansas, Government of.)

Topographical Corps:
Increase in, 873, 1474, 1607.

Internal improvements, operations of, intrusted to, 1776.

Reorganization of, recommended, 1388.

Tornado, The. (See *Virginius*, The.)

Torpedo Boats. (See Vessels, United States.)

Torpedoes:

Adoption and construction of, discussed, 5759.

Appropriation for trial with, recommended, 4304.

Tortugas. (See Dry Tortugas.)

Tory.—The terms "Whig" and "Tory" had been in use in English politics for a great many years anterior to the American Revolution. The term "Whig" designated the party opposing the royal prerogative and who were generally in favor of reforms; the term "Tory," the party upholding the prerogative and adhering to old institutions. In our colonial days the term "Tory" was applied to those who were adherents of the Crown, and the term "Whig" to the opponents thereof, and so the American sympathizers were known as Whigs, the supporters of England as Tories.

Town.—A word derived from the Anglo-Saxon word "tun," meaning "a place inclosed." The suffix still clings to the names of many English towns. In the United States the word has a varying signification. In Pennsylvania it is applied to any municipal government. In New York, Wisconsin, and most of the western states a town is a subdivision of a county, and is often called a township (q. v.), but the town is not necessarily always coextensive with the latter. In New England the town is the unit of civil organization, a county being simply an aggregation of towns.

Town Meeting.—A peculiarly democratic institution of New England and some of the newly formed western states. It is a meeting of the citizens to legislate for the town, levy taxes, elect the officers, usually a town clerk, selectmen, a treasurer, assessors, constables, overseers of the poor, and school commissioners. In some of the states the cities, by their aldermen, are authorized to transact the business formerly attended to by the town meeting. That it still has a legal existence was demonstrated as recently as 1881, when the Labor Reform Society of Boston secured a writ of mandamus to compel the city authorities to call a town meeting on petition, as required by its charter.

Towns, Seaport, protection for. (See Defenses, Public, provision for.)

Townshend Acts.—At the instance of Charles Townshend, chancellor of the exchequer, two acts were passed by the British Parliament providing for the appointment of commissioners to enforce more effectually the laws relating to taxes in the Colonies. They authorized writs of assistance and increased the duties on many articles already taxed, besides imposing others on glass, paper, colors, and tea. The object of these taxes was to support the civil government in the territories.

Township.—In the older United States counties are divided, without reference to their inhabitants, into townships varying in size from five to ten miles square. When in 1802 Col. Mansfield surveyed the Northwest Territory he divided the entire public domain into land districts, made up of a varying number of tracts each six miles square. These were called townships. These townships were again divided into thirty-six equal squares, called sections, of one square mile each and containing 640 acres. A civil township may include more or less than one township in area.

Toynbee Hall. (See Social Settlements.)

Trade, with countries bordering on the Pacific discussed, 7052, 7108.

Trade Adviser.—The office of trade adviser was established by the State Department several months after the outbreak of the Great European War, in order to assist American merchants who were experiencing difficulties with shipments of goods consigned to or from them, because of embargo and other war regulations promulgated by foreign governments. The office, which is under the supervision of the assistant secretary of state (q. v.), later broadened out into a bureau of general information and assistance to American shippers upon trade regulations and requirements of foreign governments. (See State Department.)

Trade Commission.—Under the law introduced by Mr. Covington of Maryland and approved Sept. 26, 1914, the President is authorized to appoint a commission of five members, not more than three of whom shall be members of the same political party, to take the place of the Bureau of Corporations and the Commissioners of Corporations. Property, records and employees of the bureau are transferred to the new Commission, whose duty it is to regulate commerce by preventing persons, partnerships or corporations (except banks and common carriers, regulated by other laws), from using unfair methods of competition.

Commerce is defined in the act as commerce in any territory of the United States or in the District of Columbia or between the States or Territories, or with a foreign nation. A corporation is defined as an organization, incorporated or not, having a capital stock, divided into shares or not, formed to carry on business for profit.

Whenever the Commission shall have reason to believe that any person, partnership or corporation has been using unfair methods of competition, and that a proceeding would be to the interest of the public, it shall issue a complaint and set a day for a hearing. If found guilty, orders to desist from the specified violation of the law are issued. In case of failure of the guilty party to comply with the law as pointed out by the Commission, the latter shall apply to the Circuit Court of Appeals where the corporation resides or where the competition complained of takes place. The findings of the Commission as to the facts shall be conclusive and the decree of the court final, except for review by the Supreme Court upon certiorari. The jurisdiction of the Circuit Court of Appeals in regard to orders of the Commission shall be exclusive, and orders shall be expedited and given precedence. Processes of the Commission may be served by personal delivery, registered mail or left at principal place of business.

The powers of the Commission are to (a) investigate and gather information concerning business, and practices of corporations, etc.; (b) require certified reports at any time; (c) report to the Attorney General final decrees entered against defendant corporations; (d) investigate upon direction of the President or either house; (e) make recommendations (upon application of the Attorney General), for the readjustment of the business of any corporation guilty of violation of the anti-trust laws, in order that the corporation may thereafter maintain its organization, management and conduct of business in accordance with law; (f) make public such information obtained by it, except trade secrets and names of customers, as it shall deem expedient to the public interest, make reports to Congress and recommend additional legislation; (g) classify corporations and make rules for carrying out the provisions of the law; (h) investigate trade conditions in and with foreign countries where such may affect the foreign trade of the United States.

Suits in equity before the Attorney General under the anti-trust acts may be referred to the Commission as a master in chancery to report an appropriate form of decree, and accepted at the option of the court. All departments of the government are required to furnish information relating to corporations. Agents and members of the Commission shall have access to evidence, are empowered to require attendance, administer oaths and take testimony at any place in the United States, with the aid and authority, when necessary of the Federal Courts. No person shall be excused from testifying before the Commission on the ground that his evidence might tend to degrade or criminate him, but no natural person shal be prosecuted on account of anything to which he may testify, and no natural person shall be exempt from punishment for perjury before the Commission. Refusal to testify is punishable by a fine of from $1,000 to $5,000. Failure to file reports when ordered subjects a corporation to a fine of $100 for each day of neglect. A member or employee of the Commission who reveals information imparted officially is subject to a fine of $5,000 or one year in prison.

The terms of the first Commissioners are to be three, four, five, six, and seven years, respectively, as designated by the President, and their successors are to be appointed for terms of seven years. The salary of the Commissioners is fixed at $10,000, and a Secretary is provided for at $5,000 per year.

The members of the Commission in 1917 were William J. Harris, Will H. Parry, Joseph E. Davies, William H. Colver, and John F. Fort.

Trade Commission:

Business justice could be guided by, 7916.

Created, 8151, 8158.

Establishment of, recommended, 7819.

Purpose of, 8030.

War administrative powers vested in, 8370.

Trade Dollar.—A silver coin issued by the United States from 1874 to 1878. It was coined for use in trade with China in competition with the Spanish and Mexican dollars. It was not intended for general circulation in the United States, though it was made a legal tender to the amount of $5 at the time of issue. The legal-tender provision was repealed in 1876. The weight of the trade dollar was 420 grains, while the standard American silver dollar weighed 412½ grains. An act of March 1, 1887, authorized the Treasurer to redeem in standard silver dollars all trade dollars presented during the following six months.

Trade Dollars discussed, 1399, 1463.

Trade of Foreign Powers. (See Commerce of Foreign Powers.)

Trade Information and Publicity, State Department.—In 1842, Daniel Webster, Secretary of State, assigned a clerk to the task of arranging and keeping up-to-date all commercial information from abroad which might be of service to the United States. In 1854, this work was organized as the Statistical Office of the Department of State, and in 1897 the name was changed to the Bureau of Foreign Commerce. When the Department of Commerce and Labor was organized in 1903, the Bureau of Foreign Commerce was transferred to the new department, and Secretary of State John Hay organized the Bureau of Trade Information and Publicity, to cover activities which the Department of Commerce and Labor could not advantageously prosecute. The duties of the new bureau were the supervision of trade reports and correspondence from American consuls and diplomatic officers, and also the publication of commercial information of interest. (See State Department; Consuls; Consular Service.)

Trade-Marks.—The ancient custom among merchants and manufacturers of using a special device for marking their goods or the packages containing them has long been recognized by the common law; and the right to exclusive use thereof has been sustained. The first statute providing for the protection of trade-marks in the United States by registration was the law of 1870. As this law was not restricted in its operation to trade between the states or with foreign nations, it was later held by the Supreme Court to be unconstitutional. Another general law was passed in 1905, based upon the commerce clause of the Constitution and amended in 1909. This law recognizes the right of a trader to stamp with his particular mark goods manufactured by him or selected or packed or in any way passing through his hands. The trade-mark then becomes part of the good will of a trader's business and he is protected against any use or infringement thereof by another the same as in any other property right.

The existing act provides that no trade-mark will be registered which consists of or comprises immoral or scandalous matter, or which consists of or comprises the flag or coat of arms or other insignia of the United States, or any simulation thereof, or of any state or municipality, or of any foreign nation or which consists of or comprises any design or picture that has been adopted by any fraternal society as its emblem, or of any name, distinguishing mark, character, emblem, colors, flag, or banner adopted by any institution, organization, club, or society which was incorporated in any State in the United States prior to the date of the adoption and use by the applicant; Provided, That said name, distinguishing mark, character, emblem, colors, flag, or banner was adopted and publicly used by said institution, organization, club, or society prior to the date of adoption and use by the applicant; unless it shall be shown to the satisfaction of the Commissioner of Patents that the mark was adopted and used as a trade-mark by the applicant or applicant's predecessors, from whom title is derived, at a date prior to the date of its adoption by such fraternal society as its emblem, or which trade-mark is identical with a registered or known trade-mark owned and in use by another, and appropriated to merchandise of the same descriptive properties, or which so nearly resembles a registered or known trade-mark owned and in use by another, and appropriated to merchandise of the same descriptive properties as to be likely to cause confusion or mistake in the minds of the public, or to deceive purchasers; or which consists merely in the name of an individual, firm, corporation, or association, not written, printed, impressed, or woven in some particular or distinctive manner or in association with a portrait of the individual, or merely in words or devices which are descriptive of the goods with which they are used, or of the character or quality of such goods, or merely a geographical name or term; no portrait of a living individual will be registered as a trade-mark, except by the consent of such individual evidenced by an instrument in writing; and no trade-mark will be registered which is used in unlawful business, or upon any article injurious in itself, or which has been used with the design of deceiving the public in the purchase of merchandise, or which has been abandoned. Any mark, used in commerce with foreign nations or among the several states or with Indian tribes, may be registered if it has been in actual and exclusive use as a trade-mark of the applicant, or his predecessors from whom he derived title, for ten years next preceding the passage of the act of February 20, 1905.

The fee for registration is $10; this gives exclusive right to the trade-mark for twenty years, and it may be renewed for a like period.

Aliens may register trade-marks previously registered in their own country.

Application for a trade-mark must be made to the Commissioner of Patents, setting forth a description of the trade-mark and a drawing thereof, accompanied by an affidavit to the effect that the applicant does not know of any other person who has the right to use it.

Trade-mark Treaties with Foreign Nations. —The following is a list of the Governments with which conventions for the reciprocal registration and protection of trade-marks have been entered into by the United States—Austria-Hungary, Belgium, Denmark, France, Germany, Great Britain (including colonies), Italy, Japan (including China and Korea), Luxemburg, Mexico, Rumania, Servia, Spain. The laws of Switzerland and the Netherlands being so framed as to afford reciprocal privileges to the citizens or subjects of any Government which affords similar privileges to the people of those countries, the mere exchange of diplomatic notes, giving notice of the fact, accomplishes all the purposes of a formal convention.

Trade-Marks:

Convention of South American countries for protection of, 7499.

International convention at Paris on subject of, 4714.

Treaty regarding, with—

Austria-Hungary, 4114.

Belgium, 4799, 4822.

Brazil, 4460.

France, 3967.

Germany, 4114, 4142.

Great Britain, 4408, 4419.

Italy, 4789.

Roumania, 4676.

Russia, 3887, 4220, 4247.

Spain, 4696.

Trade Relations with Foreign Countries, 7672.

Trades Unions.—The rise of a free working-class dates from the latter years of the Middle Ages. In ancient times, in well-settled communities slave labor was the rule, and in sparsely-settled communities much of the subsistence was derived from hunting, fishing and pastoral pursuits. Even through the Middle Ages, there was little work except that done in the households or on the farms; and the condition of the agricultural laborer was practically that of a serf.

In the fourteenth century in England, however, towns grew up to facilitate exchange of commodities, and there gradually flocked to them numbers of men who had become freed from their agricultural ties, and who had learned certain crafts. The Statutes of Laborers in the reign of Edward III shows the existence of a distinct class of workers, with some indication that it was becoming worthy of serious attention. In 1348, the plague devastated England, wiping out from one-third to one-half of the population, so that the workers were able to use the increased demand for labor as a means of bettering their condition.

During the next several centuries, this working-class organized itself into guilds, or associations of workingmen organized according to their trades. Although the modern trade union can hardly be said to have developed directly from these guilds, yet the indirect connection is very strong, as may be seen from the fact that the guilds of the fourteenth, fifteenth and sixteenth centuries had such familiar regulations as those limiting the number of apprentices and those providing many kinds of benefits for their members. The guilds, however, soon grew to represent the aristocracy of labor, and developed into what would be called today the middle class; and the condition of the lower classes was almost unbelievably wretched. The guilds did not survive much past Elizabethan times in their pristine strength—a decline due largely to the newer conditions of trade and commerce. All the way down to the beginning of the nineteenth century, the workers' conditions continued to be in a state not much above that of serfdom.

It was the coming of the industrial revolution, incident upon the invention of machinery, and the steam engine and upon the establishment of factories at the beginning of the nineteenth century, which began to change conditions for the laborers. On the side of actual working conditions, the new machines had decreased the demand for labor, while making possible the employment of women and children in place of the men; and on the other hand the French Revolution had filled the world with new ideals of the rights of the working-classes. In the years following the Napoleonic wars, there was little alleviation of the wretchedness in which the mass of the people lived, while at the same time they could observe the employing and trading classes becoming steadily richer and happier. Unpremeditated revolts showed the futility of endeavoring to change conditions by sporadic and unorganized efforts; and from this realization arose the modern organizations of the working-class.

The movement in England naturally was not long in reaching the United States. There is a legend that a typographical society was organized in New York City in 1795. In 1803, the journeymen shipmen of that city definitely organized, but the virtual beginning of an extensive American trade union movement may be assigned to 1825. The organizations of this period were purely local in character, but the next twenty-five years saw the growth of the amalgamation of all laborers' associations in a given locality—the so-called trades assemblies. In 1830 there was even a convention of the workingmen of New York state, and a candidate for governor was named.

The strength of the new movement may be gauged from the fact that in 1840 it was able to establish a ten-hour working day in government shipyards. In 1850, the first vigorous union of national scope was formed among the typographers; and the cigarworkers in 1874 inaugurated the practice of using a label to distinguish goods made under union conditions.

After the Civil War, a national federation of trades unions became the next logical step. In 1866, a National Labor Congress met in Baltimore, with one hundred delegates representing some sixty organizations; but many of the latter were local in their nature, and others were little more than secret or fraternal and beneficial organizations. Meetings were held until 1872, but the lack of unification among the constituent bodies and the drifting into political action finally disrupted the body in the last-mentioned year. The next year was the year of the great panic, and labor organizations suffered along with employers.

In 1874, an Industrial Congress was held in Rochester, in which the most influential bodies represented were the secret "Sovereigns of Industry" and the "Industrial Brotherhood of the United States." The Knights of Labor (q. v.) was organized in 1869, and soon became the dominant labor organization in the country, the membership in 1886 being reported as 700,000. But its influence finally paled before that of the American Federation of Labor, which was organized in 1881.

The growth of the new organization was rapid and steady. From 40,000 members in 1881, it achieved 230,000 members in 1890, from which time until 1899 the body grew but slowly. In 1899, the membership jumped to 340,000; in 1900, to 535,000; in 1901, to 785,000; in 1902, to 1,025,000; in 1903, to 1,465,000; and in 1904, to the high water mark for many years, 1,675,000. 1911 saw another upward trend, and in 1917, the membership was 2,045,793—representing 109 national and international unions, 5 departments, 45 state unions, 718 city central unions and 689 local unions. There were 21,711 local unions represented. There were 1,800 organizers. During the year it paid out in death benefits, $2,264,-000; sickness benefits of more than $1,000,-000, and a considerable amount for unemployment and strike benefits. More than 80% of the 1,317 strikes terminated were successful. In May, 1918, the membership had increased to 2,692,000.

Some of the strongest unions in the country, however, are not affiliated with the A. F. of L., notably the Bricklayers, Plasterers and Masons, and the four brotherhoods of railroad engineers, firemen, etc., and the United Garment Workers. For many years, the radical Western Federation of Miners was outside the fold, and at the present time there is nothing but enmity between the American Federation of Labor members and the I. W. W. (q. v.).

A curious relation exists between the American Federation of Labor and the Socialist Party. There are many Socialists within the A. F. of L., but they represent a minority of the organization. The Socialists, as a political body, usually support the economic struggles of the unions, although they criticise severely the present administration of the A. F. of L. The unions, on the other hand, endorse many of the planks in the political program of the Socialists. With the entrance of the United States into the European War, many of the Socialists who resigned from the Socialist Party because of its opposition to the action of their country combined with the leading officials of the A. F. of L. to form the American Alliance for Labor and Democracy. Another point of similarity between the two bodies is found in the fact that the Socialist creed preaches the international solidarity of the working-class, and is apt to be impatient of purely national alignments, whereas the strongest unions in the American Federation of Labor are those which are international in their aspects and affiliations.

There can be little doubt that the trade unions have succeeded in bettering materially the conditions of the working-classes. Primarily, they have enabled the workers to resort to collective bargaining with their employers, so that in negotiations the individual worker or group of workers will be at no unfair advantage. A tremendous amount of social legislation, national, state and municipal must also be placed to the credit of the unions, and there is seldom an election in districts where laborers are numerous where new concessions are not made to obtain the labor vote. Workers affiliated with the unions have been able to acquire shorter working-hours, higher wages, better working-conditions than those not so affiliated. And yet the fact remains that in the United States only about 8% of the workers are affiliated with the A. F. of L., with only about 12% in unions altogether. This proportion is much less than that of England, where the unions are moreover with important political representation, through the Labor Party.

The following figures show the members of the trades unions in those countries where organized labor is strongest, together with the ratio of the members to the total population. The figures are for 1913.

Australia	497,925	10%
Austria-Hungary	845,760	1½
Belgium	202,746	3
Canada	150,000	4
Denmark	152,787	6
France	1,026,302	3
Germany	3,835,660	6
Italy	971,667	3
Netherlands	220,275	4
New Zealand	71,554	7
Norway	64,108	3
Sweden	97,252	2
Switzerland	131,380	4
United Kingdom	3,928,191	9
United States	2,604,701	2½

For an account of the states which forbid intimidation of employees and the exaction of any agreement, as a condition of employment, not to join a labor organization, see the article Boycott.

Trades Unions (See also Labor):

Trading Establishments among Indians,

Trading-With-The-Enemy Act. — The chief provisions of this act, as approved by the President on October 6, 1917, were as follows :

The War Trade Board succeeds the Exports Administrative Board in all the latter's functions, including complete control over exports, under the powers created in the Espionage Act (q. v.). The War Trade Board also licenses importations, the Act giving the President the power to prohibit the importation of any article or to regulate its importation.

Under severe criminal penalties, trading without a license with a person who there is reason to believe is an enemy or an ally of enemy is made unlawful. "Trade" is defined to mean to pay, satisfy, compromise, or give security for the payment of any debt or obligation ; to draw, accept, pay, draw for acceptance or payment, or endorse any negotiable instrument ; to enter into, carry on, complete or perform any contract, agreement or obligation ; to buy, sell, loan, extend credit, trade in, deal with, exchange, transmit, transfer, assign, or otherwise receive or dispose of any form of property ; to have any form of business communication or intercourse with.

An "enemy" or "ally of enemy" is defined as a person of any nationality residing within the territory of or occupied by Germany and any of her allies, including even citizens of the United States who may be thus situated. The term includes any person doing business within such territory, wherever he reside or of whatever nationality he be. (The term "person" includes a business or corporation.) The term includes also every enemy government of the United States, and every agent of such government, wherever located. Enemy aliens (q. v.) in the United States are not included in this term, although they may be subject to internment, and the President is given power to issue licenses to trade with the enemy.

It is similarly unlawful to trade with any person whatsoever who may be acting as agent for or for the benefit of an enemy or ally of enemy.

A person who is an enemy or ally of enemy may apply for a license to do business within the United States, and may continue to do business until such application is passed upon. An enemy alien in the United States need not apply for such license unless he falls under the above definition of an enemy or an ally of the enemy. An enemy or ally of enemy granted a license to do business within the United States may be traded with by every one, but such enemy or ally of enemy may not transmit outside the United States any money or property, and may not use such money or property to establish credit inside or outside the United States for or for the benefit of an enemy or ally of enemy.

It is made unlawful to take or send outside of the United States any communication intended for an enemy or ally of enemy, and also to bring in or take out any form of communication except by mail—except through license.

A War Trade Council is created to replace the Exports Council and to act as an advisory body in all matters referred to it by the President of the War Trade Board. It is composed of the Secretaries of State, Treasury, Agriculture, Commerce and the Food Administrator, and the Chairman of the United States Shipping Board.

The Federal Trade Commission is empowered to carry out various provisions in the Act relating to patents.

The duties and scope of the Alien Property Custodian are also described in the Act, and may be consulted under the head of Alien Property Custodian.

Control over foreign exchange and transfers of bullion, etc., are also vested in the President by the Act.

A Censorship Board administers the regulations of the President concerning cable, telegraph and mail communication between the United States and foreign countries. This Board is composed of representatives of the Postmaster-general, the Secretaries of War and Navy, the War Trade Board, and the Chairman of the Committee on Public Information.

Every paper printed in a foreign language must furnish a translation to the Postmaster-general of all matter concerning the War printed by it.

It is made unlawful for any person without a license therefor to transport to or from the United States, or for any vessel of the United States registry to transport anywhere, any citizen of an enemy or ally of an enemy nation.

Various executive orders relating to the provisions of this Act may be found by consulting the Index under Wilson, Woodrow.

Trading with the Enemy Act:

Training Camp Activities, Commission on. (See War Department.)

Training Camps, Officers'. (See Army.)

Traitor.—One who commits treason. (See Treason.)

Transcontinental Highways.—In the days of the oxteam and prairie schooner, the plains and mountains were crossed by trails, usually along the lines of least resistance, keeping as close as possible to bases of supplies and water. The pioneers over what became known later as the "Santa Fe Trail" and the "Oregon Trail" were the first to leave permanent marks on routes now rapidly becoming highways between the Central-Western and the far-Western States.

Lincoln Highway.—Perhaps the most pretentious effort in this direction is that of the Lincoln Highway Association. This was formed by automobile interests of Detroit, Mich., under the leadership of Henry B. Joy to procure immediately the establishment of a continuous improved highway from the Atlantic to the Pacific, open to lawful traffic of all descriptions without toll charges, to be known as the Lincoln Highway, in memory of President Lincoln. The proposed route is from New York to Philadelphia and Pittsburg, across Northern Ohio, Indiana and Illinois, over the established roads of those states, through Iowa to Omaha, Neb., and following the course of the Platte River, it enters Wyoming, passes through Salt Lake, Utah, and by a route not yet determined, crosses the Rocky Mountains and ends at San Francisco, where connection may be made with the Pacific Highway. West of Chicago 95 per cent of the route of the Lincoln Highway is the Overland Trail. A large part of the route is designated by markers of red, white, and blue, and it is the intention of the association to have it so marked throughout its entire course. The marker is used on eight telegraph poles to the mile. Memorial arches and large signs have been erected at the entrances of the Lincoln Highway into many cities along the route.

Automobile Routes.—Five distinct and predominant routes are being developed across the Continent; gradually each will become standard, and have its special advantages, depending principally on the nature of the country, and the time of the year. These five routes may be summarized briefly as follows:

1. The "Overland Trail" crosses Illinois, Iowa, Nebraska, Wyoming, Utah and Nevada, following considerable portions of the old Oregon Trail; while there are some stretches of rough going in Wyoming, Utah and Nevada, as a whole it offers an average of fair-to-good traveling, and has hotel accommodations throughout. This is a midsummer route, analyzed in greater detail under a separate head, farther along.

2. The "Trail to Sunset" starts at Chicago and runs to Los Angeles, along the Santa Fe Trail and across New Mexico and Arizona to Southern California, thence north to San Francisco. This route offers magnificent mountain scenery, Indian pueblos and reservations, prehistoric ruins, Mexican habitations, giant desert cactus and tropical vegetation in the irrigated regions. It is a fall and early winter route, and is being rapidly improved, though there are yet several rough stretches and a lack of hotel accommodations in some parts of New Mexico and Arizona, necessitating two or three nights camping out.

3. The "Midland Trail" crosses Pennsylvania, Ohio, Indiana, Illinois, Missouri, Kansas, Colorado, Utah and Nevada. It is a most interesting route historically and crosses the Rocky Mountains amid the most magnificent scenery. It is a spring, summer and fall route, not yet fully developed in Colorado and Utah.

4. The "Northwest Trail," through Wisconsin, Minnesota, North Dakota, Montana, Idaho and Washington, should eventually be a popular midsummer route and open up a fine territory to through automobile travel. There is an abundance of fine scenery, and the progressive inhabitants of the several states traversed heartily co-operate in the road improvements necessary to the permanence and popularity of this transcontinental trunk line.

5. The "All-Southern Route," through Virginia, North Carolina, Tennessee, Arkansas, Texas, New Mexico and Arizona, though as yet only partially developed, will ultimately be a popular fall and winter route, offering many scenic attractions and climatic advantages. It was surveyed in the fall of 1913, but its publication has been held back by present and prospective developments in the territory through which it passes.

Pacific Highway.—An interstate and international automobile route extending from San Diego, Cal., northward along the Pacific Coast through Los Angeles and San Francisco, by way of Portland, Ore., to Vancouver, B. C., whence it is intended to run through British territory into Alaska. The road is being constructed and maintained by co-operation of private and state enterprise.

Trans-Mississippi Exposition. — From June 1 to Oct. 31, 1898, an exhibition of the resources of the middle west was held at Omaha, Neb. The site covered about 200 acres and the buildings were grouped around a court which extended through the middle of the grounds and surrounded a lagoon or canal which terminated in a lake, adorned by an electric fountain. The grounds were ornamented with trees, shrubs and flowers, and the buildings were covered with white staff. A special feature of ethnologic interest was the gathering of 500 Indians, representative of twenty-five tribes. The total attendance was 2,615,508, and the receipts $1,924,077.

Transportation, Miscellaneous. (See Division of Miscellaneous Transportation.)

Treason.—The Constitution of the United States declares that "treason against the United States shall consist only in levying war against them, or in adhering to their enemies, giving them aid and comfort. No person shall be convicted of treason unless on the testimony of two witnesses to the same overt act or on confession in open court" (24). The penalty is death. Conspiracy alone does not constitute treason. A motion to give Congress the sole power of defining the crimes of treason failed in the Convention of 1787. An act of Congress of July 17, 1862, provided for the liberation of the slaves of a person convicted of treason. At the close of the Civil War there were no prosecutions for treason. Most of the state constitutions contain provisions similar to that of the National Constitution. A notable instance of treason against a state was Dorr's Rebellion (q. v.) in Rhode Island in 1840-1842. Dorr was convicted, but was pardoned in 1852. A celebrated case of trial for treason is that of Aaron Burr, in 1807, which occurred at Richmond, Va., and resulted in the acquittal of Burr.

Article II, sec. 4 provides that any official of the Government convicted of treason shall be removed from office. (23) A Civil War act, dated July 17, 1862, makes the punishment, at the discretion of the court, either death or imprisonment at hard labor for not less than five years, along with a fine of not less than $10,000, and disability to hold office. No person is indictable for treason three years after the alleged act of treason was committed; nor, by constitutional interpretation, shall any one be open to the charge of treason unless he has voluntarily given actual assistance to those countries which are declared to be at war with the United States. (See Misprision of Treason.)

Treason:
Act to punish, etc., 3286, 3294.
Discussed by President Johnson, 3557.

Treasurer of the United States. (See Treasury Department.)

Treasury:
Balance deposited in national banks, 7980.
Balances against collecting and disbursing agents referred to, 1730.
Condition of, discussed. (See Finances discussed.)
Deficit in, discussed, 1955, 1959, 2079.
Experts appointed in for war risk insurance, 7979.
Fraud practiced on, 1017.
Outstanding arrears due Government discussed, 1016, 2747.
Prize money in, 2570.
Receipts in, fluctuations in, should be prevented, 1789.
Statement of. (See Finances discussed.)
Surplus in—
   Application of, to—
      Educational purposes and internal improvements recommended, 397c 444

Navy and national works recommended, 1380, 4766.

Purchase of bonds recommended, 3985.

Apportionment of, among States. (See States of the Union.)

Discussed by President—
Arthur, 4635, 4721.
Cleveland, 5093, 5165, 5361, 5372.
Fillmore, 2660, 2714.
Grant, 3985.
Harrison, Benj., 5473, 5549, 5630.
Jackson, 1014, 1077, 1380, 1458.
Jefferson, 397, 444.
Pierce, 2747, 2818.
Van Buren, 1707.

Joint resolution directing payment of, on public debt, reasons for applying pocket veto to, 5073.

Proposition to deposit, in banks throughout country discussed, 5168.

Treasury Board.—Feb. 17, 1776, the Continental Congress appointed a standing committee of five members on ways and means. They were given power over the Treasury office of accounts, the committee of claims, and some minor bureau and officials. This committee was known as the Treasury Board. Two years later provision was made for a building in which to transact the business of the board, and the Treasury office of accounts was superseded by a Comptroller, an Auditor, and a Treasurer, thus forming the germ of the present Treasury Department. The office of Superintendent of Finance (q. v.) was created to take the place of this board in 1781. After a trial of three years this office was abolished and the board reestablished and continued until 1789, when it was succeeded by the present Department.

Treasury Building:
Construction of, discussed, 1613, 1696.
Destruction of, by fire, 1248, 1336, 1344.
Papers lost in, 1248.
Erection of new, recommended, 1248, 1336.
Incendiaries of, difficulties attending conviction of, should be removed, 1492.
Plan of, discussed, 1515.

Treasury, Constitutional. (See Constitutional Treasury System.)

Treasury Department.—After the Department of State the most important executive branch of the National Government. It is more complex and extensive than any other Department, and its head officer, though ranking second to the Secretary of State, is not inferior in influence and responsibility to that Secretary.

The Treasury Department was virtually created Feb. 17, 1776, when the Continental Congress resolved: "That a standing committee of five be appointed for superintending the Treasury." April 1 of that year a Treasury Office of Accounts was established, to be carried on under the direction of the standing committee. Sept. 26, 1778, the Continental Congress established the offices of Comptroller, Auditor, Treasurer, and two Chambers of Accounts, to consist of three commissioners each, all of whom were to be appointed annually by Congress. Feb. 11, 1779, the office of Secretary of the Treasury was established (the holder to receive a salary of $2,000 annually), but on July 30, following, this office was succeeded by a Board of Treasury consisting of five commissioners and an Auditor-General assisted by six Auditors. Again, Feb. 7, 1781, it was resolved by Congress that the finances of the Confederation should be under a Superintendent of Finance (see Finances, Superintendent of), who was later assisted by a Comptroller, a Treasurer, a Register of Auditors; and, May 24, 1784, the Superintendent of Finances was superseded by the Board of Treasury, consisting of three commissioners. This ended the effort to organize the Treasury Department under the Confederation.

The present Treasury Department was established Sept. 2, 1789, during the first session of the First Congress under the Constitution; and the act, drawn by Alexander Hamilton, was constructed with such precision and comprehensiveness that few radical changes have since been found necessary. The act provided that: "There shall be a Department of the Treasury, in which shall be the following officers, namely: a Secretary of the Treasury, to be deemed the head of the Department; a Comptroller; an Auditor; a Treasurer; a Register; and an Assistant to the Secretary of the Treasury."

On May 8, 1792, the office of Assistant to the Secretary of the Treasury was superseded by the office of Commissioner of Revenue, whose duties were to collect internal revenue and direct taxes. This office was abolished by an act of Congress April 6, 1802, reestablished July 24, 1813, and again abolished Dec. 23, 1817.

The General Land Office, whose head was a Commissioner, was created in the Department of the Treasury April 25, 1812, and was transferred to the Department of the Interior in 1849. As at present organized, the work of the Department is divided among nineteen principal offices, bureaus and divisions.

As head of the Department the Secretary is charged by law with maintaining the revenue for the support of the public credit; superintending the collecting of the revenue and directing the forms of keeping and rendering public accounts; granting of warrants for all moneys drawn from the Treasury in pursuance of appropriations made by law, and for the payment of moneys into the Treasury; and annually submitting to Congress estimates of the probable revenues and disbursements of the Government. He also controls the construction of public buildings and the coinage and printing of money. There are three Assistant Secretaries. Up to 1817 the Comptroller of the Treasury revised the report of the Accountants of the other departments, but an act passed March 3, of that year, created the offices of Second, Third, Fourth, and Fifth Auditors, whose duty it was to perform this work. A Sixth Auditor was added in 1836.

In 1894 the designations and duties of the auditors were changed and definitely established as follows: That of the First Auditor, to Auditor for the Treasury Department; Second Auditor, to Auditor for the War Department; Third Auditor, to Auditor for the Interior Department; Fourth Auditor, to Auditor for the Navy Department; Fifth Auditor, to Auditor for the State and other Departments; Sixth Auditor, to Auditor for the Post-Office Department. According to the act of 1894 the offices of First and Second Comptroller were succeed-

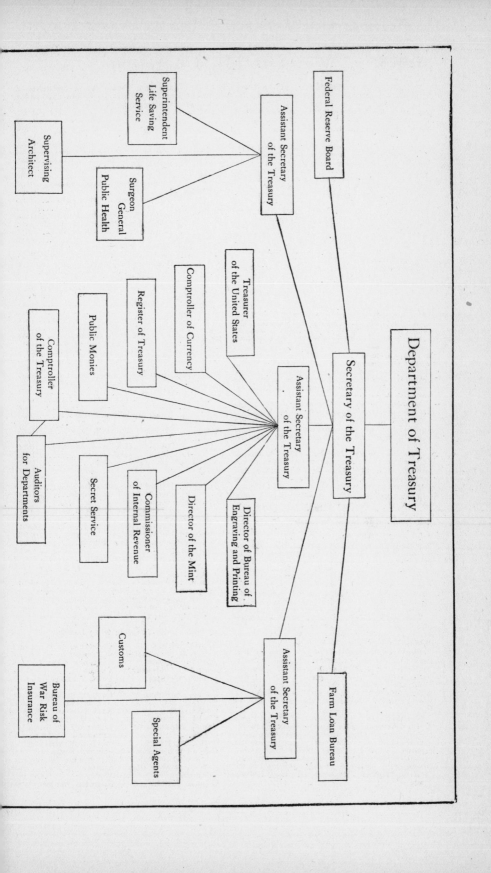

Department of Treasury

Secretary of the Treasury

Federal Reserve Board

Farm Loan Bureau

Assistant Secretary of the Treasury

Superintendent Life Saving Service

Supervising Architect

Surgeon General Public Health

Assistant Secretary of the Treasury

Treasurer of the United States

Comptroller of Currency

Register of Treasury

Public Monies

Comptroller of the Treasury

Auditors for Departments

Secret Service

Commissioner of Internal Revenue

Director of the Mint

Director of Bureau of Engraving and Printing

Assistant Secretary of the Treasury

Customs

Bureau of War Risk Insurance

Special Agents

ed by the office of Comptroller of the Treasury, whose principal duties are the rendering of decisions in cases of appeals from Auditors, heads of Departments or other officials, and the prescribing of forms for the keeping of public accounts.

Treasurer of the United States.—The Treasurer of the United States, whose office is a part of the Treasury Department. receives and disburses all public moneys deposited in the Treasury, sub-treasuries (q. v.) and in national banks that are United States depositories; is trustee for bonds that secure the national bank circulation and public deposits; has the custody of the Indian trust-fund bonds, and other public trusts; is fiscal agent for paying the interest on the public debt; and is ex-officio commissioner of the sinking fund of the District of Columbia. The duties of the Treasurer's office are distributed among eleven divisions.

Until 1894 the chief duty of the Register of the Treasury was the recording of the receipts and expenditures of the Government and the office was organized in several divisions, but in that year the number of divisions was reduced to two, viz., the Division of Loans and the Division of Notes, Coupons and Currency, the books relating to the recording of the receipts and expenditures of the Government being transferred to the Division of Bookkeeping and Warrants, of the Secretary's office. At present the office of the Treasurer is charged with the issue, exchange, transfer, and redemption of bonds and the receiving and registering of redeemed notes, certificates, coupons, etc.

Comptroller of the Currency.—The office of Comptroller of the Currency was established in 1863, its chief function being supervision of the national banks, their organization, and the issue and redemption of their notes.

Revenue-Cutter Service.—The Revenue-Cutter Service is a military arm of the Government attached to and under the direction of the Treasury Department. (See Revenue-Cutter Service.)

Secret Service.—The Secret Service Division of the Treasury Department was created in 1861, but from 1862 until 1865 it was under the State Department. In the latter year it was permanently organized as a division of the Treasury Department. It is chiefly concerned with the detection of counterfeiting and of other frauds and crimes against the Government, but in time of war the scope of its duties is somewhat enlarged. Details are also furnished for the protection of the President of the United States, and in the frequent journeyings of the present President he is always accompanied by one or more secret-service men.

The arrest of counterfeiters number about 400 annually; other arrests are for bribery, impersonating United States Government officers, perjury, etc.

Supervising Architect.—The office of Supervising Architect, charged chiefly with the erection and maintenance of Government buildings, was created in 1864. Since 1853 this work has been done by a Division of Construction with an officer of the Engineer Corps of the army at its head.

Health Bureau.—The work of the Bureau of Public Health and Marine-Hospital Service was established in 1798 but was reorganized and the office of Surgeon-General created in 1872. This official has supervision of the health of seamen, the quarantine service, and the weekly publication of "Public Health Reports of the United States."

Following is a list of the Secretaries of the Treasury with the Presidents under whom they served:

President	Secretary of the Treasury	Appointed
Washington	Alexander Hamilton, New York...	1789
"	Oliver Wolcott, Connecticut......	1795
Adams....	" "	1797
"	Samuel Dexter, Massachusetts....	1801
Jefferson...	" " ...	1801
" ...	Albert Gallatin, Pennsylvania....	1801
Madison ..	" "	1809
" ...	George W. Campbell, Tennessee...	1814
" ...	Alexander J. Dallas, Pennsylvania	1814
" ...	William H. Crawford, Georgia....	1816
Monroe....	" "	1817
J.Q.Adams	Richard Rush, Pennsylvania....	1825
Jackson....	Samuel D. Ingham, Penn........	1829
"	Louis McLane, Delaware........	1831
"	William J. Duane, Pennsylvania..	1833
"	Roger B. Taney, Maryland......	1833
"	Levi Woodbury, New Hampshire.	1834
Van Buren.	" " ..	1837
Harrison...	Thomas Ewing, Ohio............	1841
Tyler....	" "	1841
"	Walter Forward, Pennsylvania...	1841
"	John C. Spencer, New York.....	1843
"	George M. Bibb, Kentucky.....	1844
Polk.....	Robert J. Walker, Mississippi....	1845
Taylor....	W. M. Meredith, Pennsylvania...	1849
Fillmore...	Thomas Corwin, Ohio..........	1850
Pierce....	James Guthrie, Kentucky.......	1853
Buchanan..	Howell Cobb, Georgia.........	1857
" ...	Philip F. Thomas, Maryland....	1860
" ...	John A. Dix, New York........	1861
Lincoln....	Salmon P. Chase, Ohio........	1861
"	William P. Fessenden, Maine....	1864
"	Hugh McCulloch, Indiana.......	1865
Johnson...	" "	1865
Grant.....	George S. Boutwell, Mass.......	1869
" ...	Wm. A. Richardson, Mass.......	1873
" ...	Benjamin H. Bristow, Kentucky..	1874
" ...	Lot M. Morrill, Maine..........	1876
Hayes.....	John Sherman, Ohio............	1877
Garfield..	William Windom, Minnesota.....	1881
Arthur....	Charles J. Folger, New York.....	1881
"	Walter Q. Gresham, Indiana.....	1884
"	Hugh McCulloch, Indiana.......	1884
Cleveland..	Daniel Manning, New York.....	1885
" ..	Charles S. Fairchild, New York..	1887
B. Harrison	William Windom, Minnesota.....	1889
"	Charles Foster, Ohio..........	1891
Cleveland..	John G. Carlisle, Kentucky.....	1893
McKinley..	Lyman J. Gage, Illinois........	1897
Roosevelt..	" "	1901
" ..	Leslie M. Shaw, Iowa..........	1901
" ..	George B. Cortelyou, New York..	1907
Taft......	Franklin MacVeagh, Illinois.....	1909
Wilson....	William G. McAdoo, New York...	1913

For more detailed information of the scope of the activities of the Treasury Department consult the index references to the Presidents' Messages and Encyclopedic articles under the following headings:

Appropriations.
Assistant Secretaries of the Treasury.
Auditors, Treasury Department.
Banks.
Banks, National.
Bank Notes.
Banks, Pet.
Banks, Savings.
Banks, State.
Bonds.
Buildings, Public.
Bureau of Engraving and Printing.
Bureau of War Risk Insurance.
Coinage Laws.

Comptroller of the Treasury.
Currency Law.
Customs.
Debt, Public.
Duties.
Engraving and Printing.
Excise Laws.
Federal Reserve Board.
Finances.
Health Service.
Import Duties.
Life-Saving Service.
Mints.
Money.
National Banks.

Public Deposits.
Public Monies.
Reserve Banks.
Revenue-Cutter Service.
Revenue Flag.
Revenue, Internal.
Revenue, Public.
Secret Service.

Special Agents, Treasury Department.
Sub-Treasury.
Supervising Architect.
Tariff.
Taxation.

Treasury Department:

Appropriations for, transferred, 1254, 1404, 1612, 1772, 1904, 1943, 2125.

Building, picture of, frontispiece, Vol. III.

Efficiency and economy in, 7683.

Vacancy by death of head of, 5568.

Treasury Notes.—To meet the expenses of the War of 1812, $36,000,000 in Treasury notes bearing 5⅖ per cent interest were issued. They were receivable for all duties to the Government, but were not legal tender. Beginning with the panic of 1837 and extending through the Mexican War, $73,000,000 were issued, and following the panic of 1857 there was an issue of $53,-000,000. The exigencies of the Civil War required the issue of Treasury notes in large amounts. An act of Feb. 25, 1862, authorized the issue of $150,000,000 of such notes with a legal-tender character and not bearing interest. These were called greenbacks (q. v.). The United States seven-thirties, of which $830,000,-000 were issued, were a variety of Treasury note. Treasury notes were issued to pay for the monthly purchase of bullion authorized by the Sherman Act of 1890.

Treasury Notes. (See also Currency.)

Appropriation to meet outstanding, recommended, 3073.

Issuance of, 549, 2119.

Additional, discussed, 3350.

Recommended, 2989.

Payment of silver, 6078, 6176.

Redemption of, referred to, 1751.

Reissuance of, prohibition on, should be removed, 1686.

Retirement of, issued in payment of silver purchased under act of 1890, recommended, 6078, 6176.

Treasury Office of Accounts.—An important bureau under the Treasury Board as established by the Continental Congress. It was presided over by an auditor-general.

Treasury, Secretary of:

Death of, vacancy caused by, how filled, 5568.

Power of, over deposits unqualified, 1227.

Report of, 335, 464, 638, 652, 772, 800, 907, 909, 912, 1098.

Vacancy occasioned by death of, recommendations regarding filling of, 5568.

Treasury, Solicitor of, office of, established, 1090.

Operations of, referred to, 2539.

Treaties.—The modern definition of a treaty is an agreement or covenant between two or more nations or sovereignties formally signed by duly authorized commissioners and solemnly ratified by each. In ancient times terms of treaties were dictated rather than contracted. A conqueror with an army at the gates of a capital stated his terms and declared his intention of remaining and inflicting such punishment as he saw fit until he received satisfactory assurances that his wishes would be carried out.

In the fifteenth century a jurisprudence of political treaties began to grow and was closely connected with the development of European statecraft. The treaty of Westphalia, which ended the Thirty Years' War, marked the turning point between ancient and modern diplomacy. Up to this time treaty negotiations had been based upon rights which had once existed and were recognized before rupture. After the treaties of Münster and Osnabrück, the object of diplomacy was to establish a political equilibrium at the expense of preexistent rights and to maintain the *status quo*. The efforts of European diplomats during the early part of the nineteenth century were directed toward the suppression of the revolutionary spirit and the curbing of monarchical ambitions. Later the maritime rights of neutrals, suppression of slave trade, and the international emancipation of trade, navigation, arts, and labor became leading subjects for diplomatic consideration.

The popularity of the principle of arbitration marks the latest step in diplomatic progress. The proposition made by the Czar of Russia in 1898 for the general disarmament of the world and the settlement of international disputes by a court of arbitration points to a culmination of the science of diplomacy. In this connection may also be noted Secretary Bryan's peace treaties.

The first treaties of the United States were conceived before the Declaration of Indpendence was signed. Nov. 29, 1775, the Continental Congress appointed a committee on secret correspondence, charged with ascertaining whether, if the Colonies should be forced to form themselves into an independent State, France would enter into any treaty or alliance with them. On Feb. 6, 1778, two treaties were concluded in Paris with France—a treaty of alliance and a treaty of amity and commerce. On Oct. 8, 1782, a treaty of amity and commerce was concluded with the Netherlands, and April 3, 1783, a similar treaty with Sweden.

Jan. 20, 1783, an armistice with Great Britain was arranged at Versailles, followed Sept. 3 by a definitive treaty of peace, later concluded in London, recognizing the independence of the United States. This was signed by David Hartley on the part of Great Britain and by Benjamin Franklin, John Adams and John Jay on the part of the United States. Other treaties concluded before the adoption of the Constitution were a treaty of amity and commerce with Prussia, Dec. 10, 1785; a treaty of peace and friendship with Morocco in January, 1787, and a consular convention with France, Nov. 14, 1788.

In the United States the right of making and ratifying treaties is, by Article II., Section 2, of the Constitution, vested in the President under the advice and with the concurrence of two-thirds of the Senate. The right of changing the terms and conditions of a treaty before ratification is claimed by the Senate.

International law or the law of nations is very clear upon the question of treaties and of all the interpretations of its conditions. No treaty may be made which will in any way or in the slightest degree override the Constitution, or which will bind either nation to any terms or conditions that flagrantly sacrifice the interests of either, or cause the nation to do anything morally wrong in the fulfillment. A treaty becomes binding at the time of signature by duly authorized commissioners, and if the ratification is delayed, such ratification becomes retroactive; though it may be specified in the treaty that its terms become operative only upon ratification. Where an ambiguity of expression or possibility of other construction of the terms of a treaty exists, no strained interpretation is permitted and the common use of the words is followed unless this leads to an absurdity. Where two meanings are possible, that one is chosen which confers the least benefit upon the party who sought or demanded the insertion of the doubtful clause. When clauses impose hard conditions upon either party these are to be interpreted strictly so as to minimize the hard conditions; and where justice, equity, and humanity are favored by the doubtful clauses they are interpreted with broad construction, so as to confer the fullest benefits.

The term "convention" is limited to agreements which deal with subordinate questions. Treaties are classified as treaties of peace, alliance, truces, commercial treaties, extradition treaties, conventions and protocols—a name given to less formal agreements between nations. Defensive treaties are designed to defend the parties mutually against the encroachments of others. Offensive and defensive treaties or alliances obligate tLe parties to aid one another at all times during conflict of either of the parties against the encroachments of other nations. Treaties of neutrality obligate the contracting parties to take no part in conflicts between other nations.

Extradition treaties, which provide for the return of accused criminals, are described below:

When Washington was called to the Presidency he found the northern frontier of the United States occupied by British military posts and Spain making encroachments on the south. With the outbreak of the French Revolution, Spain joined England, and French sympathizers in America were attempting to fit out privateers to prey upon Spanish and English commerce. Washington was urged to cast the fortunes of the United States into one side of the struggle. To avoid any entangling alliances he sent John Jay, Chief Justice of the United States, as a special envoy to London (page 146). Nov. 19, 1794, Jay concluded the treaty which has since borne his name. In consequence of the irritating conduct of M. Genet, the French minister at Washington, Congress in 1798 abrogated the treaties and consular conventions with France. Another treaty was made in 1800, and in 1803 three conventions were signed, including the one ceding Louisiana. One of the most enduring treaties made by the United States was that of Oct. 27, 1795, with Spain, which stood for more than 100 years. This was the only treaty not swept away by the Napoleonic wars.

The treaty of Ghent, signed in 1814, was important as settling some disputed boundary questions, as well as concluding peace between the United States and England. No mention was made of the right of search and the impressment of American seamen, though these were the especial causes of the war. Other notable treaties made by the United States were the Webster-Ashburton treaty, signed at Washington in 1842, defining the northeastern boundary between Canada and the United States, and the treaty of Guadalupe Hidalgo, in 1848, concluding the Mexican War, by which Mexico ceded territory now comprising Nevada, Utah, most of Arizona, a large part of New Mexico, parts of Colorado and Wyoming, and all of California. The treaty with Japan in 1854 secured humane treatment for American sailors shipwrecked on the coast of Japan and the right to appoint a consular agent; it also led to the establishment of important trading privileges with the United States and Great Britain in 1858.

The treaties of Tientsin, concluded in 1858, and the Burlingame treaty of 1868 opened China to foreign travel and gave protection to Christians within her borders. The treaty of Washington was signed in 1871, and settled questions pending between the United States and Great Britain. It submitted the Alabama claims to a commission of arbitration and adjusted the fisheries question on a reciprocity basis. There was also a concession of important privileges by each of subjects of the other in America, and the question of the northwestern boundary of the United States was submitted to the arbitration of the German Emperor.

At the close of the Spanish-American War, in 1898, Spain was forced to relinquish Cuba and cede to the United States the island of Porto Rico, together with the Philippine Islands and Guam. Under the Constitution treaties are made a part of the supreme law of the land and they have a legal status similar to that of contracts. Numerous treaties have been made with the Indians and with various countries on the subject of extradition. (See Foreign Relations and Treaties with the various nations following descriptions of the countries.)

Treaties (see Indians); for treaties with foreign nations, see the respective countries, using list "Nations."

Alleged violation of, memorial regarding, referred to, 2003.

Assent of House to, not required, 188.

Boundary survey made under treaty of Washington, 3588.

Contract for proposed edition of, referred to, 2273.

Power to make, vested in President with consent of Senate, 187.

Priority of one over another, law in regard to, 302.

Referred to, 2538, 2540, 4851.

Request of House for correspondence regarding, declined, 186.

Return of, requested, 4888.

Withdrawn, 1888, 4922.

Trent Affair.—In the autumn of 1861 the government of the Confederate States sent J. M. Mason and John Slidel as commissioners to Great Britain and France, respectively. They went first to Havana, where they took passage on the British merchant ship Trent for St. Thomas, on their way to England. Nov. 8 the vessel was stopped in the old Bahama Channel by the U. S. S. San Jacinto, Capt. Wilkes. The Confederate commissioners were seized and taken to Boston as prisoners. Wilkes's act was in violation of the rights of neutral nations, for which the United States had always contended. The British Government promptly instructed its minister at Washington to withdraw from the United

States unless the prisoners were set at liberty and an apology tendered within seven days. The United States disavowed the act of Capt. Wilkes and set the prisoners free.

Trent, The, removal of Confederate envoys from. (See Mason and Slidell.)

Trenton, The, loss of, at Samoan Islands, 5479.

Trenton (N. J.), Battle of.—Washington's retreat through New Jersey left him with scarcely 3,000 men on the west bank of the Delaware River on Dec. 8, 1776. On the night of Dec. 13, Dr. Charles Lee was taken prisoner at Baskingridge by the British, and his army added to that of Washington gave the latter some 6,000 able-bodied soldiers. On the night of Dec. 25, 1776, Washington, with about 2,500 men, crossed the Delaware River and on the morning of the 26th attacked an outpost of 1,500 Hessians at Trenton under Col. Rahl and captured about 1,000 of them and killed 40. The American casualties were 2 killed, 2 frozen to death, and 3 wounded. The effect of this victory and that of Princeton following it was electrical. The Americans were uplifted and the British discouraged.

Trianon Decree.—A secret edict issued by Napoleon at the Grand Trianon Palace, at Versailles, Aug. 5, 1810. It placed a duty of 50 per cent on colonial products and ordered the immediate confiscation of all American vessels and merchandise brought into French ports prior to May 1, 1810, the date of the approval of the act excluding French vessels from American waters. It also ordered that until Nov. 1 American vessels were to be allowed to enter French ports, but not to unload without his permission, offering at the same time to revoke the Milan and Berlin decrees Nov. 1. The revocation was not carried into effect, and American ships and cargoes availing themselves of the promised protection were confiscated. (See also Berlin Decrees; Embargo; Milan Decree; Orders in Council.)

Tribunal of Arbitration at Paris:

Acts to give effect to award of, proclaimed, 5926, 6123.

Award of, discussed and recommendations regarding, 5958, 6062.

Case of United States at, prepared by John W. Foster, 5748.

Convention for settlement of claims under, 6097.

Discussed, 5869.

Enforcement of regulations in accordance with decision of, referred to, 6000.

Failure of negotiations of, to protect fur seals of Alaska, 6182.

Reports of agent of United States to, transmitted, 5909.

Tribute paid Algeria by United States referred to, 115, 174, 325.

Trinidad, vessels from ports of, duties on, suspended by proclamation, 4889, 6503.

Triple Alliance.—The popular name of three different political combinations of European powers: First—An alliance concluded at The Hague in 1668 between England, Holland and Sweden, having for its object the checking of the conquests of Louis XIV. Second—An alliance concluded in 1717 between England, France and Holland against Spain. With the addition of Austria in 1718 it became known as the Quadruple Alliance. Third—The Dreibund, originally formed October 7, 1879, as a dual alliance between Germany and Austria-Hungary, on the basis of mutual assistance in case of an attack by Russia on either party, and friendly neutrality in case of an attack by any other power. Italy joined this alliance and with the beginning of 1883, it has been known as the Triple Alliance. The treaty between Italy and Germany provided for common action in case of French encroachments on either power, and that between Italy and Austria-Hungary for the maintenance of a friendly neutrality in case of hostilities between France and Italy or between Russia and Austria-Hungary. (See Central Powers and European War.)

Triple Entente.—One of the political alliances or understandings between the European nations. Although published treaties bound the powers to no political or military alliance, it was generally conceded that Russia had an understanding with France that in the event of hostilities the two nations would unite against Germany. Great Britain also became a secret ally of France in her diplomatic and commercial rivalry with Germany. At the outbreak of the European War of 1914, Germany came to the assistance of Austria-Hungary when the latter was menaced by Russia, agreeably to the terms of the Triple Alliance, and France made ready to attack Germany on behalf of Russia in accordance with the Triple Entente. Italy maintained neutrality when the other members of the Alliance became involved, and Great Britain joined France and Russia in their operations against Germany on the ground of the violation of the neutrality of Belgium. (See Entente Allies and European War.)

Tripoli.—An Italian province in northern Africa, wrested from Turkey by the war of 1908 and confirmed by the Treaty of Ouchy. It is bounded on the north by the Mediterranean Sea, on the east by Egypt, on the west by Tunis and on the south by the Desert of Sahara. Its exports consist mainly of products of the Sudan brought across the Sahara by caravan. The Oasis of Fezzan and some smaller oases are within its borders. It anciently belonged to Carthage and at a later date to Rome. It was overrun and conquered by the Arabs in the seventh century and by the Turks in the sixteenth century. It became an independent state in 1713, but was reconquered by the Turks about 1835. A war occurred between Tripoli and the United States, 1801-1805 (q. v.). Area, 398,900 square miles, the population is estimated at 1,000,000.

Tripoli:

Blockade of, by United States squadron referred to, 388, 389.

Citizens of United States imprisoned in, liberated, 373.

Claims of United States against, 1025.

Corvette on coast of, destroyed by United States vessels, 353.

Ex-Bashaw of, treaty with United States relative to restoring family of, to, 418.

Tunis.—A French protectorate in northern Africa. It is one of the Barbary States. Tunis is bounded on the north and northeast by the Mediterranean Sea, on the southeast by Tripoli, on the south and southwest by the Desert of Sabara, and on the west by Algeria. It produces grain and fruits (principally dates and olives), and has important fishing interests. It is peopled by Arabs, Berbers, and Jews. Tunis formed a part of ancient Carthage, and later, as Roman Africa, it became the leading seat of Latin Christianity. It passed successively under the dominion of the Vandals, Greeks and Arabs. It was made a Turkish province in 1575. For a long time it was noted as a piratical state. It became a French protectorate in 1881. Area, 45,779 square miles; estimated population, 1,500,000.

Tunis:

Blockade of Tripoli, 388, 389.

Claims of, against United States, 388, 389.

Condolence of Bey of, on death of President Lincoln, 3565.

Consul of United States in, 169, 379, 833, 2611.

Convention with, 833.

Differences with, unsettled, 374.

Gratuity promised to, by United States partially delivered, 325.

Peace negotiations with, 389.

Questions with, regarding blockade of Tripoli, 388, 389.

Relations with, uncertain, 395.

Treaty with, 192, 253, 359, 821, 833, 852.

War with, threatened, 388.

Tunis, Treaties with.—The treaty of amity, commerce, and navigation of 1797 was in some respects modified by the latter treaty of 1824. Both, in turn, were superseded by the treaty with France regarding Tunis of May 9, 1094. By this latter the consuls of the United States residing in Tunis are no longer governed by the conditions of the former treaties, but are to be regulated in all cases by international law. The government of France agrees by this treaty to accord to the said consuls all of the rights, privileges, and immunities so provided. (See France, Treaties with.)

Turin, Italy, Hygienic Congress at, 4626.

Turkey.—The Turkish or Ottoman Empire, in southeastern Europe and in Asia and Africa, embraces a total area of 1,058,041 English square miles, with an estimated population of 31,580,000. Of this total, about 700,000 square miles, with a population exceeding 21,000,000, are directly under Turkish government.

TURKEY IN EUROPE.—Turkey in Europe occupies the eastern portion of the Balkan Peninsula and lies approximately between 40°-42° 50′ N. latitude and 26°-29° 10′ E. longitude. The only political neighbor in Europe is Bulgaria on the north and west. The southern coast is washed by the Ægean and the Sea of Marmora, and the northeast coast by the Black Sea. The principal towns are Constantinople, the capital of the Empire, with a population estimated at 1,100,000, Adrianople (120,000), Rodosto (35,000), Gallipoli (25,000), Kirk-Kilisseh, Chorlu, and Enos.

TURKEY IN ASIA.—*Anatolia* is practically coincident with Asia Minor, a peninsula of western Asia, bounded on the north by the Black Sea, on the west by the Ægean, and on the south by the Mediterranean; and separated from Turkey in Europe at the northwestern extremity by narrow straits known as the Dardanelles, which mark the entrance to the Sea of Marmora, and the Bosphorus, which forms a gateway to the Black Sea.

Physical Features.—In the western vilayets are the Granicus and Scamander, which rise in Mount Ida, 5,750 feet, the latter flowing through the plains of Troy; and the Meander, whose winding course to the Gulf of Miletus, on the Ægean coast, is the classical symbol of purposeless wandering.

Production and Industry.—The country is rich in minerals, including gold, silver, nickel, mercury, copper, iron, lead and coal, but its resources are almost entirely undeveloped; the forests of the northern mountains contain pine, fir, cedar, oak and beech, and the lower slopes and plains of the west produce figs, olives and grapes in abundance, while fruit trees flourish in the north. Cereals, cotton, rice and tobacco are cultivated, and buffaloes, camels, horses, sheep and goats form the principal wealth of the inhabitants. Carpets, rugs and cottons and mohair and silk stuffs are manufactured. Coffee, textiles and other manufactures, petroleum and salt are the principal imports. The Anatolian Railways, built by German enterprise, run from the coast to Angora, to Brusa, and to Konia, whence an extension is being built as a section of the Bagdad line (see Mesopotamia). There are also English and French lines in the west; these railways have given a great impetus to the trade of Anatolia.

Islands.—Almost all the Turkish islands have been occupied by Greece and Italy. Samothrace, Lemnos, Mitylene, Chios, Psara, Samos, Nikaria and smaller islands were seized by Greece during the Balkan War of 1912-1913; while Rhodes, Carpathos, Cos and other islands were occupied by Italy in 1912. Under the treaty of Ouchy (1912) Italy has undertaken to restore the occupied islands when all Ottoman troops have left Tripoli and Benghazi. Lemnos, Imbros, and Samothrace lie close to European Turkey, in the Ægean Sea, while Thasos, which lies near the coast of Salonica, is the personal property of the Khedive of Egypt, and is excluded from the Archipelago administration. Rhodes contains the old headquarters of the Archipelago vilayet; the island is particularly fertile, and the climate delightful, the land producing a profusion of fruits, grapes, and grain, and providing rich pastures. Mitylene, or Lesbos, north of the Gulf of Smyrna, has an area of about 680 square miles and a population estimated at 130,000, of whom all but 10,000 are Greek Christians; its products are olives, mules and cattle. Chios is about 250 square miles in extent and has a population about 70,000; its products are figs and wine. Crete, or Candia, claimed to be part of the Hellenic Kingdom at the outbreak of the war of 1912-1913, has since been incorporated by Greece. Samos, which was semi-independent, now forms part of the Hellenic Kingdom. Cyprus has been administered by Great Britain since 1878.

Turkish Armenia and Kurdistan lie between Anatolia on the north and west and Asiatic Russia and Persia on the east. Armenia occupies the northwestern corner of the Iranian Plateau, with a mountain range running diagonally from southwest to northeast and culminating in Mount Ararat (16,-920 feet), which is the meeting-point of the Armenian, Russian and Persian boundaries. Kurdistan lies between Armenia and Mesopotamia. In the Armenian plateau several rivers have their source. The Euphrates (which has a length of 1,800 miles from its source to its outflow in the Persian Gulf). The Tigris has a total length of 1,150 miles from its source to its junction with the Euphrates, 70 miles from the Persian Gulf. Other rivers are the Aras and the Churuk Su. The great lake of Van (about 2,000 square miles in area) occupies the central portion of the vilayet of that name, in Kurdistan.

Mesopotamia, or the land of the Tigris and the Euphrates, which includes the vilayets of Mosul, Bagdad, Basra, and part of the vilayet of Zor, consists of broad, undulating plains, in which wheat and barley are abundantly grown. It extends southwest to the deserts of Arabia, and southeast to the mouth of the Euphrates.

This vast district is the subject of two important schemes, both or either of which would tend to agricultural development and security. One proposal is the Bagdad (or Euphrates Valley) Railway for which a concession has been granted to a German syndicate to extend the Anatolian line from Konia, via Mosul and Bagdad, to the Persian Gulf, but there are international difficulties in the way of the completion of the line, which has not yet entered the Euphrates valley. The Mesopotamia Irrigation scheme of Sir William Willcocks will bring a vast area once more into cultivation thus reviving the prosperity of a district containing traces of close settlement in bygone days; part of the scheme is already completed, and some 300,000 acres have been made available for tillage. South of the city of Bagdad is Kerbela, the most sacred center of pilgrimage for the Shia (Persian) Muhammadans.

Syria includes several vilayets with the mutessarifliks of Jerusalem and Lebanon, extending eastward to the deserts of Arabia, and south to the Sinai Peninsula. A Franco-Turkish agreement was signed in September, 1913, under which railway and other concessions in Syria are granted to France in return for facilities for raising loans in Europe. Wheat, tobacco, fruit, and wine are produced, but, except in the Palestine littoral, there is little cultivation without irrigation.

Palestine.—Of special interest to Christians is the district known as Palestine, a strip of land along the Mediterranean shore, and lying approximately between 31° 28'-33° 20' N. latitude. Palestine is divided into the maritime plain and mountainous region of the west, and the almost unexplored region of eastern Palestine. Western Palestine contains the rivers Orontes and Jordan, of which the Orontes (170 miles) rises in the north and flows westward to the coast; while the Jordan flows almost due north and south (generally below the level of the sea) from its source, in the neighborhood of Mount Hermon, to its mouth in the Dead Sea, in a winding course of close on 200 miles, during which it flows through the Sea of Galilee. The Jordan irrigates large tracts of country during the rainy season, when it overflows its banks. Palestine now forms the mutessariflik of Jerusalem and part of the vilayet of Beyrout. The Church of the Holy Sepulchre at Jerusalem is visited annually by large bands of Christian pilgrims, principally of the Orthodox and Coptic churches, and the site of Solomon's Temple is occupied by the Mosque of Omar, which contains a relic of the Prophet and the sacrificial stone of Abraham. Recent excavations on the site of the city of Jericho have proved that the walls are still standing for the greater part of the perimeter. Damascus in Syria contains the Mosque of the Ommayedes, where is the tomb of Saladin.

The principal towns of Asiatic Turkey are Smyrna (260,000), Bagdad (150,000), Damascus (150,000), Aleppo (125,000), Beyrout (120,000), Scutari in Anatolia (80,000, and Broussa (80,000).

History.—The Ottoman Turks are descended from Asiatic tribes, who migrated westward under the pressure of the Mongol invasion, and spread from Asia Minor into southeast Europe at the beginning of the fourteenth century. The Turks captured Constantinople in 1453, and spread over the whole of the Balkan Peninsula, their name of Osmanli, or Ottoman Turks, being derived from Othman, or Osman, a notable Turkish leader in the thirteenth century. Early in the sixteenth century the Ottoman Empire was spread over Egypt and northern Africa, and penetrated northward into Hungary, a great part of which was incorporated with the Turkish dominions until 1699, when the Peace of Carlowitz freed the country from Turkish rule. In the nineteenth century the outlying African dominions, with the exception of Tripoli, broke away from their suzerain, or were occupied by other Powers, and in the latter part of the century the northern states of the Balkan Peninsula asserted their independence, under guarantees of the Christian Powers.

The revolution of 1908-1909 aimed at the restoration of the constitution granted in 1876, but withdrawn by the Sultan in 1877, from which date the rule of the Sultan was a despotism, tempered only by religious observances and the fear of a popular rising or of intervention by other Powers. The 1876 constitution, restored on July 23, 1908, consists of a monarchy and of an Assembly of two houses. During the process of constitutional reforms, which drove the Sultan Abdul Hamid (1876-1908) from the throne, war broke out between Italy and Turkey, and Tripoli and Benghazi were ceded to Italy under the Treaty of Ouchy. These events were followed in the autumn of 1912 and early months of 1913 by a disastrous war with the States of the Balkan League (Bulgaria, Montenegro, Servia, and Greece). At the outbreak of hostilities the European dominions of Turkey extended westward to the Adriatic and northward to Bosnia-Herzegovina, thus including the districts known as Macedonia, Thrace, and Albania. By the Treaty of London (1913), the northwestern boundary of European Turkey was a line drawn from Enos, on the Adriatic coast, to Midia on the Black Sea, thus excluding Adrianople, which had capitulated (after a long siege) to the Bulgarian forces. At the outbreak of the second Balkan war (in which Servia and Greece were aided against Bulgaria by Rumania), Turkey took advantage of the military difficulties of Bulgaria and reoccupied Adrianople, thus recovering a part of the lost dominions. Ruler (Sultan), Mehmed V., born Nov. 3, 1844, proclaimed April 27, 1909, in succession to Abdul Hamid II. (acceded 1876, deposed 1908). The present Sultan is the thirty-fifth in descent from Othman, the founder of the Empire, in whose line the succession is vested. During the European war of 1914, Turkey was induced to assume the offensive against Russia, and on Nov. 1, bombarded Odessa and began hostile operations in the Black Sea. In consequence the allied powers of

Russia, France and Britain dismissed the Turkish ambassadors. (See European War.)

Government.—The Turkish Parliament consists of two houses. The Senate consists of members appointed by the Sultan. The Chamber of Deputies contains 280 members, elected by delegates (chosen for the purpose by the registered voters) for a maximum of four years.

At the capital (Constantinople) there is a Court of Cassation, with a *section de requêtes*, and civil and criminal sections; a court of civil and criminal appeal; and a tribunal of first instance.

AREA AND POPULATION

Continental Divisions	Area in English Sq. Miles	Estimated Population
Turkey in Europe........	12,000	2,755,000
Turkey in Asia—		
Anatolia—		
Adana (Adana)...........	15,500	425,000
Angora (Angora).........	27,350	950,000
Archipelago (Rhodes).....	2,750	320,000
Bigha (Dardanelles)......	2,600	130,000
Broussa (Broussa)........	25,000	1,500,000
Castamuni (Castamuni)...	20,000	1,000,000
Ismid (Ismid)............	3,100	250,000
Konia (Konia)...........	40,000	1,000,000
Sivas (Sivas)............	24,000	1,100,000
Smyrna (Smyrna)........	21,000	1,500,000
Trebizond (Trebizond)....	12,500	1,000,000
	193,800	9,175,000
Armenia and Kurdistan—		
Bitlis (Bitlis)............	10,500	400,000
Diarbekir (Diarbekir).....	15,300	500,000
Erzeroum (Erzeroum).....	19,300	650,000
Mamuret el Aziz (Kharput)	12,500	600,000
Van (Van)..............	15,000	350,000
	72,600	2,500,000
Mesopotamia and Syria—		
Aleppo (Aleppo).........	31,200	1,000,000
Bagdad (Bagdad).........	42,500	600,000
Basra (Basra)...........	54,000	450,000
Beyrout (Beyrout).......	6,200	600,000
Jerusalem (Jerusalem).....	6,500	400,000
Lebanon (Tripoli)........	1,160	200,000
Mosul (Mosul)...........	35,000	400,000
Syria (Damascus)........	37,000	800,000
Zor (El Deir)............	31,000	100,000
	244,460	4,650,000
Arabia—		
Hejaz (Mecca)...........	97,000	300,000
Yemen (Sana)...........	75,000	800,000
	172,000	1,100,000
Total..............	682,960	17,425,000
Turkey in Africa—Egypt.	363,181	11,400,000
Grand Total.........	1,058,041	31,580,000

Some twenty or more races are represented in the Turkish Empire, the Osmanlis or Turks being the most numerous. Other races are Bulgarians, Vlachs, Kurds, Circassians, Armenians, Arabs, Jews, and Gipsies. Of the total population more than half are Muhammadans and about 36 per cent Christians, while 300,000 are Jews, 300,000 Druses, and 200,000 Gipsies (about equally divided between the Moslem and Christian faiths.)

Production and Industry.—Wheat is largely grown in European Turkey, in South Eastern Anatolia and in the vilayets of Basra and Syria; maize, millet and sesame are largely grown in Anatolia. The vine is very generally cultivated, and dates, figs, olives, oranges and fruit of almost every kind are grown, particularly in northern Anatolia. Basra is the principal center of the date industry, and Adrianople of the wine trade. Roses are very largely grown in Adrianople for the production of perfume. Cotton is now largely grown, and tobacco is almost universal, the trade being centered at Smyrna. The silk-worm industry is encouraged, and large quantities of silk are produced in Adrianople and in northwestern Anatolia.

The mineral wealth of Turkey is believed to be immense in both sections of the empire; gold, silver, lead, copper, iron, mercury, corundum and zinc, and coal, salt and borax are known to exist; and salt, silver, lead and copper mines are successfully exploited. Petroleum is obtained in the Adrianople coast district of the Sea of Marmora.

The principal industries are tanning and the manufacture of muslin, velvet, silks and carpets, attar of roses, and ornamental metal-work.

For the army and navy see Armies of the World and Navies of the World.

Cities.—Capital Constantinople. Population, 1,200,000. There are forty towns in the Ottoman Empire with a population exceeding 25,000.

Trade with the United States.—The value of merchandise imported into Turkey in Europe from the United States for the year 1913 was $2,217,073, and goods to the value of $9,917,890 were sent thither—a balance of $7,700,817 in favor of Turkey.

Turkey (see also Ottoman Empire):

American citizens—

Agreement respecting rights of, in, proclaimed, 4231, 4344.

Discussed, 4244, 4405.

Emigration of, to, for purpose of acquiring lands referred to, 3661.

Injuries inflicted upon in, referred to, 6090, 6147.

Privileges accorded, in, 4920.

Steps taken for protection of, in, referred to, 4321, 4627.

Treatment of religious and educational establishments of, in, discussed, 5752, 6070, 6147.

American college at Scutari exempted from taxation, 6070.

American missionaries in, protection for and treatment of, discussed, 4627, 5090, 5872, 5962, 6069, 6147.

Anatolia College partially destroyed by mobs in, and indemnity paid for discussed, 5872.

Arabian horses brought by Charles Rhind from, referred to, 1099.

Armenian subjects of—

Cruelties and atrocities committed upon, by, 5989, 6069, 6147.

Investigation of, by American consul discussed, 5989, 6069.

Referred to, 6090.

Obtaining citizenship in United States and returning to, expelled, discussed, 5872, 5962.

Treatment by, of naturalized citizens of United States of Armenian origin, 6095.

Capitulations of, 4602, 4664.

Claims of United States against, discussed, 6148, 6337.

trust." It was legal tender to the amount of 25 cents. Coinage of the 2-cent piece was discontinued in 1872.

Two-Penny Act.—A law passed in 1755 by the Virginia assembly. The principal medium of exchange had up to this time been tobacco, it being considered more substantial than the paper money of the Colony. Under the provisions of the two-penny act, or option law, all debts payable, in tobacco were made payable, at the debtor's option, in money of the Colony at the rate of 16s. 8d. per hundred-weight of tobacco. This was equivalent to 2d. a pound. On appeal to the Crown the law was vetoed.

Tygris, The, detention of, admitted by Great Britain, 2111.

Tyler and Luckett (assignees), act for relief of, vetoed, 4334.

Tyler, John.—April 6, 1841-March 3, 1835.

Fourteenth Administration—continued—Whig.

Harrison died April 4, 1841; Vice-President Tyler took oath of office April 6.

Secretary of State—
Daniel Webster (continued).
Hugh S. Legaré.
Abel P. Upshur.
John Nelson (acting).
John C. Calhoun.
Secretary of the Treasury—
Thomas Ewing (continued).
Walter Forward.
Caleb Cushing.
John C. Spencer.
George M. Bibb.
Secretary of War—
John Bell (continued).
John McLean (declined appointment).
James M. Porter (rejected by Senate).
John C. Spencer.
William Williams.
Secretary of the Navy—
George E. Badger (continued).
Abel P. Upshur.
David Henshaw (rejected by Senate).
Thomas W. Gilmer.
John Y. Mason.
Postmaster-General—
Francis Granger (continued).
Charles A. Wickliffe.
Attorney-General—
John J. Crittenden (continued).
Hugh S. Legaré.
John Nelson.

John Tyler was elected Vice-President by an electoral vote of 234—equal to that received by President Harrison. He succeeded to the position of President on the death of President Harrison, which occurred in a little more than one month after his inauguration. As this was the first break in the Presidential office since the organization of the Government, some dispute arose as to Tyler's title. Leading statesmen of both parties were actively discussing whether he was President or only Acting President. But Tyler settled the question for all time by signing his first message, "John Tyler, President."

Party Affiliation.—In the early part of his political career, Tyler was a strong supporter of President Madison's policies. In 1811 he opposed in the Virginia Assembly the recharter of the first Bank of the United States. As a member of Congress he was a strict constructionist; voted against Calhoun's internal improvement bill, the Missouri compromise, and protective tariff. In the Senate he opposed the "tariff of abominations" (1828). In 1832 he supported Jackson as the least objec-

tionable candidate, but this support was only temporary. His nomination to the Vice-Presidency with Harrison was an effort to secure for the ticket the assistance of the dissatisfied Democrats.

Finance.—The great financial event of President Tyler's administration was his famous struggle with the Whig majorities in Congress over the Fiscal Bank and Fiscal Corporation, both of which measures he vetoed. In his opening message (page 1896) he recounted the history of the United States Bank, the sub-treasury system of President Van Buren, and other financial aspects. He uttered a note of warning to Congress which passed unheeded. He said: "I shall be ready to concur with you in the adoption of such system as you may propose, reserving to myself the ultimate power of rejecting any measure which may, in my view of it, conflict with the Constitution or otherwise jeopard the prosperity of the country, a power which I could not part with, even if I would, but which I will not believe any act of yours will call into requisition." Both houses passed, and the President signed, a bill to abolish Van Buren's sub-treasury plan. The fight for the national bank then came on. President Tyler had always maintained that the Federal Government had no Constitutional right to establish a national bank within a state without first having obtained the consent of that state. Both houses passed an act incorporating a bank of the United States without providing for the consent of the states, and the President vetoed it. It failed to secure the necessary two-thirds vote and died. The "fiscal corporation" bill was then brought forward incorporating such a bank in the District of Columbia, with power to establish branches in other states. Pressure of all kinds was brought to bear upon the President to compel him to either sign this bill or to resign. But he was neither to be hoodwinked nor bullied. The bill passed both houses in September, 1841; but the President promptly vetoed it. Whereupon the majority of his Cabinet resigned, Webster alone remaining. No hoped-for embarrassment followed, for the President promptly filled the vacancies, and his nominations were at once confirmed. The great effect of the undoubted victory which Tyler won was the death-blow to paternal government.

Public Debt.—The public debt of the United States during the Tyler administration stood as follows: Jan. 1, 1842, $20,-601,226.28; 1843, $32,742,922.00; 1844, $23,461,652.50; 1845, $15,925,303.01.

Tariff.—In the second year of Tyler's administration the strife between Congress and the President was renewed. Instead of the bank question, the tariff formed the matter of dispute. The importations were insufficient to supply the Government with means, and the reduction of duties by the compromise tariff had been so great that there was not money enough to meet the expenses. A bill was passed restoring the high protective tariff of 1833 and providing that the surplus revenues that were sure to accrue therefrom should be divided among the states. The President vetoed this bill on the ground that the compromise tariff provided that the protective tariff should come to an end in 1842, and because of the provision for distributing the surplus. Congress then framed another bill based on a tariff for revenue plan, with an incidental provision for protection and distribution. The President gave great offence to Congress by vetoing this bill also. There were threats of impeachment for unwarrantable assumption of authority; but the Whigs were afraid to go

EXTENT OF THE UNITED STATES DURING THE ADMINISTRATION OF PRESIDENT TYLER, 1841-1845.

(NOT INCLUDING TERRITORIES)

MAINE 1820

VT. 1791

N.H. 1788

MASS. 1788

CONN. 1788

R.I. 1790

N.J. 1787

DEL. 1787

NEW YORK 1788

PENNSYLVANIA 1787

MD. 1788

VIRGINIA 1788

NORTH CAROLINA 1789

SOUTH CAROLINA 1788

FLORIDA 1845

MICHIGAN 1837

OHIO 1803

KENTUCKY 1792

TENNESSEE 1796

GEORGIA 1788

ALABAMA 1819

INDIANA 1816

ILLINOIS 1818

MISSISSIPPI 1817

MISSOURI 1821

ARKANSAS 1836

LOUISIANA 1812

FLAG OF 1845

before the people for election in the autumn without settling the tariff, and they were obliged to pass a bill without the distributing clause. This the President promptly signed. Later, an attempt was made to pass the distributing clause in a separate bill, but the President vetoed that. In the next Congress, the Whig majority of 25 was replaced by a Democratic majority of 61.

Internal Improvements.—Congress passed two bills for river and harbor improvements, one for the eastern part of the country, and the other for the Mississippi section. The eastern bill President Tyler vetoed (page 2183); the Mississippi bill he signed. The discrimination was on the ground that the Mississippi was a great national highway, and therein differed from all other rivers, and was on that account a feature for the consideration of the Federal Government. An attempt to override the President's veto in this matter was not successful.

Tyler, John:

Annexation of Texas, discussed by. (See Texas.)

Annual messages of, 1927, 2047, 2110, 2187.

Appointing power of President, discussed by, 1903, 1958.

Biographical sketch of, 1888.

Commissioner from Virginia to confer with President in effort to prevent war, 3193.

Day of fasting and prayer recommended by, in consequence of death of President William Henry Harrison, 1887.

Death of President William Henry Harrison announced to, 1877.

Discretionary power of President over nominations, removals, and other acts, discussed by, 1903, 1941, 1958, 2073, 2080.

Dorr's Rebellion, discussed by, and correspondence regarding, 2136, 2139, 2160.

Exchequer plan of, recommended by, 2057, 2119.

Finances discussed by, 1895, 1916, 1934, 1955, 1959, 2052, 2057, 2079, 2117, 2119, 2199.

Foreign policy, discussed by, 1890, 2049, 2064, 2160, 2169, 2171, 2176, 2190, 2193, 2206.

Hawaiian Islands, independence of, desired by United States, and control over, must not pass to foreign power, 2064.

Inaugural address of, 1889.

Internal improvements discussed by, 2183.

Large standing army unnecessary in time of peace, 1901.

Medium of exchange discussed, 1897, 1935, 2119.

Monroe Doctrine reasserted by, 2065.

Oath of office administered to, 1886.

Peace with all the world the true foundation of our policy, 2050.

Pocket vetoes of, 2108, 2182.

Portrait of, 1887.

Powers of Federal and State Governments, discussed by, 1916, 1921, 1941, 2036, 2043, 2183.

Proclamations of—

Extraordinary session of Senate, 2220.

Military expedition against Canada, 1925.

Prostration in business, referred to by, 2057.

Protest of, to action of House in adopting report assailing official conduct of, 2043.

Request of House for information in possession of, refused, 1958, 2073, 2080.

Signature of, to Webster-Ashburton Treaty, 2026.

Special session message of, 1893.

State banks, measures should be adopted respecting creation of, 1899.

State of the Union, discussed by, 1927, 2047, 2110, 2187.

Subtreasury system, discussed by, 1898, 2060.

System of government, discussed by, 2188.

Tariff discussed by, 1944, 1961, 2033, 2036, 2053, 2119.

Texas, relations with, discussed by, (See Texas.)

Veto messages of—

Appropriating proceeds of sales of public lands, reasons for applying pocket veto, 2078.

Improvement of rivers and harbors, 2183.

Incorporating Fiscal Bank, 1916.

Incorporating Fiscal Corporation, 1921.

Payment of Cherokee certificates, reasons for applying pocket veto, 2182.

Revenue cutters and steamers, 2219.

Tariff bills, 2033, 2036.

Protest of President against action of House in adopting report assailing his conduct respecting, 2043.

Testimony in contested-election cases, reasons for applying pocket veto, 2108.

War between Texas and Mexico, discussed by. (See Wars, Foreign.)

Warehousing system recommended by, 2053, 2119.

Tyranny.—The act of one ruling in a wilful manner by reason of authority, standing ready to use force or cruelty as the only sanction.

U-Boat.—A submarine; so-called from the German practice of designating their submarines by numbers attached to the letter U, the first letter of the German word, "Untersee," "under-ocean;" viz.: U-5, U-59, etc. (See Submarine.)

Ukraine.—The name (literally "borderland") of that section of southern Russia and eastern Austria inhabited by the national group describing themselves as Ukrainians, but known generally throughout the remainder of Russia as Little Russians and called in Austria the Ruthenians. That part of Ukraine which is in Russia comprises about 91% of the whole, and is included in the following governments of the Russia before the Revolution of 1917: Podolia, Kiev (Kief), Techernigov, Ekaterinoslav, Kherson, Poltava. Austrian Ukraine is part of Galicia.

Outside of Russian Poland and West Russia, Ukraine covers practically all the southern border of Russia to the Caucasus Mountains, including the northwestern part of the Black Sea shores; and its strategic position on the political map of Europe can accordingly hardly be overestimated. Indeed, students of international affairs announced even before the outbreak of the European War that if Ukraine were to become independent of Russia and of Russian influence, the power of the Pan-Russian movement would be broken.

The area of Ukraine is approximately 850,000 square kilometres, thus making it about one and one-half as large as the present German Empire. The inhabitants number some 32,000,000, of which some 28,000,000 are in Russia. This number constitutes 18½% of the entire population of Russia, and outside of the Great Russians, the Ukrainians are by far the largest of the different races comprised within the Russian Empire.

The Ukrainian language is sharply different from the Russian language, and the leaders of the Ukrainian nationalistic movement claim that there are in addition vital ethnological distinctions between the Ukrainians and the other Russian races.

From the ninth century, when a loose federation of states in the Ukraine represented probably the highest form of civilization existing at that time in the territory known to-day as Russia, until the present, Ukrainian history has been the history of a race which has kept alive its national unity in spite of cruel persecution. In the eleventh century from the invading Tartar hordes, later from the Poles, in whose country Ukraine was long incorporated, and finally from the Russians, who had gained complete possession of the country in 1793 when the final partition of Poland took place (except Galicia, which fell to Austria), the Ukrainians have suffered oppression and discrimination hardly to be surpassed in the history of Europe. In the nineteenth century, the Russian government spared few efforts to Russify the Ukraine. The native language fell under rigid and cruelly enforced restrictions, the considerable Ukrainian culture was stamped out, there was general Russian colonization, and the leaders of the Ukrainian nationalistic feeling were exiled. But around the middle of the nineteenth century, the movement for separate Ukrainian culture and political autonomy revived, and persisted, in spite of persecution, on into the twentieth century. The first Duma had 63 Ukrainian representatives, 40 of whom were formed into a political unit for national independence, and the same situation was presented in the second Duma. This was the situation of the Ukraine

in European politics when the European War broke out. Not only were the Little Russians the hereditary foes of Russia, but also the Russian espousal of the cause of a restored Poland was in violation of the Ukraine's hopes for independence; so that the sympathies of Ukraine were all with the Central Powers. Although with the outbreak of the Russian Revolution in March, 1917, much of the hostility of Ukraine toward Russia ended, yet that occurrence was seized naturally as a godsend to the movement for Ukrainian national and cultural independence. Indeed, several months before, Ukraine had responded to the Allies' statement that autonomy for subject minor nationalities was one of their war aims with a demand that this principle be applied to the Little Russians.

In June, 1917, despite the opposition of Kerensky, Ukraine decided to secede from the Russian government, and to set up a government of its own. This action received support from many of the radicals at the head of the Russian government, and, indeed, provided a sharp cause for dissent within the Russian government itself. Later developments were both military and diplomatic, but autonomy and the right to self-development were finally achieved.

The earlier years of the war saw army after army sweep back and forth through Ukraine, and the misery and suffering of the people were not surpassed in the history of the whole conflict. President Wilson even issued a special appeal for assistance on March 16, 1917 (see page 8273). The culmination of the movement for independence, however, has served to improve the condition of the Ukrainians. For the soil is very fertile, and most of the people are farmers. Before the Russian Revolution, most of the land was in the hands of the nobility, and the peasants did not hold enough to support themselves; but with the success of the Revolution, the peasants occupied and took control of the land themselves, as throughout Russia.

Umatilla, The, rewards to Osette Indians for rescuing, recommended, 4803.

Uncle Sam.—A personification of the United States Government. Several explanations have been given as to the origin of this expression, but the most plausible is the following: During the War of 1812 Elbert Anderson, an army contractor, bought large quantities of provisions for the Army and had them shipped to himself at Troy, N. Y. The shipping mark was "E. A." above and "U. S." below. One of the inspectors at Troy was Samuel Wilson, popularly known as "Uncle Sam" Wilson. A workman was asked the meaning of the initials "U. S.,, which at that time were rarely used as an abbreviation for the United States. The prompt reply was "Elbert Anderson and Uncle Sam," referring to Sam Wilson. This interpretation became current among the workmen, many of whom afterwards enlisted and communicated the explanation to their comrades from all parts of the country as the mystic cipher elicited inquiry. The story went the rounds of the press and "Uncle Sam" became the popular appellation of the Government.

Uncle Tom's Cabin.—A novel written in 1851 by Harriet Beecher Stowe. Its successful purpose was to show the evils of slavery, and its wide popularity contributed greatly to the abolition sentiment.

Underground Railroad.—A name commonly applied before the Civil War to an arrangement whereby fugitive slaves were assisted to escape to Canada. The idea originated in some one of the northern states, and the plan consisted in harboring fugitives during the day and at night conducting them to the next "station" till they finally reached the border line. This "railroad" had many branches and the stations were a night's journey apart. The principal routes were from Ket ky, across Virginia and Ohio, and from Maryland through Pennsylvania and New York. This system of aiding escaping slaves was partially organized in 1838, but did not attain its highest activity until the passage of the fugitive-slave law, about 1850.

Underwood Tariff Act.—The Tariff Act passed in 1913. (See Tariff.)

Union Flags, return of Confederate and to respective States, recommended, 5163.

Proposition withdrawn, 5164.

Union Labor Party.—A successor of the Greenback party. It was organized at Cincinnati Feb. 23, 1887, and promulgated a platform embodying the principles of the Knights of Labor. In 1891 it united with the Farmers' Alliance and other elements to form the Populist party.

Union of South Africa.—The provinces of the Union extend from the southernmost point of the African Continent to the watershed of the Limpopo River, i. e., from 34° 50'-22° S. latitude, and include all the British territory within those limits, with the exception of Basutoland and the Swaziland and Bechuanaland Protectorates, while provision is made for the future inclusion within the Union of those territories and of the territories of the British South Africa Company.

History.—The Cape of Good Hope was discovered in 1486 by Bartholomew Diaz, the commander of one of the many expeditions sent out by successive Kings of Portugal to discover an ocean route to India. Diaz merely doubled the Cape and returned home. Eleven years later, in 1497, Vasco da Gama not only doubled the Cape and landed in what is now Natal, but successfully accomplished the voyage to India. In 1652 the Netherlands East India Company took possession of the shores of Table Bay, established a fort, and occupied the adjacent lands, in order to be always ready with supplies for their passing ships. In 1814 the Cape was formally ceded to the British Crown. Natal derives its name from the fact of its discovery on Christmas Day, 1497, by the celebrated Portuguese navigator, Vasco da Gama. The first European settlement was formed (1824) by a party of Englishmen, who established themselves on the coast where Durban now stands. Natal was then a part of the great Zulu kingdom. Between 1835 and 1837 another settlement was formed by a body of Dutch Boers, who came with their wagons overland from the Cape Colony and settled in the northern districts, where to this day the Boers preponderate. In the year 1843 Natal was proclaimed British and annexed to the Cape Colony. In 1856 it was erected into a separate colony, with representative institutions, and in 1893 acquired responsible government.

The Transvaal was formed as the South African Republic by parties of Dutch Boers from the English colonies who "trekked" into the interior of the continent and wrested the land across the Vaal River from the native chiefs. The discovery of

the gold fields within its borders led to the settlement of large numbers of foreigners, and eventually to hostilities with the British Government. A war of nearly three years' duration was fought with great tenacity, and its close was marked by the inclusion of the South African Republic within the British Empire, "responsible government" being granted almost immediately.

The Orange Free State was founded, in much the same way as the Transvaal, by Boer emigrants from Cape Colony, and its independence was granted in 1854.

Government.—The Union of South Africa is constituted under the South African Act, passed by the Parliament of the United Kingdom on Sept. 20, 1909. In terms of that Act the self-governing Colonies of the Cape of Good Hope, Natal, the Transvaal, and the Orange River Colony became united on May 31, 1910, in a legislative Union under one Government under the name of the Union of South Africa, those Colonies becoming original Provinces of the Union under the names of the Cape of Good Hope, Natal, the Transvaal, and the Orange Free State respectively.

The Union Government is seized of all State property, and the Railways, Ports, Harbors, and Customs are administered by Union Commissioners for the benefit of a Consolidated Revenue Fund. The former debts of the Provinces are administered by and form a first charge upon the funds of the Union. Provision is made in the Act for the admission to the Union of Rhodesia, and for the transfer to the Union Government of the administration of protected and other native territories. The Union was inaugurated by His Royal Highness, the Duke of Connaught, in 1910. The seat of the Government is Pretoria; the capital is Cape Town. The Executive is vested in a Governor-General appointed by the Sovereign, and aided by an Executive Council, with a Legislature of two Houses. Governor-General (Pretoria), His Excellency the Rt. Hon. Viscount Gladstone.

The Senate consists of forty members. For ten years after the establishment of Union eight are nominated by the Governor-General in Council and thirty-two are elected, eight for each Province.

The House of Assembly consists of 121 elected members, fifty-one of whom represent the Cape of Good Hope, seventeen Natal, thirty-six Transvaal, and seventeen the Orange Free State. Members of both Houses must be British subjects of European descent.

AREA AND POPULATION

Provinces	Area in English Sq. Miles	Population Census of 1911
Cape of Good Hope	276,995	2,564,965
Natal	35,290	1,194,043
Transvaal	110,426	1,686,212
Orange Free State	50,389	528,174
Total	473,100	5,973,394

Ethnography.—Of the total 5,973,394 persons (1911), 3,069,392 were males, and 2,904,002 females. The increase for the Union (1904-1911) was 15.41 per cent. For the Provinces it was as follows: Cape, 6.44 per cent; Natal, 7.69 per cent; Transvaal, 32,78 per cent; Orange Free State, 36.37 per cent. The population comprised (1911) 1,276,242 Europeans or whites (591,078 females), 4,019.006 natives (1,996,-057 females) and 678,146 other colored races (316,867 females). In 1904 the figures were: Europeans, 1,116,806 (increase, 1904-1911, of 14.28 per cent; natives, 3,491,056 (increase, 1904-1911, of 15.12 per cent); and other colored races 567,962 (increase, 1904-1911, of 19.40 per cent). The total non-European increase (1904-1911) was 15.72 per cent. The proportion of Europeans in the total population in 1904 was 21.58 per cent; in 1911, 21.37 per cent.

Union Station, Washington, D. C. (See illustration opposite 6980.)

Union Veteran Legion.—Organized at Pittsburgh, Pa., March 1884, and the National Organization was perfected Nov. 17, 1886. Encampments are now organized in twenty-one states and the District of Columbia, numbering 152 encampments. The membership is over 20,000. To become a member, the applicant must have been an officer, soldier, sailor or marine of the Union army, navy, or marine corps, during the late Civil War, who volunteered prior to July 1, 1873.

United Confederate Veterans.—An association the objects and purposes of which are set forth in the constitution as finally adopted at the Houston reunion, May 23, 1895. It is a federation of all associations of Confederate veterans, soldiers and sailors. The purposes are the cultivation of ties of friendship between those who have shared common dangers, sufferings, and privations; the encouragement of the writing, by the participants therein, of narratives, episodes, occurrences, etc., of the Civil War; the collection of authentic data for an impartial history, and the preservation of war records; care for needy survivors and their dependents. Membership is by camps, and numbers about 55,000.

United Daughters of the Confederacy. —The United Daughters of the Confederacy was organized at Nashville, Tenn., Sept. 10, 1894. It is composed of the widows, wives, mothers, sisters, and lineal female descendants of men who served the Confederate cause. The objects are to unite, and to cultivate ties of friendship among such women, to keep unsullied the record of Southern achievements in the Civil War, and to develop Southern character. It has about 80,000 members in some 1,400 chapters.

United Hatters. (See Loewe vs. Lawlor, et al.)

United Labor Party.—A local political party organized in New York City in 1886. It nominated Henry George for mayor on a platform based upon his theory that values arising from the growth of society belong to the community as a whole, and that therefore land values should bear the burden of taxation (see Single Tax).

United Sons of Confederate Veterans. (See Confederate Veterans, United Sons of.)

United States.—The United States is a federal republic consisting of forty-eight states and one federal district, besides the outlying territories of Alaska, Hawaii, the Philippine Islands, Porto Rico, Guam, Tutuila Group (Samoa), Wake and other islands and the Panama Canal Zone. Continental United States occupies the southern portion of the North American Continent, between the Atlantic and Pacific Oceans, in latitude 25°-49° North and longitude 67°-124° 30′ West, its northern boundary being Canada and the southern boundary Mexico.

Physical Features.—The coast-line on both oceans has an estimated length of about 15,610 miles, besides 3,620 miles on the great lakes and 5,744 on the Gulf of Mexico. The principal river is the Mississippi-Missouri, tra-ersing the whole country from north to south, and having a course of 4,500 miles to its mouth in the Gulf of Mexico, with many large affluents, the chief of which are the Yellowstone, Nebraska, Arkansas, Ohio, and Red Rivers. The rivers flowing into the Atlantic and Pacific Oceans are comparatively small; among the former may be noticed the Hudson, Delaware, Susquehanna, Potomac, and Savannah; of the latter, the Columbia, Sacramento, and Colorado. The Mobile and Colorado of Texas fall into the Gulf of Mexico, also the Rio Grande, which partly forms the boundary with Mexico. The chain of the Rocky Mountains separates the western portion of the territory from the remainder, all communication being carried on over certain elevated passes, several of which are now traversed by railroads; west of these, bordering the Pacific coast, the Cascade Mountains and Sierra Nevada form the outer edge of a high table-land, consisting in great part of stony and sandy desert, and in which occurs the Great Salt Lake, extending to the Rocky Mountains. Eastward the country is a vast, gently undulating plain, with a general slope southward towards the marshy flats of the Gulf of Mexico, extending to the Atlantic, interrupted only by the Alleghany Mountains, in the eastern states. Nearly the whole of this plain, from the Rocky Mountains to some distance beyond the Mississippi, consists of immense treeless prairies. In the eastern states large forests of valuable timber, as beech, birch, maple, oak, pine, spruce, elm, ash, walnut; and in the south, live-oak, water-oak, magnolia, palmetto, tulip-tree, cypress, etc., still exist, the remnants of the wooded region which formerly extended over all the Atlantic slope, but into which great inroads have been made by the advance of civilization. The Mississippi valley is eminently fertile. The mineral kingdom produces in great abundance iron, copper, lead, zinc, and aluminum; the non-metallic minerals including immense quantities of coal, anthracite, petroleum, stone, cement, phosphite rock, and salt. Precious metals include gold and silver, raised mainly in Colorado, California, and Alaska (gold), and Colorado, Montana, Utah and Idaho (silver); while precious stones are worked in great variety, including the turquoise, sapphire, tourmaline, and garnet.

History.—United States history may be said to commence with the colonizing expeditions from Europe in the sixteenth and seventeenth centuries; for, although Columbus discovered America in the fifteenth century (Oct. 12, 1492), no definite European settlement was attempted until the last quarter of the sixteenth century, when England, Holland, Sweden, France, and Spain made determined efforts to bring into account the potential wealth of the newly discovered continent. Of these nationalities the English secured a paramount influence amongst the nations of Europe. In the seventeenth century a chartered company founded Jamestown (1607), and many Royalist settlements were established in the district which had been named Virginia, after Queen Elizabeth, in the previous century. But step by step with the Church and Royalist foundations in the south a similar series of Puritan and Separatist centres was established in the north. The small band of "Pilgrim Fathers" in their 180-ton *Mayflower*, from Southampton, England, to Plymouth, Massachusetts (1620), was soon followed by a stream of well-to-do merchants from Boston, Lincolnshire, and other east coast English towns, and New England became rapidly prosperous. Between these two settlements the Dutch had established themselves in New Netherlands (1621), and the Swedes in New Sweden (1638). Other English foundations were Maryland (1632), Carolina (1663), New York (1664), New Jersey (1665), and Pennsylvania (1681). Georgia (1732) was the last of the English settlements.

The Spaniards began colonizing with the second voyage of Columbus, but their settlements were mostly in Cuba, Haiti, Mexico and the islands of the Caribbean Sea and in South America. The few colonies planted on the main land were never of hardy growth. The discoveries of Cabot and Cartier opened the mouth of the St. Lawrence to French enterprise, and Champlain founded Quebec in 1608. Traversing the Great Lakes Jesuit missionaries and explorers descended the Mississippi River and established posts at St. Paul, Dubuque, Kaskaskia, and St. Louis, finally reaching New Orleans, thereby confirming the claim of France to the whole interior of the country.

A continuous struggle was waged between the English and French settlements in America, but until the War of 1754-1763 little part was taken by Great Britain in the actual campaigns. The issue of this war decided the fate of America. The British Government levied an excise tax on many articles in everyday use in the colonies. The colonists resisted in arms, and bloodshed ensued at the first engagement at Lexington, April 19, 1775, and continued until the Capitulation of Yorktown, Oct. 19, 1781, when Lord Cornwallis surrendered with the whole of his forces to General Washington. When peace was concluded, Sept. 3, 1783, between America and Great Britain, no vestige of territory over which the dispute had raged remained under British rule. On July 4, 1776, the delegates of the various American colonies adopted the Declaration of Independence. (See Revolutionary War and the various battles.)

The Declaration of Independence (q. v.) was followed by the framing of a Constitution, which was ratified in 1787 to 1790 by the thirteen Original States (Delaware, Pennsylvania, New Jersey, Georgia, Connecticut, Massachusetts, Maryland, South Carolina, New Hampshire, Virginia, New York, North Carolina, and Rhode Island). (See Admission of States.) This Constitution established a legislature of two houses, and vested the executive power in an elective President; and on April 30, 1789, George Washington entered office as the first of a line of Presidents of the United States of America.

The maritime war of Britain and France led to the outbreak of hostilities between the former and the United States, owing mainly to the rival interpretation of the law of allegiance in connection with impressment of British subjects from American ships to serve in the British Navy. On June 18, 1812, the United States declared war against Britain, in which the latter was generally successful on land and the United States almost inevitably victorious on the sea. Peace was concluded by the Treaty of Ghent, on December 24, 1814, after a purposeless war.

The war with Mexico and the civil war between the states are described under separate headings.

Government.—I the Constitution (q. v.) of Sept. 17, 1787 (to which seventeen amendments (See Amendments) have been added), the government of the United States is entrusted to three separate authorities—the Executive, the Legislative, and the Judicial.

The Executive power is vested in the President, advised and assisted by the heads of ten executive departments. The description and history of these departments will be found under the headings, State, Treasury, War, Attorney-General, Postmaster-General, Navy, Interior, Agriculture, Commerce, and Labor. (See also President.)

The Legislative power is vested in two Houses, the Senate and the House of Representatives, the President having a veto power, which may be overcome by a two-thirds vote of each House. Two Senators from each state are elected by the people thereof for the term of six years; and Representatives are chosen in each state, by popular vote for two years. The number of Representatives for each state is allotted in proportion to its population—at present one for 212,407. (See articles on Apportionment, Congress, Senate and House.)

The *Judiciary* consists of three sets of federal courts: (1) The Supreme Court at Washington, D. C., consisting of a Chief Justice and eight puisne judges, with original jurisdiction in cases affecting ambassadors, etc., or where a state is a party to the suit, and with appellate jurisdiction from inferior federal courts. (2) The Circuit Court of Appeals, dealing with appeals from district courts, and consisting of the Justice of the Supreme Court for the circuit and all the Circuit and District Judges within the circuit. (3) The District Courts, eighty-five in number, served by a District Court Judge. Besides these, the Court of Customs Appeals (q. v.) was created in 1909. (See Judiciary Courts, and Supreme Court.)

Education.—The system of public instruction extends from the kindergarten to the university. Control is vested in the state and local authorities, the only central organization being the Bureau of Education charged with statistical and advisory functions only. The number of illiterates is swollen by immigrants, and by the fact that some 44 per cent of the colored population receive no instruction. It is said that no home is beyond reach of a school, whilst in some cases pupils are conveyed to and fro at public expense. A salient feature of the American system is co-education of the sexes throughout, there being comparatively few institutions where the tuition is not dual. Powerful aid is afforded by private and philanthropic initiative. Special Schools and Professional Establishments are numerous. Leading Universities are California, the Catholic University of America, Chicago, Clark, Columbia, Cornell, Harvard, the Johns Hopkins, Michigan, Pennsylvania, Princeton, Stanford, Virginia, Wisconsin, and Yale. (See Universities.)

Articles on the co-ordinate branches of the United States government will be found alphabetically arranged in the Encyclopedic Index under the following headings:

Executive—	President
Executive	Vice-President
Executive Depts.	Capitol
Executive Mansion	Cabinet
sion	State, Dept. of

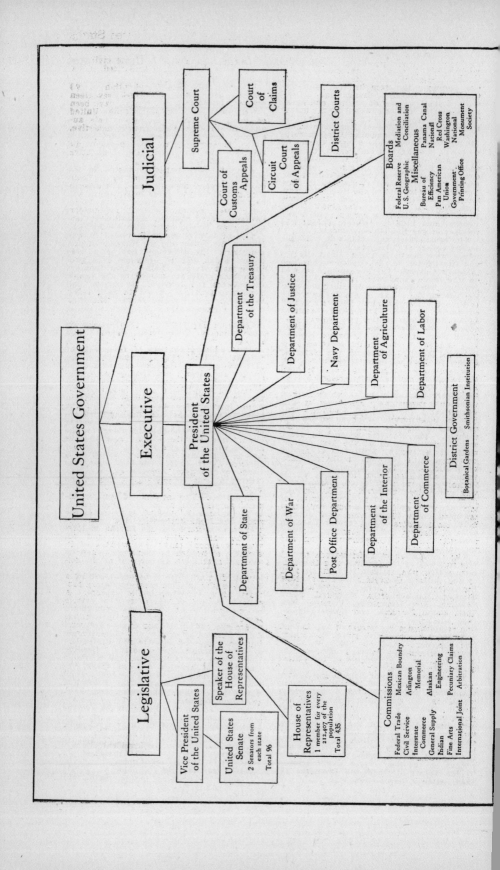

THE PROGRESS OF THE UNITED STATES IN AREA, POPULATION AND MATERIAL INDUSTRIES FROM 1800 TO 1913 IS SHOWN IN THIS TABLE WHICH IS COMPILED FROM A STATEMENT PREPARED BY THE BUREAU OF FOREIGN AND DOMESTIC COMMERCE, DEPARTMENT OF COMMERCE.

	1800	1850	1880	1900	1915a
Area b...............square miles	892,135	2,997,119	3,026,789	3,026,789	3,026,789
Population c.................no.	5,308,483	23,191,876	50,155,783	75,994,575	100,264,485
Population per square mile c....no.	6.47	7.88	16.86	25.55	33.71
Wealth d e..................dols.	....	7,135,780,000	42,642,000,000	88,517,306,775	
Wealth, per capita d e........dols.	....	307.69	850.20	1,164.79	f187,739,071,090 f1,965.00
Public debt, less cash in Treasury g............dols.	82,976,294	63,452,774	1,919,326,748	1,107,711,258	1,089,848,006
Public debt, per capita........dols.	15.63	2.74	38.27	14.52	10.82
Interest bearing debt h........dols.	82,976,294	63,452,774	1,723,993,100	1,023,478,860	969,759,090
Annual interest charge........dols.	3,402,601	3,782,393	79,633,981	33,545,130	22,936,642
Interest, per capita..........dols.	0.64	0.16	1.59	0.44	0.23
Gold coined..................dols.	317,760	31,981,739	62,308,279	99,272,943	i53,457,817
Silver coined.................dols.	224,296	1,866,100	27,411,694	36,345,321	i6,083,823
Gold in circulation j..........dols.	16,000,000	147,395,456	225,695,779	610,806,472	k600,777,874
Silver in circulation j..........dols.			68,622,345	142,050,334	k223,583,944
Gold certificates in circulation..dols.	....	....	7,963,900	200,733,019	1,076,637,759
Silver certificates in circulation.dols.	....	....	5,789,569	408,465,574	482,713,986
U. S. notes................dols.	....	....	327,895,457	313,971,545	332,035,994
National bank notes in circulation..................dols.			337,415,178	300,115,112	786,643,647
Federal Reserve notes........dols.	....	....	....	....	80,501,710
Miscellaneous currency in circulation l..................dols.	10,500,000	131,366,526	....	79,008,942	2,245,710
Total circulation of money.....dols.	26,500,000	278,761,982	973,382,228	2,055,150,998	3,585,140,626
Per capita..................dols.	5.00	12.02	19.41	26.93	35.59
National banks................no.		2,076		3,732	7,604
Capital......................dols.			455,909,565	621,536,461	1,065,891,978
Bank clearings, New York....dols.			37,182,128,621	51,964,588,564	i89,760,344,971
Total United States.........dols.				84,582,450,081	i163,975,683,000
Deposits in National banks.....dols.			833,701,034	2,458,092,758	m6,661,581,354
Deposits in savings banks.....dols.		43,431,130	819,106,973	2,389,719,954	i4,936,591,849
Depositors in savings banks.....no.		251,354	2,335,582	6,107,083	i11,109,499
Farms and farm property d...dols.		3,967,343,580	12,180,501,538	n20,439,901,164	o40,991,449,090
Farm products, value p.......dols.			2,212,450,927	4,417,069,973	p8,498,311,413
Manufacturing establishments d.no.		123,025	253,852	q207,514	q268,491
Value of products d.........dols.		1,019,106,616	5,369,579,191	q11,406,926,701	q20,672,051,870
United States Government receipts—net ordinary r.......dols.	10,848,749	43,592,889	333,526,501	567,240,852	695,663,190
Customs................dols.	9,080,933	39,668,686	186,522,065	233,164,871	209,268,107
Internal revenues.........dols.	809,397	....	124,009,374	295,327,927	s415,657,052
United States Government, disbursements, net ordinary t...dols.	10,813,971	40,948,383	264,847,637	487,713,792	731,527,572
War....................dols.	2,560,879	9,687,025	38,116,916	134,774,768	173,982,638
Navy...................dols.	3,448,716	7,904,725	13,536,985	55,953,078	141,959,853
Pensions................dols.	64,131	1,866,886	56,777,174	140,877,316	164,388,959
Interest on public debt....dols.	3,402,601	3,782,393	95,757,575	40,160,333	22,918,427
Imports of merchandise.......dols.	91,252,768	173,509,526	667,954,746	849,941,184	1,674,169,740
Per capita..................dols.	17.19	7.48	u12.51	10.93	v16.46
Exports of merchandise.......dols.	70,971,780	144,375,726	835,638,658	1,394,483,082	2,768,589,340
Per capita..................dols.	13.37	6.23	w16.43	17.76	26.70
Imports, silk, raw..............lbs.			2,562,236	11,259,310	26,030,925
Rubber, crude...............lbs.			16,826,099	49,377,138	172,068,428
Tin plates.................lbs.			379,902,880	147,963,804	10,642,237
Iron and steel, manufactures of......................dols.	....	20,145,067	71,266,699	20,478,728	22,712,660
Domestic exports, iron and steel manufactures................dols.	52,144	1,953,702	14,716,524	121,913,548	225,888,358
Domestic exports, all manufactures...................dols.		23,223,106	121,818,298	484,846,235	1,166,093,728
Farm animals, value...........dols.		544,180,516	1,576,917,556	2,228,123,134	5,969,253,000
Cattle....................no.		17,778,907	33,258,000	43,902,414	58,320,000
Horses....................no.		4,336,719	11,201,800	13,537,524	21,195,000
Sheep....................no.		21,773,220	40,765,900	41,883,065	49,956,000
Mules.....................no.		559,331	1,729,500	2,086,027	4,479,000
Swine.....................no.		30,354,213	34,034,100	37,079,356	64,618,000
Production of gold............dols.		50,000,000	36,000,000	79,171,000	i88,884,400
Silver, commercial value.....dols.		50,900	34,717,000	35,741,100	i40,348,100
Coal....................long tons		6,266,233	63,822,830	240,789,310	i458,504,890
Petroleum................gals.		....	1,104,017,166	2,672,062,218	i12,193,126,470
Pig iron...................tons		563,755	3,835,191	13,789,242	i23,332,244
Steel.....................tons			1,247,335	10,188,329	x23,513,030
Tin plates.................lbs.		....	....	849,004,022	z1,845,130,000
Copper..............long tons		650	27,000	270,588	i504,018
Wool.....................lbs.		52,516,959	232,500,000	288,636,621	i290,192,000
Wheat....................bush.		100,485,944	498,549,868	522,229,505	i878,680,000
Corn.....................bush.		592,071,104	1,717,434,543	2,105,102,516	i1,702,599,000
Cotton...................bales	153,509	2,454,442	6,605,750	10,245,602	i15,905,840
Cane sugar................lbs.		247,577,000	178,872,000	322,549,011	493,239,046
Sugar consumed............lbs.	....	....	1,979,221,478	4,477,175,236	i8,793,794,928

THE PROGRESS OF THE UNITED STATES IN AREA, POPULATION AND MATERIAL INDUSTRIES
FROM 1800 TO 1913—*Continued.*

	1800	1850	1880	1900	1915a
Cotton consumed......500-lb. bales	18,829	422,626	1,865,922	3,603,516	i5,702,639
Domestic cotton exported......lbs.		638,381,604	1,822,061,114	3,100,583,188	4,403,578,499
Railways operated..........miles		9,021	93,267	194,262	x251,984
Passengers carried..........no.				576,831,251	x1,033,679,680
Freight carried 1 mile......tons				141,596,551,161	x301,398,752,108
Revenue, ton per mile......cents				0.729	x0.729
Passenger cars...............no.				34,713	x51,700
Other cars...................no.				1,416,125	x2,393,800
American vessels built y.......tons	106,261	279,255	157,409	393,790	i316,250
Trading domestic, etc.......tons	301,919	1,949,743	2,715,224	4,338,145	i6,845,063
Trading foreign..............tons	669,921	1,585,711	1,352,810	826,694	i1,076,152
On Great Lakes..............tons		198,266	605,102	1,565,587	i2,882,922
Vessels passing through Sault Ste. Marie Canal............tons			1,734,890	22,315,834	i41,986,339
Commercial failures............no.			4,735	10,774	z10,719
Amount of liabilities........dols.			65,752,000	138,495,673	z177,106,140
Post-Offices..................no.		18,417	42,989	76,688	56,380
Receipts of P.-O. Department..dols.	280,804	5,499,985	33,315,479	102,354,579	i287,934,566
Telegrams sent (1)..........no.			29,215,509	63,167,783	(2)90,000,000
Newspapers, etc. (3)..........no.		2,526	9,723	20,806	23,167
Public schools, salaries........dols.			55,942,972	137,687,746	(4)303,537,849
Patents issued................no.		993	13,947	26,499	i41,850
Immigrants arrived (5).........no.		369,980	457,257	448,572	326,700

a Figures of 1915 are somewhat preliminary and subject to revision. *b* Exclusive of Alaska and islands belonging to the United States. *c* Census figures, relating to Continental United States; the figures for 1915 represent an estimate. *d* Census figures. *e* True valuation of real and personal property. *f* 1912. *g* 1800 to 1850, outstanding principal of the public debt, January 1. *h* Figures for the years 1800 to 1850 include the total public debt. *i* 1914. *j* Gold and silver cannot be stated separately prior to 1876. From 1862 to 1875, inclusive, gold and silver were not in circulation, except on the Pacific Coast, where it is estimated that the average specie circulation was about $25,000,000, and this estimate is continued for the three following years under the head of gold. After that period gold was available for circulation. *k* As the result of a special investigation by the Director of the Mint, a reduction of $135,000,000 was made in the estimate of gold coin in circulation on July 1, 1907, as compared with the basis of previous years, and on September 1, 1910, a reduction of $9,700,000 was made in the estimate of silver coin. *l* Includes notes of Bank of United States; State bank notes; demand notes of 1862 and 1863; fractional currency, 1870; Treasury notes of 1890-1891 to date, and currency certificates, act of June 8, 1892-1900. *m* Includes all deposits, demand and time. *n* Includes value of buildings, $3,556,639,496. The Twelfth Census was the first to collect statistics of buildings on farms. *o* Includes value of buildings, $6,325,451,528. *p* Gross value of all farm products. The figures of the various censuses are not comparable, reason for which will be found in census reports. *q* Exclusive of neighborhood industries and hand trades, included in years previous to 1905. *r* "Ordinary receipts" include receipts from customs, internal revenue, direct tax, public lands, and "miscellaneous," but do not include receipts from loans, premiums, Treasury notes, or revenues of Post-Office Department. *s* Includes corporation and income taxes, $79,-828,675 in 1915. *t* "Ordinary disbursements" include disbursements for war, navy, Indians, pensions, payments for interest, and "miscellaneous," but do not include payments for premiums, principal of public debt, or disbursements for postal service paid from revenue thereof. *u* Imports for consumption after 1850. *v* Based on general imports. *w* Domestic exports only after 1860. *x* 1913. *y* Includes canal boats and barges prior to 1880. *z* First six months. (1) Figures relate to the Western Union only and after 1900 do not include messages sent over leased wires or under railroad contracts. (2) Estimated 1912. (3) 1800 to 1850, inclusive, from census of 1880; from 1880 to 1900, inclusive, from Rowell's Newspaper Directory; after 1900 from Ayer's American Newspaper Annual. Figures for 1914 include outlying possessions. (4) Includes salaries for teachers only. Figures are for 1912. (5) 1850, total alien passengers arrived; 1850, 15 months ending December 31; after 1850, fiscal years ending June 30.

Losses sustaind by. (See Claims.)

Maritime rights of. (See Maritime Rights.)

Merchandise transported from one port to another in, over Canadian territory, discussed, 5770.

Military expeditions against. (See Illegal Combinations.)

Militia of. (See Army; Militia.)

Ministers of. (See Ministers of United States.)

Ministers to. (See the several powers.)

Mints of. (See Mint.)

Naval force on the Lakes. (See Great Lakes.)

Navigation questions. (See Navigation.)

Neutral rights of. (See Neutral Rights.)

Neutrality of. (See Neutrality.)

Northeastern boundary discussed. (See Northeastern Boundary.)

Northwestern boundary discussed. (See Northwestern Boundary.)

Outrages committed on citizens of. (See Citizens of United States.)

Panics in. (See Panics.)

Pardons granted citizens of. (See Pardons.)

Parties in, people warned against baneful effects of, 210.

Peace with other nations, hope expressed that it may be preserved, 229, 230.

Persons from foreign countries crossing borders of, and committing depredations, order regarding, 3484.

Pledge of, to Mexico. (See Mexico.)

Policy of, toward foreign powers. (See Foreign Policy.)

Political affairs of Europe not interfered with by, 2050, 2248, 2715, 4050.

Population of. (See Census.)

Powers, foreign, relations with. (See Powers, Foreign.)

Powers of. (See Powers of Federal and State Governments.)

Prefers war to tribute, 560.

Preparation for war recommended. (See War.)

Presents offered to, by—
Emperor of Morocco, 1256.
Imaum of Muscat, recommendations regarding, 1809, 2169.

Private armed vessels of, instructed to furnish aid to neutral vessels. (See Vessels, United States.)

Private claims against. (See Private Claims against United States.)

Public statutes of. (See Revised Statutes.)

Rebellions in. (See Illegal Combinations.)

Reception of letter of thanks from Greece, 950.

Recommending active and hasty preparation for war. (See War.)

Relations with foreign powers. (See Powers, Foreign.)

Relations with Texas. (See Texas.)

Resolutions of—
Pennsylvania legislature—
Pledging support to, 446, 482.

Revenue of. (See Revenue, Public.)

Revised Statutes of. (See Revised Statutes.)

Rights of, on ocean must be respected, 384.

Seat of Government of. (See District of Columbia; Seat of Government; Washington City.)

Secret agent employed by Great Britain to foment disaffection in, referred to, 483, 488.

Should not consume what it is expected to guard, 317.

Stock held by, in corporations should be sold, 1162.

Subscribes for shares in canal company. (See Chesapeake and Delaware Canal Co.)

Supported by ballot box, not musket, 1390.

Supreme Court of. (See Court, Supreme.)

System of government of discussed, 2188, 2614, 2715, 2745, 2825, 2874, 3566, 5358.

Texan forces invade territory of, 1726.

Texas, relations with. (See Texas.)

Thanks, letter of, received from Greece, 950.

Trade with foreign powers. (See Commerce.)

Transfer of Louisiana to, disagreeable to Spain, 376.

Treason, citizens punished for. (See Treason.)

Treaties of. (See Treaties.)

Troops of. (See Army; Militia.)

Unity of—
Best preserved by local self-government, 208.
Essential to liberty, 207.

Wars of. (See Algerine War; Indian Wars; Mexican War; Revolutionary War; Spanish-American War; Tripolitan War; Civil War; War of 1812.)

United States, Federal Government of. (See articles under.)

United States, The.—A famous frigate of the War of 1812. She was built at Philadelphia in 1797 and carried forty-four guns. Oct. 25, 1812, near the island of Madeira, she met and captured the British ship *Macedonian,* also of forty-four guns. Of the 300 men on the *Macedonian,* thirty-six were killed and sixty-eight wounded.

The loss on the *United States* was five killed and six wounded.

United States, The:
Combat with and capture of British frigate *Macedonian*, 506.
French seamen injured by, while firing salute, 1273.
Provision should be made for families of, 1273.

United States Bank of Pennsylvania:
Payment of bonds of, held by United States, referred to, 1726.
Suspension of, referred to, 1768.

United States Daughters of 1812.—
Membership Qualifications — Any woman over eighteen years of age of good character and a lineal descendant of an ancestor who rendered civil, military, or naval service during the War of 1812, or the period of the causes which led to that war (subsequent to the War of the Revolution), may be eligible to membership, provided the applicant be acceptable to the Society. In all the states the initiation fee is $1.

United States, European and West Virginia Land Co., agreements entered into with agents of Mexico, referred to, 3723.

United States Geographic Board. (See Geographic Board.)

United States Library. (See Library of Congress.)

United States Notes: (See also Currency.)
Act to fix amount of, and circulation of national banks vetoed, 4222.
Discussed and recommendations regarding, 6073, 6078, 6175.

United States Shipping Board.—This board was created by act of Congress approved September 7, 1916, which provides for a Shipping Board of five commissioners, to be appointed by the President, by and with the consent of the Senate, with a yearly salary of $7,500 each. The commissioners are appointed for terms of six years, and not more than three shall be of the same political party; and none of them shall have any relations with or hold stocks or bonds in any common carrier, nor engage in any other business. The Board was organized to construct merchant vessels suitable for auxiliary use in any way for naval or military purposes, but in times of peace to be operated as American merchant vessels. The Board is authorized, if it sees fit, to form a corporation or corporations better to carry out the purposes of the act, but in such corporations the Board is always to remain the majority stockholder. The Board is also to investigate the condition of the American merchant marine, and to report to Congress and to the President methods for its improvement. One of the moves made by the Board after the declaration of a state of war with Germany was to make plans for the construction of a thousand wooden ships, under the direction of General George W. Goethals, the builder of the Panama Canal.

United States vs. Peters.—A case of mandamus decided in February, 1809, by the Supreme Court of the United States, the execution of which was opposed by

the State authorities of Pennsylvania, backed by the militia. In the case of Olmstead *et al. vs.* Rittenhouse's Executrixes (q. v.) Judge Peters, of the United States district court of Pennsylvania, decided in favor of the plaintiffs, but refrained, he stated, for prudential reasons, from carrying his judgment into execution. April 2, 1803, a Pennsylvania statute was enacted forbidding the execution of the decree of the Federal court. A mandamus was then asked for against Peters. The Supreme Court granted it, Chief Justice Marshall declaring that the legislature of a State can not annul the judgment or determine the jurisdiction of a United States court. The execution of the original judgment required the payment of £11,496 9s. 9d., Pennsylvania currency, which had been placed in the custody of the State court. The Pennsylvania officials, with the militia, resisted payment for twenty-six days, when the marshal assembled a *posse comitatus* of 2,000 men, and the money was paid over without actual collision.

United States vs. Todd.—A case not printed, there having been no reporter at the time. It was possibly the first case in which the United States Supreme Court declared a Federal statute unconstitutional. Under an act of Congress passed in 1792 the name of Yale Todd was by the circuit court of Connecticut ordered to be placed upon the pension list. It was afterwards (Feb. 17, 1794) decided by the Supreme Court of the United States that the circuit court could not constitutionally make such a decree, nor could it act in the capacity of a commission not of judicial function.

Universal Expositions. (See Exhibitions.)

Universal Postal Union discussed, 4574, 4640, 5971, 6164.

Universal Military Training. (See Compulsory Military Service.)

Universal Military Training League. (See Preparedness Societies.)

Universities. (See National University; Seminaries of Learning.)

University Settlement. (See Social Settlements.)

Unlawful Expeditions. (See Illegal Combinations.)

Upper Pend d'Oreille Indians. (See Indian Tribes.)
Treaty with, 2913.

Uruguay.—Uruguay is the smallest of the South American Republics and lies between 30°-35° S. latitude and 53° 25'57" 42' W. longitude, with an eastern (Atlantic) seaboard of 120 miles, a southern shore line of 235 miles on the estuary of Rio de la Plata, and 270 miles of the Uruguay River on the west. In the north the territory is conterminous with Brazil for 450 miles.

Physical Features.—The country consists mainly (and particularly in the south and west) of undulating grassy plains. In no case do the peaks exceed 2,000 feet.

The principal river of Uruguay is the Rio Negro, flowing from northeast to southwest into the Rio de la Plata. The boundary river Uruguay is navigable from its estuary to Salto, about 200 miles north, and the Negro is also navigable for a considerable distance. On the southeast coast are several lagoons, and the northeast boundary crosses Lake Mirim.

The climate is extraordinarily healthy,

with great uniformity of temperature, the summer heat being tempered by the breezes of the Atlantic and the geographical position causing a high thermometer in winter.

History.—Uruguay resisted all attempted invasions of the Portuguese and Spaniards until the beginning of the seventeenth century, and 100 years later the Portuguese settlements were captured by the Spaniards. From 1726-1814 the country formed part of the Spanish South America and underwent many vicissitudes during the Wars of Independence. In 1814 the armies of the Argentine Confederation captured the capital and annexed the province, and it was afterward annexed by Portugal and became a province of Brazil. Aug. 25, 1825, through the heroism of the thirty-three liberators (whose memory is perpetuated in the name of one of the provinces), the country threw off the Brazilian yoke. This action led to war between Argentina and Brazil, which was settled by the mediation of the United Kingdom, Uruguay being declared an independent state in 1828.

Government.—In 1830 a Republic was inaugurated, with a Constitution of Sept. 10, 1829. The President is elected by the legislature for a term of four years and is ineligible for a consecutive period of office. President (March 1, 1915-1919), Dr. Feliciano Viera.

There is a Congress of two houses. The Senate consists of nineteen members (one for each department), elected by indirect vote for six years and renewable as to one-third every two years. The Chamber of Deputies contains seventy-five members, elected for three years by direct vote. Congress meets in annual session from February to June.

Each of the nineteen Departments has a Prefect appointed by the President, and an elective municipal council. Justice is administered in subdistrict and district courts, and in departmental courts at each provincial capital. There is a high court at Montevideo composed of three judges elected by Congress.

Education.—Primary education is free and nominally compulsory, and is, perhaps, better extended than in any other South American Republic, and there is a University at the capital.

Production and Industry.—The total area is estimated at 46,178,000 English statute acres, of which nearly 38,000,000 acres are pasture land, while 1,211,370 acres are under corn crops (wheat 683,664, maize 505,072). In 1908-1909 there were also 45,302 acres under flax producing 260,934 tons, but the flax area is diminishing. The vineyards (11,000 acres) produced close on 2,000,000 gallons of wine in 1906. Olives and tobacco are also cultivated.

The Live Stock (the rearing of which is by far the most important industry) included (1908) 8,192,602 cattle, 26,286,296 sheep, 19,951 goats, 180,999 pigs, 556,307 horses, and 17,671 mules. The extensive pasture lands are particularly suitable for cattle breeding and sheep farming, and there are many establishments for the preparation of jerked beef (tasajo) for Brazil and Cuba, and of meat extract for Europe, while the department of Paysandu sends a special brand of ox-tongues all over the world. The frozen meat industry is now developing rapidly.

The mining industry is in its infancy and awaits capital. Gold and silver, lead, copper, magnesium and lignite are indicated, and gold is produced in small quantities.

Manufactures.—The industries connected with the live stock raising constitute the chief manufactures, with the exception of flour from home-grown grain. Outside these,

Uruguay still depends very largely on imported goods.

Finance.—The national debt was stated at 133,295,145 pesos on Jan. 1, 1913. The revenue for the preceding year was 17,211,850 pesos. The peso, the unit of value, is equivalent to $1.03, United States money.

AREA AND POPULATION

Departments	Area in English Sq. Miles	Population 1909
Artigas	4,392	28,866
Canelones	1,833	91,703
Cerro Largo	5,753	46,549
Colonia	5,525	44,413
Durazno	1,744	17,379
Flores	4,763	47,699
Florida	2,192	58,243
Maldonado	1,584	30,735
Minas	4,844	53,545
Montevideo	256	317,879
Paysandú	5,115	42,256
Rio Negro	3,269	23,421
Rivera	3,700	37,292
Rocha	4,280	36,165
Salto	4,863	46,801
San José	2,687	48,546
Soriano	3,560	41,763
Tacuarembo	8,074	48,933
Treinta y Tres	3,686	30,465
Total	72,210	1,094,688

Ethnography.—In 1908 there were 890,000 Uruguayans and 200,000 foreigners (Italian 75,000, Spanish 60,000, Brazilian 30,000, Argentine 15,000, French 13,000, British 2,000, Swiss 2,000, German 1,500, others 5,000). About 4 per cent of the population is colored (negro or Indian), 10 to 12 per cent of mixed blood, and the rest white or European (mainly Italian or Spanish) descent.

Railways.—In 1911 there were 1,570 miles of railway open for traffic, all being in British hands. Three lines radiate from Montevideo, the eastern line running to Aitigas, the central line to Rivera (on the Brazilian frontier), and the western line to Mercedes, a river port on the Rio Negro. The central line also runs westward to Paysandú, and thence via Salto to the Brazilian and Argentine frontiers. A southern line runs from the capital to Minas and Maldonado. The capital has electric trams.

In 1910 there were 1,018 post-offices and 319 telegraph offices (and two wireless stations), with 6,059 miles of line, there were also 4,803 telephone stations, with 19,039 miles of lines.

Cities.—Capital Montevideo, on the northern shore of the Rio de la Plata estuary. Population (1912), 325,000. Other towns are Paysandú, Salto, Mercedes, Florida and San José.

Trade with the United States.—The value of merchandise imported into Uruguay from the United States for the year 1913 was $7,522,145, and goods to the value of $2,450,697 were sent thither—a balance of $5,071,448 in favor of the United States.

Uruguay:

American citizens aggrieved by acts of, referred to, 2014.

Treaty with, 2703, 2718, 2813, 4072

Delay in exchange of ratifications of, referred to, 2915.

Uruguay, Treaties with.—An extradition treaty was concluded with Uruguay March 11, 1905, and a naturalization convention was signed at Montevideo August 10, 1908.

Uruguay also became a party to the convention between the United States and the several republics of South and Central

America for the arbitration of pecuniary claims and the protection of inventions, etc., which was signed in Buenos Aires in 1910 and proclaimed in Washington, July 29, 1914. (See South and Central America, Treaties with.)

Usury.—A charge for the use of money in excess of the legal rate of interest. Usury is universally discredited and in many states it is a penal offense. (See Statutes of Limitations and Interest Laws.)

Utah.—One of the western group of states sometimes referred to as "Deseret," a word taken from the Book of Mormon and signifying "Honey Bee." Nickname, "Mormon State." The State extends from lat. 37° to 42° north, and from long. 109° to 114° west. It is bounded on the north by Idaho and Wyoming, on the east by Colorado and Wyoming, on the south by Arizona, and on the west by Nevada. The area is 84,990 square miles. The surface is largely mountainous and includes part of the Great Basin and all of the Great Salt Lake. The region formed a part of the territory ceded by Mexico in 1848. Agriculture, mining and manufacture, are the leading industries. Probably no other state in the Union has such a variety of resources. Irrigation has been practiced from the beginning and was once thought absolutely necessary, but in later years arid farming has achieved wonderful success. The main products of the soil are wheat, oats, barley, potatoes, sugar beets, corn, alfalfa and timothy. The yearly wool clip amounts to many millions of pounds and is continually increasing. Utah fruits are superior in sweetness, firmness, beauty and fine flavor. The most successful manufacturing industry, aside from the smelting, milling and refining of ores, is the making of beet sugar. Salt production is also extensive, as is fruit and vegetable canning. The mountains of Utah contain inexhaustible deposits of minerals of great variety; some of them unique and peculiar to the region. Silver, lead, coal and iron have been mined for many years, and gold has also been found; but copper is the great mining staple in Utah at the present time.

The first white settlements were made by the Mormons in 1847-1848. The Territory of Utah was organized in 1850. Prejudice against these people and the polygamous practices of some of them, kept Utah out of the Union for many years, though she possessed every qualification for statehood and made repeated efforts to secure it. After the issuance by the Mormon Church of its manifesto discontinuing the practice of polygamy a State Constitution was framed prohibiting plural marriages, and this instrument being approved at Washington, the State was admitted Jan. 4, 1896. The Mormons still have a majority in Utah, though in the leading cities the Gentile or non-Mormon element predominates.

With the help of irrigation, agriculture is the chief occupation of the people of Utah. In 1906 there were 300 incorporated irrigation companies in the state. The Federal Government project of irrigation includes about 80,000 acres of Utah lands. Land offices are located at Salt Lake City and Vernal. Statistics of agriculture reported to the Federal census Bureau under date of April 15, 1910, placed the number of farms in the State at 20,676, comprising 3,397,699 acres, valued, with stock and improvements, at $150,795,201. The average value of land per acre was $29.28 against $9.75 in 1900. The value of domestic animals, poultry, etc., was $28,-781,691, including 412,334 cattle, valued at $8,948,702; 115,676 horses, $9,999,835; 2,277 mules, $157,497; 64,286 swine, $445,-653; 1,827,180 sheep, $8,634,735; poultry, $327,908. The yield and value of field crops was: Corn, 8,000 acres, 280,000 bushels, $227,000; wheat, 225,000 acres, 5,025,000 bushels, $3,518,000; oats, 87,000 acres, 3,889,000 bushels, $1,828,000; rye, 5,000 acres, 78,000 bushels, $55,000; potatoes, 15,000 acres, 2,100,000 bushels, $1,-785,000; hay, 380,000 acres, 950,000 tons, $8,550,000. The State is one of the largest producers of copper. The coal production was 2,517,809 short tons. The gold mined in 1911 was 227,834 fine ounces, worth $4,-709,747, and silver, 12,679,633 fine ounces, $6,973,798. This places Utah first among the states in the production of silver. The report of the State treasurer for the biennial period 1908-10 shows receipts of $6,-157,126; expenditures, $5,153,220; balance Nov. 30, 1910, $902,739.

The number of manufacturing establishments in Utah having an annual output valued at $500 or more at the beginning of 1915 was 1,110. The amount of capital invested was $71,653,000, giving employment to 17,129 persons, using material valued at $62,234,000, and turning out finished goods worth $87,114,000. Salaries and wages paid amounted to $13,696,000.

Utah:

Admission of, into Union proclaimed, 6120.

Affairs in, correspondence regarding, referred to, 3115, 3123.

Alleged rebellion in, under leadership of Brigham Young, discussed, 2986, 3034.

Appropriation bill passed by legislature of, and vetoed, discussed and recommendations regarding, 4984.

Brigham Young, first governor of, 2985.

    Alleged rebellion under leadership of. (See Alleged Rebellion in, *ante.*)

    Removal of, and successor appointed, 2986, 3034.

Difficulties with, terminated, 3018, 3034, 3179.

Extraordinary session of legislature of, act authorizing, recommended, 4984.

Gilsonite or asphaltum in, disposition of lands containing, discussed, 6168.

Government of, discussed by President—

    Arthur, 4837.

    Buchanan, 2985, 3014, 3024, 3034.

    Fillmore, 2663.

    Hayes, 4558.

Increase in numbers and influence of non-Mormon population in, discussed, 5553.

Industrial home in, report of board on, referred to, 5186.

Information regarding, transmitted, 2678.

Judiciary of, and administration of laws in, discussed, 4162, 4204.

Vacancies in Public Offices, power of President to make provisional appointments to fill, discussed, 3190.

Vallandigham Case.—May 5, 1863, Clement L. Vallandigham, a lawyer and politician of Ohio, was arrested in accordance with orders issued by Gen. Burnside, of the United States Army, commanding the Department of Ohio. On the day following he was taken before a military commission, and subsequently tried, convicted and imprisoned for uttering opinions disloyal to the Union. May 19 the President commuted this sentence to banishment. Vallandigham applied to the Supreme Court for a writ of certiorari to review the proceedings of the commission, by which he claimed to have been unlawfully convicted. The Supreme Court, Justice Wayne delivering the opinion, decided that it had no power to review proceedings ordered by a general officer of the United States Army. Justices Nelson, Grier and Field concurred; Chief Justice Taney and Justice Miller were not present.

Valparaiso, Chile; population (1895) 220,756; sailors of the *Baltimore* assaulted at. (See *Baltimore,* The.)

Van Buren, Martin.—1837-1841.
Thirteenth Administration—Democratic.
Vice-President—R. M. Johnson.
Secretary of State—
John Forsyth (continued).
Secretary of the Treasury—
Levi Woodbury (continued).
Secretary of War—
Joel R. Poinsett.
Secretary of the Navy—
Mahlon Dickerson (continued).
James K. Paulding.
Postmaster-General—
Amos Kendall (continued).
John M. Niles.
Attorney-General—
Benjamin F. Butler (continued).
Felix Grundy.
Henry D. Gilpin.

Martin Van Buren was elected by the Democratic party in 1836. At the Democratic National Convention, held at Baltimore, May 20, he was nominated on the first ballot.

Opposition.—A rival faction of the party nominated Hugh L. White, of Tennessee. Several rival candidates were named by States as National Republican or Whig candidates. Among these were William Henry Harrison, Daniel Webster and Willie P. Mangum. Twenty-six states participated in the election, Arkansas and Michigan having been recently admitted.

Vote.—At the election held Nov. 8, the popular vote was Van Buren, 762,678; Harrison, 548,007; White, 145,396; and Webster, 42,247. The electoral vote, counted Feb. 8, 1837, gave Van Buren, 170; Harrison, 73; White, 26; Webster, 14; and Mangum, 11—all of South Carolina.

Party Affiliation.—In his youth, Van Buren was a zealous adherent of Jefferson: he was elected to the State senate of New York as a Clinton Republican; but in 1813 resumed friendly connections with Madison's administration. He disentangled the political complications that prevailed during the "era of good feeling" (1819-1821) in New York and brought about the election to the Senate of Rufus King, an old-school Federalist. Later, he became a generous supporter of Jackson, but in all of his political affiliations his conduct was marked by conservatism and moderation.

Political Complexion of Congress.—In the Twenty-fifth Congress (1837-1839) the Senate, of 52 members, was made up of 31 Democrats, 18 Whigs, and 3 Independents; and the House, of 242 members, was made up of 117 Democrats, 115 Whigs, and 10 Independents. In the Twenty-sixth Congress (1839-1841) the Senate, of 52 members, was composed of 22 Democrats, 28 Whigs, and 2 Independents; and the House, of 242 members, was made up of 103 Democrats, 132 Whigs, 6 Independents, and 1 vacancy.

Finance.—A commercial panic began in March, 1837, by the failure of Briggs & Co., of New Orleans. The panic reached its height in May, when all the banks in New York, Boston, Philadelphia and Baltimore suspended specie payments. This so much embarrassed the Government that President Van Buren convened Congress in special session in September, 1837, to consider the situation. In his Special Message (page 1541) he analyzes in detail the financial crisis and the causes which led to it. He then unfolds his plan for the institution of an independent treasury for the keeping and disbursing of Government funds. It was the return to the system in use in Washington's time and was departed from, despite the earnest warnings of Jefferson, when the United States Bank was chartered for the deposit of Government money. Congress was unwilling to sanction the plan, but the President, with unusual insistence, succeeded, near the close of his term of office, in securing the assent and cooperation to his sub-treasury plan. The Whig Congress of 1842 repealed the measure and deposited the funds in selected private banks until 1846, when the sub-treasury system was again adopted and has persisted to the present day. In his Fourth Annual Message (page 1827) the President gives a survey of the fiscal affairs of the country and says that "It will serve to illustrate more fully the principles by which I have been guided in reference to two contested points in our public policy which were earnest in their development and have been more important in their consequences than any that have arisen under our complicated and difficult, yet admirable, system of government. I allude to a national debt and a national bank. . . . Coming into office a declared enemy of both, I have earnestly endeavored to prevent a resort to either."

Public Debt.—The public debt of the United States during the administration of President Van Buren stood as follows: Jan. 1, 1838, $10,434,221.14; 1839, $3,573,343.42; 1840, $5,250,875.54; 1841, $13,594,480.75.

Commerce.—The commercial status of the United States in the year 1840 is shown by the following statistical summary: Area, 2,059,043 square miles; population, 17,069,453; population per square mile, 8.29; wealth, $7,135,780,000; money in circulation, $186,305,488; imports, $98,258,706; exports, $123,668,932; miles of railway, 2,818; vessels built, 121,203 tons; vessels in deep-sea trade, 899,765 tons; vessels in coastwise trade, 1,280,999 tons; vessels on the Great Lakes, 54,199 tons; post-offices, 13,468; immigrants arrived, 84,066.

Foreign Policy.—It is regarded as one of the most creditable features of the Van Buren administration that it was able, despite the popular wish in some quarters, to remain neutral during the rebellion in Canada. The burning of the *Caroline* in this connection caused the President to issue his proclamations of neutrality (pages 1698, 1699). In this case, as in all others,

EXTENT OF THE UNITED STATES DURING THE ADMINISTRATION OF PRESIDENT VAN BUREN, 1837-1841.

(NOT INCLUDING TERRITORIES)

MAINE 1820
VT. 1791
N.H. 1788
MASS. 1788
CONN. 1788
R.I. 1790
NEW YORK 1788
N.J. 1787
DEL. 1787
PENNSYLVANIA 1787
MD. 1788
VIRGINIA 1788
NORTH CAROLINA 1789
SOUTH CAROLINA 1788
GEORGIA 1788
MICHIGAN 1837
OHIO 1803
INDIANA 1816
KENTUCKY 1792
TENNESSEE 1796
ALABAMA 1819
ILLINOIS 1818
MISSISSIPPI 1817
MISSOURI 1821
ARKANSAS 1836
LOUISIANA 1812

FLAG OF 1841

the President consistently followed the course laid down in his Inaugural Address (page 1537) where he said: "We have no disposition, and we disclaim all right, to meddle in disputes, whether internal or foreign, that may molest other countries, regarding them in their actual state as social communities, and preserving a strict neutrality in all their controversies."
The Democrats renominated Van Buren but he was defeated by Wm. H. Harrison.

Van Buren, Martin:

Annual messages of, 1590, 1700, 1746, 1819.

Banking system discussed by, 1541, 1597, 1707.

Biographical sketch of, 1528.

Credit system, discussed by, 1541.

Death of, announced and honors to be paid memory of, 3319, 3320.

Executive authority of, over public moneys, discussed by, 1541.

Expenses of Government, discussed by, 1541, 1752, 1824.

Finances discussed by, 1541, 1596, 1686, 1706, 1751, 1757, 1789, 1822.

Fiscal operations of Government should be separated from those of individuals. (See Subtreasury System, *post.*)

Foreign policy, discussed by. 1590, 1702, 1747, 1820.

Inaugural address of, 1530.

Large standing army unnecessary in time of peace, 1607.

National and State banks discussed by, 1541, 1707, 1757, 1828.

Northeastern boundary, correspondence regarding. (See Northeastern Boundary.)

Portrait of, 1527.

Presents offered, by Imaum of Muscat, declined, 1809.

Proclamations of—
Discriminating duties on vessels of Greece suspended, 1539.
Extinguishment of Indian titles, 1538.
Extraordinary session of—
Congress, 1538.
Senate, 1857.
Facsimile of, 1549.
Levying duties on vessels of Portugal, 1589.
Neutrality in war in Canada, 1698, 1699.

Public money, views of, on custody and distribution of, 1541.

Secretary of State, 1003.

Special session message of, 1541.

State of the Union, discussed by, 1590, 1700, 1746, 1819.

Subtreasury system discussed by, 1541, 1596, 1706, 1751, 1763, 1827.

Tariff discussed, 1752.

Veto message of, act regarding distribution of Madison papers, reasons for applying pocket veto to, 1745.

33

Vancouver Island: population (1901) 26,133.

Agent sent to, referred to, 3068, 3072.

Boundary question regarding. (See Northwestern Boundary.)

Vandalia, The, loss of, at Samoan Islands, 5479.

Vanderbilt, The, presented to United States by Cornelius Vanderbilt, recommendations regarding, 3288.

Referred to, 3585.

Vatican, Peace note of Germany to, 8188.

Venezuela.—Venezuela lies on the north of the South American continent and is bounded on the north by the Caribbean Sea, west by the Republic of Colombia, east by British Guiana, and south by Brazil. The western boundary is in dispute, the area estimated by Venezuelan geographers (599,-538 square miles) lying between 1° 40′ S.-12° 26′ N. latitude and 59° 40′-73° 31′ W. longitude. Included in this area are over seventy islands off the coast, with a total area of about 14,670 square miles, the largest being Margarita, which is politically associated with Tortuga, Cubagua and Coche to form the newly constituted State of Nueva Esparta. Margarita has an area of about 400 square miles.

Physical Features.—The Eastern Andes from the southwest cross the border and reach to the Caribbean Coast, where they are prolonged by the Maritime Andes of Venezuela to the Gulf of Paria on the northeast. The main range is known as the Sierra Nevada de Merida, and contains the highest peaks in the country in Picacho de la Sierra (15,420 feet) and Salado (13,878 feet), the maritime ranges containing the Silla de Carácas (8,531 feet). Near the Brazilian border the Sierras Parima and Pacaraima and on the eastern border the Sierras de Rincote and de Usupamo enclose the republic with parallel northward spurs, between which are valleys of the Orinoco tributaries. The slopes of the mountains and foothills are covered with dense forests, but the basin of the Orinoco is mainly llanos, or level stretches of open prairie, with occasional woods.

The principal river of Venezuela is the Orinoco, exceeding 1,500 miles in length. The Orinoco is navigable for large steamers for some 700 miles, and by smaller vessels as far as the Maipures Cataract, some 200 miles further up stream. The coastal regions of Venezuela are much indented and contain many lagoons and lakes, of which Maracaibo, with an area exceeding 7,000 square miles, is the largest lake in South America.

The climate is tropical and except where modified by altitude or tempered by sea breezes is unhealthy. Yellow fever is endemic at Carácas, and plague cases have occurred there since 1908.

History.—Venezuela was visited by Columbus in 1498, and in 1499 by Alonzo de Ojeda and Amerigo Vespucci, the former naming the Gulf of Maracaibo Venezuela, or "Little Venice" (on account of the Indian pile-built settlements on the coast and shores of the lake), and the name was afterwards extended to the whole of the Orinoco basin. In 1550 the territory was formed into the captaincy-general of Carácas, and the country remainder under Spanish rule until the revolt under Simon Bolivar, a native of Carácas, who defeated the Spanish forces in the battles of Lastoguanes (1813) and Carabobo (1821), and thus secured the independence of the country. Bolivar was an untiring hero in the cause of independence, and through his efforts (and those of his adjutant Sucre) Venezuela, Ecuador and Colombia (Upper Peru) achieved their freedom from Spain, while Peru was enabled to establish its independence in consequence of his victories. He died in 1830, at the age of forty-seven, and his remains were re-interred at Carácas in 1842. Venezuela formed part of the Federal Republic at Colombia from 1822-1830, since which time it has been independent. There have been many revolutions since 1846, particularly in 1849, 1868, 1889, 1891, 1900, and 1908. In 1854 President Monagas liberated the African slaves, and in 1864 President Falcón divided the country into States and formed them into a Federal Republic.

Venezuelan Question.—Protection of the sovereignty of Venezuela by the United States through the application of the Monroe Doctrine has, on two notable occasions, called for prompt and determined action by our Presidents—Cleveland in 1895, and Roosevelt in 1902. (See Monroe Doctrine.)

The contention in 1895 was with Great Britain over the boundary between Venezuela and British Guiana. In July 1888, President Cleveland laid a statement of the dispute before the Senate (Page 5204). President Harrison, in his first annual message, expressed the hope that the question might be amicably adjusted in accordance with the historic tities of the two parties (Page 5471), but regretfully announced in his third annual message (Page 5616), that the friendly efforts of the United States in that direction had proved unavailing.

Upon his return to the Presidency, Cleveland was again confronted by the question, and in his first message announced that the controversy was still pending. (Page 5873.) In the second message during his second term he declared his determination to bring about arbitration—"a resort to which Great Britain so conspicuously favors in principle and respects in practice, and which is earnestly sought by her weaker adversary." (Page 5958.)

In July, 1895, the American Ambassador at London was instructed to communicate to the British Government the position of the United States on the question. This took the form of a protest against the enlargement of the area of the British possessions on the American continent, especially at the expense of Venezuela without the latter's consent, referring to the traditional and established policy of this Government (Page 6064), and denying the right of Great Britain to establish an arbitrary line through the territory in debate and submit to arbitration only the portion lying on one side of it.

Great Britain's reply called forth a special message from Cleveland December 17, 1895 (Page 6087), in which he laid the British reply before the Senate. The reply declared the Monroe Doctrine "inapplicable to the state of things in which we live at the present day." (Page 6088.) Cleveland firmly upheld the Monroe Doctrine, and proposed a commission of his own to determine the boundary line, and asked Congress to appropriate money to carry out the terms, whatever the consequences, which he intimated might be forcible maintenance of his contention, under the Monroe Doctrine. (Page 6090.)

Mr. Cleveland's attitude caused much excited comment throughout the country, but his position was stoutly backed by the people and newspapers of all political parties. Diplomatically, the matter was skillfully handled, and finally referred to arbitration, and it was announced to the next Congress that a general arbitration treaty with Great Britain was under way. (See page 6154.) The arbitral tribunal was appointed under the treaty of February 2, 1897, and the award was made October 3, 1899. The terms of award were announced by President McKinley in his third annual message, December 5. (See page 6380.)

(See also illustration opposite page 5485.)

The next invocation of the traditional doctrine by the United States in behalf of Venezuela was during Roosevelt's Administration. Debts due by the South American Republic to citizens of England, France, Germany, Italy, and other foreign countries, were long over-due, and payment seemed remote, if not hopeless. The creditors appealed to their respective governments for redress. England, Germany and Italy agreed upon what they termed a pacific blockade for the forcible collection of the claims. Operations began December 3, 1902, and on the 9th four Venezuelan vessels were seized and an ultimatum was sent to President Castro. Upon its rejection, two forts at Puerto Cabello and San Carlos were bombarded by the allies.

In his first message to Congress, December 3, 1901, President Roosevelt said of the Monroe Doctrine (page 6664) that there must be "no territorial aggrandizement by any non-American power at the expense of any American power on American soil. * * * We do not guarantee any state against punishment if it misconducts itself, provided that punishment does not take the form of the acquisition of territory by any non-American power."

By diplomatic interviews, all the Powers concerned, except Germany, were brought to a state of willingness to arbitrate. In the case of Germany, President Roosevelt found it necessary to intimate that Admiral Dewey, in command of the fleet, would prevent forcible occupation of the Venezuelan ports. At the same time the President informed the German Ambassador that in event the Emperor should consent to arbitration the credit for such advanced ground in international disputes would be accorded to the Emperor.

The German Ambassador conveyed personally to the President that his Majesty's government would consent to arbitration and that it had no purpose or intention to make even the smallest acquisition of territory on the South American Continent or the Islands adjacent. This voluntary and friendly declaration was afterwards repeated to the Secretary of State.

Through the offices of the diplomatic representatives of the United States at Caracas and the Government at Washington, protocols were signed whereby Venezuela agreed (see page 6794) to set apart a certain percentage of the customs receipts of two of her ports to be applied to the payment of whatever obligations might be ascertained by mixed commissions appointed for that purpose to be due from her, not only to the three powers already mentioned, whose proceedings against her had resulted in a state of war, but also to the United States, France, Spain, Belgium, the Netherlands, Norway, Sweden and Mexico, who had not employed force.

The blockading powers, however, demanded that the sums ascertained to be due their citizens by such mixed commissions should be accorded payment in full before anything was paid upon the claims of any of the so-called peace powers. The powers at this juncture asked that the question be referred to President Roosevelt for decision, but he declined, and suggested that the whole matter be submitted to the Hague Tribunal for adjudication. This was finally agreed to, and amicable settlement was reported in a special message by Roosevelt, January 23, 1905. (See page 6941.) The Hague Tribunal pronounced in favor of the allied powers.

This later incident found echo in the Third International Conference of South American Republics at Rio Janeiro in July and August, 1906, when Dr. Drago, former Minister of Foreign Affairs of Argentina, announced the adherence of South American Republics to the Monroe Doctrine, and the conference, after discussion, recommended that their delegates to the Second Peace Conference at the Hague oppose the compulsory collection by armed forces of debts due its citizens by any other government. This became known as the Drago Doctrine. (See Drago Doctrine.) Mr. Roosevelt stated the policy of the United States on this question in his sixth annual message. (Page 7060.)

Government.—The present constitution rests upon the fundamental law of August 5, 1909, under which the government is that of a Federal Republic of twenty autonomous States, a Federal District, and two Territories, with a President elected by the Federal Congress for four years and ineligible for a consecutive term of office, and a "Council of Government" of ten members (one for each two States), chosen by Congress for seven years, its members (by seniority) supplying at need a successor to the President. President (April 19. 1915-1922), General Juan Vincente Gomez, born July 24, 1859.

The Federal Congress consists of two Chambers. The Senate consists of forty members (two from each State), native born Venezuelans above thirty years of age, elected for four years. The Chamber of Deputies consists of 117 members elected for four years by direct vote in each State, in the proportion of one per 35,000 inhabitants (each State having at least one representative, irrespective of population) with other representatives for every 15,000 in excess of that number.

Each of the States has an elective President and Legislative Assembly.

Education.—Primary education is free and nominally compulsory, but little effort is made to instruct the Indians, and schools are confined to urban areas, where they were attended in 1908 by 35,777 pupils. Universities at Carácas and Mérida. About 60 per cent of the total population are absolutely illiterate.

Finance.—The revenue is derived from customs and customs surtax of 30 per cent, and excise. Salt and matches are State monopolies and are farmed out, the latter to an English company; Cigarette paper is also a farmed monopoly, and with the excise on cigarettes produces 6,000,000 bolivares. The expenditure includes 2,600,000 bolivares for amortization and service of the debt, in addition to the final payment of 7,868,600 bolivares due to certain foreign countries under the Protocol of Washington; and 9,500,000 bolivares war and marine.

The national debt was stated on June 30, 1911, to be 192,164,539 bolivares (about $36,000,000 United States money.

Production and Industry.—Agriculture and stock raising are the principal industries of the country, and most of the land is suited for these purposes. The chief agricultural products are coffee, cacao,

sugar, maize, beans, wheat, rice, potatoes, vegetables and fruit of various kinds. Cotton is now being grown successfully for three native cotton mills. The Live Stock is stated to include about 2,000,000 cattle, 1,750,000 pigs, 1,500,000 goats, and 200,000 sheep. The llanos, or grassy plains, could support many times the present estimated number with organization and development of the industry, much of the pastoral area having been abandoned since the War of Independence.

The fisheries round the coast and of the lakes are of much importance for the food of the people. Round the northern islands are important pearl fisheries, but they are only carried on in a primitive way by native fishers.

Gold, silver, copper, iron, tin, lead, mercury, sulphur, coal, asphalt and petroleum are known to exist.

Cities.—Capital, Carácas. Estimated population, 75,000. Other towns are Maracaibo (35,000), Valencia, Puerto Cabello and La Guaira, and Ciudad Bolivar.

Trade with the United States.—The value of merchandise imported into Venezuela from the United States for the year 1913 was $5,737,118, and goods to the value of $10,852,331 were sent thither—a balance of $5,115,213 in favor of the United States.

Venezuela (see also Caracas):

American citizens expelled from, 2952.

Boundary dispute with Great Britain regarding British Guiana, 5204, 5471, 5616, 5873, 5958, 6064, 6087, 6154.

Arbitration of—
Discussed, 6337, 6380.
Recommended, 6064.
Treaty for, 6154.

Monroe doctrine reasserted and attitude of United States respecting, 6064, 6087.

Civil war in, terminated, 2552.

Claims of France against, 4761.

Claims of United States against (see also Aves Island; Caracas Commission; Venezuela Steam Transportation Co.)—

Acknowledged, 2702.

Adjustment of, 6338.

Awards of commission, referred to, 4321, 4539, 4693, 4716, 4853.

Distribution of, 4421, 4629, 4807.

Convention for adjustment of, 3111, 3587, 3721, 3885, 3891, 4055, 4100, 4371, 4951, 5195, 5198, 5220, 5369, 5391, 5962.

Course pursued to enforce provisions of, 4320.

Discussed by President—
Arthur, 4761, 4807.
Cleveland, 5090, 5369.
Fillmore, 2702.
Grant, 3964, 4005, 4012, 4014, 4144, 4192, 4245, 4295, 4320.
Harrison, Benj., 5673.
Jackson, 1319.
Johnson, 3587.
Pierce, 2952.
Taylor, 2552.
Tyler, 2193.

Indemnity to be paid satisfactorily arranged, 2206.

Mixed claims commission discussed, 4432, 4761, 4920, 5471.

Termination of, 5547.

Payment of, 3444, 4295, 4320, 4321, 4359, 4629, 5873.

Objection to, 4144, 4192, 4245.

Abandoned, 4295.

Correspondence with, transmitted 5907.

Differences of, with France and Belgium, discussed, 6070.

Diplomatic relations with, 4562.

Fugitive criminals, convention with, for surrender of, 2917, 3185.

Discussed, 5962.

Import duties imposed upon American products by, 5672.

Retaliatory measures proclaimed, 5703.

Imprisonment of American citizens in, 4789, 4803, 5198.

Independence of, asserted, 613.

Minister of, to United States, grade of raised, 4718.

One hundredth anniversary of independence celebrated, 7658.

Relations of, with France, discussed, 4629.

Revolution in, followed by provisional government, referred to, 4522.

Treaty with, transmitted and discussed by President—

Buchanan, 3111, 3185.

Cleveland, 5196.

Jackson, 1444, 1450.

Johnson, 3587.

Pierce, 2917.

Van Buren, 1751.

Vessels of United States—

Seized or interfered with by, 4114, 4371, 5198, 5547, 5673, 5873, 5962, 6070.

To transport remains of Gen. Paez to, recommended, 5193.

Venezuela, Treaty with.—Apart from certain claims conventions, the only diplomatic relation between the United States and Venezuela which survives is the protocol of 1903, by which United States claims against Venezuela were submitted to arbitration. The comr sion, consisting of two members (one chosen by the President of the United States, the other by the President of Venezuela) must sit at Caracas. An umpire must be appointed to preside over the deliberations, and it was agreed that the umpire should be chosen by the queen of the Netherlands. The commissioners, acting under oath, should determine after due investigation, the justice of the claims. Should the two commissioners be unable to reach a decision, the vote of the umpire should decide the questions. Venezuela also became a party to the convention between the United States and the several leading republics of South and Central America for the arbitration of pecuniary claims and the protection of inventions, etc., which was signed

in Buenos Aires in 1910. (See South and Central America, Treaties with.)

Venezuela Steam Transportation Co., seizure and detention of steamers of, and claims arising out of, 4114, 4371, 5198, 5547, 5673, 5873, 5962.

Award in favor of, 6070.

Venice, Italy, Geographical Congress at, 4626.

Venus, Transit of. (See Naval Observatory.)

Vera Cruz (Mexico), Siege and Capture of.—March 9, 1847, Gen. Scott, who had been ordered to Mexico to conduct an expedition against its capital city by way of Vera Cruz, landed a force of 12,000 men on the beach in the vicinity of that port. By March 22 the attacking forces were in position and the siege guns mounted. Gen. Scott summoned the governor of Vera Cruz to surrender. Upon his refusal a bombardment was begun and kept up until the morning of the 26th, when overtures for surrender were made by Gen. Landero. Articles of capitulation were signed March 27. The Mexicans lost nearly 500 pieces of artillery, besides other arms and much ammunition. Five thousand prisoners were taken and paroled, and the best port of Mexico, with its famous and almost impregnable fortress of San Juan de Ulloa, was captured. The American loss was insignificant.

Vera Cruz, Occupation of.—During the Mexican revolution of 1913, Americans and other foreigners in Mexico were subjected to gross hardship and abuse. Property was seized and the owners were insulted, threatened, imprisoned, and in several instances actually met death at the hands of one or the other of the warring factions. President Wilson increased the regular troops at the border posts and sent naval vessels to the Mexican seaports to protect the lives and property of Americans and citizens of foreign countries.

On the 9th of April, 1914, a paymaster of the U. S. S. *Dolphin* landed at Iturbide bridge, Tampico, with a whaleboat and boat's crew to take off supplies. The men were unarmed and the boat carried, both at her bow and at her stern, the flag of the United States. The men were arrested, but later released, and an apology was made, but Admiral Mayo demanded that the flag of the United States be saluted with special ceremony. This was refused by President Huerta of Mexico. Citing this and a number of similar insults preceding it, President Wilson, April 20, 1914, asked Congress to approve the use of the land and naval forces of the country to enforce the fullest recognition of the rights and dignity of the United States. This was granted and Vera Cruz was occupied by the American forces. In the three days of fighting seventeen sailors and marines were killed and fifty wounded. The naval occupation was followed by a brigade of the regular army under Gen. Funston. Before attempting an advance into the interior, operations were halted by an offer of mediation between the United States and Mexico made by the diplomatic representatives of Argentina, Brazil and Chile. These met in Niagara Falls, Canada, in May. An attempt was made to adjust the differences between the two countries, but the demand for a salute to the American flag was not complied with and the American forces were withdrawn from Vera Cruz No. 23. 1914. (See illustrations opposite 7936, 7952.)

Vera Cruz, Mexico; population (1900) 960,570; battle of, referred to, 2385.

Vermont.—One of the New England States; nickname, "The Green Mountain State"; motto, "Freedom and Unity." It extends from lat. 42° 44′ to 45° 1′ north and from long. 71° 38′ to 73° 25′ west. It is bounded on the north by Quebec (Canada), on the east by New Hampshire (separated by the Connecticut River), on the south by Massachusetts, and on the west by New York (separated in part by Lake Champlain). It has an area of 9,564 square miles. Vermont is traversed from north to south by the Green Mountains. It is an agricultural state and has extensive quarries of marble and granite. The manufacture of wood-pulp is an important industry. It was explored by Champlain in 1609. The first settlement was at Brattleboro in 1724. Vermont was early claimed by both New Hampshire and New York. It was admitted to the Union in 1791.

Statistics of agriculture collected for the last Federal census, place the number of farms in the State at 32,709, comprising 4,663,577 acres, valued, with stock and improvements, at $145,399,728. The average value of land per acre was $12.52. The value of domestic animals, poultry, etc., was $22,642,686, including 430,314 cattle, valued at $11,828,892; 80,781 horses, $8,-591,357; 94,821 swine, $974,779; 118,551 sheep, $538,991; poultry, $607,787. The yield and value of the field crops for 1911 was: Corn, 46,000 acres, 1,886,000 bushels, $1,509,000; wheat, 1,000 acres, 28,000 bushels $28,000; oats, 76,000 acres; 2,660,-000 bushels, $1,569,000; potatoes, 26,000 acres, 2,730,000 bushels, $2,157,000; hay, 930,000 acres, 1,209,000 tons. $16,926,000; tobacco, 100 acres, 170,000 pounds, $27,200. The leading mineral product of the State is marble, of which Vermont produces half of the country's output. The value for the last twelve months reported for the census of 1910 was $4,679,960, while the granite output was valued at $2,451,533. Slate, lime, clay, metallic paint, soapstone, sand and gravel are also marketed. The stone production exceeds that of Pennsylvania. The manufactures include hosiery and woolen goods, wood pulp, lumber and machinery, and employ capital to the extent of $62,658,741. The output was valued at $63,083,611. The employees numbered 33,-106, and the wages paid totalled $15,221,-059. The bonded debt of the State is $135,000, and the tax rate $3.50 per $1,000. The annual receipts of the State Treasurer at last report were $1,823,390; expenditures, $1,871,166.

There are forty-seven national banks holding $7,544,364 to the credit of 21,830 depositors; and twenty-three loan and trust companies, holding $18,878,526 to the credit of 52,135 depositors. The savings banks hold $43,132,268 to the credit of 108,208 depositors.

The number of manufacturing establishments in Vermont having an annual output valued at more than $500 at the beginning of 1915 was 1,772. The amount of capital invested was $79,811,000, giving employment to 37,217 persons, using material valued at $42,555,000, and turning out finished goods worth $76,811,000. Salaries and wages paid amounted to $22,002,000.

In 1906 there were 1,073 miles of steam railways and 122 miles of electric lines. The population in 1910 was 355,956.

Vermont:

Admission of, into Union, 90.

Application made for, 87.

Constitution of United States, evidence of ratification of amendment to, 107, 166.

Officers appointed for, 91.

Vessels (see also Steamboats; Steamships; Vessels, Foreign; Vessels; United States):

American registry for American owned, 5985.

Canadian, permitted to aid disabled vessels in waters of United States, proclaimed, 5828.

Vessels, Foreign (see also under the several powers):

Appropriation for vessels detained by United States recommended, 6336.

Bond required of, 145.

Committing open hostility, right to detain for inquiry, 353.

Consular jurisdiction over crews of, in United States, 4038, 4129.

Correspondence regarding, 81.

Detained by United States, appropriation for, recommended, 6336.

Discriminating duties on—

Discussed, 5089.

Recommended, 81, 1242.

Referred to, 667, 707, 755, 866, 917, 918, 969.

Should be refunded, 1172.

Suspended by proclamation—

Austria, 1003, 1004.

Brazil, 2372.

Bremen, 606.

Chile, 2612.

China, 4552.

Cuba. (See Spain, *post.*)

France, 752, 2371, 3711, 3969, 3973, 4182.

Revoked, 4132.

Greece, 1539.

Hamburg, 607.

Hanover, 970.

Hawaiian Islands, 3713.

Italy, 942, 3021.

Japan, 4131.

Lübeck, 642.

Mecklenburg-Schwerin, 1365.

Nicaragua, 3416.

Norway, 665.

Oldenburg, 666, 1059.

Portugal, 4080.

Spain, 4128, 4810, 5075, 5155.

Revoked, 5074.

Tuscany, 1452.

Suspension terminated, 4132.

Duties on. (See Tonnage on, *post.*)

Embargo on—

For 60 days recommended, 484.

Governor requested to call forth militia if necessary to enforce, 144.

Imposed, 458.

Removed, 457, 466.

nterference with and the seizure of, by foreign powers, 138, 184, 242, 374, 477, 560, 3017.

Ironclad, referred to, 4009.

Marine railway for repair of, referred to, 1043.

Must not depart from ports of United States while dangers are threatened from belligerent nations, 421.

Northern and Northwestern lakes, passage of gunboats from tide water to, referred to, 3402.

Number of, necessary for principal seaports, 407, 455, 504.

Papers for protection of, engaged in whale fisheries, 1774.

Privileges at foreign ports denied, proclamation regarding, 3482.

Proposed distribution of, 408, 416.

Prussian abolition of duties on, 969.

Purchased for Peru, detention of, 3831, 3835.

Restrictions on, in Bosporus and Dardanelles, 4078.

Right of search. (See Right of Search.)

Sale and transfer of, while abroad, laws regarding, defective, 1755.

Sale of, referred to, 3830.

Saved from shipwreck by Neapolitan navy, 2899.

Seamen on. (See Seamen, American.)

Seized or interfered with by foreign powers, 138, 184, 242, 374, 477, 560, 3017.

Brazil, 962, 2779. (See also *Caroline*, The.)

Chile, 1822, 2051, 2116, 2193, 3445, 4289.

Colombia, 4289, 4358.

Denied privileges at foreign ports, proclamation regarding, 3482.

Denmark, 5388, 6249.

France, 138, 243, 252, 387, 490, (See also France, claims against.)

Great Britain discussed or referred to by President—
Adams, John, 242, 264, 271.
Buchanan, 3062.
Cleveland, 4990, 5198.
Fillmore, 2603, 2675, 2680.
Grant, 4068, 4070, 4114.
Jefferson, 410, 414, 420, 433, 441.
Madison, 454, 477, 481.
Polk, 2286, 2297.
Tyler, 1909, 1920, 1929, 2016, 2076, 2111, 2215, 2219.
Van Buren, 1676, 1693, 1695, 1732, 1784, 1806, 1839, 1840, 1857.
Washington, 118. (See also War of 1812 discussed.)

Haiti, 2680, 5368, 5390.

Honduras insurgents, 5869.

Mexico, 1684, 1685, 5123, 5502.

Morocco, 352, 353.

Paraguay, 2980, 3046, 3091, 3195.

Portugal, 1070, 1098, 1113, 1243.

Russia, 3794, 6336.

Spain discussed by President—
Adams, John, 243.
Arthur, 4626, 4759.
Buchanan, 2976.
Cleveland, 4919, 6068.
Fillmore, 2679, 2721.
Grant, 3986, 4052, 4189, 4195, 4196, 4210, 4276, 4290.
Hayes, 4436, 4560.
Jackson, 1112.
Pierce, 2761, 2767, 2778, 2869, 2900. (See also *Black Warrior*, The; *El Dorado*, The; *Virginius*, The.)

Venezuela, 4114, 4371, 5198, 5547, 5673, 5873, 5962.

Should be navigated exclusively by American seamen, 540.

Slaves transported by. (See African Slave Trade.)

Sold to Algiers, 237.

Steam engines for, improvement in, 2122, 2262.

Tonnage duties illegally levied on, 2948, 3049.

Tonnage duties on, referred to, 1123.

Transfer of property in, while abroad, laws regulating, referred to, 1791.

Visited by British officers, 3062.

Whaling interfered with by Russian vessels, 3794.

Veterans of Indian Wars of the United States.—Instituted by officers of the United States Army at Philadelphia, April 23, 1896. The obects are "to perpetuate the faithful services, heroism, and privations of the officers and soldiers of the Army of the United States of America, as well as of the auxiliary forces of the several states of the Union, in their successive campaigns conducted against a savage foe on our frontiers, in the interests of civilization, and for the settlement and defense of our Territories at different periods in the history of our common country since the close of the War of the Revolution; and also to collect and preserve for publication a record of these services and other historical data relating thereto, as well as to unite in a fraternal bond of union all those who are entitled to membership therein."

Veto.—The act by which the executive refuses his approval of a measure of the legislative body with which he is associated. The Constitution gives the President of the United States power to veto any act of Congress by refusing to sign the bill after its passage. In the Colonies (except Rhode Island and Connecticut) the governors had power to veto acts of the colonial legislatures. Massachusetts was the first of the original states to grant the veto power to its governor. This was in 1780. In the Convention of 1787 several veto plans were discussed, one of which proposed to associate the Supreme Court with the President in the exercise of the power. The plan finally adopted resembled that in use in Massachusetts. If the President refuses to sign an act, it is returned to the House in which it originated with his reasons for refusing his signature. That House may then proceed to reconsider the act, and if it again passes both Houses with a majority of two-thirds it becomes a law. The Constitution also provides that "if any bill shall not be returned by the President within ten days (Sundays excepted) after it shall have been presented to him, the same shall be a law in like manner as if he had signed it, unless the Congress by their adjournment prevent its return, in which case it shall not be a law" (18). The veto power was used quite sparingly by the early Presidents.

Following is the number of veto messages sent to Congress by the several Presidents. Those whose names are not mentioned sent no veto: Washington, 2; Madison, 6; Monroe, 1; Jackson, 9; Tyler, 8; Polk, 3; Pierce, 9; Buchanan, 7; Lincoln, 3; Johnson, 22; Grant, 46; Hayes, 8; Arthur, 4; Cleveland, first term, 301; Harrison, Benj., 19; Cleveland, second term, 42; McKinley, 6, and Roosevelt, 15.

Veto Messages. (See the several Presidents; the several subjects.)

Veto, Pocket.—The power of the President to prevent the enactment into law of a bill presented to him within ten days before the adjournment of Congress, without sending in a refusal to sign or his objections in writing, is known as a pocket veto.

Veto Power discussed by President— Polk, 2512.

Taylor, 2561.

Vetoes, Pension. (See Cleveland, Grover; Grant, Ulysses S.)

Vetoes, Pocket. (See the several Presidents; the several subjects.)

Vice-Admiral.—An honorary rank in the United States Navy created by Congress Dec. 21, 1864, and conferred upon David G. Farragut. At the time of its creation it was the highest grade in the Navy. Two years later (July 25, 1866) Congress created the rank of admiral and bestowed it upon Farragut, making David G. Porter vice-admiral. Oct. 17, 1870, after the death of Admiral Farragut, Porter was promoted to the vacancy and Rear-Admiral Stephen C. Rowan was made vice-admiral. On his death in 1890 the grade became extinct During the colonial period it was customary for the royal governor to be appointed vice-admiral, which made him head of the colonial admiralty courts. (See also Admiral.)

Vice-Admiral, creation of grade of, recommended, 3450, 6423.

Vice Consul.—Assistant to the Consul; or an officer appointed to perform certain special duties in the territory where there is a consul.

Vice-President of United States.—The Constitution provides for the office of Vice-President. His duty is to preside over the Senate, and in case of the removal, death, resignation, or disability of the President succeed him. His salary is $12,000 per annum. Until the adoption of the twelfth amendment, in 1804, the candidate for President receiving next to the highest number of votes was declared Vice-President. Five Vice-Presidents have succeeded to the Presidency, by reason of the death of the President, viz.: John Tyler, who succeeded William Henry Harrison in 1841; Millard Fillmore, who succeeded Zachary Taylor in 1850; Andrew Johnson, who succeeded Abraham Lincoln in 1865; Chester A. Arthur, who succeeded James A. Garfield in 1881; and Theodore Roosevelt who succeeded William McKinley in 1901. The attempt was made in 1841 to give Tyler only the title and rights of "Acting President," but he claimed the full office of President. Six Vice-Presidents have died in office, namely, George Clinton, Elbridge Gerry, William R. King, Henry Wilson, Thomas A. Hendricks and James S. Sherman. Only one resigned, John C. Calhoun.

A list of Vice-Presidents follows:

Name and Birthplace	Inaugurated
John Adams, Quincy, Mass.	1789
Thomas Jefferson, Shadwell, Va.	1797
Aaron Burr, Newark, N. J.	1801
George Clinton, Ulster Co., N. Y.	1805
Elbridge Gerry, Marblehead, Mass.	1813
Daniel D. Tompkins, Scarsdale, N. Y.	1817
John C. Calhoun, Abbeville, S. C.	1825
Martin Van Buren, Kinderhook, N. Y.	1833
Richard M. Johnson, Louisville, Ky.	1837
John Tyler, Greenway, Va.	1841
George M. Dallas, Philadelphia, Pa.	1845
Millard Fillmore, Summerhill, N. Y.	1849
William R. King, Sampson Co., N. C.	1853
John C. Breckinridge, Lexington, Ky.	1857
Hannibal Hamlin, Paris, Me.	1861
Andrew Johnson, Raleigh, N. C.	1865
Schuyler Colfax, N. Y. City, N. Y.	1869
Henry Wilson, Farmington, N. H.	1873
William A. Wheeler, Malone, N. Y.	1877
Chester A. Arthur, Fairfield, Vt.	1881
Thos. A. Hendricks, Muskingum Co., O.	1886
Levi P. Morton, Shoreham, Vt.	1889
Adlai E. Stevenson, Christian Co., Ky.	1893
Garret A. Hobart, Long Branch, N. J.	1897
Theodore Roosevelt, N. Y. City, N. Y.	1901
Charles W. Fairbanks, Unionville Center, O.	1905
James S. Sherman, Utica, N. Y.	1909
Thomas R. Marshall, No. Manchester, Ind.	1913

Vicksburg (Miss.), Siege and Capture of.—The night after the battle of the Big Black, May 17, 1863, McPherson's and McClernand's corps crossed the river on floating bridges made of bales of cotton covered with plank. Sherman, who carried the only pontoon train in the army, passed over at Bridgeport, a few miles above. The whole army then moved upon Vicksburg. Sherman, still holding the right, marched toward the Yazoo River, and on the 19th rested his right on the Mississippi, within plain view of Porter's gunboats. McPherson followed Sherman with the Seventeenth Army Corps, halting where the latter had turned off. McClernand came up by the Jackson road and deployed to the left. The investment of Vicksburg was thus complete by May 19, 1863. At this time Grant's army was over 30,000 strong. The Federal force was increased to nearly 70,000 during the siege. The Confederate garrison, commanded by Gen. Pemberton, consisted of about 25,000 or 30,000 men and 102 guns. Vicksburg's fortifications were bastioned earthworks. The place was provisioned for about two months.

On the afternoon of the 19th Grant ordered a general assault, which was repulsed with a loss to the Federals of 942. Three days later he made another attack, but the assailants succeeded merely in planting their flags on the outer slopes of the bastions. The city was found to be too strong to be taken by assault. The Federal loss on the 22d was 3,199. During the skirmishing on the 18th, 20th, and 21st of May the Union army lost 241 men. Porter assisted materially in these attacks by a constant fire from his gunboats and mortar boats. Pemberton soon began to feel the effects of the siege. By the end of May his meat rations were reduced one-half, and not long thereafter the bacon supply was entirely exhausted. There were no signs of the arrival of reenforcements and 6,000 men lay sick and wounded in the hospitals and private houses. Some of his men had been in the trenches forty-seven days and nights. Besides, they were now constantly exposed to bursting shell and the fire of sharpshooters. Thus despairing of aid, his resources about exhausted, the Confederate commander resolved to capitulate. July 3, 1863, Vicksburg was surrendered to Grant. Gen. Grant accorded magnanimous terms. The entire garrison was paroled and was allowed to depart with rations to last them beyond the Union lines. The results of the campaign were the defeat of the Confederates in several engagements, the occupation of the capital of Mississippi, and the capture of the important post of Vicksburg with its garrison and munitions of war, a loss to the Confederates of over 30,000 prisoners and several thousand killed and wounded. Among the dead were Generals Tracy, Tilghman, and Green. Grant's losses in the campaign, from the first skirmish at Port Gibson, May 1, to the surrender of Vicksburg, were 1,511 killed, 7,396 wounded, and 453 missing—a total of 9,360.

Vienna, Austria:

International Exposition in, discussed, 4142, 4190.

International Patent Congress in, 4215.

Villeré's Plantation (La.), Battle of.—

After the battle of Lake Borgne, La. (q. v.), the British expedition pushed on toward New Orleans by way of the Bayou Bienvenue and Villeré's Canal. Dec. 23, 1814, within an hour after hearing that the British were approaching, Jackson had 1,800 of his troops on the march to meet them. Half of the invading army, some 2,500 men, had approached to within nine miles of New Orleans without serious check. The schooner *Carolina* dropped down the river to a point opposite Villeré's and opened a terrible fire upon the invading army, killing or maiming 100 men in 10 minutes. The general engagement lasted about two hours. Both combatants retired from the field in the darkness. The loss of the Americans was 213, while that of the British was about 400 men.

Virgin Islands.—Formerly the Danish

West Indies. They comprise the islands of St. Thomas, St. Croix and St. John, which lie in the Caribbean Sea almost due east of Porto Rico on an important trade route to the Panama Canal, and are the northernmost and westernmost of the Lesser Antillas. Their principal product is sugar cane, although molasses, cotton and live stock are also produced. St. Thomas is an important coaling and cable station. In 1908-9, the imports were $1,566,099. Their total area is 138 square miles and their population about 25,000.

Unsuccessful attempts had been made by the United States in 1867 and in 1902 to acquire the islands. On July 25, 1916, the Government announced officially that negotiations for their purchase had been completed, and on January 18, 1917, ownership formally passed to the United States. The price paid was $25,000,000 and abandonment of any United States claims in Greenland arising from American explorations in that country. The islands are of especial value to this country because, when fortified, they will be of great service in protecting the Panama Canal.

Virginia.—One of the thirteen original

states; nicknames, "Old Dominion," "Mother of States," "Mother of Presidents"; motto, "Sic semper tyrannis" ("Be it ever thus to tyrants"). Virginia is bounded on the northwest and north by West Virginia (separated by the Alleghany Mountains), on the north and northeast by Maryland and the District of Columbia (separated by the Potomac River), on the east by the Chesapeake Bay and the Atlantic Ocean, on the south by North Carolina and Tennessee and on the southwest by Kentucky. The county of Accomac lies east of the Chesapeake. The area of the state is 42,-627 square miles. Virginia is traversed by the Blue Ridge Mountains from northeast to southwest. It is level toward the southeast. It is one of the foremost States in the Union in the production of tobacco. The State also produces largely wheat, corn, vegetables, fruit, timber, coal, iron, salt and building stone, and manufactures flour, leather, iron and tobacco.

Virginia was the first settled of the British American Colonies, the settlement having been made by the English at Jamestown in 1607. Virginia became a royal colony in 1624. It was the largest and most influential of the colonies. It took a conspicuous part in the events leading up to the Revolution. Virginia ceded to the United States all its territory beyond the Ohio River in 1784. It ratified the Constitution in 1788. This great state furnished four of the first five Presidents, and altogether five of the Presidents of the United States. It seceded from the Union April 17, 1861, and became one of the principal battle grounds of the Civil War. The state was readmitted to the Union in 1870.

Statistics of agriculture collected for the last Federal census, place the number of farms in the State at 184,018, comprising 19,495,636 acres, valued, with stock and improvements, at $635,065,383. The average value of land was $20.24, against $10.08 in 1908. The value of domestic animals, poultry, etc., was $74,891,538, including 859,067 cattle, valued at $21,124,071; 330,-424 horses, $34,857,610; 60,022 mules, $7,595,516; 767,635 swine, $4,165,640; 804,873 sheep, $3,300,026; poultry, $3,395,-962. The yield and value of the field crops for 1911 was: Corn, 1,980,000 acres, 47,-520,000 bushels, $34,690,000; wheat, 750,-000 acres 9,000,000 bushels, $8,640,000; oats, 194,000 acres, 3,880,000 bushels, $2,-095,000; rye, 48,000 acres, 552,000 bushels, $491,000; potatoes, 95,000 acres, 4,275,000 bushels, $4,104,000; hay, 437,000 acres, 280,000 tons, $5,740,000; tobacco, 160,000 acres, 128,000,000 pounds, $12,288,000. Virginia now ranks next to Kentucky (which is first) as a tobacco-growing state. There are 946 vessels engaged in fishing, employing 20,066 people. The value of the products, largely oysters, is $4,715,744. The leading minerals are coal and iron.

The number of manufacturing establishments in Virginia having an annual output valued at $500 or more at the beginning of 1915 was 5,508. The amount of capital invested was $261,501,000, giving employment to 118,109 persons, using material valued at $155,320,000, and turning out finished goods worth $264,039,000. Salaries and wages paid amounted to $56,118,000.

In 1906 there were 4,087 miles of steam railway and 497 miles of electric line. The population in 1910 was 2,061,612.

Virginia (see also Confederate States; Richmond):

Alexandria County retroceded to, by proclamation, 2320.

Application of loyal persons in, to remove within Union lines, 3360.

Authority of United States reestablished in, 3535.

Boundary line of, referred to, 125, 142.

Bounty lands of, referred to, 80.

Census of, incomplete, 654.

Claims of, for militia services in War of 1812, 806.

Elections in, troops stationed at polling places, referred to, 4367, 4372.

Lands ceded to Indians by, 108.

Loyal persons in, application of, to remove within Union lines, 3360.

Mediation of, for settlement of questions threatening Union, discussed, 3192.

Militia services in War of 1812, claims of, for, 806.

Persons in, attempting to exercise official powers of civil nature, order regarding, 3245.

Ratification of amendment to Federal Constitution by, referred to, 105, 106, 249.

Reconstruction of, recommendations regarding, 3965.

Referred to, 4000.

Time for submitting constitution to voters, proclaimed, 3967.

Referred to, 3983.

War between the States, course regarding, pursued by, 3224.

Withdrawal of, from Union, discussed, 3224.

Virginia Coupon Cases.—A series of eight cases in which the United States Supreme Court in 1884 denied the right of a state to pass laws impairing the obligation of contracts. An act of the Virginia legislature in 1871 authorized the receipt of coupons of the state's funded debt in payment of taxes and debts due the state. An act of 1882 required payment of tax dues in "gold, silver, United States Treasury notes, national-bank currency, and nothing else." The tax collectors thereupon refused to accept the coupons in payment of taxes, as authorized by the law of 1871. The court decided the law of 1882 void, and judgment was found for the plaintiff taxpayers.

Virginia Plan.—At the opening of the Convention of 1787 to amend the Articles of Confederation, Edmund Randolph, of Virginia, on behalf of his delegation, set forth the defects in the old articles and submitted a series of fifteen resolutions drawn up by Madison. This was the first plan of revision presented to the convention and is sometimes called the "Randolph Plan" or the "National Plan." It provided for representation according to population in two branches of Congress—the first chosen

by the people, the second by the state legislatures; Congressional control of taxation and commerce; Congressional veto of state enactments; an Executive chosen by Congress; a limited veto by the Executive and part of the judiciary upon acts of Congress. There were other and less important provisions. The Constitution as framed and ratified was based on the Virginia plan, but quite a number of its leading features were either rejected altogether or greatly modified.

Virginia Resolutions.—A set of nine resolutions drawn up by James Madison, then a member of the Virginia legislature, passed by that body, and signed by the governor Dec. 24, 1798. The reason for the passage of these resolutions and similar ones by Kentucky about the same time was to give expression to the feeling that had been growing since 1791 that the Federal party was endeavoring to obtain greater power than that conferred upon the Government by the Constitution. The direct cause of their adoption was the passage of the alien and sedition laws (q. v.) by Congress. The resolutions deplored the broad construction given to the Constitution, as tending toward monarchical government. They declared the Union to be a compact between the states composing it, and that when this compact was infringed, each state might interpose to protect itself. The alien and sedition laws were denounced as "palpable and alarming infractions of the Constitution." (See also Alien and Sedition Laws; Kentucky Resolutions.)

Virginius, The.—Oct. 31, 1873, the *Virginius*, an American schooner suspected of carrying men and arms from New York to the Cuban insurgents, was captured by the Spanish gunboat *Tornado* on the high seas near Jamaica. Capt. Fry and thirty-five of the crew and four Cuban passengers were executed. The affair created much ill feeling between the United States and Spain. The latter country made such reparation as lay within her power by disclaiming any intention to insult the United States, by paying an indemnity, and by surrendering 102 remaining prisoners. It was proved that the *Virginius* was not entitled to sail under our flag. She foundered at sea off Cape Fear Dec. 19, 1873, while on her way to New York. (See illustration opposite 4249.)

Virginius, The, seized by Spanish vessel and citizens of United States on, put to death, discussed, 4189, 4195, 4210.

Claims regarding, settled, 4276.

Condition of indemnity fund, referred to, 5187, 5908.

Correspondence regarding, transmitted, 4436.

Distribution of indemnity to claimants, discussed, 4290, 5122.

Orders regarding, 5077, 6339.

Visits of Foreign Commissions.—On April 20, 1917, a commission to the United States from England arrived at an American port to consult and to be consulted concerning the part to be played by the United States in the struggle against Germany. It was followed by the arrival, on April 24, of a similar commission from France; and on May 9, by the advance-guard of a similar commission from Italy. The leading figure in the English Commission was Minister

Balfour, and the leading figures in the French Commission, ex-Premier Viviani and Marshal Joffre. (For the careers of these men, look under their names in the Biographical Index.) The advance-guard of the Italian Commission was headed by Enrico Arlotta, Minister of Maritime and Railway Transportation. After consulting in Washington with the President, the Cabinet, and high officials of the United States Army and Navy, the French and English commissions paid visits to different cities of the East and Middle West, being received everywhere with acclamation. The remainder of the Italian Commission arrived in Washington on May 23, 1917. It was headed by the Prince of Udine, the eldest son of the Regent of Italy; and included in its personnel Guglielmo Marconi, the inventor of the wireless telegraph. In June, a Belgian commission arrived in the United States. It was headed by Baron Moncheur, formerly Belgian minister to the United States, Mexico, and Turkey, and later chief of the political bureau of the Belgian Foreign Office. The counsel of the commission was M. Carlier, a prominent Belgian banker; and other members were General Leclerq, Major Osterrieth, and Count d'Ursel. In the same month, a similar commission from Russia was received in the United States. It was headed by Special Ambassador Boris A. Bakhmetieff.

Viva Voce.—Vote by voice, that is, by ayes and nays. (See Acclamation.)

Volley.—The discharge from a number of guns fired simultaneously.

Volunteer Naval Reserve. (See Naval Reserve.)

Volunteer State.—A nickname for Tennessee (q. v.). (See also States); sometimes also nicknamed Big Bear State.

Vizcaya, The, mentioned, 6317.

Volunteers.—Persons who enter the military service of their own free will for temporary duty, as distinguished from regulars of a permanent military establishment. By an act passed in 1792 the American Congress recognized the existence in a number of states of volunteer organizations not included in the militia of those states. The Government has since from time to time raised volunteers for temporary purposes. Such troops are United States rather than state forces, and their officers are to be appointed by the President. A provisional force of 25,000 volunteers was authorized by Congress for the war with England in 1812. During the Mexican War 73,500 volunteers were enlisted. During the Civil War a number of calls were made for volunteers, aggregating nearly 2,800,000 enlistments. In the war with Spain over 200,000 volunteers were enlisted. (See also Militia; Army.)

Votes for President, Count of.—The electoral votes of the states are received by the President of the Senate. The two Houses meet in joint session on a day fixed by law, and the President of the Senate opens the returns and hands them to tellers, who count the votes and announce the result. In 1876 two sets of returns were received from certain states. A special electoral commission was appointed by Congress to decide which were the regular returns. In 1887 Congress passed a law providing that contests over electors should be finally decided under state laws as far as possible.

Vote of Thanks. (See Thanks of Congress.)

Wabash and Erie Canal, grant of land in aid of, to Indiana, 1725.

Wabash Indians. (See Indian Tribes.)
Instructions to commissioners in making treaty with, 6271.
Troops must be called for, to suppress, 53, 74.
Treaty with, 127.

Wabash River, act for improvement of navigation on, reasons for applying pocket veto to, 1337.

Wageworkers (see also Labor):
Condition of, discussed by President—
Roosevelt, 6903.
Compensation for when killed or injured in discharge of duty, recommended, 7206, 7213.

Wahpeton Indians. (See Indian Tribes.)

Wake and Other Islands.—The United States flag was hoisted over Wake Island in January, 1899, by Commander Taussig, of the *Bennington,* while proceeding to Guam. It is a small island in the direct route from Hawaii to Hongkong, about 2,000 miles from the first and 3,000 miles from the second.
The United States possesses a number of scattered small islands in the Pacific Ocean, some hardly more than rocks or coral reefs, over which the flag has been hoisted from time to time. They are of little present value and mostly uninhabited. The largest are Christmas, Gallego, Starbuck, Penrhyn, Phœnix, Palmyra, Howland, Baker, Johnston, Gardner, Midway, Morell, and Marcus islands. The Midway Islands are occupied by a colony of telegraphers in charge of the relay in the cable line connecting the Philippines with the United States, in all about forty persons.
The Santa Barbara group is a part of California and the Aleutian chain, extending from the peninsular of Kamchatka in Asiatic Russia to the promontory in North America which separates Bering Sea from the North Pacific, a part of Alaska.

Wakefield, Va., appropriation for approaches to monument at, to mark birthplace of Washington, recommended, 4803.

Walker vs. Jennison.—A slave case decided by the Massachusetts Supreme Court in 1783. It placed a construction upon the State constitution which soon afterwards put an end to slavery in the State. A negro servant had been whipped and imprisoned by his master, and public indignation was aroused by the offense. The owner of the slave was prosecuted. The Supreme Court, sitting in Worcester, found the defendant guilty of assault and imposed a fine upon him. The holding of the court was that the State constitution of 1870, in declaring all men free and equal, had abolished slavery in Massachusetts. As a matter of strict fact, runaway slaves were advertised for in the Boston newspapers after the decision had been promulgated. Nevertheless, the institution of slavery very soon after 1783 came to an end in Massachusetts.

Walker River Reservation, Nev., right of way for railroad through, 4736, 4776, 4953, 5178.

Walla Walla Indians. (See Indian Tribes.)

Wampum. — An Indian word meaning "white" and referring to strings of white beads worn for ornament and used as a medium of exchange. The beads were made of clam shells, through which holes had been drilled, and were strung upon a thread. Tradition says the Narragansets were the first Indians to use wampum. This is perhaps true as regards the beads made of the quahog or clam shell of the coasts of Rhode Island and Connecticut, though periwinkle shells were also used. Its use as money spread from the coast Indians inland. It was also used by the colonists of New England and the Middle States, having been deemed legal tender from 1627 to 1661. Beads of black or dark purple were rated at double the white wampum. Wampum was known to the Dutch settlers under the name of "sewon" or "zeewand." Payments were made by cutting off the desired number of beads. They were also used in the simple arithmetical calculations of the Indians.

Wanderer, The, landing of, with cargo of slaves, 3065, 3086.

War (see also Algerine War; Indian Wars; Mexican War; Revolution; Revolutionary War; Spanish-American War; Tripolitan War; Civil War; War of 1812; Wars, Foreign):
Instant redress, conferring of authority upon President to demand, recommended, 3100.
International agreement to regard private property at sea as exempt from capture by belligerents, recommended, 6338.
One-half of every century consumed in, 791.
Possibility of, with Great Britain, referred to, 2277.
Power to declare, discussed, 3100.
Preparation for, by Great Britain, 2277.
Preparation for, with—
France, recommended, 262, 268, 270, 1411.
Spain, referred to, 376.
Threatened by Tunis, 388.

War Between the States. (See Civil War.)

War Claims (see also Fourth of July Claims; Southern Claims Commissions):
Discussed, 4205, 4303, 5755.
Payment of, referred to, 4148.

War College. (See War, Department of and illustration, frontispiece, Vol. IX.)

War Department.—An Executive Department of the federal government established by act of the First Congress under the Constitution, on Aug. 7, 1789. The work then taken up by the Department was begun by the Continental Congress, that body on June 15, 1775, having elected George Washington "to command all the continental forces raised or to be raised for the defense of American liberty." An Adjutant-General, Quartermaster-General, and Commissary-General were also appointed, and on Dec. 26 of the following year Congress gave General Washington power to appoint all officers below the grade of Brigadier-General and to fill vacancies in all departments of the American Army.

In response to the recommendation of Washington, Congress, on June 13, 1776, created the Board of War, which was the germ of the modern War Department. The office of Secretary of War was created in 1781 and was filled by Henry Knox from 1784. When the War Department was formally established in 1789 he was made the first Secretary under the Constitution.

Adjutant-General.—The office of Adjutant-General was formally created by an act of Congress of March 3, 1813, there having been no regular Adjutant-General from the disbanding of the Army in 1783 up to that time. An act of March 5, 1792, created the dual office of Adjutant and Inspector-General, but on the reorganization of the Department this office was changed to that of Adjutant-General. By an act of Congress approved April 23, 1904, this office was united with the Record and Pension Office to form the office of the Military Secretary. This is the Department of records, orders and correspondence of the army and militia, the Military Secretary being charged with transmitting all orders of the Secretary of War, conducting the recruiting service, etc.

War Activities.—In addition to its peace duties, the Adjutant General's office in the first year of the war with Germany raised the volunteer enlisted strength of the Army to its maximum authorized war strength. It selected and appointed the officers to command both this force and the National Army; it selected and appointed the Army field clerks; it cared for prisoners of war and interned enemy aliens; and it kept a complete record of every man and woman going abroad in the service of the United States.

Training camps for officers were established and conducted. Appointments and commissions were prepared and distributed. The work of the recruiting service was maintained. Special orders assigning officers to duty were issued, as were all general orders, bulletins, circulars, etc. Whenever a casualty occurred in the American Expeditionary forces, the Adjutant General's office informed the family of the deceased, and kept and distributed a daily list of all in service, wounded, etc. It also established a committee on education to study the needs of the Army for trained men, to determine how such needs should be met, to secure the cooperation of the country's educational institutions, to provide the technical training of needed men, etc. The average number of pieces of mail opened and attended to every day was more than 90,000.

Inspector-General.—The Inspector-General's office was established under the Constitution by an act of March 3, 1813, although in 1777 an Inspector-General of Cavalry, and of Ordnance and Military Manufactures, had been appointed. It is the duty of the Inspector-General to inspect all military commands, stations, schools, armories, arsenals, fortifications and public works carried on by the War Department.

Judge-Advocate General.—The office of Judge-Advocate General of the Army was created in 1775, was discontinued in 1802, and existed again from 1812 to 1821. An act of March 2, 1849, authorized the President to appoint a Judge-Advocate of the Army, but in 1862 the title was changed to that of Judge-Advocate General. This

office was made head of the Bureau of Military Justice, created June 20, 1864, but by the act of July 5, 1884, the office of Judge Advocate-General and the Bureau of Military Justice were united under the designation of Judge-Advocate General's Department, of the War Department. It is the duty of the Judge-Advocate General to review the proceedings of all courts-martial, courts of inquiry and military commissions, and give opinions on legal questions arising under laws and regulations pertaining to the War Department.

Quartermaster.—The Quartermaster's office was formally organized in the War Department by an act of Congress of March 28, 1812, although provision had been made for a Quartermaster-General by the Continental Congress as early as June 16, 1775. Various enactments were also made concerning the office up to 1785, when it ceased to exist until, as stated, it was finally organized in 1812. It is the duty of the Quartermaster's Department to furnish the army with military supplies; provide transportation for troops; construct military roads and bridges; maintain national cemeteries; and provide supplies for the militia of the various states.

War Activities.—The appropriations for the Quartermaster Department in the first year of the war with Germany were $2,790,-000,000, of which $1,927,000,000 was for supply, subsistence, and transportation; $200,000,000 for barracks and quarters and $514,000,000 for the pay of the Army. Separate Divisions of Subsistence and of Supply and Equipment were created. Among the items of purchase in this year were 40,000,000 yards of bobbinet for mosquito bars; 75,000,000 yards of olive drab; 35,-000,000 yards of shelter-tent duck; 20,000,-000 woolen blankets; 35,000,000 yards of flannel shirting; 50,000,000 pairs of heavy stockings; 21,000,000 pairs of shoes.

At the beginning of the war the Department had some 3,000 motor-trucks, 450 automobiles, and 670 motorcycles. In June alone some 10,000 trucks were acquired. Other purchases in this year included 3,520 passenger cars, 6,126 motorcycles, and 5,040 bicycles. Repair shops kept pace with the production, the designs of which were soon standardized. The Cantonment Division built within three months 16 cantonments (q. v.), including 22,000 individual buildings and costing more than twice the building the Panama Canal.

Commissary-General.—The earliest legislation concerning the subsistence of the army was the resolution of the Continental Congress of June 16, 1775, creating the office of Commissary-General of Stores and Provisions. This office was succeeded on June 10, 1777, by two offices, the Commissary-General of Purchases and the Commissary-General of Issues, which acted under the direction of a committee of Congress until Nov. 25, 1779, when they were placed under the supervision of the War Board. The clothing of the troops was provided for by the ordinance of June 17, 1777, which created the office of Clothier-General, this office being placed under the direction of the War Board on April 10, 1782. An act of the Continental Congress of July 10, 1781, directed the Superintendent of Finance to procure all supplies by contract; and again on March 8, 1792, the Congress under the Constitution placed a similar duty upon the Treasury Department, which had succeeded the Superintendent of Finance. The latter act was repealed on July 16, 1798, and the Secretary of War was required to provide subsistence for the army. An act of March 16, 1802, provided for three military agents

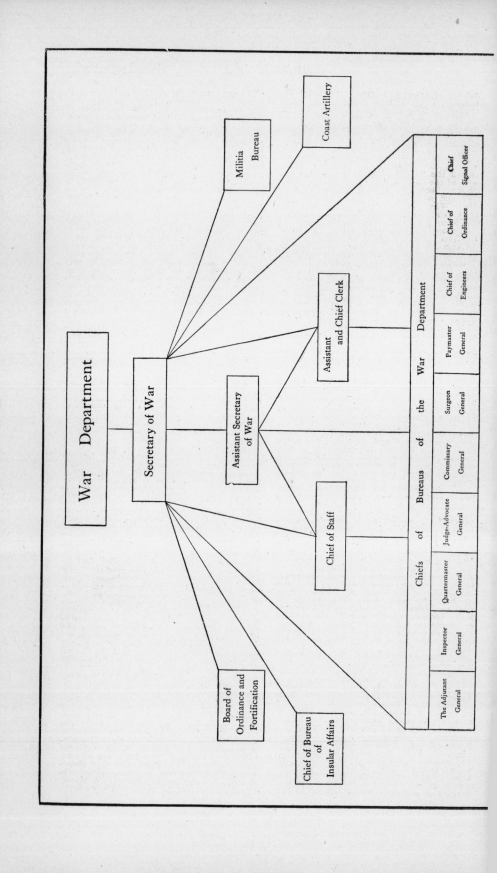

War Department

Secretary of War

- Militia Bureau
- Coast Artillery
- Assistant and Chief Clerk
- Assistant Secretary of War
- Chief of Staff
- Board of Ordinance and Fortification
- Chief of Bureau of Insular Affairs

Chiefs of Bureaus of the War Department

The Adjutant General	Inspector General	Quartermaster General	Judge-Advocate General	Commissary General	Surgeon General	Paymaster General	Chief of Engineers	Chief of Ordinance	Chief Signal Officer

to do this work, but this system was abolished by an act of March 28, 1812. which created the office of Commissary-General of Purchases. This in turn was abolished by an act of March 28, 1812, its duties transferred to the Quartermaster's Department.

The office of Commissary-General as it exists to-day was first established by an act of April 14, 1818, the head of this office being later referred to as Commissary-General of Subsistence. He provides and issues rations, and distributes articles authorized to be kept for sale to the officers and men of the army.

Provost Marshal General.—For the work of this officer in administering the provisions of the selective service law, consult the article Drafts.

Surgeon-General.—A hospital department for the army was created by Congress on July 27, 1775, its head being called Director-General and Chief Physician. By an act of March 3, 1813, the office of Physician and Surgeon-General was created and on April 14, 1818, the medical branch of the War Department was given a permanent head with the title of Surgeon-General.

Army hospitals in the first year of the war between Germany and the United States were enlarged in the United States from 7 to 63, the bed capacity from 5,000 to 88,-400. In France, hospitals were established with a bed capacity equal to from 20% to 25% of the strength of the American Expeditionary Forces.

The total strength of the personnel of the Medical Department in the first year of war was increased from 8,000 to 106,000. Of the latter number, 18,000 were officers, 7,000 were nurses, and 6,000 were in training in the ambulance service. Large army laboratories were increased from 12 to 150 and army laboratories of all sizes from 100 to 500. From the newly-established Medical Training School there had been graduated during the year 6,000 officers and 15,000 men. 150,000 psychological examinations had been made.

The Medical Department examined during this year all prospective recruits and officers. It advised on the choice and the layout of camps, on the housing, and on the feeding. It watched and studied all phases of health and disease in the camps and in the army. It undertook preventative and educational work, especially with respect to venereal disease. It developed a special mask for gas defense. Nutrition surveys of an extensive character were made. Reconstruction hospitals were established for the physical reconstruction of all permanently injured and disabled in service, with individual attention and vocational guidance and training for each case.

On War Footing.—On war footing, the Medical Service had a personnel of more than 70,000. There were more than 13,-000 commissioned officers in the Medical Reserve Corps, more than 2,600 in the Dental Reserve Corps, and more than 250 in the Sanitary Corps. New sections added to the Surgeon-General's office were on internal medicine; medical officers' training camps; medical military instruction; psychology; neurology and psychiatry; surgery; infectious diseases and laboratories; head, eye, ear, mouth and brain; military orthopedics; special hospitals and physical reconstruction; gas defense; food; office development and filing system.

Paymaster-General.—The office of Paymaster-General was provided by the resolution of Congress of June 16, 1775, but on March 23, 1787, it was merged with that of Commissioner of Army Accounts. A Pay-

master of the Army was appointed by an act of May 8, 1792, and the Pay Department was definitely organized in the War Department under an act of April 24, 1816.

Engineer Corps.—The Corps of Engineers was created on March 11, 1779, disbanded in November, 1783, but restored by the acts of May 9, 1794, and March 16, 1802. As early as July 25, 1777, however, there had been a "geographer and surveyor of roads" appointed. By an act of March 3, 1818, the appointment of topographical engineers was authorized, and in August, 1818, a Topographical Bureau was established in the War Department under the direction of the Secretary of War and the Chief Engineer. On July 5, 1838, an independent corps of topographical engineers was created, but by the act of March 3, 1863, it was merged with the Corps of Engineers. Besides those duties germane to its military nature, the Corps of Engineers conducts the river and harbor improvements.

War Activities.—At the time of the official declaration of war against Germany, the Engineer Corps office personnel consisted of 177 officers and civilian employees. One year later it consisted of 2,818 officers, enlisted men and civilian employees. During that year the Engineer troops increased from 4,125 officers and enlisted men to about 120,000, with an authorized strength of over 200,000.

During that year, units of the following classes were organized: Divisional engineers (sappers); mounted engineers (sappers for operating over extended territory); forestry (for lumbering and sawmills); railway construction; railway operation; railway maintenance; railway shop engineers; road (highway construction and maintenance); supply and shop (general supplies of all natures, except railway supplies); general construction (buildings, wharves, docks, etc.); mining (military mining); quarry; surveying, ranging and mapping; gas and flame, electrical and mechanical (installation and operation of electrical and mechanical plants); water supply, motor transportation; searchlight; pontoon bridge; clerical; labor service; replacement troops; crane operators (port terminal service); camouflage; and storekeepers and miscellaneous trades.

The first engineer troops, 1,100 strong, arrived in France less than three months after the declaration of war.

After one year of war, the Engineers' Reserve Corps consisted of about 5,500 men. The office of the Director-general of Military Railways during the first year of war placed orders for railway supplies having an aggregate weight of 754,000 long tons and a value of $142,000,000. The General Engineer Depot issued 9,500 orders for material valued at $200,000,000, including the above-mentioned amount. The Purchasing Office placed equipment equal to that required for 170 infantry divisions. Engineer depots for the receiving, storing and shipment of engineering material were established to the extent of 700,000 square feet of floor space.

Ordnance Department.—To consider ways and means of supplying the continental troops with arms and ammunition, a committee was appointed by the Continental Congress on May 27, 1775; and although a Commissioner of Artillery Stores (later called Commissioner-General of Artillery Stores) was appointed, the business of providing arms and ammunition was conducted by a secret committee of the Continental Congress and the Board of War. An act of April 2, 1794, authorized the President to appoint an officer who, under the War

Department, should perform ordnance duty, and on May 14, 1812, the Ordnance Department was formally established in the War Department. By an act of March 2, 1820, it was merged with the artillery but was reorganized as an independent bureau by an act of April 5, 1832.

War Activities.—In the first year of the war with Germany, the Ordnance Department expanded from 97 officers operating with an annual appropriation of less than $15,000,000 to 5,000 officers working under appropriations of almost $5,000,000,000. To the peace-time task of administering 11 Government arsenals was added the problem of getting quick production from more than 1,400 establishments engaged upon ordnance contracts. The Supply Division handled material amounting to 10,000 carloads monthly. The number of separate items of goods made and supplied to the troops was more than 100,000. A plant covering 13 acres was organized to manufacture recoil mechanisms after the designs furnished by the French Government. The Nitrate Division built plants and developed an industry new to the United States. Two plants for the manufacture of powder, each costing $45,000,000, were placed under construction. 1,400,000 rifles were provided; deliveries were secured on more than 17,000 machine guns; the rate of production of machine guns was increased to 225,000 yearly; the rate of production of guns of calibre of 3½ to 9 inches was increased to 15,000 yearly. 1,000,000,000 rounds of ammunition were purchased for the use of troops in cantonments alone, 23,000,000 hand grenades, 725,000 automatic pistols; 250,000 revolvers; 23,000,000 shells for heavy artillery; 430,000,000 pounds of explosives; 240,000 machine guns and 2,500,-000 rifles were among the articles of purchase. The Browning machine rifle and the Browning machine gun, heavy model, were perfected in 1918, the United States rifle, a modification of the British Enfield, having been perfected in 1917. An extensive ordnance base in France was placed under construction.

Signal Corps.—The Signal Corps was practically created June 21, 1860, when Congress authorized the addition of a signal officer to the staff of the army. The Signal Corps, by that name, was organized by an act of March 3, 1863. The duties now performed by the Weather Bureau were added to those of the Signal Corps in 1870, but in 1890 that work was transferred to the Department of Agriculture. The Chief Signal Officer has charge of all means of military communication.

War Activities.—In the first year of the war against Germany the Signal Corps was divided for administration purposes into a Division of Administration; Cable Section; Science and Research Section; Land Division, including a Pigeon Service; and the Air Division, the latter subdivided into almost 100 separate bureaus. In that year the personnel of the Air Service was increased 100 times. Schools of 11 different kinds were instituted. The average daily flight of American aviators was increased to 100,000 miles. More than 20 companies were manufacturing airplanes, 15 were engaged in the production of engines, and more than 400 were producing accessories. Branch offices were established in the chief industrial centres. For further details, see Aircraft Production, War.

The Signal Corps, in addition, took over the whole system of communications of the Army, both in France and in the United States. 1,200 miles of permanent wire were built in France, with 3,300 miles behind the battle fronts.

Aviation Service.—(See Signal Corps.)

Customs and Insular Affairs.—A Division of Customs and Insular Affairs was established in the War Department in December, 1898, for conducting the business relating to the civil government of Cuba, Puerto Rico, and the Philippine Islands. In 1900 the designation of this division was changed by Department orders to that of Division of Insular Affairs, and by an act of July 1, 1902, it was definitely established by law as a bureau of the War Department.

General Staff.—To better coordinate the various offices of the Department, the General Staff Corps was established by an act of Congress approved Feb. 14, 1903. It consists of a Chief of Staff, who took the place of the Commanding General of the Army; two general officers detailed by the President from the regular army not below the grade of brigadier-general, and forty-two officers of minor grade similarly detailed by the President. It is the duty of the General Staff Corps to prepare plans for the national defense, and for the mobilization of the military forces in time of war; to assist the Secretary of War in increasing the efficiency of the military establishment; and in case of war to act as a board of strategy. The Chief of Staff, under the direction of the President, or the Secretary of War under the direction of the President, has supervision of all troops of the line, the Adjutant-General's, Inspector-General's, Judge-Advocate General's, Quartermaster's, Subsistence, Medical, Pay, and Ordnance Departments, the Corps of Engineers, and Signal Corps.

In administering the affairs of the Department, the Secretary is aided by an Assistant Secretary, as well as by the chiefs of the various offices, bureaus, divisions and corps named above, who are officers of the regular army of the United States. Two bureaus of the Department not now in existence are: The Bureau of Refugees, Freedmen and Abandoned Lands (1865-1873), which aided in the work of reconstruction, after the Civil War; and the Bureau of the Provost-Marshal General (1863-1866), which had to do with the enrolling and calling out of the national forces and the arrest of deserters and spies. (See Army.)

An act of Congress approved April 6, 1918, creates in the Department a Second Assistant Secretary of War and a Third Assistant Secretary of War. They are appointed by the President, by and with the consent of the Senate, and receive an annual salary of $4,500, their duties being such as may be assigned by the Secretary of War or by law.

War College.—To coordinate and direct the instruction in the various service schools and to extend the opportunities for investigation and study in the army and militia Congress established the War College at Washington, and placed it under the immediate direction of the Secretary of War.

Training Camp Activities.—In April, 1917, the Secretary of War appointed a Commission to supply the normalities of life to men in the training camps and to keep the environs of the camps clean and wholesome. The Secretary of the Navy soon afterwards appointed a similar board for the Navy and both boards were placed under one chairmanship. Under the two commissions, the social and welfare work which took place in and around the camps was coordinated, along with the activities of such bodies as the Y. M. C. A., Y. W. C. A., Knights of Columbus, American Library Association, Playground and Recreation Association of America, Y. M. H. A., Y. W.

H. A., American Social Hygiene Association, and the Committee on Protective Work for Girls. 32 Liberty Theatres were constructed in the training camps. Mass athletics were developed and athletic fields constructed. The problem of prostitution was attacked, and 80 service clubs were established for the soldiers and sailors, adjacent to their camps, for their days of furlough. According to the Chairman, all "red-light" districts in the neighborhood of the camps were eliminated. For further details, see the article Y. M. C. A., *War Activities.*

War Credits Board.—This body acts on financial advances to aid contractors for supplies for the Army.

Following is a list of the Secretaries of War and the Presidents under whom they served:

President	Secretary of War	Appointed
Washington	Henry Knox, Massachusetts	1789
"	Timothy Pickering, Mass.	1795
"	James McHenry, Maryland	1795
Adams....	" "	1797
"	John Marshall, Virginia.	1800
"	Samuel Dexter, Massachusetts	1800
"	Roger Griswold, Connecticut	1801
Jefferson..	Henry Dearborn, Massachusetts.	1801
Madison...	William Eustis, Massachusetts	1809
"	John Armstrong, New York	1813
"	James Monroe, Virginia	1814
"	William H. Crawford, Georgia	1815
Monroe....	Isaac Shelby, Kentucky	1817
"	Geo. Graham (*ad. in.*), Virginia	1817
"	John C. Calhoun, S. Carolina	1817
J.Q.Adams	James Barbour, Virginia	1825
"	Peter B. Porter, New York	1828
Jackson...	John H. Eaton, Tennessee	1829
"	Lewis Cass, Michigan	1831
"	Benjamin F. Butler, New York	1837
Van Buren.	Joel R. Poinsett, South Carolina	1837
Harrison..	John Bell,* Tennessee	1841
Tyler*....	John McLean, Ohio	1841
"	John C. Spencer, New York	1841
"	James M. Porter, Pennsylvania	1843
"	William Wilkins, Pennsylvania	1844
Polk......	William L. Marcy, New York	1845
Taylor.....	George W. Crawford, Georgia	1849
"	Edward Bates, Missouri	1850
Fillmore...	Charles M. Conrad, Louisiana	1850
Pierce.....	Jefferson Davis, Mississippi	1853
Buchanan..	John B. Floyd, Virginia	1857
"	Joseph Holt, Kentucky	1861
Lincoln....	Simon Cameron, Pennsylvania	1861
"	Edwin M. Stanton, Ohio	1862
Johnson...	" "	1865
"	U. S. Grant (*ad. in.*), Illinois	1867
"	Lor. Thomas (*ad. in.*), Illinois	1868
"	John M. Schofield, New York	1868
Grant.....	John A. Rawlins, Illinois	1869
"	William T. Sherman, Ohio	1869
"	William W. Belknap, Iowa	1869
"	Alphonso Taft, Ohio	1876
"	James Don. Cameron, Penn.	1876
Hayes.....	George W. McCrary, Iowa	1877
"	Alexander Ramsey, Minnesota	1879
Garfield...	Robert T. Lincoln, Illinois	1881
Arthur....	" "	1881
Cleveland..	William C. Endicott, Mass.	1885
B. Harrison	Redfield Proctor, Vermont	1889
"	Stephen B. Elkins, West Virginia	1891
Cleveland..	Daniel S. Lamont, New York	1893
McKinley..	Russell A. Alger, Michigan	1897
"	Elihu Root, New York	1899
Roosevelt..	" "	1901
"	William H. Taft, Ohio	1904
"	Luke E. Wright, Tennessee	1908
Taft......	Jacob M. Dickinson, Tennessee	1909
"	Henry L. Stimson, New York	1911
Wilson....	Lindley M. Garrison, N. Jersey	1913
"	Newton D. Baker, Ohio	1916

*John Bell also continued by President Tyler in 1841 until appointment of successor.

For more detailed information of the scope and activities of the War Department consult the index references to the Presidents' Messages and Encyclopedic articles under the following headings:

Arms and Ammunition.	Civil War.
	Coast Artillery.
Army.	Fortifications.
Arsenals.	Indian Wars.
Artillery.	Military Academy.
Board of Ordnance and Fortification.	Military Department. Military Education.
Bureau of Insular Affairs.	Militia Bureau. Wars, Foreign.

Military Policy of America.—Secretary of War Garrison stated the policy of the Wilson administration on the subject of preparedness for defence in the following language in his report to the President in 1915:

"It is a matter of great gratification to observe that there is a realizing sense of the necessity of the adoption of a wise and sensible policy. It was inevitable that this should be the result of the consideration of this subject. In a self-governing nation the prime necessity for proper action is to secure the concentrated attention of the people; when they are all thinking about the same thing at the same time, they reach a sound and satisfactory conclusion. This subject is now receiving such concentrated attention, and a wise result will be reached when facts are realized and reason is applied. The only firm foundation is one which rests upon fact, and the only wise guide to conduct is one which proceeds from reason.

"The necessity of a nation having force commensurate with its responsibility is demonstrated by every correct process of reasoning founded upon fact. This is so whether the subject is considered in the light of the philosophy of government or of history. The use of force is the inherent essence of government. The very term itself is explicit—government—the right or power to compel obedience to law. Where there is no force to compel such obedience—that is, to govern—there, is anarchy. Individuals give up the right of unregulated action when they form themselves into or become subject to a government. The progress and advancement of that which is summed up in the word "civilization" have been made possible solely because of government. Unless the individual is secure in his person and his property, he has neither time nor inclination to devote himself to the cultivation of the mental, moral or spiritual side of his nature. That security is assured to him by government, and government can only meet its responsibility of assurance by the possession of sufficient force to secure and preserve it. In our own earlier days the continued progress of the arts of peace was constantly interrupted by the necessity of banding together to prevent destruction by aggression from without. Later, and even after many of our largest civil communities were established, the individual citizen had to be prepared to protect himself, his family and his property, against the depredations of criminals, until the community organized and prepared a police force sufficient to assure the citizen of protection.

"The identical necessity exists as to the nation. Unless the citizens thereof are assured that they can cultivate the arts of peace behind a barrier of force which will protect them from aggression and secure them in their rights, they are not free to cultivate such arts. Alike in the case of the individual, the internal municipality and the nation, there must be a realization of the responsibility and a willingness and preparation to measure up to and meet it.

War Finance Corporation.—An act of Congress approved by President Wilson on April 5, 1918, provides that the Secretary of the Treasury and four other persons shall be created a body corporate and politic in deed and in law under the name of the War Finance Corporation, to have succession for a period of ten years, provided that it close all its active business within six months after the end of the war with the Central Powers.

The capital stock is $500,000,000, all subscribed by the United States of America, subject to call upon the vote of three-fifths of the Corporation, with the approval of the Secretary of the Treasury.

The management of the Corporation is vested in the Board of Directors, of which the Secretary of the Treasury is the chairman, the other four being the four persons named in the first paragraph, and being appointed by the President by and with the consent of the Senate. No director or employee of the Corporation shall directly or indirectly participate in the discussion of any question in which his own interests are involved, or the interests of any business association with which he is directly or indirectly connected. Two of the directors first appointed shall serve for two years and two for four years, after which directors shall be appointed to serve for four years. Directors receive an annual salary of $12,000, or such amount which will make their total annual salaries from all services performed by the United States equal to $12,000.

The Corporation is authorized to make advances, upon its own terms and for not more than five years, to banks, bankers, or trust companies in the United States which shall have made since the beginning of the War and which shall have outstanding any loan or loans to any person, firm, business, or corporation whose operations are necessary or contributory to the prosecution of the War, and evidenced by notes. No such advance, however, shall exceed 75% of the value of such loans.

The Corporation is empowered, furthermore, to make such advances to any bank, banker or trust company which has given financial assistance directly or indirectly to any such person, firm, business or corporation by the purchase of its bonds or other obligations since the War, the advances not to exceed 75% of the value of such bonds or advances.

All advances shall be made upon the promissory note or notes of such banks, etc., secured by the notes, bonds, or other obligations which are the basis of any such advance, together with all the securities, if any, which such banks may hold as collateral for such notes, bonds, or other obligations.

However, the Corporation is given power to make advances up to 100% of the face value of such loan made by such bank to any such person, firm, etc., and up to 100% of the value of such bonds or other obligations purchased, provided that every such advance is secured in the manner described above and in addition by collateral security, to be furnished by the bank, of such character as may be prescribed by the Board of Directors of the War Finance Corporation, at the value at the time of such advance of at least 33% of the amount advanced by the Corporation. The Corporation retains power to require additional security at any time.

The Corporation may make advances at any time, for periods not exceeding one year, to any bank or building and loan association, on their promissory notes, whenever the Corporation deems such action helpful to the prosecution of the War or to the public interest. But such notes must be secured by the pledge of securities which in the opinion of the Corporation are 133% of the value of such advances. The rate of interest charged for such advances must be at least 1% more than the rate of discount for 90-day commercial paper contemporaneously prevailing in the Federal Reserve district in which the borrowing institution is located; but must not be more than the average rate receivable by the borrowing institution on its loans and investments made during the six months prior to the advance, except that the rate of interest shall not be less than the rate of discount on 90-day commercial paper.

The Corporation is similarly empowered to make advances to private establishments conducting business necessary for the prosecution of the War, but only for that purpose as carried out within the United States, and when such advance cannot be obtained through private sources, and not for an amount greater than 12½% of the sum of the authorized capital stock of the War Finance Corporation plus the aggregate amount of the bonds of the Corporation outstanding when the Capital Stock is paid in. All such advances must be secured by security estimated by the Directors of the Corporation as being of the value of 125% of the advance made, except in the case of a railroad under the control of the President of the United States. The rate of interest as above.

The Corporation may deal in bonds or other obligations of the United States issued or converted after Sept. 24, 1917.

The Corporation may issue bonds aggregating not more than six times its paid-in capital, to mature in from one to five years of the date of issue, as determined by the Directors with the approval of the Secretary of the Treasury.

The net earnings of the Corporation must be invested in Government securities or deposited in Federal Reserve banks, or may be used to purchase and redeem the Corporation's own bonds. Principal and interest of the Corporation's bonds are exempt from taxation except inheritance taxes, surtaxes, war profits taxes and excess profits taxes, and from the latter taxes interest on less than $5,000 worth of the bonds is exempt. The United States is not liable for securities or for the actions of the Corporation.

The original directors of the Corporation appointed by President Wilson were W. P. G. Harding, who was elected vice-chairman and general manager, Allen B. Forbes, Eugene Meyer, Jr., and Angus W. McLean.

Capital Issues Committee.—This body consists of seven members, of which at least three must be members of the Federal Reserve Board, appointed by the President, by and with the consent of the Senate. The terms of office are determined by the President, and the salaries of the members not on the Federal Reserve Board are $7,500 annually, or such amount as will make all their annual remunerations for services performed by the Government equal to $7,500 each. The President designated the first chairman, but all subsequent vacancies in the chairmanship are to be filled by the Committee.

The Committee may investigate, pass upon and determine whether it is compatible with the public interest that securities issued by any private person, firm or corporation above the amount of $100,000 since April 5, 1918, should be sold or offered for sale. The Committee, however, may not pass upon borrowing not for capital purposes or the renewing or refunding of indebtedness existing before April 5, 1918, or the resale of securities previously approved by the Committee or the securities

issued by railroads under the control of the President of the United States or the bonds of the War Finance Corporation.

No action of the Committee may be construed as carrying the approval of the Committee or of the United States upon any securities.

The original committee appointed by President Wilson consisted of Charles S. Hamlin, who was elected chairman, John Skelton Williams, Frederic A. Delano, Henry C. Flower, Frederick H. Goff, James B. Brown, John S. Drum.

War Industries Board. (See Council of National Defense.)

War Labor Board established, 8485.

War Materials, Government Requisition of.—The acts of the Sixty-fourth and Sixty-fifth Congresses which gave the President power to requisition and to contract for war materials included ships and shipping under their jurisdiction, and a statement of the powers therein granted will be found under the head of Shipbuilding, *European War Legislation.*

War Message of President Wilson, 8226.

War-Horse.—From the literal meaning, a horse used in war, the term has come to be applied to a brave soldier, or to a valiant person in any walk of life, especially to a long-favored public servant.

War of 1812.—This war grew out of the British orders in council made to destroy the commerce of France and of nations trading with France, the arbitrary impressment of American seamen, and the exercise of the right of search. These orders in council and the Berlin and Milan decrees of Napoleon subjected to capture vessels trading with England and France.

In the early part of this century European nations did not admit the right of expatriation. Great Britain held that "once an Englishman always an Englishman," and maintained the rights of search and impressment. Many of our vessels were stopped on the high seas and searched; seamen claimed to be British subjects were taken from them and forced to serve in the British navy or imprisoned for refusing to serve. Several of our men-of-war were fired upon and compelled to give up seamen in their crews. The arrogance of Great Britain was further shown by her interference with our commerce under her paper blockades. She interfered with rights which our government claimed for our vessels as neutral ships. (See Embargo Act.) The Henry affair (see Henry Documents) also increased the bitter feeling of our people. For several years previous to the war, England's action had been intolerable.

Congress passed acts known as the Embargo Act, the Nonintercourse Act, and the Nonimportation Act in an effort to check British aggressions on the commerce of the United States. The Federalists were opposed to war; the Republicans favored it. Madison, the Republican President, was personally not disposed to warlike measures, and it was asserted that he "could not be kicked into a war." Finally, however, the pressure from public and party became too strong for him. The Congress which assembled in December, 1811, was heartily disposed to resort to arms. It passed acts to increase the army, and appropriated large sums for the army and navy. Finally, on June 18, 1812, the President declared war against Great Britain. The war at first was waged along the Canadian frontier. The Americans suffered some serious re-

verses the first year in the Northwest. Detroit was surrendered by Hull, and Fort
Dearborn, on Lake Michigan, the present
site of the City of Chicago, was captured by
the British. Detroit was recovered by
Perry's splendid victory on Lake Erie in
1813. The military and naval forces of
Great Britain were greatly superior to those
of the United States. Nevertheless some
notable victories were won by the Americans
as the war progressed.

The Navy especially distinguished itself
in a remarkable series of engagements with
the enemy's ships. In 1814 the British attacked and captured Washington City and
burned the public buildings. The most
famous victory won by the Americans in
the war was that of Gen. Jackson over the
British commanded by Sir Edward M.
Pakenham, Jan. 8, 1815, at New Orleans.
This battle was fought fifteen days after
peace had been declared, but before the news
had reached New Orleans. Dec. 24, 1814,
by the treaty of Ghent (q. v.), peace was
restored. By this treaty several questions
pending between the two countries were settled, but the three principal ones, out of
which the war grew, were not mentioned.
The total number of enlistments in the
regular service was 38,187, and in the
militia 471,000. The total cost of the War
of 1812 was $107,159,003. The cost of the
Revolutionary War was $135,193,703; of
the Mexican War, $66,000,000.

War of 1812:

Alexandria, Va., retreat of British
from, 532.

American blood wantonly spilled by
Great Britain, 485.

Armistice proposed by Great Britain,
declined, 502.

Bainbridge, William, commander of
the *Constitution*, 507.

Baltimore retreat of British from, 533.

Blakely Johnston, British ship captured by vessel in command of,
534.

British attacks on Craney Island,
Fort Meigs, Sacketts Harbor, and
Sandusky, repulsed, 524.

British Government in state of war,
while United States remains in
state of peace, 489.

Brown, Jacob, victories of, over
British forces, 533.

Canada, York, reduced by American
forces, referred to, 524.

Capitol destroyed by British forces,
531.

Capture of British ship by vessel in
command of Lewis Warrington,
534.

Chauncey, Isaac, naval talents of,
commented on, 520.

Cochrane, Alex, order of, to destroy
American coast towns and districts, referred to, 530, 536.

Coffee, John, Indians defeated by
Tennessee militia under command
of, 521.

Conduct of Great Britain toward
United States, discussed, 484.

British cruiser violates American
flag, 485.

Pretended blockades without presence of adequate force, discussed, 486.

Connecticut, refusal of governor of,
to furnish militia, discussed, 501,
6268.

Constitution-Guerrière naval engagement, discussed, 502.

Constitution-Java naval engagement,
discussed, 507.

Decatur, Stephen, commander of the
United States, 506.

Deserters, pardon granted. (See Pardons.)

Destruction of American coast towns
by order of Admiral Cochrane, 536.

Detroit, Mich., surrender of, to British, 499.

Recovery of, referred to, 524.

Discussed, 484, 499, 505, 506, 507,
509, 511, 519, 525, 526, 527, 528,
530, 532, 537.

Effort of the United States to obtain
command of the Lakes, discussed,
501.

Engagement of the *United States*
with the *Macedonian* and capture
of the latter by Captain Decatur,
506.

Existence of, proclaimed, 497.

Forts Erie, George, and Malden, reduction of, by American forces, referred to, 524.

Frolic-Wasp naval engagement, discussed, 506.

Gaines, Edmund P., victories of,
over British forces, 533.

Guerrière-Constitution naval engagement, discussed, 502.

Harrison, William Henry, military
talents of, commented on, 520.

Hornet, British ship destroyed by
the, 513.

Hull, Isaac, commander of the *Constitution*, 502.

Hull, William, surrenders town and
fort of Detroit, Mich., 499.

Increase in army and militia, recommended by President Madison,
534, 538.

Indians employed by Great Britain
in, 500, 520.

Instructions to American vessels not
to interfere with neutral vessels,
529.

Intention of British commander to
lay waste American towns, proclamations regarding, 520.

Invasion of capital by British, referred to in proclamation, 530.

Jackson, Andrew, victory of volunteers under, over Indians, 521, 533.

Java-Constitution naval engagement,
discussed, 507.

Johnson, Richard M., military talents of, commented on, 520.

Jones, Jacob, commander of the *Wasp*, 506.

Lawrence, James, commander of the *Hornet*, 513.

Macdonough, Thomas, British ships captured on Lake Champlain by American squadron under, 534.

Mackinaw, Mich., attempted reduction of, by American forces, discussed, 534.

Massachusetts, refusal of governor of, to furnish militia, discussed, 501.

Mediation of Russia in, 511.
Accepted by United States, 511.
Declined by Great Britain, 519, 532.

Michigan Territory, recovery of, from British, referred to, and recommendation of assistance to the destitute, 520, 527.

Niagara Falls—
American attack near, unsuccessful, 501.
American victory on Canadian side of, 533.

Order of Admiral Cochrane to destroy American coast towns, 530, 536.

Pacific advances made to Great Britain, discussed, 502, 506.

Pardons granted deserters. (See **Pardons**.)

Peace (see also Mediation):
Mediation of Russia accepted by the United States, but declined by Great Britain, 511, 519.
Negotiations for, proposed by Great Britain should not stay preparations for war, 526.
Referred to, 536.
Terms of, proposed by President Madison declined, 502.
Treaty of, transmitted and discussed, 536, 537.
Proclamation of President Madison regarding, 545.

Pensioners of. (See Pensions, discussed.)

Perry, Oliver H., victory of naval forces under, on Lake Erie, 519.

Plattsburg, N. Y., defeat of British at, 533.

Preparation for, recommended, 479, 483.

Pretended blockade without adequate force, referred to, 486.

Proclaimed by President Madison, 497.

Proclamations of President Madison regarding, 457, 465, 476, 497, 517, 528, 543, 557, 571.

Public buildings destroyed by British forces, 530, 531.

Reduction attempted at Mackinaw, Mich., by American forces, discussed, 534.

Resolutions of—
Pennsylvania legislature—
Pledging support to Government. (See Pennsylvania.)

Retreat of British from Baltimore, 533.

Rodgers, John, frigates under command of, referred to, 502.

Scott, Winfield, victories of, over British forces, 533.

Threatened by Great Britain, referred to, 479, 489.

Threatening aspect of—
Congress convened on account of, 412.
Discussed by President Madison, 484.

Treaty of peace transmitted and discussed, 537.
Proclamation of President Madison regarding, 545.

Troops in, number and kind of, referred to, 3013.

Unfriendly policy of Great Britain, discussed, 460.

United States, engagement of the, with the *Macedonian*, 506.

Van Rensselaer, Stephen, attack of forces under, near Niagara, discussed, 501.

Vessels, American, instructed not to interfere with neutral vessels, 529.

Victories of American arms. (See Discussed, *ante*.)

Waged by Great Britain on account of extravagant views, 532.

Warrington, Lewis, British ship captured by vessel in command of, 534.

Wasp-Frolic naval engagement, discussed, 506.

York, Canada, reduction of, by American forces, referred to, 524.

War of 1917.—The title used by the Pension Bureau on May 20, 1917, to describe the conflict of the United States with Germany, as a part of the conflict which is usually described as the European War, or the Great European War.

War of Rebellion. (See Civil War.)

War of Rebellion, Official Records of:
Compilation of, appropriation for, recommended, 4304.
Publication of, plan for, recommended, 4451.

War Risk Insurance. (See Bureau of War Risk Insurance.)

War, Secretary of.—An act of the Continental Congress of Feb. 7, 1781, created the office of Secretary of War to take the place of the Board of War. Benjamin Lincoln was the first secretary, serving from 1781 to 1785, when he was succeeded by Henry Knox. Under Knox the present War Department was established. (See also War, Department of.)

War, Secretary of:
Adjutant-General of Army designated to act as, *interim*, 3819, 3861.
Clerks of, taking advantage of insolvent-debtors act, dismissed, 107.
Correspondence of, referred to, 2427.
Report of, transmitted and referred to, 291, 333, 335, 455, 622, 909, 954, 981, 995, 1018, 1036, 1089, 1097, 1128, 1113, 1444, 2055, 6345. (See also War Department.)
Suspension and removal of Secretary Stanton. (See Stanton, Edwin M.)

War Steamers:
Construction of, recommended, 2990, 3055.
Introduction of, into navies of world, referred to, 2262.

Ward Claim, referred to, 4436, 4801.

Ware vs. Hylton.—A Supreme Court case denying the right of any State or citizen to repudiate debts contracted with British subjects before the Revolutionary War. In 1796 Ware, a citizen of Great Britain, administrator of William Jones, surviving partner of Farrell & Jones, brought suit against Hylton, of Virginia, for the recovery of a debt. Hylton refused payment on the ground that the Virginia legislature of 1777 had passed an act to sequester British property and enable debtors of British subjects to pay such debts to the State loan office. The act was signed by Governor Jefferson. Hylton claimed to have complied with this statute. The United States circuit court for Virginia rendered a decree in favor of the defendant. The United States Supreme Court, however, reversed this decision on the ground that the legislature had not the power to extinguish the debt, when payment of such debts had been stipulated in the treaty of 1783. The justices rendered separate opinions to this effect. At the close of the Revolution and for a number of years afterwards there was a great deal of feeling aroused in Virginia and other States over efforts to collect British debts contracted in colonial times.

Warehouse Act.—The central purpose of the United States Warehouse Act, which became a law August 11, is to establish a form of warehouse receipt for cotton, grain, wool, tobacco and flaxseed, which will make these receipts easily and widely negotiable as delivery orders or as collateral for loans and therefore of definite assistance in financing crops. This purpose the act aims to attain by licensing and bonding warehouses under conditions which will insure the integrity of their receipts and make these receipts reliable evidence of the condition, quality, quantity and ownership of the products named which may be stored with them.
The Secretary of Agriculture is given general authority to investigate the storage, warehousing, classification, weighing and certifying of cotton, wool, grains, tobacco and flaxseed, and to classify warehouses for which licenses are applied for or issued.
He may issue to warehousemen licenses for the conduct of warehouses in which such products may be stored for interstate or foreign commerce, and also of warehouses located in places under the exclusive jurisdiction of the United States in which such products may be stored. Persons who are not warehousemen may also be licensed, subject to the same requirements as licensed warehousemen, to accept such products for storage in warehouses owned, operated or leased by any State. Licenses may be issued for periods not exceeding one year and are renewable upon a showing satisfactory to the Secretary of Agriculture. A fee not exceeding $2 may be charged for each license or renewal, and, in addition, a reasonable fee for each examination or inspection of a warehouse made upon application of the warehouseman. It is not, however, compulsory that any warehouseman be licensed by the Secretary of Agriculture.
Every applicant for a license as a warehouseman must agree to comply with the act and the rules and regulations prescribed under it. He must give a bond, with other than personal surety, to secure the performance of his obligations as a warehouseman under the laws of the place in which the warehouse is conducted, under his contracts with his depositors and under the United States Warehouse Act. The right is given to any person injured through its breach to sue in his own name on the bond for any damages sustained by him. When such bond has been given the warehouse may be designated as bonded under the United States Warehouse Act.
The Secretary of Agriculture is authorized to inspect warehouses licensed, or for which licenses are applied; to determine whether they are suitable for the proper storage of agricultural products; to prescribe the duties of licensed warehousemen with respect to their care of, and responsibility for, agricultural products; and to examine agricultural products stored in licensed warehouses. Deposits of agricultural products in such warehouses are made subject to the act and the rules and regulations under it.
Licensed warehousemen are not permitted to discriminate between persons desiring to store agricultural products in their warehouses. All agricultural products, except fungible products (such as grain and the like), of the same kind and grade, for which separate receipts are issued, must be kept that they may be separately identified and redelivered to the depositor. Warehousemen may mix grain and other fungible products, ordinarily mixed in storage, when they are of the same kind and grade and are delivered from the same mass, but may not mix such products when they are of different grades.
Original receipts must be issued for all agricultural products stored in licensed warehouses, but only when such products are actually stored at the time of the issuance of the receipts. Additional or further receipts for the same products may only be issued in place of lost or destroyed receipts, and then only under specified conditions.
The act enumerates certain facts which must be stated in all receipts issued by licensed warehousemen. They must show (a) the location of the warehouse, (b) the date of issuance, (c) the consecutive number, (d) whether the products will be delivered to the bearer, to a specified person, or to a specified person or his order, (e) the rate of storage charges, (f) a description of the product stored, including the quantity or weight, (g) the grade or other class, according to the official standards of the United States for such products, unless there be no such standard, in which event it must be stated according to some recognized standard or according to rules and regulations prescribed by the Secretary of Agriculture, (h) that they are issued subject to the United States Warehouse Act and the rules and regulations under it, (i) ownership, if any, of the products by the warehouseman, (j) any lien claimed by the ware-

houseman for advance made or liabilities incurred, (k) any other fact required by the Secretary of Agriculture, (l) the signature of the warehouseman, which may be made by his authorized agent. Unless otherwise required by the law of the State in which the warehouse is located, the grade may be omitted at the request of depositors, except in case of fungible agricultural products, if the receipts clearly show that they are not negotiable.

Warehousing System discussed by President—
Jackson, 1015.
Polk, 2405.
Tyler, 2053, 2119.

Warrior, The, illegal detention of, 2051.

Wars, Foreign:
Acheen with Netherlands, neutrality preserved by United States in, 4192.
Austria with Hungary, sympathy of American Government with latter, 2550, 2579.
Brazil with Buenos Ayres—
Peace concluded, 977.
Questions between United States and Brazil growing out of, 929, 951.
Brazil with Paraguay—
Good offices of United States tendered, 3776, 3883.
Referred to, 4078.
Canada, civil war in, neutrality of United States in, 1702, 1748.
Proclaimed, 1698, 1699.
Central America, republics in, at war with each other, 977.
Chile with Peru and Bolivia, 4522, 4563, 4628, 4717.
Claims of United States arising out of, 4913, 5083, 5369, 5544.
Conditions of peace presented by Chile, discussed, 4662, 4717, 4760.
Efforts of United States to bring about peace, discussed, 4522, 4563, 4582, 4662, 4717.
Negotiations for restoration of peace, referred to, 4676.
Terminated, 4822.
Treaty of peace discussed, 4760.
China with Japan—
Action taken by United States regarding, 5957, 6059.
Agents of United States requested to protect subjects of contestants, 5957, 6059.
Discussed by President—
Adams, John, 238.
Jefferson, 314, 349, 357.
France with China, 4823.
France with Germany—
Correspondence regarding, referred to, 4068, 4434.
Diplomatic relations resumed, 4098.
Neutrality of United States in, 4050.

Proclaimed, 4040, 4043, 4045.
Suspension of hostilities recommended by President Grant, 4055.
France with Spain—
Attempted recruiting, 2864.
Privateers, commissions not granted to, 779.
Referred to, 821.
Great Britain and France with China, neutrality preserved by United States in, 3037, 3089, 3174.
Great Britain with France, neutrality of United States proclaimed, 148.
Great Britain with Russia—
Attempts of Great Britain to draw recruits from United States, discussed, 2864.
Neutrality maintained by United States during, 2864.
Japan, civil war in, neutrality of United States in, 3888.
Proclaimed, 3712.
Mexico, civil war in—
Arrest of officer and men of United States Navy in, during, 8314.
Congress asked to permit land and naval forces to enter, during, to maintain dignity of United States, 8316.
Citizens of United States insulted in, during, 8315.
Neutrality preserved by United States in, 3444, 3581.
Proclamation revoking order forbidding export of arms to, 8309.
Mexico with Texas—
Armistice referred to, 2172.
Battle of San Jacinto, referred to, 2330.
Correspondence between President Jackson and Santa Anna regarding, 1493.
Defeat of Mexican arms, 1487.
Desire of Texas to become part of United States, 1456, 1487.
Discussed by President Tyler, 2113, 2164, 2193.
Hostilities should cease, 2113, 2164, 2194.
Independence of Texas—
Acknowledgment of, by Santa Anna referred to, 2330.
Recognition of, by United States discussed, 1484, 1500, 2113.
Interference of citizens of United States in, complained of by Mexico, 2050.
Neutrality of United States in, 1370.
Physical force, disparity of, on side of Mexico, 1487.
Referred to, 2329.
Result of, of importance to United States, 1456, 1487, 2113.

Wars of the United States.—The principal wars in which the United States has been engaged are the Revolutionary war, the war with France, war with the Barbary States (Algeria, Tunis and Tripoli), the War of 1812, the Mexican war, the Civil War, the Spanish-American war, the Indian wars, and the war with Germany. The most important conflicts with Indian tribes are described under Indian Wars. The near approach to war with France at the close of the Eighteenth Century is chronicled in the article entitled X, Y, Z Mission, and some of the minor domestic insurrections are treated under the head-

Military and Naval Forces Employed by the United States in the Several Wars Since and Including the War of the Revolution:
[Reported by the Commissioner of Pensions]

War	Dates		Troops Engaged				Individuals (estimated)
	From—	To—	Regulars	Militia and Volunteers	Navy	Total	
Revolution, war of the	April 19, 1775	April 11, 1783	130,711	58,750	15,000	309,791	
Estimated additional				105,830			184,038
Northwestern Indian war with the Miamis, Wyandots, Delawares, Potawatomies, Shawnees, Chippewas, and Ottawas. { General Harmer.	Sept. 19, 1790	Aug. 3, 1795	320	1,133		1,453 ⎫	
General St. Clair.						2,300 ⎬ 8,983	5,627
General Wayne.						5,230 ⎭	
France, war with	July 9, 1798	Sept. 30, 1800			4,593	4,593	3,216
Tripoli, Africa, war with	June 10, 1801	June 4, 1805	2,843	2,387	3,330	3,330	2,331
Northwestern Indian war, General Harrison	Sept. 11, 1811	Oct. —, 1813	250	660		910	676
Great Britain, war with, 1812	June 18, 1812	Feb. 17, 1815	85,000	471,622	20,000	576,622	286,730
Creek Indian war, Alabama	July 27, 1813	Aug. 9, 1814	600	13,181		13,781	9,048
Seminole or Florida and Georgia Indian war	Nov. 20, 1817	Oct. 31, 1818	1,000	5,911		6,911	4,643
Winnebago expedition, Wisconsin, also called La Fever Indian war (no fighting)	June —, 1827	Sept. —, 1827	900	515		1,416	1,330
Sac and Fox Indian war in Illinois	1831	1831					
Black Hawk Indian war	April 26, 1832	Sept. 21, 1832	1,339	5,126		6,465	5,900
Cherokee disturbance and removal	1833	1839		9,494		9,494	5,547
Seminole or Florida war	Dec. 23, 1835	Aug. 14, 1842	11,169	28,953		41,122	22,795
Sabine Indian disturbances, Southwestern frontier, La., Ark., and Tex. (no fighting)	April —, 1836	June —, 1836	1,323	3,106		4,429	3,365
Creek Indian disturbance in Alabama	May 5, 1836	Sept. 30, 1837	935	12,483		13,418	10,204
New York, Aroostook, and Canada (Patriot war) frontier disturbances	1838	1839		1,500		1,500	1,050
Florida war with the Seminole Indians	1842	Dec. 31, 1858					
Mexico, war with	April 24, 1846	May 30, 1848	30,954	73,776	7,500	112,230	78,718
Cayuse Indian, Oregon, Oregon volunteers	1848	1848	(¹)	1,116		1,005	1,005
Texas and New Mexico Indian war	1849	1856	1,500	1,061		2,561	4,243
Apache, Navaho, and Utah war	1849	1855	5,050	1,415			1,785
California Indian disturbance, Yuma expedition		April —, 1852	265			265	
Utah Indian disturbance	Dec. —, 1851	1853	10	530		540	540
Oregon and Washington Indian war, Rogue River, Yakima, Kilikitat, Klamath, and Salmon River	1851	Dec. 31, 1856	850	6,379		7,229	5,145
Comanche Indian war	1854			503		503	425
Seminole or Florida Indian war	Dec. 20, 1855	May 8, 1858		2,687		2,687	1,715
Rebellion, war of the (actual hostilities, however, commenced upon the firing on Fort Sumter, April 12, 1861, and ceased by the surrender of the Confederate forces under Gen. Kirby Smith, May 26, 1865)	April 15, 1861	Aug. 20, 1866	126,587	2,545,754	105,963	²2,778,304	3,212,363
Spanish-American war (actual hostilities ceased Aug. 13, 1898)	April 21, 1898	April 11, 1899	57,329	223,235	²31,959	²312,523	312,000
Philippine Islands, insurrection in	Feb. 4, 1899	July —, 1902	76,416	50,052	²13,570	²140,038	139,438
Expedition for the relief of United States legation at Peking, China	July 6, 1900	May 27, 1901	5,000	(³)	²1,913	²6,913	6,713
Occupation of Vera Cruz, Mexico	April 21, 1914	Nov. 23, 1914	6,500	(³)	3,780	10,280	10,280
War with Germany	April 6, 1917						

¹ No Regulars.   ² Officers in U. S. Marine Corps included, but not officers in U. S. Navy proper.   ³ No Volunteers.

ings: Aroostook War, Bear Flag War, Whisky Insurrection, Buckshot War, etc. The duration of the several wars and the troops engaged are shown in the table on the preceding page.

Wars of United States. (See Algerine War; Indian Wars; Mexican War; Revolutionary War; Spanish-American War; Tripolitan War; Civil War; War of 1812; European War.)

Wasco Indians. (See Indian Tribes.)

Washington, George.—1789-1797.

(FIRST TERM, 1789-1793).

First Administration—Federal.
Vice-President—John Adams.

Secretary of State—
Thomas Jefferson, from March 21, 1790.

Secretary of the Treasury—
Alexander Hamilton, from Sept. 11, 1789.

Secretary of War—
Henry Knox, from Sept. 12, 1789.

Attorney-General—
Edmund Randolph, from Sept. 26, 1789.

Postmaster-General—
Samuel Osgood, from Sept. 26, 1789.
Timothy Pickering, from Aug. 12, 1791.

The first session of the First Congress under the Constitution met in New York, April 6, 1789. Speaker of the House, F. A. Muhlenberg, of Pennsylvania.

The electoral vote was immediately counted and George Washington was found to be the unanimous choice for President. He took the oath of office April 30, and the organization of the United States government under the Constitution was begun. The first tariff bill was passed July 4. By the end of September the departments of State, War and Navy, Treasury, Post-Office and Attorney-General had been organized and the Supreme Court established.

After submitting twelve constitutional amendments to the states (ten of which were ratified, taking effect Dec. 15, 1791), Congress adjourned, and President Washington paid a visit to the northern and eastern states.

The second session of the First Congress met in New York, Jan. 4, 1790, and Washington delivered his First Annual Address (page 57). At this session Secretary Hamilton's scheme for funding the National Debt was adopted, providing (1) fund and pay the foreign debt of the Confederation ($12,000,000); (2) fund and pay the domestic debt ($40,000,000); (3) assume and pay the unpaid war debt ($21,500,000) of the states. This session also passed acts authorizing the census, the patent office and the acquisition of the District of Columbia as a permanent seat of government. Meanwhile the last of the thirteen original states had ratified the Constitution, and after amending the tariff law by increasing duties, the second session adjourned Aug. 12, 1790.

The third session of the First Congress, which met in Philadelphia, Dec. 6, 1790, passed the act incorporating the Bank of the United States, and adjourned March 3, 1791. This Congress in two years established the government on a permanent basis and provided the means to maintain it.

England further recognized the young republic by sending a minister to the capital.

The Second Congress opened at Philadelphia Oct. 24, 1791, with Jonathan Trumbull, of Connecticut, Speaker of the House. The Mint was established and an apportionment act was passed. (See Apportionment.) At the second session the President's salary was fixed at $25,000, and the electoral vote was counted, showing Washington to have received 132 (all) and John Adams 77 and George Clinton 50 as second choice.

(SECOND TERM, 1793-1797).

Second Administration—Federal.
Vice-President—John Adams.

Secretary of State—
Thomas Jefferson (continued).
Edmund Randolph, from Jan. 2, 1794.
Timothy Pickering, from Dec. 10, 1795.

Secretary of the Treasury—
Alexander Hamilton (continued).
Oliver Wolcott, from Feb. 2, 1795.

Secretary of War—
Henry Knox (continued).
Timothy Pickering, from Jan. 2, 1795.
James McHenry, from Jan. 27, 1796.

Attorney-General—
Edmund Randolph (continued).
William Bradford, from Jan. 8, 1794.
Charles Lee, from Dec. 10, 1795.

Postmaster-General—
Timothy Pickering (continued).
Joseph Habersham, from Feb. 25, 1795.

It was by perfectly natural and logical steps that Washington passed from the military leadership of the people in their struggle for independence, through the Presidency of the National Convention at Philadelphia, where months of the year 1787 were spent in framing a Constitution, to the position of first President of the United States. Speaking of Washington's eminent fitness for the office, Bancroft, in his "History of the Constitution," says: "But for him the country could not have achieved its independence; but for him it could not have formed its Union; and now but for him it could not set the Government in successful motion." The election should have been held in November, 1788; but it did not take place until the first Wednesday in January, 1789. The Constitution required that to become operative it should be ratified by nine of the thirteen states. It was not until June 21, 1788, that New Hampshire, the requisite ninth state, gave its approval; Vermont followed on the 26th of June, and New York on July 26. It was Sept. 13, 1788, before Congress passed the resolution declaring the Constitution ratified, and ordered the appointment of the electors. The interval between this date and that set for the election allowed no time for the participation of the people in the election. The electors were appointed by the legislatures of all states except that of New York, where a bitter struggle over the Constitution between the House and the Senate prevented the necessary compliance with the order, and those of North Carolina and Rhode Island, whose legislatures had not yet ratified the Constitution. There was no nomination or preparation of platform, yet when on April 6, 1789, the votes of the electors were counted in the presence of the two houses, it was found that Washington had received every vote of the ten states that had participated in the election, and that John Adams had received 34. The third highest vote was that of John Jay, who received nine.

Party Affiliation.—At no time did Washington make an avowal of party. He entered upon the duties of office with a profound veneration for the Constitution, a determination to adhere to its every pro-

EXTENT OF THE UNITED STATES DURING THE ADMINISTRATION OF PRESIDENT WASHINGTON, 1789-1797.

(NOT INCLUDING TERRITORIES)

TENNESSEE 1796

KENTUCKY 1792

GEORGIA 1788

SOUTH CAROLINA 1788

NORTH CAROLINA 1789

VIRGINIA 1788

PENNSYLVANIA 1787

NEW YORK 1788

MD. 1788

DEL 1787

N. J. 1787

VT. 1791

CONN. 1788

N. H. 1788

R. I. 1790

MASSACHUSETTS 1788

vision, and with a fixed purpose of promoting the unity of the nation. Before his election he said in a letter: "I have ever been a friend to adequate powers in Congress, without which we shall never establish a national character. . . . We are either a united people under one head and for federal purposes, or we are thirteen independent sovereignties, eternally counteracting each other." When he was consulted about the choice of a Vice-President, be expressed no preference save that he hoped it would be "a true Federalist." Even at the end of his eight years as President, after the installation of the machinery of the Government, the formulation of the policies of the country, and the application of the provisions of the Constitution to the practical duties of the administration had erected the party of which he was the head, hereafter to be known as Federalists, and that of his opponents, known for a time as Anti-Federalists—even then in his memorable Farewell Address (see page 205) he denounced party affiliation and cautioned his countrymen against its, to him, baneful effects. While he, therefore, must be regarded as the founder of a party, he, nevertheless, says: "The alternate domination of one faction over another, sharpened by the spirit of revenge natural to party dissension, which in different ages and countries has perpetrated the most horrid enormities, is itself a frightful despotism." . . . "It opens the door to foreign influence and corruption, which find a facilitated access to the Government itself through the channels of party passion."

The war between England and France had made itself felt in America through vexatious interference by both belligerents with the commerce of the United States. The French Government directed the seizure of all vessels carrying supplies to an enemy's port and Great Britain ordered her war ships to stop all vessels laden with French supplies and to turn them into British ports. War sentiment ran high in America and Washington was severely criticised for his proclamation of neutrality. These aggressions on the seas were the beginnings of a series of provocations which finally led to the second war with Great Britain in 1812. During the summer of 1793 the cornerstone of the Capitol was laid. Hamilton was the recognized leader of the Federalist party, and the followers of Jefferson began to assume the name of Republicans in opposition.

The Third Congress opened in Philadelphia Dec. 2, 1793, with F. A. Muhlenberg as Speaker of the House. Thomas Jefferson resigned from the State Department owing to his opposition to the administration, and dissensions among the Federalists themselves resulted in that party's overthrow. The Eleventh Amendment to the Constitution, securing states against suits in the United States Courts, was declared in force Jan. 8, 1798. Six ships of war were authorized—three of 44 guns and three of 38 guns. Of these the *Constitution* (44 guns), *United States* (44 guns), and the *Constellation* (38 guns) were completed. In retaliation for the English navigation acts an embargo was laid on all shipping for sixty days, and an act was passed forbidding any American vessel to supply slaves to any other nation. On account of the popular sympathy with France in her war with England it was deemed necessary to pass a neutrality law in order to avoid war with England, and John Jay was sent as envoy with a treaty. Indians in the Ohio territory, which had been giving considerable trouble, were defeated by Gen. Anthony Wayne. Stringent naturalization laws were passed at this time. Hamilton resigned his portfolio as Secretary of the Treasury in January, 1795. The Third Congress adjourned March 3, and the following summer Washington called the Senate in extra session and the Jay Treaty with England was ratified in spite of popular remonstrances against it. Treaties were also signed with the Ohio Indians, with Spain and Algiers.

The Fourth Congress met in Philadelphia Dec. 7, 1795, with Jonathan Dayton as Speaker of the House. The Jay Treaty was proclaimed March 1, 1796, and the House demanded the papers in relation thereto, and Washington refused. About this time Jefferson wrote the famous Mazzei letter (*q. v.*), which later severed the friendly letter between himself and Washington. The closing days of this session were enlivened by Fisher Ames' speech in the House on the Jay Treaty.

Political Complexion of Congress.—In the First Congress, the Senate was composed of twenty-six members, all of whom were Federalists; the House, of sixty-five members, was composed of fifty-three Federalists and twelve Democrats. In the Second Congress, the Senate was composed of seventeen Federalists and thirteen Democrats; and the House, of sixty-nine members, was made up of fifty-five Federalists and fourteen Democrats. In the second term of Washington's administration, the Third Congress was composed of a Senate of thirty-one members, of whom eighteen were Federalists and thirteen Democrats; the House, of 105 members, was made up of fifty-one Federalists and fifty-four Democrats. The Fourth Congress consisted of a Senate of thirty-two members, of whom nineteen were Federalists and thirteen Democrats; and a House of 105 members, composed of forty-six Federalists and fifty-nine Democrats.

At the third presidential election the Federals voted for John Adams and Thomas Pinckney for President and Vice-President, respectively, while the Republicans voted for Thomas Jefferson and Aaron Burr. When the votes were counted one of the great faults in the method of electing the President and Vice-President became apparent. Of the 138 votes cast for President, Adams received 71, and Jefferson, 68, and, under the Constitution, Jefferson, though a candidate for President on the opposition ticket became Vice-President. This resulted in the Twelfth Amendment to the Constitution.

Constitution.—The failure of the confederation to secure for his country that unity of government which he most desired, caused Washington great anxiety; and Shays's rebellion added greatly to his disquiet. He said in a letter to Madison, in November, 1786: "It was but the other day that we were shedding our blood to obtain the constitutions under which we now live—constitutions of our own choice and making—and now we are unsheathing the sword to overturn them." He was persuaded by his friends to head the delegation from Virginia to the convention at Philadelphia in May, 1787, and there was unanimously elected president of the convention that passed the Constitution, on Sept. 17, 1787. He immediately announced the fact to Congress by letter, in which he said: "In all our deliberations on this subject we kept steadily in our view that which appears to us the greatest interest of every true American—the consolidation of our Union—in which is involved our prosperity, felicity, safety, and, perhaps, our national existence." His firm adherence to the Constitution and his influence in interpreting it were remarked by his contemporaries. In his appointments to the several offices he acted as he himself said: "With the best intentions and fullest determination to nominate to office those persons only who, upon every consideration, were the most deserving, and who would probably execute their several functions to the interest and credit of the American Union, if such characters could be found by my exploring every avenue of information respecting their merit and pretensions that it was in my power to obtain." His regard for the Constitution seems to be epitomized in his statement in his Farewell Address (page 209): "The basis of our political system is the right of the people to make and to alter their constitutions of government. But the Constitution which at any time exists till changed by an explicit and authentic act of the whole people is sacredly obligatory on all."

Finances.—When Washington took office the finances of the country were in a deplorable state. He appointed Alexander Hamilton, of New York, Secretary of the Treasury. A loan of 3,000,000 florins (about $1,200,000) was negotiated from Holland in 1790 (see page 73), after which came Hamilton's plan for providing revenues. The first step toward the revenue was taken in the tariff bill of July 4, 1789, the preamble of which reads: "Whereas, it is necessary for the support of government, for the discharge of the debts of the United States, and the encouragement and protection of manufacturers, that duties be laid on goods, wares, and merchandise imported. Be it enacted," etc. Hamilton's plans for financing the nation and of restoring public credit involved the funding system, of which Hamilton was the originator in America, and the establishment of the Bank of the United States, the subscriptions of which were made in a single day (see page 96). Three other loans from Holland were made and are referred to by Washington with much satisfaction in his Fourth Annual Address (see page 120). The establishment of public credit was very dear to Washington. In his Second Annual Address (page 75) he expresses satisfaction at the sufficiency of the revenue provisions and adds the hope "that it will be the favorite policy with you, not merely to secure a payment of the interest of the debt funded, but as far and as fast as the growing resources of the country will permit to exonerate it of the principal itself." In his Fifth Annual Address (page 134) he says: "No pecuniary consideration is more urgent than the regular redemption and discharge of the public debt. On none can delay be more injurious or an economy of time more valuable." In his Sixth Annual Address (page 159) he again refers to this subject: "Indeed, whatsoever is unfinished in our system of public credit cannot be benefited by procrastination; and as far as may be practicable we ought to place that credit on grounds which cannot be disturbed, and to prevent that progressive accumulation of debt which must ultimately endanger all governments." His last official word on this subject is given in his Seventh Annual Address (page 177): "Congress have demonstrated their sense to be, and it were superfluous to repeat mine, that whatsoever will tend to accelerate the honorable extinction of our public debt accords as much with the true interest of our country as with the general sense of our constituents."

The attention of Congress was repeatedly called to the necessity of producing uniformity in the coins, weights, and measures of the country, to overcome the confusion resulting from the several standards in use. By the power vested in him, Washington reduced the weight of the copper cent to one pennyweight and sixteen grains, and that of the half-cent proportionately.

Public Debt.—The public debt of the United States during the years of Washington's administration stood as follows: Jan. 1, 1791, $75,463,476.52; 1792, $77,-227,924.66; 1793, $80,352,634.04; 1794, $78,427,404.77; 1795, $80,747,587.39; 1796, $83,762,172.07; 1797, $82,064,479.33.

Tariff.—The tariff act of July 4, 1789, imposed duties varying from five per cent. to ten per cent. upon iron, steel, wool, carpets, and glass; and duties of from five to twenty cents per gallon on certain liquors. An act, passed on Aug. 10, 1790, "making further provision for the payment of the debts of the United States," increased the duties upon some of the dutiable imports; and both increased and added to the duties imposed on liquors. The first case of indirect taxation in the country, other than duties on imports, was the act of March 3, 1791, "repealing after the last day of June next the duties heretofore laid upon distilled spirits imported from abroad, and laying others in their stead; and also upon spirits distilled within the United States, and for appropriating the same." The duty varied from nine to twenty-five cents a gallon according to strength; with a yearly duty of sixty cents per gallon of capacity on all stills employed. Duties on nearly all dutiable goods were slightly increased by the act of May 2, 1792, "for raising a further sum of money for the protection of the frontier, and for other purposes therein mentioned." The act of June 5, 1794, "laying certain duties upon snuff and refined sugar; also upon carriages; and retail dealers of wines, etc., were required to pay five dollars a year for license." The duty on snuff made in the country was laid at eight cents a pound; and refined sugar, two cents a pound. The act of June 7, 1794, laid additional duties on goods imported and imposed a duty upon auction sales. On March 3, 1797, an act was signed imposing stamp duties on some kinds of certificates, bills of exchange, letters patent, insurance policies, promissory notes, etc.

Opposition to the payment of excise taxes by certain distillers of western Pennsylvania necessitated sending troops to the scene of disorder, and was made the subject of three proclamations by Washington. (See Whisky Insurrection, and proclamations, pp. 116, 150 and 153.)

Commerce.—The regulation of commerce in the young republic was a task of extreme difficulty, but Washington addressed himself to the development of trade and industry with such ardor that in his Seventh Annual Address (page 176) he was able to say: "Every part of the Union displays indications of rapid and various improvement; and with burdens so light as to be scarcely perceived, with resources fully adequate to our present exigencies, with governments founded upon the general principles of rational liberty, and with mild and wholesome laws, is it too much to say that our country exhibits a spectacle of national happiness never surpassed, if ever equalled?" In Hamilton's plan for raising revenue there was included a tax on spirits. This was opposed as being a tax on a necessity, but especially because suits arising out of its imposition were triable only in Pennsylvania, thus involving great trouble and expense. The protest against the tax is known as the

Whisky Rebellion. Washington bore the defiance against that law with admirable patience and issued no fewer than three placating proclamations on the subject before resorting to force. An army of 15,-000 men was called out, but order was restored without their aid.

In the Second Annual Message (page 75) a warning is sounded for the need of better protection of American commerce by building a merchant marine, that the country be not dependent upon foreign bottoms for carrying its produce to other countries. Especial attention is called to the Mediterranean trade which was then interfered with by African pirates.

Slavery.—Washington inherited a great many slaves, and used them in his successful operations as a planter. He was, while President, the richest man in the United States. The slavery question assumed no political status in his time; but in 1786, in a letter to Mr. Morris, he said: "There is no man living who wishes more sincerely than I do to see a plan adopted for the abolition of slavery." In proof of the sincerity of this statement, all of his slaves were emancipated by his will.

Foreign Policy.—In his First Annual Message Washington (page 64) asked for provision to be made by Congress to enable him to conduct intercourse with foreign nations in a manner most conducive to public good. He adopted a firm policy of neutrality, and greatly embittered the Anti-Federalists by his refusal to aid the French revolutionists in their war against Great Britain; but consummated with the latter country the famous Jay Treaty. This spirit he embodied in his counsels that "nothing is more essential than that permanent, inveterate antipathies should be excluded and that in place of them just and amicable feelings toward all should be cultivated." His every act was regulated by the principle "that the great rule of conduct for us in regard to foreign nations is, to have in extending our commercial relations with them as little political connection as possible. Why by interweaving our destiny with that of any part of Europe entangle our peace and prosperity in the toils of European ambition, rivalship, interest, humor, or caprice?" So determined was the opposition against this policy that his famous proclamation of neutrality of April, 1793 (page 149), was denounced as "a royal edict and a daring assumption of power." Still Washington maintained this attitude even to the length of insisting upon the recall of M. Genet from America while using this country as a base and a means of making war upon Great Britain in that year. The seizure of American vessels by British cruisers fomented this opposition and Washington's act in closing the Jay Treaty exposed him to the severest censure.

Army.—Washington in his First Annual Address (page 57) urged attention to Army organization with the statement: "To be prepared for war is one of the most effectual means of preserving peace." He advocated the arming and disciplining of the people, the manufacture of military supplies, and the establishment of troops. In a special message (page 52) he had already advised that the experience and training of the "well-instructed officers and soldiers of the late Army be utilized in the development of an efficient militia." This experience he speaks of as a "resource which is daily diminishing by death and other causes. To suffer this peculiar advantage to pass away unimproved would be to neglect an opportunity which will never again occur, unless, unfortunately, we should again be involved in a long and arduous war." In his Eighth Annual Address (page 194) he urges the institution of a military academy, and adds: "However pacific the general policy of a nation may be, it ought never to be without an adequate stock of military knowledge for emergencies. The art of war is at once comprehensive and complicated, it demands much previous study, and the possession of it in its most improved and perfect state is always of great moment to the security of a nation."

Education.—In his First Annual Address (page 58) Washington urges upon Congress the necessity of making provision for the promotion of science and literature. "Knowledge," he says, "is in every country the surest basis of public happiness." He suggests efficient patronage either by aiding seminaries already established or by the institution of a national university. In his Eighth Annual Address (page 194) he says: "True it is that our country, much to its honor, contains many seminaries of learning highly respectable and useful; but the funds upon which they rest are too narrow to command the ablest professors in the different departments of liberal knowledge for the institution contemplated, though they would be excellent auxiliaries." He lays particular stress upon the "education of youth in the science of government."

Veto Messages.—In the eight years of his administration Washington issued only two veto messages. The first on April 5, 1792 (page 116), refused sanction to an act regulating the apportionment of Representatives in the several states because it was contrary to the provisions of the Constitution. The second veto message was the last message sent by Washington to Congress. It refused sanction to an act amending the military establishment because of its unfairness and injustice to the bodies of troops which it might affect (page 203).

Indian Affairs.—Washington's remarkable patience and good judgment were fully displayed in his treatment of the Indians in the uprisings that occurred among the Creeks, Wabash, Five Nations, Senecas, and Six Nations. In a special message upon treaties with the Indians (page 59) he maintains that a "due regard should be extended to these Indians whose happiness in the course of events so materially depends upon the national justice and humanity of the United States." Again (page 61), he declares that it is "important that all treaties and compacts formed by the United States with other nations, whether civilized or not, should be made with caution and executed with fidelity."

Washington, George:

Washington.—One of the Pacific coast states—nickname, "Chinook State." It extends from lat. 45° 40′ to 49° north, and from long. 117° to 124° 44′ west. It is bounded on the north by the Strait of San Juan de Fuca and British Columbia, on the east by Idaho, on the south by Oregon (partly separated by the Columbia River), and on the west by the Pacific Ocean. Area, 69,127 square miles. The Cascade Range traverses the State from north to south, west of the center. There are extensive forests, particularly in the western part, and the eastern portion produces large quantities of wheat. Gold and silver are also found in paying quantities. Salmon fishing and shipbuilding are important industries.

The country was visited as early as 1592. The mouth of the Columbia River was explored in 1792 by Captain Gray, and further explorations were conducted by Lewis and Clark in 1805. John Jacob Astor founded a trading post at the mouth of the Columbia River in 1811. The State was formed from part of the Oregon region, which was claimed by both England and America for many years. It was organized as a Territory by an act of Congress passed March 2, 1853, and admitted to the Union Nov. 11, 1889 (5460).

The arid region east of the Cascade Mountains requires irrigation for the production of full crops. During 1904, 178,000 were included in irrigation systems, and the Federal reclamation act (q. v.) provides for further irrigation as the lands are sold.

The Mount Rainier, Olympic, Washington, Wenaha, and Priest Forest Reserves have a combined area of 12,162 square miles. The total timber area is put at 34,000 square miles. The cut of the Washington lumber mills in one year was more than four billion feet, and the shipments by sea more than a billion feet. The trees are mostly fir, cedar and spruce.

Statistics of agriculture collected for the last Federal census, place the number of farms in the State at 56,192, comprising 11,712,235 acres, valued, with stock and improvements, at $637,543,411. The average value of land per acre was $44.13, against $11.68 in 1900. The value of domestic animals, poultry, etc., was $48,865,110, including 402,120 cattle, valued at $12,193,465; 280,572 horses, $29,680,849; 12,185 mules, $1,776,297; 266,135 swine, $1,674,927; 475,555 sheep, $1,931,170; poultry, $1,367,440. The yield and value of the field crops for 1911 was: Corn, 30,000 acres, 855,000 bushels, $675,000; wheat, 2,230,000 acres, 50,661,000 bushels, $35,969,000; oats, 281,000 acres, 14,528,000 bushels, $6,538,000; rye, 8,000 acres, 176,000 bushels, $141,000; potatoes, 59,000 acres, 9,440,000 bushels, $6,419,000; hay, 400,000 acres, 960,000 tons, $11,520,000.

The principal industry of the State is lumber and timber, with a capital of $40,953,816, employing 28,023 wage-earners, and turning out $49,572,512 worth of finished product from $16,325,594 raw material. The flour and feed industry is next in importance, with a capital of $6,490,492, using $12,771,390 worth of raw material, which 613 wage-earners convert into finished product valued at $14,663,612. The fisheries of the State employ nearly 3,000 boats and 4,954 persons. The value of the annual catch is $1,161,669. The State revenues for the biennial period ending Sept. 30, 1910, were $13,381,687; expenditures, $12,944,263. The bonded debt is $1,006,024. The tax rate is $31 per $1,000, and the assessed valuation is $789,912,979.

The State oyster bed reserves cover 13,683,000 acres, and salmon and many other fish are abundant.

Coal worth $7,679,801 was mined in 1907, of gold 12,689 fine ounces, silver 84,000 fine ounces, and 122,263 pounds of copper.

The industrial census of 1905 returned 2,751 manufacturing establishments, with a capital of $96,952,621, employing 48,858 persons in converting $69,166,165 worth of raw material into finished goods to the value of $128,821,667, consisting of lumber, flour, meats, fish, machinery and dairy products. There were in 1907 2,950 miles of steam railway and 330 miles of electric line. The population in 1910 was 1,141,990.

The number of manufacturing establishments in Washington having an annual output valued at $500 or more at the beginning of 1915 was 3,830. The amount of capital invested was $277,717,000, giving occupation to 78,387 persons, using material valued at $136,609,000, and turning out finished goods worth $245,327,000. Salaries and wages paid amounted to $63,207,000.

(See also "Fifty-four Forty or Fight"; Northwestern Boundary; Oregon.)

Indemnity to, recommended, 5219.
Appropriation for, 5367.
Troops sent to protect, 4933.
Geological survey of, referred to, 3016.
Indians in—
Agreement with, for relinquishment of lands, 4781.
Depredations of, referred to, 2873, 2894, 2896, 2900, 2911, 2916, 2941.
Referred to, 3015, 3016.
Lands in, set apart as public reservation by proclamation, 5810, 6209, 6215, 6218, 6219.
Light-house on coast of, point to be selected for, 3902.
Martial law in, proclamation of governor referred to, 2776.
Possessory claims in, convention with Great Britain regarding, 3380.
Unlawful combinations in, proclamations against, 4896, 5073, 5932.
Washington, The, seizure of, by British authorities, referred to, 4114.

Washington City.—The capital of the United States. It is situated in the District of Columbia, on the Potomac River, at the head of navigation, in latitude 38° 53′ N. and longitude 77° 1′ W. The site for the capital was chosen in 1790 and the seat of government was established at Washington in 1800. Washington is one of the best planned cities in the world; in addition to the usual rectangular arrangements of streets it has a number of fine wide avenues radiating in all directions from both the Capitol and the White House. At their intersections are circles laid out as small parks and most are lined with pleasant shade trees. It contains the principal public buildings in which the business of the Government is transacted.

Besides the Capitol (*q. v.*) the city contains the official residence of the President, buildings devoted to the various Departments of Government, the Congressional Library, the Smithsonian Institution, National Museum, Naval Observatory, Corcoran Art Gallery, National Soldiers' Home, Washington Monument, and many other objects of national interest. The White House, or Presidential residence, was first occupied by John Adams in 1800. The public buildings were burned by the British in 1814, and more imposing ones erected subsequently. (See also District of Columbia and Capital of United States.) Population (1910), 278,718, of which 191,532 were white and the residue colored people.

Washington City (see also District of Columbia):
Act transferring duties of trustees of colored schools in Georgetown and, vetoed, 3903.
Bridge across Potomac River at. (See District of Columbia.)
Buildings in—
Commission of inquiry relative to, referred to, 2012.
Erection of, proclamation regarding, 312.

34

On three sides of Lafayette Square, recommended, 4578.
Referred to, 356, 1911, 1957.
British invasion of, referred to in proclamation, 530.
Centennial anniversary of founding of, for capital to be held in 1900, 6347, 6404, 6456.
Conference in, of representatives of Canada and United States regarding commercial exchanges, 5675, 5678, 5748.
Conspiracy to prevent inauguration of President-elect in, referred to, 3200.
Defense of, clerks in Departments in, to be organized into companies for, 3323, 3642.
Erection of buildings in, proclamation concerning, 312.
Grand Army of Republic—
Appropriation for reception and entertainment of, in, recommended, 5672.
Order permitting members of, employed in public service to participate in parade of, 5740.
Parade of, discussed, 5763.
Improvement of Potomac flats and river front of, recommended, 4458, 4532, 4579, 4651.
Bill for, submitted, 4533.
Improvements in, recommended, 831, 909, 2710, 2837.
Insane asylum in. (See Government Hospital for Insane.)
International American Conference at, 5369, 5467.
Centennial celebration of discovery of America, resolution regarding, 5512.
Discussed, 5542.
Extradition, reports on subject of, adopted by, 5514.
Importations and exportations, recommendations of, regarding, 5506.
Intercontinental railroad, survey of route for, recommended by, 5504.
International American bank, establishment of, recommended by, 5505.
Discussed, 5560.
International American monetary union, establishment of, recommended by, 5513.
International arbitration, reports on, adopted by, 5518.
Referred to, 5623, 5874.
International bureau of information, establishment of, at, recommended by, 5506.

International law, adoption of uniform code of, recommended by, 5513.

Latin-American library, establishment of, recommended by, 5506.

Memorial tablet in State Department to commemorate meeting of, recommended by, 5514.

Patents, trade-marks, and copyrights, report of, concerning protection of, 5512.

Port dues and consular fees, recommendations of, regarding uniform system of, 5514.

Postal and cable communication, establishment of improved facilities for, recommended by, 5511.

Public health, recommendations of, for protection of, 5513.

Reciprocal commercial treaties recommended by, 5509.

Steamship service, establishment of rapid, recommended by, 5491, 5511.

Weights and measures, report of, on, 5513.

International Marine Conference at, discussed, 5180, 5370, 5468, 5493, 5498, 5543.

International Peace Congress at, discussed, 4684, 4717.

Invitation to countries of North and South America to attend, 4685.

Postponement of, referred to, 4717.

International Sanitary Conference at, discussed, 4564, 4622, 4631.

Jail erected in, 343.

Necessity for new one, 1621.

Justices of the peace in, referred to, 3800.

Loan from Maryland, payment of, guaranteed by United States, 321.

Lots in, chargeable with, 321.

Referred to, 833.

Resales of lots for deficiency in, 343.

Lots in, sale of, referred to, 833, 1838.

Monetary union International American establishment of, recommended by, and discussed, 5513.

Officers of, salary of, 343.

Pennsylvania Avenue in—

Bill for paving, vetoed, 4341.

Improvement of, referred to, 1844.

Macadamizing of, referred to, 2015.

Repavement of, referred to, 4368, 4432, 4587.

Police system for, recommended. (See District of Columbia.)

Post-office building in, erection of, recommended, 5363.

Postal Congress to be held in, discussed, recommendation regarding, 6164.

Protection for, recommendations regarding, 3323, 3642.

Public schools in. (See District of Columbia.)

Public works in, appointment of commissioners to investigate, referred to, 1904.

Recommendation for the erection of buildings on three sides of Lafayette Square, 4578.

Referred to, 253, 285, 295, 298.

Reservations in, appropriation for removing snow and ice from, recommended, 4739.

Seat of Government—

Boundaries of, referred to and proclaimed, 86, 192, 194.

Removed from Philadelphia to, 281, 295, 298, 299, 300.

Steam railway lines—

Construction of certain, urged by authorities of, 3351.

Controversies regarding occupation of streets by, discussed and referred to, 4950, 5114, 5385.

Recommendations regarding location of depots and tracks, 4459, 4579, 4651.

Street railroad companies in, report of board on amount chargeable to, referred to, 4273.

Streets in—

Bill for paving, vetoed, 4341.

Improvement of, referred to, 2015.

Macadamizing of, 2015.

Superintendent of, salary of, discussed, 343.

Surveyor of—

Report of, referred to, 356.

Salary of, discussed, 343.

Troops assembled in, by order of President Buchanan, discussed, 3200.

Water supply for, discussed, 2628, 2698, 2710, 2725, 2750, 4579, 4651, 4773.

Opinion of Judge Brewer in Great Falls land case, referred to, 3072.

Plan to take, from Great Falls of Potomac, approved, 2750.

Washington City Canal, improvement of, referred to, 3579.

Washington City (D. C.), Capture of.—
After the flight of the Americans from the field of Bladensburg Aug. 24, 1814, the British army advanced to the plain between the present Congressional Cemetery and the Capitol. Cockburn and Ross, with 200 men, rode into the city in the evening to destroy the public buildings. The unfinished Capitol, containing the Library of Congress, was fired. The President's house, the Treasury building, the arsenal, and barracks for 3,000 men were next burned. In a few hours nothing but the blackened walls remained of the public buildings, the Patent Office

alone having been spared. Only such private property as was owned or occupied by persons offensive to the British was destroyed. The President and his chief advisers fled to different points in Virginia and Maryland.

Mrs. Madison, the wife of the President, when advised of the defeat at Bladensburg, sent away the silver plate and other valuables from the Presidential mansion and at great personal risk saved from destruction the full-length portrait of Gen. Washington by Gilbert Stuart, which now adorns the Blue Room of the White House. With her sister and brother-in-law she was then conveyed to a place of safety beyond the Potomac. Commodore Tingey, in command of the navy-yard, burned the property under his control to prevent its falling into the hands of the British. The bridge over the Potomac was also destroyed. The total value of property destroyed by British and Americans in Washington was estimated at $2,000,000. On the night of the 25th Ross and Cockburn withdrew from Washington.

Washington Headquarters Association. —The purpose of this Association is to preserve the old mansion on 160th Street, near Amsterdam Avenue, New York City, which was at one time, in the War of the Revolution, the headquarters of Washington. The property is owned by the city and is under the care and direction of the Knickerbocker, Mary Washington, Colonial and Manhattan Chapters of the Daughters of the American Revolution. It is open daily to the public.

Washington Monument. — An obelisk-shaped tower of white marble erected at Washington, D. C., in honor of George Washington. The cornerstone was laid July 4, 1848, but soon the work languished and then stopped entirely. Work was resumed in 1876, and the monument was finally completed Dec. 6, 1884. It is 555 feet high and fifty-five feet square at its base. The interior walls are built of granite and contain many memorial stones from foreign nations. The entire cost of the monument was $1,187,710.
See photograph of, and appreciation, frontispiece, Vol. XVIII.

Washington Monument:
Construction of, discussed and recommendations regarding, 4430, 4532, 4579.
Dedication of, Government employees to participate in, 4879.

Washington, Treaty of.—Many treaties have been negotiated at Washington, but the one usually referred to as the treaty of Washington was negotiated between the United States and Great Britain at that city in 1871. After thirty-four meetings commissioners of the United States and England concluded a treaty between the two countries to settle pending questions. It was ratified June 17, 1871, and proclaimed to be in force July 4.

To adjust the Alabama claims it was agreed to submit them to a tribunal of arbitration, to meet at Geneva, Switzerland, and to consist of members appointed by each of the parties and by three neutral nations. Concerning the difficulties with regard to the fishing privileges of the United States vessels on the coast of British America, the treaty adjusted the differences on the basis of the reciprocity treaty of 1854, giving to persons of each nation the right of fishing on the coasts of the other. There was a mutual concession of privileges, such as that of transportation from one place to another in one country across the territory of the other without the payment of duties. Lake Michigan, the lower course of the St. Lawrence, and certain rivers in Alaska were opened to the people of both nations. It was also agreed to submit the disputed boundary line between the British possessions and the State of Washington to the arbitration of the German emperor, who, on Oct. 21, 1872, rendered a decision awarding the island of San Juan and the group of which it forms a part to the United States. (See also Alabama Claims; Geneva Tribunal.)

Washington, Treaties of. (See also Alabama Claims; Ashburton Treaty):
Of July 4, 1850, referred to, 2760.
Of May 8, 1871—
Powers to be invited to accede to rules of neutrality in, 4462.
Proclamations regarding, 4179, 4227.
Report regarding, 4086.
Referred to, 3588.

Washington Turnpike Road Co., act authorizing subscription of stock in, vetoed, 1056.

Washington's Farewell Address to be read to Army, orders regarding, 3306.

Washita River, exploration of, 387.

Wasp, The.— An American warship of eighteen guns, built at Washington in 1806. Oct. 13, 1812, the *Wasp* left the Delaware for the West Indies, under Capt. Jacob Jones, with 137 men. Five days later she fell in with six merchantmen under convoy of the British brig *Frolic*, eighteen guns and 110 men. The *Wasp* attacked, and in less than an hour the *Frolic* struck her colors after a loss of 90 men. The fight was in a heavy sea. Within two hours the *Wasp* and its prize were captured by the British frigate *Poictiers*, seventy-four guns, and the Americans were sent to Bermuda as prisoners. In 1814 the United States built a naval vessel at Newburyport and christened it the *Wasp*. It was a ship-rigged sloop of war and carried twenty-two guns and 160 men. Leaving Portsmouth May 1, 1814, under Capt. Johnson Blakely, she ran into the English Channel to look for British merchantmen. June 28 she encountered the British sloop *Reindeer*, eighteen guns and 118 men. In less than half an hour of fierce fighting the *Reindeer* struck her colors, having sustained a loss of 25 killed and 42 wounded. The American loss was 27 in all. Sept. 1, after a fight of about two hours, the *Wasp* captured the British brig *Avon*, eighteen guns. Oct. 9, in lat. 18° 35' north, long, 30° 10' west, she spoke and boarded the Swedish brig *Adams* and took off Lieut. McKnight and a master's mate of the United States ship *Essex*, on their way from Brazil to England. The *Wasp* was never heard from again.

Wasp, The:
Engagement of, with the *Frolic*, 506.
Mentioned, 6318.
Refused permission to enter ports of Paraguay by Brazilian blockade commander, 3883.

Watch-Dog.—A term of praise applied to a legislator who opposes extravagant appropriations,—usually termed "Watch-Dog of the Treasury."

"Watchful Waiting."—A term used by President Wilson with reference to our attitude in the Mexican question in his administration, 7908.

Water-Dog.—A pet name, or term of endearment, applied to sailors and other persons long experienced in life on the water.

Water Rights, policy of the Federal Government in imposing conditions in granting, 7723.

Water Supply. (See Irrigation.)

Water Witch, The, fired upon by Paraguayan fort, 2980.

Commissioner sent to demand compensation, 3050.

Demands of, acceded to, 3091.

Discussed, 3195.

Naval force sent to Paraguay, 3050.

Watervliet Arsenal, N. Y., gun factory to be established at, 5374.

Wautauga Association.—June 2, 1769, a company of North Carolina hunters formed an organization to settle the territory to the west of the Cumberland Mountains, which had been opened by the treaty of Fort Stanwix in the previous year. Their settlements were on the Wautauga, one of the tributaries of the Tennessee River, within the limits of what is now the State of Tennessee. The settlers framed a code of laws, which was signed by each of them, and the body politic thus formed was called the Wautauga Association. The tyranny of Governor Tryon, of North Carolina, caused many of the independent-spirited settlers of that Colony to cast their lot with the Wautauga Association. In 1784, at a convention held in Jonesboro, a separate state government was organized under the name of Franklin. (See also Franklin.)

Waxhaw (S. C.) Massacre.—After the capture of Charlestown, Sir Henry Clinton sent a detachment of 300 men under Col. Tarleton to disperse Col. Buford's command of 380 men, who, hearing of the fall of Charleston, had retired to a point near the North Carolina line. May 29, 1780, Tarleton, having overtaken Buford at the Waxhaw River, made a furious charge, while the Americans were awaiting flags of conference, believing hostilities suspended. Many of the Americans threw down their arms and begged for quarter; 113 were killed on the spot, 150 so badly wounded that it was impossible to move them, and only 53 were taken prisoners. Col. Buford and about 100 infantry and a few horses escaped. The British lost but 5 killed and 15 wounded.

Wea Indians. (See Indian Tribes.)

Weather Bureau.—Since 1870 the Federal Government has maintained a service having for its object the forecasting of weather conditions throughout the United States. Although originally designed for the benefit of navigation alone, an ever-broadening recognition of the practical utility of such a service has necessitated its continued extension in the interest of both agriculture and commerce. During the first twenty years of its development the work was conducted by the Signal Corps of the Army, under the direction and control of the War Department, but the demand for a strictly scientific bureau, unhampered by regulations of a military character, resulted in a re-organization of the service in 1891, and the establishment of the present Weather Bureau as a branch of the Department of Agriculture.

In the act providing for this re-organization, approved Oct. 1, 1890, the functions of the Bureau are thus summarized: "The Chief of the Weather Bureau, under the direction of the Secretary of Agriculture, shall have charge of forecasting the weather; the issue of storm warnings; the display of weather and flood signals for the benefit of agriculture, commerce, and navigation; the gaging and reporting of rivers; the maintenance and operation of seacoast telegraph lines, and the collection and transmission of marine intelligence for the benefit of commerce and navigation; the reporting of temperature and rainfall conditions for the cotton interests; the display of frost, cold-wave, and other signals; the distribution of meteorological information in the interest of agriculture and commerce, and the taking of such meteorological observations as may be necessary to establish and record the climatic conditions of the United States, or are essential for the proper execution of the foregoing duties."

Observations and Forecasts.—To the general public the Weather Bureau is probably best known through the medium of its daily forecasts and weather maps. These forecasts are based upon simultaneous observations of local weather conditions taken daily at 8 a. m. and 8 p. m. seventy-fifth meridian time, at about 200 regular observing stations scattered throughout the United States and the West Indies, and upon similar reports received daily from various points in other parts of the Northern Hemisphere. Each of the Weather Bureau stations is operated by one or more trained observers, and is equipped with mercurial barometers, thermometers, wind vanes, rain and snow gauges, and anemometers, and many of them with sunshine recorders, barographs, thermographs, and other devices which make a continuous automatic record of the local weather conditions and changes. The results of the twice-daily observations are immediately telegraphed to the central office at Washington, D. C., where they are charted for study and interpretation by experts trained to forecast the weather conditions that may be expected to prevail during the following thirty-six to forty-eight hours.

A complete telegraphic report includes the following data: Temperature, pressure (reduced to sea level), precipitation, direction of wind, state of weather, current wind velocity, maximum or minimum temperature since last observation, and kind and amount of clouds, with the direction of their movement. From these data the forecaster, by comparison with preceding reports, is able to trace the paths of storm areas from the time of their appearance to the moment of observation, and approximately determine and forecast their subsequent courses and the occurrence of other weather conditions.

Weather services similar to that of the United States are maintained by the Canadian and Mexican governments, and, by a system of interchange, daily reports are received from a number of stations in those countries. Daily observations are also received from the Azores, Iceland, the Faroe Islands, Great Britain, Germany, France, Portugal, European and Asiatic Russia, the Philippines, Hawaii, and Alaska, so that the field represented by the daily reports extends over practically the entire Northern Hemisphere.

The system for the collection and distribution of telegraphic reports of observations is so arranged that all of the principal stations in the United States receive 8 a. m. reports from a sufficient number of other stations to represent the general weather conditions over a considerable portion of the country.

Forecast centers are also established at Chicago, Ill.; New Orleans, La.; Denver, Colo.; San Francisco, Calif., and Portland, Ore. At the first three, morning forecasts only are prepared and distributed; at the last two both morning and evening forecasts. The Chicago district comprises the upper Mississippi Valley and the Northwest; the New Orleans district, Louisiana, Texas, Arkansas, and Oklahoma; the Denver district, Utah, Colorado, New Mexico, and Arizona; the San Francisco district, California and Nevada; and the Portland district, Washington, Oregon and Idaho. Forecasts are issued at Washington, D. C., for all portions of the United States not included in the aforementioned districts.

Distribution of Forecasts.—Within two hours after the morning observations have been taken the forecasts are telegraphed from the forecast centers to more than 2,300 principal distributing points, whence they are further disseminated by telegraph, telephone and mail. The forecasts reach nearly 135,000 addresses daily by mail, the greater part being delivered early in the day, and none later, as a rule, than 6 o'clock p. m. of the day of issue, and more than 3,500,000 telephone subscribers, mainly in the rural districts, receive the forecasts by telephone within an hour of the time the prediction is made. This system of forecast distribution is wholly under the supervision and at the expense of the Government, and is in addition to and distinct from the distribution effected through the press associations and the daily newspapers. The rural free mail delivery system and rural telephone lines afford means of bringing within the benefits of this system a large number of farming communities which before it was impracticable to reach with the daily forecasts. The independent rural telephone lines are being utilized to their fullest extent and this plan of distribution has been enlarged to cover the entire telephone service of many states.

The Weather Map.—The weather map is mailed immediately after the morning forecast is telegraphed. On this map the salient features of current weather conditions throughout the country are graphically represented, accompanied by a synopsis of these conditions, in addition to which complete reports from all the observing stations are presented in tabulated form. In order that all sections of the country may receive weather data, maps or bulletins containing the data in tabulated form are issued from about one hundred of the larger stations. The maps issued at Washington and other forecast centers contain detailed forecasts for the respective forecast districts, while other station maps and bulletins contain forecasts only for the localities in which they are distributed.

Climatological Service.—Although the 200 regular observing stations, each representing about 21,000 square miles of territory, furnish sufficient data upon which to base the various forecasts, observations at many intermediate points are necessary before the climatology of the United States can be properly studied. This need has given rise to the establishment of an important and interesting feature of the Weather Bureau in its Climatological Service, which is divided into forty-four local sections, each section, as a rule, covering a single state, and having for its center a regular observ-

ing station. These centers collect temperature and rainfall observations from more than 3,600 co-operative stations. During the crop-growing season (from April to September, inclusive) each section also receives weekly mail reports of weather conditions from numerous correspondents. During the same season the Central Office at Washington issues weekly a National Weather Bulletin, containing a series of charts graphically illustrating current and normal conditions of temperature and rainfall for the entire country, and a general summary of the weather for each state. There is issued at the Central Office every Tuesday during the winter a publication entitled *Snow and Ice Bulletin*, which shows the area covered by snow, the depth of snow and the thickness of ice in rivers, etc., as indicated by a large number of reports of observations made on the afternoon of the day preceding the issue of the Bulletin. This publication is of especial value to those interested in the winter wheat crop, to ice dealers, and to the manufacturers of rubber goods and all other articles the sale of which is largely affected by the presence or absence of snow and ice. During the growing season in the cotton, corn, wheat, sugar and rice-producing sections, designated centers receive telegraphic reports of rainfall and daily extremes of temperature for publication in bulletin form, each local center receiving the reports from all others.

Special Publications.—By the assistance of several thousand co-operative observers, many of whom have maintained local records for long periods, the Weather Bureau endeavors to collect special local data and thus perfect the records that are needed for the study of the relations between climate and agriculture, forestry, water resources, and other kindred subjects.

In the utilization of these meteorological data the Weather Bureau employs a staff of officials of high scientific ability who are not only engaged in the practical work already mentioned, but are also occupied in the elaboration of those fundamental principles which must necessarily play an important part in the development of meteorology and its kindred sciences. The results of these investigations are presented to the public through regular and special reports.

Among the publications of the Weather Bureau the following are worthy of special notice:

(a) *The Monthly Weather Review,* which has been published regularly since January, 1873. It contains elaborate meteorological tables and charts showing the weather conditions for the month over the United States and neighboring countries. The tables contain the details of observations made at the regular and co-operative stations of the Weather Bureau. The arrangement of the material, however, as well as the discussion of the meteorological data is according to the natural drainage areas of the country, instead of by states.

(b) *The Bulletin of the Mount Weather Research Observatory,* a publication devoted to the discussion of the scientific investigations of atmospheric phenomena, especially to those that are being carried on at the research station located at Mount Weather.

(c) A vast amount of climatological data is being prepared in a series of separates, each treating of the principal climatic features of a limited area, the complete set—106 in all—to cover the entire United States. Besides the general discussion and climatological tables, these reports will contain valuable notes furnished by the Geological Survey concerning the water power of the districts under consideration.

(d) The bulletins, published occasionally and now numbering about sixty, that contain the larger reports made by the experts of the service.

The Library of the Weather Bureau contains about 28,000 books and pamphlets, consisting principally of technical books on meteorology and allied sciences and of published climatological data from all parts of the world. It is available to all Weather Bureau officials and to students of meteorology generally, who either consult it personally or through correspondence. In addition to its general card catalogue it keeps up to date a catalogue of the meteorological contents of the principal scientific serials of the world.

The annual report of the Chief of the Bureau presents a full summary of climatic data for the United States.

Instruments and Apparatus.—The apparatus used at Weather Bureau stations for recording weather conditions is largely the result of improvements devised by the Instrument Division, to which is intrusted the care of all standards. The kites, meteorographs, self-registering instruments, and other forms of apparatus devised by the Weather Bureau are favorably known throughout the world.

The United States Government does not manufacture the instruments and apparatus employed in its meteorological work. These, in general, are purchased under formal annual contracts with responsible manufacturers, from whom instruments and apparatus of the standard Weather Bureau patterns may be procured by private parties.

Forecasts and Warnings.—The extent to which the work of the Weather Bureau affects the daily life of the people and becomes a factor in their vocations and business enterprises, already very great, is increasing yearly. Of the warnings mentioned those of storms and hurricanes, issued for the benefit of marine interests, are the most valuable.

Storm warnings are displayed at nearly 300 points along the Atlantic, Pacific, and Gulf coasts and the shores of the Great Lakes, including every port and harbor of any considerable importance, and so nearly perfect has this service become that scarcely a storm of marked danger to maritime interests has occurred for years for which ample warnings have not been issued from twelve to twenty-four hours in advance. The reports from the West Indies are especially valuable in this connection, as they enable the Bureau to forecast with great accuracy the approach of those destructive hurricanes which, during the period from July to October, are liable to sweep the Gulf and Atlantic coasts. The sailings of the immense number of vessels engaged in our ocean and lake traffic are largely determined by these warnings, and those displayed for a single hurricane are known to have detained in port on our Atlantic coast vessels valued with their cargoes at more than $30,000,000.

The warnings of those sudden and destructive temperature changes known as cold waves are probably next in importance. These warnings, which are issued from twenty-four to thirty-six hours in advance, are disseminated throughout the threatened regions by means of flags displayed at regular Weather Bureau and sub-display stations, by telegraph, telephone and mail service to all places receiving the daily forecasts and to a large number of special addresses in addition. The warnings issued for a single cold wave of exceptional severity

and extent resulted in saving more than $3,500,000 through the protection of property from injury or destruction.

The warnings of frosts and freezing weather are also of immense value, particularly to the fruit, sugar, tobacco, cranberry, and market gardening interests. The early truck-raising industry, so extensively carried on in the regions bordering on the Gulf and South Atlantic coasts and in Florida, and which has increased so greatly in the last few years is largely dependent for its success on the co-operation of the Weather Bureau in this particular, and the growers of oranges and other fruits in Florida and California have also received great benefit therefrom. The value of the orange bloom, vegetables and strawberries protected and saved on a single night in a limited district in Florida through the instrumentality of warnings of freezing weather sent out by the Bureau was reported at over $100,000.

The commerce of our rivers is greatly aided, and lives and property in regions subject to overflow are protected, by the publication of the river stages and the issue of river and flood forecasts based on reports received from about 500 special river and rainfall stations. On one occasion live stock and other movable property to the estimated value of about $15,000,000 were removed from regions in the lower Mississippi Valley that were afterward inundated, as a result of warnings issued by the Bureau a week in advance of the flood.

The value of the service was even more strongly emphasized during another great flood from March to June in the Mississippi watershed. The flood in the upper Mississippi watershed was one of the greatest in its history, while in many portions of the lower watershed the stages were the highest ever known. Yet, notwithstanding the enormous volumes of water the forecasts and warnings were accurately verified, both as to location, stage and date. Warnings were issued from four days to three weeks in advance and in no single instance did the stage that was forecast differ from that actually recorded by more than four-tenths of a foot. The average difference was about two-tenths of a foot. The value of property saved by the Weather Bureau warnings could not be accurately computed, but probably exceeded that mentioned in the preceding paragraph.

Special Benefits Derived from Reports and Warnings.—While the value of the Bureau's reports and warnings to many interests is so obvious as scarcely to need more than the brief mention already given, there are numerous special applications of the information to individual pursuits and industries that might not be suspected. An account of some of these might lead to an increased use of the data in quarters where the possibility of their application has not yet been recognized, and additional detail of the manner in which the information is utilized in a number of enterprises will doubtless be found of interest.

The railway and transportation companies make continued use of the forecasts in all of their shipments. Perishable products are protected against temperature extremes by icing or heating, as conditions may require.

The uses made of temperature forecasts in the cities are more varied than is generally supposed. With notice of an approaching cold wave greenhouses are closed and boilers fired. Fire plugs, exposed water mains, and general plumbing are protected; large stock yards drain their mains; gasoline engines are drained; work in concrete is stopped; merchants curtail advertisements or direct attention largely to cold weather articles; coal dealers supply partial orders to all customers instead of full orders to a few.

In the agricultural districts the frost and cold wave warnings are invaluable to the trucker and fruit grower, especially in the spring, when tender vegetables are protected by coverings of paper, cloth or soil.

Marine Service.—Meteorological information pertaining to the oceans is collected from about 2,000 co-operative observers on vessels of war and commerce and other sailing craft. Many vessels equipped with wireless telegraph send messages twice daily to the stations at San Francisco, Cal., and Portland, Ore., for use in the forecast work at those points. The data thus obtained are platted on daily synoptic charts for the use of the Hydrographic Office, of the Navy. Eight stations are maintained on the ocean coasts for vessel reporting and the announcement of wrecks, marine disasters and other casualties. In one year these stations reported the passing of more than 30,000 vessels.

Employees.—The conduct of the regular observation stations outside of Washington requires the constant services of about 530, and the business of the central office in Washington of about 185 employees. The annual disbursements of the Bureau amount to about $1,600,000. Original appointments are to the lowest grades, and upon certification by the Federal Civil Service Commission; promotion depends upon ability. Applicants for positions should communicate with the Civil Service Commission at Washington.

Weather Bureau:
Discussed, 5979, 6171, 6347.

Establishment of, in Department of Agriculture, recommended, 5487.

Weather-Map.—A map issued by the Weather Bureau forecasting weather conditions by such indications as wind, temperature and other elemental phenomena. (See Weather Bureau.)

Web-Foot Country.—A nickname for Oregon (q. v.). (See also States); sometimes also nicknamed Beaver State and Sunset State.

Webster-Hayne Debate.—A debate in the Senate in 1830 between Daniel Webster and Robert Y. Hayne on Constitutional interpretation.

Weehawken, The, engagement of, with the *Fingal*, referred to, 3392.

Weeks Law. (See Forest Reservations.)

Weighers and Gaugers, compensation of, referred to, 2723.

Weights and Measures:
International bureau of, establishment of, referred to, 4437.

International commission upon, at Paris, 4560.

International movement for reform of system of, referred to, 3592.

Obligatory use of metric system of, referred to, 4408.

Referred to, 166.

Report of International American Conference on, referred to, 5513.

Set of, for each State, 1477.

Uniformity of, necessity for, 58, 60, 75, 100, 561, 879.

Weldon Railroad (Va.), Seizure and Destruction of.—June 21, 1864, during Grant's operations against Petersburg and Richmond, an attempt was made to capture the Petersburg and Weldon Railroad, an important supply line for the Confederate army. The Second and Sixth Corps, under Generals Birney and Wright, cut the telegraph wires three miles south of Petersburg, but were repulsed with a loss of seven guns and many prisoners. Another and successful effort was made on Aug. 18, 1864. Lee had drawn heavily from his forces in Petersburg to resist a threatened attack on the north side of Richmond. The Fifth Army Corps, under Gen. Warren, moved from its position at the extreme left of Grant's army and struck the railroad four miles below Petersburg. Mahone's division of Lee's army tried to force Warren back, but he held his position, with a loss, after three days' fighting, of 4,543 men. By the 24th seven miles of railroad were destroyed. Aug. 25 the Second Army Corps and Gregg's cavalry, while at Reams Station destroying the railroad, were assailed. The fighting was desperate and a part of the Union line gave way after losing 5 guns and 2,400 men, three-fourths of whom were missing.

Welland Canal, controversy with Canada respecting tolls upon, discussed, 5211, 5213, 5675, 5678, 5749.

Retaliatory measures proclaimed by President Benj. Harrison, 5725.

Referred to, 5749.

Revoked by proclamation, 5812.

Settlement of, referred to, 5869.

West India Company.—In 1621 the States-General of the United Netherlands chartered the Dutch West India Company. Among other important grants it received from the Government the exclusive right of trading with a large part of the coasts of America and Africa, planting colonies building forts, employing soldiers and fleets, making treaties, and attacking the colonies and commerce of Spain and Portugal. This company planted the colony of New Netherlands in the United States, as well as the Dutch settlements in Brazil, Guiana, the West Indies, and on the Gold Coast of Africa. In 1674 the company relinquished New Netherlands to the English. Its powerful fleets took many rich prizes on the coasts of Spanish and Portuguese America. In 1624 the projector of the Dutch West India Company obtained a charter from Gustavus Adolphus, of Sweden, granting special trading privileges in America. Under its auspices settlements were made along the Delaware River.

West Indies.—The area of the West Indies is about 65,000 square miles, a little more than half that of the United Kingdom. They extend from about 27° N. latitude to 10° N. latitude. There are three independent republics—Cuba, Haiti and Santo Domingo, with an area of 72,200 square miles and a population of 3,200,000. Islands under foreign rule are: United States, 3,750 square miles; British, 2,300 square miles; Danish, 140 square miles; French, 1,350 square miles; Netherlands, 430 square miles; Venezuelan, 90 square miles.

The Bahamas consist of about 3,000 islands and reefs, of which twenty are inhabited. There is practically no running water, though there are ample underground supplies.

South of Puerto Rico the islands form a deeply submerged mountain ridge separating the Caribbean Sea from the Atlantic Ocean. Mont Pelée in Martinique, and the Souffrière, in St. Vincent, have been the scene of disastrous eruptions.

West Indies. (See also Cuba; Puerto Rico; Denmark; Danish West Indies):

Cession of islands in, to United States, treaty regarding, 3778, 3779.

Discussed, 3796, 3886.

Commerce of United States, destruction of, by pirates in, discussed, 765.

Commercial relations with, 818.

Armed vessels stationed for protection of, by, 1476.

Naval force of United States in, 650, 875, 2677.

Piracy in, 758, 765, 984, 3777.

Value of, as naval outposts, discussed, 3777. (See also St. John Island; St. Thomas Island.)

Vessels from Montserrat Island, duties on, suspended by proclamation, 4871.

West Point, N. Y.:

Military Acadamy at. (See Military Academy.)

Military Department of, discontinued, 4713.

West Virginia.—One of the central group of states. Nickname, "The Pan Handle State"; motto, "Montani semper liberi" ("Mountaineers are always freemen"). It extends from lat. 37° 12' to 40° 38' north, and from long. 77° 40' to 82° 35' west, an area of 24.170 square miles. West Virginia is bounded on the northwest by Ohio (separated by the Ohio River), on the north by Maryland and Pennsylvania (separated from the former by the Potomac), on the east and south by Virginia, and on the west by Kentucky (separated by the Big Sandy River). The state is hilly or mountainous and contains abundance of timber and coal, being, in fact, one of the leading states in the production of the latter. Of the manufacturing interests the iron and steel industry, confined almost entirely to Wheeling, is the most important.

West Virginia was originally a part of Virginia. When that state adopted the ordinance of secession, April 17, 1861, many of the people of the western and northwestern parts of the state claimed that they were not to be bound by that action. A convention was called in 1861, which resolved not to recognize the State officers who were in opposition to the National Government. This convention elected Francis H. Pierpoint governor of Virginia and called a legislature to meet at Wheeling. It also voted to erect a new state, called Kanawha, and the legislature which was called by the convention voted to recognize the new state. It was admitted to the Union as the State of West Virginia June 19, 1863 (page 3368).

The forest area of West Virginia, estimated at 18,400 square miles, covers 73 per cent. of its surface.

Statistics of agriculture collected for the last Federal census, place the number of farms in the State at 96,685, comprising 10,026,442 acres, valued with stock and improvements, at $314,738,540. The average value of land per acre was $20.65, against $12.60 in 1900. The value of domestic animals, poultry, etc., was $43,336,073, including 620,288 cattle, valued at $15,860,764; 179,991 horses, $18,583,381; 11,717 mules, $1,339.760; 328,188 swine, $2,087,392; 910,360 sheep, $3,400,901, and poultry, $1,628,700. The yield and value of the field crops of 1911 was: Corn, 707,000 acres, 18,170,000 bushels, $13,991,000; wheat, 238,000 acres, 2,737,000 bushels, $2,792,000; oats, 110,000 acres, 2,420,000 bushels, $1,355,000; rye, 17,000 acres, 187,000 bushels, $168,000; potatoes, 44,000 acres, 1,980,000 bushels, $2,059,000; hay, 648,000 acres. 428,000 tons, $8,560,000; tobacco, 15,000 acres, 11,250,000 pounds, $900,000. In 1910 the State ranked second in the amount of coal produced, taking this position away from Illinois on account of the strike among the mine-workers in the latter state. Pennsylvania is the only state producing more coal than West Virginia. The output of 1910 was 61,671,000 short tons, valued at $56,665,061. The output of 1911 fell back to 60,500,000 short tons. The state revenues for the fiscal year 1910-1911 were $5,379,699; expenditures, $5,183,416: balance on hand Sept. 30, 1911, $1,611,620. The property valuation was $1,119,828,173, and the tax rate 84 cents per $100. The State has no bonded debt.

The number of manufacturing establishments in West Virginia having an annual output valued at $500 or more at the beginning of 1915 was 2,749. The amount of capital invested was $175,727,000, giving employment to 79,278 persons, using material valued at $110,033,000, and turning out finished goods worth $193,512,000. Salaries and wages paid aggregated $51,378,000.

The business interests of the state suffered serious losses by an extensive coal miners' strike in 1914, and state-wide prohibition decreased the public revenue by $1,125,000.

West Virginia (see also Clarksburg):

Admission of, into Union, proclaimed, 3368.

Unlawful combinations in, discussed and proclamation regarding, 4399, 4424.

Westcott, Hampton, lieutenant in Navy, nomination of, and reasons therefor, 1126.

Western European Division, State Department.—This division was organized in 1909 by Secretary of State Knox. It has charge of other than administrative matters in Great Britain and Colonies, France, Belgium, Spain, Portugal, Switzerland, Norway, Sweden, Morocco, the Congo, the Netherlands, Luxemburg, Denmark and Liberia. This division of the work of the State Department (q. v.) is under the supervision of the third assistant secretary of state (q. v.).

Western Reserve.—The charters of most of the original Colonies granted territory extending from the Atlantic to the Pacific Ocean. After the Revolution the unsettled western portions were ceded to the General Government. When Connecticut made her cession the state reserved a tract of land between the forty-first parallel of latitude and Lake Erie as a foundation for her school fund. It extended 120 miles westward from the Pennsylvania boundary line, and contained 3,666,291 acres, afterwards included in Ohio. An act of Congress in 1800 authorized the President to deed to Connecticut the title to this Western Reserve, to quiet titles of settlers, on condition that the state surrender all claims to its jurisdiction. On the admission of Ohio as a state, Connecticut lost all interest in the territory. The tract was settled largely by Connecticut people.

Western Territory, instructions to governor of, regarding employment of militia against Indians, 6306.

Whale Fisheries, papers for vessels engaged in, referred to, 1774.

Whig.—A name taken by the political party in the American Colonies which favored the Revolution, as opposed to the Tories, who advocated adherence to the mother country. The name was first used in Great Britain to designate those Scotch Covenanters whose rebellion in 1699 led to the fixing the name upon any opponents of the court. The term as generally used in America, however, refers to the political party in the United States which began to develop toward the end of John Quincy Adams's administration, favoring a national bank, a protective tariff, a system of internal improvements, and in general holding to a latitudinarian construction of the Constitution. They were at first called National Republicans, and those who opposed them were known as Democratic Republicans. After the defeat of Adams, in 1828, Henry Clay became the leader of the National Republicans.

The party took the name of Whig in 1834, and in 1836, failing to unite on any candidate of their own for the Presidency, Martin Van Buren was elected by the opposition. In 1840 the Whigs elected William Henry Harrison. After the death of Harrison they quarreled with Vice-President Tyler, who had succeeded Harrison as President and had vetoed the fiscal measures passed by the Whig Congress. In 1844 they nominated Henry Clay for the Presidency, but he was defeated by James K. Polk. The annexation of Texas, the Mexican War, the Wilmot Proviso, and other phases of the slavery question caused serious dissensions in the Whig party, but they preserved their power for another term by nominating a military candidate in the person of Zachary Taylor. He was elected, but the disintegration of the Whig party had begun.

Many of the northern Whigs became Free Soilers, and by 1856 Republicans, while many temporarily joined the American or Know-Nothing party. Large numbers of the southern Whigs became Democrats. The factions of the old party united and nominated Winfield Scott for President in 1852, but he was defeated by Franklin Pierce. A small number of Whigs formed the Constitutional Union party and nominated Bell and Everett in 1860. Besides those already mentioned, the chief leaders of the party in the north were were Webster, Winthrop, Choate, Seward, Greeley, and Weed; in the south, Mangum, Badger, Bell, Berrien, Forsyth, Stephens, Toombs, Prentiss, and Crittenden, and in the west, Giddings, Ewing and Corwin.

Whisky. (See Liquors—Malt, etc.)

Whisky Insurrection.—A revolt against the enforcement of a Federal excise law by the people of four counties of western Pennsylvania.

The first bill for an excise law was beaten in Congress June 21, 1790. The project was revived the following year, and the first excise law was passed March 3, 1791. The Senators from Pennsylvania were instructed by their legislature to oppose the law, "established on principles subversive of peace, liberty, and the rights of citizens." In Pennsylvania the law was violently opposed by one Bradford and his followers and condemned by more peaceable and reflecting citizens, following the lead of Albert Gallatin, afterwards Secretary of the Treasury, minister to France, envoy extraordinary to England, etc., and William Findley and John Smiley, members of Congress. Numerous meetings were held to protest against this law, which bore with particular force upon the settlers of western Pennsylvania because of their isolated position, distance from the seaboard, and the scarcity of money in that region. In response to repeated protests Congress on May 8, 1792, passed an act reducing the duties on whisky, but, on account of the threatening attitude of some of the settlers, empowering the President to use militia in suppressing disturbances within a state, the agents of the Government sent to collect the excise having been maltreated and driven from the country and the marshals refused office room and assistance in serving writs, President Washington, by a proclamation of Sept. 15, 1792 (116), called upon the citizens to abandon their unlawful proceedings. Instead of complying, resistance to the service of writs continued and the officers were tarred and feathered. Aug. 1, 1794, a mass meeting of 7,000 armed insurgents was held on Braddock's Field, a county judge presiding, with Albert Gallatin as secretary and Bradford as the leading spirit. An emergency had now arisen. Governor Mifflin, of Pennsylvania, having declined to take the initiative, a certificate of the existence of an insurrection was obtained from a Federal judge, and on Aug. 7, 1794, President Washington again called upon the insurgents to disperse and retire peaceably to their homes on or before Sept. 1, 1794 (150). This warning was unheeded and was followed by a third proclamation on Sept. 25, 1794 (153). A requisition for 15,000 militia was issued to the governors of Pennsylvania, Virginia, Maryland, and New Jersey. A Federal commission of three and a State commission of two preceded the troops with offers of amnesty on full submission. Bradford urged armed resistance, Gallatin counseled submission. Washington accompanied the troops, which were in command of Governor Lee, of Virginia, as far as Carlisle. Alexander Hamilton, then Secretary of the Treasury, accompanied the expedition to the scene of disorder. The troops arrived in the rebellious district early in November. After giving the people time to obey the President's proclamation, Lee's force arrested many of those who failed to accept the proffered amnesty. Bradford and the more violent leaders escaped. Those captured were tried, convicted, and later pardoned by the President. The first show of Federal force had suppressed the insurrection. (See illustration opposite 162.)

Whisky Ring.—A conspiracy of distillers and United States officials formed in St. Louis, Mo., in 1872 to defraud the Government of internal-revenue taxes. By 1874 the ring had attained national proportions, with branches in Milwaukee, Chicago, Peoria, St. Louis, Cincinnati, New Orleans, San Francisco, and Washington. Distillers who refused to enter the combination were trapped into technical violations of the revenue laws, and when made liable to seizure they were given their choice between ruin and surrender to the ring. The combination became so powerful that when Secretary Bristow ordered a transfer of supervisors, which would have thrown the ring into confusion, their agents at Washington procured a countermand of the order from President Grant. After diligent effort evidence was obtained against the distillers and revenue agents. Upon this evidence the Government seized $3,500,000 worth of property and procured indictments against 238 persons. It was shown that the Treasury had been defrauded of $1,650,000 between July 1, 1874, and May 1, 1875. When the papers were laid before President Grant he indorsed them with orders to "let no guilty man escape." The most important convictions were those of John A. Joyce, special revenue agent; John McDonald, supervisor, and William O. Avery, chief clerk in the Treasury Department.

White House, The.—The site for the erection of the White House, or the "President's Palace," as it was termed on some of the earlier maps, was selected by President Washington and General L'Enfant when they laid out the city of Washington in 1792. The corner stone was placed in that year.

The plans were procured by competition, which gave the award to James Hoban, a distinguished young architect from Dublin, afterward identified for many years with the architectural work of the capital city. By the architects of today his design is considered to surpass anything of a similar style constructed in this country. The White House was so called after the home of Martha Washington in Virginia, the name being particularly appropriate, because of the fact that the free-stone of the edifice is painted white.

According to the original plan, the building was 160 feet long. It is built in the English Renaissance style. The North and South porches, constructed from designs made by Latrobe in 1803, were added twenty-five years after the first occupancy of the house; and in Jefferson's time and under his direction, terraces were built extending 150 feet east and west of the mansion. The West Terrace, enclosed in glass and otherwise disguised, became in time the Conservatory so dear to the heart of the Washington sight-seer. The East Terrace was removed about the time of the Civil War, but, happily, both of these were restored and beautified during the general reconstruction of the house in 1902.

The White House, when President Adams came to take possession of it in 1800, was neither finished nor furnished, and its surroundings were rough and unattractive, little or no effort having been made to reclaim the adjacent country from muddy and ragged woodland. From time to time Congress made small appropriations for the adornment of the Executive Mansion, and this money was spent more or less wisely by the several administrations in their efforts to make the official residence comfortable. An appropriation of fifty thousand dollars was made to President Madison after the fire of 1814, during the occupation of Washington by the British, for the purpose of refurnishing; but despite the expenditure of more than two million dollars upon the furnishing and decorating of the building during the first three-quarters of a century of its existence, it contained but few articles of value at the time of the remodelling under President Roosevelt. President Roosevelt also restored the official title "White House" to the edifice, which had been called for several previous administrations merely the "Executive Mansion."

It was originally intended that the public offices should be separate from the President's home; and previously to 1814, the Executive Departments occupied small detached buildings in the White House grounds. But of necessity the President's privacy was invaded by the business of his office, until finally, during the Civil War, President Lincoln set aside the second story of the East Wing for official business purposes. This invasion limited the accommodations for comfortable living and introduced a degree of publicity into the family life of the Chief Executive which was far from agreeable. But these and many other discomforts were at last removed in 1902-3 by the construction of the new office building and by the remodelling of the entire old building. There is now little business of an official nature conducted in the house proper, and the East Wing has been reclaimed for domestic purposes. With the exception of the outside walls, scarcely any part of the building has been left unchanged. The old flooring, long in a dangerous condition, has been replaced by new, supported upon steel beams. The latest improvements in heating, lighting, and plumbing have supplanted the old-fashioned arrangements tolerated by many administrations. In this process, it is to be regretted that many nooks and crannies of historic interest have been obliterated, but it is comforting to know that the alterations will preserve in good condition and for a much longer period the main structure and the chief beauties of the old house.

The East Room.—In viewing this magnificent apartment it is difficult to realize that it was at one time used by Mrs. John Adams as a drying-room for the family linen. The East Room was not finished until 1836, and a bare, bleak place it must have been in those early days! In former times state banquets were held there, but in more recent years it has been used chiefly for public receptions. During the administration of President Arthur this room was redecorated and refurnished, and afterward no changes of importance were made until 1902, when, with the rest of the building, it underwent almost complete transformation. Before this period the walls were hung with historical portraits, among them the Gilbert Stuart portrait of Washington, saved from the fire of 1814 by Mrs. Madison; but these were removed, as were also the pillars and beams of the old room, to give place to the present beautiful scheme of decoration. The walls and ceilings are now of white; the spaces over the doors and windows contain low-relief panels, each illustrating one of the fables of Æsop. The ceiling is most elaborate, but of delicate design; from each of its three panels hang the splendid cut-glass chandeliers, which have taken the place of the former larger, but less artistic ones. Four beautiful mantels of colored marbles are features of the recent remodelling. The draperies are of rich yellow silk.

The Blue Room.—It is in this famous apartment that the President receives his guests upon state occasions. The room is considered the handsomest in the house in point of decoration, and also in its beautiful proportions. The floor is a fine, highly polished parquetry, and the walls are covered with a heavy steel-blue silk, with yellow embroideries at the ceiling and wainscot. In the pattern of this embroidery and in the decoration of the ceiling and of the window hangings, the star is used with graceful effect. Each of the three windows is surmounted by a golden eagle. A feature of the room is the fine marble mantel with its supports representing sheaves of arrows tipped with gold bronze. When receiving in the Blue Room, the presidential party stands in front of the windows, but formerly it occupied the north end of the room. A heavy rope of silk encloses a passageway for the procession of guests, who must pass from the Red Room into the presence of the host, and thence into the Green Room. This change is one of the many that were brought about by the re-arrangement of the entire premises. During the administration of John Adams, the Blue Room was used as a sort of vestibule, its convenient location making it available for this purpose.

The Red Room.—In early times this was the anteroom to the Library and the Cabinet Room. It adjoins the State Dining Room, and by recent changes has been turned into a smoking room, except when it is required for service on receiving days. It is then used as formerly, in conjunction with the series of state parlors. Its walls are covered with dark red velvet and are hung with historical portraits. Its marble mantel is one of those which formerly adorned the State Dining Room,—the other being placed in the Green Room.

The Green Room.—In previous days the Green Room was the family dining-room. The present Private Dining Room was then used for state dinners. As in the Blue Room, the walls of the Green Room are hung with velvet; here, however, the color is an exquisite silvery green. Some of the original paintings which are reproduced in the White House Gallery of Portraits of the Presidents also adorn the walls of this room.

State and Private Dining Rooms.—The State Dining Room was enlarged in 1902 by the addition of a corridor from which the private stairway led. This necessitated the removal of that portion of the stairs. The room now measures forty by fifty feet and will accommodate as many as one hundred guests at table. The walls are of panelled oak, and the window draperies of heavy green velvet. Flemish tapestries of the sixteenth century are a feature of the room, which is further decorated by trophies of the chase in American hunting-grounds arranged around the beautifully carved cornice. The furniture is of red mahogany; it includes two tables,—the larger crescent in shape, and the smaller a rounded oblong.

An interesting feature of the furnishings of the State Dining Room is the complete service of china and cut glass, manufactured from special designs made exclusively for the White House and selected by Mrs. Roosevelt from a number submitted to her for approval. The design is simple but rich in effect, and the china is of the purest texture, the whole having been very costly. The glass, which includes many pieces, is of the best American cut.

The Private Dining Room has been remodelled in a style essentially colonial, with an attractive color scheme of ivory white and red. The ceiling is domed and the window hangings are of red velvet. The furniture in this apartment harmonizes with the general plan of decoration, it also being distinctly colonial in design.

The Library.—The room, which is oval in shape, is situated on the second story of the Executive Mansion and was once used as the President's office, but is now converted into a private sitting room. It was during President Fillmore's administration that the Library was first planned, an appropriation being made for that purpose. The low bookcases lining the walls contain over seven thousand volumes, principally literature of a historical and classical character, and chiefly of Mrs. Fillmore's own selection. She greatly deplored the lack of books in the White House and urged the need of a more extensive Library. However, it did not progress as it should have done, and is not catalogued.

The Executive Office.—From the time of President Lincoln's administration, the business of the White House began to encroach seriously upon the living quarters. The discomfort and inconvenience resulting from this combination of public and private life under one roof—and that a roof of very limited dimensions—had long been realized. Plans to relieve the situation were occasionally brought forward, but nothing was accomplished until 1902, when the reconstruction of the entire establishment took place. It was then that the one-storied and basement building was erected at the end of the West Terrace for the accommodation of the Executive Offices. The architects have placed the structure most effectively in its relation to its surroundings. It contains a Reception Room, the President's suite of rooms, the offices of the President's Secretary and Assistant Secretary, telegraph and telephone rooms and several other offices. The building is comparatively small and will probably give place to a larger one in the course of time. (See illustrations, 130, 240, 288, 711, 823, 1231, 1613, 6788.)

White Leagues referred to, 4251. (See also Klu-Klux-Klan.)

White Plains (N. Y.), Battle of.—After the battle of Harlem Heights, in which Washington was enabled to maintain his ground in the face of the British attack, Gen. Howe's war ships advanced up the East River and landed troops at Frogs Point (now Throggs Neck). His purpose was to gain a position in Washington's rear and thus cut him off from communication with his army outside of New York. About 4,000 British were sent to dislodge some 1,400 Americans who were intrenched on Chatterton Hill. After a short and sharp skirmish the Americans fell back in good order to the main body of the army, having lost but little more than half as many as their opponents. The American loss is variously stated at from 125 to 200, while the lowest official estimate of the British loss places it at 231. The following night Washington retired to a much stronger position about five miles north and Howe withdrew to Dobbs Ferry.

White Slavery.—A term applied to the enticing and incarceration of girls for immoral purposes. Exposures in Great Britain, France and the United States led to an international conference in Paris in 1902, which resulted in a treaty, afterwards ratified by nearly all the civilized governments. In March, 1910, Congress adopted what was known as the Bennett Law, making the importation of women for immoral purposes a penal offense, and, in June, 1910, Congress adopted what was known as the Mann Law, making interstate transportation of women for immoral purposes a penal offense. The constitutionality of the Mann Law was vigorously attacked, but was sustained by the Court.

Whitehall, N. Y., proclamation granting privileges of other ports to, 2540.

Wichita Indians. (See Indian Tribes.)

Wilderness (Va.), Battle of.—The rank of lieutenant-general was revived on March 2, 1864, and on the 9th of that month it was conferred upon Gen. Grant, who was given the command, under the President, of all the armies of the United States. The plan of campaign agreed upon between Grant and Sherman was to make a simultaneous advance against Lee's army in Virginia and that of Johnston in Georgia. Meade was left in control of the army of the Potomac and Sheridan placed in command of the cavalry in Virginia. Gen. B. F. Butler was made commander of the Army of the James, consisting of 38,648 men and 90 guns. May 4, 1864, Grant crossed the Rapidan with the Army of the Potomac, aggregating on May 1, according to the report of the Secretary of War, 120,380 in men and 316 guns. The Ninth Corps, 20,780 in number, was subsequently added. Lee lay on the south bank of the Rapidan with 63,984 men. The Confederate position was in the midst of a wilderness of scraggy oak, sassafras, hazel, and pine. It is a region of worn-out tobacco fields, and lies directly west of the battlefield of Chancellorsville. It was not Grant's intention to fight Lee there, but the Confederate attack early on the 5th compelled it. Lee gained ground in the two days' fighting. The battle was a bloody bush fight. More than 200,000 men fought in a vast jungle. Grant's loss amounted to over 20,000, of whom 5,000 were made prisoners. The Confederate loss was about 10,000. Grant now resolved to turn Lee's left flank and put his army between the latter and Richmond. On the night of the 7th the Federal army took up the march toward Spottsylvania Court-House. On the morning of the 8th of May the men of the opposing forces arrived almost at the same moment at the Court-House. Then occurred the great battle of Spottsylvania (q. v.). (See illustration opposite 3421.)

"Wild Cat."—The currency issued by a "Wild Cat Bank." (See "Wild Cat Banking.") During Jackson's administration and the period following, up to the institution of the National Bank System by Congress, state banks and private banks issued paper money with but little security back of them—practically mere promises to pay. This lack of soundness and stability in the banking methods of the time worked great injury to the commercial interests in the United States, and greatly retarded progress. The approbrious name "Wild Cat Banking" was applied by those seeking to reform the banking method.

Wildfire, The, capture of, by the *Mohawk*, 3124.

Wilkes's Exploring Expedition, expenditures of publication of, referred to, 3068.

Willamette Valley, etc., Wagon Road Co., lands granted to Oregon for, referred to, 4665.

William I., Emperor of Germany, death of, referred to, 5367.

William, The, captured with African negroes on board, 3126.

William and Francis, The, satisfaction to be allowed by Great Britain for detention of, 2111.

Williamsburg (Va.), Battle of.—As soon as it was discovered that the Confederates had withdrawn from Yorktown (May 5, 1862), a column was sent in pursuit. It came up with the retreating rear guard at Williamsburg. The Confederates had been reenforced from Johnston's army at Richmond. Longstreet's division, having passed beyond the town, retraced its steps to resist the attack. Hooker, of Heintzelman's division, and Smith, of Keyes's, bore the brunt of the assault, fighting from morning till late in the afternoon, vainly calling for reenforcements. The arrival of Kearny's division about 4 P. M. caused the Confederates to retire toward Richmond. The Federal loss was 2,228 men, of whom 456 were killed. The Confederate loss was 1,560, of whom 288 were killed.

Williamson's Farm (S. C.), Battle of.—One of the minor skirmishes of the Revolutionary War in the South and the first disaster to the British arms after the capture of Charleston, July 12, 1780, Capt Houk, with 115 British and Tories, was sent from the garrison at Rocky Mount to collect militia and drive back the Americans. Thomas Sumter, with 75 men, surprised and captured them. Capt. Houk was killed in the fight.

Wilmington, The, attempts of, to silence batteries at Cardenas, Cuba, 6302, 6316.

Wilmot Proviso.—President Polk, in a special message Aug. 8, 1846 (2309), made a request of Congress for money to adjust the boundary between Mexico and the United States by the purchase of certain Mexican territory outside of Texas. In accordance with this request a bill was introduced into the House appropriating $2,-000,000 for the purpose. David Wilmot, a Democrat from Pennsylvania, offered an amendment which provided "that neither slavery nor involuntary servitude shall ever exist in any part of said territory, except for crime, whereof the party shall first be duly convicted." This was the Wilmot Proviso. The bill as amended passed the House, but failed in the Senate. Early the next year another bill passed the House, appropriating $3,000,000 for the same purpose, with the Wilmot proviso, but the amendment was omitted in the Senate.

Wilson, Woodrow.—1913-1917.

Thirty-second Administration—Democratic.
Vice-President—Thomas R. Marshall.
Secretary of State—
    William Jennings Bryan.
    Robert Lansing.
Secretary of the Treasury—
    William Gibbs McAdoo.
Secretary of War—
    Lindley M. Garrison.
    Newton D. Baker.
Attorney-General—
    James Clark McReynolds.
    T. W. Gregory.
Postmaster-General—
    Albert Sidney Burleson.
Secretary of the Navy—
    Josephus Daniels.
Secretary of Interior—
    Franklin Knight Lane.
Secretary of Agriculture—
    David Franklin Houston.
Secretary of Commerce—
    William C. Redfield.
Secretary of Labor—
    William Bauchop Wilson.

The Democratic National Convention met in Baltimore, Md., June 25, 1912, and on July 6, on the forty-sixth ballot, chose Woodrow Wilson, Governor of New Jersey, as the nominee of the party. Other prominent candidates before the convention were Champ Clark, of Missouri; Judson Harmon, of Ohio, and Oscar W. Underwood, of Alabama.

Platform. — The convention reaffirmed their devotion to the principles of Democratic government formulated by Thomas Jefferson; declared that the high Republican tariff was the principal cause of the unequal distribution of wealth, and favored immediate downward revision of the rates. President Taft was denounced for his veto of the Farmers' Free List bill, and the Republican party was charged with having been faithless to its pledges of 1908. The people were appealed to for support in a demand for a tariff for revenue only. Other planks declared a private monopoly indefensible and intolerable; favored enforcement of the criminal as well as civil law against trusts and their officials; prevention of holding companies, of interlocking directors, stock watering, and discrimination in prices; legislation to restore to the Sherman Antitrust law the strength of which it was deprived by interpretation; the unhampered exercise by the states of their reserved rights; favored an income tax and the popular election of Senators; publicity of campaign contributions; presidential primaries and a single term for the President; supervision of railroad, express, telegraph and telephone companies; opposed the establishment of a central bank, and favored the revision of the banking laws; favored rural credits, and national aid to state and local roads; equal justice to capital and labor; conservation of national resources; exemption from tolls of American ships on the Panama Canal; fostering the growth of our merchant marine; independence for the Philippines; establishment of a parcel post and extension of rural free delivery.

Opposition.—The Republican party nominated President Taft for a second term, and Ex-President Roosevelt withdrew from the convention and became the nominee of the Progressive Republicans. The Socialists nominated Eugene V. Debs, the Socialist Labor Arthur E. Reimer and the Prohibitionists Eugene W. Chafin for President. A notable feature of the campaign was the split in the Republican party caused by the candidacy of Ex-President Roosevelt, who was extremely popular with the people, but opposed by the politicians and some leading newspapers.

Vote.—The popular vote showed Wilson 6,293,019; Roosevelt, 4,119,507; Taft, 3,484,956; Debs, 901,873, and Chafin, 207,-928. The combined Republican vote of Roosevelt and Taft (7,604,463) being 1,311,444 more than the vote for Wilson, thereby showed Wilson's success to have been due to the split in the Republican party. The popular vote of Wilson over Roosevelt, however, was 2,173,512. When the electoral vote was counted it showed Wilson, 435; Taft, 8, and Roosevelt, 88.

Party Problem.—The immediate task confronting Mr. Wilson was the consolidation of the Democratic Party into an effective organism. The commitment of the Party in 1896 and 1900 to the leadership of William Jennings Bryan and his free silver platform had alienated many of its ablest members, and the attack made on Mr. Clark by the Wilson forces under the leadership of Mr. Bryan at the Baltimore convention had embittered to no slight extent the powerful Clark faction. Moreover, the party had so long been out of power that practical men of affairs able to handle concrete problems were no longer as prominent in it as they had been.

Mr. Wilson's Cabinet reflected this problem By the appointment of Mr. Bryan as

Secretary of State, the cooperation of the "Peerless Leader" and his followers was assured; and even in later days when the two separated in a difference of opinion regarding foreign policy, their personal ties and political allegiance remained unbroken. The claims of the South were recognized by the appointment of a number of Southern leaders, and in the appointment of Mr. William B. Wilson as Secretary of Labor a strong bid was made for the continued support of organized labor. For the practical problems of the Commerce, Interior and Treasury Departments, President Wilson selected men with first-hand experience for their tasks.

The majority of the Democrats in Congress was so slight that any slight defection from Mr. Wilson's leadership would have proved serious, especially as a Republican taunt for years had claimed that the Democrats could never achieve power without squabbling among themselves and accomplishing little. Mr. Wilson proved himself a strong party man, especially in appointments; and before long had gained for himself an enviable reputation as a leader. Indeed, under him the executive branch of the government achieved and wielded greater power than had resided in any previous President. In thus making the administration of the country's welfare the responsibility of a party, President Wilson established in the United States to a great extent the English political system.

This increase in Presidential power represented a break with the Democratic tradition of states' rights, as did much of the reform legislation soon placed upon the statute books; and as the tariff was soon taken out of politics, the historical points of difference between the two parties began to grow indistinct. This tendency was increased by international problems and finally by the dangers of war, so that a realignment of parties in the United States along new principles became probable in the days after the War.

The many problems developing under President Wilson kept him in Washington to a greater extent than his immediate predecessors had been kept; so that he relied for points of contact with the people more upon the written than upon the spoken word. In this reliance he was aided by the eloquence and readableness of his English style, both written and spoken. Although a most attractive personality proved a strong asset to him in handling men, he showed himself unusually independent of counsel and advice, his chief adviser being Colonel E. M. House, of Texas.

Tariff.—April 8, 1913, Wilson convened Congress in extra session for the purpose of revising the tariff law in accordance with the "duty laid upon the party at the recent elections" (page 7871). The Sixty-third Congress consisted of 96 Senators, of whom 52 were Democrats; and 435 Representatives, of whom 290 were Democrats. The tariff bill introduced by Mr. Underwood, of Alabama, embodied the essential ideas of the Democratic platform—that duties should be imposed primarily to produce revenue for the government without thought of protection, and that such duties should be established by legislation that would not injure or destroy legitimate industry. One hundred items were added to the free list, including acids, salt, bread, meat, flour and meal, potatoes, paper, manufactures of leather, lumber and iron and certain machinery. Duties were imposed on seventy articles previously free.

The customs receipts for 1912 were $304,597.035, which was an average of more than 40 per cent. of the value of the

EXTENT OF THE UNITED STATES DURING THE ADMINISTRATION OF PRESIDENT WILSON, 1913-1917

(NOT INCLUDING TERRITORIES)

MAINE 1820

VT. 1791

N. H. 1788

MASS. 1788

CONN. 1788

R. I. 1790

N. Y. 1788

NEW YORK 1788

PENNSYLVANIA 1787

N. J. 1787

MD. 1788

DEL. 1787

WEST VIRGINIA 1863

VIRGINIA 1788

NORTH CAROLINA 1789

SOUTH CAROLINA 1788

GEORGIA 1788

FLORIDA 1845

OHIO 1803

MICHIGAN 1837

INDIANA 1816

KENTUCKY 1792

TENNESSEE 1796

ALABAMA 1819

MISSISSIPPI 1817

ILLINOIS 1818

WISCONSIN 1848

MISSOURI 1821

ARKANSAS 1836

LOUISIANA 1812

IOWA 1846

MINNESOTA 1858

NORTH DAKOTA 1889

SOUTH DAKOTA 1889

NEBRASKA 1867

KANSAS 1861

OKLAHOMA 1907

TEXAS 1845

MONTANA 1889

WYOMING 1890

COLORADO 1876

NEW MEXICO 1912

UTAH 1896

ARIZONA 1912

IDAHO 1890

NEVADA 1864

WASHINGTON 1889

OREGON 1859

CALIFORNIA 1850

FLAG OF 1917

imports. The estimated receipts under the new act for the fiscal year were $266,-701,000, an average of less than 30 per cent. of the estimated value of the imports. It was predicted that the deficit under the Underwood tariff would reach nearly $70,000,000. (See Import Duties.) To make up the deficiency an income tax on individuals and corporations was added to the law by authority of the Sixteenth Amendment. (See Income Tax.)

Bills were passed limiting securities issues, creating a trade commission and exempting farmers' and laborers' unions under the Sherman law.

The outbreak of the European War on August 1, 1914, had a disastrous effect upon the import trade of the United States, and tariff collections fell so markedly that internal taxes had to be greatly increased and the tariff duties themselves were finally raised. (See Corporation Tax; Internal Revenue; Tariff.) The appointment of the Tariff Commission (q. v.) finally took the Tariff out of politics.

Banking Law.—The National Monetary Commission in 1912 recommended the establishment, under federal charter, of a central reserve bank with branches in fifteen districts. The Democratic Congress rejected the principle of a central bank and embodied the opposite idea of decentralization in the Owen-Glass Federal Reserve Currency law. This divides the country into twelve districts, with a federal reserve national bank in each, to which all national banks are required to subscribe. These district banks were placed under the supervision of a Federal Reserve Board. Besides a general banking business, authority to issue currency, make loans on farming lands and an elaborate system of discounting were notable features of the law. (See Currency Law.)

Mexican Revolution.—The revolution existing in Mexico at the time of his election attracted the early attention of President Wilson, and in a special message of Aug. 27, 1913, he issued a warning and reassurance of friendship. He refused to recognize Huerta as President of the Republic because of the Mexican's assumption of power by force, without pretense of legal sanction, and through the murder of President Madero.

The rebellion in that country continued and led to abuse of Americans and other foreigners and the destruction of their property in Mexico. Finally, in April, 1914, following a series of flagrant insults to the dignity of the United States (page 7934), Wilson ordered the occupation of Vera Cruz by United States forces. (See also Mexico). At this time, however, and even later when it was necessary to send an armed force into Mexico to capture the bandit Villa, who had persistently raided United States territory, President Wilson was able to avoid open war with the republic to the south.

The failure of the United States forces to capture Villa, the continued unsettled condition of Mexico, the inability of the Administration to come to even a tentative and theoretical agreement with the Mexican government under Carranza created strong dissatisfaction with the policy of "watchful waiting" in Mexico, but there was also strong support from all classes for the President in his determination not to interfere with Mexico in the solution of her own problems. The later publication of attempts of Germany to embroil us in open hostilities with Mexico gave rise to a strong suspicion that the President's Mexican policy was directed largely by the European situation.

The early months of his administration were marked by threatened complications with Japan on account of an alien land law passed by the State of California, which Japan claimed was in violation of her treaty with the United States (page 7875).

President Wilson attacked persistently the problem of better relations between the two Americas, and left no stone untouched to remove suspicions of the motives of the United States entertained in South America. In this endeavor, much of the success he attained was due to his refusal to intervene in Mexico. He can hardly be said, however, to have succeeded in diminishing to any great extent the feeling in Central America that the United States was interfering unduly with the self-development of Central American nationalities and republics.

Toward the Filipinos also, President Wilson developed a policy of disinterestedness, and was responsible for legislation hastening the days when ultimate freedom would be granted them.

This administration saw also the acquisition of the Danish West Indies, rechristened the Virgin Islands, from Denmark.

Panama Canal.—When the Panama Canal was nearing completion the question of exempting American shipping from tolls became a matter of wide public discussion. Great Britain held that such exemption was a violation of treaty. Mr. Wilson asked Congress (page 7933) to repeal the exemption clause, and the bill to that effect was finally signed by the President on June 15, 1914.

Unofficial Advisors.—President Wilson appointed, April 2, 1915, the twelve members of the Advisory Committee on Aeronautics authorized by the naval appropriation act. The appointees are to serve without pay.

Secretary Daniels June 4, 1915, abolished the system of Naval Aids created by a Republican predecessor in office and substituted a council to be known as the Secretary's Advisory Council, to be composed of the Assistant Secretary of the Navy, the Chief of Naval Operations, the chiefs of the various bureaus, and the Commandant of the Marine Corps. The new Naval Cabinet will meet every Thursday.

An Advisory Board of sixteen civilian American inventors with Thomas Edison as chairman was announced Sept. 12. The board was made up chiefly of members of scientific societies whose members deal with those branches of science on which the navy is thought to depend for inventions.

Treasury Statement.—The fiscal year closed June 30, 1915, with an excess of ordinary disbursements over receipts of $35,864,381, and an excess of all disbursements over all receipts of $64,165,416 in the United States Treasury (including Panama Canal expenditures). The total amount from income tax collected during the year was $79,828,675, of which $36,-303,525 was collected on the last day of the fiscal year. The total treasury receipts for the year amounted to $696,598,730, as compared with $737,462,640 in 1914. The total disbursements were $760,762,147. The net balance in the general fund at the close of the fiscal year was $82,025,716. The returns for the last day of the fiscal year greatly changed the financial condition. The receipts for June 30 were $44,715,151, of which $860,236 was from customs, $7,-469,581 was from ordinary internal revenue; $36,303,525 was from income tax, and $81,809 was from miscellaneous sources. The reduction in the deficit was caused by the large collection of income tax during the year. This satisfactory condition, it was said, was largely due to the fact that the income tax came up to the estimate of $80,000,000 made by the Commissioner of Internal Revenue. This sum was sufficient to cover the large falling off in the customs revenues due to the cutting off of imports because of the European war. Internal revenue for the year, including the special war tax, amounted to $335,828,377, as against an estimate of $359,000,000 and receipts a year ago of $380,613,000. Customs for the year totaled $209,268,107, as against an estimate of $220,000,000 and receipts a year ago of $292,128,527.

Preparedness.—As the prospect that we could remain neutral throughout the European War became more and more clouded, a movement arose for the country to be prepared to the utmost of its military and industrial strength before it should become involved. This movement was aided by a belief that in our diplomatic negotiations our point of view would be strengthened by increase in our ability to sustain it at the point of the sword. The movement was led by ex-President Roosevelt, and on the whole it might be said to have had the backing of the Republican Party more than that of the Democrats. It was opposed by those who desired to keep us out of the war and to whom preparedness meant the first step toward participation.

President Wilson pursued a middle course toward preparedness. His policy will be seen by referring to the citations below. Although he put into effect great and far-reaching increases in both the Army and Navy, he nevertheless refused to sanction universal military training.

European War.—It might well be said that there was not a moment in President Wilson's administration in which it was not steeped in a problem of serious national import. Before he had completed the consolidation of his own party and the redemption of its platform pledges regarding the tariff and the currency, the Mexican problem became acute; and before that had withdrawn from the danger stage, the whole European world became involved in the greatest of all wars.

The first feeling of the American people at the outbreak of hostilities was one of horror. Our traditional policy of isolation, in spite of the implications of the Monroe Doctrine, kept us free from passions in favor of either group of belligerents. True, the invasion of Belgium in violation of treaty rights caused strong feeling against Germany, which was increased when the reports of the atrocities committed in the invaded countries were substantiated, but on the other hand we had more immigrants from Germany in our civilization than from any other country; our second largest immigrant group was the Irish, most of whom were anti-British; and the large Jewish group was by no means alone in the United States in its hatred of everything which was signified by the kingdom of the Tsar.

Before long, however, in spite of our desire to remain neutral in thought as well as in deed, and in spite of our feeling that the holocaust was due to secret diplomacy, political rivalries, imperialist and economic ambitions which seemed queerly alien to America, we became definitely involved in the problems of the war. In accordance with the rights of international law, we began to sell great quantities of military supplies to the Entente Allies, the Central Powers being unable to avail themselves of similar privileges because of England's control of the seas. Our policy was regarded by Germany as unneutral, and soon we saw

our ships sunk in Germany's submarine warfare and the lives of our citizens endangered and on occasion lost. Moreover, the consciousness that the greatest military power in the world regarded us as her enemy made us wonder what would be the result to us in our comparatively unprepared state if that power should emerge victorious in the conflict.

Furthermore, as the war continued, it became more definite to our vision not as a causeless accident in which all sides were equally to blame, but as a struggle between two sets of ideals, of systems of government, of cultures; and our own ideals, government and culture were akin to those of the Entente Allies. If German Kultur was to dominate the world, we should finally either be compelled to adopt it as our own, or else to come to grips with it ourselves.

Nevertheless, war to us seemed still the greatest of all evils, and as a whole we supported the President in his endeavors to keep us out of it, especially since the two belligerent groups seemed deadlocked and a decisive outcome improbable. But the situation altered with the extension of Germany's submarine campaign. In the first place, it was striking at the Allies' supplies, and if successful, would force them to sue for peace; in the second place, it profoundly altered the conditions which made us strong because of our isolation; and finally unless checked there would be no end to the destruction of American property on the high seas and the loss of American lives. The various steps by which President Wilson sought to modify Germany's submarine campaign, the success and the failure which attended his efforts, all will be seen by referring to the Index following. The country was sharply divided by Wilson's policy. On the one hand were those whose horror of war had been overcome by the horrors of peace and for whom the day had come when America could no longer remain at peace with honor; on the other hand were those whose horror of war still was predominant. The latter group were reinforced by the German-American element, most of whom were undeniably loyal to America but a small but noisy and powerful group of whom were rabidly pro-German. Feeling throughout the country ran high, and the divided state of public opinion was well shown by the election in November, 1916, described below.

But with the announcement of Germany's unrestrained submarine warfare, handed to the President on February 3, 1917, reluctance and doubt disappeared and, aside from the Socialists and out-and-out pacifists, every element in American life supported the country when by its dismissal of the German ambassador it showed its determination to resort to arms. The overthrow of the Tsar in Russia strengthened our faith that on the whole the Allies were representing the powers of light and on the whole the Central Powers the forces of darkness in the struggle, and our determination that the hopes for a better world order in the future should not be dissipated by the victory of the forces of darkness.

Peace Proposals.—President Wilson in a speech, May 27, 1916, before the League to Enforce Peace, held in Washington, outlined in general terms the basis on which the United States would undertake to suggest or initiate a movement for peace in Europe as follows: First, such a settlement with regard to their own immediate interests as the belligerents may agree upon. We have nothing material of any kind to ask for ourselves and are quite aware that we are in no sense or degree parties to the present quarrel. Our interest is only in peace and its future guarantees. Second, a universal association of the nations to maintain the inviolate security of the highway of the seas for the common and unhindered use of all the nations of the world and to prevent any war begun either contrary to treaty covenants or without warning and full submission of the causes to the opinion of the world— a virtual guarantee of territorial integrity and political independence.

Finally, in December, 1916, President Wilson sent a formal note to each of the European belligerents suggesting that tentative peace terms be submitted by each, to the end that an agreement might be reached. This note will be found in substance in the article European War, in the Encyclopedic Index.

In January, 1917, President Wilson delivered a heart-to-heart address to the Senate on the question of the future international organization of the nations of the world, and of the place which the United States must fill in such an organization. He declared that the struggle in Europe between comprehensive and conflicting forces was the last in which the United States could play the part of a mere onlooker, and proclaimed that the policy of the country could no longer be one of isolation. Announcing that another war like that undermining all European civilization must never be allowed to occur, he asserted that there must result an organization of nations to make peace perpetual. Accordingly, in order to prevent the entrenchment of hostile feelings which would inevitably bring on another conflict, the President declared in words which rang around the world that the peace to result from the European War must be a "Peace without Victory." The entire text of the President's address is printed on pages 8199 to 8204.

For the later developments of the European War situation as it affected the United States, see above. The situation in Mexico steadily improved, although very slowly.

Condition of United States, 1916.—The estimated population on July 1 was 102,-017,312, exclusive of territory not on the North American continent. Including outlying territories, the inhabitants of the United States numbered 112,444,620.

The wheat crop was 640,000,000 bushels and the corn crop, 2,600,000,000 bushels. The 1915 cotton crop was 5,600,000,000 bales.

The total imports were $2,197,883,510; and the exports, $4,333,658,865. These figures represent new records, but the increasing cost of living in the country had checked the spread of happiness resulting from the unparalleled prosperity. Expenditures were almost $1,050,000,000, including the expenditures for the Postal Service (more than $300,000,000) which were met by Postal revenues. There was in circulation $4,440,932,634, representing a circulation per capita of $43.00.

In 1914, there were 275,793 manufacturing establishments, employing 8,265,426 persons, representing capital of $22,790,880,-000, paying in wages and salaries more than $5,350,000,000, and producing commodities valued at $24,245,000,000.

On Nov. 17, the national banks had aggregate resources of $15,520,205,000, more than the combined resources of all the great banks of the great countries of the world. The deposits were more than $9,-000,000,000 and the reserves more than $2,400,000,000.

Legislation.—The most important internal legislative achievements of Wilson's administration are those connected with the tariff and the currency, which have been described above. A reform of vital consequence also was the federal child labor law, taking effect September 1, 1917, after which date interstate commerce was denied the products of any manufacturing establishment employing children under 14, and the products of any mine or quarry employing children under 16. A number of bills providing for increases of the army and navy are described under those heads. A series of anti-trust laws prohibited interlocking directorates and extended the powers of the Interstate Commerce Commission; but undoubtedly the most important legislation regarding industry was that concerned with the Federal Trade Commission (q. v.). A drastic shipping bill provided both for increased safety at sea and for better protection of American seamen.

With the assumption of office, President Wilson pursued a policy looking toward the decentralization of the great trusts and monopolies of the country, and the restimulation of competition. Most of his efforts in this respect were centred around the creation of the Federal Trade Commission. But the abnormal business conditions created by the outbreak of the European War radically altered the business situation in the United States, and the Administration finally was compelled to resort to all possible legitimate measures to assist American business enterprises of all natures.

Nevertheless, before the close of the second year of Mr. Wilson's administration, prosperity sharply declined. To what extent the "hard times" were due to the disturbance produced by European War conditions is a matter of individual opinion. But although production generally was decreased to a marked degree and unemployment became rife, the situation did not approach a panic condition, nor did it persist. For with their own systems of production diverted to war purposes, the belligerent European countries soon had recourse to America for assistance, speed being more essential to them than economy; and the United States in the latter half of Mr. Wilson's administration entered upon a period of affluence unprecedented in the recent history of the country. Both Capital and Labor prospered and flourished, although the well-being of the country was challenged sharply by the diversion of so large a share of its products to other countries and the consequent shortage of commodities and a rapid increase in the cost of living.

The establishment of a comprehensive system of rural credits is described under that head. There were various measures enacted to assist the American merchant marine, including the creation of the Bureau of War Risk Insurance. The administration of President Wilson saw the imposition of taxes upon incomes and corporations, taxes which became increasingly large as the European War provided the necessity for increased revenues. The popular election of United States senators was another reform dating from this administration. The filibustering tactics of certain senators regarding the question of armed neutrality brought about the adoption of a rule limiting debate in the Senate under certain conditions. In spite of increased gains, the advocates of woman suffrage and of national prohibition were unable to have Federal amendments embodying these changes in the constitution submitted to the states for ratification.

An immigration bill containing a literacy test was passed over the second veto of the President and became the law of the land.

At the close of the administration, the Federal Prohibition amendment passed Congress by the necessary two-thirds vote, and was submitted to the states for ratification.

Another notable reform of the Wilson administration was the extension of the Civil Service to all classes of postmasters. The parcel post system was made of greater public utility; and the anti-trust situation was clarified by the activities of the Federal Trade Commission.

President Wilson's administration saw also the enactment of national legislation designed to provide a normal eight-hour working-day for railroad employees. For the details of this legislation, see the article Railroads, *Eight Hour Day*.

President Wilson was married in Washington Dec. 18, 1915, to Mrs. Norman Galt, widow of a business man of that city who had died eight years before.

SECOND TERM.

Thirty-third administration—Democratic.

Vice President—
Thomas R. Marshall.
Secretary of State—
Robert Lansing.
Secretary of the Treasury—
William Gibbs McAdoo.
Carter Glass.
Secretary of War—
Newton Diehl Baker.
Attorney-General—
Thomas W. Gregory.
A Mitchell Palmer.
Postmaster-General—
Albert Sidney Burleson.
Secretary of the Navy—
Josephus Daniels.
Secretary of Interior—
Franklin Knight Lane.
Secretary of Agriculture—
David Franklin Houston.
Secretary of Commerce—
William C. Redfield.
Secretary of Labor—
William Bauchop Wilson.

Platform.—On June 15, 1916, Woodrow Wilson was re-nominated by acclamation for the Presidency by the Democratic convention in St. Louis. With little contest, Thomas R. Marshall was re-nominated for vice-president. Mr. Bryan played little or no part in the proceedings. The platform praised the achievements of Mr. Wilson's first administration, strongly commending his handling of foreign problems both with Germany and with Mexico. It re-affirmed the traditional Democratic tariff policy; and in addition, proposed a government-owned and -operated merchant marine. Preparedness, conservation, the Monroe Doctrine, a federal child labor law, ultimate independence for the Philippines, and a Federal Trade Commission were endorsed. Woman Suffrage was also endorsed, but by state action.

Opposition.—Mr. Roosevelt exerted every energy to capture the Republican nomination; but the memory of his disruption of the Republican Party by the organization of the Progressive Party four years previously was too fresh in the leaders' minds to allow him success. As soon as the Republican convention met in Chicago on June 7, it was evident that there was a strong drift to Charles Evans Hughes, formerly governor of New York, and at that time on the Supreme Bench of the United States—in spite of the American tradition that Supreme Court justices should play no part in politics and in spite of the fact that Mr. Hughes had recognized that tradition by refusing to stir a finger for nomination, or even to be quoted in con-

nection with it. The first ballot gave Mr. Hughes 253½ votes, Mr. Weeks 105, Mr. Root, 103, Mr. Cummins 85, Mr. Roosevelt 65, and Mr. LaFollette 25. Mr. Hughes was nominated on the third ballot.

The Progressive Party held its convention in Chicago at the same time, and nominated Mr. Roosevelt for the Presidency. Mr. Roosevelt, however, declined the honor, and advised that the convention endorse the nomination of Mr. Hughes; and that action saw the end of the Progressive Party as a factor in American politcs. The Prohibitionists nominated J. Frank Hanly; the Socialists, Arthur Benson.

The campaign was fought almost entirely on the question of the foreign policy of the preceding administration, Mr. Hughes, Mr. Roosevelt and the other Republican leaders assailing it as weak, un-American, and more likely to plunge the country into war than would a more vigorous assertion of American rights. The enactment of the eight-hour law for railroad employees was also denounced by Mr. Hughes as a surrender to the labor unions; and as a result, he made himself popular among business men, whereas most of the labor vote seemed to go to Mr. Wilson. The Republican promise of a federal woman suffrage amendment did not turn a majority of the women's votes to Mr. Hughes.

Re-election.—The first reports of the election indicated that the Republicans had won a sweeping victory, and that the next President of the United States would be Mr. Charles Evans Hughes. Even on the second day after the voters had gone to the polls, it seemed that Mr. Wilson had been defeated, although it was then evident that the result would be close. It was not until a week had elapsed that Mr. Wilson's re-election, by the narrow margin of 21 electoral votes, was conceded. The East went almost solidly for Mr. Hughes; and it was the West, with the scattered agricultural districts, which turned the tide in Mr. Wilson's favor. There is every evidence that the women voters of the West materially helped Mr. Wilson to his victory. The deciding state was California, where Mr. Wilson's majority was less than 4,000 in a vote of 925,000. The total Wilson popular vote was 9,116,296 as compared with 8,547,474 for his opponent. The prohibition vote gained slightly, and the Socialist vote declined sharply. For detailed account of the vote, see the article Presidential Elections. The Senate maintained a reduced Democratic majority, and the House of Representatives presented an equally divided membership.

Mr. Wilson made no change in his Cabinet from the first administration. His attention was occupied entirely by the crisis with Germany, and his policy remained uninterrupted, as indicated by his brief Second Inaugural Address (page 8221).

War with Germany.—It was constantly evident that a policy of armed neutrality would not suffice to restrain Germany's depredations against the rights of the United States, and on April 3, 1917, Congress met in special session in response to the President's summons. He addressed them that same evening; and with the consciousness that the occasion had seldom been surpassed for momentousness in the history of the world, requested recognition of a state of war with the Imperial German Government. The President defined the conflict, not so much as an endeavor to avenge American honor, as the acceptance of a gauge of battle against an ideal of government which was calculated to turn back the progress of the nobler achievements of civilization. After rehearsing the unethical principles which dominated the German government, he declared that unless those principles were once for all time overthrown, there would be no possibility of peace or even of confidence between the nations of the world. In a word, President Wilson defined the struggle as one between democracy and autocracy; and in a phrase which immediately became the battle-cry of Germany's opponents, declared that the "World must be made safe for democracy." The message was careful to explain that there was no quarrel with the German people, but only with their "irresponsible" government. The entire message may be found on pages 8226 to 8233.

Congress replied quickly to the President's leadership, and on April 6, 1917, the announcement of a state of war with Germany was signed by the President. For the prosecution of the war, see the article European War.

DOMESTIC ACHIEVEMENTS.—Although the prosecution of the war against the Central Powers naturally became the prime object of interest both to the country and to the President from the very beginning of Mr. Wilson's second administration, nevertheless certain activities of the United States not connected with the War during that period were not without importance.

The *Prohibition Movement* gained in strength, its normal arguments being strengthened by the need for the highest possible efficiency in time of war and by the example of the United States's Allies in either banning certain forms of strong drink or curtailing them. Prohibition was an issue which cut through political alignments and neither Mr. Wilson nor his party officially took part in the prohibition movement. In December, 1917, Congress passed the amendment to the United State Constitution forbidding the manufacture and sale of alcoholic liquors, and in January, 1919 the amendment was ratified by the necessary number of state legislatures, to become effective in January, 1920. However, wartime legislation of Congress had previously prohibited the sale of liquor containing more than 2¾% alcohol, from July 1, 1919 to the day when the President should declare that the demobilization of the American forces raised for the struggle against the Central Powers had been completed.

In the question of *Woman Suffrage*, however, President Wilson took a more direct interest. He used the influence at his command to endeavor to effect the passage of the Susan B. Anthony suffrage amendment to the Constitution. The invaluable services rendered by women to the war activities of the country favored the suffrage cause, the sentiment throughout the country being indicated by the granting of the vote to women in New York state by a referendum in November, 1917. Despite the President's leadership, however, equal suffrage on the whole found greater support among the Republicans than among the Democrats, largely because of the ramifications of the negro problem in the South. On May 21, 1919 the amendment to the United States Constitution prohibiting the denial of the vote to women because of their sex was passed by Congress and was submitted to the state legislatures for ratification.

In 1918 a Supreme Court decision of 5 to 4 declared unconstitutional the *Child Labor* bill passed in Mr. Wilson's first administration. However, an especial tax upon products of child labor had the effect of

accomplishing some of the purposes of the amendment.

Political issues and problems were not quiescent even during war-time. Although the President's appointments to positions of high responsibility were on the whole made without regard to political affiliation, and although the Republicans cooperated loyally with the Democrats in the passage of all necessary war legislation, yet there were many charges that politics were being played openly, both by the administration and by the opposite party. The Sixty-fifth Congress presented a Senate with a slight Democratic majority and a House of Representatives almost evenly divided; but on the whole the new national and international problems created by the war had eclipsed the old points of difference in political differences between the old parties. The concessions made to Labor, however, during the war were, justly or unjustly, laid at the door of the Wilson Administration, with the result that the business interests of the country tended to become more inimical to the Wilson Administration. However, Labor was far from satisfied with the advances it had made during Mr. Wilson's term of office and, although it tended markedly to support the Democratic Party rather than the Republican, was paying more and more attention to the possibility of organizing a political party of its own, based roughly on the model of the great British Labor Party.

Before the national elections in November, 1918, President Wilson issued an appeal to the country to show its approval of his conduct of America's efforts in the War by returning Democratic candidates. However, the results of the elections were to make the Sixty-Sixth Congress Republican in both branches. Although some observers maintained that the President's appeal had halted an even more widespread defection from the Democratic Party than actually occurred, the consensus of opinion was that he had hurt the chances of the candidates of his party by trying to make the Government, as in England, a purely partisan responsibility.

This administration saw also the rise of another agrarian political movement in the shape of the *Non-Partisan League* of the Northwest. To some extent representing the same elements which had composed the Populist movement some twenty and more years previously, its program showed more definite evidence than the latter of Socialist influence.

The crisis through which the country passed as a result of the European War also brought *Socialism* to the front as a political force to be reckoned with for the first time in the history of the United States. Most of those who opposed the Government in its prosecution of the war against the Central Powers rallied around the Socialist standard, and the publicity given by the war and by the Russian Revolution to the strength of the Socialist movement in Europe also contributed to the greatly increased number of votes which the Socialist Party polled in state, municipal and national elections. However, resentment against the attitude of the Socialist Party in the war against the Central Powers increased with the prolongation of the war and this resentment, together with the defection of many elements within the Party because of its refusal to adopt the entire Bolshevist or communist program, weakened the Socialist strength in the months directly following the termination of hostilities.

The High Cost of Living became the phenomenon of greatest national effect after the conclusion of hostilities of the Great War. Great increases in the cost of most commodities were inevitable as a result of the inflation of currency due to the war; the diversion of national production for a long period to the purely destructive purposes of war; the economic prostration of many countries of the world as a result of the war and the consequent curtailment of the world's stock of goods; the death in war of millions of workers; the necessity of heavy taxation to meet the debts of war; the removal of war-time checks upon hoarding, profiteering, and speculating; the end of the coming of hundreds of thousands of immigrants satisfied with low wages; and the great increase of wages resulting from the growth in Labor's strength during and after the war. Distress became prevalent and social unrest was marked.

The Labor Question became aggravated in the months after the termination of the hostilities of the war. Labor was as strong as never before, and was bent not only on acquiring increases in wages to correspond to the increases in the cost of living, but also in ending the open shop, in shortening the work-day, and in obtaining a share in management. Strikes were numerous and devastating.

UNITED STATES AND THE EUROPEAN WAR. MILITARY ASPECTS.—The most important aspect of the entrance of the United States into and prosecution of the war against the Central Powers was naturally the military aspect. Details of the struggle will be found under the heading European War; here only general results of the military situation can be emphasized.

The first year of America's efforts was compelled to be largely preparatory. Our military policy had always been that of a small professional army and a strong navy for defensive purposes; and as the Allies already had command of the seas when we officially joined them, our Navy could assist them only in patrol duty, submarine hunting and transport-convoying. In the latter service, the Navy proved especially effective; and United States troops and supplies were convoyed to Europe with few of the anticipated mishaps.

An effective army had to be created practically overnight. Surprisingly little opposition to the draft developed and the machinery for the new forces worked on the whole according to schedule. The training and placing of more than 1,000,000 United States troops in France before midsummer, 1918 exceeded our promises to our Allies, our program being necessarily hurried by the great German victories beginning with the spring of that year. Details of the composition of the new army will be found under the heading Drafts.

The great German offensive of 1918 called out all the resources of our Allies, so that they fell back upon United States troops for their reserves and reinforcements. Nevertheless, in spite of the preparatory role which the exigencies of the circumstances compelled, United States troops acquitted themselves no less valiantly and effectively than the veteran troops of France and Great Britain on the firing lines of northern France.

Although American troops had been stationed in the frontline trenches on a quiet sector toward the end of 1917, and although they had been utilized as reserves in the first three great German drives in the spring of 1918, it was not until the fourth German drive in July, 1918 that American forces were able to exert a decisive influence upon the conflict. In July,

1918, however, the American Expeditionary Forces played a large share in the defeat of the German drive in the Second Battle of the Marne, especially in the region around Chateau-Thierry, at the apex of the huge salient which the German forces had punched out in the previous month. In the following month, General Pershing's men rendered yeoman service in forcing back the Germans to their old positions and in September the American troops performed as a unit a major operation in the capture of the St. Mihiel salient. From that time until the signing of the armistice on November 11, 1918, American troops were largely responsible for the continued defeats inflicted upon Germany's armies in northern France.

In Russia, American troops cooperated with Japanese, British and French in armed intervention. They remained there many month after the signing of the armistice, although there was no official declaration of war upon Russia by Congress and although there were many charges that the evils of Bolshevist rule in Russia had been exaggerated and that successful armed intervention would covertly result in reestablishing the monarchist regime in Russia.

Political Aspects.—The course of President Wilson in formulating a policy which tried to keep the United States neutral during the first three years of the war and yet refused to yield any of her rights and prerogatives as a nation lent his position additional influence when finally he led the country to the fray. The remarkable hold he had obtained upon his fellow-countrymen could not but be reflected in his position among his Allies. In both Great Britain and France, the prime ministers did not reflect the views of a certain radical and intellectual minority within their countries, and this minority, with its counterpart both in the other Allies' belligerent countries and in neutral countries, placed its hopes for a new world order in President Wilson. For instance, both the British Labor Party and the French Socialists were more receptive to his words than to the words of their own premiers. The consciousness that without American assistance the German cause would have triumphed lent additional weight to the President's influence.

The policy which thus enlisted the support of those to whom the war would have been fought in vain if it ended only in a military victory without new and comprehensive rearrangements in the structure of society might be described as a policy of international political democracy. Its cornerstone was a plan for a league of nations which would not only prevent the outbreak of another great war between nations, but which would also settle racial and economic problems according to democratic principles. Races were no longer to remain under a rule distasteful to them. Minor and weak nationalities were to be protected by the organization of international justice, not by political intrigues and alliances. Diplomacy must be public. Economic privileges must be open to all. The seas must be free. Disarmament must occur to the point of domestic safety, and imperialism disappear. In a word, the old anarchy characteristic of the relations between nations was to vanish before an international organization which would approach problems no longer from the point of view of national advantage, but from the point of view of world service.

In *Mexico* internal conditions improved slowly, the country remaining far from settled.

Relations with *Japan* were clarified by the adoption of an agreement recognizing that country's privileged claims in China and her position of preeminence in the Far East.

Domestic Aspects.—The old American tradition of individualism was rudely shattered by the need for the enlistment for war purposes of every element in America's strength. Centralization was inevitable after the recognition that democracy is notoriously a poor war-maker; and almost overnight policies of state socialism were adopted by the country wherever they proved more effective than private enterprise.

Government supervision and regulation was applied to the production and consumption of food and fuel; to the production, marketing and sale of all agricultural products; to the imports and exports of the country; and to all factors in production which touched the national life in its vital parts. On the whole, food and fuel rationing and food and fuel cards were not found necessary.

The Railroads soon proved inadequate under private control to the demands made upon them; and fell under government control.

The Express Companies for similar reasons were taken over by the Government for the period of the war, as were the telephone and telegraph systems. For some months after the conclusion of actual hostilities against the Central Powers, the international cables were also taken over by the Government.

In the Shipbuilding Corporation and the War Finance Corporation the Government created and utilized private business agents of its own for its own purposes; and the same entrance into the field of what had formerly been private business was seen in the building of houses by the Government to accommodate labor for which housing accommodations around war plants were insufficient.

A definite system of *Government Insurance* replaced the old pension policy of the country with respect to its soldiers and sailors.

Censorship attempts of an official nature, however, proved alien to American feeling, and, outside of military and naval forces, the censorship applied was of a voluntary nature. On the whole the voluntary censorship was followed scrupulously by publications and individuals and proved successful.

Shipping was undoubtedly the chief concern in making available the full fighting strength of America. After delays caused by changes in and quarrels among personnel, a definite shipbuilding policy was formulated and followed with what were generally considered advantageous results.

In these fields of industrial preparedness as in all, the policy of the Administration was more and more toward centralization of power and responsibility. Bit by bit the powers of the *Council of National Defense* and its advisory committees were curtailed, and the business of the country settled under trained business executives, as heads of bodies such as the *War Industries Board.* Despite one or two charges of undue influence and favoritism, the Administration's conduct of war was unusually free from suspicion of dishonesty or graft in contracts and other forms of financial negotiations between individuals and the Government.

One of the most striking influences of the war upon domestic affairs was its enormous strengthening of the hands of *Organized Labor.* Even before asking for a declaration of war against Germany, Mr. Wilson's policy had been largely in accord with the demands of labor, especially in

the threatened railroad strike of 1916; and during the war he obtained the cooperation of the American Federation of Labor by supporting its platform on numerous occasions. The country saw that a vigorous prosecution of the war was impossible without the assistance of Labor; and on the whole acquiesced in the new concessions granted the unions. Conscription of labor was avoided.

German Influences within the United States were able to hinder the prosecution of the war very slightly. Prosecution of offenders and arrest of known agents were frequent; and accordingly with the registering of all enemy aliens, internment of all such was avoided. Enemy property in the United States was taken over by the Government for the duration of the war, through the *Alien Eenemy Custodian.*

Another striking feature of the prosecution of the war was a series of acts aimed at disloyalty, pro-Germanism, sabotage, hindering the Government in the prosecution of the war or advocating such hindrance, opposing the draft, etc. Here again the Administration pursued a middle course —these laws and the punishments meted out under them not being stringent enough to satisfy certain elements in America, while other elements complained that they were incompatible with democratic notions of tolerance and rights of conscience, even in war times.

The President at the Peace Conference in Paris.—In December, 1918, the President of the United States of America set sail for Europe to participate in the formulation of the peace terms which were to end the greatest of all wars. He returned to this country toward the end of February in the following year, sailing again for France, however, in the first week of March. He finally returned from his labors in July, 1918, having been the first President to set foot upon European soil during his incumbency of office.

Germany and her associates in the war had surrendered on the basis of the principles enunciated by President Wilson in his addresses on the war, and similarly those principles had been accepted by the associates of the United States as the platform upon which the peace must be built. In particular, the "Fourteen Points" enunciated by President Wilson in his address to Congress on January 8, 1918 became a rallying ground for the peace discussions. And President Wilson went to Europe in the hope and with the intention of effecting his program in spite of the forces opposed to it.

It cannot be said that, on the whole, he succeeded. Although received in Europe with an enthusiasm which showed him entrenched firmly in the hearts of the European masses as no other statesman of his time, the hatreds of war and the limitations of national self-seeking were obstacles which the President on many occasions could not surmount. The cornerstone of his policy, a League of Nations, was achieved, but with many limitations which served to make it of narrower scope than had been hoped. For instance, there were no effective provisions for a reduction of armaments or for the abolition of conscription; decisions of international disputes coud be reached only by unanimous vote of the nine great Powers represented on the council of the League; Great Britain retained control of the seas: there was no provision for an international police force nor for an international Supreme Court, etc. Furthermore, in the treaty proper there were awards, such as those of the Shantung peninsula in China, the northeast Adriatic sea-coast, and the Austrian Tyrol, which manifestly violated the principle of nationality. All that was claimed for the treaty was that it was the best obtainable under the circumstances, that in itself it represented a long step forward and that it was the foundation for better things.

On returning to the United States, President Wilson encountered much opposition to the treaty, chiefly in the ranks of the Republican Party. Many Senators were in favor of clauses qualifying the treaty, some were in favor of amendments and a few were in favor of complete rejection.

The *Foreign Commerce* of the United States for the fiscal year ending June 30, 1919, amounted in value to $10,320,960,839, a new record. The total value of the imports was $3,095,876,582 and that of the exports, $7,225,084,257.

For the fiscal year ending June 30, 1919, the *ordinary receipts* were $5,145,882,546. The *ordinary disbursements* were $14,935,-848,740; $3,565,835,693 represented special disbursements, chiefly through the purchase of obligations of foreign governments. The excess of public debt receipts over public debt disbursements was $13,029,280,795, obtained chiefly through the sale of Liberty and Victory Bonds and War Savings Stamps.

The *Public Debt* at the end of the fiscal year 1919 was, gross, $25,484,506,160.

Wilson, Woodrow:

Addresses—
  At—
    Baltimore, Md., 8481.
    Boston, 8690.
    Columbus, Ohio, 8784.
    Columbus statue, Genoa, Italy, 8663.
    Gettysburg, Pa., 7881.
    Guildhall, London, England, 8656.
    Hotel Biltmore, New York City, 8068.
    Independence Hall, Philadelphia, Pa., 7952.
    Indianapolis, Ind., 8024.
    Luncheon of King George, 8655.
    Luncheon of President Poincaré, 8650.
    Manchester, England, 8658.
    Manhattan Club, 8081.
    Metropolitan Opera House, New York City, 8593.
    Mount Vernon, Virginia, 8532.
    Sorbonne, Paris, 8651.
  Before—
    American Bar Association, 7991.
    American Federation of Labor, 8386.
    American soldiers in France, 8653.
    Associated Press, 8051.
    Chamber of Commerce of United States, 8034.
    Confederate veterans, 7948.
    Congress (See also Messages)—
      Annual, 7906, 8015, 8102, 8183, 8399, 8627.
      Special, 7871, 7879, 7884, 7913, 7933, 7934, 7980, 8121, 8144, 8206, 8209, 8226, 8418, 8421, 8447, 8504, 8613, 8764.

Daughters of American Revolution, 8077.
Grand Army of the Republic, 7946, 8073, 8075.
Italian Chamber of Deputies, 8661.
Labor Committee of Council of National Defense, 8248.
Naturalized citizens, 8066.
Naval Academy Graduating Class, 7949.
Naval Advisory Board, 8076.
Pan-American Financial Conference, 8071.
Peace Conference at Paris, 8664, 8665, 8669, 8681.
Senate (See also Messages), 8199, 8600, 8727.
Y. M. C. A. of Pittsburgh, Pa., 7993.
Woman Suffrage Convention, 8163.
On—
  Armed neutrality protection, 8209.
  Barry, John, unveiling of statue of, 7942.
  Columbus, 8663.
  Currency, 7871, 7879.
  Flag Day, 8276.
  Funeral of soldiers and marines killed in Mexico, 7939.
  Government control of railroads, 8419.
  High Cost of Living, 8764.
  Inauguration, 7868, 8221.
  Independence Day, 7881, 7952, 8532.
  Jackson Day, 8024.
  Liberty Loan, 8481.
  Lincoln Birthplace cession to War Department, 8160.
  Memorial Day, 8265, 8720.
  Mexico, 7884, 7934.
  Panama Canal tolls, 7933.
  Peace—
    Outlook, 8447.
    Terms and war aims, 8421, 8447, 8534, 8593.
    Without Victory, 8199.
  Railroad labor trouble, 8144.
  Red Cross, 8500.
  Renomination, 8149.
  Revenues, 7980.
  Severance of diplomatic relations with Germany, 8206.
  Submarine warfare of Germany, 8121.
  Tariff, 7871, 7879.
  Taxation needs, 8504.
  Trusts and monopolies, 7913.
  War with Germany, 8226.
To fellow-countrymen, 8249, 8311, 8535, 8556, 8627, 8726, 8783.

Central Powers. See Germany, Austria-Hungary, Bulgaria, Turkey.
Chambers of Commerce, advantages of, 8036.
Château-Thierry, American victory at, 8638, 8729.
Chemical Industry, protection urged for, 8718.
Chief of Staff given control over War Department in absence of Secretary and Assistant Secretary of War, 8362.
Child labor, prevention of, urged, 8714.
China—
    Citizens of. See Chinese.
    Emperor of, felicitations to and from, on armistice of Great War, 8625.
    Japan and, American attitude toward 1915 agreement between, 8775.
    Shantung peninsula of, award to Japan discussed, 8774.
Chinese, exclusion of, from Canal Zone, 8213.
Christianity, aggressive, discussed, 7995.
Citizens—
    American, disloyal, denounced, 8154.
    American, in Europe, relief for, 7961, 7962.
    Naturalized, disloyalty of, 8114, 8120.
    Register of those abroad to be kept by American Consuls, 8177.
    Training of, in use of arms, 8022.
Citizenship in America, meaning of, 8066.
Citizenship, requirement of Civil Service waived in special case, 8175.
Civil Service—
    Aliens, appointment of, when no citizens are available, 7959.
    Citizenship, requirement of, waived in specified case, 8175.
    Commissions, cooperation among, provisions for, 8253.
    Established in first, second, and third classes of post-offices, 8225.
    Examinations refused to recent Government employees under certain conditions, 8225.
    Former employees under, reinstated, 8276.
    Rules suspended, in—
        Appointments—
            Of aliens, 7959.
            Of war veterans, 8700, 8701.
            To military organizations sent abroad, 8262.
        Confidential positions under Trading with the Enemy Act, 8377.

Council of National Defense positions, 8253.
    Training camp activities, 8376.
    War veterans' readmission to, 8551.
Civil War soldiers, tribute to, 7946.
Claims, pecuniary, convention with South and Central American republics for arbitraton of, 7982.
Clemenceau, Premier—
    Letter from, on American war record discussed, 8721.
    Proposed as permanent chairman of Paris Peace Conference, 8664.
Cloture rule should be established in Senate, 8217.
Club life, influence of, 8081.
Coal—
    Increased production of, urged, 8566.
    Prices fixed, 8327, 8398.
Coast Guard, Treasury Department reassigned control over, 8782.
Coast line, necessity for charting, 8019.
Coastwise trade, repeal of exemption from tolls on Panama Canal for vessels in, asked, 7933.
Coconino national forest, ranger station for, 7990.
Colombia, ratification urged of treaty with, 8640.
Colon, quarantine regulations for, 7966.
Colonies, interests of, must have equal consideration with interests of claimant governments, 8424.
Colorado, domestic violence in, proclamation against, 7937.
Colorado National Forest, site for look-out station in, designated, 7966.
Columbus, Christopher, service rendered by, discussed, 8663.
Commerce, American, discussed, 8016, 8028, 8072, 8109, 8151. (See also Merchant Marine.)
Commerce, Secretary of, war administration details vested in, 8372.
Committee on Public Information. (See Public Information Committee).
Confederate soldiers, tribute to, 7948.
Congress—
    Adjournment of, denounced, 8697.
    Extra session of, called, 8709.
    Legislation of, 8045.
    Notable record of, 8015.
    Work of, commended, 8000.
Congress of Vienna—
    Denounced, 8402.
    Not to be repeated, 8449.
Conscientious objectors, regulations concerning, 8475.
Constitutional amendment for—
    Prohibition announced, 8688.
    Woman suffrage urged, 8600, 8639, 8719.

Consular Service—
American citizens to be registered by, 8177.
Currency certificates to be attached to invoices, 8176.
Regulations and forms amended, 8091, 8176, 8275.
Salaries in, regulation of, 7938.
Services rendered by, for army and navy to be free of charge, 8373.
Contraband, foodstuffs should not be classed as, 8057.
Conventions, national, composition and work of suggested, 7910.
Copyright convention with France, 8517.
Copyright privileges granted to Australia, Papua and Norfolk Island, 8480.
Corporations. (See also Monopolies)—
Income tax returns, inspection of, ordered, 7960.
Licenses asked for, in interstate trade, 8771.
Cost and economy not properly studied, 7870.
Cost of living discussed, 8765.
Council of National Defense, civil service obligations removed from, 8253.
Court-martial bill denounced, 8493.
Courts, antiquated methods of, condemned, 8030.
Credits in foreign markets, 8040.
Crops, money to move, deposited by Treasury Department, 7909.
Culebra Cut, name changed to Gaillard Cut, 8050.
Currency. (See also Federal Reserve Act)—
Antiquated system of, 7869.
Elasticity secured in, 8151.
Legislation recommended, 7879.
Reform of, urged, 7908.
Cushing attacked by German aeroplane, 8062.
Customs Service—
Collection districts designated, 7989.
Dishonest manifests in Canal Zone, fines for, 7963.
Czecho-Slovakia—
Food to be given, 8685.
Independence of—
Discussed, 8696, 8731. (See also Austria-Hungary and Nationality.)
Recognized, 8607.
Repression of, discussed, 8788.
D. A. R., Address before, 8077.
Dalmatian coast, disposition of, discussed, 8704, 8707.
Danish West Indies, payment for, 8224.
Danzig, status of, discussed, 8733.

Dardanelles must be internationalized, 8425.
Daylight Saving Law, continuance of, urged, 8757, 8760.
Deadman's Island transferred to Health Service, 7979.
Declarations of London—
Invalid during European War, 8287.
Praised and explained, 8284.
Defense, National—
Aero squadron recommended, 8106.
America not to be turned into military camp, 8021.
Armed neutrality. See Armed Neutrality.
Arms for merchant ships asked for, 8209.
Army increase—
Ordered, 8172.
Urged, 8106.
Citizen army for, discussed, 8022, 8084, 8105.
Navy the proper and natural means of, 8022.
Negligence of, denied, 8023.
Organizations, Treasury Department officials may be appointed to, 8247.
Defensive Sea Areas, established and regulated, 8234, 8236, 8240, 8338, 8531.
Democracy—
At stake in European War, 8231, 8256.
Dependent upon self-control, 8391.
Opportunities of, for service, 8473.
Democratic Party—
Acceptance of nomination by, 8149.
Continuance of, in power, urged, 8627.
Discussed, 8026, 8028, 8031.
Success, meaning of, of, 7868.
Democratization of industry urged, 8714.
Dinosaur national monument, 8087.
Diplomacy must be open and public, 8422, 8423.
Directorates, interlocking, question of, 7917.
Director General of Railroads. See Railroads.
Disarmament to the point of domestic safety essential after European War, 8424.
Disloyalty denounced, 8114, 8120, 8144, 8154.
District of Columbia—
Alien enemies barred from, 8393.
Food legislation asked for, 8771.
Draft—
Boards praised, 8385.
Discussed, 8574.
Exemption of government employees from, explained, 8320.

Lands, Indian, opened to settlement, 8047.

Lands, Public—
In Hawaii, stimulation of cultivation of, 8541.
Reclamation of, by war veterans, urged, 8642.

Law activities of Government consolidated under Justice Department, 8521.

Law, statute, and precedent, discussed, 7992.

League of Nations—
Belligerents all profess to desire, 8191.
Conditions under which America would join, 8200, 8288, 8659, 8666.
Covenant of—
Discussed, 8669-8686, 8787.
Text of, 8673-8683.
First meeting of, to be called by President Wilson, 8675.
Germany might be barred from, 8402.
Need of, discussed, 8200, 8425, 8596, 8652, 8657, 8663, 8665, 8722, 8733.

Legislation, private, discussed, 8041.

Letters patent, Germany, provision for payment of fees, on, 8269.

Liberty Day proclaimed, 8365, 8490, 8588.

Liberty Loans discussed and urged upon people, 8481, 8627, 8702.

Licensing under Food and Fuel Administrations. (See Food and Fuel Administrations.)

Lincoln, character of, discussed, 8160.

Lind, John, sent to Mexico as personal representative of, 7885.

Liquors, alcoholic content of, limited, 8415.

Lissa, island of, assigned to Italy, 8707.

Literacy test for immigrants, objections to, 8043.

Little group of wilful men in Senate denounced, 8218.

Lloyd-George, premier of Great Britain, address of, on peace terms and war aims, praised, 8422.

Lusitania, sinking of, discussed, 8062, 8290.

Lyman M. Law, sinking of, discussed, 8210.

Mails, interference with. See Great Britain.

Malt liquors, proclamations regarding manufacture of, 8583, 8699.

Mandatory principle in the League of Nations discussed, 8673, 8793.

Manzano and Zuni national forests, order combining, 7987.

March, General, permanent rank of General asked for, 8761.

Marines—
Apology by Mexicans for arrest of, 7934.
Funeral of, at Brooklyn Navy Yard, 7939.

McAdoo, Director General of Railroads, express business placed under, 8632.

McReynolds, Attorney-General, letter to, 8023.

Meat, necessity and regulations for conservation of, 8432.

Mediation in European War (See also Peace)—
Duty of America to accomplish, 8052.
Offered, 8190.

Memorial Day address, 7946, 8265.

Merchant Marine—
Defense of. See Armed Neutrality.
Discussed, 8016, 8018, 8028, 8072, 8108, 8110, 8716.
Foreign-built ships admitted to American entry, 8006, 8354.
Re-creation of, begun, 8151.

Messages to Congress. Consult the topics treated.

Messages to Fellow-Countrymen. See Addresses to Fellow-Countrymen.

Mexico—
Agreement with, for pursuit of bandits, 8131.
American troops in—
Arrest of, 7934.
Captured, release of, demanded, 8140.
Reasons for, discussed, 8134.
Use of, permission asked for, 7936.
Americans in—
Asked to leave, 7887.
Killed by Villa bandits, 8133.
Arms and ammunition shipments to—
Forbidden, 7888, 8089, 8756.
Permitted, 7928, 8090.
Bandits in, pursuit of, discussed, 8155.
Border raids and outrages, summary of, 8132.
Carrizal, encounter at, 8140.
Columbus, N. M., attacked by bandits from, 8133.
Constitutionalists, character of, 7892.
Election in, advised, 7886.
Embargo against ports of, 8091, 8136.
Gamboa, reply of, to proposals of American government, 7889.
German note to, confirmed, 8216.
Government of, de facto—
Inefficiency of, 8138.
Recognized, 8090.
Grievances against, summary of, 8132.

Investors in securities of, to be safeguarded, 8413, 8419.

Legislation concerning may be needed, 8405.

Military control suggested for, 8184.

N. Y., N. H. & H., criminal proceedings directed against, 8023.

Policy toward, discussed, 8644.

Regulation of, discussed, 8117.

Return of, to owners, date set for, 8719.

Shopmen of, demand of, for increased pay discussed, 8775.

Subsidies to, deplored, 8018.

Unified management of, benefits of, 8412, 8419.

Reclamation of waste land by soldiers urged, 8642.

Reconstruction of American industrial life unnecessary, 8640.

Red Cross, American—

Appeal for support of, 8264, 8417, 8494, 8648.

School children urged to join, 8358.

Secretaries of, to be sent to Russia, 8592.

Services of, discussed, 8501.

Red Cross, International, listing of alien enemies for, 8274.

Red Cross Week proclaimed, 8264, 8494.

Republican Party—

Defeat of, asked, 8628.

Discussed, 8025, 8150.

Research Council, National. (See National Research Council.)

Resources, natural. (See Natural Resources.)

Revenues (See also Taxation)—

Additional $100,000,000 needed, 7981.

Decrease in, announced, 7980.

Sources of, discussed, 8112.

Revolutions discussed, 8619, 8790.

Right more precious than peace, 8233.

Roosevelt, Ex-President—

Death of, announced, 8685.

Inadvisability of sending abroad in charge of volunteer regiment, 8260.

Rumania, evacuation and restoration of, essential, 8424.

Rural credits. (See Credit, Agricultural, also Farm Loan Act.)

Russia—

American sympathy for, 8423, 8469, 8501.

Convention with for protection of fur seals and sea otter, 7877.

Evacuation by foes of, necessary, 8424.

German betrayal of, denounced, 8483, 8595.

Interference with, denounced, 8424.

Intervention in, discussed, 8590, 8592.

Messages to, 8270, 8469.

Peace proposals of, discussed, 8421.

People of—

Misled 8403.

Praised, 8422, 8423.

Revolution in, praised and discussed, 8230, 8299.

Territory of, must be evacuated by foes, 8424.

Terrorism in, denounced, 8589.

Ruthenians, contribution day for stricken, proclaimed, 8273.

Saare Valley. See Sarre Valley.

Sabbath observance enjoined upon Army and Navy, 8433.

Safety at Sea—

Convention for, 8019.

International discussion of, 7912.

Sailors of United States, rights and duties of, in foreign ports, 8091.

St. Mihiel, American victory at, 8638.

Sarre Valley, problem of disposition of, discussed, 8732.

Sea areas, defensive, establishment of and regulations for, 8234, 8236, 8240.

Seamen's law, operation of suspended, 8101.

Secret treaties between Entente Allies discussed, 8703.

Security issues, control urged of, 8771.

Selective Service Law. (See Draft.)

Self-determination of Nationalities. (See Nationality.)

Senate—

Rules of, criticised, 8028, 8217.

Special session of, called, 8216.

Serbia—

Access to the sea must be granted, 8425.

Evacuation and restoration of, essential, 8424.

Freedom must be granted to, 8403.

Shantung Peninsula of China, award of, to Japan discussed, 8774.

Sheep experiment station established, 8101.

Shipping (See also Merchant Marine)—

Control of, discussed, 8642.

Control of, in ports during war, given to Secretary of Navy, 8402.

Foreign-built, admitted to American registry, 8006.

Law regarding, suspended, 8354.

Foreign interests eliminated from, 8564.

Importance of, in war against Germany, 8250.

Lack of, deplored, 8016, 8072, 8109.

Owners of, impede Government, 8313.

Purchase of, urged, 8028, 8110.

Shipping bill—

Passage of urged, 8018.

Threat against, by Senators, 8028.

Turkey—
Armistice in European War, correspondence with, concerning, 8611.
Boundaries of, to be re-arranged, 8731.
Dardenelles must be internationalized, 8425.
German domination over, must end, 8401.
Nationalities under—
Autonomy for, essential, 8401, 8425.
Help to be given, 8618.
Twin Sisters administrative site, lookout station at, 7966.
Uchida, Viscount, statement regarding Shantung Peninsula by, discussed, 8774.
Ukrainians, contribution day for, proclaimed, 8273.
Underwood, Congressman, letter to, 8000.
United States (See America.)
United States Employment Service. See Employment Service.
United States Grain Corporation organized from Food Administration Grain Corporation, 8711.
United States Tariff Commission. See Tariff Commission.
United States Wheat Director appointed, 8710.
University of Paris praised, 8651.
Utah, national monument in, 8087.
Veto messages. See topics concerned.
Virgin Islands—
Lighthouse service on, 8319.
Payment for, 8324.
Quarantine duties on, 8361.
Rules for government of, 8332, 8426.
Virginia Bill of Rights discussed, 8103.
Vocational and industrial education, promotion of, 8187.
Vocational rehabilitation of American soldiers and sailors, support urged for, 8758.
Volpna, port of, assigned to Italy, 8707.
War Department—
Control of, vested in Chief of Staff in absence of Secretary and Assistant Secretary of War, 8362.
Lincoln's birthplace presented to, 8160.
War Industries Board established and powers outlined, 8518.
War Labor Board, establishment of, 8485.
War Message, 8226.
War risk insurance, experts appointed for, 7979.
War Savings Stamps appeal for purchase of, 8519.

War, Secretary of, Governor-General of Philippines to report to, 8170.
War Trade Board—
Created and duties explained, 8367.
War Industries Board representative placed on, 8569.
War Trade Council, created, 8368.
Washington, George, foreign policy of, discussed, 8597.
Water power development discussed, 8017, 8029, 8405.
Wheat—
Conservation of, necessity and regulations for, 8432.
Control of, discussed, 8767.
Director appointed, 8710.
Prices fixed and discussed, 8346, 8457, 8577, 8580.
Whitman National Forest, enlarged, 8219.
Wireless telegraph—
Canal Zone station established, 7960.
Lands in Alaska set aside for naval radio stations, 8215.
Neutrality of, to be enforced, 7962.
Ocean-going vessels ordered to be fitted with, 7958.
Stations taken for use of government, 8006, 8241.
Woman Suffrage—
Adoption of, urged, 8375, 8600, 8639, 8719.
European War and, 8601.
Growth of movement for, 8163, 8599.
Women included in enemy alien regulations, 8491.
Women's service in the European War discussed, 8601, 8639.
World Court, establishment of, long the hope of America, 8285.
Young Men's Christian Association—
Address to, 7993.
Secretaries to be sent to Russia, 8592.
Zionist movement endorsed, 8575.
Zuni and Manzano national forests, combining, 7987.

Wilson's Creek (Mo.), Battle of.—During the summer of 1861 Confederate troops in large numbers were sent into Missouri from Arkansas, Louisiana, and Texas. Gen. Lyon was stationed at Springfield with 5,500 Federal troops. The Confederates, 20,000 strong, advanced in two columns under McCulloch and Price. During the night of Aug. 9, 1861, Sigel was sent with 1,500 men to attack the Confederate rear, nine miles distant, at Wilson's Creek, while Lyon attacked the front. Both attacks were repulsed. Sigel lost 5 of his 6 guns and more than half of his men. Lyon was killed while leading a charge. The Federal loss was 1,246 in killed, wounded, and missing. The Confederate loss was about the same.

Wines, duty on, discussed, 1131, 1321, 2127, 2250.

Winslow, The, disabled in conflict in Cardenas Bay, Cuba, 6302, 6316.

Rescued by the *Hudson*, 6302.

Thanks of Congress to officers and men of, recommended, 6302.

Wireless Telegraph.—Heinrich Hertz, of Karlsruhe, Germany, in 1888 demonstrated the existence of electric waves and devised means for producing and receiving them. Edouard Branly, of Paris, France, in 1900 brought out a sensitive detector for manifesting the presence of electric waves, to which he gave the name radio-conductor. This was improved and called a coherer by Oliver Lodge of Birmingham, England, and later perfected and used as a wireless telegraph receptor by William Marconi, of England, who patented it. The first receptor for receiving and indicating electric waves was designed by Alexander Popoff, of St. Petersburg, Russia, in 1895. Lodge later designed a syntonic system for sending and receiving, which could be tuned to the same period of oscillation by means of inductive coils and condensers. The principal systems in practical use are the Marconi, the Lodge-Muirhead, the Fessenden, the De Forest, the Telefunken, the Popp-Branly and the Paulson.

The government station at Arlington, Va., has developed a high power transmission range of 3,500 miles, conducting experiments in conjunction with the Eiffel Tower in Paris. Other high power stations are at Belmar, N. J., owned by the Marconi Company, and at Sayville, L. I., owned by the Telefunken Company, operating direct with Nauen, Germany.

Wireless Telegraph:

Ocean Going vessels ordered to be fitted with, 7958.

Order establishing station in Canal Zone for use of Navy, 7960.

Neutrality of stations ordered enforced, 7962.

Wisconsin.—One of the western group of states; nickname, "The Badger State"; motto, "Forward." It lies in the northern part of the country, between lat. 42° 27' and 47° north and long. 86° 53' and 92° 54' west, not including islands in Lake Superior and Michigan. It is bounded on the north by Lake Superior and the upper peninsula of Michigan, on the northeast and east by the upper peninsula of Michigan and Lake Michigan, on the south by Illinois, and on the west by Iowa and Minnesota (separated mostly by the Mississippi and St. Croix Rivers). The area is 56,066 square miles. Wisconsin is hilly in the north and southwest, but elsewhere is generally level. It has important agricultural, mining, and lumbering interests and extensive manufactures of flour, machinery, and beer.

Wisconsin was visited as early as 1634 by Nicollet, La Salle, and French fur traders, who established a settlement at Green Bay in 1639. It was included in the Northwest Territory till 1800, when it became a part of the Indian Territory. In 1809 it was included in Illinois Territory, and in 1818 in Michigan Territory, and in 1836 it was organized as Wisconsin Territory, and included, besides its present area, the territory now embraced in the states of Iowa and Minnesota and part of the Dakotas. It was admitted to the Union May 29, 1848.

Statistics of agriculture collected for the last Federal census place the number of farms in the state at 177,127, comprising 21,060,466 acres, valued, with stock and improvements, at $1,413,043,000. The average value of land per acre was $43.30. The domestic animals, poultry, etc., were valued at $158,454,043, including 2,678,000 cattle, valued at $67,399,858; 614,654 horses, $68,585,573; 2,872 mules, $316,066; 1,809,331 swine, $13,620,741; 929,783 sheep, $3,669,572, and poultry, $4,468,703. The yield and value of the field crops for 1911 was: corn 1,600,000 acres, 58,080,000 bushels, $34,848,000; wheat, 195,000 acres, 3,097,000 bushels, $2,788,000; oats, 2,250,000 acres, 67,050,000 bushels, $30,172,000; rye, 355,000 acres, 6,035,000 bushels, $5,069,000; potatoes, 280,000 acres, 32,480,000 bushels, $20,138,000; hay, 2,079,000 acres, 2,495,000 tons, $38,922,000; tobacco, 41,000 acres, 51,250,000 pounds, $5,125,000.

The state ranks fifth in the production of iron ore. The output in 1910 was 1,149,551 long tons, valued at $2,727,406. The amount of capital invested in manufacture is $412,647,051, and $71,471,805 is paid annually to 151,391 wage-earners. Lumber is the leading industry, with 725 establishments, capitalized at $46,543,787. The number of manufacturing establishments in Wisconsin having an annual output valued at $500 or more at the beginning of 1915 was 9,104. The amount of capital invested was $754,287,000, giving employment to 230,273 persons, using material valued at $417,415,000, and turning out finished goods worth $695,172,000. Salaries and wages paid amounted to $149,762,000.

There were in 1907, 7,292 miles of steam railway, and 776 miles of electric lines. The population in 1910 was 2,343,860.

Wisconsin:

Act for continuing certain works in, reasons for applying pocket veto to, 2460.

Boundary line with Michigan, referred to, 1846.

Constitution adopted by, transmitted, 2359, 2427.

Volunteers from, thanks of President tendered, 3442.

Wisconsin River, act regarding improvement of, vetoed, 4236.

Witnesses:

Fees of, referred to, 4730, 4770, 4836.

Protection of, from injury, recommended, 5477.

Wolverine State.—A nickname for Michigan (q. v.). (See also States); sometimes also nicknamed the Lake State.

Woman Suffrage.—The first American woman to demand the ballot so far as known, was Mistress Margaret Brent, of Maryland, in 1647. She was heir of Lord Calvert, the brother of Lord Baltimore, and executor of the estates of both in the colony, and, as representation in the Legislature was based on property, she demanded "place and voyce"—two votes—in that body. Her petition was hotly debated for several hours and finally denied.

The colonial records of Massachusetts show that women voted under the Old Province Charter from 1691 to 1780 for all elective officers. When a constitution was adopted they were excluded from a vote for Governor and Legislature but retained it for other officials. In March, 1776, Mrs. Abigail Adams wrote to her husband, John Adams, in the Continental Congress asking him to remember the ladies in the new code of laws, and in 1778, Mrs. Corbin, sister of

Richard Henry Lee, of Virginia, presented her own petition for the right to vote. The Continental Congress left the suffrage to be dealt with by the states in their constitutions and New Jersey was the only one which conferred it on women, its constitution giving the franchise to "all inhabitants worth $250, etc." In 1790 a revision of the election law used the words "he or she," thus emphasizing the inclusion of women in the electorate, but in 1807 the Legislature passed an arbitrary act limiting the suffrage to "white male citizens." This was declared to be a usurpation of authority, on the ground that the constitution could be changed only by action of the voters.

In 1826 Frances Wright, a young Scotch woman of beauty, education and wealth, came to the United States and in a series of lectures was the first to bring the question of woman suffrage thus before the public, where it met with almost universal derision. In 1836 Ernestine L. Rose, daughter of a Rabbi in Poland, made a lecture tour of America advocating the full enfranchisement of women and was the first to urge them to secure the repeal of laws which affected their interests. In the winter of 1836-7 she circulated a petition in Albany, N. Y., for a law that would enable a married woman to hold property and could get only five signatures, including men and women, but she carried these to the Legislature and addressed that body in behalf of such a law. She kept up this work steadily and by 1840 she had associated with her Elizabeth Cady Stanton, Paulina Wright Davis and Lucretia Mott. They continued their petitions and addresses to the Legislature until 1848, when the law extended property rights to married women, and thereafter they devoted themselves to working for the suffrage.

Margaret Fuller, one of a coterie of thinkers in Boston, in her writings and semi-public addresses in 1840 demanded political rights for women. In 1847 Lucy Stone, just graduated from Oberlin College, began speaking on woman's rights. Soon afterwards Lucretia Mott published a "Discourse on Woman," in answer to a lecture which Richard H. Dana was giving in many cities ridiculing the idea of political equality for women.

The first woman suffrage convention in the United States was held in the Wesleyan Chapel, at Seneca Falls, N. Y., on the 19th and 20th of July, 1848. It demanded for women equal rights with men. James Mott presided and addresses were made by Lucretia Mott and her sister, Martha C. Wright, Elizabeth Cady Stanton, Mary Ann McClintock, Frederick Douglass and several men prominent in the locality. A declaration and resolutions were discussed, the latter adopted and the former signed by one hundred men and women, some of whom withdrew their names when "the storm of ridicule began to break." This declaration stated the whole case for woman as comprehensively as it ever has been stated since; the resolutions comprised practically every demand that ever afterward was made for women, and, taken together, they formed a remarkable document.

In 1852 a bona fide woman's rights convention, with delegates present from eight states and Canada, was held in Syracuse. It brought to the front the wonderful galaxy of women whose names were henceforth connected with this movement, and here began its fifty-four years' leadership by Miss Anthony.

April 19 and 20, 1850, a woman's rights convention was held in the Second Baptist Church of Salem, Ohio. Emily Robinson,

J. Elizabeth Jones and Josephine S. Griffing were three of the leading spirits. The "Memorial to the Constitutional Convention" and the "Address to the Women of Ohio" have not been surpassed in eloquence and force in the years that have since elapsed. It is said that nearly 8,000 signatures to the memorial were secured. In 1852 the first State Suffrage Association was formed. Woman's rights conventions were held annually in Ohio thereafter until the approach of the civil war.

In May, 1850, a few women decided to call a convention to discuss exclusively the rights of women, and the time and place were fixed for Oct. 23 and 24 in Worcester, Mass., and from the holding of this convention the woman's rights movement may be said to have assumed a national aspect. Nine states were represented by speakers and among these were Garrison, Phillips, Pillsbury, Foster, Burleigh, Douglass, Channing, Mrs. Mott, Mrs. Rose, Abby Kelly, Lucy Stone, Antoinette Brown and Dr. Harriot K. Hunt, and letters were read from Emerson, Alcott, Whittier, Gerrit Smith, Joshua R. Giddings, Mrs. Swisshelm, Elizur Wright, Mrs. Stanton and others. Mrs. Davis presided. A national committee was formed, under whose management conventions were held annually in various cities, while the question was always thereafter a leading one in Massachusetts. An account of this Massachusetts convention in the *Westminster Review*, London, by Mrs. John Stuart Mill, marked the beginning of the movement for woman suffrage in Great Britain.

In 1850 the constitution of Indiana was revised and the laws for women were liberalized beyond any then existing. A woman's rights convention took place in Dublin, Ind., in October, 1851. Therefore these meetings became annual.

In June, 1852, the first woman's rights convention of Pennsylvania was held in West Chester, and was largely under the auspices of the Friends, or Quakers, among them James and Lucretia Mott.

From 1852 woman's rights conventions were held in many parts of the country. Woman suffrage was slowly gaining ground, when the breaking out of the civil war banished all other questions from the public thought. When the war was ended and the women again took up their cause they met the vast complication of the rights of the emancipated negroes, and were compelled even by those who had been their strongest supporters to yield their claims to those of negro men.

The civil, legal and political results of the fourteenth and fifteenth amendments to the national constitution tended still further to obscure and hinder the efforts to obtain the franchise for women. An Equal Rights Association had been formed to promote the interests of both negroes and white women, but in 1869 the latter were forced to recognize the necessity for a separate organization and a National Woman Suffrage Association was formed whose sole object was to secure an amendment to the national constitution which should enfranchise women. Mrs. Stanton was made president. As there was some division of sentiment at this time, a call was issued by Lucy Stone, Julia Ward Howe and others for a convention to meet in Cleveland, Ohio, the following November, and here the American Woman Suffrage Association was formed, with Henry Ward Beecher, president. It worked principally to obtain the suffrage through amendments to state constitutions. Both societies held national conventions every year thereafter. In 1890 the two bodies united under the name National American Woman Suffrage Association, and since then both methods of work have been followed. Mrs. Stanton was elected president of the new organization; Miss Anthony, vice-president-at-large; Lucy Stone, chairman Executive Committee. In 1892 Mrs. Stanton resigned her office because of advancing age; Miss Anthony was elected president and the Rev. Anna Howard Shaw, vice-president. Miss Anthony resigned the presidency in 1900 and Mrs. Carrie Chapman Catt was elected to it. In 1904 she was succeeded by Miss Shaw. National headquarters were opened in 1895. The National Association is a federation of State Suffrage Associations; the latter are composed of County Societies made up of Local Suffrage Clubs. School suffrage prevails in twenty-six states and tax-payers' suffrage in four states.

In New Zealand, Australia and Finland all women vote on exactly the same terms as all men, and in the last two countries may sit in the Parliament. In Norway women have the complete suffrage with a very slight property qualification. In Great Britain, Sweden and Iceland they vote for all officials except members of Parliament. In Canada they have the school and municipal suffrage.

Women have municipal suffrage in Ontario, Nova Scotia, Manitoba, Quebec, British Columbia, and the Northwest Territory, in Iceland, Denmark, and Sweden. In France women engaged in commerce have the right to vote for Judges of the Tribunal of Commerce. Women have some voting privileges in Cape Colony.

The International Woman Suffrage Alliance is composed of National Woman Suffrage Associations composed of twenty-two nations. Its officers are: President, Carrie Chapman Catt, New York; vice-president, Millicent Garrett Fawcett, London; second vice-president, Annie Furuhjelm, Finland; treasurer, Mrs. Stanton Colt, London; secretaries—First, Miss Martina Kramers, Holland; Mrs. Anna Lindemann, Germany; Miss Singe Bergman, Sweden.

Woman suffrage was granted in Wyoming in 1869; Colorado, 1893; Utah and Idaho, 1896; Washington, 1910; California, 1911; Kansas, Arizona and Oregon, 1912; Nevada and Montana in 1914. Five other states rejected the proposition in 1914.

Arkansas has granted the right of women to vote in primary elections, which in this Southern State is tantamount to full suffrage. In 1913, Illinois granted the right of women to vote for all offices not expressly mentioned in the Constitution of the State; and as national and municipal elections are not mentioned in state constitutions, this form of suffrage is usually known as Presidential and Municipal Suffrage. Both the Democratic and Republican parties carried planks in their platforms in the Presidential campaign of 1916 which favored the granting of the franchise to women—both favoring state action, although the Republican candidate favored Federal action. By May 1, 1917, the following states had also granted Presidential and Municipal Suffrage —North Dakota, Michigan, and Nebraska; and the following states had granted to women the right to vote in Presidential elections only—Ohio, Indiana, and Rhode Island. The Territory of Alaska has complete equal suffrage. These additions to the ranks of the equal suffrage states by May 1, 1917, gave 9,000,000 women the right to vote in Presidential elections. In November, 1916, Jeanette Rankin, Republican, was elected to the House of Representatives from Montana, thus becoming the first Congresswoman.

In 1915, equal suffrage was defeated by referendum in New York, New Jersey, Massachusetts, Pennsylvania; in 1916, in South Dakota, West Virginia, Iowa; in 1917, in Maine and Ohio.

On October 25, 1917, the Supreme Court of the state of Indiana pronounced unconstitutional the enactment of the legislature by which Presidential and Municipal suffrage had been granted to the women of that state, as noted above. The similar privilege extended by the legislature of the state of Ohio was recalled by a popular referendum on November 6, 1917, by which the male voters withdrew Presidential and Municipal suffrage from the women of that state.

On November 6, 1917, however, by a majority of approximately 100,000 of the 1,200,000 votes cast, the men of New York state granted full suffrage to the women of that, the largest state in the Union. One-tenth of the women of the country were thus enfranchised at one stroke. Practically the entire majority came from New York City.

In March, 1918, Texas gave women the right to vote in all primaries and nominating conventions.

On January 10, 1918, the House of Representatives, by vote of 274 to 136, passed a resolution submitting to the legislatures of the various states an amendment to the Constitution of the United States which would prevent the right of citizens to vote from being denied by the United States or by any state on account of sex. This was the so-called Susan B. Anthony amendment, submitted to Congress first in 1878. The vote for the amendment came from 165 Republicans; 104 Democrats; 2 Independents; 1 Socialist; 1 Prohibitionist; 1 Progressive. The vote against the amendment came from 33 Republicans; 102 Democrats; 1 Progressive.

An overwhelming majority of the advocates of woman suffrage are affiliated with the American Woman Suffrage Association, which must be distinguished from the Women's Political Union, which has changed its title to the Woman's Party. This latter organization, which believes in the political organization of women voters with only equal suffrage in view, inaugurated on March 5, 1917, a "peaceful picketing" of the White House, in their desire to persuade President Wilson to insist that Congress pass the Federal Woman Suffrage Amendment. For a period, little attention was paid to the "picketers," who kept guard at the gates of the White House with mottos inscribed upon banners; but with the entrance of the United States into the European War, public opinion became aroused at the innuendos which many of the banners cast at the President. The pickets accordingly frequently caused riots before the White House, and on their refusal to abstain from their efforts, many of their number were sent to the workhouse and later to jail for periods of from. three days to six months on the charges of obstructing traffic and disturbing the peace.

For an early cartoon of woman suffrage, see illustration opposite page 1581.

The New York State Association Opposed to Woman Suffrage has its central office in New York City. Its officers are as follows: Mrs. Arthur U. Dodge, president; Mrs. Fritz Achelis, first vice-president; Mrs. Elihu Root, Mrs. Richard Watson Gilder, Mrs. William A. Putnam, Mrs. Robert McVickar, Mrs. George D. Miller, and Mrs. William P. Northrup, vice-presidents; Mrs. Francis S. Bangs, treasurer; Mrs. George Phillips, secretary; Room 819, Engineering Societies Building, 29 West 39th St., New York City. There are also organizations in Massachusetts, Illinois, Oregon, Iowa, Washington, California, Pennsylvania and Maryland. These are founded with the object of testifying to legislative committees and through the medium of the public press that the opposition to woman suffrage is based upon what is claimed to be "the intelligent conviction of the majority of representative women in all lines of social, industrial, and domestic progress."

Woman Suffrage:

Adoption of, urged by President Wilson, 8375.

Growth of, 8163.

"Pickets" criticized, 8375.

Women included in provisions against alien enemies, 8491.

Women in Industry.—F r o m prehistoric down to modern times, a considerable share of the labor of the world has been done by women; but until the nineteenth century, practically all of that labor was done inside the home. With the invention of modern machinery, however, at the end of the eighteenth century, and the consequent coming of the Industrial Revolution in the United States in the years surrounding 1825, women became an important industrial factor in the general industrial work of the land. The invention of machinery in the first place made inevitable the production outside the home of most of the commodities which woman had been producing inside the home, and thus released her for outside work; and in the second place, the division of labor attendant upon machine operation brought into existence a number of industrial activities which required neither great skill nor physical power and persistence.

The cotton industry in the United States was the first which women entered to a large extent, although of recent years the proportion of women in that industry has decreased. In 1831, 68% of the cotton operatives were females; in 1860, 62%; in 1880, 57%; and in 1910, 44%. In all textile industries, women formed in 1850 50% of the operatives; in 1860, 53%; in 1905, 44%. At the present time, the five chief manufacturing industries in which women are present in great numbers are cotton, clothing, boots and shoes, printing and bookmaking, and tobacco. In these industries in 1905 there were 402,557 male and 482,173 female workers.

The census of 1910 showed that in the United States, of females over the age of 10 gainfully employed, the number was 8,075,772. The total number of females of that age in the country was 34,552,712, the ratio of those employed being 23.4%. In 1880, the number of females of the age of ten and over who were gainfully employed was 2,647,157, or 14.7% of those at the age. In 1880, the number of men employed at that age compared with the entire number in the United States at the same age was 78.7%, and in 1910 the ratio had increased only to 81.3%.

Of the women workers in 1910, 2,620,857 were in domestic and personal service; 1,807,050 in agricultural pursuits; 1,772,095 in manufacturing and mechanical pursuits; 1,202,352 in trade and transportation; and 673,418 in professional service. The trend of women in industry is shown by the facts that in the first above group in 1910 there were 32½% of the whole number of women workers and in 1880, 44½%; in the second group, 22½% in 1910 and 22½% in 1880; in the third group, 22% in 1910 and 24% in 1880; in

the fourth group, 15% in 1910 and 2½% in 1880; and in professional service, 8% in 1910 and 6½% in 1880.

It is also instructive to note that of the above five groups the number of men working in 1910 was in the first group 9% of the total number of men working; in the second, 36%; in the third, 30%; in the fourth, 21%; and in the fifth, 4%.

In 1910, separate occupations of women were as follows:—Dressmakers, 447,750; laundresses, 520,000; saleswomen, 257,700; typists and stenographers, 263,300; bookkeepers, 187,000; clerks, 234,250; midwives, trained and untrained nurses, 185,000; servants, 1,309,550; teachers, 478,000; telephone and telegraph operators, 96,480; milliners, 122,450; farm laborers, 1,515,425; musicians, 84,500; artists, 15,430; actresses, 12,000; doctors, 9,000; and lawyers, 560.

In 1880, of all females ten years of age and older, 15% were gainfully employed; in 1890, 17½%; in 1900, 19%; and in 1910, 23½%. In reading these figures, it must be remembered that child labor legislation during these years has been instrumental in removing many children from industry so that the proportion of women above 18 gainfully employed during those years would show an even more marked increase.

In 1900, of females between 10 and 13, 8% were gainfully employed; of those between 14 and 15, 20% were gainfully employed; of those between 16 and 20, 40% were gainfully employed; of those between 21 and 44, 26% were gainfully employed; and of those over 45, 16% were gainfully employed.

Of all the women working in 1910, 4% were between 10 and 13; 5½% between 14 and 15; 23% between 16 and 20; 52% between 21 and 44; and 15⅗% over 45.

Investigations show that women in industry receive lower wages than men, even for similar work; and receive less favorable working conditions, largely because they are comparatively unorganized. These facts have been instrumental in starting such protective legislative measures as the minimum wage and the eight-hour day, which are treated under their own headings.

For an account of the protection afforded working women by minimum wage legislation, consult the article Minimum Wage.

In the following states, women may work not more than 8 hours daily in manufacturing, mechanical, mercantile, laundry, hotel and restaurant work, etc. (certain other industries are included in some of the states): Alaska, Arizona, California, Colorado, District of Columbia, Montana, Nevada, Porto Rico (including stenographers and typists), Washington.

In the following states women may not work more than nine hours daily in the above or similar occupations: Arkansas, Idaho, Kansas, Maine, Minnesota (manufacturing, mechanical, telephone and telegraph in first class cities), Missouri, Nebraska, New York, Ohio, Oklahoma, Oregon (certain industries by order of Industrial Welfare Commission), Texas, Utah.

The following states have a ten-hour limit: Connecticut, Delaware, Georgia (cotton and woolen manufacturing), Illinois, Kentucky, Louisiana, Maryland, Massachusetts, Michigan, Minnesota (see above), Mississippi, New Hampshire (10¼), New Jersey, Oregon (see above), Pennsylvania, Rhode Island, South Dakota, Tennessee (10½), Vermont (10½) (manufacturing and mechanical), Virginia, Wisconsin, Wyoming.

South Carolina has an 11-hour limit in cotton and woolen manufacturing and a 12-hour limit in mercantile work.

The following states limit women's work

to 48 hours weekly: Alaska, California, Connecticut (restaurants and cafés), District of Columbia, Porto Rico.

The following states limit the number of hours weekly to 54: Arizona (56), Arkansas, Connecticut (55 in manufacturing only), Delaware, Maine, Massachusetts, Michigan, Minnesota (manufacturing, mechanical, telephone and telegraph in first-class cities), Missouri, Nebraska, Nevada (56), New Hampshire, New York, Ohio (50), Oregon (order of Industrial Welfare Commission—50 mercantile in Portland and 51 office in Portland), Pennsylvania, Rhode Island, Tennessee (57), Texas, Utah, Vermont (56), Wisconsin, Wyoming (52 for 6 days per week).

The following states have a 60-hour weekly limit upon women's work: California (canning only), Connecticut (58 mercantile), Georgia (cotton and woolen manufacturing), Kentucky, Louisiana, Maryland, Minnesota (58—see above), Mississippi, New Jersey, North Carolina (manufacturing), South Carolina (in industries mentioned above under this state), Wyoming (for a seven-day week).

The following states enforced a 6-day week: Alaska, Arkansas, Delaware, Massachusetts, New Jersey, New York, Ohio, Oregon (excluding telegraph, telephone and hotels, etc.), Pennsylvania.

In connection with child labor legislation (q. v.), the following states prohibit night work for girls under 18 or 21, even when there is no similar provision for boys: Arizona, Arkansas, District of Columbia, Hawaii, Indiana, Louisiana, Massachusetts, Michigan, Mississippi, New Hampshire, New York, Ohio, Oklahoma, Oregon, Pennsylvania. The following states prohibit night work (usually defined as falling between 10 P. M. and 6 A. M.): Connecticut (mercantile establishments), Indiana (manufacturing), Kansas (mercantile), Massachu-

setts, Nebraska (in cities over 5,000), New York, Oregon, Pennsylvania, Porto Rico, South Carolina (mercantile only), Utah (cities over 10,000).

Most states exempt canning from the jurisdiction of the law, many others provide for extension of the limit before Christmas, others decrease the daily and weekly hours permitted if the work is done at night, some annulled the laws during the prosecution of the war against the Central Powers, and several others have special provision for overtime on Saturdays in retail stores.

In April, 1917, the British government issued an official report regarding the employment of women in Great Britain at that time as compared with such employment at the time of the outbreak of the European War. In July, 1914, there were employed 3,298,000 women, distributed as follows:

Industries, 2,184,000; Commerce, 496,000; Local government, 198,000; Hotels, public houses, theatres, etc., 176,000; Permanent agricultural labor, 80,000; Professional, 67,500; Civil Service, 66,000; Transportation, 19,000; Finance and banking, 9,500; Government industries, 2,000.

Women, Labor of:

Discussed, 7090.

Investigation of, by Department of Commerce and Labor, 6984, 7035.

In Washington, 6983.

Wood Pulp should be relieved of tariff duty, 7099, 7346.

Wool.—The production and consumption of wool in the United States from 1840 to 1915 is set forth in the annexed table, together with the amount produced in each state in the latter year.

PRODUCTION, CONSUMPTION AND EXPORTATION OF WOOL.

[Sources: Production, 1896-1913, reports of the National Association of Wool Manufacturers, Boston; other years, reports of the Department of Agriculture.]

Period	Production	Exports of domestic	Domestic retained for consumption	Imports	Exports of foreign	Foreign retained for consumption	Total consumption, domestic and foreign
	Pounds	*Pounds*	*Pounds*	*Pounds*	*Pounds*	*Pounds*	*Pounds*
1840	35,802,114		35,802,114	9,898,740	85,528	9,813,212	45,615,326
1850	52,516,959	35,898	52,481,061	18,695,294		18,695,294	71,176,355
1860	60,264,913	1,055,928	59,208,985	26,282,955	157,064	26,125,891	85,334,876
1862-70	142,888,889	507,442	142,381,447	53,138,126	918,949	52,219,177	194,600,624
1871-80	186,275,000	152,303	186,122,697	68,030,280	3,938,616	64,091,664	250,214,361
1881-90	280,700,000	115,025	280,584,975	93,194,903	4,294,346	88,900,557	369,485,532
1891	285,000,000	291,922	284,708,078	129,303,648	2,638,123	126,665,525	411,373,603
1892	294,000,000	202,456	293,797,544	148,670,652	3,007,563	145,663,089	439,460,633
1893	303,153,000	91,858	303,061,142	172,433,838	4,218,637	168,215,201	471,276,343
1894	298,057,384	520,247	297,537,137	55,152,585	5,977,407	49,175,178	346,712,315
1895	309,748,000	4,279,109	305,468,891	206,033,906	2,343,081	203,690,825	509,159,716
1896	272,474,708	6,945,981	265,528,727	230,911,473	6,026,236	224,885,237	490,413,964
1897	259,153,251	5,271,535	253,881,716	350,852,026	3,427,834	347,424,192	601,305,908
1898	266,720,684	121,139	266,599,545	132,795,202	2,504,832	130,290,370	396,889,915
1899	272,191,330	1,683,419	270,507,911	76,736,209	12,412,916	64,323,293	334,831,204
1900	288,636,621	2,200,309	286,436,312	155,928,455	5,702,251	150,226,204	436,662,516
1901	302,502,328	199,565	302,302,763	103,583,505	3,590,502	99,993,003	402,295,766
1902	316,341,032	123,278	316,217,754	166,576,966	3,104,663	163,472,303	479,690,057
1903	287,450,000	518,919	286,931,081	177,137,796	2,992,995	174,144,801	461,075,882
1904	291,783,032	319,750	291,463,282	173,742,834	2,863,053	170,879,781	462,343,063
1905	295,488,438	123,951	295,364,487	249,135,746	2,437,697	246,698,049	542,062,536
1906	298,915,130	192,481	298,722,649	201,688,668	5,450,378	196,238,290	494,960,939
1907	298,294,750	214,840	298,079,910	203,847,545	3,231,908	200,615,637	498,695,547
1908	311,138,321	182,458	310,955,863	125,980,524	5,684,357	120,296,167	431,252,030
1909	328,110,749	28,376	328,082,373	266,409,304	3,495,599	262,913,705	590,996,078
1910	321,362,750	47,520	321,315,230	263,928,232	4,007,953	259,920,279	581,235,509
1911	318,547,900		318,547,900	137,647,641	8,205,699	129,441,942	447,989,842
1912	304,043,400		304,043,400	193,400,713	1,719,870	191,680,843	495,724,243
1913	296,175,300	770,471	295,404,829	195,293,255	4,432,404	190,860,851	486,265,680
1914	290,192,000	335,348	289,856,652	247,648,869	1,204,835	246,444,034	536,300,686
1915	288,777,000	8,158,300	280,618,700	308,083,429	7,259,934	300,823,495	581,442,195

Production Calendar Year 1915, with
Number of Fleeces and Weight
per Fleece, by States.

State	1915		
	Number of fleeces	Weight of fleece	Production
		Pounds	*Pounds*
Alabama..........	106,000	3.8	403,000
Arizona...........	950,000	6.3	5,985,000
Arkansas..........	90,000	4.5	406,000
California.........	1,900,000	6.1	11,590,000
Colorado..........	1,250,000	6.0	7,500,000
Connecticut.......	15,000	5.5	82,000
Delaware..........	5,000	5.7	28,000
Florida...........	107,000	3.1	332,000
Georgia...........	200,000	2.6	520,000
Idaho.............	1,935,000	7.9	15,286,000
Illinois...........	530,000	7.5	3,975,000
Indiana...........	725,000	6.8	4,920,000
Iowa..............	720,000	7.5	5,400,000
Kansas............	205,000	7.1	1,456,000
Kentucky..........	725,000	4.9	3,552,000
Louisiana..........	145,000	3.7	536,000
Maine.............	148,000	6.3	932,000
Maryland..........	127,000	5.9	749,000
Massachusetts.....	20,000	6.4	128,000
Michigan..........	1,170,000	6.9	8,073,000
Minnesota.........	420,000	7.0	2,940,000
Mississippi........	155,000	3.4	527,000
Missouri..........	1,050,000	6.7	7,035,000
Montana..........	3,725,000	7.7	28,682,000
Nebraska..........	240,000	7.4	1,776,000
Nevada...........	765,000	7.7	5,890,000
New Hampshire....	31,000	6.3	195,000
New Jersey........	17,000	5.6	95,000
New Mexico.......	3,325,000	5.6	18,620,000
New York.........	535,000	6.5	3,478,000
North Carolina.....	145,000	3.9	566,000
North Dakota.....	225,000	7.2	1,620,000
Ohio..............	2,110,000	6.8	14,350,000
Oklahoma.........	70,000	7.0	490,000
Oregon............	1,950,000	8.0	15,600,000
Pennsylvania......	650,000	6.2	4,030,000
Rhode Island......	5,000	5.0	25,000
South Carolina.....	29,000	4.0	116,000
South Dakota......	500,000	7.0	3,500,000
Tennessee.........	435,000	4.4	1,914,000
Texas.............	1,600,000	5.8	9,280,000
Utah..............	1,800,000	7.4	13,320,000
Vermont..........	83,000	7.1	589,000
Virginia...........	439,000	4.7	2,063,000
Washington........	460,000	8.3	3,818,000
West Virginia.....	681,000	5.0	3,405,000
Wisconsin........	550,000	7.2	3,960,000
Wyoming..........	3,630,000	8.0	29,040,000
Total..........	36,598,000	6.80	248,777,000
Pulled wool.......			40,000,000
Total product..			288,777,000

The following table exhibits in a concise
form the prices of the three grades of a standard domestic fleece wool in the seaboard markets at the beginning of each year from 1900
to 1915. In its present shape it is deemed in-
telligible to all interested in wool. In the special features of character and condition, "washed

Year	Fine	Medium	Coarse	Year	Fine	Medium	Coarse
	Cents	*Cents*	*Cents*		*Cents*	*Cents*	*Cents*
1900...	35	36½	31½	1908...	34	38	35
1901...	27	29	26	1909...	34	38	35
1902...	25½	26½	24	1910...	36	40	36
1903...	30	31	27	1911...	30	34	32
1904...	33½	32½	29½	1912...	30	32	31
1905...	34	35	36	1913...	30	36	34
1906...	34	38	36	1914...	25	30	27
1907...	34	39	36	1915...	29	36	34

Ohio fleece wool" is less subject to variation
than any other description, and therefore is
used as the basis of value in this table. Wool,
owing to its wide variety, difference in character
and condition, and liability to shrink in clean-
ing, is precluded from speculative operations
which apply to products which may be dealt in
as futures.

The business of manufacturing woolen and
worsted goods in the United States in 1914
is summed up in the following table:

	Woolen goods	Worsted goods	Total
Number of establishments.	501	298	799
Persons engaged in manufactures........	51,631	113,059	164,690
Proprietors and firm members..	316	141	457
Salaried employees....	2,150	3,391	5,541
Wage earners	49,165	109,527	158,692
Primary horsepower.......	134,597	246,623	381,220
Capital.......	$107,871,742	$281,780,836	$389,652,578
Services.....	27,726,892	58,772,968	86,499,860
Salaries.....	3,522,413	7,024,003	10,546,416
Wages.....	24,204,479	51,748,965	75,953,444
Materials.....	63,696,042	182,800,624	246,496,666
Value of products........	103,815,905	275,668,474	379,484,379
Value added by manufacture	40,119,863	92,867,850	132,987,713

The quantities and values of the different
products manufactured in 1909 are as follows:

ALL WOOL WOVEN GOODS	Square Yards	Value
Wool cloths, doeskins, cassimeres, cheviots, etc...............	40,843,979	$29,291,059
Worsted coatings, serges and suitings........	119,655.069	101,903,153
Woollen overcoatings, cloakings,kerseys,etc.	14,697,770	11,230,856
Worsted overcoatings and cloakings.......	654,404	821,688
Wool dress goods, sackings, tricots, etc., and opera and similar flannels............	29,099,956	16,385,498
Worsted dress goods, cashmeres, serges, bunting, etc........	105,801,349	54,030,376
Carriage cloths........	1,782,855	947,862
Flannels for underwear.	3,856,353	1,257,271
Blankets.............	5,137,903	3,228,797
Horse blankets.......	247,395	185,430
Woven shawls........	704,153	404,583
All other.............	463,179	167,194
Totals...........	322,944,365	$219,853,767

UNION, OR COTTON MIXED WOVEN GOODS	Square Yards	Value
Unions,tweeds,cheviots, cassimeres, etc......	18,917,478	7,780,854
Overcoatings and cloakings................	4,281,739	2,363,381
Sackings, tricots, dress goods and opera and similar flannels......	4,319,539	1,776,721
Flannels for underwear.	7,063,572	1,308,369
Blankets............	1,717,758	650,714
All other.............	1,153,265	447,934
Totals.............	37,453,351	$14,327,973

Cotton Yarn Woven Goods	Square Yards	Value
Wool fillings, cassimeres,doeskins, jeans, tweeds, coatings, etc.	45,244,866	12,107,320
Worsted fillings, cassimeres, doeskins,jeans, tweeds, coatings, etc.	29,220,252	15,009,081
Wool fillings, overcoats and cloakings	2,075,502	771,879
Satinets and linseys	5,102,460	912,182
Worsted fillings, dress goods, cashmeres and serges, mohairs, etc.	65,112,981	14,798,965
Wool fillings, dress goods and repellants.	12,916,060	2,741,816
Domett flannels and shirtings	4,571,765	911,967
Linings, Italian cloths and lastings	28,928,148	9,008,799
Blankets	9,746,841	2,684,919
Horse blankets	4,210,098	1,676,942
Carriage robes	2,889,444	1,396,595
All other	327,664	245,389
Upholstering goods and sundries		1,986,330
Woollen and worsted	1,176,542	1,528,648
All other		457,682
Partially manufactured products for sale		115,032,485
Totals	211,522,623	$181,261,999

Yarns	Pounds	Value
Woollen	28,520,493	$7,505,412
Worsted	88,323,953	80,395,543
Woollen, union or merino	10,249,625	2,143,416
Worsted, union or merino	3,761,737	3,522,812
All other	3,195,553	974,570
Worsted tops and slubbing	11,321,279	8,027,231
Noils	27,479,293	8,938,589
Waste	24,057,580	3,524,912
All other products		3,250,857
Work on materials for others		3,026,255
Totals	196,909,513	*$121,309,597

* In addition, woollen and worsted goods, to the value of $1,281,292, were made by establishments engaged primarily in the manufacture of products other than those covered by the industry designation.

Wool:
Cost of manufacturing yarn and fabrics greater in United States than in competing countries, 7680.
Cost of production in America greater than that of nearest competitor, 7680.
Proposed reduction of tariff by House would work injury to trade, 7748.
Reduction of tariff on, in accordance with report of Tariff Board would give sufficient protection to industry, 7748.
Reduction of tariff on, recommended, 7677.
Tariff, minimum *ad valorem* rate should be 35 per cent, 7747.
Tariff must offset difference in cost of production here and abroad, 7746.

Wool and Woolens, import duty on, discussed, 1247, 4247.

Wool Bill, vetoed by Taft, 7745.

Wool Taps and Yarn, low tariff on, would disrupt industry, 7747.

Wool Tariff:
Amount of capital and number of persons directly dependent upon, 7624.
Board appointed to prepare information on, 7619.
Duties on maneufactured goods in some cases prohibitory, 7679.
Duty on raw wool operates against importation of useful grades, 7678.
Minimum and valorem rate should be 35 per cent, 7747.
Rates proposed in excess of needed protection, 7622.
Revision of Schedule K (wool) of tariff law recommended, 7677.
Unanimous report of Tariff Board advises revision of, 7677.
Wilson law forced shutting down of mills, 7623.

Woolen Goods, low tariff on, would destroy fine goods industry, 7747.

Worcester vs. Georgia.—An important Supreme Court case involving the right of individual States to make laws at variance with treaties made by the Government of the United States. Samuel A. Worcester was a missionary among the Cherokees. In 1831 he was arrested by officers of the State of Georgia, tried, and sentenced to four years' imprisonment for living among the Indians in violation of an act of the State legislature which forbade any white person to reside among the Indians without a license from the governor of the State or some one authorized to issue it. Worcester pleaded authorization by the President and by the Cherokees, also the unconstitutionality of the act itself. By a writ of error the case was brought before the United States Supreme Court. That tribunal reversed the decision of the State court and rendered judgment in favor of Worcester on the ground that the Georgia act, being repugnant to the Constitution, to the treaties made by the United States with the Cherokees, and to the laws of Congress in execution thereof, was unconstitutional and void. It was held that the treaties and laws of the United States contemplate the Indian territory as completely separated from that of the States, and provide that all intercourse with the Indians shall be carried on by the Government of the Union.

Workmen's Compensation (See also Employers' Liability):
Act, urged, 7810.
Conference on, appropriation asked for, 7542.

World Court, establishment of, long the hope of America, 8285.

World's Columbian Commission:
Reports of, deposited in State Department, 6181.
Reports of, transmitted, 5567, 5669, 5769.

World's Columbian Exposition.—The idea of celebrating by an exposition the fourth centenary of the discovery of America by Columbus was conceived during the progress of the Centennial Exposition at Philadelphia in 1876. The project was widely discussed and met with general favor, New York, Washington, St. Louis, and Chicago competing for the site. In February, 1890, Congress authorized the holding of the exposition and designated Chicago as the place. A company had already been organized, with a capital of $5,-000,000, for holding the fair.

President Cleveland appointed an official board of managers, and at the close of the fair a full report was filed in the State Department.

The buildings were dedicated Oct. 21, 1892, just 400 years after the landing of Columbus. Owing to the magnitude of the enterprise the exposition did not open until May 1 following, remaining open till the 30th of the following October. It surpassed all previous world's fairs in every respect except in point of attendance, in which it fell below that of the Paris Exposition of 1889 only. Jackson Park and the Midway Plaisance, the site of the exposition, covered 633 acres of land on the shore of Lake Michigan, and of this about 190 acres were under roof. The twenty-eight main exposition buildings occupied 142½ acres, the remainder being covered by state and foreign buildings and concessions. The building devoted to the exhibition of manufactures and liberal arts was the largest in the world. It measured 1,687 by 787 feet and covered 30½ acres. The central hall, 1,280 by 380 feet, was open to the roof, a distance of 237.6 feet, without a supporting column. There were eleven acres of skylight and forty car-loads of glass in the roof, and it required 7,000,000 feet of lumber and five car-loads of nails to lay the floor. The buildings were painted by spraying machines and covered with a composition resembling marble, which gave the fair the name of the "White City."

Fifty-two foreign countries officially participated in the exposition in response to President Harrison's proclamation of Dec. 24, 1890, inviting "all the nations of the earth to take part in the commemoration of an event that is preeminent in human history and of lasting interest to mankind." (Page 5575.) The United States Government appropriations amounted to $6,-000,000. There were in all 65,422 exhibitors, 27,529,400 admissions, and the receipts amounted to $14,117,332, exceeding the expenditures by nearly $2,000,000.

See illustration opposite 5135.

World's Columbian Exposition at Chicago:

Board of management of Government exhibit designated, 5833.

Chinese artisans, admission of, to, temporarily, recommended, 5622.

Military encampment to be held during, discussed, 5669.

Proclamation respecting opening of, 5575.

Proposition to observe four hundredth anniversary of discovery of America by opening of, discussed, 5487.

Referred to, 5622.

Reports of—

Deposited in State Department, 6181.

Discussed and recommendations regarding, 5567, 5669, 5765, 5769, 6184.

Resolution of International American Conference regarding, 5512.

World Court League. (See Peace Societies.)

World's Fair. (See World's Columbian Exposition.)

World's Industrial and Cotton Centennial Exposition at New Orleans, 4773, 4802, 4804, 4863, 4923.

Board on behalf of Executive Departments designated, 4815, 4817.

Also placed in charge of Cincinnati and Louisville expositions, 4819.

Instructions to, 4819, 4820.

Proclamation regarding, 4746.

Report of board of managers of, referred to, 4953.

Württemberg.—A Kingdom of the German Empire, lying between Bavaria on the east and Baden on the west, while to the south reaches Lake Constance and the borders of the Tyrol. Though primarily an agricultural state, yielding considerable quantities of grain, beets, hops, flax and hemp, Württemberg has numerous flourishing industries. Stuttgart is the center of the publishing trade of southern Germany, and gold and silverware, clocks, pianos, surgical instruments, paper, beer and sparkling wine are largely produced both in the capital and other cities of the Kingdom. The government is a limited monarchy administered by the King and two legislative chambers. Württemberg sends four representatives to the Bundesrat and seventeen to the Reichstag. Education is compulsory, the standard of illiteracy is very low and there is an excellent university at Tübingen, founded in 1477. The King is the head of the Evangelical Church, to which 60 per cent of his subjects belong; Catholics and Jews form the rest of the population. The former Duchy and Electorate of Württemberg became a Kingdom by the peace of Pressburg in 1805 and became a state in the German Empire in 1871. Area, 7,534 square miles; population (1900), 2,169,480.

Württemberg:

Convention with, 2169.

Naturalization treaty with, 3997.

Wyandotte Constitution.—The final constitution of the State of Kansas, adopted Oct. 4, 1859. It was ratified by a vote of 10,421 to 5,530. It prohibited slavery. The governor was to be elected for two years, and Topeka was made the capital. This constitution was adopted at Wyandotte, now a part of Kansas City, Kans. (See also Lecompton Constitution; Topeka Constitution.)

Wyandotte, The, capture of the *William* by, 3126.

Wyandotte Indians. (See Indian Tribes.)

Wyoming.—One of the western group of states; motto, "Equal rights." It lies between lat. 41° and 45° north and long. 104° and 111° west. It is bounded on the north by Montana, on the east by South Dakota and Nebraska, on the south by Colorado and Utah, and on the west by Utah and Idaho. Area, 97,914 square miles. The surface being mountainous, the leading industries are stock raising and mining.

Gold, coal, iron, and petroleum are the chief minerals.

Most of the present state was included in the Louisiana Purchase. It was organized as a Territory in 1868 from areas previously in Dakota, Idaho, and Utah, but derived more remotely from the original Territories of Nebraska, Utah, and Oregon, a portion having at one time also belonged to Washington. Wyoming was admitted to the Union in 1890.

About 10,000,000 acres of Wyoming are covered with forests, and the prosperity of the state depends largely on its mineral resources and grazing lands. About 3,300 square miles are inclosed in the Yellowstone National Park (q. v.), and 2,742 reserved for the use of Indians. Most of the land is arid and unsuited to agriculture without the aid of irrigation. Under the Federal reclamation act $3,250,000 will be expended in irrigation in the valleys of the Shoshone and North Platte Rivers. Many private companies are also at work. About half the state is well fitted for cattle and sheep grazing. In July, 1911, there were 33,629,605 acres of public land unreserved and unappropriated. United States land offices are located at Buffalo, Cheyenne, Douglas, Evanston, Lander, and Sundance. (See Lands, Public.)

In 1915, the number of manufacturing establishments was 337, with an average number of wage-earners totaling 2,989, representing an investment of $29,275,000, and paying annually in wages about $2,315,000.

Statistics of agriculture collected for the last Federal census place the number of farms in the state at 10,987, comprising 8,543,010 acres, valued, with stock and improvements, at $167,189,081. The value of domestic animals, poultry, etc., was $65,-605,510, including 767,427 cattle, valued at $22,697,387; 156,062 horses, $12,426,838; 2,045 mules, $248,572; 33,947 swine, $301,-716; 5,397,161 sheep, $29,666,228, and poultry, $194,078. The yield and value of field crops for 1911 was: corn, 13,000 acres, 195,000 bushels, $148,000; wheat, 69,000 acres, 1,794,000 bushels, $1,687,000; oats, 190,000 acres, 6,555,000 bushels, $3,278,-000; rye, 2,000 acres, 40,000 bushels, $36,-000; potatoes, 10,000 acres, 420,000 bushels, $588,000; hay, 330,000 acres, 693,000 tons, $7,138,000. The coal production in 1910 exceeded all past records. The output was 7,533,088 short tons, valued at $11,706,187. During 1910 and 1911 there has been great development of the oil industry. Many new fields are being opened. The total mineral output for 1910 was $12,-110,286.

In 1917, the acreage, bushels produced, and value of the principal crops were as follows:—Wheat, 198,000; 4,206,000; $8,-412,000; Oats, 263,000; 9,470,000; $7,575,-000; Potatoes, 30,000; 4,650,000; $4,850,-000; Hay, 560,000; 950,000 tons; $16,200,-000; corn, 33,000; 650,000; $1,150,000.

In 1916, the coal production of the state was 7,900,000 net tons, valued at $12,250,-000, an increase of 28% over 1915, when the value of the production was rated at more than $10,000,000. The 1916 production of petroleum was 6,235,000 barrels; and there were mined 445,000 gross tons of iron.

The report of the State Treasurer for the fiscal year 1911 shows total receipts of $1,069,970; total expenditures, $967,568. The bonded debt is $120,000. The suffrage extends to all citizens, male and female, who can read, and who are registered as voters and have resided in the state one year and in the county sixty days next preceding the election.

The school population in 1916 was 41,831, with an enrollment of 36,630 and a teaching staff of 1,735.

About half the state is adapted for sheep-raising. The wool clip for 1910 was 36,037,500 pounds, valued at $6,342,000, a record exceeded only by Montana. The population in 1910 was 145,965; and the estimate for 1918 was 186,500.

Wyoming:

Admission of, into Union, discussed, 5553.

Chinamen injured by lawless men in, 4914, 4968, 5083.

Indemnity to, recommended, 5219.

Appropriation for, 5367.

Troops sent to protect, 4933.

Lands in, set apart for public reservation by proclamation, 5577, 5590, 6221, 6225.

Unlawful combinations in, proclamations against, 5725, 5932.

Wyoming Controversy.—In the original charter granted by Charles I. to William Penn the northern boundary of Pennsylvania was fixed at lat. 43° north. However, the proprietors of the colony accepted 42° as the northern boundary and extended the southern boundary to include the Chesapeake and Delaware bays. Connecticut claimed all the territory north of 41° in Pennsylvania, and asserted her rights by chartering the Susquehanna Company, organized in 1753, to form settlements in the disputed territory. In 1762 the company sent its first party of settlers, 200 in number, into the region, but they were driven out by the Indians, who repudiated a previous sale of their rights to Connecticut and made a sale to Pennsylvania. In 1769 the Susquehanna Company sent more colonists into the disputed country, and a desultory warfare began between them and the Pennsylvania settlers, to whom the territory had been leased. The former were several times driven out of the disputed district by the Pennsylvanias, but they finally obtained a permanent lodgment, as the Pennsylvania contestants were only lessees, while their opponents fought for their property rights. Hostilities with the mother country caused a suspension of civil strife for a time.

In 1779 an act of the Pennsylvania legislature transferred all the proprietary lands to the state. Pennsylvania brought suit against Connecticut to decide the jurisdiction over Wyoming. The case was heard by five judges at Trenton. In November, 1782, their unanimous decision, afterwards confirmed by Congress, was in favor of Pennsylvania.

Wyoming Massacre.—July 3, 1778, Col. Zebulon Butler, of the Continental army, with a force of about 300 militiamen, mostly old men and boys, marched out of Forty Fort, in the Wyoming Valley, about three miles above Wilkesbarre, Pa., to drive off an invading party of some 800 Indians and Tories under Chief Joseph Brant and the British Colonel Walter Butler. The Indians burned the forts in the upper part of the valley and forced the American militiamen to retreat in disorder. Of the 300 who left the fort in the morning the names of 162 officers and men are recorded as killed in action and the massacre which followed. Butler, the British officer in command, reported the taking of 227 scalps and only 5 prisoners. Col. Zebulon Butler with 14 men escaped from the valley.

X. Y. Z. Mission.—During the Revolution the United States secured the valuable aid of France by treaties in 1778. In 1789 monarchy was overthrown in France, and that nation soon found herself at war with England and other European nations. She desired the United States as an ally, and Genet (*see Genet, Citizen*) was sent to accomplish her purpose. His mission failed, Washington persisted firmly in preserving our neutrality, and Jay's Treaty (*which see*) was concluded with England. The course of our government angered France. In 1797 the directory, which then governed that country, gave permission to the French navy to assail our vessels. Following a policy of conciliation, in spite of French insults to our minister and the threat to our commerce, President Adams called a special session of Congress in May, 1797, and Charles Cotesworth Pinckney, John Marshall and Elbridge Gerry were sent to France to arrange matters. In the spring of the next year the President submitted to Congress dispatches that had been received from these commissioners. They had been kept waiting by Talleyrand, the minister of foreign affairs, and had been approached by three unofficial persons with what was in effect a demand for a bribe and a loan to the directory before any arrangement could be concluded with the United States. In dispatches the names of these three persons were indicated merely by the letters X., Y. and Z., and hence the whole affair came to be termed the X. Y. Z. Mission. To these demands our representatives returned a decided refusal. It is said that Pinckney made use of the phrase, "Millions for defense, but not one cent for tribute." The answer as recorded, however, was, "No, no, no; not a sixpence." About the time when these dispatches were submitted to Congress, Pinckney and Marshall were ordered to leave France, and Gerry was afterward recalled by our government. A warlike feeling instantly sprang up in the United States. The Federalists, with Adams as leader, desired to defend by force, if necessary, their policy of keeping this country from entangling foreign alliances, and desired to resent French insults. The Democrats (then called Republicans) had always favored an alliance with France and had opposed the creation of a navy for the United States. Now, however, the popular pressure could not be withstood. Bills were passed for increasing the navy and separating it from the War Department (April 30, 1798). Provision was made for a national loan and the imposition of a direct tax. The President was authorized to increase the army in case of a foreign war within three years, and soon Washington was called to be commander-in-chief of the army and Alexander Hamilton was selected as the active commander. On July 9, 1798, Congress declared the treaties with France no longer binding, and authorized our war vessels and privateers to capture armed French vessels. A few naval engagments occurred, but no event of great importance. The effect of our warlike feeling and preparations on France was excellent. American prisoners were released and the embargo which had been declared was raised on American ships. Talleyrand now hinted to our Minister to Holland, William Vans Murray, that he was willing to receive another American Minister. Adams accordingly appointed Murray, in February, 1799, and soon joined with him Oliver Ellsworth and William R. Davis. The President's action created much stir, politically, as he was considered to have become subservient to France and to have changed the former attitude of himself and the Federal party. It was some months after their appointment that our envoys arrived in Paris. Napoleon was then at the head of the government as first consul and was favorably inclined toward the United States. French commissioners were appointed, and, on Sept. 30, 1800, a friendly convention was signed. Both countries ratified it, and it was declared in force Dec. 21, 1801, and for a while the safety of our commerce was secured.

Yakama Indians. (See Indian Tribes.)

Yakima Reservation, Wash., lands on, to be used by Northern Pacific Railway, 4864, 4954, 5178.

Yale, The, mentioned, 5318.

Yancton Indians. (See Indian Tribes.)

Yanctoni Indians. (See Indian Tribes.)

Yangtse River, steamers sailing under American flag prohibited from passing through Straw Shoe Channel on, 3896, 3902.

Yankee Doodle.—A popular national air of the United States. The words are said to have been written in derision of the ill-assorted Continental troops, about 1755, by Dr. Schuckburgh, a surgeon under Gen. Amherst in the French and Indian War. The original title was "The Yankee's Return from Camp," and there are several versions. The tune has undergone various changes.

Yankee, The, mentioned, 6317.

Yankees.—A word of uncertain origin, first applied to the early English colonists, later by the English to Americans generally, and still later to Northerners by people of the South. According to common legend, Yankees is a corruption of Yengees, Yaunghees, or Yanghies, a name said to have been given by the Massachuset Indians to the English colonists in their efforts to pronounce the word "English" or the French word "Anglais." It was first applied to the New Englanders as a term of reproach by British soldiers.

Yards and Docks, Bureau of, Navy Department. (See Bureau of Yards and Docks, Navy Department.)

Yazoo Frauds.—A term applied to the sale by the State of Georgia in 1795 of her western territory, now included in Alabama and Mississippi, to four land companies, known generally as the Yazoo companies, from the district in which they operated. The land extended from the Alabama and Coosa rivers to the Mississippi, and from the thirty-first to the thirty-fifth parallel, and the price paid to the state was $500,-000, or about one and two-thirds cents per acre. It was charged that many members of the legislature who voted for the sale had been bribed. President Washington made the alleged frauds the subject of a special message (page 167). The people of the state were indignant and a party was formed to repeal the sale. In 1796 the records of the transaction were burned in the presence of the governor and legislature in accordance with what was known as the Rescinding act. Immediately numerous claims sprang up, which had to be decided by Congress.

The territory was ceded to the United States in 1802. The next year President Jefferson appointed a commission to investigate the claims, and James Madison, chairman of the commission, recommended a compromise, but Georgia refused to compensate the claimants. Their claim was sustained by the Supreme Court, however, Chief Justice Marshall holding that allegations of bribery of the legislature could not be entertained, and that purchasers from the land companies were innocent holders ; that the act of the Georgia legislature in 1796 repealing the sale of 1795 was an abrogation of contract, and therefore void. Finally an act was passed in 1814 appropriating $8,000,000 payable out of the proceeds of the sale of Mississippi lands to satisfy the Yazoo claimant.

Yellow Book.—The official publication of the French government, presenting its side of the diplomatic history which preceded the European War.

Yellow Fever (see also Contagious Diseases; International Sanitary Conference; Quarantine Regulations):

Commission to investigate causes, etc., of, recommended, 6341.

In Southern States, discussed, 4444.

Act legalizing issue of provisions to sufferers, recommended, 4452.

Yellow Peril.—The so-called perils to be feared from the yellow races, especially the Japanese. The phrase may mean the economic evils feared, rightly or wrongly, from peaceable Japanese immigration and settlement in the United States ; but it usually signifies a threatened military or naval invasion from Japan.

Yellowstone National Park. (See Parks, National.)

Yellowstone National Park, compensation to superintendent of, referred to, 4036.

York (Canada), Capture of.—The plans for the prosecution of the war with Great Britain in 1813 contemplated an invasion of Canada from both the east and the west. Gen. Harrison successfully carried out the programme in the west, routed Proctor's army, and was in possession of the territory. April 27, Gen. Dearborn, with about 1,700 men under the immediate command of Gen. Zebulon Pike, crossed Lake Ontario on Commodore Chauncey's transports and marched upon the British garrison at York (now Toronto), where Maj.-Gen. Sheaffe was in command of 800 regulars and a body of Indians. A sharp conflict ensued. The British and Indians were routed. By the explosion of a magazine Gen. Pike was killed, together with 51 other Americans and 40 British ; 180 Americans were wounded by the explosion. The American loss in the battle was 269 on land and 17 on water. The British lost, besides the prisoners, 60 killed and 89 wounded.

York, Canada, reduction of, by American forces, 524.

Yorktown, The. (See *Baltimore*, The.)

Yorktown, Va., monument at, completed and recommendations regarding, 4850.

Yorktown Centennial Celebration:

British flag to be saluted by American army and navy forces at, 4624.

Referred to, 4625.

Descendants of Baron von Steuben present at, 4626.

Representatives of French Republic and descendants of Lafayette present at, 4625.

Yorktown (Va.), Siege of, in 1781.—After the battle of Green Springs, or Jamestown, Lafayette withdrew the American army to Malvern Hill. Cornwallis hurried on toward Yorktown, which place Sir Henry Clinton designed to be held as a British post in the absence of sufficient force to hold the entire State of Virginia. By Aug. 27, 1781, the British army in Virginia, consisting of 9,433 men, was concentrated at Yorktown and Gloucester Point, just across the York River. Aug. 30 Count De Grasse arrived in Chesapeake Bay with twenty-six French ships of the line besides frigates and transports. Sept. 3 Count De St. Simon landed at Jamestown with 3,200 French troops, and the allied armies, numbering 12,000 regular troops and 4,000 militia, under Washington and Lafayette, occupied Williamsburg, about fifteen miles from Yorktown. Washington had eluded Clinton by a feint. Sept. 28 the army advanced and took a position about two miles from the British works, and on the 29th a general movement was begun to encircle the town and close in upon its defenders

On the Gloucester side the siege was maintained by the Duke de Lauzun with his legion of French cavalry and 800 marines from De Grasse's squadron, besides a body of Virginia militia under Gen. Weedon. Oct. 6 the first parallel was opened under Gen. Lincoln within 600 yards of the enemy, and heavy guns were placed in position, with the loss of 1 French officer and 16 privates. On the 11th a second parallel was established with slight loss. On the 14th the two advanced redoubts of the British were taken by storm by the American light infantry under direction of Lafayette, and the French, under Baron Vioménil. The American loss was 9 killed and 32 wounded. Three French officers were wounded. The British lost 8 killed and 17 prisoners. On the morning of the 16th an unsuccessful sortie was made on the advanced American redoubts, by about 350 British under Lieut.-Col. Abercrombie, 100 French troops being killed or wounded, with little loss and no advantage to the British.

An attempt made by Cornwallis's army to escape in boats that night was frustrated by a storm, and on the morning of Oct. 17, 1781, a flag of truce was sent to Washington, making overtures for surrender. On the 18th articles of capitulation were signed by Washington and Cornwallis. The land forces became prisoners to the Americans and the marine force to the French. The total number of British officers and men surrendered was 7,073 from the army and 900 from the navy, besides 144 guns and 6 British and 18 regimental standards. The military chest contained £2,113. The *Guadaloupe, Fowey, Benetta,* and *Vulcan,* together with 30 transports, 15 galleys, and many smaller vessels, fell into the hands of the French. The total casualties of the siege were : British, 156 killed, 326 wounded, and 70 missing ; American, 23 killed, 65 wounded ; French, 52 killed, 134 wounded.

Yorktown (Va.), Siege of, in 1862.—Nov. 1, 1861, McClellan was appointed to the chief command of the armies of the United States. He set about improving the organization and efficiency of the men, and by March 1, 1862, the forces about Washington numbered 221,987. The country was growing impatient at the inactivity of the Army, and the cry "On to Richmond" was almost universal in the North. The President directed that a move of some kind be made. The knowledge that McClellan contemplated a forward movement caused the Confederates to evacuate Manassas, Johnston withdrawing his forces to the defense of Richmond March 9, 1862. March 11 the President relieved McClellan of the command of all military departments except that of the Potomac, which had been divided into five corps, under command of Generals McDowell, Sumner, Heintzelman, Keyes, and Banks. It was decided that this army, except so much as was necessary for the protection of Washington, should move upon Richmond by way of the Virginia peninsula, lying between the James and York rivers. Fort Monroe occupies the extremity of the peninsula. Heintzelman's corps embarked March 17, and April 1 the headquarters of the Army of the Potomac was transferred to the vicinity of Fort Monroe. Yorktown was defended by Gen. Magruder with less than 8,000 Confederates. April 4 occurred the principal skirmish of the siege, in which 35 men were killed and 120 wounded on the Union side, while the Confederates lost more than 100 killed. The next month was consumed by McClellan in building fortifications and roads to take Magruder's army. May 5 the last of the Confederates retired up the peninsula.

Yosemite National Park. (See Parks, National.)

Young Men's Christian Associations.— Organizations formed to promote the welfare of young men. Although active membership is confined to those who are communicants of an evangelical church, associate membership, entitling to practically all the privileges, is open to all men.

There is hardly any field of activity in which men are engaged in which the Y. M. C. A. does not prosecute its activities. Especial attention is given to athletics and gymnastics. There are libraries; study-rooms; game-rooms; gymnasia and swimming-pools; and other rooms for rent in the more usual Y. M. C. A. building. A particular feature is the classes in all manner of subjects, both general and professional, although the night classes have to some extent been superseded in the larger cities by the evening public schools. Religious devotion and training are emphasized. There are usually separate departments for the stimulation of work among boys. Employment is found. Moreover, the associations do much field work—especially on the railroads and in the army and navy.

The movement is an international one; and there are in all countries extensive training schools for the education of Y. M. C. A. secretaries.

The movement was first organized in London by George Williams in 1844, as the result of work among the dry goods shop assistants. The first associations in North America arose in Montreal and Boston in 1851 as a result of the English experiments. The first national federation of Y. M. C. A.'s in the United States occurred in Buffalo in 1854. The progress of the movement was temporarily hindered by the Civil War, but in the following years it grew rapidly. In 1906, there were in the United States 1,761 associations, with 405,000 members. In the same year, there were throughout the world 7,794 associations, with a membership of 744,000. In 1916, there were 8,906 associations in the world, with almost 1,000,000 members; and in North America in 1917, there were 2,087 associations, with a membership of 720,468 and with 5,188 paid officials. The total operating expenses in the latter year were $21,-105,000. In addition, more than half a million was spent in foreign work and more than a million and a half in army work previously to April 6, 1917. Within the year, 85,000 men were obtained positions;

250,000 men and boys were given regular physical instruction; 83,131 pursued regular class-work in educational studies; 150,-000 pursued regular courses in Bible study; and there were more than 40,000 decisions to enter Christian life and church membership, made through Y. M. C. A. influence.

The Y. M. C. A. was extremely active among the troops of the regular army and the National Guard during the mobilization on the Mexican border in 1916. There were 42 Y. M. C. A. buildings and 6 Y. M. C. A. tents in constant operation during that period, in which 169 Y. M. C. A. secretaries were constantly active. The total attendance in Y. M. C. A. centres and at Y. M. C. A. activities was estimated at 7,871,468. Stationery was furnished to more than 5,000,000: 2,850,000 persons attended entertainments; there were more than 100,000 attendances at lectures and 680,000 at religious meetings; and some 400,000 pieces of reading matter were distributed.

Immediately upon the outbreak of the European War in August 1, 1914, the Y. M. C. A.s of the various belligerent countries became active. Two days later, the Y. M. C. A.s of the Allied countries had 250 centres in France and England among the troops; and by 1916 there were more than 1,000 such. By 1918, there were more than 500 Y. M. C. A. "huts" among the British forces in France alone.

Each hut, which costs in the neighborhood of $15,000, contains a canteen room, a large meeting and assembly hall, and a number of smaller rooms. Through the Y. M. C. A., the attempt is made to attend to all the non-military needs of the armed forces and prisoners; and the magnitude of the task may be understood when it is remembered that in 1918 the number of the individual belligerents probably exceeded 24,000,000. The Y. M. C. A. provides first for the comfort of the soldier, especially during his leisure and furlough time; and thus tries to furnish a normal channel for the outlet of his pent-up emotions. In this connection, the canteen is especially helpful. Recreation facilities of all kinds are provided, from baseball to checkers. There are reading rooms, game rooms, health talks, foreign language instruction, entertainments, religious services and prayer meetings, vocational training, and all other forms of activities which present themselves as fruitful of good results. In addition, a great amount of individual advice is given.

The insignia of the United States Y. M. C. A. workers during the war is a red triangle. The United States Y. M. C. A. became active immediately upon the entrance of the United States into the conflict, not only among the forces sent abroad, but also in the training camps. In November, 1917, a campaign for a year's budget of $35,000,-000, in addition to special donations, was successfully carried out; and it was announced that this sum would be distributed as follows:—For U. S. troops in this country, $11,000,000; for U. S. troops in France, $12,000,000; for Russian troops, $3,300,000; among the French forces, $2,650,000; among the Italian forces, $1,000,000; and in the prison camps, $1,000,000 with over $4,000,000 reserved for expansion of activities. By January 1, 1918, there were 800 Y. M. C. A. workers among the U. S. forces in France alone, and by July, 1918, there were some 5,000 officials working in the army abroad and at home for the Y. M. C. A.

Young Women's Christian Association.
—Organizations formed to promote the welfare of young women. They attempt to enter every sphere of activities in which they may be of assistance to young women, and their work is non-denominational. Particular attention is paid to physical training, and there are many classes, religious, general and professional. The movement was organized in 1855 in London, combining a Prayer Union and a Boarding Home for young women. The world federation dates from 1894. The first American organization of the Y. W. C. A. occurred in Boston in 1866, although there had been for some time organizations with different names doing similar work. In 1916, t ere were in America 933 Y. W. C. A.s, with a membership of 360,965. (Compare Young Men's Christian Associations.)

After the entrance of the United States into the European War, the Y. W. C. A. became especially active, not only in the training camps in the United States, but also in France, where it performed much reconstruction work, and assisted the Y. M. C. A. in the latter's canteens, etc. In the United States, the Y. W. C. A. "hostess huts" were especially serviceable in providing chaperonage and individual attention to women visiting, and in the vicinity of, the camps.

Ypres, Battle of. (See European War.)

Youngstown, Ohio, act for erection of public building at, vetoed, 5254.

Yucatan.—A peninsula of Mexico. It comprises the States of Yucatan and Campeche and the territory of Quintana. It is bounded on the north by the Gulf of Mexico, on the east by the Channel of Yucatan (which separates it from Cuba) and the Caribbean Sea, on the south by British Honduras and Guatemala, and on the west by the Gulf of Campeche. The surface is low. Its chief product is sisal hemp. Yucatan was discovered in 1517; was conquered by Spain, 1527-1547; became independent 1821; was annexed to Mexico 1822. In April, 1848, President Polk reiterated the "Monroe doctrine" while discussing the relations of the United States and Yucatan (2431).

Yucatan:

Acquisition of, by United States, discussed, 2431.

Aid of United States asked for, by, to suppress Indian hostilities, 2431.

Foreign powers must not take possession of, 2431.

Monroe doctrine reasserted, 2432.

Referred to, 2433, 2434, 2436.

Yukon, The, mineral wealth in, value of, 6063.

Zanesville, Ohio, act for erection of public building at, vetoed, 5016.

Zanzibar. treaty with, 5195.

Zenger's Case.—One of the most important struggles for the freedom of the press in America. John Peter Zenger was editor and publisher of the New York Weekly *Journal*, which was founded by him in 1726. His newspaper openly denounced the administration of the colonial government. For this he was brought to trial in 1735, charged with the publication of "false, scandalous, seditious libels" against the royal government of the Colony of New York. Strenuous efforts were made to secure Zenger's conviction, but no jury could be found to convict him.

Zeppelins. (See aeronautics and European war, Aerial Warfare.)
For a picture of the effects of a Zeppelin raid. see illustration opposite 8032, and description on back.

Zinc.—For many years the value of the copper mined in the Central States has exceeded that of zinc, frequently by millions of dollars, owing entirely to the greater value of the copper, for the quantity of zinc produced has been larger. Under the stimulus of extraordinary prices for both copper and zinc in 1915 the mine output of copper in the Central States increased 50,650 tons and that of zinc 47,857 tons. The value of the copper produced increased from $21,865,043 to $46,494,969, an unusual increase, but not sufficient to retain its preeminence, for the value of the recoverable zinc jumped from $17,139,264 in 1914, to $53,540,472 in 1915, "jack" thus running $7,000,000 ahead of copper. Under ordinary conditions the production of 222,548 tons of lead, valued at $20,919,512, an increase of 18,703 tons in quantity and of $5,000,000 in value, would have attracted considerable attention. An increase in value of one-third is unusual, but it appears small compared with that of either zinc or copper.

The production of silver in the Central States is always relatively unimportant. The output in 1915 amounted to 647,553 ounces, valued at $328,309, of which 585,933 ounces was derived from copper mines in Michigan.

The total value of the silver, copper, lead, and zinc mined in the Central States increased from $55,171,306 in 1914, to $121,283,262 in 1915, or about 120 per cent.

The high price of copper in 1915 benefited few companies or individuals except those interested in the comparatively small number of mines in the Lake Superior district in Michigan, for that State produced nearly all the copper credited to the Central States. Missouri reported 402,160 pounds of copper, which was derived mainly from the dressing of lead concentrates.

The average selling price of lead was less than a cent a pound more in 1915 than it was in 1914, so that lead mining was more profitable chiefly for the five or six large companies having mines in the disseminated lead region in southeastern Missouri, which produced 83 per cent of the output of the Central States. The increase in average price did not stimulate lead mining in other regions, as the only other notably increased output was due to more extensive mining of the "sheet ground" in the Joplin region, which carries considerable lead. In 1915, however, the smelters desired high-grade zinc concentrates free or nearly free from lead. Such concentrates were purchased at a base price much higher than that paid for concentrates containing over 1 per cent of lead. Moreover, high-grade zinc concentrates frequently sold for more than double the price paid for galena concentrates, so that owners of "sheet ground" and "soft ground" had no reason to rejoice over the lead content of their ore.

The largely increased and high price of zinc concentrates created a healthy boom in nearly all districts. The profits of the big operators were abnormal, but hundreds of mines worked by small companies or individuals shared in the general prosperity. Miners' wages were raised and mining machinery and supplies were liberally purchased at advanced prices. With zinc concentrates doubled and more than doubled in value any mine that would not yield a profit was indeed worthless. Producing properties or old mines with shafts and drifts that could be unwatered, where old concentrating plants could be repaired or new ones quickly built, were eagerly sought. Old dumps at abandoned mines attracted men and boys who made good wages by culling the waste rock. Tailing mills were run profitably on material that would not yield any profit when zinc concentrates sold for less than $50 a ton.

The salient facts relating to zinc and lead mining in the Central States in 1915 were the building of new mills and roasting and separating plants in the Wisconsin-Illinois region ; the increased output and the better recovery made by "flotation" in the disseminated lead district in Missouri; the more general use of thickeners, classifiers, and tables and the vastly larger yield from the "sheet ground" in southwestern Missouri; the development of the new mining territory near Picher and Cardin, in the north Miami field in Oklahoma ; and the active prospecting and mill building and the large increase in shipments of zinc carbonate in Arkansas.

According to figures of the United States Geological Survey, the production of copper from domestic ores in 1916 was 1,928,000,-000 pounds, valued at $475,000,000. The production for 1917 was 1,890,000,000 pounds, valued at $510,000,000. The output of refined copper from primary sources, both domestic and foreign, for 1917 was estimated at 2,362,000,000 pounds, as compared with 2,259,000,000 pounds for 1916. Imports of unmanufactured copper for 1916 were 462,335,000 pounds. Exports of manufactured copper for 1916 were 784,006,000 pounds.

The recoverable zinc content of ore mined in 1917 in the United States was 690,000 short tons, as compared with 702,000 short tons in 1916.

Zionism.—In the words of its founder, Dr. Theodore Herzl, the movement for the "creation of a home secured by public rights for those Jews who cannot or will not be assimilated in the country of their adoption." One branch of the Zionist movement, known as the Jewish Colonization Association, in which the leading spirit is Israel Zangwill, is willing to found this home in any suitable locality, but as a whole the Zionist movement is concerned with locating in Palestine.

The Old Testament is replete with prophecies that some day the Jews will return to their ancient home ; and from the days of the Babylonian exile, devout Jews have looked forward to the day when the Jews would once again be an autonomous race. Up to the close of the eighteenth century, when Jewish life was still almost entirely bounded by the walls of an Oriental and unmodern Ghetto, this hope, although vague, was never shaken. But at this time, under the example of Moses Mendelssohn, a definite cultural movement arose which brought the Jew out of his Ghetto and set him down as a citizen of the land of his adoption—a citizen with Jewish ties, it is true, but nonetheless a citizen bearing with interest his share in all movements of the national life of the country in which he had made a home. In the latter half of the nineteenth century, however, there occurred a tremendous Anti-Semitic movement in Europe, and the longing for a national home for the Jewish people took on new significance as a result. It is therefore natural that most orthodox or conservative Jews are Zionists and that most reformed Jews are anti-Zionists.

It was not until 1896, however, that the aims of the nationalistic impulse were put concretely. That task was performed by a brilliant journalist of Vienna, Theodore Herzl, in his book "The Jewish State." The book created a great sensation, and occasioned the formation of the first Zionist conference, held the following year in Basle, Switzerland. The aims of the movement are the acquisition of Palestine from the Turks, the rendering of the holy places extra-territorial, and the maintenance of the country autonomous under Turkish suzerainty and the guarantee of the Great Powers. The Revolution of the Young Turks in Turkey in 1908-1909 raised the hopes of the Zionists, but it was seen that those hopes had been raised in vain.

The European War affected the Zionist movement in different ways. The machinery of the organization was wrecked, along with most of its financial support ; and the Zionist leadership passed from Europe to America, where Supreme Court Justice Louis D. Brandeis was made head of the Provisional Zionist Committee. The Russian Revolution freed from persecution more than half of the 13,000,000 Jews of the world, and hence removed one of the strongest incentives, especially among non-Jews, to support the movement. On the other hand, persistent negotiations with the belligerent governments by powerful Jewish leaders seemed to have created among the Entente governments a strong sentiment for turning Palestine over to the Jews, especially if the British expedition against the Holy Land should be successful in gaining the land from the Turks and in holding it.

From the earliest days of the modern Zionist movement, pending the material acquisition of Palestine, the Zionist leaders concerned themselves largely with founding agricultural and mechanical settlements in the country, and in carrying in other ways the message of Western civilization to the inhabitants. In 1915, there were 43 agricultural colonies, all of them in a flourishing condition. One interesting feature of the Zionist movement has been the revival in Palestine of Hebrew as the language of every-day life.

Zollverein.—A union of German states for the maintenance of uniform rate of duty on imports from other countres and of free trade among themselves. It began in 1828 in an agreement between Prussia and the Grand Duchy of Hesse, and gradually developed until now it is coextensive with the German Empire, and also includes the Grand Duchy of Luxemburg.

Zollverein, The. (See Germany.)

Zona Libre.—A narrow strip of territory along the northern border of Mexico, so called because certain articles imported for consumption in it were formerly exempted from customs duties. It was first established in 1858. Imports into the zone latterly paid 10 per cent of the ordinary duties, except cattle, which paid full duty. The zone was suppressed July 1, 1905.

Zona Libre:

Discussed, 4055, 4100, 4295, 4806, 6334. Referred to, 5195.

Zuni and Manzano national forests, combined, 7987.

BIOGRAPHIC INDEX

to the

Messages and Papers of the Presidents

Abbot, Henry Larcom; soldier, civil engineer, author; b. Aug. 13, 1831, in Beverly, Mass.; General in United States Army, and prominent as an engineer; author of lectures and papers on the Defence of the Sea Coast of the United States, and Physics and Hydraulics of the Mississippi River.

Abert, James William; Major of Engineers, United States Army; b. Nov. 18, 1820, in Mount Holly, N. J.; served in Civil War, and attained rank of major; resigned in 1864; was Examiner of Patents in Washington, and later professor of mathematics and drawing in University of Missouri at Rolla.

Abert, John James; soldier, engineer; b. Sept. 17, 1788, in Shepherdton, Va.; in 1829 took charge of topographical bureau at Washington, and in 1838 became Colonel of Engineers; retired in 1861, after long and faithful service; was engaged in many of the earlier works of national engineering, and his reports prepared for the Government are standards of authority; was member of several scientific societies and one of the organizers of the National Institute of Science, which later was merged into Smithsonian Institution; died Sept. 27, 1863, in Washington.

Adair, John A. M.; b. Jay Co., Ind., Dec. 22, 1863; admitted to the bar in 1895; elected to the general assembly of Indiana in 1902, and to the 60th, 61st, 62d, 63d and 64th Congresses from Indiana.

Adams, Charles Francis; lawyer, author, member State legislature and Congress; b. Aug. 18, 1807, in Boston, Mass.; son of John Quincy Adams, sixth President of the United States, and grandson of John Adams, second President of United States; served five years in Massachusetts legislature; nominated for Vice-President on ticket with Martin Van Buren; was twice elected to Congress from Massachusetts; served as minister to England during Civil War in America; died Nov. 21, 1866, in Boston, Mass.

Adams, C. F.:
Arbitrator named by United States for Geneva Tribunal, 4139.
Correspondence regarding publications for Library of Congress transmitted, 3347.

Adams, Charles Francis, Jr., son of above; soldier, author, railroad president; b. May 27, 1835, in Boston, Mass.; officer in Union Army during Civil War; president of Union Pacific Railway; wrote works on railroads and history; bitter opponent of tariff system; died Washington, D. C., March 20, 1915.

Adams, John, biography of, 217.

Adams, John Quincy, biography of, 857.

Adams, Samuel (1722-1803); statesman; b. Boston, Mass.; as a Revolutionary leader his work was most important in the first and second Continental Congresses; was a signer of the Declaration of Independence, and a member of the ratifying Congress in Massachusetts, 1788; was lieutenant-governor of Massachusetts, 1789-94, and governor, 1794-97.

Adamson, William Charles; b. Bowdon, Ga., Aug. 13, 1854; was admitted to the bar Oct., 1876; elected to the 55th, 56th, 57th, 58th, 59th, 60th, 61st, 62d, 63d and 64th Congresses from Georgia.

Adee, Alvey A.; engineer, diplomat; b. Nov. 27, 1842, in Astoria, L. I., N. Y.; learned civil engineering; secretary to American legation in Spain, 1870 to 1877; transferred to State Department, and in 1878 became chief of diplomatic division, and in 1882 was appointed third assistant Secretary of State.

Adee, Alvey A.:
Acting Secretary of State, 5536, 6475.
Second Assistant Secretary of State, Canadian canal tolls referred to, 5678. (See also 5675.)

Adet, Pierce Auguste; French artillerist, chemist, and diplomat (1763-1832); became minister to United States in 1795; in 1797 he severed diplomatic relations between France and America with a note from the Directory stating that France would treat neutrals as they allowed themselves to be treated by English; issued inflammatory address to American people.

Adet, P. A., colors of France presented to United States by, on the occasion of the presentation of an address, dated October 21, 1794, by the committee of public safety, 181.

Agassiz, Jean Louis Rodolphe; author, educator, naturalist; b. May 28, 1807, in Switzerland; came to United States in 1846; in coast survey steamer *Bibb*, made a scientific cruise of Atlantic coast from Massachusetts to Florida; in 1848 made professor of zoology in Lawrence Scientific School, Cambridge, and founded Museum of Natural History at Cambridge; in 1871 given charge of scientific expedition on war vessel *Hassler*, which made trip around Cape Horn to San Francisco; died at Cambridge, Mass., Dec. 14, 1873.

Agassiz, J. L. R., visit of, to Brazil, referred to, 3664.

Aguinaldo, Emilio; Filipino leader; of Chinese and Tagalog parents; b. in 1870, in Cavité, Luzon; educated at College of St. Jean Lateran and University of St. Thomas, in Manila, and as protégé of Jesuit priests, studied English, French and Chinese languages at Hong Kong, and became interested in military affairs; as head of diplomatic commission to treat with Spain in 1896, he sold out the Filipino insurgents, and after a quarrel with his comrades over division of Spanish money, set up the Filipino republic, June 12, 1898, with himself as president; protested against American possession of Philippine Islands and planned to massacre Americans in Manila, but failed; attacked Americans in Manila, Feb. 4, 1899, and was defeated and driven to the mountains, where he was captured by Gen. Funston March 23, 1901.

Aguinaldo, referred to, 6408, 6414.

Aiken, Wyatt; b. Dec. 14, 1863, Abbeville Co., S. C.; was an official court stenographer in South Carolina for nineteen years; farmer all his life; during the war with Spain was a soldier; elected to the 58th, 59th, 60th, 61st, 62d, 63d and 64th Congresses from South Carolina.

Ainsworth, F. C., work of, in Record and Pension Division of War Department discussed, 5631.

Akerman, Amos T.; lawyer; Attorney General under President Grant; b. in New Hampshire in 1823; educated in the public schools of his native State and at Dartmouth College; studied law and was admitted to the bar in 1844; removed in 1850 to Elberon, Ga., where he continued the practice of his profession; identified himself with the conservative political party of Stephens, Warner, Johnson and Hill in opposition to secession, but, like many other southern conservatives, went with the majority when secession was decided upon; he was employed in the quartermaster's department of the Confederate Government; after the war joined the Republican party, supported the reconstruction policy of the government, and, in 1866, was appointed United States attorney for the district of Georgia and served in that capacity till 1870, when Grant appointed him Attorney General to succeed Ebenezer R. Hoar; resigned in 1872 and returned to Georgia and became the unsuccessful Republican candidate for United States Senator; died Dec. 21, 1880, in Cartersville, Ga.

Alden, James; naval officer; b. March 31, 1810, in Portland, Me.; as midshipman he accompanied Wilkes' exploring expedition around the world, 1838-42; commissioned commodore in 1866, and in 1868 placed in charge of Mare Island Navy Yard, San Francisco; died Feb. 6, 1877.

Aldrich, Nelson Wilmarth; b. Foster, R. I., Nov. 6, 1841; received an academic education; member of the Rhode Island general assembly in 1875-76, serving the latter year as speaker; elected to the 46th Congress and re-elected to the 47th; elected Oct. 5, 1881, to the United States Senate from Rhode Island, and re-elected 1886, 1892, 1898, and 1905. In 1908 appointed chairman of a national monetary commission to inquire into and report what changes are desirable in the laws relating to banking and currency. Upon the report of this commission was based the Aldrich-Vreeland Currency Law. Died in New York, April 16, 1915.

Alexander, Edward Porter; soldier, author, engineer; b. May 26, 1835, in Washington, Ga.; graduated at West Point in 1857; served as engineer officer in Utah expedition, 1858; professor of mathematics and engineering in West Point, 1859-60; served in Confederate Army and later as instructor in South Carolina University; became a railroad official, and wrote works on railroading.

Alexander, General E. P., settlement of question between Costa Rica and Nicaragua by, 6427.

Alexander, James, crimes charged against, 405.

Alexander, Joshua W.; b. in Cincinnati, Ohio, Jan. 22, 1852; moved to Canton, Lewis Co., Mo., and entered Christian University at Canton, Mo.; studied law and was admitted to the bar in 1875 at Gallatin, Mo.; in 1882 was elected representative to the general assembly of Missouri from Daviess County, and re-elected in 1884 and 1886; served two terms as mayor of Gallatin; elected to the 60th, 61st, 62d, 63d and 64th Congresses from Missouri.

Alger, Russell A.; soldier, lawyer, lumberman; b. Feb. 27, 1836, Lafayette, Ohio; studied law, and enlisted in Civil War as private, and in 1865 was brevetted brigadier-general and major-general for gallant conduct; elected governor of Michigan in 1884; candidate for Republican nomination for President in 1888; commander of Grand Army of Republic, 1889; appointed Secretary of War by President McKinley in 1897; one of the wealthiest men in Michigan, where he owns large lumber interests. Senator from Michigan, 1902-07; died, 1907.

Alger, R. A., thanks of President tendered Gen. Shafter through, 6574.

Allen, Alfred G.; b. near Wilmington, Ohio, July 23, 1867; attended the public schools of Wilmington, and afterward entered the law school of the Cincinnati College, from which he was graduated in 1890; since that time he has been in active practice of the law in Cincinnati; served two years as councilman at large and two years as a member of the board of sinking-fund trustees of Cincinnati; Dec. 10, 1901, married Miss Clara B. Forbes, of St. Louis, Mo., and has two children; elected to the 62d, 63d and 64th Congresses from Ohio.

Allen, Ira; soldier, author; b. April 21, 1751, in Cornwall, Conn.; was an officer in the American Army during Revolution, and was afterward instrumental in settling the boundary disputes between Vermont and neighboring states; author of "Natural and Political History of Vermont"; died Jan. 7, 1814, in Philadelphia, Pa.

Allen, Ira, claims of heir of, against Great Britain, 1268.

Allen, Walter, member of Ponca Indian Commission, 4582.

Almodovar, Duke of, communication from, regarding Spanish-American peace negotiations, 6320.

Alvarez, Manuel, acting governor of New Mexico, 2611.

Alvord, H. J., treaty with Indians concluded by, 3460.

Ambristie [Ambrister] and Arbuthnot, courts-martial of, referred to, 612.

Ames, Butler; b. Lowell, 1871; graduated from the United States Military Academy at West Point in 1894; at outbreak of Spanish war was made lieutenant and adjutant of Volunteers; at Camp Alger, near Washington, appointed acting engineer of the Second Army Corps, under General Graham, in addition to his duties as adjutant; went to Cuba and Porto Rico under General Miles; was civil administrator of Arecibo district of Porto Rico till November, 1898; served as member of the Massachusetts State legislature for three years, 1897, 1898, 1899; elected to the 58th, 59th, 60th, 61st and 62d Congresses from Massachusetts.

Ames, Fisher; author, publicist, orator, statesman; b. April 9, 1758, in Dedham, Mass.; graduated from Harvard; studied law and was a distinguished member of Massachusetts Convention for ratifying the Constitution in 1788; member of State legislature; in Congress from 1789 to 1797; was conspicuous for his eloquence and patriotism; devoutly attached to George Washington, and wrote the address to the House of Representatives to the President on his retirement from office; wrote many articles on public affairs of America, England and France; died July 4, 1808.

Ames, Fisher:
Commissioner to treat with Indians, nomination of, 250.
On committee to conduct inaugural ceremony of President Washington, 39.

Amin Bey, visit of, to United States referred to, 2655.

Anderson, Edward C., lieutenant in Navy, resignation of, referred to, 2610, 2612.

Anderson, John H., appointed to Civil Service, 6855.

Anderson, Richard Clough, Jr.; lawyer, Congressman, diplomat; b. Aug. 14, 1788, in Louisville, Ky.; practised law in Kentucky; served three terms in state assembly, of which he was chosen speaker in 1822; appointed minister to Colombia in 1823, and in 1826; when on his way to attend Congress of American Nations as envoy extraordinary, he died in Panama, July 24, 1826.

Anderson, Richard C., minister to Panama, nomination of, 886.

Anderson, Robert; soldier; b. June 14, 1805, in Louisville, Ky.; graduated from West Point in 1825; colonel of Illinois Volunteers in Black Hawk War, in 1832, and took part in Seminole and Mexican wars; major of First Artillery, and in command of Fort Sumter, S. C., in 1861, when forced to surrender to Confederate troops; attained rank of brigadier-general, and was brevetted major-general; one of the founders of National Soldiers' Home, in Washington; died Oct. 27, 1871, in Nice, France.

Anderson, Robert:
Commander of forts in Charleston Harbor, 3189.
Dispatches of, while in command of Fort Sumter referred to, 3213, 3222.
Empowered to receive volunteer troops, 3219.
Flag over Fort Sumter at evacuation of, to be raised on ruins of, by, 3484.

Anderson, Sydney; b. Goodhue County, Minn., Sept. 17, 1880; educated in the common schools of Zumbrota, Minn., and the University of Minnesota; lawyer; served as a private in Company D, Fourteenth Regiment Minnesota Volunteer Infantry, during the Spanish-American War; married and has two children; elected to the 62d, 63d and 64th Congresses from Minnesota.

Andrews, T. P., treaty with Indians concluded by, 2304.

Ansberry, Timothy T.; lawyer; b. Dec. 24, 1871, Defiance, Ohio; elected to the 60th, 61st, 62d, 63d and 64th Congresses from Ohio.

Anthony, Daniel Read, Jr.; b. Aug. 22, 1870, at Leavenworth, Kans.; admitted to the bar, but engaged in newspaper work; was mayor of Leavenworth in 1903-1905; elected to the 60th Congress to fill a vacancy caused by the election of Hon. Charles Curtis to the United States Senate; and re-elected to the 61st, 62d, 63d and 64th Congresses from Kansas.

Arbuthnot and Ambristie [Ambrister], courts-martial of, referred to, 612.

Armistead, George; soldier; b. April 10, 1780, in Newmarket, Va.; one of five brothers, all of whom took part in the War of 1812; rose successively to major of artillery by 1813; distinguished at capture of Fort George, near mouth of Niagara River, from British in 1813; brevetted lieutenant-colonel for successful defence of Fort McHenry, near Baltimore, against attack of British fleet under Admiral Cochrane, Sept. 14, 1814; presented with silver service by citizens of Baltimore; died April 25, 1818, in Baltimore, Md.

Armistead, George, mentioned, 701.

Armstrong, John; general, author, Congressman, Senator, diplomat; b. Nov. 25, 1758, in Carlisle, Pa.; officer in Revolutionary War; author of Newburgh Letters; delegate to Continental Congress in 1778 and 1787 from Pennsylvania; Secretary of State and adjutant-general; directed last Pennsylvania war against Connecticut settlers of Wyoming; United States senator from New York, 1800 to 1804; minister to France, 1804, and later to Spain; brigadier-general in 1812, and Secretary of War in 1813; died April 1, 1843, in Red Hook, N. Y.

Armstrong, John:
Communicating letter from the French minister of foreign relations showing disposition of the French people toward the people of the United States, 434, 437.

Arnold, Gerrard, reward offered for murderer of, 943.

Arnold, Samuel, implicated in murder of President Lincoln, proceedings of trial and verdict of military commission, 3532, 3533, 3534, 3540, 3545, 3546.

Arthur, Chester A., biography of, 4618.

Ashbrook, William A.; b. Johnstown, Licking Co., Ohio, July 1, 1867; 1906, was elected to the State legislature; elected to the 60th, 61st, 62d, 63d and 64th Congresses from Ohio.

Ashley, Gen., attacked by Indians, 781.

Ashton, J. Hubley; lawyer; appointed Assistant United States Attorney-general in 1864 from Pennsylvania, serving three years, and reappointed in 1868, serving one year; later connected with the court for settlement of Alabama Claims.

Ashton, J. Hubley, agent of United States before Mexican and United States Claims Commission, report of, transmitted, 4379.

Atchison, David R.; statesman; b. Frogtown, Fayette County, Ky., Aug. 11, 1807; son of a Presbyterian minister; admitted to the bar in 1830, and began practice of law in Missouri; member of State Legislature in 1834 and 1838; judge of the Platt County Circuit Court in 1841; elected United States Senator in 1843 and reelected in 1849; while senator he frequently served as president *pro tem* of the Senate: on the death of Vice-President William R. King in 1853, he became Vice-President. President Polk's term expired at noon, Sunday, March 4, 1849, and his successor, General Taylor, was not inaugurated until Monday, March 5; Senator Atchison therefore became President of the United States for one day, the law of presidential succession to members of the cabinet not yet having been enacted. Mr. Atchison died in Clinton County, Mo., Jan. 26, 1886, just one week after the approval of the essential features of the present presidential succession law. (See Presidential Succession. Also Ferry, Thomas W.)

Atkinson, Edward; author, reformer; active in matters of diet and political economy; b. Brookline, Mass., Feb. 10, 1827; author of "Industrial Progress and the Nation," "Science of Nutrition," etc.

Atkinson, Edward, international arrangement fixing rates between gold and silver coinage, report of, on, 5177.

Atkinson, Henry; soldier; b. in South Carolina, and became captain in army in 1808; made adjutant-general after War of 1812, and later appointed to command of Western army; died in June, 1842, at Jefferson Barracks, St. Louis, Mo.

Atkinson, Henry:
Mentioned, 701.
Treaty with Indians concluded by, 887.
Troops sent to suppress Indians, commanded by, 953, 1166.

Atwater, Caleb; author, lawyer, legislator; b. Dec. 25, 1778, in North Adams, Mass.; grad. from Williams College in 1804; built up law practice, and moved to Ohio in 1811; member of State legislature, and postmaster at Circleville; Indian commissioner under President Jackson; wrote a history of Ohio; died March 13, 1867, in Circleville, Ohio.

Atwater, Caleb, treaty with Indians concluded by, 1029.

Atzerodt, George A.:
Implicated in murder of President Lincoln, proceedings of trial and verdict of military commission, 3532, 3533, 3534, 3540, 3545, 3546.
Persons claiming reward for apprehension of, directed to file claims, 3551.

Augur, Christopher Colon; soldier; b. in New York in 1821; graduated from West Point in 1843; took part in Mexican War; promoted to captain in 1852, and served in Indian outbreaks in Oregon, 1855-56; served with distinction during Civil War, and in 1865 was brevetted brigadier-general and major-general; had command in Washington, 1863-66; made brigadier-general United States Army in 1869, and retired in 1885.

Augur, Christopher C., directed to assume command of Department of Missouri, 4754.

Auldjo, Thomas, vice-consul to Poole, England, nomination of, 90.

Aury, Louis De; lieutenant in New Grenada navy; b. about 1780; in command at siege of Cartagena; went to Texas with Herrero in 1816, as commander of the united fleets, and was appointed governor of Texas and Galveston Island; July, 1817, he took part in McGregor's expedition to Florida, and various South American revolts; resided in New Orleans and Havana.

Aury, Louis De, mentioned, 601.

Austin, Richard Wilson; b. at Decatur, Ala., Aug. 26, 1857; educated University of Tennessee; member of the bar; was assistant doorkeeper of the House of Representatives in the 47th Congress; United States marshal for the eastern district of Tennessee from 1897 to 1906; served as American consul at Glasgow, Scotland, from July, 1906, to November, 1907; elected to the 61st, 62d, 63d and 64th Congresses from Tennessee.

Bacon, Augustus Octavius; b. Bryan Co., Ga., Oct. 20, 1839; received a high-school education in Liberty and Troup counties; graduated at the University of Georgia; entered the Confederate army at the beginning of the war and served till its close; began the practice of law in 1866 at Macon, from which date until his election to the Senate he actively continued both in the State and Federal courts; in 1871 elected to the Georgia house of representatives, which body he served for fourteen years; during eight years he was speaker; a regent of the Smithsonian Institution; elected to the United States Senate from Georgia, in November, 1894, 1900 and 1907, having been, by a general state primary, unanimously renominated. Died in 1913.

Badger, George Edmund, statesman and Secretary of the Navy under President William H. Harrison; b. Newbern, N. C., April 17, 1795. His father was a native of Connecticut, but removed in early manhood to the South, where he became a lawyer of distinction. The son was prepared for college in the schools at Newbern, and at the age of fifteen entered Yale. With his other studies he took up law, and progressed so rapidly that at the age of twenty he was admitted to the bar. The War of 1812 was at the time disturbing the country, and Gov. Hawkins called out the militia. Badger took the field, and served as aide-de-camp to Gen. Calvin Jones, with the rank of major. He was elected to the legislature in 1816, the year of his majority, and devoted the next four years of his life to law and legislation. In 1820 he was appointed judge of the superior court, and filled the judicial bench until 1825, when he resigned and removed to Raleigh, where he continued to reside until the end of his life. In 1840 he took an active part in the Harrison presidential campaign, and soon after Mr. Harrison's inauguration was appointed Secretary of the Navy. After the death of President Harrison, and the separation of Mr. Tyler from the Whig party, Mr. Badger resigned, giving as a reason his non-agreement with the policy of Mr. Tyler. In 1846 he was elected to the United States Senate to fill an unexpired term of two years, and in 1848 reelected for a full term. In 1853 President Fillmore nominated him as a judge of the United States Supreme Court, but the nomination was not confirmed by the Senate. He was a vigorous speaker, but rarely wrote anything. He excelled in debate, and in the subjects he studied made profound research. Mr. Badger married three times, in each case forming an alliance with a distinguished family. He was prostrated by a stroke of paralysis Jan. 5, 1863, and, after a lingering illness, died May 11, 1866, at Raleigh, N. C.

Bagley, Worth, ensign in Navy, killed while attempting to silence batteries at Cardenas, Cuba, 6302, 6316.

Bailey, Edward L., reinstatement in service vetoed, 6775.

Bailey, Joseph Weldon; b. Copiah Co., Miss., Oct. 6, 1863; admitted to the bar in 1883; removed to Texas in 1885 and located at his present home; elected to the 52d, 53d, 54th, 55th, and 56th Congresses; chosen United States Senator from Texas, Jan. 23, 1901; reelected in 1907.

Bailey, Theodorus, thanks of Congress to, recommended, 3277.

Bainbridge, William, naval officer; b. May 7, 1774, at Princeton, N. J.; served as lieutenant-commander in the war with France in 1798, and was captured by the French; commanded the *Philadelphia* in the Tripolitan war and surrendered Nov. 1, 1803, after his vessel had become fast on a rock in a position where her guns could not be used; appointed commodore in 1812 and made commander of a squadron; in command of *Constitution* captured the British frigate *Java,* Dec. 29, 1812; in 1815 and 1819 commanded squadrons in the Mediterranean, returning in 1821; in command at various times of the navy yards at Charlestown, Boston, and Philadelphia; died at Philadelphia July 28, 1833.

Bainbridge, William:
 Commander of the—
  Constitution, 507.
  Philadelphia, 352, 356.
 Letter of, regarding—
  Hostile act of vessel of Morocco transmitted, 352.
  Wreck of the *Philadelphia* transmitted, 356.

Baker, Eugene M., engagement with Piegan Indians referred to, 4004.

Baker, John, imprisonment of, in New Brunswick, 963, 969, 990.
 Claims arising out of, 1687.

Baker, Marcus; geographer, mathematician, and explorer; b. Sept. 23, 1849, in Ostemo, Mich.; graduated from University of Michigan in 1870, and became professor of mathematics in Albion College, and tutor in University of Michigan; appointed to Coast and Geodetic Survey in 1873, and as assistant geographer, explored Pacific coast from Southern California to Alaska and Arctic Ocean; placed in charge of magnetic observatory, United States Signal Service, at Los Angeles, Cal., 1882; member of Board of Geographic Names, 5647.

Baldwin, Charles H.; naval officer; b. Sept. 3, 1822, in New York City; entered navy in 1839, and served on frigate *Congress* in Mexican War; in 1861 commanded steamer *Clifton;* raised to rank of rear-admiral, January, 1883, and assigned to command of Mediterranean squadron; retired in 1884; died Nov. 17, 1888, in New York City.

Baldwin, Charles H., thanks of Congress to, recommended, 3277.

Baldwin, Leon, indemnity paid by Mexico for murder of, in Durango, 5959.

Balestier, Joseph:
 Mentioned, 2688.
 Mission of, to eastern Asia referred to, 2681.

Balfour, Arthur James; b. July 25, 1848. Educated at Eton and at Trinity College, Cambridge. He was elected to Parliament in 1874, and in 1878 became private secretary to his uncle, Lord Salisbury, the Foreign Minister. His duties in this capacity laid the foundation for his comprehensive knowledge of international affairs, but he did not relinquish his keen interest in the study of philosophy, as was shown in 1879 by the publication of his well-known "Defence of Philosophic Doubt." From 1880 to 1886, he was a member of the House of Commons, but took no prominent part in the discussions, and much surprise was caused by his appointment in 1886 as Secretary for Scotland, with a seat in the Cabinet. Soon afterwards he was appointed Chief Secretary for Ireland, and created a reputation for unusual sagacity and administrative ability in that office. He also developed his ability as an orator during this period to such an extent that he became celebrated as one of the most effective speakers in Parliament. In 1891, he was made First Lord of the Treasury, and until 1895 was the leader of his Party. In 1898, he was given charge of the Foreign Office, and on the resignation of Lord Salisbury in 1902, his nephew became Prime Minister. For three and a half years the government of England during a critical period of her history lay in his hands, until his resignation in December 4, 1905, when he was succeeded by Campbell-Bannerman. He remained the leader of the Unionists, however, and received in addition many distinguished academic honors, including the Chancellorship of Edinburgh University. When the coalition Cabinet under Asquith was formed in 1915, he was made First Lord of the Admiralty, and when Lloyd-George succeeded to the Premiership in December, 1916, he was made Secretary of State for Foreign Affairs. He was the head of the English Commission which visited the United States in April, 1917, and was received with the marked honor to which his valuable services to his country so well entitled him.

Ballard, David W., governor of Idaho Territory, removal of, referred to, 3794.

Ballard, Henry E.; naval officer; b. in 1785, in Maryland; lieutenant in command of United States frigate *Constitution* in famous action with British cruisers *Cyane* and *Levant*, in Bay of Biscay, in 1815; died May 23, 1855, in Annapolis, Md.

Ballard, Henry E., commander of the *United States*, 1273.

Ballinger, Richard Achilles, of Seattle, Wash., Secretary of the Interior in President Taft's Cabinet: b. Boonesboro, Iowa, July 9, 1858; graduated from Williams College, Mass., 1884; Sept. 1, 1897, moved to Seattle, Wash.; engaged in active practice until 1904, when he was elected mayor of Seattle; 1907, Commissioner of the General Land Office; chairman of the Washington State delegation to the national convention which nominated Hon. Wm. H. Taft for the Presidency.

Balmaceda, José M., President of Chile, mentioned, 5618.

Bancroft, George; historian; b. Oct. 3, 1800, in Worcester, Mass.; educated at Exeter Academy and Cambridge University; visited Europe in 1818, and studied in Goettingen and Berlin; spent some ten years as teacher and writer; appointed collector of the Port of Boston in 1838; Secretary of the Navy in 1845; minister to Great Britain in 1846; in 1844 published first volume of "History of the United States," which later grew to twelve volumes; in 1865, by invitation of Congress, he delivered in the Capitol an oration on the death of Abraham Lincoln; appointed minister to Prussia in 1867; died in 1891.

Bancroft, George:
Death of, announced and honors to be paid memory of, 5599.

Minister to Germany, communication from, regarding political questions in Germany, transmitted, 4017.
Referred to, 4114, 4140.

Bankhead, Charles:
Correspondence regarding northeastern boundary. (See Northeastern Boundary.)
Correspondence relative to mediation offered by Great Britain in controversy between United States and France, 1436.

Bankhead, James, correspondence regarding Dorr's Rebellion, 2152, 2155, 2157, 2158.

Bankhead, John Hollis; b. Moscow, Marion (now Lamar) Co., Ala., Sept. 13, 1842; self-educated farmer; served four years in Confederate army; served in general assembly, 1865, 1866 and 1867; warden of the Alabama penitentiary, 1881-85; elected to 50th, 51st, 52d, 53d, 54th, 55th, 56th, 57th, 58th and 59th Congresses; member of the Inland Waterways Commission, 1907; appointed United States Senator to fill the vacancy caused by the death of Hon. John T. Morgan, and in July, 1907, was elected by the legislature to that position and reelected in January, 1911, for the term 1913-1919.

Banks, Nathaniel P.; soldier, legislator, governor; b. in 1816 in Waltham, Mass.; successively worked in cotton factory, lectured in public, edited country newspaper, held custom house position, practised law; member State legislature, 1849 and 1851; member of Congress in 1852, 1854, and 1856; was chosen Speaker of the House in February, 1856, after a contest of two months, on the 133d ballot; elected governor of Massachusetts, 1857, 1858, 1859; appointed Major-general of volunteers in 1861, and later to command of the Army of the Potomac: elected to Congress in 1864, 1866, 1868, 1870, 1874, 1876 and 1888; United States Marshal at Boston, 1879-1888; died in Waltham, Mass., Sept. 1, 1894.

Banks, N. P., orders issued by, at New Orleans transmitted, 3470.

Barbour, James, Secretary of War under President John Quincy Adams; b. June 10, 1775, in Orange Co., Va.; received a common school education; while serving as deputy sheriff of Orange County studied law, and in 1794 admitted to the bar; member of the Virginia house of delegates, and its speaker; United States Senator from Virginia, Anti-Democrat and State Rights, from Jan. 11 1815, to March 27, 1825, when he resigned to become Secretary of War; minister to England from May 23, 1828, to Sept. 23, 1829; died June 8, 1842, near Gordonsville, Va.

Barchfeld, Dr. Andrew Jackson; b. Pittsburg, Pa., May 18, 1863; graduated Jefferson Medical College, Philadelphia, 1884; member of the Pittsburg South Side Medical Society, Allegheny County Medical Society, Pennsylvania State Medical Society, and National Medical Association; is president of the Board of Directors, South Side Hospital, Pittsburg, and a member of the staff; elected to the 59th, 60th, 61st, 62d, 63d and 64th Congresses from Pennsylvania.

Barnhart, Henry A.; b. near Twelve Mile, a village in Cass Co., Ind.; purchased the *Rochester Sentinel* and became its publisher and editor; president and manager of the Rochester Telephone Company; president of the National Telephone Association; director of the Northern Prison at Michigan City for three years; elected to fill a vacancy in the 60th Congress, and to the 61st, 62d, 63d and 64th Congresses from Indiana.

Barnwell, Robert Woodward; Congressman, college president; b. Aug. 10, 1801, in Beaufort, S. C.; graduated from Harvard in 1821; studied law, and served in Congress, 1829-1833; president South Carolina College, 1835-1843; appointed United States Senator in 1850, to fill a vacancy; after the war he was again president of South Carolina College; died Nov. 25, 1882, in Columbia, S. C.

Barnwell, R. W., commissioner from South Carolina, mentioned, 3189.

Barron, Samuel; naval officer; b. Sept. 25, 1765, in Hampton, Va.; distinguished for gallantry in the Revolutionary navy from Virginia, in which his father, his uncle and his brother also participated; died Oct. 28, 1810, in Hampton, Va.

Barron, Samuel, correspondence regarding war with Tripoli transmitted, 379.

Barrundia, J. Martine, seizure and killing of, on the *Acapulco* and action of American minister discussed, 5544.

Conduct of Commander Reiter regarding, referred to, 5569.

Papers regarding, transmitted, 5565.

Barry, John; naval officer; b. in 1754 in Ireland; served through the Revolutionary War as a naval officer, and at the close of that war the United States began to build a new navy, and John Barry was made senior officer; in 1776 he commanded the brig *Lexington*, the first continental vessel to sail from the port of Philadelphia, and with which he made the first capture of a British war vessel accomplished by an American cruiser; later commanded the *Raleigh, Effingham, Alliance,* and others; died Sept. 30, 1803, in Philadelphia, Pa.

Barry, John;
Monument to, proposed, 6946.
Wilson speech at unveiling of, 7942.

Barry, William Taylor, Postmaster-General under President Jackson; b. Feb. 5, 1784; graduated from William and Mary College in 1803; studied law and began the practice of his profession at Lexington, Ky.; elected a Representative in the 11th Congress as a Democrat (to fill a vacancy caused by the resignation of George M. Bibb), and served from Feb. 2, 1815, until he resigned in 1816; judge of the supreme court of Kentucky; elected lieutenant-governor; appointed professor of law and politics in Transylvania University, at Lexington, in 1821; secretary of state; chief justice of the supreme court of Kentucky; appointed Postmaster-General March 9, 1829, the first Postmaster-General invited to sit in the Cabinet; resigned April 10, 1835, when he became minister to Spain; died at Liverpool, England, Aug. 30, 1835, on his way to his post; his remains were brought home and reinterred in Frankfort Cemetery with Masonic honors, Nov. 8, 1854.

Bartholdt, Richard; b. in Germany, Nov. 2, 1855; came to this country when a boy; received a classical education; learned the printing trade and became a newspaper man; was connected with several eastern papers as reporter, legislative correspondent, and editor, and was at the time of his election to Congress editor in chief of the *St. Louis Tribune;* was elected president of the Interparliamentary Union for Arbitration and Peace, and organized a group of that union in Congress; elected to the 53d, 54th, 55th, 56th, 57th, 58th, 59th, 60th, 61st, 62d and 63d Congresses from Missouri.

Bartlett, Charles Lafayette; b. Monticello, Jasper Co., Ga., Jan. 31, 1853; graduated at the University of Georgia, 1870; studied law at the University of Virginia, and was admitted to the bar 1872; elected to the house of representatives of Georgia in 1882 and 1883, and again in 1884 and 1885, and to the state senate in 1888 and 1889; elected to the 54th, 55th, 56th, 57th, 58th, 59th, 60th, 61st, 62d and 63d Congresses from Georgia.

Barton, Clara; army hospital and field nurse; b. in 1830 in North Oxford, Mass.; educated at Clinton, N. Y., and founded a free school at Bordentown, N. J.; clerk in United States Patent Office, 1854-1861; devoted herself to the care of the sick and wounded during the Civil War; did hospital work in the Franco-German War; aided the Red Cross movement; assisted the poor at Paris and Strasburg; became head of Red Cross Society in America; in 1896 she went to Turkey to aid the persecuted Armenians; during Spanish-American War she went to Cuba and had charge of distributing supplies furnished by United States Government.

Barton, Clara, president American National Red Cross, work accomplished by, in Spanish-American War discussed, 6284, 6308, 6320.

Barton, Thomas P., chargé d'affaires to France:
Correspondence regarding claims against France. (See France, claims against.)
Request of, for passports complied with, 1416.

Bashaw, Hamet, correspondence relating to Hamet Caramalli transmitted, 380.

Batchelder, J. M., mentioned as a member of the commission for the revision of the Judicial Code of the reform tribunal of Egypt, 4564.

Bates, Edward, Attorney-General under President Lincoln; b. Sept. 4, 1793, at Belmont, Goochland Co., Va.; educated at Charlotte Hall Academy, Maryland, and in 1812 obtained a midshipman's warrant but was prevented from going to sea by his mother; served as sergeant in the winter of 1812 and 1813 in a volunteer brigade; in 1814 moved to St. Louis; studied law and in 1817 admitted to the bar; circuit prosecuting attorney in 1818; member of the convention which formed the State constitution in 1820; State's attorney in 1820; member of the State house of representatives in 1822; United States district attorney, 1821-1826; elected a Representative from Missouri to the 20th Congress as an

Adams anti-Democrat; defeated for re-election to the 21st Congress; member of the State senate in 1830, and of the State house of representatives in 1834; declined a Cabinet seat tendered him by President Fillmore; in 1856 presided at the national Whig convention at Baltimore; appointed Attorney-General by President Lincoln and served from March, 1861, to September, 1864; died at St. Louis, Mo., March 25, 1869.

Bates, Brig.-Gen. John C., transmitting his report in connection with the treaty effected by him with the Sultan of Sulu, 6407.

Baumer, Julius, expulsion of, from German Empire referred to, 4460.

Bayard, James Asheton, Jr.; lawyer, member of Congress and United States Senator; b. Nov. 15, 1799, in Wilmington, Del.; his father was a member of Congress, and later Senator; his brother, Richard H., was also a Senator; he and his son, Thomas Francis, were elected to the United States Senate at the same time—1869; was a delegate to the New York convention of 1868; died June 13, 1880, in Wilmington, Del.

Bayard, James A., Jr., nomination of, as director of Bank of United States declined, 1267.

Bayard, Thomas Francis; lawyer, statesman; b. Oct. 29, 1828, in Wilmington, Del.; son of James A., Jr.; trained for mercantile life, but later adopted profession of law, which he practised in his native city; appointed United States District Attorney for Delaware in 1853, and resigned in 1854; elected to United States Senate in 1869, on same day his father was re-elected to same body; was twice re-elected; appointed Secretary of State by President Cleveland in 1885; died Sept. 28, 1898, in Dedham, Mass.

Bayard, Thomas F.:
Ambassador to Great Britain, report relating to speeches of, transmitted, 6035.
Secretary of State, 4889.
Treaty with Great Britain on subject of fisheries concluded by, 5189.

Baylor, Thomas G., member of Gun Foundry Board, 4748.

Beach, Lansing H., commissioner in marking boundary between Texas and Mexico, 4902.

Beale, Edward F.; soldier, diplomat; b. Feb. 4, 1822, in Washington, D. C.; appointed minister to Austria in 1875.

Beale, Edward F., superintendent of Indian affairs in California, accounts of, referred to, 2958, 3016.

Beaumarchais, Caron de; French wit and dramatist, lawyer, financier and author; b. in Paris in 1732; son of a watchmaker and for a time pursued his father's vocation; his skill in music procured his introduction to court; made a fortune in financial transactions with Duverny; at the outbreak of the American Revolution he contracted to supply the colonists with arms

and ammunition; in this affair he acted as secret agent of the French government; wrote "The Barber of Seville" and "The Marriage of Figaro," successful operas; favored the popular cause in French Revolution; died in 1799.

Beaumarchais, Caron de, claims of, against United States, 406, 568, 591, 696.

Beaupré, Arthur M., correspondence of, on Panama, 6758-6761.

Bedini, Gaetano; Italian cardinal; b. at Sinigaglia, May 15, 1806; went to Bologna as prolegate in 1849, and in 1853 was sent as nuncio to Brazil, with orders to visit the United States on the way and convey a friendly mission to the Government; was charged with tyrannous severity in his administration at Bologna, and his life threatened by Italian and German exiles in the United States; returned to Italy in 1854; died at Viterbo, Sept. 6, 1864.

Bedini, Gaetano, complimentary mission of, to United States, referred to, 2761.

Beecher, Henry Ward; clergyman, author; b. June 24, 1813, in Litchfield, Conn.; forty years pastor of Plymouth Church, Brooklyn, N. Y.; noted as eloquent pulpit orator; died March 8, 1887.

Beecher, Henry Ward, public address to be delivered by, at Fort Sumter, 4237.

Belknap, William Worth; soldier; Secretary of War under President Grant; b. Newburgh, N. Y., Sept. 22, 1829; son of William Goldsmith Belknap, who was prominent in the Mexican war; William W. was graduated at Princeton in 1848; studied law and was admitted to the bar in 1851; opened an office in Keokuk, Iowa, where he became prominent in Democratic politics and was elected to the state legislature; at the outbreak of the Civil War he was commissioned major of the Fifteenth Iowa Volunteers; served with distinction throughout the war under Grant, Sherman, McPherson, and others; mustered out as commander of the fourth division of the Seventeenth Army Corps; collector of internal revenue for Iowa until 1869, when Grant appointed him Secretary of War; March 7, 1876, he was charged with official corruption and impeached; charges were quashed in the Senate for lack of jurisdiction; among those best informed Belknap was believed to have been the victim of others; he was found dead in his bed in Washington, Oct. 13, 1890.

Bell, Henry Haywood; naval officer; b. about 1808, in North Carolina; early in Civil War appointed fleet captain of Western Gulf squadron; promoted to rear-admiral, July, 1866; retired 1867; died Jan. 11, 1868, in Japan.

Bell, Henry H., thanks of Congress to, recommended, 3277.

Bell, John (1797-1869); politician; b. near Nashville, Tenn.; member of Congress from Tennessee, 1827-41; speaker, 1834-35; Secretary of War under Tyler, 1841; United States Senator, 1847-59; nominated by the Constitutional Union party as candidate for the Presidency against Lincoln in 1860.

Bell, Peter Hansboro; lawyer, governor, member of Congress; b. May 18, 1812, in Culpeper, Va.; educated in Virginia and migrated to Texas in 1836; enlisted under General Houston and became inspector-general of Army of Texas; served in Mexican War as Colonel of Volunteers under General Taylor; inaugurated governor of Texas, Jan. 1, 1850; reelected in 1851, and resigned to enter Congress, where he served two terms; migrated to North Carolina and served in Confederate Army as Colonel of Volunteers during Civil War; died April 20, 1898, at Littleton, Halifax Co., N. C.

Bell, Thomas Montgomery; b. Nachoochee Valley, White Co., Ga., March 17, 1861; elected to the 59th, 60th, 61st, 62d, 63d and 64th Congresses from Georgia.

Benge, L. H., treaty with Indians negotiated by, 3592.

Benham, Alexander E. K.; naval officer; b. 1832, in New York; entered navy during Civil War; raised to rank of commander in 1867, captain in 1878, commodore in 1889, and acting rear-admiral in 1890; commander of East Indian squadron in 1891; retired in 1894.

Benham, A. E. K., action of, in protecting American interests during Brazilian insurrection, 5973.

Benner, Henry H., pension to widow of, recommended by Secretary of War, 4451.

Benson, Egbert; lawyer, author, jurist, Congressman; b. June 31, 1746, in New York City; attorney-general of New York, 1780-1789; delegate to Continental Congress, 1784-1788; member of Congress from New York, 1789-1793; judge state supreme court, 1794-1801; again elected to Congress in 1813; died Aug. 24, 1833, in Jamaica, N. Y.

Benson, Egbert:
Appointed on committee—
To conduct ceremonies of administration of oath to President Washington, 39.
To meet President Washington, 37.
Commissioner of United States to determine northeastern boundary, 191.

Benton, Thomas Hart (1782-1858); soldier and statesman; b. near Hillsboro, N. C.; removed to Tennessee; studied law, and entered the legislature; raised a volunteer company for the War of 1812; and served on General Jackson's staff; United States Senator from Missouri, 1821-51; Congressman, 1853-55.

Berard, Mary, deputy postmaster, nomination of, and reasons therefor, 2737.

Bernstein, Bernhard, claim of, against Russia, for illegal arrest and imprisonment, 4162.

Berrien, John Macpherson, Attorney-General under President Jackson; b. New Jersey, Aug. 23, 1781; in 1796 graduated from Princeton College; studied law at Sa-vannah under Hon. Joseph Clay; began the practice of law in 1799 at Louisville, then the capital of Georgia; moved to Savannah; elected solicitor of the eastern judicial circuit of Georgia in 1809; judge of the same circuit, 1810-1821; captain of the Georgia Hussars, a Savannah volunteer company, in the war of 1812-1815; State senator, 1822-1823; elected a United States Senator from Georgia as a Democrat in 1825 and served until March 9, 1829, when he resigned to accept the position of Attorney-General, Dec. 27, 1831; again elected to the United States Senate as a Whig; took his seat May 31, 1841; reelected in 1847 and resigned May 28, 1852; died at Savannah, Ga., Jan. 1, 1856.

Berry, Robert M., relief expedition under command of, 4726.

Bertholf, Ellsworth P., thanks of Congress to, recommended, 6352.

Betancourt, Gaspar A., arrest and detention of, by Spanish authorities in Cuba, 6182.

Betts, Samuel Rossiter; lawyer, jurist, member of Congress; b. June 8, 1787, in Richmond, Mass.; took part in War of 1812, and was appointed judge-advocate; represented New York in Congress, 1815-1817; appointed circuit judge for the state in 1823; judge United States district court, 1826-1867; author of "Admiralty Practice"; died Oct. 3, 1868, in New Haven, Conn.

Betts, Samuel R., decree of, regarding Spanish vessels referred to, 3795.

Beveridge, Albert J.; b. Highland Co., Ohio, Oct. 6, 1862; was admitted to the bar in 1886; elected to the United States Senate in 1899, when he ceased practice; re-elected in 1905 by the unanimous choice of his party to represent Indiana in the Senate.

Beziers, Capt., remuneration for saving American vessel requested by, 1647.

Bibb, George M., Secretary of the Treasury under President Tyler; b. Virginia in 1772; graduated from Princeton College in 1792; studied law, admitted to the bar, and commenced to practice in Kentucky; member of the state house of representatives and senate; three times elected chief justice of Kentucky; chancellor of the Louisville court of chancery; elected a United States Senator from Kentucky, serving from 1811 to 1814, when he resigned; again elected United States Senator, serving from Dec. 7, 1829, to March 3, 1835; Secretary of the Treasury for one year; resumed the practice of law at Washington, and was a clerk in the office of the Attorney-General; died at Georgetown, D. C., April 14, 1859.

Bibb, William Wyatt; governor, Congressman, Senator; b. Oct. 1, 1780, in Virginia; member of Congress from Georgia, 1806-1814; Senator, 1813-1816; appointed governor of Territory of Alabama in 1817, and elected first governor under the constitution of that state in 1819; died July 9, 1820, at Fort Jackson, Ala.

Bibb, William W., letter to Gen. Jackson transmitted, 621.

Biddle, Charles John; soldier, author, journalist, member of Congress; son of Nicholas Biddle; b. 1819 in Philadelphia, Pa.; brevetted major for gallant and meritorious service in Mexican War; Colonel of Pennsylvania Reserve Volunteers in 1861, and while in the field in Virginia was elected to Congress; author of "The Case of Major André"; died Sept. 28, 1873, in Philadelphia, Pa.

Biddle, Charles, mentioned, 2578.

Biddle, James; naval officer, soldier, diplomat; b. Feb. 28, 1783, in Philadelphia, Pa.; United States Commissioner to ratify treaty with China in 1845; visited Japan aboard United States ship *Columbus;* commanded squadron on west coast of Mexico during war with that country; had charge of naval asylum on the Schuylkill, 1838-1842; died Oct. 1, 1848, in Philadelphia.

Biddle, James, treaty with Turkey concluded by, 1093.

Bingham, Henry Harrison; b. Philadelphia, Pa., Dec. 4, 1841; was graduated at Jefferson College, 1862, A. B. and A. M., also LL. D. from Washington and Jefferson College; studied law; entered the Union Army as lieutenant and was mustered out July, 1866, having been brevetted for distinguished gallantry; received the medal of honor for special gallantry on the field of battle; postmaster of Philadelphia, March, 1867; elected to the 46th, 47th, 48th, 49th, 50th, 51st, 52d, 53d, 54th, 55th, 56th, 57th, 58th, 59th, 60th, 61st and 62d Congresses from Pennsylvania.

Bingham, John A.; lawyer, member of Congress; b. in 1815, in Pennsylvania; elected to 34th Congress from Ohio in 1854; reelected to the 35th, 36th, 39th, 40th, 41st and 42d Congresses.

Bingham, John A., special judge advocate in trial of persons implicated in assassination of President Lincoln, 3534.

Bishop, Nathan, member of Indian commission, 3977.

Bismarck, Prince von, instructions of, to German minister respecting Samoa transmitted, 5391.

Bissell, Daniel, colonel in Army, nomination of, discussed, 910.

Bissell, Wilson Shannon; lawyer; Postmaster General during President Cleveland's second term; b. London, Oneida Co., N. Y., Dec. 31, 1847; removed to Buffalo, where he attended public schools until 1863; sent to Hopkins grammar school at New Haven, and graduated Yale College 1869; returned to Buffalo and began study of law in office of Laning, Cleveland & Folsom; admitted to bar in 1871; took an active part in forwarding Grover Cleveland for Mayor of Buffalo, Governor of New York, and President of the United States; appointed Postmaster General March 6, 1893; shortened the time of carrying the mails across the continent by fourteen hours; eliminated $10,000,000 subsidies from slow steamships, and transferred the contract for printing postage stamps from private parties to the Bureau of Engraving and Printing at Washington; resigned April 4, 1895, and resumed practice of law in Buffalo, where he died Oct. 6, 1903.

Black, Frank S.; lawyer, governor, newspaper man, member of Congress; b. March 8, 1853, in Livingston, Me.; graduated from Dartmouth College, and became editor of the *Johnstown Journal;* removed to Troy, N. Y., where he did newspaper work and studied law; served the State as governor and as member of Congress.

Black, Jeremiah S.; jurist; b. Jan. 10, 1810, in Glades, Pa.; appointed presiding judge of the district in which he lived in 1842; elected to the bench of the state supreme court in 1851, and made chief justice; reelected in 1854; appointed Attorney-General of United States in 1857; was Secretary of State in 1860-1861, when he resumed the practice of law; died Aug. 9, 1883, in York, Pa.

Black, Jeremiah S.:
Counsel for President Johnson in impeachment proceedings, 3924.
Secretary of State, 3203.

Blackford, William, treaty with New Granada concluded by, 2168.

Blackmon, Frederick Leonard; b. Lime Branch, Polk County, Ga., Sept. 15, 1873; attended the public schools at Dearmanville and Choccolocco; also State Normal College at Jacksonville, Ala., and the college at Douglasville, Ga.; read law under Prof. Joe Camp, who was a lawyer and also a professor in the Douglasville College He took a course in the business college at Chattanooga, Tenn., and read law under James H. McLane, and was graduated from the university law department; admitted to the bar at Anniston, Ala., was associated with the firm of Knox, Acker, Dixon & Blackmon until elected to Congress; city attorney for Anniston four years, and served in the Alabama State Senate from 1900 until elected to Congress in 1910; chairman of the congressional committee for the fourth Alabama congressional district; married Dec. 31, 1908, has one child; nominated by the Democratic Party without opposition, and elected to the 62d, 63d and 64th Congresses from Alabama.

Blaine, James Gillespie; statesman, orator, editor; b. Jan. 31, 1830, in Washington Co., Pa.; graduated from Washington College and removed to Maine, where he edited the *Kennebec Journal* and *Portland Advertiser;* served four years in Maine legislature, two years as Speaker of the House; elected to the 38th Congress from Maine in 1862; and reelected for six succeeding terms; chosen as Speaker three terms; in 1876 he was elected United States Senator; resigned in 1881 to accept Secretary of State in President Garfield's Cabinet, serving from March till December; he was an unsuccessful candidate for President in 1884; author of "Twenty Years in Congress"; died Jan. 27, 1893, in Washington, D. C.

Blaine, James G.:
Death of, announced and honors to be paid memory of, 5820.
Secretary of State, 4603, 5450.
Correspondence regarding the *Baltimore* affair. (See *Baltimore,* The.)
Member of conference to discuss commercial relations with Canada, 5675, 5678, 5748.

Blaine, Walker G.; diplomat; son of James G.; b. in Maine, received college education, and in 1881 was appointed Third Assistant Secretary of State, and sent with W. H. Triscott as a special envoy to Peru and Chile.

Blaine, Walker, Third Assistant Secretary of State, mentioned, 4694.

Blair, Francis Preston, Jr.; soldier, lawyer, author, member of Congress; b. Feb. 19, 1821, in Lexington, Ky.; migrated to Missouri and became member of State legislature, 1852-1854; elected to 35th, 37th, and 38th Congresses; Colonel of Volunteers in 1861; appointed major-general in 1862; nominated for Vice-President on Democratic ticket in 1868 with Horatio Seymour for President; appointed United States Senator to fill a vacancy in 1871-1873; wrote "Life and Public Services of General William A. Butler"; died July 8, 1875, in St. Louis, Mo.

Blair, Frank P., Jr.:
Commission of, as major-general discussed, 3404.
Correspondence regarding assignment of command to, 3407.
Letter and advice of President Lincoln as to accepting seat in Congress or remaining in command, 3406.
Resignation of, as major-general accepted, 3407.
Withdrawal of, 3409.

Blair, Francis Preston, Sr.; journalist and politician; b. Abington, Va., in 1791; editor *Congressional Globe*, in Washington, 1830-1845; intimate friend and confidential adviser of President Jackson; supported Van Buren for the Presidency in 1848, in opposition to the regular Democratic party nominee; assisted at organization of Republican party in 1855; died Oct. 18, 1876.

Blair, Frank P., Sr., negotiations for and correspondence regarding restoration of peace, 3461.

Blair, Henry W., refusal of China to receive, as minister, 5621, 5673, 5679.

Blair, Montgomery; lawyer, judge; b. in Kentucky about 1813; brother to Francis Preston, Jr.; practised law in St. Louis, and became judge of court of common pleas; moved to Maryland about 1852; appointed Postmaster-General in March, 1861, and was removed near end of 1864; died July 27, 1883.

Blair, Montgomery, correspondence regarding resignation of Frank P. Blair, Jr., as major-general, 3407.

Blakeley, Johnston; naval officer; b. in October, 1781, in Ireland; joined the navy in 1800 and was made lieutenant in 1807, and in 1813 was appointed master commandant of the *Wasp;* June, 1814, captured British sloop, *Reindeer,* and in September the *Avon;* for these services he was promoted to captain, but the *Wasp* never returned to port and was not heard of after Oct. 9, 1814.

Blakeley, Johnston, British ship captured by vessel in command of, 534.

Blanco, Ramon, Captain-General, of Cuba, directed by Spain to suspend hostilities, referred to, 6292.

Bland, Richard Parks (1835-1899); legislator; b. near Hartford, Ky.; studied law and practised in Missouri, California, and Utah, subsequently devoting much attention to mining; represented Missouri in the House from 1873 until 1895, and then from 1897 until his death; noted as the author of the Bland Silver Bill, and 'led the free silver movement in the House; prominent candidate for the nomination for President at the Democratic National Convention of 1896.

Bland, Theodoric; soldier, member of Congress; b. in 1742, in Prince George Co., Va.; enlisted in army and became colonel of regiment of dragoons; in 1779 had command of troops at Albemarle Barracks, whence he was elected to Congress in 1780, representing Virginia in that body for three years, and was then chosen a member of Virginia legislature; member of first Congress under the constitution, having voted for its adoption; died June 1, 1790, in New York.

Bland, Theodoric:
Appointed on committee to meet Washington on his embarkation from New Jersey upon the occasion of his first inauguration, 37.

Blatchford, Richard Milford; financier, legislator, public official; b. April 23, 1798, in Stratford, Conn.; financial agent of the Bank of England in 1826; appointed to same position for Bank of United States in 1836, and assisted in winding up its affairs; member of New York legislature in 1855, and in 1859 park commissioner of New York City; fiscal agent for recruiting service at outbreak of Civil War; minister to Italy in 1862; died Sept. 3, 1875, in Newport.

Blatchford, Richard M., mentioned, 3279.

Bliss, Cornelius N.; Secretary of the Interior under President McKinley; b. Fall River, Mass., Jan. 26, 1833; finished his education in New Orleans, and in 1848 entered a dry goods importing and jobbing house in Boston; in 1867 organized the firm of Wright, Bliss & Fabyan to represent New England manufacturers; became director of Fourth National Bank, Central Trust Co., American Security Co., Equitable Life Insurance Co., Home Insurance Co., member of Union League Club; treasurer New York Hospital; declined a cabinet position under President Arthur; chairman New York State Republican Committee, 1887 and 1888; treasurer National Republican Committee in 1892; appointed Secretary of the Interior March 4, 1897, and resigned Feb. 20, 1899; long time President of the American Protective Tariff League organized to combat the influence of the Cobden Club in England and the American Tariff Reform Club in this country; died Oct. 9, 1911, in New York.

Blount, James H.; lawyer, member of Congress; b. Sept. 12, 1837, in Clinton, Ga.; graduated from University of Georgia with classical education in 1857; began practice of law in Macon, Ga.; represented Georgia in Congress from 1873 to 1893; last public service was as commissioner paramount to the Hawaiian Islands for President Cleveland; on his report Cleveland reversed the policy of Harrison toward Hawaii; died at Macon, Ga., March 8, 1903.

Blount, James H., special commissioner to Hawaiian Islands, report of, discussed, 5873, 5892.

Blow, Henry T., dispatch from, relative to commercial interests with South America, transmitted, 4014.

Boggs, Charles Stuart; naval officer; b. Jan. 28, 1811, in New Brunswick, N. J.; promoted to captain, July 16, 1862, and commodore July 25, 1866; commanded steamer *De Soto,* of North Atlantic squadron, 1867-1868; assigned to European fleet in 1869, and prepared a report on steam engines afloat; promoted to rear-admiral and appointed inspector of third lighthouse district, July 1, 1870; retired 1873; died April 22, 1888, in New Brunswick, N. J.

Boggs, Charles S., thanks of Congress to, recommended, 3277.

Bogy, Lewis V.; lawyer, legislator, railroad president; b. April 9, 1813, in St. Genevieve, Mo.; member of State legislature for several terms; Commissioner of Indian Affairs, 1867-1868; one of the projectors of the St. Louis and Iron Mountain Railroad, of which he was for two years president; elected to United States Senate in 1873, and died in St. Louis Sept. 20, 1877.

Bogy, Lewis V., mentioned, 3719.

Bolivar, Simon; South American patriot and liberator; b. at Caracas, Venezuela, in July, 1783, and inherited a large estate from his father; liberally educated in Madrid, and returned to his native land in 1809; joined the insurgents in 1811, and became a colonel under Miranda; obtained full command of the army in 1813, defeated the Spanish royalists and declared himself dictator; driven out of Venezuela in 1814 and fled to Jamaica; returned in 1816. raised another army and defeated Spaniards under Morillo in February, 1817; in 1819 took title of president, liberated New Granada, which uniting with Venezuela, formed the new republic of Colombia, of which Bolivar became first president; in 1821 and 1822 marched with his army to Peru, which, with his assistance, was soon liberated from the Spaniards; the independence of the South American republics was recognized by England and the United States; early in 1825 resigned dictatorship of Peru and went to Upper Peru, which was formed into a separate state and called Bolivia, of which he was declared perpetual dictator; also declared president of Peru for life, and again made president of Colombia; resigned in February, 1827, but the congress refused to accept his resignation; the result of his military services was the independence of three South American countries; died December, 1830, at San Pedro.

Bolivar, Simon:

Centennial celebration of birth of, at Caracas, referred to, 4716, 4760.

Delivered from assassins, medal offered President Jackson in commemoration of, declined, 1029.

Bollman, Eric; German physician; b. in Hanover, about 1770; made an unsuccessful effort to release Lafayette from prison at Olmutz, and passed some years in exile in United States; died in 1821.

Bollman, Eric, crimes charged against, 405.

Bonaparte, Charles Joseph; lawyer; b. June 9, 1851, in Baltimore, Md.; grandson of Jerome Bonaparte, brother of Napoleon I.; graduated from Harvard in 1871; practised law in his native city; appointed Secretary of the Navy, July, 1905; and later Attorney-General; active in many societies for the suppression of vice and maintenance of law and order.

Bonaparte, Charles J., mentioned, 6863.

Booher, Charles F.; b. East Groveland, Livingston Co., N. Y., Jan. 31, 1848; studied law, and went to Savannah, Mo., in 1870; was admitted to the bar in 1871; mayor of Savannah six years; elected to the 60th, 61st, 62d, 63d and 64th Congresses from Missouri.

Booth, John Wilkes; actor; assassin of President Lincoln; b. 1838 in Bel Air, Md.; after shooting the President from the stage of Ford's theatre in Washington, he fled; was pursued and shot to death in a barn near Bowling Green, Va., April 26, 1865.

Booth, John Wilkes, persons claiming reward for apprehension of, directed to file claims, 3551.

Borah, William Edgar; b. June 29, 1865, in Wayne Co., Ill.; was educated at the Kansas State University, Lawrence; admitted to practice law September, 1890, at Lyons, Kans.; elected to the United States Senate from Idaho, Jan. 15, 1907, re-elected 1913, for term ending in 1919.

Borie, Adolph E.; Secretary of the Navy under President Grant for a few months; b. Philadelphia, Nov. 25, 1809; educated in public schools of his native town and at the University of Pennsylvania; studied in Paris two years, and upon his return home entered his father's business firm of McKean, Borie & Co., engaged in trade with China and Mexico; acquired a fortune and was president of the Bank of Commerce of Philadelphia from 1848 to 1860; on the outbreak of the Civil War he gave much time and money to the enlistment and care of volunteer soldiers; one of the founders of the Union League Club of Philadelphia, the first of these institutions to be founded in the country; accepted the position of Secretary of the Navy March 5, 1869, but found that his private affairs needed his attention and resigned June 25 of the same year and was succeeded by George M. · Robeson; accompanied Gen. Grant in his tour of the world, which began in Philadelphia in 1877; died Feb. 5, 1880, in Philadelphia.

Borland, William Patterson; b. Leavenworth, Kans., Oct. 14, 1867; entered the law department of the University of Michigan at Ann Arbor, and was graduated in 1892; entered upon the practice of law at Kansas City; published in 1907 a text-book on the Law of Wills and Administrations; drafted several laws relating to city government, including the act empowering cities to regulate charges of public service corporations; was nominated Aug. 4, 1908, at a direct primary, and elected to the 61st, 62d, 63d and 64th Congresses from Missouri.

Boudinot, Elias; author, philanthropist; b. May 2, 1740, in Philadelphia, Pa.; made his home in Burlington, N. J.; first president of the American Bible Society; director of the Mint at Philadelphia, 1796-1805; author of "Second Advent of the Messiah," "The

Star in the West," an attempt to identify the American Indians with the ten lost tribes of Israel ; died Oct. 24, 1821, in Burlington, N. J.

Boudinot, Elias:
Appointed on committee to meet President Washington, 37.
Invites President Washington to meet committee at his home, 38.
Director of Mint, report of, transmitted, 303, 305.

Bourne, Jonathan, Jr.; b. New Bedford, Mass., Feb. 23, 1855 ; settled in Portland, Ore., May 16, 1878, where he was admitted to the Oregon bar in 1881 ; practiced law for only about a year, thereafter devoting his attention to mining ; president of a number of Oregon corporations and of the Bourne Cotton Mills at Fall River, Mass. ; member of State legislature during the sessions of 1885, 1886, and 1897 ; elected to the United States Senate from Oregon, for the term beginning March 4, 1907.

Boutwell, E. B., report on operations of the *John Adams,* under command of, transmitted, 2909.

Boutwell, George Sewall (1818-1905) ; politician and Cabinet officer ; b. at Brookline, Mass. ; for some years he was Democratic leader in his state ; governor, 1852-53 ; left the party when the Missouri Compromise was repealed and helped to form the Republican party, 1854 ; organized the department of internal revenue as commissioner, 1862-63 ; member of Congress, 1863-69 ; Secretary of the Treasury, 1869-73 ; United States Senator, 1873-77.

Bowell, MacKenzie, member of reciprocal trade conference between United States and Canada, 5675.

Bowen, Henry; soldier, farmer, member of Congress ; b. Dec. 26, 1841, at Maiden Spring, Va. ; educated at Emory and Henry College, Va. ; entered Confederate army and became captain ; served two terms in State legislature, and elected to Congress from Virginia in 1882 and 1886.

Bowen, Henry, correspondence regarding Dorr's Rebellion, 2145.

Bowman, Charles C.; b. Troy, N. Y., Nov. 14, 1852 ; graduated from Union College with the degree of C. E. in 1875 ; engaged in civil engineering work for the State of Massachusetts during the season of 1875 ; organized the western shipping department of the Pennsylvania Coal Co., at Pittston, Pa. ; served as superintendent of mines of the Florence Coal Co., 1883-84, and was part owner ; president of the taxpayers' association ; mayor of the city of Pittston, 1886 ; member of the select, or common, council five or six terms ; treasurer local State armory board, etc. ; elected to the Sixty-second Congress from Pennsylvania.

Boyd, Fredrico, correspondence of, on Panama, 6796, 6797.

Boynton, Michael P., imprisonment of, by authorities in Great Britain, 4602.

Boynton, Richard M., letter of Harriet M. Fisher and, to Secretary of Navy, transmitted, 3669.

36

Brace, Charles Loring; clergyman, author, philanthropist ; b. June 19, 1826, in Litchfield, Conn. ; founded Children's Aid Society, and Newsboys' Home in New York ; author of "Norsefolk," "Home Life in Germany," "The Dangerous Classes in New York," etc. ; died Aug. 11, 1890, in Switzerland.

Brace, Charles L., imprisonment of, by Austrian authorities referred to, 2689.

Bradford, William, Attorney-General under President Washington ; b. Philadelphia, Pa., Sept. 14, 1755. He was the son of Col. William Bradford, a printer, and soldier in the revolution, and great-grandson of the first printer in Philadelphia. He was educated at Princeton College, graduating in 1772, and studied law under Edward Shippen ; major of a brigade of Pensylvania Militia in the Revolution ; in 1780 he was appointed Attorney-General of Pennsylvania, and in 1784 married the daughter of Elias Boudinot, of New Jersey ; appointed a judge of the Supreme Court of Pennsylvania by Governor Mifflin ; succeeded Edmund Randolph as Attorney-General in 1794. He died Aug. 23, 1795, and was buried in Philadelphia.

Bradley, Mr., commissioner to investigate affairs of New York customhouse, 2005.

Bradley, William O.; b. near Lancaster, Ky., March 18, 1847 ; educated in the ordinary local schools ; ran away from home and joined the Union Army twice, but on account of youth was taken from the service by his father ; licensed to practice law on examination by two judges under special act of the legislature when 18 years of age, and has been engaged in the practice of law in the State and Federal courts of Kentucky and other states, the United States circuit court of appeals, and the Supreme Court of the United States ; was elected county attorney of Garrard County in 1870 ; elected governor in 1895 by a plurality of 8,912, though the Democratic plurality for President in 1892 was 40,000 ; February, 1908, was elected to the United States Senate from Kentucky.

Brady, James T.; lawyer ; b. April 9, 1815, in New York City ; appointed district attorney in 1843, and in 1845 corporation attorney ; died Feb. 9, 1869, in New York City.

Brady, James T., investigations of, at New Orleans referred to, 3583.

Branch, John, Secretary of the Navy under President Jackson ; b. Halifax Co., N. C., Nov. 4, 1782 ; graduated from the University of North Carolina in 1801 ; studied law with Judge John Haywood, and afterward practiced ; member of the State senate of North Carolina, 1811-1817, 1822, and 1834 ; was governor of North Carolina, 1817-1820 ; elected a United States Senator in 1823, and reelected in 1829 ; resigned March 9, 1829, having been appointed Secretary of the Navy ; resigned in 1831 ; elected a Representative to the 22d Congress as a Democrat ; member of the state constitutional convention in 1835 ; Democratic candidate for governor of North Carolina in 1838, and defeated by Dudley, Whig ; appointed governor of Florida by President Tyler, serving from 1844 until the election of a governor under the state constitution in 1845 ; died at Enfield, N. C., Jan. 4, 1863.

Brant, Joshua B., court of inquiry in case of, referred to, 1777.

Brandegee, Frank Bosworth; b. New London, Conn., July 8, 1864; graduated from Yale, 1885; admitted to the bar in 1888; representative in the general assembly, and for ten years was corporation counsel for the city of New London; in 1902 elected to 57th Congress to fill a vacancy, and reelected to the 58th and 59th Congresses; May 9, 1905, elected United States Senator for an unexpired term, and reelected Jan. 20, 1909, from Connecticut.

Breckenridge, John; lawyer, statesman; Attorney General under President Jefferson; b. Dec. 2, 1760, in Augusta Co., Va.; educated William and Mary College; three times chosen member of the legislature, but refused admission before the third election because of his being under age; began practice of law at Charlottesville in 1785; elected to the Third Congress, but failed to take his seat because of his removal to Kentucky in 1793, where he built up an extensive practice in contested land claims, which were the outgrowth of faulty surveys; filled several legislative and judicial positions in the new State of Kentucky; said to have been the author of the famous "Kentucky Resolutions" (q. v.); in 1801 entered the United States Senate and for four years was the spokesman of the administration; it was on his motion that the treaty purchasing Louisiana was ratified and the President directed to take possession; resigned from the Senate Dec. 25, 1805, and entered Jefferson's cabinet as Attorney General; died while in office Dec. 14, 1806.

Breckinridge, John Cabell (1821-1875); general and politician; b. near Lexington, Ky.; member of Congress from Kentucky, 1851-55; Vice-President with Buchanan, 1857-61; nominated by the southern Democrats for President against Lincoln, 1860; United States Senator from Kentucky, 1861; joined the Confederate army; Confederate secretary of war, January to April, 1865.

Breese, Kidder Randolph; naval officer; b. April 14, 1831, in Philadelphia; midshipman on Commodore Perry's Japan expedition, and was aboard the *Macedonian,* which visited northern end of Formosa to search for coal and to inquire into the captivity of Americans on that island; he served on the *San Jacinto,* which captured 1,500 slaves on the coast of Africa; took Mason and Slidell from British ship *Trent* in November, 1861; died Sept. 13, 1881.

Breese, K. Randolph, thanks of Congress to, recommended, 3277.

Brent, Charles J., refusal of Great Britain to surrender other fugitives and, discussed, 4326, 4369.

Brewer, David Josiah; jurist, associate justice United States Supreme Court; b. June 20, 1837, in Smyrna, Asia Minor; son of Rev. Joseph Brewer (Christian missionary in Turkey) and Emilia A. Field, sister of David Dudley, Cyrus W., and Justice Stephen J. Field; graduated from Yale and the Albany Law School; began practice in Leavenworth, Kans.; judge of probate and criminal courts, district court, State supreme court, United States Supreme Court; appointed associate justice United States Supreme Court to succeed Stanley Matthews, Dec. 18, 1889.

Brewer, David J., arbitrator in Venezuelan boundary dispute, 6338.

Brewer, Judge, opinion of, in Great Falls land case, referred to, 3072.

Brewster, Benjamin Harris; lawyer, jurist; b. Oct. 13, 1816, in Salem Co., N. J.; appointed by President Polk to adjudicate the claims of the Cherokee Indians against the United States; attorney-general of Pennsylvania in 1867; appointed Attorney-General by President Garfield in 1881; died April 4, 1888, in Philadelphia.

Brida, Demetrio S., mayor of Panama, 6756.

Briggs, Isaac, surveyor-general of the United States, voluntarily surveys mail road between Washington, D. C., and New Orleans, La., 364.

Bristow, Benjamin H.; Secretary of the Treasury under President Grant; b. June 20, 1832, in Elkton, Ky.; graduated Jefferson College, Pennsylvania, 1851, and began practice of law in his native town in 1853; entered the Union army at outbreak of civil war and served in the campaign against Forts Henry and Donelson, Shiloh, Pittsburg Landing, and assisted in the capture of Morgan and his band of raiders; identified with the Whig party and elected to the Kentucky Senate; after the war he opened a law office in Louisville, and in 1867 became District Attorney for Kentucky; in 1871 was appointed to the newly created office of solicitor general of the United States, and two years later was made Secretary of the Treasury, an office which he resigned in 1876 to devote himself to private practice. At the Republican National Convention in Cincinnati in 1876 Mr. Bristow was a candidate for the presidential nomination, and received 123 votes on the first ballot. He later removed to New York and continued to practice law.

Bristow, J. L.; editor; b. Wolf Co., Ky., July 22, 1861; moved back to Kansas in 1873 with his father; graduated from Baker University, in 1886; the same year he was elected clerk of the district court of Douglas County, which position he held four years; in 1890 bought the *Daily Republican* at Salina, Kans., which he edited for five years; March, 1897, appointed Fourth Assistant Postmaster-General by President McKinley; in 1900, under direction of the President, investigated the Cuban postal frauds; in 1903, under direction of President Roosevelt, conducted an extensive investigation of the Post-Office Department; in 1905 was appointed by President Roosevelt as special commissioner of the Panama Railroad; elected United States Senator in January, 1909, from Kansas.

Bristow, Pierson H., member of Board on Geographic Names, 5647.

Broadhead, James O., report of, regarding French spoliation claims transmitted, 4956.

Broglie, Duc de, correspondence regarding claims of United States against France. (See France, claims against.)

Bromberger, Max, claim of, against Mexico, 4536.

Bronski, Count de Bronno, memorial from, relative to introduction of silkworms into United States, 2584.

Brooke, George Mercer; soldier; b. in Virginia; brevetted lieutenant-colonel in 1814 for gallant conduct in the defence of Fort Erie, and colonel for distinguished services in the sortie from Fort Erie; brevetted brigadier-general in 1824 and major-general in 1848; died March 9, 1851, in San Antonio, Texas.

Brooke, George M., mentioned, 697, 894.

Brooke, John R.; soldier; b. in Pennsylvania; promoted to brigadier-general of volunteers in 1864, and brevetted major-general of volunteers; in the regular army he received brevets as colonel and brigadier-general for gallantry in several battles; during the war with Spain he was commissioned major-general.

Brooke, John R.:
Member of military commission to Puerto Rico, 6322.
Puerto Rican expedition re-enforced by corps of, 6318.

Brooks, Joseph; clergyman; b. Nov. 1, 1821, in Butler Co., Ohio; enlisted at outbreak of Civil War as chaplain 1st Missouri artillery; later assisted in raising the 11th and 33d Missouri regiments, and was transferred to the latter as chaplain; moved to Little Rock, Ark., in 1868; elected State senator in 1870, and governor in 1872; appointed postmaster of Little Rock in 1875, and held the office until his death, April 30, 1877, in Little Rock.

Brooks, Joseph, mentioned, 4273.

Brown, Aaron Vail; b. Aug. 15, 1795, in Brunswick Co., Va.; served in Tennessee legislature, and in 1839 elected to Congress, reelected 1841 and 1843; in 1845 elected governor of Tennessee; Postmaster-General in Cabinet of President Buchanan; died March 8, 1859, in Washington.

Brown, Aaron V., Postmaster-General, death of, announced and honors to be paid memory of, 3082.

Brown, George; naval officer; b. June 19, 1835; with Farragut's fleet ascended Mississippi in first attack on Vicksburg, in June, 1862; promoted to lieutenant-commander in 1862, and shortly after placed in command of ironclad *Indianola,* of the Mississippi squadron.

Brown, Jacob; soldier; b. May 9, 1775, in Bucks Co., Pa.; enlisted in War of 1812, and made brigadier-general of regular army; Jan. 24, 1814, assigned to command of Army of Niagara, as major-general; in 1821 appointed general-in-chief of regular army, which position he held till his death, Feb. 24, 1828, in Washington.

Brown, Jacob:
Death of, announced and tribute to memory of, 972.
Referred to, 914.
Victories of, over British troops, 533.

Brown, John; abolitionist; b. May 9, 1800, in Torrington, Conn.; emigrated to Kansas in 1855 and took part in anti-slavery contests in that state; planned to set free slaves in Virginia, and Oct. 16, 1859, surprised armory and arsenal at Harpers Ferry, and took forty prisoners; his band was overpowered and captured, and he was convicted in November, and hanged Dec. 2, 1859.

Brown, John, insurrection at Harpers Ferry, Va., discussed, 3084. (See also Brown's Insurrection.)

Brown, John A., second lieutenant, promotion of, to first lieutenant, discussed, 2437.

Brown, Joseph C., succeeded as Surveyor-General of Illinois by Silas Reed, 1957.

Brown, Lieut., report of, on the possibility of restraining the Navajo Indians within their reservations, transmitted, 5782.

Browning, Orville H., Secretary of the Interior under President Johnson; b. Harrison Co., Ky., in 1810; received his education at August College; admitted to practice law in 1831; moved to Quincy, Ill.; served in the Illinois Volunteers through the Black Hawk war in 1832; member of the State Senate of Illinois, 1836-1840, and of the state house of representatives, 1841-1843; one of the founders of the Republican party and a delegate to the national convention at Chicago in 1860; appointed a United States Senator from Illinois (to fill the vacancy caused by the death of Stephen A. Douglas), serving from July 4, 1861, to Jan. 30, 1863; member of the Union executive committee in 1866; appointed Secretary of the Interior in July, 1866, but only served from Sept. 1, 1866, to March 3, 1869.

Browning, O. H., correspondence of, transmitted, 3805.

Brubaker, Pharos B., capture and imprisonment of, by Honduras, 5825.

Brunot, Felix R.; merchant, philanthropist; b. Feb. 7, 1820; founded and for many years served as president of Pittsburg (Pa.) Mercantile Library.

Brunot, F. R., member of Indian Commission, 3977.

Brunswick and Luneburg, Duke of, convention with, for acquiring and inheriting property, 2826.

Brush, Robert, act for relief of, discussed, 1353.

Bryan, Nathan Philemon; b. Orange (now Lake) County, Fla., April 23, 1872; was graduated at Emory College, Oxford, Ga., in 1893; studied law at Washington and Lee University, graduating in 1895, and has since practiced law at Jacksonville; was chairman of the board of control of the Florida State Institutions of Higher Education 1905-1909; nominated for United States Senator in the Democratic primary election of Jan. 31, 1911, and elected by the legislature. His term of service will expire March 3, 1917.

Bryan, William J.; lawyer, orator; Secretary of State under President Wilson; b. March 19, 1860, at Salem, Ill.; educated at Whipple Academy and Illinois College at Jacksonville, and the Union College of Law at Chicago, and read law in the office of Hon. Lyman Trumbull; began law practice in Jacksonville, but removed to Lincoln, Neb., in 1887; elected to Congress for two succeeding terms by the Democrats and became his party's choice for United States Senator; nominated for the presidency by

the Democratic National Convention in
1896, and also by the Populists and Silver
Republicans of that year, and was defeated
by McKinley; during the Spanish-American
war he raised a regiment and was commissioned as colonel of the Third Nebraska
Infantry; renominated by the Democrats
for President in 1900, and again defeated;
established a weekly political paper in Lincoln, and made a tour of the world; nominated a third time for the presidency in
1908, and defeated; appointed Secretary of
State by President Wilson March 5, 1913.
Resigned from the Cabinet June 8, 1915,
during the controversy with Germany over
the safety of neutral ships on the high seas.

Buchanan, Frank; b. Jefferson County,
Ind., June 14, 1862; attended country
school, worked on the farm, and later became a bridge builder and structural iron
worker; became the president of the Bridge
and Structural Iron Workers' Local Union
No. 1, at Chicago, in 1898; elected the international president of the Bridge and Structural Iron Workers' Union in September,
1901; served for four successive terms and
declined to be a candidate for reelection in
1905; has been active in the general organized labor movement for years; previous to
his election to Congress was working at
the structural iron trade as inspector and
foreman; is married; never held a political
office until elected to the 62d, 63d and 64th
Congresses from Illinois.

Buchanan, James, biography of, 2960.

Buell, Don Carlos; soldier, manufacturer;
b. March 23, 1818, near Marietta, Ohio;
graduated from West Point in 1841; served
with honor in Florida and Mexican wars;
brigadier-general of volunteers in 1861;
major-general in 1862; after serving with
distinction in Civil War he became, in 1865,
president of the Green River Iron Works,
and later, until 1890, pension agent at
Louisville, Ky.

Buell, Don Carlos, second lieutenant,
proceedings in court-martial of, referred to, 2128.

Bulwer, Sir Henry Lytton, treaty between United States and Great
Britain concluded by John M. Clayton and, 2580.

Burchard, Horatio C.; merchant, lawyer;
b. Sept. 22, 1825, in Marshall, N. Y.; member Illinois legislature in 1866; elected to
Congress, 1868, 1870, 1872, 1876; Director
United States Mint in 1879; revenue commissioner for Illinois, 1885-1886.

Burchard, Horatio C., Director of Mint,
removal of, and reasons therefor,
4952.

Burgess, George Farmer; b. Wharton Co.,
Tex., Sept. 21, 1861; admitted to the bar
at Lagrange, Texas, 1882; county attorney
of Gonzales County, 1886-89; elected to
the 57th, 58th, 59th, 60th, 61st, 62d, 63d
and 64th Congresses from Texas.

Burgess, Thomas M., correspondence regarding Dorr's Rebellion, 2155.

Burleson, Albert Sidney, Postmaster-General under President Wilson; b. June 7,
1863, at San Marcos, Tex.; educated at
Agricultural and Mechanical College of
Texas, Baylor University (of Waco), and
University of Texas; admitted to the bar
in 1884; assistant city attorney of Austin

in 1885, 1886, 1887, 1888, 1889, and 1890;
appointed by the Governor of Texas attorney of the twenty-sixth judicial district in
1891; elected to said office 1892, 1894, and
1896; elected to the 56th, 57th, 58th, 59th,
60th, 61st, 62d, and 63d Congresses; appointed Postmaster-General March 4, 1913.

Burlingame, Anson; lawyer, diplomat; b.
Nov. 14, 1820, in New Berlin, N. Y.; served
in State legislature and elected to Congress
from Massachusetts; appointed minister to
Austria in 1861, and later to China; in
1867 headed a diplomatic commission from
China to the great powers of the world;
died Feb. 23, 1870, in St. Petersburg,
Russia.

Burlingame, Anson, minister to China:
Appointment of, to mission of Emperor of China referred to, 3976,
3825.

Dispatch from, transmitted, 3398,
3781.

Burnet, Daniel, member of legislative
council for Mississippi Territory,
nomination of, 445.

Burnet, Jacob; lawyer, jurist, author; b.
Feb. 22, 1770, in Newark, N. J.; member
first legislative council of Ohio; in 1821
appointed one of the judges Ohio Supreme
Court; elected to Senate of United States
to fill vacancy in 1828; in 1847 published
"Notes on Early Settlement of Northwestern Territory"; died May 10, 1853, in Cincinnati, O.

Burnet, J., correspondence regarding
removal of remains of the late President W. H. Harrison, 1906.

Burnett, John D., district attorney,
nomination of, discussed, 4960.

Burnett, John Lawson; b. Cedar Bluff,
Cherokee Co., Ala., Jan. 20, 1854; studied
law at Vanderbilt University, and was admitted to the bar in Cherokee County, Ala.,
in 1876; elected to the lower house of the
Alabama legislature in 1884, and to the
State senate in 1886; elected to the 56th,
57th, 58th, 59th, 60th, 61st, 62d, 63d and
64th Congresses from Alabama.

Burnham Hiram; soldier; b. in Maine;
distinguished at second battle of Fredericksburg and at Gettysburg for bravery and
courage; made brigadier-general in 1864,
and was conspicuous in campaign from the
Wilderness to Petersburg; killed in battle
at Newmarket, Sept. 29, 1864.

Burnham, Hiram, brigadier-general,
nomination of, referred to, 3403.

Burnside, Ambrose Everett; soldier, manufacturer; b. May 22, 1824, in Liberty,
Ind.; served on the frontier as officer of
artillery, and in 1853 resigned and turned
his attention to the manufacture of guns,
and invented the rifle which bears his name;
served with honor and distinction through
Civil War; elected governor of Rhode
Island in 1866, and in 1875 took his seat
in United States Senate from Rhode Island;
died Sept. 3, 1881, in Bristol, R. I.

Burnside, Ambrose E.:
Brigadier-general, thanks of President tendered, 3305.
Major-general, ordered to assume
command of Army of Potomac,
3325.

Burr, Aaron; soldier, statesman, Vice-President of United States; b. Feb. 6, 1756, in Newark, N. J.; appointed lieutenant-colonel in 1777, and was distinguished for ability and bravery; appointed attorney-general of New York, 1789; served in United States Senate, 1791-1797; at election for fourth President of the United States Thomas Jefferson and Burr each received 73 votes and the choice of President was made by Congress (see Vice-President), deciding in favor of Jefferson, on the thirty-sixth ballot, and Burr was elected Vice-President; July 12, 1804, mortally wounded Alexander Hamilton in duel; attempted to establish a government in Mexico which should ultimately include southwestern part of United States; tried for treason and acquitted; died Sept. 14, 1836, on Staten Island, N. Y.

Burr, Aaron:

Attempts made in Kentucky to bring to justice, 403.

Boats of, with ammunition arrested by militia, 405.

Conspiracy of, letters regarding, not received by President, 437.

Military expedition against Union planned by, 400.

Passes Fort Massac with boats, 405.

Reaches Mississippi Territory, 407.

Surrenders to officers in Mississippi Territory, 409.

Trial of—

Acquittal of, referred to, 417.

Evidence presented at, 417, 419.

Expenses incident thereto, 421, 447.

Burroughs, Marmaduke, consul at Vera Cruz, Mexico, charges preferred against, by Dr. Baldwin, 1810.

Burt, Silas W., chief examiner of Civil Service Commission, nomination of, and reasons therefor, 4745.

Burton, Theodore E.; b. Jefferson, Ashtabula Co., Ohio, Dec. 20, 1851; began the practice of law at Cleveland in 1875; author of "Financial Crises and Periods of Commercial and Industrial Depression," published in 1902; also a "Life of John Sherman"; received the degree of LL. D. from Oberlin College in 1900, and from Dartmouth College and Ohio University in 1907; Representative in the 51st, 54th, 55th, 56th, 57th, 59th, and 60th Congresses; was elected to the 61st Congress, but resigned when elected to the United States Senate by the Ohio legislature in January, 1909.

Butler, Benjamin Franklin (Massachusetts); lawyer; b. Nov. 5, 1818, in Deerfield, N. H.; served in both branches State legislature, 1853-1859; delegate to Charleston Convention, 1860; appointed brigadier-general at outbreak of Civil War in 1861; originator of phrase "contraband of war" as applied to slaves during war; served as major-general throughout war, and resumed legal practice at its close, in Lowell, Mass.; elected to Congress from Massachusetts, 1866, 1868, 1870, 1874; one of the managers of impeachment of Andrew Johnson; elected governor of Massachusetts, 1882; died Jan. 11, 1893, in Washington, D. C.

Butler, Benjamin F., Massachusetts:

Swords of Gen. Twiggs forwarded by, to President Lincoln and his recommendation that they be disposed of in reward or compliment for military service, 3346.

Butler, Benjamin Franklin (New York); lawyer; b. Dec. 14, 1795, in Kinderhook, N. Y.; appointed district attorney for Albany, 1821; elected to State legislature, 1827, and later attorney-general; served as Secretary of War, 1836-1837; Presidential elector in 1845, and twice appointed United States attorney for the southern district of New York; died Nov. 8, 1858, in Paris, France.

Butler, Benjamin F., of New York:

Correspondence regarding examination of affairs of New York custom-house referred to, 2007.

Secretary of War, nomination of, and reasons therefor, 1500.

Butler, Matthew C.:

Member of military commission to Cuba, 6322.

Statement of, regarding slaughter of American citizens in South Carolina referred to, 4329.

Butler, Pierce; soldier, statesman; b. July 11, 1744, in Ireland; delegate from South Carolina to Congress under the articles of confederation in 1778, and member of convention in 1778 which framed present constitution, and one of the signers; became Senator in 1802; resigned in 1804; died Feb. 15, 1822, in Philadelphia.

Butler, Pierce, mentioned, 3275.

Butler, Thomas S.; lawyer; b. Uwchlan, Chester Co., Pa., Nov. 4, 1855; elected to the 55th, 56th, 57th, 58th, 59th, 60th, 61st, 62d, 63d and 64th Congresses from Pennsylvania.

Byrnes, James F.; b. Charleston, S. C., May 2, 1879; received only a common school education; in 1900 was appointed official court reporter of the second circuit of South Carolina; for several years edited a newspaper; admitted to the bar, and elected solicitor of the second circuit of South Carolina; elected to the 62d, 63d and 64th Congresses from South Carolina.

Byrns, Joseph W.; b. July 20, 1869, near Cedar Hill, Robertson Co., Tenn.; graduated law department of Vanderbilt University, Nashville; three times elected a member of the lower house of the Tennessee State legislature; elected to the Tennessee State senate in 1900; elected to the 61st, 62d, 63d and 64th Congresses from Tennessee.

Cady, Heman, claim of, presented and appropriation for, recommended, 1694.

Caldwell, Charles H. B., thanks of Congress to, recommended, 3277.

Calhoun, James S.; b. in Georgia, and in 1851 was appointed first governor of the Territory of New Mexico.

Calhoun, James S., treaty with Indians concluded by, 2571.

Calhoun, J., president constitutional convention of Kansas, mentioned as forwarding c o p y of constitution framed by that body, 3002.

Calhoun, John Caldwell; author, orator, statesman, Vice-President of United States; b. March 18, 1782, in Abbeville District, S. C.; Secretary of State under Monroe and Tyler; Vice-President with John Quincy Adams; author of "A Disquisition on Government" and "The Constitution and Government of the United States"; United States Senator from 1845 till his death, March 31, 1850, in Washington, D. C.

Calhoun, John C.:
Convention with Indians concluded by, 622.
Mentioned, 2233.

Call, Richard Keith; soldier; b. 1791, in Kentucky; appointed brigadier-general of Florida militia; member of Florida legislative council in 1822, and delegate to Congress from that territory, 1823-1825; receiver at land office; governor of Florida, 1836-1839 and 1841-1844; died Sept. 14, 1862, in Tallahassee, Fla.

Call, Richard K., commander of militia in Seminole War, 1472, 1834.

Call, Dr. Samuel J., thanks of Congress recommended to, 6352.

Calvit, Thomas, member of legislative council for Mississippi Territory, nomination of, 445.

Cambon, Jules, French minister, representative of Spain in peace negotiations, 6320, 6487.

Cameron. James Donald. of Harrisburg, Pa., Secretary of War under President Grant; b. Middletown, Pa., 1833; received a classical education; student at Princeton College; entered the Middletown Bank as clerk, and became its cashier; president of the Northern Central Railway Company of Pennsylvania, 1866-1874; Secretary of War from May 22, 1876, to March 3, 1877; delegate to the national Republican convention at Cincinnati in 1876; elected a United States Senator from Pennsylvania (to fill the vacancy caused by the resignation of his father, Hon. Simon Cameron) in March, 1877; took his seat Oct. 15, 1877, and re-elected, serving until March 3, 1897.

Cameron, Simon; printer, journalist, statesman; b. March 8, 1799, in Lancaster Co., Pa.; before entering Congress was successively bank cashier and president of two railroads; elected to Senate in 1845; mentioned as candidate for President of United States in 1860; appointed Secretary of War in President Lincoln's Cabinet in 1861; resigned and was appointed minister to Russia in 1862; resigned from United States Senate during fourth term in 1877; died June 26, 1889, in Lancaster Co., Pa.

Cameron, Simon:
Ex-Secretary of War, arrest of, at suit of Pierce Butler for false imprisonment, etc., 3275.
Resolution of censure of, by House of Representatives discussed, 3278.

Campbell, Archibald, correspondence regarding northeastern boundary. (See Northeastern Boundary.)

Campbell, Bernard, claim of, against Haiti, 6100.
Settlement of, 6332.

Campbell, George Washington, Secretary of the Treasury under President Madison; b. Tennessee, 1768; graduated from Princeton College 1794; studied law and commenced practice at Nashville; elected a Representative from Tennessee to the Eighth Congress as a Democrat, and re-elected to the Ninth and Tenth Congresses; elected a United States Senator from Tennessee in place of Jenkins Whiteside, resigned, and took his seat Nov. 4, 1811, serving until Feb. 9, 1814, when he resigned; Secretary of the Treasury from Feb. 9, 1814, to Oct. 6, 1814; again elected Senator from Tennessee, serving from December 4, 1815, until 1818, when he resigned; minister to Russia 1818 to 1821; member of the French Claims Commission in 1831; died at Nashville, Tenn., Feb. 17, 1848.

Campbell, James; lawyer, jurist; Postmaster General under President Pierce; b. Sept. 1, 1812, in Philadelphia, Pa.; educated at Stockdale Academy and studied law in the office of Robert Ingram; admitted to the bar in 1834; and took part in the Dred Scott and other celebrated cases of his time; became Judge of the Court of Common Pleas in 1841, and held the office ten years, when he was elected Attorney General of Pennsylvania; March 7, 1853, he was appointed Postmaster General by President Pierce, and continued in office throughout the administration; he put into effect the three-cent postage rate, introduced the registry system, stamped envelopes and perforated postage stamps; after his term expired he resumed practice of law in Philadelphia and in 1863 was an unsuccessful candidate for United States Senator; died Jan. 23, 1893, in Philadelphia.

Campbell, John, nomination of, as Indian agent withdrawn and reasons therefor, 1037.

Campbell, John Archibald; lawyer, jurist; b. June 24, 1811, in Washington, Ga.; resigned as associate justice of United States Supreme Court in 1861, after commencement of the Civil War; strongly opposed secession of Alabama, and in 1864 did much to bring war to a close; died March 12, 1889, in Baltimore.

Campbell, John A.:
Justice Supreme Court, resignation of, referred to, 3250.
Member of commission to confer with President regarding termination of war, 2461.
Pardon applied for by, order regarding, 3550.

Campbell, Lewis D.; b. Aug. 9, 1811, in Franklin, Ohio; elected to Congress in 1848 and each succeeding Congress until 1857, when his seat was contested and the house decided against him; appointed minister to Mexico in 1865 and again elected to Congress in 1871; died Nov. 26, 1882.

Campbell, Lewis D.:
Ex-minister to Mexico, correspondence with, referred to, 3723.
Mentioned, 3642.

Campbell, Philip Pitt; b. Nova Scotia; when four years old moved with his parents to Kansas; elected to the 58th, 59th, 60th, 61st, 62d, 63d and 64th Congresses from Kansas.

Campbell, Robert; soldier, jurist; b. in 1755 in Virginia; displayed great bravery in conflicts with Cherokee Indians; commanded a regiment in battle of King's Mountains in 1780; nearly forty years a magistrate in Washington Co., Va.; moved to Tennessee in 1825; died February, 1832, near Knoxville, Tenn.

Campbell, Robert, member of Indian commission, 3977.

Candler, Ezekiel Samuel, Jr.; b. Bellville, Hamilton Co., Fla., Jan. 18, 1862, but moved with his parents to Tishomingo Co., Miss., when eight years old; moved from Iuka to Corinth, 1887, where he engaged in the practice of law; elected to the 57th, 58th, 59th, 60th, 61st, 62d, 63d and 64th Congresses from Mississippi.

Cannon, Joseph Gurney; lawyer; b. Guilford, N. C., May 7, 1836; elected to the 43d, 44th, 45th, 46th, 47th, 48th, 49th, 50th, 51st, 53d, 54th, 55th, 56th, 57th, 58th, 59th, 60th, 61st, 62d and 64th Congresses from Illinois.

Canovas del Castillo, Antonio, prime minister of Spain, assassination of, referred to, 6284.

Cantrill, James Campbell; b. Georgetown, Scott Co., Ky., July 9, 1870; elected a member of the Kentucky house of representatives, 1897 and 1899; in 1901 was elected a member of the Kentucky senate; in 1904 was elected chairman of the joint caucus of the Kentucky legislature; in 1906 Mr. Cantrill became active in the work of organizing the tobacco growers of Kentucky; 1908 he was elected president of the American Society of Equity for Kentucky, an organization for the cooperation of farmers in securing more profitable prices for their products; elected to the 61st, 62d, 63d and 64th Congresses from Kentucky.

Caramalli, Hamet:
Appeals to United States to place him on the throne of Tripoli in place of the reigning Bashaw, his younger brother, by whom he had been displaced, 380.
Referred to, 2951.

Carlin, Charles Creighton; b. Alexandria, Va., April 8, 1866; educated at the National Law University; served four years as postmaster of Alexandria; elected to the 60th Congress to fill a vacancy, and re-elected to the 61st, 62d, 63d and 64th Congresses from Virginia.

Carlisle, John Griffin, of Covington, Ky., Secretary of the Treasury under President Cleveland; b. Campbell (Kenton) County, Ky., Sept. 5, 1835; received a common school education; taught school in the county and afterwards in Covington; studied law; admitted to the bar in March, 1858; member of the State house of representatives 1859-1861; elected to the State senate in 1866 and re-elected in August, 1869; delegate at large from the State of Kentucky to the Democratic national convention at New York in July, 1868; nominated for lieutenant-governor of Kentucky in May, 1871, and elected in August of same year, serving until Sept., 1875; alternate Presidential elector for the State at large in 1876; elected to the 45th, 46th, 47th, 48th, 49th, 50th, and 51st Congresses; elected Speaker of the House of Representatives in the 48th, 49th, and 50th Congresses; resigned May 26, 1890, to become United States Senator, filling the unexpired term of James B. Beck, deceased, taking his seat May 26, 1890; resigned Feb. 4, 1893; Secretary of the Treasury 1893-1897; moved to New York City and practiced law.

Carmichael, William; diplomat; b. in Maryland; delegate to Continental Congress 1778-1780; secretary of legation with John Jay's mission to Spain, and remained there as chargé d'affaires after the return of Mr. Jay; held the position about 15 years; died February, 1795.

Carmichael, William:
Commissioner to Spain, nomination of, 107.
Recall of, from Spain, 148.
Referred to, 184.

Carnot, Marie Francois Sadi, President of France, assassination of, 5910.
Resolutions of Senate and House on, transmitted to widow of, 5957.

Carondelet, Baron de:
Authority to dispose of lands of Spain in Louisiana referred to, 651.
Validity of grant made by, to Marquis de Maison Rouge to be tested, 2013.

Carpenter, W. S., act for relief of, vetoed, 5299.

Carrington, Edward; soldier; b. Feb. 11, 1749, in Charlotte Co., Va.; active and efficient officer in the Revolution; quartermaster-general of the army of the south under Gen. Greene; delegate to Continental Congress from Virginia 1785-1786; foreman of the jury which tried Aaron Burr for treason; died Oct. 28, 1810, in Richmond, Va.

Carrington, Edward, district supervisor, nomination of, 91.

Carrington, Henry Beebe; soldier, author; b. March 2, 1824, in Wallingford, Conn.; author of "Crisis Thoughts," "Battles of the Revolution," "Apsaraka, or Indian Operations on the Plains," "The Washington Obelisk and its Voices"; general in United States Army.

Carrington, Henry B., provision for compensation to, for services rendered in Indian matters, 5499.

Carroll, Anna Ella; author, lawyer and strategist; b. Aug. 29, 1815, in Somerset Co., Mo. Her father, Thomas K. Carroll, was governor of Maryland in 1829-30. The family was related to that of Charles Carroll of Carrollton, a signer of the Declaration of Independence. Anna Ella read law in her father's office and wrote for the press. Her more important works were "The Great American Battle; or, Political Romanism," "The Star of the West," Reconstruction," "War Powers of the Government," and a pamphlet in answer to John C. Breckinridge's speech favoring secession delivered in Congress in 1861. The latter was circulated in large numbers by the War Department. At the outbreak of the civil war she freed her slaves and used her social influence to prevent Maryland from seceding from the Union. At the request of President Lincoln she went to St. Louis in 1861 to gather information on the proposed federal military expedition down the Mississippi River. After investigation she advised against the project and recommended that the heart of the confederacy be attacked by way of the Cumberland and Tennessee Rivers. Upon her advice and information Gen. Halleck sent Gen. Grant and Commodore Foote with a flotilla of gunboats and 17,000 men up the Tennessee where Fort Henry was taken, and later Fort Donelson on the Cumberland. The final capture of Vicksburg was also accomplished by following the line of attack laid out by Miss Carroll. She continued to send plans and suggestions to the War Department throughout the war. The authorship of the plan of campaign in the West was unknown except to the President and his cabinet until after the war. Miss Carroll never received adequate compensation for her services to the cause of the Union. A bill to grant her the pay of a major general was introduced in Congress in 1881, but failed of passage. She died Feb. 19, 1894, in Washington.

Carroll, Charles, of Carrollton; author, statesman; b. Sept. 20, 1737, in Annapolis, Md.; able political writer and advocate of independence; elected to Continental Congress in 1776, and signed the Declaration of Independence; devoted himself to the councils of his own state from 1778 to 1789, when he was elected Senator under the Constitution; died Feb. 14, 1832, in Baltimore, Md.; the last surviving signer of the Declaration of Independence.

Carroll, Charles, on committee to—
Conduct inaugural ceremonies of President Washington, 39.
Receive President Washington upon his arrival from New Jersey, 36.

Carson, Christopher (Kit); frontiersman, guide, and scout; b. Dec. 24, 1809, in Madison Co., Ky.; guide to Gen. Fremont in his western explorations; served in Civil War, and brevetted brigadier-general; died May 23, 1868, in Fort Lynn, Colo.

Carson, Christopher (Kit), treaty with Indians concluded by, 3827.

Carter, Charles D.; b. near Boggy Depot, an old fort in the Choctaw Nation, Aug. 16, 1869; is seven-sixteenths Chickasaw and Cherokee Indian, and nine-sixteenths Scotish-Irish; moved with his father to Mill Creek post-office and stage stand on the western frontier of the Chickasaw Nation in 1876; entered the Chickasaw Manual Labor Academy, Tishomingo, October, 1882;

September, 1892, appointed auditor of public accounts of the Chickasaw Nation; member of the Chickasaw council for the term of 1895; superintendent of schools, Chickasaw Nation, 1897; appointed mining trustee of Indian Territory by President McKinley in 1900; elected to the 60th, 61st, 62d, 63d and 64th Congresses from Oklahoma.

Carter, C. L., member of commission concluding treaty for annexation of Hawaiian Islands, 5783.

Carver, Jonathan; author, traveller; b. 1732, in Stillwater, N. Y.; explored interior of country and wrote "Travels through Interior Parts of North America"; died Jan. 31, 1780, in London, England.

Carver, Jonathan, claims of, to lands near Falls of St. Anthony, 706.

Casey, Thomas Lincoln; soldier, engineer; b. May 10, 1831, in Sacketts Harbor, N. Y.; in 1854 became assistant professor of engineering of United States Military Academy; later in command of Pacific Coast Engineer Corps; served in Civil War as staff engineer at Fort Monroe, Va.; superintended construction of permanent defenses and fortifications on coast of Maine.

Casey, Thomas L., Jr., commissioner in marking boundary between Texas and Mexico, 4902.

Cass, Lewis; author, statesman; b. Oct. 9, 1782, in Exeter, N. H.; secretary of war in President Jefferson's cabinet, ambassador to France and candidate for President in 1845; author of "Inquiries Concerning the History, Traditions and Languages of the Indians in the United States," "France: Its King and Court," and "Government"; died June 17, 1866, in Detroit, Mich.

Cass, Lewis:
Compensation paid, by Government, referred to, 2456.
Death of, announced and honors to be paid memory of, 3641.
Minister to France—
Commission of, conditional, 1449.
Nomination of, 1449.
Protest of, to treaty for suppression of slave trade, referred to, 2011.
Resignation of, mentioned, 2086.
Secretary of State, 3023.
Correspondence between President Buchanan and, referred to, 3964.
Treaty with Indians concluded by, 590, 888, 931, 961, 988, 989, 991, 996.

Castle, W. R., member of commission concluding treaty for annexation of Hawaiian Islands, 5783.

Catacazy, Constantin de, Russian minister to United States, recall of, requested, 4099.
Referred to, 4110.

Catcher, White, treaty with Indians negotiated by, 3592.

Chaffee, Gen. Adna R., authority in Philippines, 6692.

Chaffee, Earl Worden, reinstated in navy, 6937.

Chaffee, Jerome B.; financier; b. Niagara County, N. Y., April 17, 1825; received a liberal education; in 1846 moved to Adrian, Mich., subsequently settling in St. Joseph, Mo., and Elmwood, Kans., conducting a banking and real estate business in both places; moved to Colorado in 1860, where he established himself as a banker and a mining capitalist; elected to the Legislature of Colorado in 1861, 1862 and 1863, serving the last year as speaker of the house; in 1865 elected by the State Legislature of the proposed State of Colorado a United States Senator; one of the founders of the City of Denver; in 1865 became president of the First National Bank of Denver; elected to the 42d and 43d Congresses as a Republican; elected United States Senator as a Republican on the admission of Colorado as a State and served from Dec. 4, 1876, to March 3, 1879; died at Salem Center, N. Y., March 9, 1886.

Chaffee, J. B., United States Senator, mentioned, 3573.

Chamberlain, D. H.; soldier, lawyer; b. June 23, 1835, in West Brookfield, Mass.; served in Fifth Massachusetts Cavalry, 1863-1865; settled in Charleston, S. C., in 1866; elected attorney-general in 1868 and governor in 1874.

Chamberlain, D. H., letters of, regarding slaughter of American citizens in South Carolina transmitted, 4329.

Chamberlain, George Earle, b. near Natchez, Miss., Jan. 1, 1854; in 1876 he moved to Oregon, where, in 1902, he was elected governor for four years, and re-elected in 1906; in 1908 he was nominated in the primaries for United States Senator on the Democratic ticket and elected by the legislature Jan. 19, 1909, and re-elected in 1914 for the term ending 1920.

Champagny, Jean Baptiste Nompère de, mentioned, 434, 437.

Chandler, William Eaton, Secretary of the Navy under President Arthur; b. Concord, N. H., Dec. 28, 1835; received a common school education; studied law; graduated from Harvard Law School, and was admitted to the bar in 1855; appointed reporter of the decisions of the supreme court in 1859; member of the New Hampshire house of representatives in 1862, 1863, and 1864, serving as speaker during the last two years; became solicitor and judge-advocate-general of the Navy Department March 9, 1865; appointed First Assistant Secretary of the Treasury June 17, 1865, which office he resigned Nov. 30, 1867; member of the New Hampshire constitutional convention in 1876; again a member of the New Hampshire house of representatives in 1881; appointed by President Garfield Solicitor-General March 23, 1881, but was rejected by the Senate; Secretary of the Navy April 12, 1882, and served till March 7, 1885; elected to the United States Senate June 14, 1887, as a Republican, to fill the unexpired term of Austin F. Pike, deceased, serving until March 3, 1889; elected June 18, 1889, and again Jan. 16, 1895, serving until March 3, 1901; appointed in 1901 by President McKinley, president of the Spanish Claims Commission.

Chandler, Zachariah; statesman; b. Dec. 10, 1813, Bedford, N. H.; mayor of Detroit, Mich., in 1851; succeeded Lewis Cass and served three terms in United States Senate; Secretary of the Interior in President Grant's Cabinet in 1875; delegate to Philadelphia loyalists' convention in 1866; died Nov. 1, 1879, in Chicago.

Chandler, Zachariah, death of, announced and honors to be paid memory of, 4509.

Chase, Maj., *habeas corpus,* writ of, suspended in case of, 3220.

Chase, Ormond, shot by order of Mexican general, 3097.

Chase, Salmon P.; statesman; b. at Cornish, N. H., Jan. 13, 1808; graduate of Dartmouth College, and taught classical school in Washington, D. C., and studied law under William Wirt, 1826-1829, and settled in Cincinnati, 1830; practiced law; supported W. H. Harrison for President; prominent in formation of Liberty party and Freesoilers, and was counsel for defense in several fugitive slave cases; nominated Martin Van Buren for President at Buffalo in 1848; elected to United States Senate from Ohio in 1849; opposed the extension of slavery and was prominent in anti-slavery debates in Senate; elected governor of Ohio in 1855 and 1857; supported Fremont for President; received 49 votes on first ballot for nomination at Chicago convention in 1860; member of Peace Conference of 1861; Secretary of Treasury in Lincoln's Cabinet; appointed Chief Justice of United States Supreme Court to succeed Roger B. Taney, who died in 1864; presided over the court of impeachment of President Johnson; died May 7, 1873.

Chase, Salmon P.:
Chief Justice United States, death of, announced and honors to be paid memory of, 4183.
Regulations relating to trade with ports opened by proclamation signed by, 3291.

Chauncey, Isaac; naval officer; b. Feb. 20, 1772, in Black Rock, Conn.; made successful voyages to East Indies in ships of John Jacob Astor; thanked by Congress for distinguished services in actions off the coast of Tripoli; served with credit in War of 1812; made president of the Board of Navy Commissioners at Washington in 1833, which position he held till his death, Jan. 27, 1840.

Chauncey, Isaac, naval talents of, commented on, 520.

Cheek, M. A., claim of, against Siam, 6184.
Adjustment of, 6336.

Chester, John; soldier; b. Jan. 29, 1749, in Wethersfield, Conn.; appeared in colonial councils, 1772; served with distinction as captain at the battle of Bunker Hill; later colonel in Continental army until 1777; speaker of Connecticut legislature; member of council, 1788-1791, and in 1803; supervisor of district of Connecticut, 1791-1803; died Nov. 4, 1809, in Wethersford, Conn.

Chester, John, district supervisor, nomination of, 91.

Childs, Thomas; soldier; b. in 1796 in Pittsfield, Mass.; graduated West Point, 1814, and served at Fort Erie and Niagara same year; as captain in Seminole War he planned attack on Fort Drane, 1836; brevetted major and lieutenant-colonel; brevetted colonel May 9, 1846, for gallant conduct at Palo Alto and Resaca de la Palma; mentioned by General Scott as the "often-distinguished Colonel Childs"; in command at East Florida from Feb. 11, 1852, until his death from yellow fever at Fort Brooke, Tampa Bay, Oct. 8, 1853.

Childs, Thomas, gallantry of, at battle of Monterey, Mexico, 2368.

Chipman, Nathaniel; author, educator, jurist; b. Nov. 15, 1752, in Salisbury, Conn.; professor of law twenty-eight years in Middlebury College; elected judge of supreme court, 1786; chief justice, 1789; United States district judge in 1791; United States Senator from Vermont, 1797-1803; wrote "Sketches of the Principles of Government," "Reports and Dissertations"; died Feb. 13, 1843, in Tillmouth, Vt.

Chipman, Nathaniel, district judge, nomination of, 91.

Choteau, Auguste, treaty with Indians concluded by, 589.

Chouteau, Charles P., bills for relief of, vetoed, 5528, 6118.

Christie, Smith, treaty with Indians negotiated by, 3592.

Church, George E., report of, upon Ecuador, referred to, 4744.

Church, Philip, Aid-de-Camp, announced the death of Gen. Washington and communication of the President about the funeral, Dec. 21, 1799.

Churchwell, Mr., correspondence of, referred to, 3114.

Clack, John H.:
Captain in Navy, nomination of, and reasons therefor, 2032.
Master commandant, nomination of, and reasons therefor, 1106.

Claiborne, William Charles Cole; lawyer; b. 1775 in Sussex Co., Va.; judge of supreme court of Tennessee, and member of Congress two terms; appointed governor of Mississippi territory in 1801; and was commissioned to receive the Louisiana purchase on behalf of United States; and appointed governor-general, and served until 1817; elected to United States Senate, and died Dec. 23, 1817.

Claiborne, William C. C.:
Assumes government of Louisiana, 355.
Jurisdiction of, as governor of Orleans Territory extended, 465.
Letter from, regarding government of Louisiana transmitted, 355.
Orleans Territory, governor of, jurisdiction extended, 465.
Receives letter from Manuel De Salcedo, regarding Louisiana Province, 336.
Letter sent to Secretary of State, 336.

Clapp, Moses Edwin; b. Delphi, Ind., May 21, 1851; graduated from the Wisconsin Law School in 1873; county attorney of St. Croix Co., Wis.; in 1881 moved to Fergus Falls, Minn.; elected attorney-general of Minnesota in 1887, 1889, and 1891, and removed to St. Paul and made that his permanent home in 1891; elected to the United States Senate to fill a vacancy occasioned by the death of Hon. Cushman K. Davis, and took his seat Jan. 28, 1901, and reelected in 1905.

Clark, Champ; b. March 7, 1850, in Anderson Co., Ky.; 1873-74 was president of Marshall College, West Virginia; moved to Missouri in 1875; elected to the 53d, 55th, 56th, 57th, 58th, 59th, 60th, 61st, 62d, 63d and 64th Congresses from Missouri.

Clark, Charles, pardon applied for by, order regarding, 3550.

Clark, Clarence Don, b. Sandy Creek, Oswego Co., N. Y., April 16, 1851; admitted to the bar in 1874; taught school and practiced law in Delaware Co., Iowa, until 1881; moved to Evanston, Wyo., and was prosecuting attorney for Uinta County four years; elected to the 51st and 52d Congresses; elected 1895 to the United States Senate to fill a vacancy caused by the failure of the legislature to elect in 1892-93; and was re-elected in 1899 and 1905 and 1911 from Wyoming.

Clark, Daniel, officially connected with investigation of Gen. Wilkinson's conduct, 424, 427.

Clark, Edward, architect of Patent Office building, report of, on Philadelphia post-office, transmitted, 2912.

Clark, Frank W., member of board of management of Government exhibit at World's Columbian Exposition, 5833.

Clark, Frank; b. Eufaula, Ala., March 28, 1860; studied law, and was admitted to practice at Fairburn, Ga., Aug. 3, 1881; in 1884, Mr. Clark moved to Florida and located at Bartow; served three terms in the legislature of Florida; United States attorney for the southern judicial district of Florida; elected to the 59th, 60th, 61st, 62d, 63d and 64th Congresses from Florida.

Clark, John B.; soldier; b. April 17, 1802, Madison Co., Ky.; commanded regiment of mounted militia in the Black Hawk War in 1832; major-general of militia in 1848; served in State legislature and elected to Congress three terms; became colonel in Confederate army, having been expelled from the House in 1861; died Oct. 29, 1885, in Fayetteville, Mo.

Clark, John B., military services and promotion of, discussed, 2269.

Clark, William:
Exploring expedition under. (See Lewis and Clark Expedition.)
Treaty with Indians concluded by, 589, 888.

Clarke, James P.; b. Yazoo City, Miss., Aug. 18, 1854; studied law at the University of Virginia; began practice at Helena, Ark., in 1879; served in Arkansas legislature 1886-92; attorney-general of Arkansas in 1892, declined a renomination, and was elected governor in 1894; elected to the United States Senate from Arkansas 1903; re-elected in 1909, and again in 1914 for the term ending 1921.

Clay, Alexander Stephens; b. Sept. 25, 1853, in Cobb Co., Ga.; graduated from Hiawasse College in 1875; studied law and was admitted to the bar in September, 1877; in 1884-85 and 1886-87 represented Cobb County in the general assembly of the state; re-elected 1889-90; in 1892 was elected to the State Senate, and served as president of that body for two years; elected to the United States Senate from Georgia, for the term beginning March 4, 1897; re-elected in 1903 and 1909.

Clay, Clement Claiborne, Jr.; legislator; b. 1819, in Madison, Ala.; served as state judge and legislator, and was in United States Senate at outbreak of Civil War; took part in rebellion and was expelled from Senate and confined in Fortress Monroe as prisoner of state.

Clay, Clement C., Jr.:
Imprisonment of—
Arrest of, reward for, 3505.
Report of Attorney-General regarding, transmitted, 3576.
Order exempting, from arrest during journey to Washington, 3438.
Reward offered for arrest of, 3505.

Clay, Henry; orator, statesman; b. April 12, 1777, in Hanover Co., Va.; sent to United States Senate from Kentucky in 1806, and for nearly half a century was brilliant and conspicuous in the debates of that body; was thrice candidate for President, and when warned by a friend that his adherence to principle instead of party would forbid his nomination, made the historic epigram: "I would rather be right than be President"; died June 29, 1852, in Washington, D. C.

Clay, Henry:
Correspondence regarding—
Northeastern boundary. (See Northeastern Boundary.)
Pledge to Mexico, 907.
Death of, announced, 2697.
Secretary of State, 942.

Clay, James B., negotiations with Portugal for payment of claims conducted by, 2618.

Clay, John Randolph; diplomat; b. in Philadelphia, Pa., 1808; went to Russia in 1830 as secretary of legation, and in 1836 made chargé d'affaires; secretary of legation in Austria, 1838-1845, and then returned to Russia; appointed chargé d'affaires in Peru in 1847, and in 1853 raised to the rank of minister plenipotentiary to Peru, where he remained until 1860.

Clay, John R., chargé d'affaires at Lima, Peru, mentioned, 2680.

Clayton, Henry D., is a native of Barbour Co., Ala.; lawyer; served one term in the Alabama legislature; elected to the 55th, 56th, 57th, 58th, 59th, 60th, 61st, 62d and 63d Congresses from Alabama.

Clayton, John Middleton; lawyer; b. in Sussex Co., Del., July 24, 1796; member of

legislature, and later secretary of state; elected to United States Senate in 1829, 1835, 1845, and 1851; chief justice of Delaware, 1842-1845; appointed Secretary of State in President Taylor's Cabinet, in 1849, and negotiated the Clayton-Bulwer Treaty (q. v.); died Nov. 9, 1856, in Dover, Del.

Clayton, John M.:
Secretary of State, 2546.
Treaty between United States and Great Britain concluded by Sir Henry Lytton Bulwer and, 2580.

Clayton, Joshua; president of Delaware, 1789 to 1793; governor, 1793-1796; chosen United States Senator, 1798; died in Middletown, Del., Aug. 11, 1798.

Clayton, Joshua, president of Delaware, 65.

Cleary, William C., reward offered for arrest of, 3505.
Revoked, 3551.

Clendenin, David R., member of commission to try assassins of President Lincoln, etc., 3534.

Cleveland, Grover, biography of, 4882.

Clifford, Nathan, Diplomat and Attorney-General under President Polk; b. Rumney, N. H., Aug. 18, 1803; received a liberal education; studied law and commenced practice in York County in 1827; member of the state house of representatives 1830-1834, serving as speaker the last two years; attorney-general of Maine 1834-1838; elected a Representative from Maine to the 26th Congress as a Democrat; re-elected to the 27th Congress; appointed Attorney-General, serving from Dec. 23, 1846, to March 17, 1848; commissioner to Mexico, with the rank of envoy extraordinary and minister plenipotentiary, from March 18, 1848, to Sept. 6, 1849; resumed the practice of law at Portland, Me.; appointed by President Buchanan associate justice of the Supreme Court of the United States Jan. 28, 1858; died at Cornish, Me., July 25, 1881.

Clifford, Nathan, minister to Mexico, nomination of, and reason therefor, 2427.
Instructions to, referred to, 2537.
President declines to transmit to House instructions to, 2452.

Clin, Stephen, secretary of legation at Court of Great Britain, nomination of, 992.

Clinch, Duncan Lamont; soldier, legislator; b. Edgecombe Co., N. C., April 6, 1787; general in United States army, and 1843-1845 member of Congress from Georgia; died Macon, Ga., Oct. 27, 1849.

Clinch, Duncan L., troops under, in Seminole War, 1834.

Cline, Cyrus; b. Richland Co., Ohio, July 12, 1856; engaged in the banking business; elected to the 61st, 62d, 63d and 64th Congresses from Indiana.

Clinton, George; soldier, statesman; b. Ulster Co., N. Y., July 26, 1739; member of colonial assembly and of Continental Congress, 1775; voted for independence, but did not sign declaration, as he was called into military duty; brigadier-general, 1777;

governor of New York for the first eighteen consecutive years under the constitution (1777-1795), and again in 1801 ; Vice-President United States 1804, with President Jefferson, and again in 1808 with Madison ; died Washington, D. C., April 20, 1812.

Clinton, George, bronze statue of, presented by State of New York, 4214.

Clover, Richardson, member of Board on Geographic Names, 5647.

Clover, Seth, treaty with Indians concluded by, 3270.

Clymer, George; financier ; b. Philadelphia, Pa., 1739 ; one of the early continental treasurers ; member of Continental Congress and signed the Declaration of Independence ; member of Congress under articles of confederation in 1780, and under Constitution, 1789-1791, from Pennsylvania ; member of convention which formed Federal Constitution, and one of the signers ; head of Excise Department of Pennsylvania, 1791 ; sent to Georgia to negotiate treaty with the Creek and Cherokee Indians, 1796 ; later president of the Philadelphia Bank, and Academy of Fine Arts ; died in Morrisville, Pa., Jan. 23, 1813.

Clymer, George:
Commissioner to treat with Indians, nomination of, 171.
District supervisor, nomination of, 91.
Treaty with Indians concluded by, 202.

Cobb, Howell; lawyer, soldier ; b. Cherry Hill, Ga., Sept. 7, 1815 ; presidential elector, 1836 ; member of Congress, 1842-1848, speaker during latter term ; governor of Georgia, 1851-53 ; returned to Congress in 1855, and was made Secretary of the Treasury in President Buchanan's Cabinet, 1857 ; one of the leaders in the secession movement ; died Oct. 9, 1868, in New York City.

Cobb, Howell, interview with Col. Key, regarding exchange of prisoners of war, 3459.

Cochrane, Alex., order of, to British naval forces to destroy American coast towns and districts referred to, 536.

Coffee, John; soldier ; b. Prince Edward Co., Va., June 2, 1772 ; member of Congress from Georgia, 1833-1837 ; served in War of 1812 as general, and later in campaign against Indians ; died Sept. 25, 1836, in Telfair Co., Ga.

Coffee, John, Indians defeated by Tennessee militia under command of, 521.

Coffey, Titian James; lawyer, diplomat ; acting Attorney-General under President Lincoln ; b. Dec. 5, 1824 ; in Huntingdon, Pa. ; educated at home and studied law in St. Louis ; admitted to the bar in 1846 ; one of the organizers of the Republican party in Pennsylvania in 1855 ; member of Pennsylvania Legislature, 1856-60 ; author of law permitting parties to suits to testify as witnesses in their own behalf, and of the law organizing the normal school system of the State ; married Feb. 14, 1855, Mary Kerr, of Pittsburg, Pa. ; March, 1861, appointed assistant Attorney General, under Edward Bates, with whom he had

studied law ; the duties of the Attorney General devolved largely upon him even before the resignation of Mr. Bates ; wrote many of the important opinions of the office, including that under which the right of equal pay to negro soldiers with same rank as white was recognized by the government ; resigned in 1864 to resume law practice, but was appointed Secretary of Legation at St. Petersburg, Russia, and while there made a close study of European politics ; died Jan. 11, 1867, in Washington, D. C.

Coffin, George W., commander of the *Alert* in Lady Franklin Bay Expedition, 4835.

Coffin, William G., treaty with Indians concluded by, 3393, 3394.

Colbert, George, reservations sold to United States by, 616.

Colbert, Levi, reservations sold to United States, by, 616.

Colby, J. C. S., consul at Chin-Kiang, China, appointment of, discussed, 4259.

Colfax, Schuyler, Vice-President of the United States under Grant ; b. New York City, March 23, 1823 ; educated in the common schools ; became proprietor and editor of the Register at South Bend, Ind., in 1845, which he published for eighteen years ; elected in 1850 a delegate from St. Joseph County to the convention which framed the constitution of Indiana ; elected a Representative from Indiana to the 34th Congress as a Republican ; re-elected to the 35th, 36th, 37th, 38th, 39th, and 40th Congresses ; Speaker of the House of Representatives in the 38th, 39th, and 40th Congresses ; elected Vice-President of the United States on the ticket with General Grant, and served from March 4, 1869, to March 3, 1873 ; vice-president of a manufacturing company at South Bend, Ind. ; died at Mankato, Minn., Jan. 13, 1885.

Collamer, Jacob, Postmaster-General under President Taylor ; b. Troy, N. Y., 1792 ; moved with his father to Burlington, Vt. ; graduated from the University of Vermont in 1810 ; served in the war of 1812 ; studied law and practiced at Woodstock, Vt., from 1813 to 1833 ; member of the State house of representatives for several years ; judge of the superior court of Vermont 1833-1842 ; elected a Representative from Vermont to the 28th, 29th, and 30th Congresses as a Whig ; appointed Postmaster-General serving from March 7, 1849, to July 20, 1850 ; again judge of the superior court of Vermont from Nov. 8, 1850, to Oct. 3, 1854 ; elected a United States Senator from Vermont as a Republican, serving from Dec. 3, 1855, until his death, at Woodstock, Vt., No. 9, 1865.

Collier, James William; b. Glenwood plantation, near Vicksburg, Warren Co., Miss., Sept. 28, 1872 ; entered the State University and in 1894 graduated in law from that institution ; 1895 he was elected a member of the lower house of the Mississippi legislature ; elected to the 61st, 62d, 63d and 64th Congresses from Mississippi.

Collins, Edward K.; shipowner ; b. Aug. 5, 1802, in Cape Cod, Mass. ; established line of sailing packets to Liverpool, 1836 ; first steamer of Collins Line, New York to Liverpool, sailed April 27, 1849 ; died Jan. 22, 1878, in New York City.

Collins, John; statesman; b. June 8, 1717; governor of Rhode Island, 1786-89; delegate to Congress under Articles of Confederation, 1778-1783, and one of the signers of articles; member of Congress, 1789; died Newport, R. I., March 8, 1795.

Collins, John, governor of Rhode Island, etc., letter of, declaring friendship for sister States, 64.

Collins, Joseph B., act to amend act for relief of, vetoed, 4496.

Collins, Sir Richard, arbitrator in Venezuela boundary dispute, 6338.

Collins, Thomas F., claim of, against Spain, 5518

Colt, Samuel; sailor, inventor; b. Hartford, Conn., July 19, 1814; obtained patent, 1835, for pistol which should fire several shots without stopping to reload; established manufacturing plant in 1852, on tract of 250 acres at Hartford, Conn., and in 1855 the Colt Patent Firearms Company was organized; died in Hartford, Conn., Jan. 19, 1862.

Colt, Samuel, firearms invented by, 2430.

Comanos, N. D., agreement with Egypt signed by, 4849.

Comonfort, Ignacio, President of Mexico, election of, discussed, 3094.

Comstock, Cyrus Ballou; author, engineer, soldier; b. West Wrentham, Mass., Feb. 3, 1831; colonel engineers United States Army, and brevet major-general of volunteers; author of "Notes on European Surveys," "Surveys of the Northwestern Lakes," "Primary Triangulation of the United States Lake Survey."

Comstock, Cyrus B.:
Member of commission to try assassins of President Lincoln, etc., 3534.
Relieved from duty, 3534.
Mentioned, 3812.

Conger, P. H., treaty with Indians concluded by, 3901.

Conkling, Alfred; author, jurist; b. East Hampton, N. Y., Oct. 12, 1789; wrote "Treatise on Organization and Jurisdiction of Superior, Circuit, and District Courts," "Admiralty Jurisdiction," etc.; died Attica, N. Y., Feb. 5, 1874.

Conkling, Alfred, mentioned, 2770.

Conkling, Roscoe (1829-1888); politician; b. Albany, N. Y.; member of Congress from New York, 1859-63, and 1865-67; United States Senator from New York, 1867-81; President Garfield denied Conkling's claims to the control of the Federal patronage of New York State, whereupon he resigned and became a candidate for reelection on the issue raised between himself and the President, but the legislature failed to return him to the Senate, and he retired to his private practice of law; his death resulted from exposure in the memorable blizzard of 1888; his connection with the attempted nomination of Grant as President at Chicago, in 1880, is memorable.

Conner, Lieut., court-martial of, 853.

Conrad, Charles M., Secretary of War under President Fillmore; b. Winchester, Va., about 1804; moved with his father to Mississippi, and thence to Louisiana; studied law; in 1828 admitted to the bar, and commenced practice at New Orleans; member of the state house of representatives for several years; elected a United States Senator from Louisiana as a Whig in place of Alexander Mouton, resigned, serving from April 14, 1842, to March 3, 1843; delegate to the state constitutional convention in 1844; elected a representative from Louisiana to the 31st Congress as a Whig, serving from Dec. 3, 1849, to Aug. 17, 1850, when he resigned; appointed Secretary of War, serving from Aug. 13, 1850, to March 7, 1853; deputy from Louisiana in the Montgomery provisional congress of 1861; Representative from Louisiana to the 1st and 2nd Confederate Congresses, 1862-1864; died at New Orleans, Feb. 12, 1878.

Cooley, Dennis N., treaty with Indians concluded by, 3592.

Cooley, Lyman E., member of commission to consider construction of canal from Great Lakes to Atlantic Ocean, 6179.

Coolidge, Joseph, Jr., desk on which Declaration of Independence was written presented to United States by heirs of, 4540.
Letter of Robert C. Winthrop, regarding, 4541.

Copley, Ira C.; b. Knox County, Ill., Oct. 25, 1864; graduated from West Aurora High School in 1881; prepared for college at Jennings Seminary, Aurora, and graduated from Yale College in 1887, receiving the degree of bachelor of arts; graduated from Union College of Law, Chicago, in 1889; connected with the gas and electric business in Aurora; elected to the 62d, 63d and 64th Congresses from Illinois.

Cooper, Henry Allen; b. Spring Prairie, Walworth Co., Wis., Sept. 8, 1850; graduated Northwestern University 1873 and Union College of Law, Chicago, 1875; in 1880 elected district attorney of Racine County, and reelected 1882, 1884 and 1886-87; member of State senate 1887-89; elected to the 53d, 54th, 55th, 56th, 57th, 58th, 59th, 60th, 61st, 62d, 63d and 64th Congresses from Wisconsin.

Corbin, Henry Clark; soldier; b. Ohio; enlisted as volunteer in Civil War, and passed into regular army as body guard to the President; adjutant at inauguration of Garfield, Cleveland, Harrison, McKinley; served as marshal of several large parades.

Corbin, H. C.:
Delegated to entertain Prince Henry of Prussia, 6704.
Dispatch to Gen. Otis regarding force, etc., for Philippine Islands, 6580.
Instructions to Gen. Merritt through, regarding joint occupancy of Philippine Islands with insurgents, 6579

Instructions to Gen. Otis through, to avoid conflict with Philippine insurgents, 6584.

Order through to send troops to Iloilo, 6583.

Cornell, Alonzo Barton; telegrapher; b. Ithaca, N. Y., Jan. 22, 1832; associated with Prof. Morse in early development of telegraph; rose successively from operator to acting president Western Union Telegraph Co.; elected member of State legislature, 1872, and governor of New York, 1879; trustee Cornell University, founded by his father.

Cornell, A. B., naval officer at port of New York, suspension of, discussed, 4463.

Cornplanter, Seneca chief, mentioned, 103.

Cortelyou, George Bruce; Secretary of Commerce and Labor and Postmaster General under President Roosevelt; b. July 26, 1862, in New York, N. Y.; of Huguenot ancestry; educated at Hempstead Institute, State Normal School at Westfield, Mass., New England Conservatory of Music at Boston; studied music and stenography in New York; married Lily Morris Hinds of Hempstead, L. I., in 1888; appointed private secretary and stenographer to the Appraiser of the Port of New York in 1884, and later became known as a general court reporter and was especially expert as a medical stenographer; in 1889-91 was private secretary to the post-office inspector in New York, and later fourth assistant Postmaster General; while in Washington graduated from Georgetown University Law School and took a post-graduate course at Columbia University Law School; stenographer and executive clerk to Presidents Cleveland and McKinley, and was at the latter's side when he was shot in Buffalo; continued in office by President Roosevelt and when the Department of Commerce and Labor was created in February, 1903, became its first secretary; resigned in 1904 to become chairman of Republican National Committee and in 1905 entered Roosevelt's cabinet as Postmaster General; while confidential clerk for President McKinley he prepared all the Messages, papers, addresses and other State documents.

Corwin, Thomas (1794-1865); politician; b. Bourbon Co., Ky.; member of Congress, 1830-40; governor of Ohio, 1840-42; United States Senator from Ohio, 1845-50; Secretary of the Treasury under Taylor, 1850-53; member of Congress, 1859-61; and United States minister to Mexico, 1861-64; "The most brilliant and impressive of the stump-speakers of that day."

Corwin, Thomas, minister to Mexico:
Convention with Mexico proposed by, 3261, 3282.

Dispatches from, regarding war with Mexico, 3264.

Treaties with Mexico concluded by, 3264.

Costello, Mr., convicted and sentenced to imprisonment in Great Britain, 3834.

Referred to, 3897.
Released, 3902.

Covode, John; merchant; b. Westmoreland Co., Pa., March 17, 1808; member of Congress from Pennsylvania, 1855-63, and 1867-69; died Harrisburg, Pa., Jan. 11, 1871.

Covode, John, mentioned, 3571.

Cowdin, Elliot C., commissioner to Paris Exposition, report of, transmitted, 3828.

Cox, Jacob Dolson; soldier, lawyer; b. Montreal, Can., Oct. 27, 1828, of American parents; brigadier-general Ohio volunteers, 1861, and promoted to major-general; governor of Ohio, 1866-67; appointed Secretary of the Interior by President in 1869; member of Congress from Ohio, 1877-79; author of "Atlanta," "The March to the Sea," "Second Battle of Bull Run as Connected with the Fitz-John Porter Case."

Cox, Jacob D., mentioned, 3812, 3815, 3817.

Cox, Samuel Sullivan (1824-1889); editor and politician; b. Zanesville, Ohio; member of Congress from Ohio, 1857-65; from New York City, 1869-73 and 1875-85; United States minister to Turkey, 1885-86; reelected to Congress in 1888; was known as "Sunset Cox," because of a florid and exuberant description of a sunset, which was written in the *Statesman*, of Columbus, Ohio, of which he was the editor.

Cox, William Elijah; b. Dubois Co., Ind., Sept. 6, 1865; elected to the 60th, 61st, 62d, 63d and 64th Congresses from Indiana.

Cox, Zachariah, arrest and confinement of, 352.

Crabbe, Col., execution of, referred to, 3012, 3096.

Crago, Thomas S.; b. Aug. 8, 1866, at Carmichaels, Greene County, Pa., educated at Greene Academy, Waynesburg College, and Princeton University, graduating from Princeton in the class of 1893; admitted to the bar of Greene County in 1894, and later to practice in the Superior and Supreme Courts of Pennsylvania and the Circuit and District Court and Supreme Court of the United States; served as captain of Company K, Tenth Pennsylvania Volunteer Infantry, during the war with Spain and the Philippine insurrection; elected major of the Tenth Regiment National Guard of Pennsylvania, and lieutenant-colonel of this regiment; was presidential elector in the year 1900, and delegate to the Republican national convention in the year 1904; elected to the 62d and 64th Congresses from Pennsylvania.

Craig, James, alleged secret agent employed by, for fomenting disaffection in United States, 483.

Craig, Robert, mentioned, 4737.

Craig, Robert; b. Virginia; member of Congress from that state, 1829-33, 1835-41.

Craighill, W. P., Yorktown monument built under direction of, 4850.

Cranch, William; jurist, lawyer; b. Weymouth, Mass., July 17, 1769; chief justice of District of Columbia, 1805-55; author of "Reports of Cases United States Courts"; died Washington, D. C., Sept. 1, 1855.

Cranch, William:
  Commissioner of Washington City, 304.
  Oath of office administered to President Tyler by, 1886.

Crane, Thomas J., report of, on improving irrigation of Ohio River transmitted, 2685.

Crane, Winthrop Murray; b. Dalton, Mass., April 23, 1853; educated at Williston Seminary, Easthampton, Mass.; paper manufacturer; lieutenant-governor of Massachusetts, 1897-1899; governor, 1900-1902; appointed to the United States Senate Oct. 12, 1904, to fill the vacancy caused by the death of Hon. G. F. Hoar, and took his seat Dec. 6. He was elected by the legislature in January, 1905, to represent Massachusetts in the Senate and was reelected in 1907.

Craven, Thomas T., thanks of Congress to, recommended, 3277.

Crawford, Coe I., b. near Volney, Allamakee Co., Iowa, Jan. 14, 1858; graduated from the law department of the University of Iowa in 1882; located for the practice of law at Independence, Iowa, and after one year in practice went to Pierre, Dakota Territory; member of the Territorial legislature in 1889; upon the admission of South Dakota into the Union as a state, in 1889, became a member of the first State senate; elected attorney-general in 1892, and reelected in 1894; governor in 1905; nominated at the election held under the South Dakota primary law on June 9, 1908, as the Republican candidate for United States Senator, and was elected by the legislature for the term ending March 3, 1915.

Crawford, George W., Governor of Georgia and Secretary of War under President Taylor; b. Columbia County, Ga., Dec. 22, 1798; graduated from Princeton College in 1820; studied law, and in 1822 commenced practice at Augusta, Ga.; Attorney-General of the State of Georgia 1827-1831; member of the state house of representatives 1837-1842; elected a Representative from Georgia to the 27th Congress to fill the vacancy caused by the death of Richard W. Habersham, as a Whig, serving from Feb. 1, 1843, to March 3, 1843; elected governor of Georgia in 1843 and re-elected in 1845; appointed Secretary of War in 1849, but resigned the next year, on the death of President Taylor. His reputation rests largely upon his excellent administration as Governor of Georgia. He died at Belair, Ga., July 22, 1872.

Crawford, Thomas Hartley; jurist, lawyer; b. Chambersburg, Pa., Nov. 14, 1786; member of Congress from Pennsylvania, 1829-33, and elected to State legislature; commissioner of Indian affairs, 1838; judge of District of Columbia criminal court, 1845; died Washington, D. C., Jan. 27, 1868.

Crawford, T. Hartley, communication from, regarding Indian affairs, 1797, 1838, 1842.

Crawford, William Harris, jurist; Secretary of War and the Treasury under President Madison; b. Amherst County, Va., Feb. 24, 1772; moved with his father to Georgia in 1783; studied law and commenced practice at Lexington; appointed to prepare a digest of the laws of Georgia in 1799; member of the state house of representatives 1803-1807; elected a United States Senator from Georgia in place of Abraham Baldwin, deceased, serving from Dec. 9, 1807, to March 3, 1813; elected President pro tempore of the Senate March 24, 1812; declined the position of Secretary of War offered him by President Madison, and accepted the mission to France, serving from April 3, 1813, to April 22, 1815; returned home to act as agent for the sale of the land donated by Congress to La Fayette; accepted the position as Secretary of War Aug. 1, 1815, and transferred to the Treasury Oct. 22, 1816, serving until March 7, 1825; defeated as the Democratic candidate for President in 1825; on account of illness declined the request of President J. Q. Adams that he remain Secretary of the Treasury; returned to Georgia and appointed judge of the northern circuit court in 1827, which position he held until his death, at Elberton, Ga., Sept. 15, 1834.

Crawford, William H., mentioned, 1227.

Creswell, John A. J., Postmaster-General under President Grant; b. Port Deposit, Cecil Co., Md., Nov. 18, 1828. He was thoroughly educated, his parents being wealthy and ambitious for his future prospects. After studying in the schools in his neighborhood he was sent to Dickinson College, Carlisle, Pa., from which he was graduated with the highest honors in 1848. He at once began to study law, and in 1850 was admitted to practice at the bar of Maryland. Eventually he took rank as one of the foremost lawyers in Maryland. From the time when he cast his first vote as a whig, Mr. Creswell was earnest and enthusiastic in his study of politics, and in his consideration of party relations. He was a nominee from Cecil County, appointed by the whig party, to the general convention which was held in Maryland in 1850, for the purpose of remodeling the constitution of the commonwealth. In the autumn of 1861 Mr. Creswell was elected as the representative of Cecil County in the legislature of the state, and in the following year was appointed Adjutant-General of Maryland. In 1863 he was chosen a member of the United States house of representatives. There he made his mark by delivering an eloquent speech, in which he favored the abolition of slavery. In 1865 he was elected a member of the United States Senate, to fill out the unexpired term of Gov. Thomas H. Hicks, who died in Washington, Feb. 13, 1865. March 5, 1869, he was appointed Postmaster-General, being recommended for the position not only by his political friends in Maryland, but by Vice-President Colfax, Senator Ben Wade and other prominent Republicans. Mr. Creswell served in the cabinet for five years and four months, and during his administration succeeded in introducing into that department many valuable reforms. On June 22, 1874, he was appointed counsel of the United States in connection with the court of commissioners sitting on the Alabama claims, and, having resigned the postmaster-generalship a few days later, he continued to serve in that capacity until Dec. 21, 1876. Mr. Creswell died at Elkton, Dec. 23, 1896.

Curtis, Benjamin R., counsel for President Johnson in impeachment proceedings, 3924.

Curtis, Charles; b. Topeka, Kans., Jan. 25, 1860; received his education in the common schools; studied law; was admitted to the bar in 1881; elected to the 53rd, 54th, 55th, 56th, 57th, 58th, 59th, and 60th Congresses from Kansas; January, 1907, elected to United States Senate to fill out the unexpired term of Hon. J. R. Burton, resigned, and for the full term beginning March 4, 1907; again elected in 1914 for the term ending March 3, 1921.

Curtis, William Eleroy; author, diplomat; b. Akron, Ohio, Nov. 5, 1850; special envoy to South and Central American republics, the Vatican, and Spain; executive officer International American Conference; author of "United States and Foreign Powers," "Capitals of Spanish America," "Japan Sketches," etc.

Curtis, William E., mentioned, 5833.

Cushing, Caleb; lawyer, jurist, author; b. Salisbury, Mass., Jan. 17, 1800; served in the state legislature, and in Congress, 1835-43; sent by President Tyler as envoy to China, where he negotiated an important treaty; colonel of Massachusetts volunteers in Mexican War; made justice of Massachusetts Supreme Court, 1851; Attorney-General in President Pierce's Cabinet, 1853-57; author of "Historical and Political Review of the Late Revolution in France," "Practical Principles of Political Economy," "The Treaty of Washington," etc.; died Newburyport, Mass., Jan. 2, 1879.

Cushing, Caleb:
Attorney-General, mentioned, 4841.

Chief Justice Supreme Court, nomination of, withdrawn, 4213.
Minister to—
China—
Instructions to, referred to, 2134, 2218.
Transmission of commission appointing, 2134.
Treaty with China concluded by, 2205.
Spain, payment of *Virginius* claims arranged by, 4290.
Secretary of Treasury, renomination of, and reasons therefor, 2086.

Cushing, William B., thanks of Congress to, recommended, 3457.

Custer, George Armstrong; soldier; b. New Rumley, Ohio, Dec. 5, 1839; distinguished officer during Civil War, and later in campaigns against the Indians on the western plains; massacred with his entire command, near Little Big Horn River, in Montana, June 25, 1876.

Custer, George A., disaster to forces under, 4327.

Cutting, A. K., imprisonment of, by Mexican authorities, 4991, 5086, 5122.

Cutting, John B., account of, for expenditures in liberating American seamen in British ports, transmitted, 108.

Cutts, Richard D., report of, on marketable products of the sea, transmitted, 4117.

Czar of Russia. (See Russia.)

Dade, Francis Langhorn; soldier; b. Virginia; appointed lieutenant 12th infantry in 1813; captain, 1818, and brevet major, 1828; killed by Indians, near Fort King, Fla., Dec. 28, 1835.

Dade, Francis L., massacre of command of, by Seminole Indians, 1834.

Dahlberg, Gustav Isak, recommendation for indemnity to, 6457.

Dahlgren, John Adolph; naval officer; inventor, author; b. Philadelphia, Pa., Nov. 13, 1809; conducted the siege of Charleston, S. C., and made brilliant record during the Civil War; created admiral in 1863; invented Dahlgren naval gun; author of technical works on the subject of naval guns and gunnery, and maritime law; died 1870.

Dahlgren, John A.:
Rear-admiral in Navy, nomination of, 3356.
Thanks of Congress to, recommended, 3284.

Dainese, F., claim of, for salary while acting consul at Constantinople, 2957, 2958.

Dallas, Alexander J.; statesman; Secretary of the Treasury under President Madison, and previously acting Secretary of State by three successive appointments under Presidents Washington and Adams, also acting Secretary of War, 1815-16; b. June 21, 1759, in Jamaica; of Scotch parentage; educated in Edinburgh and Westminster, he read law, contracted an early marriage, returned to Jamaica and then migrated to the United States and located in Philadelphia in 1783; admitted to practice in 1785, and for a time edited the *Columbian Magazine;* was an active politician and founder of the Pennsylvania Democratic Society in 1793; besides "Features of Jay's Treaty," he published an edition of the State Laws from 1700 to 1801, and "Reports of Cases" in the United States and Pennsylvania courts before and after the Revolution (4 vols., 1790-1807). (See Supreme Court Reports.) President Jefferson appointed him United States Attorney for the Eastern District of Pennsylvania, which position he held until called by Madison to head the Treasury Department at a critical juncture; the government was practically bankrupt; Dallas advised a loan and the organization of a bank to float the same, but the bill therefor was vetoed by President Madison (page 540); Dallas then managed to allay the fears of the business world as to an extensive issue of treasury notes, and these were received at par; he succeeded, in April, 1816, in having the Bank of the United States chartered with a capital of $35,000,000; prepared the Tariff Law of 1816, under which business throughout the country received a new impetus (page 760); acting as Secretary of War subsequent to March, 1815, he reduced the army to a peace footing; published "Exposition of the Causes and Character of the War of 1812-15"; died Jan. 16, 1817, in Philadelphia.

Dallas, George Mifllin (1792-1864); statesman; b. Philadelphia; United States Senator from Pennsylvania, 1831-33; minister to Russia, 1837-39; Vice-President of the United States with Polk, 1845-49; was United States minister to England, 1856-61.

Dalton, Tristram; legislator; b. Newbury, Mass., in May, 1843, member of both branches of the Massachusetts legislature, and was chosen speaker of the house; elected to the first United States Senate under the Constitution; died Boston, May 30, 1817.

Dalton, Tristram, on committee to conduct inaugural ceremony of President Washington, 40.

Dana, E. T., arrest and maltreatment of, at Heidelberg, Baden, 2772.

Dana, Francis; lawyer, jurist; b. in Charlestown, Mass., June 13, 1743; delegate from Massachusetts to the Continental Congress, 1776-79, and in 1784 signed the Articles of Confederation; secretary of legation to Paris under John Adams; appointed minister to Russia, but not officially received; appointed minister to France, 1797, but declined; chief justice of State court, 1791-1806, when he resigned; died Cambridge, Mass., April 25, 1811.

Dana, Francis, minister to France, nomination of, and reasons therefor, 235.

Danforth, Henry G., b. June 14, 1854, in the town of Gates (now part of Rochester), Monroe County, N. Y.; educated in private schools in Rochester, at Phillips Exeter Academy, Exeter, N. H., and was graduated from Harvard College in 1877, from the Harvard Law School in 1880; was admitted to the bar in 1880; elected to the 62d, 63d and 64th Congresses from New York.

Daniel, Peter Vyvian; lawyer, jurist; b. Stafford Co., Va., April 24, 1784; served in State legislature and as lieutenant-governor; appointed judge of United States District Court for Virginia, 1836, and in 1840 was made justice of the Supreme Court of the United States; died Richmond, Va., June 30, 1860.

Daniel, Peter V., Supreme Court Justice, death of, referred to, 3250.

Daniels, Jared W., member of Indian commission, 5579.

Daniels, Josephus, Secretary of the Navy under President Wilson; b. Washington, N. C., May 18, 1862; son of Josephus and Mary (Cleves) Daniels; received an academic education in Wilson (N. C.) Collegiate Institute; a newspaper man by profession; his field of journalism began when, between the ages of fifteen and sixteen, he started a little paper in Wilson called *The Cornucopia,* of which he was the amateur editor; at the age of eighteen was the editor of the Wilson (N. C.) *Advance,* a weekly paper; admitted to the bar in 1885, but did not practice law; became editor Raleigh (N. C.) *State Chronicle* in 1885; married Addie W., daughter of Major W. H. Bagley, May 2, 1888, and has four sons; state printer for North Carolina, 1887-1893; chief clerk, Department of the Interior, 1893-1895; trustee University of North Carolina and member of the executive committee of the board of trustees; in 1894 he consolidated the *State Chronicle* and the *North Carolinian* with the *News and Observer,* and has since been its editor; has been the North Carolina member of the Democratic national committee for twenty years; nominated, confirmed, and commissioned Secretary of the Navy, March 5, 1913.

Daniels, William H., collector of customs, suspension of, referred to, 4741.

Dart, Anson, official conduct of, referred to, 3015, 3016.

Davenport, James S.; b. near Gaylesville, Cherokee County, Ala., Sept. 21, 1864; moved to Conway, Faulkner County, Ark., where he was educated in the public schools and the academy at Greenbrier, Ark., read law and was admitted to the bar; Feb. 14, 1890; in October of that year moved to Indian Territory, and continued the practice of his profession; has been twice married, in 1892 to Culielma Ross, who died in 1898, and on June 15, 1907, to Miss Byrd Ironside, both citizens by blood of the Cherokee Nation; he served two terms in the lower house of the Cherokee Legislature from 1897 to 1901, being elcted speaker the latter term, the only intermarried white man who ever held that position; was selected one of the attorneys for the Cherokee Nation and held that position until March 4, 1907; twice elected mayor of Vinita, 1903 and 1904, voluntarily retiring at the end of his second term: elected to the 60th, 62d, 63d and 64th Congresses from Oklahoma.

David, Pierre Jean, bust of Lafayette presented to Congress by, 992.

Davidson, Francis S.:
Act for relief of, 6736.
Vetoed, 6773.

Davidson, James H.; b. Colchester, Delaware Co., N. Y., June 18, 1858; graduated Albany Law School 1884 and was admitted to the bar of New York; subsequently moved to Wisconsin and commenced the practice of law at Princeton in 1887; in 1888 was elected prosecuting attorney of Green Lake County; in 1892 removed to Oshkosh; in 1895 was appointed city attorney; elected to the 55th, 56th, 57th, 58th, 59th, 60th, 61st, 62d and 64th Congresses from Wisconsin.

Davis, Charles Henry; American naval officer; b. Boston, Mass., Jan. 16, 1807; d. Washington, D. C., Feb. 18, 1877; entered the navy in 1823, became commander in 1854, and served as chief of staff and captain of the fleet in the expedition under Dupont which captured Port Royal, S. C.; in 1861; in command of the Mississippi gunboat flotilla he overcame the Confederate fleet off Port Pillow May 10, 1862; and again off Memphis June 6, 1862, on which day he received the surrender of the Confederate commander; promoted to rear-admiral Feb. 7, 1863; wrote "The Coast Survey of the United States" (1849), and "Narrative of the North Polar Expedition of the *U. S. Polaris*" (1876).

Davis, Charles Henry:
Correspondence regarding squadron at Rio Janeiro and the Paraguay difficulties, 3890.
Rear-admiral in Navy, nomination of, 3356.
Thanks of Congress to, recommended, 3284.

Davis, Charles Russell; b. Pittsfield, Ill.; moved to Lesueur Co., Minn., at an early age; admitted to the bar and practiced law for more than thirty years in Minnesota; served for two years in the house of representatives, and four years in the State senate of Minnesota; elected to the 58th, 59th, 60th, 61st, 62d, 63d and 64th Congresses from Minnesota.

Davis, Cushman Kellogg; diplomat and statesman; b. Henderson, Jefferson County, N. Y., June 16, 1838; received a common school and collegiate education, graduating from the University of Michigan in June, 1857; lawyer; first lieutenant in the Twenty-eighth Wisconsin Infantry 1862-1864; member of the Minnesota legislature in 1867; United States district attorney for Minnesota 1868-1873; governor of Minnesota 1874-1875; elected to the United States Senate as a Republican to succeed Hon. S. J. R. McMillan, and took his seat March 4, 1887; twice re-elected and served until his death, at St. Paul, Minn., Nov. 27, 1900; member of the commission which met at Paris, France, in Sept., 1898, to arrange terms of peace between the United States and Spain; died at St. Paul, Minn., Nov. 27, 1900.

Davis, Cushman K., member of Spanish-American Peace Commission, 6322.

Davis, David (1815-1886); jurist and statesman: b. in Cecil Co., Md.; associate justice of the United States Supreme Court, 1862-77; nominated for President by the Labor-Reform party against Grant, 1872; United States Senator from Illinois, 1877-83; when Arthur succeeded to the Presidency, Davis was acting Vice-President, 1881-83.

Davis, George W., member of board to consider expedition to be sent for relief of Lady Franklin Bay Expedition, 4813.

Davis, J. C. Bancroft, Acting Secretary of State, 4178.

Davis, Jefferson (1808-1889); statesman; b. in Christian Co., Ky.; graduated West Point, 1828; took part in the Black Hawk and Mexican wars: member of Congress from Mississippi, 1845-46; United States Senator from Mississippi, 1847-51; Secretary of War under Pierce, 1853-57; United States Senator, 1857-61; president of the Confederate States, 1862; arrested near Irwinsville, Ga., 1865; imprisoned in Fortress Monroe, 1865-67, and amnestied, 1868.

Davis, Jefferson:
Correspondence of governor of South Carolina with President delayed by, 3195.
Declaration of, and advisability of attempting negotiations with, discussed, 3455.
Imprisonment of, and reasons for not placing upon trial, inquired into, 3572.
Report of Attorney-General regarding, referred to, 3576.
Negotiations with, for restoration of peace discussed and correspondence regarding, 3461.
Official acts of, in Virginia declared null and void, 3535.
Reward offered for arrest of, 3505.
Persons claiming, directed to file claims, 3551.

Day, William R.; lawyer, diplomat; Secretary of State under President McKinley; commisioner to conclude the peace treaty between the United States and Spain in

1898; b. April 17, 1849, in Ravenna, Ohio; his father and his maternal grandfather and great-grandfather were eminent lawyers; he was educated in Ohio public schools and the University of Michigan; began practice in Canton, Ohio, and was offered position of U. S. District Judge by President Harrison; personal friendship for Mr. McKinley drew him into politics; and he was appointed Assistant Secretary of State under Secretary John Sherman, and upon the latter's resignation Mr. Day succeeded to the cabinet position. War had been declared against Spain, and it was due to Secretary Day's skill in diplomacy that the conflict was confined to the two nations directly concerned. When Spain asked peace terms Mr. Day signed the protocol providing for a commission of five members to meet at Paris to conclude the final terms. He presided over the commission, and signed a treaty of peace Dec. 10, 1898, and upon his return to the United States, was appointed U. S. Circuit Judge of the Sixth Judicial Circuit, and in February, 1903, became an associate Justice of the Supreme Court. Mr. Day married in Canton, Ohio, and had four sons, William L., Luther, Stephen and Rufus.

Day, William R.:
President of Spanish-American Peace Commission, 6322.
Secretary of State, 6476.

Dearborn, Henry (father of H. A. S. Dearborn), Secretary of War under President Jefferson; b. Hampton, N. H., Feb. 23, 1751; received a public school education; studied medicine; began practicing in 1772; captain during the Revolutionary War; moved to Monmouth, Me., in June, 1784; elected brigadier-general of militia in 1787; and made major-general in 1789; appointed United States marshal for the district of Maine in 1789; elected a Representative from one of the Maine districts of Massachusetts to the 3d Congress as a Democrat, and reelected to the 4th Congress, serving from Dec. 2, 1793, until March 3, 1797; appointed Secretary of War, and served from March 4, 1801, until March 7, 1809; appointed collector of the port of Boston by President Madison in 1809, which position he held until Jan. 27, 1812, when he was appointed senior major-general in the United States Army; in command at the capture of York (now Toronto), April 27, 1813; recalled from the frontier July 6, 1813, and placed in command of the city of New York; appointed minister plenipotentiary to Portugal by President Monroe, and served from May 7, 1822, until June 30, 1824, when, by his own request, he was recalled; returned to Roxbury, Mass., where he died June 6, 1829.

De Camp, John, thanks of Congress to, recommended, 3277.

Decatur, Stephen; naval officer; b. Sinnepuxent, Md., January, 1779; entered navy 1798; February, 1804, entered the harbor of Tripoli with a small party and burned the American frigate *Philadelphia,* which had been captured by Barbarian; for this act he was promoted to captain; active in War of 1812, as commander of *United States* and *President;* commander of squadron sent to Mediterranean, 1815, and captured two Algerine war vessels and dictated treaty of peace to Dey of Algiers; killed in a duel near Bladensburg, Md., March 22, 1820, by Commodore James Barron.

Decatur, Stephen:
Captain in Navy, advancement of, to grade of, referred to, 362.
Claims of, arising from recapture of the *Philadelphia,* 1025.
Commander of the *United States,* 506.

De Haven, Lieut. Edwin J., expedition commanded by, in search of Sir John Franklin and companions, return of, 2668.

De Kalb, Baron Johann, claims of representatives of, for services rendered United States in Revolutionary War, 1270.

Delafield, Richard, member of board to examine quotas of States under call for troops, 3476.

Delano, Columbus, Secretary of the Interior under President Grant; b. Shoreham, Vt., in 1809; moved to Mount Vernon, Ohio, in 1817; received an academic education; studied law, and in 1831 admitted to the bar; elected a Representative from Ohio to the 29th Congress as a Whig; defeated by two votes at the Whig state convention in 1847 as a candidate for the nomination for governor; delegate to the Republican national convention at Chicago which nominated Lincoln and Hamlin; served as state commissary-general of Ohio in 1861; defeated by two votes for the United States Senate in 1862; member of the state house of representatives in 1863; delegate to the Republican national convention at Baltimore which nominated Lincoln and Johnson; elected to the 39th Congress as a Republican; reelected to the 40th Congress; George W. Morgan, Democrat, obtained the certificate of election, but was voted out of his seat June 3, 1868, and Mr. Delano recognized; appointed Secretary of the Interior, Nov. 1, 1870, which position he held until Oct. 19, 1875, when he resigned.

Delfosse, M. Maurice, selection of, as commissioner on fisheries question with Great Britain referred to, 4438.

De Long, George W., death of, in *Jeannette* expedition, 4726.
Remains of, removed to United States, 4834.

De Martens, M. F., arbitrator, in Venezuelan boundary dispute, 6338.

Denby, Charles:
Member of Commission to Philippine Islands, 6584.
Minister to China, regulations for consular courts promulgated by, 5388.

Dennison, William, Governor of Ohio (1860-62), and postmaster-general under President Lincoln; b. Cincinnati, Nov. 23, 1815. He was graduated from Miami University in 1835, was admitted to the bar in 1840, and settled at Columbus, Ohio, where after some years of legal practice, he became president of a bank and of a railroad, and was sent to the legislature in 1848-50. In 1856 he was a member of the Pittsburgh convention which organized the Republican party, and of that which met at Philadelphia, June 17th, and nominated J. C. Frémont. As governor in 1860-62 he was

ve-y active in supporting the war by raising troops and supplies, as well as in protecting the border; some of his measures
at this time were thought to be at least
extra-constitutional. It was through .Gov.
Dennison's efforts that West Virginia was
saved to the Union. He assured the Unionists of that state that if they would break
off from old Virginia and adhere to the
Union, 'he would send the necessary military force to protect them. When it became
necessary to redeem this pledge, Gov. Dennison sent Ohio militia, who, uniting with
the loyal citizens, drove the Confederates
out of West Virginia. When the general
government was about to refund to Ohio
money used for military purposes, the state
auditor and the attorney-general decided
that this money could not legally be used
again for military purposes. Gov. Dennison, therefore, through 'his personal agents,
caused it to be collected from the federal
government, and used it for military purposes instead of turning it into the Ohio
state treasury. It was again refunded to
Ohio, again collected by his agents, and
was thus used over and over again, so that
he intercepted in all $1,077,600. It was a
high-handed measure, but justifiable on the
ground of public necessity. He presented
satisfactory accounts, and vouchers to the
legislature for every dollar, and no shadow
was ever cast upon 'him or his officers who
disbursed it. In 1864 he presided over the
national convention of his party at Baltimore, and was called into the cabinet by
President Lincoln in October, 1864, as postmaster-general. This post he held until
July, 1866. He reappeared in the political
field as a member of the national convention
of 1880 and a candidate for United States
Senator, but was not elected. He was a
benefactor of Dennison University, founded
in 1831 at Granville, Ohio. Gov. Dennison
died June 15, 1882.

**Denniston, William H., act for relief
of,** vetoed, 4222.

Dent, Stanley Hubert, Jr.; b. Eufaula,
Ala., Aug. 16, 1869; graduated from the
Southern University, of Greensboro, Ala.,
with the degree of A. B., in 1886, and in
1889 was graduated in law from the University of Virginia; elected to the 61st Congress from Alabama, receiving 10,754 votes,
none being cast against him, and re-elected
to the 62d Congress without opposition; and
later to the 63d and 64th Congresses.

Depew, Chauncey Mitchell; b. Peekskill,
N. Y., April 23, 1834; graduated from Yale
College in 1856, and in 1887 received the
degree of LL. D. from his alma mater; admitted to the bar in 1858, elected to the
assembly in 1861 and 1862; in 1863 candidate for secretary of state, and reversed
the Democratic success of 1862, being elected by 30,000 majority; in 1866 appointed
attorney for the New York & Harlem Railroad Company; made general counsel of the
New York Central & Hudson River Railroad
Company in 1875; president of the New
York Central & Hudson River Railroad in
1885; resigned in 1899 to become chairman
of the boards of directors of the New York
Central, the Lake Shore, the Michigan Central, and the New York, Chicago & St.
Louis Railroad companies; elected to the
United States Senate from New York in
1899; re-elected 1905.

De Poiery, Mr., captain by brevet, nomination of, and reasons therefor, 67.

Derrick, W. S., Acting Secretary of
State, 2613.

Dewey, George; Admiral of the Navy; b.
Montpelier, Vt., Dec. 26, 1837; graduated
Annapolis Naval Academy, 1858, and assigned to Mediterranean squadron; served
throughout Civil War in navy of lower Mississippi River and Gulf of Mexico, and later
with North Atlantic squadron; commander
of *Narragansett,* 1870; had charge of Pacific
survey and Secretary of Lighthouse Board,
1872-82; captain-commander of the *Dolphin,*
of White Squadron, 1884; commodore, 1896;
assigned to Asiatic squadron, Nov. 30, 1897;
April, 1898, following British declaration of
neutrality, left port of Hong Kong, arriving at Manila Bay April 30, with nine vessels and 1,694 men; May 1, destroyed the
Spanish fleet of thirteen vessels and reduced the.five batteries defending the city;
raised to rank of acting rear-admiral, and
received vote of thanks and sword; Congress, 1899, re-created rank of Admiral, and
President McKinley appointed Dewey to the
office previously held only by Farragut and
Porter. Admiral Dewey died Jan. 16, 1917.

Dewey, George:
Attack of American land forces and
capture of Manila assisted by
squadron under, 6319.

Thanks of President tendered,
6568.

Member of Philippine Commission,
6584.

Spanish fleet destroyed in Manila
Bay by American squadron under, 6297, 6315.

Appointed acting rear-admiral,
6297, 6568.

Sword to be presented to, 6302.

Thanks of Congress to, 6298.

Recommended, 6297.

Reply of, 6302.

Thanks of President tendered,
6568.

Referred to, 6297.

Suggestions from, regarding force,
etc., for Philippine Islands requested by President, 6580.

Devens, Charles, Attorney-General under
President Hayes; b. Charlestown, Middlesex Co., Mass., April 4, 1820, the son of
Charles and Mary Lithgow Devens, and
grandson of Richard Devens, a revolutionary patriot. His maternal grandfather was
Col. Arthur Lithgow, of Augusta, Me.
Charles entered Harvard, from which he
was graduated in 1838. He subsequently
studied law in the Harvard Law School,
and afterward with Hubbard & Watts of
Boston. In 1841 he was admitted to the
bar, and at once began the practice of his
profession at Northfield, later removing to
Greenfield. In 1848-49 he served as a
member of the state senate, and from the
latter year until 1853 as United States marshal for the district of Massachusetts.
When the Civil War broke out he enlisted
in the cause of the Union, and on April 19.
1861, was unanimously elected major of the
third battalion rifles—three full companies.
with which he at once proceeded to the
front. On July 26th of the same year
Major Devens was made colonel of the
fifteenth regiment Massachusetts volunteers.
He was brevetted brigadier-general during
the siege of Yorktown, and took command

of a brigade in Couch's division, fourth army corps. Gen. Devens was severely wounded at the battle of Fair Oaks, but would not leave the field until the fall of night terminated the hostilities for the day. At the battle of Antietam his horse was shot from under him, and for gallant conduct while in command of a brigade at Fredericksburg he was complimented by the general commanding the division. At the request of Gen. Grant, Gen. Devens in April, 1865, was commissioned major-general by brevet for gallantry and good conduct at the capture of Richmond. He was mustered out of service, at his own request, at Washington, in June, 1866, after a brilliant military career of five years and three months. He was elected national commander of the G. A. R. to succeed Gen. Burnside, and has also served as commander of the Military Order Loyal Legion of Massachusetts, as well as of the military societies of the army of the Potomac and of the James, and of the sixth army corps. In 1867 Gov. Bullock appointed Gen. Devens one of the judges of the superior court of Massachusetts, and in 1873 Gov. Washburn made him one of the judges of the supreme court. On March 10, 1877, he became a member of President Hayes's cabinet, taking the portfolio of Attorney-General. Upon returning to Massachusetts, Gen. Devens was reappointed to the supreme bench by Gov. Long.

Dexter, John S., district supervisor, nomination of, 91.

Dexter, Samuel, Secretary of War under President John Adams; b. Massachusetts, May 14, 1761; graduated from Harvard College in 1781; studied law and admitted to the bar; member of the state house of representatives, 1788-1790, elected a Representative from Massachusetts to the 3d Congress as a Federalist; elected to the United States Senate, serving from Dec. 2, 1799, until he resigned in June, 1800; appointed Secretary of War, May 13, 1800, and Secretary of the Treasury, Dec. 31, 1800; declined the mission to Spain offered him by President Madison; while on his way home with his family from Washington, D. C., died at Athens, N. Y., May 3, 1816; published The Progress of Science (a poem), 1780, also Speeches and Political Papers, and several other political pamphlets.

Diaz, A. J., arrest and imprisonment of, by Cuban authorities, 5516.

Diaz, Porfirio, revolution in Mexico and installation of, as President, 4419, 6333.

Dick, Charles; lawyer; b. Akron, Ohio, Nov. 3, 1858; served in the Eighth Ohio Volunteer Infantry in Cuba in the war with Spain; represented the Nineteenth Ohio District in the 55th, 56th, 57th, and 58th Congresses; instrumental in securing the enactment of the Dick Militia law, and raising pay of army and navy; elected March 2, 1904, United States Senator for the short and long terms from Ohio.

Dickerson, Mahlon (brother of Philemon Dickerson), Secretary of the Navy under Presidents Jackson and Van Buren; born at Hanover, N. J., April 17, 1770; graduated from Princeton College in 1789; studied law and in 1773 was admitted to the bar; began the practice of his profes-

sion at Philadelphia; quartermaster-general of Pennsylvania, 1805-1808; recorder of the city court of Philadelphia, 1808-1810; returned to New Jersey; member of the state house of representatives in 1814; governor of New Jersey, 1815-17; elected United States Senator from New Jersey as a State Rights Democrat; serving from December 1, 1817, to March 2, 1833; appointed Secretary of the Navy June 30, 1834, and reappointed by President Van Buren; United States district judge of the district of New Jersey; delegate to the state constitutional convention in 1844; president of the American Institute, 1846-1848; died at his home in Succasunna, Morris County, N. J., Oct. 5, 1853.

Dickinson, Don. McDonald, Postmaster-general under President Cleveland, born Jan. 17, 1846, at Port Ontario, Oswego Co., N. Y. His ancestors were among the early settlers of Massachusetts, and his father and grandfather natives of the state. The first of the family who came to America was John Dickinson, a member of the Continental congress of 1774, president of the executive council, and one of the founders of Dickson College, Carlisle, Pa., to whom Jonathan Dickinson, chief justice of the province of Pennsylvania in 1719, was also related in the direct line. The father of Mr. Dickinson in 1820 explored the shores of lakes Erie, Huron and Michigan in a birch-bark canoe, and in 1848 removed to Michigan, settling in St. Clair county, where his son received his primary education in the public schools, and entering the law department of the University of Michigan, was graduated before reaching his majority. The interval prior to his admission to the bar he spent in studying the management of cases and the practical application of the philosophy and logis of law. In 1867 he entered upon a successful and lucrative practice, being concerned in all of the leading cases under the bankruptcy act of that year. In 1872 he entered political life, and in 1876, as chairman of the state democratic central committee, conducted the Tilden campaign, being brought into close relations with that statesman until his death. As member of the national democratic committee in 1884-85, he enjoyed the full confidence and esteem of President Cleveland, who in 1888 called him to a seat in his cabinet, being the fourth representative of Michigan to be honored thus.

Dickinson, Jacob McGavock, of Nashville, Tenn., Secretary of War in President Taft's Cabinet; b. Jan. 30, 1851, Columbus, Miss.; graduated from the University of Nashville; studied law at Columbia College, New York, in Paris, and at the University of Leipzig; L.L. D., Columbia University of New York, University of Illinois and Yale; Assistant Attorney-General of the United States from Feb. 13, 1895, to March 8, 1897; in 1903 appeared as counsel for the United States before the Alaskan Boundary Tribunal in London; Assistant Professor of Latin in the University of Nashville; served several times by special appointment as judge on the Supreme Bench of Tennessee; was General Counsel of the Illinois Central Railroad Company at the time of appointment as Secretary of War.

Dickson, James C., receiver of public moneys, nomination of, withdrawn and reasons therefor, 1040.

Dickson, Walter, outrages committed on family of, in Palestine, 3015.

Dies, Martin; b. in Jackson Parish, La., March 13, 1870; moved to Texas with his parents in 1876; elected county judge of Tyler County in 1894; district attorney of the first judicial district of Texas in 1898; elected to the 61st, 62d, 63d and 64th Congresses from Texas.

Dillingham, William Paul; b. Waterbury, Vt., Dec. 12, 1843; admitted to the bar in 1867; member of the Vermont house of representatives in 1876 and again in 1884; a state senator in 1878 and again in 1880; governor of Vermont from 1888 to 1890; Oct. 18, 1900, was elected United States Senator from Vermont to fill a vacancy caused by the death of Justic S. Morrill; Oct. 15, 1902, elected to succeed himself, and re-elected Oct. 21, 1908, for the term ending March 3, 1915.

Dingle, W. B., arrest and maltreatment of, at Heidelberg, Baden, 2772.

Dingley, Nelson, Jr. (1832-1899); statesman; b. Durham, Me.; for thirty years (1856-86) he was editor of the *Lewiston Journal;* sat in the State Legislature, 1862-73; and was speaker, 1863-64; governor of Maine, 1874-75; sat in Congress, 1881-99; framed the Dingley tariff bill of 1897.

Dinsmore, Silas, commissioner to treat with Indians, 423.

Dix, John Adams; soldier, statesman; b. Boscawen, N. H., July 24, 1798; joined the army in 1812 and served through the second war with England; while serving in the army studied law, and in 1828 resigned his commission as captain and took up practice of law at Cooperstown, N. Y.; served as adjutant-general and secretary of state of New York; was elected to the state legislature and United States Senator; appointed Secretary of the Treasury, Jan. 9, 1861; while in this position, with the Confederacy organized and the authority of the Federal Government defied in the South, he sent to Lieutenant Caldwell in the revenue service at New Orleans the historic message: "If any one attempts to haul down the American flag, shoot him on the spot"; organized and sent into service during the Civil War seventeen regiments of militia; major-general of volunteers, June, 1861; as commander of the Seventh Army Corps he secured control of the whole country between the Pamunkey and Rappahannock rivers, and cut off Gen. Lee's communication with Richmond, and had the Confederate capital almost at his mercy in June, 1863, when he was ordered to fall back to the defense of Washington; during the draft riots in New York, in 1863, he was appointed commander of the Department of the East and succeeded in subduing the disorder and restoring business confidence; first president of the Union Pacific Railway Company, 1863-68; served through the Civil War, and was appointed minister to France; and later was elected governor of New York, 1872; died New York City, April 21, 1879.

Dix, John A.:
Applications to go south across military lines to be made to, 3302.
Authority given to, while commanding at Baltimore, 3313.
Commissioner to examine cases of State prisoners, 3310.
Mentioned, 3279.
Prisoners of war released to report to, 3303.

Dixon, Lincoln; b. Vernon, Jennings Co., Ind., Feb. 9, 1860; elected prosecuting attorney for the sixth judicial circuit of the state in 1884; re-elected in 1886, 1888, and 1890; was elected to the 59th, 60th, 61st, 62d, 63d and 64th Congresses from Indiana.

Dobbin, James Cochrane, Secretary of the Navy under President Pierce; born at Fayetteville, N. C., in 1814; graduated from the University of North Carolina in 1832; studied law, and admitted to the bar in 1825; began practicing at Fayetteville; elected a Representative from North Carolina to the Twenty-ninth Congress as a Democrat; declined to be a candidate for re-election; member of the house of commons in 1848, 1850, and 1852, and in 1850 was speaker; delegate to the national Democratic convention at Baltimore in 1852; Secretary of the Navy from March 7, 1853, to March 6, 1857; died at Fayetteville, N. C., Aug. 4, 1857.

Dodge, Grenville M.; engineer, soldier; b. Danvers, Mass., April 12, 1831; received a liberal education and graduated at the military university, Norwich, Vt.; studied civil engineering; chief engineer of the Union Pacific Railroad; entered the Union Army as a captain and left the service as a major-general; elected a Representative from Iowa to the 40th Congress as a Republican; located in New York City, but still retained residence in Iowa; president of Society of Army of Tennessee; president of New York commandery of Loyal Legion; president of commission to inquire into the management of the war with Spain; extensively interested in western railroad building and management; vice-president of the Grant Monument Association.

Dodge Henry (father of Augustus C. Dodge); soldier and statesman; b. Vincennes, Ind., Oct. 12, 1782; received a limited education; emigrated to Missouri; served in the Black Hawk and other Indian wars; left the army as colonel of the First United States Dragoons July, 1836; governor of Wisconsin from July 4, 1836, to 1841; elected a delegate from Wisconsin to the 27th Congress as a Democrat; re-elected to the 28th Congress; again appointed governor of Wisconsin, Feb. 6, 1846; elected United States Senator from Wisconsin as a Democrat, and re-elected, serving from June 23, 1848, to March 3, 1857.

Dodge, Henry, troops in Indian campaign under command of, 1332.

Dodge, William E.; merchant; b. Hartford, Conn., Sept. 4, 1805; received a liberal education; moved to New York in 1818; became a clerk in a store, and in 1826 commenced business on his own account; established the house of Phelps, Dodge & Co., of which he was the head for forty years; delegate to the peace convention in 1861; claimed to have been elected a Representative from New York to the 39th Congress (James Brooks having received the certificate of election and taken his seat), and on April 6, 1866, the House decided that Mr. Dodge was entitled to the seat, serving from April 6, 1866, to March 3, 1867; died Feb. 9, 1883, at New York City.

Dodge, William E., member of Indian commission, 3977.

Dole, Sanford Ballard; judge of the supreme court of Hawaii, head of the provisional government of Hawaii, and president of the republic of Hawaii from the

overthrow of the kingdom till the annexation of the islands to the United States;
b. Hawaii, April 23, 1844, of American
parents; admitted to the bar in Boston, and
returned to Hawaii; the provisional government, of which he was the head, negotiated a treaty of annexation with the
United States, but President Cleveland withdrew the treaty and requested President
Dole to relinquish to the queen her authority in the islands; Dole refused and later
(1898) visited the United States and Congress passed an act annexing the islands to
the United States.

Dole, Sanford B.:
 Member of commission to recommend
 legislation for Hawaiian Islands,
 6333.
 Minister of foreign affairs of provisional government of Hawaii, letter from, transmitted, 5906, 5907.
 Sovereignty of Hawaiian Islands
 transferred to United States by,
 6332.

Dole, William P., treaty with Indians
 concluded by, 3393, 3394, 3395, 3400,
 3402, 3411, 3413.

Dolliver, Jonathan Prentiss; b. near
Kingwood, Preston Co., Va., (now W. Va.),
Feb. 6, 1858; graduated in 1875 from the
West Virginia University; was admitted to
the bar in 1878; elected to the 51st Con-
gress from Iowa; member of the House
also in the 52d, 53d, 54th, 55th, and 56th
Congresses; Aug. 23, 1900, appointed United
States Senator to fill a vacancy; elected
Jan. 21, 1902, to succeed himself; re-elect-
ed, 1907, senator from Iowa; died in 1911.

Donaldson, Edward, thanks of Congress
 to, recommended, 3277.

Donaldson, Joseph, Jr., treaty with Algiers concluded by, 184.

Donelson, Andrew J., minister to Germany, nomination of, 2455.
 Recall of, referred to, 2549.

Doremus, Frank E.; b. Venango County,
Pa., Aug. 31, 1865; served in the Legislature of Michigan 1891-2; has been assistant
corporation counsel and controller of the
city of Detroit; elected to the 62d, 63d
and 64th Congresses from Michigan.

Dorn, Andrew J., commissioner for the
 United States, treaty made by, with
 the Senecas, August, 1854, 2829.

Doty, James Duane; statesman; b. New
York in 1799; received a common school
education; moved to Menasha, Wis.; elected
a delegate from Wisconsin to the 25th and
26th Congresses; governor of Wisconsin
1841-1844; elected a Representative from
Wisconsin to the 31st Congress as a Democrat and to the 32d Congress as a Free-soil
Democrat; appointed treasurer of Utah and
governor of that Territory in 1864 by President Lincoln; died at Salt Lake City, June
13, 1865.

Doty, James D.:
 Mentioned, 3397.
 Treaty with Indians concluded by,
 1912.

Doughton, Robert L.; b. Laurel Springs,
N. C., Nov. 7, 1863; educated in the public
schools and at Laurel Springs High School;
farmer, stock raiser, and banker; president
of the Deposit and Savings Bank of North
Wilkesboro, N. C.; elected to the state senate from the thirty-fifth senatorial district
November, 1908; elected to the 62d, 63d
and 64th Congresses from North Carolina.

Douglas, James, governor of Vancouver Island, repayment of sum advanced by, recommended, 3067.

Douglas, Stephen Arnold (1813-1861);
politician; b. Brandon, Vt.; elected judge
of the supreme court of Illinois, 1841; member of Congress from Illinois, 1843-47;
United States Senator, 1847-61; author of
the "Squatter sovereignty" doctrine, and
reported the Kansas-Nebraska bill, 1854;
nominated by the Democratic party in 1860
against Lincoln for the Presidency; he was
known as the "Little Giant."

Douglass, Frederick, recorder of deeds,
 District of Columbia, resignation of,
 referred to, 5116.

Drexel, Joseph W., chairman of executive committee on pedestal of Statue
 of Liberty Enlightening the World,
 4982.

Driscoll, Daniel A.; b. Buffalo, N. Y.,
March 6, 1875; elected to the 61st, 62d,
63d and 64th Congresses from New York.

Drum, Richard C., Adjutant-General:
 Union and Confederate flags, return
 of, to respective States, recommended by, 5163.
 Proposition withdrawn, 5164.

Duane, William J.; printer, editor, author, lawyer; Secretary of the Treasury
under President Jackson; b. 1780, in Clon-
mel, Ireland; part of his boyhood was
spent in India, but his father came to
America in 1795, and edited a paper, the
Aurora, published in Philadelphia; the son
learned the printing trade and devoted some
years to the business, and also studied
law; admitted to the bar in 1815; he was
deeply interested in education, and his legal
ability won him fame and fortune; he was
selected by Stephen Girard to draw the
will by which that noted philanthropist
bequeathed some $6,000,000 to educational
and eleemosynary institutions in Philadelphia; every effort was made by Girard's
relatives to break the will, but the terms
were so explicit that not a flaw could be
found in it; Mr. Duane's wide reputation as
a lawyer induced President Jackson to appoint him in 1833 Secretary of the Treasury upon the refusal of Secretary McLane
to remove the public deposits from the
Bank of the United States upon the order
of the President; Mr. Duane, after his appointment, also refused to remove the deposits, and Jackson removed him from the
office and appointed Roger B. Taney, who
acceded to the President's demands; Mr.
Duane resumed the practice of law in Philadelphia, where he died Sept. 27, 1865; he
published "Narrative and Correspondence
Concerning the Removal of the Deposits,"
1838; "The Law of Nations Investigated,"
1809; "Letters on Internal Improvements,"
1811.

Dullye, Eugene, expulsion of, from
 Prussia, 3123.

Dunbar, William, appointed to explore Washita River, 387.

Dunham, Aaron, district supervisor, nomination of, 91.

Dunlap, Robert P.; lawyer; b. Maine in 1789; graduated from Bowdoin College in 1815; studied law; began practicing at Brunswick, Me.; member of the State house of representatives 1821-1823 and of the State senate 1823-1832; president of the State senate four years; an executive councilor in 1833; governor of Maine 1834-1838; elected a Representative from Maine to the 28th Congress as a Democrat, and re-elected to the 29th Congress; collector of customs at Portland, Me., 1848-49; president of the board of overseers of the Bowdoin College; died at Brunswick, Me., Oct. 20, 1859.

Dunlap, Robert P.:
Correspondence regarding imprisonment of Ebenezer S. Greely, 1575, 1622.

Correspondence regarding northeastern boundary. (See Northeastern Boundary.)

Du Pont, Henry Algernon; b. Eleutherean Mills, Newcastle Co., Del., July 30, 1838; entered the University of Pennsylvania at Philadelphia in 1855, and United States Military Academy July 1, 1856; commissioned second lieutenant, Engineers, 1861; first lieutenant, Artillery, 1861; served with honor throughout Civil War; twice brevetted for gallant and meritorious services, and awarded a medal by Congress; resigned from the army, 1875, and became president and general manager of the Wilmington and Northern Railroad Company; elected United States Senator June 13, 1906, from Delaware to serve the unexpired portion of the term beginning March 4, 1905.

Dupont, Samuel F.:
Mentioned, 3279.

Thanks of Congress to, recommended, 3265, 3271.

Dupre, Henry G.; b. Opelousas, St. Landry Parish, La., July 28, 1873; educated in the public schools at Opelousas and graduated in 1892 from the Tulane University of Louisiana, at New Orleans, with the degree of bachelor of arts; subsequently received the degree of bachelor of laws from the same institution; served as assistant city attorney of New Orleans from 1900 to 1910; elected to the House of Representatives of Louisiana; re-elected in 1904 and in 1908; elected speaker of the House of Representatives of Louisiana for the session of 1908; elected to the Sixty-first Congress Nov. 8, 1910, to fill the unexpired term occasioned by the death of the Hon. Samuel L. Gilmore; re-elected to the 62d, 63d and 64th Congresses.

Dyer, Leonidas C.; b. Warren County, Mo., June 11, 1871; educated in the public schools, Central Wesleyan College, at Warrenton,. Mo., and the law department of the Washington University, city of St. Louis; served as assistant circuit attorney of St. Louis; served in the Spanish War; elected to the 62d, 63d and 64th Congresses from Missouri.

Eads, James Buchanan; engineer; b. May 23, 1820, in Lawrenceburgh, Ind.; became self-supporting at an early age in St. Louis, and during his spare time applied himself to the study of engineering and allied sciences without the aid of school or teacher; while clerk on a Mississippi River steamboat he invented the diving-bell boat to recover cargoes from sunken vessels, and, later, a larger boat, to pump sand and water from sunken vessels and raise the cargo intact. These inventions proved successful and profitable and Mr. Eads in 1845 established a glass factory in St. Louis, the first west of Ohio; in 1856 he proposed to Congress a plan to remove all snags, sunken hulks, wrecks and other obstructions from the western rivers; the measure passed the house but failed in the senate for want of time. At the outbreak of civil war he was engaged by President Lincoln to construct light draught gunboats to patrol western and southern rivers. Inside a hundred days he had built eight iron-clad steamboats carrying 107 large guns. These were the first iron-clads built in the United States, and were used in the capture of Fort Henry Feb. 6, 1862 (q. v.), more than a month before the *Merrimac* and *Monitor* were finished; later constructed six turreted iron vessels, in which 11-inch and 15-inch guns, worked by steam, were loaded and fired every forty-five seconds, on a different plan from those of Ericsson and Coles, constituting the first manipulation of heavy artillery by steam. Eads' next important achievement was the design and construction, from 1867 to 1874, of the steel arch bridge over the Mississippi at St. Louis, a marvel of engineering skill. In 1874 he began the work of deepening the mouth of the Mississippi by building parallel jetties out into the sea across the bar of sediment that had been deposited by the spreading waters. This problem had baffled the skill of engineers for forty years; the price agreed upon was $5,250,-000, and to secure the first payment half the work had to be executed. President Grant (page 4362) and President Hayes (page 4524) made reports on the progress of the work which was completed in 1879; published a plan for a ship railway across the Isthmus of Tehuantepec, Mexico, by which ships and their cargoes could be safely and inexpensively transported from ocean to ocean; engaged to devise improvements for St. John's River, Florida; Sacramento River, California; the harbor of Toronto, Canada;; the port of Vera Cruz, Mexico; visited the great rivers and canals of Europe, Asia and Africa; received degree of LL.D. from University of Michigan; first American to receive the Albert medal (British); died March 16, 1887, in Nassau, N. P.

Eads, James B.:
Grants to, for construction of jetties in Mississippi River, order regarding, 4282.

Improvement of South Pass of Mississippi River, under, discussed, 4362, 4524.

Eaton, Dorman B., chairman Civil Service Commission, report of, discussed, 4588.

Eaton, John, publication of second edition of Second Arctic Expedition suggested by, 4666.

Eaton, John Henry; Secretary of War under President Jackson; b. Tennessee in 1800; received a liberal education; studied law and admitted to the bar; practiced at Nashville; elected United States Senator from Tennessee (in place of George W. Campbell, resigned), and unanimously re-elected, serving from Nov. 16, 1818, to March, 1829, when he resigned; appointed Secretary of War; resigned June 18, 1831; appointed governor of Florida 1834-1836; minister to Spain 1836-1840; died at Washington, D. C., Nov. 17, 1856.

Eaton, John H., treaty with Indians concluded by, 1271.

Eaton, William:
Correspondence regarding war with Tripoli transmitted, 379.

Eckert, T. T., negotiations for, and correspondence regarding restoration of peace, 3461.

Edgcomb, Willard W., treaty with Orange Free State concluded by, 4116.

Edmunds, George F.; lawyer, President *pro tem* of Senate; b. Feb. 1, 1828, in Richmond, Vt.; received a public school education and the instruction of a private tutor; studied and practiced law; member of the State legislature of Vermont in 1854, 1855, 1857, 1858, and 1859, serving three years as speaker; a member of the State senate, and its presiding officer *pro tempore* in 1861 and 1862; appointed to the United States Senate as a Republican to fill the vacancy caused by the death of Solomon Foot, and took his seat April 5, 1866; in the Senate he had charge of the tenure of office act, and was active in the impeachment proceedings against President Johnson; he helped to secure the passage of the reconstruction measures; sided with Grant in his difficulties with Sumner, Schurz, and Trumbull; member of the Electoral Commission in 1876-77; with Senator Thurman he pushed through the Pacific Railroads funding act; was the sponsor in the Senate of the act for the suppression of polygamy in Utah; when Vice-President Arthur became President Senator Edmunds was elected President *pro tempore* of the Senate; at the Republican National Conventions held in Chicago in 1880 he received 34 votes for the nomination for President of the United States, and four years later received 93; elected by the legislature for the remainder of the term ending March 4, 1869; re-elected for the terms ending in 1875, 1881, 1887, and 1893; resigned Nov. 1, 1891; member of the electoral commission of 1876; after leaving the United States Senate he moved to Philadelphia, Pa., where he engaged in the practice of law.

Edwards, Charles Gordon; b. Tattnall Co., Ga., July 2, 1878; educated at Gordon Institute, Barnesville, Ga., Agricultural College, Lake City, Fla., and the University of Georgia, graduating B. L. from the latter 1898; moved to Savannah; Oct. 11, 1906, elected to the 60th, 61st, 62d, 63d and 64th Congresses from Georgia.

Edwards, Ninian; lawyer, jurist; b. in Montgomery Co., Md., March, 1775; moved to Kentucky and was twice elected to the legislature; later judge of the general court of Kentucky, of the circuit court, of the court of appeals, and finally chief justice of the state, all before reaching his thirty-second year; appointed by President Madison to be governor of Illinois Territory in 1809, to which office he was three times reappointed; when Illinois was admitted to the Union, he was elected to the United States Senate, serving from 1818-24; elected governor in 1826, serving till 1831; died of cholera in Belleville, Ill., July 20, 1833.

Edwards, Ninian:
Minister to Mexico, examination of, by committee referred to, 808.
Treaty with Indians concluded by, 589.

Egan, Patrick, minister to Chile. (See *Baltimore*, The.)

Ehrman, Felix, consular correspondence of, 6788, 6792.

Ekin, James A., member of commission to try assassins of President Lincoln, etc., 3534.

Elder, Samuel S., member of Gun Foundry Board, 4748.

Elkins, Stephen Benton; b. Perry Co., Ohio, Sept. 26, 1841; was admitted to the bar in 1864, and went to New Mexico, and began the practice of law; was a member of the Territorial legislative assembly of New Mexico in 1864-65; elected to the 43d and 44th Congresses; later moved to West Virginia and devoted himself to business affairs; appointed Secretary of War Dec. 17, 1891, in President Harrison's Cabinet; in 1894 was elected to the United States Senate from West Virginia, and re-elected in 1901 and 1907.

Ellerbe, James Edwin; b. near Marion, S. C., Jan. 12, 1867; entered Wofford College, at Spartanburg, S. C., 1884, spending three years; graduated, 1887; A. B.; elected to the state legislature; elected to the 59th, 60th, 61st and 62d Congresses from South Carolina without opposition.

Ellery, Charles, lieutenant in Navy, nomination of, and reasons therefor, 1129.

Ellicott, Andrew, United States commissioner for running line between United States and Spanish possessions, 962.

Ellis, Albert G., treaty with Indians concluded by, 2529.

Ellis, Powhatan, Minister to Mexico:
Mentioned, 1790.
Nomination of, 1537.

Ellsworth, Oliver (1745-1807); jurist and statesman; b. Windsor, Conn.; represented Connecticut in the United States Senate, 1789-96; received 11 electoral votes for President in the third electoral college, 1796; chief justice of the United States Supreme Court, 1796-1800; minister extraordinary to France, 1799.

Ellsworth, Oliver, minister to France, nomination of, 274.

Emerson, John B., petition of, regarding use of his invention referred to, 2528.

Emery, A. H., compensation to, for services in perfecting testing machine recommended, 4540.

Emmons, G. T., reports on Alaskan Indians, 7071.

Emory, U. H., map of Texas compiled by, 2166.

Emory, W. H., report on survey of boundary between Mexico and United States transmitted, 2915.

Emory, William H., commander of the *Bear* in Lady Franklin Bay Expedition, 4835.

Endicott, William Crowninshield, Secretary of War under President Cleveland; born in Salem, Mass., Nov. 19, 1826. He was the son of William Putnam and Mary (Crowninshield) Endicott. He is descended directly from Gov. John Endicott, who came to Salem in 1628, and on his mother's side is a grandson of the Hon. Jacob Crowninshield, who was a well-known member of congress in the early part of this century. Mr. Endicott was educated in Salem schools and in 1843 entered Harvard, from which he was graduated in 1847. Soon after graduating he studied law in the office of Nathaniel J. Lord, then the leading member of the Essex bar, and in the Harvard Law School at Cambridge. He was called to the bar in 1850, and began the practice of law in Salem in 1851. He was a member of the Salem common council in 1852, and in 1853 he entered into partnership with Jairus W. Perry (who is well known throughout the country as the author of "Perry and Trusts") under the firm name of Perry & Endicott. From 1857 to 1864 he was solicitor of the city of Salem. In 1884 he was the Democratic candidate for governor of Massachusetts, but was defeated. In 1885 he became secretary of war, and held office to the end of Mr. Cleveland's term. Mr. Endicott is president of the Peabody Academy of Science in Salem, which position he has held since 1868, and is a member of the corporation of Harvard, and one of the trustees of the Peabody Education Fund.

Endicott, William C., Secretary of War:
Union and Confederate flags, return of, and Confederate flags, return of, to respective states recommended, 5163.
Proposition withdrawn, 5164.

Eno, Amos F., secretary of Arkansas, appointment of, revoked, 3377.

Ericsson, John; engineer, inventor; b. Langbanshyttan, Sweden, July 31, 1803; appointed cadet in the Swedish corps of engineers, 1814, and rose to the rank of captain; early displayed precocious talent as an inventor; made many improvements in the application of artificial draught to locomotives, and in 1829 built an engine which, in competition with Stephenson's locomotive, ran a mile in 56 seconds, and inaugurated the era of rapid railway travel; English indifference to his inventions caused him to move to America in 1839; here he applied the screw propeller principle to steamboats, and in 1843 to United States war ships; originated the range-finder; discarded the breaching for heavy guns, and placed the machinery of war vessels below the water line, and protected it with coal bunkers; made the first practical application of twin screw propellers; the success of his ironclad *Mon-*

Faben, J. W., Dominican minister, mentioned, 4017.

Fairbanks, Charles Warren; lawyer, legislator, and twenty-sixth Vice-President of the United States; b. Union Co., Ohio, 1852; removed to Indianapolis, 1874, and admitted to the bar in that year; elected United States Senator, 1897, to succeed Daniel W. Voorhees, and re-elected, 1903; Joint High Commissioner at Quebec to adjust Canadian difficulties, 1898; Vice-President of the United States with Roosevelt, 1905-1909.

Fairchild, Charles Stebbins, Secretary of the Treasury under President Cleveland; born in Cazenovia, N. Y., April 30, 1842. His father was Sidney T. Fairfield, for many years attorney for the New York Central R. R., and one of the leading men of central New York. Young Fairchild studied at the common schools and at the Oneida Conference Seminary at Cazenovia, where he prepared for a university course, and went to Harvard in 1859, graduating in the class of 1863. He determined to follow the legal profession, entered the Harvard Law School, and completed the prescribed course in 1865, receiving the degree of Bachelor of Laws. He then removed to Albany, where he continued his legal studies, and in 1866 was admitted to the bar; April 1, 1887, President Cleveland appointed him secretary of the treasury. He continued to fill that office until the close of Mr. Cleveland's administration in March, 1889.

Fairchild, Lucius:
Letter of, and memorial relative to Paris Exposition transmitted, 3668.
Member of Cherokee Commission, 5481.

Fairfield, John, correspondence regarding northeastern boundary. (See Northeastern Boundary.)

Faris-El-Hakim, maltreatment of, in Egypt, and indemnity for, referred to, 3278.

Farman, Mr., mentioned, 4564.

Farnsworth, Hiram W., treaty with Indians, concluded by, 3277, 3413.

Farr, John R.; b. Scranton, Pa., July 18, 1857; educated in public schools, School of the Lackawanna, Scranton, Pa., Phillips Academy, Andover, Mass., and Lafayette College, Easton, Pa.; newsboy, printer, publisher, in the real estate business; served in the Pennsylvania House of Representatives, 1891, 1893, 1895, 1897, 1899; speaker session of 1899; author of free school book and compulsory education laws; elected to the 62d, 63d and 64th Congresses from Pennsylvania.

Farragut, David Glasgow; Admiral of the Navy; b. Campbells Station, near Knoxville, Tenn., July 5, 1801; entered the navy as midshipman, 1810; promoted to commander in 1841; ordered to Vera Cruz in Mexican War too late for service; began operations during Civil War, against New Orleans, April 24, 1862; opened the lower Mississippi and twice ran the batteries at Vicksburg; July 16, 1862, Congress created the rank of rear-admiral, and conferred it with thanks upon Farragut; Aug. 5, 1864, he passed the fortifications and floating batteries of Mobile Bay, and maintained a blockade of the city till November; for this exploit he was presented by the citizens of New York with $50,000 to buy a home, and Congress created the higher rank of vice-admiral, and the President nominated Rear-Admiral Farragut for the office; July 25, 1865, the exalted rank of admiral was established, and the Senate confirmed Farragut therein; in command on James River at fall of Richmond; died in Portsmouth, N. H., Aug. 14, 1870, and buried in Woodlawn Cemetery, New York.

Farragut, David G.:
Thanks of Congress to, recommended, 3276.
Thanks of President tendered, 3440.

Farwell, John V., member of Indian commission, 3977.

Fauchet, Mr., attempted seizure of, by commander of the *Africa,* 3344.

Faure, President, death of, 6367.

Fay, Theodore S., mentioned, 2205.

Fergusson, Harvey B.; b. Sept. 9, 1848, in Pickens County, Ala.; educated at Washington and Lee University, graduating with the degree of M. A. in 1874; and in the law department in 1875; practiced law in Wheeling, W. Va., from 1876 to 1882; removed in 1882 to New Mexico; residing at Albuquerque; delegate in the 55th Congress; member of the Democratic national committee from 1896 to 1904; elected as Representative in Congress from New Mexico at the first state election on Nov. 7, 1911, and again to the 63d and 64th Congresses.

Ferris, Scott; b. Nov. 7, 1877, Neosho, Newton Co., Mo.; graduated from Kansas City School of Law, 1901; elected to the legislature of Oklahoma in 1904, representing the twenty-second district; elected to the 60th, 61st, 62d, 63d and 64th Congresses from Oklahoma.

Ferry, Thomas W.; lumberman, legislator; b. June 1, 1827, in Mackinac, Mich.; received a public school education; engaged in lumber business with his father and brothers at Grand Haven; member of the house of representatives of Michigan, 1850; State senate, 1856; vice-president for Michigan in the Chicago Republican Convention, 1860; appointed 1864 to represent Michigan on the board of managers of the Gettysburg Soldiers' National Cemetery, and reappointed 1867; elected to 39th, 40th, and 41st Congresses, and reelected to the 42d Congress, but did not take his seat, having been elected to the United States Senate to succeed Jacob M. Howard, Republican; took his seat in the Senate March 4, 1871; chosen President *pro tempore* March 9 and 19, and again Dec. 20, 1875, and by the death of Vice-President Wilson became acting Vice-President, serving as such until March 4, 1877; actually President from 12 o'clock noon Sunday, March 4, 1877, till the same hour next day, when President Hayes was inaugurated; represented President Grant at the opening of the Centennial Exposition in Philadelphia, July 4, 1876; reelected a Senator Jan. 17, 1877; reelected President *pro tempore* of the Senate March 5, 1877, Feb. 26, 1878, April 17, 1878, and March 3, 1879; died in 1896.

Folger, Charles J.; lawyer, jurist; Secretary of the Treasury under President Arthur; b. April 16, 1818, in Nantucket, Mass.; removed when a boy to Geneva, N. Y.; graduated Hobart College, studied law and was admitted to the bar in 1839; gave evidence of judicial ability while serving as a justice of the peace in Geneva; in 1844 appointed Judge of the Court of Common Pleas in Ontario County, later Master in Chancery until the Chancery Court was abolished in 1846; County Judge of Ontario County 1851 to 1855; was a Silas Wright Democrat and a Barn Burner, but when the Republican party was formed he became active in its work and was elected to the State Senate in 1861, serving eight years, most of the time leader of his party; member of the State Constitutional Convention of 1867; was a bitter opponent of Governor Reuben E. Fenton; became prominent in the contest between the Gould and Vanderbilt interests for control of the Erie Railroad; in the Senate he was the author of the famous protective labor bill, which guaranteed freedom of action to labor men; appointed Assistant Treasurer of the United States at New York by President Grant; in 1870 was elected an Associate Justice of the Court of Appeals, and in 1880 became Chief Justice; in 1881 appointed by President Arthur to be Secretary of the Treasury; he was nominated for Governor of New York by the Republicans and defeated by Grover Cleveland; died Sept. 4, 1884.

Folger, Charles J., Secretary of Treasury, death of, announced and honors to be paid memory of, 4821.

Fonseca, Manuel D., President of Brazil, mentioned, 5617.

Foote, Andrew H.:
Thanks of Congress to, recommended, 3283.
Thanks of President tendered, 3305.

Ford, Henry, railroad concession to, 6770.

Fordney, Joseph Warren; b. Blackford Co., Ind., Nov. 5, 1853; located in Saginaw in 1869; was vice-president of the Saginaw Board of Trade; elected alderman in 1895, and re-elected in 1897; elected to the 56th, 57th, 58th, 59th, 60th, 61st, 62d, 63d and 64th Congresses from Michigan.

Forsyth, John; lawyer; b. Fredericksburg, Va., Oct. 22, 1780; he was attorney-general of the State, and a representative in Congress from Georgia, 1813-18 and 1823-27; United States Senator from Georgia, 1818-19, and for the term 1829-37; governor of Georgia in 1827, 1828 and 1829; minister to Spain, 1819-22; and was Secretary of State under President Jackson; died Washington City, Oct. 21, 1841.

Forsyth, John, Secretary of State:
Correspondence regarding—
Canadian outrages, 1618.
Claims against France. (See France, claims against.)
Northeastern boundary. (See Northeastern Boundary.)
Letter of, regarding treaty with France, 1345.
Outrages perpetrated by Canadians against the United States, Correspondence of, concerning, 1618.

Fort, Governor G. F. (N. J.), inaugural address quoted, 7515.

Forward, Oliver, treaty with Indians concluded by, 940.

Forward, Walter; lawyer, jurist; b. Connecticut, in 1786; elected to Congress from Pennsylvania, where he continued till 1825; appointed first comptroller of the treasury, 1841, holding this position until appointed by President Tyler, Secretary of the Treasury; many years presiding judge of the district court of Allegheny Co., Pa.; died Pittsburg, Pa., Nov. 24, 1852.

Forward, Walter, Secretary of Treasury, resignation of, mentioned, 2087.

Foss, George Edmund; b. Berkshire, Franklin Co., Vt., July 2, 1863; graduated from Harvard College in 1885; admitted to the bar and began the practice of law in Chicago; elected to the 54th, 55th, 56th, 57th, 58th, 59th, 60th, 61st, 62d and 64th Congresses from Illinois.

Foster, Charles; merchant; Secretary of the Treasury under President Benjamin Harrison; b. April 12, 1828, near Tiffin, Ohio; began to attend the public schools at the age of four years, and at twelve entered the Norwalk (Ohio) Academy; sickness in the family prevented his completion of the course of study and at nineteen he took entire charge of his father's store; extended liberal credit to families of soldiers in the civil war and was active in securing enlistments; the Foster mercantile business continued to expand under his direction for more than half a century; he was an ardent Republican, and in 1870 was elected to Congress by a majority of 726 in a district which had previously been Democratic by 1,800, and which at the same election gave a majority for the Democratic State ticket; he proved to be an able and industrious legislator and was reelected in 1872, 1874 and 1876; elected Governor of Ohio in 1879 after an exciting canvass in which he was dubbed "Calico Charlie" on account of his having been in the drygoods business; the idea was utilized as a feature of the campaign and calico became the keynote in the decorations; bands and marching clubs were uniformed in calico and whole towns were decorated with it; calico neckties became the rage, and newspapers were printed upon calico instead of paper; he was reelected two years later by an increased majority; defeated for Senator in 1890, and also for Congress; appointed Secretary of the Treasury by President Harrison in 1891; he adjusted the fifty-million-four-and-a-half-per cent. loan by continuing $25,364,500 at two per cent. interest and redeemed the remainder.

Foster, Charles, member of Sioux Commission, 5480.

Foster, C. W., member of board to examine quotas of States under call for troops, 3476.

Foster, George E., member of reciprocal trade conference between United States and Canada, 5675.

Foster, John Watson; lawyer, diplomat; b. Petersburg, Ind., March 2, 1836; served throughout the Civil War, rising to the rank of colonel and brevet brigadier-general; appointed minister to Mexico in

1873; transferred to St. Petersburg in 1880, and in 1883 appointed minister to Spain; served as Secretary of State in President Benjamin Harrison's Cabinet, 1892-96.

Foster, John W.:
Counsel for United States in Bering Sea question, 5748.
Member of reciprocal trade conference between United States and Canada, 5675.
Secretary of State, 5724.
Treaty for annexation of Hawaiian Island signed by, 5783.

Foster, Martin D.; b. near West Salem, Edwards, Co., Ill., Sept. 3, 1861; began the study of medicine in the Eclectic Medical Institute at Cincinnati, Ohio, graduating in 1882, also graduating from the Hahnemann Medical College at Chicago, Ill., in 1894, and began the practice of medicine in Olney, Ill., in 1882; was member of the Board of United States Examining Surgeons from 1885 to 1889, and from 1893 to 1897; elected to the 60th, 61st, 62d, 63d and 64th Congresses from Illinois.

Foster, Robert S., member of court to try assassins of President Lincoln, etc., 3534.

Foster, Stephen C., correspondence regarding northeastern boundary. (See Northeastern Boundary.)

Fox, Henry S., correspondence regarding—
Northeastern boundary. (See Northeastern Boundary.)
Outrages committed by Canadians on American frontiers, 1618.

Francis, David R.; merchant; Secretary of the Interior under President Cleveland; b. Oct. 1, 1850, in Richmond, Ky.; educated at Richmond Academy and Washington University at St. Louis; began commercial life in the wholesale grocery business in St. Louis and in 1877 established a commission business and engaged in the exportation of grain; President of the St. Louis Merchants' Exchange in 1884; elected Mayor of St. Louis in 1885, and Governor of Missouri in 1888; in 1896 President Cleveland appointed him Secretary of the Interior; for the purpose of taking practical charge of the Louisiana Purchase Exposition, held in St. Louis in 1904, Mr. Francis was made president of a company having twenty-four standing committees; the State of Missouri appropriated $1,000,000 for a State exhibit, the city of St. Louis $5,-000,000, the federal government $5,000,-000, and by private subscription another $5,000,000 was raised; to the management of this vast enterprise Mr. Francis devoted his time and energy without compensation.

Francis, John Brown; b. Philadelphia, Pa., May 31, 1794; on the death of his father he was reared by Nicholas Brown, of Providence, R. I., receiving a classical education and graduated from Brown University in 1808; attended the Litchfield Law School; never practiced; became interested in agricultural pursuits; secretary of the State Agricultural Society; a representative from Warwick in the State legislature in 1824, 1826-1828 and 1832; elected gov-

ernor in 1832 as a Jackson and Antimasonic candidate, serving until 1838; State senator in 1843; chancellor of Brown University 1841-1854; elected United States Senator (vice William Sprague, resigned), as a Law and Order candidate, serving from Feb. 7, 1844, to March 3, 1845; again State senator in 1847, 1849 and 1852-1854; died at Warwick, R. I., Aug. 9, 1864.

Francis, John B., correspondence regarding Dorr's Rebellion, 2141.

Francis, William B.; b. Updegraff, Jefferson County, Ohio, of German and Irish parentage; admitted to practice law in 1889; practiced in all State and Federal courts; delegate to the Democratic national convention at St. Louis in 1904; elected to the 62d, 63d and 64th Congresses from Ohio.

Franklin, Benjamin; author, printer, philosopher; b. Boston, Mass., Jan. 17, 1706; published "Poor Richard's Almanac," 1732-37, and later established a newspaper, and after that a magazine; he was the father and patron of the American Philosophical Society; postmaster of Philadelphia, and Postmaster-General for the Colonies; for his scientific investigations into the nature of lightning he was elected F. R. S. in 1775; was active in founding what later became the University of Pennsylvania; as early as 1754 he proposed a scheme of union for the thirteen colonies under a central government; served the American colonies as commissioner to England, where he secured the repeal of the stamp act, and did much to avert the revolution, but when his efforts at conciliation failed, became one of the signers of the Declaration of Independence, which he helped draft; acted as a diplomatic agent of the United States at Paris during Revolution; delegate in 1787 to the convention which drew up the United States Constitution; president of the Supreme Council of Pennsylvania (in effect governor of the State) 1785-88; died at Philadelphia, April 17, 1790.

Franklin, Benjamin, letter from President and decree of National Assembly of France on death of, 87.

Franklin, John; British rear-admiral; b. Spilsby, Lincolnshire, England, April 16, 1786; joined the navy in childhood and served at Copenhagen, Trafalgar and New Orleans (1815); led Arctic expeditions, 1818, 1819, 1825 and 1845; elected F. R. S., 1823, and knighted in 1829; set out in command of the *Erebus* and *Terror* (1845) in search of a northwest passage between the Atlantic and Pacific oceans north of America; after three years, no tidings having been received of the expedition, relief ships were sent out, and traces of the party were found, but it was not until 1859 that Captain McClintock, in command of the *Fox*, sent out by Lady Franklin in search of her husband, found a paper from one of the ships bearing the legend: "Sir John Franklin died June 11, 1847."

Franklin, Sir John, expedition in search of missing ships under command of:
Recommended, 2563.
Referred to, 2624.
Return of, under De Haven, 2668.
Token of thankfulness offered American officers in, by Great Britain, 2897.

Franklin, Samuel R., president of International Marine Conference at Washington, 5493.

Frear, Walter F., member of commission to recommend legislation for Hawaiian Islands, 6333.

Frear, William H., claim of, against France, 5198.

Frederick III., Emperor of Germany, death of, referred to, 5367.

Frederick, Empress Dowager, of Germany, death of, referred to, 6680.

Freeman, Mr., exploration of Red River by, discussed, 396.

Frelinghuysen, Frederick Theodore; lawyer; b. Millstone, N. J., Aug. 4, 1817; graduated Rutgers College, and admitted to the bar in 1839; appointed attorney-general of New Jersey, 1861 and 1866; United States Senator, 1866-69, and elected for full term beginning 1871; took prominent part in proceedings to impeach Andrew Johnson, and was selected to reply to the last annual message sent by the latter to Congress (p. 3870); refused President Grant's appointment as minister to England in 1870; appointed Secretary of State by President Arthur, 1881; died Newark, N. J., May 20, 1885.

Frelinghuysen, Frederick T., Secretary of State, 4710.

Frémont, John Charles; soldier, explorer; b. Savannah, Ga., Jan. 21, 1813; graduate Charleston (S. C.) College; became lieutenant of engineers in the War Department and conducted government explorations in the Rocky Mountains and California; in 1845, while heading an exploration expedition to the Pacific slope, he encountered the Mexican general, De Castro, who was proceeding to expel the American settlers from California; the settlers joined Frémont's forces, overcame the Mexicans, and declared themselves independent, with Frémont as governor; he joined with the naval forces of Commodore Stockton, who had been sent to conquer California; one of the first Senators from California, 1849-51; first Republican candidate for President, unsuccessfully opposing James Buchanan; surveyed a travel route from the Mississippi to San Francisco; appointed major-general of volunteers, May 14, 1861; served in Missouri and the Shenandoah Valley and resigned 1864; retired 1890, and died July 13, 1890.

Frémont, John C.:
Assigned to command of Mountain Department, 3312.

Court-martial in case of, 2430.
Death of, announced and honors to be paid memory of, 5541.
Mountain howitzer taken by, on Oregon expedition referred to, 2127.
Public accounts of, referred to, 2918.

Fromentin, Eligius; jurist; b. France; received a classical education; studied law; admitted to the bar and practiced at New Orleans; United States Senator from Louisiana from May 24, 1813, to March 3, 1819; appointed judge of the criminal court at New Orleans in 1821; appointed United States district judge for the district of Florida in January, 1822, but soon resigned and resumed the practice of law at New Orleans; his wife died of yellow fever and he also died within twenty-four hours at New Orleans, Oct. 6. 1822.

Fromentin, Eligius, misunderstanding of, with Andrew Jackson, 682.

Fruchier, John, impressed into military service of France, case of, 5199.

Frye, William Pierce; b. Lewiston, Me., Sept. 2, 1831; graduated at Bowdoin College; studied and practiced law; was a member of the state legislature in 1861, 1862 and 1867; mayor of the city of Lewiston in 1866-67; was attorney-general of the State of Maine in 1867, 1868 and 1869; received the degree of LL.D. from Bates College in July, 1881, and the same degree from Bowdoin College in 1889; representative in the 42d, 43d, 44th, 45th, 46th and 47th Congresses; was elected March 15, 1881, to the United States Senate from Maine to succeed James G. Blaine; appointed Secretary of State, March 18, 1881; was reelected in 1883, 1888, 1895, 1901 and again in 1907; was a member of the commission which met in Paris, September, 1898, to adjust terms of peace between the United States and Spain.

Frye, William P., member of Spanish-American Peace Commission, 6322.

Fuller, Charles E.; b. near Belvidere, Ill.; admitted to the bar of Illinois in 1870; served five terms in State legislature; raised a regiment for the Spanish-American War in 1898, and was commissioned colonel by Governor Tanner, but the regiment was never called into service; elected to the 58th, 59th, 60th, 61st, 62d and 64th Congresses from Illinois.

Fuller, Melville W., arbitrator in Venezuelan boundary dispute, 6338.
Member of Court of Arbitration, appointed, 6432.

Gadsden, James; soldier, diplomat; b. Charleston, S. C., May 15, 1788; appointed inspector-general of the army in 1820, with rank of colonel; minister to Mexico in 1853, and negotiated for the purchase of the strip of country just north of Mexico and now forming part of Arizona and New Mexico for $10,000,000; died Charleston, S. C., Dec. 26, 1858.

Gadsden, James:
Mentioned, 2770.
Rejection of nomination of, as colonel discussed, 695, 702.

Gage, Lyman J.; banker; Secretary of the Treasury under Presidents McKinley and Roosevelt; b. June 28, 1836, in De Ruyter, N. Y.; educated in Rome (N. Y.) Academy, and began life as a postal clerk; went to Chicago in 1855 and became a bank clerk, and finally president of the First National Bank of that city; was largely instrumental in securing for Chicago the World's Columbian Exposition and became its first president; during his term as Secretary of the Treasury the Spanish-American War broke out, and Mr. Gage recommended the issue of $200,000,000 of 3 per cent. bonds; the description of the cause and cure of financial panics, in his report for 1898, is one of the clearest expositions of the subject ever written; resigned from Roosevelt's cabinet and retired to private life, settling in San Diego, Cal.

Gaillard, John; statesman; b. St. Stephens District, S. C., Sept. 5, 1765; received a liberal education; elected a United States Senator from South Carolina (in place of Pierce Butler, resigned), serving from Jan. 31, 1805, until he died, at Washington, D. C., Feb. 26, 1826; President pro tempore of the Senate in the 11th, 13th, 14th, 15th, 16th, 17th and 18th Congresses.

Gaillard, John, letter of President Monroe to, referred to, 573.

Gaines, Edmund Pendleton; soldier; b. Culpepper Co., Va., March 20, 1777; entered the army in 1799, and was frequently promoted until he was made a major-general for the gallantry at Fort Erie in 1814; died New Orleans, La., June 6, 1849.

Gaines, Edmund P.:
Calls of, for volunteers or militia discussed, 2298, 2300.
Court of inquiry in case of, and opinion of, discussed, 1511.
Inspection reports of, referred to, 995.
Mentioned, 697.
Requisition of, for volunteers in Indian war not sanctioned by President, 1453.
Settlement of accounts of, referred to, 2130.
Victories of, over British troops, 533.

Gaines, John P.; native of Walton, Ky.; received a thorough English education; studied law and admitted to the bar at Walton, where he began practice; served in the Mexican war as major; captured at Incarnacion in January, 1847, and while in captivity elected a Representative from Kentucky to the 13th Congress as a Whig; governor of Oregon Territory 1850-1853; died in Oregon in 1858.

Gaines, John P., correspondence regarding seat of government of Oregon, 2684.

Gale, George, district supervisor, nomination of, 91.

Gallagher, Thomas; b. Concord, N. H., in 1850; moved to Chicago in 1866; elected to the 61st, 62d, 63d and 64th Congresses from Illinois.

Gallatin, Albert; author, banker, diplomat, statesman; b. Geneva, Switzerland, Jan. 29, 1761; elected United States Senator from Pennsylvania in 1795; at the expiration of his term he was appointed Secretary of the Treasury; became president of the National Bank of New York, and was active in the establishment of the New York University; his writings have been collected in six volumes and deal with the subjects of banking and currency, the Mexican War and its cost, the Indian tribes of North and Central America; died Astoria, N. Y., Aug. 12, 1849.

Gallatin, Albert:
Commissioner to settle boundary question with Georgia, 329.

Gallinger, Jacob H.; b. Cornwall, Ontario, March 28, 1837; received a common school and academic education; was a printer in early life; studied medicine and was graduated with honors in 1858, and followed the profession of medicine and surgery from April, 1862, until he entered Congress; was a member of the house of representatives of New Hampshire in 1872, 1873, and 1891; member of the constitutional convention in 1876; member of the State senate in 1878, 1879 and 1880; was surgeon-general of New Hampshire with the rank of brigadier-general in 1879-80; received the honorary degree of A. M. from Dartmouth College in 1885; elected to the 49th and 50th Congresses, and declined renomination to the 51st Congress, United States Senator from New Hampshire, for the term beginning March 4, 1891; re-elected in 1897, 1903 and in 1909, for the term ending March 3, 1915.

Gannett, Henry, member of Board on Geographic Names, 5647.

Ganon, N., correspondence regarding unlawful expedition in New York, 1616.

Garcia, Manuel, act granting pension to, vetoed, 5286.

Gardner, Augustus Peabody; b. Nov. 5, 1865; Member of the Massachusetts State Senate for two terms; served during the Spanish-American war; elected to the 57th Congress to fill a vacancy; and to the 58th, 59th, 60th, 61st, 62d, 63d and 64th Congresses from Massachusetts.

Gardner, Obadiah; b. Sept. 13, 1852, in what is now the town of Grant, St. Clair County, Mich.; moved to Maine at the age of 12 years; attended common schools; paid his way through Eastman's Business College, Poughkeepsie, N. Y., also at Coburn Classical Institute, Waterville, Me.; engaged in business in Rockland, Me.; since 1872 has been member of city government; member Maine Board of Agriculture; master Maine State Grange from 1897 to 1907, during which time the membership was increased 35,540; in 1908 received the unanimous nomination for Governor of Maine by the Democrats; polled the largest vote ever given to a Democrat on a straight party ticket, coming within 7,000 votes of election; appointed Chairman of Board of States Assessors April 1, 1911, for six years; appointed United States Senator Sept. 23, 1811. by Gov. Plaisted to fill the vacancy caused by the death of the Hon. William P. Frye.

Gardoqui, Don Diego, commercial relations with Spain, letter of, concerning, 113.

Garesché, J. P., assistant adjutant-general, order regarding Missouri militia, 3243.

Garfield, James A., biography of, 4593.

Garland, Augustus H., Attorney-General under President Cleveland; was born in Tipton County, Tenn., June 11, 1832; his parents moved to Arkansas in 1833; educated at St. Mary's College and St. Joseph's College in Kentucky; studied law and admitted to practice in 1853 at Washington, Ark., where he then lived; moved to Little Rock in 1856; delegate to the state convention that passed the ordinance of secession in 1861; member of the provisional congress that met at Montgomery, Ala., in May, 1861, and subsequently of the Confederate Congress, serving in both houses, and being in the senate when the war closed; elected to the United States Senate from Arkansas for the term beginning March 4, 1867, but not admitted to his seat; made the test-oath case as to lawyers in the Supreme Court of the United States and gained it (see Garland ex parte, 4 Wallace); followed the practice of law until the fall of 1874, when elected governor of Arkansas without opposition; elected in January, 1876, by the legislature of Arkansas, without opposition, to the United States Senate as a Democrat to succeed Powell Clayton. Republican, and took his seat March 5, 1877; re-elected in 1883; resigned in 1885 to accept the position of Attorney-General; died at Washington, D. C., Jan. 26, 1899.

Garland, John, gallantry of, at battle of Monterey, Mexico, referred to, 2368.

Garner, John Nance; b. Red River Co., Tex., Nov. 22, 1869; member of the Texas House of Representatives for four years; elected to the 58th, 59th, 60th, 61st, 62d, 63d and 64th Congresses from Texas.

Garrett, Finis James; b. Aug. 26, 1875, near Ore Springs, in Weakley Co., Tenn.; studied law and was admitted to the bar in 1899; elected to the 59th, 60th, 61st, 62d, 63d and 64th Congresses from Tennessee.

Garrett, William H., treaty with Indians concluded by, 2775.

Garrison, Lindley Miller, Secretary of War under President Wilson; born in Camden, N. J., Nov. 28, 1864; B. L. University of Pennsylvania 1886; admitted to the bar 1886; practiced in Philadelphia until 1888; admitted to the bar of New Jersey in 1888; practiced until June 15, 1904; became vice chancellor of New Jersey on that day and served until the 5th day of March, 1913, resigning the office to become Secretary of War, March 5, 1913.

Gary, James A.; manufacturer; Postmaster General under President McKinley; b. Oct. 22, 1833, in New London Co., Conn.; attended school at Rockhill Institute, Ellicott City, Md., and Allegheny College, Meadville, Pa.; in 1861 engaged in the cotton manufacturing business with his father in Baltimore; exerted strong influence in behalf of the Union cause in Maryland; was a candidate on the Republican ticket for Congress and later for Governor, but defeated; active in Republican politics and represented his State in many national conventions of his party, and served sixteen consecutive years on the National Committee; he was an efficient Postmaster General, but failing health compelled him to resign in 1898. He was married in Baltimore and has one son and seven daughters.

Gates, William, major, United States Army:
Nomination of, discussed, 1488.
Trial solicited by, 1489.

Geary, John W., referred to, 2980, 2995.

George V, coronation of, 7668.

Geronimo; an Apache chief, of the tribe of Chiricahua Indians; during 1884 and 1885 headed a band of hostile Indians who terrorized New Mexico and Arizona; Gen. Crook succeeded in bringing the Indians to terms of surrender, but before they could be carried out the Indians escaped to the mountains; Gen. Crook was succeeded by Gen. Nelson A. Miles, and he waged such a vigorous campaign against the Indians that they were forced to accept his terms of surrender, and Geronimo and his principal supporters were imprisoned in Fort Pickens, Fla.; Geronimo was afterwards taken to Fort Sill., Okla., where he was held a prisoner:

Geronimo:
Mentioned, 5495.
Surrender of Apaches under, to Gen. Miles, discussed, 5099.

Gerry, Commander, mentioned, 2838.

Gerry, Elbridge (1744-1814); statesman and fifth Vice-President of the United States; b. Marblehead, Mass.; member Massachusetts Legislature, 1772; elected to the Continental Congress, 1776; signed the Declaration of Independence, and served on several important committees; chairman of the treasury board, 1780; member of the convention which formulated the Federal Constitution, 1787; member of Congress, 1790-95; acted with Pinckney and Marshall on the X. Y. Z. mission to France, 1797, and when they were dismissed from France, Gerry was asked to remain; joined the Democratic party, and was elected Governor of Massachusetts, 1810; Vice-President with Madison, 1812, and died in office.

Gibson, Walter M., held in duress by Dutch authorities at Batavia, 2828, 2831.

Giddings, Joshua Reed; author, lawyer, diplomat; b. Athens, Pa., Oct. 6, 1795; moved to Ohio and was elected to the legislature of that State in 1826; member of Congress from Ohio, 1838-59; recognized for many years as the leader of the antislavery party; appointed consul-general to British North America, 1861; his collected writings include speeches in Congress, "The Exiles of Florida," "The Rebellion: "Its Authors and Its Causes," and "Essays of Pacificus"; died Montreal, Canada, May 27, 1864.

Gilbert, Henry C., treaty with Indians concluded by, 2829, 2884, 2954.

Gillespie, Capt., dispatch to consul at Monterey forwarded and destroyed by, 2428.

Gillett, Frederick Huntington; b. Westfield, Mass., Oct. 16, 1851; graduated at Amherst College, 1874, and Harvard Law School, 1877; admitted to the bar, 1877, assistant attorney-general of Massachusetts from 1879 to 1882; elected to the Massachusetts house of representatives in 1890 and 1891; elected to the 53d, 54th, 55th, 56th, 57th, 58th, 59th, 60th, 61st, 62d, 63d and 64th Congresses from Massachusetts.

Gillis, James M., mentioned, 3279. Observations of, referred to, 2776.

Gillmore, Quincy A., ceremonies at Fort Sumter to be conducted by, in absence of Gen. Sherman, 3484.

Gilmer, Thomas W., Secretary of the Navy under President Tyler; a native of Virginia; attended the public schools; studied law; admitted to the bar; commenced practice at Charlottesville; for several years state representative, two years of which time was speaker; Governor of Virginia 1840-41; elected a representative from Virginia to the Twenty-seventh Congress as Whig; re-elected to the Twenty-eighth Congress as a Democrat serving until February 15, 1844, when he was appointed Secretary of the Navy; killed by the bursting of a gun on board the U. S. steamer *Princeton*, near Washington, D. C., Feb. 28, 1844.

Gilmer, Thomas W., Secretary of Navy, death of, announced and honors to be paid memory of, 2132, 2186.

Gilpin, Henry D.; lawyer, author; Attorney General under President Van Buren; b. April 14, 1801, in Lancaster, England; in 1816 the family settled in Philadelphia, and Henry was sent to the University of Pennsylvania, took a law course and was admitted to practice in 1822; he had previously filled the position of secretary of the Chesapeake and Delaware Canal Company, which owed its existence to his grandfather; the family were all affiliated with the Society of Friends; Henry D.'s legal reputation was enhanced by his management of an important international case growing out of the rival claims of two Portuguese ministers, each of whom had been accredited to this country by one of the two conflicting governments of Portugal; his skilled handling of this case won the admiration of President Jackson and the confidence of the Supreme Court; appointed United States District Attorney at Philadelphia in 1832, a position he held five years, at the same time serving as a government director of the United States Bank; assisted President Jackson in suppressing the Bank's monopoly; appointed by Van Buren Solicitor of the Treasury in 1837, and in 1840 Attorney General of the United States, though yet less than forty years of age; retired from political life at the end of Van Buren's administration and devoted himself to the pursuit of literature, art and social life; edited the *Atlantic Souvenir*, a literary and art journal; published the "Biography of the Signers of the Declaration of Independence," contributed to the *American Quarterly Review, Democratic Review*, and *North American Review*; superintended the publication of the "Madison Papers," authorized by Congress (1840); wrote "Opinions of the Attorneys General of the United States," 1840; "Autobiography of Walter Scott, Compiled from Passages in His Writings"; "Life of Martin Van Buren"; at his death in Philadelphia, Jan. 9, 1860, he bequeathed both money and collections to historical societies.

Gilpin, Henry D., director of Bank of United States, nomination of, and reasons therefor, 1260.

Glass, Carter; b. Lynchburg, Va., Jan. 4, 1858; publisher of the *Daily News* and *The Daily Advance;* member of Virginia State Senate, 1899-1903; resigned from Virginia State Senate to contest for seat in Congress; was elected to the 57th, 58th, 59th, 60th, 61st, 62d, 63d and 64th Congresses from Virginia.

Glendy, William M., captain in Navy, nomination for promotion withdrawn and reasons therefor, 4000.

Godwin, Hannibal Lafayette; b. Nov. 3, 1873, near Dunn, Harnett Co., N. C.; educated in the schools at Trinity College, Durham, N. C.; read law at the University of North Carolina and was admitted to the bar, 1896; member of the State Senate of North Carolina 1903; elected to the 60th, 61st, 62d, 63d and 64th Congresses from North Carolina.

Goff, Nathan, Jr., Secretary of the Navy under President Hayes; born in Clarksburg, W. Va., on Feb. 9, 1843; educated at the Northwestern Virginia Academy, Georgetown College, and the University of the City of New York; admitted to the bar in 1865; elected a member of the West Virginia legislature in 1867; appointed United States attorney for the district of West Virginia in 1868, to which position he was reappointed in 1872, 1876, and 1880; resigned the district attorneyship in Jan., 1881, when he was appointed Secretary of the Navy; in March, 1881, President Garfield reappointed him district attorney for West Virginia, which position he again resigned in July, 1882; he enlisted in the Union Army in June, 1861, in the Third Regiment Virginia Volunteer Infantry; served as lieutenant of Company G, also as adjutant of said regiment, and as major of the Fourth Virginia Volunteer Cavalry; Republican candidate for Congress in 1870 in the First West Virginia district, as also in the year 1874; candidate of the Republican party for governor of West Virginia in 1876 and defeated by Hon. H. M. Mathews; elected to the Forty-eighth Congress as a Republican, and re-elected to the Forty-ninth and Fiftieth Congresses; in 1888 elected governor of West Virginia on the face of the returns by a plurality of 130 votes; the election was contested by A. B. Fleming, the Democratic candidate, who was seated as governor by a majority vote of the legislature; appointed United States circuit judge of the fourth circuit March 17, 1892, by President Harrison.

Goldsborough, Louis M.; rear admiral; b. Feb. 18, 1805, in Washington, D. C.; appointed midshipman at the age of seven years; served under Bainbridge and Stewart; married a daughter of William Wirt and resided for some years on a tract of land in Florida owned by his father-in-law; commanded a company of cavalry and an armed steamer in the Seminole War; made a naval commander in 1840; member of commission to explore California and Oregon in 1849; Superintendent of the Naval Academy, 1853-57; squadron commander during Civil War; received thanks of Congress for his services in co-operation with Gen. Burnside for the capture of Roanoke Island; advanced to rear admiral in 1862, and retired in 1873; died Feb. 20, 1877.

Goldsborough, Louis M.:
Thanks of Congress to, recommended 3266.
Thanks of President tendered, 3305.

Good, James William; b. Sept. 24, 1866, Linn Co., Iowa; graduated from Coe College, Cedar Rapids, and the law department of the University of Michigan; elected to the 61st, 62d, 63d and 64th Congresses from Iowa.

Goodwin, William Shields; b. Warren, Ark., May 2, 1866, son of T. M. and Esther (Shields) Goodwin, of Gwinnett and Milton counties, Ga., respectively; educated in the public schools of his home town, at Farmers' Academy, near Duluth, Ga., and at a business college in Atlanta, Ga., universities of Arkansas and Mississippi; is a lawyer; in 1897 married Miss Sue Meek, of Warren, Ark.; in 1895 was member of Arkansas General Assembly; in 1900 was Democratic Presidential Elector; in 1905 and 1907 was State Senator; since 1907 has been a member of the Board of Trustees of the University of Arkansas; was elected to the 62d, 63d and 64th Congresses from Arkansas.

Gordan, George W., correspondence regarding slave trade referred to, 2287, 2538.

Gordon, William W., member of military commission of Puerto Rico, 6322.

Gore, Christopher; statesman; b. Boston, Mass., Sept. 21, 1758; graduated from Harvard College in 1776; studied law; admitted to the bar and began practice at Boston; United States attorney for the district of Massachusetts 1789-1796; commissioner to England 1796-1803; chargé d'affaires at London 1803-4; a member of the State house of representatives and State senate; governor of Massachusetts 1809 and 1810; elected a United States Senator from Massachusetts, serving from May 28, 1813, to 1816, when he resigned; a trustee of Harvard University; died at Waltham, Mass., March 1, 1827.

Gore, Christopher, commissioner of United States under treaty with Great Britain, 188.

Gore, Thomas Pryor, b. Webster Co., Miss., Dec. 10, 1870; graduated from the Law Department of Cumberland University, Lebanon, Tenn., 1892; moved to Texas in 1896 and to Oklahoma in 1901; served one term in the Territorial Senate; nominated for the United States Senate in State Primary, June 8, 1907; elected by the Legislature Dec. 11; re-elected for a full term by the Legislature Jan. 20, 1909, to represent Oklahoma.

Gorman, Arthur Pue (1839-1906); statesman; b. Maryland; United States Senator, 1881-99, 1903-06; recognized leader of the Democratic party for over thirty years; opposed the Force bill, 1889; helped to remodel the Wilson Tariff bill, 1894; an expert on the trans-Isthmian Canal question, and favored the Nicaraguan route.

Gorostiza, Manuel E. de, pamphlet issued by, regarding troops under Gen. Gaines, 1646.

Goward, Gustavus, report of, on Samoan Islands transmitted, 4473.

Graham, James D., report of, as commissioner in northeastern boundary. (See Northeastern Boundary.)

Graham, James M.; b. Ireland, April 14, 1852; came to Sangamon Co., Ill., in 1868; admitted to bar in 1885; served one term as Member of the House of Representatives in General Assembly of Illinois; elected to the 61st, 62d, 63d and 64th Congresses from Illinois.

Graham, John, commissioner to South America, 617.

Graham, William Alexander (brother of James Graham), Secretary of the Navy under President Fillmore; born in Lincoln County, N. C., Sept. 5, 1804; received a classical education; graduated from the University of North Carolina in 1824; studied law at Newbern; admitted to the bar and began practicing at Hillsboro; member of the house of commons of North Carolina 1833-1840; elected a United States Senator (vice Robert Strange, resigned), serving from Dec. 10, 1840, to March 3, 1843; elected governor of North Carolina in 1844 as a Whig; re-elected in 1846; after declining the mission to Spain, in 1849, was Secretary of the Navy from July 20, 1850, until March 7, 1853; Whig candidate for Vice-President in 1852; Senator in the Second Confederate Congress; delegate to the Philadelphia Union convention in 1866; died at Saratoga Springs,, N. Y., Aug. 11, 1875.

Granger, Francis (son of Gideon Granger), Postmaster-General under President W. H. Harrison; born at Suffield, Conn., Dec. 1, 1792; pursuing classical studies, he graduated from Yale College in 1811; studied law; admitted to the bar in 1816, commencing practice at Canandaigua, N. Y.; member of the state house of representatives 1826-1831; twice candidate of the National Republicans for governor of New York and defeated; delegate to the National Anti-Masonic convention at Philadelphia September 11, 1830; defeated as the National Republican candidate for Vice-President in 1831; elected a Representative from New York to the Twenty-fourth Congress as a Whig; defeated as the Whig candidate for the Twenty-fifth Congress by Mark A. Sibley; elected to the Twenty-sixth Congress; appointed Postmaster-General, serving from March 6, 1841, to September 18, 1841; elected to the Twenty-seventh Congress as a Whig (vice John Greig, resigned), serving from December, 7, 1841, to March 3, 1843; his "silver gray" hair was assumed as a name by a portion of the Whig party in New York; delegate to the peace convention in 1861; died at Canandaigua, N. Y., Aug. 28, 1868.

Granger, Gideon; lawyer, statesman, author; Postmaster General under Presidents Jefferson and Madison; b. July 19, 1767, in Suffield, Conn.; graduated from Yale in 1787, and after studying law took up practice in his native town; when twenty-five years of age he was elected to the Connecticut Legislature and reelected annually till 1801; was recognized as leader in the legislature; draughted and assisted in passing the common school law of Connecticut; served as Postmaster General during Jefferson's two terms and part of that of Madison, resigning in 1814; removed to New York and became a warm supporter of De Witt Clinton; elected to the New York Senate that he might aid in promoting the construction of the Erie Canal, but was compelled by failing health to resign; author of "Political Essays," originally published in periodicals under the *nom de plume* of "Epaminondas" and "Algernon Sydney"; delivered a model Fourth of July oration at Suffield in 1797; died Dec. 31, 1822, in Canandaigua, N. Y.

Granger, Gordon, thanks of President tendered, 3440.

Grant, Julia Dent, swords and testimonials of Gen. Grant offered Government by, recommendations regarding, 4857.

Schedule of articles, 4859.

Grant, Lewis A., brigadier-general, nomination of, referred to, 3403.

Grant, U. S., biography of, 3957.

Grasse, Marquis de, mentioned, 6932.

Gray, Finly H., b. July 24, 1864, in Fayette County, Ind.; obtained common school education only; began the study and practice of law alone in Connersville, in 1893; elected Mayor of Connersville in 1904; reelected in 1909; elected to the 62d, 63d and 64th Congresses from Indiana.

Gray, George; diplomat; b. Newcastle, Del., May 4, 1840; graduated from Princeton College when nineteen years old, receiving the degree of A. B., and in 1862 the degree of A.M.; after studying law with his father, Andrew C. Gray, he spent a year in the Harvard Law School, and admitted to practice in 1863; appointed attorney-general of the State of Delaware in 1879 by Governor Hall, and reappointed attorney-general in 1884 by Governor Stockley; delegate to the national Democratic convention at St. Louis in 1876, at Cincinnati in 1880, and at Chicago in 1884; elected to the United States Senate as a Democrat to fill the vacancy caused by the appointment of Thomas F. Bayard as Secretary of State, and took his seat March 19, 1885; reelected in 1887 and took his seat March 4, 1887; reelected in 1893, serving until March 3, 1899; member of the commission which met at Quebec, August, 1898, to settle difference between United States and Canada, and later of the commission which met at Paris in September, 1898, to arrange terms of peace between United States and Spain; in October, 1902, appointed chairman of the commission to investigate conditions of the coal strike in Pennsylvania.

Gray, George, member of Spanish-American Peace Commission, 6322.

Gray, William E., refusal of Great Britain to surrender other fugitives and, discussed, 4368.

Greeley, Horace (1811-1872); journalist and author; b. Amherst, N. H.; founded the *New York Tribune,* 1841; sat in Congress for New York, 1848-49; took a leading part in the anti-slavery movement; and was the unsuccessful nominee of the fused Liberal Republicans and Democrats for the Presidency in 1872 against Grant.

Greeley, Horace, Messrs. Clay, Thompson, Holcomb, and Sanders accompanied to Washington on peace mission by, 3438.

Greely, Adolphus Washington; author, explorer; b. Newburyport, Mass., March 27, 1844; served through the Civil War, and was commissioned captain and brevetted major and honorably discharged 1867; later as lieutenant in the regular army he was detailed to construct telegraph lines on the Indian and Mexican frontiers; Dec. 11, 1886, commissioned brigadier-general and made chief signal officer; assigned to command an arctic expedition to establish one of the circumpolar stations, in which work eleven natives co-operated; Aug. 12, 1881, landed twenty-six persons within 496 miles of the pole, and added about 6,000 square miles of land, hitherto unknown, to the maps; after the loss of their ship and enduring hunger and hardship, Greely and the few survivors of his party were rescued by relief parties sent after them; Greely was highly honored for his discoveries.

Greely, A. W., expedition fitted out for relief of Lady Franklin Bay Expedition under, discussed, 4835.

Board to consider expedition to be sent, 4813.

Offer of rewards for rescue of, discussed, 4795.

Recommended, 4693, 4787.

Vessel presented by Great Britain to United States to aid in, 4791.

Return of, 4917.

Recommended, 4855.

Greely, Ebenezer S., arrest and imprisonment of, by authorities of New Brunswick, correspondence regarding, 1575, 1622.

Claims arising out of, 1687.

Green, Charles L., passed assistant surgeon in Navy, court-martial of, referred to, 3998.

Green, Duff, employment of, in Europe, 2180, 2181, 2213.

Greene, William Stedman; b. Tremont, Tazewell Co., Ill., April 28, 1841; removed to Fall River with his parents in 1844; commenced business as auctioneer, real estate and insurance agent in 1866; elected Mayor of Fall River in 1880, 1886, 1895, 1896, 1897, and declined re-election; in July, 1888, was appointed by Governor Ames General Superintendent of Prisons for the State, and served until 1893, when he was removed by the Democratic Governor for political reasons; appointed Postmaster and entered upon his duties April 1, 1898; resigned this position and was elected to Congress, May 31, 1898, to fill an unexpired term in the 55th Congress; also elected to the 56th, 57th, 58th, 59th, 60th, 61st, 62d, 63d and 64th Congresses from Massachusetts.

Greenough, Horatio, statue of Washington executed by, 1910.

Greer, James A., member of board to consider expeditions for relief of Lady Franklin Bay Expedition, 4813.

Gregg, Alexander White; lawyer; graduated King College, at Bristol, Tenn., and law department of the University of Virginia; elected to the 58th, 59th, 60th, 61st, 62d, 63d and 64th Congresses from Texas.

Gregory, J. Shaw, treaty with Indians concluded by, 3263.

Gregory, Thomas W.; lawyer, Attorney-General under President Wilson; b. Nov. 6, 1861, in Crawfordsville, Miss.; graduated Southwestern Presbyterian University, Clarksville, Tenn., 1888; attended the University of Virginia and the University of Texas; admitted to the bar in 1885, and practiced in Austin, Tex., until 1913, when he was appointed special assistant to Attorney General McReynolds in the investigation of the affairs of the New York, New Haven and Hartford Railroad; upon the appointment of McReynolds to the Supreme Court he was succeeded as Attorney general by Mr. Gregory Sept. 3, 1914.

Greiner, John, treaty with Indians concluded by, 2727.

Grenfel, George St. Leger, papers touching case of, transmitted, 3661.

Gresham, Walter Quinton (1832-1895); statesman and Cabinet officer; b. Lanesville, Ind.; began the practice of law 1853; entered the Union army at the outbreak of the Civil War; brevetted major-general of volunteers 1865; Postmaster-General, 1882-84; Secretary of the Treasury, 1884; Secretary of State under Cleveland, 1893.

Gresham, Walter Q., Secretary of State, 5827.

Death of, announced and honors to be paid memory of, 6022, 6046.

Griest, William Walton; manufacturer of iron, president of railway and lighting companies, and a newspaper publisher; elected to the 61st, 62d, 63d and 64th Congresses from Pennsylvania.

Griffin, Walter T., report of, transmitted, 5769.

Griggs, John W.; lawyer; Attorney General under President McKinley; b. July 10, 1849, in Newton, N. J.; educated at Newton Collegiate Institute and at Lafayette College, Easton, Pa.; took up law practice in Paterson, N. J., and became president of a national bank, and was elected a State Assemblyman, Senator and finally Governor, being the first Republican to hold that office in thirty years; succeeded Joseph McKenna as Attorney General Jan. 31, 1898, and resigned March 31, 1901.

Griswold Roger, was born May 21, 1762, at Lyme, Conn.; pursued classical studies, graduating from Yale College in 1780; studied law, admitted to the bar in 1783 and began practice at Norwich; returned to Lyme in 1794; elected a Representative from Connecticut to the 4th, 5th, 6th, 7th, and 8th Congresses as a Federalist; appointed judge of the Supreme Court of Connecticut in 1807; Presidential elector

on the Pinckney and King ticket; Lieutenant-Governor of Connecticut 1809-11, and Governor from 1811 until his death Oct. 25, 1812, at Lyme, Conn.

Griswold, Stanley, conduct of, while secretary of Michigan Territory, referred to, 430.

Groesbeck, William S.; attorney; b. New York City, July 24, 1815; received an academic education nad studied law; admitted to the bar; began practice at Cincinnati, Ohio; member of the State constitutional convention in 1851; commissioner to codify the laws of Ohio in 1852; elected a Representative from Ohio to the 35th Congress as a Democrat; member of the peace conference in 1861; State senator in 1862; delegate to the national Union convention at Philadelphia in 1866; one of President Johnson's counsel in his impeachment trial; died in 1897.

Groesbeck, William S., counsel for President Johnson in impeachment proceedings, 3947.

Grogan, Mr., capture and imprisonment of, by Canadians, 1828.

Grosvenor, Charles H., brevet brigadier-general, acts and proceedings of, declared null and void, 3548.

Grundy, Felix, Attorney-General under President Van Buren; born in Berkeley County, Va., Sept. 11, 1777; when two years old moved to Brownsville, Pa.; thence in 1780 to Kentucky; received an academic education; studied law; admitted to the bar and practiced; member of the Kentucky constitutional convention in 1799; member of the state legislature 1800-1805; chosen judge of the supreme court of Kentucky in 1806; soon afterwards made chief justice; moved to Nashville, Tenn., in 1807; elected a Representative from Tennessee as a War Democrat to the Twelfth and Thirteenth Congresses; resigned in 1814; member of the Tennessee house of representatives 1815-1819; elected a United States Senator from Tennessee (vice John H. Eaton, resigned), serving from Dec. 7, 1829, to July 4, 1838, when he resigned; appointed Attorney-General July 5, 1838, resigning Dec. 1, 1840, to become United States Senator; having doubts as to his eligibility, returned to Tennessee to become an "inhabitant" of the state, and was again elected Dec. 14, 1840, but died at Nashville, Tenn, Dec. 19, 1840.

Guernsey, Frank Edward; b. Oct. 15, 1866, Dover, Piscataquis Co., Me.; studied law and was admitted to the bar at Dover in 1890; was elected treasurer of Piscataquis County in 1890, and re-elected twice, serving until Dec. 31, 1896; member of the Maine House of Representatives in 1897 and 1899, and a member of the Maine Senate in 1903; elected to fill a vacancy in the 60th Congress, and to the 61st, 62d, 63d and 64th Congresses from Maine.

Guerra, Jesus, demand of Mexico for extradition of, refused, 6333.

Guest, John, thanks of Congress to, recommended, 3277.

Guiteau, Charles J., President Garfield assassinated by, 4967.

Gurovits, Odon, report of, on Navajo Indians transmitted, 5782.

Guthrie, James, Secretary of the Treasury under President Pierce; b. Nelson County, Ky., Dec. 5th, 1792; educated at McAllister's Academy, Bardstown, Ky.; entered the Mississippi trade; also studied and practiced law at Bardstown, Ky.; appointed Commonwealth attorney in 1820 and moved to Louisville; member of the state legislature for several years, serving in both branches; delegate and chosen president of the Kentucky constitutional convention; president of the University of Louisville, the Louisville and Portland Canal Company, and the Louisville and Nashville Railroad Company; appointed Secretary of the Treasury in 1853; elected United States Senator from Kentucky as a Democrat, serving from March 4, 1865, to Feb. 7, 1868, when he resigned on account of illness; died at Louisville, Ky., March 13, 1869.

Gutte, Isidore, claim of, to vessel condemned by Salvador and subsequently presented to United States, 4988.

Gwin, Samuel, register of land office:
Nomination of, and reasons therefor, 1137, 1170, 1198.
Official conduct of, charges affecting, 1447.

Gwin, William M.:
Immigration plans of, referred to, 3571.
Mentioned, 2570.

Habersham, Joseph, soldier and Postmaster-General under Presidents Washington, John Adams and Jefferson; b. Savannah, Ga., July 28, 1751; his father, James, came from England to Savannah with Whitefield, the English evangelist, in 1738, and taught school for some years, but became a merchant in 1744, and was subsequently prominent in civil affairs. He raised the first cotton in the state, and sent the first few bales of cotton to England that went out from Georgia; three of his sons were zealous patriots, and Joseph was a member of the first committee appointed by the friends of liberty in his native colony, in July, 1774; in 1775 (June 11), with others, he seized the powder in the arsenal at Savannah, for the use of the colonists; during the same month 'he was made a member of the Georgia committee of safety. In July of that year he commanded a party which captured a British government vessel, having on board 15,000 pounds of powder; during the following Jan., and while a member of the colonial assembly, he raised a party of volunteers, which took Gov. Wright a prisoner, and confined him to his 'house under guard. Appointed (Feb. 4, 1776) major of the 1st Georgia battery, he defended Savannah from a naval attack early in March. In the winter of 1778, after the capture of Savannah by the British, he removed his family to Virginia, but participated in the unsuccessful attack upon that city while it was in the hands of the British in September, 1779; he was lieutenant-colonel at the close of the war; in 1785-86 he was a delegate from Georgia to the Continental Congress, and speaker of the state assembly in 1785, and in 1790; President Washington appointed him U. S. Postmaster-General in 1795, and he was continued in office by Presidents John Adams and Jefferson until 1801, when he resigned the position to become president (1802) of the United States Branch Bank at Savannah, which presidency he held until his death at Savannah Nov. 17, 1815. A county of his native state bears his name.

Hale, C. H., treaty with Indians concluded by 3403.

Hale, Eugene; b. Turner, Oxford Co., Me., June 9, 1836; received an academic education; studied law, was admitted to the bar in 1857, and commenced practice at the age of twenty; was a member of the Legislature of Maine in 1867, 1868 and 1880; was elected to the 41st, 42d, and 43d Congresses; appointed Postmaster-General by President Grant in 1874, but declined; was re-elected to the 44th and 45th Congresses, was tendered a Cabinet appointment as Secretary of the Navy by President Hayes, and declined; received the degree of LL. D. from Bates College, from Colby University, and from Bowdoin College; was elected to the United States Senate to succeed Hannibal Hamlin, for the term beginning March 4, 1881; was re-elected in 1887, 1893, 1899 and in 1905 to represent Maine.

Hale, John Parker (1806-1873); statesman; b. at Dover, N. H.; a member of Congress, 1843-45; United States Senator, 1847-53, and 1855-65; nominated for President by the Liberal party in 1847; and by the Free-Soil Democrats in 1852; in the latter part of his political career he was a Republican; United States minister to Spain, 1865-69; in the early days he stood almost alone in the Senate as an anti-slavery Democrat.

Hale, W. J., claim of, against Argentine Republic, 4806.

Hall, Charles F., publication of second edition of Second Arctic Expedition made by, suggested, 4666.

Hall, Nathan K., Postmaster-General under President Fillmore; b. Marcellus, N. Y., March 10, 1810; received an academic education; studied law at Buffalo with Millard Fillmore; admitted to the bar in 1832; commenced practice under the firm name of Fillmore, Hall & Haven; member of the state house of representatives in 1846; elected a Representative from New York to the Thirtieth Congress as a Whig; appointed Postmaster-General, serving from July 23, 1850, to Aug. 31, 1852; appointed United States district judge for the western district of New York, holding the position until he died, at Buffalo, N. Y., March 2, 1874.

Halleck, Henry Wager; soldier, author; b. Westernville, N. Y., Jan. 16, 1815; grad. U. S. Military Acad., 1839; ordered to Monterey, Cal., 1847, which he fortified and maintained as rendezvous of Pacific-squadron; and took an active part in Mexican War; member of the convention which, in 1849, framed the constitution for California; engaged in practice of law and in mining and railroad work in California and became major-general of state militia; on the breaking out of the Civil War was appointed Major-General of U. S. army on recommendation of Gen. Winfield Scott; his effective work in the west during the early months of the rebellion resulted in his being placed in command of the Department of the Mississippi, which included all the country between the Allegheny and Rocky Mountains; July 23, 1863, was appointed by President Lincoln general-in-chief of the armies of the United States, with headquarters at Washington; later transferred to the Pacific coast, and after the close of the war to the division of the south with headquarters at Louisville, Ky.; for his lectures and writings on the science of war he was honored with college degrees; among his published works was a translation of the "Political and Military History of Napoleon"; died Louisville, Ky., Jan. 9, 1872.

Halleck, Henry W.:

Lieutenant in Engineer Corps, report of, on means of national defense, 2213.

Major-general—

Assigned to command of Department of Mississippi, 3312.

Assigned to command of land forces of United States, 3317.

Relieved from command and assigned to duty as chief of staff, 3435.

Halpine, William G., Fenian prisoner, release of, referred to, 4114.

Hamed, Mahommed, treaty between Turkey and United States concluded by, 1093.

Hamill, James A.; b. in Jersey City, N. J., March 30, 1877; was admitted to the bar of New Jersey, 1900; elected in 1902 a member of the New Jersey house of assembly, where he served four consecutive one-year terms; elected to the 60th, 61st, 62d, 63d and 64th Congresses from New Jersey.

Hamilton, Alexander; statesman; b. in the West Indies, Jan. 11, 1757; entered the army as an artillery officer and became an aide-de-camp to lieutenant-colonel; delegate to the Continental Congress from New York in 1782 and 1783, and under the constitution in 1787 and 1788; member of the convention which framed the Constitution and by his writings, signed "Publius," did much to secure its adoption, but was the only member from New York who signed that instrument; appointed secretary of the treasury 1789 and continued in that office until 1795, when he resigned; had a difficulty with Aaron Burr in 1804, and in a duel between the two fought at Weehawken, N. J., he received a fatal wound from which he died the next day, July 12, 1804.

Hamilton, Alexander, commissioner of land titles in East Florida, report of, transmitted to the House by President Monroe, 812.

Hamilton, Andrew J.; statesman; b. Madison County, Ala., Jan. 28, 1815; received a liberal education; studied law and admitted to the bar; clerk of the county court; moved to Texas in 1846 and resumed the practice of law at Lagrange; Presidential elector on the Buchanan and Breckenridge ticket in 1856; elected a Representative from Texas to the 36th Congress as a Republican; appointed by President Lincoln military governor of Texas in 1862; appointed provisional governor by President Johnson in 1865; delegate to the loyalists' convention at Philadelphia in 1866; died at Austin, Tex., April 10, 1875.

Hamilton, Andrew J., provisional governor of Texas, appointed with authority to arrange and direct a convention of delegates to be chosen by only loyal citizens of the State and by none others, 3519.

Hamilton, Charles S., brevet second lieutenant, promotion of, to second lieutenant recommended, 2296.

Hamilton, Edward L.; b. Niles, Mich., Dec. 9, 1857; admitted to the bar in 1884; elected to the 55th, 56th, 57th, 58th, 59th, 60th, 61st, 62d, 63d and 64th Congresses from Michigan.

Hamilton, James A., correspondence regarding northeastern boundary. (See Northeastern Boundary.)

Hamilton, Paul; financier, Governor of South Carolina, Secretary of the Navy under President Madison; b. Oct. 16, 1762, in St. Paul's parish, S. C.; although a young man he was of great service during the Revolution; from 1799 to 1804 was Comptroller of South Carolina, displaying remarkable capacity for financial affairs and systematizing the finances of the State; Governor, 1804-06; appointed Secretary of the Navy by President Madison in 1809; while Hamilton was Secretary authority was given for the construction of four ships of seventy-four guns each, six frigates and six sloops of war, and a war debt of $21,000,000 was created; the success of the navy is recorded elsewhere; Mr. Hamilton resigned in December, 1812, and died June 30, 1816, at Beaufort, S. C.

Hamlin, Courtney Walker; b. at Brevard, N. C., Oct. 27, 1858; elected to the 58th,

60th, 61st, 62d, 63d and 64th Congresses from Missouri.

Hamlin, Hannibal; statesman; b. Paris, Me., Aug. 27, 1809; member of the Maine legislature, 1836-40, and speaker of the house 1837, 1839 and 1840; elected to the 28th and 29th Congresses, and again became a member of the State legislature in 1847; elected to the United State Senate 1848 to fill a vacancy of four years and in 1851 was re-elected for the full term; elected governor of Maine, in 1857 and resigned the same year to return to the Senate; resigned from the Senate Jan. 1, 1861, having been elected Vice-President on the ticket with President Lincoln; presided over the senate during Lincoln's first term, and after the election of Lincoln and Johnson, was made Collector of the Port of Boston, which he resigned in 1866; again elected to the Senate in 1869, and for the fifth time in 1875; declined reelection in 1881, after a service of twenty-five years in the Senate; minister to Spain under President Garfield; died July 4, 1891, at Bangor, Me., the third Vice-President to die on the nation's birthday.

Hamlin, Hannibal, death of, announced and honors to be paid memory of, 5609.

Hammond Samuel; engineer, soldier; b. Richmond County, Va., Sept. 21, 1757; received a liberal education; served in the Revolutionary Army; after independence was established settled at Savannah; surveyor-general of Georgia; served in the Creek war and commanded a corps of Georgia volunteers; member of the State house of representatives; elected a Representative from Georgia to the 8th Congress as a Democrat; civil and military governor of upper Louisiana Territory 1805-1824; receiver of public moneys at St. Louis; moved in 1824 to South Carolina; a member of the State legislature; surveyor-general in 1825; secretary of State of South Carolina 1831-1835; died near Augusta, Ga., Sept. 11, 1842.

Hammond, Samuel, colonel commandant, commissioned, 364.

Hancock, John; patriot, statesman; b. Quincy, Mass., Jan. 12, 1737; pursuing classical studies, graduated from Harvard College in 1754; trained to a business career in his uncle's large counting-room, whose large fortune and business he inherited; several years was one of the selectmen of Boston; member of the provincial legislature 1766-1772; active in pre-Revolutionary movements, and, with Samuel Adams, was exempted from pardon in Governor Gage's proclamation of June 12, 1775; Delegate from Massachusetts to the Continental Congress 1775-1780 and 1785-86, serving as President of the Continental Congress May 27, 1775-October, 1777; served as senior major-general of Massachusetts militia during the Revolutionary war; member of the Massachusetts constitutional convention of 1780; governor of Massachusetts 1780-1785 and 1787, until his death at Quincy, Oct. 8, 1793.

Hancock, John, governor of Massachusetts, letter of, regarding eastern boundary transmitted, 65.

Hancock, John; jurist; b. of Virginia parents, in Jackson County, Ala., Oct. 29, 1824; educated partly in Alabama and partly in Tennessee; studied law at Winchester,

Tenn.; admitted to the bar in 1846; settled in Texas in 1847, practicing his profession there until August, 1851; elected to the district bench of the State and served as judge until 1855, when he resigned and resumed practice and planting; member of the State legislature in 1860 and 1861, when he refused to take the oath of allegiance to the Confederate States and was expelled; elected a member of the State constitutional convention of 1866; engaged in the practice of his profession, planting and stock raising; elected a Representative to the 42d, 43d and 44th Congresses, and re-elected to the 48th Congress as a Democrat; after the expiration of his term in Congress he resumed the practice of law at Austin, Tex., and died there July 19, 1893.

Hancock, Winfield Scott; soldier; b. Montgomery Square, Pa., Feb. 14, 1824; grad. West Point, 1844, and served with distinction in Mexican War; commissioned brigadier-general in 1861; commanded the second army corps in left center of the battle of Gettysburg, his conduct in this campaign calling forth the thanks of Congress; his gallantry and efficiency in the Wilderness, Spottsylvania, and at Petersburg earned for him his promotion to major-general; after the war he was stationed at Governors Island, New York harbor; nominated for president by the Democrats in 1880, but was defeated by Garfield; died Governors Island, Feb. 9, 1886.

Hancock, Winfield S.:
   Death of, announced and honors to be paid memory of, 5077.
   Department of South merged in Department of East under command of, 4754.
   Ordered to execute sentence of military court in case of assassins of President Lincoln, 3546.
   Patriotic conduct of, recognition of, by Congress recommended, 3793.

Handy, Moses P., special commissioner to Paris Exposition, death of, referred to, 6329.

Hanna, Marcus Alonzo (1837-1904); politician and business man; b. Lisbon, Ohio; prominent as a delegate to the National Republican Conventions after 1884, and is given credit for securing the nomination and election of President McKinley, in whose campaign Hanna was chairman of the Republican Committee 1896; in 1897 he was appointed United States Senator to succeed John Sherman, and was returned again in 1898; was an influential supporter and adviser of the administration.

Hannen, Sir Nicholas John, arbitrator of Cheek claim against Siam, 6336.

Hanson, Grafton D., restoration of, to rank in Army recommended, 2368.

Hardee, William J., major by brevet, nomination of and reasons therefor, 2443.

Hardy, Rufus; b. Dec. 16, 1855, Monroe Co., Miss.; admitted to the bar in 1875; elected county attorney of Navarro Co., Tex., in 1880 and 1882; district attorney, thirteenth judicial district, 1884 and 1886; district judge of the same district, 1888 and 1892; elected to the 60th,

61st, 62d, 63d and 64th Congresses from Texas.

Harlan, James, Secretary of the Interior under President Johnson; b. Clark County, Ill., Aug. 25, 1820; received a classical education, graduating from the Indiana Asbury University in 1845; studied law; removed to Iowa; superintendent of public instruction in 1847; president of the Iowa Wesleyan University; elected a United States Senator from Iowa as a Whig in May, 1855; the seat having been declared vacant on the ground of an informality in his election, again elected for the remainder of the term in 1857, and re-elected in 1860, serving until March, 1865, having been appointed Secretary of the Interior; resigned this position in 1866, having been elected to the United States Senate as a Republican for the term beginning in 1867, and served until March 3, 1873; delegate to the peace convention in 1861; delegate to the Philadelphia Loyalist convention of 1866; presiding judge of court of commissioners of Alabama claims 1882-1885; editor of Washington *Chronicle*; died at Mount Pleasant, Iowa, Oct. 5, 1899.

Harmon, Judson; Attorney General under President Cleveland; b. Feb. 3, 1846, in Newton, O.; son of a Baptist minister, who conducted his early education until he entered Denison University, where he was graduated in 1866; studied law under Hon. George Hoadly and at Cincinnati Law School and began practice in 1869 in Cincinnati; married in 1870 Olive Scobey, of Hamilton, Ohio; supported Horace Greeley for President in the campaign of 1872; judge of the Superior Court of Cincinnati 1878-1887; appointed Attorney General June 8, 1895, to succeed Richard Olney, who became Secretary of State; many of his opinions and papers are highly regarded, particularly his reply to Bryan's attack on the President's authority to suppress interference with functions of the government; during his term as Attorney General he argued many important cases in the Supreme Court, and took an active part in the international and other complications which marked the latter part of Cleveland's second administration.

Harmon, Judson, Attorney-General, order to, respecting indebtedness of Pacific railroads, 6233.

Harmount, E. Hertzberg, Dominican consul-general in London, mentioned, 4017.

Harney, William Selby; soldier; b. near Haysboro, Tenn., Aug. 27, 1800; commissioned second lieutenant in the regular army Feb. 13, 1818; served in the Black Hawk and Seminole Indian Wars and in the Mexican War; brevetted brigadier-general for gallantry at Cerro Gordo; served in later campaigns against the Indians on the western plains; relieved of his command and placed on the retired list at the outbreak of the Civil War and brevetted major-general for long and faithful service; died Orlando, Fla., May 9, 1889.

Harney, William S.:
   Correspondence of, referred to, 3110.
   Sioux Indians—
      Report of, on, 3897.
      Stipulations with, recommendations regarding, 2912.
   Visit of, to San Juan Island discussed, 3093.

Academy, Wilbur, Oreg., 1884-1886; president of the Oregon State Normal School at Drain, 1888-1891; the remainder of his educational work has been in connection with Willamette University; elected to the 60th, 61st, 62d, 63d and 64th Congresses from Oregon.

Hay, James; b. in Millwood, Clarke Co., Va.; was educated at private schools in Maryland and Virginia, at the University of Pennsylvania and Washington and Lee University, Virginia, from which latter institution he graduated in law in 1877; moved to Harrisonburg, Va., 1877; elected attorney for the Commonwealth in 1883, 1887, 1891 and 1895; elected to the House of Delegates of Virginia in 1885, 1887, and 1889; elected to the Virginia State Senate in 1893; elected to the 55th, 56th, 57th, 58th, 59th, 60th, 61st, 62d, 63d and 64th Congresses from Virginia.

Hay, John; lawyer, editor, diplomat, author; b. Salem, Ind., Oct. 8, 1838; became Private Secretary to President Lincoln in 1861, adjutant and aide-de-camp during Civil War, and was brevetted colonel; employed as an editorial writer on the New York *Tribune* during the years 1870 to 1875; secretary of legation at Paris, France, 1865-67; at Madrid, Spain, 1869-70; chargé d'affaires at Vienna, Austria, 1867-69; First Assistant Secretary of State in the Hayes administration; Ambassador to Great Britain 1897-98; appointed Secretary of State in the Cabinet of President McKinley, 1898; among his writings published in book form are "Pike County Ballads," which include "Jim Bludso" and "Little Breeches"; "Castillian Days," "History of the Administration of Abraham Lincoln," in collaboration with John C. Nicolay.

Hay, John, Secretary of State, 6492.
  Authorized to confer with Great Britain and Germany concerning Samoa, 6596.
  Correspondence of, with Gen. Reyes, 6854.
  Death of, announced, 6955.
  Signs Panama Canal Treaty, 6823.

Hayes, Everis Anson, b. Waterloo, Jefferson Co., Wis., March 10, 1855; graduated from both the literary and law departments of the University of Wisconsin, receiving the degrees of B. L. and LL. B.; in 1887 he removed to Santa Clara Co., Cal., and there engaged in fruit raising and mining, and, with his brother, became publisher and proprietor of the San Jose *Daily Morning Mercury* and *Evening Herald;* elected to the 59th, 60th, 61st, 62d, 63d and 64th Congresses from California.

Hayes, Rutherford B., biography of, 4391.

Hayne, Isaac W., bearer of letter from Governor Pickens to President Buchanan, 3195.

Hayne, Robert Young (1791-1840); statesman and orator; b. Parish of St. Paul, S. C.; admitted to the bar 1812; speaker of the Legislature of South Carolina, 1818; Attorney-General of the State 1818-23; United States Senator 1823-32; engaged in the famous debate with Webster on the "States Rights" question; Governor of South Carolina 1832-34 and favored moderate nullification.

Hazen, William B., member of board to consider expeditions to be sent for relief of Lady Franklin Bay Expedition, 4813.

Head, Lafayette, treaty with Indians concluded by, 3393.

Heap, Samuel D., convention with Tunis signed by, 833.

Heflin, James Thomas, b. at Louina, Randolph Co., Ala., April 9, 1869; studied law at Lafayette, Ala., and was admitted to the bar in 1893; elected Mayor of Lafayette 1893, holding this office two terms; served in Legislature and was elected Secretary of State in 1902; later to the 58th, 59th, 60th, 61st, 62d, 63d and 64th Congresses from Alabama.

Heine, William, consular clerk, removal of, and reason therefor, 4110.

Helgesen, H. T., b. near Decorah, Winneshiek county, Iowa, June 26, 1857; educated in the Decorah public schools, normal institute and business college; after graduating he entered the mercantile business; moved to Milton, N. Dak., where he operated an extensive lumber and hardware business, and extensively engaged in farming; member of the board of regents of the State University in 1889 he became the first commissioner of agriculture and labor in the newly admitted state of North Dakota; in the general election held November, 1910, was elected to the 62d, 63d and 64th Congresses from North Dakota.

Helm, Harvey; b. Danville, Boyle Co., Ky.; graduated A. B., Central University of Kentucky; admitted to the bar 1892; elected to State Assembly 1893; Lincoln county attorney 1897 and 1900; Member of the 60th, 61st, 62d, 63d and 64th Congresses from Kentucky.

Hempstead, Christopher, consul at Belize, British Honduras, mentioned, 2574.

Hendricks, Thomas Andrews (1811-1885); statesman and twenty-first Vice-President of the United States; b. at Zanesville, Ohio; began the practice of law in Indiana, and became Member of Congress 1851-55; United States Senator 1863-69; Governor of Indiana 1873-77; unsuccessful candidate for Vice-President with Tilden 1876; elected Vice-President with Cleveland 1884, but died in November of his first year.

Hendricks, Thomas A., Vice-President, death of announced and honors to be paid memory of, 4904, 4905, 4909.

Henry, B. H., report of agent to Fiji Islands to investigate claim of, transmitted, 6098.

Henry, E. Stevens, b. in Gill, Mass., in 1836, moving when 13 years old with his parents to Rockville, Conn.; was a representative in the Lower House of the Connecticut General Assembly of 1883; State Senator in 1887-88; treasurer of the State of Connecticut from 1889 to 1893; elected to the 54th, 55th, 56th, 57th, 58th, 59th, 60th, 61st and 62d Congresses from Connecticut.

Henry, John, alleged secret agent of Great Britain in United States for fomenting disaffection, 483.

Henry, Patrick; statesman, orator; b. Studley, Va., May 29, 1736; chosen in 1765 to the Virginia Assembly and elected a delegate from Virginia to the Continental Congress 1774-76; elected Governor of Virginia in 1776 and declined re-election; delegate to the Richmond Convention (q. v.) in 1777; served in the State Assembly from 1780 to 1791, and was again elected Governor in 1796, but declined to serve; died Red Hill, Va., June 6, 1799.

Henry, Patrick, minister to France, nomination of, 274.

Henry of Prussia, Prince, reception of, in United States, 6703.

Henry, Robert Lee; b. May 12, 1864, in Linden, Cass Co., Tex.; graduated M. A. from the Southwestern University of Texas in 1885, valedictorian of his class; elected Mayor of Texarkana in 1890; resigned the mayoralty to become Assistant Attorney-General, holding the latter office for nearly three years; was elected to the 55th, 56th, 57th, 58th, 59th, 60th, 61st and 62d Congresses from Texas.

Henshaw, David; politician, merchant, writer; Secretary of the Navy under President Tyler; b. April 2, 1791, in Leicester, Mass.; educated at the public schools and Leicester Academy; apprenticed to a drug house in Boston and continued in that business till 1829; became interested in politics and New England railroads; wrote political articles for the press; member of both branches of Massachusetts legislature, and member of Congress; appointed Collector of the Port of Boston in 1830; nominated for Secretary of the Navy by President Tyler, but served only a few months as the Senate refused to confirm the appointment; died Nov. 11, 1862.

Hensley, Walter L., b. Jefferson County, Mo., Sept. 3, 1871; educated in the public schools of his county and the law departments of the Missouri University; admitted to the bar in 1894; elected to the 62d, 63d and 64th Congresses from Missouri.

Hepner, George, treaty with Indians concluded by, 2830.

Herbert, Hilary A., Secretary of the Navy under President Cleveland; b. Laurensville, S. C., March 12, 1834; moved to Greenville, Butler County, Ala., in 1846; attended the University of Alabama in 1853-54; and the University of Virginia in 1855-56; studied law and admitted to the bar; entered the Confederate service as captain; promoted to the colonelcy of the Eighth Alabama Volunteers; disabled at the battle of the Wilderness, May 6, 1864; continued the practice of law at Greenville, Ala., until 1872, when he moved to Montgomery, where he afterwards practiced; elected a Representative from Alabama to the 45th, 46th, 47th, 48th, 49th, 50th, 51st, and 52d Congresses as a Democrat; Secretary of the Navy 1893-1897; located at Washington, D. C., and practiced law.

Herbert, Michael H., Canadian canal tolls referred to, 5675, 5678.

Hering, Rudolph, on committee to report upon sewerage system in District of Columbia, 5487, 5514.

Hermosa, William L., report of, on exploration of valley of the Amazon, transmitted, 2724, 2762.

Herold, David E.:
Implicated in assassination of President Lincoln, proceedings of trial and verdict of military commission, 3532, 3533, 3534, 3540, 3545, 3546.
Persons claiming reward for apprehension of, directed to file claims, 3551.

Herran, Dr. Tomas, correspondence of, concerning Panama, 6761.

Herschell, Lord, arbitrator in Venezuelan boundary dispute, 6338.

Hewitt, Abram Stevens; manufacturer, scientist, philanthropist; b. Haverstraw, N. Y., July 31, 1822; received his elementary education in the public schools of New York City, where he gained a prize scholarship to Columbia College, whence he graduated at the head of his class in 1842; acting professor of mathematics in 1843; studied law and admitted to practice in the State supreme court in October, 1845; his eyesight failing, he engaged in the iron business, and under the firm of Cooper & Hewitt established extensive iron works, mainly in New Jersey and Pennsylvania; appointed one of the ten United States scientific commissioners to visit the French Exposition Universelle of 1867 and made a report on iron and steel, which was published by Congress and has been translated into most foreign languages; organized and managed the Cooper Union for the Advancement of Science and Art, designed especially for the education of the working classes; elected to the 44th, 45th, 47th, 48th and 49th Congresses as a Democrat; mayor of New York City, 1887-88; died Jan. 18, 1903, at New York City.

Hewitt, Abram S., commissioner to Paris Universal Exhibition, 3798.

Heyburn, Weldon Brinton; b. Delaware Co., Pa., May 23, 1852; admitted to the bar in 1876; in 1883-84 moved to Shoshone Co., Idaho; he was a member of the convention which framed the constitution of the State of Idaho; chairman of the judiciary committee of that body; was elected to the United States Senate from Idaho for the term beginning March 4, 1903, and was re-elected Jan. 13, 1909.

Higginson, Francis J., expedition to Puerto Rico convoyed by fleet under, 6318.

Hill, Charles E., claim of, against China, referred to, 4436, 4801.

Hill, Ebenezer J.; b. Redding, Conn., Aug. 4, 1845; in 1862 he received from Yale University the honorary degree of master of arts; in 1863 he joined the army as a civilian, and remained until the close of the war; elected to the 54th, 55th, 56th, 57th, 58th, 59th, 60th, 61st, 62d, 63d and 64th Congresses from Connecticut.

Hinds, Asher Crosby; b. Benton, Me., Feb. 6, 1863; graduated from Colby College 1883; began newspaper work in Portland in 1884; Speaker's Clerk, United States House of Representatives, 1890-91; clerk at Speaker's table, United States House of Representatives, 1895-1911; elected to the 62d, 63d and 64th Congresses from Maine.

Hise, Elijah; statesman; b. Kentucky, July 4, 1802; defeated as Democratic candidate for lieutenant-governor in 1836; chargé d'affaires to Guatemala, March 31, 1848, to June 21, 1849; Presidential elector on the Democratic ticket in 1856; elected a Representative from Kentucky to the 39th Congress as a Democrat (vice Henry Grider, deceased), serving from Dec. 3, 1866, to 1867; re-elected to the 40th Congress; died at Russellville, Ky., May 8, 1867.

Hise, Elijah, treaty concluded by, with—
Guatemala, 2572, 2686.
Nicaragua, 2572, 2602.

Hitchcock, Ethan Allen (1835-1909); diplomat and cabinet officer; b. Mobile, Ala.; settled in business in St. Louis until 1860; thence in China until 1872; diplomatic representative in Russia as Minister 1897-98, and as the first Ambassador there 1898-99; Secretary of the Interior under McKinley until 1907.

Hitchcock, Frank Harris, Postmaster-General in President Taft's Cabinet; b. Amherst, Ohio, Oct. 5, 1867; has resided in Massachusetts from early boyhood; graduated from Harvard University in 1891; First Assistant Postmaster-General from 1905 to 1908; Chairman of the Republican National Committee in 1908 and conducted the Presidential campaign of that year.

Hitchcock, Gilbert M.; b. Omaha, Neb., Sept. 18, 1859; educated in public schools and by study in Germany and a law course at University of Michigan; graduated 1881; established the Omaha *Evening World* in 1885, which later became, under his management, the Omaha *Morning, Evening* and *Sunday World-Herald;* elected to the 58th, 60th and 61st Congresses from Nebraska; nominated in Democratic primaries for United States Senator, August, 1910; under the Oregon plan was elected and confirmed by the Legislature Jan. 18, 1911; his term will expire March 3, 1917.

Hitt, Robert Roberts; b. Urbana, Ohio, Jan. 16, 1834; moved to Ogle County, Ill., in 1837; educated at Rock River Seminary (now Mount Morris College) and at De Pauw University; reported Lincoln-Douglas debates in 1858; first secretary of legation and chargé d'affaires ad interim at Paris from December, 1874, until March, 1881; Assistant Secretary of State in 1881; regent of the Smithsonian Institution and chairman of the Committee of Foreign Affairs; commissioner to the Hawaiian Islands in 1898; elected to the 47th Congress Nov. 7, 1882, to fill the vacancy occasioned by the death of Hon. R. M. A. Hawk; elected to the 48th, 49th, 50th, 51st, 52d, 53d, 54th, 55th, 56th, 57th and 58th Congresses as a Republican.

Hitt, Robert R., member of commission to Hawaiian Islands, 6333.

Hoar, Ebenezer Rockwood (1816-1895); jurist and statesman; b. at Concord, Mass.; Judge of the Massachusetts Supreme Court 1859-69; Attorney-General of the United States under Grant 1869-70; Member of the Joint High Commission which negotiated the treaty of Washington 1871 with Great Britain; Member of Congress from Massachusetts 1873-75.

Hoar, Ebenezer R., member of commission to settle questions with Great Britain, 4075.

Hoar, George Frisbie (1826-1904); statesman; b. at Concord, Mass.; associated with the Free-Soil party, and later with the Republican party; Member of Congress from Massachusetts 1869-77; Member of the Hayes-Tilden Electoral Commission 1877; United States Senator 1877-1904; noted for his consistent oppositon to "imperialism."

Hobart, Garret Augustus (1844-1899); statesman and twenty-fourth Vice-President of the United States; b. Long Branch, N. J.; began the practice of law 1869; member of the State Legislature 1872; State Senator 1876, and became President of the State Senate 1881; and 1896 he was elected Vice-President of the United States with McKinley.

Hobby, James M., first assistant engineer, advancement in grade of, recommended, 3411.

Hobson, Richmond Pearson; b. Greensboro, Ala., Aug. 17, 1870; was educated at the Southern University, the United States Naval Academy, the French National School of Naval Design; is a naval architect and lecturer; served in the United States Navy from 1885 to 1903; received the degree of LL. D. from Southern University, June, 1906; elected to the 60th, 61st and 62d Congresses from Alabama.

Hobson, Richmond P., sinking of the *Merrimac* in Santiago Harbor, Cuba, by, 6305, 6316.
Thanks of Congress to, and promotion of, recommended, 6306.

Hodgson, Daniel B., recognition of services of, in battle of Manila Bay, Philippine Islands, recommendations regarding, 6305.

Hodgson, William B., conduct of, while in Constantinople, referred to, 2011.

Holcombe, James P., order exempting, from arrest during journey to Washington, 3438.

Holden, William W., provisional governor of North Carolina, appointed, 3510.

Holmes, Theophilus Hunter; soldier; b Clinton, N. C., Nov. 13, 1894; graduated United States Military Academy 1829; engaged in frontier service in the Seminole war and in the occupation of Texas; promoted to captain in the Mexican war and brevetted major for gallantry at Monterey; on the breaking out of the war he resigned from the army (April 22, 1861) and went to North Carolina and organized the State militia, and when the secession ordinance was passed became a brigadier-general in the Confederate army; after the war he returned to his home and died in Fayetteville, N. C., June 21, 1880.

Holmes, Theophilus H.:
Gallant conduct of, in Mexican War, 2370.
Major by brevet, nomination of, and correspondence regarding, 2369.

Holsey, Robert, act granting pension to, vetoed, 5026.

Holt, Joseph; lawyer, jurist; b. Breckenridge Co., Ky., Jan. 6, 1807; engaged in
law practice at Louisville, Ky., 1832-36,
and in Vicksburg, Miss., 1836-42; removed
to Washington and became Commissioner
of Patents 1857-59; Postmaster-General
1859-60; Secretary of War 1860-61; President Lincoln appointed him, in 1862, Judge-
Advocate General of the Army; declined
the Cabinet positions of Attorney-General
and Secretary of War; conducted the trials
of Fitz-John Porter (charged with disobedience of orders) and of the assassins of
President Lincoln; brevetted major-general
for "faithful, meritorious and distinguished" services in the bureau of military justice
during the war; died Washington, D. C.,
Aug. 1, 1894.

Holt, Joseph:
Judge-advocate in trial of persons implicated in assassination of President Lincoln, 3534.
Secretary of War, authorized to perform duties of, 3190.

Hood, John B., victories of Federals
over Confederate forces under, referred to, 3442.

Hooker, Joseph:
Commander of corps in Army, 3325.
Ordered to take military possession
of railroads, 3379.

Hoover, Herbert C.; b. West Branch,
Iowa, on August 10, 1874. In 1895 was
graduated from Leland Stanford University
in the department of mining engineering.
During the following years he was associated with geological and mining enterprises in different quarters of the globe, and
saw service in the Boxer Rebellion in China
in 1900. In London at the outbreak of the
Great European War, he was made executive director of the Belgian Relief Work,
and continued in that capacity until the
entrance of his own country into the war
brought him back in 1917 to the United
States as director of the National Food Commission created by the Government.

Hopkins, George W.; statesman; b.
Goochland County, Va., Feb. 22, 1804; received a common school education; studied
law and began practice at Lebanon, Va.;
a member of the State house of representatives 1833-34; elected a Representative
from Virginia to the 24th, 25th, 26th, 27th,
28th and 29th Congresses as a Democrat;
chargé d'affaires to Portugal March 3,
1847, to Oct. 18, 1849; again a member of
the State house of representatives in 1849;
judge of the circuit court; elected to the
35th Congress; again elected a member of
the State house of representatives; died
March 2, 1861.

Hopkins, George W., chargé d'affaires
at Lisbon, Portugal, mentioned, 2550.

Hopkinson, Joseph (son of Francis Hopkinson); b. Philadelphia, Pa., Nov. 12,
1770; graduated from the University of
Pennsylvania in 1786; studied law and in
1791 admitted to practice; began the practice of his profession at Easton, Pa.; elected a Representative from Pennsylvania to
the 14th and 15th Congresses; moved to
Bordentown, N. J., and after three years returned to Philadelphia, Pa.; judge of the
United States district court for Easton, Pa.,
1828-1842; delegate to the State constitutional convention in 1837; died at Philadelphia Jan. 15, 1842.

Hopkinson, Joseph, commissioner to
treat with Indians, nomination of,
256.

Horton, Benjamin J., telephone concession in Puerto Rico, 6732.

Houard, John E., imprisonment of, by
Spanish authorities referred to, 4116.

Houston, David Franklin, Secretary of
Agriculture under President Wilson; b.
Monroe, Union County, N. C., Feb. 17,
1866; son of William Henry and Cornelia
Anne (Stevens) Houston; A. B., South
Carolina College 1887; A. M., Harvard
1892; (LL. D., Tulane 1903, University of
Wisconsin, 1906, Yale 1913); married
Helen Beall, of Austin, Tex., December 11,
1895; tutor in ancient languages South
Carolina College and graduate student
1887-88; superintendent of city schools
Spartanburg, S. C., 1888-1891; graduate
student political science, Harvard 1891-
1894; adjunct professor 1894-1897, associate
professor 1897-1900, professor political
science 1900-1902, and dean of faculty
1899-1902, University of Texas; president
Agricultural and Mechanical College of
Texas 1902-1905; president University of
Texas 1905-1908; chancellor Washington
University, St. Louis, since September 24,
1908; member Southern Educational Board;
trustee John F. Slater Fund; member Rockefeller Sanitary Commission; fel-
fow Texas State Historical Society; member American Economic Association; president Harvard Graduate Club 1893-94;
author: A Critical Study of Nullification
in South Carolina, etc.; took office as Secretary of Agriculture March 6, 1913.

Houston, Sam; soldier, statesman; b.
Rockbridge Co., Va., March 2, 1793; enlisted in the army in 1813, and served under Gen. Jackson in the war with the Creek
Indians; distinguished himself for bravery
on various occasions and at the conclusion
of the war found himself lieutenant; studied
law in Nashville, and after holding several
minor offices in Tennessee was elected to
Congress in 1823 and served till 1827, when
he became Governor of Tennessee; in 1829,
before the expiration of his gubernatorial
term he resigned his office and went to take
up his abode among the Cherokee Indians
in Arkansas; in 1832 he went to Texas on
the invitation of President Jackson to arrange treaties with the Comanches and
other Indians; joined in the Texas revolution and was made commander of the military forces; fought the Mexicans with such
vigor that the independence of the Texans
was conceded and Houston became the first
President of the new republic; after an intervening term in Congress he was again
elected President of Texas in 1841, while
continually advocating annexation to the
United States; in 1846 his hopes were realized and Texas became a state of the union,
and Houston was sent to the United States
Senate; continued in the Senate until 1859,
when he was elected Governor of Texas;
advised against secession and was denounced
therefor as a traitor to the South; vetoed
a resolution recognizing the authority of
the Texas State Convention of Jan. 28,
1861, and the resolution was passed over
his veto and the State seceded from the
union by a vote of 167 to 7; as Governor
he submitted to the will of the people, but
declined to take the oath of allegiance to
the Confederacy, and was deposed from his
office of Governor; likewise refused a commission of major-general in Federal Army
tendered by President Lincoln; died in
Huntsville, Texas, July 26, 1863.

Houston, Sam:
Commander of Texan army, 1493.
President of Republic of Texas, 2172.

Houston, William Cannon; b. Bedford
Co., Tenn., March 17, 1852; elected to the
Legislature in 1876; admitted to the bar in
1878; again elected to the Legislature in
1880 and 1882; elected Circuit Judge in
1894 and 1898; elected to the 59th, 60th,
61st, 62d, 63d and 64th Congresses from
Tennessee.

Howard, E. A., agent of Ponca Indians,
4583.

Howard, John Eager; soldier, statesman;
b. Baltimore, June 4, 1752; received a liberal education; served in the Revolutionary
war and colonel when peace was declared;
Delegate from Maryland to the Continental
Congress 1787-88; governor of Maryland
1789-1792; member of the State senate
1795; elected a United States Senator from
Maryland vice R. Potts, resigned, serving
from Dec. 7, 1796, to March 3, 1803; died
at Baltimore, Md., Oct. 12, 1827.

Howard, John E., legislative acts of
Maryland received from, transmitted,
63.

Howard, Lieut., report of, regarding
services of Apache Indians transmitted, 5495.

Howard, Oliver Otis; soldier, author; b.
Leeds, Me., Nov. 8, 1830; graduated Bowdoin College, A. B., 1850; A. M., 1853;
graduated U. S. Military Academy, 1854;
served through the civil war, rising successively from lieutenant to major-general;
retired Nov. 8, 1894; author of "Donald's
School Days," "Chief Joseph of the Nez
Perces," "Life of Zachary Taylor," and
articles on subjects connected with the civil
war.

Howard, Oliver O., Commissioner of
Freedmen's Bureau:
Directed to effect arrangement between freedmen and landowners,
3549.

Report of his observations of the
condition of the seceded States
and of the operations of the Freedmen's Bureau therein, referred to,
3571.

Howard, William Schley; b. Kirkwood,
Dekalb County, Ga., June 29, 1875; attended Neel's Academy until 12 years of
age; was a page in the House of Representatives of Georgia in 1888-89; calendar
clerk of the House in 1890-91; appointed
Private Secretary to United States Senator
Patrick Walsh, of Georgia, in 1893; studied
law at night and was admitted to the bar
at Wrightsville, Ga., 1895; enlisted in the
Third Georgia Volunteer Infantry on July
2, 1898, serving during the Spanish-American war as Sergeant; on his return from
the war moved back to Dekalb county and
began the practice of his profession; elected
to the House of Representatives of Georgia
in 1899; introduced what is now known as
the Howard franchise tax act, the first of
its kind introduced in the South; married
Miss Lucia Augusta du Vinage, of Texas,
in 1905; elected to the 62d, 63d and 64th
Congresses from Georgia.

Howe, Albion P., member of court to
try assassins of President Lincoln,
3534.

Howe, Haughwout, records of association founded for purposes of aiding
soldiers of Civil War offered to
United States, 4798.

Howe, S. D., treaty with Indians concluded by, 3403.

Howe, Samuel G., imprisonment of, in
Prussia, 1136.

Howe, Timothy O.; Postmaster-General
under President Arthur; b. Livermore, Me.,
Feb. 24, 1816; received a liberal education;
studied law and practiced; served one
term in the state legislature; moved to
Wisconsin in 1845; elected judge of the
circuit and supreme courts of Wisconsin
in 1850 and resigned in 1855; elected a
United States Senator from Wisconsin as
a Union Republican and re-elected two
terms, serving from 1861-1869; appointed
one of the delegates to the International
Monetary conference in Paris in 1881; appointed Postmaster-General in 1881; died
at Kenosha, Wis., March 25, 1883.

Howe, Timothy O., Postmaster-General,
death of, announced and honors to
be paid memory of, 4747.

Howell, Joseph; b. Feb. 17, 1857, in
Boxelder Co., Utah; attended Utah University; Mayor of Wellsville, and a Member
of the Board of Regents of Utah University;
served three terms in the Territorial Legislature and one in the State Senate; elected
to the 58th, 59th, 60th, 61st, 62d, 63d and
64th Congresses from Utah.

Howison, Henry L., member of Board
on Geographic Names, 5647.

Hubbard, Commander J., report of, on
revolution in Panama, 6838.

Hubbard, Samuel Dickinson; Postmaster-
General under President Fillmore; b. Middletown, Conn., August 10, 1779; pursued
classical studies and graduated from Yale
College in 1819; studied law, but devoted
himself to manufacturing; elected a Representative from Connecticut to the 29th
Congress as a Whig; re-elected to the 30th
Congress; Postmaster-General Aug. 31,
1852, to March 7, 1853; died at Middletown, Conn., Oct. 8, 1855.

Huebschmann, Francis, treaties with Indians concluded by, 2773, 2896.

Huggins, Samuel, wounding and rob-
bing of, by Mexican soldiers, referred
to, 4376.

Hughes, Charles James, Jr.; b. Kingston, Richmond, Mo., Feb. 16, 1853; graduated from Richmond (Mo.) College in
1871; received the degree of LL. D. both
from the University of Missouri and the
University of Denver; began the practice
of law in August, 1877; Senator Hughes,
while engaging generally in the practice
of law, has given special attention to mining and irrigation litigation; for many
years professor of mining law in the University of Denver; elected United States
Senator from Colorado Jan. 20, 1909.

Hughes, William; b. in 1872; served in the Spanish-American War; elected to the 58th, 60th, 61st and 62d Congresses from New Jersey.

Hull, Cordell; b. Oct. 2, 1871, Overton (now Pickett) Co., Tenn.; graduated law department of Cumberland University, Lebanon, Tenn.; member of the lower house of the Tennessee Legislature two terms; served in the Spanish-American War, with the rank of captain; later was first appointed by the Governor, and afterwards elected Judge of the Fifth Judicial Circuit of Tennessee; elected to the 60th, 61st, 62d, 63d and 64th Congresses from Tennessee.

Hull, Isaac; naval officer; b. Derby, Conn., March 9, 1773; took to the sea in early life and joined United States Navy March 9, 1798; in 1804 he commanded the brig *Argus*, one of the vessels of Commodore Preble's fleet in the Mediterranean; made captain in 1806 and put in command of the frigate *Constitution;* his capture and destruction of the British frigate *Guerrière*, Aug. 19, 1812, was the first naval victory of the second war with England and won fame and fortune for Hull; Congress voted him a gold medal and $50,000; later commanded the *Ohio*, flagship of the European squadron; retired in 1841 and died in Philadelphia, Pa., Feb. 13, 1843.

Hull, Isaac:
Letters of Andrew Stevenson to, referred to, 1953.
Victory of the *Constitution* under command of, over the *Guerrière*, 502.

Hull, William; soldier; b. Derby, Conn., June 24, 1753; graduated Yale 1772, and admitted to the bar in 1775; captain of a company of militia in the uprising against England; was an active officer during the Revolutionary War, and at its close was second in command of the only regiment not disbanded, Gen. Heath being its colonel; in 1784 he was ordered to take possession of the frontier forts of Niagara, Detroit, Mackinac, and others on the great lakes, but they were not surrendered until after the Jay treaty was signed; appointed governor of Michigan Territory by President Jefferson in 1805; at the outbreak of the War of 1812 the Territory was unprepared for hostilities and Hull was defeated and taken a prisoner to Montreal; later exchanged and convicted of cowardice and neglect of duty by a court-martial; he was sentenced to death, but pardoned by President Madison; published a vindication in 1824; died Newton, Mass., Nov. 29, 1825.

Hull, William:
Letter of, regarding Indians referred to, 421.
Official conduct of, referred to, 430.
Surrenders fort and town of Detroit to the British, 500.
Treaty with Indians concluded by, 422.

Hulsemann, Chevalier, chargé d'affaires of Austria, withdrawal of, referred to, 2690.

Humphrey, William E.; b. March 31, 1862, near Alamo, Montgomery Co., Ind.; graduated Wabash College, Crawfordsville,

Ind., 1887; was admitted to the bar and practiced law at Crawfordsville; in 1893 moved to Seattle, Wash.; in 1898 was elected to the office of corporation counsel of Seattle; re-elected in 1900; elected to the 58th, 59th, 60th, 61st, 62d, 63d and 64th Congresses from Washington.

Humphreys, Benjamin Grubb; b. Claiborne Co., Miss., Aug. 17, 1865; studied law, and was admitted to the bar November, 1891; when war was declared against Spain, in April, 1898, he raised a company and was elected first lieutenant; served under Maj.-Gen. Fitzhugh Lee in Florida during the entire war, being mustered out with his regiment at Columbia, Tenn., Dec. 22, 1898; elected to the 58th, 59th, 60th, 61st, 62d, 63d and 64th Congresses from Mississippi.

Humphreys, David, minister to Portugal, nomination of, 90.

Hunt, Alexander C., treaty with Indians concluded by, 3663, 3827.

Hunt, William H.; lawyer; Secretary of the Navy under President Garfield; b. in 1824 in Charleston, S. C.; after a public school education he entered Yale College, Class '43, and remained there but two years; went to New Orleans and began the practice of law; before the war he was Whig in politics, during the war a staunch Union man, and later a Republican; appointed Attorney General of Louisiana to fill a vacancy in 1876, and claimed to have been elected to that office the following year, but the Democratic State officers were recognized by President Hayes; Mr. Hunt was later made judge of the United States Court of Claims; March 5, 1881, President Garfield appointed him Secretary of the Navy; upon the reorganization of the cabinet by President Arthur he retired in favor of William E. Chandler; in 1882 he was appointed Minister to Russia, and died Feb. 27, 1884, in St. Petersburg.

Hunter, David; soldier; b. Washington, D. C., July 21, 1802; graduated U. S. Military Academy, 1822; served in the Mexican War, and in February, 1861, was assigned to accompany President-elect Lincoln from Springfield, Ill., to Washington; made brigadier-general and served through the Civil War and was mustered out as brigadier-general in 1866; retired from the regular service six months later; died Washington, D. C., Feb. 2, 1886.

Hunter, David:
Command of corps formerly under Gen. Burnside, assumed by, 3325.
Member of court to try assassins of President Lincoln, etc., 3534.
Proclamation of, for freedom of slaves in certain States declared void, 3292.

Hunter, Lieut., report of, on establishment of steamship lines referred to, 2173.

Hunter, Robert M. T.; statesman; b. Essex County, Va., April 21, 1809; received a liberal education and graduated from the University of Virginia; studied law, and in 1830 admitted to the bar; elected a Representative from Virginia to the 25th, 26th and 27th Congresses; defeated for re-election; served as Speaker of the House in the 26th Congress; defeated for the 28th Congress; elected to the 29th Congress; elected a United States Senator from Virginia, serving from 1847 until he withdrew when Virginia seceded, and in July, 1861, was expelled; delegate from Virginia to the Confederate provincial congress at Richmond; Confederate State Senator from Virginia to the 1st Confederate Congress; Confederate Secretary of State; elected State treasurer of Virginia in 1877; died in Essex County, Va., July 18, 1887.

Hunter, Robert M. T., member of commission to confer with President regarding termination of war, 3461.

Hunter, William; physician, diplomat; b. Newport, R. I., Nov. 26, 1774; graduated from Brown University in 1791; studied medicine in London; returned to Newport and in 1796 admitted to the bar; served several years in the State house of representatives; elected a United States Senator from Rhode Island and re-elected, serving from Nov. 25, 1811, to March 3, 1821; commissioned chargé d'affaires to Brazil June 28, 1834, and minister plenipotentiary Sept. 13, 1841, serving until Dec. 9, 1843; died at Newport, R. I., Dec. 3, 1849.

Hunter, W., Acting Secretary of State, 3487, 3504.

Hunter, W. M., court-martial of, 889.

Huntington, Samuel (about 1732-1796); politician; b. at Norwich, Conn.; member of Congress, 1777, and signer of the Declaration of Independence; governor of Connecticut, 1786-96; received the two electoral votes from his own state in the first election for President in 1789.

Hurlburt, Stephen A.; diplomat; b. Charleston, S. C., Nov. 29, 1815; received a thorough education; studied law; admitted to the bar in 1837; served in the Florida war; moved to Belvidere, Ill., in 1845; Whig delegate to the constitutional convention of Illinois in 1847; Presidential elector on the Whig ticket in 1848 and on the Republican ticket in 1868; member of the legislature in 1859, 1861 and 1867; served in the Union Army 1861-1865, being appointed brigadier-general of volunteers May 27, 1861, and major-general in Sept. 1862; minister resident to the United States of Colombia 1869-1872; elected a Representative from Illinois to the 43d and 44th Congresses as a Republican; appointed minister to Peru in 1881, becoming prominent in Secretary Blaine's Peruvian-Chilean policy; died at Lima, Peru, March 27, 1882.

Hurlbut, Stephen A., minister to Bogota, mentioned, 4011.

Hutchins, Charles, treaty with Indians concluded by, 3403.

Ingalls, John J.; author, journalist, lawyer, statesman, orator; b. Dec. 29, 1833, at Middleton, Essex Co., Mass.; educated in public schools of Haverhill and graduated Williams College 1855; admitted to the bar in 1857 and the following year moved to Atchison, Kan., and entered actively into the political discussions which distraught the territory at the time; delegate to the Wyandotte Conventon in 1859, and secretary of the territorial council; secretary of State Senate in 1861 and in the following year elected to that body; became editor of the Atchison *Champion*; unsuccessful candidate for Lieutenant Governor on the Republican ticket in 1862 and 1864; engaged in the practice of law and journalism till 1873, when he was elected to the United States Senate and served for eighteen consecutive years; he was an eloquent and convincing speaker; from 1889 to 1891 he was president *pro tem.* of the Senate, where his proficiency in parliamentary procedure was strikingly apparent; after leaving the Senate wrote for the press and practiced law until his death, Aug. 16, 1900.

Ingham, Samuel D., Secretary of the Treasury under President Jackson; b. Pennsylvania Sept. 16, 1779; attended the public schools; manager of a paper mill at Easton, N. J., for several years; member of the state legislature of Pennsylvania for three years; prothonotary at Philadelphia; elected a Representative from Pennsylvania to the 13th, 14th, and 15th Congresses as a Jackson Democrat, resigning July 6, 1818; elected a Representative to the 17th Congress, vice Samuel Moore, resigned; re-elected to the 18th, 19th, and 20th Congresses; Secretary of the Treasury from March 6, 1829, serving until Aug. 8, 1831, when he resigned; died at Trenton, N. J., June 5, 1860.

Innis, James, commissioner appointed by United States under treaty with Great Britain, 188-

Iredell, James (1751-1799); politician and jurist; b. Lewes, England; justice of the United States Supreme Court, 1790-1799; in the third electoral college he received three votes for President.

Iredell, James (1788-1853); politician and jurist; b. at Edenton, N. C.; governor of North Carolina, 1827-28; and United States Senator, 1828-31.

Irion, R. A., secretary of state of Republic of Texas, convention signed by, 1686.

Irvine, Callender, commissary-general of purchases, nomination of, discussed, 992.

Irwin, James T., act granting pension to, vetoed, 5044.

Irwin, John, commanding American naval forces at Honolulu, reports of, referred to, 5906.

Irwin, Walter R., treaty with Indians concluded by, 3896.

Izard, Ralph; patriot, statesman; b. near Charleston, S. C., in 1742; received classical education and graduated from Cambridge University, England; Delegate from South Carolina to the Continental Congress 1781-1783; elected United States Senator from South Carolina 1789-1795; appointed by the Continental Congress commissioner to Tuscany; recalled June 8, 1779; pledged his large estate in South Carolina for the payment of ships of war to be used in the Revolution; died near Charleston, S. C., May 30, 1804.

Izard, Ralph, on committee to conduct inaugural ceremonies of President Washington, 40.

Jackson, Andrew, biography of, 998.

Jackson, Henry R., minister to Mexico, resignation of, 5123.

Jacobs, Richard T., lieutenant-governor of Kentucky, arrest and imprisonment of, 3460.

Jacobs, Stephen, district attorney, nomination of, 91.

Jacoway, Henderson M., b. Dardanelle, Yell County, Ark., Nov. 7, 1870, and is the third son of Judge W. D. Jacoway; graduated from the Dardanelle High School at the age of 16 years and from the Winchester Literary College, Winchester, Tenn., in 1892; in 1898 graduated from law department of Vanderbilt University, receiving a degree of LL. B.; served as secretary of the Dawes Commission during the Cleveland administration; elected to the office of prosecuting attorney in 1904, and re-elected in 1906. Sept. 19, 1907, married Miss Margaret H. Cooper, daughter of Hon. S. B. Cooper, of Beaumont, Tex.; was elected to the 62d Congress from Arkansas, carrying every county in the district and nearly every voting precinct and re-elected to the 63d and 64th Congresses.

Jacques, William H., member of Gun Foundry Board, 4748.

James, Ollie M.; b. Crittenden Co., Ky., July 27, 1871; was admitted to the bar in 1891; was one of the attorneys for Governor Goebel in his celebrated contest for governor of the State of Kentucky; elected to the 58th, 59th, 60th, 61st, and 62d Congresses from Kentucky; elected to the United States Senate for term ending 1920.

James, Thomas L.; printer, publisher, editor; Postmaster General under President Garfield; b. March 29, 1831, in Utica, N. Y.; left school at the age of fifteen and was apprenticed to a local printer; at twenty he became a partner in publishing the Madison County (N. Y.) *Journal*; the paper was Whig in politics, and as editor Mr. James attracted the attention of the leading men of the State; in 1861 he was appointed to a position in the office of the Collector of the Port of New York and in 1873 President Grant made him postmaster at New York; he declined the office of Collector of the Port, tendered by President Hayes, and was reappointed Postmaster; he declined the Republican nomination for Mayor of New York and Postmaster General under Hayes; March 5, 1881, Garfield named him for Postmaster General and he accepted the place; he found the service disorganized, many of the employees dishonest and an annual deficit of $2,000,000; under his executive direction abuses were corrected, frauds punished and the service was made self-sustaining; declined to serve in Arthur's cabinet, returned to New York and entered the banking business.

Jarvis, Charles, correspondence regarding northeastern boundary. (See Northeastern Boundary.)

Jay, John (1745-1829); jurist and statesman; b. New York City; represented the State of New York in Congress, 1774-77, and drew up the constitution of New York, 1777; United States minister to Spain, 1780-82; peace commissioner with Adams and Franklin at Paris, 1783; secretary for foreign affairs, 1784-89; first chief justice of the Supreme Court of the United States, 1789-95; concluded with England the treaty of 1794, known as Jay's Treaty, which conveyed to the United States the military posts of the northwest, erected the eastern boundary, provided for the payment of English debts and the settlement of American claims, restricted the United States trade with the West Indies, and defined the conditions of neutrality at sea; Jay was an unsuccessful candidate for governor of New York 1792; was special minister to Great Britain, 1794-95 and governor of New York, 1795-1801.

Jay, John, minister to Great Britain, nomination of, 146.

Jefferson, Thomas, biography of, 307.

Jenckes, Thomas A.; statesman; b. Cumberland, R. I., Nov. 2, 1818; graduated from Brown University in 1838; studied law, and in 1840 admitted to the bar; began practice at Providence; clerk in the State legislature 1840-1844; secretary of the State constitutional convention in 1842; adjutant-general 1845-1855; member of the State legislature 1854-1859; commissioner to revise the laws of the State in 1855; elected a Representative from Rhode Island to the 38th, 39th, 40th and 41st Congresses as a Republican; defeated as a Republican candidate to the 42d Congress; died at Cumberland, R. I., Nov. 4, 1875.

Jenckes, Thomas A., correspondence regarding Dorr's Rebellion, 2149.

Jenkins, Capt. (See *Baltimore*, The.)

Jesup, Thomas S., commander of forces in Seminole War, 1472.

Report of, referred to, 1697.

Jewell, Marshall, Governor of Connecticut (1869-70 and 1871-72), and Postmaster-General under President Grant; b. Winchester, N. H., Oct. 20, 1825; his American ancestry goes back to Thomas Jewell, who was granted land at Wollaston, Mass., shortly after the settlement of Massachusetts; he received a common school education and learned tanning under his father; in 1873, after having served two terms as governor, he was appointed minister to Russia, whence he was recalled to be made Postmaster-General in 1874; he was chairman of the Republican National Committee during the campaign that ended with Garfield's election to the presidency; he died at Hartford, Feb. 10, 1883.

Jewett, Milo A., consul of United States at Sivas, Turkey, directed to investigate Armenian atrocities, 5991.

Joffre, Joseph Jacques Césaire; b. near the Pyrenees in France in 1852. As a youth entered the Ecole Polytechnique (the French Military Academy) as a student of military engineering; and saw service during the Franco-Prussian War in 1870 as a sub-lieutenant of artillery in a Paris fortification. He became prominently and favorably known as a deep student of military engineering, and was made a captain in 1876. In 1885 he was active in the Indo-Chinese campaign, and was appointed a major in 1889. As a result of his brilliant services in Timbuctoo in 1894, he was made a lieutenant-colonel and was awarded the Legion of Honor. His thorough mastery of military science soon brought him appointment as professor in the Ecole de Guerre (School of

Jones, Roger; soldier; b. Washington, D. C., Feb. 25, 1831; graduated U. S. Military Academy, 1847; served on the Texas frontier and in New Mexico, and at the outbreak of the Civil War was promoted to the rank of captain, and received the thanks of President Lincoln and Secretary Cameron; served throughout the war, and rose to the rank of brigadier-general; died Fortress Monroe, Va., Jan. 26, 1889.

Jones, Roger:

Correspondence regarding Dorr's Rebellion, 2157.

Mentioned, 702.

Orders respecting funeral honors to—

Adams, John, 914.

Harrison, W. H., 1880.

Jefferson, 914.

Lafayette, 1314.

Jones, Thomas, proceedings of, in taking possession of Monterey, Mexico, discussed, 2080.

Jones, Wesley L., b. near Bethany, Ill., Oct. 9, 1863, three days after the death of his father, a private in the Civil War; his mother maintained herself and children by her own labor; he did all kinds of farm work, hiring out by the month when 10 years of age; attended public schools in winter; worked during the summer until he was 16, when he entered Southern Illinois College, teaching to pay his way; working in the harvest fields during the summer; admitted to the bar on examination in 1886; elected to the 56th, 57th, 58th, 59th, and 60th Congresses as one of the Representatives-at-large from the State of Washington; the legislature of 1907 for Washington enacted a direct primary law in which provision was made for expressing the party choice for United States Senator by popular vote; he became a candidate and was successful by a large majority, and was duly elected to the United States Senate.

Jones, William, Secretary of the Navy under President Madison; b. Philadelphia, Pa., in 1760; received a liberal education; served in the Revolutionary war; entered the Continental Naval service; moved to Charleston, S. C.; returned to Pennsylvania; elected a Representative from that state to the 7th Congress as a Democrat; Secretary of the Navy Jan. 12, 1813-Dec. 7, 1814; collector of customs at Philadelphia; died at Bethlehem, Pa., Sept. 5, 1831.

Jones, William, Secretary of Navy:

Duties of Secretary of Treasury discharged by, during the absence of Albert Gallatin, one of the commissioned envoys to treat with Great Britain and Russia in 1813.

Jones, William Atkinson; b. Warsaw, Va., March 21, 1849; elected to the 52d, 53d, 54th, 55th, 56th, 57th, 58th, 59th, 60th, 61st, 62d, 63d and 64th Congresses from Virginia.

Juarez, Benito P., President of Mexico:

Demonstration by Congress of United States of Colombia in honor of, referred to, 3575.

Government formed by, discussed, 3095.

Referred to, 3175, 3577.

Jussen, Edmund, act for relief of, vetoed, 4168.

Kahn, Julius; b. Feb. 28, 1861, at Kuppenheim, Grand Duchy of Baden, Germany; immigrated to California with his parents in 1866; in 1892 was elected to the legislature of the State of California; in January, 1894, was admitted to the bar by the supreme court of California; was elected to the 56th, 57th, 59th, 60th, 61st, 62d, 63d and 64th Congresses from California.

Kalakaua, David, King of Hawaiian Islands:
Coronation of, discussed, 4761.
Death of, in United States, discussed, 5623.
Visit of, to United States, 4630.

Kalanianaole, J. Kuhio; b. March 26, 1871, at Koloa, island of Kauai, Hawaii; was educated in Honolulu, the United States, and England; is a capitalist; was employed in the office of minister of the interior and in the custom-house under the monarchy; cousin to the late King Kalakaua and Queen Liliuokalani, monarchs of the then Kingdom of Hawaii, and nephew of Queen Kapaiolani, consort of Kalakaua; created prince by royal proclamation in 1884; married Elizabeth Kahanu Kaauwai, daughter of a chief of the island of Maui, Oct. 8, 1896; elected delegate to the 58th, 59th, 60th, 61st, and 62d Congresses from Waikiki, district of Honolulu, island of Oahu.

Kasson, John A., report of, on commercial relations with Cuba, 6294.

Kautz, August V., member of court to try assassins of President Lincoln, etc., 3534.

Kearny, Philip, major-general in Army, nomination of, and reasons therefor, 3362.

Keiley, Anthony M.; jurist; b. New Jersey, in 1835; graduated Randolph Macon College, in Virginia; founded and carried on the Norfolk *Virginian,* and the *Index and News,* of Petersburg; appointed by President Cleveland envoy extraordinary and minister plenipotentiary to Italy in 1885; but the appointment was cancelled on account of the objections of the Italian government, and he was accredited to Austria, but he was declared *persona non grata* at Vienna, and he resigned; in 1886 President Cleveland appointed him to the International Court in Egypt, maintained by the leading countries to adjudicate international questions; died in Paris, France, Jan. 24, 1905.

Keiley, A. M.:
Minister to Austria-Hungary, appointment of, and refusal of Government to receive, discussed, 4910.
Minister to Italy and Austria-Hungary, appointment of, referred to, 4951.

Keim, D. B. R., report of, on consular affairs and amount paid to, referred to, 4123, 4160, 4161.

Keith, Charles B., treaty with Indians concluded by, 3284.

Kelley, Mr., commissioner to investigate affairs of New York custom-house, 2005.

Kellogg, William P.:
Candidate for governor of Louisiana, election disturbances discussed. (See Louisiana, elections in.)
Mentioned, 4177.

Kendall, Amos; lawyer, editor, author; Postmaster General under President Jackson; b. Aug. 16, 1789, in Dunstable, Mass.; attended school at New Ipswich, N. H., and graduated from Dartmouth College in 1811; studied law in Groton, Mass.; travelled by way of Washington, D. C., to Kentucky, where he became a tutor in private families, including that of Henry Clay; admitted to the bar in Kentucky and made postmaster at Georgetown in 1814; became sole editor of the *Argus of Western America* at Frankfort, Ky., in 1816, and was interested in promoting the cause of education; appointed by President Jackson Fourth Auditor of the Treasury, 1829; acquired great influence in the administration and was largely the means of having the *Globe* newspaper supersede the *Telegraph* as the official organ; appointed Postmaster General in 1835; he found the department disorganized, corrupt and heavily in debt; within a year the debts were cleared, but Mr. Kendall had incurred the hostility of powerful mail contractors, who obtained judgments against him for claims he considered invalid; he started successively *Kendall's Expositor* and the *Union Democrat,* both of which failed; for the judgments against him he was imprisoned within the bounds of the District of Columbia; Congress later paid the claims and abolished the law of imprisonment for debt in the District; his reputation was established as an honest man and a pure, faithful, inflexible public officer; when he left the Post Office Department he received the most gratifying testimony to that effect from those who had associated with him; he later declined a foreign mission tendered by President Polk, and in 1845, associated with Prof. S. F. B. Morse in the development of the telegraph; this business brought him an ample fortune, which he devoted largely to benevolences; in 1860 he published in the *Washington Evening Star* a series of vigorous protests against the secession of the Southern States; at the outbreak of the Civil War he placed his house and grounds in Washington at the disposal of the government for the use of troops and spent a year in Trenton, N. J.; he published an incomplete "Life of Andrew Jackson"; died Nov. 12, 1869, in Washington.

Kennedy, Charles A.; b. Montrose, Iowa, March 24, 1869; mayor of his native town for four years; in 1903 he was elected to the Iowa legislature, serving two terms; elected to the 60th, 61st, 62d, 63d and 64th Congresses from Iowa.

Kennedy, John P.; Secretary of the Navy under President Fillmore; b. Baltimore, Md., Oct. 25, 1795; received a classical education; graduated from Baltimore College in 1812; studied law, and admitted to the bar in 1816; commenced practice at Baltimore; served in the war of 1812; State representative 1820-1822; appointed secretary to the legation at Chile, January 27, 1823, but resigned; defeated for the 25th Congress, but subsequently elected to the same Congress as a Representative from

Maryland (vice Isaac McKim, deceased), serving from April 30, 1838, to 1839; defeated for the 26th Congress; Presidential elector on the Whig ticket in 1840; elected to the 27th and 28th Congresses; Secretary of the Navy July 22, 1852, to March 7, 1853; died at Newport, R. I., Aug. 18, 1870.

Kennon, Beverly, court-martial of, referred to, 811.

Kent, Edward, correspondence regarding northeastern boundary. (See Northeastern Boundary.)

Kent, William; b. Chicago, Ill., March 29, 1864, and is the son of Albert E. and Adaline Elizabeth (Dutton) Kent; his parents moved to California in 1871 and settled in Marin County; preliminary education received in private schools in California and at Hopkin's Grammar School, New Haven, Conn.; entered Yale in 1883 and graduated in 1887, with the degree of A. B.; M. A. (honorary), Yale, 1908; located in Chicago to look after his father's business interests; in 1890 entered into partnership with his father, under the firm name of A. E. Kent & Son; was married to Elizabeth Thacher of Ojai Valley, Cal., Feb. 26, 1890; owner of real estate and business interests in Chicago, as well as in California; member of the firm of Kent & Burke, cattle dealers, Genoa, Nebr.; active in civic affairs; member of the Chicago City Council from 1895 to 1897; president of the Municipal Voters' League of Chicago, 1899-1900, and a member of its executive committee from 1897 to 1904; member of the Illinois Civil Service Association and of the Civil Service Reform League of Chicago; member of the following clubs: Union League; University; City (Chicago); Yale (New York) University; Bohemian (San Francisco); Graduates (Yale); sought the Republican nomination for Congress as a Progressive against Duncan E. McKinlay, and defeated the latter under the direct primary law of California; was elected to the 62d, 63d and 64th Congresses from California.

Kenyon, William S.; b. Elyria, Ohio, June 10, 1869; educated at Iowa College, Grinnell, Iowa, and law school of the State University of Iowa; was prosecuting attorney for Webster County, Iowa, for five years; district judge for two years; general attorney Illinois Central Railroad Co. for three years; Assistant to the Attorney-General of the United States for one year; elected to the United States Senate April 12, 1911, to succeed the Hon. Lafayette Young, who was appointed United States Senator Nov. 12, 1910, to fill the vacancy caused by the death of Hon. Jonathan P. Dolliver, and took his seat April 24, 1911.

Kern, John Worth; b. Dec. 20, 1849, in Howard County, Ind.; educated in the common schools, Normal College at Kokomo, Ind., and graduated from the law department of the University of Michigan with degree of bachelor of laws, class 1869; by profession, a lawyer, practising at Kokomo, Ind., until 1885, since that time at Indianapolis; member of bar of Supreme Court of the United States and member of American Bar Association; was reporter of the Indiana Supreme Court from 1885 to 1889, and edited and published 17 volumes of Indiana Reports—volumes 100 to 116, inclusive; member of Indiana State Senate 1893-1897; city solicitor of Indianapolis,

1897-1901; special assistant United States district attorney 1892-4; Democratic candidate for governor in 1900 and 1904; Democratic candidate for Vice-President in 1908; married and has three children; was nominated as the party's candidate for United States Senator by a unanimous vote of the Democratic State convention in 1910, and elected Jan. 18, 1911.

Kernan, John D., member of Strike Commission, 5983.

Kerr, Joseph, commissioner for Cumberland road, 406.

Kerr, J. Bozman, chargé d'affaires in Nicaragua, mentioned, 2687, 2695.

Kerr, Michael C.; b. Titusville, Pa., March 15, 1827; received a liberal education and graduated from Louisville University in 1851; admitted to the bar and began practice at New Albany, Ind., in 1852; elected city attorney in 1854; elected prosecuting attorney of Floyd County in 1855; member of the State legislature in 1856 and 1857; elected reporter of the supreme court of Indiana in 1862; elected a Representative from Indiana to the 39th, 40th, 41st and 42d Congresses as a Democrat; defeated for the 43d Congress; elected to the 44th Congress and elected its Speaker; died at Rockbridge Alum Springs, Va., Aug. 19, 1876.

Kerr, Michael C., Speaker of House of Representatives, death of, announced, 4352.

Key, David McKendree; Postmaster-General under President Hayes; b. Greene County, Tenn., Jan. 27, 1824; raised on a farm in Monroe County; attended the common schools; graduated from Hiawassee College in 1850; studied law, admitted to the bar, and began practice at Chattanooga in 1853; Presidential elector on the Democratic ticket in 1856 and on the Breckinridge and Lane ticket in 1860; served in the Confederate army as lieutenant-colonel in the Civil War; member of the state constitutional convention in 1870; chancellor of the third chancery district 1870-1875; defeated as the Democratic candidate to the 43d Congress; appointed a United States Senator from Tennessee as a Democrat (vice Andrew Johnson, deceased), serving from December 6, 1875, to January 29, 1877; defeated for re-election; Postmaster-General March 12, 1877, to 1880; resigned to accept United States judgeship of the eastern district of Tennessee; retired Jan. 26, 1894; died at Chattanooga, Tenn., Feb. 3, 1900.

Key, Francis Scott; American lawyer and song writer; b. Frederick County, Md., Aug. 1, 1779; educated at St. John's College, Annapolis, and commenced the practice of law in Frederic City; became district attorney for the District of Columbia. As a song writer he is remembered by his "Star-Spangled Banner," a popular national lyric suggested and partly written while the author was detained aboard the British fleet during the bombardment of Fort McHenry, near Baltimore, of which he was a witness; d. Baltimore, Jan. 11, 1843. A collection of his miscellaneous poems was published in 1856.

Key, Thomas M., interview with Gen. Cobb regarding exchanging of prisoners of war, 3459.

nental army at Cambridge, Mass., April
19, 1775, and rendered efficient service
in the early days of the Revolution;
during the winter of 1775-76, he transported fifty-five pieces of ordnance
and 2,300 pounds of lead from Ticonderoga to Cambridge; made brigadier-
general of artillery in 1776; after the war
he founded the Society of Cincinnati; appointed Secretary of War by Congress,
1785, and on the inauguration of Washington as President was retained in the
Cabinet; resigned Jan. 2, 1795, the compensation of the office not being sufficient to support his family; removed to
Maine and engaged in farming; died at
Thomaston, Me., Oct. 25, 1802.

Knox, Henry:
Commissioner appointed by United
States under treaty with Great
Britain, 188.
Commissioner to treat with Indians,
70.
Proceedings of Cabinet were signed
by him as attendant adviser of
President Jefferson.

Knox, Philander Chase; Secretary of
State under President Taft; b. Brownsville, Pa., May 6, 1853; admitted to the
bar in 1875; assistant United States district attorney for the western district of
Pennsylvania in 1876; made Attorney-
General in the Cabinet of President Mc-
Kinley in 1901 and of President Roosevelt Dec. 16, 1901; resigned that office
June 30, 1904, to accept appointment as
United States Senator from Pennsylvania,
to fill a vacancy caused by the death of
Hon. M. S. Quay, and took his seat Dec.
6; elected by the legislature January,
1905, for the term ending March 3, 1911;
resigned as Senator March 4, 1909, to
accept the position of Secretary of State.

Kock, Bernard, agreement with, for
emigration of negroes canceled, 3368.

Konop, Thomas F.; b. Franklin, Ke-
waunee County, Wis., Aug. 17, 1879; at-
tended a country school and high school,
Two Rivers, Wis.; and the State Normal
School at Oshkosh; studied law at the
Northern Illinois College of Law and at

the State University of Nebraska, from
which last-named institution he received
his degree of LL. B. in 1904; admitted to
the bar in Wisconsin; served three terms
as district attorney of his county. Mr.
Konop was nominated for Congress in
September, 1910, on the Democratic ticket
in a district safely Republican by 5,000;
after a hard campaign of two months, during which he visited every corner of his
district, he was elected by a plurality of 5
votes, the Republican State ticket carrying the district at the same time; elected
to the 62d, 63d and 64th Congresses from
Wisconsin.

Kosciusko, statue of, at Washington,
D. C., 5934.

Kossuth, Louis; an eminent Hungarian
patriot, orator and statesman; born of a
noble family at Monok, county of Zem-
plin, 1802; studied law and joined the
popular party in opposing the despotic
rule of Austria; imprisoned in 1837-40
for having offended the government by his
writings; elected to the Diet in 1847, and
acquired a high reputation as an orator;
he induced the Diet to vote the perfect
equality of civil rights and public burdens for all classes, and to extend the
right of suffrage; became minister of
finance in the cabinet formed in April,
1848; in April, 1849, the Hungarians renounced allegiance to Austria and chose
Kossuth dictator; Russian intervention on
behalf of Austria prevented the establishment of a Hungarian republic; Kossuth
went to Turkey, where he was imprisoned,
but later liberated through the intervention of the United States and England;
visited England and the United States in
1857, where he was greeted with enthusiasm; died Turin, Italy, March 20, 1894.

Kossuth, Louis:
Liberation of, and companions re-
ferred to, 2647, 2655.
Misunderstanding of, with Capt.
Long referred to, 2682.

Koszta, Martin, seizure and imprisonment of, by Austrian brig of war
and subsequent release of, discussed, 2742.
Referred to, 2764, 2770, 2771.

La Blanche, Alcée:
Chargé d'Affaires to Republic of Texas, nomination of, 1501.
Convention at Houston, Tex., signed by, 1686.

Ladd, Edward H., claim of, against Colombia, 4804.

Lafayette, George W.:
First copperplate of Declaration of Independence bequeathed to Congress by father of, letter of, presenting, 1342.
Resolutions of Congress on death of father of, transmitted to, 1343.
Reply of, to, 1344.

Lafayette, Marquis de; French solder and statesman; b. Chavagnac, near Brioude, Auvergne, Sept. 6, 1757; educated at the College of Louis le Grand, Paris, and became an officer of the guards; learning of the Declaration of Independence of the American colonists, he determined to aid them; with 11 companions he arrived in America, April 14, 1777, and volunteered his services to Congress without pay; he was given a major-general's commission, and became a member of Washington's staff; served valiantly through the Revolution and secured for the American cause financial assistance and the reinforcement of a fleet and 6,000 troops under Rochambeau; returned to France, and two days after the destruction of the Bastile (July 15, 1789), saved the lives of the King and Queen; resigned his titles on the adoption of the French constitution; one of the three major-generals during the coalitions against France, in 1792; visited the United States on invitation of the President at the request of Congress, and was received with enthusiastic delight; was presented a section of land and $200,000, his fortune having been swept away; died Paris, May 20, 1834.

Lafayette, Marquis de:
Bust of, presented to Congress, 992.
"Citizen of France, but friend of United States," 1313.
Death of—
Announced, 1273.
Funeral honors to be paid memory of, 1314.
Resolutions of Congress on, transmitted to family of, 1343.
Reply of George W. Lafayette, 1344.
Tribute to memory of, 1314.
Declaration of Independence, first copperplate of, bequeathed to Congress by, letter of son presenting, 1342.
Mentioned, 6932.
Services of, to America discussed and provision for, recommended, 828.
Visit of, to United States, 874.
Declines invitation to be conveyed in United States ship of war, 827.
Writes concerning claims of—
Baron De Kalb, 1270.
French citizens, 1198.

Lafean, Daniel Franklin; b. York, Pa., Feb. 7, 1861; actively engaged in the manufacturing business and banking; elected to the 58th, 59th, 60th, 61st, 62d, 63d and 64th Congresses from Pennsylvania.

Lafferty, A. W.; b. Audrain County, Mo., June 10, 1875; attended the law department of the Missouri State University, admitted to the bar of the Supreme Court of Missouri, and practiced law at Montgomery City, Mo.; served three years with the rank of captain in the Missouri National Guard and one term as prosecuting attorney; in 1909 he was given the degree of LL. B. by the law department of the Missouri University; appointed special agent of the General Land Office, and was sent to Oregon, arriving at Portland the 1st of March, 1905; resigned as special agent of the Land Office and re-entered the private practice of law; instituted litigation in the Federal court in Oregon to compel the Oregon and California Railroad Company to sell 2,300,000 acres of lands granted to it by act of Congress in accordance with the terms of the grant, which require that the lands shall be sold by the railroad company to actual settlers only in quantities not greater than a quarter section to any one settler, and at prices not exceeding $2.50 per acre; became a candidate for Congress in 1910 as a Progressive Republican, favoring greater liberality to homesteaders and the giving to Oregon the benefit of her own natural resources; was elected to the 62d, 63d and 64th Congresses from Oregon.

Lafitte, Jean. (See Barrataria, Island of.)

La Follotte, Robert Marion; b. at Primrose, Dane Co., Wis., June 14, 1855; graduated from the State University of Wisconsin, 1879; admitted to the bar in 1880; elected a member of the 49th, 50th, and 51st Congresses; elected governor of Wisconsin in 1900, 1902, and 1904; elected to the United States Senate from Wisconsin, Jan. 25, 1905.

La Follette, William L.; b. Boone Co., Ind., Nov. 30, 1860, and went West at the age of 16 years, settling in eastern Washington; engaged in fruit, grain, and stock raising for 30 years, and served one term in the Washington legislature and on various appointive commissions; elected to the 62d, 63d and 64th Congresses from Washington.

Lamar, Lucius Quintus Cincinnatus, Secretary of the Interior under President Cleveland; b. Putnam County, Ga., Sept. 1, 1825; moved to Oxford, Miss.; graduated from Emory College, Oxford, Ga.; in 1845 studied law at Macon, and admitted to the bar in 1847; returned to Oxford, Miss., in 1849; served a year as professor of mathematics at the University of Mississippi; moved to Covington, Ga., and elected a State representative in 1853; returned to Lafayette County Miss.; elected a Representative from Mississippi to the 35th Congress as a Democrat, and re-elected to the 36th, serving until his retirement, Jan. 12, 1861, to become a member of the secession convention of Mississippi; served in the Confederate army as lieutenant-colonel and colonel; in 1863 entered the diplomatic service of the Confederacy on a special mission to Russia; in 1866 elected professor of political economy and social science at the University of Mississippi, and in 1867 professor of law; elected a Representative from Mississippi to the 43d Congress and also to the 44th; United States Senator from Mississippi 1877 to March 6, 1885, resigning to accept the Secretaryship of Interior; in December, 1887, appointed associate justice of the United States Supreme Court; died at Vineville, Ga., Jan. 23, 1893.

Lambert, William, astronomical observations by, 680, 688, 789.

Lamont, Daniel Scott, journalist and Secretary of War under President Cleveland; b. McGrawville, Cortland Co., N. Y., Feb. 9, 1851; he came of Scotch-Irish ancestry, who emigrated to this country and devoted themselves to farming; from such lineage sprung Andrew Jackson, John C. Calhoun, Horace Greeley, and many others of the most eminent men of America; young Lamont's father was a well-to-do farmer, and the boy, after having studied in the Cortland Normal College, was sent to Union College, Schenectady, N. Y., but did not graduate; he left college before the end of the course in order to enter the profession of journalism, for which he possessed both taste and predilection; he purchased an interest in the *"Democrat,"* a paper published at the county seat of his native county, and became its editor, at the same time interesting himself warmly in politics; for a time the young man held a position on the staff of the Albany *"Argus,"* and he thus became known to many of the most influential politicians of the state. When Grover Cleveland was elected governor of New York, he met young Lamont; and, having had occasion to make use of his knowledge and ability in the preparation of his first message, offered him an honorary position on his military staff, which gave him the title of colonel; Gov. Cleveland next appointed Lamont his private secretary, in which position the latter made himself so useful and valuable, that when Mr. Cleveland became President he took Lamont with him to the White House; it was Mr. Lamont, who, when private secretary to Gov. Cleveland, originated the phrase "Public office a public trust." He used this as a headline in compiling a pamphlet of Mr. Cleveland's speeches and addresses; the expression used by Mr. Cleveland was, "Public officials are the trustees of the people," and it was employed in his letter accepting the nomination for the office of mayor of Buffalo.

Lander, Frederick W., activity and enterprise manifested by, commended, 3305.

Landreau, John C., claim of, against Peru referred to, 4463.

Lane, Franklin Knight, Secretary of the Interior under President Wilson; b. Charlottetown, Prince Edward Islands, Canada, July 15, 1864; son of Dr. C. S. and C. W. H. Lane; removed to California during childhood; educated at the University of California 1886; married Anne Wintermute, of Tacoma, Wash., April 11, 1893; engaged in newspaper work in college days and later was reporter, New York correspondent for western papers, and part owner and editor of the Tacoma *Daily News;* admitted to the bar in California in 1889; corporation counsel for city of San Francisco three terms, 1897-1902; candidate for governor of California 1902; party vote of

legislature of California for United States Senator 1903; member Interstate Commerce Commission December, 1905, to March, 1913; formerly member permanent international railway commission, representing United States Government; took office as Secretary of the Interior March 5, 1913.

Lane, Henry S.; b. Montgomery County, Ky., Feb. 24, 1811; received a public school education; studied law and began practicing at Crawfordsville, Ind.; served in the State senate; elected a Representative from Indiana to the 26th Congress, vice T. A. Howard, resigned; re-elected to the 27th Congress; served in the Mexican war as lieutenant-colonel of volunteers; elected governor of Indiana in 1860; served two days and resigned to become a United States Senator from Indiana 1861-1867; delegate to the Republican national convention at Chicago in 1868 and at Cincinnati in 1876; died at Crawfordsville, Ind., June 11, 1881.

Lane, Henry S., member of Indian commission, 3977.

Lane, James H., brigadier-general, United States Army, appointment of, referred to, 3236.

Langdon, John; statesman; b. Portsmouth, N. H., June 25, 1741; chosen delegate to Congress from New Hampshire, 1775-76; captain of volunteers in Vermont and Rhode Island; speaker of the house of representatives of New Hampshire, 1776-77, and judge of the court of common pleas; again appointed delegate to Congress in 1783, and repeatedly a member of the legislature, and speaker; elected governor in 1788; United States Senator, 1789-91; again from 1805 to 1808 and in 1810 and 1811, he was governor; died at Portsmouth, N. H., Sept. 18, 1819.

Langdon, John:
Appointed on committee to meet President Washington, 36
Washington's election certified by, as President of Senate, 35.

Langley, John Wesley; b. Floyd Co., Ky.; attended the law departments of the National, Georgetown, and Columbian (now George Washington) universities for an aggregate period of eight years and was awarded the first prize in two of them; had conferred on him the degrees of bachelor of laws, master of laws, doctor of the civil law, and master of diplomacy; served two terms in the Kentucky legislature; elected to the 60th, 61st, 62d, 63d and 64th Congresses from Kentucky.

Lardner, James L., thanks of Congress to, recommended, 3284.

Larkin, T. O., dispatch forwarded to, and destroyed by Capt. Gillespie, 2428.

Larned, Samuel, treaty with Peru-Bolivian Confederation concluded by, 1563.

Larrabee, Charles F., member of Indian commission, 5579.

Larrinaga, Tulio; of San Juan; b. Trujillo Alto, Jan. 15, 1847; educated in the Seminario Consiliar of San Ildefonso, at San Juan, where he received the degree

Lee, Robert Edward, soldier, son of General Henry Lee (Light Horse Harry); b. Jan. 19, 1807, at Stratford House, Westmoreland County, Va.; graduated United States Military Academy, West Point, 1829; served in the Mexican War as chief engineer on the staff of Gen. Winfield Scott; superintendent of West Point Military Academy (1852-1855); in command military department of Texas 1860; resigned from the army April 25, 1861, after Virginia had seceded from the Union; and became major-general of the state forces, later a general in the Confederate army, and finally Commander-in-chief of all the forces of the Southern States. Throughout the entire war 'he maintained with skill and valor the cause he believed to be just, and at last, when overcome by the Federal army, he surrendered to General Grant at Appomattox, Va., April 9, 1865, thus ending the Civil War. He advised his soldiers to accept the proffered parole, return to their homes and be good citizens. After the war he was made President of Washington College at Lexington, Va., where he died Oct. 12, 1870. A beautiful mausoleum was erected over his tomb at Lexington, and an equestrian statue commemorates 'his name in Richmond, Va.

Lee, Robert E.; b. Schuylkill County, Pa., and educated in the common schools of Pottsville; elected to the 62d, 63d and 64th Congresses from Pennsylvania.

Lee, Samuel P., thanks of Congress to, recommended as a naval officer commanding one of the vessels engaged in the operations under Flag-Officer Farragut at Forts Jackson and St. Philip, at New Orleans, 1862, 3277.

Legarda, Benito; b. Manila, Sept. 27, 1853; was educated in the Jesuits' College and St. Thomas University of Manila, from the latter of which he received the degree of LL. B.; held some honorific positions during the Spanish régime; joined Aguinaldo when he landed in Cavite shortly after Admiral Dewey had destroyed the Spanish fleet, 1898; member of Aguinaldo's cabinet at Malolos and vice-president of the Filipino congress; resigned these positions to return to Manila in December, 1898; cooperated with live interest in the establishment of peace during and after the war between the Filipinos and Americans; Feb. 1, 1901, appointed by President McKinley a member of the Philippine Commission; elected by the Philippine legislature to be a Resident Commissioner of the Philippine Islands in the United States, November, 1907.

Legare, Hugh Swinton, Attorney-General under President Tyler; b. Charleston, S. C., Jan. 2, 1789; graduated from the College of South Carolina in 1814; studied law; visited Paris and Edinburgh; admitted to the bar at Charleston, S. C., in 1822; state representative 1820-1822 and 1824-30; Attorney-general of South Carolina 1830-1832; chargé d'affaires to Brussels 1832-1836; elected a Representative from South Carolina to the 25th Congress as a Union Democrat; defeated for the 26th Congress; Attorney-General from Sept. 13, 1841, until his death, at Boston, Mass., June 20, 1843.

Leggett, Mortimer D., Commissioner of Patents, recommendation of, referred to, 4115.

Leib, R. J., consul at Tangier, disposition of presents given by Emperor of Morocco discussed, 1256.

Lennox, David, attacked while discharging duties of marshal, 151.

Lenroot, Irvine L.; b. Superior Co., Wis., Jan. 31, 1869; became court reporter, studied law, and was admitted to the bar in 1897; elected to the Wisconsin legislature in 1900, 1902, and 1904; elected speaker of the assembly in 1903 and 1905; elected to the 61st, 62d, 63d and 64th Congresses from Wisconsin.

Letcher, John; b. Lexington, Rockbridge County, Va., March 28, 1813; studied at Washington College and at Randolph-Macon College; studied law and commenced practice at Lexington in 1839; Presidential elector on the Democratic ticket in 1848; delegate to the State constitutional convention of 1850; elected a Representative from Virginia to the 32d, 33d, 34th and 35th Congresses as a Democrat; governor of Virginia 1860-1864; turned over the entire forces of the State to the Confederacy before its secession; died at Lexington, Va., Jan. 26, 1884.

Letcher, John, official acts of, in Virginia declared null and void, 3535.

Lever, Asbury Francis; b. Jan. 5, 1875, near Springhill, Lexington Co., S. C.; graduated in law at the Georgetown University in 1899, and admitted to practice in his state by the supreme court; elected to the state legislature from Lexington County; elected to the 58th, 59th, 60th, 61st, 62d, 63d and 64th Congresses from South Carolina.

Levy, David (afterwards David Levy Yulee); b. St. Thomas, West Indies, in 1811; pursued classical studies and studied law in Virginia; moved to Florida in 1824, becoming a planter; elected a Delegate from Florida to the 27th and 28th Congresses as a Democrat; changed his name to David Levy Yulee; delegate to the first State constitutional convention; twice elected a United States Senator from Florida as a Democrat, serving from Dec. 1, 1845, to 1851, and from 1855 until his retirement, Jan. 1, 1861; president of the Atlantic and Gulf Railroad; served in the Confederate Congress; prisoner of state at Fort Pulaski in 1865; died at New York City Oct. 10, 1886.

Levy, Jefferson M.; b. in his district, son of Capt. Jonas P. Levy, and nephew of Commodore Uriah P. Levy, a distinguished naval officer of the last generation, who was mainly instrumental in the abolition of flogging in the United States Navy; graduated from the University of New York, studied law; one of the founders of the Democratic Club of New York; studied law; member Chamber of Commerce and Board of Trade and Transportation of New York; Commodore Levy, in 1830, at the suggestion of President Jackson, became the owner of Monticello, the home of Thomas Jefferson, and at his uncle's death Mr. Levy became, and still remains, the owner; the homestead is maintained by Mr. Levy in keeping with its distinguished traditions. Mr. Levy was elected to the 56th and 62d Congresses from New York.

Lewis, David J.; b. May 1, 1869, at Nuttals Bank, Center County, Pa., near Osceola, Clearfield County; began coal mining at 9 years of age and learned to read at Sunday school; continued at mining until 1892, when he was admitted to the bar of Allegheny County, having pursued his occupation as a miner and his studies in law and Latin at the same time; elected to the Maryland senate in 1901, and to the 62d. 63d and 64th Congresses from Maryland.

Liliuokalani, Queen of Hawaiian Islands:

Referred to, 5623.

Restoration of, to throne, discussed, 5783.

Surrender of sovereignty of, discussed, 5903.

Lincoln, Abraham, biography of, 3204.

Lincoln, Benjamin, commissioner to treat with Indians, nomination of, 52.

Lincoln. Levi: b. Worcester, Mass., Oct. 25, 1782; graduated from Harvard College in 1802; studied law, commencing practice in 1805; Democratic State senator in 1812 and State representative 1814-1822; delegate to the State constitutinoal convention in 1820; elected lieutenant-governor in 1823; appointed associate justice of the supreme court in 1824; governor 1825-1834; elected a Representative from Massachusetts to the 23d Congress as a Whig, vice John Davis, resigned; elected to the 24th, 25th and 26th Congresses, serving from March 5, 1834, to 1841; collector of Boston in 1841; president of the State senate; Presidential elector on the Whig ticket in 1848; first mayor of Worcester in 1848; member of numerous historical and agricultural societies; died at Worcester, Mass., May 29, 1868.

Lincoln, Levi, commissioner to settle boundary question with Georgia, 329.

Lincoln, Robert T.; Secretary of War under President Garfield, and Minister to England; b. Aug. 1, 1843, in Springfield, Ill., eldest child of President Lincoln; educated in a private school of Springfield, and at Illinois State University; later spent a year at Phillips Academy, Exeter, N. H., graduated from Harvard in 1864; took a course in law and was appointed a captain of volunteers; saw service in the final campaign of the Civil War, ending at Appomattox; resumed the study of law in Chicago and was admitted to the bar in 1867; took an active part in local politics and worked for the election of Grant, Blaine and Garfield for the presidency; appointed Secretary of War in 1881 by President Garfield; on the accession of Arthur to the presidency he was the only one of Garfield's cabinet who was requested to remain in office, which he did to the close of the administration; President Harrison appointed him Minister to England.

Lind, John; b. Sweden, March 25, 1854; received a public school education; attended the State University at Minneapolis; taught school read law, and admitted to the bar in 1877; appointed receiver of the Tracy land office in 1881; elected to the 50th, 51st and 52d Congresses as a Republican; served in the Spanish war as quartermaster of the Twelfth Minnesota Regiment of Volunteers; elected governor of Minnesota in 1898 as a Democrat; elected to the 58th Congress; sent to Mexico on mission of peace by President Wilson during insurrection in 1913.

Lind, John, sent as representative to Mexico, 7885.

Instructions to, 7885.

Proposals rejected, 7887.

Lindbergh, Charles A.; b. in Sweden and brought by his parents to Melrose, Minn., in his first year; an extensive writer for magazines and newspapers on political economy; has always taken great interest in farming; elected to the 60th, 61st, 62d, 63d and 64th Congresses from Minnesota.

Linthicum, John C.; b. Linthicum, Anne Arundel County, Md., Nov. 26, 1867; received his early education in the public schools of that county and of Baltimore city, later entering the State Normal School, from which he graduated in 1886, when he became principal of Braddock School, Frederick County, and later taught school in his native county of Anne Arundel; returning to Baltimore he took a special course in the historical and political department of Johns Hopkins University, after which he entered the University of Maryland school of law, from which he obtained his degree of LL. B. in 1890; practiced law in the city of Baltimore; elected to the house of delegates from Baltimore; chairman of the city delegation, chairman of the elections committee, a member of the judiciary committee and of the printing committee, and performed valuable service for the state and city; elected to the state senate; appointed in 1908 by Governor Crothers as judge-advocate-general; elected to the 62d, 63d and 64th Congresses from Maryland.

Lippitt, Henry F.; b. Providence, Oct. 12, 1856; received an academical education, graduating from Brown University, with the degree of A. B.; entered the cotton manufacturing business, in which he has served in various capacities from day operative to general manager; he has been a director in the Mechanics' National Bank, of Providence, in several of the mill mutual insurance companies, and vice-president of the People's Savings Bank, of Providence; colonel on the staff of Governor Taft of Rhode Island in 1888-89; was elected, 1911, to the United States Senate from Rhode Island.

Livermore, W. R., commissioner in marking boundary line between Texas and Mexico, 4902.

Livingston, Edward; lawyer, jurist, author; b. Clermont, N. Y., May 26, 1764; representative in Congress from New York City, 1795-1802; United States Attorney for the district of New York, and in 1801 Governor Clinton appointed him mayor of New York City; contracted yellow fever during the epidemic in 1803, and on his recovery found his fiscal affairs had been so badly managed by his agent as to be hopeless; he confessed judgment to the United States in the sum of $100,000; gave up all his property and went to New Orleans and began the practice of law; was a member of the Louisiana legislature and represented the state in the 18th, 19th, and 20th Congresses, and in the Senate from 1829 to 1831, when he resigned to accept the position of Secretary of State; appointed minister to France in 1833; his "Penal Code" is considered a monument to his profound learning, and his "Criminal Jurisprudence" is a standard law book; died Rhinebeck, N. Y., May 23, 1836.

Livingston, Edward:
Minister to France—
Correspondence regarding claims
against France. (See France,
claims against.)
Referred to, 1407.
Instructed to quit France if claims
are not paid, 1354.
Official conduct of, complimentary
letter concerning, 1404.
Resignation of, transmitted, 1403.
Secretary of State, 1219.
Correspondence relating to north-
eastern boundary. (See North-
eastern Boundary.)

Livingston, Joseph W., consul at San
Juan de Nicaragua, mentioned, 2573.

Livingston, Robert R.; statesman, diplomat; b. New York City, Nov. 27, 1746;
graduated from King's College in 1765;
studied law, and commenced practice in
New York; city recorder 1773-1775; member of the colonial assembly 1775; Delegate from New York to the Continental Congress 1775-1777 and 1779-1781; secretary
of foreign affairs August, 1781, to August,
1783; delegate to the State constitutional
convention in April, 1777; chancellor of
New York State 1777-1801; minister plenipotentiary to France 1801-1804; prominent
in local affairs; died at Clermont, N. Y.,
Feb. 26, 1813.

Livingston, Robert R., minister to negotiate treaty with France, nomination
of, 339.

Lloyd, James Tighlman; b. Carona, Lewis
Co., Mo., Aug. 28, 1857; admitted to the
bar, and practiced his profession in Lewis
County until 1885, when he located at
Shelbyville; elected to the 55th Congress,
to fill a vacancy; elected to the 56th,
57th, 58th, 59th, 60th, 61st, 62d, 63d and
64th Congresses from Missouri.

Lloyd-George, David; b. in Manchester,
England, on January 17, 1863, but at the
age of 1 year was taken to live in Wales.
He studied for the bar, and became a solicitor before he was twenty years old. As a
Non-Conformist, he early was attracted to
politics, and at a by-election was elected to
a seat in the House of Commons in 1890.
During the next ten years, he became noted
in Parliament as a trenchant Parliamentary
fighter, his radical views on social questions
endearing him to the working-classes. He
bitterly opposed the Boer War during 1899-
1902, and his opposition made him unpopular
to the extent that he was mobbed when he
attempted to speak in Birmingham in 1900.
When the Liberals were returned to power
in 1905, he was made President of the
Board of Trade, and earned fame for himself, not only by his efficient administration
of that office, but also by his settlement of
the severe railroad strike of 1906. When
Asquith became Premier in 1908, he was
made Chancellor of the Exchequer, and proceeded to outline a comprehensive series of
social reforms for England, including
schemes for old-age pensions and national
insurance. To provide revenue for this program, he introduced his famous budget of
1909-10, in which large taxes were laid upon
the unearned increment of land, and upon
other possessions of the wealthy classes.
The budget was eventually thrown out by
the House of Lords, as a result of which the
veto powers of the House of Lords were cur-

tailed. When the coalition Cabinet was
formed in 1915, he became the Minister of
Munitions, and on December 7, 1916, succeeded Asquith as Prime Minister.

Lobeck; C. O.; b. Andover, Ill., April 6,
1852; educated at Andover, at high school,
Geneseo, Ill., and one year at German
Wallace College, Berea, Ohio, and, later
a term at Dyhrenfurth Commercial College, Chicago; from 1875 to 1892 was a
commercial traveler, selling dry goods and
hardware; member of the Travelers'
Protective Association; entered political
life in 1892, being elected state senator
(Omaha district), Nebraska; became a
Silver Republican, supporting Mr. Bryan;
in 1897 elected a councilman of Omaha,
city comptroller of Omaha; was Democratic presidential elector for Nebraska in
1900; nominated at the primary election
Aug. 16, 1910, over four competitors and
was elected to the 62d, 63d and 64th Congresses from Nebraska.

Lodge, Henry Cabot; b. Boston, Mass.,
May 12, 1850; graduated from Harvard
College in 1871, receiving the degree of
LL. B., and Ph. D. from Harvard University for his thesis on "The Land Law
of the Anglo-Saxons;" has published
"Short History of the English Colonies in
America;" "Life of Alexander Hamilton;"
"Life of Daniel Webster;" edited the
works of Alexander Hamilton in 9
volumes; published "Studies in History;"
"Life of Washington," 2 volumes; member of the Massachusetts Historical Society, the Virginia Historical Society, the
American Academy of Arts and Science,
the New England Historic and Genealog-
ical Society; has received the degree of
doctor of laws from Williams College,
Clark University, Yale University, and
Harvard University; Regent of the Smithsonian Institution; served in house of representatives of Massachusetts; elected to
the 50th, 51st, 52d, and 53d Congresses;
took his seat in the Senate March 4, 1893;
re-elected 1899 and 1905 to represent Massachusetts.

Long, John C., misunderstanding with
Louis Kossuth referred to, 2682.

Long, John D.:
Report of, on number of lives lost by
sinking of the *Maine*, 6296.
Thanks of President tendered Commodore Dewey by, 6568.

Longworth, Nicholas; b. Cincinnati, O.,
Nov. 5, 1869; graduated A. B. from Harvard University, 1891; graduated Cincinnati Law School, 1894; admitted to the
bar, 1894; elected to the Ohio house of
representatives, 1899, and to state senate,
1901; elected to the 58th, 59th, 60th, 61st,
62d and 64th Congresses from Ohio.

Loomis, F. B., reports of, during Panama Revolution, 6752-6755.

Loud, George Alvin, lumberman of Au
Sable; b. June 18, 1852, in Bracebridge,
Geauga Co., Ohio; engaged in the lumber business; during the Spanish-American
War, while making a trip around the
world on the revenue cutter *McCulloch*,
under commission of six months as paymaster, was present and participated in
the battle of Manila. Later was sent
by the governor in charge of the hospital
train, through the southern camps and
hospitals, to bring home the sick soldiers
of Michigan regiments; elected to the
58th, 59th, 60th, 61st, 62d and 64th Congresses from Michigan.

McAdoo, William Gibbs, Secretary of the Treasury under President Wilson; b. near Marietta, Ga., Oct. 31, 1863; son of William G. McAdoo, M. A. LL. D., who was a judge, soldier in the Mexican and Civil Wars, district attorney general of Tennessee, and adjunct professor of English and history in the University of Tennessee; removed from Georgia to Tennessee; studied at the University of Tennessee; admitted to the bar at the age of 21; practiced law in Chattanooga until 1892, when he removed to New York and continued the practice of his profession; conceived the Hudson River tunnel system; organized the company which built it and was its president from 1902 to 1913; delegate to the Baltimore convention in 1912; vice chairman of the Democratic National Committee and acting chairman during the greater part of the campaign of 1912; married Sarah Houston Fleming, of Chattanooga, Tenn., who died February, 1912, and is the father of six children—three sons and three daughters; appointed Secretary of the Treasury March 5. 1913; was married May 7, 1914, to Miss Eleanor Randolph Wilson, daughter of the President.

McArthur, Duncan, treaty with Indians concluded by, 590.

McCall, Samuel Walker; b. East Providence, R. I., Feb. 28, 1851; admitted to the bar, practicing in Boston; served as editor in chief of the Boston *Daily Advertiser;* member of the Massachusetts house of representatives of 1888, 1889, and 1892; author of biography of Thaddeus Stevens, "American Statesmen Series"; elected to the 53d, 54th, 55th, 56th, 57th, 58th, 59th, 60th, 61st and 62d Congresses from Massachusetts.

McCalla, Bowman H., member of board to consider expedition to be sent for relief of Lady Franklin Bay Expedition, 4813.

McCallum, D. C., military director and superintendent of railroads, appointed, 3302.

McClellan, Capt., Florida volunteers under command of, referred to, 2430.

McClellan, George Brinton; soldier, author; b. Philadelphia, Pa., Dec. 3, 1826; entered West Point as an instructor, and prepared a manual on "Bayonet Exercise," which became a text-book in military service; at the outbreak of the Rebellion he was appointed major-general of Ohio volunteers, and soon after to same rank in the regular army, and on the retirement of Gen. Scott was made general-in-chief of the United States army; commanded the Army of the Potomac in the Peninsular campaign; resigned from the army in 1864; Democratic candidate for President in opposition to President Lincoln in 1864; governor of New Jersey, 1878-81; published books on military subjects; died Oct. 29, 1885.

McClellan, George B.:
Command of Army of United States assumed by, 3241.
Plans of, approved, 3312.
Referred to, 3257.
Death of, announced and honors to be paid memory of, 4904.

Relieved of command of Army of Potomac, and Major-General Burnside ordered to take command of that Army. He in turn to be succeeded by Major-General Hunter, 3325.
Relieved of command of other departments, retaining command of Department of Potomac, 3312.
Report of, on Dominican Republic, transmitted, 4071.
Resignation of, as major-general accepted, 3443.

McClelland, Robert, Secretary of the Interior under President Pierce; b. Greencastle, Pa., Aug. 1, 1807; graduated from Dickinson College, Carlisle, Pa., in 1829; admitted to the bar in Chambersburg in 1831; moved to Pittsburg. thence in 1833 to Monroe, Mich.; delegate to the state constitutional conventions of 1835 and 1867; state representative 1838-1843, the last year as speaker of the house; elected a Representative from Michigan to the 28th, 29th, and 30th Congresses as a Democrat; delegate to the national Democratic conventions of 1848, 1852, and 1868; governor of Michigan 1851-1853; resigning; Secretary of the Interior 1853-1857; died at Detroit, Mich., Aug. 27, 1880.

McCook, Anson G.; soldier; b. Steubenville, Ohio, Oct. 10, 1835; received a common school education; in the spring of 1854 crossed the plains to California; returned in the autumn of 1859, and at the outbreak of the rebellion was engaged in the study of law; entered the Union Army as captain in the Second Regiment of Ohio Infantry, and was at the first battle of Bull Run; on the reorganization of the regiment was commissioned major and afterwards promoted to lieutenant-colonel and colonel, serving with the regiment in the Army of the Cumberland; at the muster out of the regiment commissioned colonel of the One hundred and ninety-fourth Ohio Infantry, and at the close of the war brevetted brigadier-general; appointed assessor of internal revenue in the seventeenth Ohio district in November, 1865; moved to New York in May, 1873; elected to the 45th, 46th and 47th Congresses as a Republican.

McCook, Anson G., letter of, regarding statue of Gen. Garfield to be erected in Washington transmitted, 4795.

McCook, Edward M., brigadier-general in Army, nomination of, referred to, 3403.

McCord, Victor H., claim of, against Peru, 5988, 6092, 6335.

McCrary, George Washington, Secretary of War under President Hayes; b. near Evansville, Ind., Aug. 29, 1835; moved to what is now Iowa in 1836; attended public schools; studied law, commencing practice at Keokuk in 1856; elected state representative in 1857 and state senator in 1861; elected a Representative from Iowa to the 41st, 42d, 43d, and 44th Congresses as a Republican; Secretary of War March 12, 1877 to 1879; judge of the eighth judicial district 1879-1884; moved to Kansas City, Mo., becoming consulting attorney for the Atchison, Topeka and Santa Fe Railroad Company; died at St. Joseph, Mo., June 23, 1895.

McCrea, Lieut., interpreter at trial and investigation into the Chilean outrage upon the sailors of the *Baltimore*, 5620, 5650, 5662, 5747, 5750.

McCulloch, Ben, sent to Utah during troubles with Mormons, 3036.

McCulloch, Hugh; lawyer, banker; Secretary of the Treasury under Presidents Lincoln, Johnson and Arthur; b. Dec. 7, 1808, in Kennebunk, Me.; educated at Saco Academy and Bowdoin College; taught school and studied law; in 1833 went to Fort Wayne, Ind., and began practice; became a manager of the State Bank of Indiana, and gained a high reputation as a financier; in 1863 Secretary Chase appointed him Comptroller of the Currency, and upon the retirement of William Pitt Fessenden President Lincoln made him Secretary of the Treasury, reappointed him for the second term, and after the death of Lincoln was retained by Andrew Johnson throughout his term; was connected with the banking house of Jay Cooke & Co., and successful in negotiating loans for the government and funding the debts of the Southern States; in 1884, when Walter Q. Gresham resigned, President Arthur appointed him again Secretary of the Treasury, a place he held to the end of the administration; died May 24, 1895, at his country place in Maryland, near Washington.

McCulloch, Hugh, correspondence of, transmitted, 3804.

McDaniel, James, treaty with Indians concluded by, 3592.

McDermott, James Thomas; b. Grand Rapids, Mich., Feb. 13, 1872; in 1893 he moved to Chicago, where he followed his vocation as a telegraph operator until 1906, when he was elected to the 60th Congress; was re-elected to the 61st, 62d, 63d and 64th Congresses from Illinois.

McEldery, Hugh, director of Bank of United States, nomination of, and reasons therefor, 1260.

McEnery, Samuel Douglas; b. Monroe, La., May 28, 1837; educated at Spring Hill College, Mobile, Ala., the United States Naval Academy, and the University of Virginia; graduated from State and National Law School, Poughkeepsie, N. Y.; served in the Confederate Army, in the war between the States; elected lieutenant-governor in 1879, and on the death of Governor Wiltz, October, 1881, succeeded him in the executive office; elected in 1884; defeated by Gen. Francis T. Nicholls in 1888, who appointed his opponent, S. D. McEnery, to be associate justice of the Supreme Court in 1888 for the term of twelve years; elected to the United States Senate from Louisiana for the term beginning March 4, 1897; re-elected in 1902 and again for the term commencing March 4, 1909.

McEnery, Samuel D., candidate for governor of Louisiana, election disturbances discussed, 4261.

McElvain, John, treaty with Indians concluded by, 1029.

McGarrahan, William, act to submit title of, to lands to Court of Private Land Claims, vetoed, 5680.

McGillicuddy, Daniel J.; b. Aug. 27, 1859, in Lewiston, Me.; graduate of Bowdoin College, 1881; member of Maine legislature 1884-85; mayor of Lewiston, 1887, 1890, and 1902; elected to the 62d, 63d and 64th Congresses from Maine.

McGregor, Gen., commission to, discussed, 601.

McGrew, John F., member of legislative council for Mississippi Territory, nomination of, 445.

McGuire, Bird; b. Belleville, Ill., in 1864; taken to Kansas in childhood, and there educated; in 1895 moved to Pawnee Co., Okla., and practiced law; in 1897 was appointed assistant United States attorney for Oklahoma Territory, in which capacity he served until his nomination for Congress as delegate from the Territory of Oklahoma; served as such in the 58th and 59th Congresses; elected to the 60th Congress, 1907, his term of service beginning upon the admission of Oklahoma as a state, and re-elected to the 61st Congress from Oklahoma.

McHenry, James, Secretary of War under President Washington; b. Ireland, Nov. 16, 1753; aide-de-camp to General Lafayette during the Revolution; Delegate from Maryland to the Continental Congress 1783-1786 and the Federal constitutional convention in 1787; Secretary of War, Jan. 29, 1796, to May 13, 1800; died at Baltimore, Md., May 8, 1816.

McIntosh, Lachlan, naval officer at Savannah, Ga., nomination of, and reasons therefor, 50.

McKee, John:
Instructions to, regarding possession of Florida, 491.
Mentioned, 473.

McKeever, Isaac, captain in navy, nomination of, and reasons therefor, 1745.

McKenna, Joseph, Attorney-General under President McKinley; b. Philadelphia, Pa., Aug. 10, 1843; went to California with his parents in Jan., 1855; district attorney of Solano County for two terms, commencing in March, 1866; served in the California legislature in the session of 1875 and 1876; unsuccessful Republican candidate for Congress in 1876 from the 3rd district, and again the unsuccessful candidate in 1879; elected to the 49th Congress as a Republican; re-elected to the 50th, 51st and 52d Congresses; Attorney-General and subsequently a justice of the Supreme Court.

McKenney, Thomas L., treaty with Indians concluded by, 931, 960, 961, 996.

McKenzie, John C., b. Woodbine Township, Jo Daviess County, Ill., Feb. 18, 1860; educated in the common schools; taught school, farmed, then read law; admitted to the bar and practised his profession; served four years as member Illinois State Claims Commission under Gov. John R. Tanner; two terms in the House and three terms in the Senate of the Illinois General Assembly, one term as president pro tem. of the Senate, and elected to the 62d, 63d and 64th Congresses from Illinois.

Maclauchlan, J. A., correspondence regarding imprisonment of Ebenezer S. Greely, 1575, 1828.

Macomb, Alexander; soldier, author; b. Detroit, Mich., April 3, 1782; active in the War of 1812, becoming major-general in command of the army in 1828; author of "Treatise on Martial Law," "Treatise on Practice of Courts-Martial," and "Pontiac," a drama; died Washington, D. C., June 25, 1841.

Macomb, Alexander:
Letter of, on British fortifications on northern frontier of United States, 1815.
Mentioned, 701.
President court of inquiry, 1508.
Papers transmitted to, 1510, 1511.

Macomb, William H., commander in Navy, advancement in grade of, recommended, 3458.

MacVeagh, Franklin, of Chicago, Ill., Secretary of the Treasury in President Taft's Cabinet; b. Chester Co., Pa.; graduated at Yale, 1862; Columbia Law School, New York, 1864; nominated by the Democrats of Illinois, 1894, for United States Senator and made a canvass of the state, but was defeated in the legislature; member of the executive committee, National Civic Federation.

MacVeagh, Wayne; lawyer, statesman; Attorney General under President Garfield; b. April 19, 1833, in Phœnixville, Pa.; educated in Pottstown, Pa., and graduated from Yale College in 1853; studied law in West Chester, Pa., and admitted to the bar; apt in debate and industrious he soon made a wide reputation as a lawyer and was for some years counsel to the Pennsylvania Railroad Company; served a short time in the Civil War; in 1863 he was chairman of the Republican State Committee of Pennsylvania; in 1870 President Grant appointed him Minister to Turkey; he actively opposed the regular Republican organization in Pennsylvania, of which his father-in-law, Simon Cameron, was the leader; appointed Attorney General by President Garfield March 5, 1881, but resigned on the accession of Arthur to the Presidency.

Madden, Martin B.; b. March 20, 1855; elected to the 59th, 60th, 61st, 62d, 63d and 64th Congresses from Illinois.

Madison, James, biography of, 450.

Madison, Dolly P.:
Correspondence with President Jackson on death of her husband, 1479.
Writings of her husband on Constitutional Convention referred to, 1479.
Correspondence regarding publication of, 1481.

Madrazo, Don Juan, claims of, against United States, 1268.
Attorney-General declines to give opinion on, 1450.

Magoon, Charles E., appointed Canal Commissioner, 7400.

Maher, James P.; b. Brooklyn, N. Y., Nov. 3, 1865; educated in St. Patrick's Academy, Brooklyn; upon graduating he entered as an apprentice in the hatters' trade. In 1887 went to Danbury, Conn., to work at his trade as a journeyman hatter; in 1894 was elected president of the Danbury Hat Makers' Society, and in 1897 was elected national treasurer of the United Hatters of North America; elected to the 62d, 63d and 64th Congresses from New York.

Maison Rouge, Marquis de, validity of grant to, by Baron de Carondelet, to be tested, 2013.

Malietoa, King of Samoan Islands, 5545, 5871, 5963.
Death of, 6336.

Mallory, Stephen R.; b. Trinidad in 1813 on his father's vessel, sailing from Bridgeport, Conn.; located at Key West in 1821; attended schools in Connecticut and New York; studied law at Key West, and commenced practice there in 1833; appointed by President Jackson customs inspector at Key West; county judge of Monroe County; appointed collector of the port of Key West in 1845; elected and re-elected a United States Senator from Florida as a Democrat, serving from 1851 until his retirement Jan. 21, 1861; secretary of the navy of the Confederate States; at the close of the civil war was arrested and imprisoned for treason, but released in 1867; moved to Pensacola, Fla., where he died Nov. 9, 1873.

Mallory, Stephen R., imprisonment of, report of Attorney-General regarding, transmitted, 3576.

Malmros, Oscar, reports of, during Panama Revolution, 6752-6755.

Mann, Ambrose Dudley; diplomat; b. Hanover Court House, Va., April 26, 1801; resigned from U. S. Military Academy to take up study of law; appointed consul to Bremen, Germany, by President Tyler in 1842, and negotiated important treaties with German states; commissioner to Hungary, 1849, and by appointment of President Fillmore became minister to Switzerland, and negotiated a reciprocity treaty with that republic; joined the Southern Confederacy and was sent to England and France on special mission by seceding states; made his home in Europe after the Civil War; died Paris, France, Nov. 20, 1889.

Mann, A. Dudley:
Special agent to Hungary, correspondence of, referred to, 2579.
Treaty with Swiss Confederation concluded by, 2634.

Mann, James B.; b. 1856; graduate of the University of Illinois, and the Union College of Law in Chicago; elected to the 55th, and each succeeding Congress, including the 64th from Illinois.

Manning, Daniel (1831-1887); an American Democratic politician and Cabinet officer; b. in Albany, N. Y.; had large influence in Cleveland's election to the governorship of New York, and to the Presidency; Secretary of the Treasury under Cleveland, 1885-87.

Martin, Alexander; b. New Jersey in 1740; graduated from Princeton College in 1756; studied law, and commenced practice in North Carolina in 1772; member of the colonial assembly; colonel in the Revolutionary war; State senator 1779-1782, 1785-1788; governor 1782-1785 and 1789-1792; delegate to the State convention for the adoption of the Federal Constitution; United States Senator from North Carolina 1793-1799; died at Danbury, N. C., in November, 1807.

Martin, Alexander, legislative act of North Carolina received from, transmitted, 64.

Martin, Henry W., treaty with Indians concluded by, 3395.

Martin, Morgan L., treaty with Indians concluded by, 2529.

Martin, Thomas Staples; b. Scottsville, Albemarle Co., Va., July 29, 1847; soon after leaving the University of Virginia he commenced the study of law by a course of private reading at home, and was licensed to practice in 1869; Dec. 19, 1893, was elected Senator from Virginia for the term commencing March 4, 1895; re-elected in 1899 and 1905.

Martine, James E.; b. in the city of New York, August, 1850; attended the public schools, but owing to the death of his father was compelled to leave school at the age of 13 years; never held public office; at the primary election for United States Senator he was chosen to represent New Jersey.

Martinez, F. P., Mexican Minister, mentioned, 1790.

Marty, Martin, member of Chippewa Commission, 5500.

Marvin, William, provisional governor of Florida, appointed, 3527.

Mason, John Y., Secretary of the Navy under Presidents Tyler and Polk and Attorney-General under President Polk; b. Greensville, Va., April 18, 1799; graduated from the University of North Carolina in 1816; studied law, commencing practice at Hicksford, Va.; state representative 1819-1829; United States district judge for eastern Virginia; elected a Representative from Virginia to the 22nd, 23d, and 24th Congresses as a Democrat, resigning January 11, 1837; elected judge of the Virginia general court; delegate to the state constitutional conventions of 1828 and 1849; Secretary of the Navy March 14, 1844-45, and Sept. 9, 1846-1849; Attorney-General March 5, 1845, to Sept. 9, 1846; minister to England Jan. 22, 1854, until his death, at Paris, France, Oct. 3, 1859.

Mason, Otis T., member of Board on Geographic Names, 5647.

Mataafa, insurrection in Samoan Islands under, 5871, 5963. Arrangements for return of, and other exiles, 6336.

Mather, Thomas, treaty with Indians concluded by, 889.

Matlock, Gideon C., treaty with Indians concluded by, 2304.

Matthews, Edmund O., member of Gun Foundry Board, 4748.

Matthews, George, instructions to, regarding possessions of Florida, 491. Unauthorized conduct of, discussed and powers given, revoked, 492.

Matthews, James C., recorder of deeds, District of Columbia, nomination of, and reasons therefor, 5116.

Matthews, John; jurist; b. Charleston, S. C., in 1744; studied law; associate judge of the State supreme court in 1776; Delegate from South Carolina to the Continental Congress 1778-1782; governor 1782-83; judge of the court of equity in 1784; died at Charleston, S. C., Nov. 17, 1802.

Matthews, John, district supervisor, nomination of, 91.

Maury, Matthew F.:
Immigration plans of, referred to, 3571.
Improvement in science of nautical affairs by, 2670.

Maximilian (Ferdinand Maximilian Joseph):
Capture and execution of, referred to, 3725.
Decrees of—
Declaring blockade of ports proclaimed void, 3631.
Reestablishing slavery in Mexico referred to, 3569.
Organization for purpose of avenging death of, referred to, 3780.

Maxwell, Hugh, authority issued to, to arrest unlawful expeditions, 2697.

Maybrick, Florence E., imprisonment of, in Great Britain, 6101.

Maynard, Horace; statesman, diplomatist; Postmaster General under President Hayes; b. Aug. 30, 1814, in Westboro, Mass.; educated in his native town and graduated at Amherst College as valedictorian of his class in 1838; went to Tennessee and taught school and studied law at Knoxville, and was admitted to practice in 1844; for three terms (1857-63) he represented the Second Tennessee district in Congress, and was a stout supporter of the Union; Attorney General of Tennessee 1863-65, and for seven years thereafter again member of Congress; appointed by President Grant Minister to Turkey in 1875, and after five years in that position, was made Postmaster General by President Hayes, and served till the end of the administration; prominently identified with educational work and the Presbyterian Church in Tennessee; died May 3, 1882, at Knoxville.

Mayson, F. G., lieutenant in Marine Corps, appointment of, referred to, 2273.

Mead, Cowles; elected representative in Congress from Georgia in 1805, but his seat was successfully contested by Thomas Spalding; appointed secretary of Mississippi Territory in 1806.

Mead, Cowles:
Arrival of Aaron Burr in Mississippi announced by, 407.
Surrender of Aaron Burr announced by, 409.

Meade, George Gordon; soldier; b. Cadiz, Spain, Dec. 31, 1815; graduated U. S. Military Academy, 1835; served in the Seminole War; resigned from the army and engaged in surveying and engineering; 1845-47 served in the Mexican War; made surveys of lakes, rivers and harbors as lieutenant of engineers in government service; commissioned brigadier-general of volunteers, Aug. 31, 1861; served through the Civil War; but his name will ever be connected with the battle of Gettysburg, where he commanded on the 1st, 2nd, and 3d days of July, 1863, and the victory which produced such decided results; promoted to major-general in 1864, and as a special honor was given command of the grand review which took place in Washington at the close of the war; died Philadelphia, Pa., Nov. 6, 1872.

Meade, George G.:
Instructions to, referred to, 3826.
Order to, regarding suppression of military expedition, 3631.

Meade, Richard W., U. S. N.:
Agreement with great chief of Tutuila concluded by, 4122.
Imprisonment of, by Spain and claim arising out of, 594.
Mentioned, 5833.

Medill, William; b. Newcastle County, Del., in 1805; received a liberal education; studied law, and commenced practice in Lancaster County, Ohio, in 1832; member of the State legislature; elected a Representative from Ohio to the 26th and 27th Congresses as a Democrat; Second Assistant Postmaster-General in 1845; Indian Commissioner Oct. 28, 1845, to May 29, 1850; delegate to the Ohio constitutional convention of 1850; lieutenant-governor of Ohio 1851-52, and governor 1854-55; First Comptroller of the Treasury March 26, 1857, to April 10, 1861; died at Lancaster, Ohio, Sept. 2, 1865.

Medill, William, treaty with Indians concluded by, 2521.

Meigs, Montgomery C.; soldier, civil engineer; b. Augusta, Ga., May 3, 1816; graduate U. S. Military Academy, 1836; engaged in engineering work and construction of forts and government buildings; made quartermaster-general U. S. Army, 1861, which office he continued to hold until his retirement in 1882; died Washington, D. C., Jan. 2, 1892.

Meigs, Montgomery C.:
Act making appropriation for Government expenses, including work to be superintended by, discussed, 3128.
Appointed on commission to examine subject of reorganization of Army, 4352.
Report of, on—
Extension of Capitol, transmitted, 2917, 3110.
Error in, referred to, 2918.

Water supply for Washington City, 2725.

Meigs, Return Jonathan, Postmaster-General under President Madison; b. Middletown, Conn., in November, 1765; graduated from Yale College in 1785; studied law, and commenced practice at Marietta, Ohio; served in the Indian war; judge of the Ohio supreme court; elected a United States Senator from Ohio as a Democrat, serving from January 6, 1809, to his resignation, May 1, 1810; governor of Ohio 1810-1814; Postmaster-General March 17, 1814, to June 26, 1823; died at Marietta, Ohio, March 29, 1825.

Meigs, Return J., treaty with Indians concluded by, 834.

Menard, Pierre, treaty with Indians concluded by, 988, 989, 991, 1029.

Meredith, William M; lawyer; Secretary of the Treasury under President Taylor; b. June 8, 1799, in Philadelphia, Pa.; son of wealthy and accomplished parents and a precocious youth, graduating from the University of Pennsylvania at the age of thirteen years; studied law and was admitted to the bar, but for many years never had a case; at the age of twenty-five he was elected to the State Legislature, where he became leader of the Whigs; from 1834 to 1839 he was a member of the Select Council of Philadelphia, and in 1837 and 1872 of the State Constitutional Convention; candidate for United States Senator in 1845; President Taylor appointed him Secretary of the Treasury in 1849, and upon the death of Taylor he resumed law practice in Philadelphia; between 1840 and 1872 he was one of the most prominent lawyers in Philadelphia, in marked contrast with his early career; in 1870 he was appointed by President Grant to be senior counsel for the United States in the Geneva Tribunal of Arbitration; died Aug. 17, 1873, in Philadelphia.

Meriwether, David; b. Virginia in 1755; received a liberal education; served in the Revolutionary war; located at Wilkes County, Ga.; elected a Representative from Georgia to the 7th, 8th and 9th Congresses as a Democrat, serving from Dec. 6, 1802, to 1807; appointed a commissioner to the Creek Indians in 1804; Presidential elector in 1812; died near Athens, Ga., Nov. 16, 1822.

Meriwether, David, treaties with Indians concluded by, 589, 2884.

Meriwether, David; b. Louisa County, Va., Oct. 30, 1800; attended the common schools; engaged in fur trading near Council Bluffs, Iowa; became a farmer in Kentucky; in 1832 elected a State representative and served a number of years; delegate to the State constitutional convention of 1849; State secretary of state; appointed a United States Senator from Kentucky (vice Henry Clay, deceased), serving from July 6, 1852, until Sept. 1, 1852; governor of New Mexico May 6, 1853, to Jan. 5, 1855; died near Louisville, Ky., April 4, 1893.

Merritt, Wesley; soldier; b. New York City, June 16, 1836; graduated U. S. Military Academy, 1860; brevetted major for gallant and meritorious services at Gettysburg; promoted to major-general, 1895, and appointed to command in the Philippines and made military governor in 1898; retired, 1900.

Merritt, Wesley:
Directed to aid in executing laws in Indian Territory, 5483.
Expeditions to Philippine Islands under command of, 6315.
Attack upon and surrender of Manila, 6319.
Thanks of President tendered, 6579.
Instructions of President regarding military occupation of islands, 6569, 6571, 6572.
Joint occupancy with insurgents not to be permitted, 6579.

Metcalf, Victor Howard, Secretary of Commerce and Labor under President Roosevelt; born at Utica, Oneida County, N. Y., Oct. 10, 1853; graduated from the Utica Free Academy, also from Russell's Military Academy, New Haven, Conn., and then entered the class of 1876, Yale; left the academic department of Yale in his junior year and entered the Yale Law School, graduating therefrom in 1876; admitted to practice in the supreme court of Connecticut in June, 1876, and in the supreme court of New York in 1877; practiced law in Utica, N. Y., for two years, and then moved to California, locating in Oakland; formed a law partnership in 1881 with George D. Metcalf, under the firm name of Metcalf & Metcalf; elected to the 56th, 57th, and 58th Congresses, when he was appointed Secretary of Commerce and Labor.

Meyer, George von Lengerke, Postmaster-General and Secretary of the Navy under President Taft; b. Boston, June 24, 1858; graduated from Harvard University in 1879; member of the Massachusetts House of Representatives, 1892-1896; speaker, 1894-1896; ambassador to Italy, 1900; transferred to Russia, 1905; recalled, 1907, to enter the Cabinet as Postmaster-General, holding that post until March 6, 1909, when he took oath of office as Secretary of the Navy.

Michel, F., donation of buildings and grounds to United States for mint proposed by, 4311.

Mifflin, Thomas; soldier; b. Philadelphia, Pa., in 1744; attended Philadelphia College; visited Europe in 1765; returned and engaged in business; member of the colonial legislature in 1772-73; Delegate from Pennsylvania to the Continental Congress 1774-1776 and 1782-1784; served with distinction in the Revolution as major, reaching the rank of major-general Feb. 19, 1777; opposed Washington toward the last of the struggle; speaker of the State house of representatives in 1785; delegate to the Federal constitutional convention of 1787; president of the supreme executive council of Pennsylvania, October, 1788, to October, 1790; president of the State constitutional convention of 1790; governor of Pennsylvania 1791-1800; died at Lancaster, Pa., Jan. 20, 1800.

Mifflin, Thomas, letter of, referred to, 256.

Mileo, Nicolino, impressment of, into service of and punishment by Italy, referred to, 5673.

Miles, Dixon S., court of inquiry in case of, referred to, 3260.

Miles, Nelson Appleton; soldier, author; b. Westminster, Mass., Aug. 8, 1839; served during Civil War as a brigadier-general of volunteers; promoted to major-general, 1890, and successfully conducted campaigns against the Indians, and on several occasions prevented war with the Indians by judicious and humane settlement of difficulties without the use of military power; legislatures of Kansas, Montana, New Mexico and Arizona passed unanimous votes of thanks for his services on their borders; in the War with Spain, in 1898, he mobilized the regular army of 25,000 men and organized 200,000 volunteers for emergency; took command at Santiago, Cuba, July 11, 1908, and led an army of occupation to Porto Rico; wrote "Military Europe," "Observations Abroad," "From New England to the Golden Gate," etc.

Miles, Nelson A.:
Authorized to perform duties of Secretary of War in emergency, 6604.
Member of Ponca Indian Commission, 4582.
Outbreaks among Sioux, suppressed by, 6426.
Puerto Rican campaign under command of, 6318.
Surrender of Indians to, 5099.

Milledge, John; b. Savanah, Ga., in 1757; served in the Revolutionary struggle; attorney-general of Georgia in 1780; elected a Representative from Georgia to the 2d Congress (vice Anthony Wayne, whose seat was declared vacant), serving from Nov. 22, 1792, to March 2, 1793; elected to the 4th, 5th and 7th Congresses, resigning in May, 1802; governor 1802-1806; elected a United States Senator from Georgia, serving from Dec. 11, 1806, until his resignation in 1809; died at Sand Hill, Ga., Feb. 9, 1818.

Milledge, John, letter of President Madison to, regarding taking of oath, 451.

Miller, Clarence Benjamin; b. March 13, 1872, Goodhue Co., Minn., graduated from the University of Minnesota law department, 1900; member of the Minnesota legislature, 1907; elected to the 61st, 62d, 63d and 64th Congresses from Minnesota.

Miller, James, governor of Arkansas, legalization of official acts of, recommended, 801.

Miller, Joseph N., joint resolution annexing Hawaiian Islands delivered to President Dole by, 6332.

Miller, Washington D., secretary to President Houston, of Texas, 2172.

Miller, William, refuge given to, by the *St. Louis*, 1133.

Miller, William Henry Harrison, Attorney-General under President Benjamin Harrison; b. Augusta, Oneida Co., N. Y., Sept. 6, 1840; his ancestry is English and Scotch; he grew up on his father's farm, attending the country schools and Whitestown Seminary, and was graduated from Hamilton College in 1861; after teaching school at Maumee City, O., for a short time, he enlisted in May, 1862, in the 84th Ohio infantry, a three-months' regiment; being mustered out in September, he took up the study of law in the office of Chief Justice Waite; he read law during his leisure and was admitted to the bar at Peru in 1865 ; he practiced in that city for a short time, holding the office of county school examiner, the only office he ever held until appointed attorney-general; in conducting business before the federal courts at Indianapolis, Mr. Miller formed the acquaintance of Gen. Harrison, and on the retirement of Albert G. Porter from the firm of Porter, Harrison & Hines in 1874, he was invited to enter that firm; from then till his appointment as attorney-general Mr. Miller was exclusively engaged in the practice of the law ; as his was one of the two or three leading firms of Indiana, he was engaged in the most important litigation before the United States courts and the supreme court of the state.

In the Terry case his bold and fortunate action early attracted public attention; on hearing that there was danger that David S. Terry, a very prominent and somewhat notorious lawyer of California, would attack Justice Field, of the United States Supreme Court, when the latter should go on the California circuit, Mr. Miller promptly directed the U. S. marshal to protect him. In compliance with this order a deputy marshal was detailed to attend Justice Field. Terry was killed in the very act of making a deadly assault on the venerable justice. The authority of the deputy marshal being questioned and an attempt made to prosecute him by the authorities of California, Mr. Miller avowed the act and directed the defense of the deputy marshal, on the ground that independently of all statutes, it was the constitutional duty of the executive to protect the judiciary. On this high plane the case was fought and the Attorney-General was sustained both in the United States Circuit and Supreme Courts.

Miramon, Miguel:

President of Mexico, election of, discussed, 3095, 3175.

Property of American citizens confiscated by, 3120.

Mitchell, David B., instructions to, regarding possession of Florida, 493, 495.

Mitchell, John, agent for American prisoners of war at Halifax, Nova Scotia, 507.

Mizner, Lansing B., minister to Guatemala, action of, regarding seizure of Gen. Barrundia, and subsequent recall of, discussed, 5544.

Papers regarding, transmitted, 5565.

Monahan, Thomas R., arrest and imprisonment of, by Mexican authorities, 4852.

Mondell, Frank Wheeler; b. St. Louis, Mo., Nov. 6, 1860; engaged in mercantile pursuits, stock raising, mining and railway construction in various Western States and Territories; settled in Wyoming in 1887, and took an active part in the establishment and building of the town of Newcastle and the development of the Cambria mines; elected mayor of Newcastle in 1888, and served until 1895; elected a member of the first State senate in 1890; elected to the 54th Congress; served as Assistant Commissioner of the General Land Office from Nov. 15, 1897, to March 3, 1899; elected to the 54th. 56th. 57th, 58th, 59th. 60th. 61st. 62d, 63d and 64th Congresses from Wyoming.

Money, Hernando de Soto, lawyer and planter ; b. Aug. 26, 1839, in Holmes Co., Miss., educated at the University of Mississippi ; served in the Confederate army ; elected to the 44th, 45th, 46th, 47th, 48th, 53d and 54th Congresses ; January, 1896, elected to the Senate for the term beginning March 4, 1899 ; was appointed to the United States Senate Oct. 8, 1897, to fill a vacancy ; elected by the legislature of Mississippi, March 3, 1899 ; elected to succeed himself for the term beginning March 4, 1905.

Monroe, James, biography of, 572.

Monson, Sir Edmund, award of, as arbitrator in claim of Carlos Butterfield & Co. against Denmark, 5545.

Montgomery, Alexander, member of legislative council for Mississippi Tertory, nomination of, 445.

Montgomery, William, brigadier-general, nomination of, referred to, 1094.

Montgomery, William R., court-martial in case of, referred to, 2893.

Montt, Jorge, President of Chile, mentioned, 5619. (See also *Baltimore,* The.)

Moody, William H., Secretary of the Navy under President Roosevelt: b. Newbury, Mass., Dec. 23, 1853 ; graduated from Phillips Academy, Andover, Mass., in 1872, and from Harvard University in 1876 ; lawyer by profession ; district attorney for the eastern district of Massachusetts from 1890 to 1895 ; elected to the 54th Congress as a Republican, at a special election, to fill the vacancy caused by the death of Gen. William Cogswell ; re-elected to the 55th, 56th, and 57th Congresses ; resigned April 30, 1902, having been appointed Secretary of the Navy May 1, 1902.

Moon, John Austin; lawyer ; was three times appointed and twice elected judge of the fourth judicial circuit of Tennessee ; elected to the 55th, 56th, 57th, 58th, 59th, 60th, 61st, 62d, 63d and 64th Congresses from Tennessee.

Mooney, James, seizure of Vicenzo Rebello by, in New Orleans, La., 4653.

Moore, Alfred, commissioner to treat with Indians, nomination of, 250.

Moore, John B., Acting Secretary of State, 6481.

Moore, J. Hampton; b. Woodbury, N. J., March 8, 1864 ; law student in Philadelphia, 1877 to 1880 ; Chief Bureau of Manufactures, Department of Commerce and Labor, 1905 ; president Atlantic Deeper Waterways Association, 1808-9 ; elected to the 59th Congress for an unexpired term, and to the 60th, 61st and 62d Congress from Pennsylvania.

Moore, Thomas, commissioner for Cumberland road, 406.

Moore, Thomas P.; b. Charlotte County, Va., in 1797 ; received a public school education : an officer in the war of 1812 ; elected a Representative from Kentucky to the 18th Congress as a Jackson Democrat ; re-elected to the 19th and 20th Congresses, serving from Dec. 1, 1823, until March 3, 1829; appointed by President Jackson minister plenipotentiary to the United States of Colombia March 13, 1829, and served until April 16, 1833; returned to Kentucky and received a certificate of election as a Representative to the 23d Congress as a Democrat, having received 3,099 votes against 3,055 votes for R. P. Letcher, Whig, but the House, after much discussion, rejected some of the votes given to each candidate and declared that Letcher had 11 majority; appointed lieutenant-colonel of the Third United States Dragoons in the war with Mexico, serving from March 3, 1847, to July 31, 1848; a delegate from Mercer County to the Kentucky constitutional convention of 1849-50; died at Harrodsburg, Ky., July 21, 1853.

Moore, Thomas P., minister to Colombia, judgment and discretion of, discussed, 1030.

Mora, Antonio M., claim of, against Spain, 5677, 5910, 5962, 5989, 5998. Payment and distribution of, 6069.

Morales, Don John Bonaventure, authority to dispose of lands of Spain in Louisiana, referred to, 651.

Morgan, Dick Thompson; b. Prairie Creek, Vigo Co., Ind., Dec. 6, 1853; entered Union Christian College at Meron, Ind., from which institution he graduated in 1876, B. S.; in 1880, graduated from the Central Law School of Indianapolis, Ind., member of the lower house of the Indiana legislature, 1880-81; appointed register of the United States land office at Woodward, Okla., by President Roosevelt, in 1904, and served until May 1, 1908; elected to the 61st, 62d and 64th Congresses from Oklahoma.

Morgan, John T.; b. Athens, McMinn County, Tenn., June 20, 1824; received an academic education, chiefly in Alabama, to which State he emigrated when nine years old; studied law; admitted to the bar in 1845 and practiced until elected to the Senate; Presidential elector in 1860 for the State at large, and voted for Breckenridge and Lane; delegate in 1861 from Dallas County to the State convention which passed the ordinance of secession; joined the Confederate army in May, 1861; after the war resumed the practice of his profession at Selma; Presidential elector for the State at large in 1876, and voted for Tilden and Hendricks; elected to the United States Senate as a Democrat, and took his seat March 5, 1877; re-elected in 1882, 1888, 1894, and Nov. 17, 1900, for the term expiring 1907; member of a commission to prepare a system of laws for the Hawaiian Islands.

Morgan, John T.:
Argument of, in Senate on canal construction, referred to, 5624.
Member of commission to Hawaiian Islands, 6333.

Morrill, Ashley C., treaty at the Old Crossing of Red Lake River, Minnesota, with the chiefs of the Red Lake and Pembina bands of Chippewa Indians (1864), concluded by, 3397.

Morrill, Lot M., Secretary of the Treasury under Presidents Grant and Hayes; b.

Belgrade, Me., May 3, 1813; a student at Waterville College, Maine; studied and practiced law; member of the state legislature in 1854 and 1856, presiding over the senate the last year; governor of Maine 1858-1860; elected a United States Senator from Maine as a Republican (to fill the vacancy created by the election of Hannibal Hamlin to the Vice-Presidency) and took his seat Jan. 17, 1861; re-elected in 1863; appointed in Dec. 1869, and afterwards elected by the legislature, to fill the vacancy occasioned by the death of William Pitt Fessenden, re-elected as a Republican in 1871; served until July 7, 1876, when he became Secretary of the Treasury, serving until March 8, 1877; appointed by President Hayes collector of customs at Portland, Me., in 1877; died at Augusta, Me., Jan. 10, 1883.

Morris, George W., thanks of Congress to, recommended, 3345.

Morris, Gouverneur (1752-1815); statesman; b. Morrisiania, N. Y.; began the practice of law, 1771; member of the Continental Congress, 1777-80; on the committee that drafted the Constitution, 1787; as assistant superintendent of finance, 1781-85, he planned the present system of coinage; sat at the Constitutional Convention from Pennsylvania, 1787; United States minister to France, 1792-94; United States Senator from New York, 1800-1803.

Morris, Gouverneur:
Minister to France, recall of, requested, 147.
Successor of, appointed, 148.
Treaty with Great Britain, appointed to conclude, 88.

Morris, Henry, thanks of Congress to, recommended, 3277.

Morris, Lewis R., United States Marshal, nomination of, 91.

Morrison, Martin Andrew; b. Frankfort, Ind., April 15, 1862; graduated from the University of Virginia, receiving the degree of Bachelor of Laws; from Butler University, in June, 1887, received the degree of Master of Arts; engaged in the practice of law; elected to the 61st, 62d, 63d and 64th Congresses from Indiana.

Morse, Freeman H., report of, on foreign maritime commerce of United States, etc., transmitted, 3831.

Morton, J. Sterling; farmer, editor; Secretary of Agriculture under President Cleveland; originator of Arbor Day under State patronage; b. April 22, 1832, in Adams, Jefferson Co., N. Y.; taken by his parents to Michigan in infancy and educated at a private school in Monroe and at a Methodist Seminary at Albion; graduated Michigan University 1854, married and went to Nebraska the same year and joined the company which laid out Nebraska City; took up a half section of public land adjoining the town and established thereon Arbor Lodge, which was his home for the remainder of his life; he also established the Nebraska City *News*, a Democratic paper; appointed by President Buchanan Secretary of the Territory in 1858, and became Governor upon the resignation of William A. Richardson; defeated for Governor after the admission of the State to the Union; was four times Democratic candidate for Governor; and twice defeated for Congress; member of State Legislature and his party's standing choice for United States Senator; appointed by President Cleveland Secretary of Agriculture; in 1872 he induced the Governor of Nebraska to set apart a day for the ceremonious planting of trees throughout the State; in recognition of his advocacy of the plan, his birthday was proclaimed a State holiday to be devoted to tree-planting and studying the benefits of arboriculture; this example was followed by other States until the custom has become well-nigh universal; died April 28, 1902.

Morton, J. Sterling, death of, 6705.

Morton, Levi Parsons (1824——); banker, and twenty-second Vice-President of United States; b. at Shoreham, Vt.,; was United States minister to France, 1881-85; Vice-President with Harrison, 1889-93, and governor of the State of New York, 1895-96.

Morton, Oliver P., death of, announced and honors to be paid memory of, 5043.

Morton, Paul; Secretary of the Navy under President Roosevelt; railroad manager and financier; b. May 22, 1857, in Detroit, Mich.; son of J. Sterling Morton, who was Secretary of Agriculture under President Cleveland; educated in public schools of Nebraska, and at the age of sixteen began work as an office boy in the office of the Burlington and Missouri River Railroad at Burlington, Iowa; married Oct. 13, 1880, Charlotte Goodridge of Chicago; advanced rapidly in knowledge and ability to manage railroad, coal and iron affairs and Jan. 1, 1896, became vice-president of the Atchison, Topeka and Santa Fé Railroad; developed advanced ideas in railroad management, strongly favoring uniformity in freight rates and the abolition of discriminating rates among shippers, advocated publicity in the affairs of great corporations seeking to sell their stocks and bonds to the public; during the strike on the C., B. & Q. Railroad in 1888 he openly avowed his sympathy with the engineers and firemen and favored granting their demands; became a champion of irrigation of the arid lands of the West; President Roosevelt appointed him Secretary of the Navy to succeed William H. Moody, resigned, in July, 1904; retired at the end of one year to become President of the Equitable Assurance Society of New York.

Moss, Ralph W.; b. Center Point, Clay Co., Ind., April 21, 1862; elected to the Indiana State senate in 1904, serving four years; elected to the 61st, 62d, 63d and 64th Congresses from Indiana.

Motley, John Lothrop; lawyer, historian, author, diplomat; b. Boston, Mass., April 15, 1814; graduated Harvard College, 1831; studied in Germany, and was admitted to the bar in 1836; wrote "The Rise and Fall of the Dutch Republic," published in 1856; appointed minister to Austria by President Lincoln in 1861; minister to England by President Grant in 1869; published "History of the United Netherlands," "The Life and Death of John of Barneveld"; besides historical works and essays for magazines,

he wrote "Morton's Hope" and "Merry Mount," romances; died Dorsetshire, England, May 29, 1877.

Motley, John L.:
Mentioned, 4014.
Minister to—
Austria—
Conversations and opinions of, referred to, 3664.
Removal of, referred to, 3780.
Resignation of, referred to, 3661.
Great Britain, recall of, referred to, 4070.

Mott, Luther W.; b. Oswego, Nov. 30, 1874; educated at the Oswego High School and Harvard College, graduated from the latter in 1896; in the banking business at Oswego, and has been president of the New York State Bankers' Association; elected to the 62d, 63d and 64th Congresses from New York.

Moultrie, William; soldier; b. South Carolina in 1731; member of militia organized for defence against Cherokee Indian raids; member of Provincial Congress, 1775; made brigadier-general in 1776, and in 1779 defeated a superior force of British near Beaufort, and defended Charleston, S. C.,; taken prisoner by the British and exchanged for Gen. Burgoyne; major-general, 1782; governor of South Carolina, 1785-86 and 1794-96; died Charleston, S. C., Sept. 27, 1805.

Mudd, Samuel A., implicated in assassination of President Lincoln, proceedings of trial and verdict of military commission, 3532, 3533, 3534, 3540, 3545, 3546.

Mulvihill, Thomas, petition of, for repossession of lands conveyed to United States by, 4739, 4778.

Murat, Joachim, commerce of United States, depredations committed on, by, 1269.

Murray, William Vans; diplomat; b. Cambridge, Md., in 1762; received a liberal education; studied law in the Temple, at London, and began practice at his home in 1785; served as a member of the Maryland State legislature; elected a Representative from Maryland to the 2d, 3d and 4th Congresses as a Federalist; minister resident to the Netherlands 1797-1801; died at Cambridge, Md., Dec. 11, 1803.

Murray, William Vans, minister to France, nomination of, 272, 274.

Myers, Henry L.; b. Oct. 9, 1862, in Cooper County, Mo.; educated in private schools in Missouri; taught school and studied law; licensed to practice law in his native state; in 1893 moved to Hamilton, Mont., and there engaged in the practice of law; has served as prosecuting attorney, State senator, and district judge; was serving his second term in the last-named position when, on March 2, 1911, he was elected United States Senator from Montana, for the term beginning March 4, 1911.

Nagel, Charles; Secretary of Commerce and Labor under President Taft; b. Aug. 9, 1849, in Colorado Co., Tex.; member of the Missouri legislature, 1881-1883; president of the St. Louis city council, 1893-1897; member St. Louis Law School faculty since 1886; board of trustees of Washington University; national committeeman from Missouri in 1908.

Nairne, John, vessel under, ordered from and forbidden to reenter waters of United States, 391.

Nash, Thomas, was charged with murder and piracy on the British frigate *Hermoine.* He was surrendered to Great Britain, 1799.

Neighbors, Robert S., mentioned, 3249.

Nelson, John, Attorney-General under President Tyler; b. Frederick, Md., June 1, 1791; graduated from William and Mary College in 1811; studied law and began practice in his native town; held several local offices; elected a Representative from Maryland to the 17th Congress; minister to Naples Oct. 24, 1831, to Oct. 15, 1832; Attorney-General, 1843-1845; died at Baltimore, Md., Jan. 8, 1860.

Nelson, John Mandt; b. Burke, Dane Co., Wis., Oct. 10, 1870; graduate University of Wisconsin, 1892, and law department of the University of Wisconsin, 1896; elected to the 59th Congress to fill a vacancy and to the 60th, 61st, 62d, 63d and 64th Congresses from Wisconsin.

Nelson, Knute; b. Norway, Feb. 2, 1843; came to the United States in 1849, to Minnesota in 1871; was a private and noncommissioned officer during the War of the Rebellion; admitted to the bar in 1867; member of the Wisconsin legislature in 1868 and 1869; county attorney of Douglas Co., Minn., in 1872, 1873 and 1874; State senator in 1875, 1876, 1877 and 1878; member of the board of regents of the State University Feb. 1, 1882, to Jan. 1, 1893; member of the 48th, 49th and 50th Congresses from Minnesota; elected governor of Minnesota in 1892; elected United States Senator for the term commencing March 4, 1895; reelected in 1901 and 1907.

Nelson, Samuel, associate justice, Supreme Court, member of commission to settle questions with Great Britain, 4075.

Nelson, Thomas A. R., counsel for President Johnson in impeachment proceedings, 3924.

Neville, John, attacked while discharging duties as revenue inspector, 151.

Newcomb, Frank H., thanks of Congress to, recommended, 6302.

Newcomb, Simon, report of, on improvements in astronomical observatories, etc., referred to, 4790.

Newlands, Francis Griffith; b. Natchez, Miss., Aug. 28, 1848; attended the Columbian College Law School at Washington, went to San Francisco, where he entered upon the practice of law and continued until 1888, when he became a citizen of the State of Nevada; elected to the 53d, 54th, 55th, 56th and 57th Congresses; elected to the United States Senate for the term beginning March 4, 1903. In the general election of 1908 Mr. Newlands submitted nis candidacy for reelection to a popular vote, under the election law of Nevada, and received a large majority over the votes of all competitors. The legislature, being pledged in advance by the party platforms to carry out the popular will, thereupon, without opposition, reelected him United States Senator from Nevada, for the term ending March 3, 1915.

Nicholas, Emperor. (See Russia.)

Nichols, Edward F., thanks of Congress to, recommended, 3277.

Nicks, John, removal of, from office, explanation regarding, 1094.

Nico, Econchatta, claim of, for losses sustained, 1683.

Nicoll, Francis H., memorial of, presented to Congress, 1037.

Niles, John Milton, Postmaster-General under President Van Buren; b. Windsor, Conn., Aug. 20, 1787; received a liberal education; studied law and began practice at Hartford, Conn.; established the Hartford *Times;* county judge 1821-1826; member of the state house of representatives in 1826; postmaster at Hartford in 1829; appointed a United States Senator from Connecticut (vice Nathan Smith, deceased) as a Whig, and subsequently elected, serving from Dec. 21, 1835, to March 3, 1839; Postmaster-General 1840-41; again elected a United States Senator; serving from 1843 to 1849; died at Hartford, Conn., May 31, 1856.

Nixon, George S.; b. April 2, 1860, in Placer Co., Cal.; entered the employ of a railroad company and studied telegraphy; transferred to Nevada, where he served three years as a telegraph operator, and in 1884 accepted a clerical position in a bank at Reno; largely interested in banking, mining, stock raising, and farming; served as a member of the Nevada legislature in 1891; elected to the United States Sena e from Nevada for the term beginning March 4, 1905.

Noah, M. Mordecai, surveyor of customs, renomination of, 1043.

Noble, John Willock, Secretary of the Interior under President Benjamin Harrison; b. Lancaster, Ohio, Oct. 26, 1831; his father was a native of Pennsylvania, and his mother, Catherine McDill, of Maryland; after obtaining a good preparatory education in the public schools of Cincinnati, he spent one year at Miami University, and then entered the junior class at Yale, from which institution he was graduated in 1851, before he had attained the age of twenty years; he then studied law under the instruction of Henry Stanberry (afterward attorney-general in the cabinet of President Johnson) and of his brother, Henry C. Noble, and was admitted to the bar in 1855 at St. Louis, Mo. He began the practice of law there, but in 1856 removed to Keokuk, Iowa.; in Aug., 1861, he was made a first lieutenant in the 3d regiment of Iowa cavalry, and subsequently became adjutant; he did valiant service at the battle of Pea Ridge in the spring of 1862 and was present at the surrender of Vicksburg, and at the battle of Tupela, Miss.; he also took part in the successful raids made by Gen. James H. Wilson, the storming of Selma, Ala., the capture of Columbus, Ga., and in numerous minor engagements. For a time he was judge advocate-general of the army of the southwest, and the department of Missouri, under Gen. Samuel R. Curtis, but soon returned to his regiment, with which he served four years; he rose by regular promotion in his own regiment to be colonel, and was breveted brigadier-general by congress "for distinguished and meritorious services in the field"; after the close of the war Gen. Noble resumed the practice of law in St. Louis; there he encountered great opposition in enforcing the provisions of the internal revenue laws, especially from dealers in whiskey and tobacco, who were very rebellious in that state; among the offenders brought to justice by him at this period, were the noted counterfeiters Biebusch and Burke; shortly after, when in Washington, President Grant invited him to the White House, and in the presence of his assembled cabinet thanked him "for the faithful manner in which he had performed the duties of his office"; in Iowa, Mr. Noble, before the war, had practiced at the same bar, state and federal, with Samuel F. Miller, afterward justice of the United States supreme court, Gen. W. W. Belknap, and George W. McCrary, each afterward secretary of war, and John F. Dillon, afterward judge of the United States circuit court, and other able lawyers. His ability as an attorney and his marked individuality as a public-spirited citizen gave him a national reputation, and in 1889 President Harrison appointed him secretary of the interior, a position for which his successful experience and marked executive abilities especially fitted him. His administration of the duties of this responsible office has been characterized by decision of purpose and a comprehensive knowledge of public affairs, nowhere more marked than in his settlement of questions arising from the opening to settlers of some of the Indian reservations and the organization of the territory of Oklahoma, where the rush for land gave rise to conflict for claims.

Noland, N. B., claims of, against Peru, 6099.

Norris, P. W., petition of, for compensation for services rendered transmitted, 4669.

Nourse, Joseph E., publication of second edition of Second Arctic Expedition recommended by, 4666.

Nye, Frank Mellen; b. Shirley, Piscataquis Co., Me., March 7, 1852; member of the Wisconsin assembly 1884-85; elected to the 60th, 61st, and 62d Congresses from Minnesota.

Nye, James W.; b. Madison County, N. Y., June 10, 1815; received a common school education; studied law and practiced; held several local offices; defeated as the Antislavery candidate for the 39th Congress; moved to Syracuse, N. Y.; appointed governor of Nevada Territory in 1861; elected a United States Senator from Nevada as a Republican and re-elected, serving from Dec. 4, 1865, to March 3, 1873; a short time after leaving the United States Senate his reason became impaired, and he died at White Plains, N. Y., Dec. 25, 1876.

Nye, James W., governor of Nevada Territory, letter of, transmitted, 3405.

Oakes, D. C., treaty with Indians concluded by, 3663.

O'Brien, Richard, letter of, regarding bombardment of Tripoli, 363.

O'Donnell, Patrick, trial, conviction, and execution of, by Great Britain, 4782.

Oehler, G. F., treaty with Indians concluded by, 2953.

O'Fallon, Benjamin, treaty with Indians concluded by, 887.

O'Fallon, James, armed force levied by, referred to and proclamation against, 93.

Offley, David, treaty with Turkey concluded by, 1093.

Ogden, Herbert G., member of Board on Geographic Names, 5647.

Ogden, Peter V., crimes charged against, 405.

Ogden, Thomas L., treaty with Indians concluded by, 940.

O'Gorman, James A.; b. New York City, May 5, 1860; educated in the public schools, the College of the City of New York and the law department of the New York University, graduating with LL.B. in 1882; admitted to the bar in 1882; served as justice of the district court, justice of the supreme court, State of New York; elected United States Senator from New York, March 31, 1911.

O'Laughlin, Michael, implicated in assassination of President Lincoln, proceedings of trial and verdict of military commission, 3532, 3533, 3534, 3540, 3545, 3546.

Oldfield, William A., lawyer; b. Franklin, Izard Co., Ark., Feb. 4, 1874; when war broke out between the United States and Spain, in 1898, enlisted as a private; promoted to first sergeant, and later to first lieutenant, and was mustered out with that rank in 1899; elected to the 61st, 62d, 63d and 64th Congresses from Arkansas.

Oliver, George Tener, b. County Tyrone, Ireland, Jan. 6, 1848, while his parents were visiting in that country, they at the time being residents of Allegheny City, Pa.; studied law and was admitted to the bar of Allegheny county in 1871; after an active practice of ten years, he retired and engaged in iron and steel manufacturing; president of the Youngstown Car Manufacturing Company, at Youngstown, Ohio; connected as a director with several financial and industrial corporations in Pittsburg; in 1900 purchased the Pittsburgh Gazette, and later in the same year acquired the controlling interest in the Pittsburgh Chronicle-Telegraph; in 1906 the Pittsburgh Gazette and the Pittsburgh Times which are now published under the name of the Gazette-Times, and he is the principal owner of both papers; elected March 17, 1909, to the United States Senate from Pennsylvania.

Olmstead, Gideon, sailor, resident of Connecticut during the Revolutionary War; captured at sea by a British vessel and placed aboard the British sloop *Active*, carrying stores from Jamaica to the British in New York; he and three over Americans overpowered the British crew and took possession of the ship; while making for Little Egg Harbor they were captured by the *Convention* of Philadelphia and the privateer *Girard*, and taken before the Pennsylvania State Court of Admiralty; this court divided the prize into four parts, giving Olmstead and his companions, who had made the capture, only one-fourth; they appealed to Congress, and the Committee on Appeals decided in their favor, but the Pennsylvania Court refused to yield, and directed the ship to be sold and the money paid into the state court to await final decision; the case dragged along until 1809, when the Pennsylvania authorities offered armed resistance to the United States Marshal at Philadelphia; he called to his assistance a *posse comitatus* of 2,000 men; before an actual conflict between state and federal officials occurred the matter was adjusted and the money ($18,000) paid to the United States Marshal; Olmstead died at East Hartford, Conn., Feb. 7, 1845, aged 96 years.

Olmstead, Gideon:

Correspondence with governor of Pennsylvania in regard to case of, 462.

Resolutions of Pennsylvania legislature protesting against Supreme Court decision in case of, 456.

Olney, Richard; lawyer; Attorney General and Secretary of State under President Cleveland; b. Sept. 15, 1835, in Oxford, Mass.; educated at Leicester Academy and graduated Brown University, 1856, and LL.B. Harvard Law School 1858; began practice in Boston and soon was looked upon as an authority on wills and estates; later achieved a reputation as a railroad and corporation lawyer; appointed by President Cleveland in 1893 Attorney General, and upon the death of Walter Q. Gresham in 1895 he was transferred to Secretary of State.

Olney, Richard, Secretary of State, 6024.

Onis, Louis de, letter of, to Captain-General of Caracas transmitted, 473.

Ord, Edward O. C., negotiations of, for and correspondence regarding restoration of peace, 3461.

Orr, B. G., contract of, with Government to furnish supplies, 598.

Orr, James L., commissioner from South Carolina, mentioned, 3189.

Osgood, Samuel, Postmaster-General under President Washington; b. at Andover, Mass., Feb. 14, 1748; graduated from Harvard College in 1770; studied theology; merchant; served several years as a member of the state house of representatives; member of the provincial congress; entered the revolutionary army as captain and left the service as colonel and assistant quarter-master; delegate from Massachusetts to the Continental Congress; first commissioner of the United States Treasury 1785-1789; Postmaster-General 1789-1791; moved to New York City; member of the state house of representatives 1800-1802; supervisor of New York 1801-1803; naval officer at the port of New York, where he died August 12, 1813.

Padgett, Lemuel Phillips; b. Nov. 28, 1855, in Columbia, Tenn.; was elected to the state senate and served one term; elected to the 57th, 58th, 59th, 60th, 61st, 62d, 63d and 64th Congresses from Tennessee.

Paez, José Antonio, vessel to transport remains of, to Venezuela, recommended, 5193.

Page, Carroll Smalley, b. Westfield, Vt., Jan. 10, 1843; is LL. D. of Norwich University; represented Hyde Park in the House of Representatives, 1869-87, and Lamoille County in the state senate, 1874-76; governor of the state, 1890-92; elected to the United State Senate from Vermont, Oct. 21, 1908, to fill a vacancy caused by the death of Hon. Redfield Proctor.

Page, Robert Newton; b. Cary, Wake Co., N. C., Oct. 26, 1859; elected to the legislature of 1901; elected to the 58th, 59th, 60th, 61st, 62d, 63d and 64th Congresses from North Carolina.

Page, Thomas J., claim of, against Argentina adjusted, 6324.

Pageot, A., French chargé d'affaires: Announces intention to return to France, 1420.
Correspondence regarding claims against France. (See France, claims against.)

Palmer, Joel, treaty with Indians concluded by, 2762, 2836, 2839, 2913, 2914, 2956.

Palmer, John McAuley (1817-1900); soldier and politician; b. Eagle Creek, Scott Co., Ky.; settled in Illinois in 1831; entered the State Senate as a Democrat 1852; joined the Republican party; served through the Civil War; Governor of Illinois, 1868; United States Senator, 1890; nominated for the Presidency of the United States by the Gold Democrats in 1900.

Palmer, Jonathan, inspector of revenue, nomination of, revoked, 419.

Palmerston, Lord, correspondence regarding—
Imprisonment of Ebenezer S. Greely, 1575, 1622.
Northeastern boundary. (See Northeastern Boundary.)

Parke, John G., negotiations for any correspondence regarding restoration of peace, 3161.

Parker, Foxhall A., commander of Home Squadron, mentioned, 2676.

Parker, Peter, commissioner to China, mentioned, 3062, 3113.

Parker, Willis W., inspector and collector, nomination of, 390.

Parks, Gorham, correspondence regarding African slave trade, 2538.

Parsons, Justin W., murder of, in Turkey, referred to, 4627.

Parsons, Lewis E., provisional governor of Alabama, appointed, 3521.

Parsons, Theophilus; jurist; b. Feb. 24, 1750. in Byfield, Essex Co., Mass.; grad-

uated Harvard 1769; admitted to the bar at Falmouth, Mass. (now Portland, Me.), in 1774; he soon built up a lucrative practice which extended throughout all New England; was an influential Federal leader; member of the celebrated "Essex Junto," composed of citizens of Massachusetts who Opposed the adoption of the State constitution in 1778; in 1788 gave active support to the convention to ratify the Constitution of the United States, being the author of the "Conciliatory Resolutions" offered by John Hancock in the convention; appointed in 1801 by President John Adams to fill out the unexpired term of Charles Lee as Attorney General; in 1806 was appointed Chief Justice of the Supreme Court of Massachusetts, which office he held until his death in Boston Oct. 30, 1813; his rulings and decisions were especially luminous on the laws of pleading, marine insurance and real estate; a collection of his opinions has been published under the title "Commentaries on the Laws of the United States."

Patten, Thomas G.; b. New York City, Sept. 12, 1861; educated at Mount Pleasant Academy, Ossining, N. Y., and Columbia College; president of the New York and Long Branch Steamboat Co.; never held public office until elected to the 62d, 63d and 64th Congresses from New York.

Patterson, Eliza W., act for relief of, permitted to become law and reasons therefor, 4806.

Patterson, William, associate justice, Supreme Court, nomination of, void, 129.

Paulding, Hiram, arrest of William Walker and associates in Nicaragua by, 2997.
Referred to, 3001, 3017.

Paulding, James K.; author; Secretary of the Navy under President Van Buren; b. Dutchess Co., N. Y., Aug. 22, 1778; had little education, but upon entering the employment of an uncle in New York City, associated with the best families of the day, including among his intimates Washington Irving, Gouverneur Kemble and Henry Brevoort; wrote political sketches and satires for the local press; his works were so full of patriotic spirit that President Madison was attracted to him and appointed him Secretary of the newly created Board of Navy Commissioners in 1815; resigned in 1823 and returned to New York, where he had been appointed Naval Agent; held this position until 1838, when President Van Buren appointed him Secretary of the Navy; he ended his political career March 4, 1841; among his principal literary works were "Inchiquin the Jesuit's Letters on American Literature and Politics," "The Backwoodsman," "Salamagundi Papers," "John Bull in America," "The Dutchman's Fireside," "Life of Washington," "Westward, Ho"; died April 6, 1860, at his estate Hyde Park, N. Y.

Pauls, George, death of, referred to, and appropriation to widow of, recommended, 5494.

Pauncefote, Lord, British Ambassador: Agreement between United States and Great Britain for *modus vivendi* regarding Bering Sea fisheries, signed by, 5581.

Communications in regard to Venezuelan boundary, transmitted by, 6087.

Death of, 6705.

Payne, Henry Clay (1843-1904); politician and Cabinet officer; b. Ashfield, Mass.; removed to Milwaukee and entered politics as a Republican; succeeded Charles Emery Smith as Postmaster-General in Roosevelt's Cabinet, 1902.

Payne, John Howard, minister to Tunis, nomination of, referred to, 2611.

Payne, Lewis:
Implicated in assassination of President Lincoln, proceedings of trial and verdict of military commission, 3532, 3533, 3534, 3540, 3545, 3546.
Persons claiming reward for apprehension of, directed to file claims, 3551.

Payne, Sereno Elisha; b. Hamilton, N. Y., June 26, 1843; graduated University of Rochester, 1864; admitted to the bar in 1866; elected to the 48th Congress from New York and re-elected to each succeeding Congress since, including the 64th, thus entitling him to the honor of being the oldest continuous member of Congress. Died in Washington, Dec. 10, 1914.

Paynter, Thomas H.; b. Lewis Co., Ky., Dec. 9, 1861; educated in Rand's Academy and Center College, Danville, Ky.; studied law; admitted to the bar in 1872; elected to the 51st, 52d, and 53d Congresses; elected Judge of the Court of Appeals of Kentucky in Noember, 1894, for an eight-year term and to accept which he resigned in January, 1895, as a member of the 53d Congress; was re-elected judge of the court of appeals in 1902, which position he held until Aug. 1, 1906, when he resigned; elected to the United States Senate for the term beginning March 4, 1907, from Kentucky.

Peabody, Charles A., provisional judge for Louisiana, appointed, 3323.

Peabody, George, medal presented to, referred to, 3897.

Peace, Samuel, ensign in Navy, nomination of, and reasons therefor, 3357.

Pearce, James A.; lawyer, legislator; b. Dec 8, 1804, in Alexandria, Va.; educated in his native town and graduated College of New Jersey 1822; studied law in Baltimore and began practice in Cambridge, but later removed to Louisiana and engaged in sugar planting; after three years he returned and resumed the practice of law in Kent Co., Md.; elected to the House of Delegates in 1831 and two years later was elected to Congress, where he served almost continuously until 1843, when he was elected to the United States Senate; during his long service as Senator he was especially interested in the Library of Congress, tne Smithsonian Institution, the Coast Survey and educational matters; he was offered an appointment as United States Judge for Maryland and was also nominated and confirmed as Secretary of the Interior by President Fillmore, but declined both these offices; while still Sen-

ator he died Dec. 20, 1862, at Chesterton, Md.

Peck, Ferdinand W., commissioner-general to Paris Exposition, 6330.

Pedersen, Peder, Danish minister, mentioned, 911.

Pelletier, Antonio, imprisonment of, in Haiti, and claims arising out of, discussed, 3829, 4665, 4918, 5120.

Pendergrast, Garret J., correspondence with, while commander of the *Boston*, 2302.

Pendleton, George H.; diplomat; b. Cincinnati, Ohio, July 25, 1825; received an academic education in the schools of Cincinnati and afterwards in Europe; studied law, admitted to the bar and began practice at Cincinnati; member of the State senate of Ohio in 1854 and 1855; Representative from Ohio to the 35th, 36th, 37th and 38th Congresses; Democratic candidate for Vice-President on the ticket headed by George B. McClellan in 1864; Democratic candidatc for governor of Ohio in 1869; elected to the United States Senate as a Democrat and took his seat March 18, 1879, serving until March 3, 1885; minister to Germany in 1885; died Nov. 24, 1898, at Brussels, Belgium.

Pendleton, George H., report of, on diseases of swine in Germany referred to, 5197.

Penrose, Boies; b. Philadelphia, Nov. 1, 1860; graduated from Harvard College in 1881; read law with Wayne MacVeagh and was admitted to the bar in 1883; practiced his profession in Philadelphia; member of the State Legislature, 1884-91; elected to the United States Senate from Pennsylvania for the term beginning March 4, 1897; re-elected in 1903 and 1909.

Perkins, Benjamin W., claim of, against Russia, 3826.

Perry, Benjamin F., provisional governor of South Carolina, appointed, 3524.

Perry, Matthew Calbraith; naval officer; b. about 1821; made lieutenant, 1848, and served for several years in the coast survey; commissioned captain 1867, and placed on retired list; died New York City, Nov. 16, 1873.

Perry, Matthew C.:
Directed to protect rights of American fishermen in British possessions, 2694.
Report of, on light-houses of England and France, 1819.

Perry, Oliver Hazard; naval officer; b. South Kingston, R. I., Aug. 21, 1785; commissioned midshipman 1799; served in the Mediterranean fleet in campaign of 1801-03, against pirates; after the surrender of Gen. Hull, at Detroit, Perry asked to be put in command on the lakes, then in undisputed possession of the English; built a fleet on Lake Erie in 1813, consisting of eight vessels, and with about 500 men defeated the British fleet of six vessels fully manned, and sent the laconic message to Gen. Harrison: "We have met the enemy, and they are ours"; rendered further service on the great lakes, in the defense of Baltimore, and in the Mediterranean; he was highly honored for his achievements; died of yellow fever at Trinidad, in the West Indies, Aug. 23, 1819, while in command of the *John Adams*; his remains were transferred to Newport, R. I., Dec. 4, 1826.

Perry, Oliver H.:
Death of, referred to, 631.
Victory of naval forces under, on Lake Erie discussed, 519.

Perry, Rodger, commander in Navy, nomination of, and reasons therefor, 3354.

Pershing, John Joseph; b. in Linn Co., Mo., Sept. 13, 1860. Was graduated from the United States Military Academy in 1886. In 1892 was appointed a first lieutenant, and a major of volunteers in 1899. In 1901 he was made a captain of cavalry, and in 1906 was raised to the rank of brigadier-general by President Roosevelt. He saw service during the Indian campaign of 1886, and during the Spanish-American War. His achievements in annihilating the Moro rebellions in the Philippines in 1913 won him distinction, and he was made commander of the United States troops sent into Mexico in 1916 to capture Villa. On May 19, 1917, President Wilson announced that General Pershing would lead the division of the United States regular army to leave for France within a few days of the announcement.

Phelps, John Smith; b. Simsbury, Conn., Dec. 22, 1814; graduated from Trinity College, Hartford, Conn.; studied law, and began practice at Simsbury; moved to Springfield, Mo., in 1843; served in the Missouri State house of representatives; elected a Representative from Missouri to the 29th, 30th, 31st, 32d, 33d, 34th, 35th, 36th and 37th Congresses as a Democrat; colonel in the Union Army; military governor of Arkansas; defeated as the Democratic candidate for the 38th Congress; governor of Missouri 1877-1881; died at St. Louis, Mo., Nov. 20, 1886.

Phelps, John S., military governor of Arkansas, appointment of, revoked, 3377.

Pickens, Andrew:
Commissioner to treat with Indians, nomination of, 171.
Treaty with Indians concluded by 202.

Pickens, Francis W.; diplomat; b. Tagaloo, S. C., April 7, 1805; received a liberal education; studied law, and in 1829 began practice in Edgefield District; engaged in planting; served several years as a member of the State house of representatives; elected a Representative from South Carolina to the 23d Congress as a Nullifier; re-elected to the 24th, 25th, 26th and 27th Congresses; member of the State house of representatives in 1844; delegate to the national Democratic convention at Cincinnati in 1856; minister to Russia 1858-1860; elected Confederate governor of South Carolina and took an active part in the rebellion; died at Edgefield, S. C., Jan. 25, 1869.

Pickens, Francis W., correspondence of, with President Buchanan referred to, 3195.

Pickering, John, district judge, complaint against, 344.

Pickering Timothy, Postmaster-General, Secretary of State and Secretary of War under President Washington; b. at Salem, Mass., July 17, 1745; graduated from Harvard College in 1763; studied law and began practice at Salem; appointed a judge of the court of common pleas for Essex County in 1775 and judge of the provincial maritime court; entered the Revolutionary Army as colonel; appointed Adjutant-General May 24, 1777; elected by Congress Quarter-Master General; Postmaster-General 1791-1794; appointed Secretary of War January 2, 1794, and Secretary of State December 10, 1795, holding the last position until May 10, 1800; farmer in Pennsylvania; returned to Massachusetts in 1802; defeated candidate for the Eighth Congress; elected a United States Senator from Massachusetts; re-elected, serving from October 17, 1803, to March 3, 1811; defeated for re-election by J. V. Varnum in 1811; member of the executive council; elected a representative from Massachusetts to the 13th and 14th Congresses as a Federalist; returned to his farm near Wenham, Mass.; died at Salem, Mass., Jan. 29, 1829.

Pickering, Timothy:
Commissioner of United States, nomination of, 290.
Mentioned, 103, 114.
Secretary of State, 239.

Pickett, George E., major-general, Confederate army, application for pardon of, 3657.

Pickett, J. C., chargé d'affaires at Lima, Peru, mentioned, 2294.

Pierce, Franklin, biography of, 2728.

Pierce, Henry A., dispatch of, relative to annexation of Hawaiian Islands, referred to, 4085.

Pierce, John, killed by shot from the *Leander,* 390.

Pierpont, Francis H., governor, to be aided in restoring Virginia into Union, 3535.

Pierrepont, Edwards, Attorney-General under President Grant; b. at North Haven, Conn., March 4, 1817, the son of Giles Pierrepont and Eunice, daughter of Jonathan Munson, and great-grandson of Joseph Pierrepont, who settled in North Haven, his father having given a valuable property to the town for public use. Edwards Pierrepont was graduated from Yale College in the class of 1837, having been prepared for college by the Rev. Noah Porter, afterward the president of Yale. He received the oration honor at his graduation, which was one of the highest class honors. In 1840 he was graduated from the New Haven Law School, and began the practice of his profession at Columbus, Ohio, in partnership with P. C. Wilcox, of that city. In 1846 he removed to New York city. He was appointed minister to Russia in 1873, but declined the office. In 1875 he accepted the portfolio of attorney-general. In 1876 he was appointed envoy extraordinary and minister plenipotentiary to the Court of St. James. He died in New York City March 6, 1892.

Pierrepont, Edwards, commissioner to examine cases of State prisoners, 3310.

Pike, Zebulon M., report of, on exploration of Mississippi River referred to, 396, 436.

Pillow, Gideon J., courts of inquiry in case of, referred to, 2444, 2454.

Pinckney, Charles Cotesworth (1746-1825); politician; b. Charleston, S. C.; fought with the continental army in the Revolutionary War; member of the Constitutional Convention of 1787; special envoy to France on the "X. Y. Z. mission"; Federalist candidate for Vice-President, 1800, and for President, 1804 and 1808.

Pinckney, Charles C.:
Minister to France and envoy extraordinary, nomination of, 235.
Minister to negotiate treaty with Spain, nomination of, 339.
President Jefferson notified of election by, 308.

Pinckney, Thomas; soldier, lawyer, jurist; b. Charleston, S. C., Oct. 23, 1750; Governor of South Carolina, 1787-89; Minister to Great Britain, 1792-94, and in the latter year went on a mission to Spain, where he made the treaty of St. Ildefonso, securing to the United States the free navigation of the Mississippi River; returned to Charleston in 1796, and was elected to Congress, 1799-1801; died Charleston, S. C., Nov. 2, 1828.

Pinckney, Thomas, mentioned, 886, 962.
Minister to negotiate with Spain, nomination of, 164.

Pinkney, William; attorney-general under President Madison; b. Annapolis, Md., March 17, 1764; member of convention which ratified the Federal Constitution; representative in Congress from 1789 to 1792; member State Legislature in 1795; sent to England in 1806 as envoy extraordinary, and in 1807 raised to the rank of minister plenipotentiary; attorney-general of Maryland in 1811, and representative in Congress in 1815-16; later he was sent as minister to Russia and as envoy to Naples; elected to the United States Senate in 1819, and continued in that position till his death, in Washington, Feb. 25, 1822.

Pinkney, William:
Commissioner appointed by United States under treaty with Great Britain, 188.
Minister to Russia, nomination of, 557.
Minister to settle questions with Great Britain, nomination of, 390.
Letter received by Secretary of State from, 456.

Piron, Pierce, claims of, against United States, 2585.

Pitcairn, Joseph, vice-consul to Paris, nomination of, 165.

Poindexter, George; lawyer, jurist; b. Louisa Co., Va., 1779; moved to Mississippi, and was made attorney-general; delegate to Congress from that territory from 1807 to 1813, when he was appointed Federal Judge of the territory; representative in Congress from 1817 to 1819, and was second governor of Mississippi under the constitution 1819-21; United States Senator 1830-35; died Jackson, Miss., Sept. 5, 1853.

Poindexter, George:
Commissioner to investigate affairs of New York custom-house, 2005.
Notes and bills discounted at Bank of United States for benefit of, inquired into, 1346.

Poinsett, Joel Roberts; author, scientist; b. Charleston, S. C., March 2, 1779; representative in Congress from South Carolina, 1821-25; appointed minister to Mexico and was Secretary of War under President Van Buren; was a botanist of some note, the genus Poinsettia having been named in his honor; author of "Notes on Mexico," made in 1822; died in Statesburg, S. C., Dec. 14, 1851.

Poinsett, Joel R.:
Correspondence regarding Canadian outrages on American frontier, 1618.
Minister to Mexico, recall of, requested, 1010.
Letter of, to Mr. Clay, regarding pledge to Mexico, referred to, 907.
Referred to, 910.
Reports regarding Canadian outrages on American frontier, 1618.

Polk, James K., biography of, 2221.

Polk, William, district supervisor, nomination of, 91.

Pomerene, Atlee; b. Berlin, Holmes County, Ohio, Dec. 6, 1863; attended village school; later went to Vermillion Institute, Hayesville, Ohio, where he was tutor of Latin and Greek for one year; graduate of Princeton College in 1884 and of the Cincinnati Law School in 1886; received the degrees of A. B. and A. M. at Princeton and degree of B. L. at the Cincinnati Law School; located at Canton, Ohio, in the practice of law in 1886; elected prosecuting attorney of Stark County in 1896; member of the honorary tax commission of Ohio, appointed by Gov. Andrew L. Harris in 1906; chairman of the Ohio State Democratic Convention at Dayton, Ohio, held in June, 1910, which nominated him for lieutenant-governor on the ticket with Gov. Judson Harmon; elected lieutenant-governor 1910, and the general assembly on Jan. 10, 1911, elected him United States Senator from Ohio.

Pope, Benjamin F., assistant surgeon in Army, nomination of, and reasons therefor, 4275.

Pope, John; soldier, author; b. Louisville, Ky., March 16, 1822; prominent officer during Civil War; made major-general in regular army 1882, assigned to Department of the Pacific 1884, and retired in 1886; published a valuable work on "Explorations from the Red River to the Rio Grande," and a memoir entitled: "Campaign in Virginia"; died Sept. 23, 1892.

Pope, John:
Directed to assume command of Military Division of Pacific and Department of California, 4754.
Instructions to, referred to, 3826.
Mentioned, 3345.

Porter, David; naval officer, author; b. Boston, Mass., Feb. 1, 1780; became captain of the frigate *Essex*, July, 1812, and within the year captured the British man-of-war *Alert* and a number of English merchant ships; in 1813 he cruised to the Pacific Ocean in the *Essex* and took many prizes; the *Essex* was attacked near Valparaiso, in March, 1814, by two British vessels, and, after a long and desperate resistance, captured; naval commissioner 1815-23; chargé d'affaires in Turkey 1831; minister resident at Constantinople 1839; died at Pera, 1843; he was the father of Admiral David D. Porter and Commodore William D. Porter.

Porter, David:
Frigate in command of, surrenders to British, 534.
Mentioned, 845.
Naval talents of, commented on, 782.

Porter, David Dixon; Admiral of the Navy; b. Chester, Pa., near Philadelphia, June 8, 1813; entered the navy as midshipman, 1829; made lieutenant 1841, and served in Mexican War; commander, 1861, of mortar boats and gunboats on lower Mississippi; co-operated with Gen. Grant in operations against Vicksburg, for which he was promoted to rear-admiral July 4, 1863; commanded naval forces, which reduced Fort Fisher Jan. 15, 1865; appointed vice-admiral, July 25, 1866; admiral Aug. 15, 1870; died at Washington, D. C., Feb. 16, 1891, and was buried in Arlington Cemetery.

Porter, David D.:
Admiral of Navy, death of, announced and honors to be paid memory of, 5569, 5600.
Captain in Navy, nomination of, 3356.
Rear-admiral in Navy, nomination of, 3393.
Thanks of Congress to, recommended, 3277, 3284, 3352.

Porter, Fitz-John; soldier; b. Portsmouth, N. H., June 13, 1822; graduated West Point, 1845; served in Mexican War; brevetted brigadier-general and served in Civil War until November, 1862, when he was arrested and placed under court-martial, which resulted in his dismissal from the army; reinstated by act of Congress, 1886; after his retirement from the army he was appointed commissioner of public works in New York City, and later police commissioner; at the expiration of his term in that office he was appointed fire commissioner, also cashier of New York post-office and assistant receiver of the New Jersey Central Railroad.

Porter, Fitz-John:
Act for relief of, vetoed, 4808.
Appeal of, referred to, 4857.
Proceedings and report of board in case of, referred to, 4474.

Relieved from command of corps, 3325.
Sentence of court-martial in case of, in part remitted, 4712.

Porter, Horace, member of court to try assassins of President Lincoln, etc., 3534.
Relieved from duty, 3534.

Porter, James M.; lawyer, soldier; b. Jan. 6, 1793, in Selma, Pa.; educated for the law and served throughout the War of 1812; after the war he built up a large practice in eastern Pennsylvania and New Jersey; member of the Pennsylvania Constitutional Convention in 1838; appointed Secretary of War by President Tyler in 1843, but the Senate refused to confirm the appointment; one of the founders of Lafayette College and for twenty-five years president of its Board of Trustees; he was a prominent Mason; died Nov. 11, 1862, in Easton, Pa.

Porter, Peter Buel; Secretary of War under President John Quincy Adams; b. at Salisbury, Conn., Aug. 4, 1773; graduated from Yale College in 1791; studied law and began practice at Canandaigua, N. Y.; held various local offices; elected a representative from New York to the 11th and 12th Congresses as a Democrat; served as a major-general in the war of 1812; elected to the 14th Congress, serving from Dec. 4, 1815, to 1816, when he resigned; secretary of state of New York 1815-16; appointed Secretary of War, serving from 1828 to 1829; died at Niagara Falls, N. Y., March 20, 1844.

Porter, Stephen G.; b. Salem, Columbiana County, Ohio, May 18, 1869; moved to Allegheny, Pa., in 1877; received a common and high school education; studied medicine two years; read law and was admitted to the Allegheny County bar in 1893; never held any office until he was elected to the 62d, 63d and 64th Congresses from Pennsylvania.

Potter, Elisha R.; b. Kingston, R. I., June 20, 1811; graduated from Harvard College in 1830; served several years as a member of the State house of representatives; adjutant-general of the State in 1835 and 1836; elected a Representative from Rhode Island to the 28th Congress as a Whig; State commissioner of public schools 1849-1854, when he resigned; judge of the Rhode Island supreme court, March 16, 1868, to his death, April 10, 1882.

Potter, Elisha R., correspondence regarding Dorr's Rebellion, 2141, 2148, 2149.

Powell, Joseph W., naval cadet, to be made ensign for attempting to rescue force of the *Merrimac*, 6306.

Powell, L. E., treaty with Indians concluded by, 2521.

Powell, Lazarus W.; b. Henderson County, Ky., Oct. 6, 1812; graduated from St. Joseph College, Bardstown, in 1833; studied law, and in 1835 began practice; served in the State legislature as a member in 1836; a Presidential elector on the Polk and Dallas ticket in 1844; governor of Kentucky 1851-1855; elected a United States Senator from Kentucky as a Democrat, serving from 1859 to 1865; delegate to the national Union convention at Philadelphia in 1866; died near Henderson, Ky., July 3, 1867.

Powell, Lazarus W., sent to Utah during troubles with Mormons, 3036.

Powers, Caleb, b. Whitley County, Ky., Feb. 1, 1869; attended Union College, Barbourville, Ky.; State University, Lexington, Ky.; Centre College, Danville, Ky., and the Valparaiso Indiana University, Valparaiso, Ind., where he graduated in law and was admitted to the bar in 1894; elected superintendent of public schools for Knox County, Ky., in 1894, and re-elected in 1897; in 1899 was elected secretary of state for the State of Kentucky. During the contests for state offices at this time, Senator William Goebel, the Democratic contestant for governor, was shot and killed by an unknown assassin; and upon the heels of that followed Mr. Powers' long persecution with which the public is familiar. After having served eight years, three months and three days in the jails of Kentucky he was given his freedom and was nominated and elected to the 62d, 63d and 64th Congresses from Kentucky.

Powers, Hiram, American sculptor, negotiations with, regarding work of art for Capitol, 2910.

Preble, Edward; naval officer; b. Portland, Me., Aug. 15, 1761; made midshipman in navy, 1779; commodore of the Mediterranean squadron, 1803, in command of the Constitution; exacted from the Emperor of Morocco a renewal of the treaty of 1786; bombarded the city of Tripoli, 1804; for his services in the Mediterranean he was voted a gold medal by Congress; died Portland, Me., Aug. 25, 1807.

Preble, Edward:

Energy and judgment displayed by, 365.

Medal presented to, March 3, 1805, for gallantry, mentioned, 352.

Preble, George Henry; naval officer; b. Portland, Me., Feb. 25, 1816; midshipman, Oct. 10, 1835; served in China and in the Mexican War; took part in the operations against New Orleans and the lower Mississippi as far north as Vicksburg and off Mobile Bay, in the Civil War; promoted rear-admiral, Sept. 30, 1876, and retired 1878; died Brookline, Mass., March 1, 1885.

Preble, George H.:

Commander in Navy, nomination of, and reasons therefor, 3354.

Thanks of Congress to, recommended, 3277.

Preston, William B.; lawyer, statesman; Secretary of the Navy under President Taylor; b. Nov. 25, 1805, in Smithfield, Va.; graduated from the University of Virginia and admitted to the bar; entered political life quite young and served a number of terms in the Virginia House of Delegates and the State Senate; was elected to Congress as a Whig; March 8, 1849, President Taylor appointed him Secretary of the Navy; upon the death of Taylor he retired from politics; in 1861 he was elected a member of the Secession Convention, and being a Union man, opposed the secession of the State, as long as there was any hope for the opposition, but went with the majority and was elected to the Confederate Senate in 1861, and was a member of that body until his death, which occurred Nov. 16, 1862, at Smithfield, Va.

Prince of Wales, visit of, to United States, 3171.

Prioleau, Samuel, claim of representatives of, refused and reasons therefor, 2826.

Proctor, Redfield, Secretary of War under President Benjamin Harrison; b. at Proctorsville, Vt., June 1, 1831, of English stock, descended from Robert Proctor, who came from London to Salem, Mass., in 1635; graduated from Dartmouth College in 1851, and from the Albany Law School in 1859; enlisted in the Third Regiment of Vermont Volunteers in 1861, of which he was appointed quartermaster with the rank of lieutenant; served on the staff of Gen. William F. (Baldy) Smith as brigade and division quartermaster; promoted major of the Fifth Regiment and colonel of the Fifteenth; after being mustered out returned to Vermont and engaged in the practice of law, and later became interested in the devolpment of the marble industry; representative in the State Legislature in 1867-68 and 1888; member of the State Senate and president pro tem of that body in 1874-75; lieutenant-governor of the state from 1876 to 1878, and governor from 1878 to 1880; delegate to the Republican national convention of 1884, and chairman of the Vermont delegation in the same conventions of 1888 and 1896; appointed Secretary of War in March. 1889; resigned from the cabinet in Nov., 1891, to accept the appointment as United States Senator as a Republican, to succeed George F. Edmunds, and was elected by the Vermont Legislature Oct. 18, 1892, to fill both the unexpired and full terms; elected Oct. 18, 1898, to succeed himself for the term beginning March 4, 1899, and ending March 3, 1905.

Proctor, Redfield, resignation of, as Secretary of War and appointment as United States Senator from Vermont referred to, 5630.

Pujo, Arsene Paulin; b. Dec. 16, 1861, near Lake Charles, Calcasieu Parish, of the marriage of Paul Pujo, of Tarbes, France, to Miss Eloise M. Le Bleu; admitted to the bar Oct. 23, 1886, by the supreme court of Louisiana; elected to the 58th, 59th, 60th and 61st Congresses from Louisiana.

Pulaski, Count Casimir, brigadier-general in Army, service rendered by and compensation to, referred to, 5124.

Statue of, at Washington, D. C., 6860.

Purvis, H. W., report of, on slaughter of American citizens in South Carolina, 4329.

Putnam, Rufus, treaty with Indians concluded by, 127.

Putnam, William L., treaty with Great Britain on subject of fisheries concluded by, 5189.

Queen, Walter W., thanks of Congress to, recommended, 3277.

Quiggle, Chloe, act granting pension to, vetoed, 5233.

Quezon, Manuel L.; b. Baler, Province of Tayabas, Philippines, Aug. 19, 1878; received his primary and secondary education in the College of San Juan de Letran, obtaining the degree of bachelor of arts and expert land surveyor; studied law in the University of St. Thomas, and was admitted to the Filipino bar in April, 1903. During the revolution was a major of the Philippine army, and was detailed to Gen. Aguinaldo's staff; under the American Government he held the office of prosecuting attorney for the Province of Mindoro, and was subsequently transferred to the Province of Tayabas with the same office. May 15, 1909, the Philippine Legislature elected him Resident Commissioner of the Philippine Islands in the United States to succeed Hon. Pablo Ocampo de Leon.

Radcliffe, William, compensation to, 6866.

Rainey, Henry T.; b. Aug. 20, 1860, at Carrollton, Ill.; graduated from Union College of Law, Chicago, in 1885, receiving the degree of B. L.; soon afterwards admitted to the bar; elected to 58th, 59th, 60th, 61st, 62d, 63d and 64th Congresses from Illinois.

Raker, John E.; b. near Knoxville, Knox County, Ill., Feb. 22, 1863; in 1873 moved with his parents to Lassen County, Cal.; worked on the ranch and farm and attended the public schools and the State Normal School at San Jose, Cal., 1882-1884; studied law and was admitted to the bar in the fall of 1885; engaged in many important suits involving water rights and land matters, as well as many noted criminal cases; district attorney for Modoc county four years, 1895-1898; judge of the Superior Court of California in the county of Modoc in 1902 and re-elected in 1908; resigned Dec. 19, 1910; admitted to the Supreme Court of Oregon, the United States Circuit and District Courts of California, United States Court of Appeals, and the Supreme Court of the United States; elected to the 62d, 63d and 64th Congresses from California.

Ramsay, David, arrest and maltreatment of, at Heidelberg, Baden, 2772.

Ramsey, Alexander; lawyer; b. Harrisburg, Pa., Sept. 8, 1815; admitted to the Pennsylvania bar and practiced in Harrisburg, which district he represented in the 28th and 29th Congresses, 1843-47; appointed territorial governor of Minnesota, 1849, and made important treaties with the Indians of the section; mayor of St. Paul, 1855-57, and governor of Minnesota, 1860-63; from 1863 to 1875 he was United States Senator, and President Hayes appointed him Secretary of War, 1879-81; died St. Paul, Minn., April 22, 1903.

Ramsey, Alexander:

Superintendent of Indian affairs in Minnesota, misconduct of, referred to, 2760.

Treaty with Indians concluded by, 3397.

Ramsden, Fred W., British consul at Santiago, Cuba, services of, to United States and subsequent death of, referred to, 6331.

Randall Alexander Williams, Postmaster-General under President Johnson, and eighth Governor of Wisconsin; b. Ames, Montgomery Co., N. Y., Oct. 31, 1819, the son of Phineas Randall, a native of Massachusetts, and resident of Montgomery county, N. Y.; and subsequently of Waukesha, Wis. Alexander passed through college, studied law, and began the practice of his profession in 1840, in Waukesha. He was appointed postmaster at Waukesha, and in 1847 was elected a member of the convention that framed the constitution. In 1855 he was a member of the State Assembly, an unsuccessful competitor for the attorney-generalship, and was chosen judge, to fill an unexpired term of the Milwaukee Circuit Court. In 1857 he was elected Governor of Wisconsin, re-elected in 1859, occupying the gubernatorial chair at the outbreak of the war. He declared at once the loyalty of Wisconsin to the Union, and the purpose of her people to fight for its integrity in such a way as to draw national attention, and his prompt and efficient measures, well seconded by all, augmented the useful service of the state, and gave her character and standing. He assembled the legislature in extra session, but before it could act, he organized the Second regiment, using for this purpose the public funds before a lawful appropriation had been made; but when the legislature convened it upheld him in what he had done. When his term as governor expired in 1861 he contemplated entering the army, but was prevailed upon by President Lincoln to accept the post of minister to Italy, where he remained for a year and returning home became first assistant to Postmaster-General Dennison; in 1866 President Johnson appointed him post-postmaster-general, and he served in that capacity to the end of that administration. He died July 25, 1872, in Elmira, N. Y.

Randall, Alex W., correspondence of, transmitted, 3804.

Randall, Samuel J., statesman; Speaker of the House of Representatives; b. Philadelphia, Oct. 10, 1828; received an academic education; engaged in mercantile pursuits; member of the city councils of Philadelphia four years; Member of the State Senate of Pennsylvania in 1858-59; elected to the 38th, 39th, 40th, 41st, 42d, 43d, 44th, 45th and 46th Congresses as a Democrat; elected Speaker of the House for the last session of the 44th, for the 45th and 46th Congresses; re-elected to the 47th, 48th, 49th, 50th and 51st Congresses; died at Washington, D. C., April 13, 1890.

Randolph, Edmund; statesman; b. Williamsburg, Pa., Aug. 10, 1753; graduated College William and Mary; delegate to the Continental Congress from Virginia, 1779-83; in 1788 was a member of the convention which framed the Constitution of the United States, but voted against its adoption; governor of Virginia, 1788; appointed Attorney-General of the United States, 1789, and in 1794 Secretary of State in Washington's Cabinet; died Clarke Co., Va., Sept. 13, 1813.

Randolph, Edmund, Attorney-General, proceedings of Cabinet were signed by, Aug. 5, 1793.

Randolph, Edmund J., Attorney-General and Secretary of State under President Washington; b. Virginia, Aug. 10, 1753; received a liberal education, studied law, and began practice at Williamsburg; served in the Revolutionary Army; Attorney-General of Virginia in 1776; Delegate from Virginia to the Continental Congress, 1779-1782; Governor of Virginia, 1786-1788; member of the convention that framed the Federal Constitution; appointed Attorney-General Sept. 26, 1789; transferred to the State Department as Secretary of State, January 2, 1794, but was invited to resign in August, 1795, having lost the confidence of the President; died in Clarke County, Va., Sept. 13, 1813.

Randolph, John, Jr., letter of, demanding that certain of the navy officers who had insulted him, be punished, 291.

Rankin, Jeanette; the first Congresswoman, was born in Montana in 1878. She is a graduate of the University of Montana, and of the New York School of Philanthropy. She was known for many years throughout her state and the West as an ardent worker in the cause of equal suffrage, and was elected to Congress on the Republican ticket in the elections held in November, 1916, taking her seat in the House of Representatives when the Sixty-fifth Congress assembled in special session on April 2, 1917.

Ransom, George M., thanks of Congress to, recommended, 3277.

Rauch, George Washington; b. Warren, Huntington Co., Ind., Feb. 22, 1876; admitted to the bar in 1902, and began the practice of law at Marion, Ind.; elected to the 60th, 61st, 62d, 63d and 64th Congresses from Indiana.

Rawlins, John Aaron; soldier; Secretary of War under President Grant; b. East Galena, Ill., Feb. 13, 1831; after seeing much service in the field he rose by degrees to the rank of major-general by brevet in 1865; served as chief of staff to the general commanding the armies, and on the accession of Gen. Grant to the Presidency, he was appointed Secretary of War; died Washington, D. C., Sept. 9, 1869.

Rawlins, John A.:
Secretary of War, death of, announced and honors to be paid memory of, 3978.
Statue of, recommendations regarding erection of, 4124.

Ray, James B., treaty with Indians concluded by, 931.

Rayner, Isidor; b. Baltimore, April 11, 1850; educated at the University of Maryland, and the University of Virginia; admitted to the bar in 1870 and has held the following public offices: In 1878 he was elected to the Maryland Legislature for two years; in 1885 he was elected to the State Senate for four years; in 1886, to the 50th Congress, and later to the 52d and 53d Congresses; attorney-general of Maryland, 1889-1903; elected to the United States Senate from Maryland for the term beginning March 4, 1905.

Read, John, agent of United States, referred to, 328.

Rebello Vicenzo, seizure of at New Orleans, 4653.

Rector, Wharton:
Conviction of, for crimes committed referred to, 1039.
Indian agent, renomination of, and reasons therefor, 1045.

Redfield, William Cox, Secretary of Commerce under President Wilson; b. June 18, 1858, at Albany, N. Y.; was married at Brooklyn, N. Y., in 1885, to Elise M. Fuller, of Brooklyn, N. Y.; they have two children; in 1867 his parents moved to Pittsfield, Mass, in which city he received his education in the grammar and high schools; engaged in the manufacture of iron and steel forgings, tools, etc., from 1885 to 1905; was commissioner of public works for the borough of Brooklyn; in 1910 was elected to the 62d Congress; from 1907 until his appointment as Secretary of Commerce was vice-president and a director of the American Blower Company, Detroit,

Manufacturers of engines, heating, ventilating, drying and cooling apparatus; was also president of the American Manufacturers' Export Association, and is still president of the National Society for the Promotion of Industrial Education; he made a business journey around the world in 1910-11 to study industrial conditions generally, his itinerary taking him to Hawaii, Japan, the Philippines, Honghong, Java, Singapore, Burma, India, France, England and Holland; he is the author of a book entitled "The New Industrial Day"; appointed Secretary of Commerce March 4, 1913.

Reed, Silas, surveyor of Missouri and Illinois:
Nomination of, and reasons therefor, 1956.
Error in, corrected, 1957.
Official conduct of, referred to, 2212, 2214.

Reed, Thomas Brackett (1839-1902); politician; b. Portland, Me.; practiced law after 1865, and was active in politics in his native State; member of Congress, 1877-99, and Speaker of the House during the terms of 1889-91, 1895-97, and 1897-99; originator of the famous Reed rules, governing House procedure.

Reed, William Bradford; lawyer, diplomat; b. Philadelphia, Pa., June 30, 1806; attorney-general of Pennsylvania, 1838; United States Minister to China, 1857 and 1858 and negotiated the treaty which was ratified in 1861; died New York City, Feb. 18, 1886.

Reed, William B.:
Commissioner to China, instructions to, referred to, 3015.
Dispatches of, regarding convention with China, referred to, 3071.

Reeves, Benjamin H., treaty with Indians concluded by, 889.

Reid, Samuel C., battle sword of father offered to United States by, 5119.

Reid, Whitelaw, member of Spanish-American Peace Commission, 6322.

Reiter, George C., conduct of, in connection with arrest and killing of Gen. Barrundia, referred to, 5569.

Rennels, Hiram G., receiver of public money, nomination of, 1040.

Renshaw, William B., thanks of Congress to, recommended, 3277.

Renwick, James, report of, as commissioner on northeastern boundary. (See Northeastern Boundary.)

Reyes, Rafael, correspondence of, concerning Panama, 6852.

Reynolds, Alexander W., assistant quartermaster, nomination of, and reasons therefor, 2996.

Reynolds, John C., directed to accompany ex-President Jackson home, 1540.

Reynolds, Thomas C., report of, on commerce of Nicaragua, Honduras and Salvador, 5116.

Rhind, Charles:
Arabian horses received by, from Turkey, referred to, 1099.
Treaty with Turkey concluded by, 1093.

Rice, Francis W., arrest and imprisonment of, at Acapulco, Mexico, 2834, 2837.

Rice, Henry M.; b. Waitsfield, Vt., Nov. 29, 1816; received a liberal education; resided in the Territories of Iowa, Wisconsin and Minnesota; elected a Delegate from Minnesota Territory to the 33d and 34th Congresses as a Democrat; elected a United States Senator from Minnesota, serving from May 12, 1858, to March 3, 1863; elected treasurer of Ramsay County in 1878; died in 1894.

Rice, Henry M., member of Chippewa Commission, 5500.

Richardson, Israel B., major-general in Army, nomination of, and reasons therefor, 2697.

Richardson, James D., statesman and author; b. Rutherford Co., Tenn., March 10, 1843, and was a student at Franklin College, near Nashville, when the civil war began. Although he was only 18 years old at the time he entered the Confederate Army as a private. At the end of the first year of the war he was made adjutant of the Forty-fifth Tennessee Infantry, in which capacity he served for three years. At the close of the war he read law, and in 1867, began practice in Murfreesboro. He was elected to the lower house of the Tennessee Legislature, taking his seat in October, 1871, and was elected Speaker of the House on the first day of the session, although he was only 28 years old at the time. The following year he was elected to the State Senate and was a delegate to the Democratic National Conventions of 1876, 1896 and 1900. He became a Member of Congress in 1885 and served the Fifth District of Tennessee in that capacity for twenty years. He was the Democratic nominee for Speaker of the House of the 56th and 57th Congresses. Among the committees on which he served was the Committee on War Claims, in which he had much influence. Mr. Richardson was prominent in Masonic circles, in which he attained the thirty-third degree, and was Grand Master of the order in his state in 1873 and 1874. In 1901 he was elected Sovereign Grand Commander of the Southern Jurisdiction, Scottish Rite Masons. He was the editor and compiler of "Messages and Papers of the Presidents" and of "Messages and Papers of the Confederacy." He died at Murfreesboro, Tenn., July 24, 1914.

Richardson, James D., resolution authorizing compilation of Messages and Papers of the Presidents by. (See Prefatory Note, Volume One.)

Richardson, William; b. Athens, Limestone Co., Ala.; was in the Confederate army; was severely wounded at battle of Chickamauga and paroled in April, 1865, in Marietta, Ga.; representative in the general assembly of Alabama, 1865-67; judge of the court of probate and county court of Madison County, Ala.; elected to fill an unexpired term in the 56th Congress; elected to the 57th, 58th, 59th, 60th, 61st, 62d and 63d Congresses from Alabama.

Richardson, William Adams, financier and jurist, Secretary of the Treasury under President Grant; b. Tyngsborough, Mass., Nov. 2, 1821, the sixth in descent from Ezekiel Richardson, the first of the family to settle in New England. William A. was graduated from Harvard in 1843, studied law with his brother Daniel and received the degree of LL. B. in 1846; assisted Judge Joel Parker in revising the general statutes of Massachusetts; appointed Assistant Secretary of the Treasury in 1869, and as financial agent abroad conducted the delivery in London of more than $130,000,000 United States bonds of the five per cent loan there negotiated through him; in 1873 he was appointed Secretary of the Treasury to succeed Mr. Boutwell, who had been elected Senator from Massachusetts. One of Mr. Richardson's most important acts as Secretary was the transfer of the Geneva award money, $15,500,-000, from London to Washington without causing any stir in the financial circles of either country. In the financial panic of 1873 he kept the treasury from becoming involved by preventing ill-advised employment of the public money. He resigned the treasury to become Judge of the Court of Claims. In 1881 and 1891 he edited the supplement to the Revised Statutes of the United States, and established the style since pursued in that work. He was a lecturer on law in Georgetown University, LL. D. of Columbian University, and D. C. Dartmouth, Howard and Georgetown.

Richmond, James C., application of, for redress of wrongs, 2772.

Riddells, Bennett, consul to Chihuahua, Mexico, nomination of, and reasons therefor, 2587.

Riel, Louis, trial and execution of, by authorities of British North America, report regarding, transmitted, 5449.

Rigny, M. de, correspondence regarding claims against France. (See France, claims against.)

Riley, Bennett:
Correspondence regarding affairs in California, referred to, 2584.
Mentioned, 2570.

Riley, Frank B., American sailor, alleged killing of, in Genoa, Italy, 5769.

Riley, Patrick, deputy United States marshal, assaulted in Boston, 2637.
Proclamation regarding, 2645.

Riordan, Daniel J.; b. in Hester street, New York City, 1870; elected to the State Senate in 1902, 1904 and 1906; elected a member of the 56th Congress to serve unexpired term, and to the 60th, 61st, 62d, 63d and 64th Congresses from New York.

Roberts, Edmund, treaty with Siam concluded by, 1272.

Roberts, E. E.; b. Pleasant Grove, Sutter County, Cal., Dec. 12, 1870; educated in the public rural schools and in the State Normal School at San José; studied law and was elected district attorney of Ormsby County, Nev., in 1900; re-elected in 1902, 1904 and 1906, and again re-elected in 1908, being indorsed by all parties; was nominated at the primary election for Representative in Congress, and later elected to the 62d, 63d and 64th Congresses from Nevada.

Roberts, Ernest W.; b. East Madison, Me., Nov. 22, 1858; graduated at Boston University Law School, and admitted to the bar in 1881; elected a member of the Massachusetts house of representatives of 1894, 1895 and 1896; member of the Massachusetts Senate of 1897 and 1898, and to the 56th, 57th, 58th, 59th, 60th, 61st, 62d, 63d and 64th Congresses from Massachusetts.

Roberts, Joseph, first lieutenant, promotion of captain discussed, 2437.

Robertson, James; pioneer; b. Brunswick Co., Va., June 28, 1742; joined Daniel Boone's third expedition across the Alleghanies, and planted corn in Wautauga County, N. C., which he thought was part of Virginia, but which proved to be part of the Cherokee Indian lands, for which it was necessary to obtain a lease; joined in 1772 by Capt. John Sevier; they held the place against the Indians, and in 1779 they made a second settlement on the present site of Nashville, Tenn.; defended the settlements against many attacks of Indians and Spanish; appointed brigadier-general in United States army by President Washington, 1790, and Indian commissioner; died in the Chickasaw region of Tennessee, Sept. 1, 1814.

Robertson, James, nominated:
Brigadier-general of militia of Miro District, Ohio, Feb. 22, 1791.
Commissioner to treat with Indians, 423.

Robertson, John, commissioner from Virginia to confer with States in effort to prevent war, 3193.

Robertson, Thomas J., slaughter of American citizens in South Carolina referred to, 4329.

Robeson, George M., Secretary of the Navy under President Grant; was born at Oxford, N. J., in 1827; received an academic education; graduated from Princeton College in 1847; studied law; admitted to the bar in 1850 and practiced at Newark and afterwards at Camden; appointed prosecutor of the pleas for Camden County in 1858; appointed attorney-general of New Jersey in 1867, and served until he resigned, June 22, 1869, to accept the position of Secretary of the Navy, which he held until 1877; resumed the practice of law; elected to the 46th Congress as a Republican; re-elected to the 47th Congress; died Sept. 27, 1897.

Robinson, Benjamin F., treaty with Indians concluded by, 2953.

Rochambeau, Comte de:
Compensation prayed for by descendants of, 1198, 1270, 1273, 1348.
Letter of Marquise de Lafayette regarding, transmitted, 1198.
Mentioned, 6932.

Rochester, William B., secretary to Congress of Nations, nomination of, 886.

Rockhill, William W., member of board of management of Government exhibit at World's Columbian Exposition, 5833.
Mentioned, 6678.

Rodenberg, William A.; lawyer; b. near Chester, Randolph Co., Ill., Oct. 30, 1865; elected to the 56th Congress a member of the United States Civil Service Commission by President McKinley, March, 1901; resigned April, 1902, in order to again make the race for Congress; elected to the 58th, 59th, 60th, 61st, 62d and 64th Congresses from Illinois.

Rodgers, John; naval officer; b. Hartford Co., Md., July 11, 1771; joined the navy, 1798, and shipped on the Constitution; assigned by Capt. Truxton to take the captured *L'Insurgente* into port; commanded the *John Adams*, off Tripoli, 1802-03, and captured the Moorish ship *Meshonda;* succeeded Commodore Barron in command of the Mediterranean squadron, 1805, and exacted favorable treaties from the Barbary states; on breaking out of the second war with England, he was made captain of the *President*, and served through the war, taking many prizes; died Philadelphia, Pa., Aug. 1, 1838.

Rodgers, John, I:
American frigate under command of, attacked by British vessel, 477.
Correspondence regarding war with Tripoli, 379.
Frigates under command of, referred to, 502.
Gallant enterprise of, in destroying corvette on the coast of Tripoli, 353.
Report of, regarding docks and wharf referred to, 769.

Rodgers, John, II.; naval officer; son of above; b. Hartford Co., Md., Aug. 8, 1812; warranted midshipman, 1828, and served aboard the *Constellation*, 1829-32; served in surveying, exploring and map-making expeditions; served through the Civil War, and made rear-admiral, 1869; took the monitor *Monadnock* through the Straits of Magellan to San Francisco, 1866, and commanded Asiatic squadron, 1870-72; died Washington, D. C., May 5, 1882.

Rodgers, John, II:
Rear-admiral, mentioned, 4666.
Thanks of Congress to, recommended, 3392.

Rodney, Caesar A., Attorney-General under President Jefferson and Madison; b. Dover, Del., Jan. 4, 1772; received a liberal education; studied law; began practice at Wilmington, Del.; elected a Representative from Delaware to the 8th Congress as a Democrat; appointed Attorney-General by President Jefferson and continued by President Madison, serving from 1807 to 1811; served in the war of 1812; sent to South America by President Monroe as one of the commissioners to investigate and report on the propriety of recognizing the independence of the Spanish-American Republics; elected to the 17th Congress, serving from Dec. 3, 1821, to Jan. 24, 1822; elected to the United States Senate, and served until Jan. 27, 1823, when he resigned, having been appointed minister plenipotentiary to Buenos Ayres; died at his post June 10, 1824.

Ruggles, Samuel B., delegate to International Monetary Conference at Paris, report of, transmitted, 4013.

Ruiz, Ricardo, arrest, imprisonment, and death of, in Cuba, 6184.

Rush, Richard; lawyer; author, diplomat; b. Philadelphia, Pa., Aug. 29, 1780; appointed Attorney-General in 1814; minister to England, 1817, serving until 1825; Secretary of the Treasury under John Quincy Adams; candidate for Vice-President on the ticket with John Adams and in 1847 was appointed minister to France, remaining in office ten years; published, in 1833, "A Residence at the Court of St. James," and later, "Familiar Letters of Washington"; died Philadelphia, July 30, 1859.

Rush, Richard:
Acting Secretary of State, 605.
Correspondence of, regarding cession of lands for light-houses referred to, 845.

Rush, William Henry, imprisonment of, in Cuba referred to, 2538.

Rusk, Jeremiah McL.; Secretary of Agriculture under President Benjamin Harrison; b. Morgan County, Ohio, June 17, 1830; received a limited education; moved to Vernon County, Wis., in 1853; held various local offices; member of the Wisconsin State Legislature in 1862; major of the Twenty-fifth Wisconsin Volunteers in July, 1862; promoted to the colonelcy; brevetted brigadier-general at the close of the war; elected bank comptroller of Wisconsin 1866-67, and again elected for 1868-69; elected a Representative from Wisconsin to the 42d, 43d and 44th Congresses as a Republican; Secretary of Agriculture March 5, 1889, to March 5, 1893; died in 1893.

Rusk, Jeremiah McL., Secretary of Agriculture, mentioned, 5763.

Russell, John E., member of commission to consider construction of canal from Great Lakes to Atlantic Ocean, 6179.

Russell, John H., thanks to Congress to, recommended, 3277.

Russell, John M., consul to St. Petersburg, nomination of, 165.

Russell, Jonathan; lawyer, diplomat; b. Providence, R. I., Feb. 27, 1771; graduate Rhode Island College, A. B., 1791; A. M., 1794; after having been chargé d'affaires at Paris and London he was appointed, Jan. 8, 1814, to negotiate a treaty of peace with Great Britain at Ghent; minister plenipotentiary to Sweden, 1814-18; member of 17th and 18th Congresses from Massachusetts, 1821-25; died Milton, Mass., Feb. 17, 1832.

Russell, Jonathan:
Letter of, regarding treaty of Ghent discussed, 707, 711.
Minister to Sweden, nomination of, 515.
Pacific advances made by United States to Great Britain referred to, 506.

Russell, Joseph J.; b. Mississippi Co., Mo., Aug. 23, 1854; educated in the public schools and in the Charleston Academy; graduated from law school, Missouri State University, in 1880, with degree LL. B.; elected prosecuting attorney in 1880 and 1882; in 1884 was a Cleveland elector for his district; in 1886 and 1888 elected to the state legislature, and in his last term was speaker of the House; in 1892 was a delegate to the Democratic national convention; judge advocate-general on Gov. Dockery's staff; permanent chairman of Democratic state convention in 1910; elected to the 60th, 62d, 63d and 64th Congresses from Missouri.

Russell, Lord John, letter of, regarding treaty of Washington referred to, 2884.

Ryan, William A. C., indemnity paid by Spain on account of execution of, referred to, 4408.

Minister to—
Brazil, correspondence regarding slave trade, referred to, 2765.
Great Britain, member of commission to settle questions with latter, 4075.

Schley, Winfield Scott; naval officer; b. Richfield Farm, Frederick Co., Md., Oct. 9, 1839; graduated U. S. Naval Academy, 1860; served during the Civil War with Farragut on the lower Mississippi, and then went to the China station; commanded an expedition in 1884 which rescued Lieut. A. W. Greely and six companions from imminent death in the arctic regions; Feb. 6, 1898, promoted commodore, and later selected to command the flying squadron to protect the Atlantic coast; joined Sampson's fleet blockading Santiago, Cuba, and on July 3, 1898, during the absence of Sampson, the Spanish fleet attempted to escape; Schley commanded the movements of the American fleet. and before the return of Sampson had destroyed the enemy's vessels; retired Oct. 9, 1901; died New York City, Oct. 2, 1911.

Schley, Winfield S.:
Lady Franklin Bay expedition under command of, 4835.
Member of military commission to Puerto Rico, 6322.
Sailors of the *Baltimore,* under command of, assaulted at Valparaiso, Chile. (See *Baltimore,* The.)
Santiago Harbor shelled by American squadron under, 6316.
Spanish fleet attempting to escape from Santiago Harbor, destroyed by American squadron under direction of, 6317. (See Enc. Art., Santiago Harbor, Battle of.)

Schmidt, Conrad, arrest and detention of, at Bremen, 2772.

Schofield, John McAllister; soldier; b. Gerry, N. Y., Sept. 29, 1831; graduated U. S. Military Academy, 1853; professor of physics in Washington University, Missouri, at outbreak of Civil War, and took an active part in military operations in Missouri and Tennessee, attaining the rank of major-general of volunteers; honorably mustered out of the volunteer service, Sept. 1, 1866, and on June 2, 1868, succeeded Edwin M. Stanton as Secretary of War, and served in Johnson's and Grant's Cabinets till March 12, 1869; promoted to major-general U. S. A., March 4, 1869; lieutenant-general, Feb. 5, 1895, and retired Sept. 29, 1895.

Schofield, John M.:
Directed to assume command of—
Army, 5353.
Military Division of Missouri, 4120.
Lieutenant-general, revival of grade of, in behalf of, recommended, 5968.
Retirement of, from Army, discussed, 6056.
Secretary of War, appointment of, referred to, 3862.

Schoolcraft, Henry R., results of Indian investigations by, referred to, 2609.

Schriver, Ed., correspondence of, transmitted, 3810.

Schuetze, William H., report of, on transmission of testimonials by, to Russian subjects aiding survivors of *Jeannette* expedition, 5120.

Schurman, Jacob G., commissioner to Philippine Islands, 6584.

Schurz, Carl; writer, soldier; b. Liblar, Germany, March 2, 1829; received a classical education; emigrated to the United States in 1852 and located in New York; delegate to the Chicago convention of 1860; appointed minister to Spain in 1861, but soon afterwards resigned; appointed brigadier-general of volunteers in the Union Army; engaged in newspaper work after the war in Missouri; delegate to the Chicago convention in 1868; elected a United States Senator from Missouri as a Republican 1869-1875; Secretary of the Interior 1877-1881; editor of New York *Evening Post* 1881-1884; contributed to *Harper's Weekly* 1892-1898; president of the National Civil Service Reform League 1892-1901; died in New York City, May 14, 1906.

Schurz, Carl, report of, on conditions in the South, transmitted, 3571.

Schwan, Theodore, Puerto Rican expedition reenforced by brigade of, 6318.

Scott, Charles, expedition against Wabash Indians commanded by, 104.

Scott, Lieut.-Col. L. K., claim of, against United States, 6826.

Scott, Martin, promotion of, in military service, discussed, 2269.

Scott, Nathan Bay; b. Guernsey Co., Ohio; served in the Civil War, and after the war engaged in the manufacture of glass at Wheeling, W. Va.; elected to the United States Senate from West Virginia in 1899; reelected in 1905.

Scott, Winfield (1786-1866); soldier and politician; b. near Petersburg, Va.; after admission to the bar, 1806, he entered the United States army as captain of the light artillery, 1808; in the War of 1812 he fought at Queenstown Heights, 1812; Chippewa and Lundy's Lane, 1814, and was made brigadier-general and brevet major-general in that year; in the nullification troubles, 1832, he commanded in South Carolina; fought against the Seminoles and Creeks, 1835-37; helped settle the boundary dispute with Great Britain over the line between Maine and New Brunswick, 1838; major-general and commander-in-chief of the army, 1841; took chief command in Mexico, 1847; won the battles of Cerro Gordo, Contreras, Churubusco, Molino del Rey. and Chapultepec; nominated as Whig candidate for President, 1852, and was defeated by Pierce; appointed brevet lieutenant-general. 1847; helped settle the San Juan question with Great Britain, 1859.

Scott, Winfield:
British fortifications on northern frontier, letter of, on, 1804.
Commander of—
Army in war with Mexico, assignment of command to, and subsequent recall of, discussed, 2298, 2431.

Whig, and later Republican, United States Senator, 1849-61; in a speech at Rochester, 1858, he characterized the struggle between freedom and slavery as "an irrepressible conflict"; candidate for the Republican nomination for President, 1860; Secretary of State, 1861-69; wounded by an accomplice of Booth, 1865; traveled extensively between 1869 and 1871; was a consistent supporter of Johnson's reconstruction policy; his diplomatic services to his country include a most tactful handling of the "Trent affair"; withdrawal of the French troops from Mexico; and the cession of Alaska to the United States by Russia in 1867.

Seward, William H.:
Correspondence regarding Dorr's Rebellion, 2151.
Death of, announced and honors to be paid memory of, 4137.
Letters addressed by, to governors of certain States, referred to, 5200.
Memory of, death of, and honors to be paid to the, 4137.
Report on wounding of, 3792.
Secretary of State, 3215, 3510.
Wounding of, by assassins announced, 3485, 3486, 3487.
Military commission to try persons implicated in, and proceedings of, 3532, 3533, 3534, 3540, 3545, 3546.
Report on, referred to, 3792.
Reward offered for alleged instigators of, 3505.

Seymour, Horatio (1810-1886); politician; b. at Pompey Hill, Onondaga Co., N. Y., practiced law after 1832; elected to the New York States assembly, 1841; mayor of Utica, 1842; speaker of the State assembly, 1845; Democratic candidate for governor, 1850, and defeated; elected to the office for the term of 1853-55; defeated for governor, 1854, for having vetoed a prohibition bill in that year; reelected for the term of 1863-65; during this term the draft riots occurred in New York City, 1863; Democratic national chairman, 1864 and 1868; unsuccessful Democratic candidate for governor, 1868; nominated as the Democratic candidate for Presidency to oppose Grant in 1868.

Shackerly, Peter, claims of orphan child of, 1693.

Shackleford, Dorsey W.; b. Aug. 27, 1853; elected to the 56th, 57th, 58th, 59th, 60th, 61st, 62d, 63d and 64th Congresses from Missouri.

Shafter, William Rufus; soldier; b., Galesburg, Mich., Oct. 16, 1835; enlisted in the Civil War, 1861, and mustered out brigadier-general of volunteers, March 13, 1865; entered the regular army, 1867, and upon the outbreak of hostilities with Spain, in 1898, given command of the expedition sent to Cuba; arrived at Daiquiri June 21, took Siboney, Guasimas, El Caney, and San Juan Hill, and finally, July 14, all the Spanish troops in Eastern Cuba surrendered to him, and he remained in possession till peace was declared; retired with the rank of major-general, Feb. 2, 1901.
39

Shafter, William R.:
Army under, lands near Santiago, Cuba, 6317.
Operations of, around and subsequent capitulation of Santiago, 6317.
Thanks of President tendered, 6574, 6577.

Shakespeare, H. O., appointed representative to foreign countries to investigate causes, cure, etc., of cholera, 4902.
Report of, referred to, 5565.

Sharkey, William L., provisional governor of Mississippi, appointed, 3512.

Sharp, Solomon, authority to accept present from British officers, referred to, 3404.

Sharpe, George H., report of, on assassination of President Lincoln and attempted assassination of Secretary Seward transmitted, 3792.

Shaw, Leslie M.; banker, lawyer; Secretary of the Treasury under President Roosevelt; b. Nov. 2, 1848, in Morristown, Vt.; his early education was received in his native town, and, removing to Iowa in 1869, was graduated from Cornell College, at Mt. Vernon, and from Iowa College of Law in 1876; removed to Denison, Iowa, and went into the banking business; came into political prominence through his reply to W. J. Bryan's free silver theories; elected Governor of Iowa in 1897 and 1899; soon became known as a sound speaker on political and financial questions, and when Secretary Gage retired from the Treasury Mr. Shaw was appointed; he was called upon in 1902, 1903, 1905 and 1906 to relieve the stringency in the money market, and established what his successors continued as a treasury "relief fund"; when his term expired March 4, 1907, became President of the Carnegie Trust Company of New York; President of the International Monetary Conference at Indianapolis in 1898; active in affairs of the Methodist Church.

Shelby, Isaac; pioneer, patriot, soldier, first and fifth governor of Kentucky, Secretary of War under President Monroe; b. Dec. 11, 1750, near North Mountain, Frederick Co., Md.; removed with his father to the present site of Bristol, Tenn., in 1771 and engaged in farming and cattle raising on a large scale; compelled to defend their property against the Indians both father and son received military commissions in the Revolution; Isaac was largely employed in engineer work and convoying stores; active in military operations in Virginia and the Carolinas with Gen. Marion; after the Revolution he settled on his farm, "Traveler's Rest," in Lincoln Co. (Ky.), then part of Virginia; took part in the movement to set up a separate territory and became the first governor of Kentucky in 1791; served as a presidential elector every four years from 1800 to 1820; during 1812-13 under his patriotic calls thirty-seven regiments, a total of more than 16,000 men, volunteered for service against the British and Indians; later he sent 2,200 men to Gen. Jackson at New Orleans and promised 10,000 more should they be needed; died July 18, 1826, on his estate in Kentucky; counties in nine states have been named in his honor.

Shonts, Theodore P., Chairman Panama Canal Commission, 7020.

Short, William; diplomat; b. Spring Garden, Surry Co., Va., Sept. 30, 1759; graduated William and Mary College, 1779; went to France with Jefferson as secretary of legation in 1784; appointed by Washington chargé d'affaires, and transferred to The Hague as minister resident, 1794, and to Madrid as commissioner plenipotentiary and concluded several important treaties with Spain; died Philadelphia, Dec. 5, 1849.

Short, William:
Commissioner to Spain, nomination of, 107.
Referred to, 184.
Nomination of, as minister to—
France, 50.
Russia, 449.
Spain, 148.

Shriver, David, superintendent of Cumberland road, 816.

Shufeldt, Robert Wilson; naval officer; b. Red Hook, N. J., Feb. 21, 1822; entered the service as midshipman, 1839; appointed consul-general to Cuba by President Lincoln in 1861, and served two years in Havana, when he resigned and took part in the naval operations of the South Atlantic and Gulf coast squadrons; engaged in promoting a transit route across the Isthmus of Tehuantepec in 1861 and in 1870-71; was promoted to rear-admiral, 1883, and retired Feb. 21, 1884; died Washington, D. C., Nov. 7, 1895.

Shufeldt, Robert W.:
Consul-general at Havana, 3344.
Correspondence regarding Johanna Island, referred to, 4536.
Cruise of, around the world, referred to, 4693.

Sibley, George C., treaty with Indians concluded by, 889.

Sierra, Justo, communication from, regarding suffering in Yucatan resulting from Indian insurrections, 2431.

Sieyès, Emmanuel Joseph, letter of, on death of Benjamin Franklin, 87.

Simmons, F. M.; b. Jan. 20, 1854, in Jones Co., N. C.,; graduated at Trinity College, that State, with the degree of A. B., in June, 1873; admitted to the bar in 1875; in 1886 was elected a member of the 50th Congress; received the degree of LL.D. from Trinity College, N. C., June, 1901; elected to the United States Senate for the term beginning March 4, 1901; reelected in 1907 and 1913 to represent North Carolina.

Simmons, James Fowler; b. Little Compton, R. I., Sept. 10, 1795; received a classical education; farmer; served in the lower branch of the State legislature 1828-1841; United States Senator from Rhode Island 1841-1847; again elected, serving from Dec. 7, 1857, to December, 1862, when he resigned; died at Johnson, R. I., July 10, 1864.

Simmons, James F., correspondence regarding Dorr's Rebellion, 2158.

Simpson, Edward, member of Gun Foundry Board, 4748.

Simpson, Slingsby, vessel under, ordered from and forbidden to reenter waters of United States, 391.

Sims, Thetus Willrette; b. April 25, 1852, in Wayne Co., Tenn.; graduated law department of the Cumberland University, at Lebanon, Tenn., June, 1876; elected to the 55th, 56th, 57th, 58th, 59th, 60th, 61st, 62d, 63d and 64th Congresses from Tennessee.

Sisson, Thomas Upton; b. Sept. 22, 1869; in Attala Co., Miss., graduated at the Southwestern Presbyterian University at Clarkesville, Tenn., taking the degree of A. B. in 1889; graduated in law at Cumberland University, Lebanon, Tenn., and was admitted to the bar at Memphis, Tenn., in 1894; moved from Memphis to Winona, Miss., in 1895; served in the State senate; elected to the 61st Congress from Mississippi, without opposition, and reelected to the 62d, 63d and 64th Congresses.

Sitgreave, Samuel, commissioner of United States, nomination of, 290.

Sitting Bull:
Disturbances caused by, discussed, 4576.
Surrender of, discussed, 4625, 4637.

Slacum, George W., report of, relating to African slave trade transmitted, 2268.

Slayden, James I.; b. in Kentucky; attended Washington and Lee University, Lexington, Va.; member of the twenty-third legislature of Texas, but declined reelection; elected to the 55th and all subsequent Congresses including the 64th from Texas.

Slemp, Campbell Bascom; b. Lee Co., Va., Sept. 4, 1870; served as page in the Virginia house of representatives, and was graduated from the Virginia Military Institute; elected to the 60th Congress to fill a vacancy and reelected to the 61st, 62d, 63d and 64th Congresses from Virginia.

Slidell, John; b. New York in 1793; received a liberal education; studied law and began practice at New Orleans; United States district attorney 1829-1833; elected a Representative from Louisiana to the 28th Congress as a State Rights Democrat; reelected to the 29th Congress, and resigned Nov. 10, 1845, having been appointed minister to Mexico, but that Government refused to accept him; elected United States Senator from Louisiana (vice Pierre Soulé, resigned) and re-elected, serving from 1853 to 1861; retired from the Senate and afterwards expelled; arrested at Habana on the English mail steamer *Trent* while on his way to England, and brought to the United States and confined in Fort Warren; soon released, and sailed for England Jan. 1, 1862; died at London, July 29, 1871.

Slidell, John:
Confederate envoy to France, removal of, from British steamer *Trent*, 3262, 3263, 3264, 3267, 3268.
Mission to Mexico for adjustment of differences discussed, 2288, 2415.

Sloan, Charles H.; b. Monticello, Iowa, May 2, 1863; graduated Iowa State Agricultural College, 1884, and moved to Nebraska same year; twice elected prosecuting attorney of Fillmore County; elected to the Nebraska State Senate; elected to the 62d, 63d and 64th Congresses from Nebraska.

Sloat, John D., commander of the *St. Louis,* 1133.

Smith, Albert, commissioner, on northeastern boundary, 2023.

Smith, Albert N., thanks of Congress to, recommended, 3277.

Smith, Caleb Blood, Secretary of the Interior under President Lincoln; b. Boston, Mass., April 16, 1808; accompanied his parents to Ohio in 1814; graduated from the Miami University; studied law and began practice at Connersville, Ind.; founded and edited the *Indiana Sentinel* in 1832; state representative 1833-1836, the last year as Speaker; elected a Representative from Indiana to the 28th, 29th and 30th Congresses; Presidential Elector in 1840; moved to Cincinnati, Ohio, where he practiced law; Presidential Elector on the Fremont ticket in 1856; Secretary of the Interior 1861-62, and resigned to become judge for the district of Indiana; died at Indianapolis, Ind., Jan. 7, 1884.

Smith, Caleb B., ex-Secretary of Interior, death of, announced and honors to be paid, memory of, 3432.

Smith, Charles B.; b. Erie Co., N. Y., Sept. 14, 1870; went to Arcade Academy, where he completed full course and was graduated; for several years worked, alternately at farming, railroad telegraphing, and newspaper work; became a reporter on the Buffalo *Courier,* of which he later in life was made editor-in-chief. Appointed managing editor of the Buffalo *Times,* the Buffalo *Evening Enquirer* and the Buffalo *Morning Courier;* during his connection with the Buffalo *Times,* acted as Albany correspondent of that publication, and at the same time one of the associate editors of the Albany *Argus;* owner and editor of the Niagara Falls *Journal;* elected to the 62d, 63d and 64th Congresses from New York.

Smith, Charles E.; editor; Postmaster General under President McKinley; b. Feb. 18, 1842, in Mansfield, Conn.; educated in Albany, N. Y.; served as military secretary and judge advocate general in the early years of the Civil War; in 1865, purchased the Albany *Express* and later became editor of the *Journal;* became prominent in Republican party and later wrote platforms and resolutions; in 1880 went to Philadelphia and became editor and part owner of the *Press;* appointed by President Harrison Minister to Russia; succeeded James A. Gary as Postmaster General in 1898, and established rural free delivery. Mr. Smith was twice married and had no children. He died Jan. 19, 1908, in Philadelphia.

Smith, Daniel; b. Fauquier County, Va., about 1740; one of the earliest settlers in Tennessee; appointed by President Washington secretary of the territory south of the Ohio River Jan. 7, 1790; a general of militia; appointed a United States Senator from Tennessee (in place of Andrew Jackson, resigned), serving from Dec. 3,

1798, to March 3, 1799; elected a Senator from Tennessee, serving from Dec. 2, 1805, to 1809, when he resigned; died in Sumner County, Tenn., July 16, 1818.

Smith, Daniel, treaty with Indians concluded by, 834.

Smith, Ellison DuRant; merchant and planter; b. Aug. 1, 1866, Lynchburg, Sumter (now Lee) Co., S. C., entered Wofford College, Spartanburg, S. C., from which institution he graduated in 1889; at Wofford he won gold medals in debate, science, and literature in his sophomore, junior, and senior years; member of the legislature from Sumter County, 1896 to 1900; began the cotton movement in 1901, which resulted in the organization of the Farmers' Protective Association; became a national figure on account of addresses at New Orleans, Birmingham, Dallas, and Shreveport; was nominated for United States Senator from South Carolina at a primary election in September, 1908; elected, 1909, for the term beginning March 4; reelected in 1914.

Smith, Emory, trial and conviction of Crawford Keys for murder of, 3659.

Smith, General, negotiations of, at New Orleans referred to, 3583.

Smith, Hoke; b. Sept. 2, 1855, in Newton, N. C., educated principally by his father, Dr. H. H. Smith, who was a professor in the University of North Carolina; read law while teaching school, and has been actively engaged in practice for 30 years; married Dec. 19, 1883, to Miss Birdie Cobb; Secretary of the interior from March 4, 1893, to Sept. 1, 1896; was governor of Georgia from July, 1907, to July 1909, and from July 1, 1911, to Nov. 15, 1911; elected to the Senate July 12, 1911, and resigned as governor Nov. 15, 1911; reelected to the Senate for term ending March 3, 1921.

Smith, Isaac, commissioner to conclude treaty with Indians, nomination of, 203.

Smith, John, alleged associate of Aaron Burr, 420.

Smith, John Jay, imprisonment of, by Mexican authorities referred to, 4376.

Smith, J. M. C.; in early life learned painter and mason trade; was educated in Charlotte (Mich.) High School and the University of Michigan; lawyer by profession, president of the First National Bank of Charlotte, and is interested in farming; has been prosecuting attorney, alderman and member of the constitutional convention of 1908; was elected to the 62d, 63d and 64th Congresses from Michigan.

Smith, J. S., dispatches of, relative to imprisonment of Davis Hatch, referred to, 4113.

Smith, John Walter; b. Snow Hill, Feb. 5, 1845; educated at private schools and at Union Academy, and engaged in the lumber business in Maryland, Virginia, and North Carolina; president of the First National Bank of Snow Hill, and director in many business and financial institutions; elected to represent Worcester County in the senate of Maryland in 1889, and was successively reelected in 1893 and 1897; was president of the State senate during the session of 1894; was nominated and elected to Congress from Maryland, 1898; was elected governor of Maryland by over 12,000 plurality in 1899; served from 1900 to 1904; was nominated by direct vote of the members of the Democratic party of Maryland on Nov. 5, 1907, by a plurality of 17,931, at the first primary election held in his State for United States Senator, to serve the term beginning March 4, 1909, and was thereafter elected United States Senator for that term by the general assembly of the State; he was elected United States Senator at the same session of the Maryland legislature on March 24 to fill the vacancy occasioned by the death of Hon. William Pinkney Whyte for the unexpired term ending March 3, 1909; reelected 1914, for term ending March 3, 1921.

Smith, Melancton, thanks of Congress to, recommended, 3277.

Smith, Noah, district supervisor, nomination of, 91.

Smith, Persifor F., correspondence regarding affairs in California referred to, 2584.

Smith, Robert; b. Peterboro, N. H., June 12, 1802; attended the public schools; farmer, moved to Illinois and located at Alton; served in the State house of representatives 1836-1840; elected a Representative from Illinois to the 28th, 29th and 30th Congresses as a Democrat; elected to the 35th Congress; died at Alton, Ill., Dec. 21, 1867.

Smith, Robert; lawyer; Secretary of the Navy and Attorney General under President Jefferson, and Secretary of State under President Madison; b. November, 1757, in Lancaster, Pa.; educated in the public schools and graduated Princeton in 1781; served in the Revolutionary War and was present at the battle of the Brandywine; after the war he studied law and began practice in Baltimore; State Senator in Maryland, 1793, and Member of the House of Delegates 1796-1800; also member of the Baltimore City Council; appointed Secretary of the Navy by President Jefferson Jan. 26, 1802, and served until 1805, when he was made Attorney General; held this office until 1809, when Madison appointed him Secretary of State; resigned in 1811, and declined the proffered appointment as Minister to Russia; President of a branch of the American Bible Society and the Maryland Agricultural Society; died Nov. 26, 1842, in Baltimore.

Smith, Robert, Secretary of State, 457.

Smith, Thomas A., official conduct of, referred to, 970.

Smith, W. H., correspondence regarding Dorr's Rebellion, 2147.

Smith, Watson, thanks of Congress to, recommended, 3277.

Smith, William, official acts of, in Virginia, declared null and void, 3535.

Smith, William Alden; b. Dowagiac, Mich., May 12, 1859; studied law, and was admitted to the bar in 1883; was honored with the degree of master of arts by Dartmouth College in June, 1901; is president and principal owner of the Grand Rapids *Herald;* elected to the 54th, 55th, 56th,

57th, 58th and 59th Congresses, and was unopposed for a seventh term and unanimously re-elected to the 60th Congress; elected to the United States Senate from Michigan for the term beginning March 4, 1907; re-elected 1913 for term ending March 3, 1919.

Smith, William F., special commissioner to investigate administration in military division bordering on Mississippi River, appointed, 3474.

Smith, William Robert; b. Aug. 18, 1863, Smith Co., Tex.; studied law in Tyler, Tex.; admitted to the bar in 1885; appointed by the governor judge of the thirty-second judicial district of Texas, to fill a vacancy; re-elected to the same office in 1898 and 1900, without opposition; elected to the 58th, 59th, 60th, 61st, 62d, 63d and 64th Congresses from Texas.

Smith, William S., district supervisor, nomination of, 91.

Smithson, James. (See Smithsonian Institution.)

Smoot, Reed; b. Jan. 10, 1862, at Salt Lake City, Utah; educated at the State University and Brigham Young Academy; is a banker and woollen manufacturer; elected to the United States Senate from Utah, March 5, 1903, and for the term of six years to begin March 4, 1909; re-elected in 1914 for term ending March 3, 1921.

Southard, Samuel L., served as Secretary of War and as Secretary of the Treasury under President John Quincy Adams; b. Baskingridge, N. J., June 9, 1787; graduated from Princeton College in 1804; studied law and began practice at Kensington, N. J.; appointed law reporter by the state legislature; served one week as a member of the state legislature, when he resigned to become associate justice of the supreme court of New Jersey; Presidential elector in 1820; elected a United States Senator from New Jersey (vice J. J. Wilson, resigned) as a Whig, serving from Feb. 16, 1821, to March 3, 1823; Acting Secretary of the Treasury March 7, 1825, to July 1, 1825; also for a short time was Secretary of War; Attorney-General of New Jersey; Governor of New Jersey in 1832; again elected a United States Senator, serving from December 2, 1833, to May 3, 1842, when he resigned; died at Fredericksburg, Va., June 26, 1842.

Spangler, Edward, implicated in assassination of President Lincoln, proceedings of trial and verdict of military commission, 3532, 3533, 3534, 3540, 3545, 3546.

Sparkman, Stephen M.; lawyer; b. in Hernando County, Fla., July 29, 1849; read law and was admitted to practice in 1872; was state's attorney for the sixth judicial circuit from 1878 to 1887; elected to the 54th, 55th, 56th, 57th, 58th, 59th, 60th, 61st, 62d, 63d and 64th Congresses.

Sparrow, Thomas W., claims of, against Peru, 6099.

Spear, Edward, lieutenant of artillery, nominations of, and reasons therefor, 55.

Speed, James, Attorney-General under President Lincoln; b. Jefferson county, Ky., March 11, 1812. His ancestors were early pioneers of Kentucky, and prominent promoters of all measures that helped to build up the material interests of the new territory. He was graduated from St. Joseph's College, Bardstown, Ky., in 1828, and was for a time clerk in the circuit and county courts. He studied law at Transylvania University, was admitted to the bar and began practice at Louisville in 1833, becoming one of the most distinguished jurists in Kentucky, occupying for a time the position of professor of law in the Louisville University. His well-known opposition to slavery prevented him from having any strong political influence in pro-slavery days, but his consistent and upright course brought him a great measure of public esteem and confidence. In 1841 he was elected to the State Legislature, but in 1849 he suffered a defeat in the state constitutional convention as the "emancipation" candidate against James Guthrie, candidate for the pro-slavery party. In the discussions that ensued in Kentucky upon the question of secession, Mr. Speed threw the weight of his influence on the Union side, and to his earnest efforts is largely ascribed the decision of the state convention against secession. On the breaking out of the war, President Lincoln, who had been the life-long friend of Mr. Speed's family, called upon him to assist in organizing the national troops in his native state, making him mustering officer of volunteers for the first call for 75,000 men in 1861. July 1863, he was selected by President Lincoln as the successor of Edward Bates as Attorney-General, which position he resigned after the death of Mr. Lincoln, not being in accord with President Johnson's administration. He died at his home in Kentucky, June 25, 1887.

Speight, Jesse; b. Greene County, N. C., Sept. 22, 1795; received a public school education; served several terms in both branches of the state legislature, and for a number of years was speaker of the house; elected a Representative from North Carolina to the 21st, 22nd, 23rd, and 24th Congresses as a Democrat; moved to Plymouth, Miss., and elected to the state house of representatives and chosen speaker; elected a United States Senator from Mississippi as a Democrat, serving from Dec. 1, 1845, to May 1, 1847, when he died, at Columbus, Miss.

Speight, J., correspondence regarding interference in elections, 1315.

Spencer, John Canfield, Secretary of War and the Treasury under President Tyler; b. Hudson, N. Y., Jan. 8, 1788; graduated from Union College in 1806; studied law, and in 1809 began practice at Canandaigua, N. Y.; served in the war of 1812; postmaster at Canandaigua; assistant attorney-general for the western part of New York in 1815; elected a Representative from New York to the 15th Congress as a Democrat; member of the state house of representatives 1820-21, and one year as Speaker; State Senator 1824-1828; again a member of the State House of Representatives in 1832; Secretary of State; appointed Secretary of War. Oct. 12, 1841, serving until March 3, 1843, when he was transferred to the Treasury Department, resigning May 3, 1844; died at Albany, N. Y., May 18, 1855.

Spencer, John C.:
    Associate Justice Supreme Court,

    nomination of, and reasons therefor, 2181.
Correspondence regarding Dorr's Rebellion, 2152, 2153, 2155, 2157.

Sprague, William, correspondence regarding Dorr's Rebellion, 2158.

Stanbery, Henry; lawyer; Attorney-General under President Johnson; b. New York City, Feb. 20, 1803; graduated Washington (Pa.) College, 1819; moved to Ohio and engaged in practice of law, 1824-46, and became the first attorney-general of Ohio, 1846-51; appointed Attorney General in Cabinet of President Johnson, 1866; died New York City, June 25, 1881.

Stanbery, Henry:
Counsel for President Johnson in impeachment proceedings, 3924.
Special commissioner to investigate administration in military division on Mississippi River, 3474.

Standley, John S., delegate to the Choctaws for treaty purposes, mentioned, 5668.

Stanly, Edward; b. Newbern, N. C., about 1811; studied law and admitted to the bar; served three terms in the house of commons of the state legislature and one term as speaker; attorney-general of North Carolina in 1847; elected a Whig Representative to the 25th, 26th, and 27th Congresses; elected to the 31st and 32d Congresses; moved to California and practiced law; for a few months military governor of North Carolina in 1862, but resigned and returned to California; died at San Francisco, Cal., July 12, 1872.

Stanly, Edward, military governor of North Carolina, authority and action of, referred to, 3281.

Stanton, Edwin McMasters (1814-1869); jurist and statesman; b. Steubenville, Ohio; Attorney-General from December, 1860, until March, 1861; Secretary of War under Lincoln, 1862, and until his removal by Johnson, 1867; restored by the Senate in January, 1868; President Johnson's attempt to remove him again in February of the same year led to the President's impeachment; Stanton resigned on the acquittal in May, 1868; four days prior to his death he was made an associate justice of the Supreme Court.

Stanton, Edwin M.:
Correspondence of, relative to the restoration of peace, 3461.
Death of, announced and honors to be paid memory of, 4047.
Discussion of, and orders concerning the suspension of, as Secretary of War and transfer of records to Gen. U. S. Grant, 3754, 3781, 3801.
Negotiations for and correspondence regarding restoration of peace, 3461.
Secretary of War—
    Removal of, discussed and orders regarding, 3819, 3820, 3861.
    Suspension of, discussed and orders regarding, 3754, 3781, 3801.

Stevens, Thaddeus (1793-1868) ; statesman ; b. in Caledonia Co., Vt. ; after studying law he removed to Gettysburg, Pa., 1816 ; entered the legislature of Pennsylvania ; Whig member of Congress, 1849-53 ; changed his political views and was Republican member of Congress, 1859-68, becoming one of the leaders of the radical wing of that party ; consistent opponent of slavery and an advocate of reconstruction ; manager of the impeachment proceedings of President Johnson in 1868.

Stevenson, Adlai Ewing; politician and twenty-third Vice-President of United States ; b. Christian Co., Ky., in 1835 ; removed to Bloomington, Ill., and was a member of Congress, 1875-77 and 1879-81 ; elected Vice-President with Cleveland, 1893-97, and was an unsuccessful candidate for re-election in 1900.

Stevenson, Andrew; diplomat ; b. Culpepper Co., Va., 1784 ; admitted to the bar and became a representative in the legislature, 1804-20 ; member of the 18th to 23d Congresses from Dec. 1, 1823, to June 2, 1834, from Virginia ; minister to Great Britain, 1836-41 ; died Albemarle Co., Va., June 25, 1857.

Stevenson, Andrew, minister to Great Britain:
Correspondence regarding—
Imprisonment of E. S. Greely, 1575, 1622.
Northeastern boundary. (See Northeastern Boundary.)
Nomination of, discussed, 1272.

Stewart, Alexander T.; merchant ; b. Oct. 12, 1803, in Lisburne, near Belfast, Ireland ; educated in Belfast and at Trinity College, Dublin, with the idea of entering the ministry, but the death of his father interfered with his plans and he went to New York in 1823 ; maintained himself as a tutor for some time, until by the death of his grandfather he inherited $3,000 or $4,000 ; with this capital he entered the drygoods business, and, in 1848, erected a marble building at Broadway and Chambers street in New York, which was for many years celebrated as the finest drygoods store in the country ; at the outbreak of the civil war he was a multimillionaire, and in 1862 completed a stone and iron store building at Broadway and Tenth street, for his expanding business ; by making large purchases he gained control of the cotton market, and, securing the output of several large woolen mills in New York and New England, he manufactured uniforms and clothing for the troops which were being hurried to the front ; he became a warm personal friend of General Grant, and when the latter became President he tendered the position of Secretary of the Treasury to Mr. Stewart, and after his unanimous confirmation by the Senate it was found to be contrary to law to appoint a government contractor to a federal position ; Mr. Stewart made many investments in real estate and at the time of his death owned the Grand Union Hotel at Saratoga Springs, and a large estate at Garden City, L. I., and was worth perhaps $40,000,000 ; died April 10, 1876, in New York.

Stewart, Alexander T., nomination and confirmation of, as Secretary of Treasury, discussed, 3962.
Withdrawal of message, 3963.

Stewart, Charles:
Charges against, discussed, 847.
Court-martial of, referred to, 889.
Nomination of, discussed, 3063.

Stewart, William A., imprisonment, conviction, and release of, at Valparaiso, Chile, 2772.

Stickney, Amos, report of, on protection of levees, referred to, 4797.

Stickney, William, member of Ponca Indian Commission, 4582.

Stivers, Charles B., joint resolution declaring retirement of, from Army legal, etc., vetoed, 5526.

Stockton, Robert Field; naval officer ; b. Princeton, N. J., Aug. 20, 1795 ; entered navy as midshipman Sept. 1, 1811, aboard the *President;* on duty with the Mediterranean squadron in the Algerine War ; founded the colony of Liberia in West Africa ; promoted to commander-in-chief of the Pacific squadron, October, 1845 ; with Col. John C. Frémont captured Los Angeles, Cal., Aug. 13, 1846, and established civil government ; was elected Senator from New Jersey in 1851, and resigned in 1853 ; died at Princeton, N. J., Oct. 7, 1866.

Stockton, Robert F.:
Captain in Navy, nomination of, and reasons therefore, 1745.
Construction of the *Princeton* under direction of, referred to, 2130.

Stoddert, Benjamin, Secretary of the Navy under President John Adams, and for a short time acted as Secretary of War ; b. in Charles County, Md., in 1751, a descendant of an old Scotch family. His grandfather settled in Maryland about 1675, and his father, Capt. James Stoddert, was an officer in the old French and Indian war, and was killed at the defeat of Gen. Braddock. Benjamin Stoddert was brought up as a merchant, but on the outbreak of the war of the revolution joined the army ; was made captain of cavalry, and served actively and with distinction up to the time of the battle of Brandywine, when he held the rank of major. In that engagement he was severely wounded and was obliged to retire. He was secretary of the board of war, in which position he continued until the end of 1781. After the declaration of peace he settled in Georgetown, D. C., in business of general merchandizing, and was very successful. In May, 1798, he was appointed secretary of the navy by President Adams to succeed George Cabot, being the second to occupy that position, and the first to formate a naval force for the defence of the infant states. He continued in the naval department until March 4, 1801. Afterward for a time he was acting secretary of war. At the close of Adams' administration he devoted himself to settling his business affairs, which had been neglected, and he soon afterward retired to private life. He died in Bladensburg, Md., Dec. 18, 1813.

Stone, Claudius U.; b. Menard Co., Ill., May 11, 1879 ; educated in the public schools and later completed commercial and college courses ; served as a corporal in Company K, Fourth Illinois Volunteer Infantry, for 12 months during the Spanish-American War. Four months of this time he spent in Cuba ; in 1902 he was chosen county superintendent of schools of Peoria

County; in 1909 he was chosen president of the association of county superintendents of schools of the state; is state historian of the United Spanish-American War Veterans; studied law, was admitted to the bar and formed a partnership with Judge L. O. Eagleton; married in 1902 to Miss Genevieve C. Francis; elected to the 62d, 63d and 64th Congresses from Illinois.

Stone, William J.; b. May 7, 1848, in Madison County, Ky.; graduated from Missouri University, which later conferred upon him the degree of LL. D.; admitted to the bar in 1869; prosecuting attorney of Vernon County; Representative in the 49th, 50th and 51st Congresses; governor of Missouri, 1893-1897; elected to the United States Senate from Missouri for the term beginning March 4, 1903, and re-elected in 1909 and 1914, for term ending March 3, 1921.

Stone, William, report of, on slaughter of American citizens in South Carolina, transmitted, 4329.

Storer, George W., conduct of, referred to, 2528.

Straus, Oscar S.; diplomatist; b. Dec. 23, 1850, in Otterberg, Rhenish Bavaria; brought to America by his parents in 1854 and settled in Talbotton, Ga.; after three years the family moved to New York and established the importing house of L. Straus & Son; Oscar attended Columbia Grammar School two years and then entered Columbia College, graduating in 1871; began the practice of law in 1873; appointed Minister to Turkey by President Cleveland in 1887; reappointed by Presidents Harrison and McKinley; he was of great service to Christian missionary societies in securing for them privileges and immunities in Turkey; gained high favor from the Sultan, who offered to decorate him with the highest order of the empire, but was prevented by the law which forbids foreign representatives accepting presents; he has been the recipient of honorary degrees by several colleges.

Street, George F., correspondence regarding northeastern boundary. (See Northeastern Boundary.)

Stringham, Silas H., thanks of Congress to, recommended, 3284.

Stuart, Alexander H. H., Secretary of the Interior under President Fillmore; b. Staunton, Va., April 2, 1807; graduated from William and Mary College; studied law, and in 1828 began practice at Staunton; served in the state house of representatives 1836-1838; elected a representative from Virginia to the 27th Congress as a Whig; Presidential elector on the Clay ticket in 1844 and the Taylor ticket in 1848; Secretary of the Interior 1850-1853; member of the State Senate 1857-1861; delegate to the National Union convention in 1866; claimed to have been elected a Representative from Virginia to the 9th Congress, but not admitted to his seat; died at Staunton, Va., Feb. 13, 1891.

Stuart, Charles B., report of waterway, referred to, 3402.

Stuart, George H., member of Indian commission, 3977.

Sullivan, John T., director of Bank of United States, nomination of, and reasons therefor, 1260.

Sulloway, Cyrus Adams; b. Grafton, N. H., June 8, 1839; studied law, admitted to the bar in 1863; member of the New Hampshire house of representatives in 1872-73 and from 1887 to 1893, inclusive; elected to the 54th, 55th, 56th, 57th, 58th, 59th, 60th, 61st, 62d and 64th Congresses from New Hampshire.

Sumner, Charles (1811-1874); statesman, b. Boston, Mass.; after a period of foreign travel, 1837-40, he became a strong opponent of slavery; at first a Whig, he became a Free-Soiler in 1848, and was an unsuccessful candidate for Congress; elected United States Senator from Massachusetts by Free-Soilers and Democrats, 1851; re-elected as a Republican in 1857, 1863 and 1869; from 1856 to 1859 he was not in his seat in the Senate; was an ardent anti-slavery worker; chairman of foreign affairs, 1861, until his removal, 1871, for opposing Grant's scheme for annexing Santo Domingo; supported the Civil Rights Bill; and bitterly opposed Grant's re-election in 1872.

Sumner, Edwin V., treaty with Indians concluded by, 2727.

Suplee, Edwin M., report of, on Navajo Indians, transmitted, 5782.

Surratt, John H.:
Discovery and arrest of, referred to, 3657, 3659.
Reward offered for arrest of, revoked, 3551.
Trial of, referred to, 3799.

Surratt, Mary E., implicated in assassination of President Lincoln, proceedings of trial of, and verdict of military commission, 3532, 3533, 3534, 3540, 3545, 3546.

Sutherland, George; b. March 25, 1862, in Buckinghamshire, England; studied law at the University of Michigan, being admitted to practice in the supreme court of that State in March, 1883; State Senator in the first State legislature of Utah; elected to the 57th Congress; declined renomination to the 58th; elected to the United States Senate by the Utah Legislature for the term beginning March 4, 1905; re-elected in 1911, for term ending March 3, 1917.

Swanson, Claude A.; b. Swansonville, Pittsylvania County, Va., March 31, 1862; attended public school until he attained the age of 16, then attended the Virginia Polytechnic Institute for one session; matriculated at Randolph-Macon College, Ashland, Va., and remained there three sessions, graduating with the degree of A. B. in 1885; studied law at the University of Virginia, graduating with the degree of B. L. in 1886; practiced law at Chatham, Va., until he was nominated and elected to the 53d Congress; re-elected to the 54th, 55th, 56th, 57th, 58th and 59th Congresses; was a candidate in the Democratic primary for governor of the State of Virginia in 1905; was nominated and elected in November, 1905; resigned his seat in Congress and was inaugurated and served as governor of Virginia until Feb. 1, 1910;

on Aug. 1, 1910, he was appointed by Gov. William Hodges Mann to fill the vacancy in the United States Senate occasioned by the death of Senator John Warwick Daniel for the remainder of his unexpired term, ending March 3, 1911; reappointed by Gov. Mann from March 4, 1911, until the meeting of the General Assembly of Virginia; elected to fill the unexpired term beginning March 4, 1911, and ending March 4, 1917.

Swartwout, Samuel, crimes charged against, 405.

Default of, referred to, 1709, 1723.

Thanks of Congress to, recommended, 3277.

Switzer, Robert M.; b. March 6, 1863, near Gallipolis, Ohio, and his education consisted of instruction in the country district schools, a few terms at the Gallia Academy, and about five terms at Rio Grande College, all in his native county; has always lived in Gallia county, Ohio, at or near Gallipolis; was admitted to the practice of law in the courts of Ohio in 1892, and has been continuously engaged in the practice of law at Gallipolis, Ohio; elected prosecuting attorney; elected to the 62d, 63d and 64th Congresses from Ohio.

Sylvester, Isaac A., appropriation for payment of claim of, recommended, 4668.

Symmes, John Cleves; jurist, soldier; b. Long Island, N. Y., July 21, 1742, removed to New Jersey, chairman of the Committee of Safety of Sussex Co., 1774; one of the committee which framed the first State Constitution; distinguished himself in the revolutionary army and became colonel; in 1787 headed an organization which purchased a tract of 1,000 acres of land along the Ohio and Miami rivers and founded the settlements of North Bend and Cincinnati; appointed by Congress one of the three judges of the Northwest Territory in 1788; died Cincinnati, Feb. 26, 1814.

Symmes, John C.:

Lands lying within patent of, referred to, 807.

Lands on Great Miami purchased by, referred to, 105.

Trescot, William H.:

    Mentioned, 4561.

    Special envoy extraordinary to Peru, Chile, and Bolivia, referred to, 4694.

Taft, Alphonso; jurist, diplomatist; Secretary of State and Attorney General under President Grant, Minister to Austria and Russia; b. Nov. 5, 1814, at Townsend, Vt.; educated in the country schools and when nineteen years old entered Yale College and graduated in 1833; taught school, tutored and studied law and in 1838, admitted to the bar in New Haven, Conn.; went to Cincinnati, where he built up a lucrative law practice; was an influential factor in making Cincinnati a great railroad center as well as energetic in educational and other public matters; in 1856 was a member of the convention which nominated John C. Fremont for President, and later judge of the Supreme Court of Cincinnati; he was defeated for member of Congress and for Governor of Ohio; warmly supported Hayes for President; in March, 1876 President Grant appointed him Secretary of War and three months later transferred him to the office of Attorney General, where he remained until the close of the administration; resumed law practice until in 1882 when Arthur appointed him Minister to Austria, whence he was transferred to Russia in 1884; went to South America for his health, and on returning died May, 1891, in San Diego, Cal.

Taft, Lydia A., act granting pension to, vetoed, 6106.

Taft, William H., biography of, 7661.

Taney, Roger Brooke (1777-1864); jurist and cabinet officer; b. Calvert Co., Md.; began the practice of law 1799 and became a leading Federalist; attorney-general of Maryland 1827; changed his politics and supported Andrew Jackson, who made him attorney-general 1831-1833; as secretary of the treasury he removed the deposits from the United States Bank, which his predecessor, William J. Duane, had refused to do; when Congress assembled it refused to sanction his appointment; his nomination as associate justice of the Supreme Court was not confirmed by the Senate; on the death of John Marshall, in 1836, Taney was appointed chief justice of the Supreme Court of the United States, where, in 1857, he gave his famous decision in the Dred Scott case; he was for long the main bulwark of slavery throughout the Union.

Tappan, Samuel F., treaty with Indians concluded by, 3834.

Tate, James H., consul at Buenos Ayres, nomination of, and reasons therefor, 2271.

Taussig, Edward D., member of board of management of Government exhibit at World's Columbian Exposition, 5833.

Taylor, David, claim of, referred to, 2678.

Taylor, Edward Thomas; b. Metamora, Woodford Co., Ill., June 19, 1858; moved to Leadville, Colo., and graduated from the law department of the University of Michigan in 1884, receiving the degree of LL. B.; 1896 was elected state senator, and served twelve years in that capacity, and has the reputation of having been the author of more important laws and constitutional amendments than any person that ever sat in any legislature of any state in the Union during the entire history of this Government—over forty general statutes and five

separate constitutional amendments that were adopted by a general vote of the people; elected to the 61st, 62d, 63d, and 64th Congresses from Colorado at large.

Taylor, George Washington; b. Jan. 16, 1849, in Montgomery Co., Ala.; was admitted to practice law at Mobile, Ala., November, 1871; entered the army as a Confederate soldier at the age of fifteen years, in November, 1864, being then a student at the academy in Columbia, S. C., and served till the end of the war; elected to general assembly of Alabama in 1878, and served one term; elected to the 55th, 56th, 57th, 58th, 59th, 60th, 61st, 62d, and 63d Congresses from Alabama.

Taylor, John, commissioner to treat with Indians, nomination of, 326.

Taylor, Margaret S., resolution of Congress on death of husband, transmitted to, 2598.

Taylor, N. P., register in land office at St. Louis, conduct of, referred to, 2010.

Taylor, Nathaniel G., treaty with Indians concluded by, 3827.

Taylor, Robert Love; lawyer; b. July 31, 1850, at Happy Valley, Carter Co., Tenn., at the place on the Wautauge River where the first fort was established by John Sevier; elected to the 46th Congress in 1878; elected governor of Tennessee 1886, and reelected in 1888; elected governor for a third term in 1896; represented the district in Congress represented before him by his father, Nathaniel G. Taylor, and after him by his brother, Alfred A. Taylor, the latter of whom he defeated for governor in 1886; nominated for United States Senate in the Democratic primary election, May, 1906, and elected in January, 1907.

Taylor, Zachary, biography of, 2541.

Teller, Henry M.; lawyer; Secretary of the Interior under President Arthur; b. May 23, 1830, in Allegany Co., N. Y.; his father was a well-to-do farmer and gave him a good education; after leaving school he studied law, moved to Illinois and practiced three years; in 1861 he went to Colorado and settled in Central City, the chief mining town of the territory; affiliated with the Republicans in politics, and when the State was admitted to the Union was elected to the United States Senate, where he served until 1882, when he was appointed Secretary of the Interior by President Arthur; March 3, 1885, he retired from the cabinet and immediately took his seat in the Senate to which he had been elected to succeed Nathaniel P. Hill; he was again chosen in 1891; died Feb. 23, 1914.

Terrill, William R., brigadier-general in Army, nomination of, and reasons therefor, 3362.

Terry, Alfred H., report of, on disaster to forces under Gen. Custer transmitted, 4327.

Terry, David S., assault by, upon Justice Field, discussed, 5477.

Terry, Elias S., commissioner to adjudicate claim of David Taylor, 2678.

Thacher, John M., report of, on International Patent Congress referred to, 4215.

Thayer, Sylvanus, brevet colonel in Army, nomination of, and reasons therefor, 1696.

Thomas, Francis; b. Frederick County, Md., Feb. 3, 1799; graduated from St. John's College, Annapolis; studied law, and began practice at Frankville; member of the state house of representatives 1822, 1827, and 1829, the last year as speaker; elected a Representative from Maryland to the 22d Congress as a Democrat; again elected to the 23d, 24th, 25th, and 26th Congresses; president of the Chesapeake and Ohio Canal for two years; governor of Maryland 1841-44; a delegate in 1850 to the state constitutional convention; elected a Representative to the 37th Congress as a Union Republican; re-elected to the 38th, 39th, and 40th Congresses; collector of internal revenue 1870-1872; minister to Peru from 1872 to 1875; died Jan. 22, 1876, near Franklinville, Md.

Thomas, Francis, agreement with Peru, signed by, 4212.

Thomas, George H., statue of, to be unveiled, 4509.

Thomas, Lorenzo; soldier; Secretary of War *ad interim;* b. Oct. 26, 1804, in New Castle, Del.; his father and grandfather were respectively soldiers in the War of 1812 and the Revolution; Lorenzo was graduated from the Military Academy at West Point in 1823, and served in the Florida war until 1837; assistant Adjutant General in Washington till the breaking out of the Mexican War, during which he was chief of staff to Gen. William O. Butler (1846-1848); brevetted lieutenant colonel for gallantry at Monterey; returned to the adjutant general's office and when the Civil War broke out was chief of staff to Gen. Winfield Scott; brevetted brigadier general 1861, and served as adjutant general during the Civil War; brevetted major general in 1865; Feb. 28, 1868, President Johnson appointed him Secretary of War to succeed Edwin M. Stanton, removed; the impeachment of the President prevented this order from going into effect, and Thomas never entered upon the duties of the office. He died March 2, 1875, in Washington.

Thomas, Lorenzo, Secretary of War *ad interim,* directed to act as, 3819, 3861.

Thomas, Philip Francis; Secretary of the Treasury under President Buchanan; b. Talbot County, Md., Sept. 12. 1810; received a liberal education; studied law, and began practice at Easton. Md., in 1831; member of the State constitutional convention in 1836; member of the State house of delegates 1838, 1843 and 1845; elected a Representative from Maryland to the 26th Congress; elected Governor of Maryland in 1847; appointed Commissioner of Patents Feb. 16, 1860; Secretary of the Treasury, 1860-61; elected a United States Senator from Maryland, but was not admitted to his seat; elected a Representative to the 44th Congress as a Democrat; died at Baltimore, Md., Oct. 2, 1890.

Thompson, Clark W., treaty with Indians concluded by, 3411.

Thompson, Elizabeth, Carpenter's painting of Lincoln and Cabinet at reading of Emancipation Proclamation presented to Congress by, 4435.

Thompson, Jacob; Secretary of the Interior under President Buchanan; b. Caswell County, N. C., May 15, 1810; graduated from the University of North Carolina, and afterwards served as a tutor; studied law, and in 1835 began practice in Mississippi; elected a Representative from Mississippi to the 26th Congress as a Democrat on a general ticket; re-elected to the 27th, 28th, 29th, 30th and 31st Congresses; declined a re-election; Secretary of the Interior, March 6, 1857, until he resigned, Jan. 8, 1861; served in the Confederate army; governor of Mississippi 1862-1864; special agent of the Confederate Government in Canada; died at Memphis, Tenn., March 24, 1885.

Thompson, Jacob:
Order exempting from arrest during journey to Washington, 3438.
Reward offered for arrest of, 3505. Revoked, 3551.

Thompson, Richard W.; Secretary of the Navy under President Hayes; b. Culpeper County, Va., June 9, 1809; received a classical education; moved to Kentucky in 1831; clerk in a store; moved to Lawrence County, Ind.; taught school; studied law, and in 1834 began practicing at Bedford, Ind.; member of the State house of representatives 1834-35; State Senator 1836-37; elected a representative from Indiana to the 27th Congress as a Whig; Presidential elector in 1840 on the Harrison and Tyler ticket; elected to the 30th Congress as a Whig; declined a renomination; declined the Austrian mission; declined the recordership of the General Land Office offered him by President Fillmore; delegate to the national Republican convention of 1869 at Chicago; Presidential elector on the Lincoln and Johnson ticket in 1864; delegate to the national Republican convention at Chicago in 1868. and at Cincinnati in 1876; Secretary of the Navy March 12, 1877-1881, resigning to become chairman of the American Committee of the Panama Canal Company; director of the Panama Railroad Company; died Feb. 9, 1900.

Thompson, Richard W., claim of, for alleged services to Menominee Indians, 2839.

Thompson, Smith; lawyer, jurist; Secretary of the Navy under President Monroe; b. Jan. 17, 1768, in Stanford, Dutchess Co., N. Y.; received a liberal education and was graduated at Princeton in 1788; studied law under Chancellor Kent in Poughkeepsie, and was admitted to the bar in 1792; began practice in Troy, but returned to Poughkeepsie and in 1800 was elected to the State Legislature and the following year a delegate to the Constitutional Convention; associate justice of the State Supreme Court 1802-1814; Chief Justice 1814-1818, when President Monroe appointed him Secretary of the Navy to succeed B. M. Crowninshield; resigned in 1823 to become a Justice of the United States Supreme Court, a position he held until his death Dec. 18, 1843. in Poughkeepsie.

Thomson, Charles, informs Washington of his election as President, 34.

Thorn, Owen, claim of, against Great Britain referred to, 3964.

Thornton, Sir Edward, umpire of commission to adjudicate differences between Mexico and United States, 4359.

Thornton, James S., lieutenant-commander in Navy, advancement in grade of, recommended, 3458.

Thornton, John R.; b. Iberville Parish, La., Aug. 25, 1846; resided in Rapides Parish, La., since 1853; left Louisiana State University in 1863 and volunteered in Confederate States Army, in which he served as private until close of Civil War; followed agriculture for an occupation until 1877, when he was licensed by the Supreme Court of Louisiana to practice law, and has followed that profession ever since; served as judge of Rapides Parish, La., from 1878 to 1880; member of the last state constitutional convention of Louisiana in 1898; member of the board of supervisors, Louisiana State University; one of the three Louisiana commissioners to conference on uniform laws for the United States, and vice-president of that body; member of the American Bar Association and one of the local council of that body in Louisiana; appointed Aug. 27, 1910, by the governor of Louisiana as United States Senator in place of Hon. S. D. McEnery, deceased, and elected Dec. 7, 1910, for term ending March 3, 1915.

Thornton, William, commissioner of Washington City, 304.

Thrasher, John S.:
Imprisonment of, at Havana, 2676.
Trial and sentence of, referred to, 2677.

Thurston, Lorin A.:
Hawaiian minister to United States, recall of, discussed, 6065.
Member of commission concluding treaty for annexation of Hawaiian Islands, 5783.
Representative of provisional government of Hawaiian Islands, referred to, 5906.

Tilden, Samuel Jones (1814-1886); lawyer and statesman; b. New Lebanon, N. Y.; after his admission to the bar, in 1841, he entered politics as a Democrat; elected to the assembly of New York, 1845; member of the constitutional convention, 1846; professed Free-Soiler views, 1848; defeated as the Democratic candidate for attorney-general, 1855; chairman of the Democratic state committee, 1866; opposed the "Tweed Ring"; Democratic governor of New York, 1875-76; foremost in the reform of canal management; ran as Democratic candidate for the presidency against Hayes, 1876, and received a plurality of 25,224 over Hayes, who was declared elected by the Electoral Commission.

Tillinghast, Joseph L., correspondence regarding Dorr's Rebellion, 2158.

Tillman, Benjamin Ryan; b. Edgefield Co., S. C., Aug. 11, 1847; received an academic education; quit school in 1864 to join the Confederate army; began the agitation in 1886 for industrial and technical

education, which culminated in the establishment of the Clemson Agricultural and Mechanical College, at Calhoun's old home, Fort Hill; the demand for educational reform broadened into a demand for other changes in state affairs, and he was put forward by the farmers as a candidate for governor in 1890, and was elected; re-elected in 1892; elected Senator in 1895 from South Carolina; re-elected in 1901 and in 1907 and 1913 for term ending March 3, 1919.

Tilson, John Quillin; b. Clearbranch, Tenn., April 5, 1866; graduated from the Yale Law School in 1893; served in the Spanish-American War as lieutenant of volunteers; in 1904 he was elected a representative in the Connecticut general assembly; was re-elected in 1906, and was speaker of the Connecticut house of representatives during the session of 1907; elected to the 61st, 62d, and 64th Congresses from Connecticut.

Tipton, John; b. Sevier County, Tenn., Aug. 14, 1786; moved to Indiana, where he bought a small farm, paying for it by splitting rails; served with the "Yellow Jackets" in the Tippecanoe campaign; sheriff of Harrison County, Ind., in 1815; served in the state house of representatives in 1821; elected a United States Senator from Indiana, vice James Noble, deceased; again elected for a full term and served from Jan. 3, 1832, until he died, April 5, 1839, at Logansport, Ind.

Tipton, John, treaty with Indians concluded by, 931, 964.

Tobey, E. S., member of Indian commission, 3977.

Tod, David, minister to Rio de Janeiro, mentioned, 2562.

Tompkins, C. H., member of court to try assassins of President Lincoln, etc., 3534.

Tompkins, Daniel D. (1774-1825); statesman and sixth Vice-President of the United States; b. Scarsdale, N. Y.; began the practice of law, 1797; associate justice of the New York Supreme Court, 1804-1807; governor of New York, 1807-17; prorogued the legislature for ten months to prevent the establishment of the Bank of North America in New York City; was an ardent supporter of the War of 1812; greatly furthered the abolition of slavery in his state, 1817; twice elected Vice-President of the United States, 1817-25.

Tompkins, Daniel D., governor of New York, accounts of, referred to, 789, 802, 809.

Totten, Joseph G., correspondence regarding water supply for Washington and Georgetown, 2698.

Toucey, Isaac; Attorney-General under President Polk, and Secretary of the Treasury under Buchanan; b. Newtown, Conn., Nov. 5, 1796; received a classical education; studied law, and in 1818 began practice at Hartford; State Attorney for Hartford County 1822-1825; elected a Representative from Connecticut to the 24th and 25th Congresses as a Democrat; defeated as the Democratic candidate for re-election; again attorney for Hartford County 1842-1844; defeated as the Democratic candidate for governor of Connecticut in 1845, and again in 1846; elected to the Legislature; again defeated for governor in 1847; Attorney-General 1848-49; State Senator in 1850, and a member of the house of representatives in 1852; elected a United States Senator from Connecticut as a Democrat, serving from May 14, 1852, to March 3, 1857; Secretary of the Navy under President Buchanan 1857-1861; died at Hartford, Conn., July 30, 1869.

Tousig, Simon, claim of, to protection of United States, 2761.

Tower, Charlemagne, lawyer, coal operator and ironmaster, bibliophile; b. Paris, Oneida County, N. Y., April 18, 1809; educated at Chenango, Clinton and Utica academies; and graduated Harvard, 1830, where he was a classmate and intimate friend of Charles Sumner; studied law under Hermanus Bleecker of Albany; removed to Pennsylvania in 1848, and for twenty years was engaged in litigation over titles to coal lands; perfected title to the lands now owned by the Philadelphia and Reading railway; at the outbreak of the civil war he raised a company of volunteers, which he equipped and led to the front; became owner of large tracts of coal lands in Pennsylvania, and organized the Lehigh and Wilkesbarre Coal Co.; actively interested in building the Northern Pacific railroad; the crowning achievement of his life was the development of the valuable iron mines of the Vermilion Range in Minnesota; between 1875 and 1885 he acquired title to vast deposits of iron ore ninety miles northeast of Duluth, Minn., and seventy miles north of Lake Superior; though past seventy years of age he capitalized the undertaking himself and organized the Minnesota Iron Company and the Duluth and Iron Range Railroad Company; also built a 70-mile railroad from Lake Vermilion to Two Harbors, on Lake Superior; the first shipment of 68,000 tons of ore was made to Cleveland in 1884; soon the town of Tower sprang up on Lake Vermilion; in 1892, 600,000 tons of ore was shipped from the range; this proved to be one of the most valuable developments in the United States; these large mining and railroad properties were later absorbed by a large syndicate of which Mr. Tower was the head. He devoted much time to the collection of rare and valuable books, especially Americana, and formed the most complete collection of the colonial laws of America, which at his death, in Waterville, N. Y., July 24, 1889, was bequeathed to the Pennsylvania Historical Society. His son, Charlemagne Tower, Jr., served as Ambassador to Germany in 1902.

Towner, Horace M.; b. Belvidere, Ill., Oct. 23, 1855; educated at the public and high schools of Belvidere, Chicago University, and Union College of Law; married to Harriet Elizabeth Cole in 1887; admitted to the bar in 1877, and practiced law in Corning until 1890; elected judge of the third judicial district of Iowa in 1890, and served until Jan. 1, 1911; for ten years lecturer on constitutional law in the State University of Iowa, from which he received the degree of LL. B.; served as president of the Iowa State Bar Association; elected to the 62d, 63d, and 64th Congresses from Iowa.

Townsend, Charles Elroy; b. Concord, Jackson Co., Mich., Aug. 15, 1856; admitted to the Jackson bar to practice law in 1895; elected to the 58th, 59th, 60th,

and 61st Congresses from Michigan; nominated for United States Senator at the primaries in 1910 and elected by the legislature in 1911 for the term which will expire March 3, 1917.

Townsend, E. D., Asst. Adj.-Gen., signed order for release of Clement C. Clay, Jr., April 17, 1866.

Towson, Nathan, appointment of, to artillery discussed, 681.
Rejection of, discussed, 695, 702.

Tracy, Benjamin Franklin; Secretary of the Navy under President Benjamin Harrison; b. Owego, N. Y., April 26, 1830. His father, Benjamin, a man of marked integrity and enterprise, was a pioneer in the settlement of the southern tier of counties in the State of New York. Young Tracy began his education at the common school in Owego and entered Owego Academy where he studied for several years, acquiring an excellent English education. He then entered the law office of N. W. Davis, being admitted to the bar in May, 1851. November, 1853, as a candidate upon the Whig ticket, he was elected by a surprisingly large majority district attorney for Tioga county, at that time a democratic stronghold. He was re-elected in 1856. During the civil war he recruited two regiments, and as colonel took part in the battle of Spottsylvania, and later commanded the prison camp at Elmira, N. Y. In 1866, as United States District Attorney, he gave especial attention to the prevention of frauds by whiskey distillers, and drew up a law which resulted in increasing the revenue of distilled spirits from $13,000,000 to $50,000,000 in one year.

Tracy, Benjamin F., Secretary of Navy, mentioned, 5759.

Trenholm, George A., pardon applied for by, order regarding, 3550.

Trescot, William Henry; diplomat; b. Charleston, S. C., Nov. 10, 1822; graduated Charleston College, 1840, and admitted to the bar in 1843; appointed secretary of legation at London, 1852, and in 1860 was made assistant secretary of state; commissioner to revise the treaty with China in 1880, and to negotiate a commercial treaty with Mexico in 1882; died Pendleton, S. C., May 4, 1898.

Tribble, Samuel J.; b. in Franklin Co., Ga.; received college and legal education at the University of Georgia; located in Athens, Ga., engaged in the practice of law; elected to the 62d, 63d, and 64th Congresses from Georgia.

Trimble, Alexandria, demand of Mexico for extradition of, 4791.

Trist, Nicholas P.; lawyer, diplomatist; b. Charlottesville, Va., June 2, 1800; entered United States Military Academy at West Point, where, at the age of nineteen, he became acting assistant professor of French; left before graduation and took up the study of law under Thomas Jefferson, whose granddaughter he subsequently married; in 1828 appointed first clerk in the Treasury Department, and the following year private secretary to President Andrew Jackson; consul at Havana 1834-36; assistant Secretary of State in 1845; three years later sent as peace commissioner to Mexico, and on Feb. 2, 1848, signed the treaty of

Guadaloupe Hidalgo (q. v.) ; continued the practice of law .until 1870, when President Grant appointed him postmaster at Alexandria, Va., where he died Feb. 11, 1874.

Trist, N. P.:

Commissioner to Mexico—

Conduct of, discussed, 2423, 2424.

Dispatches from, referred to, 2426, 2427.

Recall of, discussed, 2423, 2424.

Terms of authority given to draw money from Treasury referred to, 2426.

Treaty with Mexico concluded by, discussed and recommendations regarding, 2423, 2424.

Consul at Havana—

Correspondence regarding slave trade referred to, 1909.

Malpractices of, referred to, 1845.

Troup, Robert, treaty with Indians concluded by, 940.

Truman, Benjamin C., report of, on condition of Southern people referred to, 3584.

Tuck, Somerville P., report of, regarding French spoliation claims referred to, 4956, 4982, 5199.

Tucker, Beverly, reward offered for arrest of, 3505.

Revoked, 3551.

Tucker, Thomas, appointed on committee to meet President Washington, 37

Tudor, William:

Correspondence of, while consul to Peru and chargé d'affaires to Brazil referred to, 1500, 1587.

Mentioned, 996.

Turreau, Gen., letter of, concerning arrival of Cuban exiles in United States, referred to, 456.

Turtle, Thomas, member of Board on Geographic Names, 5647.

Tuttle, William E., Jr.; b. Horseheads, N. Y., Dec. 10, 1870; was graduated from Elmira Free Academy in 1887, and was a student at Cornell University two years; engaged in the lumber business; was elected to the 62d, 63d, and 64th Congresses from New Jersey.

Twiggs, David E., swords formerly property of, placed at disposal of Congress, 3346.

Tyler, John, biography of, 1888.

Tyner, James N.; Postmaster-General under President Grant; b. Brookville, Ind., Jan. 17, 1826; received an academic education, graduating in 1844; spent ten years in business; studied law, and began its practice at Peru, Ind.; secretary of the State Senate for four successive sessions, commencing in 1857; Presidential elector in 1860; special agent of the Post-Office Department 1861-1866; elected a Representative from Indiana as a Republican to the 41st Congress at a special election (occasioned by the election of D. D. Pratt to the United States Senate), and re-elected to the 42d and 43d Congresses; appointed by President Grant governor of Colorado, but declined; accepted the position of Second Assistant Postmaster-General, serving from Feb. 26, 1875, to July 12, 1876, and Postmaster-General, serving from July 12, 1876, to March 3, 1877; appointed by President Hayes First Assistant Postmaster-General, serving from March 16, 1877, to his resignation in October, 1881; assistant attorney-general for the Post-Office Department 1889-1893, and from May, 1897, to 1903; delegate to the International Postal Congresses at Paris in 1878, and at Washington in 1897.

Uhl, Edwin F., Acting Secretary of State, 6018.

Underwood, Oscar W.; b. Louisville, Jefferson Co., Ky., May 6, 1862; was educated at Rugby School, Louisville, Ky., and the University of Virginia; moved to Birmingham, Ala., and began practice of law; elected to the 54th, 55th, 56th, 57th, 58th, 59th, 60th, 61st, 62d, and 63d Congresses from Alabama, and in 1914 elected to represent the state in the United States Senate.

Upshur, Abel Parker (1790-1844); statesman and cabinet officer; b. in Northampton Co., Va.; secretary of the navy under Tyler 1841-43; secretary of state to succeed Webster, 1843; representative of the extreme States-Rights and pro-slavery school of Southern politics.

Upshur, Abel P., death of, announced and honors to be paid memory of, 2132, 2186.

Usher, John Palmer, Secretary of the Interior under President Lincoln and Johnson; b. Brookfield, N. Y., Jan. 9, 1816. His descent is traced from Hezekiah Usher, who settled in Cambridge, Mass., about 1639, and purchased in England the press and type for printing Eliot's Bible. His great-great-grandfather was John Usher, lieutenant-governor of New Hampshire under Gov. Andros. Mr. Usher was admitted to the supreme court of the state of New York, and as solicitor in the court of chancery in the same state Jan. 18, 1839. In 1840 he removed to Terre Haute, Ind., and was admitted to practice in the supreme court of the United States in 1859. In the meantime he served in the state legislature, and was for a short time attorney-general of the state under Gov. Morton. He was appointed first assistant secretary of the interior by President Lincoln March 20, 1862, and on the resignation of Caleb B. Smith, succeeded him as secretary Jan. 8, 1863, resigning his post May 15, 1865, one month after the inauguration of President Johnson. He then returned to the practice of his profession, and became, subsequently, consulting attorney for the eastern division of the Union Pacific Railroad Company. He died in Philadelphia April 13, 1889.

Usher, John P., treaty with Indians concluded by, 3394.

Utter, George H.; b. Plainfield, N. J., July 24, 1854; printer by trade and publisher of *Westerly Sun;* fitted for college at Alfred (N. Y.) Academy and Westerly High School; graduated from Amherst College in 1877; aide on staff of Gov. Bourn (1883-1885); member of Rhode Island House of Representatives (1885-89), the last year being speaker; member of the Rhode Island Senate (1889-1891); Secretary of State (1891-1894); lieutenant-governor in 1904 and governor in 1905 and 1906; elected to the 62d Congress from Rhode Island. Died in Providence, R. I., Nov. 3, 1912.

Vaca, Antonio, private land claim of, 4694.

Vallandigham, Clement Laird (1820-1871) ; Democratic politician ; b. New Lisbon, Ohio ; member of Congress, 1858-63 ; leader of the "Copperheads" of the North during the Civil War ; arrested by United States under Burnside and banished to the Confederate lines, 1863, going thence to Canada ; unsuccessful candidate for governor of Ohio, 1863 ; prominent at the national Democratic convention of 1863, and took a large part in the nomination of McClellan ; in the Grant-Greeley contest of 1872 he proposed a union of all of the forces opposed to Grant.

Van Bokkelene, Mr., imprisonment and release of, by Haitien authorities, discussed, 4918.

Claim arising out of, 5369, 5545.

Van Buren, Martin, biography of, 1528.

Vanderbilt, Cornelius; financier ; b. Port Richmond, Staten Island, N. Y., May 27, 1794 ; started business in 1811 by transporting government employees between New York City and Staten Island ; in 1815 became part owner of a schooner and in 1815 captain of a canal boat running between New York and Philadelphia ; later established steamboat lines on Long Island Sound and the Hudson River ; and in 1851 established a route to San Francisco, via Nicaragua ; in 1855 established a line of steamers between New York and Havre ; sold all his steamboat interests in 1859, and bought stocks of New York railroads ; elected president of New York Central Railroad in 1869 ; interested in Western Union Telegraph and other valuable stocks estimated to be worth $60,000,000 to $100,-000,000 ; died New York City, Jan. 4, 1877.

Vanderbilt, Cornelius:
Appropriation to, for carrying ocean mails between Atlantic and Pacific coasts, recommended, 3184.
Ocean Steamer *Vanderbilt*, presented to United States by, recommendations regarding, 3288.
Referred to, 3585.

Vanderbilt, William H., deed of trust and correspondence of, respecting swords of Gen. Grant offered to Government, 4858, 4862.

Vandershie, Daniel, treaty with Indians concluded by, 3274.

Van de Venter, Christopher, correspondence with Gen. Jackson, referred to, 618.

Van Rensselaer, Rensselaer, commander-in-chief of unlawful expedition in New York, 1616.

Van Rensselaer, Stephen, attack of forces under, near Niagara, discussed, 501.

Van Valkenburg, Robert B.; soldier ; b. Steuben County, N. Y., Sept. 4, 1821 ; received a liberal education ; studied law, and began practicing at Bath, N. Y.; member of the state house of representatives 1852, 1857, and 1858 ; organized seventeen regiments for the civil war ; elected a Representative from New York to the 37th and 38th Congresses as a Republican ; took the field as colonel of the One hundred and seventh Regiment of New York Volunteers, and was its commander at the battle of

Antietam ; minister to Japan 1866-1869 ; died at Suwanee Springs, Fla., Aug. 2, 1888.

Van Valkenburg, Robert B.:
Mentioned, 3793.
Minister to Japan, correspondence regarding cooly trade, referred to, 3837.

Vaughan, Charles R., correspondence regarding northeastern boundary. (See Northeastern Boundary.)

Vilas, William F.; Postmaster-General under President Cleveland ; b. Chelsea, Orange County, Vt., July 9, 1840 ; moved with his father's family to Wisconsin, and settled at Madison, June 4, 1851 ; graduated from the State University in 1858 ; from the law department of the University of Albany, N. Y., in 1860 ; admitted to the bar by the supreme court of New York and by the supreme court of Wisconsin in the same year, and began the practice of law at Madison, July 9, 1860 ; captain of Company A, Twenty-third Regiment Wisconsin Infantry Volunteers, and afterwards major and lieutenant-colonel of the regiment ; professor of law of the law department of the State university ; regent of the university 1880-1885 ; one of three revisers appointed by the supreme court of Wisconsin in 1875 who prepared the existing revised body of the statute law adopted in 1878 ; member of assembly in the Wisconsin legislature in 1885 ; delegate to the Democratic national conventions of 1876, 1880, 1884, and permanent chairman of the latter ; Postmaster-General from March 7, 1885, to January 16, 1888, and Secretary of the Interior to March 6, 1889 ; elected Jan. 28, 1891, United States Senator as a Democrat for the term of 1891-1897 ; edited several Wisconsin Supreme Court Reports ; resumed the practice of law.

Viollier, Lewis W., consular clerk, removal of, from office and reasons therefor, 4067.

Viviani, René; b. in French North Africa in 1863. Early identified himself with the Socialist movement, and from 1893 to 1902 was a member of the Chamber of Deputies from the Sorbonne district of Paris. Again in 1906 he was elected a deputy, and in the same year was made Minister of Labor in the Cabinet under Clémenceau, holding the same office under the premiership of Briand until 1910. From 1913 to 1914 he was Minister of Public Instruction, and in June, 1914, became premier himself, and hence was at the head of the French administration at the outbreak of the European War. He resigned as premier in October, 1915, and became Minister of Justice. In 1916, with Briand as premier, he was appointed Minister of Justice and Public Instruction, and in April, 1917 was the head of the French commission which visited the United States to consult upon war matters.

Volstead, Andrew J.; b. Goodhue Co., Minn., in 1860 ; mayor of Granite Falls, and for fourteen years county attorney of Yellow Medicine County ; elected to the 58th, 59th, 60th, 61st, 62d, 63d, and 64th Congresses from Minnesota.

Von Scholten, Maj.-Gen., Danish minister to United States, correspondence with Secretary of State, referred to, 1094.

Von Steuben, presentation of replica of, to Germany, 7669.

1888; moved to Tacoma, Wash., where he finished reading law and was admitted to the bar; elected to the Washington State Senate in 1896, and re-elected in 1900; elected to the 62d and 64th Congresses from Washington.

Ward, Frederick T., death of, while in military service of China, 3353.

Ward, John Elliot; diplomat; b. Sunbury, Ga., Oct. 2, 1814; admitted to the bar in 1835; solicitor-general of Georgia, 1836-38; member of legislature, 1839, 1845, and 1853; appointed minister to China, 1858, and resigned in 1861 because of his secession views.

Ward, John E., minister to China:
Appointment of, 3089.
Refusal of, to submit to humiliating ceremonies in approaching sovereign, 3090.

Ward, Samuel, special agent to Mexico, mentioned, 2770.

Warner, William; b. Lafayette Co., Wis., June 11, 1840; enlisted in 1862 in the Civil War, and was promoted to major; located in Kansas City, Mo., in 1865 and engaged in the practice of law; elected to Congress in 1884, and re-elected in 1886; elected commander-in-chief of the Grand Army of the Republic in 1888; appointed United States district attorney for the western district of Missouri in 1870, 1882, 1898, and in 1902; recipient of degree of LL. D. from the University of Michigan; elected to the United States Senate from Missouri, March 18, 1905.

Warner, William, member of Sioux Commission, 5480.

Warren, Francis Emory; b. Hinsdale, Mass., June 20, 1844; served as private and noncommissioned officer in Civil War; received the Congressional medal of honor for gallantry on battlefield at the siege of Port Hudson; president of the senate of Wyoming legislature in 1873-74, and member of the senate in 1884-85; mayor of the city of Cheyenne, and served three terms as treasurer of Wyoming; appointed governor of Wyoming by President Arthur in 1885, and removed by President Cleveland in 1886; again appointed governor of Wyoming by President Harrison in 1889, and served until the Territory was admitted as a state, when he was elected the first governor; elected to the United States Senate, Nov. 18, 1890; re-elected in 1895, 1901, 1907, and 1913 for term ending March 3, 1919.

Warren, John, arrest and trial of, in Great Britain, 3827.
Convicted and sentenced to imprisonment, 3834.
Referred to, 3897.
Released, 3902.

Warrington, Lewis; naval officer; b. Williamsburg, Va., Nov. 3, 1782; entered navy as midshipman, 1800; attached to *Chesapeake;* served in the Mediterranean, 1803-1806; earned a gold medal and the thanks of Congress for his gallant achievements in War of 1812; died Washington, D. C., Oct. 12, 1851.

Warrington, Lewis:
British ship captured by vessel in command of, 534.
Energy displayed by, in suppressing piracies, 876.

Warrior, The, illegal detention of, 2051.

Washburn, Charles A., minister to Paraguay, controversy with President of Paraguay, discussed, 3883.

Washburne, Elihu Benjamin (1816-1887); politician; b. Livermore, Me.; admitted to the bar, 1840; settled in Galena, Ill.; member of Congress, 1853-69; chairman of the committee of commerce, 1855-65; called the "Watch Dog of the Treasury" on account of his rigid economy in handling public funds; secretary of state under Grant, 1869; resigned on account of ill-health; minister to France, where he remained during the siege of Paris.

Washburne, Elihu B.:
Death of, announced and honors to be paid memory of, 5165.
Minister to France, metric convention signed by, 4312.

Washington, Bushrod, commissioner to treat with Indians, nominations of, 250.

Washington, George, biography of, 33.

Washington, John, treaty with Indians concluded by, 2571.

Washington, Martha; the wife of the first President of the United States was b. Martha Dandridge, Kent County, Va., May, 1732. Descended from a highly respected Welsh clergyman her youth had every advantage of good birth, high social position and intercourse with refined society, and she was carefully trained in all the accomplishments common to young ladies of the period. She had an agreeable personality, a refined face and winning manners. In her seventeenth year she was married to Daniel Parke Custis. It was a love match and the young couple went to live at a plantation known as the White House, on the Pamunkey River, in Kent County. Three children were born of this union, and in a few years the eldest son and his father died, leaving Mrs. Custis and the two other children well provided for. Besides large landed estates her fortune included £45,000 in money. She was still young and beautiful, and had many admirers. After three years of widowhood she was married to George Washington in the White House amid scenes of old-time Virginia hospitality amid a joyous assemblage of relatives and friends. Soon after the wedding the Washingtons went to live at Mount Vernon. During the Revolution Mrs. Washington spent the winters with her husband in his headquarters and the summers at Mount Vernon. Martha Custis, her daughter, died at the age of seventeen and John Custis, her son, died at the age of sixteen just after the close of the Revolutionary war, through which he served. Of the years in which she figured as the social head of the nation it is needless to speak. The elegant simplicity and the austere statefulness of the public entertainments of early official social life are familiar to all and the Washingtons led for eight years. Martha Custis Washington died in 1801, two years after her husband, and was buried beside him in the family vault at Mount Vernon.

of A. B. and that of A. M. in 1871 ; studied law at Columbia Law School, and was graduated in 1869, receiving the degree of LL. B. ; was admitted to the bar of Rhode Island and of New York in 1869 ; governor of Rhode Island, 1885-1887 ; elected to the United States Senate from Rhode Island, June 13, 1894 ; re-elected in 1900, and again for the term ending March 3, 1913.

Wetmore, Prosper M., naval agent, accounts of, referred to, 2682.

Weyler, Valeriano, reconcentration policy of, in Cuba, discussed, 6256, 6283, 6284, 6308.

Referred to, 6285.

Wharton, William F., Acting Secretary of State, 5581.

Agreement between United States and Great Britain for *modus vivendi* regarding Bering Sea fisheries signed by, 5581.

Wheaton, Henry:

Referred to, 2205.

Treaty concluded by, with—

Denmark, 1044.

Zollverein, 2169.

Wheeler, Joseph; soldier ; of Wheeler, Ala. ; b. Augusta, Ga., Sept. 10, 1836 ; graduated from West Point in 1859 ; lieutenant of cavalry, and served in New Mexico ; resigned in 1861 ; lieutenant of artillery in the Confederate army ; successively promoted to the command of a regiment, brigade, division, and army corps, and in 1862 assigned to the command of the army corps of cavalry of the Western Army, continuing in that position till the war closed ; by joint resolution of the Confederate Congress received the thanks of that body for successful military operations, and for the defense of the city of Aiken received the thanks of the State of South Carolina ; May 11, 1864, became the senior cavalry general of the Confederate armies ; appointed professor of philosophy Louisiana State Seminary in 1866, which he declined ; lawyer and planter ; appointed major-general of volunteers by President McKinley May 4, 1898, and assigned to command of Cavalry Division, U. S. Army ; on June 24, with 900 men, fought and defeated Lieutenant-General Linares at Las Guasimas, the enemy having over 2,000 regular Spanish troops ; at the battle of San Juan, July 1 and 2, senior officer in immediate command on the field, and senior member of commission which negotiated the surrender of Santiago and 23,000 Spanish soldiers ; assigned to command of United States forces at Montauk, Long Island, Aug. 18, and on Oct. 5 assigned to the command of the Fourth Army Corps ; Aug. 31, 1899, in command of First Brigade, Second Division, Eighth Corps, in the Philippines ; engaged with enemy at Santa Rita Sept. 9 and also on Sept. 16, also in capture of Porac, Sept. 28, and in the various engagements with the enemy at Angeles, Oct. 10 to 17, inclusive ; in the advance upon and capture of Bamban, Nov. 11, and the minor expeditions to Camiling, Nov. 23, and expedition to Sulipa and San Ignacio ; elected as a Democrat to the 47th, 49th, 50th, 51st, 52d, 53d, 54th, and 55th Congresses, and re-elected to the 56th Congress ; failed to qualify to fill his place ; retired in 1900 as a brigadier-general of the Regular Army.

Wheeler, Joseph, operations of cavalry division under, around Santiago, Cuba, discussed, 6395.

Wheeler, William Almon (1819-1887) ; statesman and nineteenth Vice-President ; b. Malone, N. Y. ; began the practice of law, 1845 ; district attorney of Franklin Co., N. Y., 1846-49 ; Whig representative to the state assembly, 1848-59 ; state senator, 1858-59 ; Republican member of Congress, 1861-63 and 1869-77 ; by the "Wheeler Compromise" in 1874 he adjusted the difficulty with Louisiana ; Republican candidate for Vice-President with Hayes, 1876, and declared elected, 1877 ; served from 1877-1881.

Wheelock, John E., arrest and imprisonment of, in Venezuela, 4789, 4803.

Whipple, John, correspondence regarding Dorr's Rebellion, 2140, 2141.

Whitacre, John J.; b. Dec. 28, 1860 ; elected to the 62d Congress from Ohio, Nov. 8, 1910.

Whitby, Henry, British officer, proclamation for arrest of, for murder of American citizen, 390.

White, Alexander, commissioner of Washington City, 302.

White, Alexander; statesman ; b. Franklin, Tenn., Oct. 16, 1816 ; moved to Alabama ; received an academic education ; served in the Seminole War in 1836 ; studied law and practiced ; elected a representative from Alabama to the 32d Congress as a Union Whig, defeating Samuel F. Rice, State Rights Democrat ; member of State Constitutional Convention in 1865 ; member General Assembly in 1872 ; elected Representative-at-large to the 43d Congress ; defeated for re-election ; appointed an associate justice of the United States Court for the territory of Utah in 1875.

White, George; b. Elmira, N. Y., Aug. 21, 1872 ; attended the common schools of Titusville, Pa., and graduated from the High School in 1891, and in that year entered Princeton University, graduating in the class of 1895 with the degree of B. A. ; entered the oil business ; mined in the Klondike, 1898-1901 ; elected to the legislature and represented Washington Co., Ohio, from 1905 to 1908 ; elected to the 62d, 63d, and 64th Congresses from Ohio.

White, Joseph L., counsel of ship canal company, 2676.

White, Joseph M., employment of, to compile land laws in Florida, 994.

White, William, imprisonment of, in Buenos Ayres, 632.

Whitely, Simeon, treaty with Indians concluded by, 3393.

Whiting, Joseph B., member of Chippewa Commission, 5500.

Whitney, William Collins (1841-1904) ; financier and politician ; b. Conway, Mass. ; in 1871, he took an active part against the "Tweed Ring" in New York ; was corporation counsel of New York City, 1875-82 ; Secretary of the Navy, 1885-89 ; a strong supporter of Cleveland, whose presidential campaign he managed in 1892 ; it was his masterly management that secured both nomination and election of Cleveland under peculiarly adverse conditions; his great work as financier was the consolidation of the traction lines in New York City.

Whittlesey, Elisha, commissioner to adjudicate claims of David Taylor, 2678.

Wickersham, George Woodward; Attorney-General under President Taft; b. Pittsburgh, Pa., Sept. 19, 1858; graduated law department of the University of Pennsylvania, 1880; admitted to the Philadelphia bar and practiced there until 1882, when he removed to New York City.

Wickersham, James; lawyer; b. Aug. 24, 1857; appointed United States district judge of Alaska, 1900, and resigned to take effect Jan. 1, 1908; elected delegate to the 61st, 62d, and 63d Congresses from Alaska.

Wickliffe, Charles A.; Postmaster-General under President Tyler; b. Bardstown, Ky., June 8, 1788; received a liberal education; studied law and began practice at Bardstown; state representative 1812-13 and 1822-23; elected a representative from Kentucky to the 18th Congress as a Clay Democrat; re-elected to the 19th, 20th, 21st and 22d Congresses; elected to the State house of representatives in 1834, and speaker; lieutenant-governor of Kentucky in 1836; became governor at the death of Gov. Clark in 1839; Postmaster-General 1841-1845; sent on a secret mission by President Polk to the Republic of Texas in 1845; elected a Representative from Kentucky to the 37th Congress as a Union Whig; delegate to the national Democratic convention at Chicago in 1864; died in Howard County, Md., Oct. 31, 1869.

Wilcox, Orlando B., negotiations for and correspondence regarding restoration of peace, 3463.

Wilder, W. C., member of commission concluding treaty of annexation of Hawaiian Islands, 5783.

Wilkes, Charles; naval officer; b. New York, April 3, 1798; joined the navy as midshipman Jan. 1, 1818; conducted an expedition to explore the southern Pacific Ocean, 1838-42; in 1861, while cruising in the *San Jacinto*, he intercepted the British steamer *Trent* and took from her two confederate commissioners who were on their way to England, and placed them under the custody of Federal authorities at Fort Warren; between 1862 and 1866 he was employed chiefly in blockade duty on the South Atlantic coast; made rear-admiral, 1866, and soon after retired; died Washington, D. C., Feb. 8, 1877.

Wilkes, Charles:
Commander of exploring expedition, report of, on Oregon Territory referred to, 2013.
Removal of Mason and Slidell from British vessel. (See Mason and Slidell.)

Wilkes's Exploring Expedition, expenditures of publication of, referred to, 3068.

Wilkinson, James; soldier; b. Maryland, 1757, and joined the Revolutionary Army, 1778; appointed secretary of the board of war, of which Gen. Gates was president; settled in Kentucky after the war, and engaged in expeditions against the Indians; governor of Louisiana Territory, 1805-06; appointed major-general in 1813 and made unsuccessful efforts to occupy Canada; on the reorganization of the army in 1815 he was discharged and migrated to Mexico, where he died Dec. 28, 1825.

Wilkinson, James:
Aaron Burr's insurrection, troops sent to suppress, commanded by, 401.
Conduct and commercial transactions of, inv stigated, 423.
No intimation found of corrupt receipt of money by, 427.
Expeditions against Wabash Indians commanded by, 104.
Mentioned, 405.

Williams, Eli, commissioner for Cumberland road, 406.

Williams, George H.; b. New Lebanon, N. Y., March 23, 1823; received a liberal education; studied law; moved to Iowa, where he began the practice of his profession; judge of the first judicial district of Iowa 1847-1852; Presidential elector in 1852; chief justice of the Territory of Oregon in 1853 and again in 1857, resigning; member of the constitutional convention of Oregon in 1858; elected a United States Senator from Oregon as a Union Republican 1865-1871; Attorney-General of the United States 1872-1875; nominated by President Grant Chief Justice of the Supreme Court of the United States, but the name was withdrawn.

Williams, George H., member of commission to settle questions with Great Britain, 4075.

Williams, John Sharp; b. July 30, 1854, at Memphis, Tenn.; received a fair education at private schools, the Kentucky Military Institute, near Frankfort, Ky., the University of the South, Sewanee, Tenn., the University of Virginia, and the University of Heidelberg, in Baden, Germany; subsequently studied law under Profs. Minor and Southall at the University of Virginia; in December, 1878, moved to Yazoo City, Miss., where he engaged in the practice of his profession and the varied pursuits of a cotton planter; delegate to the Chicago convention which nominated Cleveland and Stevenson; served as temporary chairman of the Democratic national convention in 1904; was elected to the 53d, 54th, 55th, 56th, 57th, 58th, and 59th Congresses, and re-elected to the 60th Congress, receiving all the votes cast. He had no opposition either for renomination or election; was the candidate of his party for the office of Speaker in the 58th, 59th, and 60th Congresses. On Aug. 1, 1907, Mr. Williams was chosen at a primary election to be the candidate of the Democratic party for the United States Senate from Mississippi, and on Jan. 23, 1908, elected by the legislature to succeed Hon. H. D. Money. His term will expire March 8, 1917.

Windom, William, Secretary of Treasury, death of, announced and honors to be paid memory of, 5599. Referred to, 5568.

Wines, E. C., commissioner to International Congress on Prevention of Crimes, report of, referred to, 4115.

Winslow, Ezra D., refusal of Great Britain to surrender other fugitives and, 4325, 4369.

Winslow, John A., thanks of Congress to, recommended, 3457.

Winthrop, Robert C., correspondence respecting presentation to United States of desk upon which Declaration of Independence was written, 4540.

Wirt, William, lawyer, author, orator; Attorney General under Presidents Monroe and John Quincy Adams; b. Nov. 8, 1772, in Bladensburg, Md.; his parents, Swiss-German, died he was a child and he was reared by an uncle and educated at Georgetown, D. C., and at the private school of the Rev. James Hunt in Montgomery Co., Md.; admitted to the bar in 1792, and began practice in Culpeper Courthouse, Va., and wrote on topics of the time; upon the death of his wife in 1799, went to Richmond and was made Clerk of the House of Delegates, and in 1802 Chancellor of the Eastern District; in 1803 published "Letters of a British Spy," which ran to ten editions; in 1807 President Jefferson appointed him counsel for the Government in the trial of Aaron Burr for treason, and one of his speeches in that memorable trial has ever since been regarded as a classic example of American oratory; appointed by President Madison District Attorney for Virginia in 1816, and by President Monroe to be Attorney General in 1817 and continued through the administration of John Quincy Adams; Judge Story regarded him as "among the ablest and most eloquent of the bar of the Supreme Court"; he was counsel for the defense in the celebrated Dartmouth College case (q. v.), in which he was opposed by Daniel Webster; among his addresses was one on the death of Jefferson and Adams, and one at Rutgers College, which was reproduced in England, France and Germany; candidate for President on the Anti-Masonic ticket in 1832, and received a popular vote of 33,108, and the electoral vote of Vermont; died Feb. 18, 1834, in Washington.

Wise, Henry Augustus; naval officer; b. Brooklyn, N. Y., May 12, 1819; entered the navy as midshipman, 1834; served in the Seminole War and on the Pacific coast during the Mexican War; flag lieutenant of Mediterranean squadron, 1852-54; conveyed the Japanese ambassadors home in frigate Niagara, 1861; promoted to captain and chief of naval ordnance bureau with rank of commander in December, 1866; died at Naples, Italy, April 2, 1869.

Wise, Henry A., minister to—

Brazil—

    Correspondence of, referred to, 2426, 2428, 2538.

    Dispatches from, regarding slave trade, 2215.

France, nomination of, and reasons therefor, 2086.

Witherspoon, Samuel A.; b. May 4, 1855, in Lowndes Co., Miss.; educated at the University of Mississippi and was graduated in 1876; for three years a tutor of Latin in the State University, and that institution has conferred upon him the degree of A. B., A. M., and LL. D.; was married on the 17th day of June, 1880, to Miss Sue E. May, of Versailles, Ky. In the election to the 62d Congress from Mississippi was the nominee of the Democratic party and had no opponent. He was also reelected to 63d and 64th Congresses.

Wolcott, Oliver, Jr.; lawyer, financier, seventh Governor of Connecticut, Secretary of the Treasury under Presidents Washington and Adams; b. Jan. 11, 1760, in Litchfield, Conn.; educated by his mother and at Litchfield grammar school; graduated Yale 1778; studied law in his native town and served in the War of the Revolution; admitted to the bar in 1781 and went to Hartford and became Controller of Public Accounts; when the federal government was reorganized under the Constitution in 1789 he was made auditor of the United States Treasury, and later Controller; refused the presidency of the United States Bank in 1791; succeeded Alexander Hamilton as Secretary of the Treasury in 1795; and continued throughout the administration of Washington and into that of John Adams; resigned Nov. 8, 1800, and was appointed judge of the United States Supreme Court for the district of Connecticut, Vermont and New York; one of the founders of the Merchants Bank of New York and the Bank of North America; returned to Litchfield in 1815 and engaged in manufacture of woolen goods and became a strong advocate of protection to home industries; although a member of the Congregational Church he was active in securing the repeal of the law taxing all other religious denominations for the support of the Congregational Church; elected Lieutenant Governor in 1817, and Governor the following year, serving until 1827; died June 1, 1833, in New York and was buried in Litchfield.

Wolcott, Oliver, commissioner of United States, nomination of, 290.

Wolford, Frank, Presidential elector of Kentucky, arrest and imprisonment of, 3460.

Wood, John E., correspondence of, referred to, 3014.

Wood, Leonard; b. Winchester, N. H., on Oct. 9, 1860. Was graduated from the Harvard Medical School in 1884, and in 1886 became an assistant surgeon, with the rank of first lieutenant, in the United States army. In the same year, he saw service in the Indian campaigns in Arizona and New Mexico. In 1891, he was made a surgeon in the army, with the rank of captain. During the Spanish-American War, he and Theodore Roosevelt recruited the volunteer regiment familiarly known as the "Rough Riders," and he was rewarded for his services by being created a colonel in 1898. From 1899 to 1902, he was military governor of Cuba, and was made a brigadier-general. In 1903, he was made a major-general, and in 1908 was given command of the Department of the East, to be transferred in 1917 to the Department of the Southeast.

Wood, Lafayette B., brevet second lieutenant, promotion of, to second lieutenant, recommended, 2296.

Woodbury, Levi, Secretary of the Navy under President Jackson and of the Treasury under President Van Buren; b. Francistown, N. H., Dec. 22, 1789; graduated from Dartmouth College in 1809; studied law and began practice at Francistown; appointed judge of the superior court of New Hampshire in 1816; moved to Portsmouth; governor of New Hampshire 1823-24; State representative 1825 and speaker; a United States Senator as a Democrat 1825-1831; State senator 1831, but declined; Secretary of the Navy 1831, and in 1834 transferred to the Treasury Department, serving until 1841; appointed chief justice of the superior court of New Hampshire, but declined; again a member of the United States Senate 1841-1845; resigned, having been appointed a justice of the Supreme Court of the United States (vice Joseph Story, deceased), serving until he died at Portsmouth, N. H., Sept. 4, 1851.

Woodbury, Levi, Secretary of Treasury in 1836, issued an order regarding the circulation of small bank notes and certain rules to reduce the number of by payment in specie.

Correspondence respecting interference in elections and pay of soldiers, 1315.

Woodford, Stewart L.; statesman; b. New York City Sept. 3, 1835; graduated from Columbia College in 1854; studied law, and began practice in New York City; assistant attorney for the United States at New York City in 1861; served in the Union Army; lieutenant-colonel of the One hundred and twenty-seventh New York Volunteers and later colonel, and brigadier-general; first Union military commander of Charleston, S. C., and of Savannah, Ga.; lieutenant-governor of New York in 1866; president of the electoral college in 1872; elected a Representative from New York to the Forty-third Congress as a Republican, but resigned July 1, 1874, having been appointed United States attorney for the southern district of New York.

Woodford, Stewart L., minister to Spain mentioned, 6257, 6284, 6286.
Withdrawal of, 6312.

Woodruff, Wilford, letter of, advising Mormons to refrain from contracting marriages forbidden by law, referred to, 5553.

Woodworth, Selim E., thanks of Congress to, recommended, 3277.

Wool, John Ellis; soldier; b. Newburgh, N. Y., Feb. 20, 1784; engaged in business as bookseller in Troy, N. Y., and later studied law, which he abandoned to enlist as captain in the army in April, 1812; he rendered distinguished service during the second war with England and in 1816 was made inspector-general with rank of colonel; appointed brigadier-general in 1841; actively supported Gen. Taylor in Mexican War, and received the thanks of Congress and a sword for his valor; placed in command of Fort Monroe, Va., August, 1861; was promoted to major-general, 1862, and placed on the retired list Aug. 1, 1863; died Troy, N. Y., Nov. 10, 1869.

Wool, John E.:
Correspondence regarding Department of Pacific, 2429, 2431, 3014.

Inquiry in case of, 1589.
Thanks of President tendered to, and the forces under his command in bringing about the surrender of Norfolk, and the evacuation of batteries, 3313.

Wooster, David, monument to memory of, information regarding, 801.

Worcester, Dean C., member of commission to Philippine Islands, 6584.

Worden, John Lorimer; naval officer; b. Westchester Co., N. Y., March 12, 1818; entered navy as midshipman Jan. 10, 1834; commanded the iron-clad *Monitor* in her fight with the *Merrimac* off Hampton Roads, March 9, 1862; promoted Captain, 1863, and did duty at New York in connection with the iron-clads; commissioned rear-admiral Nov. 20, 1872; retired Dec. 23, 1886; died Oct. 18, 1897.

Worden, John L.:
Captain in Navy, nomination of, 3352.
Imprisonment of, 3235.
Thanks of Congress to, recommended, 3344.
Thanks of President tendered, 3313.

Worden, L. J., act for relief of, vetoed, 5247.
Consideration and return of, discussed, 5249.

Works, John D.; b. Ohio Co., Ind., March 29, 1847; was reared on a farm until sixteen and a half years of age, when he enlisted in the army, serving eighteen months, until the close of the Civil War; educated in the common schools of Indiana; is a lawyer and practiced his profession for fifteen years at Vevay, Ind.; in 1883 moved to California; served one term as a member of the legislature of Indiana in 1879; was judge of the Superior Court of San Diego Co., Cal., and a justice of the Supreme Court of that state; for a short time, in 1910, a member of the City Council of the city of Los Angeles, Cal., and its president; member of the American Bar Association more than twenty years; elected United States Senator for California by the legislature of that state for the term ending March 3, 1917.

Worrell, Edward, consul at Matanzas, correspondence regarding estates of deceased American citizens in Cuba, 2893.

Worthington, Nicholas E., member of Strike Commission, 5983.

Wright, Carroll D., member of Strike Commission, 5983.

Wright, Isaac H., naval agent, appointment of, referred to, 2272.

Wright, John C.; journalist; b. Wethersfield, Conn., in 1783; received a liberal education; printer; studied law, and began practice at Steubenville, Ohio; judge of the state supreme court; elected a Representative from Ohio to the 18th, 19th, and 20th Congresses; defeated for re-election; engaged in newspaper work and for some years proprietor of the Cincinnati *Gazette;* delegate to the peace congress; died at Washington, D. C., Feb. 13, 1861.

APPENDIX

THE SIXTY-FIFTH CONGRESS

DELEGATIONS BY STATES

[Names of Democrats in roman type; Republicans in *italics;* Socialist in Roman with *; Progressives in LARGE AND SMALL CAPITALS; Independent in CAPITALS; Prohibitionist in *ITALIC CAPITALS.*]

ALABAMA.
SENATORS.

John H. Bankhead. | Oscar W. Underwood.

REPRESENTATIVES.

[Democrats, 10.]

1. O. L. Gray.
2. S. Hubert Dent, Jr.
3. H. B. Steagall.
4. Fred L. Blackmon.
5. J. Thomas Heflin.
6. W. B. Oliver.
7. John L. Burnett.
8. E. B. Almon.
9. Geo. Huddleston.
10. W. B. Bankhead.

ARIZONA.
SENATORS.

Henry F. Ashurst. | Marcus A. Smith.

REPRESENTATIVE.

[Democrat, 1.]
At Large—Carl Hayden.

ARKANSAS.
SENATORS.

William F. Kirby. | Joe T. Robinson.

REPRESENTATIVES.

[Democrats, 7.]

1. Thaddeus H. Caraway.
2. William A. Oldfield.
3. J. N. Tillman.
4. Otis T. Wingo.
5. H. M. Jacoway.
6. Samuel M. Taylor.
7. William S. Goodwin.

CALIFORNIA.
SENATORS.

J. D. Phelan. | *Hiram Johnson.*

REPRESENTATIVES.

[Democrats, 4; Republicans, 6; Prohibitionist, 1.]

1. Clarence F. Lea.
2. John E. Raker.
3. *Charles F. Curry.*
4. *Julius Kahn.*
5. *John I. Nolan.*
6. *J. A. Elston.*
7. *Denver S. Church.*
8. *Everis A. Hayes.*
9. *C. H. RANDALL.*
10. *Henry Z. Osborne.*
11. William Kettner.

COLORADO.
SENATORS.

Charles S. Thomas. | John F. Shaforth.

REPRESENTATIVES.

[Democrats, 3; Republican, 1.]

1. B. C. Hilliard.
2. *Charles B. Timberlake.*
3. Edward Keating.
4. Edward T. Taylor.

CONNECTICUT.
SENATORS.

Frank B. Brandegee. | *George P. McLean.*

REPRESENTATIVES.

[Democrat, 1; Republicans, 4.]

1. Augustus Lonergan.
2. *R. R. Freeman.*
3. *J. Q. Tilson.*
4. *E. J. Hill.*
5. *J. P. Glynn.*

DELAWARE.
SENATORS.

Josiah O. Wolcott. | Williard Saulsbury.

REPRESENTATIVE.

[Democrat, 1.]
At Large—Albert F. Polk.

FLORIDA.
SENATORS.

Duncan U. Fletcher. | Park Trammel.

REPRESENTATIVES.

[Democrats, 4.]

1. H. J. Drake.
2. Frank Clark.
3. Walter Kehoe.
4. W. J. Sears.

GEORGIA.
SENATORS.

Thomas W. Hardwick. | Hoke Smith.

REPRESENTATIVES.

[Democrats, 12.]

1. J. W. Overstreet.
2. Frank Park.
3. Charles R. Crisp.
4. William C. Adamson.
5. William S. Howard.
6. James W. Wise.
7. Gordon Lee.
8. C. H. Brand.
9. Thomas M. Bell.
10. Carl Vinson.
11. John R. Walker.
12. W. W. Larsen.

IDAHO.
SENATORS.

William E. Borah. | *James H. Brady.*

REPRESENTATIVES.

[Republicans, 2.]
At Large—*Burton I. French, Addison T. Smith.*

ILLINOIS.
SENATORS.

J. Hamilton Lewis. | *Lawrence Y. Sherman.*

REPRESENTATIVES.

[Democrats, 6; Republicans, 21.]

At Large—*Medill McCormick, William E. Mason.*

1. *Martin B. Madden.*
2. *James R. Mann.*
3. *W. W. Wilson.*
4. Charles Martin.
5. Adolph J. Sabath.
6. James McAndrews.
7. Niels Juul.
8. Thomas Gallagher.
9. *Fred A. Britten.*
10. *G. E. Foss.*
11. *Ira C. Copley.*
12. *C. E. Fuller.*
13. *John C. McKenzie.*
14. *William J. Graham.*
15. *E. J. King.*
16. *Clifford Ireland.*
17. *J. A. Sterling.*
18. *Joseph G. Cannon.*
19. *W. B. McKinley.*
20. Henry T. Rainey.
21. *L. E. Wheeler.*
22. *W. A. Rodenburg.*
23. Martin D. Foster.
24. *T. S. Williams.*
25. *E. E. Denison.*

INDIANA.
SENATORS.

James E. Watson. | Harry S. New.

REPRESENTATIVES.
[Democrats, 4; Republicans, 9.]

1. George K. Denton.
2. Oscar E. Bland.
3. William E. Cox.
4. Lincoln Dixon.
5. Everett Sanders.
6. D. W. Comstock.
7. Merrill Moores.
8. A. H. Vestal.
9. Fred S. Purnell.
10. W. R. Wood.
11. Milton Krauss.
12. L. W. Fairfield.
13. Henry A. Barnhart.

IOWA.
SENATORS.

Albert B. Cummins. | William S. Kenyon.

REPRESENTATIVES.
[Republicans, 11.]

1. Charles A. Kennedy.
2. H. E. Hull.
3. B. E. Sweet.
4. Gilbert N. Haugen.
5. James W. Good.
6. C. W. Ramseyer.
7. C. C. Dowell.
8. Horace M. Towner.
9. William R. Green.
10. Frank P. Woods.
11. George C. Scott.

KANSAS.
SENATORS.

Charles Curtis. | William H. Thompson.

REPRESENTATIVES.
[Democrats, 5; Republicans, 3.]

1. Daniel R. Anthony, Jr.
2. E. C. Little.
3. Philip P. Campbell.
4. Dudley Doolittle.
5. Guy T. Helvering.
6. John R. Connolly.
7. Jouett Shouse.
8. W. A. Ayres.

KENTUCKY.
SENATORS.

J. C. W. Beckham. | Ollie M. James.

REPRESENTATIVES.
[Democrats, 9; Republicans, 2.]

1. Alben W. Barkley.
2. D. H. Kinchloe.
3. Robt. Y. Thomas, Jr.
4. Ben Johnson.
5. Swagar Sherley.
6. Arthur B. Rouse.
7. J. C. Cantrill.
8. Harvey Helm.
9. W. J. Fields.
10. John W. Langley.
11. Caleb Powers.

LOUISIANA.
SENATORS.

Robert F. Broussard. | Joseph E. Ransdell.

REPRESENTATIVES
[Democrats, 7; Progressive, 1.]

1. Albert Estopinal.
2. H. Garland Dupre.
3. W. P. Martin.
4. John T. Watkins.
5. Riley Wilson.
6. J. Y. Sanders.
7. Ladislas Lazaro.
8. James B. Aswell.

MAINE.
SENATORS.

Bert M. Fernald. | Frederick Hale.

REPRESENTATIVES.
[Republicans, 4.]

1. Louis B. Goodall.
2. Wallace H. White, Jr.
3. John A. Peters.
4. Ira G. Hersey.

MARYLAND.
SENATORS.

John Walter Smith. | Joseph G. France.

REPRESENTATIVES.
[Democrats, 4; Republicans, 2.]

1. J. D. Price.
2. J. Fred. C. Talbott.
3. Charles P. Cady.
4. J. Charles Linthicum
5. S. E. Mudd.
6. Frederick N. Zihlman

MASSACHUSETTS.
SENATORS.

Henry Cabot Lodge. | John W. Weeks.

REPRESENTATIVES.
[Democrats, 4; Republicans, 11; Independent, 1.]

1. Allen T. Treadway.
2. Frederick H. Gillett.
3. Calvin D. Paige.
4. Samuel E. Winslow.
5. John J. Rogers.
6. Augustus P. Gardner.
7. M. F. Phelan.
8. F. W. Dallinger.
9. A. T. FULLER.
10. P. F. Tague.
11. G. H. Tinkham.
12. J. A. Gallivan.
13. W. H. Carter.
14. Richard Olney, 2d.
15. William S. Greene.
16. Joseph Walsh.

MICHIGAN.
SENATORS.

William Alden Smith. | Charles E. Townsend.

REPRESENTATIVES.
[Democrat, 1; Republicans, 12.]

1. Frank E. Doremus.
2. Mark R. Bacon.
3. J. M. C. Smith.
4. Edward L. Hamilton.
5. Carl E. Mapes.
6. P. H. Kelley.
7. Louis C. Cranton.
8. Joseph W. Fordney.
9. J. C. McLaughlin.
10. Gilbert R. Currie.
11. F. D. Scott.
12. W. F. James.
13. C. A. Nichols.

MINNESOTA.
SENATORS.

Knute Nelson. | Frank B. Kellogg.

REPRESENTATIVES.
[Democrat, 1; Republicans, 8; Progressive, 1.]

1. Sydney Anderson.
2. F. F. Ellsworth.
3. Charles R. Davis.
4. C. C. Van Dyke.
5. Ernest Lundeen.
6. Harold Knutson.
7. Andrew J. Volstead.
8. Clarence B. Miller.
9. Halvor Steenerson.
10. THOMAS D. SCHALL

MISSISSIPPI.
SENATORS.

John Sharp Williams. | James K. Vardaman.

REPRESENTATIVES.
[Democrats, 8.]

1. Ezekiel S. Candler, Jr.
2. Hubert D. Stephens.
3. Benj. G. Humphreys
4. Thomas U. Sisson.
5. William W. Venable.
6. B. P. Harrison.
7. Percy E. Quin.
8. James W. Collier.

MISSOURI.
SENATORS.

William J. Stone. | James A. Reed.

REPRESENTATIVES.
[Democrats, 14; Republicans, 2.]

1. Milton A. Romjue.
2. William W. Rucker.
3. J. W. Alexander.
4. Charles F. Booher.
5. William P. Borland.
6. C. C. Dickinson.
7. C. W. Hamlin.
8. D. W. Shackleford.
9. Champ Clark.
10. J. E. Meeker.
11. William L. Igoe.
12. L. C. Dyer.
13. Walter L. Hensley.
14. Joseph J. Russell.
15. Perl D. Decker.
16. Thomas L. Rubey.

MONTANA.
SENATORS.

Henry L. Meyers. | Thomas J. Walsh.

REPRESENTATIVES.
[Democrat, 1; Republican, 1.]

At Large—John M. Evans, Miss Jeanette Rankin.

NEBRASKA.
SENATORS.

Gilbert M. Hitchcock. | George W. Norris.

REPRESENTATIVES.
[Democrats, 3; Republicans, 3.]

1. C. F. Reavis.
2. C. O. Lobeck.
3. Dan V. Stephens.
4. Charles H. Sloan.
5. A. C. Shallenberger.
6. Moses P. Kinkaid.

NEVADA.
SENATORS.
Francis G. Newlands. | Key Pittman.

REPRESENTATIVE.
[Republican, 1.]
At Large—*E. E. Roberts.*

NEW HAMPSHIRE.
SENATORS.
Jacob H. Gallinger. | Henry F. Hollis.

REPRESENTATIVES.
[Republicans, 2.]
1. *C. A. Sullaway.*[2] | 2. *E. H. Wasson.*

NEW JERSEY.
SENATORS.
Joseph S. Frelinghuysen | William Hughes.

REPRESENTATIVES.
[Democrats, 3; Republicans, 9.]

1. *William J. Browning*	7. *Dow H. Drukker.*
2. *Isaac Bacharach.*	8. *E. W. Gray.*
3. Thomas J. Scully.	9. *R. W. Parker.*
4. *E. C. Hutchinson.*	10. *Fred Lehlbach.*
5. *J. H. Capstick.*	11. John J. Egan.
6. *John R. Ramsey.*	12. James A. Hamill.

NEW MEXICO.
SENATORS.
Andrieus A. Jones | *Albert B. Fall.*

REPRESENTATIVE.
[Democrat, 1.]
At Large—W. B. Walton.

NEW YORK.
SENATORS.
J. W. Wadsworth, Jr. | *William M. Calder.*

REPRESENTATIVES.
[Democrats, 16; Republicans, 26; Socialist, 1.]

1. *Frederick C. Hicks.*	23. Daniel C. Oliver.
2. C. P. Caldwell.	24. *Benj. L. Fairchild.*
3. James V. Flynn.	25. *J. W. Husted.*
4. Harry H. Dale.	26. *Edmund Platt.*
5. James P. Maher.	27. *C. B. Ward.*
6. *F. W. Rowe.*	28. *R. B. Sanford.*
7. John J. Fitzgerald.	29. *James S. Parker.*
8. Daniel J. Griffin.	30. George R. Lunn.
9. *O. W. Swift.*	31. *Bertram H. Snell.*
10. *R. L. Haskell.*	32. *Luther W. Mott.*
11. Daniel J. Riordan.	33. *H. P. Snyder.*
12. M. M. London.*	34. *G. W. Fairchild.*
13. C. D. Sullivan.	35. *W. W. Magee.*
14. *F. H. La Guardia.*[1]	36. *Norman J. Gould.*
15. Michael F. Conry.	37. *H. H. Pratt.*
16. Peter J. Dooling.	38. *Thomas B. Dunn.*
17. John F. Carew.	39. *Archie D. Sanders.*
18. *George B. Francis.*	40. *S. W. Dempsey.*
19. *Walter M. Chandler.*	41. Charles B. Smith.
20. *Isaac Seigel.*	42. *William F. Waldow.*
21. Murray Hulbert.	43. *Charles M.Hamilton*
22. Henry Bruckner.	

NORTH CAROLINA.
SENATORS.
F. M. Simmons. | Lee S. Overman.

REPRESENTATIVES.
[Democrats, 10.]

1. John H. Small.	6. Hannibal L.Godwin
2. Claude Kitchen.	7. L. D. Robinson.
3. George Hood.	8. R. L. Doughton.
4. Edward W. Pou.	9. Edwin Y. Webb.
5. Charles M. Stedman	10. Zeb. Weaver.

[1]—Died March 2, 1917.
[2]—Died March 11, 1912.

NORTH DAKOTA.
SENATORS.
Porter J. McCumber. | *Asle J. Gronna.*

REPRESENTATIVES.
[Republicans, 3.]
1. *Henry T. Helgesen.* | 3. *Patrick D. Norton*
2. *George M. Young.*

OHIO.
SENATORS.
Warren G. Harding. | Atlee Pomerene.

REPRESENTATIVES.
[Democrats, 13; Republicans, 9.]

1. *Nicholas Longworth.*	12. C. Brumbaugh.
2. *Victor Heintz.*	13. A. W. Overmyer.
3. Warren Gard.	14. E. R. Bathrick.
4. Benj. F. Welty.	15. George White.
5. John S. Snook.	16. *R. C. McCulloch.*
6. *C. C. Kearns.*	17. W. A. Ashbrook.
7. *Simon D. Fess.*	18. *D. A. Hollingworth.*
8. J. A. Key.	19. *J. G. Cooper.*
9. Isaac R. Sherwood.	20. William Gordon.
10. *Robert M. Switzer.*	21. Robert Crosser.
11. Horatio C.Claypool.	22. *H. I. Emerson.*

OKLAHOMA.
SENATORS.
Thomas P. Gore. | Robert L. Owen.

REPRESENTATIVES.
[Democrats, 6; Republicans, 2.]

1. *T. A. Chandler.*	5. J. B. Thompson.
2. W. W. Hastings.	6. Scott Ferris.
3. C. D. Carter.	7. J. V. McClintic.
4. T. D. McKeown.	8. *D. T. Morgan.*

OREGON.
SENATORS.
George E. Chamberlain. | Harry Lane.

REPRESENTATIVES.
[Republicans, 3.]
1. *Willis C. Hawley.* | 3. *C. N. McArthur.*
2. *Nicholas J. Sinnott.* |

PENNSYLVANIA.
SENATORS.
Boies Penrose. | *Philander C. Knox.*

REPRESENTATIVES.
[Democrats, 7; Republicans, 29.]
At Large—*T. S. Crago, M. H. Garland, Joseph McLaughlin, John R. K. Scott.*

1. *William S. Vare.*	17. *B. K. Focht.*
2. *George S. Graham.*	18. *Aaron S. Kreider.*
3. *J. Hampton Moore.*	19. *John M. Rose.*
4. *George W. Edmonds*	20. Andrew R.Brodbeck
5. *P. E. Costello.*	21. *C. H. Rowland.*
6. *G. P. Darrow.*	22. *Edwin E. Robbins.*
7. *Thomas S. Butler.*	23. Bruce F. Sterling.
8. *H. W. Watson.*	24. *Henry W. Temple.*
9. *William W. Griest.*	25. *Henry A. Clark.*
10. *John R. Farr.*	26. H. J. Steele.
11. *G. W. Templeton.*	27. *Nathan L. Strong.*
12. *R. D. Heaton.*	28. *O. D. Bleakley.*
13. A. G. Dewalt.	29. *Stephen G. Porter.*
14. *L. T. McFadden.*	30. *M. C. Kelly.*
15. *Edgar R. Kiess.*	31. *J. M. Morin.*
16. John V. Lesher.	32. *Guy E. Campbell.*

RHODE ISLAND.
SENATORS.
Peter G. Gerry. | *LeBaron B. Colt.*

REPRESENTATIVES.
[Democrat, 1; Republicans, 2.]
1. G. F. O'Shaunessy. | 3. *Ambrose Kennedy.*
2. *W. R. Stiness.*

SOUTH CAROLINA.

SENATORS.

Benjamin R. Tillman. | Ellison D. Smith.

REPRESENTATIVES.
[Democrats, 7.]

1. Richard S. Whaley.
2. James F. Byrnes.
3. Fred H. Dominick.
4. Sam. J. Nicholls.
5. W. F. Stevenson.
6. J. Willard Ragsdale.
7. Asbury F. Lever.

SOUTH DAKOTA.

SENATORS.

Thomas Sterling. | Ed. S. Johnson.

REPRESENTATIVES.
[Republicans, 2; Democrat, 1.]

1. *Charles H. Dillon.*
2. *R. C. Johnson.*
3. H. L. Gandy.

TENNESSEE.

SENATORS.

K. D. McKellar. | John K. Shields.

REPRESENTATIVES.
[Democrats, 8; Republicans, 2.]

1. *Sam R. Sells.*
2. *Richard W. Austin.*
3. John A. Moon.
4. Cordell Hull.
5. William C. Houston.
6. Joseph W. Byrns.
7. Lemuel P. Padgett.
8. Thetus W. Sims.
9. Finis J. Garrett.
10. Hubert Fisher.

TEXAS.

SENATORS.

Charles A. Culberson. | Morris Sheppard.

REPRESENTATIVES.
[Democrats, 18.]

At Large—Daniel E. Garrett, Jeff. McLemore.

1. Eugene Black.
2. Martin Dies.
3. James Young.
4. Sam Rayburn.
5. H. W. Summers.
6. Rufus Hardy.
7. A. W. Gregg.
8. Joe H. Eagle.
9. J. J. Mansfield.
10. J. P. Buchanan.
11. Tom Connally.
12. James C. Wilson.
13. Marvin Jones.
14. James L. Slayden.
15. John N. Garner.
16. Thomas L. Blanton

UTAH.

SENATORS.

Reed Smoot. | William H. King.

REPRESENTATIVES.
[Democrats, 2.]

1. M. H. Welling.
2. J. H. Mays.

VERMONT.

SENATORS.

William P. Dillingham. | *Carroll S. Page.*

REPRESENTATIVES.
[Republicans, 2.]

1. *Frank L. Greene.*
2. *P. H. Dale.*

VIRGINIA.

SENATORS.

Thomas S. Martin. | Claude A. Swanson.

REPRESENTATIVES.
[Democrats, 9; Republican, 1.]

1. William A. Jones.
2. E. E. Holland.
3. A. J. Montague.
4. Walter A. Watson.
5. Edward W. Saunders.
6. Carter Glass.
7. T. W. Harrison.
8. Charles C. Carlin.
9. *C. Bascom Slemp.*
10. Henry D. Flood.

WASHINGTON.

SENATORS.

Wesley L. Jones. | *Miles Poindexter.*

REPRESENTATIVES.
[Republicans, 4; Democrat, 1.]

1. *John F. Miller.*
2. *L. H. Hadley.*
3. *A. Johnson.*
4. *William L. La Follette.*
5. C. C. Dill.

WEST VIRGINIA.

SENATORS.

Howard Sutherland. | *Nathan Goff.*

REPRESENTATIVES.
[Democrats, 2; Republicans, 4.]

1. M. M. Neely.
2. George M. Bowers.
3. Stuart F. Reed.
4. Harry C. Woodyard.
5. Ed. Cooper.
6. Adam B. Littlepage.

WISCONSIN.

SENATORS.

Robert M. La Follette. | Paul O. Husting.

REPRESENTATIVES.
[Republicans, 11.]

1. *Henry A. Cooper.*
2. *Edward Voight.*
3. *John M. Nelson.*
4. *William J. Cary.*
5. *William H. Stafford.*
6. *J. H. Davidson.*
7. *John J. Esch.*
8. *Edward E. Browne.*
9. *David G. Classon.*
10. *James A. Frear.*
11. *Irvine L. Lenroot.*

WYOMING.

SENATORS.

John D. Kendrick. | *Francis E. Warren.*

REPRESENTATIVE.
[Republican, 1.]

At Large—*Frank W. Mondell.*

ALASKA.

DELEGATE.

Charles A. Sulzer.

HAWAII.

DELEGATE.

J. Kalanianaole.

PHILIPPINES.

RESIDENT COMMISSIONERS.

—— —— | Manuel Earnshaw.

PORTO RICO.

RESIDENT COMMISSIONER.

—— ——

RECAPITULATION.

SENATE.

Democrats	54
Republicans	42
Total	**96**

HOUSE.

Democrats	215
Republicans	2..
Progressives	2
Independent	1
Socialist	1
Prohibitionist	1
Total	**435**
Total joint ballot	531

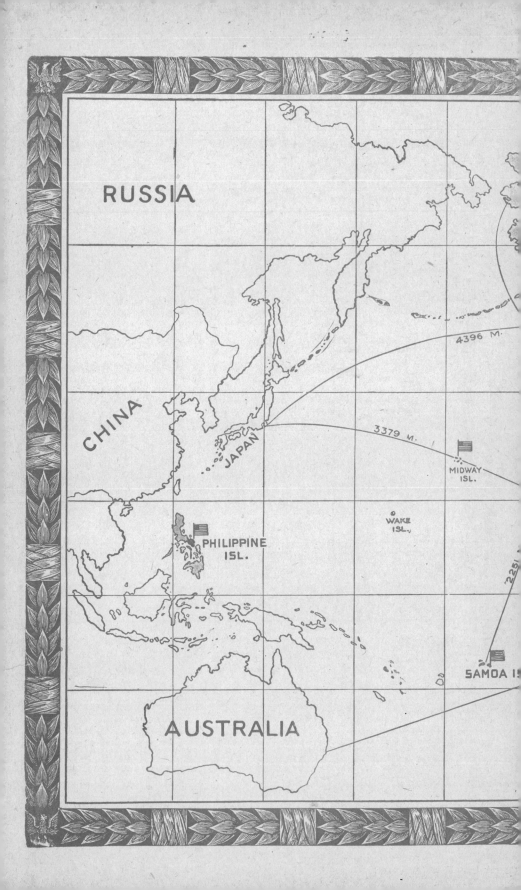